6th EDITION

5-28-9,10,11

Principles of Financial Accounting

516 Mondop
476, 9553
H-718 4631541
SYED Shafiq

Jerry J. Weygandt PhD, CPA

Arthur Andersen Alumni Professor of Accounting
University of Wisconsin
Madison, Wisconsin

Donald E. Kieso PhD, CPA

KPMG Peat Marwick
 Emeritus Professor of Accountancy
Northern Illinois University
DeKalb, Illinois

Paul D. Kimmel PhD, CPA

Associate Professor of Accounting
University of Wisconsin—Milwaukee
Milwaukee, Wisconsin

www.wiley.com/college/weygandt

 JOHN WILEY & SONS, INC.

NEW YORK • CHICHESTER • WEINHEIM • BRISBA  *SINGAPORE*

D1307597

Dedicated to
our mothers-in-law,
Maxyne Stottrup, Mathilda Reichenbacher, Rhojeanne Thompson,
and their daughters,
Enid, Donna, and Merlynn.

Special Dedication to
Walter G. Kell
Scholar-athlete, husband, father, teacher, author, gentleman, and friend

EXECUTIVE EDITOR   *Brent Gordon*
SENIOR DEVELOPMENT EDITOR   *Nancy Perry*
ASSOCIATE EDITOR   *Cynthia Taylor*
SENIOR MARKETING MANAGER   *Clancy Marshall*
PRODUCTION SERVICES MANAGER   *Jeanine Furino*
NEW MEDIA EDITOR   *David Kear*
PRODUCTION COORDINATOR   *Elm Street Publishing Services, Inc.*
ART DIRECTOR   *Dawn L. Stanley*
TEXT DESIGNER   *Sheree Goodman*
COVER DESIGNER   *Dawn L. Stanley*
PHOTO EDITOR   *Sara Wight*
PHOTO RESEARCHER   *Elyse Rieder*
ILLUSTRATION EDITOR   *Sandra Rigby*
ART STUDIO   *Precision Graphics*
COVER PHOTO   *James Bareham/Stone*

This book was set in Times Ten by York Graphic Services and printed and bound by Von Hoffmann Press. The cover was printed by Von Hoffmann Press.

Recognizing the importance of preserving what has been written, it is a policy of John Wiley & Sons, Inc. to have books of enduring value published in the United States printed on acid-free paper, and we exert our best efforts to that end.

The paper in this book was manufactured by a mill whose forest management programs include sustained yield harvesting of its timberlands. Sustained yield harvesting principles ensure that the number of trees cut each year does not exceed the amount of new growth.

We are grateful for permission to use the following material: The Lands' End logo throughout the text and the Lands' End 2000 Annual Report in Appendix A. Lands' End is a registered trademark of Lands' End Direct Merchants, Inc. Used with permission. The Abercrombie & Fitch 2000 Annual Report in Appendix B: Printed with permission of Abercrombie & Fitch Co.

ISBN 0-471-41288-0

Printed in the United States of America

10 9 8 7 6 5 4 3

STUDENT TO STUDENT

Greetings!

Congratulations on your decision to take on one of the most challenging and satisfying courses offered . . . Accounting. As your semester progresses, I am sure that you will have a very good understanding of the accounting field and all that it involves. To help you through your class, here are some tips that I used to achieve academic success:

- Read ahead! Before going over a chapter in the classroom, take the time to read over the chapter so that while the professor is introducing the material you will already have an understanding of the objectives. Start with the *Concepts for Review*, the *Feature Story*, the *Study Objectives*, and the *Preview*; they will help you focus on the main points of the chapter. Then, as you read the chapter and follow the examples, you will be able to comprehend the material by yourself.

- Review! Once your instructor has presented the chapter material in class, be sure to re-read the chapter, concentrating on any areas that seem confusing. Look at the *Study Objectives* in the margins again and do the *Before You Go On* exercises to check whether you have understood and learned the material in each section. Look closely at the *Demonstration Problems* and answer the *Self-Study Questions* at the end of the chapter.

- Do the homework! I cannot over-stress the importance of doing the problems. The problems at the end of each chapter are the best way to gauge your understanding of the chapter material. If you can answer the problems in the chapter with confidence, you will be confident with the material.

- Use a highlighter! This textbook belongs to you, and if you are planning a career in business you will want to keep this book for reference material. Highlighting any material you feel is important in the chapter, or any material you are struggling with, will help you concentrate on those areas when you come back to the chapter review.

- Stay current! Accounting is a course where you build a foundation, and subsequent lessons stand on that foundation. Do not allow yourself to fall behind. Staying current with the lessons being taught in class is a crucial key to success in the course.

I hope that you will find these tips helpful and that your experience in accounting will be as rewarding as my own.

I wish you success,

Robert H. McNamara

Robert H. McNamara
Suffolk County Community College

THE RECORDING PROCESS

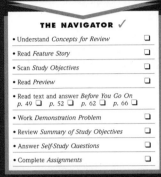

THE NAVIGATOR ✓

- Understand *Concepts for Review* ❑
- Read *Feature Story* ❑
- Scan *Study Objectives* ❑
- Read *Preview* ❑
- Read text and answer *Before You Go On*
  p. 49 ❑ p. 52 ❑ p. 62 ❑ p. 66 ❑
- Work *Demonstration Problem* ❑
- Review *Summary of Study Objectives* ❑
- Answer *Self-Study Questions* ❑
- Complete *Assignments* ❑

The Navigator is a learning system designed to guide you through each chapter and help you succeed in learning the material. It consists of (1) a checklist at the beginning of the chapter, which outlines text features and study skills you will need, and (2) a series of check boxes that prompt you to use the learning aids in the chapter and set priorities as you study.

The **Feature Story** helps you picture how the chapter topic relates to the real world of accounting and business. Throughout the chapter, references to the Feature Story will help you put new ideas in context, organize them, and remember them. The problem called **A Look Back at Our Feature Story** toward the end of the chapter helps you pull together the ideas learned in the chapter. Many Feature Stories end with the **URL** of the company cited in the story.

*C*ONCEPTS FOR REVIEW

Before studying this chapter, you should know or, if necessary, review:

a. What are assets, liabilities, owner's capital, owner's drawings, revenues, and expenses. (Ch. 1, pp. 13–14)

b. Why assets equal liabilities plus owner's equity. (Ch. 1, p. 12)

c. What transactions are and how they affect the basic accounting equation. (Ch. 1, pp. 15–20)

☑ THE NAVIGATOR

Concepts for Review, listed at the beginning of each chapter, are the accounting concepts you learned in previous chapters that you will need to know in order to understand the topics you are about to learn. Page references are provided if you need to review before reading the chapter.

*F*EATURE STORY

No Such Thing As a Perfect World

When she got a job doing the accounting for **Forster's Restaurants**, Tanis Anderson had almost finished her business administration degree at Simon Fraser University. But even after Tanis completed her degree requirements, her education still continued—this time, in the real world.

Tanis's responsibilities include paying the bills, tracking food and labor costs, and managing the payroll for **The Mug and Musket**, a popular destination restaurant in Surrey, British Columbia. "My title is Director of Finance," she laughs, "but really that means I take care of whatever needs doing!"

The use of judgment is a big part of the job. As Tanis says, "I learned all the fundamentals in my business classes, but school prepares you for a perfect world, and there is no such thing."

She feels fortunate that her boss understands her job is a learning experience as well as a responsibility. "Sometimes he's let me do something he knew perfectly well was a mistake so I can learn something through experience," she admits.

To help others gain the benefits of her real-world learning, Tanis is

always happy to help students in the area who want to use Forster's as the subject of a project or report. "It's the least I can do," she says.

☑ THE NAVIGATOR

Study Objectives at the beginning of each chapter give you a framework for learning the specific concepts and procedures covered in the chapter. Each study objective reappears in the margin at the point where the concept is discussed. Finally, you can review all the study objectives in the **Summary** at the end of the chapter.

*S*TUDY OBJECTIVES

After studying this chapter, you should be able to:

1. Explain what an account is and how it helps in the recording process.
2. Define debits and credits and explain how they are used to record business transactions.
3. Identify the basic steps in the recording process.
4. Explain what a journal is and how it helps in the recording process.
5. Explain what a ledger is and how it helps in the recording process.
6. Explain what posting is and how it helps in the recording process.
7. Prepare a trial balance and explain its purposes.

☑ THE NAVIGATOR

The **Preview** begins by linking the Feature Story with the major topics of the chapter. It is followed by a graphic outline of major topics and subtopics that will be discussed. This narrative and visual preview gives you a mental framework upon which to arrange the new information you are learning.

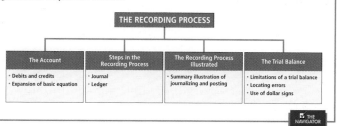

PREVIEW OF CHAPTER 2

In Chapter 1, we analyzed business transactions in terms of the accounting equation. The cumulative effects of these transactions were presented in tabular form. Imagine a restaurant and gift shop such as **The Mug and Musket** using the same tabular format as Softbyte to keep track of every one of its transactions. In a single day, this restaurant and gift shop engages in hundreds of business transactions. To record each transaction this way would be impractical, expensive, and unnecessary. Instead, a set of procedures and records are used to keep track of transaction data more easily.

This chapter introduces and illustrates these basic procedures and records. The content and organization of Chapter 2 are as follows.

THE RECORDING PROCESS

The Account	Steps in the Recording Process	The Recording Process Illustrated	The Trial Balance
• Debits and credits • Expansion of basic equation	• Journal • Ledger	• Summary illustration of journalizing and posting	• Limitations of a trial balance • Locating errors • Use of dollar signs

THE NAVIGATOR

A **CD** icon at various places throughout the book refers you to the CD that came with your textbook. On the CD, you will find *further discussion and examples,* an *Accounting Cycle Tutorial,* additional *Demonstration Problems, Self-Tests,* and *Key Term Matching Activities* to help you study, and additional *real-world cases.*

STUDY OBJECTIVE 1

Explain what an account is and how it helps in the recording process.

Accounting Cycle Tutorial—The Recording Process

THE ACCOUNT

An **account** is an individual accounting record of increases and decreases in a specific asset, liability, or owner's equity item. For example, Softbyte (the company discussed in Chapter 1) would have separate accounts for Cash, Accounts Receivable, Accounts Payable, Service Revenue, Salaries Expense, and so on. In its simplest form, an account consists of three parts: (1) the title of the account, (2) a left or debit side, and (3) a right or credit side. Because the alignment of these parts of an account resembles the letter T, it is referred to as a **T account**. The basic form of an account is shown in Illustration 2-1.

Illustration 2-1

Basic form of account

Title of Account	
Left or debit side	Right or credit side
Debit balance	Credit balance

T Account

THE LEDGER

The entire group of accounts maintained by a company is called the ledger. The ledger keeps in one place all the information about changes in specific account balances.

Companies may use various kinds of ledgers, but every company has a general ledger. A **general ledger** contains all the assets, liabilities, and owner's equity accounts, as shown in Illustration 2-15. A business can use a looseleaf binder or card file for the ledger. Each account is kept on a separate sheet or card. Whenever we use the term ledger in this textbook without a modifying adjective, we mean the general ledger.

STUDY OBJECTIVE 5

Explain what a ledger is and how it helps in the recording process.

General Ledger

Individual Assets	Individual Liabilities	Individual Owner's Equity
Equipment Land Supplies Cash	Interest Payable Salaries Payable Accounts Payable Notes Payable	Salaries Expense Service Revenue J. Lind, Drawing J. Lind, Capital

Illustration 2-15

The general ledger

Study Objectives reappear in the margins at the point where the topic is discussed. End-of-chapter assignments are keyed to study objectives.

Color illustrations visually reinforce important concepts and therefore often contain material that may appear on exams.

The ledger should be arranged in the order in which accounts are presented in the financial statements, beginning with the balance sheet accounts. First in order are the asset accounts, followed by liability accounts, owner's capital, owner's drawing, revenues, and expenses. Each account is numbered for easier identification.

The ledger provides management with the balances in various accounts. For example, the Cash account shows the amount of cash that is available to meet current obligations. Amounts due from customers can be found by examining Accounts Receivable, and amounts owed to creditors can be found by examining Accounts Payable.

Accounting in Action boxes give you more glimpses into the real world of business. These high-interest boxes are classified by three types of issues—business, ethics, and international—each identified by its own icon. New in this edition, **e-Business Insights** describe how e-business technology is expanding the services provided by accountants.

62   CHAPTER 2 The Recording Process

ACCOUNTING IN ACTION   *Business Insight*

E-business is having a tremendous impact on how companies share information within the company, and with people outside the company, such as suppliers, creditors, and investors. A new type of software, Extensible Markup Language (XML), is enabling the creation of a universal way to exchange data. An organization called XBRL.org is using XML to develop an internationally accepted framework called the Extensible Business Reporting Model (XBRL). The organization is comprised of representatives from industry, accounting firms, investment houses, bankers, regulators, and others. The goal of this organization is to establish a framework that "the global business information supply chain will use to create, exchange, and analyze financial reporting information including, but not limited to, regulatory filings such as annual and quarterly financial statements, general ledger information, and audit schedules."

Before You Go On sections follow each key topic. *Review It* questions prompt you to stop and review the key points you have just studied. If you cannot answer these questions, you should go back and read the section again.

Review It questions marked with the Lands' End icon ask you to find information in Lands' End's 2000 Annual Report, which is packaged with this text and excerpted in Appendix A at the end of the text.

Brief *Do It* exercises ask you to put your newly acquired knowledge to work. They outline an *Action Plan* necessary to complete the exercise, and the accompanying *Solution* helps you see how the problem should be solved. (The *Do It* exercises are keyed to similar homework exercises.)

Accounts Receivable   371

BEFORE YOU GO ON...

▶ *REVIEW IT*
1. What is the primary criticism of the direct write-off method?
2. Explain the difference between the percentage of sales and the percentage of receivables methods.
3. **Lands' End** has a generous customer return policy. What accounting treatment does Lands' End use for customer returns? (*Hint:* Review Lands' End's notes.) The answer to this question is provided on page 396.

▶ *DO IT*
Brule Co. has been in business 5 years. The ledger at the end of the current year shows: Accounts Receivable $30,000, Sales $180,000, and Allowance for Doubtful Accounts with a debit balance of $2,000. Bad debts are estimated to be 10% of receivables. Prepare the entry to adjust the Allowance for Doubtful Accounts.

ACTION PLAN
• Report receivables at their cash (net) realizable value.
• Estimate the amount the company does not expect to collect.
• Consider the existing balance in the allowance account when using the percentage of receivables basis.

SOLUTION
The following entry should be made to bring the balance in the Allowance for Doubtful Accounts up to a balance of $3,000 (0.1 × $30,000):

Bad Debts Expense	5,000	
Allowance for Doubtful Accounts		5,000
(To record estimate of uncollectible accounts)		

Related exercise material: BE9-3, BE9-4, BE9-5, BE9-6, BE9-7, E9-2, E9-3, and E9-4.

THE NAVIGATOR

---

50   CHAPTER 2 The Recording Process

The Recording Process

Analyze each transaction   Enter transaction in a journal   Transfer journal information to ledger accounts

Illustration 2-12
The recording process

Infographics, a special type of illustration, pictorially link concepts to the real world and provide visual reminders of key concepts.

The basic steps in the recording process occur repeatedly. The analysis of transactions was illustrated in Chapter 1. Further examples will be given in this and later chapters. The other steps in the recording process are explained in the next sections.

Technology in Action examples show how computer technology is used in accounting and business.

TECHNOLOGY IN ACTION

Computerized and manual accounting systems basically parallel one another. Most of the procedures are handled by electronic circuitry in computerized systems. They seem to occur invisibly. But, to fully comprehend how computerized systems operate, you need to understand manual approaches for processing accounting data.

Technology in Action boxes show how computers are used by accountants and by users of accounting information.

THE JOURNAL

Transactions are initially recorded in chronological order in a **journal** before being transferred to the accounts. Thus, the journal is referred to as the book of original entry. For each transaction the journal shows the debit and credit effects on specific accounts. Companies may use various kinds of journals, but every company has the most basic form of journal, a **general journal**. Typically, a general journal has spaces for dates, account titles and explanations, references, and two amount columns. Whenever we use the term journal in this textbook without a

STUDY OBJECTIVE 4
Explain what a journal is and how it helps in the recording process.

Key Terms and concepts are printed in blue where they are first explained in the text, and they are defined again in the end-of-chapter glossary.

The Basics of Adjusting Entries   101

revenues. In fact, an accrued expense on the books of one company is an accrued revenue to another company. For example, the $200 accrual of fees by Pioneer is an accrued expense to the client that received the service.

Adjustments for accrued expenses are needed for two purposes: (1) to record the obligations that exist at the balance sheet date, and (2) to recognize the expenses that apply to the current accounting period. Prior to adjustment, both liabilities and expenses are understated. Thus, **the adjusting entry for accrued expenses results in a debit (increase) to an expense account and a credit (increase) to a liability account**.

ACCRUED INTEREST. Pioneer Advertising Agency signed a $5,000, 3-month note payable on October 1. The note requires interest at an annual rate of 12%. The amount of the interest accumulation is determined by three factors: (1) the face value of the note, (2) the interest rate, which is always expressed as an annual rate, and (3) the length of time the note is outstanding. In this instance, the total interest due on the $5,000 note at its due date 3 months hence is $150 ($5,000 × 12% × 3/12), or $50 for one month. The formula for computing interest and its application to Pioneer Advertising Agency for the month of October[2] are shown in Illustration 3-12. Note that the time period is expressed as a fraction of a year.

> **HELPFUL HINT**
> Interest is a cost of borrowing money that accumulates with the passage of time.

> **Helpful Hints** in the margins are like having an instructor with you as you read. They further clarify concepts being discussed.

Illustration 3-12
Formula for computing interest

Face Value of Note	×	Annual Interest Rate	×	Time in Terms of One Year	=	Interest
$5,000	×	12%	×	1/12	=	$50

The accrued expense adjusting entry at October 31 is:

Oct. 31	Interest Expense	50	
	Interest Payable		50
	(To record interest on notes payable)		

A	=	L	+	OE
		+50		−50

> **Accounting equation analyses** have been inserted in the margin next to key journal entries. They help you understand the impact of an accounting transaction on the financial statements.

After this adjusting entry is posted, the accounts show:

Interest Expense		Interest Payable	
10/31 Adj. 50			10/31 Adj. 50

Illustration 3-13
Interest accounts after adjustment

Interest Expense shows the interest charges for the month. The amount of interest owed at the statement date is shown in Interest Payable. It will not be paid until the note comes due at the end of 3 months. The Interest Payable account is used instead of crediting (increasing) Notes Payable. The reason for using the two accounts is to disclose the two types of obligations (interest and principal) in the accounts and statements. **If this adjusting entry is not made, liabilities and interest**

> **Financial statements** appear throughout the book. Those from real companies are identified by a logo or related photo. Often, numbers or categories are highlighted in colored type to draw your attention to key information.

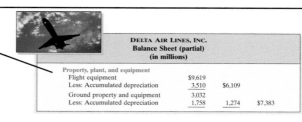

DELTA AIR LINES, INC.
Balance Sheet (partial)
(in millions)

Property, plant, and equipment			
Flight equipment	$9,619		
Less: Accumulated depreciation	3,510	$6,109	
Ground property and equipment	3,032		
Less: Accumulated depreciation	1,758	1,274	$7,383

Illustration 4-20
Property, plant, and equipment section

Intangible Assets

Intangible assets are noncurrent resources that do not have physical substance. They are recorded at cost, and this cost is expensed over the useful life of the intangible asset. Intangible assets include patents, copyrights, and trademarks or

For example, **Lands' End** reported in its 2000 Annual Report a beginning inventory of $219,686,000, and cost of goods sold for the year ended January 28, 2000, of $727,291,000. The inventory turnover formula and computation for Lands' End are shown below.

Illustration 6-28
Inventory turnover formula and computation for **Lands' End**

LANDS' END
DIRECT MERCHANTS

Cost of Goods Sold	÷	Average Inventory	=	Inventory Turnover
$727,291,000	÷	$\frac{\$219,686,000 + \$162,193,000}{2}$	=	3.8 times

> One technique for determining the meaning of the information on financial statements is **ratio analysis**. Throughout this text, you will analyze key financial ratios using data from Lands' End's financial statements. (Also, Chapter 19 addresses the topic of financial statement analysis in detail.)

A variant of the inventory turnover ratio is the **average days to sell inventory**. For example, the inventory turnover for Lands' End of 3.8 times divided into 365 is approximately 96 days. This is the approximate age of the inventory.

There are typical levels of inventory in every industry. Companies that are able to keep their inventory at lower levels and higher turnovers and still satisfy customer needs are the most successful.

The last **Before You Go On** exercise takes you back for a critical look at the chapter-opening Feature Story.

BEFORE YOU GO ON...

▶ *REVIEW IT*
1. What is a trial balance and what is its primary purpose?
2. How is a trial balance prepared?
3. What are the limitations of a trial balance?

A LOOK BACK AT OUR FEATURE STORY

Refer back to the Feature Story about The Mug and Musket at the beginning of the chapter, and answer the following questions.
1. What accounting entries would Tanis likely make to record (a) the receipt of cash from a customer in payment of their bill, (b) payment of a utility bill, and (c) payment of wages for the waiters?
2. How did Tanis's job as Director of Finance help in her studies as she finished her business administration degree?

SOLUTION
1. Tanis would likely make the following entries.
   (a) Cash
           Food Sales Revenue
               (Receipt of payment for food services)
   (b) Utility Expense
           Cash
               (Payment of electric bill)
   (c) Salaries (or Wages) Expense
           Cash
               (Paid waiters' wages)
2. As a result of her accounting position, Tanis was able to relate the subject matter as well as much of the assignment material in her business courses to a real-world context. From her job, she knew how bills were paid, how supplies were determined, how employees were hired, managed, evaluated, and paid.

THE NAVIGATOR

DEMONSTRATION PROBLEM

Bob Sample opened the Campus Laundromat on September 1, 2002. During the first month of operations the following transactions occurred.

Sept. 1 Invested $20,000 cash in the business.
      2 Paid $1,000 cash for store rent for the month of September.
      3 Purchased washers and dryers for $25,000, paying $10,000 in cash and signing a $15,000, 6-month, 12% note payable.
      4 Paid $1,200 for one-year accident insurance policy.
     10 Received bill from the *Daily News* for advertising the opening of the laundromat $200.
     20 Withdrew $700 cash for personal use.
     30 Determined that cash receipts for laundry services for the month were $6,200.

The chart of accounts for the company is the same as in Pioneer Advertising Agency except for the following: No. 154 Laundry Equipment and No. 610 Advertising Expense.

Instructions

(a) Journalize the September transactions. (Use J1 for the journal page number.)
(b) Open ledger accounts and post the September transactions.
(c) Prepare a trial balance at September 30, 2002.

Additional Demonstration Problem

Demonstration Problems review the chapter material. These sample problems provide you with *Action Plans* that list the strategies needed to solve the problem and with *Solutions*. The *CD icon* tells you there is an additional demonstration problem you can work through on the CD that came with your textbook.

SOLUTION TO DEMONSTRATION PROBLEM

(a)

	GENERAL JOURNAL			**J1**
Date	**Account Titles and Explanation**	**Ref.**	**Debit**	**Credit**
2002				
Sept. 1	Cash	101	20,000	
	Bob Sample, Capital	301		20,000
	(Owner's investment of cash in business)			
2	Rent Expense	729	1,000	
	Cash	101		1,000
	(Paid September rent)			
3	Laundry Equipment	154	25,000	
	Cash	101		10,000
	Notes Payable	200		15,000
	(Purchased laundry equipment for cash and 6-month, 12% note payable)			
4	Prepaid Insurance	130	1,200	
	Cash	101		1,200
	(Paid one-year insurance policy)			
10	Advertising Expense	610	200	
	Accounts Payable	201		200
	(Received bill from *Daily News* for advertising)			
20	Bob Sample, Drawing	306	700	
	Cash	101		700
	(Withdrew cash for personal use)			
30	Cash	101	6,200	
	Service Revenue	400		6,200
	(Received cash for services provided)			

ACTION PLAN
- Make separate journal entries for each transaction.
- In journalizing, make sure debits equal credits.
- In journalizing, use specific account titles taken from the chart of accounts.
- Provide appropriate description of journal entry.
- Arrange ledger in statement order, beginning with the balance sheet accounts.
- Post in chronological order.
- Use numbers in the reference column to indicate the amount has been posted.
- In the trial balance, list accounts in the order in which they appear in the ledger.
- List debit balances in the left column, and credit balances in the right column.

The **Summary of Study Objectives** relates the study objectives to the key points in the chapter. It gives you another opportunity to review as well as to see how all the key topics within the chapter are related.

The **Glossary** defines all the terms and concepts introduced in the chapter. Page references help you find any terms you need to study further. The *CD icon* tells you that there is a Key Term Matching Activity on the CD that came with your textbook that will help you master the material.

Self-Study Questions 69

SUMMARY OF STUDY OBJECTIVES

1. *Explain what an account is and how it helps in the recording process.* An account is a record of increases and decreases in specific asset, liability, and owner's equity items.

2. *Define debits and credits and explain how they are used to record business transactions.* The terms debit and credit are synonymous with left and right. Assets, drawings, and expenses are increased by debits and decreased by credits. Liabilities, owner's capital, and revenues are increased by credits and decreased by debits.

3. *Identify the basic steps in the recording process.* The basic steps in the recording process are: (a) analyze each transaction in terms of its effects on the accounts, (b) enter the transaction information in a journal, (c) transfer the journal information to the appropriate accounts in the ledger.

4. *Explain what a journal is and how it helps in the recording process.* The initial accounting record of a transaction is entered in a journal before the data are entered in the accounts. A journal (a) discloses in one place the complete effects of a transaction, (b) provides a chronological record

of transactions, and (c) prevents or locates errors because the debit and credit amounts for each entry can be readily compared.

5. *Explain what a ledger is and how it helps in the recording process.* The entire group of accounts maintained by a company is referred to as the ledger. The ledger keeps in one place all the information about changes in specific account balances.

6. *Explain what posting is and how it helps in the recording process.* Posting is the procedure of transferring journal entries to the ledger accounts. This phase of the recording process accumulates the effects of journalized transactions in the individual accounts.

7. *Prepare a trial balance and explain its purposes.* A trial balance is a list of accounts and their balances at a given time. Its primary purpose is to prove the equality of debits and credits after posting. A trial balance also uncovers errors in journalizing and posting and is useful in preparing financial statements.

THE NAVIGATOR

Key Term Matching Activity

GLOSSARY

Account A record of increases and decreases in specific asset, liability, or owner's equity items. (p. 44).

Chart of accounts A list of accounts and the account numbers that identify their location in the ledger. (p. 56).

Compound entry A journal entry that involves three or more accounts. (p. 52).

Credit The right side of an account. (p. 45).

Debit The left side of an account. (p. 45).

Double-entry system A system that records in appropriate accounts the dual effect of each transaction. (p. 45).

General journal The most basic form of journal. (p. 50).

General ledger A ledger that contains all asset, liability, and owner's equity accounts. (p. 53).

Journal An accounting record in which transactions are initially recorded in chronological order. (p. 50).

Journalizing The entering of transaction data in the journal. (p. 50).

Ledger The entire group of accounts maintained by a company. (p. 53).

Posting The procedure of transferring journal entries to the ledger accounts. (p. 54).

Simple entry A journal entry that involves only two accounts. (p. 51).

T account The basic form of an account. (p. 44).

Three-column form of account A form with columns for debit, credit, and balance amounts in an account. (p. 54).

Trial balance A list of accounts and their balances at a given time. (p. 64).

Chapter 2 Self-Test

SELF-STUDY QUESTIONS

Answers are at the end of the chapter.

(SO 1) 1. Which of the following statements about an account is true?
a. In its simplest form, an account consists of two parts.
b. An account is an individual accounting record of increases and decreases in specific asset, liability, and owner's equity items.
c. There are separate accounts for specific assets and liabilities but only one account for owner's equity items.
d. The left side of an account is the credit or decrease side.

2. Debits: (SO 2)
a. increase both assets and liabilities.
b. decrease both assets and liabilities.
c. increase assets and decrease liabilities.
d. decrease assets and increase liabilities.

3. A revenue account: (SO 2)
a. is increased by debits.
b. is decreased by credits.
c. has a normal balance of a debit.
d. is increased by credits.

---

70 CHAPTER 2 The Recording Process

(SO 2) 4. Accounts that normally have debit balances are:
a. assets, expenses, and revenues.
b. assets, expenses, and owner's capital.
c. assets, liabilities, and owner's drawings.
d. assets, owner's drawings, and expenses.

(SO 3) 5. Which of the following is *not* part of the recording process?
a. Analyzing transactions.
b. Preparing a trial balance.
c. Entering transactions in a journal.
d. Posting transactions.

(SO 4) 6. Which of the following statements about a journal is false?
a. It is not a book of original entry.
b. It provides a chronological record of transactions.
c. It helps to locate errors because the debit and credit amounts for each entry can be readily compared.
d. It discloses in one place the complete effect of a transaction.

(SO 5) 7. A ledger:
a. contains only asset and liability accounts.
b. should show accounts in alphabetical order.
c. is a collection of the entire group of accounts maintained by a company.
d. is a book of original entry.

8. Posting:
a. norma
b. transfe
c. is an
d. transf

9. A trial ba
a. is a lis
b. proves
transa
c. will n
d. proves

10. A trial ba
a. a corr
b. the pu
plies
c. a $100
Drawi
d. a $450
ited to
and cr

QUESTIONS

1. Describe the parts of a T account.

2. "The terms *debit* and *credit* mean increase and decrease, respectively." Do you agree? Explain.

3. José Amaro, a fellow student, contends that the double-entry system means each transaction must be recorded twice. Is José correct? Explain.

4. Teresa Alvarez, a beginning accounting student, believes debit balances are favorable and credit balances are unfavorable. Is Teresa correct? Discuss.

5. State the rules of debit and credit as applied to (a) asset accounts, (b) liability accounts, and (c) the owner's equity accounts (revenue, expenses, owner's drawing, and owner's capital).

6. What is the normal balance for each of the following accounts? (a) Accounts Receivable. (b) Cash. (c) Owner's Drawing. (d) Accounts Payable. (e) Service Revenue. (f) Salaries Expense. (g) Owner's Capital.

7. Indicate whether each of the following accounts is an asset, a liability, or an owner's equity account and whether it has a normal debit or credit balance: (a) Accounts Receivable, (b) Accounts Payable, (c) Equipment, (d) Owner's Drawing, (e) Supplies.

8. For the following transactions, indicate the account debited and the account credited.
(a) Supplies are purchased on account.
(b) Cash is received on signing a note payable.
(c) Employees are paid salaries in cash.

9. Indicate whether the following accounts generally will have (a) debit entries only, (b) credit entries only, or (c) both debit and credit entries.

(1) Cash.
(2) Accounts Receivable.
(3) Owner's Drawing.
(4) Accounts Payable.
(5) Salaries Expense.
(6) Service Revenue.

10. What are the basic steps in the recording process?

11. What are the advantages of using a journal in the recording process?

12. (a) When entering a transaction in the journal, should the debit or credit be written first?
(b) Which should be indented, the debit or credit?

13. Describe a compound entry, and provide an example.

14. (a) Should business transaction debits and credits be recorded directly in the ledger accounts?
(b) What are the advantages of first recording transactions in the journal and then posting to the ledger?

15. The account number is entered as the last step in posting the amounts from the journal to the ledger. What is the advantage of this step?

16. Journalize the following business transactions.
(a) Doris Wang invests $9,000 cash in the business.
(b) Insurance of $800 is paid for the year.
(c) Supplies of $1,500 are purchased on account.
(d) Cash of $7,500 is received for services rendered.

17. (a) What is a ledger?
(b) What is a chart of accounts and why is it important?

18. What is a trial balance and what are its purposes?

19. Kap Shin is confused about how accounting information flows through the accounting system. He believes the flow of information is as follows.
(a) Debits and credits posted to the ledger.
(b) Business transaction occurs.

Self-Study Questions are a practice test, keyed to Study Objectives, that gives you an opportunity to check your knowledge of important topics. Answers appear on the last page of the chapter. The *CD icon* tells you that there is an additional Self-Test on the CD that came with your textbook to help you master the material.

Questions allow you to explain your understanding of concepts and relationships covered in the chapter.

(c) Information entered in the journal.
(d) Financial statements are prepared.
(e) Trial balance is prepared.
Is Kap correct? If not, indicate to Kap the proper flow of the information.

20. Two students are discussing the use of a trial balance. They wonder whether the following errors, each consid-ered separately, would prevent the trial balance from balancing.
(a) The bookkeeper debited Cash for $600 and credited Wages Expense for $600 for payment of wages.
(b) Cash collected on account was debited to Cash for $900 and Service Revenue was credited for $90. What would you tell them?

BRIEF EXERCISES

BE2-1 For each of the following accounts indicate the effects of (a) a debit and (b) a credit on the accounts and (c) the normal balance of the account.

Indicate debit and credit effects and normal balance.
(SO 2)

1. Accounts Payable.
2. Advertising Expense.
3. Service Revenue.
4. Accounts Receivable.
5. B. C. Jardine, Capital.
6. B. C. Jardine, Drawing.

BE2-2 Transactions for the H. J. Oslo Company for the month of June are presented below. Identify the accounts to be debited and credited for each transaction.

Identify accounts to be debited and credited.
(SO 2)

June 1 H. J. Oslo invests $3,000 cash in a small welding business of which he is the sole proprietor.
2 Purchases equipment on account for $900.
3 $500 cash is paid to landlord for June rent.
12 Bills J. Kronsnoble $300 for welding work done on account.

BE2-3 Using the data in BE2-2, journalize the transactions. (You may omit explanations.)

Journalize transactions.
(SO 4)

BE2-4 Tage Shumway, a fellow student, is unclear about the basic steps in the recording process. Identify and briefly explain the steps in the order in which they occur.

Identify and explain steps in recording process.
(SO 3)

BE2-5 J. A. Norris has the following transactions during August of the current year. Indicate (a) the effect on the accounting equation and (b) the debit-credit analysis illustrated on pages 57–61 of the text.

Indicate basic and debit-credit analysis.
(SO 4)

Aug. 1 Opens an office as a financial advisor, investing $6,000 in cash.
4 Pays insurance in advance for 6 months, $1,800 cash.
16 Receives $800 from clients for services rendered.
27 Pays secretary $500 salary.

BE2-6 Using the data in BE2-5, journalize the transactions. (You may omit explanations.)

Journalize transactions.
(SO 4)

BE2-7 Selected transactions for the Gonzales Company are presented in journal form below. Post the transactions to T accounts. Make one T account for each item and determine each account's ending balance.

Post journal entries to T accounts.
(SO 6)

J1

Date	Account Titles and Explanation	Ref.	Debit	Credit
May 5	Accounts Receivable		5,000	
	Service Revenue			5,000
	(Billed for services provided)			
12	Cash		2,400	
	Accounts Receivable			2,400
	(Received cash in payment of account)			
15	Cash		2,000	
	Service Revenue			2,000
	(Received cash for services provided)			

nal entries for the Gonzales Company are presented in BE2-7. Post the standard form of account.

er balances given below, prepare a trial balance for the P. J. Carland 002. List the accounts in the order shown on page 65 of the text. All ac-mal.
$7,000, Cash $6,800, P. J. Carland, Capital $20,000, P. J. Carland, Draw-$17,000, Service Revenue $6,000, Accounts Receivable $3,000, Salaries ent Expense $1,000.

nced bookkeeper prepared the following trial balance. Prepare a correct all account balances are normal.

GOMEZ COMPANY
Trial Balance
December 31, 2002

	Debit	Credit
Cash	$18,800	
Prepaid Insurance		$ 3,500
Accounts Payable		3,000
Unearned Revenue	4,200	
P. Gomez, Capital		15,000
P. Gomez, Drawing		4,500
Service Revenue		25,600
Salaries Expense	18,600	
Rent Expense		2,400
	$41,600	$54,000

EXERCISES

Identify debits, credits, and normal balances.
(SO 2)

E2-1 Selected transactions for A. Mane, an interior decorator, in her first month of business, are as follows.

Jan. 2 Invested $10,000 cash in business.
3 Purchased used car for $4,000 cash for use in business.
9 Purchased supplies on account for $500.
11 Billed customers $1,800 for services performed.
16 Paid $200 cash for advertising start of business.
20 Received $700 cash from customers billed on January 11.
23 Paid creditor $300 cash on account.
28 Withdrew $1,000 cash for personal use of owner.

Instructions
For each transaction indicate the following.
(a) The basic type of account debited and credited (asset, liability, owner's equity).
(b) The specific account debited and credited (cash, rent expense, service revenue, etc.).
(c) Whether the specific account is increased or decreased.
(d) The normal balance of the specific account.

Use the following format, in which the January 2 transaction is given as an example.

	Account Debited				Account Credited			
	(a)	(b)	(c)	(d)	(a)	(b)	(c)	(d)
Date	Basic Type	Specific Account	Effect	Normal Balance	Basic Type	Specific Account	Effect	Normal Balance
Jan. 2	Asset	Cash	Increase	Debit	Owner's Equity	A. Mane, Capital	Increase	Credit

Brief Exercises help you focus on one Study Objective at a time and thus help you build confidence in your basic skills and knowledge. A pencil icon in any of the end-of-chapter materials marks an exercise or problem that will help you practice business writing skills. (Keyed to Study Objectives.)

Exercises, which are more difficult than Brief Exercises, help you continue to build confidence in your ability to use the material learned in the chapter. (Keyed to Study Objectives.)

Accounts Receivable	$ 8,642	Prepaid Insurance	$ 1,968
Accounts Payable	8,396	Repair Expense	961
Cash	?	Service Revenue	10,610
Delivery Equipment	49,360	I. M. Tardy, Drawing	700
Gas and Oil Expense	758	I. M. Tardy, Capital	44,636
Insurance Expense	523	Salaries Expense	4,428
Notes Payable	21,450	Salaries Payable	815

Instructions
Prepare a trial balance with the accounts arranged as illustrated in the chapter and fill in the missing amount for Cash.

PROBLEMS: SET A

P2-1A Frontier Park was started on April 1 by C. J. Sanculi. The following selected events and transactions occurred during April.

Journalize a series of transactions.
(SO 2, 4)

Apr. 1 Sanculi invested $40,000 cash in the business.
  4 Purchased land costing $30,000 for cash.
  8 Incurred advertising expense of $1,800 on account.
  11 Paid salaries to employees $1,500.
  12 Hired park manager at a salary of $4,000 per month, effective May 1.

Each Problem helps you pull together and apply several concepts from the chapter. Two sets of Problems—A and B—are keyed to the same Study Objectives and provide additional opportunities to apply concepts learned in the chapter.

General Ledger Problems, identified by an icon, are selected problems that can be solved using the *General Ledger Software* package.

Problems marked with the **Peachtree** icon can be worked using *Peachtree Complete® Accounting to Accompany Accounting Principles, Sixth Edition*. A separate student workbook that includes the newly released software is available for purchase.

Marginal check figures provide a key number part way through your problem solution, to help you know you're on the right track with your work.

Spreadsheet Problems, identified by an icon, are selected problems that can be solved using the spreadsheet software *Solving Accounting Principles Problems Using Excel and Lotus 1-2-3 for Windows*.

---

78   CHAPTER 2   The Recording Process

Trial balance totals $26,630

Instructions
Prepare a correct trial balance. Note: The chart of accounts includes the following: T. Santos, Drawing, and Supplies. (*Hint:* It helps to prepare the correct journal entry for the transaction described and compare it to the mistake made.)

Journalize transactions, post, and prepare a trial balance.
(SO 2, 4, 6, 7)

P2-5A   The Lake Theater is owned by Avtar Sandhu. All facilities were completed on March 31. At this time, the ledger showed: No. 101 Cash $6,000; No. 140 Land $10,000; No. 145 Buildings (concession stand, projection room, ticket booth, and screen) $8,000; No. 157 Equipment $6,000; No. 201 Accounts Payable $2,000; No. 275 Mortgage Payable $8,000; and No. 301 Avtar Sandhu, Capital $20,000. During April, the following events and transactions occurred.

Apr. 2 Paid film rental of $800 on first movie.
  3 Ordered two additional films at $500 each.
  9 Received $1,800 cash from admissions.
  10 Made $2,000 payment on mortgage and $1,000 on accounts payable.
  11 Lake Theater contracted with R. Thoms Company to operate the concession stand. Thoms is to pay 17% of gross concession receipts (payable monthly) for the right to operate the concession stand.
  12 Paid advertising expenses $300.
  20 Received one of the films ordered on April 3 and was billed $500. The film will be shown in April.
  25 Received $4,200 cash from admissions.
  29 Paid salaries $1,600.
  30 Received statement from R. Thoms showing gross concession receipts of $1,000 and the balance due to The Lake Theater of $170 ($1,000 × 17%) for April. Thoms paid one-half of the balance due and will remit the remainder on May 5.
  30 Prepaid $900 rental on special film to be run in May.

In addition to the accounts identified above, the chart of accounts shows: No. 112 Accounts Receivable, No. 136 Prepaid Rentals, No. 405 Admission Revenue, No. 406 Concession Revenue, No. 610 Advertising Expense, No. 632 Film Rental Expense, and No. 726 Salaries Expense.

Instructions

Trial balance totals $33,670

(a) Enter the beginning balances in the ledger as of April 1. Insert a check mark (✓) in the reference column of the ledger for the beginning balance.
(b) Journalize the April transactions.
(c) Post the April journal entries to the ledger. Assume that all entries are posted from page 1 of the journal.
(d) Prepare a trial balance on April 30, 2002.

PROBLEMS: SET B

Journalize a series of transactions.
(SO 2, 4)

P2-1B   Surepar Miniature Golf and Driving Range was opened on March 1 by Jane McInnes. The following selected events and transactions occurred during March:

Mar. 1 Invested $50,000 cash in the business.
  3 Purchased Lee's Golf Land for $38,000 cash. The price consists of land $23,000, building $9,000, and equipment $6,000. (Make one compound entry.)
  5 Advertised the opening of the driving range and miniature golf course, paying

---

80   CHAPTER 2   The Recording Process

Prepare a correct trial balance.
(SO 7)

P2-4B   The trial balance of Thom Wargo Co. shown below does not balance.

THOM WARGO CO.
Trial Balance
June 30, 2002

	Debit	Credit
Cash		$ 3,840
Accounts Receivable	$ 3,231	
Supplies	800	
Equipment	3,000	
Accounts Payable		2,666
Unearned Revenue	2,200	
T. Wargo, Capital		9,000
T. Wargo, Drawing	800	
Service Revenue		2,380
Salaries Expense	3,400	
Office Expense	910	
	$14,341	$17,886

Each of the listed accounts has a normal balance per the general ledger. An examination of the ledger and journal reveals the following errors.

1. Cash received from a customer on account was debited for $570, and Accounts Receivable was credited for the same amount. The actual collection was for $750.
2. The purchase of a typewriter on account for $340 was recorded as a debit to Supplies for $340 and a credit to Accounts Payable for $340.
3. Services were performed on account for a client for $890. Accounts Receivable was debited for $890, and Service Revenue was credited for $89.

25   Billed customers $3,000 for cleaning services.
31   Paid gas and oil for month on truck $200.
31   Withdrew $900 cash for personal use.

The chart of accounts for Terry's Window Washing contains the following accounts: No. 101 Cash, No. 112 Accounts Receivable, No. 128 Cleaning Supplies, No. 130 Prepaid Insurance, No. 157 Equipment, No. 158 Accumulated Depreciation—Equipment, No. 201 Accounts Payable, No. 212 Salaries Payable, No. 301 Terry Duffy, Capital, No. 306 Terry Duffy, Drawing, No. 350 Income Summary, No. 400 Service Revenue, No. 633 Gas & Oil Expense, No. 634 Cleaning Supplies Expense, No. 711 Depreciation Expense, No. 722 Insurance Expense, No. 726 Salaries Expense.

Instructions

(a) Journalize and post the July transactions. Use page J1 for the journal and the three-column form of account.

(b) Trial balance $16,900   (b) Prepare a trial balance at July 31 on a work sheet.

(c) Adjusted trial balance $18,600   (c) Enter the following adjustments on the work sheet and complete the work sheet.
(1) Services provided but unbilled and uncollected at July 31 were $1,100.
(2) Depreciation on equipment for the month was $200.
(3) One-twelfth of the insurance expired.
(4) An inventory count shows $600 of cleaning supplies on hand at July 31.
(5) Accrued but unpaid employee salaries were $400.

(d) Net income $4,200;   (d) Prepare the income statement and owner's equity statement for July and a classified balance sheet at July 31.
Total assets $15,100

(e) Journalize and post adjusting entries. Use page J2 for the journal.

(f) Journalize and post closing entries and complete the closing process. Use page J3 for the journal.

(g) Post-closing trial balance $15,300   (g) Prepare a post-closing trial balance at July 31.

COMPREHENSIVE PROBLEM: CHAPTERS 2 TO 4

Bill Murphy opened Bill's Window Washing on July 1, 2002. During July, the following transactions were completed.

July 1   Invested $10,000 cash in the business.
1   Purchased a used truck for $8,000, paying $3,000 cash and the balance on account.
3   Purchased cleaning supplies for $800 on account.
5   Paid $2,400 on a one-year insurance policy, effective July 1.
12   Billed customers $3,500 for cleaning services.
18   Paid $1,000 of amount owed on truck, and $400 of amount owed on cleaning supplies.
20   Paid $1,600 for employee salaries.
21   Collected $1,400 from customer billed on July 12.

> In selected chapters, a **Comprehensive Problem** follows the A and B Problem sets. The Comprehensive Problem pulls together and uses topics you have learned over several chapters.

31   Received statement from M. Brewer showing gross receipts from concessions of $8,000 and the balance due to Sabo Theater of $1,200 ($8,000 × 15%) for March. Brewer paid one-half the balance due and will remit the remainder on April 5.
31   Received $15,000 cash from admissions.

In addition to the accounts identified above, the chart of accounts includes: No. 112 Accounts Receivable, No. 405 Admission Revenue, No. 406 Concession Revenue, No. 610 Advertising Expense, No. 632 Film Rental Expense, and No. 726 Salaries Expense.

Instructions

(a) Enter the beginning balances in the ledger. Insert a check mark (✓) in the reference column of the ledger for the beginning balance.

(b) Journalize the March transactions.

(c) Post the March journal entries to the ledger. Assume that all entries are posted from page 1 of the journal.

(d) Prepare a trial balance on March 31, 2002.   Trial balance totals $118,900

BROADENING YOUR PERSPECTIVE

FINANCIAL REPORTING AND ANALYSIS

FINANCIAL REPORTING PROBLEM: Lands' End, Inc.

BYP2-1 The financial statements of **Lands' End, Inc.** are presented in Appendix A. The notes accompanying the statements contain the following selected accounts, stated in thousands of dollars.

Accounts Payable	$ 74,510	Income Taxes Payable	$ 10,255
Accounts Receivable	17,753	Interest Expense	1,890
Property, Plant, and Equipment	283,139	Inventory	162,193

Instructions

(a) Answer the following questions.
(1) What is the increase and decrease side for each account?
(2) What is the normal balance for each account?

(b) Identify the probable other account in the transaction and the effect on that account when:
(1) Accounts Receivable is decreased.
(2) Accounts Payable is decreased.
(3) Inventory is increased.

(c) Identify the other account(s) that ordinarily would be involved when:
(1) Interest Expense is increased.
(2) Property, Plant, and Equipment is increased.

COMPARATIVE ANALYSIS PROBLEM: Lands' End vs. Abercrombie & Fitch

BYP2-2 Lands' End's financial statements are presented in Appendix A. Abercrombie & Fitch's financial statements are presented in Appendix B.

Instructions

(a) Based on the information contained in the financial statements, determine the normal balance of the listed accounts for each company.

Lands' End	Abercrombie & Fitch
1. Inventory	1. Accounts Receivable
2. Property, Plant, and Equipment	2. Cash and Equivalents
3. Accounts Payable	3. Cost of Goods Sold
4. Interest Expense	4. Sales (revenue)

> The **Broadening Your Perspective** section helps you pull together various concepts covered in the chapter and apply them to real-world business decisions.

> The **Financial Reporting Problem** directs you to study various aspects of the financial statements in Lands' End's 2000 Annual Report, which is packaged with the text and excerpted in Appendix A at the end of the text.

> A **Comparative Analysis Problem** offers the opportunity to compare and contrast the financial reporting of Lands' End with that of a competitor, Abercrombie & Fitch, whose financial statements are excerpted in Appendix B.

INTERPRETING FINANCIAL STATEMENTS: A Global Focus

BYP2-3 **Doman Industries Ltd.**, whose products are sold in 30 countries worldwide, is an integrated Canadian forest products company.

Doman sells the majority of its lumber products in the United States and a significant amount of its pulp products in Asia. Doman also has loans from other countries. For example, on June 18, 1999, the Company borrowed US$160 million at an annual interest rate of 12%. Doman must repay this loan, and interest, in U.S. dollars.

One of the challenges global companies face is to make themselves attractive to investors from other countries. This is difficult to do when different accounting rules in different countries blur the real impact of earnings. For example, in 1998 Doman reported a loss of $2.3 million, using Canadian accounting rules. Had it reported under U.S. accounting rules, its loss would have been $12.1 million.

Many companies that want to be more easily compared with U.S. and other global competitors have switched to U.S. accounting principles. Canadian National Railway, Corel, Cott, Inco, and the Thomson Corporation are but a few examples of large Canadian companies whose financial statements are now presented in U.S. dollars, which adhere to U.S. GAAP, or are reconciled to U.S. GAAP.

Instructions

(a) Identify advantages and disadvantages that companies should consider when switching to U.S. reporting standards.

(b) Suppose you wish to compare Doman Industries to a U.S.-based competitor. Do you believe the use of country-specific accounting policies would hinder your comparison? If so, explain how.

(c) Suppose you wish to compare Doman Industries to a Canadian-based competitor. If the companies chose to apply generally acceptable Canadian accounting policies differently, how could this affect your comparison of their financial results?

(d) Do you see any significant distinction between comparing statements prepared using generally accepted accounting principles of different countries and comparing statements prepared using generally accepted accounting principles of the same country (e.g., U.S.) but that apply the principles differently?

EXPLORING THE WEB

BYP2-4 Much information about specific companies is available on the World Wide Web. Such information includes basic descriptions of the company's location, activities, industry, financial health, and financial performance.

Address: biz.yahoo.com/i *(or go to www.wiley.com/college/weygandt)*

Steps:

1. Type in a company name, or use index to find company name.
2. Choose **Profile**. Perform instructions (a)–(c) below.
3. Click on the company's specific industry to identify competitors. Perform instructions

---

Interpreting Financial Statements: A Global Focus asks you to apply concepts presented in the chapter to specific situations faced by actual foreign companies.

Exploring the Web exercises guide you to Internet sites where you can find and analyze information related to the chapter topic. The Internet sites referred to in the Exploring the Web exercises can be accessed directly, or by going through the textbook's Web site at **www.wiley.com/college/weygandt**. At the book's Web site you also can find many other valuable resources and activities, such as additional Internet exercises, Interactive Quizzing, and PowerPoint slides.

The **Group Decision Cases** require teams of students to evaluate a manager's decision or choose from among alternative courses of action. They help prepare you for the business world by giving you practice in solving problems with colleagues.

GROUP DECISION CASE

BYP2-5 Lucy Lars operates Lucy Lars Riding Academy. The academy's primary sources of revenue are riding fees and lesson fees, which are paid on a cash basis. Lucy also boards horses for owners, who are billed monthly for boarding fees. In a few cases, boarders pay in advance of expected use. For its revenue transactions, the academy maintains the following accounts: No. 1 Cash, No. 5 Boarding Accounts Receivable, No. 27 Unearned Boarding Revenue, No. 51 Riding Revenue, No. 52 Lesson Revenue, and No. 53 Boarding Revenue.

The academy owns 10 horses, a stable, a riding corral, riding equipment, and office equipment. These assets are accounted for in accounts No. 11 Horses, No. 12 Building, No. 13 Riding Corral, No. 14 Riding Equipment, and No. 15 Office Equipment.

For its expenses, the academy maintains the following accounts: No. 6 Hay and Feed Supplies, No. 7 Prepaid Insurance, No. 21 Accounts Payable, No. 60 Salaries Expense, No. 61 Advertising Expense, No. 62 Utilities Expense, No. 63 Veterinary Expense, No. 64 Hay and Feed Expense, and No. 65 Insurance Expense.

Communication Activities help you build business communication skills by asking you to engage in real-world business situations using writing, speaking, or presentation skills.

COMMUNICATION ACTIVITY

BYP2-6 Merlynn's Maid Company offers home cleaning service. Two recurring transactions for the company are billing customers for services rendered and paying employee salaries. For example, on March 15, bills totaling $6,000 were sent to customers and $2,000 was paid in salaries to employees.

Instructions

Write a memo to your instructor that explains and illustrates the steps in the recording process for each of the March 15 transactions. Use the format illustrated in the text under the heading, "The Recording Process Illustrated" (p. 57).

Through the **Ethics Cases**, you will reflect on typical ethical dilemmas, learn how to analyze such situations, and decide on an appropriate course of action.

ETHICS CASE

BYP2-7 Megan Menard is the assistant chief accountant at Hokey Company, a manufacturer of computer chips and cellular phones. The company presently has total sales of $20 million. It is the end of the first quarter. Megan is hurriedly trying to prepare a general ledger trial balance so that quarterly financial statements can be prepared and released to management and the regulatory agencies. The total credits on the trial balance exceed the debits by $1,000. In order to meet the 4 p.m. deadline, Megan decides to force the debits and credits into balance by adding the amount of the difference to the Equipment account. She chose Equipment because it is one of the larger account balances; percentage-wise, it will be the least misstated. Megan "plugs" the difference! She believes that the difference will not affect anyone's decisions. She wishes that she had another few days to find the error but realizes that the financial statements are already late.

Instructions

(a) Who are the stakeholders in this situation?

(b) What are the ethical issues involved in this case?

(c) What are Megan's alternatives?

Answers to Self-Study Questions provide feedback on your understanding of concepts.

Answers to Self-Study Questions

1. b   2. c   3. d   4. d   5. b   6. a   7. c   8. d   9. a   10. c

---

Answers to *Review It* Questions based on the Lands' End financial statements provide feedback to your search for information in the Lands' End Annual Report.

LANDS'END

Answer to *Lands' End* Review It Question 4, p. 49

Cash—debit; Accounts Payable—credit; Interest Expense—debit.

After you complete your homework assignments, it's a good idea to go back to **The Navigator** checklist at the start of the chapter to see if you have used all the study aids of the chapter.

✓ *Remember to go back to the Navigator box on the chapter-opening page and check off your completed work.*

This questionnaire aims to find out something about your preferences for the way you work with information. You will have a preferred learning style and one part of that learning style is your preference for the intake and the output of ideas and information.

Circle the letter of the answer that best explains your preference. Circle more than one if a single answer does not match your perception. Leave blank any question that does not apply.

1. You are about to give directions to a person who is standing with you. She is staying in a hotel in town and wants to visit your house later. She has a rental car. Would you
   a. draw a map on paper?
   b. tell her the directions?
   c. write down the directions (without a map)?
   d. pick her up at the hotel in your car?

2. You are not sure whether a word should be spelled "dependent" or "dependant." Do you
   c. look it up in the dictionary?
   a. see the word in your mind and choose by the way it looks?
   b. sound it out in your mind?
   d. write both versions down on paper and choose one?

3. You have just received a copy of your itinerary for a world trip. This is of interest to a friend. Would you
   b. call her immediately and tell her about it?
   c. send her a copy of the printed itinerary?
   a. show her on a map of the world?
   d. share what you plan to do at each place you visit?

4. You are going to cook something as a special treat for your family. Do you
   d. cook something familiar without the need for instructions?
   a. thumb through the cookbook looking for ideas from the pictures?
   c. refer to a specific cookbook where there is a good recipe?

5. A group of tourists has been assigned to you to find out about wildlife reserves or parks. Would you
   d. drive them to a wildlife reserve or park?
   a. show them slides and photographs?
   c. give them pamphlets or a book on wildlife reserves or parks?
   b. give them a talk on wildlife reserves or parks?

6. You are about to purchase a new CD player. Other than price, what would most influence your decision?
   b. The salesperson telling you what you want to know.
   c. Reading the details about it.
   d. Playing with the controls and listening to it.
   a. Its fashionable and upscale appearance.

7. Recall a time in your life when you learned how to do something like playing a new board game. Try to avoid choosing a very physical skill, e.g., riding a bike. How did you learn best? By
   a. visual clues — pictures, diagrams, charts?
   c. written instructions?
   b. listening to somebody explaining it?
   d. doing it or trying it?

8. You have an eye problem. Would you prefer that the doctor
   b. tell you what is wrong?
   a. show you a diagram of what is wrong?
   d. use a model to show what is wrong?

9. You are about to learn to use a new program on a computer. Would you
   d. sit down at the keyboard and begin to experiment with the program's features?
   c. read the manual that comes with the program?
   b. call a friend and ask questions about it?

10. You are staying in a hotel and have a rental car. You would like to visit friends whose address/location you do not know. Would you like them to
    a. draw you a map on paper?
    b. tell you the directions?
    c. write down the directions (without a map)?
    d. pick you up at the hotel in their car?

11. Apart from price, what would most influence your decision to buy a particular book?
    d. You have used a copy before.
    b. A friend talking about it.
    c. Quickly reading parts of it.
    a. The appealing way it looks.

12. A new movie has arrived in town. What would most influence your decision to go (or not go)?
    b. You heard a radio review about it.
    c. You read a review about it.
    a. You saw a preview of it.

13. Do you prefer a lecturer or teacher who likes to use
    c. a textbook, handouts, readings?
    a. flow diagrams, charts, graphs?
    d. field trips, labs, practical sessions?
    b. discussion, guest speakers?

Count your choices:

a.	b.	c.	d.
V	A	R	K

Now match the letter or letters you have recorded most to the same letter or letters in the Learning Styles Chart. You may have more than one learning style preference—many people do. Next to each letter in the chart are suggestions that will refer you to different learning aids throughout this text.

LEARNING STYLES CHART

  VISUAL

INTAKE: TO TAKE IN THE INFORMATION	TO MAKE A STUDY PACKAGE	TEXT FEATURES THAT MAY HELP YOU THE MOST	OUTPUT: TO DO WELL ON EXAMS
• Pay close attention to charts, drawings, and handouts your instructor uses. • Underline. • Use different colors. • Use symbols, flow charts, graphs, different arrangements on the page, white space.	Convert your lecture notes into "page pictures." To do this: • Use the "Intake" strategies. • Reconstruct images in different ways. • Redraw pages from memory. • Replace words with symbols and initials. • Look at your pages.	**The Navigator** **Feature Story** **Preview** **Infographics/Illustrations** **Photos** **Accounting in Action** **Accounting Equation Analyses** **Key Terms in blue** **Words in bold** **Demonstration Problem/Action Plan** **Questions/Exercises/Problems** **Financial Reporting Problem** **Comparative Analysis Problem** **Interpreting Financial Statements** **Exploring the Web**	• Recall your "page pictures." • Draw diagrams where appropriate. • Practice turning your visuals back into words.

  AURAL

INTAKE: TO TAKE IN THE INFORMATION	TO MAKE A STUDY PACKAGE	TEXT FEATURES THAT MAY HELP YOU THE MOST	OUTPUT: TO DO WELL ON EXAMS
• Attend lectures and tutorials. • Discuss topics with students and instructors. • Explain new ideas to other people. • Use a tape recorder. • Leave spaces in your lecture notes for later recall. • Describe overheads, pictures, and visuals to somebody who was not in class.	You may take poor notes because you prefer to listen. Therefore: • Expand your notes by talking with others and with information from your textbook. • Tape record summarized notes and listen. • Read summarized notes out loud. • Explain your notes to another "aural" person.	**Preview** **Infographics/Illustrations** **Accounting in Action** **Review It/Do It/Action Plan** **Summary of Study Objectives** **Glossary** **Demonstration Problem/Action Plan** **Self-Study Questions** **Questions/Exercises/Problems** **Financial Reporting Problem** **Comparative Analysis Problem** **Exploring the Web** **Group Decision Case** **Communication Activity** **Ethics Case**	• Talk with the instructor. • Spend time in quiet places recalling the ideas. • Practice writing answers to old exam questions. • Say your answers out loud.

SOURCE: Adapted from VARK pack. © Copyright Version 2.0 (2000) held by Neil D. Fleming, Christchurch, New Zealand and Charles C. Bonwell, Green Mountain Falls, COLORADO 80819 (719) 684-9261. This material may be used for faculty or student development if attribution is given. It may not be published in either paper or electronic form without consent of the authors. There is a VARK website at www.active-learning-site.com.

READING/WRITING

INTAKE: TO TAKE IN THE INFORMATION	TO MAKE A STUDY PACKAGE	TEXT FEATURES THAT MAY HELP YOU THE MOST	OUTPUT: TO DO WELL ON EXAMS
• Use lists and headings. • Use dictionaries, glossaries, and definitions. • Read handouts, textbooks, and supplementary library readings. • Use lecture notes.	• Write out words again and again. • Reread notes silently. • Rewrite ideas and principles into other words. • Turn charts, diagrams, and other illustrations into statements.	**The Navigator** **Feature Story** **Study Objectives** **Preview** **Review It/Do It/Action Plan** **Summary of Study Objectives** **Glossary** **Self-Study Questions** **Questions/Exercises/Problems** **Writing Problems** **Financial Reporting Problem** **Comparative Analysis Problem** **Interpreting Financial Statements: Global Focus** **Exploring the Web** **Group Decision Case** **Communication Activity**	• Write exam answers. • Practice with multiple-choice questions. • Write paragraphs, beginnings and endings. • Write your lists in outline form. • Arrange your words into hierarchies and points.

  KINESTHETIC

INTAKE: TO TAKE IN THE INFORMATION	TO MAKE A STUDY PACKAGE	TEXT FEATURES THAT MAY HELP YOU THE MOST	OUTPUT: TO DO WELL ON EXAMS
• Use all your senses. • Go to labs, take field trips. • Listen to real-life examples. • Pay attention to applications. • Use hands-on approaches. • Use trial-and-error methods.	You may take poor notes because topics do not seem concrete or relevant. Therefore: • Put examples in your summaries. • Use case studies and applications to help with principles and abstract concepts. • Talk about your notes with another "kinesthetic" person. • Use pictures and photographs that illustrate an idea.	**The Navigator** **Feature Story** **Preview** **Infographics/Illustrations** **Review It/Do It/Action Plan** **Summary of Study Objectives** **Demonstration Problem/ Action Plan** **Self-Study Questions** **Questions/Exercises/Problems** **Financial Reporting Problem** **Comparative Analysis Problem** **Interpreting Financial Statements: Global Focus** **Exploring the Web** **Group Decision Case** **Communication Activity**	• Write practice answers. • Role-play the exam situation.

 For all learning styles: Be sure to use the CD to enhance your understanding of the concepts and procedures of the text. In particular, use the **Study Skills Tips**, **Interactive Navigator**, **Accounting Cycle Tutorial**, **Additional Demonstration Problems**, **Interactive Self-Tests**, and **Key Term Matching Activities**.

The Accounting Principles Web Site at http://www.wiley.com/college/weygandt

This resource and learning tool serves as a launching pad for you to numerous activities, resources, and related sites. On the Web site, you'll find Exploring the Web activities, Internet Exercises, Interactive Quizzing, Learning Styles Assessment, and more. In addition, there are links to companies discussed in the text and items available for downloading such as the PowerPoint Presentations.

NEW Accounting Principles, Interactive Learning Edition

The Interactive Learning Edition (ILE) combines the full text with interactive learning tools to accommodate various learning styles. This dynamic *ebook* offers an active approach to learning that enables you to do things like take detailed notes in the program's text, highlight important information as you read the text, consult a hypertext glossary by simply rolling over key words in the text, search the text, and view additional media such as animations and videos.

Working Papers Volume I: Chapters 1–13 and Volume II: Chapters 14–27

Working Papers are partially completed accounting forms for all end-of-chapter exercises, problems, and cases. A convenient resource for organizing and completing homework assignments, the Working Papers demonstrate how to correctly set up solution formats and are tied directly to textbook assignments.

NEW Electronic Working Papers

Available on a CD-ROM, these Excel-formatted, partially completed accounting forms can be used for end-of-chapter exercises, problems, and cases.

Problem-Solving Survival Guide Volume I: Chapters 1–13 and Volume II: Chapters 14–27

The Problem-Solving Survival Guide tutorial is designed to improve your success rate in solving accounting principles homework assignments and exam questions. The Problem-Solving Survival Guide also provides additional insight and tips on how to study accounting. Each chapter includes an overview of key chapter topics and a review of chapter study objectives; purpose statements for each question, case, or exercise and a direct link to study objectives; and tips to alert you to common pitfalls and misconceptions, as well as reminders of concepts and principles to help solve problems. A selection of multiple-choice exercises and cases representative of common exam questions or homework assignments enhance your proficiency, and detailed solutions and explanations assist you in the approach, setup, and completion of problems.

This new edition also features an online companion powered by WILEY eGrade. This online version includes all of the wonderful resources and tips for solving accounting principles homework assignments and exam questions as the print version, within an interactive Web environment. It provides you with immediate scoring and individualized feedback on your work. The *eGrade* **Student Learning Guide**, automatically bundled with the Problem-Solving Survival Guide, helps you in getting started with the *eGrade* Online Assessment System.

Student Study Guide Volume I: Chapters 1–13 and Volume II: Chapters 14–27

The Student Study Guide is a comprehensive review of accounting and a powerful tool for you to use in the classroom, guiding you through chapter content, tied to study objectives, and providing resources for use during lectures. This is an excellent resource when preparing for exams.

Each chapter of the Student Study Guide includes study objectives and a chapter review consisting of 20 to 30 key points; a demonstration problem linked to study objectives in the textbook; and additional opportunities for you to practice your knowledge and skills through true/false, multiple-choice, and matching questions related to key terms and exercises linked to study objectives. Solutions to the exercises explain the hows and whys so you get immediate feedback.

NEW A Reader's Guide to Accounting Principles: Strategies for Successful Reading and Supplemental Glossary

With this guide, you will learn reading strategies that will increase your comprehension, help you remember information better, and make your experience reading *Accounting Principles* more successful.

Business Extra Web Site at http://www.wiley.com/college/businessextra

The Business Extra Web site gives you instant access to a wealth of current articles dealing with all aspects of financial and managerial accounting. The articles are organized by topic, and discussion questions follow each article. The Business Extra password card is available for purchase.

NEW WSJ.com at
http://www.wiley.com/college/wsjseries

Get "street smart" using *The Wall Street Journal*! WSJ.com contains articles and activities that put you at the cutting edge of today's business world. *The Journal* offers essential tools for business success, including resources for research and advice on career development. The WSJ.com password card is available for purchase.

Practice Sets

Practice sets expose you to a real-world simulation of maintaining a complete set of accounting records for a business. You'll find that practice sets reinforce the concepts and procedures learned in each chapter of the textbook. They also show you how concepts and procedures are brought together to generate the accounting information that is essential in assessing the financial position and operating results of a company. The practice sets available are:

- Campus Cycle Shop
- Heritage Home Furniture
- University Bookstore, Inc.
- *NEW* Custom Party Associates

General Ledger Software

The General Ledger Software program allows you to solve selected end-of-chapter text problems, which are identified by an icon in the margin of the text, using a computerized accounting system. The software allows you to complete the Campus Cycle Shop, Heritage Home Furniture, University Bookstore, Inc., and Custom Party Associates practice sets on a computer.

NEW Peachtree Complete® Accounting Problems and Software

The Peachtree Complete® Accounting Problems are selected problems denoted by the Peachtree logo that can be solved using *Peachtree Complete® Accounting to Accompany Accounting Principles, Sixth Edition*. A separate student workbook that includes the newly released software is available.

Solving Accounting Principles Problems Using Excel and Lotus 1-2-3

These electronic spreadsheet templates (available in either Excel or Lotus) allow you to complete selected end-of-chapter exercises and problems, identified by an icon in the margin of the text. The manuals, which include the disks, guide you step-by-step from an introduction to computers and Excel or Lotus, to completing preprogrammed spreadsheets, to designing your own spreadsheets.

ACKNOWLEDGMENTS

During the course of the development of *Accounting Principles*, Sixth Edition, the authors benefited greatly from feedback from numerous instructors and students of accounting principles courses throughout the country, including many users of the Fifth Edition of the text. Their criticism, constructive suggestions, and innovative ideas helped focus the revision on the needs of the students. We are indebted to the contributions of the following accounting professionals.

Reviewers and Focus Group Participants for Prior Editions of Accounting Principles

Hector Agostini, Middlesex Community College; Linda Alderson, Cabrillo College; Marilyn Allan, Central Michigan University; Walter Allen, North Virginia Community College; Melody Ashenfelter, Southwestern Oklahoma State University; Peter Barton, University of Wisconsin-Whitewater; Abdul Baten, North Virginia Community College; Don Baynham, Eastfield College; Janet Becker, University of Pittsburgh-Johnstown; Steven Becker, University of Wisconsin-Platteville; Harold Bland, Roosevelt University; Dennis Bolen, Augustana College; Lana Bone, West Valley College; Nancy Boyd, Middle Tennessee State University; Eugene Braun, North Virginia Community College; Russell Breslaur, Chabot College; William Brooks, Southwestern Oklahoma State University; Virginia Brunell, Diablo Valley College; Jim Bryant, Catonsville Community College; Terry Bullock, College of DuPage; Ashley Burrowes, California State University-Bakersfield; Madeline Carlin, University of Pittsburgh; Lloyd Carroll, Borough of Manhattan Community College; Janet Cassagio, Nassau Community College; Randy Castello, West Valley College; Ed Castelloe, Lincoln Land Community College; Barbara Chiapetta, Nassau Community College; Joan Cook, Milwaukee Area Technical College; John Corradetti, Joliet Junior College; Sharon Cotton, Schoolcraft College; Carolyn Craig, Shepherd College; Mark Dawson, Indiana University of Pennsylvania; Michael Deda, Fairleigh Dickinson University; Irene Douma, Montclair State College; Charles Downing, Massasoit Community College; Roger DuFresne, Northern Essex Community College; Dean Eiteman, Indiana University of Pennsylvania; David Erlich, Queens College; Cecelia Fewox, Trident Technical College; Carl Fisher, Foothills College; Michael Foland, Belleville Area College; Jeannie Folk, College of DuPage; Mary Kathryn Gardner, Johnson & Wales University; Angelo Gazzola, University of Wisconsin-Fox Valley; Robert Giacoletti, Eastern Kentucky University; Debra Goorbin, Westchester Community College; Ed Gordon, Triton College; W. Michael Gough, DeAnza College; Janet Grange, Chicago State University; Don Green, State University of New York-Farmingdale; Gloria Halpern, Montgomery College; Margie Hamilton, Lewis & Clark Community College; Clo Hampton, West Valley College; Ken Hardy, Catonsville Community College; Patricia Harrison, University of New Orleans; John Hartwick, Bucks County Community College; Nabil Hassan, Wright State University; Alene Helling, Stark Technical College; Keith Hendrick, Wallace State College; Thomas Hofmeister, Northwestern Business School; Lou Jacoby, Saginaw Valley State University; Joe Kederabek, Baldwin-Wallace College; Janice Kelley, St. Louis Community College; Robert Kirsch, Bowling Green State University; Shirly Kleiner, Johnson County Community College; Carol Klinger, Queens College; Jeanette Klosterman, Hutchinson Community College; Roann Kopel, Eastern Illinois University; John Lannen, Salem State College; Doug Larson, Salem State College; Kathy Larson, Middlesex Community College; Larry Larson, Triton College; Robyn Lawrence, University of Scranton; Bruce Leauby, LaSalle University; Marcella Lecky, University of Southwestern Louisiana; Henri LeClerc, Suffolk Community College; Paul Lisowski, Edinboro University; Garry Lym, Golden Gate University; Johnnie Mapp, Norfolk State University; Mary Maury, St. John's University; Jean McKenzie, Fergus Falls Community College; Noel McKeon, Florida Community College-Jacksonville; Greg Mostyn, Mission College; Rhonda Mulkonen, University of South Dakota; Deborah Niemer, Oakland Community College-Royal Oak; Betty Nolen, Floyd Junior College; Cletus O'Drobinak, South Suburban College; Lynn Mazzola Paluska, Nassau Community College; Deanne Pannell, Pellissippi State Technical College; Sandra Penn, Wayne State University; Wayne Pfingsten, Belleville Area College; Rose Marie Pilcher, Abilene Christian University; Beverly Piper, Ashland University; Paul Polachek, Loyola University of Chicago; Kay Poston, Arizona State University-West Campus; Charles Reilly, Suffolk Community College; Bill Reynolds, St. Charles Community College; James Rosa, Queensborough Community College; Victoria Rymer, University of Maryland; Stephen Schaefer, Contra Costa College; Nancy Sheridan, Bucks County Community College; Barry Smith, DeAnza College; Jerome Spallino, Westmoreland Community College; Melvin Stinnett, Oklahoma Christian University; John Sullivan, North Shore Community College; Carolyn Strikler, Ohlone College; Lynda Thompson, Massasoit Community College; Cynthia Tomes, Des Moines Area Community College-Urban Campus; Karen Ulbrich, Parkland College; DuWayne Wacker, University of North Dakota; Janis Waivio, Delta College; Daniel Ward, Southwest Louisiana State University; Michael Watters, New Mexico State University; John Wells, Triton College; Robert Wernagel, College of the Mainland; Kathleen Wessman, Montgomery College; Chris Widmer, Tidewater Community College; Steven Wong, San Jose City College.

Reviewers and Focus Group Participants for Accounting Principles, Sixth Edition

Victoria Beard, University of North Dakota; Ken Couvillion, San Joaquin Delta College; Linda Dening, Jefferson Community College; Albert Fisher, Community College of Southern Nevada; George Gardner, Bemidji State University; Marc Giullian, University of Louisiana-Lafayette; Kathy Horton, College of DuPage; Margaret Hoskins, Henderson State University; Inam Hussain, Purdue University; Sharon Johnson, Kansas City Community College; J. Suzanne King, University of Charleston; Terry Kubichan, Old Dominion University; Melanie Mackey, Ocean County College; Jamie O'Brien, South Dakota State University; Shelly Ota, Leeward Community College; Peter J. Poznanski, Cleveland State University; David Ravetch, University of California-Los Angeles; Paul J. Shinal, Cayuga Community College; Beverly Terry, Central Piedmont Community College.

Student Reviewers for Prior Editions of Accounting Principles—Schools

Appalachian State University, College of Lake County, Hofstra University, Massasoit Community College, Nassau Community College, North Carolina A & M University, Ocean County Community College, Ohlone State College, Phoenix College, Providence College, Queensborough Community College, University of Maine-Bangor, University of Scranton, University of Southwestern Louisiana, University of Texas-San Antonio, Wake Forest Technical College.

Student Reviewers for Accounting Principles, Sixth Edition

Special thanks go to Kathy Horton and the students of the *College of DuPage* and to Alphonse J. Ruggiero and the students of *Suffolk County Community College.*

Reviewers of Supplements for Prior Editions of Accounting Principles

Jim Benedum, Milwaukee Area Technical College; Joan Cook, Milwaukee Area Technical College; Gaspare Di-Lorenzo, Gloucester County College; David Erlach, Queens College; Mark Holtzman, Hofstra University; Phil Kishimori, Leeward Community College; Lynn Koshiyama, University of Alaska-Anchorage; Laura Ruff, Milwaukee Area Technical College; Nathan Saltzberg, Milwaukee Area Technical College; Anita Singer, Kings College; Daniel Small, Jay Sargeant Reynolds Community College; David Zaumeyer, Rutgers University.

General Ledger Software Advisory Board

Denise Bloom, Upper Iowa University; Kevin Dooley, Kapiolani Community College; Peter Doran, North Shore Community College; Jeannie Folk, College of DuPage; Carolyn Harris, University of Texas-San Antonio; Molly Linksz, Anne Arundel Community College; Shelly Ota, Leeward Community College; Patricia A. Robinson, Johnson & Wales University; Robert R. Rovegno, Suffolk Community College; Alphonse J. Ruggiero, Suffolk Community College; Karen Russom, North Harris Community College; Lynda Thompson, Massasoit Community College; Anne Tippitt, Tarrant County Junior College-South Campus.

Special Thanks

Special thanks to Barbara Trenholm, University of New Brunswich, for her insights, and a very special thank you to Ann Torbert for her outstanding editorial efforts and other contributions that raised the quality of this book.

We also sincerely appreciate the work of the supplement authors for the Sixth Edition: Marianne Bradford, Bryant College; Mel Coe, DeVry Institute of Technology—Atlanta; Joan Cook, Milwaukee Area Technical College; Denise M. English, Boise State University; Larry Falcetto, Emporia State University; Patricia Fedje, Minot State University; Sarah L. Frank, University of West Florida; Jessica Frazier, Eastern Kentucky University; Candace Humphrey, Northeast Iowa Community College; Marilyn Hunt, University of Central Florida; Doug Kieso, University of California—Irvine; David R. Koeppen, Boise State University; Gary Lubin, Merck; Sally Nelson, Northeast Iowa Community College; Rex A. Schildhouse, University of Phoenix—San Diego Campus; David Schwinghamer, Collège Ahuntsic, Montreal; Dick Wasson, Southwestern College.

We also thank those who have assured the accuracy of our supplements: Jack Borke, University of Wisconsin-Platteville; Denise M. English, Boise State University; Marc Giullian, University of Louisiana—Lafayette; Jennifer Laudermilch, Coopers & Lybrand; David R. Koeppen, Boise State University; Laura Ruff, Milwaukee Area Technical College—West; Alice Sineath, Forsyth Technical College; Teresa Speck, St. Mary's University; Chris Tomas, Northeast Iowa Community College; Beth M. Woods, CPA.

In addition, special recognition goes to Ivan Pagan of the University of Wisconsin-Madison and Jo Koehn of Central Missouri State University for their work in applying Bloom's Taxonomy; to Karen Huffman of Palomar College for her assessment of the text's pedagogy and suggestions on how to increase its helpfulness to students; to Gary R. Morrison of Wayne State University for his review of the instructional design; to Nancy Galli of Palomar College for her work on learning styles; and to Wayne Higley of Buena Vista University for his technical proofing.

We also thank the editorial, marketing, production, design, and illustration staff of John Wiley & Sons. The following individuals were particularly helpful: Brent Gordon, Nancy Perry, David Kear, Susan Elbe, Joe Heider, Clancy Marshall, Cynthia Taylor, Summer Macey, Robert Meador, Steve Kazlauskas, Alida Setford, Jeanine Furino, Dawn Stanley, Madelyn Lesure, Sandra Rigby, Sara Wight, Mary Ann Benson, Alison Bamert, Sarah Warfield, Lenore Belton, Jaime Perea, and Marsheela Evans. In addition, a note of gratitude to Ginger Yarrow, Barb Lange, and Jennifer Wood of Elm Street Publishing Services and Jackie Henry of York Graphic Services for their help on this project.

Finally, our thanks for the support provided by Will Pesce, President and Chief Executive Officer, and Bonnie Lieberman, Senior Vice-President of the College Division. Suggestions and comments from users—instructors and students alike—will be appreciated.

Jerry J. Weygandt
Donald E. Kieso
Paul D. Kimmel

BRIEF CONTENTS

Jerry J. Weygandt, PhD, CPA, is Arthur Andersen Alumni Professor of Accounting at the University of Wisconsin — Madison. He holds a Ph.D. in accounting from the University of Illinois. Articles by Professor Weygandt have appeared in the *Accounting Review, Journal of Accounting Research, Accounting Horizons, Journal of Accountancy*, and other academic and professional journals. These articles have examined such financial reporting issues as accounting for price-level adjustments, pensions, convertible securities, stock option contracts, and interim reports. Professor Weygandt is author of other accounting and financial reporting books and is a member of the American Accounting Association, the American Institute of Certified Public Accountants, and the Wisconsin Society of Certified Public Accountants. He has served on numerous committees of the American Accounting Association and as a member of the editorial board of the *Accounting Review*; he also has served as President and Secretary-Treasurer of the American Accounting Association. In addition, he has been actively involved with the American Institute of Certified Public Accountants and has been a member of the Accounting Standards Executive Committee (AcSEC) of that organization. He has served on the FASB task force that examined the reporting issues related to accounting for income taxes and is presently a trustee of the Financial Accounting Foundation. Professor Weygandt has received the Chancellor's Award for Excellence in Teaching and the Beta Gamma Sigma Dean's Teaching Award. He is on the board of directors of M & I Bank of Southern Wisconsin and the Dean Foundation. He is the recipient of the Wisconsin Institute of CPA's Outstanding Educator's Award and the Lifetime Achievement Award. In 2001 he received the American Accounting Association's Outstanding Accounting Educator Award.

Donald E. Kieso, PhD, CPA, received his bachelor's degree from Aurora University and his doctorate in accounting from the University of Illinois. He has served as chairman of the Department of Accountancy and is currently the KPMG Peat Marwick Emeritus Professor of Accountancy at Northern Illinois University. He has public accounting experience with Price Waterhouse & Co. (San Francisco and Chicago) and Arthur Andersen & Co. (Chicago) and research experience with the Research Division of the American Institute of Certified Public Accountants (New York). He has done postdoctorate work as a Visiting Scholar at the University of California at Berkeley and is a recipient of NIU's Teaching Excellence Award and four Golden Apple Teaching Awards. Professor Kieso is the author of other accounting and business books and is a member of the American Accounting Association, the American Institute of Certified Public Accountants, and the Illinois CPA Society. He has served as a member of the Board of Directors of the Illinois CPA Society, the AACSB's Accounting Accreditation Committees, the State of Illinois Comptroller's Commission, as Secretary-Treasurer of the Federation of Schools of Accountancy, and as Secretary-Treasurer of the American Accounting Association. Professor Kieso is currently serving on the Board of Trustees and Executive Committee of Aurora University, as a member of the Board of Directors of Castle BancGroup Inc., and as Treasurer and Director of Valley West Community Hospital. From 1989 to 1993 he served as a charter member of the national Accounting Education Change Commission. In 1988 he received the Outstanding Accounting Educator Award from the Illinois CPA Society, in 1992 he received the FSA's Joseph A. Silvoso Award of Merit and the NIU Foundation's Humanitarian Award for Service to Higher Education, in 1995 he received a Distinguished Service Award from the Illinois CPA Society, and in 2000 he was awarded the Community Citizen of the Year Award by Rotary International.

Paul D. Kimmel, PhD, CPA, received his bachelor's degree from the University of Minnesota and his doctorate in accounting from the University of Wisconsin. He is an Associate Professor at the University of Wisconsin — Milwaukee, and has public accounting experience with Deloitte & Touche (Minneapolis). He was the recipient of the UWM School of Business Advisory Council Teaching Award, the Reggie Taite Excellence in Teaching Award, and a three-time winner of the Outstanding Teaching Assistant Award at the University of Wisconsin. He is also a recipient of the Elijah Watts Sells Award for Honorary Distinction for his results on the CPA exam. He is a member of the American Accounting Association and has published articles in *Accounting Review, Accounting Horizons, Issues in Accounting Education, Journal of Accounting Education*, as well as other journals. His research interests include accounting for financial instruments and innovation in accounting education. He has published papers and given numerous talks on incorporating critical thinking into accounting education, and helped prepare a catalog of critical thinking resources for the Federated Schools of Accountancy.

ACCOUNTING IN ACTION

1

THE NAVIGATOR ✓

- Understand *Concepts for Review* ❑
- Read *Feature Story* ❑
- Scan *Study Objectives* ❑
- Read *Preview* ❑
- Read text and answer *Before You Go On*
  p. 9 ❑   *p. 14* ❑   *p. 21* ❑   *p. 25* ❑
- Work *Demonstration Problem* ❑
- Review *Summary of Study Objectives* ❑
- Answer *Self-Study Questions* ❑
- Complete *Assignments* ❑

The Navigator is a learning system designed to prompt you to use the learning aids in the chapter and set priorities as you study.

CONCEPTS FOR REVIEW

Before studying this chapter, you should know or, if necessary, review:

a. How to use the study aids in this book. (Student Owner's Manual, pages iv-xiii)

b. How you learn best. (Student Owner's Manual, pages xiv–xvi)

c. The nature of the special student supplements that accompany this textbook. (Student Owner's Manual, pages xvii–xviii)

Concepts for Review highlight concepts from your earlier reading that you need to understand before starting the new chapter.

☑ THE NAVIGATOR

FEATURE STORY

Things Rarely Go the Way You Plan

As the Scottish poet Robert Burns said, "The best laid schemes o' mice an' men gang aft a'gley." Or, in plain English, things rarely go the way you plan. Take, for example, the life of Gary Comer. Gary wanted to start a company, he liked to sail, and he knew how to write ad copy for catalogs. So in 1963 Gary founded a company that sold sailing gear by catalog. Until 1975 the company, located in Chicago, was primarily a struggling sailing-gear company. That year, 28 pages of its 30-page catalog were devoted to sailing. Only two years later a shift had begun. By then, 13 pages of its 40-page catalog were devoted to clothing.

In the nearly 40 years since the company was founded, much has changed: The company no longer sells sailing gear, it is no longer headquartered in Chicago, and Gary no longer writes his own ad copy. Instead, the copy for the 260 million catalogs that his company distributes annually is written by some of the 7,200 people Gary now employs.

His company, **Lands' End, Inc.**, still relies on catalogs to generate most of its $1 billion in annual sales. In the future the company wants to be able to sell its goods throughout the world, and to do so using retail stores, catalogs, or the Internet—whatever it takes to get the goods out the door and onto the customers' backs.

Although things do not always go as planned, *lack* of planning is often a recipe for disaster. Lands' End did not become one of the largest mail-order companies in the world without careful planning. Its managers are constantly working to increase revenues and minimize costs. Careful consideration must be given to many types of decisions: what new products to sell and which to discontinue, how to finance current operations and expansion, where to locate, and whether to buy or rent properties.

The information needed for these decisions is provided by the company's accounting system. In addition, the company must report its results to the investors and creditors who provide it with the funds it needs to operate. A company communicates its past performance and its plans for the future in its annual report. A copy of the Lands' End, Inc. 2000 Annual Report accompanies this text. In this book you will learn how the accounting information in the annual report was determined, and how to use such information to make business decisions of all sorts.

www.landsend.com

STUDY OBJECTIVES

After studying this chapter, you should be able to:

1. Explain what accounting is.
2. Identify the users and uses of accounting.
3. Understand why ethics is a fundamental business concept.
4. Explain the meaning of generally accepted accounting principles and the cost principle.
5. Explain the meaning of the monetary unit assumption and the economic entity assumption.
6. State the basic accounting equation, and explain the meaning of assets, liabilities, and owner's equity.
7. Analyze the effects of business transactions on the basic accounting equation.
8. Understand what the four financial statements are and how they are prepared.

1

The opening story about **Lands' End, Inc.** highlights the importance of having good financial information to make effective business decisions. Whatever one's pursuits or occupation, the need for financial information is inescapable. You cannot earn a living, spend money, buy on credit, make an investment, or pay taxes without receiving, using, or dispensing financial information. Good decision making depends on good information.

The purpose of this chapter is to show you that accounting is the system used to provide useful financial information. The content and organization of Chapter 1 are as follows.

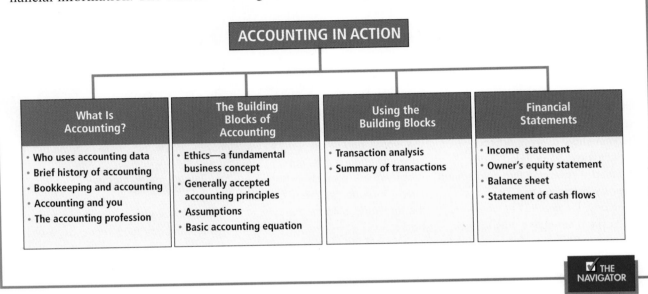

The **Preview** describes and outlines the major topics and subtopics you will see in the chapter.

WHAT IS ACCOUNTING?

STUDY OBJECTIVE 1

Explain what accounting is.

Essential terms are printed in blue when they first appear, and are defined in the end-of-chapter glossary.

Accounting is an information system that **identifies**, **records**, and **communicates** the economic events of an organization to interested users. Let's take a closer look at these three activities.

1. **Identifying** economic events involves selecting the **economic activities relevant to a particular organization**. The sale of goods by **Lands' End**, the providing of services by **Sprint**, the payment of wages by **Ford Motor Company**, and the collection of ticket and broadcast money and the payment of expenses by major league sports teams are examples of economic events.

2. Once identified, economic events are **recorded** to provide a history of the organization's financial activities. Recording consists of keeping a **systematic**, **chronological diary of events**, measured in dollars and cents. In recording, economic events are also classified and summarized.

3. The identifying and recording activities are of little use unless the information is **communicated** to interested users. Financial information is communicated through **accounting reports**, the most common of which are called **financial statements**. To make the reported financial information meaningful, accountants report the recorded data in a standardized way. Information resulting

from similar transactions is accumulated and totaled. For example, all sales transactions of **Lands' End** are accumulated over a certain period of time and reported as one amount in the company's financial statements. Such data are said to be reported **in the aggregate**. By presenting the recorded data in the aggregate, the accounting process simplifies a multitude of transactions and makes a series of activities understandable and meaningful.

A vital element in communicating economic events is the accountant's ability to **analyze** and **interpret** the reported information. Analysis involves the use of ratios, percentages, graphs, and charts to highlight significant financial trends and relationships. Interpretation involves **explaining the uses**, **meaning**, **and limitations of reported data**. Appendix A of this textbook illustrates the financial statements and accompanying notes and graphs from **Lands' End, Inc.**; Appendix B illustrates the financial statements of **Abercrombie & Fitch Co.** We refer to these statements at various places throughout the text. At this point, they probably strike you as complex and confusing. By the end of this course, you'll be surprised at your ability to understand and interpret them.

In summary, the accounting process may be summarized as follows.

References throughout the chapter tie the accounting concepts you are learning to the story that opened the chapter.

Illustration 1-1

Accounting process

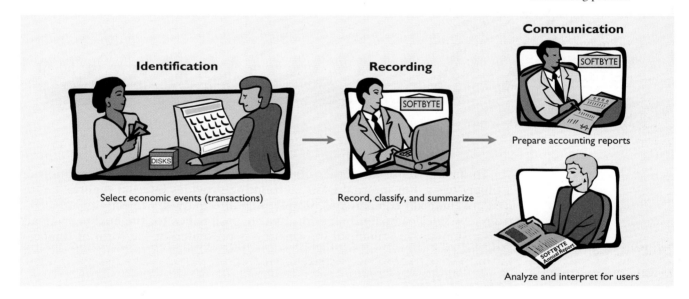

Identification — Select economic events (transactions)

Recording — Record, classify, and summarize

Communication — Prepare accounting reports

Analyze and interpret for users

Accounting should consider the needs of the users of financial information. Therefore, you should know who these users are and something about their needs for information.

WHO USES ACCOUNTING DATA

Because it communicates financial information, accounting is often called "the language of business." The information that a user of financial information needs depends upon the kinds of decisions the user makes. The differences in the decisions divide the users of financial information into two broad groups: internal users and external users.

STUDY **OBJECTIVE 2**

Identify the users and uses of accounting.

Internal Users

Illustration 1-2

Questions asked by internal users

Internal users of accounting information are managers who plan, organize, and run a business. These include **marketing managers**, **production supervisors**, **finance directors**, **and company officers**. In running a business, managers must answer many important questions, as shown in Illustration 1-2.

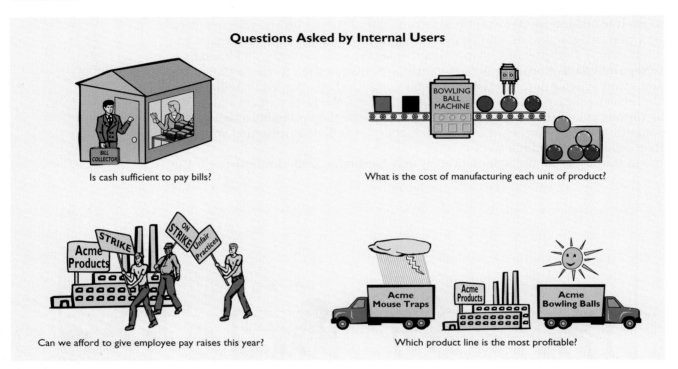

Questions Asked by Internal Users

Is cash sufficient to pay bills?

What is the cost of manufacturing each unit of product?

Can we afford to give employee pay raises this year?

Which product line is the most profitable?

To answer these and other questions, users need detailed information on a timely basis. For internal users, accounting provides **internal reports**. Examples are financial comparisons of operating alternatives, projections of income from new sales campaigns, and forecasts of cash needs for the next year. In addition, summarized financial information is presented in the form of financial statements.

External Users

HELPFUL HINT
The IRS requires businesses to retain records that can be audited. Also, the Foreign Corrupt Practices Act requires public companies to keep records.

There are several types of **external users** of accounting information. **Investors** (owners) use accounting information to make decisions to buy, hold, or sell stock. **Creditors** such as suppliers and bankers use accounting information to evaluate the risks of granting credit or lending money. Some questions that may be asked by investors and creditors about a company are shown in Illustration 1-3.

The information needs and questions of other external users vary considerably. **Taxing authorities**, such as the Internal Revenue Service, want to know whether the company complies with the tax laws. **Regulatory agencies**, such as the Securities and Exchange Commission and the Federal Trade Commission, want to know whether the company is operating within prescribed rules. **Customers** are interested in whether a company will continue to honor product warranties and support its product lines. **Labor unions** want to know whether the owners can pay increased wages and benefits. **Economic planners** use accounting information to forecast economic activity.

Illustration 1-3

Questions asked by
external users

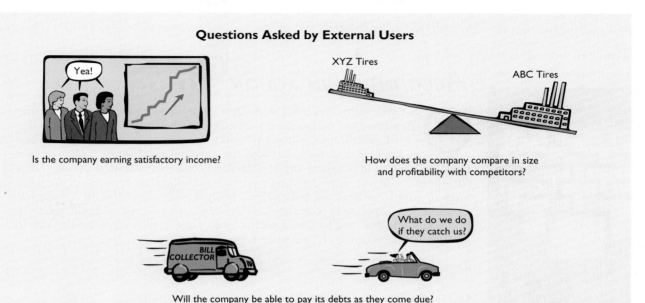

Questions Asked by External Users

Is the company earning satisfactory income?

How does the company compare in size and profitability with competitors?

Will the company be able to pay its debts as they come due?

---

*A*CCOUNTING IN ACTION   *International Insight*

When the chief engineer of Irkutsk Energo, a public utility in Moscow, addressed a gathering of international investors, he provided them with all kinds of financial information about the company. The reason: Russians are learning that corporate openness lures much-needed foreign investment. But foreign investors have been reluctant to invest because Russian firms have been secretive (and sometimes deceptive) about their financial affairs. Now, however, things may change because firms such as Irkutsk Energo have enjoyed stock price surges after providing candid accounting information. In short, good accounting information may help Russia solve some of its economic problems.

SOURCE: The Wall Street Journal, June 9, 1995, p. A-6.

Accounting in Action examples illustrate important and interesting accounting situations in business.

BRIEF HISTORY OF ACCOUNTING

The **origins of accounting** are generally attributed to the work of Luca Pacioli, an Italian Renaissance mathematician. Pacioli was a close friend and tutor to Leonardo da Vinci and a contemporary of Christopher Columbus. In his text *Summa de Arithmetica, Geometria, Proportione et Proportionalite,* Pacioli described a system to ensure that financial information was recorded efficiently and accurately.

With the advent of the **industrial age** in the nineteenth century and, later, the emergence of large corporations, a separation of the owners from the managers of businesses took place. As a result, the need to report the financial status of the enterprise became more important, to ensure that managers acted in accord with owners' wishes. Also, transactions between businesses became more complex, making necessary improved approaches for reporting financial information.

Our economy has now evolved into a post-industrial age—**the information age**—in which many "products" are information services. The computer has been the driver of the information age.

*A*CCOUNTING IN ACTION ∧ *Business Insight*

E-business involves much more than simply selling goods over the Internet. According to Lou Gerstner, **IBM's** CEO, "e-business is all about cycle time, speed, globalization, enhanced productivity, reaching new customers, and sharing knowledge across institutions for competitive advantage." Many accountants are involved in designing and implementing computer systems, including systems for e-business. In fact, in recent years e-business consulting has been one of the largest areas of growth for large accounting firms. Many accountants choose to communicate their computer expertise to potential customers by gaining professional certification. Certification is accomplished by taking professional exams, such as those provided by the Institute for Certification of Computing Professionals *(www.aitp.org)*.

DISTINGUISHING BETWEEN BOOKKEEPING AND ACCOUNTING

Many individuals mistakenly consider bookkeeping and accounting to be the same. This confusion is understandable because the accounting process **includes the bookkeeping function**. However, accounting also includes much more. **Bookkeeping usually involves only the recording of economic events**. It is therefore just one part of the accounting process. In total, **accounting involves the entire process of identifying**, **recording**, **and communicating economic events**.

Accounting may be further divided into financial accounting and managerial accounting. **Financial accounting** is the field of accounting that provides economic and financial information for investors, creditors, and other external users. **Managerial accounting** provides economic and financial information for managers and other internal users. Financial accounting is covered in Chapters 1–19 of this text. Managerial accounting is discussed in Chapters 20–27.

ACCOUNTING AND YOU

One question frequently asked by students of accounting is, "How will the study of accounting help me?" It should help you a great deal, because a working knowledge of accounting is desirable for virtually every field of endeavor. Some examples of how accounting is used in other careers include:

General management: Imagine running **General Motors**, a major hospital, a school, a **McDonald's** franchise, a bike shop. All general managers need to understand accounting data in order to make wise business decisions.

Marketing: A marketing specialist develops strategies to help the sales force be successful. But making a sale is meaningless unless it is a profitable sale. Marketing people must be sensitive to costs and benefits, which accounting helps them quantify and understand.

Finance: Do you want to be a banker, an investment analyst, a stock broker? These fields rely heavily on accounting. In all of them you will regularly examine and analyze financial statements. In fact, it is difficult to get a good job in a finance function without two or three courses in accounting.

Real estate: The most prevalent career in real estate is that of a broker, a person who sells real estate. Because a third party—the bank—is almost always involved in financing a real estate transaction, brokers must understand the numbers involved: Can the buyer afford to make the payments to the bank? Does the cash flow from an industrial property justify the purchase price? What are the tax benefits of the purchase?

Accounting is useful even for occupations you might think completely unrelated. If you become a doctor, a lawyer, a social worker, a teacher, an engineer, an architect, or an entrepreneur—you name it—a working knowledge of accounting is relevant. You will need to understand financial reports in any enterprise you are associated with.

THE ACCOUNTING PROFESSION

What would you do if you join the accounting profession? You probably would work in one of three major fields—public accounting, private accounting, or not-for-profit accounting.

Careers in Accounting

This **CD icon** informs you of additional resources available on the CD that came with your text.

Public Accounting

In **public accounting**, you would offer expert service to the general public in much the same way that a doctor serves patients and a lawyer serves clients. A major portion of public accounting involves **auditing**. In this area, a certified public accountant (CPA) examines the financial statements of companies and expresses an opinion as to the fairness of presentation. When the presentation is fair, users consider the statements to be **reliable**. For example, **Lands' End** investors would demand audited financial statements before extending it financing.

Taxation is another major area of public accounting. The work performed by tax specialists includes tax advice and planning, preparing tax returns, and representing clients before governmental agencies such as the Internal Revenue Service.

A third area in public accounting is **management consulting**. It ranges from the installing of basic accounting systems to helping companies determine whether they should use the space shuttle for high-tech research and development projects.

Private Accounting

Instead of working in public accounting, you might choose to be an employee of a business enterprise. In **private (or managerial) accounting**, you would be involved in one of the following activities.

1. **General accounting**—recording daily transactions and preparing financial statements and related information.
2. **Cost accounting**—determining the cost of producing specific products.
3. **Budgeting**—assisting management in quantifying goals concerning revenues, costs of goods sold, and operating expenses.
4. **Accounting information systems**—designing both manual and computerized data processing systems.
5. **Tax accounting**—preparing tax returns and doing tax planning for the company.
6. **Internal auditing**—reviewing the company's operations to see if they comply with management policies and evaluating the efficiency of operations.

You can see that within a specific company, private accountants perform as wide a variety of duties as the public accountant.

Illustration 1-4 presents the general career paths in public and private accounting.

Illustration 1-4

Career paths in public and private accounting

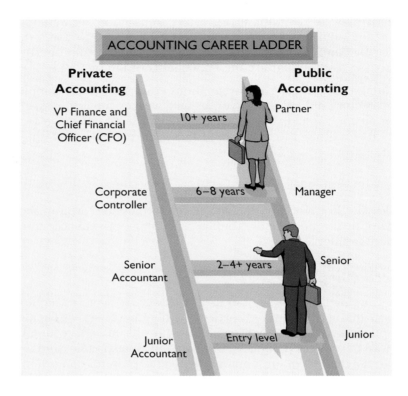

Not-for-Profit Accounting

Like businesses that exist to make a profit, not-for-profit organizations also need sound financial reporting and control. Donors to such organizations as the **United Way**, the **Ford Foundation**, and the **Red Cross** want information about how well the organization has met its financial objectives and whether continued support is justified. Hospitals, colleges, and universities must make decisions about allocating funds. Local, state, and federal governmental units provide financial information to legislators, citizens, employees, and creditors. At the federal level, the largest employers of accountants are the **Internal Revenue Service**, the **General Accounting Office**, the **Federal Bureau of Investigation**, and the **Securities and Exchange Commission**.

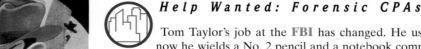

ACCOUNTING IN ACTION *Business Insight*

Help Wanted: Forensic CPAs

Tom Taylor's job at the **FBI** has changed. He used to pack a .357 magnum; now he wields a No. 2 pencil and a notebook computer. Taylor, age 37, for two years an FBI agent, is a forensic accountant, somebody who sniffs through company books to ferret out white-collar crime. Demand for this service has surged in the past few years. In one recent year, a recruiter for San Diego's **Robert Half International**, a head-hunting firm, had requests for more than 1,000 such snoops.

Qualifications: a CPA with FBI, IRS, or similar government experience. Interestingly, despite its macho image, the FBI has long hired mostly accountants and lawyers as agents.

BEFORE YOU GO ON...

▶ *REVIEW IT*

1. What is accounting?
2. Who uses accounting information?
3. What is the difference between bookkeeping and accounting?
4. How can you use your accounting knowledge?
5. If you join the accounting profession, in what three major fields do you have a choice of a job?
6. What types of services are provided by public accountants?
7. What activities might you be involved in if you work in private accounting?
8. Name five not-for-profit organizations.

Before You Go On questions at the end of major text sections offer an opportunity to stop and reexamine the key points you have studied.

THE BUILDING BLOCKS OF ACCOUNTING

Every profession develops a body of theory consisting of principles, assumptions, and standards. Accounting is no exception. Just as a doctor follows certain standards in treating a patient's illness, an accountant follows certain standards in reporting financial information. For these standards to work, a fundamental business concept is followed—ethical behavior.

ETHICS—A FUNDAMENTAL BUSINESS CONCEPT

Wherever you make your career—whether in accounting, marketing, management, finance, government, or elsewhere—your actions will affect other people and organizations. The standards of conduct by which one's actions are judged as right or wrong, honest or dishonest, fair or not fair, are **ethics**. Imagine trying to carry on a business or invest money if you could not depend on the individuals you deal with to be honest. If managers, customers, investors, co-workers, and creditors all consistently lied, effective communication and economic activity would be impossible. Information would have no credibility.

Fortunately most individuals in business are ethical. Their actions are both legal and responsible, and they consider the organization's interests in their decision making. However, sometimes public officials and business executives act unethically. For example, a former chief of the finance committee of the **House of Representatives** was indicted for possible illegal behavior; **Sears** was accused of widespread customer overcharging on car repairs; **Woolworth Corp.** executives were dismissed because they reported false income numbers. As one business leader noted: "We are all embarrassed by the events that make *The Wall Street Journal* read like the *Police Gazette*."

To sensitize you to ethical situations and to give you practice at solving ethical dilemmas, we have included in the book three types of ethics materials: (1) marginal notes that provide helpful hints for developing ethical sensitivity, (2) Ethics in Accounting boxes that highlight ethics situations and issues, and (3) at the end of the chapter, an ethics case simulating a business situation. In the process of analyzing these ethics cases and your own ethical experiences, you should apply the three steps outlined in Illustration 1-5.

STUDY OBJECTIVE **3**

Understand why ethics is a fundamental business concept.

Illustration 1-5

Steps in analyzing ethics cases

Solving an Ethical Dilemma

1. Recognize an ethical situation and the ethical issues involved.

Use your personal ethics to identify ethical situations and issues. Some businesses and professional organizations provide written codes of ethics for guidance in some business situations.

2. Identify and analyze the principal elements in the situation.

Identify the *stakeholders*—persons or groups who may be harmed or benefited. Ask the question: What are the responsibilities and obligations of the parties involved?

3. Identify the alternatives, and weigh the impact of each alternative on various stakeholders.

Select the most ethical alternative, considering all the consequences. Sometimes there will be one right answer. Other situations involve more than one right solution; these situations require an evaluation of each and a selection of the best alternative.

GENERALLY ACCEPTED ACCOUNTING PRINCIPLES

STUDY OBJECTIVE 4

Explain the meaning of generally accepted accounting principles and the cost principle.

The accounting profession has developed standards that are generally accepted and universally practiced. This common set of standards is called **generally accepted accounting principles (GAAP)**. These standards indicate how to report economic events.

Two organizations are primarily responsible for establishing generally accepted accounting principles. The first is the **Financial Accounting Standards Board (FASB)**. This private organization establishes broad reporting standards of general applicability as well as specific accounting rules. The second standards-setting group is the **Securities and Exchange Commission (SEC)**. The SEC is a governmental agency that requires companies to file financial reports following generally accepted accounting principles. In situations where no principles exist, the SEC often mandates that certain guidelines be used. In general, the FASB and the SEC work hand in hand to assure that timely and useful accounting principles are developed.

> **INTERNATIONAL NOTE**
>
> The standards-setting processes in Canada, Mexico, and the United States are similar in most respects. All three have relatively open deliberations on new rules, and they support efforts to follow international standards. The use of similar accounting principles within North America has implications for the success of the North American Free Trade Agreement (NAFTA).

One important principle is the **cost principle**, which states that assets should be recorded at their cost. **Cost is the value exchanged at the time something is acquired.** If you buy a house today, the cost is the amount you pay for it, say $200,000. If you sell the house in two years for $230,000, the sales price is its **market value**—the value determined by the market for homes at that time. At the time of acquisition, cost and fair market value are the same. In subsequent periods, cost and fair market value may vary, **but the cost amount continues to be used in the accounting records**.

To see the importance of the cost principle, consider the following example. At one time, **Greyhound Corporation** had 128 bus stations nationwide that cost approximately $200 million. The current market value of the stations is now close to $1 billion. But, until the bus stations are actually sold, estimates of their market values are subjective—they are informed estimates. So, under the cost principle, the bus stations are recorded and reported at $200 million, not $1 billion.

ALTERNATIVE TERMINOLOGY
The cost principle is often referred to as the *historical cost principle.*

As the Greyhound example indicates, cost has an important advantage over other valuations: Cost is **reliable**. The values exchanged at the time something is acquired generally can be **objectively measured** and can be **verified**. Critics argue that cost is often not relevant and that market values provide more useful information. Despite this shortcoming, cost continues to be used in the financial statements because of its reliability.

STUDY OBJECTIVE 5

Explain the meaning of the monetary unit assumption and the economic entity assumption.

ASSUMPTIONS

In developing generally accepted accounting principles, certain basic assumptions are made. These assumptions provide a foundation for the accounting process.

Two main assumptions are the **monetary unit assumption** and the **economic entity assumption**.

Monetary Unit Assumption

The monetary unit assumption requires that only transaction data that can be expressed in terms of money be included in the accounting records. This assumption enables accounting to quantify (measure) economic events. The monetary unit assumption is vital to applying the cost principle discussed earlier. This assumption does prevent some relevant information from being included in the accounting records. For example, the health of the owner, the quality of service, and the morale of employees would not be included because they cannot be quantified in terms of money.

An important part of the monetary unit assumption is the added assumption that the unit of measure remains sufficiently constant over time. However, the assumption of a stable monetary unit has been challenged because of the significant decline in the purchasing power of the dollar. For example, what used to cost $1.00 in 1960 costs over $4.00 in 2001. In such situations, adding, subtracting, or comparing 1960 dollars with 2001 dollars is highly questionable. The profession has recognized this problem and encourages companies to disclose the effects of changing prices.

Economic Entity Assumption

An economic entity can be any organization or unit in society. It may be a business enterprise (such as General Electric Company), a governmental unit (the state of Ohio), a municipality (Seattle), a school district (St. Louis District 48), or a church (Southern Baptist). The economic entity assumption requires that the activities of the entity be kept separate and distinct from the activities of its owner and all other economic entities. To illustrate, Sally Rider, owner of Sally's Boutique, should keep her personal living costs separate from the expenses of the Boutique. Lands' End, L.L. Bean, and Eddie Bauer are segregated into separate economic entities for accounting purposes.

ACCOUNTING IN ACTION *Ethics Insight*

 A violation of the economic entity assumption contributed to the resignation by the chief executive of **W. R. Grace and Company**. Investors were angered to learn that company funds were used for personal medical care, a Manhattan apartment, and a personal chef for the company's chief. Funds were also used to support a hotel interest owned by the chief executive's son.

We will generally discuss the economic entity assumption in relation to a business enterprise, which may be organized as a proprietorship, partnership, or corporation.

PROPRIETORSHIP. A business owned by one person is generally a **proprietorship**. The owner is often the manager/operator of the business. Small service-type businesses (plumbing companies, beauty salons, and auto repair shops), farms, and small retail stores (antique shops, clothing stores, and used-book stores) are often sole proprietorships. **Usually only a relatively small amount of money (capital) is necessary to start in business as a proprietorship. The owner**

(proprietor) **receives any profits, suffers any losses, and is personally liable for all debts of the business.** There is no legal distinction between the business as an economic unit and the owner, but the accounting records of the business activities are kept separate from the personal records and activities of the owner.

PARTNERSHIP.   A business owned by two or more persons associated as partners is a **partnership.** In most respects a partnership is like a proprietorship except that more than one owner is involved. Typically a partnership agreement (written or oral) sets forth such terms as initial investment, duties of each partner, division of net income (or net loss), and settlement to be made upon death or withdrawal of a partner. Each partner generally has unlimited personal liability for the debts of the partnership. **Like a proprietorship, for accounting purposes the partnership affairs must be kept separate from the personal activities of the partners.** Partnerships are often used to organize retail and service-type businesses, including professional practices (lawyers, doctors, architects, and certified public accountants).

CORPORATION.   A business organized as a separate legal entity under state corporation law and having ownership divided into transferable shares of stock is a **corporation.** The holders of the shares (stockholders) **enjoy limited liability;** that is, they are not personally liable for the debts of the corporate entity. Stockholders **may transfer all or part of their shares to other investors at any time** (i.e., sell their shares). The ease with which ownership can change adds to the attractiveness of investing in a corporation. Because ownership can be transferred without dissolving the corporation, the corporation **enjoys an unlimited life**.

Although the combined number of proprietorships and partnerships in the United States is more than four times the number of corporations, the revenue produced by corporations is nine times greater. Most of the largest enterprises in the United States—for example, **Exxon Mobil**, **General Motors**, **Wal-Mart**, **Citigroup**, and **Lands' End, Inc.**—are corporations.

BASIC ACCOUNTING EQUATION

STUDY OBJECTIVE 6

State the basic accounting equation, and explain the meaning of assets, liabilities, and owner's equity.

**Accounting Cycle Tutorial—
Analyzing Business Transactions**

Illustration 1-6

The basic accounting equation

Other essential building blocks of accounting are the categories into which economic events are classified. The two basic elements of a business are what it owns and what it owes. **Assets** are the resources owned by a business. For example, Lands' End's competitor **Abercrombie & Fitch** has total assets of approximately $458 million. Liabilities and owner's equity are the rights or claims against these resources. Thus, a company such as Abercrombie & Fitch that has $458 million of assets also has $458 million of claims against those assets. Claims of those to whom money is owed (creditors) are called **liabilities**. Claims of owners are called **owner's equity**. For example, Abercrombie & Fitch has liabilities of $147 million and owners' equity of $311 million. This relationship of assets, liabilities, and owner's equity can be expressed as an equation as follows.

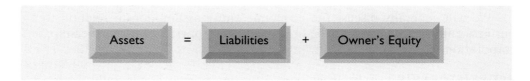

Assets = Liabilities + Owner's Equity

This relationship is referred to as the **basic accounting equation.** Assets must equal the sum of liabilities and owner's equity. Because creditors' claims must be paid before ownership claims if a business is liquidated, liabilities are shown before owner's equity in the basic accounting equation.

The accounting equation applies to all **economic entities** regardless of size, nature of business, or form of business organization. It applies to a small proprietorship such as a corner grocery store as well as to a giant corporation such as Kellogg or General Mills. The equation provides the **underlying framework** for recording and summarizing the economic events of a business enterprise.

Let's look in more detail at the categories in the basic accounting equation.

Assets

As noted above, **assets** are resources owned by a business. They are used in carrying out such activities as production, consumption, and exchange. The common characteristic possessed by all assets is the capacity to provide future services or benefits. In a business enterprise, that service potential or future economic benefit eventually results in cash inflows (receipts) to the enterprise.

For example, the enterprise Campus Pizza owns a delivery truck that provides economic benefits from its use in delivering pizzas. Other assets of Campus Pizza are tables, chairs, jukebox, cash register, oven, mugs and silverware, and, of course, cash.

Liabilities

Liabilities are claims against assets. That is, **liabilities are existing debts and obligations**. For example, businesses of all sizes usually borrow money and purchase merchandise on credit. Campus Pizza, for instance, purchases cheese, sausage, flour, and beverages on credit from suppliers. These obligations are called **accounts payable**. Campus Pizza also has a **note payable** to First National Bank for the money borrowed to purchase the delivery truck. Campus Pizza may also have **wages payable** to employees and **sales and real estate taxes payable** to the local government. All of these persons or entities to whom Campus Pizza owes money are its **creditors**.

Most claims of creditors attach to the entity's **total** assets rather than to the specific assets provided by the creditor. Creditors may legally force the liquidation of a business that does not pay its debts. In that case, the law requires that creditor claims be paid before ownership claims.

Owner's Equity

The ownership claim on total assets is known as **owner's equity**. It is equal to total assets minus total liabilities. Here is why: The assets of a business are supplied or claimed by either creditors or owners. To find out what belongs to owners, we subtract the creditors' claims (the liabilities) from assets. The remainder is the owner's claim on the assets—the owner's equity. Since the claims of creditors must be paid before ownership claims, owner's equity is often referred to as **residual equity**.

INCREASES IN OWNER'S EQUITY.   In a proprietorship, owner's equity is increased by owner's investments and revenues.

Investments by Owner. **Investments by owner** are the assets the owner puts into the business. These investments increase owner's equity.

Revenues. **Revenues** are the **gross increase in owner's equity resulting from business activities entered into for the purpose of earning income**. Generally, revenues result from the sale of merchandise, the performance of services, the rental of property, and the lending of money.

Revenues usually result in an increase in an asset. They may arise from different sources and are identified by various names depending on the nature of the business. Campus Pizza, for instance, has two categories of sales revenues—pizza sales and beverage sales. Common sources of revenue are: sales, fees, services, commissions, interest, dividends, royalties, and rent.

DECREASES IN OWNER'S EQUITY. In a proprietorship, owner's equity is decreased by owner's drawings and expenses.

Drawings. An owner may withdraw cash or other assets for personal use. These withdrawals could be recorded as a direct decrease of owner's equity. However, it is generally considered preferable to use a separate classification called drawings to determine the total withdrawals for each accounting period. **Drawings decrease owner's equity.**

Expenses. Expenses are the cost of assets consumed or services used in the process of earning revenue. They are **decreases in owner's equity that result from operating the business.** Expenses represent actual or expected cash outflows (payments). Like revenues, expenses take many forms and are identified by various names depending on the type of asset consumed or service used. For example, Campus Pizza recognizes the following expenses: cost of ingredients (meat, flour, cheese, tomato paste, mushrooms, etc.); cost of beverages; wages expense; utility expense (electric, gas, and water expense); telephone expense; delivery expense (gasoline, repairs, licenses, etc.); supplies expense (napkins, detergents, aprons, etc.); rent expense; interest expense; and property tax expense.

In summary, owner's equity is increased by an owner's investments and by revenues from business operations. In contrast, owner's equity is decreased by an owner's withdrawals of assets and by expenses. These relationships are shown in Illustration 1-7. Net income results when revenues exceed expenses. A net loss occurs when expenses exceed revenues.

Illustration 1-7

Increases and decreases in owner's equity

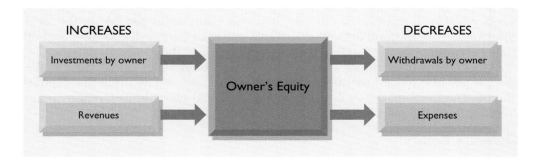

Review It questions marked with this icon require that you use Lands' End's 2000 Annual Report.

BEFORE YOU GO ON...

▶ *REVIEW IT*

1. Why is ethics a fundamental business concept?
2. What are generally accepted accounting principles? Give an example.
3. Explain the monetary unit and the economic entity assumptions.
4. The accounting equation is: Assets = Liabilities + Owner's Equity. Replacing the words in that equation with dollar amounts, what is **Lands' End's** accounting equation at January 28, 2000? (*Hint:* Owner's equity is equivalent to stockholders' equity. The answer to this question is provided on page 41.)
5. What are assets, liabilities, and owner's equity?

▶ *DO IT*

Classify the following items as investment by owner (I), owner's drawings (D), revenues (R), or expenses (E). Then indicate whether the following items increase or decrease owner's equity: (1) rent expense, (2) service revenue, (3) drawings, and (4) salaries expense.

ACTION PLAN
• Review the rules for changes in owner's equity: Investments and revenues increase owner's equity. Expenses and drawings decrease owner's equity.
• Understand the sources of revenue: the sale of merchandise, performance of services, rental of property, and lending of money.

- Understand what causes expenses: the consumption of assets or services.
- Recognize that drawings are withdrawals of cash or other assets from the business for personal use.

SOLUTION
1. Rent expense is classified as an expense (E); it decreases owner's equity.
2. Service revenue is classified as revenue (R); it increases owner's equity.
3. Drawings is classified as owner's drawings (D); it decreases owner's equity.
4. Salaries expense is classified as an expense (E); it decreases owner's equity.

Related exercise material: BE1-1, BE1-2, BE1-3, BE1-4, BE1-5, BE1-6, BE1-7, BE1-9, E1-1, E1-2, E1-3, E1-4, E1-6, and E1-7.

USING THE BUILDING BLOCKS

Transactions (often referred to as business transactions) are the economic events of an enterprise that are recorded. Transactions may be identified as external or internal. **External transactions involve economic events between the company and some outside enterprise.** For example, Campus Pizza's purchase of cooking equipment from a supplier, payment of monthly rent to the landlord, and sale of pizzas to customers are external transactions. **Internal transactions are economic events that occur entirely within one company.** The use of cooking and cleaning supplies illustrates internal transactions for Campus Pizza.

A company may carry on many activities that do not in themselves represent business transactions. Hiring employees, answering the telephone, talking with customers, and placing orders for merchandise are examples. Some of these activities, however, may lead to business transactions: Employees will earn wages, and merchandise will be delivered by suppliers. Each event must be analyzed to find out if it has an effect on the components of the basic accounting equation. If it does, it will be recorded in the accounting process. Illustration 1-8 demonstrates the transaction identification process.

STUDY OBJECTIVE 7

Analyze the effects of business transactions on the basic accounting equation.

Illustration 1-8

Transaction identification process

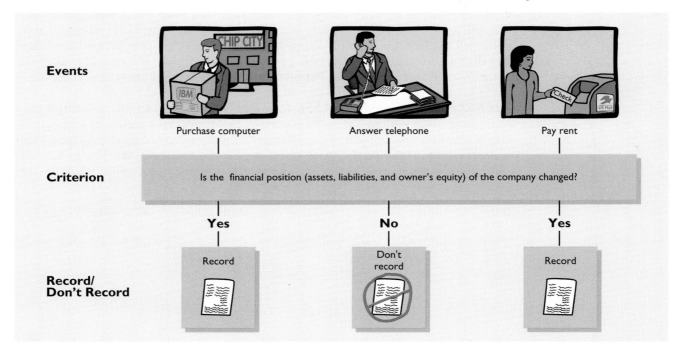

The equality of the basic equation must be preserved. Therefore, each transaction must have a dual effect on the equation. For example, if an asset is increased, there must be a corresponding:

1. Decrease in another asset, or
2. Increase in a specific liability, or
3. Increase in owner's equity.

It follows that two or more items could be affected when an asset is increased. For example, as one asset is increased $10,000, another asset could decrease $6,000 and a specific liability could increase $4,000. Any change in a liability or ownership claim is subject to similar analysis.

TRANSACTION ANALYSIS

The following examples are business transactions for a computer programming business during its first month of operations. You will want to study these transactions until you are sure you understand them. They are not difficult, but they are important to your success in this course. The ability to analyze transactions in terms of the basic accounting equation is essential for an understanding of accounting.

TRANSACTION (1). INVESTMENT BY OWNER.   Ray Neal decides to open a computer programming service which he names Softbyte. On September 1, 2002, he invests $15,000 cash in the business. This transaction results in an equal increase in assets and owner's equity. The asset Cash increases $15,000, as does the owner's equity, identified as R. Neal, Capital. The effect of this transaction on the basic equation is:

	Assets	=	Liabilities	+	Owner's Equity	
	Cash	=			R. Neal, Capital	
(1)	+$15,000	=			+$15,000	Investment

Observe that the equality of the basic equation has been maintained. Note also that the source of the increase in owner's equity (Investment) is indicated. Why does this matter? Because investments by the owner do not represent revenues, and they are excluded in determining net income. Therefore it is necessary to make clear that the increase is an investment rather than revenue from operations.

TRANSACTION (2). PURCHASE OF EQUIPMENT FOR CASH.   Softbyte purchases computer equipment for $7,000 cash. This transaction results in an equal increase and decrease in total assets, though the composition of assets changes: Cash is decreased $7,000, and the asset Equipment is increased $7,000. The specific effect of this transaction and the cumulative effect of the first two transactions are:

		Assets		=	Liabilities	+	Owner's Equity
		Cash	Equipment	=			R. Neal, Capital
	Old Bal.	$15,000					$15,000
(2)		−7,000	+$7,000				
	New Bal.	$ 8,000	$7,000	=			$15,000
		$15,000					

Observe that total assets are still $15,000, and Neal's equity also remains at $15,000, the amount of his original investment.

TRANSACTION (3). PURCHASE OF SUPPLIES ON CREDIT.   Softbyte purchases for $1,600 from Acme Supply Company computer paper and other supplies expected to last several months. Acme agrees to allow Softbyte to pay this bill next month, in October. This transaction is referred to as a purchase on account or a credit purchase. Assets are increased because of the expected future benefits of using the paper and supplies, and liabilities are increased by the amount due Acme Company. The asset Supplies is increased $1,600, and the liability Accounts Payable is increased by the same amount. The effect on the equation is:

		Assets			=	Liabilities	+	Owner's Equity
						Accounts		R. Neal,
		Cash +	Supplies +	Equipment =		Payable	+	Capital
	Old. Bal.	$8,000		$7,000				$15,000
(3)			+$1,600			+$1,600		
	New Bal.	$8,000 +	$1,600 +	$7,000	=	$1,600	+	$15,000
			$16,600				$16,600	

Total assets are now $16,600. This total is matched by a $1,600 creditor's claim and a $15,000 ownership claim.

TRANSACTION (4). SERVICES PROVIDED FOR CASH.   Softbyte receives $1,200 cash from customers for programming services it has provided. This transaction represents Softbyte's principal revenue-producing activity. Recall that **revenue increases owner's equity**. In this transaction, Cash is increased $1,200, and R. Neal, Capital is increased $1,200. The new balances in the equation are:

			Assets				=	Liabilities	+	Owner's Equity	
								Accounts		R. Neal,	
		Cash	+	Supplies	+	Equipment	=	Payable	+	Capital	
	Old Bal.	$8,000		$1,600		$7,000		$1,600		$15,000	
(4)		+1,200								+1,200	Service Revenue
	New Bal.	$9,200	+	$1,600	+	$7,000	=	$1,600	+	$16,200	
				$17,800					$17,800		

The two sides of the equation balance at $17,800. The source of the increase in owner's equity is indicated as Service Revenue. Service revenue is included in determining Softbyte's net income.

TRANSACTION (5). PURCHASE OF ADVERTISING ON CREDIT.   Softbyte receives a bill for $250 from the *Daily News* for advertising but postpones payment of the bill until a later date. This transaction results in an increase in liabilities and a decrease in owner's equity. The specific items involved are Accounts Payable and R. Neal, Capital. The effect on the equation is:

		Assets			=	Liabilities	+	Owner's Equity	
		Cash	+ Supplies	+ Equipment =		Accounts Payable	+	R. Neal, Capital	
	Old Bal.	$9,200	$1,600	$7,000		$1,600		$16,200	
(5)						+250		−250	Advertising Expense
	New Bal.	$9,200 +	$1,600 +	$7,000	=	$1,850	+	$15,950	
			$17,800				$17,800		

The two sides of the equation still balance at $17,800. Owner's equity is decreased when the expense is incurred, and the specific cause of the decrease (advertising expense) is noted. Expenses do not have to be paid in cash at the time they are incurred. When payment is made at a later date, the liability Accounts Payable will be decreased and the asset Cash will be decreased [see Transaction (8)]. The cost of advertising is considered an expense, as opposed to an asset, because the benefits have been used. This expense is included in determining net income.

TRANSACTION (6). SERVICES PROVIDED FOR CASH AND CREDIT.
Softbyte provides $3,500 of programming services for customers. Cash of $1,500 is received from customers, and the balance of $2,000 is billed on account. This transaction results in an equal increase in assets and owner's equity. Three specific items are affected: Cash is increased $1,500; Accounts Receivable is increased $2,000; and R. Neal, Capital is increased $3,500. The new balances are as follows.

		Assets				=	Liabilities	+	Owner's Equity	
		Cash +	Accounts Receivable	+ Supplies	+ Equipment =		Accounts Payable	+	R. Neal, Capital	
	Old Bal.	$9,200		$1,600	$7,000		$1,850		$15,950	
(6)		+1,500	+$2,000						+3,500	Service Revenue
	New Bal.	$10,700 +	$2,000	+ $1,600 +	$7,000	=	$1,850	+	$19,450	
			$21,300					$21,300		

Why increase owner's equity $3,500 when only $1,500 has been collected? Because the inflow of assets resulting from the earning of revenues does not have to be in the form of cash. Remember that owner's equity is increased when revenues are earned; in Softbyte's case revenues are earned when the service is provided. When collections on account are received later, Cash will be increased and Accounts Receivable will be decreased [see Transaction (9)].

TRANSACTION (7). PAYMENT OF EXPENSES. Expenses paid in cash for September are store rent $600, salaries of employees $900, and utilities $200. These payments result in an equal decrease in assets and owner's equity. Cash is decreased $1,700, and R. Neal, Capital is decreased by the same amount. The effect of these payments on the equation is:

		Assets				=	Liabilities	+	Owner's Equity	
	Cash +	Accounts Receivable +	Supplies +	Equipment	=		Accounts Payable	+	R. Neal, Capital	
Old Bal.	$10,700	$2,000	$1,600	$7,000	=		$1,850	+	$19,450	
(7)	−1,700								−600	Rent Expense
									−900	Salaries Expense
									−200	Utilities Expense
New Bal.	$ 9,000 +	$2,000 +	$1,600 +	$7,000	=		$1,850	+	$17,750	
			$19,600					$19,600		

The two sides of the equation now balance at $19,600. Three lines are required in the analysis to indicate the different types of expenses that have been incurred.

TRANSACTION (8).   PAYMENT OF ACCOUNTS PAYABLE.   Softbyte pays its $250 *Daily News* advertising bill in cash. Remember that the bill was previously recorded [in Transaction (5)] as an increase in Accounts Payable and a decrease in owner's equity. This payment "on account" decreases the asset Cash by $250 and also decreases the liability Accounts Payable by $250. The effect of this transaction on the equation is:

			Assets			=	Liabilities	+	Owner's Equity
	Cash +	Accounts Receivable +	Supplies +	Equipment	=	Accounts Payable	+	R. Neal, Capital
Old Bal.	$9,000	$2,000	$1,600	$7,000	=	$1,850	+	$17,750
(8)	−250					−250		
New Bal.	$8,750 +	$2,000 +	$1,600 +	$7,000	=	$1,600	+	$17,750
			$19,350				$19,350	

Observe that the payment of a liability related to an expense that has previously been recorded does not affect owner's equity. The expense was recorded in Transaction (5) and should not be recorded again.

TRANSACTION (9).   RECEIPT OF CASH ON ACCOUNT.   The sum of $600 in cash is received from customers who have previously been billed for services [in Transaction (6)]. This transaction does not change total assets, but it changes the composition of those assets. Cash is increased $600 and Accounts Receivable is decreased $600. The new balances are:

			Assets			=	Liabilities	+	Owner's Equity
	Cash +	Accounts Receivable +	Supplies +	Equipment	=	Accounts Payable	+	R. Neal, Capital
Old Bal.	$8,750	$2,000	$1,600	$7,000	=	$1,600	+	$17,750
(9)	+600	−600						
New Bal.	$9,350 +	$1,400 +	$1,600 +	$7,000	=	$1,600	+	$17,750
			$19,350				$19,350	

Note that a collection on account for services previously billed and recorded does not affect owner's equity. Revenue was already recorded in Transaction (6) and should not be recorded again.

TRANSACTION (10). WITHDRAWAL OF CASH BY OWNER. Ray Neal withdraws $1,300 in cash from the business for his personal use. This transaction results in an equal decrease in assets and owner's equity. Both Cash and R. Neal, Capital are decreased $1,300, as shown below.

		Assets					=	**Liabilities**	+	**Owner's Equity**	
		Cash	+	Accounts Receivable	+ Supplies +	Equipment	=	Accounts Payable	+	R. Neal, Capital	
	Old Bal.	$9,350		$1,400	$1,600	$7,000		$1,600		$17,750	
(10)		−1,300								−1,300	Drawings
	New Bal.	$8,050	+	$1,400 +	$1,600 +	$7,000	=	$1,600	+	$16,450	
				$18,050						$18,050	

Observe that the effect of a cash withdrawal by the owner is the opposite of the effect of an investment by the owner. **Owner's drawings are not expenses.** Like owner's investment, they are excluded in determining net income.

SUMMARY OF TRANSACTIONS

The September transactions of Softbyte are summarized in Illustration 1-9. The transaction number, the specific effects of the transaction, and the balances after each transaction are indicated. The illustration demonstrates some significant facts listed on the next page.

Illustration 1-9

Tabular summary of Softbyte transactions

		Assets				= **Liabilities** +		**Owner's Equity**	
Transaction	Cash	+ Accounts Receivable	+ Supplies +	Equipment =	Accounts Payable	+	R. Neal, Capital	
(1)	+$15,000						+$15,000	Investment
(2)	−7,000			+$7,000				
	8,000		+	7,000 =			15,000	
(3)			+$1,600		+$1,600			
	8,000		+ 1,600 +	7,000 =	1,600	+	15,000	
(4)	+1,200						+1,200	Service Revenue
	9,200		+ 1,600 +	7,000 =	1,600	+	16,200	
(5)					+250		−250	Advertising Expense
	9,200		+ 1,600 +	7,000 =	1,850	+	15,950	
(6)	+1,500	+$2,000					+3,500	Service Revenue
	10,700 +	2,000	+ 1,600 +	7,000 =	1,850	+	19,450	
(7)	−1,700						−600	Rent Expense
							−900	Salaries Expense
							−200	Utilities Expense
	9,000 +	2,000	+ 1,600 +	7,000 =	1,850	+	17,750	
(8)	−250				−250			
	8,750 +	2,000	+ 1,600 +	7,000 =	1,600	+	17,750	
(9)	+600	−600						
	9,350 +	1,400	+ 1,600 +	7,000 =	1,600	+	17,750	
(10)	−1,300						−1,300	Drawings
	$ 8,050 +	$1,400	+ $1,600 +	$7,000 =	$1,600	+	$16,450	
			$18,050			$18,050		

1. Each transaction must be analyzed in terms of its effect on:
   (a) the three components of the basic accounting equation.
   (b) specific types (kinds) of items within each component.

2. The two sides of the equation must always be equal.

3. The causes of each change in the owner's claim on assets must be indicated in the owner's equity column.

There! You made it through transaction analysis. If you feel a bit shaky on any of the transactions, it might be a good idea at this point to get up, take a short break, and come back again for a 10- to 15-minute review of the transactions, to make sure you understand them before you go on to the next section.

BEFORE YOU GO ON...

▶ *REVIEW IT*

1. What is an example of an external transaction? What is an example of an internal transaction?

2. If an asset increases, what are the three possible effects on the basic accounting equation?

▶ *DO IT*

A tabular analysis of the transactions made by Roberta Mendez & Co., a certified public accounting firm, for the month of August is shown below. Each increase and decrease in owner's equity is explained.

	Assets			=	Liabilities	+		Owner's Equity	
			Office		Accounts			R. Mendez,	
	Cash	+	Equipment	=	Payable	+		Capital	
1.	+$25,000						+25,000	Investment	
2.			+7,000		+7,000				
3.	+8,000						+8,000	Service Revenue	
4.	−850						−850	Rent Expense	

Describe each transaction that occurred for the month.

ACTION PLAN
- Analyze the tabular analysis to determine the nature and effect of each transaction.
- Keep the accounting equation always in balance.
- Remember that a change in an asset will require a change in another asset, a liability, or in owner's equity.

SOLUTION

1. The owner invested $25,000 of cash in the business.
2. The company purchased $7,000 of office equipment on credit.
3. The company received $8,000 of cash in exchange for services performed.
4. The company paid $850 for this month's rent.

Related exercise material: BE1-4, BE1-5, BE1-6, BE1-7, E1-2, E1-3, E1-4, E1-6, and E1-7.

☑ THE NAVIGATOR

FINANCIAL STATEMENTS

STUDY OBJECTIVE **8**

Understand what the four financial statements are and how they are prepared.

After transactions are identified, recorded, and summarized, four financial statements are prepared from the summarized accounting data:

1. An **income statement** presents the revenues and expenses and resulting net income or net loss for a specific period of time.
2. An **owner's equity statement** summarizes the changes in owner's equity for a specific period of time.
3. A **balance sheet** reports the assets, liabilities, and owner's equity at a specific date.
4. A **statement of cash flows** summarizes information about the cash inflows (receipts) and outflows (payments) for a specific period of time.

HELPFUL HINT

The income statement, owner's equity statement, and statement of cash flows are all for a *period* of time, whereas the balance sheet is for a *point* in time.

Each statement provides management, owners, and other interested parties with relevant financial data.

The financial statements of Softbyte are shown in Illustration 1-10. The statements are interrelated: **(1) Net income of $2,750 shown on the income statement is added to the beginning balance of owner's capital in the owner's equity statement. (2) Owner's capital of $16,450 at the end of the reporting period shown in the owner's equity statement is reported on the balance sheet. (3) Cash of $8,050 on the balance sheet is reported on the statement of cash flows.**

Also, every set of financial statements is accompanied by explanatory notes and supporting schedules that are an integral part of the statements. Examples of these notes and schedules are illustrated in later chapters of this textbook.

Be sure to carefully examine the format and content of each statement. The essential features of each are briefly described in the following sections.

INCOME STATEMENT

ALTERNATIVE TERMINOLOGY
The income statement is sometimes referred to as the *statement of operations, earnings statement,* or *profit and loss statement.*

Softbyte's income statement reports the revenues and expenses for a specific period of time (in this case, "For the Month Ended September 30, 2002"). Its income statement is prepared from the data appearing in the owner's equity column of Illustration 1-9.

On the income statement, revenues are listed first, followed by expenses. Finally net income (or net loss) is determined. Although practice varies, we have chosen in our illustrations and homework solutions to list expenses in order of magnitude. Alternative formats for the income statement will be considered in later chapters.

Note that investment and withdrawal transactions between the owner and the business are not included in the measurement of net income. For example, the withdrawal by Ray Neal of cash from Softbyte was not regarded as a business expense, as explained earlier.

OWNER'S EQUITY STATEMENT

Softbyte's owner's equity statement reports the changes in owner's equity for a specific period of time. The time period is the same as that covered by the income statement. Data for the preparation of the owner's equity statement are obtained from the owner's equity column of the tabular summary (Illustration 1-9) and from the income statement. The beginning owner's equity amount is shown on the first line of the statement. Then, the owner's investments, net income, and the owner's drawings are identified. The information in this statement indicates the reasons why owner's equity has increased or decreased during the period.

SOFTBYTE
Income Statement
For the Month Ended September 30, 2002

Revenues		
Service revenue		$4,700
Expenses		
Salaries expense	$900	
Rent expense	600	
Advertising expense	250	
Utilities expense	200	
Total expenses		1,950
Net income		$2,750

①

SOFTBYTE
Owner's Equity Statement
For the Month Ended September 30, 2002

R. Neal, Capital, September 1		$ –0–
Add: Investments	$15,000	
Net income	2,750	17,750
		17,750
Less: Drawings		1,300
R. Neal, Capital, September 30		$16,450

SOFTBYTE
Balance Sheet
September 30, 2002

Assets

Cash	$ 8,050
Accounts receivable	1,400
Supplies	1,600
Equipment	7,000
Total assets	$18,050

Liabilities and Owner's Equity

Liabilities	
Accounts payable	$ 1,600
Owner's equity	
R. Neal, Capital	16,450
Total liabilities and owner's equity	$18,050

② ③

SOFTBYTE
Statement of Cash Flows
For the Month Ended September 30, 2002

Cash flows from operating activities		
Cash receipts from revenues	$3,300	
Cash payments for expenses	(1,950)	
Net cash provided by operating activities		1,350
Cash flows from investing activities		
Purchase of equipment		(7,000)
Cash flows from financing activities		
Investments by owner	$15,000	
Drawings by owner	(1,300)	13,700
Net increase in cash		8,050
Cash at the beginning of the period		0
Cash at the end of the period		$8,050

Illustration 1-10

Financial statements and their interrelationships

HELPFUL HINT
The heading of each statement identifies the company, the type of statement, and the specific date or time period covered by the statement.

HELPFUL HINT
Note that final sums are double-underlined, and negative amounts are presented in parentheses.

HELPFUL HINT
Net income is computed first and is needed to determine the ending balance in owner's equity. The ending balance in owner's equity is needed in preparing the balance sheet. The cash shown on the balance sheet is needed in preparing the statement of cash flows.

What if Softbyte reported a net loss in its first month? Let's assume that during the month of September 2002, Softbyte lost $10,000. The presentation in the owner's equity statement of a net loss appears in Illustration 1-11.

Illustration 1-11

Presentation of net loss

SOFTBYTE Owner's Equity Statement For the Month Ended September 30, 2002		
R. Neal, Capital, September 1		$ – 0 –
Add: Investments		15,000
		15,000
Less: Drawings	$ 1,300	
Net loss	10,000	11,300
R. Neal, Capital, September 30		$ 3,700

Any additional investments are reported as investments in the owner's equity statement.

BALANCE SHEET

Softbyte's balance sheet reports the assets, liabilities, and owner's equity at a specific date (in this case, September 30, 2002). The balance sheet is prepared from the column headings and the month-end data shown in the last line of the tabular summary (Illustration 1-9). Observe that the assets are listed at the top, followed by liabilities and owner's equity. Total assets must equal total liabilities and owner's equity. In the Softbyte balance sheet, only one liability, accounts payable, is reported. In most cases, there will be more than one liability. When two or more liabilities are involved, a customary way of listing is as follows.

Illustration 1-12

Presentation of liabilities

Liabilities	
Notes payable	$10,000
Accounts payable	63,000
Salaries payable	18,000
Total liabilities	$91,000

The balance sheet is like a snapshot of the company's financial condition at a specific moment in time (usually the month-end or year-end).

ACCOUNTING IN ACTION Business Insight

Why do companies choose the particular year-ends that they do? Not every company uses December 31 as the accounting year-end. Many companies choose to end their accounting year when inventory or operations are at a low. This is advantageous because compiling accounting information requires much time and effort by managers, so they would rather do it when they aren't as busy operating the business. Also, inventory is easier and less costly to count when it is low. Some companies whose year-ends differ from December 31 are **Delta Air Lines**, June 30; **Walt Disney Productions**, September 30; **Kmart Corp.**, January 31; and **Dunkin' Donuts Inc.**, October 31.

STATEMENT OF CASH FLOWS

Softbyte's statement of cash flows provides information on the cash receipts and payments for a specific period of time. The statement of cash flows reports (1) the cash effects of a company's operations during a period, (2) its investing transactions, (3) its financing transactions, (4) the net increase or decrease in cash during the period, and (5) the cash amount at the end of the period.

> **HELPFUL HINT**
> Investing activities pertain to investments made by the company, not investments made by the owner.

Reporting the sources, uses, and net increase or decrease in cash is useful because investors, creditors, and others want to know what is happening to a company's most liquid resource. The statement of cash flows, therefore, provides answers to the following simple but important questions.

1. Where did the cash come from during the period?
2. What was the cash used for during the period?
3. What was the change in the cash balance during the period?

Softbyte's statement of cash flows is provided in Illustration 1-10.

As shown in the statement, cash increased $8,050 during the period. Net cash flow provided from operating activities increased cash $1,350. Cash flow from investing transactions decreased cash $7,000. And cash flow from financing transactions increased cash $13,700. At this time, you need not be concerned with how these amounts are determined. Chapter 18 will examine the statement of cash flows in detail.

BEFORE YOU GO ON...

▶ *REVIEW IT*
1. What are the income statement, statement of owner's equity, balance sheet, and statement of cash flows?
2. How are the financial statements interrelated?

A LOOK BACK AT OUR FEATURE STORY

Refer back to the Feature Story about **Lands' End** at the beginning of the chapter, and answer the following questions.
1. If you were interested in investing in Lands' End, what would the balance sheet and income statement tell you?
2. Would you request audited financial statements? Explain.
3. Will the financial statements show the market value of the company? Explain.

A Look Back exercises refer to the chapter-opening Feature Story. These exercises help you analyze that real-world situation in terms of the accounting topic of the chapter.

SOLUTION
1. The balance sheet reports the assets, liabilities, and owner's equity of the company. The income statement presents the revenues and expenses and resulting net income (or net loss) for a specific period of time. The balance sheet is like a snapshot of the company's financial condition at a point in time. The income statement indicates the profitability of the company. Also, the sources of the company's revenues and its expenses are provided in the income statement.
2. You should request **audited** financial statements—statements that a CPA has examined and expressed an opinion as to the fairness of presentation. You should not make decisions without having audited financial statements.
3. The financial statements will not show the market value of the company. One important principle of accounting is the cost principle, which states that assets should be recorded at cost. Cost has an important advantage over other valuations: it is reliable.

> ☑ THE NAVIGATOR

Demonstration Problems are a final review of the chapter. The **Action Plan** gives tips about how to approach the problem, and the **solution** demonstrates both the form and content of complete answers.

DEMONSTRATION PROBLEM

Mary Malone opens her own law office on July 1, 2002. During the first month of operations, the following transactions occurred.

1. Invested $10,000 in cash in the law practice.
2. Paid $800 for July rent on office space.
3. Purchased office equipment on account $3,000.
4. Provided legal services to clients for cash $1,500.
5. Borrowed $700 cash from a bank on a note payable.
6. Performed legal services for client on account $2,000.
7. Paid monthly expenses: salaries $500, utilities $300, and telephone $100.

Instructions

(a) Prepare a tabular summary of the transactions.

(b) Prepare the income statement, owner's equity statement, and balance sheet at July 31 for Mary Malone, Attorney at Law.

ACTION PLAN

- Remember that assets must equal liabilities and owner's equity after each transaction.
- Investments and revenues increase owner's equity.
- Expenses decrease owner's equity.
- The income statement shows revenues and expenses for a period of time.
- The owner's equity statement shows the changes in owner's equity for a period of time.
- The balance sheet reports assets, liabilities, and owner's equity at a specific date.

SOLUTION TO DEMONSTRATION PROBLEM

(a)

Trans-action	Cash	+ Accounts Receivable	+ Equipment	= Notes Payable	+ Accounts Payable	+ Mary Malone, Capital	
(1)	+$10,000					+$10,000	Investment
(2)	−800					−800	Rent Expense
	9,200			=		9,200	
(3)			+$3,000		+$3,000		
	9,200	+	3,000	=	3,000	+ 9,200	
(4)	+1,500					+1,500	Service Revenue
	10,700	+	3,000	=	3,000	+ 10,700	
(5)	+700			+$700			
	11,400	+	3,000	= 700	+ 3,000	+ 10,700	
(6)		+$2,000				+2,000	Service Revenue
	11,400 +	2,000	+ 3,000	= 700	+ 3,000	+ 12,700	
(7)	−900					−500	Salaries Expense
						−300	Utilities Expense
						−100	Telephone Expense
	$10,500 +	$2,000	+ $3,000	= $700	+ $3,000	+ $11,800	

Assets = Liabilities + Owner's Equity

(b)

MARY MALONE
Attorney at Law
Income Statement
For the Month Ended July 31, 2002

Revenues		
Service revenue		$3,500
Expenses		
Rent expense	$800	
Salaries expense	500	
Utilities expense	300	
Telephone expense	100	
Total expenses		1,700
Net income		$1,800

CHAPTER

28

7. *Analyze*
   accounting
   dual effe
   dividua
   decre
   ity.

8.

MARY MALONE
Attorney at Law
Owner's Equity Statement
For the Month Ended July 31, 2002

Mary Malone, Capital, July 1		$ –0–
Add: Investments	$10,000	
Net income	1,800	11,800
Mary Malone, Capital, July 31		$11,800

MARY MALONE
Attorney at Law
Balance Sheet
July 31, 2002

Assets

Cash	$10,500
Accounts receivable	2,000
Equipment	3,000
Total assets	$15,500

Liabilities and Owner's Equity

Liabilities	
Notes payable	$ 700
Accounts payable	3,000
Total liabilities	3,700
Owner's equity	
Mary Malone, Capital	11,800
Total liabilities and owner's equity	$15,500

☑ THE NAVIGATOR

first
fore) to
ous types of a
rials that appear at
each chapter. Knowing
purpose of the different assignments will help you appreciate what each contributes to
your accounting skills and
competencies.

SUMMARY OF STUDY OBJECTIVES

1. *Explain what accounting is.* Accounting is an information system that identifies, records, and communicates the economic events of an organization to interested users.

2. *Identify the users and uses of accounting.* The major users and uses of accounting are: (a) Management uses accounting information in planning, controlling, and evaluating business operations. (b) Investors (owners) decide whether to buy, hold, or sell their financial interests on the basis of accounting data. (c) Creditors (suppliers and bankers) evaluate the risks of granting credit or lending money on the basis of accounting information. Other groups that use accounting information are taxing authorities, regulatory agencies, customers, labor unions, and economic planners.

3. *Understand why ethics is a fundamental business concept.* Ethics are the standards of conduct by which actions are judged as right or wrong. If you cannot depend on the honesty of the individuals you deal with, effective communication and economic activity would be impossible, and information would have no credibility.

4. *Explain the meaning of generally accepted accounting principles and the cost principle.* Generally accepted accounting principles are a common set of standards used by accountants. The cost principle states that assets should be recorded at their cost.

5. *Explain the meaning of the monetary unit assumption and the economic entity assumption.* The monetary unit assumption requires that only transaction data capable of being expressed in terms of money be included in the accounting records. The economic entity assumption requires that the activities of each economic entity be kept separate from the activities of its owner and other economic entities.

6. *State the basic accounting equation, and explain the meaning of assets, liabilities, and owner's equity.* The basic accounting equation is:

$$\text{Assets} = \text{Liabilities} + \text{Owner's Equity}$$

Assets are resources owned by a business. Liabilities are creditorship claims on total assets. Owner's equity is the ownership claim on total assets.

he effects of business transactions on the basic equation. Each business transaction must have a [effect] on the accounting equation. For example, if an [in-] asset is increased, there must be a corresponding (1) [decrea]se in another asset, or (2) increase in a specific liabil[ity, o]r (3) increase in owner's equity.

[U]nderstand what the four financial statements are and [h]ow they are prepared. An income statement presents the revenues and expenses of a company for a specified pe-riod of time. An owner's equity statement summarizes the changes in owner's equity that have occurred for a spe-cific period of time. A balance sheet reports the assets, li-abilities, and owner's equity of a business at a specific date. A statement of cash flows summarizes information about the cash inflows (receipts) and outflows (payments) for a specific period of time.

Key Term Matching Activity

GLOSSARY

Accounting The information system that identifies, records, and communicates the economic events of an organization to interested users. (p. 2).

Assets Resources owned by a business. (p. 13).

Auditing The examination of financial statements by a cer-tified public accountant in order to express an opinion as to the fairness of presentation. (p. 7).

Balance sheet A financial statement that reports the assets, liabilities, and owner's equity at a specific date. (p. 22).

Basic accounting equation Assets = Liabilities + Owner's Equity. (p. 12).

Bookkeeping A part of accounting that involves only the recording of economic events. (p. 6).

Corporation A business organized as a separate legal entity under state corporation law, having ownership divided into transferable shares of stock. (p. 12).

Cost principle An accounting principle that states that as-sets should be recorded at their cost. (p. 10).

Drawings Withdrawal of cash or other assets from an unin-corporated business for the personal use of the owner(s). (p. 14).

Economic entity assumption An assumption that requires that the activities of the entity be kept separate and distinct from the activities of its owner and all other economic entities. (p. 11).

Ethics The standards of conduct by which one's actions are judged as right or wrong, honest or dishonest, fair or not fair. (p. 9).

Expenses The cost of assets consumed or services used in the process of earning revenue. (p. 14).

Financial accounting The field of accounting that provides economic and financial information for investors, creditors, and other external users. (p. 6).

Financial Accounting Standards Board (FASB) A private organization that establishes generally accepted accounting principles. (p. 10).

Generally accepted accounting principles (GAAP) Com-mon standards that indicate how to report economic events. (p. 10).

Income statement A financial statement that presents the revenues and expenses and resulting net income or net loss of a company for a specific period of time. (p. 22).

Investments by owner The assets put into the business by the owner. (p. 13).

Liabilities Creditorship claims on total assets. (p. 13).

Management consulting An area of public accounting that involves financial planning and control and the development of accounting and computer systems. (p. 7).

Managerial accounting The field of accounting that provides economic and financial information for managers and other internal users. (p. 6)

Monetary unit assumption An assumption stating that only transaction data that can be expressed in terms of money be included in the accounting records. (p. 11).

Net income The amount by which revenues exceed ex-penses. (p. 14).

Net loss The amount by which expenses exceed revenues. (p. 14).

Owner's equity The ownership claim on total assets. (p. 13).

Owner's equity statement A financial statement that sum-marizes the changes in owner's equity for a specific period of time. (p. 22).

Partnership An association of two or more persons to carry on as co-owners of a business for profit. (p. 12).

Private (or managerial) accounting An area of accounting within a company that involves such activities as cost account-ing, budgeting, and accounting information systems. (p. 7).

Proprietorship A business owned by one person. (p. 11).

Public accounting An area of accounting in which the ac-countant offers expert service to the general public. (p. 7).

Revenues The gross increase in owner's equity resulting from business activities entered into for the purpose of earn-ing income. (p. 13).

Securities and Exchange Commission (SEC) A governmen-tal agency that requires companies to file financial reports in accordance with generally accepted accounting principles. (p. 10).

Statement of cash flows A financial statement that summa-rizes information about the cash inflows (receipts) and cash outflows (payments) for a specific period of time. (p. 22).

Taxation An area of public accounting that involves tax ad-vice, tax planning, and preparing tax returns. (p. 7).

Transactions The economic events of an enterprise that are recorded by accountants. (p. 15).

SELF-STUDY QUESTIONS

Answers are at the end of the chapter.

(SO 1) **1.** Which of the following is *not* a step in the accounting process?
- a. identification.
- c. recording.
- b. verification.
- d. communication.

(SO 2) **2.** Which of the following statements about users of accounting information is *incorrect*?
- a. Management is an internal user.
- b. Taxing authorities are external users.
- c. Present creditors are external users.
- d. Regulatory authorities are internal users.

(SO 2) **3.** Services provided by a public accountant include:
- a. auditing, taxation, and management consulting.
- b. auditing, budgeting, and management consulting.
- c. auditing, budgeting, and cost accounting.
- d. internal auditing, budgeting, and management consulting.

(SO 4) **4.** The cost principle states that:
- a. assets should be initially recorded at cost and adjusted when the market value changes.
- b. activities of an entity are to be kept separate and distinct from its owner.
- c. assets should be recorded at their cost.
- d. only transaction data capable of being expressed in terms of money be included in the accounting records.

(SO 5) **5.** Which of the following statements about basic assumptions is *incorrect*?
- a. Basic assumptions are the same as accounting principles.
- b. The economic entity assumption states that there should be a particular unit of accountability.
- c. The monetary unit assumption enables accounting to measure economic events.
- d. An important part of the monetary unit assumption is the stable monetary unit assumption.

6. Net income will result during a time period when: (SO 6)
- a. assets exceed liabilities.
- b. assets exceed revenues.
- c. expenses exceed revenues.
- d. revenues exceed expenses.

7. Performing services on account will have the following (SO 7) effects on the components of the basic accounting equation:
- a. increase assets and decrease owner's equity.
- b. increase assets and increase owner's equity.
- c. increase assets and increase liabilities.
- d. increase liabilities and increase owner's equity.

8. As of December 31, 2002, Stoneland Company has as- (SO 7) sets of $3,500 and owner's equity of $2,000. What are the liabilities for Stoneland Company as of December 31, 2002?
- a. $1,500.
- b. $1,000.
- c. $2,500.
- d. $2,000.

9. On the last day of the period, Genesis Company buys a (SO 8) $900 machine on credit. This transaction will affect the:
- a. income statement only.
- b. balance sheet only.
- c. income statement and owner's equity statement only.
- d. income statement, owner's equity statement, and balance sheet.

10. The financial statement that reports assets, liabilities, (SO 8) and owner's equity is the:
- a. income statement.
- b. owner's equity statement.
- c. balance sheet.
- d. statement of cash flow.

QUESTIONS

1. "Accounting is ingrained in our society and it is vital to our economic system." Do you agree? Explain.

2. Identify and describe the steps in the accounting process.

3. (a) Who are internal users of accounting data?(b) How does accounting provide relevant data to these users?

4. What uses of financial accounting information are made by (a) investors and (b) creditors?

5. "Bookkeeping and accounting are the same." Do you agree? Explain.

6. John Alcorn Travel Agency purchased land for $85,000 cash on December 10, 2002. At December 31, 2002, the land's value has increased to $93,000. What amount should be reported for land on John Alcorn's balance sheet at December 31, 2002? Explain.

7. What is the monetary unit assumption? What impact does inflation have on the monetary unit assumption?

8. What is the economic entity assumption?

9. What are the three basic forms of business organizations for profit-oriented enterprises?

10. Kathy Mendoza is the owner of a successful printing shop. Recently her business has been increasing, and Kathy has been thinking about changing the organization of her business from a proprietorship to a corporation. Discuss some of the advantages Kathy would enjoy if she were to incorporate her business.

11. What is the basic accounting equation?

12. (a) Define the terms assets, liabilities, and owner's equity. (b) What items affect owner's equity?

13. Which of the following items are liabilities of Design Jewelry Stores?
    - (a) Cash.
    - (b) Accounts payable.
    - (c) Drawings.
    - (d) Accounts receivable.
    - (e) Supplies.
    - (f) Equipment.
    - (g) Salaries payable.
    - (h) Service revenue.
    - (i) Rent expense.

14. Can a business enter into a transaction in which only the left side of the basic accounting equation is affected? If so, give an example.

15. Are the following events recorded in the accounting records? Explain your answer in each case.
    - (a) The owner of the company dies.
    - (b) Supplies are purchased on account.
    - (c) An employee is fired.
    - (d) The owner of the business withdraws cash from the business for personal use.

16. Indicate how the following business transactions affect the basic accounting equation.
    - (a) Paid cash for janitorial services.
    - (b) Purchased equipment for cash.
    - (c) Invested cash in the business.
    - (d) Paid accounts payable in full.

17. Listed below are some items found in the financial statements of Alberto Rivera Co. Indicate in which financial statement(s) the following items would appear.
    - (a) Service revenue.
    - (b) Equipment.
    - (c) Advertising expense.
    - (d) Accounts receivable.
    - (e) Alberto Rivera, Capital.
    - (f) Wages payable.

18. In February 2002, Joe Kirby invested an additional $10,000 in his business, Kirby's Pharmacy, which is organized as a proprietorship. Kirby's accountant, Lance Jones, recorded this receipt as an increase in cash and revenues. Is this treatment appropriate? Why or why not?

19. "A company's net income appears directly on the income statement and the owner's equity statement, and it is included indirectly in the company's balance sheet." Do you agree? Explain.

20. King Enterprises had a capital balance of $168,000 at the beginning of the period. At the end of the accounting period, the capital balance was $198,000.
    - (a) Assuming no additional investment or withdrawals during the period, what is the net income for the period?
    - (b) Assuming an additional investment of $13,000 but no withdrawals during the period, what is the net income for the period?

21. Summarized operations for Kaustav Sen Co. for the month of July are as follows.

    Revenues earned: for cash $35,000; on account $70,000.

    Expenses incurred: for cash $26,000; on account $40,000.

    Indicate for Kaustav Sen Co. (a) the total revenues, (b) the total expenses, and (c) net income for the month of July.

BRIEF EXERCISES

Use basic accounting equation.
(SO 6)

BE1-1 Presented below is the basic accounting equation. Determine the missing amounts.

	Assets	=	Liabilities	+	Owner's Equity
(a)	$80,000		$50,000		?
(b)	?		$45,000		$70,000
(c)	$94,000		?		$62,000

Use basic accounting equation.
(SO 6)

BE1-2 Given the accounting equation, answer each of the following questions.
- (a) The liabilities of Weber Company are $100,000 and the owner's equity is $252,000. What is the amount of Weber Company's total assets?
- (b) The total assets of Kafka Company are $170,000 and its owner's equity is $80,000. What is the amount of its total liabilities?
- (c) The total assets of Motzek Co. are $600,000 and its liabilities are equal to one half of its total assets. What is the amount of Motzek Co.'s owner's equity?

Use basic accounting equation.
(SO 6)

BE1-3 At the beginning of the year, Gilles Company had total assets of $820,000 and total liabilities of $500,000. Answer the following questions.
- (a) If total assets increased $150,000 during the year and total liabilities decreased $80,000, what is the amount of owner's equity at the end of the year?
- (b) During the year, total liabilities increased $100,000 and owner's equity decreased $70,000. What is the amount of total assets at the end of the year?
- (c) If total assets decreased $90,000 and owner's equity increased $120,000 during the year, what is the amount of total liabilities at the end of the year?

Determine effect of transactions on basic accounting equation.
(SO 7)

BE1-4 Presented below are three business transactions. On a sheet of paper, list the letters (a), (b), (c) with columns for assets, liabilities, and owner's equity. For each column, indicate whether the transactions increased (+), decreased (−), or had no effect (NE) on assets, liabilities, and owner's equity.

(a) Purchased supplies on account.

(b) Received cash for providing a service.

(c) Paid expenses in cash.

BE1-5 Follow the same format as BE1-4 above. Determine the effect on assets, liabilities, and owner's equity of the following three transactions.

Determine effect of transactions on basic accounting equation.
(SO 7)

(a) Invested cash in the business.

(b) Withdrawal of cash by owner.

(c) Received cash from a customer who had previously been billed for services provided.

BE1-6 Classify each of the following items as owner's drawing (D), revenue (R), or expense (E).

Determine effect of transactions on owner's equity.
(SO 7)

____**(a)** Advertising expense

____**(b)** Commission revenue

____**(c)** Insurance expense

____**(d)** Salaries expense

____**(e)** Farve, Drawing

____**(f)** Rent revenue

____**(g)** Utilities expense

BE1-7 Presented below are three transactions. Mark each transaction as affecting owner's investment (I), owner's drawings (D), revenue (R), expense (E), or not affecting owner's equity (NOE).

Determine effect of transactions on owner's equity.
(SO 7)

____**(a)** Received cash for services performed

____**(b)** Paid cash to purchase equipment

____**(c)** Paid employee salaries.

BE1-8 In alphabetical order below are balance sheet items for Cheng Company at December 31, 2002. Kim Cheng is the owner of Cheng Company. Prepare a balance sheet, following the format of Illustration 1-10.

Prepare a balance sheet.
(SO 8)

Accounts payable	$80,000
Accounts receivable	$72,500
Cash	$39,000
Kim Cheng, Capital	$31,500

BE1-9 Indicate whether each of the following items is an asset (A), liability (L), or part of owner's equity (OE).

Identify assets, liabilities, and owner's equity.
(SO 6)

____**(a)** Accounts receivable

____**(b)** Salaries payable

____**(c)** Equipment

____**(d)** Office supplies

____**(e)** Owner's investment

____**(f)** Notes payable

BE1-10 Indicate whether the following items would appear on the income statement (IS), balance sheet (BS), or owner's equity statement (OE).

Determine where items appear on financial statements.
(SO 8)

____**(a)** Notes payable

____**(b)** Advertising expense

____**(c)** H. Bruns, Capital

____**(d)** Cash

____**(e)** Service revenue

Exercises

E1-1 Robbins Cleaners has the following balance sheet items.

Classify accounts as assets, liabilities, and owner's equity.
(SO 6)

Accounts payable	Accounts receivable
Cash	Notes payable
Cleaning equipment	Salaries payable
Cleaning supplies	J. Robbins, Capital

Instructions

Classify each item as an asset, liability, or owner's equity.

E1-2 Selected transactions for Green Acres Lawn Care Company are listed below.

Analyze the effect of transactions.
(SO 6, 7)

1. Made cash investment to start business.

2. Paid monthly rent.

3. Purchased equipment on account.
4. Billed customers for services performed.
5. Withdrew cash for owner's personal use.
6. Received cash from customers billed in (4).
7. Incurred advertising expense on account.
8. Purchased additional equipment for cash.
9. Received cash from customers when service was performed.

Instructions

List the numbers of the above transactions and describe the effect of each transaction on assets, liabilities, and owner's equity. For example, the first answer is: (1) Increase in assets and increase in owner's equity.

Analyze the effect of transactions on assets, liabilities, and owner's equity.
(SO 6, 7)

E1-3   Kidman Computer Timeshare Company entered into the following transactions during May 2002.

1. Purchased computer terminals for $21,500 from Digital Equipment on account.
2. Paid $4,000 cash for May rent on storage space.
3. Received $15,000 cash from customers for contracts billed in April.
4. Provided computer services to Fisher Construction Company for $3,000 cash.
5. Paid Northern States Power Co. $11,000 cash for energy usage in May.
6. Kidman invested an additional $32,000 in the business.
7. Paid Digital Equipment for the terminals purchased in (1) above.
8. Incurred advertising expense for May of $1,200 on account.

Instructions

Indicate with the appropriate letter whether each of the transactions above results in:

(a) an increase in assets and a decrease in assets.
(b) an increase in assets and an increase in owner's equity.
(c) an increase in assets and an increase in liabilities.
(d) a decrease in assets and a decrease in owner's equity.
(e) a decrease in assets and a decrease in liabilities.
(f) an increase in liabilities and a decrease in owner's equity.
(g) an increase in owner's equity and a decrease in liabilities.

Analyze transactions and compute net income.
(SO 7)

E1-4   An analysis of the transactions made by Roberta Mendez & Co., a certified public accounting firm, for the month of August is shown below. Each increase and decrease in owner's equity is explained.

	Cash	+ Accounts Receivable	+ Supplies	+ Office Equipment	= Accounts Payable	+ Owner's Equity R. Mendez, Capital	
1.	+$12,000					+$12,000	Investment
2.	−2,000			+$5,000	+$3,000		
3.	−750		+$750				
4.	+2,600	+$3,700				+6,300	Service Revenue
5.	−1,500				−1,500		
6.	−2,000					−2,000	Drawings
7.	−650					−650	Rent Expense
8.	+450	−450					
9.	−2,900					−2,900	Salaries Expense
10.					+500	−500	Utilities Expense

Instructions

(a) ▭▭▭▶ Describe each transaction that occurred for the month.
(b) Determine how much owner's equity increased for the month.
(c) Compute the amount of net income for the month.

Prepare an income statement and owner's equity statement.
(SO 8)

E1-5   An analysis of transactions for Roberta Mendez & Co. was presented in E1-4.

Instructions

Prepare an income statement and an owner's equity statement for August and a balance sheet at August 31, 2002.

E1-6 The Padre Company had the following assets and liabilities on the dates indicated.

Determine net income (or loss).
(SO 7)

December 31	Total Assets	Total Liabilities
2002	$400,000	$250,000
2003	$460,000	$305,000
2004	$590,000	$400,000

Padre began business on January 1, 2002, with an investment of $100,000.

Instructions

From an analysis of the change in owner's equity during the year, compute the net income (or loss) for:

(a) 2002, assuming Padre's drawings were $15,000 for the year.

(b) 2003, assuming Padre made an additional investment of $50,000 and had no drawings in 2003.

(c) 2004, assuming Padre made an additional investment of $15,000 and had drawings of $20,000 in 2004.

E1-7 Two items are omitted from each of the following summaries of balance sheet and income statement data for two proprietorships for the year 2002, Neve Campbell and Maxim Enterprises.

Analyze financial statements items.
(SO 6, 7)

	Neve Campbell	Maxim Enterprises
Beginning of year:		
Total assets	$ 97,000	$129,000
Total liabilities	80,000	(c)
Total owner's equity	(a)	95,000
End of year:		
Total assets	160,000	180,000
Total liabilities	120,000	50,000
Total owner's equity	40,000	130,000
Changes during year in owner's equity:		
Additional investment	(b)	25,000
Drawings	24,000	(d)
Total revenues	215,000	100,000
Total expenses	175,000	85,000

Instructions

Determine the missing amounts.

E1-8 The following information relates to Stanley Tucci Co. for the year 2002.

Prepare income statement and owner's equity statement.
(SO 8)

Stanley Tucci, Capital, January 1, 2002	$ 48,000	Advertising expense	$ 1,800
Stanley Tucci, Drawing during 2002	5,000	Rent expense	10,400
Service revenue	57,500	Utilities expense	3,100
Salaries expense	28,000		

Instructions

After analyzing the data, prepare an income statement and an owner's equity statement for the year ending December 31, 2002.

E1-9 Glenn Close is the bookkeeper for Amaro Company. Glenn has been trying to get the balance sheet of Amaro Company to balance. Amaro's balance sheet is as follows.

Correct an incorrectly prepared balance sheet.
(SO 8)

AMARO COMPANY
Balance Sheet
December 31, 2002

Assets		Liabilities	
Cash	$20,500	Accounts payable	$20,000
Supplies	8,000	Accounts receivable	(8,500)
Equipment	46,000	Amaro, Capital	67,500
Amaro, Drawing	4,500	Total liabilities and	
Total assets	$79,000	owner's equity	$79,000

Compute net income and prepare a balance sheet.
(SO 8)

Instructions
Prepare a correct balance sheet.

E1-10 Kap Shin is the sole owner of Bear Park, a public camping ground near the Lake Mead National Recreation Area. Kap has compiled the following financial information as of December 31, 2002.

Revenues during 2002—camping fees	$160,000	Market value of equipment	$140,000
Revenues during 2002—general store	47,000	Notes payable	60,000
Accounts payable	11,000	Expenses during 2002	150,000
Cash on hand	20,000	Supplies on hand	2,500
Original cost of equipment	115,500		

Instructions
(a) Determine Kap Shin's net income from Bear Park for 2002.
(b) Prepare a balance sheet for Bear Park as of December 31, 2002.

Prepare an income statement.
(SO 8)

E1-11 Presented below is financial information related to the 2002 operations of Hockenberry Cruise Company.

Maintenance expense	$ 77,000
Property tax expense (on dock facilities)	10,000
Salaries expense	142,000
Advertising expense	3,500
Ticket revenue	325,000

Instructions
Prepare the 2002 income statement for Hockenberry Cruise Company.

Prepare an owner's equity statement.
(SO 8)

E1-12 Presented below is information related to the sole proprietorship of Mark Garland, attorney.

Legal service revenue—2002	$360,000
Total expenses—2002	211,000
Assets, January 1, 2002	85,000
Liabilities, January 1, 2002	62,000
Assets, December 31, 2002	168,000
Liabilities, December 31, 2002	70,000
Drawings—2002	?

Instructions
Prepare the 2002 owner's equity statement for Mark Garland's legal practice.

PROBLEMS: SET A

Analyze transactions and compute net income.
(SO 6, 7)

P1-1A Affleck's Repair Shop was started on May 1 by B. Affleck. A summary of May transactions is presented below.

1. Invested $10,000 cash to start the repair shop.
2. Purchased equipment for $5,000 cash.
3. Paid $400 cash for May office rent.
4. Paid $500 cash for supplies.
5. Incurred $250 of advertising costs in the *Beacon News* on account.
6. Received $4,100 in cash from customers for repair service.
7. Withdrew $500 cash for personal use.
8. Paid part-time employee salaries $1,000.
9. Paid utility bills $140.
10. Provided repair service on account to customers $850.
11. Collected cash of $120 for services billed in transaction (10).

Instructions

(a) Ending capital $12,660

(a) Prepare a tabular analysis of the transactions, using the following column headings: Cash, Accounts Receivable, Supplies, Equipment, Accounts Payable, and B. Affleck, Capital. Revenue is called Service Revenue.

(b) From an analysis of the column B. Affleck, Capital, compute the net income or net loss for May.

(b) Net income $3,160

P1-2A Judi Dench opened a veterinary business in Nashville, Tennessee, on August 1. On August 31, the balance sheet showed Cash $9,000, Accounts Receivable $1,700, Supplies $600, Office Equipment $6,000, Accounts Payable $3,600, and J. Dench, Capital $13,700. During September the following transactions occurred.

Analyze transactions and prepare income statement and owner's equity statement.
(SO 6, 7, 8)

1. Paid $2,900 cash on accounts payable.
2. Collected $1,300 of accounts receivable.
3. Purchased additional office equipment for $2,100, paying $800 in cash and the balance on account.
4. Earned revenue of $6,300, of which $2,500 is paid in cash and the balance is due in October.
5. Withdrew $600 cash for personal use.
6. Paid salaries $700, rent for September $900, and advertising expense $300.
7. Incurred utility expenses for month on account $170.
8. Received $7,000 from Capital Bank—money borrowed on a note payable.

Instructions
(a) Prepare a tabular analysis of the September transactions beginning with August 31 balances. The column headings should be as follows: Cash + Accounts Receivable + Supplies + Office Equipment = Notes Payable + Accounts Payable + J. Dench, Capital.

(a) Ending capital $17,330

(b) Prepare an income statement for September, an owner's equity statement for September, and a balance sheet at September 30.

(b) Net income $4,230
Total assets $26,500

P1-3A On May 1, Dennis Chambers started Skyline Flying School, a company that provides flying lessons, by investing $45,000 cash in the business. Following are the assets and liabilities of the company on May 31, 2002, and the revenues and expenses for the month of May.

Prepare income statement, owner's equity statement, and balance sheet.
(SO 8)

Cash	$ 6,500	Notes Payable	$30,000
Accounts Receivable	7,200	Rent Expense	1,200
Equipment	64,000	Repair Expense	400
Lesson Revenue	8,600	Fuel Expense	2,500
Advertising Expense	500	Insurance Expense	400
		Accounts Payable	800

Dennis Chambers made no additional investment in May, but he withdrew $1,700 in cash for personal use.

Instructions
(a) Prepare an income statement and owner's equity statement for the month of May and a balance sheet at May 31.
(b) Prepare an income statement and owner's equity statement for May assuming the following data are not included above: (1) $900 of revenue was earned and billed but not collected at May 31, and (2) $3,300 of fuel expense was incurred but not paid.

(a) Net income $3,600
Owner's equity $46,900
Total assets $77,700
(b) Net income $1,200
Owner's equity $44,500

P1-4A Ron Salem started his own delivery service, Salem Deliveries, on June 1, 2002. The following transactions occurred during the month of June.

Analyze transactions and prepare financial statements.
(SO 7, 8)

June 1 Ron invested $10,000 cash in the business.
2 Purchased a used van for deliveries for $10,000. Ron paid $2,000 cash and signed a note payable for the remaining balance.
3 Paid $500 for office rent for the month.
5 Performed $1,400 of services on account.
9 Withdrew $200 cash for personal use.
12 Purchased supplies for $150 on account.
15 Received a cash payment of $750 for services provided on June 5.
17 Purchased gasoline for $100 on account.
20 Received a cash payment of $1,500 for services provided.
23 Made a cash payment of $500 on the note payable.
26 Paid $250 for utilities.
29 Paid for the gasoline purchased on account on June 17.
30 Paid $500 for employee salaries.

Instructions

(a) Ending capital $11,350

(a) Show the effects of the previous transactions on the accounting equation using the following format.

	Assets				Liabilities		Owner's Equity
Date	Cash +	Accounts Receivable +	Supplies +	Delivery Van	= Notes Payable +	Accounts Payable +	R. Salem, Capital

Include explanations for any changes in the R. Salem, Capital account in your analysis.

(b) Net income $1,550
(c) Cash $8,200

(b) Prepare an income statement for the month of June.
(c) Prepare a balance sheet at June 30, 2002.

Determine financial statement amounts and prepare owner's equity statements.
(SO 7, 8)

P1-5A   Financial statement information about four different companies is as follows.

	Zarle Company	Wasicsko Company	McCain Company	Russe Company
January 1, 2002				
Assets	$ 84,000	$110,000	(g)	$170,000
Liabilities	50,000	(d)	75,000	(j)
Owner's equity	(a)	60,000	50,000	90,000
December 31, 2002				
Assets	(b)	147,000	200,000	(k)
Liabilities	55,000	65,000	(h)	80,000
Owner's equity	58,000	(e)	130,000	180,000
Owner's equity changes in year				
Additional investment	(c)	15,000	10,000	15,000
Drawings	25,000	(f)	14,000	20,000
Total revenues	350,000	420,000	(i)	520,000
Total expenses	320,000	385,000	342,000	(l)

Instructions

(a) Determine the missing amounts.
(b) Prepare the owner's equity statement for Wasicsko Company.
(c) ▭▭▭▶   Write a memorandum explaining the sequence for preparing financial statements and the interrelationship of the owner's equity statement to the income statement and balance sheet.

Problems: Set B

Analyze transactions and compute net income.
(SO 6, 7)

P1-1B   On April 1, Dolly Parton established Matrix Travel Agency. The following transactions were completed during the month.

1. Invested $10,000 cash to start the agency.
2. Paid $400 cash for April office rent.
3. Purchased office equipment for $2,500 cash.
4. Incurred $300 of advertising costs in the *Chicago Tribune,* on account.
5. Paid $600 cash for office supplies.
6. Earned $9,500 for services rendered: $1,000 cash is received from customers, and the balance of $8,500 is billed to customers on account.
7. Withdrew $200 cash for personal use.
8. Paid *Chicago Tribune* amount due in transaction (4).
9. Paid employees' salaries $2,200.
10. Received $8,000 in cash from customers who have previously been billed in transaction (6).

Instructions

(a) Ending capital $16,400

(a) Prepare a tabular analysis of the transactions using the following column headings: Cash, Accounts Receivable, Supplies, Office Equipment, Accounts Payable, and Dolly Parton, Capital.

(b) From an analysis of the column Dolly Parton, Capital, compute the net income or net loss for April.

(b) Net income $6,600

P1-2B Michelle Pfeiffer opened a law office, Michelle Pfeiffer, Attorney at Law, on July 1, 2002. On July 31, the balance sheet showed Cash $4,000, Accounts Receivable $1,500, Supplies $500, Office Equipment $5,000, Accounts Payable $4,200, and Michelle Pfeiffer, Capital $6,800. During August the following transactions occurred.

Analyze transactions and prepare income statement and owner's equity statement.
(SO 6, 7, 8)

1. Collected $1,400 of accounts receivable.
2. Paid $2,700 cash on accounts payable.
3. Earned revenue of $7,500 of which $3,000 is collected in cash and the balance is due in September.
4. Purchased additional office equipment for $1,000, paying $400 in cash and the balance on account.
5. Paid salaries $2,500, rent for August $900, and advertising expenses $350.
6. Withdrew $550 in cash for personal use.
7. Received $2,000 from Standard Federal Bank—money borrowed on a note payable.
8. Incurred utility expenses for month on account $250.

Instructions
(a) Prepare a tabular analysis of the August transactions beginning with July 31 balances. The column headings should be as follows: Cash + Accounts Receivable + Supplies + Office Equipment = Notes Payable + Accounts Payable + Michelle Pfeiffer, Capital.
(b) Prepare an income statement for August, an owner's equity statement for August, and a balance sheet at August 31.

(a) Ending capital $9,750

(b) Net income $3,500
Total assets $14,100

P1-3B On June 1, Cindy Crawford started Divine Cosmetics Co., a company that provides individual skin care treatment, by investing $26,200 cash in the business. Following are the assets and liabilities of the company at June 30 and the revenues and expenses for the month of June.

Prepare income statement, owner's equity statement, and balance sheet.
(SO 8)

Cash	$12,000	Notes Payable	$13,000
Accounts Receivable	4,000	Accounts Payable	1,200
Service Revenue	7,500	Supplies Expense	1,600
Cosmetic Supplies	2,000	Gas and Oil Expense	800
Advertising Expense	500	Utilities Expense	300
Equipment	25,000		

Cindy made no additional investment in June, but withdrew $1,700 in cash for personal use during the month.

Instructions
(a) Prepare an income statement and owner's equity statement for the month of June and a balance sheet at June 30, 2002.
(b) Prepare an income statement and owner's equity statement for June assuming the following data are not included above: (1) $800 of revenue was earned and billed but not collected at June 30, and (2) $100 of gas and oil expense was incurred but not paid.

(a) Net income $4,300
Owner's equity $28,800
Total assets $43,000
(b) Net income $5,000
Owner's equity $29,500

P1-4B Julie Spengel started her own consulting firm, Spengel Consulting, on May 1, 2002. The following transactions occurred during the month of May.

Analyze transactions and prepare financial statements.
(SO 7, 8)

May 1 Spengel invested $8,000 cash in the business.
2 Paid $800 for office rent for the month.
3 Purchased $500 of supplies on account.
5 Paid $50 to advertise in the *County News*.
9 Received $1,000 cash for services provided.
12 Withdrew $700 cash for personal use.
15 Performed $3,300 of services on account.
17 Paid $2,500 for employee salaries.
20 Paid for the supplies purchased on account on May 3.
23 Received a cash payment of $2,000 for services provided on account on May 15.
26 Borrowed $5,000 from the bank on a note payable.
29 Purchased office equipment for $2,400 on account.
30 Paid $150 for utilities.

Instructions

(a) Ending capital $8,100

(a) Show the effects of the previous transactions on the accounting equation using the following format.

	Assets				Liabilities		Owner's Equity
Date	Cash +	Accounts Receivable +	Supplies +	Office Equipment =	Notes Payable +	Accounts Payable +	J. Spengel, Capital

Include explanations for any changes in the J. Spengel, Capital account in your analysis.

(b) Net income $800

(c) Cash $11,300

(b) Prepare an income statement for the month of May.

(c) Prepare a balance sheet at May 31, 2002.

Determine financial statement amounts and prepare owner's equity statements.
(SO 7, 8)

P1-5B Financial statement information about four different companies is as follows.

	Yanni Company	Selara Company	Candlebox Company	Winans Company
January 1, 2002				
Assets	$ 75,000	$90,000	(g)	$150,000
Liabilities	50,000	(d)	75,000	(j)
Owner's equity	(a)	60,000	54,000	90,000
December 31, 2002				
Assets	(b)	117,000	180,000	(k)
Liabilities	55,000	62,000	(h)	80,000
Owner's equity	45,000	(e)	110,000	140,000
Owner's equity changes in year				
Additional investment	(c)	8,000	10,000	15,000
Drawings	10,000	(f)	12,000	10,000
Total revenues	350,000	400,000	(i)	500,000
Total expenses	335,000	385,000	360,000	(l)

Instructions

(a) Determine the missing amounts. (*Hint:* For example, to solve for (a), Assets − Liabilities = Owner's equity = $25,000.)

(b) Prepare the owner's equity statement for Yanni Company.

(c) [pencil icon] Write a memorandum explaining the sequence for preparing financial statements and the interrelationship of the owner's equity statement to the income statement and balance sheet.

BROADENING YOUR PERSPECTIVE

FINANCIAL REPORTING AND ANALYSIS

FINANCIAL REPORTING PROBLEM: Lands' End, Inc.

BYP1-1 The actual financial statements of **Lands' End**, as presented in the company's 2000 Annual Report, are contained in Appendix A (at the back of the textbook).

Instructions

Refer to Lands' End's financial statements and answer the following questions.

(a) What were Lands' End's total assets at January 28, 2000? At January 29, 1999?

(b) How much cash (and cash equivalents) did Land's End have on January 28, 2000?

(c) What amount of accounts payable did Lands' End report on January 28, 2000? On January 29, 1999?

(d) What were Lands' End's net sales in 1998? In 1999? In 2000?

(e) What is the amount of the change in Lands' End's net income from 1999 to 2000?

COMPARATIVE ANALYSIS PROBLEM: Lands' End vs. Abercrombie & Fitch

BYP1-2 **Lands' End's** financial statements are presented in Appendix A. **Abercrombie & Fitch's** financial statements are presented in Appendix B.

Instructions

(a) Based on the information contained in these financial statements, determine the following for each company.

   (1) Total assets at January 28, 2000, for Lands' End and at January 29, 2000, for Abercrombie & Fitch.

   (2) Accounts (notes) receivable, net at January 28, 2000, for Lands' End and at January 29, 2000, for Abercrombie & Fitch.

   (3) Net sales for year ended in 2000.

   (4) Net income for year ended in 2000.

(b) What conclusions concerning the two companies can be drawn from these data?

INTERPRETING FINANCIAL STATEMENTS: A Global Focus

BYP1-3 Today companies must compete in a global economy. **Nestlé**, a Swiss company, is the largest food company in the world. If you were interested in broadening your investment portfolio, you might consider investing in Nestlé. However, investing in international companies can pose some additional challenges. Consider the following excerpts from the notes to Nestlé's financial statements.

NESTLÉ
Notes to the Financial Statements (partial)
(a) The Group accounts comply with International Accounting Standards (IAS) issued by the International Accounting Standards Committee (IASC) and with the Standards Interpretations issued by the Standards Interpretation Committee of the IASC (SIC).
(b) The accounts have been prepared under the historical cost convention and on an accrual basis. All significant consolidated companies have a 31st December accounting year end. All disclosures required by the 4th and 7th European Union company law directives are provided.
(c) On consolidation, assets and liabilities of Group companies denominated in foreign currencies are translated into Swiss francs at year-end rates. Income and expense items are translated into Swiss francs at the annual average rates of exchange or, where known or determinable, at the rate on the date of the transaction for significant items.

Instructions

Discuss the implications of each of these items in terms of the effect it might have (positive or negative) on your ability to compare Nestlé to a U.S. food company such as Tootsie Roll or Hershey Foods. (*Hint:* In preparing your answer review the discussion of principles and assumptions in financial reporting on pages 10 and 11.)

EXPLORING THE WEB

BYP1-4 This exercise will familiarize you with skill requirements, job descriptions, and salaries for accounting careers.

Address: **www.cob.ohio-state.edu/dept/fin/jobs/account.htm** *(or go to*
       www.wiley.com/college/weygandt)

Instructions

Go to the site shown above. Answer the following questions.

(a) What are the three broad areas of accounting (from "Skills and Requirements")?
(b) List eight skills required in accounting.
(c) How do the three accounting areas differ in terms of these eight required skills?
(d) Explain one of the key job functions in accounting.
(e) Based on the *Smart Money* survey, what is the salary range for a junior staff accountant with Deloitte & Touche?

CRITICAL THINKING

GROUP DECISION CASE

BYP1-5 Jill and Mark Illster, local golf stars, opened the Chip-Shot Driving Range on March 1, 2002, by investing $10,000 of their cash savings in the business. A caddy shack was constructed for cash at a cost of $4,000, and $800 was spent on golf balls and golf clubs. The Illsters leased five acres of land at a cost of $1,000 per month and paid the first month's rent. During the first month, advertising costs totaled $750, of which $150 was unpaid at March 31, and $400 was paid to members of the high-school golf team for retrieving golf balls. All revenues from customers were deposited in the company's bank account. On March 15, Jill and Mark withdrew a total of $800 in cash for personal living expenses. A $100 utility bill was received on March 31 but was not paid. On March 31, the balance in the company's bank account was $7,550.

Jill and Mark thought they had a pretty good first month of operations. But, their estimates of profitability ranged from a loss of $2,450 to net income of $2,100.

Instructions

With the class divided into groups, answer the following.

(a) How could the Illsters have concluded that the business operated at a loss of $2,450? Was this a valid basis on which to determine net income?
(b) How could the Illsters have concluded that the business operated at a net income of $2,100? (*Hint:* Prepare a balance sheet at March 31.) Was this a valid basis on which to determine net income?
(c) Without preparing an income statement, determine the actual net income for March.
(d) What was the revenue earned in March?

COMMUNICATION ACTIVITY

BYP1-6 Sarah Rankin, the bookkeeper for New York Company, has been trying to get the balance sheet to balance. The company's balance sheet is as follows.

NEW YORK COMPANY
Balance Sheet
For the Month Ended December 31, 2002

Assets		Liabilities	
Equipment	$20,500	Thompson, Capital	$23,000
Cash	9,000	Accounts receivable	(6,000)
Supplies	2,000	Thompson, Drawing	(2,000)
Accounts payable	(6,000)	Notes payable	10,500
	$25,500		$25,500

Instructions

Explain to Sarah Rankin in a memo why the original balance sheet is incorrect, and what should be done to correct it.

ETHICS CASE

BYP1-7 After numerous campus interviews, Warren Filler, a senior at Great Northern College, received two office interview invitations from the Baltimore offices of two large firms.

Both firms offered to cover his out-of-pocket expenses (travel, hotel, and meals). He scheduled the interviews for both firms on the same day, one in the morning and one in the afternoon. At the conclusion of each interview, he submitted to both firms his total out-of-pocket expenses for the trip to Baltimore: mileage $70 (280 miles at $0.25), hotel $130, meals $36, parking and tolls $18, for a total of $254. He believes this approach is appropriate. If he had made two trips, his cost would have been two times $254. He is also certain that neither firm knew he had visited the other on that same trip. Within ten days Warren received two checks in the mail, each in the amount of $254.

Instructions

(a) Who are the stakeholders (affected parties) in this situation?
(b) What are the ethical issues in this case?
(c) What would you do in this situation?

Answers to Self-Study Questions

1. b   **2.** d   **3.** a   **4.** c   **5.** a   **6.** d   **7.** b   **8.** a   **9.** b   **10.** c

Answer to *Lands' End* Review It Question 4, p. 14

Lands' End's accounting equation is:

Assets		Liabilities		Owner's (Stockholders') Equity
$456,196,000	=	$159,989,000	+	$296,207,000

Remember to go back to the Navigator box on the chapter-opening page and check off your completed work.

THE RECORDING PROCESS

THE NAVIGATOR ✓

- Understand *Concepts for Review* ❏
- Read *Feature Story* ❏
- Scan *Study Objectives* ❏
- Read *Preview* ❏
- Read text and answer *Before You Go On*
  p. 49 ❏   p. 52 ❏   p. 62 ❏   p. 66 ❏
- Work *Demonstration Problem* ❏
- Review *Summary of Study Objectives* ❏
- Answer *Self-Study Questions* ❏
- Complete *Assignments* ❏

*C*ONCEPTS FOR REVIEW

Before studying this chapter, you should know or, if necessary, review:

a. What are assets, liabilities, owner's capital, owner's drawings, revenues, and expenses. (Ch. 1, pp. 13–14)

b. Why assets equal liabilities plus owner's equity. (Ch. 1, p. 12)

c. What transactions are and how they affect the basic accounting equation. (Ch. 1, pp. 15–20)

☑ THE NAVIGATOR

No Such Thing As a Perfect World

When she got a job doing the accounting for **Forster's Restaurants**, Tanis Anderson had almost finished her business administration degree at Simon Fraser University. But even after Tanis completed her degree requirements, her education still continued—this time, in the real world.

Tanis's responsibilities include paying the bills, tracking food and labor costs, and managing the payroll for **The Mug and Musket**, a popular destination restaurant in Surrey, British Columbia. "My title is Director of Finance," she laughs, "but really that means I take care of whatever needs doing!"

The use of judgment is a big part of the job. As Tanis says, "I learned all the fundamentals in my business classes, but school prepares you for a perfect world, and there is no such thing."

She feels fortunate that her boss understands her job is a learning experience as well as a responsibility. "Sometimes he's let me do something he knew perfectly well was a mistake so I can learn something through experience," she admits.

To help others gain the benefits of her real-world learning, Tanis is

always happy to help students in the area who want to use Forster's as the subject of a project or report. "It's the least I can do," she says.

THE NAVIGATOR

After studying this chapter, you should be able to:

1. Explain what an account is and how it helps in the recording process.
2. Define debits and credits and explain how they are used to record business transactions.
3. Identify the basic steps in the recording process.
4. Explain what a journal is and how it helps in the recording process.
5. Explain what a ledger is and how it helps in the recording process.
6. Explain what posting is and how it helps in the recording process.
7. Prepare a trial balance and explain its purposes.

THE NAVIGATOR

In Chapter 1, we analyzed business transactions in terms of the accounting equation. The cumulative effects of these transactions were presented in tabular form. Imagine a restaurant and gift shop such as **The Mug and Musket** using the same tabular format as Softbyte to keep track of every one of its transactions. In a single day, this restaurant and gift shop engages in hundreds of business transactions. To record each transaction this way would be impractical, expensive, and unnecessary. Instead, a set of procedures and records are used to keep track of transaction data more easily.

This chapter introduces and illustrates these basic procedures and records. The content and organization of Chapter 2 are as follows.

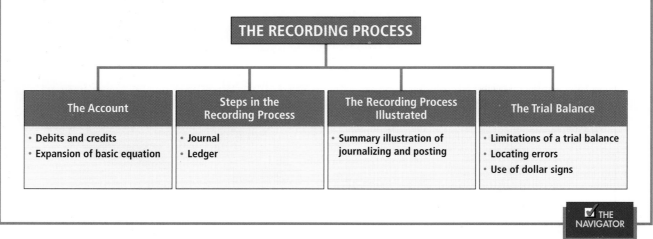

THE RECORDING PROCESS			
The Account	**Steps in the Recording Process**	**The Recording Process Illustrated**	**The Trial Balance**
• Debits and credits • Expansion of basic equation	• Journal • Ledger	• Summary illustration of journalizing and posting	• Limitations of a trial balance • Locating errors • Use of dollar signs

☑ THE NAVIGATOR

STUDY OBJECTIVE 1

Explain what an account is and how it helps in the recording process.

Accounting Cycle Tutorial—Recording Business Transactions

THE ACCOUNT

An **account** is an individual accounting record of increases and decreases in a specific asset, liability, or owner's equity item. For example, Softbyte (the company discussed in Chapter 1) would have separate accounts for Cash, Accounts Receivable, Accounts Payable, Service Revenue, Salaries Expense, and so on. In its simplest form, an account consists of three parts: (1) the title of the account, (2) a left or debit side, and (3) a right or credit side. Because the alignment of these parts of an account resembles the letter T, it is referred to as a **T account**. The basic form of an account is shown in Illustration 2-1.

Illustration 2-1

Basic form of account

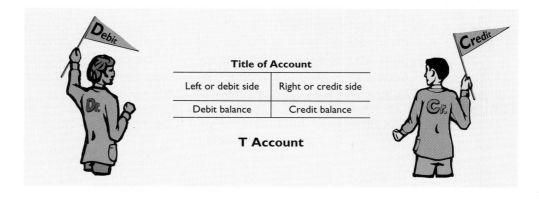

Title of Account	
Left or debit side	Right or credit side
Debit balance	Credit balance

T Account

The T account is a standard shorthand in accounting that helps make clear the effects of transactions on individual accounts. We will use it often throughout this book to explain basic accounting relationships. (Note that when we are referring to a specific account, we capitalize its name.)

DEBITS AND CREDITS

The term **debit** means left, and **credit** means right. They are commonly abbreviated as Dr. for debit and Cr. for credit.[1] These terms are directional signals: They indicate which side of a T account a number will be recorded on. Entering an amount on the left side of an account is called **debiting** the account; making an entry on the right side is **crediting** the account.

The procedure of having debits on the left and credits on the right is an accounting custom, or rule (like the custom of driving on the right-hand side of the road in the United States). **This rule applies to all accounts.** When the totals of the two sides are compared, an account will have a **debit balance** if the total of the debit amounts exceeds the credits. An account will have a **credit balance** if the credit amounts exceed the debits.

The recording of debits and credits in an account is shown in Illustration 2-2 for the cash transactions of Softbyte. The data are taken from the cash column of the tabular summary in Illustration 1-9.

STUDY OBJECTIVE 2

Define debits and credits and explain how they are used to record business transactions.

Illustration 2-2

Tabular summary compared to account form

HELPFUL HINT

At this point, don't think about increases and decreases in relation to debits and credits. As you'll soon learn, the effects of debits and credits depend on the type of account involved.

In the tabular summary every positive item represents a receipt of cash; every negative amount represents a payment of cash. Notice that in the account form the increases in cash are recorded as debits, and the decreases in cash are recorded as credits. Having increases on one side and decreases on the other helps in determining the total of each side of the account as well as the overall balance in the account. The account balance, a debit of $8,050, indicates that Softbyte has had $8,050 more increases than decreases in cash.

Debit and Credit Procedure

In Chapter 1 you learned the effect of a transaction on the basic accounting equation. Remember that each transaction must affect two or more accounts to keep the basic accounting equation in balance. In other words, for each transaction debits must equal credits in the accounts. The equality of debits and credits provides the basis for the **double-entry system** of recording transactions.

Under the double-entry system the dual (two-sided) effect of each transaction is recorded in appropriate accounts. This universally used system provides a logical method for recording transactions. It also offers a means of proving the

HELPFUL HINT

Debits must equal credits for each transaction.

---

[1]These terms and their abbreviations come from the Latin words *debere* (Dr.) and *credere* (Cr.).

accuracy of the recorded amounts. If every transaction is recorded with equal debits and credits, then the sum of all the debits to the accounts must equal the sum of all the credits.

The double-entry system for determining the equality of the accounting equation is much more efficient than the plus/minus procedure used in Chapter 1. There, it was necessary after each transaction to compare total assets with total liabilities and owner's equity to determine the equality of the two sides of the accounting equation.

ASSETS AND LIABILITIES. We know that both sides of the basic equation (Assets = Liabilities + Owner's equity) must be equal. It follows that increases and decreases in assets and liabilities must be recorded opposite from each other. In Illustration 2-2, increases in cash—an asset—were entered on the left side, and decreases in cash were entered on the right side. Therefore, increases in liabilities must be entered on the right or credit side, and decreases in liabilities must be entered on the left or debit side. The effects that debits and credits have on assets and liabilities are summarized as follows.

Illustration 2-3

Debit and credit effects—assets and liabilities

Debits	Credits
Increase assets	Decrease assets
Decrease liabilities	Increase liabilities

> **HELPFUL HINT**
> The normal balance for an account is always the same as the increase side.

Debits to a specific asset account should exceed the credits to that account. Credits to a liability account should exceed debits to that account. The **normal balance** of an account is on the side where an increase in the account is recorded. Thus, asset accounts normally show debit balances, and liability accounts normally show credit balances. The normal balances can be diagrammed as follows.

Illustration 2-4

Normal balances—assets and liabilities

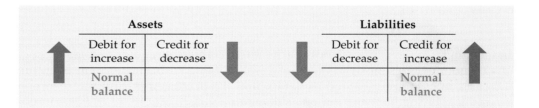

Knowing the normal balance in an account may help you trace errors. For example, a credit balance in an asset account such as Land or a debit balance in a liability account such as Wages Payable would indicate recording errors. Occasionally, an abnormal balance may be correct. The Cash account, for example, will have a credit balance when a company has overdrawn its bank balance (i.e., written a "bad" check).

OWNER'S EQUITY. As indicated in Chapter 1, owner's equity is increased by owner's investments and by revenues. It is decreased by owner's drawings and by expenses. In a double-entry system, accounts are kept for each of these types of transactions, as explained below.

Owner's Capital. Investments by owners are credited to the Owner's Capital account. Credits increase this account and debits decrease it. For example, when cash is invested in the business, Cash is debited (increased) and Owner's Capital is credited (increased). When the owner's investment in the business is reduced, Owner's Capital is debited (decreased).

The rules of debit and credit for the Owner's Capital account are stated as follows.

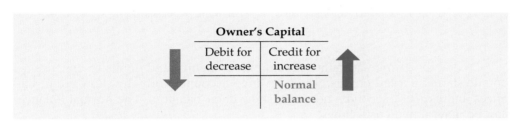

Debits	Credits
Decrease Owner's Capital	Increase Owner's Capital

Illustration 2-5

Debit and credit effects— Owner's Capital

The normal balance in this account can be diagrammed as follows.

Owner's Capital

Debit for decrease	Credit for increase
	Normal balance

Illustration 2-6

Normal balance—Owner's Capital

Owner's Drawing. An owner may withdraw cash or other assets for personal use. Withdrawals could be debited directly to Owner's Capital to indicate a decrease in owner's equity. However, it is preferable to establish a separate account, called the Owner's Drawing account. This separate account makes it easier to determine total withdrawals for each accounting period. **The drawing account decreases owner's equity. It is not an income statement account like revenues and expenses.** Owner's Drawing is increased by debits and decreased by credits. Normally, the drawing account will have a debit balance.

The rules of debit and credit for the drawing account are stated as follows.

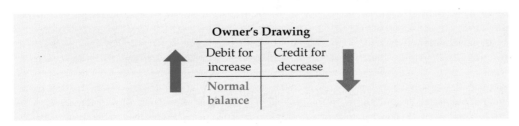

Debits	Credits
Increase Owner's Drawing	Decrease Owner's Drawing

Illustration 2-7

Debit and credit effects— Owner's Drawing

The normal balance can be diagrammed as follows.

Owner's Drawing

Debit for increase	Credit for decrease
Normal balance	

Illustration 2-8

Normal balance—Owner's Drawing

Revenues and Expenses. Remember that the ultimate purpose of earning revenues is to benefit the owner(s) of the business. When revenues are earned, owner's equity is increased. Therefore, **the effect of debits and credits on revenue accounts is the same as their effect on Owner's Capital**. Revenue accounts are increased by credits and decreased by debits.

Expenses have the opposite effect: expenses decrease owner's equity. Since expenses are the negative factor in computing net income, and revenues are the positive factor, it is logical that the increase and decrease sides of expense accounts should be the reverse of revenue accounts. Thus, expense accounts are increased by debits and decreased by credits.

The effect of debits and credits on revenues and expenses can be stated as follows.

Illustration 2-9

Debit and credit effects—revenues and expenses

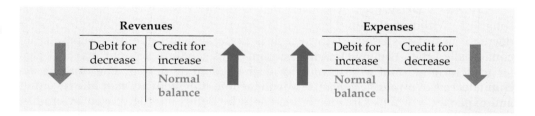

Debits	Credits
Decrease revenues	Increase revenues
Increase expenses	Decrease expenses

Credits to revenue accounts should exceed debits, and debits to expense accounts should exceed credits. Thus, revenue accounts normally show credit balances and expense accounts normally show debit balances. The normal balances can be diagrammed as follows.

Illustration 2-10

Normal balances—revenues and expenses

Revenues		Expenses	
Debit for decrease	Credit for increase	Debit for increase	Credit for decrease
	Normal balance	Normal balance	

EXPANSION OF BASIC EQUATION

You have already learned the basic accounting equation. Illustration 2-11 expands this equation to show the accounts that comprise owner's equity. In addition, the debit/credit rules and effects on each type of account are illustrated. Study this diagram carefully. It will help you understand the fundamentals of the double-entry system. Like the basic equation, the expanded basic equation must be in balance (total debits equal total credits).

Illustration 2-11

Expanded basic equation and debit/credit rules and effects

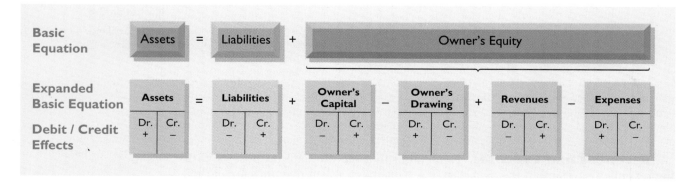

▶ *REVIEW IT*

1. What do the terms debit and credit mean?
2. What are the debit and credit effects on assets, liabilities, and owner's capital?
3. What are the debit and credit effects on revenues, expenses, and owner's drawing?
4. What are the normal balances for **Lands' End's** Cash, Accounts Payable, and Interest Expense accounts? The answers to this question are provided on page 84.

▶ *DO IT*

Kate Browne has just rented space in a shopping mall in which she will open a beauty salon, to be called "Hair It Is." Long before opening day and before purchasing equipment, hiring employees, and remodeling the space, Kate has been advised to set up a double-entry set of accounting records in which to record all of her business transactions.

Identify the balance sheet accounts that Kate will likely need to record the transactions needed to open her business. Indicate whether the normal balance of each account is a debit or a credit.

ACTION PLAN

• Determine the types of accounts needed: Kate will need asset accounts for each different type of asset she invests in the business, and liability accounts for any debts she incurs.
• Understand the types of owner's equity accounts: Only Owner's Capital will be needed when Kate begins the business. Other owner's equity accounts will be needed later.

SOLUTION: Kate would likely need the following accounts in which to record the transactions necessary to ready her beauty salon for opening day: Cash (debit balance); Equipment (debit balance); Supplies (debit balance); Accounts Payable (credit balance); if she borrows money, Notes payable (credit balance); K. Browne, Capital (credit balance).

Related exercise material: BE2-1, BE2-2, E2-1, E2-3, and E2-10.

*S*TEPS IN THE RECORDING PROCESS

In practically every business, the basic steps in the recording process are:

1. Analyze each transaction for its effects on the accounts.
2. Enter the transaction information in a journal (book of original entry).
3. Transfer the journal information to the appropriate accounts in the ledger (book of accounts).

STUDY OBJECTIVE **3**

Identify the basic steps in the recording process.

Although it is possible to enter transaction information directly into the accounts without using a journal or ledger, few businesses do so.

The sequence of events in the recording process begins with the transaction. Evidence of the transaction is provided by a **business document**, such as a sales slip, a check, a bill, or a cash register tape. This evidence is analyzed to determine the effects of the transaction on specific accounts. The transaction is then entered in the journal. Finally, the journal entry is transferred to the designated accounts in the ledger. The sequence of events in the recording process is shown in Illustration 2-12.

The Recording Process

| Analyze each transaction | Enter transaction in a journal | Transfer journal information to ledger accounts |

Illustration 2-12

The recording process

The basic steps in the recording process occur repeatedly. The analysis of transactions was illustrated in Chapter 1. Further examples will be given in this and later chapters. The other steps in the recording process are explained in the next sections.

Technology in Action examples show how computer technology is used in accounting and business.

TECHNOLOGY IN ACTION

 Computerized and manual accounting systems basically parallel one another. Most of the procedures are handled by electronic circuitry in computerized systems. They seem to occur invisibly. But, to fully comprehend how computerized systems operate, you need to understand manual approaches for processing accounting data.

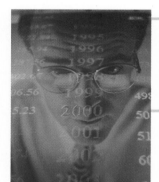

STUDY OBJECTIVE 4

Explain what a journal is and how it helps in the recording process.

THE JOURNAL

Transactions are initially recorded in chronological order in a **journal** before being transferred to the accounts. Thus, the journal is referred to as the book of original entry. For each transaction the journal shows the debit and credit effects on specific accounts. Companies may use various kinds of journals, but every company has the most basic form of journal, a **general journal**. Typically, a general journal has spaces for dates, account titles and explanations, references, and two amount columns. Whenever we use the term journal in this textbook without a modifying adjective, we mean the general journal.

The journal makes several significant contributions to the recording process:

1. It discloses in one place the complete effects of a transaction.
2. It provides a chronological record of transactions.
3. It helps to prevent or locate errors because the debit and credit amounts for each entry can be readily compared.

Journalizing

Entering transaction data in the journal is known as **journalizing**. Separate journal entries are made for each transaction. A complete entry consists of: (1) the date of the transaction, (2) the accounts and amounts to be debited and credited, and (3) a brief explanation of the transaction.

Illustration 2-13 shows the technique of journa...
actions of Softbyte. These transactions were: Sep...
$15,000 cash in the business, and computer equipme...
cash. The numbered J1 indicates that these two entri...
page of the journal.

GENERAL JOURNAL

Date	Account Titles and Explanation	R...
2002 Sept. 1	Cash R. Neal, Capital (Owner's investment of cash in business)	
1	Computer Equipment Cash (Purchase of equipment for cash)	

The standard form and content of journal entries are as follows.

1. The date of the transaction is entered in the Date column. The date re...
   should include the year, month, and day of the transaction.
2. The debit account title (that is, the account to be debited) is entered first a...
   the extreme left margin of the column headed "Account Titles and Explanation," and the amount of the debit is recorded in the Debit column.
3. The credit account title (that is, the account to be credited) is indented and
   entered on the next line in the column headed "Account Titles and Explanation," and the amount of the credit is recorded in the Credit column.
4. A brief explanation of the transaction is given on the line below the credit account title.
5. A space is left between journal entries. The blank space separates individual
   journal entries and makes the entire journal easier to read.
6. The column titled Ref. (which stands for reference) is left blank when the
   journal entry is made. This column is used later when the journal entries are
   transferred to the ledger accounts. At that time, the ledger account number
   is placed in the Reference column to indicate where the amount in the journal entry was transferred.

It is important to use correct and specific account titles in journalizing. Since
most accounts appear later in the financial statements, wrong account titles lead
to incorrect financial statements. Some flexibility exists initially in selecting account titles. The main criterion is that each title must appropriately describe the
content of the account. For example, the account title used for the cost of delivery trucks may be Delivery Equipment, Delivery Trucks, or Trucks. Once a company chooses the specific title to use, all later transactions involving the account
should be recorded under that account title.[2]

If an entry involves only two accounts, one debit and one credit, it is considered a **simple entry**. Some transactions, however, require more than two accounts

---

[2]In homework problems, when specific account titles are given, they should be used. When account titles are not given, you may select account titles that identify the nature and content of each
account. The account titles used in journalizing should not contain explanations such as Cash Paid
or Cash Received.

52

ompound

700

1,200

se 400

r wages and adver-

try correct? No. It is ect in form because both ts should be listed before e credit. It is incorrect in content because the debit amounts do not equal the credit amount.

Vhen three or more accounts are required in one journal entry, erred to as a **compound entry**. To illustrate, assume that on July 1, pany purchases a delivery truck costing $14,000 by paying $8,000 ie balance on account (to be paid later). The compound entry is as

GENERAL JOURNAL **J1**

Date	Account Titles and Explanation	Ref.	Debit	Credit
2002				
July 1	Delivery Equipment		14,000	
	Cash			8,000
	Accounts Payable			6,000
	(Purchased truck for cash with balance on account)			

In a compound entry, the total debit and credit amounts must be equal. Also, the standard format requires that all debits be listed before the credits.

BEFORE YOU GO ON...

REVIEW IT

1. What is the sequence of the steps in the recording process?
2. What contribution does the journal make to the recording process?
3. What is the standard form and content of a journal entry made in the general journal?

DO IT

In establishing her beauty salon, Hair It Is, Kate Browne engaged in the following activities:

1. Opened a bank account in the name of Hair It Is and deposited $20,000 of her own money in this account as her initial investment.
2. Purchased equipment on account (to be paid in 30 days) for a total cost of $4,800.
3. Interviewed three persons for the position of beautician.

In what form (type of record) should Kate record these three activities? Prepare the entries to record the transactions.

ACTION PLAN

- Understand which activities need to be recorded and which do not. Any that have economic effects should be recorded in a journal.
- Analyze the effects of transactions on asset, liability, and owner's equity accounts.

SOLUTION: Each transaction that is recorded is entered in the general journal. The three activities would be recorded as follows.

1. Cash	20,000	
K. Browne, Capital		20,000
(Owner's investment of cash in business)		
2. Equipment	4,800	
Accounts Payable		4,800
(Purchase of equipment on account)		
3. No entry because no transaction has occurred.		

Related exercise material: BE2-3, BE2-5, BE2-6, E2-2, E2-4, E2-6, E2-7, and E2-8.

THE NAVIGATOR

THE LEDGER

The entire group of accounts maintained by a company is called the **ledger**. The ledger keeps in one place all the information about changes in specific account balances.

Companies may use various kinds of ledgers, but every company has a general ledger. A **general ledger** contains all the assets, liabilities, and owner's equity accounts, as shown in Illustration 2-15. A business can use a looseleaf binder or card file for the ledger. Each account is kept on a separate sheet or card. Whenever we use the term ledger in this textbook without a modifying adjective, we mean the general ledger.

STUDY OBJECTIVE 5

Explain what a ledger is and how it helps in the recording process.

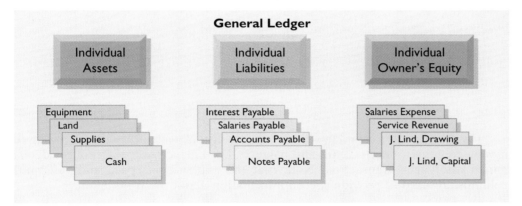

Illustration 2-15

The general ledger

The ledger should be arranged in the order in which accounts are presented in the financial statements, beginning with the balance sheet accounts. First in order are the asset accounts, followed by liability accounts, owner's capital, owner's drawing, revenues, and expenses. Each account is numbered for easier identification.

The ledger provides management with the balances in various accounts. For example, the Cash account shows the amount of cash that is available to meet current obligations. Amounts due from customers can be found by examining Accounts Receivable, and amounts owed to creditors can be found by examining Accounts Payable.

ACCOUNTING IN ACTION   *Business Insight*

In his autobiography Sam Walton described the double-entry accounting system he began the **Wal-Mart** empire with: "We kept a little pigeonhole on the wall for the cash receipts and paperwork of each [Wal-Mart] store. I had a blue binder ledger book for each store. When we added a store, we added a pigeonhole. We did this at least up to twenty stores. Then once a month, the bookkeeper and I would enter the merchandise, enter the sales, enter the cash, and balance it."

SOURCE: Sam Walton, *Made in America* (New York: Doubleday, 1992), p. 53.

Standard Form of Account

The simple T-account form used in accounting textbooks is often very useful for illustration purposes. However, in practice, the account forms used in ledgers are much more structured. A widely used form is shown in Illustration 2-16, using assumed data from a cash account.

Illustration 2-16

Three-column form of account

	CASH					No. 101
Date	**Explanation**	**Ref.**	**Debit**	**Credit**	**Balance**	
2002						
June 1			25,000		25,000	
2				8,000	17,000	
3			4,200		21,200	
9			7,500		28,700	
17				11,700	17,000	
20				250	16,750	
30				7,300	9,450	

This form is often called the **three-column form of account** because it has three money columns—debit, credit, and balance. The balance in the account is determined after each transaction. Note that the explanation space and reference columns are used to provide special information about the transaction.

Posting

STUDY OBJECTIVE **6**

Explain what posting is and how it helps in the recording process.

The procedure of transferring journal entries to the ledger accounts is called **posting**. Posting involves the following steps.

1. In the ledger, enter in the appropriate columns of the account(s) debited the date, journal page, and debit amount shown in the journal.
2. In the reference column of the journal, write the account number to which the debit amount was posted.
3. In the ledger, enter in the appropriate columns of the account(s) credited the date, journal page, and credit amount shown in the journal.
4. In the reference column of the journal, write the account number to which the credit amount was posted.

These four steps are diagrammed in Illustration 2-17 (on page 55) using the first journal entry of Softbyte. The boxed numbers indicate the sequence of the steps.

Posting should be performed in chronological order. That is, all the debits and credits of one journal entry should be posted before proceeding to the next journal entry. Postings should be made on a timely basis to ensure that the ledger is up to date.[3]

The reference column **in the journal** serves several purposes. The numbers in this column indicate the entries that have been posted. After the last entry has been posted, this column should be scanned to see that all postings have been made.

The reference column **of a ledger** account indicates the journal page from which the transaction was posted. The explanation space of the ledger account is used infrequently because an explanation already appears in the journal. It generally is used only when detailed analysis of account activity is required.

HELPFUL HINT

How can one tell whether all postings have been completed? Answer: Scan the reference column of the journal to see whether there are any blanks opposite account titles. If there are no blanks, all postings have been made.

---

[3]In homework problems, it will be permissible to journalize all transactions before posting any of the journal entries.

Illustration 2-17

Posting a journal entry

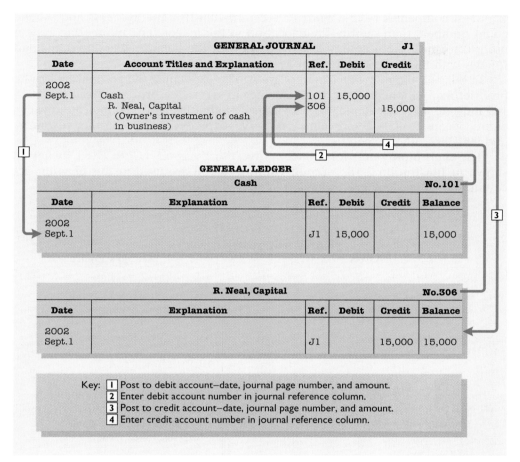

	GENERAL JOURNAL			J1
Date	Account Titles and Explanation	Ref.	Debit	Credit
2002 Sept.1	Cash	101	15,000	
	R. Neal, Capital	306		15,000
	(Owner's investment of cash in business)			

GENERAL LEDGER

Cash   No.101

| Date | Explanation | Ref. | Debit | Credit | Balance |
| 2002 Sept.1 | | J1 | 15,000 | | 15,000 |

R. Neal, Capital   No.306

| Date | Explanation | Ref. | Debit | Credit | Balance |
| 2002 Sept.1 | | J1 | | 15,000 | 15,000 |

Key: 1 Post to debit account—date, journal page number, and amount.
2 Enter debit account number in journal reference column.
3 Post to credit account—date, journal page number, and amount.
4 Enter credit account number in journal reference column.

TECHNOLOGY IN ACTION

Determining what to record is the most critical (and for most businesses the most expensive) point in the accounting process. In computerized systems, after this phase is completed, the input and all further processing just boil down to merging files and generating reports. Programmers and management information system types with good accounting backgrounds (such as they should gain from a good principles textbook) are better able to develop effective computerized systems.

Chart of Accounts

The number and type of accounts used differ for each enterprise. The number of accounts depends on the amount of detail desired by management. For example, the management of one company may want one account for all types of utility expense. Another may keep separate expense accounts for each type of utility, such as gas, electricity, and water. Similarly, a single proprietorship like Softbyte will have fewer accounts than a corporate giant like **Ford Motor Company**. Softbyte may be able to manage and report its activities in twenty to thirty accounts, while Ford requires thousands of accounts to keep track of its worldwide activities.

Most companies have a **chart of accounts** that lists the accounts and the account numbers that identify their location in the ledger. The numbering system used to identify the accounts usually starts with the balance sheet accounts and follows with the income statement accounts.

In this and the next two chapters, we will be explaining the accounting for the proprietorship Pioneer Advertising Agency (a service enterprise). Accounts 101–199 indicate asset accounts; 200–299 indicate liabilities; 301–350 indicate owner's equity accounts; 400–499, revenues; 601–799, expenses; 800–899, other revenues; and 900–999, other expenses.

The chart of accounts for Pioneer Advertising Agency (C. R. Byrd, owner) is shown in Illustration 2-18. Accounts shown in red are used in this chapter; accounts shown in black are explained in later chapters.

Illustration 2-18

Chart of accounts

CHART OF ACCOUNTS
Pioneer Advertising Agency

Assets	Owner's Equity
101 Cash	301 C. R. Byrd, Capital
112 Accounts Receivable	306 C. R. Byrd, Drawing
126 Advertising Supplies	350 Income Summary
130 Prepaid Insurance	
157 Office Equipment	**Revenues**
158 Accumulated Depreciation—Office Equipment	400 Service Revenue
Liabilities	**Expenses**
200 Notes Payable	631 Advertising Supplies Expense
201 Accounts Payable	711 Depreciation Expense
209 Unearned Revenue	722 Insurance Expense
212 Salaries Payable	726 Salaries Expense
230 Interest Payable	729 Rent Expense
	905 Interest Expense

You will notice that there are gaps in the numbering system of the chart of accounts for Pioneer Advertising. Gaps are left to permit the insertion of new accounts as needed during the life of the business.

THE RECORDING PROCESS ILLUSTRATED

Illustrations 2-19 through 2-28 show the basic steps in the recording process, using the October transactions of the Pioneer Advertising Agency. Its accounting period is a month. A basic analysis and a debit-credit analysis precede the journalizing and posting of each transaction. For simplicity, the T-account form is used in the illustrations instead of the standard account form.

Study the transaction analyses in Illustrations 2-19 through 2-28 carefully. **The purpose of transaction analysis is first to identify the type of account involved, and then to determine whether a debit or a credit to the account is required.** You should always perform this type of analysis before preparing a journal entry. Doing so will help you understand the journal entries discussed in this chapter as well as more complex journal entries to be described in later chapters.

Keep in mind that every journal entry affects one or more of the following items: assets, liabilities, owner's capital, owner's drawing, revenues, or expenses. By becoming skilled at transaction analysis, you will be able to recognize quickly the impact of any transaction on these six items.

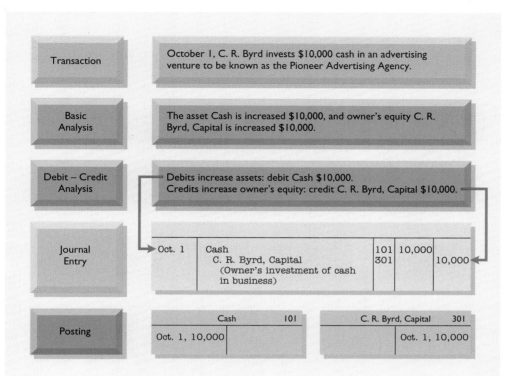

Illustration 2-19

Investment of cash by owner

HELPFUL HINT
To correctly record a transaction, you must carefully analyze the event and translate that analysis into debit and credit language.
First: Determine what type of account is involved.
Second: Determine what items increased or decreased and by how much.
Third: Translate the increases and decreases into debits and credits.

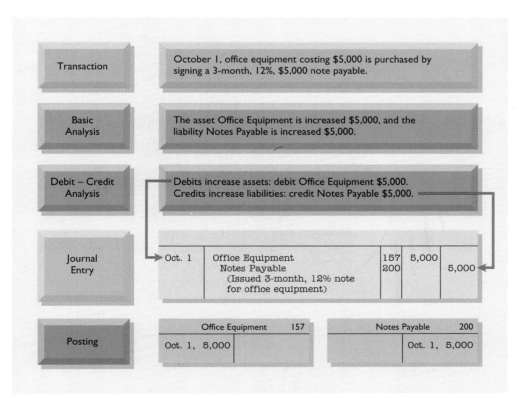

Illustration 2-20

Purchase of office equipment

Illustration 2-21

Receipt of cash for future service

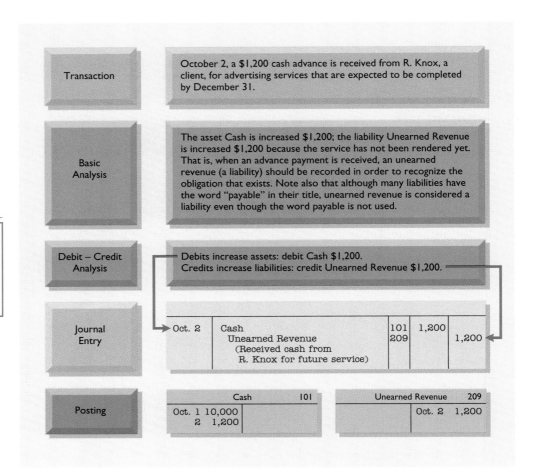

HELPFUL HINT
When the revenue is earned, the Unearned Revenue account is debited (decreased), and a revenue account is credited (increased).

Illustration 2-22

Payment of monthly rent

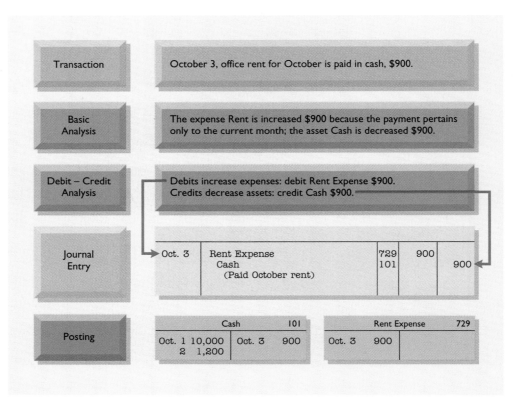

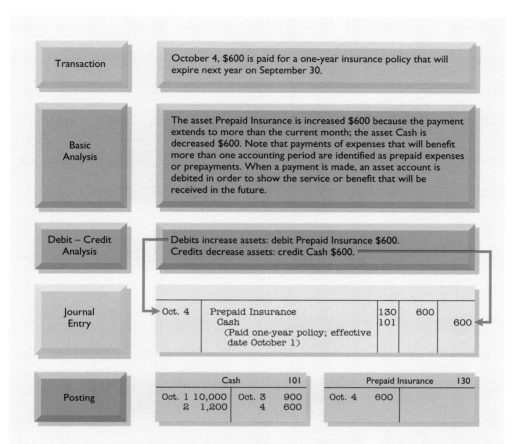

Illustration 2-23

Payment for insurance

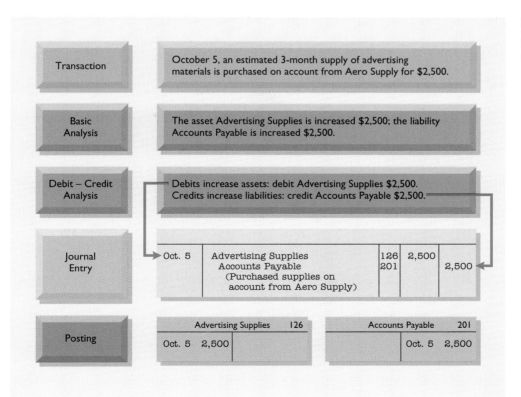

Illustration 2-24

Purchase of supplies on credit

Illustration 2-25

Hiring of employees

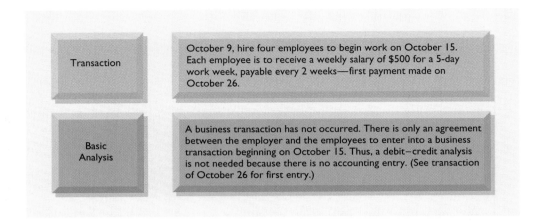

Illustration 2-26

Withdrawal of cash by owner

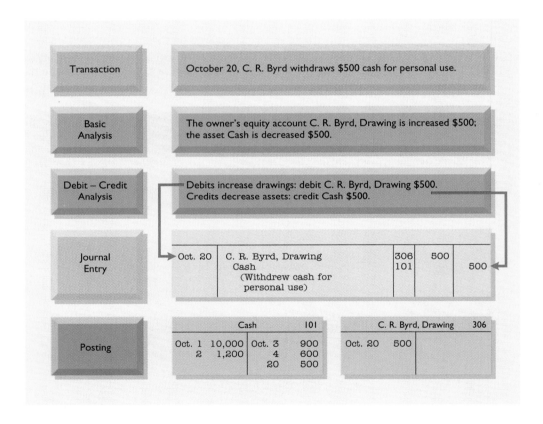

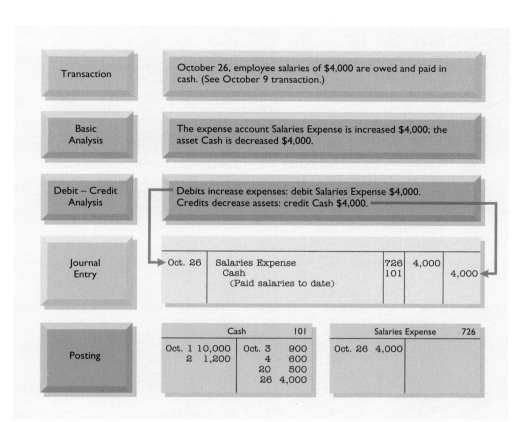

Illustration 2-27
Payment of salaries

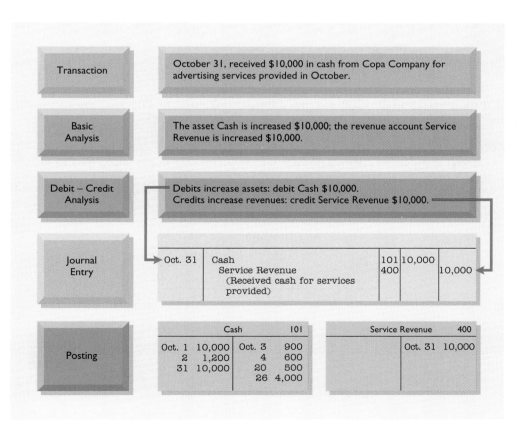

Illustration 2-28
Receipt of cash for services provided

ACCOUNTING IN ACTION ∧ *Business Insight*

E-business is having a tremendous impact on how companies share information within the company, and with people outside the company, such as suppliers, creditors, and investors. A new type of software, Extensible Markup Language (XML), is enabling the creation of a universal way to exchange data.

An organization called XBRL.org is using XML to develop an internationally accepted framework called the Extensible Business Reporting Model (XBRL). The organization is comprised of representatives from industry, accounting firms, investment houses, bankers, regulators, and others. The goal of this organization is to establish a framework that "the global business information supply chain will use to create, exchange, and analyze financial reporting information including, but not limited to, regulatory filings such as annual and quarterly financial statements, general ledger information, and audit schedules."

SOURCE: www.XBRL.org.

BEFORE YOU GO ON...

▶ *REVIEW IT*
1. How does journalizing differ from posting?
2. What is the purpose of (a) the ledger and (b) a chart of accounts?

▶ *DO IT*
Kate Brown recorded the following transactions in a general journal during the month of March.

Cash	2,280	
Service Revenue		2,280
Wages Expense	400	
Cash		400
Utilities Expense	92	
Cash		92

Post these entries to the Cash account of the general ledger to determine the ending balance in cash. The beginning balance in cash on March 1 was $600.

ACTION PLAN
- Recall that posting involves transferring the journalized debits and credits to specific accounts in the ledger.
- Determine the ending balance by netting the total debits and credits.

SOLUTION

Cash

3/1	600		400
	2,280		92
3/31 Bal.	2,388		

Related exercise material: BE2-7, BE2-8, E2-2, E2-5, and E2-8.

☑ THE NAVIGATOR

SUMMARY ILLUSTRATION OF JOURNALIZING AND POSTING

The journal for Pioneer Advertising Agency for October is shown in Illustration 2-29. The ledger is shown in Illustration 2-30, on page 64, with all balances in color.

	GENERAL JOURNAL			Page J1
Date	**Account Titles and Explanation**	**Ref.**	**Debit**	**Credit**
2002				
Oct. 1	Cash	101	10,000	
	C. R. Byrd, Capital	301		10,000
	(Owner's investment of cash in business)			
1	Office Equipment	157	5,000	
	Notes Payable	200		5,000
	(Issued 30-month, 12% note for office equipment)			
2	Cash	101	1,200	
	Unearned Revenue	209		1,200
	(Received cash for future services)			
3	Rent Expense	729	900	
	Cash	101		900
	(Paid October rent)			
4	Prepaid Insurance	130	600	
	Cash	101		600
	(Paid one-year policy; effective date October 1)			
5	Advertising Supplies	126	2,500	
	Accounts Payable	201		2,500
	(Purchased supplies on account from Aero Supply)			
20	C. R. Byrd, Drawing	306	500	
	Cash	101		500
	(Withdrew cash for personal use)			
26	Salaries Expense	726	4,000	
	Cash	101		4,000
	(Paid salaries to date)			
31	Cash	101	10,000	
	Service Revenue	400		10,000
	(Received cash for services provided)			

Illustration 2-29

General journal entries

Cash   No. 101

Date	Explanation	Ref.	Debit	Credit	Balance
2002					
Oct. 1		J1	10,000		10,000
2		J1	1,200		11,200
3		J1		900	10,300
4		J1		600	9,700
20		J1		500	9,200
26		J1		4,000	5,200
31		J1	10,000		15,200

Advertising Supplies   No. 126

Date	Explanation	Ref.	Debit	Credit	Balance
2002					
Oct. 5		J1	2,500		2,500

Prepaid Insurance   No. 130

Date	Explanation	Ref.	Debit	Credit	Balance
2002					
Oct. 4		J1	600		600

Office Equipment   No. 157

Date	Explanation	Ref.	Debit	Credit	Balance
2002					
Oct. 1		J1	5,000		5,000

Notes Payable   No. 200

Date	Explanation	Ref.	Debit	Credit	Balance
2002					
Oct. 1		J1		5,000	5,000

Accounts Payable   No. 201

Date	Explanation	Ref.	Debit	Credit	Balance
2002					
Oct. 5		J1		2,500	2,500

Unearned Revenue   No. 209

Date	Explanation	Ref.	Debit	Credit	Balance
2002					
Oct. 2		J1		1,200	1,200

C. R. Byrd, Capital   No. 301

Date	Explanation	Ref.	Debit	Credit	Balance
2002					
Oct. 1		J1		10,000	10,000

C. R. Byrd, Drawing   No. 306

Date	Explanation	Ref.	Debit	Credit	Balance
2002					
Oct. 20		J1	500		500

Service Revenue   No. 400

Date	Explanation	Ref.	Debit	Credit	Balance
2002					
Oct. 31		J1		10,000	10,000

Salaries Expense   No. 726

Date	Explanation	Ref.	Debit	Credit	Balance
2002					
Oct. 26		J1	4,000		4,000

Rent Expense   No. 729

Date	Explanation	Ref.	Debit	Credit	Balance
2002					
Oct. 3		J1	900		900

Illustration 2-30

General ledger

THE TRIAL BALANCE

STUDY OBJECTIVE 7

Prepare a trial balance and explain its purposes.

HELPFUL HINT

A trial balance is so named because it is a test to see if the sum of the debit balances equals the sum of the credit balances.

A **trial balance** is a list of accounts and their balances at a given time. Customarily, a trial balance is prepared at the end of an accounting period. The accounts are listed in the order in which they appear in the ledger; debit balances are listed in the left column and credit balances in the right column.

The primary purpose of a trial balance is to prove (check) that the debits equal the credits after posting. In other words, the sum of the debit account balances in the trial balance should equal the sum of the credit account balances. **If the debits and credits do not agree, the trial balance can be used to uncover errors in journalizing and posting. In addition, it is useful in the preparation of financial statements,** as will be explained in the next two chapters.

The steps for preparing a trial balance are:

1. List the account titles and their balances.
2. Total the debit and credit columns.
3. Prove the equality of the two columns.

The trial balance prepared from Pioneer Advertising's ledger is shown below.

Illustration 2-31

A trial balance

PIONEER ADVERTISING AGENCY **Trial Balance** **October 31, 2002**		
	Debit	**Credit**
Cash	$15,200	
Advertising Supplies	2,500	
Prepaid Insurance	600	
Office Equipment	5,000	
Notes Payable		$ 5,000
Accounts Payable		2,500
Unearned Revenue		1,200
C. R. Byrd, Capital		10,000
C. R. Byrd, Drawing	500	
Service Revenue		10,000
Salaries Expense	4,000	
Rent Expense	900	
	$28,700	$28,700

HELPFUL HINT
To sum a column of figures is sometimes referred to as *to foot* the column. The column is then said to be *footed*.

Note that the total debits ($28,700) equal the total credits ($28,700). Account numbers are sometimes shown to the left of the account titles in the trial balance.

A trial balance is a necessary checkpoint for uncovering certain types of errors before you proceed to other steps in the accounting process. For example, if only the debit portion of a journal entry has been posted, the trial balance would bring this error to light.

LIMITATIONS OF A TRIAL BALANCE

A trial balance does not guarantee freedom from recording errors, however. **It does not prove that all transactions have been recorded or that the ledger is correct.** Numerous errors may exist even though the trial balance columns agree. For example, the trial balance may balance even when (1) a transaction is not journalized, (2) a correct journal entry is not posted, (3) a journal entry is posted twice, (4) incorrect accounts are used in journalizing or posting, or (5) offsetting errors are made in recording the amount of a transaction. In other words, as long as equal debits and credits are posted, even to the wrong account or in the wrong amount, the total debits will equal the total credits.

LOCATING ERRORS

The procedure for preparing a trial balance is relatively simple. However, if the trial balance does not balance, locating an error in a manual system can be time-consuming, tedious, and frustrating. Errors generally result from mathematical mistakes, incorrect postings, or simply transcribing data incorrectly.

What do you do if you are faced with a trial balance that does not balance? First determine the amount of the difference between the two columns of the trial balance. After this amount is known, the following steps are often helpful:

1. If the error is $1, $10, $100, or $1,000, re-add the trial balance columns and recompute the account balances.
2. If the error is divisible by 2, scan the trial balance to see whether a balance equal to half the error has been entered in the wrong column.

*E***THICS NOTE**

Auditors are required to differentiate *errors* from *irregularities* when evaluating the accounting system. An error is the result of an unintentional mistake; as such, it is neither ethical nor unethical. An irregularity, on the other hand, is an intentional misstatement, which is viewed as unethical.

3. If the error is divisible by 9, retrace the account balances on the trial balance to see whether they are incorrectly copied from the ledger. For example, if a balance was $12 and it was listed as $21, a $9 error has been made. Reversing the order of numbers is called a transposition error.

4. If the error is not divisible by 2 or 9 (for example, $365), scan the ledger to see whether an account balance of $365 has been omitted from the trial balance, and scan the journal to see whether a $365 posting has been omitted.

TECHNOLOGY IN ACTION

In a computerized system, the trial balance is often only one column (no debit or credit columns), and the accounts have plus and minus signs associated with them. The final balance therefore is zero. Any errors that develop in a computerized system will undoubtedly involve the initial recording rather than some error in the posting or preparation of a trial balance.

USE OF DOLLAR SIGNS

Note that dollar signs do not appear in the journals or ledgers. Dollar signs are usually used only in the trial balance and the financial statements. Generally, a dollar sign is shown only for the first item in the column and for the total of that column. A single line is placed under the column of figures to be added or subtracted; the total amount is double underlined to indicate the final sum.

BEFORE YOU GO ON...

▶ *REVIEW IT*
1. What is a trial balance and what is its primary purpose?
2. How is a trial balance prepared?
3. What are the limitations of a trial balance?

A LOOK BACK AT OUR FEATURE STORY

Refer back to the Feature Story about **The Mug and Musket** at the beginning of the chapter, and answer the following questions.
1. What accounting entries would Tanis likely make to record (a) the receipt of cash from a customer in payment of their bill, (b) payment of a utility bill, and (c) payment of wages for the waiters?
2. How did Tanis's job as Director of Finance help in her studies as she finished her business administration degree?

SOLUTION
1. Tanis would likely make the following entries.
   (a) Cash
       Food Sales Revenue
         (Receipt of payment for food services)
   (b) Utility Expense
       Cash
         (Payment of electric bill)
   (c) Salaries (or Wages) Expense
       Cash
         (Paid waiters' wages)
2. As a result of her accounting position, Tanis was able to relate the subject matter as well as much of the assignment material in her business courses to a real-world context. From her job, she knew how bills were paid, how supplies were determined, how employees were hired, managed, evaluated, and paid.

☑ THE NAVIGATOR

DEMONSTRATION PROBLEM

Additional Demonstration Problem

Bob Sample opened the Campus Laundromat on September 1, 2002. During the first month of operations the following transactions occurred.

Sept. 1 Invested $20,000 cash in the business.
      2 Paid $1,000 cash for store rent for the month of September.
      3 Purchased washers and dryers for $25,000, paying $10,000 in cash and signing a $15,000, 6-month, 12% note payable.
      4 Paid $1,200 for one-year accident insurance policy.
    10 Received bill from the *Daily News* for advertising the opening of the laundromat $200.
    20 Withdrew $700 cash for personal use.
    30 Determined that cash receipts for laundry services for the month were $6,200.

The chart of accounts for the company is the same as in Pioneer Advertising Agency except for the following: No. 154 Laundry Equipment and No. 610 Advertising Expense.

Instructions

(a) Journalize the September transactions. (Use J1 for the journal page number.)
(b) Open ledger accounts and post the September transactions.
(c) Prepare a trial balance at September 30, 2002.

SOLUTION TO DEMONSTRATION PROBLEM

(a)

GENERAL JOURNAL   J1

Date	Account Titles and Explanation	Ref.	Debit	Credit
2002				
Sept. 1	Cash	101	20,000	
	Bob Sample, Capital	301		20,000
	(Owner's investment of cash in business)			
2	Rent Expense	729	1,000	
	Cash	101		1,000
	(Paid September rent)			
3	Laundry Equipment	154	25,000	
	Cash	101		10,000
	Notes Payable	200		15,000
	(Purchased laundry equipment for cash and 6-month, 12% note payable)			
4	Prepaid Insurance	130	1,200	
	Cash	101		1,200
	(Paid one-year insurance policy)			
10	Advertising Expense	610	200	
	Accounts Payable	201		200
	(Received bill from *Daily News* for advertising)			
20	Bob Sample, Drawing	306	700	
	Cash	101		700
	(Withdrew cash for personal use)			
30	Cash	101	6,200	
	Service Revenue	400		6,200
	(Received cash for services provided)			

ACTION PLAN

- Make separate journal entries for each transaction.
- In journalizing, make sure debits equal credits.
- In journalizing, use specific account titles taken from the chart of accounts.
- Provide appropriate description of journal entry.
- Arrange ledger in statement order, beginning with the balance sheet accounts.
- Post in chronological order.
- Use numbers in the reference column to indicate the amount has been posted.
- In the trial balance, list accounts in the order in which they appear in the ledger.
- List debit balances in the left column, and credit balances in the right column.

(b) **GENERAL LEDGER**

Cash					No. 101
Date	Explanation	Ref.	Debit	Credit	Balance
2002 Sept. 1		J1	20,000		20,000
2		J1		1,000	19,000
3		J1		10,000	9,000
4		J1		1,200	7,800
20		J1		700	7,100
30		J1	6,200		13,300

Accounts Payable					No. 201
Date	Explanation	Ref.	Debit	Credit	Balance
2002 Sept. 10		J1		200	200

Bob Sample, Capital					No. 301
Date	Explanation	Ref.	Debit	Credit	Balance
2002 Sept. 1		J1		20,000	20,000

Prepaid Insurance					No. 130
Date	Explanation	Ref.	Debit	Credit	Balance
2002 Sept. 4		J1	1,200		1,200

Bob Sample, Drawing					No. 306
Date	Explanation	Ref.	Debit	Credit	Balance
2002 Sept. 20		J1	700		700

Laundry Equipment					No. 154
Date	Explanation	Ref.	Debit	Credit	Balance
2002 Sept. 3		J1	25,000		25,000

Service Revenue					No. 400
Date	Explanation	Ref.	Debit	Credit	Balance
2002 Sept. 30		J1		6,200	6,200

Notes Payable					No. 200
Date	Explanation	Ref.	Debit	Credit	Balance
2002 Sept. 3		J1		15,000	15,000

Advertising Expense					No. 610
Date	Explanation	Ref.	Debit	Credit	Balance
2002 Sept. 10		J1	200		200

Rent Expense					No. 729
Date	Explanation	Ref.	Debit	Credit	Balance
2002 Sept. 2		J1	1,000		1,000

(c)

CAMPUS LAUNDROMAT
Trial Balance
September 30, 2002

	Debit	Credit
Cash	$13,300	
Prepaid Insurance	1,200	
Laundry Equipment	25,000	
Notes Payable		$15,000
Accounts Payable		200
Bob Sample, Capital		20,000
Bob Sample, Drawing	700	
Service Revenue		6,200
Advertising Expense	200	
Rent Expense	1,000	
	$41,400	$41,400

SUMMARY OF STUDY OBJECTIVES

1. Explain what an account is and how it helps in the recording process. An account is a record of increases and decreases in specific asset, liability, and owner's equity items.

2. Define debits and credits and explain how they are used to record business transactions. The terms debit and credit are synonymous with left and right. Assets, drawings, and expenses are increased by debits and decreased by credits. Liabilities, owner's capital, and revenues are increased by credits and decreased by debits.

3. Identify the basic steps in the recording process. The basic steps in the recording process are: (a) analyze each transaction in terms of its effects on the accounts, (b) enter the transaction information in a journal, (c) transfer the journal information to the appropriate accounts in the ledger.

4. Explain what a journal is and how it helps in the recording process. The initial accounting record of a transaction is entered in a journal before the data are entered in the accounts. A journal (a) discloses in one place the complete effects of a transaction, (b) provides a chronological record

of transactions, and (c) prevents or locates errors because the debit and credit amounts for each entry can be readily compared.

5. Explain what a ledger is and how it helps in the recording process. The entire group of accounts maintained by a company is referred to as the ledger. The ledger keeps in one place all the information about changes in specific account balances.

6. Explain what posting is and how it helps in the recording process. Posting is the procedure of transferring journal entries to the ledger accounts. This phase of the recording process accumulates the effects of journalized transactions in the individual accounts.

7. Prepare a trial balance and explain its purposes. A trial balance is a list of accounts and their balances at a given time. Its primary purpose is to prove the equality of debits and credits after posting. A trial balance also uncovers errors in journalizing and posting and is useful in preparing financial statements.

☑ THE NAVIGATOR

Key Term Matching Activity

GLOSSARY

Account A record of increases and decreases in specific asset, liability, or owner's equity items. (p. 44).

Chart of accounts A list of accounts and the account numbers that identify their location in the ledger. (p. 56).

Compound entry A journal entry that involves three or more accounts. (p. 52).

Credit The right side of an account. (p. 45).

Debit The left side of an account. (p. 45).

Double-entry system A system that records in appropriate accounts the dual effect of each transaction. (p. 45).

General journal The most basic form of journal. (p. 50).

General ledger A ledger that contains all asset, liability, and owner's equity accounts. (p. 53).

Journal An accounting record in which transactions are initially recorded in chronological order. (p. 50).

Journalizing The entering of transaction data in the journal. (p. 50).

Ledger The entire group of accounts maintained by a company. (p. 53).

Posting The procedure of transferring journal entries to the ledger accounts. (p. 54).

Simple entry A journal entry that involves only two accounts. (p. 51).

T account The basic form of an account. (p. 44).

Three-column form of account A form with columns for debit, credit, and balance amounts in an account. (p. 54).

Trial balance A list of accounts and their balances at a given time. (p. 64).

Chapter 2 Self-Test

SELF-STUDY QUESTIONS

Answers are at the end of the chapter.

(SO 1) **1.** Which of the following statements about an account is true?
a. In its simplest form, an account consists of two parts.
b. An account is an individual accounting record of increases and decreases in specific asset, liability, and owner's equity items.
c. There are separate accounts for specific assets and liabilities but only one account for owner's equity items.
d. The left side of an account is the credit or decrease side.

2. Debits: (SO 2)
a. increase both assets and liabilities.
b. decrease both assets and liabilities.
c. increase assets and decrease liabilities.
d. decrease assets and increase liabilities.

3. A revenue account: (SO 2)
a. is increased by debits.
b. is decreased by credits.
c. has a normal balance of a debit.
d. is increased by credits.

(SO 2) **4.** Accounts that normally have debit balances are:
   a. assets, expenses, and revenues.
   b. assets, expenses, and owner's capital.
   c. assets, liabilities, and owner's drawings.
   d. assets, owner's drawings, and expenses.

(SO 3) **5.** Which of the following is *not* part of the recording process?
   a. Analyzing transactions.
   b. Preparing a trial balance.
   c. Entering transactions in a journal.
   d. Posting transactions.

(SO 4) **6.** Which of the following statements about a journal is false?
   a. It is not a book of original entry.
   b. It provides a chronological record of transactions.
   c. It helps to locate errors because the debit and credit amounts for each entry can be readily compared.
   d. It discloses in one place the complete effect of a transaction.

(SO 5) **7.** A ledger:
   a. contains only asset and liability accounts.
   b. should show accounts in alphabetical order.
   c. is a collection of the entire group of accounts maintained by a company.
   d. is a book of original entry.

8. Posting: (SO 6)
   a. normally occurs before journalizing.
   b. transfers ledger transaction data to the journal.
   c. is an optional step in the recording process.
   d. transfers journal entries to ledger accounts.

9. A trial balance: (SO 7)
   a. is a list of accounts with their balances at a given time.
   b. proves the mathematical accuracy of journalized transactions.
   c. will not balance if a correct journal entry is posted twice.
   d. proves that all transactions have been recorded.

10. A trial balance will not balance if: (SO 7)
   a. a correct journal entry is posted twice.
   b. the purchase of supplies on account is debited to Supplies and credited to Cash.
   c. a $100 cash drawing by the owner is debited to Owner's Drawing for $1,000 and credited to Cash for $100.
   d. a $450 payment on account is debited to Accounts Payable for $45 and credited to Cash for $45.

Questions

1. Describe the parts of a T account.

2. "The terms *debit* and *credit* mean increase and decrease, respectively." Do you agree? Explain.

3. José Amaro, a fellow student, contends that the double-entry system means each transaction must be recorded twice. Is José correct? Explain.

4. Teresa Alvarez, a beginning accounting student, believes debit balances are favorable and credit balances are unfavorable. Is Teresa correct? Discuss.

5. State the rules of debit and credit as applied to (a) asset accounts, (b) liability accounts, and (c) the owner's equity accounts (revenue, expenses, owner's drawing, and owner's capital).

6. What is the normal balance for each of the following accounts? (a) Accounts Receivable. (b) Cash. (c) Owner's Drawing. (d) Accounts Payable. (e) Service Revenue. (f) Salaries Expense. (g) Owner's Capital.

7. Indicate whether each of the following accounts is an asset, a liability, or an owner's equity account and whether it has a normal debit or credit balance: (a) Accounts Receivable, (b) Accounts Payable, (c) Equipment, (d) Owner's Drawing, (e) Supplies.

8. For the following transactions, indicate the account debited and the account credited.
   (a) Supplies are purchased on account.
   (b) Cash is received on signing a note payable.
   (c) Employees are paid salaries in cash.

9. Indicate whether the following accounts generally will have (a) debit entries only, (b) credit entries only, or (c) both debit and credit entries.

(1) Cash. (4) Accounts Payable.
(2) Accounts Receivable. (5) Salaries Expense.
(3) Owner's Drawing. (6) Service Revenue.

10. What are the basic steps in the recording process?

11. What are the advantages of using a journal in the recording process?

12. (a) When entering a transaction in the journal, should the debit or credit be written first?
   (b) Which should be indented, the debit or credit?

13. Describe a compound entry, and provide an example.

14. (a) Should business transaction debits and credits be recorded directly in the ledger accounts?
   (b) What are the advantages of first recording transactions in the journal and then posting to the ledger?

15. The account number is entered as the last step in posting the amounts from the journal to the ledger. What is the advantage of this step?

16. Journalize the following business transactions.
   (a) Doris Wang invests $9,000 cash in the business.
   (b) Insurance of $800 is paid for the year.
   (c) Supplies of $1,500 are purchased on account.
   (d) Cash of $7,500 is received for services rendered.

17. (a) What is a ledger?
   (b) What is a chart of accounts and why is it important?

18. What is a trial balance and what are its purposes?

19. Kap Shin is confused about how accounting information flows through the accounting system. He believes the flow of information is as follows.
   (a) Debits and credits posted to the ledger.
   (b) Business transaction occurs.

(c) Information entered in the journal.

(d) Financial statements are prepared.

(e) Trial balance is prepared.

Is Kap correct? If not, indicate to Kap the proper flow of the information.

20. Two students are discussing the use of a trial balance. They wonder whether the following errors, each consid-

ered separately, would prevent the trial balance from balancing.

(a) The bookkeeper debited Cash for $600 and credited Wages Expense for $600 for payment of wages.

(b) Cash collected on account was debited to Cash for $900 and Service Revenue was credited for $90.

What would you tell them?

*B*RIEF EXERCISES

BE2-1 For each of the following accounts indicate the effects of (a) a debit and (b) a credit on the accounts and (c) the normal balance of the account.

1. Accounts Payable. DR
2. Advertising Expense. DR
3. Service Revenue. CR
4. Accounts Receivable. DR
5. B. C. Jardine, Capital. CR investment
6. B. C. Jardine, Drawing. DR

Indicate debit and credit effects and normal balance.
(SO 2)

BE2-2 Transactions for the H. J. Oslo Company for the month of June are presented below. Identify the accounts to be debited and credited for each transaction.

June 1 H. J. Oslo invests $3,000 cash in a small welding business of which he is the sole proprietor.

 2 Purchases equipment on account for $900.

 3 $500 cash is paid to landlord for June rent.

 12 Bills J. Kronsnoble $300 for welding work done on account.

Identify accounts to be debited and credited.
(SO 2)

BE2-3 Using the data in BE2-2, journalize the transactions. (You may omit explanations.)

BE2-4 [pencil icon] Tage Shumway, a fellow student, is unclear about the basic steps in the recording process. Identify and briefly explain the steps in the order in which they occur.

BE2-5 J. A. Norris has the following transactions during August of the current year. Indicate (a) the effect on the accounting equation and (b) the debit-credit analysis illustrated on pages 57–61 of the text.

Aug. 1 Opens an office as a financial advisor, investing $6,000 in cash.

 4 Pays insurance in advance for 6 months, $1,800 cash.

 16 Receives $800 from clients for services rendered.

 27 Pays secretary $500 salary.

Journalize transactions.
(SO 4)
Identify and explain steps in recording process.
(SO 3)
Indicate basic and debit-credit analysis.
(SO 4)

BE2-6 Using the data in BE2-5, journalize the transactions. (You may omit explanations.)

BE2-7 Selected transactions for the Gonzales Company are presented in journal form below. Post the transactions to T accounts. Make one T account for each item and determine each account's ending balance.

Journalize transactions.
(SO 4)
Post journal entries to T accounts.
(SO 6)

J1

Date	Account Titles and Explanation	Ref.	Debit	Credit
May 5	Accounts Receivable		5,000	
	Service Revenue			5,000
	(Billed for services provided)			
12	Cash		2,400	
	Accounts Receivable			2,400
	(Received cash in payment of account)			
15	Cash		2,000	
	Service Revenue			2,000
	(Received cash for services provided)			

*Post journal entries to stan-
dard form of account.*
(SO 6)
Prepare a trial balance.
(SO 7)

BE2-8   Selected journal entries for the Gonzales Company are presented in BE2-7. Post the transactions using the standard form of account.

BE2-9   From the ledger balances given below, prepare a trial balance for the P. J. Carland Company at June 30, 2002. List the accounts in the order shown on page 65 of the text. All account balances are normal.

   Accounts Payable $7,000, Cash $6,800, P. J. Carland, Capital $20,000, P. J. Carland, Drawing $1,200, Equipment $17,000, Service Revenue $6,000, Accounts Receivable $3,000, Salaries Expense $4,000, and Rent Expense $1,000.

*Prepare a correct trial
balance.*
(SO 7)

BE2-10   An inexperienced bookkeeper prepared the following trial balance. Prepare a correct trial balance, assuming all account balances are normal.

GOMEZ COMPANY
Trial Balance
December 31, 2002

	Debit	Credit
Cash	$18,800	
Prepaid Insurance		$ 3,500
Accounts Payable		3,000
Unearned Revenue	4,200	
P. Gomez, Capital		15,000
P. Gomez, Drawing		4,500
Service Revenue		25,600
Salaries Expense	18,600	
Rent Expense		2,400
	$41,600	$54,000

EXERCISES

*Identify debits, credits, and
normal balances.*
(SO 2)

E2-1   Selected transactions for A. Mane, an interior decorator, in her first month of business, are as follows.

Jan.	2	Invested $10,000 cash in business.
	3	Purchased used car for $4,000 cash for use in business.
	9	Purchased supplies on account for $500.
	11	Billed customers $1,800 for services performed.
	16	Paid $200 cash for advertising start of business.
	20	Received $700 cash from customers billed on January 11.
	23	Paid creditor $300 cash on account.
	28	Withdrew $1,000 cash for personal use of owner.

Instructions
For each transaction indicate the following.

(a) The basic type of account debited and credited (asset, liability, owner's equity).
(b) The specific account debited and credited (cash, rent expense, service revenue, etc.).
(c) Whether the specific account is increased or decreased.
(d) The normal balance of the specific account.

   Use the following format, in which the January 2 transaction is given as an example.

	Account Debited				Account Credited			
Date	**(a)** Basic Type	**(b)** Specific Account	**(c)** Effect	**(d)** Normal Balance	**(a)** Basic Type	**(b)** Specific Account	**(c)** Effect	**(d)** Normal Balance
Jan. 2	Asset	Cash	Increase	Debit	Owner's Equity	A. Mane, Capital	Increase	Credit

E2-2   Data for A. Mane, interior decorator, are presented in E2-1.

Journalize transactions and post using standard account form.
(SO 4)

Instructions
Journalize the transactions using journal page J1. (You may omit explanations.)

E2-3   Presented below is information related to Marx Real Estate Agency.

Analyze transactions and determine their effect on accounts.
(SO 2)

Oct. 1   Lynn Marx begins business as a real estate agent with a cash investment of
          $10,000.
       2   Hires an administrative assistant.
       3   Purchases office furniture for $1,900, on account.
       6   Sells a house and lot for B. Rollins; bills B. Rollins $3,200 for realty services
          provided.
      27   Pays $700 on the balance related to the transaction of October 3.
      30   Pays the administrative assistant $1,500 in salary for October.

Instructions
Prepare the debit-credit analysis for each transaction as illustrated on pages 57–61.

E2-4   Transaction data for Marx Real Estate Agency are presented in E2-3.

Journalize transactions.
(SO 4)

Instructions
Journalize the transactions. (You may omit explanations.)

E2-5   Selected transactions from the journal of J. L. Kang, investment broker, are presented
below.

Post journal entries and prepare a trial balance.
(SO 6, 7)

Date	Account Titles and Explanation	Ref.	Debit	Credit
Aug. 1	Cash		2,000	
	J. L Kang, Capital			2,000
	(Owner's investment of cash in business)			
10	Cash		2,400	
	Service Revenue			2,400
	(Received cash for services provided)			
12	Office Equipment		4,000	
	Cash			1,000
	Notes Payable			3,000
	(Purchased office equipment for cash and notes payable)			
25	Accounts Receivable		1,600	
	Service Revenue			1,600
	(Billed for services provided)			
31	Cash		900	
	Accounts Receivable			900
	(Receipt of cash on account)			

Instructions
(a) Post the transactions to T accounts.
(b) Prepare a trial balance at August 31, 2002.

E2-6   The T accounts on the next page summarize the ledger of Kim Landscaping Company
at the end of the first month of operations.

Journalize transactions from account data and prepare a trial balance.
(SO 4, 7)

Cash			No. 101
4/1	5,000	4/15	600
4/12	900	4/25	1,500
4/29	400		
4/30	800		

Unearned Revenue			No. 205
		4/30	800

Accounts Receivable			No. 112
4/7	3,200	4/29	400

J. Kim, Capital			No. 301
		4/1	5,000

Supplies			No. 126
4/4	1,800		

Service Revenue			No. 400
		4/7	3,200
		4/12	900

Accounts Payable			No. 201
4/25	1,500	4/4	1,800

Salaries Expense		No. 726
4/15	600	

Instructions

(a) Prepare the complete general journal (including explanations) from which the postings to Cash were made.

(b) Prepare a trial balance at April 30, 2002.

Journalize transactions from account data and prepare a trial balance.
(SO 4, 7)

E2-7   Presented below is the ledger for Holly Co.

Cash			No. 101
10/1	6,000	10/4	400
10/10	650	10/12	1,500
10/10	5,000	10/15	250
10/20	500	10/30	300
10/25	2,000	10/31	500

Holly, Capital			No. 301
		10/1	6,000
		10/25	2,000

Holly, Drawing			No. 306
10/30	300		

Accounts Receivable			No. 112
10/6	800	10/20	500
10/20	940		

Service Revenue			No. 407
		10/6	800
		10/10	650
		10/20	940

Supplies			No. 126
10/4	400		

Store Wages Expense		No. 628
10/31	500	

Furniture			No. 149
10/3	2,000		

Rent Expense		No. 729
10/15	250	

Notes Payable			No. 200
		10/10	5,000

Accounts Payable			No. 201
10/12	1,500	10/3	2,000

Instructions

(a) Reproduce the journal entries for the transactions that occurred on October 1, 10, and 20, and provide explanations for each.

(b) Determine the October 31 balance for each of the accounts above, and prepare a trial balance at October 31, 2002.

similar to this in the test

E2-8 Selected transactions for Craig Stevenson Company during its first month in business are presented below.

Prepare journal entries and post using standard account form.
(SO 4, 6)

Sept. 1 Invested $10,000 cash in the business.
5 Purchased equipment for $10,000 paying $5,000 in cash and the balance on account.
25 Paid $3,000 cash on balance owed for equipment.
30 Withdrew $500 cash for personal use.

Stevenson's chart of accounts shows: No. 101 Cash, No. 157 Equipment, No. 201 Accounts Payable, No. 301 Craig Stevenson, Capital, No. 306 Craig Stevenson, Drawing.

Instructions

(a) Journalize the transactions on page J1 of the journal.
(b) Post the transactions using the standard account form.

E2-9 The bookkeeper for John Castle's Equipment Repair made a number of errors in journalizing and posting, as described below.

Analyze errors and their effects on trial balance.
(SO 7)

1. A credit posting of $400 to Accounts Receivable was omitted.
2. A debit posting of $750 for Prepaid Insurance was debited to Insurance Expense.
3. A collection on account of $100 was journalized and posted as a debit to Cash $100 and a credit to Service Revenue $100.
4. A credit posting of $300 to Property Taxes Payable was made twice.
5. A cash purchase of supplies for $250 was journalized and posted as a debit to Supplies $25 and a credit to Cash $25.
6. A debit of $485 to Advertising Expense was posted as $458.

Instructions
For each error:

(a) Indicate whether the trial balance will balance.
(b) If the trial balance will not balance, indicate the amount of the difference.
(c) Indicate the trial balance column that will have the larger total.

Consider each error separately. Use the following form, in which error (1) is given as an example.

Error	(a) In Balance	(b) Difference	(c) Larger Column
(1)	No	$400	debit

E2-10 The accounts in the ledger of Tardy Delivery Service contain the following balances on July 31, 2002.

Prepare a trial balance
(SO 2, 7)

Accounts Receivable	$ 8,642	Prepaid Insurance	$ 1,968
Accounts Payable	8,396	Repair Expense	961
Cash	?	Service Revenue	10,610
Delivery Equipment	49,360	I. M. Tardy, Drawing	700
Gas and Oil Expense	758	I. M. Tardy, Capital	44,636
Insurance Expense	523	Salaries Expense	4,428
Notes Payable	21,450	Salaries Payable	815

Instructions
Prepare a trial balance with the accounts arranged as illustrated in the chapter and fill in the missing amount for Cash.

PROBLEMS: SET A

P2-1A Frontier Park was started on April 1 by C. J. Sanculi. The following selected events and transactions occurred during April.

Journalize a series of transactions.
(SO 2, 4)

Peachtree

Apr. 1 Sanculi invested $40,000 cash in the business.
4 Purchased land costing $30,000 for cash.
8 Incurred advertising expense of $1,800 on account.
11 Paid salaries to employees $1,500.
12 Hired park manager at a salary of $4,000 per month, effective May 1.

13 Paid $1,500 cash for a one-year insurance policy.
17 Withdrew $600 cash for personal use.
20 Received $5,700 in cash for admission fees.
25 Sold 100 coupon books for $25 each. Each book contains 10 coupons that entitle the holder to one admission to the park.
30 Received $5,900 in cash admission fees.
30 Paid $900 on account for advertising incurred on April 8.

Sanculi uses the following accounts: Cash; Prepaid Insurance; Land; Accounts Payable; Unearned Admission Revenue; C. J. Sanculi, Capital; C. J. Sanculi, Drawing; Admission Revenue; Advertising Expense; and Salaries Expense.

Instructions
Journalize the April transactions.

Journalize transactions, post, and prepare a trial balance.
(SO 2, 4, 6, 7)

P2-2A Iva Holz is a licensed CPA. During the first month of operations of her business, the following events and transactions occurred.

May 1 Holz invested $30,000 cash.
    2 Hired a secretary-receptionist at a salary of $1,000 per month.
    3 Purchased $1,500 of supplies on account from Read Supply Company.
    7 Paid office rent of $900 cash for the month.
   11 Completed a tax assignment and billed client $1,100 for services rendered.
   12 Received $3,500 advance on a management consulting engagement.
   17 Received cash of $1,200 for services completed for H. Arnold Co.
   31 Paid secretary-receptionist $1,000 salary for the month.
   31 Paid 40% of balance due Read Supply Company.

Iva uses the following chart of accounts: No. 101 Cash, No. 112 Accounts Receivable, No. 126 Supplies, No. 201 Accounts Payable, No. 205 Unearned Revenue, No. 301 Iva Holz, Capital, No. 400 Service Revenue, No. 726 Salaries Expense, and No. 729 Rent Expense.

Instructions

Trial balance totals $36,700

(a) Journalize the transactions.
(b) Post to the ledger accounts.
(c) Prepare a trial balance on May 31, 2002.

Journalize and post transactions, prepare a trial balance, and determine elements of financial statements.
(SO 2, 4, 6, 7)

P2-3A Leo Mataruka owns and manages a computer repair service, which had the following trial balance on December 31, 2001 (the end of its fiscal year).

BYTE REPAIR SERVICE
Trial Balance
December 31, 2001

Cash	$ 8,000	
Accounts Receivable	15,000	
Parts Inventory	13,000	
Prepaid Rent	3,000	
Shop Equipment	21,000	
Accounts Payable		$19,000
Leo Mataruka, Capital		41,000
	$ 60,000	$60,000

Summarized transactions for January 2002 were as follows.

1. Advertising costs, paid in cash, $1,000.
2. Additional repair parts inventory acquired on account $3,000.
3. Miscellaneous expenses, paid in cash, $2,000.
4. Cash collected from customers on account $13,000.
5. Cash paid to creditors on account $15,000.

6. Repair parts used during January $4,000. (*Hint:* Debit this to Repair Parts Expense.)
7. Repair services performed during January: for cash $4,000; on account $9,000.
8. Wages for January, paid in cash, $3,000.
9. Rent expense for January recorded. However, no cash was paid out for rent during January. A rent payment had been made for 3 months, in advance, on December 1, 2001, in the amount of $4,500.
10. Leo's drawings during January were $2,000.

Instructions

(a) Explain why the December 31, 2001, balance in the Prepaid Rent account is $3,000. (Refer to the Trial Balance and item (9) above.)
(b) Open T accounts for each of the accounts listed in the trial balance, and enter the opening balances for 2002.
(c) Prepare journal entries to record each of the January transactions.
(d) Post the journal entries to the accounts in the ledger. (Add accounts as needed.)
(e) Prepare a trial balance as of January 31, 2002.
(f) Determine the total assets as of January 31, 2002. (It is not necessary to prepare a balance sheet. Simply list the relevant amounts from the trial balance and calculate the total.)
(g) Determine the net income or loss for the month of January 2002. (It is not necessary to prepare an income statement. Simply list the relevant amounts from the trial balance, and calculate the amount of the net income or loss.)

Trial balance totals $61,000

P2-4A   The trial balance of the Santos Company shown below does not balance.

Prepare a correct trial balance.
(SO 7)

SANTOS COMPANY
Trial Balance
May 31, 2002

	Debit	Credit
Cash	$ 3,850	
Accounts Receivable		$ 2,750
Prepaid Insurance	700	
Equipment	12,000	
Accounts Payable		4,500
Property Taxes Payable	560	
T. Santos, Capital		11,700
Service Revenue	8,690	
Salaries Expense	4,200	
Advertising Expense		1,100
Property Tax Expense	800	
	$30,800	$20,050

Your review of the ledger reveals that each account has a normal balance. You also discover the following errors.

1. The totals of the debit sides of Prepaid Insurance, Accounts Payable, and Property Tax Expense were each understated $100.
2. Transposition errors were made in Accounts Receivable and Service Revenue. Based on postings made, the correct balances were $2,570 and $8,960, respectively.
3. A debit posting to Salaries Expense of $200 was omitted.
4. A $700 cash drawing by the owner was debited to T. Santos, Capital for $700 and credited to Cash for $700.
5. A $520 purchase of supplies on account was debited to Equipment for $520 and credited to Cash for $520.
6. A cash payment of $450 for advertising was debited to Advertising Expense for $45 and credited to Cash for $45.
7. A collection from a customer for $210 was debited to Cash for $210 and credited to Accounts Payable for $210.

Trial balance totals $26,630

Instructions

Prepare a correct trial balance. Note: The chart of accounts includes the following: T. Santos, Drawing, and Supplies. (*Hint:* It helps to prepare the correct journal entry for the transaction described and compare it to the mistake made.)

Journalize transactions, post, and prepare a trial balance.
(SO 2, 4, 6, 7)

P2-5A The Lake Theater is owned by Avtar Sandhu. All facilities were completed on March 31. At this time, the ledger showed: No. 101 Cash $6,000; No. 140 Land $10,000; No. 145 Buildings (concession stand, projection room, ticket booth, and screen) $8,000; No. 157 Equipment $6,000; No. 201 Accounts Payable $2,000; No. 275 Mortgage Payable $8,000; and No. 301 Avtar Sandhu, Capital $20,000. During April, the following events and transactions occurred.

Apr. 2 Paid film rental of $800 on first movie.
3 Ordered two additional films at $500 each.
9 Received $1,800 cash from admissions.
10 Made $2,000 payment on mortgage and $1,000 on accounts payable.
11 Lake Theater contracted with R. Thoms Company to operate the concession stand. Thoms is to pay 17% of gross concession receipts (payable monthly) for the right to operate the concession stand.
12 Paid advertising expenses $300.
20 Received one of the films ordered on April 3 and was billed $500. The film will be shown in April.
25 Received $4,200 cash from admissions.
29 Paid salaries $1,600.
30 Received statement from R. Thoms showing gross concession receipts of $1,000 and the balance due to The Lake Theater of $170 ($1,000 × 17%) for April. Thoms paid one-half of the balance due and will remit the remainder on May 5.
30 Prepaid $900 rental on special film to be run in May.

In addition to the accounts identified above, the chart of accounts shows: No. 112 Accounts Receivable, No. 136 Prepaid Rentals, No. 405 Admission Revenue, No. 406 Concession Revenue, No. 610 Advertising Expense, No. 632 Film Rental Expense, and No. 726 Salaries Expense.

Instructions

Trial balance totals $33,670

(a) Enter the beginning balances in the ledger as of April 1. Insert a check mark (✓) in the reference column of the ledger for the beginning balance.
(b) Journalize the April transactions.
(c) Post the April journal entries to the ledger. Assume that all entries are posted from page 1 of the journal.
(d) Prepare a trial balance on April 30, 2002.

*P*ROBLEMS: *SET B*

Journalize a series of transactions.
(SO 2, 4)

P2-1B Surepar Miniature Golf and Driving Range was opened on March 1 by Jane McInnes. The following selected events and transactions occurred during March:

Mar. 1 Invested $50,000 cash in the business.
3 Purchased Lee's Golf Land for $38,000 cash. The price consists of land $23,000, building $9,000, and equipment $6,000. (Make one compound entry.)
5 Advertised the opening of the driving range and miniature golf course, paying advertising expenses of $1,600.
6 Paid cash $1,480 for a one-year insurance policy.
10 Purchased golf clubs and other equipment for $2,600 from Palmer Company payable in 30 days.
18 Received $800 in cash for golf fees earned.
19 Sold 100 coupon books for $15 each. Each book contains 10 coupons that enable the holder to one round of miniature golf or to hit one bucket of golf balls.
25 Withdrew $500 cash for personal use.
30 Paid salaries of $600.
30 Paid Palmer Company in full.
31 Received $500 cash for fees earned.

Jane McInnes uses the following accounts: Cash; Prepaid Insurance; Land; Buildings; Equipment; Accounts Payable; Unearned Revenue; Jane McInnes, Capital; Jane McInnes, Drawing; Golf Revenue; Advertising Expense; and Salaries Expense.

Instructions
Journalize the March transactions.

P2-2B   Patricia Perez is a licensed architect. During the first month of the operation of her business, the following events and transactions occurred.

Journalize transactions, post, and prepare a trial balance.
(SO 2, 4, 6, 7)

April 1   Invested $20,000 cash.
       1   Hired a secretary-receptionist at a salary of $300 per week payable monthly.
       2   Paid office rent for the month $800.
       3   Purchased architectural supplies on account from Halo Company $1,500.
      10   Completed blueprints on a carport and billed client $900 for services.
      11   Received $500 cash advance from R. Welk for the design of a new home.
      20   Received $1,500 cash for services completed and delivered to P. Donahue.
      30   Paid secretary-receptionist for the month $1,500.
      30   Paid $600 to Halo Company on account.

Patricia uses the following chart of accounts: No. 101 Cash, No. 112 Accounts Receivable, No. 126 Supplies, No. 201 Accounts Payable, No. 205 Unearned Revenue, No. 301 Patricia Perez, Capital, No. 400 Service Revenue, No. 726 Salaries Expense, and No. 729 Rent Expense.

Instructions
(a) Journalize the transactions.
(b) Post to the ledger accounts.
(c) Prepare a trial balance on April 30, 2002.

Trial balance totals $23,800

P2-3B   Bablad Brokerage Services was formed on May 1, 2002. The following transactions took place during the first month.

Journalize transactions, post, and prepare a trial balance and financial statements.
(SO 2, 4, 6, 7)

Transactions on May 1:
 1. Jacob Bablad invested $120,000 cash in the company, as its sole owner.
 2. Hired two employees to work in the warehouse. They will each be paid a salary of $2,000 per month.
 3. Signed a 2-year rental agreement on a warehouse; paid $48,000 cash in advance for the first year. (*Hint:* The portion of the cost related to May 2002 is an expense for this month.)
 4. Purchased furniture and equipment costing $70,000. A cash payment of $20,000 was made immediately; the remainder will be paid in 6 months.
 5. Paid $3,000 cash for a one-year insurance policy on the furniture and equipment. (*Hint:* The portion of the cost related to May 2002 is an expense for this month.)

Transactions during the remainder of the month:
 6. Purchased basic office supplies for $1,000 cash.
 7. Purchased more office supplies for $2,000 on account.
 8. Total revenues earned were $30,000—$10,000 cash and $20,000 on account.
 9. Paid $800 to suppliers on account.
10. Collected $5,000 from customers on account.
11. Received utility bills in the amount of $400, to be paid next month.
12. Paid the monthly salaries of the two employees, totalling $4,000.

Instructions
(a) Prepare journal entries to record each of the events listed.
(b) Post the journal entries to T accounts.
(c) Prepare a trial balance as of May 31, 2002.
(d) Prepare an income statement and a statement of owner's equity for Bablad Brokerage Services for the month ended May 31, 2002, and a balance sheet as of May 31, 2002.

Trial balance totals $201,600

Prepare a correct trial balance.
(SO 7)

P2-4B The trial balance of Thom Wargo Co. shown below does not balance.

THOM WARGO CO.
Trial Balance
June 30, 2002

	Debit	Credit
Cash		$ 3,840
Accounts Receivable	$ 3,231	
Supplies	800	
Equipment	3,000	
Accounts Payable		2,666
Unearned Revenue	2,200	
T. Wargo, Capital		9,000
T. Wargo, Drawing	800	
Service Revenue		2,380
Salaries Expense	3,400	
Office Expense	910	
	$14,341	$17,886

Each of the listed accounts has a normal balance per the general ledger. An examination of the ledger and journal reveals the following errors.

1. Cash received from a customer on account was debited for $570, and Accounts Receivable was credited for the same amount. The actual collection was for $750.
2. The purchase of a typewriter on account for $340 was recorded as a debit to Supplies for $340 and a credit to Accounts Payable for $340.
3. Services were performed on account for a client for $890. Accounts Receivable was debited for $890, and Service Revenue was credited for $89.
4. A debit posting to Salaries Expense of $600 was omitted.
5. A payment on account for $206 was credited to Cash for $206 and credited to Accounts Payable for $260.
6. The withdrawal of $500 cash for Wargo's personal use was debited to Salaries Expense for $500 and credited to Cash for $500.

Instructions

Trial balance totals $16,581

Prepare a correct trial balance. (*Hint:* It helps to prepare the correct journal entry for the transaction described and compare it to the mistake made.)

Journalize transactions, post, and prepare a trial balance.
(SO 2, 4, 6, 7)

P2-5B The Sabo Theater, owned by Adam Sabo, will begin operations in March. The Sabo will be unique in that it will show only triple features of sequential theme movies. As of February 28, the ledger of Sabo showed: No. 101 Cash $16,000; No. 140 Land $42,000; No. 145 Buildings (concession stand, projection room, ticket booth, and screen) $18,000; No. 157 Equipment $16,000; No. 201 Accounts Payable $12,000; and No. 301 A. Sabo, Capital $80,000. During the month of March the following events and transactions occurred.

Mar. 2 Acquired the three *Star Wars* movies (*Star Wars, The Empire Strikes Back,* and *The Return of the Jedi*) to be shown for the first 3 weeks of March. The film rental was $9,000; $3,000 was paid in cash and $6,000 will be paid on March 10.

3 Ordered the first three *Star Trek* movies to be shown the last 10 days of March. It will cost $300 per night.

9 Received $6,500 cash from admissions.

10 Paid balance due on *Star Wars* movies rental and $3,000 on February 28 accounts payable.

11 Sabo Theater contracted with M. Brewer Company to operate the concession stand. Brewer is to pay 15% of gross concession receipts (payable monthly) for the right to operate the concession stand.

12 Paid advertising expenses $800.

20 Received $7,200 cash from admissions.

20 Received the *Star Trek* movies and paid the rental fee of $3,000.

31 Paid salaries of $4,800.

31 Received statement from M. Brewer showing gross receipts from concessions of
$8,000 and the balance due to Sabo Theater of $1,200 ($8,000 × 15%) for March.
Brewer paid one-half the balance due and will remit the remainder on April 5.

31 Received $15,000 cash from admissions.

In addition to the accounts identified above, the chart of accounts includes: No. 112 Accounts
Receivable, No. 405 Admission Revenue, No. 406 Concession Revenue, No. 610 Advertising
Expense, No. 632 Film Rental Expense, and No. 726 Salaries Expense.

Instructions

(a) Enter the beginning balances in the ledger. Insert a check mark (✓) in the reference column of the ledger for the beginning balance.
(b) Journalize the March transactions.
(c) Post the March journal entries to the ledger. Assume that all entries are posted from page 1 of the journal.
(d) Prepare a trial balance on March 31, 2002.

Trial balance totals $118,900

BROADENING YOUR PERSPECTIVE

FINANCIAL REPORTING AND ANALYSIS

FINANCIAL REPORTING PROBLEM: Lands' End, Inc.

BYP2-1 The financial statements of **Lands' End, Inc.** are presented in Appendix A. The
notes accompanying the statements contain the following selected accounts, stated in thousands
of dollars.

Accounts Payable	$ 74,510	Income Taxes Payable	$ 10,255
Accounts Receivable	17,753	Interest Expense	1,890
Property, Plant, and Equipment	283,139	Inventory	162,193

Instructions

(a) Answer the following questions.

(1) What is the increase and decrease side for each account?
(2) What is the normal balance for each account?

(b) Identify the probable other account in the transaction and the effect on that account when:

(1) Accounts Receivable is decreased.
(2) Accounts Payable is decreased.
(3) Inventory is increased.

(c) Identify the other account(s) that ordinarily would be involved when:

(1) Interest Expense is increased.
(2) Property, Plant, and Equipment is increased.

COMPARATIVE ANALYSIS PROBLEM: Lands' End vs. Abercrombie & Fitch

BYP2-2 **Lands' End's** financial statements are presented in Appendix A. **Abercrombie &
Fitch's** financial statements are presented in Appendix B.

Instructions

(a) Based on the information contained in the financial statements, determine the normal balance of the listed accounts for each company.

Lands' End	Abercrombie & Fitch
1. Inventory	1. Accounts Receivable
2. Property, Plant, and Equipment	2. Cash and Equivalents
3. Accounts Payable	3. Cost of Goods Sold
4. Interest Expense	4. Sales (revenue)

(b) Identify the other account ordinarily involved when:

(1) Accounts Receivable is increased.
(2) Accrued Payroll is decreased.
(3) Property, Plant, and Equipment is increased.
(4) Interest Expense is increased.

INTERPRETING FINANCIAL STATEMENTS: A Global Focus

BYP2-3 **Doman Industries Ltd.**, whose products are sold in 30 countries worldwide, is an integrated Canadian forest products company.

Doman sells the majority of its lumber products in the United States and a significant amount of its pulp products in Asia. Doman also has loans from other countries. For example, on June 18, 1999, the Company borrowed US$160 million at an annual interest rate of 12%. Doman must repay this loan, and interest, in U.S. dollars.

One of the challenges global companies face is to make themselves attractive to investors from other countries. This is difficult to do when different accounting rules in different countries blur the real impact of earnings. For example, in 1998 Doman reported a loss of $2.3 million, using Canadian accounting rules. Had it reported under U.S. accounting rules, its loss would have been $12.1 million.

Many companies that want to be more easily compared with U.S. and other global competitors have switched to U.S. accounting principles. **Canadian National Railway**, **Corel**, **Cott**, **Inco**, and the **Thomson Corporation** are but a few examples of large Canadian companies whose financial statements are now presented in U.S. dollars, which adhere to U.S. GAAP, or are reconciled to U.S. GAAP.

Instructions

(a) Identify advantages and disadvantages that companies should consider when switching to U.S. reporting standards.

(b) Suppose you wish to compare Doman Industries to a U.S.-based competitor. Do you believe the use of country-specific accounting policies would hinder your comparison? If so, explain how.

(c) Suppose you wish to compare Doman Industries to a Canadian-based competitior. If the companies chose to apply generally acceptable Canadian accounting policies differently, how could this affect your comparison of their financial results?

(d) Do you see any significant distinction between comparing statements prepared using generally accepted accounting principles of different countries and comparing statements prepared using generally accepted accounting principles of the same country (e.g., U.S.) but that apply the principles differently?

EXPLORING THE WEB

BYP2-4 Much information about specific companies is available on the World Wide Web. Such information includes basic descriptions of the company's location, activities, industry, financial health, and financial performance.

Address: **biz.yahoo.com/i** *(or go to www.wiley.com/college/weygandt)*

Steps:

1. Type in a company name, or use index to find company name.
2. Choose **Profile**. Perform instructions (a)–(c) below.
3. Click on the company's specific industry to identify competitors. Perform instructions (d)–(g) below.

Instructions

Answer the following questions.

(a) What is the company's industry?
(b) What was the company's total sales?
(c) What was the company's net income?
(d) What are the names of four of the company's competitors?
(e) Choose one of these competitors.
(f) What is this competitor's name? What were its sales? What was its net income?
(g) Which of these two companies is larger by size of sales? Which one reported higher net income?

CRITICAL THINKING

GROUP DECISION CASE

BYP2-5   Lucy Lars operates Lucy Lars Riding Academy. The academy's primary sources of revenue are riding fees and lesson fees, which are paid on a cash basis. Lucy also boards horses for owners, who are billed monthly for boarding fees. In a few cases, boarders pay in advance of expected use. For its revenue transactions, the academy maintains the following accounts: No. 1 Cash, No. 5 Boarding Accounts Receivable, No. 27 Unearned Boarding Revenue, No. 51 Riding Revenue, No. 52 Lesson Revenue, and No. 53 Boarding Revenue.

The academy owns 10 horses, a stable, a riding corral, riding equipment, and office equipment. These assets are accounted for in accounts No. 11 Horses, No. 12 Building, No. 13 Riding Corral, No. 14 Riding Equipment, and No. 15 Office Equipment.

For its expenses, the academy maintains the following accounts: No. 6 Hay and Feed Supplies, No. 7 Prepaid Insurance, No. 21 Accounts Payable, No. 60 Salaries Expense, No. 61 Advertising Expense, No. 62 Utilities Expense, No. 63 Veterinary Expense, No. 64 Hay and Feed Expense, and No. 65 Insurance Expense.

Lucy makes periodic withdrawals of cash for personal living expenses. To record Lucy's equity in the business and her drawings, two accounts are maintained: No. 50 Lucy Lars, Capital, and No. 51 Lucy Lars, Drawing.

During the first month of operations an inexperienced bookkeeper was employed. Lucy Lars asks you to review the following eight entries of the 50 entries made during the month. In each case, the explanation for the entry is correct.

Date	Account	Debit	Credit
May 1	Cash	18,000	
	Lucy Lars, Capital		18,000
	(Invested $18,000 cash in business)		
5	Cash	250	
	Riding Revenue		250
	(Received $250 cash for lessons provided)		
7	Cash	500	
	Boarding Revenue		500
	(Received $500 for boarding of horses beginning June 1)		
14	Riding Equipment	80	
	Cash		800
	(Purchased desk and other office equipment for $800 cash)		
15	Salaries Expense	400	
	Cash		400
	(Issued check to Lucy Lars for personal use)		
20	Cash	148	
	Riding Revenue		184
	(Received $184 cash for riding fees)		
30	Veterinary Expense	75	
	Accounts Payable		75
	(Received bill of $75 from veterinarian for services rendered)		
31	Hay and Feed Expense	1,700	
	Cash		1,700
	(Purchased an estimated 2 months' supply of feed and hay for $1,700 on account)		

Instructions

With the class divided into groups, answer the following.

    (a) Identify each journal entry that is correct. For each journal entry that is incorrect, prepare the entry that should have been made by the bookkeeper.

    (b) Which of the incorrect entries would prevent the trial balance from balancing?

    (c) What was the correct net income for May, assuming the bookkeeper reported net income of $4,500 after posting all 50 entries?

    (d) What was the correct cash balance at May 31, assuming the bookkeeper reported a balance of $12,475 after posting all 50 entries (and the only errors occurred in the items listed above)?

COMMUNICATION ACTIVITY

BYP2-6 Merlynn's Maid Company offers home cleaning service. Two recurring transactions for the company are billing customers for services rendered and paying employee salaries. For example, on March 15, bills totaling $6,000 were sent to customers and $2,000 was paid in salaries to employees.

Instructions

Write a memo to your instructor that explains and illustrates the steps in the recording process for each of the March 15 transactions. Use the format illustrated in the text under the heading, "The Recording Process Illustrated" (p. 57).

ETHICS CASE

BYP2-7 Megan Menard is the assistant chief accountant at Hokey Company, a manufacturer of computer chips and cellular phones. The company presently has total sales of $20 million. It is the end of the first quarter. Megan is hurriedly trying to prepare a general ledger trial balance so that quarterly financial statements can be prepared and released to management and the regulatory agencies. The total credits on the trial balance exceed the debits by $1,000. In order to meet the 4 p.m. deadline, Megan decides to force the debits and credits into balance by adding the amount of the difference to the Equipment account. She chose Equipment because it is one of the larger account balances; percentage-wise, it will be the least misstated. Megan "plugs" the difference! She believes that the difference will not affect anyone's decisions. She wishes that she had another few days to find the error but realizes that the financial statements are already late.

Instructions

    (a) Who are the stakeholders in this situation?

    (b) What are the ethical issues involved in this case?

    (c) What are Megan's alternatives?

Answers to Self-Study Questions

1. b   **2.** c   **3.** d   **4.** d   **5.** b   **6.** a   **7.** c   **8.** d   **9.** a   **10.** c

Answer to *Lands' End* Review It Question 4, p. 49

Cash—debit; Accounts Payable—credit; Interest Expense—debit.

☑ *Remember to go back to the Navigator box on the chapter-opening page and check off your completed work.*

ADJUSTING THE ACCOUNTS

3

CONCEPTS FOR REVIEW

Before studying this chapter, you should know or, if necessary, review:

   a. What a double-entry system is. (Ch. 2, p. 45)

   b. How to increase or decrease assets, liabilities, and owner's equity using debit and credit procedures. (Ch. 2, pp. 45–48)

   c. How to journalize a transaction. (Ch. 2, pp. 50–52)

   d. How to post a transaction. (Ch. 2, pp. 54–56)

   e. How to prepare a trial balance. (Ch. 2, pp. 64–66)

THE NAVIGATOR

Timing Is Everything

In Chapter 1 you learned a neat little formula: Net income = Revenues − Expenses. And in Chapter 2 you learned some nice, orderly rules for recording corporate revenue and expense transactions. Guess what? Things are not really that nice and neat. In fact, it is often difficult to determine in what time period some revenues and expenses should be reported. And, in measuring net income, timing is everything.

There are rules that give guidance on these issues. But occasionally these rules are overlooked, misinterpreted, or even intentionally ignored. Consider the following examples.

• **McKesson HBOC**, one of the largest prescription drug distributors, restated its first-quarter, 1999, earnings because $26.2 million included in healthcare software sales weren't final and should not have been recorded. This negative surprise caused McKesson's share price to plummet 48 percent overnight, from $65.75 to $34.50, wiping out $9 billion in the market value of its stock.

• **Cambridge Biotech Corp.**, which develops vaccines and diagnostic tests for humans and animals, said that it reported revenue from transactions that "don't appear to be bona fide."

• **Media Vision Technology Inc.**, a maker of sound and animation equipment for computers, was accused of operating a "phantom" warehouse to hide inventory for returned products already recorded as sales.

• **Penguin USA**, a book publisher, said that it understated expenses in a number of years because it failed to report expenses for discounts given to customers for paying early.

In each case, accrual accounting concepts were violated. That is, revenues or expenses were not recorded in the proper period, which had a substantial impact on reported income. Their timing was off!

After studying this chapter, you should be able to:

1. Explain the time period assumption.
2. Explain the accrual basis of accounting.
3. Explain why adjusting entries are needed.
4. Identify the major types of adjusting entries.
5. Prepare adjusting entries for prepayments.
6. Prepare adjusting entries for accruals.
7. Describe the nature and purpose of an adjusted trial balance.

In Chapter 2 we examined the recording process through the preparation of the trial balance. Before we will be ready to prepare financial statements from the trial balance, additional steps need to be taken. The timing mismatch between revenues and expenses of the four companies mentioned in our Feature Story illustrates the types of situations that make these additional steps necessary. For example, long-lived assets purchased or constructed in prior accounting years are being used to produce goods and provide services in the current year. What portion of these assets' costs, if any, should be recognized as an expense of the current period? Before financial statements can be prepared, this and other questions relating to the recognition of revenues and expenses must be answered. With the answers in hand, we can then adjust the relevant account balances.

The content and organization of Chapter 3 are as follows.

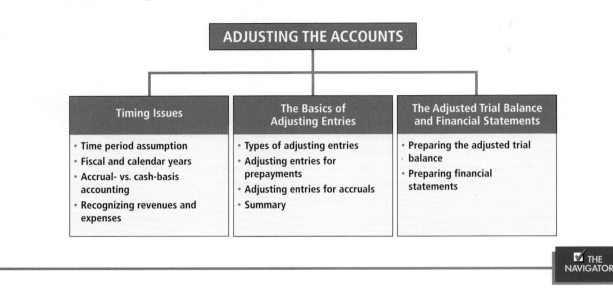

*T*IMING ISSUES

STUDY OBJECTIVE 1

Explain the time period assumption.

No adjustments would be necessary if we could wait to prepare financial statements until a company ended its operations. At that point, we could easily determine its final balance sheet and the amount of lifetime income it earned. The following anecdote illustrates one way to compute lifetime income.

> A grocery store owner from the old country kept his accounts payable on a spindle, accounts receivable on a note pad, and cash in a cigar box. His daughter, having just passed the CPA exam, chided the father: "I don't understand how you can run your business this way. How do you know what your profits are?"
>
> "Well," the father replied, "when I got off the boat 40 years ago, I had nothing but the pants I was wearing. Today your brother is a doctor, your sister is a college professor, and you are a CPA. Your mother and I have a nice car, a well-furnished house, and a lake home. We have a good business, and everything is paid for. So, you add all that together, subtract the pants, and there's your profit."

SELECTING AN ACCOUNTING TIME PERIOD

Although the old grocer may be correct in his evaluation, it is impractical to wait so long for the results of operations. All entities, from the corner grocery, to a global company like **Kellogg**, to your college or university, find it desirable and necessary to report the results of their activities more frequently. For example, management usually wants monthly financial statements, and the Internal Revenue Service requires all businesses to file annual tax returns. Therefore, **accountants divide the economic life of a business into artificial time periods**. This convenient assumption is referred to as the **time period assumption**.

Many business transactions affect more than one of these arbitrary time periods. For example, Farmer Brown's milking machine bought in 1998 and the airplanes purchased by **Delta Air Lines** five years ago are still in use today. Therefore we must determine the relevance of each business transaction to specific accounting periods. Doing so may involve subjective judgments and estimates.

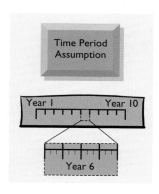

ALTERNATIVE TERMINOLOGY
The time period assumption is also called the *periodicity assumption*.

FISCAL AND CALENDAR YEARS

Both small and large companies prepare financial statements periodically in order to assess their financial condition and results of operations. **Accounting time periods are generally a month, a quarter, or a year.** Monthly and quarterly time periods are called **interim periods**. Most large companies are required to prepare both quarterly and annual financial statements.

An accounting time period that is one year in length is referred to as a **fiscal year**. A fiscal year usually begins with the first day of a month and ends twelve months later on the last day of a month. The accounting period used by most businesses coincides with the **calendar year** (January 1 to December 31). Companies whose fiscal year differs from the calendar year include **Delta Air Lines**, June 30; **Walt Disney Productions**, September 30; and **Kmart Corp.**, January 31. Sometimes a company's year-end will vary from year to year. For example, **Lands' End's** fiscal year ends on the Friday closest to January 31, which was January 29 in 1999 and January 28 in 2000.

ACCRUAL- VS. CASH-BASIS ACCOUNTING

What you will learn in this chapter is **accrual-basis accounting**. Under the accrual basis, transactions that change a company's financial statements are recorded **in the periods in which the events occur**. For example, using the accrual basis to determine net income means recognizing revenues when earned (rather than when the cash is received). It also means recognizing expenses when incurred (rather than when paid). Information presented on an accrual basis reveals relationships likely to be important in predicting future results. Under accrual accounting, revenues are recognized when services are performed, so trends in revenues are thus more meaningful for decision-making.

An alternative to the accrual basis is the cash basis. Under **cash-basis accounting**, revenue is recorded when cash is received, and an expense is recorded when cash is paid. The cash basis often leads to misleading financial statements. It fails to record revenue that has been earned but for which the cash has not been received. Also, expenses are not matched with earned revenues. **Cash-basis accounting is not in accordance with generally accepted accounting principles (GAAP).**

STUDY OBJECTIVE **2**

Explain the accrual basis of accounting.

*I*NTERNATIONAL NOTE

Although different accounting standards are often used in other major industrialized countries, accrual-basis accounting is followed by all these countries.

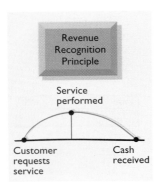

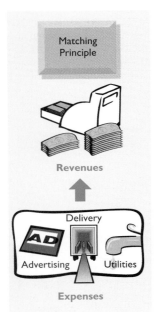

Most companies use accrual-basis accounting. Individuals and some small companies use cash-basis accounting. The cash basis is justified for small businesses because they often have few receivables and payables. Accountants are sometimes asked to convert cash-basis records to the accrual basis. As you might expect, extensive adjusting entries are required for this task.

RECOGNIZING REVENUES AND EXPENSES

Determining the amount of revenues and expenses to be reported in a given accounting period can be difficult. To help in this task, accountants have developed two principles as part of generally accepted accounting principles (GAAP): the revenue recognition principle and the matching principle.

The **revenue recognition principle** dictates that revenue be recognized in the accounting period in which it is earned. **In a service enterprise, revenue is considered to be earned at the time the service is performed.** To illustrate, assume that a dry cleaning business cleans clothing on June 30 but customers do not claim and pay for their clothes until the first week of July. Under the revenue recognition principle, revenue is earned in June when the service is performed, rather than in July when the cash is received. At June 30, the dry cleaner would report a receivable on its balance sheet and revenue in its income statement for the service performed.

Accountants follow the approach of "let expenses follow revenues." That is, expense recognition is tied to revenue recognition. In the preceding example, this principle means that the salary expense incurred in performing the cleaning service on June 30 should be reported in the income statement for the same period in which the service revenue is recognized. The critical issue in expense recognition is when the expense makes its contribution to revenue. This may or may not be the same period in which the expense is paid. If the salary incurred on June 30 is not paid until July, the dry cleaner would report salaries payable on its June 30 balance sheet. The practice of expense recognition is referred to as the **matching principle** because it dictates that efforts (expenses) be matched with accomplishments (revenues).

$\mathcal{A}$CCOUNTING IN ACTION *Business Insight*

Suppose you are a filmmaker like George Lucas and spend $11 million to produce a film such as *Star Wars*. Over what period should the cost be expensed? It should be expensed over the economic life of the film. But what is its economic life? The filmmaker must estimate how much revenue will be earned from box office sales, video sales, television, and games and toys—a period that could be less than a year or more than 20 years, as is the case for Twentieth Century Fox's *Star Wars*. Originally released in 1977, and rereleased in 1997, domestic revenues total nearly $500 million for *Star Wars* and continue to grow. This situation demonstrates the difficulty of properly matching expenses to revenues.

SOURCE: Star Trek Newsletter, 22.

Once the economic life of a business has been divided into artificial time periods, the revenue recognition and matching principles can be applied. This one assumption and two principles thus provide guidelines as to when revenues and expenses should be reported. These relationships are shown in Illustration 3-1.

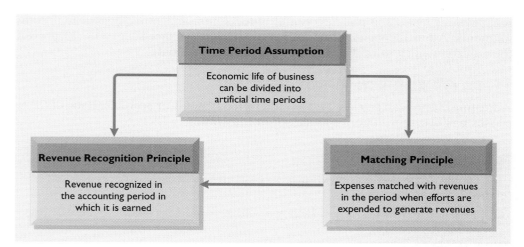

Illustration 3-1

GAAP relationships in revenue and expense recognition

BEFORE YOU GO ON...

▶ *REVIEW IT*
1. What is the relevance of the time period assumption to accounting?
2. What are the revenue recognition and matching principles?

THE BASICS OF ADJUSTING ENTRIES

In order for revenues to be recorded in the period in which they are earned, and for expenses to be recognized in the period in which they are incurred, adjusting entries are made at the end of the accounting period. In short, **adjusting entries are needed to ensure that the revenue recognition and matching principles are followed**.

Adjusting entries make it possible to report on the balance sheet the appropriate assets, liabilities, and owner's equity at the statement date and to report on the income statement the proper net income (or loss) for the period. However, the trial balance—the first pulling together of the transaction data—may not contain up-to-date and complete data. This is true for the following reasons.

1. Some events are not journalized daily because it is inexpedient to do so. Examples are the consumption of supplies and the earning of wages by employees.

2. Some costs are not journalized during the accounting period because they expire with the passage of time rather than through recurring daily transactions. Examples are equipment deterioration, and rent and insurance.

3. Some items may be unrecorded. An example is a utility service bill that will not be received until the next accounting period.

Adjusting entries are required every time financial statements are prepared. The starting point is an analysis of each account in the trial balance to determine whether it is complete and up-to-date. The analysis requires a thorough understanding of the company's operations and the interrelationship of accounts. Preparing adjusting entries is often an involved process. The company may need to make inventory counts of supplies and repair parts. It may need to prepare supporting

STUDY OBJECTIVE 3

Explain why adjusting entries are needed.

Accounting Cycle Tutorial—Making Adjusting Entries

HELPFUL HINT
Adjusting entries are needed to enable financial statements to be in conformity with GAAP.

schedules of insurance policies, rental agreements, and other contractual commitments. Adjustments are often prepared after the balance sheet date. However, the adjusting entries are dated as of the balance sheet date.

TYPES OF ADJUSTING ENTRIES

Adjusting entries can be classified as either prepayments or accruals. Each of these classes has two subcategories as shown in Illustration 3-2.

Prepayments
1. **Prepaid Expenses.** Expenses paid in cash and recorded as assets before they are used or consumed.
2. **Unearned Revenues.** Cash received and recorded as liabilities before revenue is earned.

Accruals
1. **Accrued Revenues.** Revenues earned but not yet received in cash or recorded.
2. **Accrued Expenses.** Expenses incurred but not yet paid in cash or recorded.

Specific examples and explanations of each type of adjustment are given on the following pages. Each example is based on the October 31 trial balance of Pioneer Advertising Agency, from Chapter 2, reproduced in Illustration 3-3.

PIONEER ADVERTISING AGENCY Trial Balance October 31, 2002		
	Debit	**Credit**
Cash	$15,200	
Advertising Supplies	2,500	
Prepaid Insurance	600	
Office Equipment	5,000	
Notes Payable		$ 5,000
Accounts Payable		2,500
Unearned Revenue		1,200
C. R. Byrd, Capital		10,000
C. R. Byrd, Drawing	500	
Service Revenue		10,000
Salaries Expense	4,000	
Rent Expense	900	
	$28,700	$28,700

We assume that Pioneer Advertising uses an accounting period of one month. Thus, monthly adjusting entries will be made. The entries will be dated October 31.

ADJUSTING ENTRIES FOR PREPAYMENTS

As indicated earlier, prepayments are either prepaid expenses or unearned revenues. Adjusting entries for prepayments are required to record the portion of the prepayment that represents the **expense incurred or the revenue earned** in the current accounting period.

If an adjustment is needed for prepayments, the asset and liability are overstated and the related expense and revenue are understated before the adjustment. For example, in the trial balance, the balance in the asset Advertising Supplies shows only supplies purchased. This balance is overstated; a related expense account, Advertising Supplies Expense, is understated because the cost of supplies used has not been recognized. Thus the adjusting entry for prepayments will **decrease a balance sheet account** (Advertising Supplies) and **increase an income statement account** (Advertising Supplies Expense). The effects of adjusting entries for prepayments are graphically depicted in Illustration 3-4.

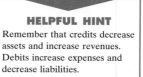

HELPFUL HINT
Remember that credits decrease assets and increase revenues. Debits increase expenses and decrease liabilities.

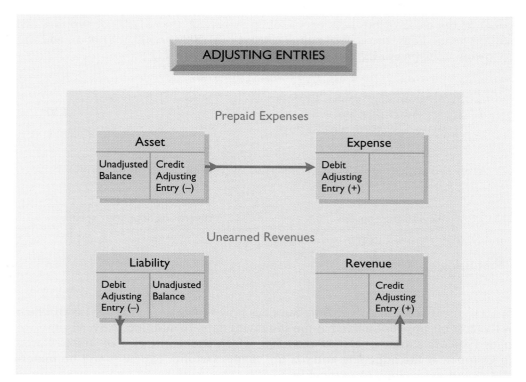

Illustration 3-4

Adjusting entries for prepayments

Prepaid Expenses

As stated on page 92, expenses paid in cash and recorded as assets before they are used or consumed are called **prepaid expenses**. When a cost is prepaid, an asset account is debited to show the service or benefit that will be received in the future. Prepayments often occur in regard to insurance, supplies, advertising, and rent. In addition, prepayments are made when buildings and equipment are purchased.

Prepaid expenses expire either with the passage of time (e.g., rent and insurance) or through use and consumption (e.g., supplies). The expiration of these costs does not require daily journal entries, which would be unnecessary and impractical. Instead, it is customary to postpone recognizing cost expirations until financial statements are prepared. At each statement date, adjusting entries are made for two purposes: (1) to record the expenses that apply to the current accounting period, and (2) to show the unexpired costs in the asset accounts.

Prior to adjustment, assets are overstated and expenses are understated. **Thus, the prepaid expense adjusting entry results in a debit (increase) to an expense account and a credit (decrease) to an asset account.**

SUPPLIES.   Businesses use various types of supplies. For example, a CPA firm will have **office supplies** such as stationery, envelopes, and accounting paper. An advertising firm will have **advertising supplies** such as graph paper, video film, and

Supplies

Oct.5

Supplies purchased; record asset

Oct.31

Supplies used; record supplies expense

poster paper. Supplies are generally debited to an asset account when they are acquired. In the course of operations, supplies are depleted, but recognition of supplies used is deferred until the adjustment process. At that point, a physical inventory (count) of supplies is taken. The difference between the balance in the Supplies (asset) account and the cost of supplies on hand represents the supplies used (expense) for the period.

Pioneer Advertising Agency purchased advertising supplies costing $2,500 on October 5. A debit (increase) was made to the asset Advertising Supplies. This account shows a balance of $2,500 in the October 31 trial balance. An inventory count at the close of business on October 31 reveals that $1,000 of supplies are still on hand. Thus, the cost of supplies used is $1,500 ($2,500 − $1,000), and the following adjusting entry is made.

Equation analyses summarize the effects of the transaction on the accounting equation.

Equation Analysis
A = L + OE
−1,500 −1,500

Oct. 31	Advertising Supplies Expense	1,500	
	Advertising Supplies		1,500
	(To record supplies used)		

After the adjusting entry is posted, the two supplies accounts show:

Illustration 3-5

Supplies accounts after adjustment

Advertising Supplies				Advertising Supplies Expense		
10/5	2,500	10/31 **Adj.**	**1,500**	10/31 **Adj.**	**1,500**	
10/31 Bal.	1,000					

The asset account Advertising Supplies now shows a balance of $1,000, which is the cost of supplies on hand at the statement date. In addition, Advertising Supplies Expense shows a balance of $1,500, which equals the cost of supplies used in October. **If the adjusting entry is not made, October expenses will be understated and net income overstated by $1,500. Also, both assets and owner's equity will be overstated by $1,500 on the October 31 balance sheet.**

ACCOUNTING IN ACTION *Business Insight*

The costs of product advertising are sometimes considered prepayments. As a manager for **Procter & Gamble** noted, "If we run a long ad campaign for soap and bleach, we sometimes report the costs as prepayments if we think we'll receive sales benefits from the campaign down the road." Presently it is a judgment call whether these costs should be prepayments or expenses in the current period. It is difficult to develop guidelines consistent with the matching principle because situations vary widely across companies. Outlays for advertising can be substantial. Recent big advertising spenders: **Sears, Roebuck and Co.** spent $1.28 billion, **Nike** $978 million, and **McDonald's** $503 million.

INSURANCE. Most companies have fire and theft insurance on merchandise and equipment, personal liability insurance for accidents suffered by customers, and automobile insurance on company cars and trucks. The cost of insurance protection is determined by the payment of insurance premiums. The minimum term of coverage is usually one year, but three- to five-year terms are available and offer lower annual premiums. Insurance premiums normally are charged to the asset account Prepaid Insurance when paid. At the financial statement date it is necessary to debit (increase) Insurance Expense and credit (decrease) Prepaid Insurance for the cost that has expired during the period.

On October 4, Pioneer Advertising Agency paid $600 for a one-year fire insurance policy. The effective date of coverage was October 1. The premium was charged to Prepaid Insurance when it was paid, and this account shows a balance of $600 in the October 31 trial balance. Analysis reveals that $50 ($600 ÷ 12) of insurance expires each month. Thus, the following adjusting entry is made.

Oct. 31	Insurance Expense	50	
	Prepaid Insurance		50
	(To record insurance expired)		

After the adjusting entry is posted, the accounts show:

Prepaid Insurance				Insurance Expense		
10/4	600	10/31 **Adj.**	50	10/31 **Adj.**	50	
10/31 Bal.	550					

Illustration 3-6

Insurance accounts after adjustment

The asset Prepaid Insurance shows a balance of $550. This amount represents the unexpired cost for the remaining eleven months of coverage. The $50 balance in Insurance Expense is equal to the insurance cost that has expired in October. **If this adjustment is not made, October expenses will be understated by $50 and net income overstated by $50. Also, both assets and owner's equity will be overstated by $50 on the October 31 balance sheet.**

DEPRECIATION. A business enterprise typically owns productive facilities such as buildings, equipment, and vehicles. Because these assets provide service for a number of years, each is recorded as an asset, rather than an expense, in the year it is acquired. As explained in Chapter 1, such assets are recorded at cost, as required by the cost principle. The term of service is referred to as the useful life.

According to the matching principle, a portion of the cost of a long-lived asset should be reported as an expense during each period of the asset's useful life. Depreciation is the allocation of the cost of an asset to expense over its useful life in a rational and systematic manner.

Need for Depreciation Adjustment. From an accounting standpoint, acquiring productive facilities is viewed essentially as a long-term prepayment for services. The need for periodic adjusting entries for depreciation is, therefore, the same as that for other prepaid expenses: to recognize the cost that has expired (expense) during the period and to report the unexpired cost (asset) at the end of the period.

At the time an asset is acquired, its useful life cannot be known with certainty. The asset may be useful for a longer or shorter time than expected, depending on such factors as actual use, deterioration due to the elements or obsolescence. Thus, you should recognize that **depreciation is an estimate** rather than a factual measurement of the cost that has expired. A common procedure in computing depreciation expense is to divide the cost of the asset by its useful life. For example, if cost is $10,000 and useful life is expected to be 10 years, annual depreciation is $1,000.[1]

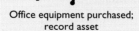
---

[1] Additional consideration is given to computing depreciation expense in Chapter 10.

For Pioneer Advertising, depreciation on the office equipment is estimated to be $480 a year, or $40 per month. Accordingly, depreciation for October is recognized by the following adjusting entry.

A	=	L	+	OE
−40				−40

Oct. 31	Depreciation Expense	40	
	Accumulated Depreciation—Office Equipment		40
	(To record monthly depreciation)		

After the adjusting entry is posted, the accounts show:

Illustration 3-7

Accounts after adjustment for depreciation

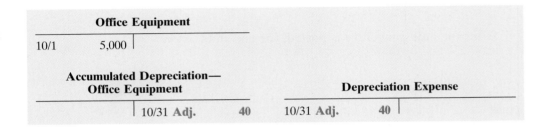

The balance in the accumulated depreciation account will increase $40 each month. After journalizing and posting the adjusting entry at November 30, the balance will be $80; at December 31, $120; and so on.

Statement Presentation. Accumulated Depreciation—Office Equipment is a contra asset account. A **contra asset account** is one that is offset against an asset account on the balance sheet. This accumulated depreciation account appears just after Office Equipment on the balance sheet. Its normal balance is a credit. An alternative would be to credit (decrease) Office Equipment directly for the depreciation each month. But use of the contra account provides disclosure of **both the original cost** of the equipment **and the total cost that has expired to date**. In the balance sheet, Accumulated Depreciation—Office Equipment is deducted from the related asset account as follows.

> **HELPFUL HINT**
> All contra accounts have increases, decreases, and normal balances opposite to the account to which they relate.

Illustration 3-8

Balance sheet presentation of accumulated depreciation

Office equipment	$5,000	
Less: Accumulated depreciation—office equipment	40	**$4,960**

ALTERNATIVE TERMINOLOGY
Book value is sometimes referred to as *carrying value* or *unexpired cost.*

The difference between the cost of any depreciable asset and its related accumulated depreciation is referred to as the **book value** of that asset. In Illustration 3-8, the book value of the equipment at the balance sheet date is $4,960. You should realize that the book value is generally different from the market value (the price at which the asset could be sold in the marketplace). The reason the two are different is that depreciation is a means of cost allocation, not a matter of valuation.

Depreciation expense also identifies that portion of the asset's cost that has expired in October. As in the case of other prepaid adjustments, the omission of this adjusting entry would cause total assets, total owner's equity, and net income to be overstated and depreciation expense to be understated.

If the company owns additional equipment, such as delivery or store equipment, or if it has buildings, depreciation expense is recorded on each of those items. Related accumulated depreciation accounts also are established, such as: Accumulated Depreciation—Delivery Equipment; Accumulated Depreciation—Store Equipment; and Accumulated Depreciation—Buildings.

Unearned Revenues

Unearned Revenues

Oct.2

Thank you in advance for your work

I will finish by Dec. 31

≈ $1,200

Cash is received in advance; liability is recorded

Oct.31

Service is provided; revenue is recorded

As stated on page 92, cash received and recorded as liabilities before revenue is earned is called **unearned revenues**. Such items as rent, magazine subscriptions, and customer deposits for future service may result in unearned revenues. Airlines such as United, American, and Delta treat receipts from the sale of tickets as unearned revenue until the flight service is provided. Similarly, college tuition received prior to the start of a semester is considered unearned revenue. Unearned revenues are the opposite of prepaid expenses. Indeed, unearned revenue on the books of one company is likely to be a prepayment on the books of the company that has made the advance payment. For example, if identical accounting periods are assumed, a landlord will have unearned rent revenue when a tenant has prepaid rent.

When the payment is received for services to be provided in a future accounting period, an unearned revenue account (a liability) should be credited (increased) to recognize the obligation that exists. Later, unearned revenues are earned by providing service to a customer. It may not be practical to make daily journal entries as the revenue is earned. In such cases, recognition of earned revenue is delayed until the end of the period. Then an adjusting entry is made to record the revenue that has been earned and to show the liability that remains. In the typical case, liabilities are overstated and revenues are understated prior to adjustment. Thus, **the adjusting entry for unearned revenues results in a debit (decrease) to a liability account and a credit (increase) to a revenue account**.

Pioneer Advertising Agency received $1,200 on October 2 from R. Knox for advertising services expected to be completed by December 31. The payment was credited to Unearned Revenue; this account shows a balance of $1,200 in the October 31 trial balance. Analysis reveals that $400 of those fees was earned in October. The following adjusting entry is made.

ALTERNATIVE TERMINOLOGY
Unearned revenue is sometimes referred to as *deferred revenue*.

Oct. 31	Unearned Revenue	400	
	Service Revenue		400
	(To record revenue for services provided)		

A	=	L	+	OE
		−400		+400

After the adjusting entry is posted, the accounts show:

Unearned Revenue				Service Revenue			
10/31 **Adj.**	400	10/2	1,200			10/31 Bal.	10,000
		10/31 Bal.	800			31 **Adj.**	400

Illustration 3-9

Revenue accounts after prepayments adjustment

The liability Unearned Revenue now shows a balance of $800. This amount represents the remaining prepaid advertising services to be performed in the future. At the same time, Service Revenue shows total revenue of $10,400 earned in October. **If this adjustment is not made, revenues and net income would be understated by $400 in the income statement. Also, liabilities would be overstated and owner's equity would be understated by $400 on the October 31 balance sheet.**

ACCOUNTING IN ACTION  *Business Insight*

Many early dot-com investors focused almost entirely on revenue growth instead of net income. Many early dot-com companies earned most of their revenue from selling advertising space on their Web sites. To boost reported revenue, some sites began swapping ad space. Company A would put an ad for its Web site on company B's Web site, and company B would put an ad for its Web site on company A's Web site. No money ever changed hands, but each company recorded revenue (for the value of the space that it gave up on its site) and expense (for the value of its ad that it placed on the other company's site). This practice did little to boost net income and resulted in no additional cash inflow—but it did boost *reported* revenue. This practice was quickly put to an end because accountants felt that it did not meet the criteria of the revenue recognition principle.

BEFORE YOU GO ON...

▶ *REVIEW IT*

1. What are the four types of adjusting entries?
2. What is the effect on assets, owner's equity, expenses, and net income if a prepaid expense adjusting entry is not made?
3. What is the effect on liabilities, owner's equity, revenues, and net income if an unearned revenue adjusting entry is not made?
4. Using the Eleven-Year Consolidated Financial Summary of **Lands' End's** financial statements, what was the amount of depreciation and amortization expense for 2000 and for 1999? The answer to this question is provided on page 131.

LANDS' END
DIRECT MERCHANTS

▶ *DO IT*

The ledger of Hammond, Inc. on March 31, 2002, includes the following selected accounts before adjusting entries.

	Debit	Credit
Prepaid Insurance	3,600	
Office Supplies	2,800	
Office Equipment	25,000	
Accumulated Depreciation—Office Equipment		5,000
Unearned Revenue		9,200

An analysis of the accounts shows the following.

1. Insurance expires at the rate of $100 per month.
2. Supplies on hand total $800.
3. The office equipment depreciates $200 a month.
4. One-half of the unearned revenue was earned in March.

Prepare the adjusting entries for the month of March.

ACTION PLAN
- Make adjusting entries at the end of the period for revenues earned and expenses incurred in the period.
- Don't forget to make adjusting entries for prepayments. Failure to adjust for prepayments leads to overstatement of the asset or liability and related understatement of the expense or revenue.

SOLUTION

1. Insurance Expense	100	
Prepaid Insurance		100
(To record insurance expired)		

2. Office Supplies Expense	2,000	
Office Supplies		2,000
(To record supplies used)		
3. Depreciation Expense	200	
Accumulated Depreciation—Office Equipment		200
(To record monthly depreciation)		
4. Unearned Revenue	4,600	
Service Revenue		4,600
(To record revenue for services provided)		

*Related exercise material: BE3-3, BE3-4, BE3-5, BE3-6, E3-2, E3-3, E3-4,
E3-5, E3-6, E3-7, E3-8, and E3-9.*

ADJUSTING ENTRIES FOR ACCRUALS

The second category of adjusting entries is **accruals**. Adjusting entries for accruals are required to record revenues earned and expenses incurred in the current accounting period that have not been recognized through daily entries.

An accrual adjustment is needed when various accounts are understated: the revenue account and the related asset account, and/or the expense account and the related liability account. Thus, the adjusting entry for accruals will **increase both a balance sheet and an income statement account**. Adjusting entries for accruals are graphically depicted in Illustration 3-10.

STUDY OBJECTIVE 6

Prepare adjusting entries for accruals.

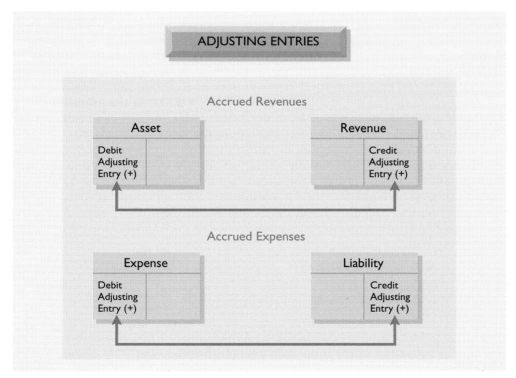

Illustration 3-10

Adjusting entries for accruals

Accrued Revenues

Oct.31

Revenue and receivable are recorded for unbilled services

Nov.

Cash is received; receivable is reduced

Accrued Revenues

As explained on page 92, revenues earned but not yet received in cash or recorded at the statement date are *accrued revenues*. Accrued revenues may accumulate (accrue) with the passing of time, as in the case of interest revenue and rent revenue. Or they may result from services that have been performed but neither billed nor collected, as in the case of commissions and fees. The former are unrecorded because the earning of interest and rent does not involve daily transactions. The latter may be unrecorded because only a portion of the total service has been provided.

An adjusting entry is required for two purposes: (1) to show the receivable that exists at the balance sheet date, and (2) to record the revenue that has been earned during the period. Prior to adjustment both assets and revenues are understated. Thus, **an adjusting entry for accrued revenues results in a debit (increase) to an asset account and a credit (increase) to a revenue account**.

In October Pioneer Advertising Agency earned $200 for advertising services that were not billed to clients before October 31. Because these services have not been billed, they have not been recorded. The following adjusting entry is made.

A	=	L	+	OE
+200				+200

Oct. 31	Accounts Receivable	200	
	Service Revenue		200
	(To record revenue for services provided)		

After the adjusting entry is posted, the accounts show:

Illustration 3-11

Receivable and revenue accounts after accrual adjustment

Accounts Receivable		**Service Revenue**	
10/31 **Adj.** 200		10/31 10,000	
		31 400	
		31 **Adj.** 200	
		10/31 Bal. 10,600	

The asset Accounts Receivable shows that $200 is owed by clients at the balance sheet date. The balance of $10,600 in Service Revenue represents the total revenue earned during the month ($10,000 + $400 + $200). **If the adjusting entry is not made, the following will all be understated: assets and owner's equity on the balance sheet, and revenues and net income on the income statement.**

In the next accounting period, the clients will be billed. The entry to record the billing should recognize that a portion has already been recorded in the previous month's adjusting entry. To illustrate, assume that bills totaling $3,000 are mailed to clients on November 10. Of this amount, $200 represents revenue earned in October and recorded as Service Revenue in the October 31 adjusting entry. The remaining $2,800 represents revenue earned in November. Thus, the following entry is made.

A	=	L	+	OE
+2,800				+2,800

Nov. 10	Accounts Receivable	2,800	
	Service Revenue		2,800
	(To record revenue for services provided)		

This entry records service revenue between November 1 and November 10. The subsequent collection of revenue from clients (including the $200 earned in October) will be recorded with a debit (increase) to Cash and a credit (decrease) to Accounts Receivable.

Accrued Expenses

As indicated on page 92, expenses incurred but not yet paid or recorded at the statement date are called **accrued expenses**. Interest, rent, taxes, and salaries can be accrued expenses. Accrued expenses result from the same causes as accrued revenues. In fact, an accrued expense on the books of one company is an accrued revenue to another company. For example, the $200 accrual of fees by Pioneer is an accrued expense to the client that received the service.

Adjustments for accrued expenses are needed for two purposes: (1) to record the obligations that exist at the balance sheet date, and (2) to recognize the expenses that apply to the current accounting period. Prior to adjustment, both liabilities and expenses are understated. Thus, **the adjusting entry for accrued expenses results in a debit (increase) to an expense account and a credit (increase) to a liability account**.

ACCRUED INTEREST.   Pioneer Advertising Agency signed a $5,000, 3-month note payable on October 1. The note requires interest at an annual rate of 12%. The amount of the interest accumulation is determined by three factors: (1) the face value of the note, (2) the interest rate, which is always expressed as an annual rate, and (3) the length of time the note is outstanding. In this instance, the total interest due on the $5,000 note at its due date 3 months hence is $150 ($5,000 × 12% × 3/12), or $50 for one month. The formula for computing interest and its application to Pioneer Advertising Agency for the month of October[2] are shown in Illustration 3-12. Note that the time period is expressed as a fraction of a year.

> **HELPFUL HINT**
> Interest is a cost of borrowing money that accumulates with the passage of time.

Illustration 3-12

Formula for computing interest

The accrued expense adjusting entry at October 31 is:

Oct. 31	Interest Expense	50	
	Interest Payable		50
	(To record interest on notes payable)		

A	=	L	+	OE
		+50		−50

After this adjusting entry is posted, the accounts show:

Interest Expense			Interest Payable		
10/31	Adj.	50		10/31	Adj.	50

Illustration 3-13

Interest accounts after adjustment

Interest Expense shows the interest charges for the month. The amount of interest owed at the statement date is shown in Interest Payable. It will not be paid until the note comes due at the end of 3 months. The Interest Payable account is used instead of crediting (increasing) Notes Payable. The reason for using the two accounts is to disclose the two types of obligations (interest and principal) in the accounts and statements. **If this adjusting entry is not made, liabilities and interest expense will be understated, and net income and owner's equity will be overstated.**

ACCRUED SALARIES.   Some types of expenses are paid for after the services have been performed. Examples are employee salaries and commissions. At

---

[2]The computation of interest will be considered in more depth in later chapters.

Pioneer Advertising, salaries were last paid on October 26; the next payday is November 9. As shown in the calendar in Illustration 3-14, three working days remain in October (October 29–31).

Illustration 3-14

Calendar showing Pioneer's pay periods

At October 31, the salaries for the last three days of the month represent an accrued expense and a related liability. The employees receive total salaries of $2,000 for a five-day work week, or $400 per day. Thus, accrued salaries at October 31 are $1,200 ($400 × 3). The adjusting entry is:

A	=	L	+	OE
		+1,200		−1,200

Oct. 31	Salaries Expense			1,200	
	Salaries Payable				1,200
	(To record accrued salaries)				

After this adjusting entry is posted, the accounts show:

Illustration 3-15

Salary accounts after adjustment

Salaries Expense				Salaries Payable		
10/26	4,000				10/31 **Adj.**	1,200
31 **Adj.**	1,200					
10/31 Bal.	5,200					

After this adjustment, the balance in Salaries Expense of $5,200 (13 days × $400) is the actual salary expense for October. (The employees started work on October 15.) The balance in Salaries Payable of $1,200 is the amount of the liability for salaries owed as of October 31. **If the $1,200 adjustment for salaries is not recorded, Pioneer's expenses will be understated $1,200, and its liabilities will be understated $1,200.**

At Pioneer Advertising, salaries are payable every two weeks. The next payday is November 9, when total salaries of $4,000 will again be paid. The payment will consist of $1,200 of salaries payable at October 31 plus $2,800 of salaries expense for November (seven working days as shown in the November calendar × $400). Therefore, the following entry is made on November 9.

A	=	L	+	OE
−4,000		−1,200		−2,800

Nov. 9	Salaries Payable			1,200	
	Salaries Expense			2,800	
	Cash				4,000
	(To record November 9 payroll)				

This entry does two things: (1) It eliminates the liability for Salaries Payable that was recorded in the October 31 adjusting entry. (2) It records the proper amount of Salaries Expense for the period between November 1 and November 9.

TECHNOLOGY IN ACTION

 In many computer systems, the adjusting process is handled like any other transaction, with the accountant inputting the adjustment at the time required. The main difference between adjusting entries and regular transactions is that with adjusting entries, one part of the computer system may perform the required calculation for such items as depreciation or interest and then "feed" these figures to the journalizing process.

Such systems are also able to display information before and after changes were made. Management may be interested in such information to highlight the impact that adjustments have on the various accounts and financial statements.

BEFORE YOU GO ON...

▶ *REVIEW IT*

1. If an accrued revenue adjusting entry is not made, what is the effect on assets, owner's equity, revenues, and net income?
2. If an accrued expense adjusting entry is not made, what is the effect on liabilities, owner's equity, and interest expense?

▶ *DO IT*

Calvin and Hobbs are the new owners of Micro Computer Services. At the end of August 2002, their first month of ownership, Calvin and Hobbs are trying to prepare monthly financial statements. They have the following information for the month.

1. At August 31, Calvin and Hobbs owed employees $800 in salaries that will be paid on September 1.
2. On August 1, Calvin and Hobbs borrowed $30,000 from a local bank on a 15-year mortgage. The annual interest rate is 10%.
3. Service revenue unrecorded in August totaled $1,100.

Prepare the adjusting entries needed at August 31, 2002.

ACTION PLAN

- Make adjusting entries at the end of the period for revenues earned and expenses incurred in the period.
- Don't forget to make adjusting entries for accruals. Adjusting entries for accruals will increase both a balance sheet and an income statement account.

SOLUTION

1. Salaries Expense	800	
Salaries Payable		800
(To record accrued salaries)		
2. Interest Expense	250	
Interest Payable		250
(To record interest)		
($30,000 × 10% × 1/12 = $250)		
3. Accounts Receivable	1,100	
Service Revenue		1,100
(To record revenue for services provided)		

Related exercise material: BE3-7, E3-2, E3-3, E3-4, E3-5, E3-6, E3-7, E3-8, and E3-9.

☑ THE NAVIGATOR

SUMMARY OF BASIC RELATIONSHIPS

The four basic types of adjusting entries are summarized in Illustration 3-16. Take some time to study and analyze the adjusting entries shown in the summary. Be sure to note that **each adjusting entry affects one balance sheet account and one income statement account**.

Illustration 3-16

Summary of adjusting entries

Type of Adjustment	Reason for Adjustment	Accounts before Adjustment	Adjusting Entry
1. Prepaid expenses	Prepaid expenses originally recorded in asset accounts have been used.	Assets overstated Expenses understated	Dr. Expenses Cr. Assets
2. Unearned revenues	Unearned revenues initially recorded in liability accounts have been earned.	Liabilities overstated Revenues understated	Dr. Liabilities Cr. Revenues
3. Accrued revenues	Revenues have been earned but not yet received in cash or recorded.	Assets understated Revenues understated	Dr. Assets Cr. Revenues
4. Accrued expenses	Expenses have been incurred but not yet paid in cash or recorded.	Expenses understated Liabilities understated	Dr. Expenses Cr. Liabilities

The journalizing and posting of adjusting entries for Pioneer Advertising Agency on October 31 are shown in Illustrations 3-17 and 3-18. All adjustments are identified in the ledger by the reference J2 because they have been journalized on page 2 of the general journal. A center caption entitled "Adjusting Entries" may be inserted between the last transaction entry and the first adjusting entry to identify these entries. When reviewing the general ledger in Illustration 3-18, note that the adjustments are highlighted in color.

Illustration 3-17

General journal showing adjusting entries

HELPFUL HINT
(1) Adjusting entries should not involve debits or credits to cash. (2) Evaluate whether the adjustment makes sense. For example, an adjustment to recognize supplies used should increase supplies expense. (3) Double-check all computations.

	GENERAL JOURNAL			**J2**
Date	**Account Titles and Explanation**	**Ref.**	**Debit**	**Credit**
2002 Oct. 31	Adjusting Entries			
	Advertising Supplies Expense	631	1,500	
	Advertising Supplies	126		1,500
	(To record supplies used)			
31	Insurance Expense	722	50	
	Prepaid Insurance	130		50
	(To record insurance expired)			
31	Depreciation Expense	711	40	
	Accumulated Depreciation—Office Equipment	158		40
	(To record monthly depreciation)			
31	Unearned Revenue	209	400	
	Service Revenue	400		400
	(To record revenue for services provided)			
31	Accounts Receivable	112	200	
	Service Revenue	400		200
	(To record revenue for services provided)			
31	Interest Expense	905	50	
	Interest Payable	230		50
	(To record interest on notes payable)			
31	Salaries Expense	726	1,200	
	Salaries Payable	212		1,200
	(To record accrued salaries)			

Cash No. 101

Date	Explanation	Ref.	Debit	Credit	Balance
2002					
Oct. 1		J1	10,000		10,000
2		J1	1,200		11,200
3		J1		900	10,300
4		J1		600	9,700
20		J1		500	9,200
26		J1		4,000	5,200
31		J1	10,000		15,200

Accounts Receivable No. 112

Date	Explanation	Ref.	Debit	Credit	Balance
2002					
Oct. 31	Adj. entry	J2	200		200

Advertising Supplies No. 126

Date	Explanation	Ref.	Debit	Credit	Balance
2002					
Oct. 5		J1	2,500		2,500
31	Adj. entry	J2		1,500	1,000

Prepaid Insurance No. 130

Date	Explanation	Ref.	Debit	Credit	Balance
2002					
Oct. 4		J1	600		600
31	Adj. entry	J2		50	550

Office Equipment No. 157

Date	Explanation	Ref.	Debit	Credit	Balance
2002					
Oct. 1		J1	5,000		5,000

Accumulated Depreciation—Office Equipment No. 158

Date	Explanation	Ref.	Debit	Credit	Balance
2002					
Oct. 31	Adj. entry	J2		40	40

Notes Payable No. 200

Date	Explanation	Ref.	Debit	Credit	Balance
2002					
Oct. 1		J1		5,000	5,000

Accounts Payable No. 201

Date	Explanation	Ref.	Debit	Credit	Balance
2002					
Oct. 5		J1		2,500	2,500

Unearned Revenue No. 209

Date	Explanation	Ref.	Debit	Credit	Balance
2002					
Oct. 2		J1		1,200	1,200
31	Adj. entry	J2	400		800

Salaries Payable No. 212

Date	Explanation	Ref.	Debit	Credit	Balance
2002					
Oct. 31	Adj. entry	J2		1,200	1,200

Interest Payable No. 230

Date	Explanation	Ref.	Debit	Credit	Balance
2002					
Oct. 31	Adj. entry	J2		50	50

C. R. Byrd, Capital No. 301

Date	Explanation	Ref.	Debit	Credit	Balance
2002					
Oct. 1		J1		10,000	10,000

C. R. Byrd, Drawing No. 306

Date	Explanation	Ref.	Debit	Credit	Balance
2002					
Oct. 20		J1	500		500

Service Revenue No. 400

Date	Explanation	Ref.	Debit	Credit	Balance
2002					
Oct. 31		J1		10,000	10,000
31	Adj. entry	J2		400	10,400
31	Adj. entry	J2		200	10,600

Advertising Supplies Expense No. 631

Date	Explanation	Ref.	Debit	Credit	Balance
2002					
Oct. 31	Adj. entry	J2	1,500		1,500

Depreciation Expense No. 711

Date	Explanation	Ref.	Debit	Credit	Balance
2002					
Oct. 31	Adj. entry	J2	40		40

Insurance Expense No. 722

Date	Explanation	Ref.	Debit	Credit	Balance
2002					
Oct. 31	Adj. entry	J2	50		50

Salaries Expense No. 726

Date	Explanation	Ref.	Debit	Credit	Balance
2002					
Oct. 26		J1	4,000		4,000
31	Adj. entry	J2	1,200		5,200

Rent Expense No. 729

Date	Explanation	Ref.	Debit	Credit	Balance
2002					
Oct. 3		J1	900		900

Interest Expense No. 905

Date	Explanation	Ref.	Debit	Credit	Balance
2002					
Oct. 31	Adj. entry	J2	50		50

Illustration 3-18

General ledger after adjustment

THE ADJUSTED TRIAL BALANCE AND FINANCIAL STATEMENTS

After all adjusting entries have been journalized and posted, another trial balance is prepared from the ledger accounts. This is called an adjusted trial balance. Its purpose is to **prove the equality** of the total debit balances and the total credit balances in the ledger after all adjustments have been made. The accounts in the adjusted trial balance contain all data that are needed for the preparation of financial statements.

PREPARING THE ADJUSTED TRIAL BALANCE

The adjusted trial balance for Pioneer Advertising Agency is presented in Illustration 3-19. It has been prepared from the ledger accounts in Illustration 3-18. The amounts affected by the adjusting entries are highlighted in color. Compare these amounts to those in the unadjusted trial balance in Illustration 3-3 on page 92.

Illustration 3-19

Adjusted trial balance

PIONEER ADVERTISING AGENCY	Dr.	Cr.
Adjusted Trial Balance		
October 31, 2002		
Cash	$15,200	
Accounts Receivable	200	
Advertising Supplies	1,000	
Prepaid Insurance	550	
Office Equipment	5,000	
Accumulated Depreciation—Office Equipment		$ 40
Notes Payable		5,000
Accounts Payable		2,500
Unearned Revenue		800
Salaries Payable		1,200
Interest Payable		50
C. R. Byrd, Capital		10,000
C. R. Byrd, Drawing	500	
Service Revenue		10,600
Salaries Expense	5,200	
Advertising Supplies Expense	1,500	
Rent Expense	900	
Insurance Expense	50	
Interest Expense	50	
Depreciation Expense	40	
	$30,190	$30,190

PREPARING FINANCIAL STATEMENTS

Financial statements can be prepared directly from the adjusted trial balance.
Illustrations 3-20 and 3-21 show the interrelationships of data in the adjusted trial
balance and the financial statements.

As shown in Illustration 3-20, the income statement is first prepared from the
revenue and expense accounts. The owner's equity statement is derived from the
owner's capital and drawing accounts and the net income (or net loss) from the
income statement. As shown in Illustration 3-21, the balance sheet is then prepared from the asset and liability accounts and the ending owner's capital balance
as reported in the owner's equity statement.

Illustration 3-20

Preparation of the income
statement and owner's
equity statement from the
adjusted trial balance

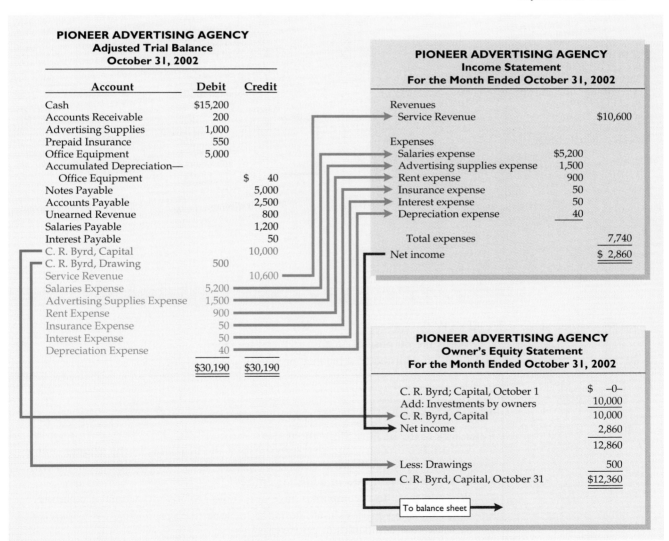

Illustration 3-21

Preparation of the balance
sheet from the adjusted trial
balance

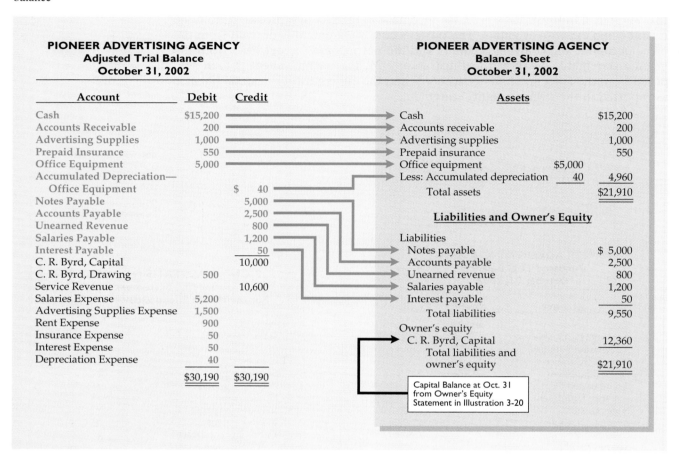

▶ *REVIEW IT*

1. What is the purpose of an adjusted trial balance?
2. How is an adjusted trial balance prepared?

A LOOK BACK AT OUR FEATURE STORY

Refer back to the Feature Story about **McKesson HBOC**, **Cambridge Biotech**, **Media Vision Technology**, and **Penguin USA** at the beginning of the chapter, and answer the following questions.

1. What are the purposes of adjusting entries?
2. What do these four companies have in common relative to accrual accounting?
3. What adjusting entries should be made for long-lived productive assets purchased by these four companies in prior years?
4. What other types of adjusting entries do you believe these companies might make?

SOLUTION

1. Adjusting entries are necessary to make the financial statements complete and accurate. Adjusting entries are made to record revenues in the period in which they are earned and to recognize expenses in the period in which they are incurred. Therefore, adjustments ensure that the revenue recognition and matching principles are followed.

2. Each of the companies misstated net income by either overstating revenues (sales) or understating expenses. They failed to properly **time** the reporting of revenues or expenses.

3. The purchase and use of long-lived assets in the production of revenue requires the systematic allocation of their cost over their useful lives by recording depreciation expense periodically.

4. (a) Accrued expenses: rent, salaries, utilities, interest, taxes.
   (b) Accrued revenues: interest earned, rent, commissions, fees.
   (c) Prepaid expenses: insurance, rent, supplies, advertising.
   (d) Unearned revenues: rent, subscriptions, customer deposits, and prepayments.

☑ THE NAVIGATOR

DEMONSTRATION PROBLEM

Terry Thomas opens the Green Thumb Lawn Care Company on April 1. At April 30, the trial balance shows the following balances for selected accounts.

Additional Demonstration Problem

Prepaid Insurance	$ 3,600
Equipment	28,000
Notes Payable	20,000
Unearned Revenue	4,200
Service Revenue	1,800

Analysis reveals the following additional data.

1. Prepaid insurance is the cost of a 2-year insurance policy, effective April 1.

2. Depreciation on the equipment is $500 per month.

3. The note payable is dated April 1. It is a 6-month, 12% note.

4. Seven customers paid for the company's 6 months' lawn service package of $600 beginning in April. These customers were serviced in April.

5. Lawn services provided other customers but not billed at April 30 totaled $1,500.

Instructions
Prepare the adjusting entries for the month of April. Show computations.

SOLUTION TO DEMONSTRATION PROBLEM

GENERAL JOURNAL   **J1**

Date	Account Titles and Explanation	Ref.	Debit	Credit
	Adjusting Entries			
Apr. 30	Insurance Expense		150	
	Prepaid Insurance			150
	(To record insurance expired:			
	$3,600 ÷ 24 = $150 per month)			
30	Depreciation Expense		500	
	Accumulated Depreciation—Equipment			500
	(To record monthly depreciation)			

ACTION PLAN

• Note that adjustments are being made for one month.

• Make computations carefully.

• Select account titles carefully.

• Make sure debits are made first and credits are indented.

• Check that debits equal credits for each entry.

30	Interest Expense		200	
	Interest Payable			200
	(To record interest on notes payable: $20,000 × 12% × 1/12 = $200)			
30	Unearned Revenue		700	
	Service Revenue			700
	(To record service revenue: $600 ÷ 6 = $100; $100 per month × 7 = $700)			
30	Accounts Receivable		1,500	
	Service Revenue			1,500
	(To record revenue for services provided)			

SUMMARY OF STUDY OBJECTIVES

1. Explain the time period assumption. The time period assumption assumes that the economic life of a business can be divided into artificial time periods.

2. Explain the accrual basis of accounting. Accrual-basis accounting means that events that change a company's financial statements are recorded in the periods in which the events occur, rather than in the periods in which the company receives or pays cash.

3. Explain why adjusting entries are needed. Adjusting entries are made at the end of an accounting period. They ensure that revenues are recorded in the period in which they are earned and that expenses are recognized in the period in which they are incurred.

4. Identify the major types of adjusting entries. The major types of adjusting entries are prepaid expenses, unearned revenues, accrued revenues, and accrued expenses.

5. Prepare adjusting entries for prepayments. Prepayments are either prepaid expenses or unearned revenues. Adjusting entries for prepayments are required at the statement date to record the portion of the prepayment that represents the expense incurred or the revenue earned in the current accounting period.

6. Prepare adjusting entries for accruals. Accruals are either accrued revenues or accrued expenses. Adjusting entries for accruals are required to record revenues earned and expenses incurred in the current accounting period that have not been recognized through daily entries.

7. Describe the nature and purpose of an adjusted trial balance. An adjusted trial balance shows the balances of all accounts, including those that have been adjusted, at the end of an accounting period. Its purpose is to show the effects of all financial events that have occurred during the accounting period.

Key Term Matching Activity

GLOSSARY

Accrual-basis accounting Accounting basis in which transactions that change a company's financial statements are recorded in the periods in which the events occur. (p. 89).

Accrued expenses Expenses incurred but not yet paid in cash or recorded. (p. 100).

Accrued revenues Revenues earned but not yet received in cash or recorded. (p. 99).

Adjusted trial balance A list of accounts and their balances after all adjustments have been made. (p. 106).

Adjusting entries Entries made at the end of an accounting period to ensure that the revenue recognition and matching principles are followed. (p. 91).

Book value The difference between the cost of a depreciable asset and its related accumulated depreciation. (p. 96).

Calendar year An accounting period that extends from January 1 to December 31. (p. 89).

Cash-basis accounting Accounting basis in which revenue is recorded when cash is received and an expense is recorded when cash is paid. (p. 89).

Contra asset account An account that is offset against an asset account on the balance sheet. (p. 96).

Depreciation The allocation of the cost of an asset to expense over its useful life in a rational and systematic manner. (p. 95).

Fiscal year An accounting period that is one year in length. (p. 89).

Interim periods Monthly or quarterly accounting time periods. (p. 89).

Matching principle The principle that efforts (expenses) be matched with accomplishments (revenues). (p. 90).

Prepaid expenses Expenses paid in cash and recorded as assets before they are used or consumed. (p. 93).

Revenue recognition principle The principle that revenue be recognized in the accounting period in which it is earned. (p. 90).

Time period assumption An assumption that the economic life of a business can be divided into artificial time periods. (p. 89).

Unearned revenues Cash received and recorded as liabilities before revenue is earned. (p. 97).

Useful life The length of service of a productive facility. (p. 95).

APPENDIX *Alternative Treatment of Prepaid Expenses and Unearned Revenues*

In our discussion of adjusting entries for prepaid expenses and unearned revenues, we illustrated transactions for which the initial entries were made to balance sheet accounts. In the case of prepaid expenses, the prepayment was debited to an asset account. In the case of unearned revenue, the cash received was credited to a liability account. Some businesses use an alternative treatment: (1) At the time an expense is prepaid, it is debited to an expense account. (2) At the time of a receipt for future services, it is credited to a revenue account. The circumstances that justify such entries and the different adjusting entries that may be required are described below. The alternative treatment of prepaid expenses and unearned revenues has the same effect on the financial statements as the procedures described in the chapter.

STUDY OBJECTIVE 8

Prepare adjusting entries for the alternative treatment of prepayments.

*P*REPAID EXPENSES

Prepaid expenses become expired costs either through the passage of time (e.g., insurance) or through consumption (e.g., advertising supplies). If, at the time of purchase, the company expects to consume the supplies before the next financial statement date, **it may be more convenient initially to debit (increase) an expense account rather than an asset account**.

Assume that Pioneer Advertising expects that all of the supplies purchased on October 5 will be used before the end of the month. A debit of $2,500 to Advertising Supplies Expense (rather than to the asset account Advertising Supplies) on October 5 will eliminate the need for an adjusting entry on October 31, if all the supplies are used. At October 31, the Advertising Supplies Expense account will show a balance of $2,500, which is the cost of supplies used between October 5 and October 31.

But what if the company does not use all the supplies, and an inventory of $1,000 of advertising supplies remains on October 31? Obviously, an adjusting entry is needed. Prior to adjustment, the expense account Advertising Supplies Expense is overstated $1,000, and the asset account Advertising Supplies is understated $1,000. Thus the following adjusting entry is made.

Oct. 31	Advertising Supplies	1,000	
	Advertising Supplies Expense		1,000
	(To record supplies inventory)		

A	=	L	+	OE
+1,000				+1,000

After posting the adjusting entry, the accounts show:

Advertising Supplies		Advertising Supplies Expense	
10/31 **Adj.** 1,000		10/5 2,500	10/31 **Adj.** 1,000
		10/31 **Bal.** 1,500	

Illustration 3A-1

Prepaid expenses accounts after adjustment

After adjustment, the asset account Advertising Supplies shows a balance of $1,000, which is equal to the cost of supplies on hand at October 31. In addition, Advertising Supplies Expense shows a balance of $1,500, which is equal to the cost of supplies used between October 5 and October 31. If the adjusting entry is not made, expenses will be overstated and net income will be understated by $1,000 in the October income statement. Also, both assets and owner's equity will be understated by $1,000 on the October 31 balance sheet.

A comparison of the entries and accounts for advertising supplies is shown in Illustration 3A-2.

Illustration 3A-2

Adjustment approaches—a comparison

Prepayment Initially Debited to Asset Account (per chapter)			Prepayment Initially Debited to Expense Account (per appendix)		
Oct. 5	Advertising Supplies	2,500	Oct. 5	Advertising Supplies	
	Accounts Payable	2,500		Expense	2,500
				Accounts Payable	2,500
Oct. 31	Advertising Supplies		Oct. 31	Advertising Supplies	1,000
	Expense	1,500		Advertising Supplies	
	Advertising Supplies	1,500		Expense	1,000

After posting the entries, the accounts appear as follows.

Illustration 3A-3

Comparison of accounts

(per chapter) Advertising Supplies				(per appendix) Advertising Supplies			
10/5	2,500	10/31 **Adj.**	1,500	10/31 **Adj.**	1,000		
10/31 **Bal.**	1,000						
Advertising Supplies Expense				**Advertising Supplies Expense**			
10/31 **Adj.**	1,500			10/5	2,500	10/31 **Adj.**	1,000
				10/31 **Bal.**	1,500		

Note that the account balances under each alternative are the same at October 31: Advertising Supplies $1,000, and Advertising Supplies Expense $1,500.

UNEARNED REVENUES

Unearned revenues become earned either through the passage of time (e.g., unearned rent) or through providing the service (e.g., unearned fees). Similar to the case for prepaid expenses, a revenue account may be credited (increased) when cash is received for future services.

To illustrate, assume that Pioneer Advertising received $1,200 for future services on October 2. The services were expected to be performed before October 31.[3] In such a case, Service Revenue is credited. If revenue is in fact earned before October 31, no adjustment is needed.

---

[3]This example focuses only on the alternative treatment of unearned revenues. In the interest of simplicity, the entries to Service Revenue pertaining to the immediate earning of revenue ($10,000) and the adjusting entry for accrued revenue ($200) have been ignored.

However, if at the statement date $800 of the services have not been performed, an adjusting entry is required. The revenue account Service Revenue is overstated $800, and the liability account Unearned Revenue is understated $800. Thus, the following adjusting entry is made.

Oct. 31	Service Revenue	800	
	Unearned Revenue		800
	(To record unearned revenue)		

HELPFUL HINT
The required adjusted balances here are Service Revenue $400 and Unearned Revenue $800.

A	=	L	+	OE
		+800		−800

After posting the adjusting entry, the accounts show:

Unearned Revenue		Service Revenue			
	10/31 **Adj.** 800	10/31 **Adj.** 800	10/2	1,200
			10/31 **Bal.** 400

Illustration 3A-4

Unearned revenue accounts after adjustment

The liability account Unearned Revenue shows a balance of $800. This is equal to the services that will be provided in the future. In addition, the balance in Service Revenue equals the services provided in October. If the adjusting entry is not made, both revenues and net income will be overstated by $800 in the October income statement. Also, liabilities will be understated by $800, and owner's equity will be overstated by $800 on the October 31 balance sheet.

A comparison of the entries and accounts for service revenue earned and unearned is shown in Illustration 3A-5.

Unearned Revenue Initially Credited to Liability Account (per chapter)			Unearned Revenue Initially Credited to Revenue Account (per appendix)		
Oct. 2	Cash	1,200	Oct. 2	Cash	1,200
	Unearned Revenue	1,200		Service Revenue	1,200
Oct. 31	Unearned Revenue	400	Oct. 31	Service Revenue	800
	Service Revenue	400		Unearned Revenue	800

Illustration 3A-5

Adjustment approaches— a comparison

After posting the entries, the accounts appear as follows.

(per chapter) Unearned Revenue		(per appendix) Unearned Revenue	
10/31 **Adj.** 400	10/2 1,200		10/31 **Adj.** 800
	10/31 **Bal.** 800		

Service Revenue		Service Revenue			
	10/31 **Adj.** 400	10/31 **Adj.** 800	10/2	1,200
			10/31 **Bal.** 400

Illustration 3A-6

Comparison of accounts

Note that the balances in the accounts are the same under the two alternatives: Unearned Revenue $800, and Service Revenue $400.

SUMMARY OF ADDITIONAL ADJUSTMENT RELATIONSHIPS

The use of alternative adjusting entries requires additions to the summary of basic relationships presented earlier in Illustration 3-16. The additions are shown in color in Illustration 3A-7.

Alternative adjusting entries **do not apply** to accrued revenues and accrued expenses because **no entries occur before these types of adjusting entries are made**. Therefore, the entries in Illustration 3-16 for these two types of adjustments remain unchanged.

Illustration 3A-7

Summary of basic relationships for prepayments

Type of Adjustment	Reason for Adjustment	Account Balances before Adjustment	Adjusting Entry
1. Prepaid expenses	(a) Prepaid expenses initially recorded in asset accounts have been used.	Assets overstated Expenses understated	Dr. Expenses Cr. Assets
	(b) Prepaid expenses initially recorded in expense accounts have not been used.	**Assets understated Expenses overstated**	**Dr. Assets Cr. Expenses**
2. Unearned revenues	(a) Unearned revenues initially recorded in liability accounts have been earned.	Liabilities overstated Revenues understated	Dr. Liabilities Cr. Revenues
	(b) Unearned revenues initially recorded in revenue accounts have not been earned.	**Liabilities understated Revenues overstated**	**Dr. Revenues Cr. Liabilities**

SUMMARY OF STUDY OBJECTIVE FOR APPENDIX

8. Prepare adjusting entries for the alternative treatment of prepayments. Prepayments may be initially debited to an expense account. Unearned revenues may be credited to a revenue account. At the end of the period, these accounts may be overstated. The adjusting entries for prepaid expenses are a debit to an asset account and a credit to an expense account. Adjusting entries for unearned revenues are a debit to a revenue account and a credit to a liability account.

*Note: All asterisked Questions, Exercises, and Problems relate to material in the appendix to the chapter.

Chapter 3 Self-Test

SELF-STUDY QUESTIONS

Answers are at the end of the chapter.

(SO 1) **1.** The time period assumption states that:
  a. revenue should be recognized in the accounting period in which it is earned.
  b. expenses should be matched with revenues.
  c. the economic life of a business can be divided into artificial time periods.
  d. the fiscal year should correspond with the calendar year.

(SO 2) **2.** The principle dictating that efforts (expenses) be matched with accomplishments (revenues) is the:
  a. matching principle.
  b. cost principle.
  c. periodicity principle.
  d. revenue recognition principle.

3. One of the following statements about the accrual basis (SO 2) of accounting is *false*. That statement is:
  a. Events that change a company's financial statements are recorded in the periods in which the events occur.
  b. Revenue is recognized in the period in which it is earned.
  c. This basis is in accord with generally accepted accounting principles.
  d. Revenue is recorded only when cash is received, and expense is recorded only when cash is paid.

(SO 3) **4.** Adjusting entries are made to ensure that:
a. expenses are recognized in the period in which they are incurred.
b. revenues are recorded in the period in which they are earned.
c. balance sheet and income statement accounts have correct balances at the end of an accounting period.
d. all of the above.

(SO 4) **5.** Each of the following is a major type (or category) of adjusting entries *except:*
a. prepaid expenses.
b. accrued revenues.
c. accrued expenses.
d. earned revenues.

(SO 5) **6.** The trial balance shows Supplies $1,350 and Supplies Expense $0. If $600 of supplies are on hand at the end of the period, the adjusting entry is:

a. Supplies | 600 |
   Supplies Expense | | 600
b. Supplies | 750 |
   Supplies Expense | | 750
c. Supplies Expense | 750 |
   Supplies | | 750
d. Supplies Expense | 600 |
   Supplies | | 600

(SO 5) **7.** Adjustments for unearned revenues:
a. decrease liabilities and increase revenues.
b. have an assets and revenues account relationship.
c. increase assets and increase revenues.
d. decrease revenues and decrease assets.

(SO 6) **8.** Adjustments for accrued revenues:
a. have a liabilities and revenues account relationship.

b. have an assets and revenues account relationship.
c. decrease assets and revenues.
d. decrease liabilities and increase revenues.

9. Kathy Siska earned a salary of $400 for the last week of (SO 6) September. She will be paid on October 1. The adjusting entry for Kathy's employer at September 30 is:

a. No entry is required.
b. Salaries Expense | 400 |
   Salaries Payable | | 400
c. Salaries Expense | 400 |
   Cash | | 400
d. Salaries Payable | 400 |
   Cash | | 400

10. Which of the following statements is *incorrect* concern- (SO 7) ing the adjusted trial balance?
a. An adjusted trial balance proves the equality of the total debit balances and the total credit balances in the ledger after all adjustments are made.
b. The adjusted trial balance provides the primary basis for the preparation of financial statements.
c. The adjusted trial balance lists the account balances segregated by assets and liabilities.
d. The adjusted trial balance is prepared after the adjusting entries have been journalized and posted.

*11. The trial balance shows Supplies $0 and Supplies Expense (SO 8) $1,500. If $800 of supplies are on hand at the end of the period, the adjusting entry is:
a. Debit Supplies $800 and credit Supplies Expense $800.
b. Debit Supplies Expense $800 and credit Supplies $800.
c. Debit Supplies $700 and credit Supplies Expense $700.
d. Debit Supplies Expense $700 and credit Supplies $700.

QUESTIONS

1. (a) How does the time period assumption affect an accountant's analysis of business transactions?
(b) Explain the terms *fiscal year, calendar year,* and *interim periods.*

2. State two generally accepted accounting principles that relate to adjusting the accounts.

3. Bon Barone, a lawyer, accepts a legal engagement in March, performs the work in April, and is paid in May. If Barone's law firm prepares monthly financial statements, when should it recognize revenue from this engagement? Why?

4. Why do accrual-basis financial statements provide more useful information than cash-basis statements?

5. In completing the engagement in (3) above, Barone incurs $4,500 of expenses in March, which are paid in April. How much expense should be deducted from revenues in the month the revenue is recognized? Why?

6. "Adjusting entries are required by the cost principle of accounting." Do you agree? Explain.

7. Why may a trial balance not contain up-to-date and complete financial information?

8. Distinguish between the two categories of adjusting entries, and identify the types of adjustments applicable to each category.

9. What is the debit/credit effect of a prepaid expense adjusting entry?

10. "Depreciation is a valuation process that results in the reporting of the fair market value of the asset." Do you agree? Explain.

11. Explain the differences between depreciation expense and accumulated depreciation.

12. Shen Company purchased equipment for $15,000. By the current balance sheet date, $7,000 had been depreciated. Indicate the balance sheet presentation of the data.

13. What is the debit/credit effect of an unearned revenue adjusting entry?

14. A company fails to recognize revenue earned but not yet received. Which of the following accounts are involved in the adjusting entry: (a) asset, (b) liability, (c) revenue, or (d) expense? For the accounts selected, indicate whether they would be debited or credited in the entry.

15. A company fails to recognize an expense incurred but not paid. Indicate which of the following accounts is debited and which is credited in the adjusting entry: (a) asset, (b) liability, (c) revenue, or (d) expense.

16. A company makes an accrued revenue adjusting entry for $800 and an accrued expense adjusting entry for $600. How much was net income understated prior to these entries? Explain.

17. On January 9, a company pays $5,000 for salaries, of which $2,000 was reported as Salaries Payable on December 31. Give the entry to record the payment.

18. For each of the following items before adjustment, indicate the type of adjusting entry (prepaid expense, unearned revenue, accrued revenue, and accrued expense) that is needed to correct the misstatement. If an item could result in more than one type of adjusting entry, indicate each of the types.
   (a) Assets are understated.
   (b) Liabilities are overstated.

(c) Liabilities are understated.
(d) Expenses are understated.
(e) Assets are overstated.
(f) Revenue is understated.

19. One-half of the adjusting entry is given below. Indicate the account title for the other half of the entry.
   (a) Salaries Expense is debited.
   (b) Depreciation Expense is debited.
   (c) Interest Payable is credited.
   (d) Supplies is credited.
   (e) Accounts Receivable is debited.
   (f) Unearned Service Revenue is debited.

20. "An adjusting entry may affect more than one balance sheet or income statement account." Do you agree? Why or why not?

21. Why is it possible to prepare financial statements directly from an adjusted trial balance?

*22. The Alpha Company debits Supplies Expense for all purchases of supplies and credits Rent Revenue for all advanced rentals. For each type of adjustment, give the adjusting entry.

BRIEF EXERCISES

Indicate why adjusting entries are needed.
(SO 3)

BE3-1 The ledger of Hilo Company includes the following accounts. Explain why each account may require adjustment.
   (a) Prepaid Insurance   (c) Unearnd Revenue
   (b) Depreciation Expense   (d) Interest Payable

Identify the major types of adjusting entries.
(SO 4)

BE3-2 Riko Company accumulates the following adjustment data at December 31. Indicate (a) the type of adjustment (prepaid expense, accrued revenues and so on), and (b) the accounts before adjustment (overstated or understated).
   1. Supplies of $100 are on hand.
   2. Services provided but unbilled total $900.
   3. Interest of $200 has accumulated on a note payable.
   4. Rent collected in advance totaling $800 has been earned.

Prepare adjusting entry for supplies.
(SO 5)

BE3-3 Sain Advertising Company's trial balance at December 31 shows Advertising Supplies $8,700 and Advertising Supplies Expense $0. On December 31, there are $1,700 of supplies on hand. Prepare the adjusting entry at December 31, and using T accounts, enter the balances in the accounts, post the adjusting entry, and indicate the adjusted balance in each account.

Prepare adjusting entries for depreciation.
(SO 5)

BE3-4 At the end of its first year, the trial balance of Shuey Company shows Equipment $25,000 and zero balances in Accumulated Depreciation—Equipment and Depreciation Expense. Depreciation for the year is estimated to be $5,000. Prepare the adjusting entry for depreciation at December 31, post the adjustments to T accounts, and indicate the balance sheet presentation of the equipment at December 31.

Prepare adjusting entries for prepaid expense.
(SO 5)

BE3-5 On July 1, 2002, Cheng Co. pays $15,000 to Wanzo Insurance Co. for a 3-year insurance contract. Both companies have fiscal years ending December 31. For Cheng Co., journalize and post the entry on July 1 and the adjusting entry on December 31.

Prepare adjusting entry for unearned revenue.
(SO 5)

BE3-6 Using the data in BE3-5, journalize and post the entry on July 1 and the adjusting entry on December 31 for Wanzo Insurance Co. Wanzo uses the accounts Unearned Insurance Revenue and Insurance Revenue.

BE3-7 The bookeeper for Rosenberg Company asks you to prepare the following accrued adjusting entries at December 31.

1. Interest on notes payable of $300 is accrued.
2. Services provided but unbilled total $1,250.
3. Salaries earned by employees of $900 have not been recorded.

Use the following account titles: Service Revenue, Accounts Receivable, Interest Expense, Interest Payable, Salaries Expense, and Salaries Payable.

Prepare adjusting entries for accruals.
(SO 6)

BE3-8 The trial balance of Hoi Company includes the following balance sheet accounts. Identify the accounts that require adjustment. For each account that requires adjustment, indicate **(a)** the type of adjusting entry (prepaid expenses, unearned revenues, accrued revenues, and accrued expenses) and **(b)** the related account in the adjusting entry.

Analyze accounts in an adjusted trial balance.
(SO 7)

Accounts Receivable	Interest Payable
Prepaid Insurance	Unearned Service Revenue
Accumulated Depreciation—Equipment	

BE3-9 The adjusted trial balance of Lumas Company at December 31, 2002, includes the following accounts: S. Lumas, Capital $15,600; S. Lumas, Drawing $6,000; Service Revenue $38,400; Salaries Expense $13,000; Insurance Expense $2,000; Rent Expense $4,000; Supplies Expense $1,500; and Depreciation Expense $1,300 Prepare an income statement for the year.

Prepare an income statement from an adjusted trial balance.
(SO 7)

BE3-10 Partial adjusted trial balance data for Lumas Company is presented in BE3-9. The balance in S. Lumas, Capital is the balance as of January 1. Prepare an owner's equity statement for the year assuming net income is $16,600 for the year.

Prepare an owner's equity statement from an adjusted trial balance.
(SO 7)

*BE3-11 Lam Company records all prepayments in income statement accounts. At April 30, the trial balance shows Supplies Expense $2,800, Service Revenue $9,200, and zero balances in related balance sheet accounts. Prepare the adjusting entries at April 30 assuming **(a)** $1,000 of supplies on hand and **(b)** $800 of service revenue should be reported as unearned.

Prepare adjusting entries under alternative treatment of prepayments.
(SO 8)

EXERCISES

E3-1 On numerous occasions, proposals have surfaced to put the federal government on the accrual basis of accounting. This is no small issue. If this basis were used, it would mean that billions in unrecorded liabilities would have to be booked, and the federal deficit would increase substantially.

Distinguish between cash and accrual basis of accounting.
(SO 2)

Instructions

(a) What is the difference between accrual-basis accounting and cash-basis accounting?

(b) Why would politicians prefer the cash basis over the accrual basis?

(c) Write a letter to your senator explaining why the federal government should adopt the accrual basis of accounting.

E3-2 Jawson Company accumulates the following adjustment data at December 31.

1. Services provided but unbilled total $750.
2. Store supplies of $300 have been used.
3. Utility expenses of $225 are unpaid.
4. Unearned revenue of $260 has been earned.
5. Salaries of $900 are unpaid.
6. Prepaid insurance totaling $350 has expired.

Identify types of adjustments and account relationships.
(SO 4, 5, 6)

Instructions

For each of the above items indicate the following.

(a) The type of adjustment (prepaid expense, unearned revenue, accrued revenue, or accrued expense).

(b) The accounts before adjustment (overstatement or understatement).

E3-3 The ledger of Easy Rental Agency on March 31 of the current year includes the following selected accounts before adjusting entries have been prepared.

Prepare adjusting entries from selected account data.
(SO 5, 6, 7)

	Debit	Credit
Prepaid Insurance	$ 3,600	
Supplies	2,800	
Equipment	25,000	
Accumulated		
Depreciation—Equipment		$ 8,400
Notes Payable		20,000
Unearned Rent		9,900
Rent Revenue		60,000
Interest Expense	–0–	
Wage Expense	14,000	

An analysis of the accounts shows the following.
1. The equipment depreciates $250 per month.
2. One-third of the unearned rent was earned during the quarter.
3. Interest of $500 is accrued on the notes payable.
4. Supplies on hand total $650.
5. Insurance expires at the rate of $300 per month.

Instructions
Prepare the adjusting entries at March 31, assuming that adjusting entries are made quarterly. Additional accounts are: Depreciation Expense, Insurance Expense, Interest Payable, and Supplies Expense.

Prepare adjusting entries.
(SO 5, 6, 7)

E3-4 Karen Tong, D.D.S., opened a dental practice on January 1, 2002. During the first month of operations the following transactions occurred.

1. Performed services for patients who had dental plan insurance. At January 31, $875 of such services was earned but not yet billed to the insurance companies.
2. Utility expenses incurred but not paid prior to January 31 totaled $520.
3. Purchased dental equipment on January 1 for $80,000, paying $20,000 in cash and signing a $60,000, 3-year note payable. The equipment depreciates $400 per month. Interest is $500 per month.
4. Purchased a one-year malpractice insurance policy on January 1 for $12,000.
5. Purchased $1,600 of dental supplies. On January 31, determined that $700 of supplies were on hand.

Instructions
Prepare the adjusting entries on January 31. Account titles are: Accumulated Depreciation—Dental Equipment, Depreciation Expense, Service Revenue, Accounts Receivable, Insurance Expense, Interest Expense, Interest Payable, Prepaid Insurance, Supplies, Supplies Expense, Utilities Expense, and Utilities Payable.

Prepare adjusting entries.
(SO 5, 6, 7)

E3-5 The trial balance for Pioneer Advertising Agency is shown in Illustration 3-3, p. 92. In lieu of the adjusting entries shown in the text at October 31, assume the following adjustment data.

1. Advertising supplies on hand at October 31 total $1,100.
2. Expired insurance for the month is $100.
3. Depreciation for the month is $50.
4. Unearned revenue in October totals $600.
5. Services provided but unbilled at October 31 are $300.
6. Interest accrued at October 31 is $70.
7. Accrued salaries at October 31 are $1,400.

Instructions
Prepare the adjusting entries for the items above.

Prepare correct income statement
(SO 2, 5, 6, 7)

E3-6 The income statement of Weller Co. for the month of July shows net income of $1,400 based on Service Revenue $5,500, Wages Expense $2,300, Supplies Expense $1,200, and Utilities Expense $600. In reviewing the statement, you discover the following.

1. Insurance expired during July of $400 was omitted.
2. Supplies expense includes $500 of supplies that are still on hand at July 31.
3. Depreciation on equipment of $150 was omitted.

4. Accrued but unpaid wages at July 31 of $300 were not included.

5. Services provided but unrecorded totaled $1,100.

Instructions

Prepare a correct income statement for July.

E3-7   A partial adjusted trial balance of Cordero Company at January 31, 2002, shows the following.

Analyze adjusted data.
(SO 4, 5, 6, 7)

CORDERO COMPANY
Adjusted Trial Balance
January 31, 2002

	Debit	Credit
Supplies	$ 850	
Prepaid Insurance	2,400	
Salaries Payable		$ 800
Unearned Revenue		750
Supplies Expense	950	
Insurance Expense	400	
Salaries Expense	1,800	
Service Revenue		2,000

Instructions

Answer the following questions, assuming the year begins January 1.

(a) If the amount in Supplies Expense is the January 31 adjusting entry, and $850 of supplies was purchased in January, what was the balance in Supplies on January 1?

(b) If the amount in Insurance Expense is the January 31 adjusting entry, and the original insurance premium was for one year, what was the total premium and when was the policy purchased?

(c) If $2,500 of salaries was paid in January, what was the balance in Salaries Payable at December 31, 2001?

(d) If $1,600 was received in January for services performed in January, what was the balance in Unearned Revenue at December 31, 2001?

E3-8   Selected accounts of Felipe Company are shown below.

Journalize basic transactions and adjusting entries.
(SO 5, 6, 7)

Supplies Expense

7/31	700		

Supplies

7/1 Bal.	1,100	7/31	700
7/10	200		

Salaries Payable

		7/31	1,200

Accounts Receivable

7/31	500		

Unearned Revenue

7/31	900	7/1 Bal.	1,500
		7/20	750

Salaries Expense

7/15	1,200		
7/31	1,200		

Service Revenue

		7/14	3,000
		7/31	900
		7/31	500

Instructions

After analyzing the accounts, journalize **(a)** the July transactions and **(b)** the adjusting entries that were made on July 31. (*Hint:* July transactions were for cash.)

E3-9   The trial balances before and after adjustment for Tang Company at the end of its fiscal year are presented below.

Prepare adjusting entries from analysis of trial balances.
(SO 5, 6, 7)

TANG COMPANY
Trial Balance
August 31, 2001

	Before Adjustment		After Adjustment	
	Dr.	**Cr.**	**Dr.**	**Cr.**
Cash	$10,400		$10,400	
Accounts Receivable	8,800		9,500	
Office Supplies	2,300		700	
Prepaid Insurance	4,000		2,500	
Office Equipment	14,000		14,000	
Accumulated Depreciation—Office Equipment		$ 3,600		$ 4,800
Accounts Payable		5,800		5,800
Salaries Payable		–0–		1,100
Unearned Rent		1,500		600
T. Tang, Capital		15,600		15,600
Service Revenue		34,000		34,700
Rent Revenue		11,000		11,900
Salaries Expense	17,000		18,100	
Office Supplies Expense	–0–		1,600	
Rent Expense	15,000		15,000	
Insurance Expense	–0–		1,500	
Depreciation Expense	–0–		1,200	
	$71,500	$71,500	$74,500	$74,500

Instructions

Prepare the adjusting entries that were made.

Prepare financial statements from adjusted trial balance.
(SO 5, 6, 7)

E3-10   The adjusted trial balance for Tang Company is given in E3-9.

Instructions

Prepare the income and owner's equity statements for the year and the balance sheet at August 31.

Record transactions on accrual basis; convert revenue to cash receipts.
(SO 5, 6)

E3-11   The following data are taken from the comparative balance sheets of Breakers Billiards Club, which prepares its financial statements using the accrual basis of accounting.

December 31	2002	2001
Fees receivable from members	$12,000	$ 9,000
Unearned fees revenue	17,000	22,000

Fees are billed to members based upon their use of the club's facilities. Unearned fees arise from the sale of gift certificates, which members can apply to their future use of club facilities. The 2002 income statement for the club showed that fees revenue of $153,000 was earned during the year.

Instructions

(*Hint:* You will probably find it helpful to use T accounts to analyze this data.)

(a) Prepare journal entries for each of the following events that took place during 2002.

　(1) Fees receivable from 2001 were all collected.
　(2) Gift certificates outstanding at the end of 2001 were all redeemed.
　(3) An additional $30,000 worth of gift certificates were sold during 2002. A portion of these were used by the recipients during the year; the remainder were still outstanding at the end of 2002.
　(4) Fees for 2002 were billed to members.
　(5) Fees receivable for 2002 (i.e., those billed in item [4] above) were partially collected.

(b) Determine the amount of cash received by the club, with respect to fees, during 2002.

*E3-12   At Devereaux Company, prepayments are debited to expense when paid, and unearned revenues are credited to revenue when received. During January of the current year, the following transactions occurred.

Journalize transactions and adjusting entries using appendix.
(SO 8)

Jan. 2   Paid $1,800 for fire insurance protection for the year.
      10   Paid $1,700 for supplies.
      15   Received $5,100 for services to be performed in the future.

On January 31, it is determined that $1,500 of the services fees have been earned and that there are $800 of supplies on hand.

Instructions
 (a) Journalize and post the January transactions. (Use T accounts.)
 (b) Journalize and post the adjusting entries at January 31.
 (c) Determine the ending balance in each of the accounts.

PROBLEMS: SET A

P3-1A   Han Solo started his own consulting firm, Solo Company, on June 1, 2002. The trial balance at June 30 is as follows.

Prepare adjusting entries, post to ledger accounts, and pre-pare adjusted trial balance.
(SO 5, 6, 7)

SOLO COMPANY
Trial Balance
June 30, 2002

Account Number		Debit	Credit
100	Cash	$ 7,750	
110	Accounts Receivable	6,000	
120	Prepaid Insurance	2,400	
130	Supplies	2,000	
135	Office Equipment	15,000	
200	Accounts Payable		$ 4,500
230	Unearned Service Revenue		4,000
300	H. Solo, Capital		21,750
400	Service Revenue		7,900
510	Salaries Expense	4,000	
520	Rent Expense	1,000	
		$38,150	$38,150

In addition to those accounts listed on the trial balance, the chart of accounts for Solo Company also contains the following accounts and account numbers: No. 136 Accumulated Depreciation—Office Equipment, No. 210 Utilities Payable, No. 220 Salaries Payable, No. 530 Depreciation Expense, No. 540 Insurance Expense, No. 550 Utilities Expense, and No. 560 Supplies Expense.

Other data:

1. Supplies on hand at June 30 are $1,300.
2. A utility bill for $150 has not been recorded and will not be paid until next month.
3. The insurance policy is for a year.
4. $2,500 of unearned service revenue has been earned at the end of the month.
5. Salaries of $1,500 are accrued at June 30.
6. The office equipment has a 5-year life with no salvage value. It is being depreciated at $250 per month for 60 months.
7. Invoices representing $3,000 of services performed during the month have not been recorded as of June 30.

Instructions

(a) Prepare the adjusting entries for the month of June. Use J3 as the page number for your journal.

(b) Post the adjusting entries to the ledger accounts. Enter the totals from the trial balance as beginning account balances and place a check mark in the posting reference column.

(c) Prepare an adjusted trial balance at June 30, 2002.

Prepare adjusting entries, adjusted trial balance, and financial statements.

(SO 5, 6, 7)

P3-2A Muddy River Resort opened for business on June 1 with eight air-conditioned units. Its trial balance before adjustment on August 31 is as follows.

MUDDY RIVER RESORT
Trial Balance
August 31, 2002

Account Number		Debit	Credit
101	Cash	$ 19,600	
126	Supplies	3,300	
130	Prepaid Insurance	6,000	
140	Land	25,000	
143	Cottages	125,000	
149	Furniture	26,000	
201	Accounts Payable		$ 6,500
208	Unearned Rent		7,400
275	Mortgage Payable		80,000
301	P. Javorek, Capital		100,000
306	P. Javorek, Drawing	5,000	
429	Rent Revenue		80,000
622	Repair Expense	3,600	
726	Salaries Expense	51,000	
732	Utilities Expense	9,400	
		$273,900	$273,900

In addition to those accounts listed on the trial balance, the chart of accounts for Muddy River Resort also contains the following accounts and account numbers: No. 112 Accounts Receivable, No. 144 Accumulated Depreciation—Cottages, No. 150 Accumulated Depreciation—Furniture, No. 212 Salaries Payable, No. 230 Interest Payable, No. 620 Depreciation Expense—Cottages, No. 621 Depreciation Expense—Furniture, No. 631 Supplies Expense, No. 718 Interest Expense, and No. 722 Insurance Expense.

Other data:

1. Insurance expires at the rate of $400 per month.
2. A count on August 31 shows $900 of supplies on hand.
3. Annual depreciation is $4,800 on cottages and $2,400 on furniture.
4. Unearned rent of $5,100 was earned prior to August 31.
5. Salaries of $400 were unpaid at August 31.
6. Rentals of $800 were due from tenants at August 31. (Use Accounts Receivable.)
7. The mortgage interest rate is 12% per year. (The mortgage was taken out on August 1.)

Instructions

(c) Adj. trial balance $277,700

(d) Net income $15,300 Ending capital balance $110,300 Total assets $200,300

(a) Journalize the adjusting entries on August 31 for the 3-month period June 1–August 31.

(b) Prepare a ledger using the three-column form of account. Enter the trial balance amounts and post the adjusting entries. (Use J1 as the posting reference.)

(c) Prepare an adjusted trial balance on August 31.

(d) Prepare an income statement and an owner's equity statement for the 3 months ending August 31 and a balance sheet as of August 31.

Prepare adjusting entries and financial statements.

(SO 5, 6, 7)

P3-3A Grant Advertising Agency was founded by Thomas Grant in January of 1998. Presented on the next page are both the adjusted and unadjusted trial balances as of December 31, 2002.

Debits		Credits	
Cash	$ 9,500	Notes Payable	$ 17,000
Accounts Receivable	14,000	Accounts Payable	9,000
Equipment	45,000	Jill Jay, Capital	25,000
Insurance Expense	1,800	Graphic Revenue	52,100
Salaries Expense	30,000	Consulting Revenue	6,000
Supplies Expense	3,700		
Advertising Expense	1,900		
Rent Expense	1,500		
Utilities Expense	1,700		
	$109,100		$109,100

Analysis reveals the following additional data.

1. The $3,700 balance in Supplies Expense represents supplies purchased in January. At June 30, $1,300 of supplies was on hand.
2. The note payable was issued on February 1. It is a 12%, 6-month note.
3. The balance in Insurance Expense is the premium on a one-year policy, dated March 1, 2002.
4. Consulting fees are credited to revenue when received. At June 30, consulting fees of $1,100 are unearned.
5. Graphic revenue earned but unbilled at June 30 totals $2,000.
6. Depreciation is $2,000 per year.

Instructions

(a) Journalize the adjusting entries at June 30. (Assume adjustments are recorded every 6 months.)

(b) Prepare an adjusted trial balance.

(c) Prepare an income statement and owner's equity statement for the 6 months ended June 30 and a balance sheet at June 30.

(b) Adj. trial balance
$112,950

(c) Net income $19,050
Ending capital $44,050
Total assets $72,000

PROBLEMS: SET B

P3-1B Julie Brown started her own consulting firm, Astromech Consulting, on May 1, 2002. The trial balance at May 31 is as follows.

Prepare adjusting entries, post to ledger accounts, and prepare an adjusted trial balance.
(SO 5, 6, 7)

ASTROMECH CONSULTING
Trial Balance
May 31, 2002

Account Number		Debit	Credit
101	Cash	$ 6,500	
110	Accounts Receivable	4,000	
120	Prepaid Insurance	3,600	
130	Supplies	1,500	
135	Office Furniture	12,000	
200	Accounts Payable		$ 3,500
230	Unearned Service Revenue		3,000
300	J. Brown, Capital		19,100
400	Service Revenue		6,000
510	Salaries Expense	3,000	
520	Rent Expense	1,000	
		$31,600	$31,600

In addition to those accounts listed on the trial balance, the chart of accounts for Astromech Consulting also contains the following accounts and account numbers: No. 136 Accumulated Depreciation—Office Furniture, No. 210 Travel Payable, No. 220 Salaries Payable, No. 530 Depreciation Expense, No. 540 Insurance Expense, No. 550 Travel Expense, and No. 560 Supplies Expense.

Other data:

1. $500 of supplies have been used during the month.
2. Travel expense incurred but not paid on May 31, 2001, $200.
3. The insurance policy is for 2 years.
4. $1,000 of the balance in the unearned service revenue account remains unearned at the end of the month.
5. May 31 is a Wednesday, and employees are paid on Fridays. Astromech Consulting has two employees, who are paid $500 each for a 5-day work week.
6. The office furniture has a 5-year life with no salvage value. It is being depreciated at $200 per month for 60 months.
7. Invoices representing $2,000 of services performed during the month have not been recorded as of May 31.

Instructions
(a) Prepare the adjusting entries for the month of May. Use J4 as the page number for your journal.
(b) Post the adjusting entries to the ledger accounts. Enter the totals from the trial balance as beginning account balances and place a check mark in the posting reference column.
(c) Prepare an adjusted trial balance at May 31, 2002.

Prepare adjusting entries, adjusted trial balance, and financial statements.
(SO 5, 6, 7)

P3-2B   The Roach Motel opened for business on May 1, 2002. Its trial balance before adjustment on May 31 is as follows.

ROACH MOTEL
Trial Balance
May 31, 2002

Account Number		Debit	Credit
101	Cash	$ 2,500	
126	Supplies	1,900	
130	Prepaid Insurance	2,400	
140	Land	15,000	
141	Lodge	70,000	
149	Furniture	16,800	
201	Accounts Payable		$ 5,300
208	Unearned Rent		3,600
275	Mortgage Payable		35,000
301	Sara Sutton, Capital		60,000
429	Rent Revenue		9,200
610	Advertising Expense	500	
726	Salaries Expense	3,000	
732	Utilities Expense	1,000	
		$113,100	$113,100

In addition to those accounts listed on the trial balance, the chart of accounts for Roach Motel also contains the following accounts and account numbers: No. 142 Accumulated Depreciation—Lodge, No. 150 Accumulated Depreciation—Furniture, No. 212 Salaries Payable, No. 230 Interest Payable, No. 619 Depreciation Expense—Lodge, No. 621 Depreciation Expense—Furniture, No. 631 Supplies Expense, No. 718 Interest Expense, and No. 722 Insurance Expense.

Other data:

1. Insurance expires at the rate of $200 per month.
2. A count of supplies shows $900 of unused supplies on May 31.
3. Annual depreciation is $3,600 on the lodge and $3,000 on furniture.

4. The mortgage interest rate is 12%. (The mortgage was taken out on May 1.)
5. Unearned rent of $1,500 has been earned.
6. Salaries of $300 are accrued and unpaid at May 31.

Instructions
(a) Journalize the adjusting entries on May 31.
(b) Prepare a ledger using the three-column form of account. Enter the trial balance amounts and post the adjusting entries. (Use J1 as the posting reference.)
(c) Prepare an adjusted trial balance on May 31.
(d) Prepare an income statement and an owner's equity statement for the month of May and a balance sheet at May 31.

(c) Adj. trial balance
$114,300
(d) Net income $3,800
Ending capital balance
$63,800
Total assets $106,850

P3-3B Otaki Co. was organized on July 1, 2002. Quarterly financial statements are prepared. The unadjusted and adjusted trial balances as of September 30 are shown below.

Prepare adjusting entries and financial statements.
(SO 5, 6, 7)

OTAKI CO.
Trial Balance
September 30, 2002

	Unadjusted		Adjusted	
	Dr.	**Cr.**	**Dr.**	**Cr.**
Cash	$ 6,700		$ 6,700	
Accounts Receivable	400		1,100	
Prepaid Rent	1,500		900	
Supplies	1,200		1,000	
Equipment	15,000		15,000	
Accumulated Depreciation—Equipment				$ 350
Notes Payable		$ 5,000		5,000
Accounts Payable		1,510		1,510
Salaries Payable				400
Interest Payable				50
Unearned Rent		900		500
Yosuke Otaki, Capital		14,000		14,000
Yosuke Otaki, Drawing	600		600	
Commission Revenue		14,000		14,700
Rent Revenue		400		800
Salaries Expense	9,000		9,400	
Rent Expense	900		1,500	
Depreciation Expense			350	
Supplies Expense			200	
Utilities Expense	510		510	
Interest Expense			50	
	$35,810	$35,810	$37,310	$37,310

Instructions
(a) Journalize the adjusting entries that were made.
(b) Prepare an income statement and an owner's equity statement for the 3 months ending September 30 and a balance sheet at September 30.
(c) If the note bears interest at 12%, how many months has it been outstanding?

(b) Net income $3,490
Ending capital $16,890
Total assets $24,350

P3-4B A review of the ledger of Zieger Company at December 31, 2002, produces the following data pertaining to the preparation of annual adjusting entries.

Prepare adjusting entries
(SO 5, 6)

1. Prepaid Insurance $12,300. The company has separate insurance policies on its buildings and its motor vehicles. Policy B4564 on the building was purchased on July 1, 2001, for $9,000. The policy has a term of 3 years. Policy A2958 on the vehicles was purchased on January 1, 2002, for $4,800. This policy has a term of 2 years.

2. Unearned Subscriptions $49,000. The company began selling magazine subscriptions in 2002 on an annual basis. The selling price of a subscription is $50. A review of subscription contracts reveals the following.

1. Insurance expense $5,400

2. Subscription revenue $7,000

Subscription Date	Number of Subscriptions
October 1	200
November 1	300
December 1	480
	980

3. Interest expense $1,600

4. Salaries expense $3,240

3. Notes Payable $40,000. This balance consists of a note for 6 months at an annual interest rate of 12%, dated September 1.

4. Salaries Payable $0. There are eight salaried employees. Salaries are paid every Friday for the current week. Five employees receive a salary of $600 each per week, and three employees earn $800 each per week. December 31 is a Wednesday. Employees do not work weekends. All employees worked the last 3 days of December.

Instructions

Prepare the adjusting entries at December 31, 2002.

Journalize transactions and follow through accounting cycle to preparation of financial statements.
(SO 5, 6, 7)

P3-5B On November 1, 2002, the account balances of Thao Equipment Repair were as follows.

No.	Debits		No.	Credits	
101	Cash	$ 2,790	154	Accumulated Depreciation	$ 500
112	Accounts Receivable	2,510	201	Accounts Payable	2,100
126	Supplies	2,000	209	Unearned Service Revenue	1,400
153	Store Equipment	10,000	212	Salaries Payable	500
			301	P. Thao, Capital	12,800
		$17,300			$17,300

During November the following summary transactions were completed.

Nov. 8 Paid $1,100 for salaries due employees, of which $600 is for November.
10 Received $1,200 cash from customers on account.
12 Received $1,400 cash for services performed in November.
15 Purchased store equipment on account $3,000.
17 Purchased supplies on account $1,500.
20 Paid creditors on account $2,500.
22 Paid November rent $300.
25 Paid salaries $1,000.
27 Performed services on account and billed customers for services rendered $900.
29 Received $550 from customers for future service.

Adjustment data consist of:

1. Supplies on hand $1,600.
2. Accrued salaries payable $500.
3. Depreciation for the month is $120.
4. Unearned service revenue of $1,250 is earned.

Instructions

(a) Enter the November 1 balances in the ledger accounts.
(b) Journalize the November transactions.
(c) Post to the ledger accounts. Use J1 for the posting reference. Use the following accounts: No. 407 Service Revenue, No. 615 Depreciation Expense, No. 631 Supplies Expense, No. 726 Salaries Expense, and No. 729 Rent Expense.

(d) Trial balance $21,650
(f) Adj. trial balance $22,270
(g) Net loss $870; Ending capital $11,930; Total assets $17,230

(d) Prepare a trial balance at November 30.
(e) Journalize and post adjusting entries.
(f) Prepare an adjusted trial balance.
(g) Prepare an income statement and an owner's equity statement for November and a balance sheet at November 30.

BROADENING YOUR PERSPECTIVE

*F*INANCIAL REPORTING AND ANALYSIS

FINANCIAL REPORTING PROBLEM: Lands' End, Inc.

BYP3-1 The financial statements of Lands' End are presented in Appendix A at the end of this textbook.

Instructions
(a) Using the consolidated financial statements and related information, identify items that may result in adjusting entries for prepayments.
(b) Using the consolidated financial statements and related information, identify items that may result in adjusting entries for accruals.
(c) Using the Eleven-Year Consolidated Financial Summary, what has been the trend since 1990 for depreciation and amortization expense?

COMPARATIVE ANALYSIS PROBLEM: Lands' End vs. Abercrombie & Fitch

BYP3-2 Lands' End's financial statements are presented in Appendix A. Abercrombie & Fitch's financial statements are presented in Appendix B.

Instructions
Based on information contained in these financial statements, determine the following for each company.
(a) Net increase (decrease) in property, plant, and equipment (net) from 1999 to 2000.
(b) Increase (decrease) in selling, general, and administrative expenses from 1999 to 2000.
(c) Increase (decrease) in accounts payable from 1999 to 2000.
(d) Increase (decrease) in net income from 1999 to 2000.
(e) Increase (decrease) in cash and cash equivalents from 1999 to 2000.

INTERPRETING FINANCIAL STATEMENTS: A Global Focus

BYP3-3 Hoescht Marion Roussel (HMR) is one of the world's largest research-based pharmaceutical companies. It is headquartered in Frankfurt, Germany. It conducts research in Germany, France, and the United States. Its financial statements are based on the International Accounting Standards of the International Accounting Standards Committee.

Instructions
Answer each of the following questions.
(a) The statement of cash flows reports interest paid during 1998 of $344 million, while the income statement reports interest expense of $721 million. What might explain this difference? Give an example of the journal entry that you would expect to see that would cause this difference (ignore amounts).
(b) Among its liabilities, the company reports provisions for litigation and environmental protection. What types of litigation and environmental protection costs might this company incur? What are the possible points in time that litigation costs might be expensed? At what point do you think these costs should be expensed on the income statement in order to provide proper matching of revenues and expenses? What challenges to matching does litigation present?
(c) The notes to the company's financial statements state that the company records revenues "at the time of shipment of products or performance of services." Is this consistent with the revenue recognition practices described in this chapter? What considerations might you want to take into account in determining whether this is the appropriate approach to recognize revenues?

EXPLORING THE WEB

BYP3-4 A wealth of accounting-related information is available via the Internet. For example the Rutgers Accounting Web offers access to a great variety of sources.

Address: **www.rutgers.edu/accounting/raw** ***(or go to www.wiley.com/college/weygandt)***

Steps: Click on **Accounting Resources**, or click on **RAW's Features**. (*Note:* Once on this page, you may have to click on the **text only** box to access the available information.)

Instructions
(a) List the categories of information available through the **Accounting Resources** page.
(b) Select any one of these categories and briefly describe the types of information available.

CRITICAL THINKING

GROUP DECISION CASE

BYP3-5 The Happy Travel Court was organized on April 1, 2001, by Nancy Fox. Nancy is a good manager but a poor accountant. From the trial balance prepared by a part-time bookkeeper, Nancy prepared the following income statement for the quarter that ended March 31, 2002.

HAPPY TRAVEL COURT
Income Statement
For the Quarter Ended March 31, 2002

Revenues		
Travel court rental revenue		$95,000
Operating expenses		
Advertising	$ 5,200	
Wages	29,800	
Utilities	900	
Depreciation	800	
Repairs	4,000	
Total operating expenses		40,700
Net income		$54,300

Nancy knew that something was wrong with the statement because net income had never exceeded $20,000 in any one quarter. Knowing that you are an experienced accountant, she asks you to review the income statement and other data.

You first look at the trial balance. In addition to the account balances reported above in the income statement, the ledger contains the following additional selected balances at March 31, 2002.

Supplies	$ 5,200
Prepaid Insurance	7,200
Notes Payable	12,000

You then make inquiries and discover the following.

1. Travel court rental fees include advanced rentals for summer month occupancy $30,000.
2. There were $1,300 of supplies on hand at March 31.
3. Prepaid insurance resulted from the payment of a one-year policy on January 1, 2002.
4. The mail on April 1, 2002, brought the following bills: advertising for week of March 24, $110; repairs made March 10, $260; and utilities, $180.
5. There are four employees, who receive wages totaling $350 per day. At March 31, 2 days' wages have been incurred but not paid.
6. The note payable is a 3-month, 10% note dated January 1, 2002.

Instructions

With the class divided into groups, answer the following.

(a) Prepare a correct income statement for the quarter ended March 31, 2002.

(b) Explain to Nancy the generally accepted accounting principles that she did not recognize in preparing her income statement and their effect on her results.

COMMUNICATION ACTIVITY

BYP3-6 In reviewing the accounts of Marylee Co. at the end of the year, you discover that adjusting entries have not been made.

Instructions

Write a memo to Mary Lee Virgil, the owner of Marylee Co., that explains the following: the nature and purpose of adjusting entries, why adjusting entries are needed, and the types of adjusting entries that may be made.

ETHICS CASE

BYP3-7 Die Hard Company is a pesticide manufacturer. Its sales declined greatly this year due to the passage of legislation outlawing the sale of several of Die Hard's chemical pesticides. In the coming year, Die Hard will have environmentally safe and competitive chemicals to replace these discontinued products. Sales in the next year are expected to greatly exceed any prior year's. The decline in sales and profits appears to be a one-year aberration. But even so, the company president fears a large dip in the current year's profits. He believes that such a dip could cause a significant drop in the market price of Die Hard's stock and make the company a takeover target.

To avoid this possibility, the company president calls in Becky Freeman, controller, to discuss this period's year-end adjusting entries. He urges her to accrue every possible revenue and to defer as many expenses as possible. He says to Becky, "We need the revenues this year, and next year can easily absorb expenses deferred from this year. We can't let our stock price be hammered down!" Becky didn't get around to recording the adjusting entries until January 17, but she dated the entries December 31 as if they were recorded then. Becky also made every effort to comply with the president's request.

Instructions

(a) Who are the stakeholders in this situation?

(b) What are the ethical considerations of (1) the president's request and (2) Becky's dating the adjusting entries December 31?

(c) Can Becky accrue revenues and defer expenses and still be ethical?

Answers to Self-Study Questions

1. c   **2.** a   **3.** d   **4.** d   **5.** d   **6.** c   **7.** a   **8.** b   **9.** b   **10.** c   **11.** a

Answer to *Lands' End* Review It Question 4, p. 98

2000 depreciation and amortization expense is $20.7 million; 1999 depreciation and amortization expense is $18.7 million.

✓ *Remember to go back to the Navigator box on the chapter-opening page and check off your completed work.*

COMPLETION OF THE ACCOUNTING CYCLE

THE NAVIGATOR ✓

- Understand *Concepts for Review* ❑
- Read *Feature Story* ❑
- Scan *Study Objectives* ❑
- Read *Preview* ❑
- Read text and answer *Before You Go On*
  p. 140 ❑   *p.* 150 ❑   *p.* 156 ❑
- Work *Demonstration Problem* ❑
- Review *Summary of Study Objectives* ❑
- Answer *Self-Study Questions* ❑
- Complete *Assignments* ❑

CONCEPTS FOR REVIEW

Before studying this chapter, you should know or, if necessary, review:

   a. How to apply the revenue recognition and matching principles.
(Ch. 3, pp. 90–91)

   b. How to make adjusting entries. (Ch. 3, pp. 91–103)

   c. How to prepare an adjusted trial balance. (Ch. 3, p. 106)

   d. How to prepare a balance sheet, income statement, and owner's
equity statement. (Ch. 3, pp. 107–108)

☑ THE NAVIGATOR

Everyone Likes to Win

When Ted Castle was a hockey coach at the University of Vermont, his players were self-motivated by their desire to win. Hockey was a game you either won or lost. But at **Rhino Foods, Inc.**, a specialty-bakery-foods company he founded in Burlington, Vermont, he discovered that manufacturing-line workers were not so self-motivated. Ted thought, what if he turned the food-making business into a game, with rules, strategies, and trophies?

Ted knew that in a game knowing the score is all-important. He felt that only if the employees know the score—know exactly how the business is doing daily, weekly, monthly—could he turn food-making into a game. But Rhino is a closely held, family-owned business, and its financial statements and profits were confidential. Should Ted open Rhino's books to the employees?

A consultant he was working with put Ted's concerns in perspective. The consultant said, "Imagine you're playing touch football. You play for an hour or two, and the whole time I'm sitting there with a book, keeping score. All of a sudden I blow the whistle, and I say, 'OK, that's it. Everybody go home.' I close my book and walk away. How would you feel?" Ted opened his books and revealed the financial statements to his employees.

The next step was to teach employees the rules and strategies of how to win at making food. The first lesson: "Your opponent at Rhino is expenses. You must cut and control expenses." Ted and his staff distilled those lessons into daily scorecards (production reports and income statements) that keep Rhino's employees up-to-date on the game. At noon each day, Ted posts the previous day's results at the entrance to the production room. Everyone checks whether they made or lost money on what they produced the day before. And it's not just an academic exercise; there's a bonus check for each employee at the end of every four-week "game" that meets profitability guidelines. Everyone can be a winner!

Rhino has flourished since the first game, three years ago. Employment has nearly tripled to 58, while both revenues and profits have grown by about 600 percent.

☑ THE NAVIGATOR

STUDY OBJECTIVES

After studying this chapter, you should be able to:

1. Prepare a work sheet.
2. Explain the process of closing the books.
3. Describe the content and purpose of a post-closing trial balance.
4. State the required steps in the accounting cycle.
5. Explain the approaches to preparing correcting entries.
6. Identify the sections of a classified balance sheet.

☑ THE NAVIGATOR

As was true at **Rhino Foods, Inc.** financial statements can help employees understand what is happening in the business. In Chapter 3, we prepared financial statements directly from the adjusted trial balance. However, with so many details involved in the end-of-period accounting procedures, it is easy to make errors. Locating and correcting errors can cost much time and effort. One way to minimize errors in the records and to simplify the end-of-period procedures is to use a work sheet.

In this chapter we will explain the role of the work sheet in accounting as well as the remaining steps in the accounting cycle, most especially, the closing process, again using Pioneer Advertising Agency as an example. Then we will consider (1) correcting entries and (2) classified balance sheets. The content and organization of Chapter 4 are as follows.

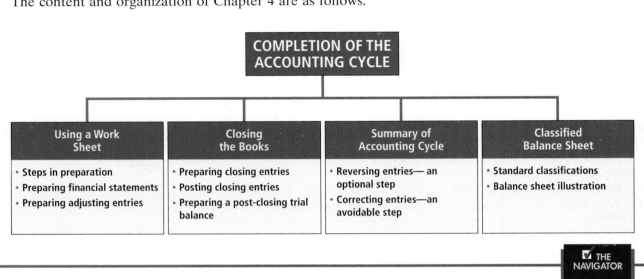

USING A WORK SHEET

STUDY OBJECTIVE 1

Prepare a work sheet.

A **work sheet** is a multiple-column form that may be used in the adjustment process and in preparing financial statements. As its name suggests, the work sheet is a working tool. **A work sheet is not a permanent accounting record**; it is neither a journal nor a part of the general ledger. The work sheet is merely a device used to make it easier to prepare adjusting entries and the financial statements. In small companies with relatively few accounts and adjustments, a work sheet may not be needed. In large companies with numerous accounts and many adjustments, it is almost indispensable.

The basic form of a work sheet and the procedure (five steps) for preparing it are shown in Illustration 4-1. Each step must be performed in the prescribed sequence.

Illustration 4-1

Form and procedure for a work sheet

The use of a work sheet is optional. When one is used, financial statements are prepared from the work sheet. The adjustments are entered in the work sheet columns and are then journalized and posted after the financial statements have been prepared. Thus, management and other interested parties can receive the financial statements at an earlier date when a work sheet is used.

STEPS IN PREPARING A WORK SHEET

We will use the October 31 trial balance and adjustment data of Pioneer Advertising in Chapter 3 to illustrate the preparation of a work sheet. Each step of the process is described below and demonstrated in Illustrations 4-2 and 4-3A, B, C, and D following page 138.

STEP 1. PREPARE A TRIAL BALANCE ON THE WORK SHEET.   All ledger accounts with balances are entered in the account title space. Debit and credit amounts from the ledger are entered in the trial balance columns. The work sheet trial balance for Pioneer Advertising Agency is shown in Illustration 4-2.

STEP 2. ENTER THE ADJUSTMENTS IN THE ADJUSTMENTS COLUMNS.

Turn over the first transparency, Illustration 4-3A. When a work sheet is used, all adjustments are entered in the adjustments columns. In entering the adjustments, applicable trial balance accounts should be used. If additional accounts are needed, they are inserted on the lines immediately below the trial balance totals. Each adjustment is indexed and keyed; this practice facilitates the journalizing of the adjusting entry in the general journal. **The adjustments are not journalized until after the work sheet is completed and the financial statements have been prepared.**

The adjustments for Pioneer Advertising Agency are the same as the adjustments illustrated on page 104. They are keyed in the adjustments columns of the work sheet as follows.

(a) An additional account Advertising Supplies Expense is debited $1,500 for the cost of supplies used, and Advertising Supplies is credited $1,500.

(b) An additional account Insurance Expense is debited $50 for the insurance that has expired, and Prepaid Insurance is credited $50.

(c) Two additional depreciation accounts are needed. Depreciation Expense is debited $40 for the month's depreciation, and Accumulated Depreciation— Office Equipment is credited $40.

(d) Unearned Revenue is debited $400 for services provided, and Service Revenue is credited $400.

(e) An additional account Accounts Receivable is debited $200 for services provided but not billed, and Service Revenue is credited $200.

(f) Two additional accounts relating to interest are needed. Interest Expense is debited $50 for accrued interest, and Interest Payable is credited $50.

(g) Salaries Expense is debited $1,200 for accrued salaries, and an additional account Salaries Payable is credited $1,200.

Note in the illustration that after all the adjustments have been entered, the adjustments columns are totaled and the equality of the column totals is proved.

STEP 3. ENTER ADJUSTED BALANCES IN THE ADJUSTED TRIAL BALANCE COLUMNS.
Turn over the second transparency, Illustration 4-3B. The adjusted balance of an account is obtained by combining the amounts entered in the first four columns of the work sheet for each account. For example, the Prepaid Insurance account in the trial balance columns has a $600 debit balance and a $50 credit in the adjustments columns. The result is a $550 debit balance recorded in the adjusted trial balance columns. **For each account on the work sheet, the amount in the adjusted trial balance columns is the account balance that will appear in the ledger after the adjusting entries have been journalized and posted.** The balances in these columns are the same as those in the adjusted trial balance in Illustration 3-19 (page 106).

After all account balances have been entered in the adjusted trial balance columns, the columns are totaled and their equality is proved. The agreement of the column totals facilitates the completion of the work sheet. If these columns are not in agreement, the financial statement columns will not balance and the financial statements will be incorrect.

STEP 4. EXTEND ADJUSTED TRIAL BALANCE AMOUNTS TO APPROPRIATE FINANCIAL STATEMENT COLUMNS.
Turn over the third transparency, Illustration 4-3C. The fourth step is to extend adjusted trial balance amounts to the income statement and balance sheet columns of the work sheet. Balance sheet accounts are entered in the appropriate balance sheet debit and credit columns. For instance, Cash is entered in the balance sheet debit column, and Notes Payable is entered in the credit column. Accumulated Depreciation is extended to the balance sheet credit column. The reason is that accumulated depreciation is a contra-asset account with a credit balance.

Because the work sheet does not have columns for the owner's equity statement, the balance in owner's capital is extended to the balance sheet credit column. In addition, the balance in owner's drawing is extended to the balance sheet debit column because it is an owner's equity account with a debit balance.

The expense and revenue accounts such as Salaries Expense and Service Revenue are entered in the appropriate income statement columns.

All of these extensions are shown in Illustration 4-3C.

HELPFUL HINT
Every adjusted trial balance amount must be extended to one of the four statement columns. Debit amounts go to debit columns and credit amounts go to credit columns.

STEP 5. TOTAL THE STATEMENT COLUMNS, COMPUTE THE NET INCOME (OR NET LOSS), AND COMPLETE THE WORK SHEET.
Turn over the fourth transparency, Illustration 4-3D. Each of the financial statement columns must be totaled. The net income or loss for the period is then found by computing the dif-

ference between the totals of the two income statement columns. If total credits exceed total debits, net income has resulted. In such a case, as shown in Illustration 4-3D, the words "Net Income" are inserted in the account titles space. The amount then is entered in the income statement debit column and the balance sheet credit column. **The debit amount balances the income statement columns, and the credit amount balances the balance sheet columns.** In addition, the credit in the balance sheet column indicates the increase in owner's equity resulting from net income.

If, instead, total debits in the income statement columns exceed total credits, a net loss has occurred. The amount of the net loss is entered in the income statement credit column and the balance sheet debit column.

After the net income or net loss has been entered, new column totals are determined. The totals shown in the debit and credit income statement columns will match. The totals shown in the debit and credit balance sheet columns will also match. If either the income statement columns or the balance sheet columns are not equal after the net income or net loss has been entered, an error has been made in the work sheet. The completed work sheet for Pioneer Advertising Agency is shown in Illustration 4-3D.

> **HELPFUL HINT**
> All pairs of columns must balance for a work sheet to be complete.

*T*ECHNOLOGY IN ACTION

The work sheet can be computerized using an electronic spreadsheet program. The Excel supplement for this textbook is one of the most popular versions of such spreadsheet packages. With a program like Excel, you can produce any type of work sheet (accounting or otherwise) that you could produce with paper and pencil on a columnar pad. The tremendous advantage of an electronic work sheet over the paper-and-pencil version is the ability to change selected data easily. When data are changed, the computer updates the balance of your computations instantly. More specific applications of electronic spreadsheets will be noted as we proceed.

PREPARING FINANCIAL STATEMENTS FROM A WORK SHEET

After a work sheet has been completed, all the data that are required for the preparation of financial statements are at hand. The income statement is prepared from the income statement columns. The balance sheet and owner's equity statement are prepared from the balance sheet columns. The financial statements prepared from the work sheet for Pioneer Advertising Agency are shown in Illustration 4-4. At this point, adjusting entries have not been journalized and posted. Therefore, the ledger does not support all financial statement amounts.

The amount shown for owner's capital on the work sheet is the account balance **before considering drawings and net income (or loss).** When there have been no additional investments of capital by the owner during the period, this amount is the balance at the beginning of the period.

Using a work sheet, financial statements can be prepared before adjusting entries are journalized and posted. **However, the completed work sheet is not a substitute for formal financial statements.** Data in the financial statement columns of the work sheet are not properly arranged for statement purposes. Also, as noted above, the financial statement presentation for some accounts differs from their statement columns on the work sheet. **A work sheet is essentially a working tool of the accountant; it is not distributed to management and other parties.**

Accounting Cycle Tutorial— Preparing Financial Statements and Closing the Books

(**Note:** Text continues on page 139, following acetate overlays.)

Illustration 4-2

Preparing a trial balance

PIONEER ADVERTISING AGENCY
Work Sheet
For the Month Ended October 31, 2002

Account Titles	Trial Balance Dr.	Trial Balance Cr.	Adjustments Dr.	Adjustments Cr.	Adjusted Trial Balance Dr.	Adjusted Trial Balance Cr.	Income Statement Dr.	Income Statement Cr.	Balance Sheet Dr.	Balance Sheet Cr.
Cash	15,200									
Advertising Supplies	2,500									
Prepaid Insurance	600									
Office Equipment	5,000									
Notes Payable		5,000								
Accounts Payable		2,500								
Unearned Revenue		1,200								
C. R. Byrd, Capital		10,000								
C. R. Byrd, Drawing	500									
Service Revenue		10,000								
Salaries Expense	4,000									
Rent Expense	900									
Totals	28,700	28,700								

Include all accounts with balances from ledger.

Trial balance amounts are taken directly from ledger accounts.

Illustration 4-4

Financial statements from a
work sheet

PIONEER ADVERTISING AGENCY Income Statement For the Month Ended October 31, 2002		
Revenues		
Service revenue		$10,600
Expenses		
Salaries expense	$5,200	
Advertising supplies expense	1,500	
Rent expense	900	
Insurance expense	50	
Interest expense	50	
Depreciation expense	40	
Total expenses		7,740
Net income		$ 2,860

PIONEER ADVERTISING AGENCY Owner's Equity Statement For the Month Ended October 31, 2002		
C. R. Byrd, Capital, October 1		$ –0–
Add: Investments	$10,000	
Net income	2,860	12,860
		12,860
Less: Drawings		500
C. R. Byrd, Capital, October 31		$12,360

PIONEER ADVERTISING AGENCY Balance Sheet October 31, 2002		
Assets		
Cash		$15,200
Accounts receivable		200
Advertising supplies		1,000
Prepaid insurance		550
Office equipment	$5,000	
Less: Accumulated depreciation	40	4,960
Total assets		$21,910
Liabilities and Owner's Equity		
Liabilities		
Notes payable		$ 5,000
Accounts payable		2,500
Interest payable		50
Unearned revenue		800
Salaries payable		1,200
Total liabilities		9,550
Owner's equity		
C. R. Byrd, Capital		12,360
Total liabilities and owner's equity		$21,910

PREPARING ADJUSTING ENTRIES FROM A WORK SHEET

A work sheet is not a journal, and it cannot be used as a basis for posting to ledger accounts. To adjust the accounts, it is necessary to journalize the adjustments and post them to the ledger. **The adjusting entries are prepared from the adjustments columns of the work sheet.** The reference letters in the adjustments columns and the explanations of the adjustments at the bottom of the work sheet help identify the adjusting entries. However, writing the explanation to the adjustments at the bottom of the work sheet is not required. As indicated previously, the journalizing and posting of adjusting entries **follows** the preparation of financial statements when a work sheet is used. The adjusting entries on October 31 for Pioneer Advertising Agency are the same as those shown in Illustration 3-17 (page 104).

B E F O R E Y O U G O O N . . .

▶ *REVIEW IT*
1. What are the five steps in preparing a work sheet?
2. How is net income or net loss shown in a work sheet?
3. How does a work sheet relate to preparing financial statements and adjusting entries?

▶ *DO IT*
Susan Elbe is preparing a work sheet. Explain to Susan how the following adjusted trial balance accounts should be extended to the financial statement columns of the work sheet: Cash; Accumulated Depreciation; Accounts Payable; Julie Kerr, Drawing; Service Revenue; and Salaries Expense.

ACTION PLAN
• Extend asset balances to the balance sheet debit column. Extend liability balances to the balance sheet credit column. Extend accumulated depreciation to the balance sheet credit column.
• Extend the drawing account to the balance sheet debit column.
• Extend expenses to the income statement debit column.
• Extend revenue accounts to the income statement credit column.

SOLUTION
  Income statement debit column—Salaries Expense
  Income statement credit column—Service Revenue
  Balance sheet debit column—Cash; Julie Kerr, Drawing
  Balance sheet credit column—Accumulated Depreciation; Accounts Payable
 As indicated in the Technology in Action box on page 137, the work sheet is an ideal application for electronic spreadsheet software like Microsoft Excel and LOTUS 1–2–3.

Related exercise material: BE4-1, BE4-2, BE4-3, E4-1, E4-2, E4-4, and E4-5.

☑ THE NAVIGATOR

CLOSING THE BOOKS

STUDY OBJECTIVE 2

Explain the process of closing the books.

At the end of the accounting period, the accounts are made ready for the next period. This is called **closing the books**. In closing the books, it is necessary to distinguish between temporary and permanent accounts. **Temporary** or **nominal accounts** relate only to a given accounting period. They include all income statement accounts and owner's drawing. All temporary accounts are closed. In contrast, **permanent** or **real accounts** relate to one or more future accounting periods. They consist of all balance sheet accounts, including owner's capital. Permanent accounts are not closed. Instead, their balances are carried forward into the next accounting period. Illustration 4-5 identifies the accounts in each category.

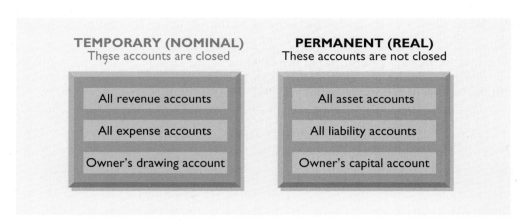

Illustration 4-5

Temporary versus permanent accounts

> **HELPFUL HINT**
> A contra-asset account, such as accumulated depreciation, is a permanent account also.

PREPARING CLOSING ENTRIES

At the end of the accounting period, the temporary account balances are transferred to the permanent owner's equity account, owner's capital, through the preparation of closing entries.[1] **Closing entries** formally recognize in the ledger the transfer of net income (or net loss) and owner's drawing to owner's capital. The results of these entries are shown in the owner's equity statement. **These entries also produce a zero balance in each temporary account. These accounts are then ready to accumulate data in the next accounting period separate from the data of prior periods.** Permanent accounts are not closed.

Journalizing and posting closing entries is a required step in the accounting cycle. (See Illustration 4-12 on page 148.) This step is performed after financial statements have been prepared. In contrast to the steps in the cycle that you have already studied, closing entries are generally journalized and posted **only at the end of a company's annual accounting period**. This practice facilitates the preparation of annual financial statements because all temporary accounts will contain data for the entire year.

In preparing closing entries, each income statement account could be closed directly to owner's capital. However, to do so would result in excessive detail in the permanent owner's capital account. Instead, the revenue and expense accounts are closed to another temporary account, **Income Summary**; only the net income or net loss is transferred from this account to owner's capital.

Closing entries are journalized in the general journal. A center caption entitled Closing Entries, inserted in the journal between the last adjusting entry and the first closing entry, identifies these entries. Then the closing entries are posted to the ledger accounts.

Closing entries may be prepared directly from the adjusted balances in the ledger, from the income statement and balance sheet columns of the work sheet, or from the income and owner's equity statements. Separate closing entries could be prepared for each nominal account, but the following four entries accomplish the desired result more efficiently:

1. Debit each revenue account for its balance, and credit Income Summary for total revenues.

2. Debit Income Summary for total expenses, and credit each expense account for its balance.

3. Debit Income Summary and credit Owner's Capital for the amount of net income.

---

[1] Closing entries for a partnership and for a corporation are explained in Chapters 13 and 14, respectively.

HELPFUL HINT

Owner's Drawing is closed directly to Capital and *not* to Income Summary because Owner's Drawing is not an expense.

4. Debit Owner's Capital for the balance in the Owner's Drawing account, and credit Owner's Drawing for the same amount.

The four entries are referenced in the diagram of the closing process shown in Illustration 4-6 and in the journal entries in Illustration 4-7. The posting of closing entries is shown in Illustration 4-8.

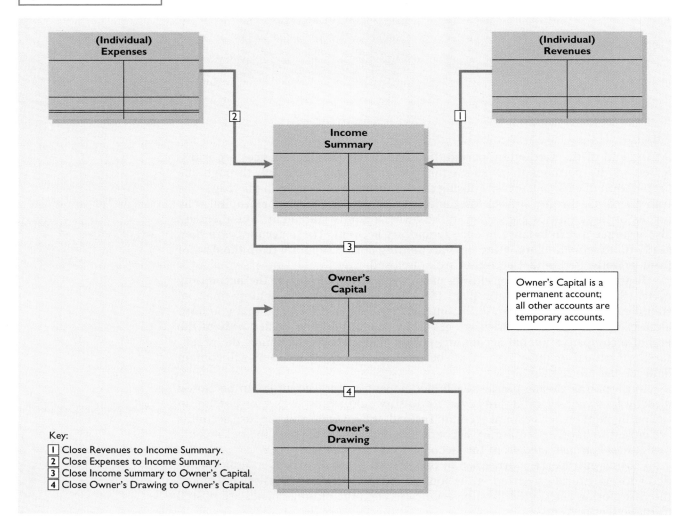

Key:
1 Close Revenues to Income Summary.
2 Close Expenses to Income Summary.
3 Close Income Summary to Owner's Capital.
4 Close Owner's Drawing to Owner's Capital.

Illustration 4-6

Diagram of closing process—proprietorship

If there were a net loss because expenses exceeded revenues, entry 3 in Illustration 4-6 would be reversed: Credit Income Summary and debit Owner's Capital.

Accounting in Action *Business Insight*

Until Sam Walton had opened twenty Wal-Mart stores, he used what he called the "ESP method" of closing the books. ESP was a pretty basic method: If the books didn't balance, Walton calculated the amount by which they were off and entered that amount under the heading ESP—which stood for "Error Some Place." As Walton noted, "It really sped things along when it came time to close those books."

SOURCE: Sam Walton, *Made in America* (New York: Doubleday Publishing Company, 1992), p. 53.

Closing Entries Illustrated

In practice, closing entries are generally prepared only at the end of the annual accounting period. However, to illustrate the journalizing and posting of closing entries, we will assume that Pioneer Advertising Agency closes its books monthly. The closing entries at October 31 are shown in Illustration 4-7.

GENERAL JOURNAL				J3
Date	**Account Titles and Explanation**	**Ref.**	**Debit**	**Credit**
	Closing Entries			
	(1)			
2002				
Oct. 31	Service Revenue	400	10,600	
	Income Summary	350		10,600
	(To close revenue account)			
	(2)			
31	Income Summary	350	7,740	
	Advertising Supplies Expense	631		1,500
	Depreciation Expense	711		40
	Insurance Expense	722		50
	Salaries Expense	726		5,200
	Rent Expense	729		900
	Interest Expense	905		50
	(To close expense accounts)			
	(3)			
31	Income Summary	350	2,860	
	C. R. Byrd, Capital	301		2,860
	(To close net income to capital)			
	(4)			
31	C. R. Byrd, Capital	301	500	
	C. R. Byrd, Drawing	306		500
	(To close drawings to capital)			

Illustration 4-7

Closing entries journalized

> **HELPFUL HINT**
> Income Summary is a very descriptive title: total revenues are closed to Income Summary; total expenses are closed to Income Summary; and the balance in the Income Summary is a net income or net loss.

Note that the amounts for Income Summary in entries (1) and (2) are the totals of the income statement credit and debit columns, respectively, in the work sheet.

A couple of cautions in preparing closing entries: (1) Avoid unintentionally doubling the revenue and expense balances rather than zeroing them. (2) Do not close owner's drawing through the Income Summary account. **Owner's drawing is not an expense, and it is not a factor in determining net income.**

POSTING CLOSING ENTRIES

The posting of the closing entries and the ruling of the accounts are shown in Illustration 4-8. Note that all temporary accounts have zero balances after posting the closing entries. In addition, you should realize that the balance in owner's capital (C. R. Byrd, Capital) represents the total equity of the owner at the end of the accounting period. This balance is shown on the balance sheet and is the ending capital reported on the owner's equity statement, as shown in Illustration 4-4 on page 139. **The Income Summary account is used only in closing.** No entries are journalized and posted to this account during the year.

As part of the closing process, the **temporary accounts** (revenues, expenses, and owner's drawing) in T-account form are totaled, balanced, and double-ruled as shown in Illustration 4-8. The **permanent accounts** (assets, liabilities, and owner's capital) are not closed: A single rule is drawn beneath the current period entries, and the account balance carried forward to the next period is entered below the single rule. (For example, see C. R. Byrd, Capital.)

> **HELPFUL HINT**
> The balance in Income Summary before it is closed must equal the net income or net loss for the period.

Illustration 4-8

Posting of closing entries

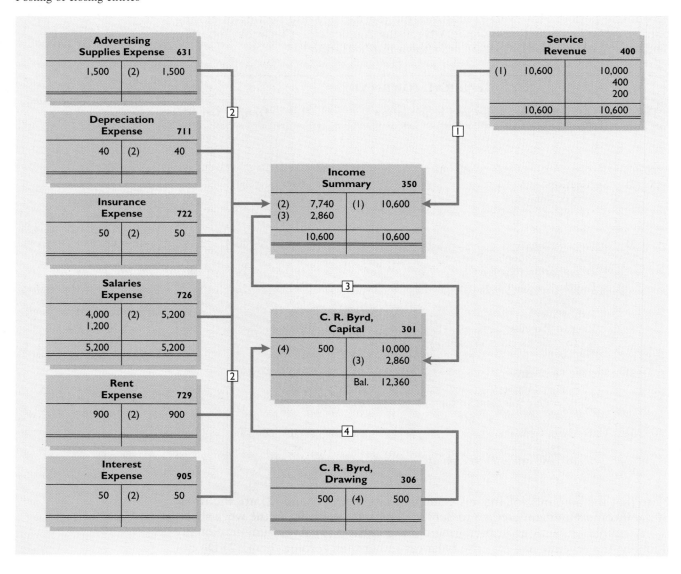

ACCOUNTING IN ACTION   Business Insight

Technology has dramatically changed the accounting process. When Larry Carter became chief financial officer of **Cisco Systems**, closing the quarterly accounts would take up to ten days. Within four years he got it down to two days and halved the cost of finance, to 1 percent of sales. Now he is aiming to be able to do a "virtual close"—closing within a day on any day in the quarter.

This is not just showing off. Knowing exactly where you are all of the time, says Mr. Carter, allows you to respond faster than your competitors. But it also means that the 600 people who used to spend 10 days a quarter tracking transactions can now be more usefully employed on things such as mining data for business intelligence.

SOURCE: Excerpted from "Business and the Internet," *The Economist*, June 26, 1999, p. 12.

PREPARING A POST-CLOSING TRIAL BALANCE

STUDY OBJECTIVE **3**

Describe the content and purpose of a post-closing trial balance.

After all closing entries have been journalized and posted, another trial balance, called a **post-closing trial balance**, is prepared from the ledger. The post-closing trial balance lists permanent accounts and their balances after closing entries have been journalized and posted. **The purpose of this trial balance is to prove the equality of the permanent account balances that are carried forward into the next accounting period.** Since all temporary accounts will have zero balances, **the post-closing trial balance will contain only permanent—balance sheet—accounts.**

The procedure for preparing a post-closing trial balance again consists entirely of listing the accounts and their balances. The post-closing trial balance for Pioneer Advertising Agency is shown in Illustration 4-9. These balances are the same as those reported in the company's balance sheet in Illustration 4-4.

PIONEER ADVERTISING AGENCY Post-Closing Trial Balance October 31, 2002		
	Debit	**Credit**
Cash	$15,200	
Accounts Receivable	200	
Advertising Supplies	1,000	
Prepaid Insurance	550	
Office Equipment	5,000	
Accumulated Depreciation—Office Equipment		$ 40
Notes Payable		5,000
Accounts Payable		2,500
Unearned Revenue		800
Salaries Payable		1,200
Interest Payable		50
C. R. Byrd, Capital		12,360
	$21,950	$21,950

Illustration 4-9

Post-closing trial balance

HELPFUL HINT

Will total debits in a post-closing trial balance equal total assets on the balance sheet? Answer: No. Accumulated depreciation is deducted from assets on the balance sheet but added to the credit balance total in a post-closing trial balance.

The post-closing trial balance is prepared from the permanent accounts in the ledger. The permanent accounts of Pioneer Advertising are shown in the general ledger in Illustration 4-10 on page 146. Remember that the balance of each permanent account is computed after every posting. Therefore, no additional work on these accounts is needed as part of the closing process.

A post-closing trial balance provides evidence that the journalizing and posting of closing entries have been properly completed. It also shows that the accounting equation is in balance at the end of the accounting period. However, like the trial balance, it does not prove that all transactions have been recorded or that the ledger is correct. For example, the post-closing trial balance will balance if a transaction is not journalized and posted or if a transaction is journalized and posted twice.

The remaining accounts in the general ledger are temporary accounts (shown in Illustration 4-11 on page 147). After the closing entries are correctly posted, each temporary account has a zero balance. These accounts are double-ruled to finalize the closing process.

(Permanent Accounts Only)

GENERAL LEDGER

Cash					No. 101
Date	Explanation	Ref.	Debit	Credit	Balance
2002					
Oct. 1		J1	10,000		10,000
2		J1	1,200		11,200
3		J1		900	10,300
4		J1		600	9,700
20		J1		500	9,200
26		J1		4,000	5,200
31		J1	10,000		15,200

Accounts Receivable					No. 112
Date	Explanation	Ref.	Debit	Credit	Balance
2002					
Oct. 31	Adj. entry	J2	200		200

Advertising Supplies					No. 126
Date	Explanation	Ref.	Debit	Credit	Balance
2002					
Oct. 5		J1	2,500		2,500
31	Adj. entry	J2		1,500	1,000

Prepaid Insurance					No. 130
Date	Explanation	Ref.	Debit	Credit	Balance
2002					
Oct. 4		J1	600		600
31	Adj. entry	J2		50	550

Office Equipment					No. 157
Date	Explanation	Ref.	Debit	Credit	Balance
2002					
Oct. 1		J1	5,000		5,000

Accumulated Depreciation—Office Equipment					No. 158
Date	Explanation	Ref.	Debit	Credit	Balance
2002					
Oct. 31	Adj. entry	J2		40	40

Notes Payable					No. 200
Date	Explanation	Ref.	Debit	Credit	Balance
2002					
Oct. 1		J1		5,000	5,000

Accounts Payable					No. 201
Date	Explanation	Ref.	Debit	Credit	Balance
2002					
Oct. 5		J1		2,500	2,500

Unearned Revenue					No. 209
Date	Explanation	Ref.	Debit	Credit	Balance
2002					
Oct. 2		J1		1,200	1,200
31	Adj. entry	J2	400		800

Salaries Payable					No. 212
Date	Explanation	Ref.	Debit	Credit	Balance
2002					
Oct. 31	Adj. entry	J2		1,200	1,200

Interest Payable					No. 230
Date	Explanation	Ref.	Debit	Credit	Balance
2002					
Oct. 31	Adj. entry	J2		50	50

C. R. Byrd, Capital					No. 301
Date	Explanation	Ref.	Debit	Credit	Balance
2002					
Oct. 1		J1		10,000	10,000
31	Closing entry	J3		2,860	12,860
31	Closing entry	J3	500		12,360

Note: The permanent accounts for Pioneer Advertising Agency are shown here; the temporary accounts are shown in Illustration 4-11. Both permanent and temporary accounts are part of the general ledger; they are segregated here to aid in learning.

Illustration 4-10

General ledger, permanent accounts

SUMMARY OF THE ACCOUNTING CYCLE

STUDY OBJECTIVE 4

State the required steps in the accounting cycle.

The steps in the accounting cycle are shown in Illustration 4-12 on page 148. From the graphic you can see that the cycle begins with the analysis of business transactions and ends with the preparation of a post-closing trial balance. The steps in the cycle are performed in sequence and are repeated in each accounting period.

(Temporary Accounts Only)

GENERAL LEDGER

C. R. Byrd, Drawing — No. 306

Date	Explanation	Ref.	Debit	Credit	Balance
2002					
Oct. 20		J1	500		500
31	Closing entry	J3		500	–0–

Income Summary — No. 350

Date	Explanation	Ref.	Debit	Credit	Balance
2002					
Oct. 31	Closing entry	J3		10,600	10,600
31	Closing entry	J3	7,740		2,860
31	Closing entry	J3	2,860		–0–

Service Revenue — No. 400

Date	Explanation	Ref.	Debit	Credit	Balance
2002					
Oct. 31		J1		10,000	10,000
31	Adj. entry	J2		400	10,400
31	Adj. entry	J2		200	10,600
31	Closing entry	J3	10,600		–0–

Advertising Supplies Expense — No. 631

Date	Explanation	Ref.	Debit	Credit	Balance
2002					
Oct. 31	Adj. entry	J2	1,500		1,500
31	Closing entry	J3		1,500	–0–

Depreciation Expense — No. 711

Date	Explanation	Ref.	Debit	Credit	Balance
2002					
Oct. 31	Adj. entry	J2	40		40
31	Closing entry	J3		40	–0–

Insurance Expense — No. 722

Date	Explanation	Ref.	Debit	Credit	Balance
2002					
Oct. 31	Adj. entry	J2	50		50
31	Closing entry	J3		50	–0–

Salaries Expense — No. 726

Date	Explanation	Ref.	Debit	Credit	Balance
2002					
Oct. 26		J1	4,000		4,000
31	Adj. entry	J2	1,200		5,200
31	Closing entry	J3		5,200	–0–

Rent Expense — No. 729

Date	Explanation	Ref.	Debit	Credit	Balance
2002					
Oct. 3		J1	900		900
31	Closing entry	J3		900	–0–

Interest Expense — No. 905

Date	Explanation	Ref.	Debit	Credit	Balance
2002					
Oct. 31	Adj. entry	J2	50		50
31	Closing entry	J3		50	–0–

Note: The temporary accounts for Pioneer Advertising Agency are shown here; the permanent accounts are shown in Illustration 4-10. Both permanent and temporary accounts are part of the general ledger; they are segregated here to aid in learning.

Illustration 4-11

General ledger, temporary accounts

Steps 1–3 may occur daily during the accounting period, as explained in Chapter 2. Steps 4–7 are performed on a periodic basis, such as monthly, quarterly, or annually. Steps 8 and 9, closing entries, and a post-closing trial balance, are usually prepared only at the end of a company's **annual** accounting period.

There are also two optional steps in the accounting cycle. As you have seen, a work sheet may be used in preparing adjusting entries and financial statements. In addition, reversing entries may be used as explained below.

REVERSING ENTRIES—AN OPTIONAL STEP

Some accountants prefer to reverse certain adjusting entries at the beginning of a new accounting period. A **reversing entry** is made at the beginning of the next accounting period. It is the exact opposite of the adjusting entry made in the previous period. **The preparation of reversing entries is an optional bookkeeping procedure that is not a required step in the accounting cycle.** Accordingly, we have chosen to cover this topic in an appendix at the end of the chapter.

Illustration 4-12

Steps in the accounting cycle

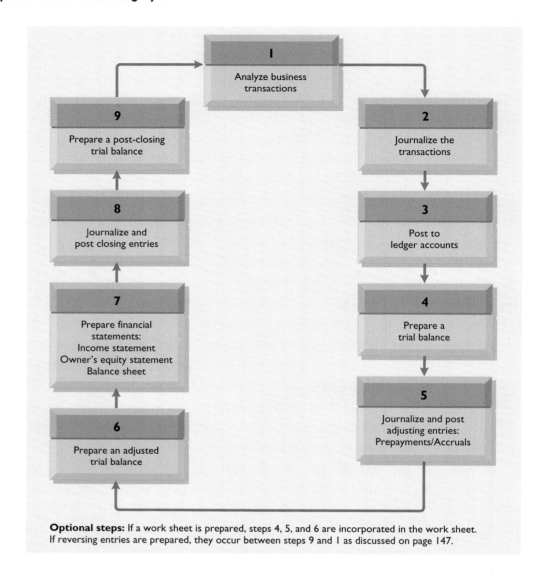

Optional steps: If a work sheet is prepared, steps 4, 5, and 6 are incorporated in the work sheet. If reversing entries are prepared, they occur between steps 9 and 1 as discussed on page 147.

CORRECTING ENTRIES—AN AVOIDABLE STEP

STUDY OBJECTIVE 5

Explain the approaches to preparing correcting entries.

Unfortunately, errors may occur in the recording process. Errors should be corrected **as soon as they are discovered** by journalizing and posting **correcting entries**. If the accounting records are free of errors, no correcting entries are necessary.

You should recognize several differences between correcting entries and adjusting entries. First, adjusting entries are an integral part of the accounting cycle. Correcting entries, on the other hand, are unnecessary if the records are free of errors. Second, **adjustments are journalized and posted only at the end of an accounting period. In contrast, correcting entries are made whenever an error is discovered.** Finally, adjusting entries always affect at least one balance sheet account and one income statement account. In contrast, correcting entries may involve any combination of accounts in need of correction. **Correcting entries must be posted before closing entries.**

To determine the correcting entry, it is useful to compare the incorrect entry with the correct entry. Doing so helps identify the accounts and amounts that should—and should not—be corrected. After comparison, a correcting entry is made to correct the accounts. This approach is illustrated in the following two cases.

CASE 1.   On May 10, a $50 cash collection on account from a customer is journalized and posted as a debit to Cash $50 and a credit to Service Revenue $50. The error is discovered on May 20, when the customer pays the remaining balance in full.

Incorrect Entry (May 10)			Correct Entry (May 10)		
Cash	50		Cash	50	
Service Revenue		50	Accounts Receivable		50

Illustration 4-13

Comparison of entries

A comparison of the incorrect entry with the correct entry reveals that the debit to Cash $50 is correct. However, the $50 credit to Service Revenue should have been credited to Accounts Receivable. As a result, both Service Revenue and Accounts Receivable are overstated in the ledger. The following correcting entry is required.

	Correcting Entry		
May 20	Service Revenue	50	
	Accounts Receivable		50
	(To correct entry of May 10)		

Illustration 4-14

Correcting entry

A	=	L	+	OE
−50				−50

CASE 2.   On May 18, office equipment costing $450 is purchased on account. The transaction is journalized and posted as a debit to Delivery Equipment $45 and a credit to Accounts Payable $45. The error is discovered on June 3, when the monthly statement for May is received from the creditor.

Incorrect Entry (May 18)			Correct Entry (May 18)		
Delivery Equipment	45		Office Equipment	450	
Accounts Payable		45	Accounts Payable		450

Illustration 4-15

Comparison of entries

A comparison of the two entries shows that three accounts are incorrect. Delivery Equipment is overstated $45; Office Equipment is understated $450; and Accounts Payable is understated $405. The correcting entry is:

	Correcting Entry		
June 3	Office Equipment	450	
	Delivery Equipment		45
	Accounts Payable		405
	(To correct entry of May 18)		

Illustration 4-16

Correcting entry

A	=	L	+	OE
+450				
−45		+405		

*E*THICS NOTE

Citigroup once reported a correcting entry reducing reported revenue by $23 million, while firing 11 employees. Company officials did not specify why the employees had apparently intentionally inflated the revenue figures, although it was noted that their bonuses were tied to their unit's performance.

Instead of preparing a correcting entry, **it is possible to reverse the incorrect entry and then prepare the correct entry.** This approach will result in more entries and postings than a correcting entry, but it will accomplish the desired result.

ACCOUNTING IN ACTION *Business Insight*

Yale Express, a short-haul trucking firm, turned over much of its cargo to local truckers for delivery completion. Yale collected the entire delivery charge and, when billed by the local trucker, sent payment for the final phase to the local trucker. Yale used a cutoff period of 20 days into the next accounting period in making its adjusting entries for accrued liabilities. That is, it waited 20 days to receive the local truckers' bills to determine the amount of the unpaid but incurred delivery charges as of the balance sheet date.

On the other hand, **Republic Carloading**, a nationwide, long-distance freight forwarder, frequently did not receive transportation bills from truckers to whom it passed on cargo until months after the year-end. In making its year-end adjusting entries, Republic waited for months in order to include all of these outstanding transportation bills.

When Yale Express merged with Republic Carloading, Yale's vice president employed the 20-day cutoff procedure for both firms. As a result, millions of dollars of Republic's accrued transportation bills went unrecorded. When the erroneous procedure was detected and correcting entries were made, these and other errors changed a reported profit of $1.14 million into a loss of $1.88 million!

BEFORE YOU GO ON...

▶ *REVIEW IT*
1. How do permanent accounts differ from temporary accounts?
2. What four different types of entries are required in closing the books?
3. What is the content and purpose of a post-closing trial balance?
4. What are the required and optional steps in the accounting cycle?

▶ *DO IT*
The work sheet for Hancock Company shows the following in the financial statement columns: R. Hancock, Drawing $15,000, R. Hancock, Capital $42,000, and net income $18,000. Prepare the closing entries at December 31 that affect owner's capital.

ACTION PLAN
• Remember to make closing entries in the correct sequence.
• Make the first two entries to close revenues and expenses.
• Make the third entry to close net income to owner's capital.
• Make the final entry to close owner's drawing to owner's capital.

SOLUTION

Dec. 31	Income Summary	18,000	
	R. Hancock, Capital		18,000
	(To close net income to capital)		
Dec. 31	R. Hancock, Capital	15,000	
	R. Hancock, Drawing		15,000
	(To close drawings to capital)		

Related exercise material: BE4-4, BE4-5, BE4-6, BE4-8, E4-3, E4-6, E4-8, and E4-9.

☑ THE NAVIGATOR

CLASSIFIED BALANCE SHEET

The financial statements illustrated up to this point were purposely kept simple. We classified items as assets, liabilities, and owner's equity in the balance sheet, and as revenues and expenses in the income statement. **Financial statements, however, become more useful to management, creditors, and potential investors when the elements are classified into significant subgroups.** In the remainder of this chapter we will introduce you to the primary balance sheet classifications. The classified income statement will be presented in Chapter 5. The classified financial statements are what Ted Castle, owner of **Rhino Foods, Inc.,** gave to his employees to understand what was happening in the business.

STUDY OBJECTIVE 6

Identify the sections of a classified balance sheet.

STANDARD CLASSIFICATIONS

A **classified balance sheet** usually contains these standard classifications:

Assets	Liabilities and Owner's Equity
Current assets	Current liabilities
Long-term investments	Long-term liabilities
Property, plant, and equipment	Owner's (Stockholders') equity
Intangible assets	

Illustration 4-17

Standard balance sheet classifications

These sections help the financial statement user determine such matters as (1) the availability of assets to meet debts as they come due and (2) the claims of short- and long-term creditors on total assets. A classified balance sheet also makes it easier to compare companies in the same industry, such as **GM**, **Ford**, and **DaimlerChrysler** in the automobile industry. Each of the sections is explained below.

A complete set of specimen financial statements for **Lands' End, Inc.** is shown in Appendix A at the back of the book.

Current Assets

Current assets are cash and other resources that are reasonably expected to be realized in cash or sold or consumed in the business within one year of the balance sheet date or the company's operating cycle, whichever is longer. For example, accounts receivable are current assets because they will be realized in cash through collection within one year. A prepayment such as supplies is a current asset because of its expected use or consumption in the business within one year.

The **operating cycle** of a company is the average time that is required to go from cash to cash in producing revenues. The term "cycle" suggests a circular flow, which in this case, starts and ends with cash. For example, in municipal transit companies, the operating cycle would tend to be short since services are provided entirely on a cash basis. On the other hand, the operating cycle in manufacturing companies is longer: they purchase goods and materials, manufacture and sell products, bill customers, and collect cash. This is a cash to cash cycle that may extend for several months. Most companies have operating cycles of less than one year. More will be said about operating cycles in later chapters.

In a service enterprise, it is customary to recognize four types of current assets: (1) cash, (2) short-term investments such as U.S. government bonds,

INTERNATIONAL NOTE

Other countries use a different format for the balance sheet. In Great Britain, for example, property, plant, and equipment are reported first on the balance sheet; assets and liabilities are netted and grouped into net current and net total assets.

(3) receivables (notes receivable, accounts receivable, and interest receivable), and (4) prepaid expenses (insurance and supplies). **These items are listed in the order of liquidity.** That is, they are listed in the order in which they are expected to be converted into cash. This arrangement is illustrated below in the presentation of **UAL, Inc. (United Airlines).**

Illustration 4-18

Current assets section

UNITED AIRLINES	UAL, INC, (UNITED AIRLINES) Balance Sheet (partial) (in millions)
Current assets	
Cash	$ 310
Short-term investments	379
Receivables	1,284
Aircraft fuel, spare parts, and supplies	340
Prepaid expenses	368
Other current assets	254
Total current assets	$2,935

A company's current assets are important in assessing the company's short-term debt-paying ability, as explained later in the chapter.

Long-Term Investments

HELPFUL HINT
Long-term investments are investments *made by* the business—not investments by the owner *in* the business. Investments by the owner in the business are reported as part of owner's (stockholders') equity (see p. 155).

Like current assets, **long-term investments** are resources that can be realized in cash. However, the conversion into cash is not expected within one year or the operating cycle, whichever is longer. In addition, long-term investments are not intended for use or consumption within the business. This category, often just called "investments," normally includes stocks and bonds of other corporations. **Deluxe Corporation** reported the following in its balance sheet.

Illustration 4-19

Long-term investments section

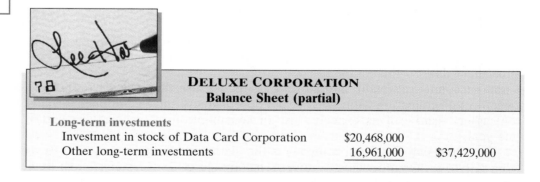

DELUXE CORPORATION Balance Sheet (partial)		
Long-term investments		
Investment in stock of Data Card Corporation	$20,468,000	
Other long-term investments	16,961,000	$37,429,000

Property, Plant, and Equipment

ALTERNATIVE TERMINOLOGY
Property, plant, and equipment are sometimes referred to as *plant assets* or *fixed assets.*

Property, plant, and equipment are tangible resources of a relatively permanent nature that are used in the business and not intended for sale. This category includes land, buildings, machinery and equipment, delivery equipment, and furniture and fixtures. Assets subject to depreciation should be reported at cost less accumulated depreciation. This practice is illustrated in the following presentation of **Delta Air Lines**.

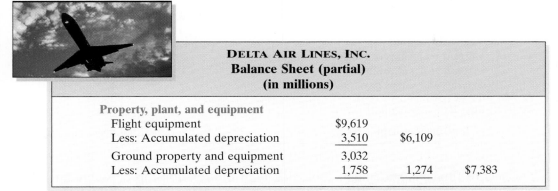

DELTA AIR LINES, INC. Balance Sheet (partial) (in millions)			
Property, plant, and equipment			
Flight equipment	$9,619		
Less: Accumulated depreciation	3,510	$6,109	
Ground property and equipment	3,032		
Less: Accumulated depreciation	1,758	1,274	$7,383

Illustration 4-20

Property, plant, and equipment section

Intangible Assets

Intangible assets are noncurrent resources that do not have physical substance. They are recorded at cost, and this cost is expensed over the useful life of the intangible asset. Intangible assets include patents, copyrights, and trademarks or trade names that give the holder **exclusive right** of use for a specified period of time. Their value to a company is generally derived from the rights or privileges granted by governmental authority.

In its balance sheet, **Brunswick Corporation** reported the following.

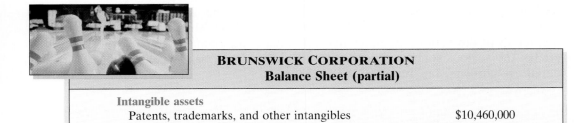

BRUNSWICK CORPORATION Balance Sheet (partial)	
Intangible assets	
Patents, trademarks, and other intangibles	$10,460,000

Illustration 4-21

Intangible assets section

Current Liabilities

Listed first in the liabilities and owner's equity section of the balance sheet are current liabilities. **Current liabilities** are obligations that are reasonably expected to be paid from existing current assets or through the creation of other current liabilities. As in the case of current assets, the time period for payment is one year or the operating cycle, whichever is longer. Current liabilities include (1) debts related to the operating cycle, such as accounts payable and wages and salaries payable, and (2) other short-term debts, such as bank loans payable, interest payable, taxes payable, and current maturities of long-term obligations (payments to be made within the next year on long-term obligations).

The arrangement of items within the current liabilities section has evolved through custom rather than from a prescribed rule. Notes payable is usually listed first, followed by accounts payable. Other items are then listed in any order. The current liabilities section adapted from the balance sheet of **UAL, Inc. (United Airlines)** is as follows.

Illustration 4-22

Current liabilities section

Liquidity

Illiquidity

UAL, INC. (UNITED AIRLINES) Balance Sheet (partial) (in thousands)	
Current liabilities	
Notes payable	$ 297,518
Accounts payable	382,967
Current maturities of long-term obligations	81,525
Unearned ticket revenue	432,979
Salaries and wages payable	435,622
Taxes payable	80,390
Other current liabilities	240,652
Total current liabilities	$1,951,653

Users of financial statements look closely at the relationship between current assets and current liabilities. This relationship is important in evaluating a company's **liquidity**—its ability to pay obligations that are expected to become due within the next year or operating cycle. When current assets exceed current liabilities at the balance sheet date, the likelihood for paying the liabilities is favorable. When the reverse is true, short-term creditors may not be paid, and the company may ultimately be forced into bankruptcy.

Long-Term Liabilities

ALTERNATIVE TERMINOLOGY
Long-term liabilities are also called *long-term debt* or *noncurrent liabilities.*

Obligations expected to be paid after one year or an operating cycle, whichever is longer, are classified as **long-term liabilities**. Liabilities in this category include bonds payable, mortgages payable, long-term notes payable, lease liabilities, and obligations under employee pension plans. Many companies report long-term debt maturing after one year as a single amount in the balance sheet. They then show the details of the debt in the notes that accompany the financial statements. Others list the various sources of long-term liabilities. In its balance sheet, **Consolidated Freightways, Inc.** reported the following.

CONSOLIDATED FREIGHTWAYS, INC. Balance Sheet (partial) (in thousands)	
Long-term liabilities	
Bank notes payable	$10,000
Mortgage payable	2,900
Bonds payable	53,422
Other long-term debt	9,597
Total long-term liabilities	$75,919

Illustration 4-23

Long-term liabilities section

Owner's Equity

The content of the owner's equity section varies with the form of business organization. In a proprietorship, there is one capital account. In a partnership, there is a capital account for each partner. For a corporation, owners' equity is divided into two accounts—Capital Stock and Retained Earnings. Investments of assets in the business by the stockholders are recorded by debiting an asset account and crediting the Capital Stock account. Income retained for use in the business is recorded in the Retained Earnings account. The Capital Stock and Retained Earnings accounts are combined and reported as **stockholders' equity** on the balance sheet. (We'll learn more about these corporation accounts in later chapters.)

In its balance sheet, **Dell Computer Corporation** recently reported its owners' (stockholders') equity section as follows.

DELL COMPUTER CORPORATION ($ in thousands)	
Stockholders' equity	
Common stock, 2,543,000,000 shares	$1,781,000
Retained earnings	540,000
Total stockholders' equity	$2,321,000

Illustration 4-24

Stockholders' equity section

CLASSIFIED BALANCE SHEET, ILLUSTRATED

An unclassified, report form balance sheet of Pioneer Advertising Agency was presented in Illustration 3-21 on page 108. Using the same adjusted trial balance accounts at October 31, 2002, we can prepare the classified balance sheet shown in Illustration 4-25. For illustrative purposes, assume that $1,000 of the notes payable is due currently and $4,000 is long-term.

The balance sheet is most often presented in **report form**, with assets listed above liabilities and owner's equity. The balance sheet may also be presented in **account form**: the assets section is placed on the left and the liabilities and owner's equity sections on the right, as shown in Illustration 4-25.

PIONEER ADVERTISING AGENCY Balance Sheet October 31, 2002					
Assets			**Liabilities and Owner's Equity**		
Current assets			Current liabilities		
Cash		$15,200	Notes payable		$1,000
Accounts receivable		200	Accounts payable		2,500
Advertising supplies		1,000	Unearned revenue		800
Prepaid insurance		550	Salaries payable		1,200
Total current assets		16,950	Interest payable		50
Property, plant, and equipment			Total current liabilities		5,550
Office equipment	$5,000		Long-term liabilites		
Less: Accumulated depreciation	40	4,960	Notes payable		4,000
Total assets		$21,910	Total liabilities		9,550
			Owner's equity		
			C. R. Byrd, Capital		12,360
			Total liabilities and owner's equity		$21,910

Illustration 4-25

Classified balance sheet in account form

Another, more complete example of a classified balance sheet is presented in report form in Illustration 4-26.

Illustration 4-26

Classified balance sheet in report form

FRANKLIN CORPORATION Balance Sheet October 31, 2002			
Assets			
Current assets			
Cash		$ 6,600	
Short-term investments		2,000	
Accounts receivable		7,000	
Inventories		4,000	
Supplies		2,100	
Prepaid insurance		400	
Total current assets			$22,100
Long-term investments			
Investment in stock of Walters Corp.			7,200
Property, plant, and equipment			
Land		10,000	
Office equipment	$ 24,000		
Less: Accumulated depreciation	5,000	19,000	29,000
Intangible assets			
Patents			3,100
Total assets			$61,400
Liabilities and Owner's Equity			
Current liabilities			
Notes payable		$11,000	
Accounts payable		2,100	
Unearned revenue		900	
Salaries payable		1,600	
Interest payable		450	
Total current liabilities			$16,050
Long-term liabilities			
Notes payable		1,300	
Mortgage payable		10,000	
Total long-term liabilities			11,300
Total liabilities			27,350
Owner's equity			
B. Franklin, Capital			34,050
Total liabilities and owner's equity			$61,400

BEFORE YOU GO ON...

▶ *REVIEW IT*

1. What are the major sections in a classified balance sheet?

2. Using the **Lands' End, Inc.** annual report, determine its current liabilities at January 28, 2000, and January 29, 1999. Were current liabilities higher or lower than current assets in these two years? The answer to this question is provided on page 180.

3. What is the difference between the report form and the account form of the classified balance sheet?

LOOK BACK AT OUR FEATURE STORY

Refer back to the Feature Story about **Rhino Foods, Inc.** at the beginning of the chapter, and answer the following questions.

1. What is the lesson of the Rhino Foods story and Ted Castle's innovations?
2. How did Rhino's employees' knowledge of financial statements, especially production reports and the income statement, contribute to their effectiveness as employees?

SOLUTION

1. If you give employees equity in the company and provide them with the training and the information to understand the financial consequences of their decisions and actions, they will act more responsibly and make a greater contribution to the sales and income of the company. In other words, they begin to think like owners.

2. By understanding the income statement, they now recognize the impact of revenues and expenses in arriving at net income—as well as how productivity and expenses affect their bonuses.

 THE NAVIGATOR

DEMONSTRATION PROBLEM

At the end of its first month of operations, Watson Answering Service has the following unadjusted trial balance.

Additional Demonstration Problem

WATSON ANSWERING SERVICE
August 31, 2002
Trial Balance

	Debit	Credit
Cash	$ 5,400	
Accounts Receivable	2,800	
Prepaid Insurance	2,400	
Supplies	1,300	
Equipment	60,000	
Notes Payable		$40,000
Accounts Payable		2,400
Ray Watson, Capital		30,000
Ray Watson, Drawing	1,000	
Service Revenue		4,900
Salaries Expense	3,200	
Utilities Expense	800	
Advertising Expense	400	
	$77,300	$77,300

Other data consist of the following:

1. Insurance expires at the rate of $200 per month.
2. There are $1,000 of supplies on hand at August 31.
3. Monthly depreciation on the equipment is $900.
4. Interest of $500 on the notes payable has accrued during August.

Instructions

(a) Prepare a work sheet.

(b) Prepare a classified balance sheet assuming $35,000 of the notes payable are long-term.

(c) Journalize the closing entries.

ACTION PLAN

• In completing the work sheet, be sure to (a) key the adjustments, (b) start at the top of the adjusted trial balance columns and extend adjusted balances to the correct statement columns, and (c) enter net income (or net loss) in the proper columns.

• In preparing a classified balance sheet, know the contents of each of the sections.

• In journalizing closing entries, remember that there are only four entries and that owner's drawing is closed to owner's capital.

SOLUTION TO DEMONSTRATION PROBLEM

(a)

WATSON ANSWERING SERVICE
Work Sheet
For the Month Ended August 31, 2002

Account Titles	Trial Balance Dr.	Trial Balance Cr.	Adjustments Dr.	Adjustments Cr.	Adjusted Trial Balance Dr.	Adjusted Trial Balance Cr.	Income Statement Dr.	Income Statement Cr.	Balance Sheet Dr.	Balance Sheet Cr.
Cash	5,400				5,400				5,400	
Accounts Receivable	2,800				2,800				2,800	
Prepaid Insurance	2,400			(a) 200	2,200				2,200	
Supplies	1,300			(b) 300	1,000				1,000	
Equipment	60,000				60,000				60,000	
Notes Payable		40,000				40,000				40,000
Accounts Payable		2,400				2,400				2,400
Ray Watson, Capital		30,000				30,000				30,000
Ray Watson, Drawing	1,000				1,000				1,000	
Service Revenue		4,900				4,900		4,900		
Salaries Expense	3,200				3,200		3,200			
Utilities Expense	800				800		800			
Advertising Expense	400				400		400			
Totals	77,300	77,300								
Insurance Expense			(a) 200		200		200			
Supplies Expense			(b) 300		300		300			
Depreciation Expense			(c) 900		900		900			
Accumulated Depreciation—Equipment				(c) 900		900				900
Interest Expense			(d) 500		500		500			
Interest Payable				(d) 500		500				500
Totals			1,900	1,900	78,700	78,700	6,300	4,900	72,400	73,800
Net Loss								1,400	1,400	
Totals							6,300	6,300	73,800	73,800

Explanation: (a) Insurance expired, (b) Supplies used, (c) Depreciation expensed, (d) Interest accrued.

(b)

WATSON ANSWERING SERVICE
Balance Sheet
August 31, 2002

Assets

Current assets		
Cash		$ 5,400
Accounts receivable		2,800
Prepaid insurance		2,200
Supplies		1,000
Total current assets		11,400
Property, plant, and equipment		
Equipment	$60,000	
Less: Accumulated depreciation—equipment	900	59,100
Total assets		$70,500

Liabilities and Owner's Equity

Current liabilities		
Notes payable	$ 5,000	
Accounts payable	2,400	
Interest payable	500	
Total current liabilities	7,900	
Long-term liabilities		
Notes payable	35,000	
Total liabilities	42,900	
Owner's equity		
Ray Watson, Capital	27,600*	
Total liabilities and owner's equity	$70,500	

*Ray Watson, Capital, $30,000 less drawings $1,000 and net loss $1,400.

(c)

Aug. 31	Service Revenue	4,900	
	Income Summary		4,900
	(To close revenue account)		
31	Income Summary	6,300	
	Salaries Expense		3,200
	Depreciation Expense		900
	Utilities Expense		800
	Interest Expense		500
	Advertising Expense		400
	Supplies Expense		300
	Insurance Expense		200
	(To close expense accounts)		
31	Ray Watson, Capital	1,400	
	Income Summary		1,400
	(To close net loss to capital)		
31	Ray Watson, Capital	1,000	
	Ray Watson, Drawing		1,000
	(To close drawings to capital)		

☑ THE NAVIGATOR

SUMMARY OF STUDY OBJECTIVES

1. Prepare a work sheet. The steps in preparing a work sheet are: (a) prepare a trial balance on the work sheet, (b) enter the adjustments in the adjustments columns, (c) enter adjusted balances in the adjusted trial balance columns, (d) extend adjusted trial balance amounts to appropriate financial statement columns, and (e) total the statement columns, compute net income (or net loss), and complete the work sheet.

2. Explain the process of closing the books. Closing the books occurs at the end of an accounting period. The process is to journalize and post closing entries and then rule and balance all accounts. In closing the books, separate entries are made to close revenues and expenses to Income Summary, Income Summary to Owner's Capital, and Owner's Drawings to Owner's Capital. Only temporary accounts are closed.

3. Describe the content and purpose of a post-closing trial balance. A post-closing trial balance contains the balances in permanent accounts that are carried forward to the next accounting period. The purpose of this trial balance is to prove the equality of these balances.

4. State the required steps in the accounting cycle. The required steps in the accounting cycle are: (a) analyze business transactions, (b) journalize the transactions, (c) post to ledger accounts, (d) prepare a trial balance, (e) journalize and post adjusting entries, (f) prepare an adjusted trial balance, (g) prepare financial statements, (h) journalize and post closing entries, and (i) prepare a post-closing trial balance.

5. Explain the approaches to preparing correcting entries. One approach for determining the correcting entry is to compare the incorrect entry with the correct entry. After comparison, a correcting entry is made to correct the accounts. An alternative to a correcting entry is to reverse the incorrect entry and then prepare the correct entry.

6. Identify the sections of a classified balance sheet. In a classified balance sheet, assets are classified as current assets; long-term investments; property, plant, and equipment; and intangibles. Liabilities are classified as either current or long-term. There is also an owner's equity section, which varies with the form of business organization.

Key Term Matching Activity

GLOSSARY

Classified balance sheet A balance sheet that contains a number of standard classifications or sections. (p. 151).

Closing entries Entries made at the end of an accounting period to transfer the balances of temporary accounts to a permanent owner's equity account, Owner's Capital. (p. 141).

Correcting entries Entries to correct errors made in recording transactions. (p. 148).

Current assets Cash and other resources that are reasonably expected to be realized in cash or sold or consumed in the business within one year or the operating cycle, whichever is longer. (p. 151).

Current liabilities Obligations reasonably expected to be paid from existing current assets or through the creation of other current liabilities within the next year or operating cycle, whichever is longer. (p. 153).

Income Summary A temporary account used in closing revenue and expense accounts. (p. 141).

Intangible assets Noncurrent resources that do not have physical substance. (p. 153).

Liquidity The ability of a company to pay obligations that are expected to become due within the next year or operating cycle. (p. 154).

Long-term investments Resources not expected to be realized in cash within the next year or operating cycle. (p. 152).

Long-term liabilities Obligations expected to be paid after one year. (p. 154).

Operating cycle The average time required to go from cash to cash in producing revenues. (p. 151).

Permanent (real) accounts Balance sheet accounts whose balances are carried forward to the next accounting period. (p. 140).

Post-closing trial balance A list of permanent accounts and their balances after closing entries have been journalized and posted. (p. 145).

Property, plant, and equipment Assets of a relatively permanent nature that are being used in the business and not intended for sale. (p. 152).

Reversing entry An entry made at the beginning of the next accounting period that is the exact opposite of the adjusting entry made in the previous period. (p. 147).

Stockholders' equity The ownership claim of shareholders on total assets. It is to a corporation what owner's equity is to a proprietorship. (p. 155).

Temporary (nominal) accounts Revenue, expense, and drawing accounts whose balances are transferred to owner's capital at the end of an accounting period. (p. 140).

Work sheet A multiple-column form that may be used in the adjustment process and in preparing financial statements. (p. 134).

 APPENDIX *Reversing Entries*

STUDY OBJECTIVE 7

Prepare reversing entries.

After the financial statements are prepared and the books are closed, it is often helpful to reverse some of the adjusting entries before recording the regular transactions of the next period. Such entries are called reversing entries. **A reversing entry is made at the beginning of the next accounting period and is the exact opposite of the adjusting entry made in the previous period.** The recording of reversing entries is an **optional** step in the accounting cycle.

The purpose of reversing entries is to simplify the recording of a subsequent transaction related to an adjusting entry. In Chapter 3, you may recall, the payment of salaries after an adjusting entry resulted in two debits: one to Salaries Payable and the other to Salaries Expense. With reversing entries, the entire subsequent payment can be debited to Salaries Expense. **The use of reversing entries does not change the amounts reported in the financial statements. What it does is simplify the recording of subsequent transactions.**

*I*LLUSTRATION OF REVERSING ENTRIES

Reversing entries are most often used to reverse two types of adjusting entries: accrued revenues and accrued expenses. They are seldom made for prepaid expenses and unearned revenues. To illustrate the optional use of reversing entries for accrued expenses, we will use the salaries expense transactions for Pioneer Advertising Agency. The transaction and adjustment data are as follows.

1. October 26 (initial salary entry): $4,000 of salaries earned between October 15 and October 26 are paid.
2. October 31 (adjusting entry): Salaries earned between October 29 and October 31 are $1,200. These will be paid in the November 9 payroll.
3. November 9 (subsequent salary entry): Salaries paid are $4,000. Of this amount, $1,200 applied to accrued wages payable and $2,800 was earned between November 1 and November 9.

The comparative entries with and without reversing entries are shown in Illustration 4A-1.

Illustration 4A-1

Comparative entries— not reversing vs. reversing

	When Reversing Entries Are Not Used (per chapter)				When Reversing Entries Are Used (per appendix)		
	Initial Salary Entry				*Initial Salary Entry*		
Oct. 26	Salaries Expense	4,000		Oct. 26	Salaries Expense	4,000	
	Cash		4,000		Cash		4,000
	Adjusting Entry				*Adjusting Entry*		
Oct. 31	Salaries Expense	1,200		Oct. 31	**Salaries Expense**	1,200	
	Salaries Payable		1,200		**Salaries Payable**		1,200
	Closing Entry				*Closing Entry*		
Oct. 31	Income Summary	5,200		Oct. 31	**Income Summary**	5,200	
	Salaries Expense		5,200		**Salaries Expense**		5,200
	Reversing Entry				*Reversing Entry*		
Nov. 1	No reversing entry is made.			Nov. 1	**Salaries Payable**	1,200	
					Salaries Expense		1,200
	Subsequent Salary Entry				*Subsequent Salary Entry*		
Nov. 9	Salaries Payable	1,200		Nov. 9	**Salaries Expense**	4,000	
	Salaries Expense	2,800			**Cash**		4,000
	Cash		4,000				

The first three entries are the same whether or not reversing entries are used. The last two entries are different. The November 1 **reversing entry** eliminates the $1,200 balance in Salaries Payable that was created by the October 31 adjusting entry. The reversing entry also creates a $1,200 credit balance in the Salaries Expense account. As you know, it is unusual for an expense account to have a credit balance. The balance is correct in this instance, though, because it anticipates that the entire amount of the first salary payment in the new accounting period will be debited to Salaries Expense. This debit will eliminate the credit balance, and the resulting debit balance in the expense account will equal the salaries expense incurred in the new accounting period ($2,800 in this example).

TECHNOLOGY IN ACTION

Using reversing entries in a computerized accounting system is more efficient than in a manual system. The reversing entry saves writing a program to locate the amount accrued from the preceding period and making the more complicated entry in the current period. That is, the computer does not have to be programmed to determine whether any accrued items exist.

Illustration 4A-2

Postings with reversing entries

When reversing entries are made, all cash payments of expenses can be debited to the expense account. This means that on November 9 (and every payday) Salaries Expense can be debited for the amount paid without regard to any accrued salaries payable. Being able to make the same entry each time simplifies the recording process: Subsequent transactions can be recorded as if the related adjusting entry had never been made.

The posting of the entries with reversing entries is shown in Illustration 4A-2.

Salaries Expense					Salaries Payable				
10/26 Paid	4,000	10/31 Closing	5,200		11/1 Reversing	1,200	10/31 Adjusting	1,200
31 Adjusting	1,200							
	5,200		5,200					
11/9 Paid	4,000	11/1 Reversing	1,200					

Reversing entries may also be made for accrued revenue adjusting entries. For Pioneer Advertising, the adjusting entry was: Accounts Receivable (Dr.) $200 and Service Revenue (Cr.) $200. Thus, the reversing entry on November 1 is:

A	=	L	+	OE
−200				−200

Nov. 1	Service Revenue	200	
	Accounts Receivable		200
	(To reverse October 31 adjusting entry)		

When the accrued fees are collected, Cash is debited and Service Revenue is credited.

SUMMARY OF STUDY OBJECTIVE FOR APPENDIX

7. Prepare reversing entries. Reversing entries are the opposite of the adjusting entries made in the preceding period. They are made at the beginning of a new accounting period to simplify the recording of later transactions related to the adjusting entries. In most cases, only accrued adjusting entries are reversed.

*Note: All asterisked Questions, Exercises, and Problems relate to material in the appendix to the chapter.

Chapter 4 Self-Test

SELF-STUDY QUESTIONS

Answers are at the end of the chapter.

(SO 1) **1.** Which of the following statements is *incorrect* concerning the work sheet?
 a. The work sheet is essentially a working tool of the accountant.
 b. The work sheet is distributed to management and other interested parties.

 c. The work sheet cannot be used as a basis for posting to ledger accounts.
 d. Financial statements can be prepared directly from the work sheet before journalizing and posting the adjusting entries.

2. In a work sheet, net income is entered in the following (SO 1) columns:

a. income statement (Dr) and balance sheet (Dr).
b. income statement (Cr) and balance sheet (Dr).
c. income statement (Dr) and balance sheet (Cr).
d. income statement (Cr) and balance sheet (Cr).

(SO 2) **3.** An account that will have a zero balance after closing entries have been journalized and posted is:
a. Service Revenue.
b. Advertising Supplies.
c. Prepaid Insurance.
d. Accumulated Depreciation.

(SO 2) **4.** When a net loss has occurred, Income Summary is:
a. debited and Owner's Capital is credited.
b. credited and Owner's Capital is debited.
c. debited and Owner's Drawing is credited.
d. credited and Owner's Drawing is debited.

(SO 2) **5.** The closing process involves separate entries to close (1) expenses, (2) drawings, (3) revenues, and (4) income summary. The correct sequencing of the entries is:
a. (4), (3), (2), (1)
b. (1), (2), (3), (4)
c. (3), (1), (4), (2)
d. (3), (2), (1), (4)

(SO 3) **6.** Which types of accounts will appear in the post-closing trial balance?
a. Permanent (real) accounts.
b. Temporary (nominal) accounts.
c. Accounts shown in the income statement columns of a work sheet.
d. None of the above.

(SO 4) **7.** All of the following are required steps in the accounting cycle *except*:
a. journalizing and posting closing entries.
b. preparing financial statements.
c. journalizing the transactions.
d. preparing a work sheet.

8. Cash of $100 received at the time the service was pro- (SO 5) vided was journalized and posted as a debit to Cash $100 and a credit to Accounts Receivable $100. Assuming the incorrect entry is not reversed, the correcting entry is:
a. debit Service Revenue $100 and credit Accounts Receivable $100.
b. debit Accounts Receivable $100 and credit Service Revenue $100.
c. debit Cash $100 and credit Service Revenue $100.
d. debit Accounts Receivable $100 and credit Cash $100.

9. In a classified balance sheet, assets are usually classified (SO 6) using the following categories:
a. current assets; long-term assets; property, plant, and equipment; and intangible assets.
b. current assets; long-term investments; property, plant, and equipment; and other assets.
c. current assets; long-term investments; tangible assets; and intangible assets.
d. current assets; long-term investments; property, plant, and equipment; and intangible assets.

10. Current assets are listed: (SO 6)
a. by liquidity.
b. by importance.
c. by longevity.
d. alphabetically.

*11. On December 31, Regis Company correctly made an ad- (SO 7) justing entry to recognize $2,000 of accrued salaries payable. On January 8 of the next year, total salaries of $3,400 were paid. Assuming the correct reversing entry was made on January 1, the entry on January 8 will result in a credit to Cash $3,400 and the following debit(s):
a. Salaries Payable $1,400, and Salaries Expense $2,000.
b. Salaries Payable $2,000 and Salaries Expense $1,400.
c. Salaries Expense $3,400.
d. Salaries Payable $3,400.

THE
NAVIGATOR

QUESTIONS

1. "A work sheet is a permanent accounting record and its use is required in the accounting cycle." Do you agree? Explain.

2. Explain the purpose of the work sheet.

3. What is the relationship, if any, between the amount shown in the adjusted trial balance column for an account and that account's ledger balance?

4. If a company's revenues are $125,000 and its expenses are $113,000, in which financial statement columns of the work sheet will the net income of $12,000 appear? When expenses exceed revenues, in which columns will the difference appear?

5. Why is it necessary to prepare formal financial statements if all of the data are in the statement columns of the work sheet?

6. Identify the account(s) debited and credited in each of the four closing entries, assuming the company has net income for the year.

7. Describe the nature of the Income Summary account and identify the types of summary data that may be posted to this account.

8. What are the content and purpose of a post-closing trial balance?

9. Which of the following accounts would not appear in the post-closing trial balance? Interest Payable; Equipment; Depreciation Expense; Kathy Ho, Drawing; Unearned Revenue; Accumulated Depreciation—Equipment; and Service Revenue.

10. Distinguish between a reversing entry and an adjusting entry. Are reversing entries required?

11. Indicate, in the sequence in which they are made, the three required steps in the accounting cycle that involve journalizing.

12. Identify, in the sequence in which they are prepared, the three trial balances that are often used to report financial information about a company.

13. How do correcting entries differ from adjusting entries?

14. What standard classifications are used in preparing a classified balance sheet?

15. What is meant by the term "operating cycle?"

16. Define current assets. What basis is used for arranging individual items within the current assets section?

17. Distinguish between long-term investments and property, plant, and equipment.

18. How do current liabilities differ from long-term liabilities?

19. (a) What is the term used to describe the owner's equity section of a corporation? (b) Identify the two owner's equity accounts in a corporation and indicate the purpose of each.

20. How does a report form balance sheet differ from an account form balance sheet?

*21. Clearwater Company prepares reversing entries. If the adjusting entry for interest payable is reversed, what type of an account balance, if any, will there be in Interest Payable and Interest Expense after the reversing entry is posted?

*22. At December 31, accrued salaries payable totaled $4,500. On January 10, total salaries of $8,000 are paid. (a) Assume that reversing entries are made at January 1. Give the January 10 entry, and indicate the Salaries Expense account balance after the entry is posted. (b) Repeat part (a) assuming reversing entries are not made.

*B*RIEF *EXERCISES*

List the steps in preparing a work sheet.
(SO 1)

BE4-1 The steps in using a work sheet are presented in random order below. List the steps in the proper order by placing numbers 1–5 in the blank spaces.

  (a) ____ Prepare a trial balance on the work sheet.
  (b) ____ Enter adjusted balances.
  (c) ____ Extend adjusted balances to appropriate statement columns.
  (d) ____Total the statement columns, compute net income (loss), and complete the work sheet.
  (e) ____ Enter adjustment data.

Prepare partial work sheet.
(SO 1)

BE4-2 The ledger of Giovanni Company includes the following unadjusted balances: Prepaid Insurance $4,000, Service Revenue $58,000, and Salaries Expense $25,000. Adjusting entries are required for **(a)** expired insurance $1,200; **(b)** services provided $900, but unbilled and uncollected; and **(c)** accrued salaries payable $800. Enter the unadjusted balances and adjustments into a work sheet and complete the work sheet for all accounts. *Note:* You will need to add the following accounts: Accounts Receivable, Salaries Payable, and Insurance Expense.

Identify work sheet columns for selected accounts.
(SO 1)

BE4-3 The following selected accounts appear in the adjusted trial balance columns of the work sheet for Gordon Company: Accumulated Depreciation; Depreciation Expense; B. Gordon, Capital; B. Gordon, Drawing; Service Revenue; Supplies; and Accounts Payable. Indicate the financial statement column (income statement Dr., balance sheet Cr., etc.) to which each balance should be extended.

Prepare closing entries from ledger balances.
(SO 2)

BE4-4 The ledger of Benson Company contains the following balances: D. Benson, Capital $30,000; D. Benson, Drawing $2,000; Service Revenue $50,000; Salaries Expense $26,000; and Supplies Expense $4,000. Prepare the closing entries at December 31.

Post closing entries; rule and balance T accounts.
(SO 2)

BE4-5 Using the data in BE4-4, enter the balances in T accounts, post the closing entries, and rule and balance the accounts.

Journalize and post closing entries using the three-column form of account.
(SO 2)

BE4-6 The income statement for Edgebrook Golf Club for the month ending July 31 shows Green Fee Revenue $14,000, Salaries Expense $8,200, Maintenance Expense $2,500, and Net Income $3,300. Prepare the entries to close the revenue and expense accounts. Post the entries to the revenue and expense accounts, and complete the closing process for these accounts using the three-column form of account.

Identify post-closing trial balance accounts.
(SO 3)

BE4-7 Using the data in BE4-3, identify the accounts that would be included in a post-closing trial balance.

List the required steps in the accounting cycle in sequence.
(SO 4)

BE4-8 The steps in the accounting cycle are listed in random order below. List the steps in proper sequence, assuming no work sheet is prepared, by placing numbers 1–9 in the blank spaces.

  (a) ____ Prepare a trial balance.
  (b) ____ Journalize the transactions.

(c) ____ Journalize and post closing entries.
(d) ____ Prepare financial statements.
(e) ____ Journalize and post adjusting entries.
(f) ____ Post to ledger accounts.
(g) ____ Prepare a post-closing trial balance.
(h) ____ Prepare an adjusted trial balance.
(i) ____ Analyze business transactions.

BE4-9 At Piccola Company, the following errors were discovered after the transactions had been journalized and posted. Prepare the correcting entries.

Prepare correcting entries.
(SO 5)

1. A collection on account from a customer for $780 was recorded as a debit to Cash $780 and a credit to Service Revenue $780.
2. The purchase of store supplies on account for $1,730 was recorded as a debit to Store Supplies $1,370 and a credit to Accounts Payable $1,370.

BE4-10 The balance sheet debit column of the work sheet for Salsa Company includes the following accounts: Accounts Receivable $12,500; Prepaid Insurance $3,600; Cash $18,400; Supplies $5,200, and Marketable Securities $8,200. Prepare the current assets section of the balance sheet, listing the accounts in proper sequence.

Prepare the current assets section of a balance sheet.
(SO 6)

*BE4-11 At October 31, Orlaida Company made an accrued expense adjusting entry of $800 for salaries. Prepare the reversing entry on November 1, and indicate the balances in Salaries Payable and Salaries Expense after posting the reversing entry.

Prepare reversing entries.
(SO 7)

EXERCISES

E4-1 The adjusted trial balance columns of the work sheet for Jose Tortilla Company are as follows.

Complete work sheet.
(SO 1)

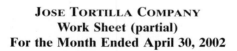

JOSE TORTILLA COMPANY
Work Sheet (partial)
For the Month Ended April 30, 2002

Account Titles	Adjusted Trial Balance Dr.	Adjusted Trial Balance Cr.	Income Statement Dr.	Income Statement Cr.	Balance Sheet Dr.	Balance Sheet Cr.
Cash	15,052					
Accounts Receivable	7,840					
Prepaid Rent	2,280					
Equipment	23,050					
Accumulated Depreciation		4,921				
Notes Payable		5,700				
Accounts Payable		5,972				
J. Tortilla, Capital		33,960				
J. Tortilla, Drawing	3,650					
Service Revenue		12,590				
Salaries Expense	9,840					
Rent Expense	760					
Depreciation Expense	671					
Interest Expense	57					
Interest Payable		57				
Totals	63,200	63,200				

Instructions
Complete the work sheet.

Prepare financial statements from work sheet.
(SO 1, 6)

E4-2   Work sheet data for Jose Tortilla Company are presented in E4-1. The owner did not make any additional investments in the business in April.

Instructions

Prepare an income statement, an owner's equity statement, and a classified balance sheet.

Journalize and post closing entries and prepare a post-closing trial balance.
(SO 2, 3)

E4-3   Work sheet data for the Jose Tortilla Company are presented in E4-1.

Instructions

(a) Journalize the closing entries at April 30.
(b) Post the closing entries to Income Summary and J. Tortilla, Capital. Use T accounts.
(c) Prepare a post-closing trial balance at April 30.

Prepare adjusting entries from a work sheet and extend balances to work sheet columns.
(SO 1)

E4-4   The adjustments columns of the work sheet for Gilberto Company are shown below.

	Adjustments	
Account Titles	**Debit**	**Credit**
Accounts Receivable	600	
Prepaid Insurance		400
Accumulated Depreciation		1,000
Salaries Payable		500
Service Revenue		600
Salaries Expense	500	
Insurance Expense	400	
Depreciation Expense	1,000	
	2,500	2,500

Instructions

(a) Prepare the adjusting entries.
(b) Assuming the adjusted trial balance amount for each account is normal, indicate the financial statement column to which each balance should be extended.

Derive adjusting entries from work sheet data.
(SO 1)

E4-5   Selected work sheet data for Karen Allman Company are presented below.

Account Titles	Trial Balance		Adjusted Trial Balance	
	Dr.	**Cr.**	**Dr.**	**Cr.**
Accounts Receivable	?		34,000	
Prepaid Insurance	26,000		18,000	
Supplies	9,000		?	
Accumulated Depreciation		12,000		?
Salaries Payable		?		6,000
Service Revenue		88,000		95,000
Insurance Expense			?	
Depreciation Expense			10,000	
Supplies Expense			4,000	
Salaries Expense	?		49,000	

Instructions

(a) Fill in the missing amounts.
(b) Prepare the adjusting entries that were made.

E4-6 The adjusted trial balance of Mozart Company at the end of its fiscal year is:

Journalize and post closing entries and prepare a post-closing trial balance.
(SO 2, 3)

MOZART COMPANY
Adjusted Trial Balance
July 31, 2002

No.	Account Titles	Debits	Credits
101	Cash	$ 14,940	
112	Accounts Receivable	8,780	
157	Equipment	15,900	
167	Accumulated Depreciation		$ 5,400
201	Accounts Payable		4,220
208	Unearned Rent Revenue		1,800
301	W.A. Mozart, Capital		45,200
306	W.A. Mozart, Drawing	14,000	
404	Commission Revenue		65,100
429	Rent Revenue		6,500
711	Depreciation Expense	4,000	
720	Salaries Expense	55,700	
732	Utilities Expense	14,900	
		$128,220	$128,220

Instructions

(a) Prepare the closing entries using page J15.

(b) Post to W.A. Mozart, Capital and No. 350 Income Summary accounts. (Use the three-column form.)

(c) Prepare a post-closing trial balance at July 31.

E4-7 The adjusted trial balance for Mozart Company is presented in E4-6.

Prepare financial statements.
(SO 6)

Instructions

(a) Prepare an income statement and an owner's equity statement for the year. Mozart did not make any capital investments during the year.

(b) Prepare a classified balance sheet at July 31.

E4-8 Selected accounts for Eden Salon are presented below. All June 30 postings are from closing entries.

Prepare closing entries and an owner's equity statement.
(SO 2)

Salaries Expense				Service Revenue				Barbara Eden, Capital			
6/10	3,200	6/30	8,800	6/30	15,600	6/15	7,200	6/30	2,500	6/1	12,000
6/28	5,600					6/24	8,400			6/30	2,300
										Bal.	11,800

Supplies Expense				Rent Expense				Barbara Eden, Drawing			
6/12	800	6/30	1,500	6/1	3,000	6/30	3,000	6/13	1,000	6/30	2,500
6/24	700							6/25	1,500		

Instructions

(a) Prepare the closing entries that were made.

(b) Post the closing entries to Income Summary.

Prepare correcting entries.
(SO 5)

E4-9 Lipizzan Company has an inexperienced accountant. During the first 2 weeks on the job, the accountant made the following errors in journalizing transactions. All entries were posted as made.

1. A payment on account of $830 to a creditor was debited to Accounts Payable $380 and credited to Cash $380.
2. The purchase of supplies on account for $600 was debited to Equipment $60 and credited to Accounts Payable $60.
3. A $400 withdrawal of cash for T. Lipizzan's personal use was debited to Salaries Expense $400 and credited to Cash $400.

Instructions
Prepare the correcting entries.

Prepare a classified balance sheet.
(SO 6)

E4-10 The adjusted trial balance for Bristol Bowling Alley at December 31, 2002, contains the following accounts.

Debits		Credits	
Building	$128,800	Amy Bristol, Capital	$115,000
Accounts Receivable	14,520	Accumulated Depreciation—Building	45,600
Prepaid Insurance	4,680	Accounts Payable	13,480
Cash	20,840	Mortgage Payable	93,600
Equipment	62,400	Accumulated Depreciation—Equipment	18,720
Land	61,200	Interest Payable	2,600
Insurance Expense	780	Bowling Revenues	14,180
Depreciation Expense	7,360		$303,180
Interest Expense	2,600		
	$303,180		

Instructions
(a) Prepare a classified balance sheet; assume that $13,600 of the mortgage payable will be paid in 2003.
(b) ▭▭▭▭▷ Comment on the liquidity of the company.

Prepare closing and reversing entries.
(SO 2, 4, 7)

*E4-11 On December 31, the adjusted trial balance of Becky Employment Agency shows the following selected data.

Accounts Receivable	$24,000	Commission Revenue	$92,000
Interest Expense	7,800	Interest Payable	2,000

Analysis shows that adjusting entries were made to (1) accrue $5,000 of commission revenue and (2) accrue $2,000 interest expense.

Instructions
(a) Prepare the closing entries for the temporary accounts at December 31.
(b) Prepare the reversing entries on January 1.
(c) Post the entries in (a) and (b). Rule and balance the accounts. (Use T accounts.)
(d) Prepare the entries to record (1) the collection of the accrued commissions on January 10 and (2) the payment of all interest due ($2,700) on January 15.
(e) Post the entries in (d) to the temporary accounts.

PROBLEMS: SET A

P4-1A Darth Vader began operations as a private investigator on January 1, 2002. The trial balance columns of the work sheet for Darth Vader P.I. at March 31 are as follows.

Prepare work sheet, financial statements, and adjusting and closing entries.
(SO 1, 2, 3, 6)

DARTH VADER P.I.
Work Sheet
For the Quarter Ended March 31, 2002

Account Titles	Trial Balance Dr.	Trial Balance Cr.
Cash	11,400	
Accounts Receivable	5,620	
Supplies	1,050	
Prepaid Insurance	2,400	
Equipment	30,000	
Notes Payable		10,000
Accounts Payable		12,350
D. Vader, Capital		20,000
D. Vader, Drawing	600	
Service Revenue		13,620
Salaries Expense	2,200	
Travel Expense	1,300	
Rent Expense	1,200	
Miscellaneous Expense	200	
	55,970	55,970

87300

Other data:

1. Supplies on hand total $750.
2. Depreciation is $500 per quarter.
3. Interest accrued on 6-month note payable, issued January 1, $300.
4. Insurance expires at the rate of $150 per month.
5. Services provided but unbilled at March 31 total $750.

Instructions

(a) Enter the trial balance on a work sheet and complete the work sheet.
(b) Prepare an income statement and owner's equity statement for the quarter and a classified balance sheet at March 31. D. Vader did not make any additional investments in the business during the quarter ended March 31, 2002.
(c) Journalize the adjusting entries from the adjustments columns of the work sheet.
(d) Journalize the closing entries from the financial statement columns of the work sheet.

(a) Adjusted trial balance $57,520

(b) Net income $7,920
Total assets $49,970

P4-2A The adjusted trial balance columns of the work sheet for Shmi Skywalker Company is as follows.

Complete work sheet; prepare financial statements, closing entries, and post-closing trial balance.
(SO 1, 2, 3, 6)

Peachtree

SHMI SKYWALKER COMPANY
Work Sheet
For the Year Ended December 31, 2002

Account No.	Account Titles	Adjusted Trial Balance Dr.	Adjusted Trial Balance Cr.
101	Cash	20,800	
112	Accounts Receivable	15,400	
126	Supplies	2,300	
130	Prepaid Insurance	4,800	
151	Office Equipment	44,000	
152	Accumulated Depreciation—Office Equipment		18,000
200	Notes Payable		20,000
201	Accounts Payable		8,000

Account No.	Account Titles	Adjusted Trial Balance Dr.	Adjusted Trial Balance Cr.
212	Salaries Payable		3,000
230	Interest Payable		1,000
301	S. Skywalker, Capital		36,000
306	S. Skywalker, Drawing	12,000	
400	Service Revenue		79,000
610	Advertising Expense	12,000	
631	Supplies Expense	3,700	
711	Depreciation Expense	6,000	
722	Insurance Expense	4,000	
726	Salaries Expense	39,000	
905	Interest Expense	1,000	
	Totals	165,000	165,000

Instructions

(a) Net income $13,300

(b) Current assets $43,300
Current liabilities $22,000

(e) Post-closing trial balance
$87,300

(a) Complete the work sheet by extending the balances to the financial statement columns.

(b) Prepare an income statement, owner's equity statement, and a classified balance sheet. $10,000 of the notes payable become due in 2003. S. Skywalker did not make any additional investments in the business during 2002.

(c) Prepare the closing entries. Use J14 for the journal page.

(d) Post the closing entries. Use the three-column form of account. Income Summary is No. 350.

(e) Prepare a post-closing trial balance.

Prepare financial statements, closing entries, and post-closing trial balance. (SO 1, 2, 3, 6)

P4-3A The completed financial statement columns of the work sheet for Panaka Company are shown below.

PANAKA COMPANY
Work Sheet
For the Year Ended December 31, 2002

Account No.	Account Titles	Income Statement Dr.	Income Statement Cr.	Balance Sheet Dr.	Balance Sheet Cr.
101	Cash			10,200	
112	Accounts Receivable			7,500	
130	Prepaid Insurance			1,800	
157	Equipment			28,000	
167	Accumulated Depreciation				8,600
201	Accounts Payable				12,000
212	Salaries Payable				3,000
301	O. Panaka, Capital				34,000
306	O. Panaka, Drawing			7,200	
400	Service Revenue		44,000		
622	Repair Expense	3,200			
711	Depreciation Expense	2,800			
722	Insurance Expense	1,200			
726	Salaries Expense	36,000			
732	Utilities Expense	3,700			
	Totals	46,900	44,000	54,700	57,600
	Net Loss		2,900	2,900	
		46,900	46,900	57,600	57,600

Instructions

(a) Net loss $2,900
Ending capital $23,900
Total assets $38,900

(a) Prepare an income statement, owner's equity statement, and a classified balance sheet. O. Panaka made an additional investment in the business of $4,000 during 2002.

(b) Prepare the closing entries.

(c) Post the closing entries and rule and balance the accounts. Use T accounts. Income Summary is No. 350.

(d) Prepare a post-closing trial balance.

(d) Post-closing trial balance
$47,500

P4-4A   Wookie Amusement Park has a fiscal year ending on September 30. Selected data from the September 30 work sheet are presented below.

Complete work sheet; prepare classified balance sheet, entries, and post-closing trial balance.
(SO 1, 2, 3, 6)

WOOKIE AMUSEMENT PARK
Work Sheet
For the Year Ended September 30, 2002

	Trial Balance		Adjusted Trial Balance	
	Dr.	**Cr.**	**Dr.**	**Cr.**
Cash	41,400		41,400	
Supplies	18,600		1,200	
Prepaid Insurance	31,900		3,900	
Land	80,000		80,000	
Equipment	120,000		120,000	
Accumulated Depreciation		36,200		43,000
Accounts Payable		14,600		14,600
Unearned Admissions Revenue		3,700		1,700
Mortgage Payable		50,000		50,000
I.M. Wookie, Capital		109,700		109,700
I.M. Wookie, Drawing	14,000		14,000	
Admissions Revenue		277,500		279,500
Salaries Expense	105,000		105,000	
Repair Expense	30,500		30,500	
Advertising Expense	9,400		9,400	
Utilities Expense	16,900		16,900	
Property Taxes Expense	18,000		21,000	
Interest Expense	6,000		12,000	
Totals	491,700	491,700		
Insurance Expense			28,000	
Supplies Expense			17,400	
Interest Payable				6,000
Depreciation Expense			6,800	
Property Taxes Payable				3,000
Totals			507,500	507,500

Instructions

(a) Prepare a complete work sheet.

(b) Prepare a classified balance sheet. (*Note:* $10,000 of the mortgage payable is due for payment in the next fiscal year.)

(c) Journalize the adjusting entries using the work sheet as a basis.

(d) Journalize the closing entries using the work sheet as a basis.

(e) Prepare a post-closing trial balance.

(a) Net income $32,500
(b) Total current assets
$46,500

(e) Post-closing trial balance
$246,500

P4-5A   Ewok-Ackbar opened Ewok's Carpet Cleaners on March 1. During March, the following transactions were completed.

Complete all steps in accounting cycle.
(SO 1, 2, 3, 4, 6)

Peachtree

Mar. 1   Invested $10,000 cash in the business.

1   Purchased used truck for $6,000, paying $4,000 cash and the balance on account.

3   Purchased cleaning supplies for $1,200 on account.

5   Paid $1,800 cash on one-year insurance policy effective March 1.

14   Billed customers $2,800 for cleaning services.

18   Paid $1,500 cash on amount owed on truck and $500 on amount owed on cleaning supplies.

20   Paid $1,500 cash for employee salaries.

21   Collected $1,600 cash from customers billed on March 14.

28   Billed customers $2,500 for cleaning services.
31   Paid gas and oil for month on truck $200.
31   Withdrew $700 cash for personal use.

The chart of accounts for Ewok's Carpet Cleaners contains the following accounts: No. 101 Cash, No. 112 Accounts Receivable, No. 128 Cleaning Supplies, No. 130 Prepaid Insurance, No. 157 Equipment, No. 158 Accumulated Depreciation—Equipment, No. 201 Accounts Payable, No. 212 Salaries Payable, No. 301 A. Ewok, Capital, No. 306, A. Ewok, Drawing, No. 350 Income Summary, No. 400 Service Revenue, No. 633 Gas & Oil Expense, No. 634 Cleaning Supplies Expense, No. 711 Depreciation Expense, No. 722 Insurance Expense, No. 726 Salaries Expense.

Instructions

(b) Trial balance $16,500
(c) Adjusted trial balance $17,850

(a) Journalize and post the March transactions. Use page J1 for the journal and the three-column form of account.
(b) Prepare a trial balance at March 31 on a work sheet.
(c) Enter the following adjustments on the work sheet and complete the work sheet.
   (1) Earned but unbilled revenue at March 31 was $600.
   (2) Depreciation on equipment for the month was $250.
   (3) One-twelfth of the insurance expired.
   (4) An inventory count shows $400 of cleaning supplies on hand at March 31.
   (5) Accrued but unpaid employee salaries were $500.

(d) Net income $2,500
   Total assets $13,500

(d) Prepare the income statement and owner's equity statement for March and a classified balance sheet at March 31.
(e) Journalize and post adjusting entries. Use page J2 for the journal.
(f) Journalize and post closing entries and complete the closing process. Use page J3 for the journal.

(g) Post-closing trial balance $13,750

(g) Prepare a post-closing trial balance at March 31.

Analyze errors and prepare correcting entries.
(SO 5)

P4-6A   Bob Thebeau, CPA, was retained by Doneright TV Repair to prepare financial statements for April 2002. Thebeau accumulated all the ledger balances per Doneright's records and found the following.

DONERIGHT TV REPAIR
Trial Balance
April 30, 2002

	Debit	Credit
Cash	$ 4,100	
Accounts Receivable	3,200	
Supplies	800	
Equipment	10,600	
Accumulated Depreciation		$ 1,350
Accounts Payable		2,100
Salaries Payable		500
Unearned Revenue		890
B. Thebeau, Capital		12,900
Service Revenue		5,450
Salaries Expense	3,300	
Advertising Expense	400	
Miscellaneous Expense	290	
Depreciation Expense	500	
	$23,190	$23,190

Bob Thebeau reviewed the records and found the following errors.

1. Cash received from a customer on account was recorded as $950 instead of $590.
2. A payment of $30 for advertising expense was entered as a debit to Miscellaneous Expense $30 and a credit to Cash $30.

3. The first salary payment this month was for $1,900, which included $500 of salaries payable on March 31. The payment was recorded as a debit to Salaries Expense $1,900 and a credit to Cash $1,900. (No reversing entries were made on April 1.)

4. The purchase on account of a typewriter costing $340 was recorded as a debit to Supplies and a credit to Accounts Payable for $340.

5. A cash payment of repair expense on equipment for $86 was recorded as a debit to Equipment $68 and a credit to Cash $68.

Instructions

(a) Prepare an analysis of each error showing (1) the incorrect entry, (2) the correct entry, and (3) the correcting entry. Items 4 and 5 occurred on April 30, 2002.

(b) Prepare a correct trial balance.

Trial balance $22,690

Pᴙᴏʙʟᴇᴍs: SET B

P4-1B The trial balance columns of the work sheet for Phantom Roofing at March 31, 2002, are as follows.

Prepare a work sheet, financial statements, and adjusting and closing entries.
(SO 1, 2, 3, 6)

Pʜᴀɴᴛᴏᴍ Rᴏᴏꜰɪɴɢ
Work Sheet
For the Month Ended March 31, 2002

Account Titles	Trial Balance	
	Dr.	Cr.
Cash	2,500	
Accounts Receivable	1,600	
Roofing Supplies	1,100	
Equipment	6,000	
Accumulated Depreciation—Equipment		1,200
Accounts Payable		1,100
Unearned Revenue		300
Z. Phantom, Capital		7,000
Z. Phantom, Drawing	600	
Service Revenue		3,000
Salaries Expense	700	
Miscellaneous Expense	100	
	12,600	12,600

Other data:

1. A physical count reveals only $220 of roofing supplies on hand.
2. Depreciation for March is $200.
3. Unearned revenue amounted to $200 after adjustment on March 31.
4. Accrued salaries are $400.

Instructions

(a) Enter the trial balance on a work sheet and complete the work sheet.

(b) Prepare an income statement and owner's equity statement for the month of March and a classified balance sheet at March 31. Z. Phantom did not make any additional investments in the business in March.

(c) Journalize the adjusting entries from the adjustments columns of the work sheet.

(d) Journalize the closing entries from the financial statement columns of the work sheet.

(a) Adjusted trial balance $13,200
(b) Net income $820
Total assets $8,920

Complete work sheet; prepare financial statements, closing entries, and post-closing trial balance.
(SO 1, 2, 3, 6)

P4-2B The adjusted trial balance columns of the work sheet for Boss Nass Company, owned by Boss Nass, are as follows.

Boss Nass Company
Work Sheet
For the Year Ended December 31, 2002

Account No.	Account Titles	Adjusted Trial Balance Dr.	Cr.
101	Cash	13,600	
112	Accounts Receivable	15,400	
126	Supplies	1,500	
130	Prepaid Insurance	2,800	
151	Office Equipment	34,000	
152	Accumulated Depreciation—Office Equipment		8,000
200	Notes Payable		16,000
201	Accounts Payable		6,000
212	Salaries Payable		3,000
230	Interest Payable		500
301	Boss Nass, Capital		25,000
306	Boss Nass, Drawing	10,000	
400	Service Revenue		88,000
610	Advertising Expense	12,000	
631	Supplies Expense	5,700	
711	Depreciation Expense	4,000	
722	Insurance Expense	5,000	
726	Salaries Expense	42,000	
905	Interest Expense	500	
	Totals	146,500	146,500

Instructions

(a) Net income $18,800

(b) Current assets $33,300;
   Current liabilities $19,500

(e) Post-closing trial balance
   $67,300

(a) Complete the work sheet by extending the balances to the financial statement columns.
(b) Prepare an income statement, owner's equity statement, and a classified balance sheet. (*Note:* $10,000 of the notes payable become due in 2003.) Boss Nass did not make any additional investments in the business during the year.
(c) Prepare the closing entries. Use J14 for the journal page.
(d) Post the closing entries. Use the three-column form of account. Income Summary is No. 350.
(e) Prepare a post-closing trial balance.

Prepare financial statements, closing entries, and post-closing trial balance.
(SO 1, 2, 3, 6)

P4-3B The completed financial statement columns of the work sheet for Nute Gunray Company are shown below.

Nute Gunray Company
Work Sheet
For the Year Ended December 31, 2002

Account No.	Account Titles	Income Statement Dr.	Cr.	Balance Sheet Dr.	Cr.
101	Cash			16,600	
112	Accounts Receivable			13,500	
130	Prepaid Insurance			3,500	
157	Equipment			26,000	
167	Accumulated Depreciation				5,600
201	Accounts Payable				11,300
212	Salaries Payable				3,000
301	Nute Gunray, Capital				36,000
306	Nute Gunray, Drawing			12,000	
400	Service Revenue		59,000		
622	Repair Expense	1,800			
711	Depreciation Expense	2,600			

Account No.	Account Titles	Income Statement Dr.	Income Statement Cr.	Balance Sheet Dr.	Balance Sheet Cr.
722	Insurance Expense	2,200			
726	Salaries Expense	35,000			
732	Utilities Expense	1,700			
	Totals	43,300	59,000	71,600	55,900
	Net Income	15,700			15,700
		59,000	59,000	71,600	71,600

Instructions

(a) Prepare an income statement, owner's equity statement, and a classified balance sheet.

(b) Prepare the closing entries. Nute did not make any additional investments during the year.

(c) Post the closing entries and rule and balance the accounts. Use T accounts. Income Summary is No. 350.

(d) Prepare a post-closing trial balance.

(a) Ending capital $39,700; Total current assets $33,600

(d) Post-closing trial balance $59,600

P4-4B   Rebecca Sherrick Management Services began business on January 1, 2002, with a capital investment of $120,000. The company manages condominiums for owners (Service Revenue) and rents space in its own office building (Rent Revenue). The trial balance and adjusted trial balance columns of the work sheet at the end of the first year are as follows.

Complete work sheet; prepare classified balance sheet, entries, and post-closing trial balance. (SO 1, 2, 3, 6)

REBECCA SHERRICK MANAGEMENT SERVICES
Work Sheet
For the Year Ended December 31, 2002

Account Titles	Trial Balance Dr.	Trial Balance Cr.	Adjusted Trial Balance Dr.	Adjusted Trial Balance Cr.
Cash	14,500		14,500	
Accounts Receivable	23,600		23,600	
Prepaid Insurance	3,100		1,600	
Land	56,000		56,000	
Building	106,000		106,000	
Equipment	48,000		48,000	
Accounts Payable		10,400		10,400
Unearned Rent Revenue		5,000		1,800
Mortgage Payable		100,000		100,000
R. Sherrick, Capital		120,000		120,000
R. Sherrick, Drawing	20,000		20,000	
Service Revenue		75,600		75,600
Rent Revenue		23,000		26,200
Salaries Expense	30,000		30,000	
Advertising Expense	17,000		17,000	
Utilities Expense	15,800		15,800	
Totals	334,000	334,000		
Insurance Expense			1,500	
Depreciation Expense—Building			2,500	
Accumulated Depreciation—Building				2,500
Depreciation Expense—Equipment			3,900	
Accumulated Depreciation—Equipment				3,900
Interest Expense			10,000	
Interest Payable				10,000
Totals			350,400	350,400

Instructions

(a) Prepare a complete work sheet.

(b) Prepare a classified balance sheet. (*Note:* $10,000 of the mortgage payable is due for payment next year.)

(a) Net income $21,100

(b) Total current assets $39,700

(e) Post-closing trial balance
    $249,700

(c) Journalize the adjusting entries.
(d) Journalize the closing entries.
(e) Prepare a post-closing trial balance.

Complete all steps in accounting cycle.
(SO 1, 2, 3, 4, 6)

P4-5B   Terry Duffy opened Terry's Window Washing on July 1, 2002. During July the following transactions were completed.

July	1	Duffy invested $9,000 cash in the business.
	1	Purchased used truck for $6,000, paying $3,000 cash and the balance on account.
	3	Purchased cleaning supplies for $900 on account.
	5	Paid $1,200 cash on one-year insurance policy effective July 1.
	12	Billed customers $2,500 for cleaning services.
	18	Paid $1,000 cash on amount owed on truck and $500 on amount owed on cleaning supplies.
	20	Paid $1,200 cash for employee salaries.
	21	Collected $1,400 cash from customers billed on July 12.
	25	Billed customers $3,000 for cleaning services.
	31	Paid gas and oil for month on truck $200.
	31	Withdrew $900 cash for personal use.

The chart of accounts for Terry's Window Washing contains the following accounts: No. 101 Cash, No. 112 Accounts Receivable, No. 128 Cleaning Supplies, No. 130 Prepaid Insurance, No. 157 Equipment, No. 158 Accumulated Depreciation—Equipment, No. 201 Accounts Payable, No. 212 Salaries Payable, No. 301 Terry Duffy, Capital, No. 306 Terry Duffy, Drawing, No. 350 Income Summary, No. 400 Service Revenue, No. 633 Gas & Oil Expense, No. 634 Cleaning Supplies Expense, No. 711 Depreciation Expense, No. 722 Insurance Expense, No. 726 Salaries Expense.

Instructions

(a) Journalize and post the July transactions. Use page J1 for the journal and the three-column form of account.

(b) Trial balance $16,900
(c) Adjusted trial balance
    $18,600

(b) Prepare a trial balance at July 31 on a work sheet.
(c) Enter the following adjustments on the work sheet and complete the work sheet.
   (1) Services provided but unbilled and uncollected at July 31 were $1,100.
   (2) Depreciation on equipment for the month was $200.
   (3) One-twelfth of the insurance expired.
   (4) An inventory count shows $600 of cleaning supplies on hand at July 31.
   (5) Accrued but unpaid employee salaries were $400.

(d) Net income $4,200;
    Total assets $15,100

(d) Prepare the income statement and owner's equity statement for July and a classified balance sheet at July 31.
(e) Journalize and post adjusting entries. Use page J2 for the journal.
(f) Journalize and post closing entries and complete the closing process. Use page J3 for the journal.

(g) Post-closing trial balance
    $15,300

(g) Prepare a post-closing trial balance at July 31.

COMPREHENSIVE PROBLEM: CHAPTERS 2 TO 4

Bill Murphy opened Bill's Window Washing on July 1, 2002. During July, the following transactions were completed.

July	1	Invested $10,000 cash in the business.
	1	Purchased a used truck for $8,000, paying $3,000 cash and the balance on account.
	3	Purchased cleaning supplies for $800 on account.
	5	Paid $2,400 on a one-year insurance policy, effective July 1.
	12	Billed customers $3,500 for cleaning services.
	18	Paid $1,000 of amount owed on truck, and $400 of amount owed on cleaning supplies.
	20	Paid $1,600 for employee salaries.
	21	Collected $1,400 from customer billed on July 12.

25   Billed customers $2,500 for cleaning services.
31   Paid gas and oil for the month on the truck, $300.
31   Withdrew $400 cash for personal use.

The chart of accounts for Bill's Window Washing contains the following accounts: No. 101 Cash, No. 112 Accounts Receivable, No. 128 Cleaning Supplies, No. 130 Prepaid Insurance, No. 157 Equipment, No. 158 Accumulated Depreciation—Equipment, No. 201 Accounts Payable, No. 212 Salaries Payable, No. 301, Bill Murphy, Capital, No. 306 Bill Murphy, Drawing, No. 350 Income Summary, No. 400 Service Revenue, No. 633 Gas & Oil Expense, No. 634 Cleaning Supplies Expense, No. 711 Depreciation Expense, No. 722 Insurance Expense, No. 726 Salaries Expense.

Instructions
(a) Journalize and post the July transactions. Use page J1 for the journal.
(b) Prepare a trial balance at July 31 on a work sheet.   (b) T/B totals $20,400
(c) Enter the following adjustments on the work sheet, and complete the work sheet.
   (1) Earned but unbilled fees at July 31 were $1,300.
   (2) Depreciation on equipment for the month was $200.
   (3) One-twelfth of the insurance expired.
   (4) An inventory count shows $200 of cleaning supplies on hand at July 31.
   (5) Accrued but unpaid employee salaries were $300.
(d) Prepare the income statement and statement of owner's equity for July, and a classified   (d) NI $4,100
balance sheet at July 31, 2002.   T/A $18,400
(e) Journalize and post the adjusting entries. Use page J2 for the journal.
(f) Journalize and post the closing entries, and complete the closing process. Use page J3 for the journal.
(g) Prepare a post-closing trial balance at July 31.   (g) T/B totals $18,600

BROADENING YOUR PERSPECTIVE

FINANCIAL REPORTING AND ANALYSIS

FINANCIAL REPORTING PROBLEM: Lands' End, Inc.

BYP4-1   The financial statements of **Lands' End, Inc.** are presented in Appendix A at the end of this textbook.

Instructions
Answer the following questions using the Consolidated Balance Sheet and the Notes to Consolidated Financial Statements section.

(a) What were Lands' End's total current assets at January 28, 2000 and January 29, 1999?
(b) Are assets that Lands' End's included under current assets listed in proper order? Explain.
(c) How are Lands' End's assets classified?
(d) What are "cash equivalents"?
(e) What were Lands' End's total current liabilities at January 28, 2000 and January 29, 1999?

COMPARATIVE ANALYSIS PROBLEM: Lands' End vs. Abercrombie & Fitch

BYP4-2   **Lands' End's** financial statements are presented in Appendix A. **Abercrombie & Fitch's** financial statements are presented in Appendix B.

Instructions
(a) Based on the information contained in these financial statements, determine each of the following for Lands' End at January 28, 2000, and for Abercrombie & Fitch at January 29, 2000.
   (1) Total current assets.
   (2) Net amount of property, plant, and equipment (land, buildings, and equipment).
   (3) Total current liabilities.
   (4) Total stockholders' (shareholders') equity.
(b) What conclusions concerning the companies' respective financial positions can be drawn from these data?

INTERPRETING FINANCIAL STATEMENTS: A Global Focus

BYP4-3 **Mo och Comsjo AB (MoDo)** is one of Europe's largest forest products companies. It has production facilities in Sweden, France, and Great Britain. Its headquarters is in Stockholm, Sweden. Its statements are presented in conformity with the standards issued by the Swedish Standards Board. Its financial statements are presented to be harmonized (that is, to have minimal difference in methods) with member countries of the European Union. The balance sheet on the next page was taken from a recent annual report.

Instructions

List all differences that you notice between MoDo's balance sheet presentation (format and terminology) and the presentation of U.S. companies shown in the chapter. For differences in terminology, list the corresponding terminology used by U.S. companies.

EXPLORING THE WEB

BYP4-4 Numerous companies have established home pages on the Internet, e.g., **Boston Beer Company (www.samadams.com), Ford Motor Company (www.ford.com),** and **Kodak (www.kodak.com).** You may have noticed company Internet addresses in television commercials or magazine advertisements.

Instructions

Examine the home pages of any two companies and answer the following questions.

(a) What type of information is available?
(b) Is any accounting-related information presented?
(c) Would you describe the home page as informative, promotional, or both? Why?

CRITICAL THINKING

GROUP DECISION CASE

BYP4-5 Everclean Janitorial Service was started 2 years ago by Bonnie Harris. Because business has been exceptionally good, Bonnie decided on July 1, 2002, to expand operations by acquiring an additional truck and hiring two more assistants. To finance the expansion, Bonnie obtained on July 1, 2002, a $25,000, 10% bank loan, payable $10,000 on July 1, 2003, and the balance on July 1, 2004. The terms of the loan require the borrower to have $10,000 more current assets than current liabilities at December 31, 2002. If these terms are not met, the bank loan will be refinanced at 15% interest. At December 31, 2002, the accountant for Everclean Janitorial Service Inc. prepared the following balance sheet.

EVERCLEAN JANITORIAL SERVICE
Balance Sheet
December 31, 2002

Assets		Liabilities and Owner's Equity	
Current assets		Current liabilities	
Cash	$ 6,500	Notes payable	$10,000
Accounts receivable	9,000	Accounts payable	2,500
Janitorial supplies	5,200	Total current liabilities	12,500
Prepaid insurance	4,800	Long-term liability	
Total current assets	25,500	Notes payable	15,000
Property, plant, and equipment		Total liabilities	27,500
Cleaning equipment (net)	22,000	Owner's equity	
Delivery trucks (net)	34,000	Bonnie Harris, capital	54,000
Total property, plant, and equipment	56,000		
Total assets	$81,500	Total liabilities and owner's equity	$81,500

Bonnie presented the balance sheet to the bank's loan office on January 2, 2003, confident that the company had met the terms of the loan. The loan officer was not impressed. She said,

MODO Consolidated Balance Sheet at December 31 (Swedish kronor, in millions)	1998	1997
Assets		
Fixed assets		
Intangible assets		
Goodwill, leases and similar rights	32	69
Tangible assets		
Forest land	4,585	4,560
Buildings, other land and land installations	2,565	2,049
Machinery and equipment	13,216	12,814
Fixed plants under construction and		
advance payments	341	128
	20,707	19,551
Financial assets		
Shares and participations		
Associate companies	89	129
Other shares and participations	59	48
Other long-term receivables	44	49
	192	226
	20,931	19,846
Current assets		
Inventories, etc.	3,648	3,620
Current receivables	4,614	4,600
Short-term placements	780	1,189
Cash in bank	461	447
	9,503	9,856
	30,434	29,702
Equity and Liabilities		
Equity		
Restricted equity		
Share capital	4,443	4,443
Restricted reserves	7,819	5,985
Non-restricted equity		
Non-restricted reserves	3,611	4,513
Profit for the year	2,504	1,434
	18,377	16,375
Minority interests	5	5
Provisions		
Interest-bearing		
Pension provisions	135	1,544
Interest-free		
Tax provisions	3,228	3,815
Other provisions	240	239
	3,603	5,598
Liabilities		
Financial liabilities	4,249	3,961
Operating liabilities	4,200	3,763
	8,449	7,724
	30,434	29,702
Pledged assets	445	481
Contingent liabilities	233	182

"We need financial statements audited by a CPA." A CPA was hired and immediately realized that the balance sheet had been prepared from a trial balance and not from an adjusted trial balance. The adjustment data at the balance sheet date consisted of the following.

(1) Earned but unbilled janitorial services were $5,000.
(2) Janitorial supplies on hand were $2,500.
(3) Prepaid insurance was a 3-year policy dated January 1, 2002.
(4) December expenses incurred but unpaid at December 31, $300.
(5) Interest on the bank loan was not recorded.
(6) The amounts for property, plant, and equipment presented in the balance sheet were reported net of accumulated depreciation (cost less accumulated depreciation). These amounts were $4,000 for cleaning equipment and $5,000 for delivery trucks as of January 1, 2002. Depreciation for 2000 was $2,000 for cleaning equipment and $5,000 for delivery trucks.

Instructions
With the class divided into groups, answer the following.
(a) Prepare a correct balance sheet.
(b) Were the terms of the bank loan met? Explain.

COMMUNICATION ACTIVITY

BYP4-6 The accounting cycle is important in understanding the accounting process.

Instructions
Write a memo to your instructor that lists the steps of the accounting cycle in the order in which they should be completed. Complete your memo with a paragraph that explains the optional steps in the cycle.

ETHICS CASE

BYP4-7 As the controller of TellTale Perfume Company, you discover a misstatement that overstated net income in the prior year's financial statements. The misleading financial statements appear in the company's annual report which was issued to banks and other creditors less than a month ago. After much thought about the consequences of telling the president, Eddie Lieman, about this misstatement, you gather your courage to inform him. Eddie says, "Hey! What they don't know won't hurt them. But, just so we set the record straight, we'll adjust this year's financial statements for last year's misstatement. We can absorb that misstatement better in this year than in last year anyway! Just don't make such a mistake again."

Instructions
(a) Who are the stakeholders in this situation?
(b) What are the ethical issues in this situation?
(c) What would you do as a controller in this situation?

Answers to Self-Study Questions

1. b **2.** c **3.** a **4.** b **5.** c **6.** a **7.** d **8.** b **9.** d **10.** a **11.** c

Answers to *Lands' End* Review It Question 2, p. 156

Current liabilities in 2000 were $150,872,000. Current liabilities in 1999 were $205,283,000. In both 2000 and 1999, current liabilities were less than current assets.

Remember to go back to the Navigator box on the chapter-opening page and check off your completed work.

ACCOUNTING FOR MERCHANDISING OPERATIONS

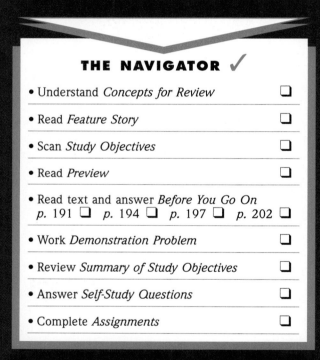

THE NAVIGATOR ✓

- Understand *Concepts for Review* ☐

- Read *Feature Story* ☐

- Scan *Study Objectives* ☐

- Read *Preview* ☐

- Read text and answer *Before You Go On*
  p. 191 ☐   *p.* 194 ☐   *p.* 197 ☐   *p.* 202 ☐

- Work *Demonstration Problem* ☐

- Review *Summary of Study Objectives* ☐

- Answer *Self-Study Questions* ☐

- Complete *Assignments* ☐

*C*ONCEPTS FOR REVIEW

Before studying this chapter, you should know or, if necessary, review:

   a. How to close revenue, expense, and drawing accounts. (Ch. 4, pp. 140–144)

   b. The steps in the accounting cycle. (Ch. 4, pp. 146–148)

THE NAVIGATOR

Selling Dollars for 85 Cents

For most of the last decade **Wal-Mart** has set the rules of the retail game. Entrepreneur Scott Blum, CEO of **Buy.com**, has a different game plan. He is selling consumer products at or below cost. Buy.com is trying to create an outlet synonymous with low prices—in the hope of becoming the leading e-commerce portal on the Internet. He plans to make up the losses from sales by selling advertising on the company's Web site.

As if the idea of selling below cost weren't unusual enough, Blum has added another twist to merchandising: He doesn't want to handle inventory. So he has wholesalers and distributors ship the products directly to his Web site customers.

Buy.com's slogan, "The lowest prices on earth," may be the most eye-catching sales pitch ever. The company is ruthlessly committed to being the price leader—even if it means losing money on every sale. Its own computers search competitors' Web sites to make sure that

Buy.com has the lowest prices on the Internet.

The amount of available capital (cash) is the natural limit to a business model in which money is lost on every sale. During the 3-month period ended June 30, 2000, Buy.com still had not generated a net positive cash flow, and it reported a net loss of $32.8 million. At June 30, 2000, the company had $140 million in cash, so even if it loses money on each sale, Buy.com should be able to run for a while.

Consider the implications if Buy.com is successful. Buy.com's success could change the very way wholesalers and distributors view their businesses. Its success may have an impact on all kinds of retailers—starting with Buy.com itself. If Buy.com proves that the ad space on a product order form—its Web site—is almost as valuable as the product being ordered, another virtual reseller is sure to enter the

market with even lower prices. In addition, Wal-Mart is also experimenting with Internet retailing.

Of course, there is one big winner if Buy.com succeeds: you. It has never been a better time to be a customer.

Source: J. William Gurley, "Buy.com May Fail, But If It Succeeds, Retailing May Never Be the Same," *Fortune*, January 11, 1999, pp. 150–152.

www.buy.com

After studying this chapter, you should be able to:

1. Identify the differences between a service enterprise and a merchandiser.
2. Explain the entries for purchases under a perpetual inventory system.
3. Explain the entries for sales revenues under a perpetual inventory system.
4. Explain the steps in the accounting cycle for a merchandiser.
5. Distinguish between a multiple-step and a single-step income statement.
6. Explain the computation and importance of gross profit.

As indicated in the Feature Story, **Buy.com** is an unusual merchandiser because it does not have its own inventory. Like traditional merchandisers such as Wal-Mart, though, it generates revenues by selling goods to customers rather than performing services. Merchandisers that purchase and sell directly to consumers—such as **Kmart**, **Safeway**, and **Toys "R" Us**—are called **retailers**. In contrast, merchandisers that sell to retailers are known as **wholesalers**. For example, retailer **Walgreens** might buy goods from wholesaler **McKesson HBOC**; **Office Depot** might buy office supplies from wholesaler **United Stationers**.

The steps in the accounting cycle for a merchandiser are the same as the steps for a service enterprise. But merchandisers use additional accounts and entries that are required in recording merchandising transactions.

The content and organization of Chapter 5 are as follows.

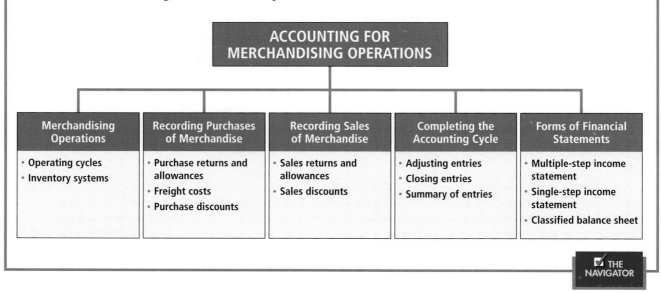

MERCHANDISING OPERATIONS

STUDY OBJECTIVE 1

Identify the differences between a service enterprise and a merchandiser.

Measuring net income for a merchandiser is conceptually the same as for a service enterprise. That is, net income (or loss) results from the matching of expenses with revenues. For a merchandiser, the primary source of revenues is the sale of merchandise. This revenue source is often referred to as **sales revenue** or **sales**. Unlike expenses for a service company, expenses for a merchandiser are divided into two categories: (1) the cost of goods sold and (2) operating expenses.

The **cost of goods sold** is the total cost of merchandise sold during the period. This expense is directly related to the revenue recognized from the sale of the goods. Sales revenue less cost of goods sold is called **gross profit** on sales. For example, when a calculator costing $15 is sold for $25, the gross profit is $10. Merchandisers report gross profit on sales in the income statement.

After gross profit is calculated, operating expenses are deducted to determine net income (or net loss). **Operating expenses** are expenses incurred in the process of earning sales revenue. Examples of operating expenses are sales salaries, advertising expense, and insurance expense. The operating expenses of a merchandiser include many of the expenses found in a service company.

The income measurement process for a merchandiser is diagrammed in Illustration 5-1. The items in the three blue boxes are peculiar to a merchandiser. They are not used by a service company.

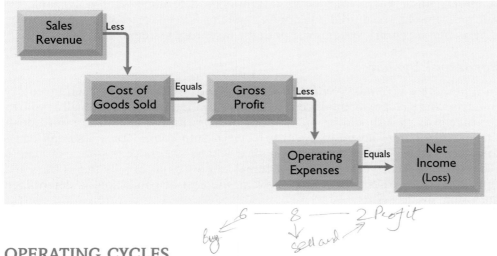

Illustration 5-1

Income measurement process for a merchandiser

OPERATING CYCLES

The operating cycle of a merchandiser differs from that of a service company, as shown in Illustration 5-2. The operating cycle of a merchandiser ordinarily is longer than that of a service company. The purchase of merchandise inventory

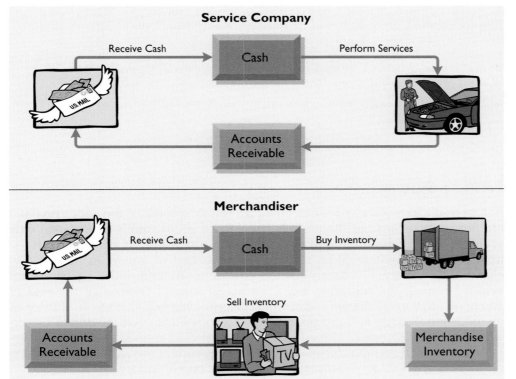

Illustration 5-2

Operating cycles for a service company and a merchandiser

and its eventual sale lengthen the cycle. Note that the added asset account for a merchandising company is an **inventory** account. It is usually entitled Merchandise Inventory. Merchandise inventory is reported as a current asset on the balance sheet.

INVENTORY SYSTEMS

A merchandiser keeps track of its inventory to determine what is available for sale and what has been sold. One of two systems is used to account for inventory: a **perpetual inventory system** or a **periodic inventory system**.

Perpetual System

In a **perpetual inventory system**, detailed records of the cost of each inventory purchase and sale are maintained. This system continuously—perpetually—shows the inventory that should be on hand for every item. For example, a Ford dealership has separate inventory records for each automobile, truck, and van on its lot. With the use of bar codes and optical scanners, a grocery store can keep a daily running record of every box of cereal and every jar of jelly that it buys and sells. Under a perpetual inventory system, the cost of goods sold is **determined each time a sale occurs**.

TECHNOLOGY IN ACTION

What's in a bar code? First, the bar code usually doesn't contain descriptive data (just as your Social Security number or car's license plate number doesn't have anything about your name or where you live). For example, the bar codes found on food items at grocery stores don't contain the price or description of the food item. Instead, the bar code has a 12-digit "product number" in it. When read by a bar code reader and transmitted to the computer, the computer finds the disk file item record(s) associated with that item number. In the disk file is the price, vendor name, quantity on-hand, description, and so on. The computer does a "price lookup" by reading the bar code, and then it creates a register of the items and adds the price to the subtotal of the groceries sold. It also subtracts the quantity from the "on-hand" total.

SOURCE: Excerpted from *A Bar Code Primer,* © 1997 Worth Data.

Periodic System

In a **periodic inventory system**, detailed inventory records of the goods on hand are not kept throughout the period. The cost of goods sold is **determined only at the end of the accounting period**—that is, periodically. At that time, a physical inventory count is taken to determine the cost of goods on hand (Merchandise Inventory). To determine the cost of goods sold under a periodic inventory system, the following steps are necessary: (1) Determine the cost of goods on hand at the beginning of the accounting period. (2) Add to it the cost of goods purchased. (3) Subtract the cost of goods on hand at the end of the accounting period.

Illustration 5-3 graphically compares the sequence of activities and the timing of the cost of goods sold computation under the two inventory systems.

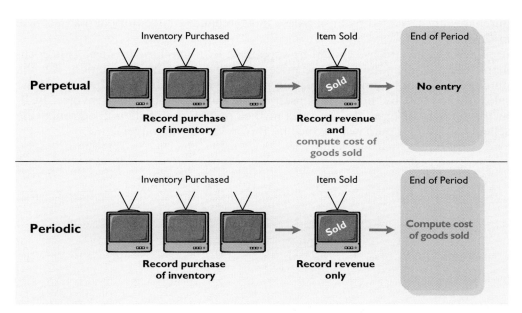

Illustration 5-3

Comparing periodic and
perpetual inventory systems

Additional Considerations

Perpetual systems have traditionally been used by companies that sell merchandise with high unit values. Examples are automobiles, furniture, and major home appliances. The widespread use of computers and electronic scanners now enables many more companies to install perpetual inventory systems. The perpetual inventory system is so named because the accounting records continuously—perpetually—show the quantity and cost of the inventory that should be on hand at any time.

A perpetual inventory system provides better control over inventories than a periodic system. The inventory records show the quantities that should be on hand. So, the goods can be counted at any time to see whether the amount of goods actually on hand agrees with the inventory records. Any shortages uncovered can be investigated immediately. A perpetual inventory system does require additional clerical work and additional cost to maintain the subsidiary records. But a computerized system can minimize this cost. Much of **Wal-Mart's** success is attributed to its sophisticated perpetual inventory system. When snowboard maker **Morrow Snowboards Inc.** issued shares of stock to the public for the first time, some investors expressed reluctance to invest in Morrow. They were concerned about a number of accounting control problems. To reduce investor concerns, Morrow implemented a perpetual inventory system to improve its control over inventory.

Because the perpetual inventory system is growing in popularity and use, we illustrate it in this chapter. The periodic system, still widely used, is described in the next chapter.

RECORDING PURCHASES OF MERCHANDISE

Purchases of inventory may be made for cash or on account (credit). Purchases are normally recorded when the goods are received from the seller. Every purchase should be supported by business documents that provide written evidence of the transaction. Each cash purchase should be supported by a canceled check or a cash register receipt indicating the items purchased and amounts paid. Cash

STUDY OBJECTIVE 2

Explain the entries for
purchases under a
perpetual inventory system.

purchases are recorded by an increase in Merchandise Inventory and a decrease in Cash.

Each credit purchase should be supported by a **purchase invoice**. This document indicates the total purchase price and other relevant information. But the purchaser does not prepare a separate purchase invoice. Instead, the copy of the sales invoice sent by the seller is used by the buyer as a purchase invoice. In Illustration 5-4, for example, the sales invoice prepared by Sellers Electronix (the seller) is used as a purchase invoice by Beyer Video (the buyer).

Illustration 5-4

Sales invoice used as purchase invoice by Beyer Video

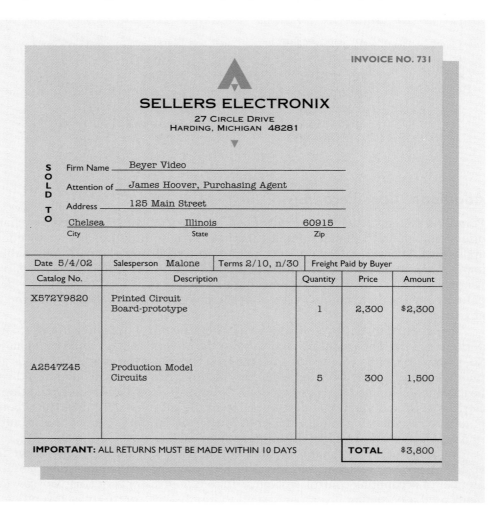

			INVOICE NO. 731

SELLERS ELECTRONIX

27 CIRCLE DRIVE
HARDING, MICHIGAN 48281

S O L D T O

Firm Name ___ Beyer Video ___

Attention of ___ James Hoover, Purchasing Agent ___

Address ___ 125 Main Street ___

Chelsea ___ Illinois ___ 60915 ___
City / State / Zip

Date 5/4/02	Salesperson Malone	Terms 2/10, n/30	Freight Paid by Buyer		
Catalog No.	Description		Quantity	Price	Amount
X572Y9820	Printed Circuit Board-prototype		1	2,300	$2,300
A2547Z45	Production Model Circuits		5	300	1,500

IMPORTANT: ALL RETURNS MUST BE MADE WITHIN 10 DAYS   **TOTAL** $3,800

The associated entry for Beyer Video for the invoice from Sellers Electronix is:

A	=	L +	OE
+3,800		+3,800	

May 4	Merchandise Inventory	3,800	
	Accounts Payable		3,800
	(To record goods purchased on account from Sellers Electronix)		

Under the perpetual inventory system, purchases of merchandise for sale are recorded in the Merchandise Inventory account. Thus, a retailer of general merchandise such as **Wal-Mart** would debit Merchandise Inventory for clothing, sporting goods, and anything else purchased for resale to customers.

Not all purchases are debited to Merchandise Inventory, however. Purchases of assets acquired for use and not for resale (such as supplies, equipment, and similar items) are recorded as increases to specific asset accounts rather than to Merchandise Inventory. Wal-Mart would increase Supplies to record the purchase of materials used to make shelf signs or for cash register receipt paper.

PURCHASE RETURNS AND ALLOWANCES

A purchaser may be dissatisfied with the merchandise received. The goods may be damaged or defective, of inferior quality, or perhaps they do not meet the purchaser's specifications. In such cases, the purchaser may return the goods to the seller. The purchaser is granted credit if the sale was made on credit, or a cash refund if the purchase was for cash. This transaction is known as a **purchase return**. Or the purchaser may choose to keep the merchandise if the seller is willing to grant an allowance (deduction) from the purchase price. This transaction is known as a **purchase allowance**.

Assume that Beyer Video returned goods costing $300 to Sellers Electronix on May 8. The entry by Beyer Video for the returned merchandise is:

May 8	Accounts Payable	300	
	Merchandise Inventory		300
	(To record return of goods received		
	from Sellers Electronix)		

A	=	L	+	OE
−300		−300		

Beyer Video increased Merchandise Inventory when the goods were received. So, Beyer Video decreases Merchandise Inventory when it returns the goods or when it is granted an allowance.

FREIGHT COSTS

The sales agreement should indicate whether the seller or the buyer is to pay the cost of transporting the goods to the buyer's place of business. When a common carrier such as a railroad, trucking company, or airline is used, the transportation company prepares a freight bill (often called a bill of lading) in accordance with the sales agreement. Freight terms are expressed as either **FOB shipping point** or **FOB destination**. The letters FOB mean **free on board**. Thus, FOB shipping point means that goods are placed free on board the carrier by the seller, and the buyer pays the freight costs. Conversely, **FOB destination** means that the goods are placed free on board to the buyer's place of business, and the seller pays the freight. For example, the sales invoice in Illustration 5-4 on page 188 indicates that the buyer (Beyer Video) pays the freight charges.

> **HELPFUL HINT**
> Freight terms may be stated by location. A Chicago seller may use "FOB Chicago" for FOB shipping point and the buyer's city for FOB destination.

When the purchaser directly incurs the freight costs, the account Merchandise Inventory is debited. For example, if upon delivery of the goods on May 6, Beyer Video pays Acme Freight Company $150 for freight charges, the entry on Beyer Video's books is:

May 6	Merchandise Inventory	150	
	Cash		150
	(To record payment of freight on goods		
	purchased)		

A	=	L	+	OE
+150				
−150				

In contrast, **freight costs incurred by the seller on outgoing merchandise are an operating expense to the seller**. These costs increase an expense account titled Freight-out or Delivery Expense. If the freight terms on the invoice in Illustration

5-4 had required that Sellers Electronix pay the $150 freight charges, the entry by Sellers Electronix would have been:

A	=	L	+	OE
−150				−150

May 4	Freight-out (or Delivery Expense)	150	
	Cash		150
	(To record payment of freight on goods sold)		

When the freight charges are paid by the seller, the seller will usually establish a higher invoice price for the goods to cover the expense of shipping.

ACCOUNTING IN ACTION *Business Insight*

It can cost a lot to convert from traditional business to e-commerce. For example, when **Borders**, the second largest seller of books, went online, it had to build an entirely new $15 million distribution center. The reason? It previously shipped large orders of books to its stores. Instead, it now has to distribute tiny orders to individual customers. The distribution costs of online sales can be suprisingly high—as much as 15 percent of sales.

PURCHASE DISCOUNTS

The credit terms of a purchase on account may permit the buyer to claim a cash discount for prompt payment. The buyer calls this cash discount a **purchase discount**. This incentive offers advantages to both parties: The purchaser saves money, and the seller is able to shorten the operating cycle by converting the accounts receivable into cash earlier.

The **credit terms** specify the amount of the cash discount and time period during which it is offered. They also indicate the length of time in which the purchaser is expected to pay the full invoice price. In the sales invoice in Illustration 5-4, credit terms are 2/10, n/30. This is read "two-ten, net thirty." It means that a 2 percent cash discount may be taken on the invoice price, less ("net of") any returns or allowances, if payment is made within 10 days of the invoice date (the **discount period**). If payment is not made in that time, the invoice price, less any returns or allowances, is due 30 days from the invoice date. Or, the discount period may extend to a specified number of days after the month in which the sale occurs. For example, 1/10 EOM (end of month) means that a 1 percent discount is available if the invoice is paid within the first 10 days of the next month.

The seller may elect not to offer a cash discount for prompt payment. In that case, credit terms will specify only the maximum time period for paying the balance due. For example, the time period may be stated as n/30, n/60, or n/10 EOM. These mean, respectively, that the net amount must be paid in 30 days, 60 days, or within the first 10 days of the next month.

When an invoice is paid within the discount period, the amount of the discount decreases Merchandise Inventory. Inventory is recorded at its cost and, by paying within the discount period, the merchandiser has reduced its cost. To illustrate, assume Beyer Video pays the balance due of $3,500 (gross invoice price of $3,800 less purchase returns and allowances of $300) on May 14, the last day of the discount period. The cash discount is $70 ($3,500 × 2%), and the amount of cash paid by Beyer Video is $3,430 ($3,500 − $70). The entry to record the May 14 payment by Beyer Video is:

HELPFUL HINT
The term *net* in "net 30" means the remaining amount due after subtracting any sales returns and allowances and partial payments.

May 14	Accounts Payable	3,500	
	Cash		3,430
	Merchandise Inventory		70
	(To record payment within discount period)		

A	=	L	+	OE
−3,430		−3,500		
−70				

If Beyer Video failed to take the discount and instead made full payment on June 3, Beyer Video's entry would be:

June 3	Accounts Payable	3,500	
	Cash		3,500
	(To record payment with no discount taken)		

A	=	L	+	OE
−3,500		−3,500		

ACCOUNTING IN ACTION   Business Insight

In the 1990s, **Sears** wielded its retail clout by telling its suppliers that, rather than pay its obligations in the standard 30-day period, it would now pay in 60 days. This practice is often adopted by firms that are experiencing a shortage of cash. A Sears spokesperson insisted, however, that Sears did not have cash problems. Rather, it was simply utilizing "vendor-financed inventory methods to improve its return on investment." Supplier trade groups were outspoken critics of Sears's policy. They suggested that consumers would be the ultimate victims, because the financing costs would eventually be passed on to them.

A merchandiser usually should take all available discounts. Passing up the discount may be viewed as **paying interest** for use of the money. For example, if Beyer Video passed up the discount, it would be like paying an interest rate of 2 percent for the use of $3,500 for 20 days. This is the equivalent of an annual interest rate of approximately 36.5 percent (2% × 365/20). Obviously, it would be better for Beyer Video to borrow at prevailing bank interest rates of 8 percent to 12 percent than to lose the discount.

HELPFUL HINT
So as not to miss purchase discounts, unpaid invoices should be filed by due dates. This procedure helps the purchaser remember the discount date, prevents early payment of bills, and maximizes the time that cash can be used for other purposes.

BEFORE YOU GO ON...

▶ *REVIEW IT*

1. How does the measurement of net income in a merchandising company differ from that in a service enterprise?

2. In what ways is a perpetual inventory system different from a periodic system?

3. Under the perpetual inventory system, what entries are made to record purchases, purchase returns and allowances, purchase discounts, and freight costs?

☑ THE NAVIGATOR

RECORDING SALES OF MERCHANDISE

Sales revenues, like service revenues, are recorded when earned. This is done in accord with the revenue recognition principle. Typically, sales revenues are earned when the goods are transferred from the seller to the buyer. At this point the sales transaction is completed, and the sales price has been established.

STUDY OBJECTIVE 3

Explain the entries for sales revenues under a perpetual inventory system.

Sales may be made on credit or for cash. Every sales transaction should be supported by a **business document** that provides written evidence of the sale. **Cash register tapes** provide evidence of cash sales. A **sales invoice**, like the one that was shown in Illustration 5-4 (page 188), provides support for a credit sale. The original copy of the invoice goes to the customer. A copy is kept by the seller for use in recording the sale. The invoice shows the date of sale, customer name, total sales price, and other relevant information.

Two entries are made for each sale. The first entry records the sale: Cash (or Accounts Receivable, if a credit sale) is increased by a debit, and Sales is increased by a credit at the selling (invoice) price of the goods. The second entry records the cost of the merchandise sold: Cost of Goods Sold is increased by a debit, and Merchandise Inventory is decreased by a credit for the cost of those goods. As a result, the Merchandise Inventory account will show at all times the amount of inventory that should be on hand.

To illustrate a credit sales transaction, Sellers Electronix's sale of $3,800 on May 4 to Beyer Video (see Illustration 5-4, page 188) is recorded as follows. (Assume the merchandise cost Sellers Electronix $2,400.)

A	=	L	+	OE
+3,800				+3,800

May	4	Accounts Receivable	3,800	
		Sales		3,800
		(To record credit sale to Beyer Video per invoice #731)		

A	=	L	+	OE
−2,400				−2,400

	4	Cost of Goods Sold	2,400	
		Merchandise Inventory		2,400
		(To record cost of merchandise sold on invoice #731 to Beyer Video)		

Gross profit is: 3800 1400

HELPFUL HINT

The Sales account is credited only for sales of goods held for resale. Sales of assets not held for resale (such as equipment or land) are credited directly to the asset account.

For internal decision-making purposes, merchandisers may use more than one sales account. For example, Sellers Electronix may keep separate sales accounts for its TV sets, videocassette recorders, and microwave ovens. By using separate sales accounts for major product lines, company management can monitor sales trends more closely and respond more strategically to changes in sales patterns. For example, if TV sales are increasing while microwave oven sales are decreasing, the company could reevaluate its advertising and pricing policies on each of these items.

However, on its income statement presented to outside investors, a merchandiser would normally provide only a single sales figure—the sum of all of its individual sales accounts. This is done for two reasons. First, providing detail on individual sales accounts would add length to the income statement. Second, companies do not want their competitors to know the details of their operating results.

SALES RETURNS AND ALLOWANCES

We now look at the "flipside" of purchase returns and allowances, which are **sales returns and allowances** recorded on the books of the seller. Sellers Electronix's entries to record credit for returned goods involve two entries: (1) The first is an increase in Sales Returns and Allowances and a decrease in Accounts Receivable at the $300 selling price. (2) The second is an increase in Merchandise Inventory (assume a $140 cost) and a decrease in Cost of Goods Sold. The entries are as follows.

HELPFUL HINT

If the customer is sent cash, then credit Cash rather than Accounts Receivable.

May 8	Sales Returns and Allowances	300	
	Accounts Receivable		300
	(To record credit granted to Beyer Video for returned goods)		

A	=	L	+	OE
−300				−300

8	Merchandise Inventory	140	
	Cost of Goods Sold		140
	(To record cost of goods returned)		

A	=	L	+	OE
+140				+140

If goods are returned because they are damaged or defective, then the entry to Merchandise Inventory and Cost of Goods Sold should be for the estimated value of the returned goods, rather than their cost. For example, if the goods returned to Sellers Electronix were defective and had a scrap value of $50, Merchandise Inventory would be debited for $50, and Cost of Goods Sold would be credited for $50.

Sales Returns and Allowances is a **contra revenue account** to Sales. The normal balance of Sales Returns and Allowances is a debit. A contra account is used, instead of debiting Sales, to disclose in the accounts the amount of sales returns and allowances. This information is important to management. Excessive returns and allowances suggest inferior merchandise, inefficiencies in filling orders, errors in billing customers, and mistakes in delivery or shipment of goods. Also, a debit recorded directly to Sales could distort comparisons between total sales in different accounting periods.

> **HELPFUL HINT**
> Remember that the increases, decreases, and normal balances of contra accounts are the opposite of the accounts to which they correspond.

ACCOUNTING IN ACTION *Business Insight*

Returned goods can represent 15 percent of total sales volume. Most companies do a poor job of dealing with returned goods, often destroying perfectly good merchandise. A new piece of software developed by cosmetic company **Estee Lauder** may change this. When boxes of Estee Lauder lipstick and other products arrive back from a retailer, each barcode is scanned, and each item's expiration date and condition are determined. It is then either scrapped or sorted for resale to employees, in "seconds" stores, or in developing countries. The system paid for its $1.5 million development cost in 9 months because it enabled the company to resell two-and-a-half times as many items, at less than half the cost of the old system.

SOURCE: "Cash from Trash," *The Economist,* February 6, 1999.

SALES DISCOUNTS

As mentioned in our discussion of purchase transactions, the seller may offer the customer a cash discount for the prompt payment of the balance due. From the seller's point of view, this is called a **sales discount**. Like a purchase discount, a sales discount is based on the invoice price less returns and allowances, if any. The Sales Discounts account is debited for discounts that are taken. The entry by Sellers Electronix to record the cash receipt on May 14 from Beyer Video within the discount period is:

May 14	Cash	3,430	
	Sales Discounts	70	
	Accounts Receivable		3,500
	(To record collection within 2/10, n/30 discount period from Beyer Video)		

A	=	L	+	OE
+3,430				−70
−3,500				

Like Sales Returns and Allowances, Sales Discounts is a **contra revenue account** to Sales. Its normal balance is a debit. This account is used, instead of debiting Sales, to disclose cash discounts taken by customers. If the discount is not taken, Sellers Electronix debits Cash for $3,500 and credits Accounts Receivable for the same amount at the date of collection.

·BEFORE YOU GO ON...

▶ *REVIEW IT*

1. Under a perpetual inventory system, what are the two entries that must be recorded at the time of each sale?
2. Why is it important to use the Sales Returns and Allowances account, rather than simply reducing the Sales account, when goods are returned?

▶ *DO IT*

On September 5, De La Hoya Company buys merchandise on account from Junot Diaz Company. The selling price of the goods is $1,500, and the cost to Diaz Company was $800. On September 8 defective goods with a selling price of $200 and a scrap value of $80 are returned. Record the transaction on the books of both companies.

ACTION PLAN

- Purchaser: Record purchases of inventory at its cost and directly reduce the Merchandise Inventory account for returned goods.
- Seller: Record both the sale and the cost of goods sold at the time of the sale. Record returns in a contra account, Sales Returns and Allowances.

SOLUTION

De La Hoya Company

Sept. 5	Merchandise Inventory		1,500	
	Accounts Payable			1,500
	(To record goods purchased on account)			
8	Accounts Payable		200	
	Merchandise Inventory			200
	(To record return of defective goods)			

Junot Diaz Company

Sept. 5	Accounts Receivable		1,500	
	Sales			1,500
	(To record credit sale)			
5	Cost of Goods Sold		800	
	Merchandise Inventory			800
	(To record cost of goods sold on account)			
8	Sales Returns and Allowances		200	
	Accounts Receivable			200
	(To record credit granted for receipt of returned goods)			
8	Merchandise Inventory		80	
	Cost of Goods Sold			80
	(To record scrap value of goods returned)			

Related exercise material: BE5-1, BE5-2, BE5-3, BE5-4, E5-1, E5-2, E5-3, and E5-4.

☑ THE NAVIGATOR

COMPLETING THE ACCOUNTING CYCLE

Up to this point, we have illustrated the basic entries in recording transactions relating to purchases and sales in a perpetual inventory system. Now we consider the remaining steps in the accounting cycle for a merchandiser. Each of the required steps described in Chapter 4 for a service company applies to a merchandising company. Use of a worksheet by a merchandiser (an optional step) is shown in the appendix to this chapter.

STUDY OBJECTIVE 4

Explain the steps in the accounting cycle for a merchandiser.

ADJUSTING ENTRIES

A merchandiser generally has the same types of adjusting entries as a service company. But a merchandiser using a perpetual system will require one additional adjustment to make the records agree with the actual inventory on hand. Here's why: At the end of each period, a merchandiser using a perpetual system will take a physical count of its goods on hand for control purposes. A company's unadjusted balance in Merchandise Inventory will usually not agree with the actual amount of inventory on hand at year-end. The perpetual inventory records may be incorrect due to a variety of causes such as recording errors, theft, or waste. As a result, the perpetual records need adjustment to ensure that the recorded inventory amount agrees with the actual inventory on hand. **This involves adjusting Merchandise Inventory and Cost of Goods Sold.**

For example, suppose that the records of Sellers Electronix report an unadjusted balance in Merchandise Inventory of $40,500. Through a physical count, the company determines that its actual merchandise inventory on hand at year-end is $40,000. The adjusting entry would be to debit Cost of Goods Sold for $500 and to credit Merchandise Inventory for $500.

> **HELPFUL HINT**
> The steps required to determine the actual inventory on hand are discussed in Chapter 6.

CLOSING ENTRIES

For a merchandiser, like a service enterprise, all accounts that affect the determination of net income are closed to Income Summary. In journalizing, all temporary accounts with debit balances are credited, and all temporary accounts with credit balances are debited, as shown below for Sellers Electronix. Cost of goods sold is a new account that must be closed to Income Summary.

> **HELPFUL HINT**
> The easiest way to prepare the first two closing entries is to identify the temporary accounts by their balances and then prepare one entry for the credits and one for the debits.

Dec. 31	Sales	480,000	
	Income Summary		480,000
	(To close income statement accounts with		
	credit balances)		
31	Income Summary	450,000	
	Sales Returns and Allowances		12,000
	Sales Discounts		8,000
	Cost of Goods Sold		316,000
	Store Salaries Expense		45,000
	Rent Expense		19,000
	Freight-out		7,000
	Advertising Expense		16,000
	Utilities Expense		17,000
	Depreciation Expense		8,000
	Insurance Expense		2,000
	(To close income statement accounts with		
	debit balances)		

31	Income Summary		30,000	
	R.A. Lamb, Capital			30,000
	(To close net income to capital)			
31	R.A. Lamb, Capital		15,000	
	R.A. Lamb, Drawing			15,000
	(To close drawings to capital)			

After the closing entries are posted, all temporary accounts have zero balances. In addition, R.A. Lamb, Capital has a credit balance of $98,000: beginning balance + net income − drawings ($83,000 + $30,000 − $15,000).

SUMMARY OF MERCHANDISING ENTRIES

The entries for the merchandising accounts using a perpetual inventory system are summarized in Illustration 5-5.

Illustration 5-5

Daily recurring and adjusting and closing entries

	Transactions	Daily Recurring Entries	Dr.	Cr.
Sales Transactions	Selling merchandise to customers.	Cash or Accounts Receivable Sales	XX	XX
		Cost of Goods Sold Merchandise Inventory	XX	XX
	Granting sales returns or allowances to customers.	Sales Returns and Allowances Cash or Accounts Receivable	XX	XX
		Merchandise Inventory Cost of Goods Sold	XX	XX
	Paying freight costs on sales; FOB destination.	Freight-out Cash	XX	XX
	Receiving payment from customers within discount period.	Cash Sales Discounts Accounts Receivable	XX XX	XX
Purchase Transactions	Purchasing merchandise for resale.	Merchandise Inventory Cash or Accounts Payable	XX	XX
	Paying freight costs on merchandise purchased; FOB shipping point.	Merchandise Inventory Cash	XX	XX
	Receiving purchase returns or allowances from suppliers.	Cash or Accounts Payable Merchandise Inventory	XX	XX

	Paying suppliers within discount period.	Accounts Payable
		   Merchandise Inventory
		   Cash
			XX	XX
				XX

	Events	Adjusting and Closing Entries	Dr.	Cr.
	Adjust because book amount is higher than the inventory amount determined to be on hand.	Cost of Goods Sold Merchandise Inventory	XX	XX
	Closing temporary accounts with credit balances.	Sales Income Summary	XX	XX

	Closing temporary accounts with debit balances.	Income Summary
		   Sales Returns and Allowances
		   Sales Discounts
		   Cost of Goods Sold
		   Freight-out
		   Expenses
			XX	XX
				XX
				XX
				XX
				XX

BEFORE YOU GO ON...

▶ *REVIEW IT*

1. Why is an adjustment to the Merchandise Inventory account usually needed?
2. What merchandising account(s) will appear in the post-closing trial balance?

▶ *DO IT*

The trial balance of Revere Clothing Company at December 31 shows Merchandise Inventory $25,000, Sales $162,400, Sales Returns and Allowances $4,800, Sales Discounts $3,600, Cost of Goods Sold $110,000, Rental Revenue $6,000, Freight-out $1,800, Rent Expense $8,800, and Salaries and Wages Expense $22,000. Prepare the closing entries for the above accounts.

ACTION PLAN

• Close all temporary accounts with credit balances to Income Summary by debiting these accounts.

• Close all temporary accounts with debit balances to Income Summary by crediting these accounts.

SOLUTION: The two closing entries are:

Dec. 31	Sales	162,400	
	Rental Revenue	6,000	
	Income Summary		168,400
	(To close accounts with credit balances)		
Dec. 31	Income Summary	151,000	
	Cost of Goods Sold		110,000
	Sales Returns and Allowances		4,800
	Sales Discounts		3,600
	Freight-out		1,800
	Rent Expense		8,800
	Salaries and Wages Expense		22,000
	(To close accounts with debit balances)		

Related exercise material: BE5-7, E5-5, and E5-6.

☑ THE NAVIGATOR

FORMS OF FINANCIAL STATEMENTS

Two forms of the income statement are widely used by merchandisers. Also, merchandisers use the classified balance sheet, introduced in Chapter 4. The use of these financial statements by merchandisers is explained below.

STUDY OBJECTIVE 5

Distinguish between a multiple-step and a single-step income statement.

MULTIPLE-STEP INCOME STATEMENT

The **multiple-step income statement** is so named because it shows the steps in determining net income (or net loss). It shows two main steps: (1) Cost of goods sold is subtracted from net sales, to determine gross profit. (2) Operating expenses are deducted from gross profit, to determine net income. These steps relate to the company's principal operating activities. A multiple-step statement also distinguishes between **operating** and **non-operating activities**. This distinction provides users with more information about a company's income performance. The statement also highlights intermediate components of income and shows subgroupings of expenses.

Income Statement Presentation of Sales

The multiple-step income statement begins by presenting sales revenue. As contra revenue accounts, sales returns and allowances, and sales discounts are deducted from sales to arrive at **net sales**. The sales revenues section for Sellers Electronix, using assumed data, is as follows.

Illustration 5-6

Computation of net sales

SELLERS ELECTRONIX Income Statement (partial)		
Sales revenues		
Sales		$480,000
Less: Sales returns and allowances	$12,000	
Sales discounts	8,000	20,000
Net sales		**$460,000**

This presentation discloses the key aspects of the company's principal revenue-producing activities.

Gross Profit

STUDY OBJECTIVE 6

Explain the computation and importance of gross profit.

From Illustration 5-1, you learned that cost of goods sold is deducted from sales revenue to determine **gross profit**. Sales revenue used for this computation is **net sales**. On the basis of the sales data presented in Illustration 5-6 (net sales of $460,000) and the cost of goods sold under the perpetual inventory system (assume $316,000), the gross profit for Sellers Electronix is $144,000, computed as follows.

Illustration 5-7

Computation of gross profit

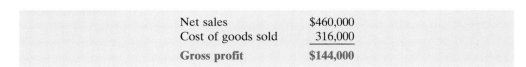

Net sales	$460,000
Cost of goods sold	316,000
Gross profit	**$144,000**

A company's gross profit may also be expressed as a percentage. This is done by dividing the amount of gross profit by net sales. For Sellers Electronix the **gross profit rate** is 31.3 percent, computed as follows.

Illustration 5-8

Gross profit rate formula and computation

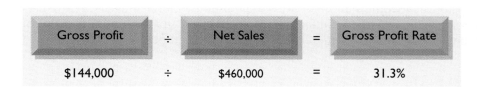

Gross Profit	÷	Net Sales	=	Gross Profit Rate
$144,000	÷	$460,000	=	31.3%

The gross profit rate is generally considered to be more useful than the gross profit amount. The rate expresses a more meaningful (qualitative) relationship between net sales and gross profit. For example, a gross profit of $1,000,000 may be impressive. But, if it is the result of a gross profit rate of only 7 percent, it is not so impressive. The gross profit rate tells how many cents of each sales dollar go to gross profit.

Gross profit represents the **merchandising profit** of a company. It is not a measure of the overall profitability, because operating expenses have not been deducted. But the amount and trend of gross profit is closely watched by management and other interested parties. They compare current gross profit with amounts reported in past periods. They also compare the company's gross profit rate with rates of competitors and with industry averages. Such comparisons provide information about the effectiveness of a company's purchasing function and the soundness of its pricing policies.

Operating Expenses and Net Income

Operating expenses are the third component in measuring net income for a merchandiser. As indicated earlier, these expenses are similar in merchandising and service enterprises. At Sellers Electronix, operating expenses were $114,000. The firm's net income is determined by subtracting operating expenses from gross profit. Thus, net income is $30,000, as shown below.

Gross profit	$144,000	
Operating expenses	**114,000**	
Net income	$ 30,000	

Illustration 5-9

Operating expenses in computing net income

The net income amount is the "bottom line" of a company's income statement.

Nonoperating Activities

Nonoperating activities consist of (1) revenues and expenses from auxiliary operations and (2) gains and losses that are unrelated to the company's operations. The results of nonoperating activities are shown in two sections: "Other revenues and gains" and "Other expenses and losses." For a merchandiser, these sections will typically include the following items.

Nonoperating Activities	
Other revenues and gains	**Other expenses and losses**
Interest revenue from notes receivable and marketable securities	Interest expense on notes and loans payable
Dividend revenue from investments in capital stock	Casualty losses from recurring causes such as vandalism and accidents
Rent revenue from subleasing a portion of the store	Loss from the sale or abandonment of property, plant, and equipment
Gain from the sale of property, plant, and equipment	Loss from strikes by employees and suppliers

Illustration 5-10

Items reported in nonoperating sections

The nonoperating activities are reported in the income statement immediately after the company's primary operating activities. These sections are shown in Illustration 5-11, using assumed data for Sellers Electronix.

Illustration 5-11

Multiple-step income statement—nonoperating sections and subgroupings of operating expenses

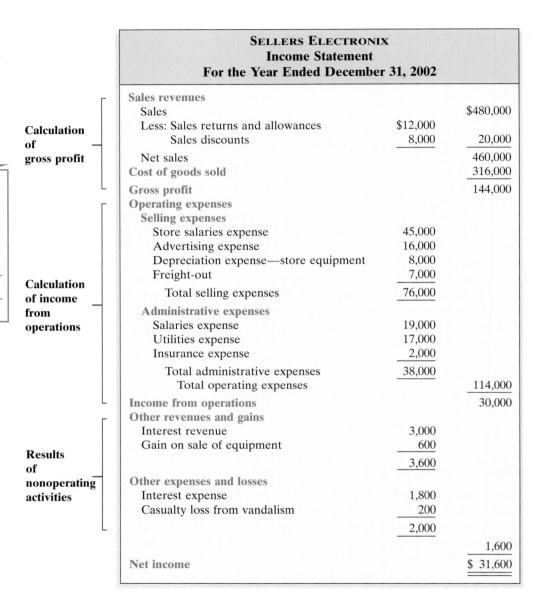

SELLERS ELECTRONIX			
Income Statement			
For the Year Ended December 31, 2002			
Sales revenues			
Sales			$480,000
Less: Sales returns and allowances		$12,000	
Sales discounts		8,000	20,000
Net sales			460,000
Cost of goods sold			316,000
Gross profit			144,000
Operating expenses			
Selling expenses			
Store salaries expense		45,000	
Advertising expense		16,000	
Depreciation expense—store equipment		8,000	
Freight-out		7,000	
Total selling expenses		76,000	
Administrative expenses			
Salaries expense		19,000	
Utilities expense		17,000	
Insurance expense		2,000	
Total administrative expenses		38,000	
Total operating expenses			114,000
Income from operations			30,000
Other revenues and gains			
Interest revenue		3,000	
Gain on sale of equipment		600	
		3,600	
Other expenses and losses			
Interest expense		1,800	
Casualty loss from vandalism		200	
		2,000	
			1,600
Net income			$ 31,600

Calculation of gross profit

Calculation of income from operations

Results of nonoperating activities

When the two nonoperating sections are included, the label "**Income from operations**" (or Operating income) precedes them. It clearly identifies the results of the company's normal operations. Income from operations is determined by subtracting cost of goods sold and operating expenses from net sales.

In the nonoperating activities sections, items are generally reported at the net amount. Thus, if a company received a $2,500 insurance settlement on vandalism losses of $2,700, the loss is reported at $200. Note, too, that the results of the two nonoperating sections are netted. The difference is added to or subtracted from income from operations to determine net income. It is not uncommon for companies to combine these two nonoperating sections into a single "Other revenues and expenses" section.

ACCOUNTING IN ACTION *Business Insight*

During a recent quarter, the earnings of computer chip maker Intel shot up 79 percent. But enthusiasm about the huge jump was dampened by the fact that some analysts questioned the earnings figure. The analysts were concerned because included in the ordinary earnings figure were a variety of special items and "one-time" gains from sales of investments. The analysts would prefer that these items were reported separately, under "Other revenues and expenses." In evaluating the company, some analysts simply ignore the investment gains.

Subgrouping of Operating Expenses

In larger companies, operating expenses are often subdivided into selling expenses and administrative expenses, as illustrated in Illustration 5-11. **Selling expenses** are those associated with making sales. They include expenses for sales promotion as well as expenses of completing the sale, such as delivery and shipping. **Administrative expenses** (sometimes called general expenses) relate to general operating activities such as personnel management, accounting, and store security.

When subgroupings are made, some expenses may have to be prorated (e.g., 70% to selling and 30% to administrative expenses). For example, if a store building is used for both selling and general functions, building expenses such as depreciation, utilities, and property taxes will need to be allocated.

Any reasonable classification of expenses that serves to inform those who use the statement is satisfactory. The present tendency in statements prepared for management's internal use is to present in considerable detail expense data grouped along lines of responsibility.

SINGLE-STEP INCOME STATEMENT

Another income statement format is the **single-step income statement**. The statement is so named because only one step, subtracting total expenses from total revenues, is required in determining net income (or net loss).

In a single-step statement, all data are classified under two categories: (1) revenues and (2) expenses. The **revenues** category includes both operating revenues and other revenues and gains. The **expenses** category includes cost of goods sold, operating expenses, and other expenses and losses. A condensed single-step statement for Sellers Electronix is shown in Illustration 5-12.

> **ETHICS NOTE**
>
> At the end of a celebratory lunch the employees of a sales department each gave the manager $10, and he paid the bill with his charge card. During the next week you notice that the manager reported the full amount of the lunch bill on his expense report (and requested reimbursement). When this question was posed to the CEO of Intel, he suggested that an appropriate action would be to report the problem anonymously to the internal audit staff for investigation. What would you do? Does it make a difference if the company is large or small?

Illustration 5-12

Single-step income statement

SELLERS ELECTRONIX Income Statement For the Year Ended December 31, 2002		
Revenues		
Net sales		$460,000
Interest revenue		3,000
Gain on sale of equipment		600
Total revenues		463,600
Expenses		
Cost of goods sold	$316,000	
Selling expenses	76,000	
Administrative expenses	38,000	
Interest expense	1,800	
Casualty loss from vandalism	200	
Total expenses		432,000
Net income		$ 31,600

There are two primary reasons for using the single-step format: (1) A company does not realize any type of profit or income until total revenues exceed total expenses, so it makes sense to divide the statement into these two categories. (2) The format is simpler and easier to read than the multiple-step format. But for homework problems, the single-step format should be used only when it is specifically requested.

CLASSIFIED BALANCE SHEET

In the balance sheet, merchandise inventory is reported as a current asset immediately below accounts receivable. Recall from Chapter 4 that items are listed under current assets in their order of liquidity. Merchandise inventory is less liquid than accounts receivable because the goods must first be sold and then collection must be made from the customer. Illustration 5-13 presents the assets section of a classified balance sheet for Sellers Electronix.

HELPFUL HINT
Merchandise inventory is a current asset because it is expected to be sold within one year or the operating cycle, whichever is longer.

Illustration 5-13

Assets section of a classified balance sheet (partial)

HELPFUL HINT
The $40,000 is the cost of the inventory on hand, not its expected selling price.

SELLERS ELECTRONIX Balance Sheet (partial) December 31, 2002		
Assets		
Current assets		
Cash		$ 9,500
Accounts receivable		16,100
Merchandise inventory		40,000
Prepaid insurance		1,800
Total current assets		67,400
Property, plant, and equipment		
Store equipment	$80,000	
Less: Accumulated depreciation—store equipment	24,000	56,000
Total assets		$123,400

BEFORE YOU GO ON...

► *REVIEW IT*

1. Determine **Lands' End's** gross profit rate for 2000 and 1999. Indicate whether it increased or decreased from 1999 to 2000. The answer to this question is provided on page 221.
2. What are nonoperating activities, and how are they reported in the income statement?
3. How does a single-step income statement differ from a multiple-step income statement?

 LOOK BACK AT OUR FEATURE STORY

Refer back to the Feature Story about **Buy.com** at the beginning of the chapter, and answer the following questions.

1. What is the business of Buy.com? What makes it attractive to consumers?
2. How much inventory does Buy.com carry?
3. How does Buy.com's operating cycle differ from those of other retailers because of its unique merchandising system?

4. In what way might Buy.com's unique method of merchandising affect the general ledger accounts used?

5. How does Buy.com expect to sell products below cost and still remain in business long term?

SOLUTION

1. Buy.com is a Web retailer that sells and delivers goods directly from wholesalers to consumers. Buy.com's slogan is, "The lowest prices on earth." The company is committed to being the price leader—even if it means losing money on every sale.

2. Buy.com has no inventory. It is a *virtual* corporation that advertises on a Web site and places orders with wholesalers who deliver direct to customers from whom Buy.com has taken orders.

3. Buy.com's operating cycle is more like that of a service company than a merchandiser because it carries no inventory. Therefore, the operating cycle is abbreviated—cash to accounts receivable to cash.

4. Buy.com's general ledger will contain no Merchandise Inventory account and may or may not contain the following accounts: Freight-in, Freight-out, Purchase Returns and Allowances, Sales Returns and Allowances, Purchase Discounts, and Sales Discounts. The use of these accounts depends on the agreement Buy.com has with it suppliers (the wholesalers and distributors who deliver direct to customers) and with its customers.

5. Buy.com is trying to create a brand synonymous with low price. If it becomes the leading e-commerce portal, its site becomes valuable ad space. Buy.com hopes to make up its deficit through advertising revenues.

☑ THE NAVIGATOR

DEMONSTRATION PROBLEM

The adjusted trial balance columns of the work sheet for the year ended December 31, 2002, for Dykstra Company are as follows.

Additional Demonstration Problem

Debit		Credit	
Cash	14,500	Accumulated Depreciation	18,000
Accounts Receivable	11,100	Notes Payable	25,000
Merchandise Inventory	29,000	Accounts Payable	10,600
Prepaid Insurance	2,500	Gene Dykstra, Capital	81,000
Store Equipment	95,000	Sales	536,800
Gene Dykstra, Drawing	12,000	Interest Revenue	2,500
Sales Returns and Allowances	6,700		673,900
Sales Discounts	5,000		
Cost of Goods Sold	363,400		
Freight-out	7,600		
Advertising Expense	12,000		
Store Salaries Expense	56,000		
Utilities Expense	18,000		
Rent Expense	24,000		
Depreciation Expense	9,000		
Insurance Expense	4,500		
Interest Expense	3,600		
	673,900		

Instructions

Prepare an income statement assuming Dykstra Company does not use subgroupings for operating expenses.

ACTION PLAN

- Remember that the key components of the income statement are net sales, cost of goods sold, gross profit, total operating expenses, and net income (loss). Report these components in the right-hand column of the income statement.

- Put nonoperating items after income from operations.

SOLUTION TO DEMONSTRATION PROBLEM

DYKSTRA COMPANY
Income Statement
For the Year Ended December 31, 2002

Sales revenues			
Sales			$536,800
Less: Sales returns and allowances	$6,700		
Sales discounts	5,000		11,700
Net sales			525,100
Cost of goods sold			363,400
Gross profit			161,700
Operating expenses			
Store salaries expense	56,000		
Rent expense	24,000		
Utilities expense	18,000		
Advertising expense	12,000		
Depreciation expense	9,000		
Freight-out	7,600		
Insurance expense	4,500		
Total operating expenses			131,100
Income from operations			30,600
Other revenues and gains			
Interest revenue	2,500		
Other expenses and losses			
Interest expense	3,600		1,100
Net income			$ 29,500

---

*S*UMMARY OF *STUDY OBJECTIVES*

1. *Identify the differences between a service enterprise and a merchandiser.* Because of inventory, a merchandiser has sales revenue, cost of goods sold, and gross profit. To account for inventory, a merchandiser must choose between a perpetual inventory system and a periodic inventory system.

2. *Explain the entries for purchases under a perpetual inventory system.* The Merchandise Inventory account is debited for all purchases of merchandise, freight-in, and other costs, and it is credited for purchase discounts and purchase returns and allowances.

3. *Explain the entries for sales revenues under a perpetual inventory system.* When inventory is sold, Accounts Receivable (or Cash) is debited, and Sales is credited for the **selling price** of the merchandise. At the same time, Cost of Goods Sold is debited, and Merchandise Inventory is credited for the **cost** of the inventory items sold.

4. *Explain the steps in the accounting cycle for a merchandiser.* Each of the required steps in the accounting cycle for a

service enterprise applies to a merchandiser. A work sheet is again an optional step. Under a perpetual inventory system, the Merchandise Inventory account must be adjusted to agree with the physical count.

5. *Distinguish between a multiple-step and a single-step income statement.* A multiple-step income statement shows numerous steps in determining net income, including nonoperating activities sections. In a single-step income statement all data are classified under two categories, revenues or expenses, and net income is determined by one step.

6. *Explain the computation and importance of gross profit.* Gross profit is computed by subtracting cost of goods sold from net sales. Gross profit represents the merchandising profit of a company. The amount and trend of gross profit are closely watched by management and other interested parties.

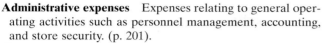

GLOSSARY

Administrative expenses   Expenses relating to general operating activities such as personnel management, accounting, and store security. (p. 201).

Contra revenue account   An account that is offset against a revenue account on the income statement. (p. 193).

Cost of goods sold   The total cost of merchandise sold during the period. (p. 184).

FOB destination   Freight terms indicating that the goods will be placed free on board at the buyer's place of business, and the seller pays the freight costs. (p. 189).

FOB shipping point   Freight terms indicating that goods are placed free on board the carrier by the seller, and the buyer pays the freight costs. (p. 189).

Gross profit   The excess of net sales over the cost of goods sold. (p. 184).

Income from operations   Income from a company's principal operating activity; determined by subtracting cost of goods sold and operating expenses from net sales. (p. 200).

Multiple-step income statement   An income statement that shows numerous steps in determining net income (or net loss). (p. 197).

Net sales   Sales less sales returns and allowances and sales discounts. (p. 198).

Operating expenses   Expenses incurred in the process of earning sales revenues that are deducted from gross profit in the income statement. (p. 184).

Other expenses and losses   A nonoperating activities section of the income statement that shows expenses from auxiliary operations and losses unrelated to the company's operations. (p. 199).

Other revenues and gains   A nonoperating activities section of the income statement that shows revenues from auxiliary operations and gains unrelated to the company's operations. (p. 199).

Periodic inventory system   An inventory system in which detailed records are not maintained throughout the accounting period and the cost of goods sold is determined only at the end of an accounting period. (p. 186).

Perpetual inventory system   An inventory system in which the cost of each inventory item is maintained throughout the accounting period and detailed records continuously show the inventory that should be on hand. (p. 186).

Purchase discount   A cash discount claimed by a buyer for prompt payment of a balance due. (p. 190).

Purchase invoice   A document that supports each credit purchase. (p. 188).

Sales discount   A reduction given by a seller for prompt payment of a credit sale. (p. 193).

Sales invoice   A document that supports each credit sale. (p. 192).

Sales revenue (sales)   Primary source of revenue in a merchandising company. (p. 184).

Selling expenses   Expenses associated with making sales. (p. 201).

Single-step income statement   An income statement that shows only one step in determining net income (or net loss). (p. 201).

APPENDIX *Work Sheet for a Merchandiser*

USING A WORK SHEET

As indicated in Chapter 4, a work sheet enables financial statements to be prepared before the adjusting entries are journalized and posted. The steps in preparing a work sheet for a merchandiser are the same as they are for a service enterprise (see page 135). The work sheet for Sellers Electronix is shown in Illustration 5A-1 (on page 206). The unique accounts for a merchandiser using a perpetual inventory system are shown in capital letters in red.

STUDY OBJECTIVE 7

Prepare a work sheet for a merchandiser.

TRIAL BALANCE COLUMNS

Data for the trial balance are obtained from the ledger balances of Sellers Electronix at December 31. The amount shown for Merchandise Inventory, $40,500, is the year-end inventory amount from the perpetual inventory system.

Illustration 5A-1

Work sheet for
merchandiser

SELLERS ELECTRONIX
Work Sheet
For the Year Ended December 31, 2002

	Trial Balance Dr.	Trial Balance Cr.	Adjustments Dr.	Adjustments Cr.	Adjusted Trial Balance Dr.	Adjusted Trial Balance Cr.	Income Statement Dr.	Income Statement Cr.	Balance Sheet Dr.	Balance Sheet Cr.
Cash	9,500				9,500				9,500	
Accounts Receivable	16,100				16,100				16,100	
MERCHANDISE INVENTORY	40,500			(a) 500	40,000				40,000	
Prepaid Insurance	3,800			(b) 2,000	1,800				1,800	
Store Equipment	80,000				80,000				80,000	
Accumulated Depreciation		16,000		(c) 8,000		24,000				24,000
Accounts Payable		20,400				20,400				20,400
R.A. Lamb, Capital		83,000				83,000				83,000
R.A. Lamb, Drawing	15,000				15,000				15,000	
SALES		480,000				480,000		480,000		
SALES RETURNS AND ALLOWANCES	12,000				12,000		12,000			
SALES DISCOUNTS	8,000				8,000		8,000			
COST OF GOODS SOLD	315,500		(a) 500		316,000		316,000			
Freight-out	7,000				7,000		7,000			
Advertising Expense	16,000				16,000		16,000			
Rent Expense	19,000				19,000		19,000			
Store Salaries Expense	40,000		(d) 5,000		45,000		45,000			
Utilities Expense	17,000				17,000		17,000			
Totals	599,400	599,400								
Insurance Expense			(b) 2,000		2,000		2,000			
Depreciation Expense			(c) 8,000		8,000		8,000			
Salaries Payable				(d) 5,000		5,000				5,000
Totals			15,000	15,000	612,400	612,400	450,000	480,000	162,400	132,400
Net Income							30,000			30,000
Totals							480,000	480,000	162,400	162,400

Key: (a) Adjustment to inventory on hand, (b) Insurance expired, (c) Depreciation expense, (d) Salaries accrued.

ADJUSTMENTS COLUMNS

A merchandiser generally has the same types of adjustments as a service company. As you see in the work sheet, adjustments (b), (c), and (d) are for insurance, depreciation, and salaries. These adjustments were also required for Pioneer Advertising Agency, as illustrated in Chapters 3 and 4. Adjustment (a) was required to adjust the perpetual inventory carrying amount to the actual count.

After all adjustments data are entered on the work sheet, the equality of the adjustments column totals is established. The balances in all accounts are then extended to the adjusted trial balance columns.

ADJUSTED TRIAL BALANCE

The adjusted trial balance shows the balance of all accounts after adjustment at the end of the accounting period.

INCOME STATEMENT COLUMNS

The accounts and balances that affect the income statement are transferred from the adjusted trial balance columns to the income statement columns. For Sellers Electronix, Sales of $480,000 is shown in the credit column. The contra revenue accounts Sales Returns and Allowances $12,000 and Sales Discounts $8,000 are shown in the debit column. The difference of $460,000 is the net sales shown on the income statement (Illustration 5-11).

Finally, all the credits in the income statement column should be totaled and compared to the total of the debits in the income statement column. If the credits exceed the debits, the company has net income. In Sellers Electronix's case there was net income of $30,000. If the debits exceed the credits, the company would report a net loss.

BALANCE SHEET COLUMNS

The major difference between the balance sheets of a service company and a merchandiser is inventory. For Sellers Electronix, the ending inventory amount of $40,000 is shown in the balance sheet debit column. The information to prepare the owner's equity statement is also found in these columns. That is, the capital account of R. A. Lamb is $83,000. The drawings for R. A. Lamb are $15,000. Net income results when the total of the debit column exceeds the total of the credit column in the balance sheet columns. A net loss results when the total of the credits exceeds the total of the debit balances.

SUMMARY OF STUDY OBJECTIVE

7. Prepare a work sheet for a merchandiser. The steps in preparing a work sheet for a merchandiser are the same as they are for a service company. The unique accounts for a merchandiser are Merchandise Inventory, Sales, Sales Returns and Allowances, Sales Discounts, and Cost of Goods Sold.

Note: All **asterisked** Questions, Exercises, and Problems relate to material in the appendix to the chapter.

Chapter 5 Self-Test

SELF-STUDY QUESTIONS

Answers are at the end of the chapter.

(SO 1) **1.** Gross profit will result if:
   a. operating expenses are less than net income.
   b. sales revenues are greater than operating expenses.
   c. sales revenues are greater than cost of goods sold.
   d. operating expenses are greater than cost of goods sold.

(SO 2) **2.** Under a perpetual inventory system, when goods are purchased for resale by a company:
   a. purchases on account are debited to Merchandise Inventory.
   b. purchases on account are debited to Purchases.
   c. purchase returns are debited to Purchase Returns and Allowances.
   d. freight costs are debited to Freight-out.

(SO 3) **3.** The sales accounts that normally have a debit balance are:
   a. Sales Discounts.
   b. Sales Returns and Allowances.
   c. both (a) and (b).
   d. neither (a) nor (b).

4. A credit sale of $750 is made on June 13, terms 2/10, (SO 3) net/30. A return of $50 is granted on June 16. The amount received as payment in full on June 23 is:
   a. $700.
   b. $686.
   c. $685.
   d. $650.

5. Which of the following accounts will normally appear in (SO 3) the ledger of a merchandising company that uses a perpetual inventory system?
   a. Purchases.
   b. Freight-in.
   c. Cost of Goods Sold.
   d. Purchase Discounts.

(SO 5) **6.** The multiple-step income statement for a merchandiser shows each of the following features *except*:
   a. gross profit.
   b. cost of goods sold.
   c. a sales revenue section.
   d. investing activities section.

(SO 6) **7.** If sales revenues are $400,000, cost of goods sold is $310,000, and operating expenses are $60,000, the gross profit is:
   a. $30,000.
   b. $90,000.
   c. $340,000.
   d. $400,000.

(SO 5) **8.** In a single-step income statement:
   a. gross profit is reported.
   b. cost of goods sold is not reported.

   c. sales revenues and "other revenues and gains" are reported in the revenues section of the income statement.
   d. operating income is separately reported.

9. Which of the following appears on both a single-step and (SO 5) a multiple-step income statement?
   a. sales.
   b. gross profit.
   c. income from operations.
   d. cost of goods sold.

*10. In a work sheet, Merchandise Inventory is shown in the (SO 7) following columns:
   a. Adjusted trial balance debit and balance sheet debit.
   b. Income statement debit and balance sheet debit.
   c. Income statement credit and balance sheet debit.
   d. Income statement credit and adjusted trial balance debit.

Questions

1. (a) "The steps in the accounting cycle for a merchandising company are different from the accounting cycle for a service enterprise." Do you agree or disagree? (b) Is the measurement of net income for a merchandiser conceptually the same as for a service enterprise? Explain.

2. Why is the normal operating cycle for a merchandiser likely to be longer than for a service company?

3. (a) How do the components of revenues and expenses differ between a merchandiser and a service enterprise? (b) Explain the income measurement process in a merchandising company.

4. How does income measurement differ between a merchandiser and a service company?

5. When is cost of goods sold determined in a perpetual inventory system?

6. Distinguish between FOB shipping point and FOB destination. Identify the freight terms that will result in a debit to Merchandise Inventory by the purchaser and a debit to Freight-out by the seller.

7. Explain the meaning of the credit terms 2/10, n/30.

8. Goods costing $2,000 are purchased on account on July 15 with credit terms of 2/10, n/30. On July 18 a $200 credit memo is received from the supplier for damaged goods. Give the journal entry on July 24 to record payment of the balance due within the discount period using a perpetual inventory system.

9. Joan Hollins believes revenues from credit sales may be earned before they are collected in cash. Do you agree? Explain.

10. (a) What is the primary source document for recording (1) cash sales, (2) credit sales, and (3) sales returns and allowances? (b) Using XXs for amounts, give the journal entry for each of the transactions in part (a).

11. A credit sale is made on July 10 for $900, terms 2/10, n/30. On July 12, $100 of goods are returned for credit. Give the journal entry on July 19 to record the receipt of the balance due within the discount period.

12. Explain why the Merchandise Inventory account will usually require adjustment at year-end.

13. Prepare the closing entries for the Sales account, assuming a balance of $200,000 and the Cost of Goods Sold account with a $130,000 balance.

14. What merchandising account(s) will appear in the post-closing trial balance?

15. Frank Voris Co. has sales revenue of $115,000, cost of goods sold of $70,000, and operating expenses of $20,000. What is its gross profit?

16. Elizabeth Sherrick Company reports net sales of $800,000, gross profit of $570,000, and net income of $200,000. What are its operating expenses?

17. Identify the distinguishing features of an income statement for a merchandising company.

18. Identify the sections of a multiple-step income statement that relate to (a) operating activities, and (b) nonoperating activities.

19. Distinguish between the types of functional groupings of operating expenses. What problem is created by these groupings?

20. How does the single-step form of income statement differ from the multiple-step form?

*21. Indicate the columns of the work sheet in which (a) merchandise inventory and (b) cost of goods sold will be shown.

BRIEF EXERCISES

BE5-1 Presented below are the components in Sang Nam Company's income statement. Determine the missing amounts.

Compute missing amounts in determining net income.
(SO 1)

	Sales	Cost of Goods Sold	Gross Profit	Operating Expenses	Net Income
(a)	$75,000	?	$31,500	?	$10,800
(b)	$108,000	$70,000	?	?	$29,500
(c)	?	$71,900	$99,600	$39,500	?

BE5-2 Keo Company buys merchandise on account from Cesar Company. The selling price of the goods is $800, and the cost of the goods is $560. Both companies use perpetual inventory systems. Journalize the transaction on the books of both companies.

Journalize perpetual inventory entries.
(SO 2, 3)

BE5-3 Prepare the journal entries to record the following transactions on Rowen Company's books using a perpetual inventory system.

Journalize sales transactions.
(SO 3)

(a) On March 2, Rowen Company sold $800,000 of merchandise to Mosquera Company, terms 2/10, n/30. The cost of the merchandise sold was $580,000.

(b) On March 6, Mosquera Company returned $120,000 of the merchandise purchased on March 2 because it was defective. The cost of the returned merchandise was $90,000.

(c) On March 12, Rowen Company received the balance due from Mosquera Company.

BE5-4 From the information in BE5-3, prepare the journal entries to record these transactions on Mosquera Company's books under a perpetual inventory system.

Journalize purchase transactions.
(SO 2)

BE5-5 Rafeul Huda Company provides the following information for the month ended October 31, 2002: Sales on credit $280,000, cash sales $100,000 sales discounts $11,000, sales returns and allowances $20,000. Prepare the sales revenues section of the income statement based on this information.

Prepare sales revenues section of income statement.
(SO 3)

BE5-6 At year-end the perpetual inventory records of Kren Company showed merchandise inventory of $98,000. The company determined, however, that its actual inventory on hand was $97,100. Record the necessary adjusting entry.

Prepare adjusting entry for merchandise inventory.
(SO 4)

BE5-7 Prasad Company has the following merchandise account balances: Sales $180,000, Sales Discounts $2,000, Cost of Goods Sold $105,000, and Merchandise Inventory $40,000. Prepare the entries to record the closing of these items to Income Summary.

Prepare closing entries for merchandise accounts.
(SO 4)

BE5-8 ✏▷ Explain where each of the following items would appear on (1) a multiple-step income statement, and on (2) a single-step income statement: **(a)** gain on sale of equipment, **(b)** casualty loss from vandalism, and **(c)** cost of goods sold.

Contrast presentation in multiple-step and single-step income statements.
(SO 5)

BE5-9 Assume Cajon Company has the following account balances: Sales $500,000, Sales Returns and Allowances $15,000, Cost of Goods Sold $350,000, Selling Expenses $70,000, and Administrative Expenses $40,000. Compute the following: **(a)** net sales, **(b)** gross profit, and **(c)** income from operations.

Compute net sales, gross profit, and income from operations.
(SO 3, 5, 6)

*BE5-10 Presented below is the format of the work sheet presented in the chapter.

Identify work sheet columns for selected accounts.
(SO 7)

Trial Balance		Adjustments		Adjusted Trial Balance		Income Statement		Balance Sheet	
Dr.	Cr.	Dr.	Cr.	Dr.	Cr.	Dr.	Cr.	Dr.	Cr.

Indicate where the following items will appear on the work sheet: **(a)** Cash, **(b)** Merchandise Inventory, **(c)** Sales, **(d)** Cost of goods sold.

Example:
Cash: Trial balance debit column; Adjusted trial balance debit column; and Balance sheet debit column.

EXERCISES

Journalize purchases transactions.
(SO 2)

E5-1 Information related to Munoz Co. is presented below.

1. On April 5, purchased merchandise from Freeman Company for $17,000 terms 2/10, net/30, FOB shipping point.
2. On April 6 paid freight costs of $900 on merchandise purchased from Freeman.
3. On April 7, purchased equipment on account for $26,000.
4. On April 8, returned damaged merchandise to Freeman Company and was granted a $3,000 allowance.
5. On April 15 paid the amount due to Freeman Company in full.

Instructions

(a) Prepare the journal entries to record these transactions on the books of Munoz Co. under a perpetual inventory system.
(b) Assume that Munoz Co. paid the balance due to Freeman Company on May 4 instead of April 15. Prepare the journal entry to record this payment.

Journalize perpetual inventory entries.
(SO 2, 3)

E5-2 On September 1, Roth Office Supply had an inventory of 30 pocket calculators at a cost of $20 each. The company uses a perpetual inventory system. During September, the following transactions occurred.

Sept. 6 Purchased 80 calculators at $19 each from Lanza Co. for cash.
9 Paid freight of $80 on calculators purchased from Lanza Co.
10 Returned 2 calculators to Lanza Co. for $40 credit (including freight) because they did not meet specifications.
12 Sold 26 calculators costing $20 (including freight) for $31 each to Really Big Book Store, terms n/30.
14 Granted credit of $31 to Really Big Book Store for the return of one calculator that was not ordered.
20 Sold 30 calculators costing $20 for $31 each to Mallik Card Shop, terms n/30.

Instructions
Journalize the September transactions.

Prepare purchase and sale entries and closing entries.
(SO 2, 3)

E5-3 On June 10, Kogan Company purchased $6,000 of merchandise from R. Rego Company FOB shipping point, terms 2/10, n/30. Kogan pays the freight costs of $300 on June 11. Damaged goods totaling $400 are returned to R. Rego for credit on June 12. The scrap value of these goods is $200. On June 19, Kogan pays R. Rego Company in full, less the purchase discount. Both companies use a perpetual inventory system.

Instructions

(a) Prepare separate entries for each transaction on the books of Kogan Company.
(b) Prepare separate entries for each transaction for Rego Company. The merchandise purchased by Kogan on June 10 had cost Rego $3,000.

Journalize sales transactions.
(SO 3)

E5-4 Presented below are transactions related to R. Garg Company.

1. On December 3, R. Garg Company sold $480,000 of merchandise to G. Wallace Co., terms 2/10, n/30, FOB shipping point. The cost of the merchandise sold was $320,000.
2. On December 8, G. Wallace Co. was granted an allowance of $25,000 for merchandise purchased on December 3.
3. On December 13, R. Garg Company received the balance due from G. Wallace Co.

Instructions

(a) Prepare the journal entries to record these transactions on the books of R. Garg Company using a perpetual inventory system.
(b) Assume that R. Garg Company received the balance due from G. Wallace Co. on January 2 of the following year instead of December 13. Prepare the journal entry to record the receipt of payment on January 2.

Prepare sales revenues section and closing entries.
(SO 3, 4, 5)

E5-5 The adjusted trial balance of Dimitry Company shows the following data pertaining to sales at the end of its fiscal year October 31, 2002: Sales $800,000, Freight-out $12,000, Sales Returns and Allowances $25,000, and Sales Discounts $15,000.

Instructions

(a) Prepare the sales revenues section of the income statement.

(b) Prepare separate closing entries for (1) sales, and (2) the contra accounts to sales.

E5-6 Presented is information related to Croce Co. for the month of January 2002.

Prepare adjusting and closing entries.
(SO 4)

Ending inventory per		Salary expense	$ 61,000
perpetual records	$ 21,600	Sales discounts	8,000
Ending inventory actually		Sales returns and allowances	13,000
on hand	21,200	Sales	350,000
Cost of goods sold	208,000		
Freight-out	7,000		
Insurance expense	12,000		
Rent expense	20,000		

Instructions

(a) Prepare the necessary adjusting entry for inventory.

(b) Prepare the necessary closing entries.

E5-7 In its income statement for the year ended December 31, 2002, Berman Company reported the following condensed data.

Prepare multiple-step and single-step income statements.
(SO 5)

Administrative expenses	$ 435,000	Selling expenses	$ 490,000
Cost of goods sold	1,289,000	Loss on sale of equipment	10,000
Interest expense	70,000	Net sales	2,350,000
Interest revenue	45,000		

Instructions

(a) Prepare a multiple-step income statement.

(b) Prepare a single-step income statement.

E5-8 An inexperienced accountant for Chinchilla Company made the following errors in recording merchandising transactions.

Prepare correcting entries for sales and purchases.
(SO 2, 3)

1. A $175 refund to a customer for faulty merchandise was debited to Sales $175 and credited to Cash $175.
2. A $200 credit purchase of supplies was debited to Merchandise Inventory $200 and credited to Cash $200.
3. An $80 sales discount was debited to Sales.
4. A cash payment of $30 for freight on merchandise purchases was debited to Freight-out $300 and credited to Cash $300.

Instructions

Prepare separate correcting entries for each error, assuming that the incorrect entry is not reversed. (Omit explanations.)

E5-9 Presented below is financial information for two different companies.

Compute missing amounts.
(SO 5, 6)

	Amoruso Company	Tamburri Company
Sales	$90,000	(d)
Sales returns	(a)	$ 5,000
Net sales	83,000	95,000
Cost of goods sold	56,000	(e)
Gross profit	(b)	38,000
Operating expenses	15,000	(f)
Net income	(c)	15,000

Instructions

Determine the missing amounts.

Complete work sheet.
(SO 7)

*E5-10   Presented below are selected accounts for Garland Company as reported in the work sheet at the end of May 2002.

Accounts	Adjusted Trial Balance		Income Statement		Balance Sheet	
	Dr.	Cr.	Dr.	Cr.	Dr.	Cr.
Cash	9,000					
Merchandise Inventory	80,000					
Sales		450,000				
Sales Returns and Allowances	10,000					
Sales Discounts	7,000					
Cost of Goods Sold	250,000					

Instructions

Complete the work sheet by extending amounts reported in the adjusted trial balance to the appropriate columns in the work sheet. Do not total individual columns.

Problems: Set A

Journalize purchase and sales transactions under a perpetual inventory system.
(SO 2, 3)

P5-1A   Travel Warehouse distributes suitcases to retail stores and extends credit terms of 1/10, n/30 to all of its customers. At the end of July, Travel's inventory consisted of 40 suitcases purchased at $30 each. During the month of July the following merchandising transactions occurred.

July 1   Purchased 50 suitcases on account for $30 each from Suitcase Manufacturers, FOB destination, terms 1/15, n/30. The appropriate party also made a cash payment of $100 for freight on this date.
3   Sold 40 suitcases on account to Luggage World for $50 each.
9   Paid Suitcase Manufacturers in full.
12   Received payment in full from Luggage World.
17   Sold 30 suitcases on account to The Travel Spot for $50 each.
18   Purchased 60 suitcases on account for $1,700 from Vacation Manufacturers, FOB shipping point, terms 2/10, n/30. The appropriate party also made a cash payment of $100 for freight on this date.
20   Received $300 credit (including freight) for 10 suitcases returned to Vacation Manufacturers.
21   Received payment in full from The Travel Spot.
22   Sold 40 suitcases on account to Vacations-Are-Us for $50 each.
30   Paid Vacation Manufacturers in full.
31   Granted Vacations-Are-Us $250 credit for 5 suitcases returned costing $150.

Travel Warehouse's chart of accounts includes the following: No. 101 Cash, No. 112 Accounts Receivable, No. 120 Merchandise Inventory, No. 201 Accounts Payable, No. 401 Sales, No. 412 Sales Returns and Allowances, No. 414 Sales Discounts, No. 505 Cost of Goods Sold.

Instructions

Journalize the transactions for the month of July for Travel Warehouse using a perpetual inventory system.

P5-2A Hubbs Distributing Company completed the following merchandising transactions in the month of April. At the beginning of April, the ledger of Hubbs showed Cash of $9,000 and M. Hubbs, Capital of $9,000.

Journalize, post, and prepare a partial income statement. (SO 2, 3, 5, 6)

Peachtree

Apr. 2 Purchased merchandise on account from Leshner Supply Co. $5,900, terms 2/10, n/30.

4 Sold merchandise on account $5,200, FOB destination, terms 2/10, n/30. The cost of the merchandise sold was $4,100.

5 Paid $200 freight on April 4 sale.

6 Received credit from Leshner Supply Co. for merchandise returned $300.

11 Paid Leshner Supply Co. in full, less discount.

13 Received collections in full, less discounts, from customers billed on April 4.

14 Purchased merchandise for cash $4,400.

16 Received refund from supplier on cash purchase of April 14, $500.

18 Purchased merchandise from Testa Distributors $4,200, FOB shipping point, terms 2/10, n/30.

20 Paid freight on April 18 purchase $100.

23 Sold merchandise for cash $6,400. The merchandise sold had a cost of $5,120.

26 Purchased merchandise for cash $2,300.

27 Paid Testa Distributors in full, less discount.

29 Made refunds to cash customers for defective merchandise $90. The returned merchandise had a scrap value of $30.

30 Sold merchandise on account $3,700, terms n/30. The cost of the merchandise sold was $3,000.

Hubbs Company's chart of accounts includes the following: No. 101 Cash, No. 112 Accounts Receivable, No. 120 Merchandise Inventory, No. 201 Accounts Payable, No. 301 M. Hubbs, Capital, No. 401 Sales, No. 412 Sales Returns and Allowances, No. 414 Sales Discounts, No. 505 Cost of Goods Sold, and No. 644 Freight-out.

Instructions
(a) Journalize the transactions using a perpetual inventory system.
(b) Enter the beginning cash and capital balances, and post the transactions. (Use J1 for the journal reference.)
(c) Prepare the income statement through gross profit for the month of April 2002.

(c) Gross profit $2,916

P5-3A Gitler Department Store is located near the Village shopping mall. At the end of the company's fiscal year on December 31, 2002, the following accounts appeared in two of its trial balances.

Prepare financial statements and adjusting and closing entries. (SO 4, 5)

	Unadjusted	Adjusted		Unadjusted	Adjusted
Accounts Payable	$ 79,300	$ 79,300	Interest Payable		$ 8,000
Accounts Receivable	50,300	50,300	Interest Revenue	$ 4,000	4,000
Accumulated Depr.—Building	42,100	52,500	Merchandise Inventory	75,000	75,000
Accumulated Depr.—Equipment	29,600	42,900	Mortgage Payable	80,000	80,000
Building	190,000	190,000	Office Salaries Expense	32,000	32,000
Cash	23,000	23,000	Prepaid Insurance	9,600	2,400
L. Gitler, Capital	176,600	176,600	Property Taxes Expense		4,800
Cost of Goods Sold	412,700	412,700	Property Taxes Payable		4,800
Depr. Expense—Building		10,400	Sales Salaries Expense	76,000	76,000
Depr. Expense—Equipment		13,300	Sales	628,000	628,000
L. Gitler, Drawing	28,000	28,000	Sales Commissions Expense	11,000	15,500
Equipment	110,000	110,000	Sales Commissions Payable		4,500
Insurance Expense		7,200	Sales Returns and Allowances	8,000	8,000
Interest Expense	3,000	11,000	Utilities Expense	11,000	11,000

Analysis reveals the following additional data.

1. Insurance expense and utilities expense are 60% selling and 40% administrative.
2. $20,000 of the mortgage payable is due for payment next year.
3. Depreciation on the building and property tax expense are administrative expenses; depreciation on the equipment is a selling expense.

Instructions

(a) Net income $30,100
    Capital $178,700
    Total assets $355,300

(a) Prepare a multiple-step income statement, an owner's equity statement, and a classified balance sheet.
(b) Journalize the adjusting entries that were made.
(c) Journalize the closing entries that are necessary.

Journalize, post, and prepare a trial balance.
(SO 2, 3, 4)

Peachtree

P5-4A Mike Young, a former professional tennis star, operates Mike's Tennis Shop at the Jackson Lake Resort. At the beginning of the current season, the ledger of Mike's Tennis Shop showed Cash $2,500, Merchandise Inventory $1,700, and M. Young, Capital $4,200. The following transactions were completed during April.

Apr. 4 Purchased racquets and balls from Sampras Co. $640, FOB shipping point, terms 3/10, n/30.
6 Paid freight on purchase from Sampras Co. $40.
8 Sold merchandise to members $1,150, terms n/30. The merchandise sold had a cost of $750.
10 Received credit of $40 from Sampras Co. for a damaged racquet that was returned.
11 Purchased tennis shoes from Alan Sports for cash, $300.
13 Paid Sampras Co. in full.
14 Purchased tennis shirts and shorts from Tiger's Sportswear $700, FOB shipping point, terms 2/10, n/60.
15 Received cash refund of $50 from Alan Sports for damaged merchandise that was returned.
17 Paid freight on Tiger's Sportswear purchase $30.
18 Sold merchandise to members $800, terms n/30. The cost of the merchandise sold was $530.
20 Received $500 in cash from members in settlement of their accounts.
21 Paid Tiger's Sportswear in full.
27 Granted an allowance of $30 to members for tennis clothing that did not fit properly.
30 Received cash payments on account from members, $675.

The chart of accounts for the tennis shop includes the following: No. 101 Cash, No. 112 Accounts Receivable, No. 120 Merchandise Inventory, No. 201 Accounts Payable, No. 301 M. Young, Capital, No. 401 Sales, No. 412 Sales Returns and Allowances, No. 505 Cost of Goods Sold.

Instructions

(a) Journalize the April transactions using a perpetual inventory system.
(b) Enter the beginning balances in the ledger accounts and post the April transactions. (Use J1 for the journal reference.)

(c) Total debits $6,150

(c) Prepare a trial balance on April 30, 2002.

Complete accounting cycle beginning with a work sheet.
(SO 4, 5, 6, 7)

*P5-5A The trial balance of Brennan Fashion Center contained the following accounts at November 30, the end of the company's fiscal year.

BRENNAN FASHION CENTER
Trial Balance
November 30, 2002

	Debit	Credit
Cash	$ 28,700	
Accounts Receivable	33,700	
Merchandise Inventory	45,000	
Store Supplies	5,500	
Store Equipment	85,000	
Accumulated Depreciation—Store Equipment		$ 18,000
Delivery Equipment	48,000	
Accumulated Depreciation—Delivery Equipment		6,000
Notes Payable		51,000
Accounts Payable		48,500
C. Brennan, Capital		110,000
C. Brennan, Drawing	12,000	
Sales		759,200
Sales Returns and Allowances	4,200	
Cost of Goods Sold	497,400	
Salaries Expense	140,000	
Advertising Expense	26,400	
Utilities Expense	14,000	
Repair Expense	12,100	
Delivery Expense	16,700	
Rent Expense	24,000	
Totals	$992,700	$992,700

Adjustment data:
1. Store supplies on hand totaled $3,500.
2. Depreciation is $9,000 on the store equipment and $7,000 on the delivery equipment.
3. Interest of $11,000 is accrued on notes payable at November 30.
4. Merchandise inventory actually on hand is $44,400.

Other data:
1. Salaries expense is 70% selling and 30% administrative.
2. Rent expense and utilities expense are 80% selling and 20% administrative.
3. $30,000 of notes payable are due for payment next year.
4. Repair expense is 100% administrative.

Instructions
(a) Enter the trial balance on a work sheet, and complete the work sheet.
(b) Prepare a multiple-step income statement and owner's equity statement for the year and a classified balance sheet as of November 30, 2002.
(c) Journalize the adjusting entries.
(d) Journalize the closing entries.
(e) Prepare a post-closing trial balance.

(a) Adj. trial balance
$1,019,700
Net loss $5,200
(b) Gross profit $257,000
Total assets $203,300

PROBLEMS: SET B

P5-1B   Dazzle Book Warehouse distributes hardback books to retail stores and extends credit terms of 2/10, n/30 to all of its customers. At the end of May, Dazzle's inventory consisted of 240 books purchased at $1,200. During the month of June the following merchandising transactions occurred.

Journalize purchase and sale transactions under a perpetual inventory system.
(SO 2, 3)

June 1	Purchased 130 books on account for $5 each from Reader's World Publishers, FOB destination, terms 1/10, n/30. The appropriate party also made a cash payment of $50 for the freight on this date.
3	Sold 140 books on account to the Book Nook for $10 each.
6	Received $50 credit for 10 books returned to Reader's World Publishers.
9	Paid Reader's World Publishers in full, less discount.
15	Received payment in full from the Book Nook.
17	Sold 120 books on account to Read-A-Lot Bookstore for $10 each.
20	Purchased 120 books on account for $5 each from Read More Publishers, FOB destination, terms 2/15, n/30. The appropriate party also made a cash payment of $50 for the freight on this date.
24	Received payment in full from Read-A-Lot Bookstore.
26	Paid Read More Publishers in full, less discount.
28	Sold 110 books on account to Readers Bookstore for $10 each.
30	Granted Readers Bookstore $150 credit for 15 books returned costing $75.

Dazzle Book Warehouse's chart of accounts includes the following: No. 101 Cash, No. 112 Accounts Receivable, No. 120 Merchandise Inventory, No. 201 Accounts Payable, No. 401 Sales, No. 412 Sales Returns and Allowances, No. 414 Sales Discounts, No. 505 Cost of Goods Sold.

Instructions
Journalize the transactions for the month of June for Dazzle Book Warehouse using a perpetual inventory system.

Journalize, post, and prepare partial income statement.
(SO 2, 3, 5, 6)

P5-2B Eagle Hardware Store completed the following merchandising transactions in the month of May. At the beginning of May, the ledger of Eagle showed Cash of $5,000 and J. Eagle, Capital of $5,000.

May 1	Purchased merchandise on account from Lathrop Wholesale Supply $6,000, terms 2/10, n/30.
2	Sold merchandise on account $4,700, terms 2/10, n/30. The cost of the merchandise sold was $3,100.
5	Received credit from Lathrop Wholesale Supply for merchandise returned $200.
9	Received collections in full, less discounts, from customers billed on sales of $4,500 on May 2.
10	Paid Lathrop Wholesale Supply in full, less discount.
11	Purchased supplies for cash $900.
12	Purchased merchandise for cash $2,400.
15	Received refund for poor quality merchandise from supplier on cash purchase $230.
17	Purchased merchandise from Kumar Distributors $1,900, FOB shipping point, terms 2/10, n/30.
19	Paid freight on May 17 purchase $250.
24	Sold merchandise for cash $6,200. The merchandise sold had a cost of $4,340.
25	Purchased merchandise from Tsai Inc. $1,000, FOB destination, terms 2/10, n/30.
27	Paid Kumar Distributors in full, less discount.
29	Made refunds to cash customers for defective merchandise $100. The returned merchandise had a scrap value of $20.
31	Sold merchandise on account $1,600, terms n/30. The cost of the merchandise sold was $1,120.

Eagle Hardware's chart of accounts includes the following: No. 101 Cash, No. 112 Accounts Receivable, No. 120 Merchandise Inventory, No. 126 Supplies, No. 201 Accounts Payable, No. 301 J. Eagle, Capital, No. 401 Sales, No. 412 Sales Returns and Allowances, No. 414 Sales Discounts, No. 505 Cost of Goods Sold.

Instructions

(a) Journalize the transactions using a perpetual inventory system.

(b) Enter the beginning cash and capital balances and post the transactions. (Use J1 for the journal reference.)

(c) Prepare an income statement through gross profit for the month of May 2002.

(c) Gross profit $3,770

P5-3B Forcina Department Store is located in midtown Metropolis. During the past several years, net income has been declining because of suburban shopping centers. At the end of the company's fiscal year on November 30, 2002, the following accounts appeared in two of its trial balances.

Prepare financial statements and adjusting and closing entries.
(SO 4, 5)

	Unadjusted	Adjusted		Unadjusted	Adjusted
Accounts Payable	$ 47,310	$ 47,310	Interest Revenue	$ 5,000	$ 5,000
Accounts Receivable	11,770	11,770	Merchandise Inventory	36,200	36,200
Accumulated Depr.—Delivery Equip.	15,680	19,680	Notes Payable	46,000	46,000
Accumulated Depr.—Store Equip.	32,300	41,800	Prepaid Insurance	13,500	4,500
Cash	8,000	8,000	Property Tax Expense		3,500
N. Forcina, Capital	84,200	84,200	Property Taxes Payable		3,500
Cost of Goods Sold	633,220	633,220	Rent Expense	19,000	19,000
Delivery Expense	8,200	8,200	Salaries Expense	120,000	120,000
Delivery Equipment	57,000	57,000	Sales	850,000	850,000
Depr. Expense—Delivery Equip.		4,000	Sales Commissions Expense	8,000	12,750
Depr. Expense—Store Equip.		9,500	Sales Commissions Payable		4,750
N. Forcina, Drawing	12,000	12,000	Sales Returns and Allowances	10,000	10,000
Insurance Expense		9,000	Store Equip.	125,000	125,000
Interest Expense	8,000	8,000	Utilities Expense	10,600	10,600

Analysis reveals the following additional data.

1. Salaries expense is 70% selling and 30% administrative.
2. Insurance expense is 50% selling and 50% administrative.
3. Rent expense, utilities expense, and property tax expense are administrative expenses.
4. Notes payable are due in 2005.

Instructions

(a) Prepare a multiple-step income statement, an owner's equity statement, and a classified balance sheet.

(b) Journalize the adjusting entries that were made.

(c) Journalize the closing entries that are necessary.

(a) Net income $7,230
Capital $79,430
Total assets $180,990

P5-4B Gregory Scott, a former professional golf star, operates Greg's Pro Shop at Bay Golf Course. At the beginning of the current season on April 1, the ledger of Greg's Pro Shop showed Cash $2,500, Merchandise Inventory $3,500, and G. Scott, Capital $6,000. The following transactions were completed during April.

Journalize, post, and prepare a trial balance.
(SO 2, 3, 4)

Apr. 5 Purchased golf bags, clubs, and balls on account from Hardy Co. $1,600, FOB shipping point, terms 2/10, n/60.

  7 Paid freight on Hardy purchase $80.

  9 Received credit from Hardy Co. for merchandise returned $100.

  10 Sold merchandise on account to members $1,100, terms n/30. The merchandise sold had a cost of $730.

  12 Purchased golf shoes, sweaters, and other accessories on account from Titleist Sportswear $660, terms 1/10, n/30.

  14 Paid Hardy Co. in full, less discount.

  17 Received credit from Titleist Sportswear for merchandise returned $60.

  20 Made sales on account to members $700, terms n/30. The cost of the merchandise sold was $490, less discount.

  21 Paid Titleist Sportswear in full.

  27 Granted an allowance to members for clothing that did not fit properly $30.

  30 Received payments on account from members $1,200.

The chart of accounts for the pro shop includes the following: No. 101 Cash, No. 112 Accounts Receivable, No. 120 Merchandise Inventory, No. 201 Accounts Payable, No. 301 G. Scott, Capital, No. 401 Sales, No. 412 Sales Returns and Allowances, No. 505 Cost of Goods Sold.

Instructions

(a) Journalize the April transactions using a perpetual inventory system.

(b) Enter the beginning balances in the ledger accounts and post the April transactions. (Use J1 for the journal reference.)

(c) Prepare a trial balance on April 30, 2002.

(c) Total debits $7,800

Complete accounting cycle beginning with a work sheet. (SO 4, 5, 6, 7)

*P5-5B The trial balance of Graham Wholesale Company contained the following accounts at December 31, the end of the company's fiscal year.

GRAHAM WHOLESALE COMPANY
Trial Balance
December 31, 2002

	Debit	Credit
Cash	$ 25,400	
Accounts Receivable	37,600	
Merchandise Inventory	90,000	
Land	92,000	
Buildings	197,000	
Accumulated Depreciation—Buildings		$ 54,000
Equipment	83,500	
Accumulated Depreciation—Equipment		42,400
Notes Payable		50,000
Accounts Payable		37,500
M. Graham, Capital		267,800
M. Graham, Drawing	10,000	
Sales		904,100
Sales Discounts	4,600	
Cost of Goods Sold	709,900	
Salaries Expense	69,800	
Utilities Expense	19,400	
Repair Expense	5,900	
Gas and Oil Expense	7,200	
Insurance Expense	3,500	
Totals	$1,355,800	$1,355,800

Adjustment data:

1. Depreciation is $10,000 on buildings and $9,000 on equipment. (Both are administrative expenses.)
2. Interest of $7,000 is due and unpaid on notes payable at December 31.
3. Merchandise inventory actually on hand is $89,200.

Other data:

1. Salaries are 80% selling and 20% administrative.
2. Utilities expense, repair expense, and insurance expense are 100% administrative.
3. $15,000 of the notes payable are payable next year.
4. Gas and oil expense is a selling expense.

Instructions

(a) Adj. trial balance total $1,381,800
Net income $57,000
(b) Gross profit $188,800
Total assets $409,300

(e) Total debits $524,700

(a) Enter the trial balance on a work sheet, and complete the work sheet.

(b) Prepare a multiple-step income statement and owner's equity statement for the year, and a classified balance sheet at December 31, 2002.

(c) Journalize the adjusting entries.

(d) Journalize the closing entries.

(e) Prepare a post-closing trial balance.

BROADENING YOUR PERSPECTIVE

*F*INANCIAL REPORTING AND ANALYSIS

FINANCIAL REPORTING PROBLEM: Lands' End, Inc.

BYP5-1 The financial statements of **Lands' End, Inc.** are presented in Appendix A at the end of this textbook.

Instructions
Answer the following questions using the Consolidated Statement of Earnings.

(a) What was the percentage change in (1) sales and in (2) net income from 1998 to 1999 and from 1999 to 2000?

(b) What was the company's gross profit rate in 1998, 1999, and 2000?

(c) What was the company's percentage of net income to net sales in 1998, 1999, and 2000? Comment on any trend in this percentage.

COMPARATIVE ANALYSIS PROBLEM: Lands' End vs. Abercrombie & Fitch

BYP5-2 **Lands' End's** financial statements are presented in Appendix A. **Abercrombie & Fitch's** financial statements are presented in Appendix B.

Instructions
(a) Based on the information contained in these financial statements, determine each of the following for each company.
  (1) Gross profit for 2000.
  (2) Gross profit rate for 2000.
  (3) Operating income for 2000.
  (4) Percent change in operating income from 1999 to 2000.

(b) What conclusions concerning the relative profitability of the two companies can be drawn from these data?

INTERPRETING FINANCIAL STATEMENTS: A Global Focus

BYP5-3 In August 1999 it was announced that two giant French retailers, **Carrefour SA** and **Promodes SA**, would merge. A headline in *The Wall Street Journal* blared, "French Retailers Create New Wal-Mart Rival." While **Wal-Mart's** total sales would still exceed those of the combined company, Wal-Mart's international sales are far less than those of the combined company. This is a serious concern for Wal-Mart, since its primary opportunity for future growth lies outside of the United States.

Below are basic financial data for the combined corporation (in French francs) and Wal-Mart (in U.S. dollars). Even though their results are presented in different currencies, by employing ratios we can make some basic comparisons.

	Carrefour/ Promodes (in billions)	Wal-Mart (in billions)
Sales	Fr 298.0	$137.6
Cost of goods sold	274.0	108.7
Operating expenses	9.6	22.4
Net income	5.5	4.4
Total assets	155.0	50.0
Average total assets	140.4	47.7
Current assets	63.5	21.1
Current liabilities	85.8	16.8
Total liabilities	114.2	28.9

Instructions
Compare the two companies by answering the following.

(a) Calculate the gross profit rate for each of the companies, and discuss their relative abilities to control cost of goods sold.

(b) Calculate the operating expense to sales ratio (operating expenses ÷ sales), and discuss the companies' relative abilities to control operating expenses.

(c) What concerns might you have in relying on this comparison?

EXPLORING THE WEB

BYP5-4 No financial decision maker should ever rely solely on the financial information reported in the annual report to make decisions. It is important to keep abreast of financial news. This activity demonstrates how to search for financial news on the Web.

Address: biz.yahoo.com/i *(or go to www.wiley.com/college/weygandt)*

Steps:

1. Type in either Lands' End or Abercrombie & Fitch.
2. Choose **News**.
3. Select an article that sounds interesting to you.

Instructions

(a) What was the source of the article? (For example, Reuters, Businesswire, PR Newswire.)

(b) Pretend that you are a personal financial planner and that one of your clients owns stock in the company. Write a brief memo to your client, summarizing the article and explaining the implications of the article for their investment.

CRITICAL THINKING

GROUP DECISION CASE

BYP5-5 Three years ago, Kathy Webb and her brother-in-law John Utley opened FedCo Department Store. For the first two years, business was good, but the following condensed income results for 2001 were disappointing.

FEDCO DEPARTMENT STORE
Income Statement
For the Year Ended December 31, 2001

Net sales		$700,000
Cost of goods sold		546,000
Gross profit		154,000
Operating expenses		
Selling expenses	$100,000	
Administrative expenses	25,000	125,000
Net income		$ 29,000

Kathy believes the problem lies in the relatively low gross profit rate (gross profit divided by net sales) of 22%. John believes the problem is that operating expenses are too high.

Kathy thinks the gross profit rate can be improved by making both of the following changes:

1. Increase average selling prices by 17%. This increase is expected to lower sales volume so that total sales will increase only 6%.
2. Buy merchandise in larger quantities and take all purchase discounts. These changes are expected to increase the gross profit rate by 3%.

Kathy does not anticipate that these changes will have any effect on operating expenses.

John thinks expenses can be cut by making both of the following changes.

1. Cut 2001 sales salaries of $60,000 in half and give sales personnel a commission of 2% of net sales.
2. Reduce store deliveries to one day per week rather than twice a week; this change will reduce 2001 delivery expenses of $30,000 by 40%.

John feels that these changes will not have any effect on net sales.

Kathy and John come to you for help in deciding the best way to improve net income.

Instructions

With the class divided into groups, answer the following.

(a) Prepare a condensed income statement for 2002 assuming (1) Kathy's changes are implemented and (2) John's ideas are adopted.
(b) What is your recommendation to Kathy and John?
(c) Prepare a condensed income statement for 2002 assuming both sets of proposed changes are made.

COMMUNICATION ACTIVITY

BYP5-6   The following situation is in chronological order.

1. Dexter decides to buy a surfboard.
2. He calls Surfing USA Co. to inquire about their surfboards.
3. Two days later he requests Surfing USA Co. to make him a surfboard.
4. Three days later, Surfing USA Co. sends him a purchase order to fill out.
5. He sends back the purchase order.
6. Surfing USA Co. receives the completed purchase order.
7. Surfing USA Co. completes the surfboard.
8. Dexter picks up the surfboard.
9. Surfing USA Co. bills Dexter.
10. Surfing USA Co. receives payment from Dexter.

Instructions
In a memo to the president of Surfing USA Co., explain the following.

(a) When should Surfing USA Co. record the sale?
(b) Suppose that with his purchase order, Dexter is required to make a down payment. Would that change your answer?

ETHICS CASE

BYP5-7   Rita Pelzer was just hired as the assistant treasurer of Yorkshire Store. The company is a specialty chain store with nine retail stores concentrated in one metropolitan area. Among other things, the payment of all invoices is centralized in one of the departments Rita will manage. Her primary responsibility is to maintain the company's high credit rating by paying all bills when due and to take advantage of all cash discounts.

Jamie Caterino, the former assistant treasurer who has been promoted to treasurer, is training Rita in her new duties. He instructs Rita that she is to continue the practice of preparing all checks "net of discount" and dating the checks the last day of the discount period. "But," Jamie continues, "we always hold the checks at least 4 days beyond the discount period before mailing them. That way we get another 4 days of interest on our money. Most of our creditors need our business and don't complain. And, if they scream about our missing the discount period, we blame it on the mail room or the post office. We've only lost one discount out of every hundred we take that way. I think everybody does it. By the way, welcome to our team!"

Instructions
(a) What are the ethical considerations in this case?
(b) Who are the stakeholders that are harmed or benefitted in this situation?
(c) Should Rita continue the practice started by Jamie? Does she have any choice?

Answers to Self-Study Questions

1. c   **2.** a   **3.** c   **4.** b   **5.** c   **6.** d   **7.** b   **8.** c   **9.** d   **10.** a

Answer to *Lands' End* Review It Question 1, p. 202

For Lands' End, the 2000 gross profit rate is 44.9% ($593 ÷ $1,320). The 1999 gross profit rate was 45% ($617 ÷ $1,371). The rate therefore decreased by 0.1% from 1999 to 2000. All this information was provided in Lands' End's management discussion and analysis section. It also could be computed from the income statement presented.

Remember to go back to the Navigator box on the chapter-opening page and check off your completed work.

INVENTORIES

THE NAVIGATOR ✓

- Understand *Concepts for Review* ❑
- Read *Feature Story* ❑
- Scan *Study Objectives* ❑
- Read *Preview* ❑
- Read text and answer *Before You Go On*
  p. 227 ❑   p. 233 ❑   p. 242 ❑   p. 247 ❑
- Work *Demonstration Problems* ❑
- Review *Summary of Study Objectives* ❑
- Answer *Self-Study Questions* ❑
- Complete *Assignments* ❑

*C*ONCEPTS FOR REVIEW

Before studying this chapter, you should know or, if necessary, review:

   a. The cost principle (Ch. 1, p. 10) and matching principle of accounting.
   (Ch. 3, p. 90)

   b. How to record purchases, sales, and cost of goods sold under a
   perpetual inventory system. (Ch. 5, pp. 187–194)

   c. How to prepare financial statements for a merchandiser. (Ch. 5,
   pp. 197–202)

☑ THE
NAVIGATOR

Taking Stock—from Backpacks to Bicycles

Backpacks and jackets sporting the jagged peaks of the **Mountain Equipment Co-op (MEC)** logo are a familiar sight on hiking trails and campuses. Sales of these popular items help the Vancouver-based co-op to finance its primary goal: to provide members with products and services for wilderness recreational activities at a reasonable cost.

MEC has five retail stores across Canada and a huge market in catalogue sales around the world. It ships everything from climbing ropes, kayaks, and bike helmets to destinations as far away as Japan and South America.

Keeping financial track of the flow of these items is a responsibility of Fara Jumani, a member of the inventory costing group at MEC and a part-time college student. "We have

tens of thousands of items in inventory, and we are adding new ones all the time," says Ms. Jumani. "Because we make a lot of our own clothing goods, we also have a lot of in-house inventory—fabric and supplies that will be used to make products."

MEC tracks the cost of its inventory using the average cost of the various items in inventory, weighted by the number purchased at each different unit cost. (This procedure is called the weighted average cost method.) "Because costs tend to fluctuate," explains Ms. Jumani, "that method best captures our overall costs."

Unlike most retail operations, MEC is not out to make a profit. As

a co-op, it exists to serve its members. "But we have to stay fiscally healthy to do that," points out Ms. Jumani. "If we go bankrupt, we won't be serving anyone." Accounting for inventory—from backpacks to bicycles—is an important part of MEC's fiscal fitness routine.

☑ THE NAVIGATOR

$\mathcal{S}$ TUDY OBJECTIVES

After studying this chapter, you should be able to:

1. Describe the steps in determining inventory quantities.
2. Prepare the entries for purchases and sales of inventory under a periodic inventory system.
3. Determine cost of goods sold under a periodic inventory system.
4. Identify the unique features of the income statement for a merchandiser using a periodic inventory system.
5. Explain the basis of accounting for inventories, and describe the inventory cost flow methods.
6. Explain the financial statement and tax effects of each of the inventory cost flow methods.
7. Explain the lower of cost or market basis of accounting for inventories.
8. Indicate the effects of inventory errors on the financial statements.
9. Compute and interpret inventory turnover.

☑ THE NAVIGATOR

As indicated in the opening story about **Mountain Equipment Co-op**, careful accounting for inventory is necessary to stay in business. In this chapter we will explain the methods used in determining the cost of inventory on hand at the balance sheet date. We also will discuss differences in perpetual and periodic inventory systems, and the effects of inventory errors on a company's financial statements.

The content and organization of Chapter 6 are as follows.

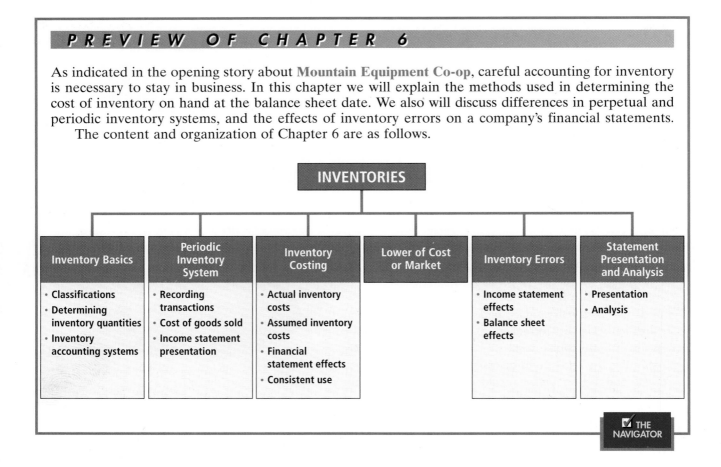

*I*NVENTORY BASICS

In our economy, inventories are an important barometer of business activity. The U.S. Commerce Department publishes monthly inventory data for retailers, wholesalers, and manufacturers. The amount of inventories and the time required to sell the goods on hand are two closely watched indicators. During downturns in the economy, there is an initial buildup of inventories, as it takes longer to sell existing quantities. Inventories generally decrease with an upturn in business activity. A delicate balance must be maintained between too little inventory and too much. A company with too little inventory to meet demand will have dissatisfied customers and sales personnel. One with too much inventory will be burdened with unnecessary carrying costs.

Inventories affect both the balance sheet and the income statement. In the **balance sheet** of merchandising companies, inventory is frequently the most significant current asset. Of course, its amount and relative importance can vary, even for companies in the same industry. For example, **Wal-Mart** reported inventory of $17 billion, representing 81% of total current assets. For the same period, **J.C. Penney Company** reported $6 billion of inventory, representing 54% of total current assets. In the **income statement**, inventory is vital in determining the results of operations for a particular period. Also, gross profit (net sales less cost of goods sold) is closely watched by management, owners, and other interested parties (as explained in Chapter 5).

CLASSIFYING INVENTORY

How a company classifies its inventory depends on whether the firm is a merchandiser or a manufacturer. A **merchandiser's** inventory consists of many different items. For example, in a grocery store, canned goods, dairy products, meats, and produce are just a few of the inventory items on hand. These items have two common characteristics: (1) They are owned by the company, and (2) they are in a form ready for sale in the ordinary course of business. Only one inventory classification, **merchandise inventory**, is needed to describe the many different items that make up the total inventory.

A **manufacturer's** inventories are also owned by the company, but some goods may not yet be ready for sale. As a result, inventory is usually classified into three categories: finished goods, work in process, and raw materials. For example, **General Motors** classifies vehicles completed and ready for sale as **finished goods**. The vehicles in various stages of production are classified as **work in process**. The steel, glass, upholstery, and other components that are on hand waiting to be used in production are **raw materials**.

The accounting principles and concepts discussed in this chapter apply to inventory classifications of both merchandising and manufacturing companies. In this chapter we will focus on merchandise inventory.

> **HELPFUL HINT**
> Regardless of the classification, all inventories are reported under current assets on the balance sheet.

DETERMINING INVENTORY QUANTITIES

Many businesses take a physical inventory count on the last day of the year. Businesses using the periodic inventory system must make such a count to determine the inventory on hand at the balance sheet date and to compute cost of goods sold. Even businesses using a perpetual inventory system must take a physical inventory at some time during the year.

Determining inventory quantities consists of two steps: (1) taking a physical inventory of goods on hand, and (2) determining the ownership of goods.

STUDY OBJECTIVE 1

Describe the steps in determining inventory quantities.

Taking a Physical Inventory

Taking a physical inventory involves actually counting, weighing, or measuring each kind of inventory on hand. In many companies, taking an inventory is a formidable task. Retailers such as **Kmart**, **Home Depot**, or your favorite music store have thousands of different inventory items. An inventory count is generally more accurate when goods are not being sold or received during the counting. So, companies often "take inventory" when the business is closed or when business is slow. Many retailers, for example, close early on a chosen day in January—after the holiday sales and returns—to count inventory.

To minimize errors in taking the inventory, a company should adhere to **internal control** principles and practices that safeguard inventory:

1. The counting should be done by employees who do not have custodial responsibility for the inventory.
2. Each counter should establish the authenticity of each inventory item. For example, does each box contain a 25-inch television set? Does each storage tank contain gasoline?
3. There should be a second count by another employee.
4. Prenumbered inventory tags should be used. All inventory tags should be accounted for.
5. At the end of the count, a designated supervisor should check that all inventory items are tagged and that no items have more than one tag.

After the physical inventory is taken, the quantity of each kind of inventory is listed on **inventory summary sheets**. To ensure accuracy, the listing should be verified by a second employee. Later, unit costs will be applied to the quantities in order to determine a total cost of the inventory—which is the topic of later sections.[1]

ACCOUNTING IN ACTION Business Insight

Failure to observe the foregoing internal control procedures contributed to the Great Salad Oil Swindle. In this case, management intentionally overstated its salad oil inventory, which was stored in large holding tanks. Three procedures contributed to overstating the oil inventory: (1) Water added to the bottom of the holding tanks caused the oil to float to the top. Inventory-taking crews who viewed the holding tanks from the top observed only salad oil. In fact, as much as 37 out of 40 feet of many of the holding tanks contained water. (2) The company's inventory records listed more holding tanks than it actually had. The company repainted numbers on the tanks after inventory crews examined them, so the crews counted the same tanks twice. (3) Underground pipes pumped oil from one holding tank to another during the inventory taking. Therefore, the same salad oil was counted more than once. Although the salad oil swindle was unusual, it demonstrates the complexities involved in assuring that inventory is properly counted.

Determining Ownership of Goods

Before we can begin to calculate the cost of inventory, we need to consider the ownership of goods. Specifically, we need to be sure that we have not included in the inventory any goods that do not belong to the company.

GOODS IN TRANSIT. Goods are considered **in transit** when they are in the hands of a public carrier (such as a railroad, trucking, or airline company) at the statement date. Goods in transit should be included in the inventory of the party that has legal title to the goods. Legal title is determined by the terms of sale, as shown in Illustration 6-1 and described below.

1. **FOB (free on board) shipping point:** Ownership of the goods passes to the buyer when the public carrier accepts the goods from the seller.
2. **FOB destination:** Legal title to the goods remains with the seller until the goods reach the buyer.

Illustration 6-1

Terms of sale

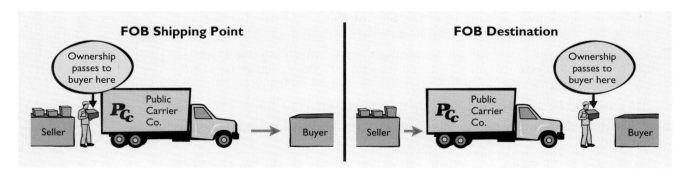

---

[1]To estimate the cost of inventory when a physical inventory cannot be taken (the inventory is destroyed) or when it is inconvenient (during interim periods), estimating methods are applied. These methods (gross profit method and retail inventory method) are discussed in Appendix 6B.

Inventory quantities may be seriously miscounted if goods in transit at the statement date are ignored. Assume that Hargrove Company has 20,000 units of inventory on hand on December 31. It also has the following goods in transit: (1) **sales** of 1,500 units shipped December 31 FOB destination, and (2) **purchases** of 2,500 units shipped FOB shipping point by the seller on December 31. Hargrove has legal title to both the units sold and the units purchased. If units in transit are ignored, inventory quantities would be understated by 4,000 units (1,500 + 2,500).

TECHNOLOGY IN ACTION

Many companies have invested large amounts of time and money in automated inventory systems. One of the most sophisticated is **Federal Express's** Digitally Assisted Dispatch System (DADS). It uses hand-held "Super-Trackers" to transmit data about the packages and documents to the firm's computer system. Based on bar codes, the system allows the firm to know where any package is at any time to prevent losses and to fulfill the firm's delivery commitments. More recently, FedEx's software enables customers to track shipments on their own PCs.

CONSIGNED GOODS. In some lines of business, it is customary to acquire merchandise on consignment. Under such an arrangement, the holder of the goods (the *consignee*) does not own the goods. Ownership remains with the shipper of the goods (the *consignor*) until the goods are actually sold to a customer. Because consigned goods are not owned by the consignee, they should not be included in the consignee's physical inventory count. But, the consignor should include merchandise held by the consignee as part of its inventory.

INVENTORY ACCOUNTING SYSTEMS

One of two basic systems of accounting for inventories may be used: **(1) the perpetual inventory system,** or **(2) the periodic inventory system**. Chapter 5 discussed and illustrated the perpetual inventory system. This chapter discusses and illustrates the periodic inventory system. Appendix 6A compares the periodic inventory system with the perpetual inventory system. Appendix 6C continues coverage of the perpetual inventory system.

Some businesses find it either unnecessary or uneconomical to invest in a computerized perpetual inventory system. As illustrated in Chapter 5, a perpetual inventory system keeps track of inventory in number of units **and** in dollar costs per unit. Many small merchandising business managers still feel that a perpetual inventory system costs more than it is worth. These managers can control merchandise and manage day-to-day operations either without detailed inventory records or with a perpetual **units only** inventory system.

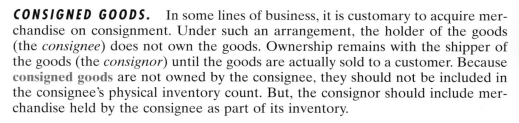

BEFORE YOU GO ON...

▶ *REVIEW IT*
1. What steps are involved in determining inventory quantities?
2. How is ownership determined for goods in transit at the balance sheet date?
3. Who has title to consigned goods?

▶ *DO IT*
Hasbeen Company completed its inventory count. It arrived at a total inventory value of $200,000. You have been informed of the information listed below. Discuss how this information affects the reported cost of inventory.

1. Goods held on consignment for Falls Co., costing $15,000, were included in the inventory.
2. Purchased goods of $10,000 which were in transit (terms: FOB shipping point) were not included in the count.
3. Sold inventory with a cost of $12,000 which was in transit (terms: FOB shipping point) was not included in the count.

ACTION PLAN
- Apply the rules of ownership to goods held on consignment.
- Apply the rules of ownership to goods in transit FOB shipping point.

SOLUTION
The goods of $15,000 held on consignment should be deducted from the inventory count. The goods of $10,000 purchased FOB shipping point should be added to the inventory count. Sold goods of $12,000 which were in transit FOB shipping point should not be included in the ending inventory. Thus, inventory should be carried at $195,000.

Related exercise material: BE6-4, E6-1, and E6-4.

PERIODIC INVENTORY SYSTEM

STUDY OBJECTIVE 2

Prepare the entries for purchases and sales of inventory under a periodic inventory system.

In a **periodic inventory system**, revenues from the sale of merchandise are recorded when sales are made, in the same way as in a perpetual system. But, no attempt is made on the date of sale to record the cost of the merchandise sold. Instead, a physical inventory count is taken at the end of the period. This count determines (1) the cost of the merchandise on hand and (2) the cost of the goods sold during the period. There is another key difference: Under a periodic system, purchases of merchandise are recorded in a Purchases account rather than a Merchandise Inventory account. Also, under a periodic system, it is customary to record the following in separate accounts: purchase returns and allowances, purchase discounts, and freight-in on purchases. That way, accumulated amounts for each are known.

RECORDING TRANSACTIONS

To illustrate the recording of merchandise transactions under a periodic inventory system, we will use the purchase/sale transactions between Sellers Electronix and Beyer Video discussed in Chapter 5.

RECORDING PURCHASES OF MERCHANDISE

On the basis of the sales invoice (Illustration 5-4 shown on page 188) and receipt of the merchandise ordered from Sellers Electronix, Beyer Video records the $3,800 purchase as follows.

HELPFUL HINT
Be careful not to fall into the trap of debiting purchases of equipment or supplies to Purchases.

A	=	L	+	OE
		+3,800		−3,800

May 4	Purchases		3,800	
	Accounts Payable			3,800
	(To record goods purchased on account, terms 2/10, n/30)			

Purchases is a temporary account whose normal balance is a debit.

Purchase Returns and Allowances

Some of the merchandise received from Sellers Electronix is inoperable. Beyer Video returns $300 worth of the goods and prepares the following entry to recognize the purchase return.

May 8	Accounts Payable	300	
	Purchase Returns and Allowances		300
	(To record return of inoperable goods		
	purchased from Sellers Electronix)		

A	=	L	+	OE
		−300		+300

Purchase Returns and Allowances is a temporary account whose normal balance is a credit.

Freight Costs

When the purchaser directly incurs the freight costs, the account Freight-in is debited. For example, upon delivery of the goods on May 6, Beyer pays Acme Freight Company $150 for freight charges on its purchase from Sellers Electronix. The entry on Beyer's books is:

May 9	Freight-in	150	
	Cash		150
	(To record payment of freight, terms FOB		
	shipping point)		

A	=	L	+	OE
−150				−150

ALTERNATIVE TERMINOLOGY
Freight-in is frequently called *transportation-in*.

Like Purchases, Freight-in is a temporary account whose normal balance is a debit. **Freight-in is part of cost of goods purchased**. In accordance with the cost principle, cost of goods purchased should include any freight charges necessary to bring the goods to the purchaser. Freight costs are not subject to a purchase discount. Purchase discounts apply only on the invoice cost of the merchandise.

Purchase Discounts

On May 14 Beyer Video pays the balance due on account to Sellers Electronix. Beyer takes the 2% cash discount allowed by Sellers for payment within 10 days. The payment and discount are recorded by Beyer Video as follows.

May 14	Accounts Payable	3,500	
	Purchase Discounts		70
	Cash		3,430
	(To record payment to Sellers Electronix		
	within the discount period)		

A	=	L	+	OE
−3,430		−3,500		+70

Purchase Discounts is a temporary account whose normal balance is a credit.

RECORDING SALES OF MERCHANDISE

The sale of $3,800 of merchandise to Beyer Video on May 4 (sales invoice No. 731, Illustration 5-4 on page 188) is recorded by Sellers Electronix as follows.

May 4	Accounts Receivable	3,800	
	Sales		3,800
	(To record credit sales per invoice #731 to		
	Beyer Video)		

A	=	L	+	OE
+3,800				+3,800

Sales Returns and Allowances

Based on the receipt of returned goods from Beyer Video on May 8, Sellers Electronix records the $300 sales return as follows.

A = L + OE
−300   −300

	May 8	Sales Returns and Allowances	300	
		Accounts Receivable		300
		(To record return of goods from Beyer Video)		

Sales Discounts

On May 15, Sellers Electronix receives payment of $3,430 on account from Beyer Video. Sellers honors the 2% cash discount and records the payment of Beyer's account receivable in full as follows.

A = L + OE
+3,430   −70
−3,500

	May 15	Cash	3,430	
		Sales Discounts	70	
		Accounts Receivable		3,500
		(To record collection from Beyer Video within 2/10, n/30 discount period)		

COMPARISON OF ENTRIES— PERPETUAL VS. PERIODIC

For purposes of comparison, the periodic inventory system entries above are shown in Illustration 6A-1 (in Appendix 6A on page 250) next to those from Chapter 5 (pages 188–193) under the perpetual inventory system for both Sellers Electronix and Beyer Video.

COST OF GOODS SOLD

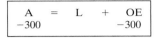

STUDY OBJECTIVE **3**

Determine cost of goods sold under a periodic inventory system.

As the entries above indicate, under a periodic inventory system a running account of the changes in inventory is not recorded as either purchases or sales transactions occur. Neither the daily amount of merchandise on hand is known nor is the cost of goods sold. **To determine the cost of goods sold under a periodic inventory system**, three steps are required: (1) Record purchases of merchandise (as shown above). (2) Determine the cost of goods purchased. (3) Determine the cost of goods on hand at the beginning and end of the accounting period. The cost of goods on hand must be determined by a physical inventory count and application of the cost to the items counted in the inventory. In this section, we look in more detail at this process.

DETERMINING COST OF GOODS PURCHASED

Earlier in this chapter we used four accounts to record the purchase of inventory under a periodic inventory system. These accounts are:

Illustration 6-2

Normal balances: cost of goods purchased accounts

Account	Normal Balance
Purchases	Debit
Purchase Returns and Allowances	Credit
Purchase Discounts	Credit
Freight-in	Debit

All of these accounts are **temporary accounts**. They are used to determine the cost of goods sold, which is an expense disclosed on the income statement. Therefore, the balances in these accounts must be reduced to zero at the end of each accounting period. Information about cost of goods sold can then be accumulated for the next accounting period.

The procedure for determining the cost of goods purchased is as follows.

1. The accounts with credit balances (Purchase Returns and Allowances, Purchase Discounts) are subtracted from Purchases. The result is **net purchases**.

2. Freight-in is then added to net purchases. The result is **cost of goods purchased**.

To illustrate, assume that Sellers Electronix shows the following balances for the accounts above: Purchases $325,000; Purchase Returns and Allowances $10,400; Purchase Discounts $6,800; and Freight-in $12,200. Net purchases is $307,800, and cost of goods purchased is $320,000, as computed in Illustration 6-3.

Purchases		$325,000
(1) Less: Purchase returns and allowances	$10,400	
Purchase discounts	6,800	17,200
Net purchases		307,800
(2) Add: Freight-in		12,200
Cost of goods purchased		**$320,000**

Illustration 6-3

Computation of net purchases and cost of goods purchased

Determining Cost of Goods on Hand

To **determine the cost of inventory on hand, Sellers Electronix must take a physical inventory**. Taking a physical inventory involves:

1. Counting the units on hand for each item of inventory.
2. Applying unit costs to the total units on hand for each item.
3. Totaling the costs for each item of inventory, to determine the total cost of goods on hand.

A physical inventory should be taken at or near the balance sheet date.

The account Merchandise Inventory is used to record the cost of inventory on hand at the balance sheet date. This amount becomes the beginning inventory for the next accounting period. For Sellers Electronix, the balance in Merchandise Inventory at December 31, 2001, is $36,000. This amount is also the January 1, 2002, balance in Merchandise Inventory. During the year, **no entries are made to Merchandise Inventory**. At the end of the year, entries are made to eliminate the beginning inventory and to record the ending inventory. We will assume that Sellers Electronix's ending inventory on December 31, 2002, is $40,000.

Computing Cost of Goods Sold

We have now reached the point where we can compute cost of goods sold. Doing so involves two steps:

1. Add the cost of goods purchased to the cost of goods on hand at the beginning of the period (beginning inventory). The result is the **cost of goods available for sale**.

2. Subtract the cost of goods on hand at the end of the period (ending inventory) from the cost of goods available for sale. The result is the **cost of goods sold**.

ALTERNATIVE TERMINOLOGY
Some use the term *cost of sales* instead of *cost of goods sold*.

For Sellers Electronix the cost of goods available for sale is $356,000, and the cost of goods sold is $316,000, as shown below.

Illustration 6-4

Computation of cost of goods available for sale and cost of goods sold

	Beginning inventory	$ 36,000
(1)	Add: Cost of goods purchased	320,000
	Cost of goods available for sale	356,000
(2)	Less: Ending inventory	40,000
	Cost of goods sold	**$316,000**

Gross profit, operating expenses, and net income are computed and reported in a periodic inventory system in the same manner as under a perpetual inventory system, as shown in Illustration 6-5. (See also Chapter 5, Illustration 5-11, page 200).

Illustration 6-5

Income statement for a merchandiser using a periodic inventory system

SELLERS ELECTRONIX
Income Statement
For the Year Ended December 31, 2002

Sales revenue			
Sales			$480,000
Less: Sales returns and allowances		$ 12,000	
Sales discounts		8,000	20,000
Net sales			460,000
Cost of goods sold			
Inventory, January 1		36,000	
Purchases	$325,000		
Less: Purchase returns and allowances	$10,400		
Purchase discounts	6,800	17,200	
Net purchases		307,800	
Add: Freight-in		12,200	
Cost of goods purchased		320,000	
Cost of goods available for sale		356,000	
Inventory, December 31		40,000	
Cost of goods sold			316,000
Gross profit			144,000
Operating expenses			
Store salaries expense		45,000	
Rent expense		19,000	
Utilities expense		17,000	
Advertising expense		16,000	
Depreciation expense—store equipment		8,000	
Freight-out		7,000	
Insurance expense		2,000	
Total operating expenses			114,000
Net income			**$ 30,000**

HELPFUL HINT

The far right column identifies the major subdivisions of the income statement. The next column identifies the primary items comprising cost of goods sold of $316,000 and operating expenses of $114,000; in addition, contra revenue items of $20,000 are reported. The third column explains cost of goods purchased of $320,000. The fourth column reports contra purchase items of $17,200.

Chapter 6 — Completing the Accounting Cycle, Periodic Inventory System

STUDY OBJECTIVE 4

Identify the unique features of the income statement for a merchandiser using a periodic inventory system.

INCOME STATEMENT PRESENTATION

The income statement for merchandisers under a periodic inventory system contains three features not found in the income statement of a service enterprise.

These features are: (1) a sales revenue section, (2) a cost of goods sold section, and (3) gross profit. These same three features appear for a merchandiser under a perpetual inventory system. But, under a periodic inventory system, the cost of goods sold section generally will contain more detail. Using assumed data for specific operating expenses, the income statement for Sellers Electronix using a periodic inventory system is shown in Illustration 6-5. Whether the periodic or the perpetual inventory system is used, merchandise inventory is reported at the same amount in the current assets section.

ALTERNATIVE TERMINOLOGY
Gross profit is sometimes referred to as *merchandising profit* or *gross margin*.

BEFORE YOU GO ON...

▶ *REVIEW IT*
1. Name two basic systems of accounting for inventory.
2. Identify the three steps in determining cost of goods sold.
3. What accounts are used in determining the cost of goods purchased?
4. What is included in cost of goods available for sale?

▶ *DO IT*
Aerosmith Company's accounting records show the following at year-end: Purchase Discounts $3,400; Freight-in $6,100; Sales $240,000; Purchases $162,500; Beginning Inventory $18,000; Ending Inventory $20,000; Sales Discounts $10,000; Purchase Returns $5,200; and Operating Expenses $57,000. Compute the following amounts for Aerosmith Company: net sales, cost of goods purchased, cost of goods sold, gross profit, and net income.

ACTION PLAN
• Understand the relationships of the cost components in measuring net income for a merchandising company.
• Compute net sales.
• Compute cost of goods purchased.
• Compute cost of goods sold.
• Compute gross profit.
• Compute net income.

SOLUTION
Net sales: $240,000 − $10,000 = $230,000.
Cost of goods purchased: $162,500 − $5,200 − $3,400 + $6,100 = $160,000.
Cost of goods sold: $18,000 + $160,000 − $20,000 = $158,000.
Gross profit: $230,000 − $158,000 = $72,000.
Net income: $72,000 − $57,000 = $15,000.

Related exercise material: BE6-2, BE6-3, E6-2, and E6-3.

THE NAVIGATOR

*I*NVENTORY COSTING UNDER A PERIODIC INVENTORY SYSTEM

All expenditures needed to acquire goods and to make them ready for sale are included as inventoriable costs. **Inventoriable costs** may be regarded as a pool of costs that consists of two elements: (1) the cost of the beginning inventory and (2) the cost of goods purchased during the year. The sum of these two equals the cost of goods available for sale.

Conceptually, the costs of the purchasing, receiving, and warehousing departments (whose efforts make the goods available for sale) should also be included

STUDY OBJECTIVE 5

Explain the basis of accounting for inventories, and describe the inventory cost flow methods.

in inventoriable costs. But, there are practical difficulties in allocating these costs to inventory. So these costs are generally accounted for as **operating expenses** in the period in which they are incurred.

Inventoriable costs are allocated either to ending inventory or to cost of goods sold. Under a periodic inventory system, the allocation is made at the end of the accounting period. First, the costs for the ending inventory are determined. Next, the cost of the ending inventory is subtracted from the cost of goods available for sale, to determine the cost of goods sold.

To illustrate, assume that General Suppliers has a cost of goods available for sale of $120,000. This amount is based on a beginning inventory of $20,000 and cost of goods purchased of $100,000. The physical inventory indicates that 5,000 units are on hand. The costs applicable to the units are $3.00 per unit. The allocation of the pool of costs is shown in Illustration 6-6. As shown, the $120,000 of goods available for sale are allocated $15,000 to ending inventory (5,000 × $3.00) and $105,000 to cost of goods sold.

HELPFUL HINT

Under a perpetual inventory system, described in Chapter 5, the allocation of costs is recognized continuously as purchases and sales are made.

Illustration 6-6

Allocation (matching) of pool of costs

	Pool of Costs	
	Cost of Goods Available for Sale	
Beginning inventory		$ 20,000
Cost of goods purchased		100,000
Cost of goods available for sale		**$120,000**

Step 1			**Step 2**	
Ending Inventory			**Cost of Goods Sold**	
Units	**Unit Cost**	**Total Cost**	Cost of goods available for sale	$120,000
			Less: Ending inventory	15,000
5,000	$3.00	**$15,000**	Cost of goods sold	**$105,000**

USING ACTUAL PHYSICAL FLOW COSTING— SPECIFIC IDENTIFICATION

Costing of the inventory is complicated because specific items of inventory on hand may have been purchased at different prices. For example, a company may experience several increases in the cost of identical goods within a given year. Or, unit costs may decline. Under such circumstances, how should different unit costs be allocated between the ending inventory and cost of goods sold?

One answer is to use specific identification of the units purchased. This method tracks the **actual physical flow** of the goods. **Each item of inventory is marked, tagged, or coded with its "specific" unit cost.** At the end of the year the specific costs of items still in inventory make up the total cost of the ending inventory. Assume, for example, that Southland Music Company purchases three 46-inch television sets at costs of $700, $750, and $800, respectively. During the year, two sets are sold at $1,200 each. At December 31, the $750 set is still on hand. The ending inventory is $750, and the cost of goods sold is $1,500 ($700 + $800). This is shown graphically in Illustration 6-7.

Specific identification is possible when a company sells a limited variety of high-unit-cost items that can be clearly identified from purchase through sale. Examples are automobile dealerships (cars, trucks, and vans), music stores (pianos and organs), and antique shops (tables and cabinets).

HELPFUL HINT

What gross profit will Southland Music report? Answer: $900 (Sales $2,400 − CGS $1,500).

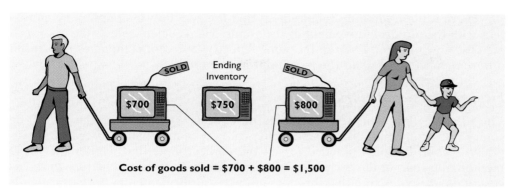

Illustration 6-7

Specific identification method

But what if we cannot specifically identify particular inventory items? For example, drug, grocery, and hardware stores sell thousands of relatively low-unit-cost items of inventory. These are often indistinguishable from one another. It may be impossible or impractical to track each item's cost. In that case (as the next section will show), we must make assumptions about which units were sold.

The general rule is this: When feasible, specific identification is the ideal method of allocating cost of goods available for sale. It reports ending inventory at actual cost and matches the actual cost of goods sold against sales revenue.

However, specific identification may enable management to manipulate net income. To see how, assume that a music store has three identical Steinway grand pianos, purchased at different costs. When selling one piano, management could maximize net income by selecting the piano with the lowest cost to match against revenues. Or, it could minimize net income (and lower its taxes) by selecting the highest-cost piano.

HELPFUL HINT
A major disadvantage of the specific identification method is that management may be able to manipulate net income through specific identification of items sold.

USING ASSUMED COST FLOW METHODS—FIFO, LIFO, AND AVERAGE COST

Because specific identification is often impractical, other cost flow methods are allowed. These assume flows of costs that may be unrelated to the physical flow of goods. For this reason we call them **assumed cost flow methods** or **cost flow assumptions**. They are:

1. First-in, first-out (FIFO).
2. Last-in, first-out (LIFO).
3. Average cost.

To illustrate these three inventory cost flow methods, we will assume that Bow Valley Electronics uses a **periodic inventory system**. The information shown in Illustration 6-8 relates to its Z202 Astro Condenser.

*I*NTERNATIONAL NOTE
A survey of accounting standards in 21 major industrial countries found that all three methods were permissible. In Ireland and the U.K., LIFO is permitted only in extreme circumstances.

Illustration 6-8

Inventoriable units and costs for Bow Valley Electronics

BOW VALLEY ELECTRONICS
Z202 Astro Condensers

Date	Explanation	Units	Unit Cost	Total Cost
1/1	Beginning inventory	100	$10	$ 1,000
4/15	Purchase	200	11	2,200
8/24	Purchase	300	12	3,600
11/27	Purchase	400	13	5,200
	Total	1,000		$12,000

During the year, 550 units were sold, and 450 units are on hand at 12/31.

There is no accounting requirement that the cost flow assumption be consistent with the physical movement of the goods. Management selects the appropriate cost flow method. Even in the same industry, different companies may reach different conclusions as to the most appropriate method.

First-in, First-out (FIFO)

The **FIFO method** assumes that the **earliest goods** purchased are the first to be sold. FIFO often parallels the actual physical flow of merchandise because it generally is good business practice to sell the earliest units first. Under the FIFO method, the **costs** of the earliest goods purchased are the first to be recognized as cost of goods sold. (Note that this does not necessarily mean that the earliest units *are* sold first, but that the costs of the earliest units are recognized first. In a bin of picture hangers at the hardware store, for example, no one really knows, nor would it matter, which hangers are sold first.) The allocation of the cost of goods available for sale at Bow Valley Electronics under FIFO is shown in Illustrations 6-9 and 6-10.

Illustration 6-9

Allocation of costs — FIFO method

Pool of Costs

Cost of Goods Available for Sale

Date	Explanation	Units	Unit Cost	Total Cost
1/1	Beginning inventory	100	$10	$ 1,000
4/15	Purchase	200	11	2,200
8/24	Purchase	300	12	3,600
11/27	Purchase	400	13	5,200
	Total	1,000		$12,000

HELPFUL HINT

Note the sequencing of the allocation: (1) Compute ending inventory. (2) Determine cost of goods sold.

	Step 1				**Step 2**	
	Ending Inventory				**Cost of Goods Sold**	
Date	Units	Unit Cost	Total Cost			
11/27	400	$13	$5,200	Cost of goods available for sale		$12,000
8/24	50	12	600	Less: Ending inventory		5,800
Total	450		$5,800	Cost of goods sold		$ 6,200

Illustration 6-10

FIFO—First costs in are first costs out in computing cost of goods sold

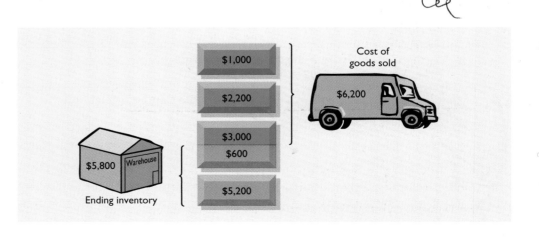

Note that the ending inventory is based on the latest units purchased. That is, **under FIFO, the cost of the ending inventory is found by taking the unit cost of the most recent purchase and working backward until all units of inventory are costed**.

We can verify the accuracy of the cost of goods sold by recognizing that the **first units acquired are the first units sold**. The computations for the 550 units sold are shown in Illustration 6-11.

Date	Units		Unit Cost		Total Cost
1/1	100	×	$10	=	$1,000
4/15	200	×	11	=	2,200
8/24	250	×	12	=	3,000
Total	550				$6,200

Illustration 6-11

Proof of cost of goods sold

Last-in, First-out (LIFO)

The **LIFO method** assumes that the **latest goods** purchased are the first to be sold. LIFO seldom coincides with the actual physical flow of inventory. Only for goods in piles, such as hay, coal, or produce at the grocery store would LIFO match the physical flow of inventory. Under the LIFO method, the **costs** of the latest goods purchased are the first to be assigned to cost of goods sold. The allocation of the cost of goods available for sale at Bow Valley Electronics under LIFO is shown in Illustration 6-12.

Illustration 6-12

Allocation of costs—LIFO method

Pool of Costs

Cost of Goods Available for Sale

Date	Explanation	Units	Unit Cost	Total Cost
1/1	Beginning inventory	100	$10	$ 1,000
4/15	Purchase	200	11	2,200
8/24	Purchase	300	12	3,600
11/27	Purchase	400	13	5,200
	Total	1,000		$12,000

Step 1				**Step 2**	
Ending Inventory				**Cost of Goods Sold**	

Date	Units	Unit Cost	Total Cost		
1/1	100	$10	$1,000	Cost of goods available for sale	$12,000
4/15	200	11	2,200	Less: Ending inventory	5,000
8/24	150	12	1,800	Cost of goods sold	$ 7,000
Total	450		$5,000		

> **HELPFUL HINT**
> The costs allocated to ending inventory ($5,000) plus the costs allocated to CGS ($7,000) must equal CGAS ($12,000).

Illustration 6-13 graphically displays the LIFO cost flow.

Under the LIFO method, **the cost of the ending inventory is found by taking the unit cost of the oldest goods and working forward until all units of inventory are costed**. As a result, the first costs assigned to ending inventory are the costs of the beginning inventory. Proof of the costs allocated to cost of goods sold is shown in Illustration 6-14.

Illustration 6-13

LIFO—Last costs in are first costs out in computing cost of goods sold

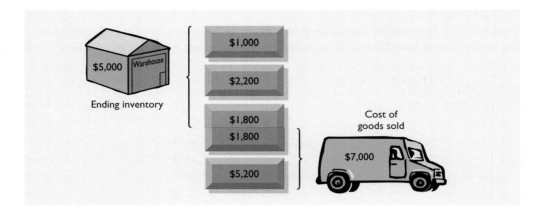

Illustration 6-14

Proof of cost of goods sold

Date	Units		Unit Cost		Total Cost
11/27	400	×	$13	=	$5,200
8/24	150	×	12	=	1,800
Total	550				**$7,000**

Under a periodic inventory system, **all goods purchased during the period are assumed to be available for the first sale, regardless of the date of purchase**.

Average Cost

The **average cost method** assumes that the goods available for sale have the same (average) cost per unit. Generally such goods are identical. Under this method, the cost of goods available for sale is allocated on the basis of the **weighted-average unit cost**. The formula and a sample computation of the weighted-average unit cost are as follows.

Illustration 6-15

Formula for weighted-average unit cost

The weighted-average unit cost is then applied to the units on hand. This computation determines the cost of the ending inventory. The allocation of the cost of goods available for sale at Bow Valley Electronics using average cost is shown in Illustrations 6-16 and 6-17.

To verify the cost of goods sold data in Illustration 6-16, multiply the units sold by the weighted-average unit cost (550 × $12 = $6,600). Note that this method does not use the average of the **unit costs**. That average is $11.50 ($10 + $11 + $12 + $13 = $46; $46 ÷ 4). Instead, the average cost method uses the average **weighted** by the quantities purchased at each unit cost.

Pool of Costs
Cost of Goods Available for Sale

Date	Explanation	Units	Unit Cost	Total Cost
1/1	Beginning inventory	100	$10	$ 1,000
4/15	Purchase	200	11	2,200
8/24	Purchase	300	12	3,600
11/27	Purchase	400	13	5,200
	Total	1,000		$12,000

Step 1 — Ending Inventory	Step 2 — Cost of Goods Sold
$12,000 ÷ 1,000 = $12.00	Cost of goods available for sale $12,000
	Less: Ending inventory 5,400
Units × Unit Cost = Total Cost	Cost of goods sold $ 6,600
450 × $12.00 = $5,400	

Illustration 6-16

Allocation of costs—average cost method

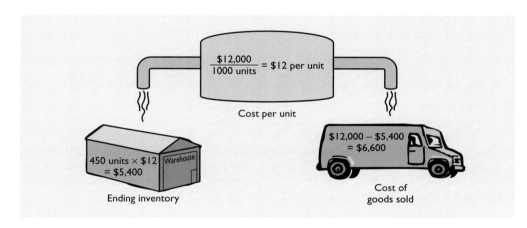

Illustration 6-17

Average cost—the average cost of the goods available for sale during the period is the cost used to compute cost of goods sold

FINANCIAL STATEMENT EFFECTS OF COST FLOW METHODS

Each of the three cost flow methods is acceptable. For example, **Black and Decker Manufacturing Company** and **Wendy's International** currently use the FIFO method. **Campbell Soup Company, Kroger Co.,** and **Walgreen Drugs** use LIFO. **Bristol-Myers-Squibb Co.** and **Motorola, Inc.** use the average cost method. A company may also use more than one cost flow method at the same time. **Del Monte Corporation** uses LIFO for domestic inventories and FIFO for foreign inventories. Illustration 6-18 shows the use of the three methods in the 600 largest U.S. companies. Companies adopt different inventory cost flow methods for various reasons. Usually, one of the following factors is involved:

1. Income statement effects.
2. Balance sheet effects.
3. Tax effects.

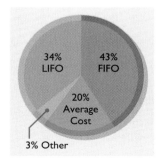

Illustration 6-18

Use of cost flow methods in major U.S. companies

STUDY OBJECTIVE 6

Explain the financial statement and tax effects of each of the inventory cost flow methods.

Income Statement Effects

To understand why companies might choose a particular cost flow method, let's compare their effects on the financial statements of Bow Valley Electronics. The condensed income statements in Illustration 6–19 assume that Bow Valley sold its 550 units for $11,500, and its operating expenses were $2,000. Its income tax rate is 30%.

Illustration 6-19

Comparative effects of cost flow methods

BOW VALLEY ELECTRONICS Condensed Income Statements			
	FIFO	**LIFO**	**Average Cost**
Sales	$11,500	$11,500	$11,500
Beginning inventory	1,000	1,000	1,000
Purchases	11,000	11,000	11,000
Cost of goods available for sale	12,000	12,000	12,000
Ending inventory	**5,800**	**5,000**	**5,400**
Cost of goods sold	6,200	7,000	6,600
Gross profit	5,300	4,500	4,900
Operating expenses	2,000	2,000	2,000
Income before income taxes[2]	3,300	2,500	2,900
Income tax expense (30%)	990	750	870
Net income	**$ 2,310**	**$ 1,750**	**$ 2,030**

The cost of goods available for sale ($12,000) is the same under each of the three inventory cost flow methods. But the ending inventory is different in each method, and this difference affects cost of goods sold. Each dollar of difference in ending inventory therefore results in a corresponding dollar difference in income before income taxes. For Bow Valley, there is an $800 difference between FIFO and LIFO.

In a period of rising prices, FIFO produces a higher net income. This happens because the expenses matched against revenues are the lower unit costs of the first units purchased. In a period of rising prices (as is the case here), FIFO reports the highest net income ($2,310) and LIFO the lowest ($1,750); average cost falls in the middle ($2,030). To management, higher net income is an advantage: It causes external users to view the company more favorably. Also, if management bonuses are based on net income, FIFO will provide the basis for higher bonuses.

Some argue that the use of LIFO in a period of rising prices enables the company to avoid reporting **paper or phantom profit** as economic gain. To illustrate, assume that Kralik Company buys 200 XR492s at $20 per unit on January 10. It buys 200 more on December 31 at $24 each. During the year, it sells 200 units at $30 each. The results under FIFO and LIFO are shown in Illustration 6-20.

> **HELPFUL HINT**
> If prices are falling, the results from the use of FIFO and LIFO are reversed: FIFO will report the lowest net income and LIFO the highest.

Illustration 6-20

Income statement effects compared

	FIFO	**LIFO**
Sales (200 × $30)	$6,000	$6,000
Cost of goods sold	**4,000** (200 × $20)	**4,800** (200 × $24)
Gross profit	$2,000	$1,200

---

[2]It is assumed that Bow Valley is a corporation, and corporations are required to pay income taxes.

Under LIFO, the company has recovered the current replacement cost ($4,800) of the units sold. The gross profit in economic terms under LIFO is real. Under FIFO, the company has recovered only the January 10 cost ($4,000). To replace the units sold, it must reinvest $800 (200 × $4) of the gross profit. Thus, $800 of the gross profit under FIFO is phantom, or illusory. As a result, reported net income under FIFO is also overstated in real terms.

Balance Sheet Effects

A major advantage of FIFO is that in a period of rising prices, the costs allocated to ending inventory will be close to their current cost. For Bow Valley, for example, 400 of the 450 units in the ending inventory are costed at the November 27 unit cost of $13.

A major shortcoming of LIFO is that in a period of rising prices, the costs allocated to ending inventory may be understated in terms of current cost. This is true for Bow Valley: The cost of the ending inventory includes the $10 unit cost of the beginning inventory. The understatement becomes even greater if the inventory includes goods purchased in one or more prior accounting periods.

Tax Effects

We have seen that both inventory on the balance sheet and net income on the income statement are higher when FIFO is used in a period of rising prices. Why, then, would a company use LIFO? The reason is that LIFO results in the lowest income taxes during times of rising prices. The lower net income reported by LIFO translates to a lower tax liability. For example, at Bow Valley Electronics, income taxes are $750 under LIFO, compared to $990 under FIFO. The tax saving of $240 makes more cash available for use in the business.

ACCOUNTING IN ACTION *Business Insight*

Most small firms use the FIFO method. But fears of rising prices often cause firms to switch to LIFO. For example, **Chicago Heights Steel Co.** boosted cash "by 5% to 10% by lowering income taxes" when it switched to LIFO. Electronic games distributor **Atlas Distributing Inc.** considered a switch "because the costs of our games, made in Japan, are rising 15% a year," said Joseph Serpico, treasurer. When inflation heats up, the number of companies choosing LIFO rises dramatically.

USING INVENTORY COST FLOW METHODS CONSISTENTLY

Whatever cost flow method a company chooses, it should be used consistently from one period to another. Consistent application makes financial statements more comparable over successive time periods. In contrast, using FIFO in one year and LIFO in the next would make it difficult to compare the net incomes of the two years.

Although consistent application is preferred, a company *may* change its method of inventory costing. Such a change and its effects on net income should be disclosed in the financial statements. A typical disclosure is shown in Illustration 6-21, using information from recent financial statements of **Quaker Oats Company**.

Illustration 6-21

Disclosure of change in cost flow method

QUAKER OATS COMPANY
Notes to the Financial Statements

Note 1 Effective July 1, the Company adopted the LIFO cost flow assumption for valuing the majority of U.S. Grocery Products inventories. The Company believes that the use of the LIFO method better matches current costs with current revenues. The effect of this change on the current year was to decrease net income by $16.0 million.

*A*CCOUNTING IN ACTION *International Insight*

U.S. companies typically choose between LIFO and FIFO. Many choose LIFO because it reduces inventory profits and taxes. However, the international community recently considered rules that would ban LIFO entirely and force companies to use FIFO. This proposal was defeated, but the issue will not go away.

The issue is sensitive. As John Wulff, controller for **Union Carbide** noted, "We were in support of the international effort up until the proposal to eliminate LIFO." Wulff says that if Union Carbide had been suddenly forced to switch from LIFO to FIFO, its reported $632 million pretax income would have jumped by $300 million. That would have increased Carbide's income tax bill by as much as $120 million. Given this, do you believe that accounting principles and rules should be the same around the world?

BEFORE YOU GO ON...

▶ *REVIEW IT*
1. How do the cost and matching principles apply to inventoriable costs?
2. How are the three assumed cost flow methods applied in allocating inventoriable costs?
3. What factors should be considered by management in selecting an inventory cost flow method?
4. Which inventory cost flow method produces (a) the highest net income in a period of rising prices, and (b) the lowest income taxes?
5. What amount is reported by **Lands' End** in its 2000 Annual Report as inventories at January 28, 2000? Which inventory cost flow method does Lands' End use? The answer to this question is provided on p. 273.

LANDS' END
DIRECT MERCHANTS

▶ *DO IT*
The accounting records of Shumway Ag Implement show the following data.

Beginning inventory	4,000 units at $3
Purchases	6,000 units at $4
Sales	5,000 units at $12

Determine the cost of goods sold during the period under a periodic inventory system using (a) the FIFO method, (b) the LIFO method, and (c) the average cost method.

ACTION PLAN
• Understand the periodic inventory system.
• Compute the cost of goods sold under the periodic inventory system using the FIFO cost flow method.

- Compute the cost of goods sold under the periodic inventory system using the LIFO cost flow method.
- Compute the cost of goods sold under the periodic inventory system using the average cost method.

SOLUTION
(a) FIFO: (4,000 @ $3) + (1,000 @ $4) = $12,000 + $4,000 = $16,000.
(b) LIFO: 5,000 @ $4 = $20,000.
(c) Average cost: [(4,000 @ $3) + (6,000 @ $4)] ÷ $10,000 = ($12,000 + $24,000) ÷ 10,000 =
            $3.60 per unit; 5,000 @ $3.60 = $18,000.

Related exercise material: BE6-6, BE6-7, E6-5, E6-6, and E6-7.

 THE NAVIGATOR

VALUING INVENTORY AT THE LOWER OF COST OR MARKET (LCM)

Inventory values sometimes fall due to changes in technology or in fashion. When the value of inventory is lower than its cost, the inventory is written down to its market value. This is done by valuing the inventory at the **lower of cost or market (LCM)** in the period in which the decline occurs. LCM is an example of the **conservatism** constraint: When choosing among alternatives, the best choice is the method that is least likely to overstate assets and net income.

Under the LCM basis, "market" is defined as **current replacement cost**, not selling price. For a merchandiser, "market" is the cost of purchasing the same goods at the present time from the usual suppliers in the usual quantities.

Assume that Len's TV has the following lines of merchandise with costs and market values as indicated. LCM produces the following result.

STUDY OBJECTIVE 7

Explain the lower of cost or market basis of accounting for inventories.

	Cost	Market	Lower of Cost or Market
Television sets			
Consoles	$ 60,000	$ 55,000	$ 55,000
Portables	45,000	52,000	45,000
Total	105,000	107,000	
Video equipment			
Recorders	48,000	45,000	45,000
Movies	15,000	14,000	14,000
Total	63,000	59,000	
Total inventory	$168,000	$166,000	$159,000

Illustration 6-22

Computation of lower of cost or market

The amount entered in the final column is the lower of the cost or market amount for **each item**. LCM is applied to the items in inventory after one of the costing methods (specific identification, FIFO, LIFO, or average cost) has been applied to determine cost.

*I*NVENTORY *ERRORS*

STUDY OBJECTIVE 8

Indicate the effects of inventory errors on the financial statements.

Unfortunately, errors occasionally occur in taking or costing inventory. Some errors are caused by counting or pricing the inventory incorrectly. Others occur because of improper recognition of the transfer of legal title to goods in transit. When errors occur, they affect both the income statement and the balance sheet.

INCOME STATEMENT EFFECTS

Remember that both the beginning and ending inventories are used to determine cost of goods sold in a periodic system. The ending inventory of one period automatically becomes the beginning inventory of the next period. Inventory errors thus affect the determination of cost of goods sold and net income.

The effects on cost of goods sold can be determined by using the following formula. First enter the incorrect data in the formula. Then substitute the correct data, and find the difference between the two CGS amounts.

Illustration 6-23

Formula for cost of goods sold

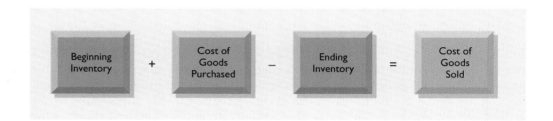

If beginning inventory is understated, cost of goods sold will be understated. If ending inventory is understated, cost of goods sold will be overstated. The effects of inventory errors on the current year's income statement are shown in Illustration 6-24.

Illustration 6-24

Effects of inventory errors on current year's income statement

Inventory Error	Cost of Goods Sold	Net Income
Beginning inventory understated	Understated	Overstated
Beginning inventory overstated	Overstated	Understated
Ending inventory understated	Overstated	Understated
Ending inventory overstated	Understated	Overstated

ETHICS NOTE

Inventory fraud includes pricing inventory at amounts in excess of their actual value, or claiming to have inventory when no inventory exists. Inventory fraud is usually done to overstate ending inventory, which understates cost of goods sold and creates higher income.

An error in ending inventory in the current period will have a **reverse effect on net income of the next period**. This is shown in Illustration 6-25 on the next page. Note that understating ending inventory in 2002 understates beginning inventory in 2003 and overstates net income in 2003.

Over the two years, total net income is correct. The errors offset one another. Notice that for 2002 and 2003 total income using incorrect data is $35,000 ($22,000 + $13,000). This is the same as the total income of $35,000 ($25,000 + $10,000) using correct data. Also note in this example that an error in the beginning inventory does not result in a corresponding error in the ending inventory. The correctness of the ending inventory depends entirely on the accuracy of taking and costing the inventory at the balance sheet date.

Condensed Income Statement

	2002		2003	
	Incorrect	**Correct**	**Incorrect**	**Correct**
Sales	$80,000	$80,000	$90,000	$90,000
Beginning inventory	$20,000	$20,000	**$12,000**	**$15,000**
Cost of goods purchased	40,000	40,000	68,000	68,000
Cost of goods available for sale	60,000	60,000	80,000	83,000
Ending inventory	**12,000**	**15,000**	23,000	23,000
Cost of goods sold	48,000	45,000	57,000	60,000
Gross profit	32,000	35,000	33,000	30,000
Operating expenses	10,000	10,000	20,000	20,000
Net income	$22,000	$25,000	$13,000	$10,000

($3,000)
Net income
understated

$3,000
Net income
overstated

Total income for
2 years correct

Illustration 6-25

Effects of inventory errors on two years' income statements

BALANCE SHEET EFFECTS

The effect of ending-inventory errors on the balance sheet can be determined by the basic accounting equation: Assets = Liabilities + Owner's equity. Errors in the ending inventory have the following effects on these components.

Ending Inventory Error	Assets	Liabilities	Owner's Equity
Overstated	Overstated	None	Overstated
Understated	Understated	None	Understated

Illustration 6-26

Ending inventory error— balance sheet effects

The effect of an error in ending inventory on the next period was shown in Illustration 6-25. If the error is not corrected, total net income for the two periods would be correct. Thus, total owner's equity reported on the balance sheet at the end of the next period will also be correct.

STATEMENT PRESENTATION AND ANALYSIS

PRESENTATION

As indicated in Chapter 5, inventory is classified as a current asset after receivables in the balance sheet. In a multiple-step income statement, cost of goods sold is subtracted from sales. There also should be disclosure of (1) the major inventory classifications, (2) the basis of accounting (cost, or lower of cost or market), and (3) the costing method (FIFO, LIFO, or average).

Lands' End, for example, in its January 28, 2000, balance sheet reported inventory of $162,193,000 under current assets. The accompanying notes to the financial statements, as shown in Illustration 6-27, disclosed the following information.

Illustration 6-27

Inventory disclosures by **Lands' End**

LANDS' END, INC.
Notes to the Financial Statements

Note 1. Summary of significant accounting policies

Inventory

Inventory, primarily merchandise held for resale, is stated at last-in, first-out (LIFO) cost, which is lower than market.

As indicated in this brief note, Lands' End values its inventories at the lower of cost or market using the LIFO method.

ANALYSIS

The amount of inventory carried by a company has significant economic consequences. And inventory management is a double-edged sword that requires constant attention. On the one hand, management wants to have a great variety and quantity on hand so that customers have a wide selection and items are always in stock. But such a policy may incur high carrying costs (e.g., investment, storage, insurance, obsolescence, and damage). On the other hand, low inventory levels lead to stockouts and lost sales.

Common ratios used to manage and evaluate inventory levels are inventory turnover and a related measure, average days to sell the inventory.

Inventory turnover measures the number of times on average the inventory is sold during the period. Its purpose is to measure the liquidity of the inventory. The inventory turnover is computed by dividing cost of goods sold by the average inventory during the period. Unless seasonal factors are significant, average inventory can be computed from the beginning and ending inventory balances. For example, **Lands' End** reported in its 2000 Annual Report a beginning inventory of $219,686,000, and cost of goods sold for the year ended January 28, 2000, of $727,291,000. The inventory turnover formula and computation for Lands' End are shown below.

STUDY OBJECTIVE 9

Compute and interpret inventory turnover.

Illustration 6-28

Inventory turnover formula and computation for **Lands' End**

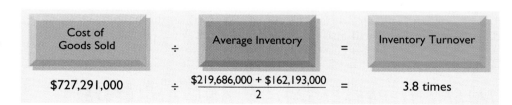

A variant of the inventory turnover ratio is the **average days to sell inventory**. For example, the inventory turnover for Lands' End of 3.8 times divided into 365 is approximately 96 days. This is the approximate age of the inventory.

There are typical levels of inventory in every industry. Companies that are able to keep their inventory at lower levels and higher turnovers and still satisfy customer needs are the most successful.

BEFORE YOU GO ON...

▶ *REVIEW IT*

1. Why is it appropriate to report inventories at the lower of cost or market?
2. How do inventory errors affect financial statements?
3. What does inventory turnover reveal?

A LOOK BACK AT OUR FEATURE STORY

Refer back to the Feature Story concerning Mountain Equipment Co-op (MEC) at the beginning of the chapter, and answer the following questions.

1. Why does MEC use the weighted average cost flow method to determine inventory?
2. Should MEC consider changing from the periodic weighted average cost method to a perpetual inventory system to track inventory costs? List the advantages and disadvantages of such a change.

SOLUTION

1. MEC uses the weighted average cost flow method because of fluctuations in costs of these inventory items.
2. MEC would find a perpetual inventory method useful to monitor its large number of inventory items. This is important with catalogue sales. When customers call to place an order, MEC would know immediately whether the item is in stock. Also, large fluctuations in the cost of each inventory item could be tracked to ensure that selling prices are adjusted where necessary to recover cost and any desired markup. A disadvantage of the perpetual inventory method would be the need for more recordkeeping than under the current periodic inventory method. Scanners and new computing equipment might also be required. Also, full disclosure would have to be made in the notes to the financial statements in the year of the change.

☑ THE NAVIGATOR

DEMONSTRATION PROBLEM 1

Gerald D. Englehart Company has the following inventory, purchases, and sales data for the month of March.

Additional Demonstration Problem

Inventory:	March 1	200 units @ $4.00	$ 800
Purchases:			
	March 10	500 units @ $4.50	2,250
	March 20	400 units @ $4.75	1,900
	March 30	300 units @ $5.00	1,500
Sales:			
	March 15	500 units	
	March 25	400 units	

The physical inventory count on March 31 shows 500 units on hand.

Instructions

Under a **periodic inventory system**, determine the cost of inventory on hand at March 31 and the cost of goods sold for March under the (a) first-in, first-out (FIFO) method, (b) last-in, first-out (LIFO) method, and (c) average cost method.

ACTION PLAN

• Compute the cost of inventory under the periodic FIFO method by allocating to the units on hand the **latest costs**.

• Compute the cost of inventory under the periodic LIFO method by allocating to the units on hand the **earliest costs**.

• Compute the cost of inventory under the periodic average cost method by allocating to the units on hand a **weighted-average cost**.

SOLUTION TO DEMONSTRATION PROBLEM 1

The cost of goods available for sale is $6,450, as follows.

Inventory:		200 units @ $4.00	$ 800
Purchases:			
	March 10	500 units @ $4.50	2,250
	March 20	400 units @ $4.75	1,900
	March 30	300 units @ $5.00	1,500
Total cost of goods available for sale			$6,450

Under a **periodic inventory system**, the cost of goods sold under each cost flow method is as follows.

FIFO Method

Ending inventory:

Date	Units	Unit Cost	Total Cost	
March 30	300	$5.00	$1,500	
March 20	200	4.75	950	$2,450

Cost of goods sold: $6,450 − $2,450 = $4,000

LIFO Method

Ending inventory:

Date	Units	Unit Cost	Total Cost	
March 1	200	$4.00	$ 800	
March 10	300	4.50	1,350	$2,150

Cost of goods sold: $6,450 − $2,150 = $4,300

Weighted-Average Cost Method

Weighted-average unit cost: $6,450 ÷ 1,400 = $4.607
Ending inventory: 500 × $4.607 = $2,303.50

Cost of goods sold: $6,450 − $2,303.50 = $4,146.50

SUMMARY OF STUDY OBJECTIVES

1. Describe the steps in determining inventory quantities. The steps in determining inventory quantities are (1) taking a physical inventory of goods on hand and (2) determining the ownership of goods in transit.

2. Prepare the entries for purchases and sales of inventory under a periodic inventory system. In recording purchases, entries are required for (a) cash and credit purchases, (b) purchase returns and allowances, (c) purchase discounts, and (d) freight costs. In recording sales, entries are required for (a) cash and credit sales, (b) sales returns and allowances, and (c) sales discounts.

3. Determine cost of goods sold under a periodic inventory system. The steps in determining cost of goods sold are (a) record the purchases of merchandise, (b) determine the cost of goods purchased, and (c) determine the cost of goods on hand at the beginning and end of the accounting period.

4. Identify the unique features of the income statement for a merchandiser using a periodic inventory system. The income statement for a merchandiser contains three sections: sales revenue, cost of goods sold, and operating expenses. The cost of goods sold section under a periodic inventory system generally reports beginning and ending inventory, cost of goods purchased, and cost of goods available for sale.

5. Explain the basis of accounting for inventories, and describe the inventory cost flow methods. The primary basis of accounting for inventories is cost. Cost includes all expenditures necessary to acquire goods and to make them ready for sale. Inventoriable costs include (1) the cost of beginning inventory and (2) the cost of goods purchased. The inventory cost flow methods are: specific identification, FIFO, LIFO, and average cost.

6. *Explain the financial statement and tax effects of each of the inventory cost flow methods.* The cost of goods available for sale may be allocated to cost of goods sold and ending inventory by specific identification or by a method based on an assumed cost flow. These methods have different effects on financial statements during periods of changing prices. When prices are rising, FIFO results in lower cost of goods sold and higher net income than the average cost and the LIFO methods. LIFO results in the lowest income taxes (because of lower net income). In the balance sheet, FIFO results in an ending inventory that is closest to current value. The inventory under LIFO is the farthest from current value.

7. *Explain the lower of cost or market basis of accounting for inventories.* The lower of cost or market (LCM) basis is used when the current replacement cost (market) is less than cost. Under LCM, the loss is recognized in the period in which the price decline occurs.

8. *Indicate the effects of inventory errors on the financial statements.* In the income statement of the current year: (a) An error in beginning inventory will have a reverse effect on net income (overstatement of inventory results in understatement of net income); and (b) an error in ending inventory will have a similar effect on net income (overstatement of inventory results in overstatement of net income). If ending inventory errors are not corrected in the next period, their effect on net income for that period is reversed, and total net income for the two years will be correct. In the balance sheet, ending inventory errors will have the same effect on total assets and total stockholders' equity and no effect on liabilities.

9. *Compute and interpret inventory turnover.* Inventory turnover is calculated as cost of goods sold divided by average inventory. It can be converted to average days in inventory by dividing 365 days by the inventory turnover ratio. A higher turnover or lower average days in inventory suggests that management is trying to keep inventory levels low relative to sales.

☑ THE NAVIGATOR

Key Term Matching Activity

Glossary

Average cost method Inventory costing method that assumes that the goods available for sale have the same (average) cost per unit; generally the goods are identical. (p. 238).

Consigned goods Goods shipped by a consignor, who retains ownership, to another party called the consignee. (p. 227).

Cost of goods available for sale The sum of the beginning merchandise inventory plus the cost of goods purchased. (p. 231).

Cost of goods purchased The sum of net purchases plus freight-in. (p. 231).

Cost of goods sold The total cost of merchandise sold during the period, determined by subtracting ending inventory from the cost of goods available for sale. (p. 231).

Current replacement cost The amount that would be paid at the present time to acquire an identical item. (p. 243).

First-in, first-out (FIFO) method Inventory costing method that assumes that the costs of the earliest goods acquired are the first to be recognized as cost of goods sold. (p. 236).

Inventoriable costs The pool of costs that consists of two elements: (1) the cost of the beginning inventory and (2) the cost of goods purchased during the period. (p. 233).

Inventory turnover A measure of the number of times on average the inventory is sold during the period; computed by dividing cost of goods sold by the average inventory during the period. (p. 246).

Last-in, first-out (LIFO) method Inventory costing method that assumes that the costs of the latest units purchased are the first to be allocated to cost of goods sold. (p. 237).

Lower of cost or market (LCM) basis Method of valuing inventory that recognizes the decline in the value when the current purchase price (market) is less than cost. (p. 243).

Net purchases Purchases less purchase returns and allowances and purchase discounts. (p. 231).

Periodic inventory system An inventory system in which inventoriable costs are allocated to ending inventory and cost of goods sold at the end of the period. Cost of goods sold is computed at the end of the period by subtracting the ending inventory (costs are assigned based on a physical count of items on hand) from the cost of goods available for sale. (p. 228).

Specific identification method An actual, physical flow inventory costing method in which items still in inventory are specifically costed to arrive at the total cost of the ending inventory. (p. 234).

▶ **APPENDIX 6A** *Comparison of Entries—Perpetual vs. Periodic*

The periodic inventory system entries shown in this chapter are reproduced in the righthand column of Illustration 6A-1 on the next page. (They are printed in red.) In the middle column (printed in blue) are the entries from Chapter 5 (pages 188–193) for the perpetual inventory system for both Sellers Electronix and Beyer Video. Having these entries side-by-side should help you compare the differences. The entries that are different in the two inventory systems are highlighted.

Illustration 6A-1

Comparison of journal entries under perpetual and periodic inventory systems

ENTRIES ON BEYER VIDEO'S BOOKS

Transaction	Perpetual Inventory System		Periodic Inventory System	

May 4 Purchase of merchandise on credit.	Merchandise Inventory
	    Accounts Payable
		3,800
		3,800
			Purchases
			    Accounts Payable
				3,800
				3,800

May 8 Purchase returns and allowances.	Accounts Payable
	    Merchandise Inventory
		300
		300
			Accounts Payable
			    Purchase Returns
			    and Allowances
				300
				
				300

May 9 Freight costs on purchase.	Merchandise Inventory
	    Cash
		150
		150
			Freight-in
			    Cash
				150
				150

May 14 Payment on account with a discount.	Accounts Payable
	    Cash
	    Merchandise Inventory
		3,500
		3,430
		70
			Accounts Payable
			    Cash
			    Purchase Discounts
				3,500
				3,430
				70

ENTRIES ON SELLERS ELECTRONIX'S BOOKS

Transaction	Perpetual Inventory System		Periodic Inventory System	

May 4 Sale of merchandise on credit.	Accounts Receivable
	    Sales
		3,800
		3,800
			Accounts Receivable
			    Sales
				3,800
				3,800

	Cost of Goods Sold Merchandise Inventory	2,400 2,400	No entry for cost of goods sold	

May 8 Return of merchandise sold.	Sales Returns and
	Allowances
	    Accounts Receivable
		
		300
		300
			Sales Returns and
			Allowances
			    Accounts Receivable
				
				300
				300

	Merchandise Inventory Cost of Goods Sold	140 140	No entry	

May 15 Cash received on account with a discount.	Cash
	Sales Discounts
	    Accounts Receivable
		3,430
		70
		3,500
			Cash
			Sales Discounts
			    Accounts Receivable
				3,430
				70
				3,500

APPENDIX 6B *Estimating Inventories*

STUDY OBJECTIVE 10

Describe the two methods of estimating inventories.

We assumed in the chapter that a company would be able to physically count its inventory. But what if it cannot? What if the inventory were destroyed by fire, for example? In that case, we would use an estimate.

Two circumstances explain why inventories are sometimes estimated. First, management may want monthly or quarterly financial statements, but a physical inventory is taken only annually. Second, a casualty such as fire, flood, or earthquake may make it impossible to take a physical inventory. The need for estimating inventories is associated primarily with a periodic inventory system because of the absence of detailed inventory records.

There are two widely used methods of estimating inventories: (1) the gross profit method and (2) the retail inventory method.

GROSS PROFIT METHOD

The **gross profit method** estimates the cost of ending inventory by applying a gross profit rate to net sales. It is used in preparing monthly financial statements under a periodic system. This method is relatively simple but effective. It will detect large errors. Accountants, auditors, and managers frequently use the gross profit method to test the reasonableness of the ending inventory amount.

To use this method, a company needs to know its net sales, cost of goods available for sale, and gross profit rate. With the gross profit rate, the company can estimate its gross profit for the period. The formulas for using the gross profit method are given in Illustration 6B-1.

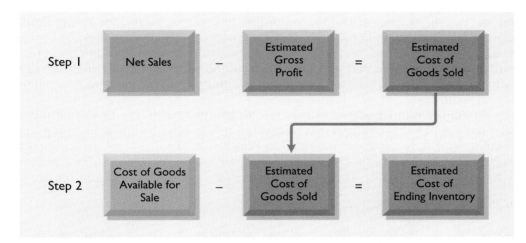

Illustration 6B-1

Gross profit method formulas

To illustrate, assume that Williams Company wishes to prepare an income statement for the month of January. Its records show net sales $200,000, beginning inventory $40,000, and cost of goods purchased $120,000. In the preceding year, the company realized a 30% gross profit rate. It expects to earn the same rate this year. Given these facts and assumptions, the estimated cost of the ending inventory at January 31 can be computed under the gross profit method as follows.

Illustration 6B-2

Example of gross profit method

Step 1:

Net sales	$200,000
Less: Estimated gross profit (30% × $200,000)	60,000
Estimated cost of goods sold	**$140,000**

Step 2:

Beginning inventory	$ 40,000
Cost of goods purchased	120,000
Cost of goods available for sale	160,000
Less: Estimated cost of goods sold	140,000
Estimated cost of ending inventory	**$ 20,000**

The gross profit method is based on the assumption that the gross profit rate will remain constant. But it may not remain constant, because of a change in merchandising policies or in market conditions. In such cases, the rate should be adjusted to reflect current operating conditions. In some cases, a more accurate estimate can be obtained by applying this method on a department or product-line basis.

The gross profit method should not be used in preparing a company's financial statements at the end of the year. These statements should be based on a physical inventory count.

RETAIL INVENTORY METHOD

A retail store such as **Kmart, Ace Hardware,** or **Wal-Mart** has thousands of different types of merchandise at low unit costs. In such cases it is difficult and time-consuming to apply unit costs to inventory quantities. An alternative is to use the **retail inventory method** to estimate the cost of inventory. In most retail concerns, a relationship between cost and sales price can be established. The cost-to-retail percentage is then applied to the ending inventory at retail prices to determine inventory at cost.

To use the retail inventory method, a company's records must show both the cost and retail value of the goods available for sale. The formulas for using the retail inventory method are presented in Illustration 6B-3.

Illustration 6B-3

Retail inventory method formulas

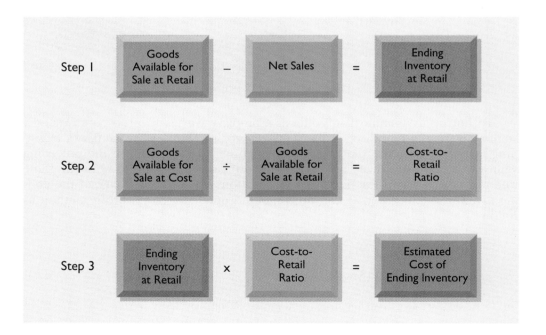

The logic of the retail method can be demonstrated by using unit-cost data. Assume that 10 units purchased at $7 each are marked to sell for $10 per unit. Thus, the cost-to-retail ratio is 70% ($70 ÷ $100). If 4 units remain unsold, their retail value is $40 (4 × $10), and their cost is $28 ($40 × 70%). This amount agrees with the total cost of goods on hand on a per unit basis (4 × $7).

The application of the retail method for Lacy Co. is shown in Illustration 6B-4. Note that it is not necessary to take a physical inventory to determine the estimated cost of goods on hand at any given time.

	At Cost	At Retail	
Beginning inventory	$14,000	$ 21,500	
Goods purchased	61,000	78,500	
Goods available for sale	$75,000	100,000	
Net sales		70,000	
(1) **Ending inventory at retail**		$ 30,000	
(2) **Cost-to-retail ratio = ($75,000 ÷ $100,000) = 75%**			
(3) **Estimated cost of ending inventory = ($30,000 × 75%)**	**$22,500**		

Illustration 6B-4

Example of retail inventory method

The retail inventory method also facilitates taking a physical inventory at the end of the year. The goods on hand can be valued at the prices marked on the merchandise. The cost-to-retail ratio is then applied to the goods on hand at retail to determine the ending inventory at cost.

The major disadvantage of the retail method is that it is an averaging technique. It may produce an incorrect inventory valuation if the mix of the ending inventory is not representative of the mix in the goods available for sale. Assume, for example, that the cost-to-retail ratio of 75% for Lacy Co. consists of equal proportions of inventory items that have cost-to-retail ratios of 70%, 75%, and 80%. If the ending inventory contains only items with a 70% ratio, an incorrect inventory cost will result. This problem can be minimized by applying the retail method on a department or product-line basis.

> **HELPFUL HINT**
> In determining inventory at retail, selling prices on the units are used. Tracing actual unit costs to invoices is unnecessary.

SUMMARY OF STUDY OBJECTIVE FOR APPENDIX 6B

10. *Describe the two methods of estimating inventories.* The two methods of estimating inventories are the gross profit method and the retail inventory method. Under the gross profit method, a gross profit rate is applied to net sales to determine estimated cost of goods sold. Estimated cost of goods sold is then subtracted from cost of goods available for sale to determine the estimated cost of the ending inventory.

Under the retail inventory method, a cost-to-retail ratio is computed by dividing the cost of goods available for sale by the retail value of the goods available for sale. This ratio is then applied to the ending inventory at retail to determine the estimated cost of the ending inventory.

GLOSSARY FOR APPENDIX 6B

Gross profit method   A method for estimating the cost of the ending inventory by applying a gross profit rate to net sales. (p. 251).

Retail inventory method   A method used to estimate the cost of the ending inventory by applying a cost-to-retail ratio to the ending inventory at retail. (p. 252).

APPENDIX 6C *INVENTORY COST FLOW METHODS IN PERPETUAL INVENTORY SYSTEMS*

Each of the inventory cost flow methods described in the chapter for a periodic inventory system can be used in a perpetual inventory system. To illustrate the application of the three assumed cost flow methods (FIFO, LIFO, and average cost), we will use the data shown below and in this chapter for Bow Valley Electronics' product Z202 Astro Condenser.

STUDY OBJECTIVE 11

Apply the inventory cost flow methods to perpetual inventory records.

Illustration 6C-1

Inventoriable units and costs

	BOW VALLEY ELECTRONICS Z202 Astro Condensers				
Date	Explanation	Units	Unit Cost	Total Cost	Balance in Units
1/1	Beginning inventory	100	$10	$ 1,000	100
4/15	Purchases	200	11	2,200	300
8/24	Purchases	300	12	3,600	600
9/10	Sales	550			50
11/27	Purchases	400	13	5,200	450
				$12,000	

FIRST-IN, FIRST-OUT (FIFO)

Under FIFO, the cost of the earliest goods on hand prior to each sale is charged to cost of goods sold. The cost of goods sold on September 10 consists of the units on hand January 1 and the units purchased April 15 and August 24. The inventory on a FIFO method perpetual system is shown in Illustration 6C-2.

Illustration 6C-2

Perpetual system—FIFO

Date	Purchases	Sales	Balance
January 1			(100 @ $10) $1,000
April 15	(200 @ $11) $2,200		(100 @ $10) ⎫ $3,200 (200 @ $11) ⎭
August 24	(300 @ $12) $3,600		(100 @ $10) ⎫ (200 @ $11) ⎬ $6,800 (300 @ $12) ⎭
September 10		(100 @ $10) (200 @ $11) (250 @ $12)	(50 @ $12) $ 600
		$6,200	
November 27	(400 @ $13) $5,200		(50 @ $12) ⎫ **$5,800** (400 @ $13) ⎭

The ending inventory in this situation is $5,800. The cost of goods sold is $6,200 [(100 @ $10) + (200 @ $11) + (250 @ $12)].

The results under FIFO in a perpetual system are the **same as in a periodic system**. See Illustration 6-9 on page 236. There, similarly, the ending inventory is $5,800 and cost of goods sold is $6,200. Regardless of the system, the first costs in are the costs assigned to cost of goods sold.

LAST-IN, FIRST-OUT (LIFO)

Under the LIFO method using a perpetual system, the cost of the most recent purchase prior to sale is allocated to the units sold. The cost of the goods sold on September 10 consists of all the units from the August 24 and April 15 purchases and 50 of the units in beginning inventory. The ending inventory on a LIFO method is computed in Illustration 6C-3.

Date	Purchases		Sales	Balance	
January 1				(100 @ $10)	$1,000
April 15	(200 @ $11)	$2,200		(100 @ $10) } $3,200 (200 @ $11)	
August 24	(300 @ $12)	$3,600		(100 @ $10) (200 @ $11) } $6,800 (300 @ $12)	
September 10			(300 @ $12) (200 @ $11) (50 @ $10)	(50 @ $10)	$ 500
			$6,300		
November 27	(400 @ $13)	$5,200		(50 @ $10) } $5,700 (400 @ $13)	

Illustration 6C-3

Perpetual system—LIFO

The use of LIFO in a perpetual system will usually produce cost allocations that differ from using LIFO in a periodic system. In a perpetual system, the latest units incurred **prior to each sale** are allocated to cost of goods sold. In contrast, in a periodic system, the latest units incurred **during the period** are allocated to cost of goods sold. Thus, when a purchase is made after the last sale, the LIFO periodic system will apply this purchase to the previous sale. See Illustration 6-14 on page 238. There, the proof shows the 400 units @ $13 purchased on November 27 applied to the sale of 550 units on September 10. As shown above under the LIFO perpetual system, the 400 units @ $13 purchased on November 27 are all applied to the ending inventory.

The ending inventory in this LIFO perpetual example is $5,700 and cost of goods sold is $6,300. Compare these amounts to the LIFO periodic illustration where the ending inventory is $5,000 and cost of goods sold is $7,000.

AVERAGE COST

The average cost method in a perpetual inventory system is called the **moving-average method.** Under this method a new average is computed **after each purchase**. The average cost is computed by dividing the cost of goods available for sale by the units on hand. The average cost is then applied to: (1) the units sold, to determine the cost of goods sold, and (2) the remaining units on hand, to determine the ending inventory amount. The application of the average cost method by Bow Valley Electronics is shown in Illustration 6C-4.

Date	Purchases		Sales	Balance	
January 1				(100 @ $10)	$1,000
April 15	(200 @ $11)	$2,200		(300 @ $10.667)	$3,200
August 24	(300 @ $12)	$3,600		(600 @ $11.333)	$6,800
September 10			(550 @ $11.333)	(50 @ $11.333)	$ 567
			($6,233)		
November 27	(400 @ $13)	$5,200		(450 @ $12.816)	$5,767

Illustration 6C-4

Perpetual system—average cost method

As indicated above, **a new average is computed each time a purchase is made.** On April 15, after 200 units are purchased for $2,200, a total of 300 units costing $3,200 ($1,000 + $2,200) are on hand. The average unit cost is $10.667 ($3,200 ÷ 300). On August 24, after 300 units are purchased for $3,600, a total of 600 units costing $6,800 ($1,000 + $2,200 + $3,600) are on hand at an average cost per unit of $11.333 ($6,800 ÷ 600). This unit cost of $11.333 is used in costing sales until another purchase is made, when a new unit cost is computed. Thus, the unit cost of the 550 units sold on September 10 is $11.333, and the total cost of goods sold is $6,233. On November 27, following the purchase of 400 units for $5,200, there are 450 units on hand costing $5,767 ($567 + $5,200), with a new average cost of $12.816 ($5,767 ÷ 450).

Compare this moving-average cost under the perpetual inventory system to Illustration 6-16 on page 239 showing the weighted-average method under a periodic inventory system.

Additional Demonstration Problem

DEMONSTRATION PROBLEM 2

Demonstration Problem 1 on pages 247–248 showed cost of goods sold computations under a periodic inventory system. Now let's assume that Gerald D. Englehart Company uses a perpetual inventory system. The company has the same inventory, purchases, and sales data for the month of March as shown earlier.

Inventory:	March 1	200 units @ $4.00	$ 800
Purchases:	March 10	500 units @ $4.50	2,250
	March 20	400 units @ $4.75	1,900
	March 30	300 units @ $5.00	1,500
Sales:	March 15	500 units	
	March 25	400 units	

The physical inventory count on March 31 shows 500 units on hand.

Instructions
Under a **perpetual inventory system**, determine the cost of inventory on hand at March 31 and the cost of goods sold for March under the (a) first-in, first-out (FIFO) method, (b) last-in, first-out (LIFO) method, and (c) average cost method.

SOLUTION TO DEMONSTRATION PROBLEM 2

The cost of goods available for sale is $6,450, as follows.

Inventory:		200 units @ $4.00	$ 800
Purchases:	March 10	500 units @ $4.50	2,250
	March 20	400 units @ $4.75	1,900
	March 30	300 units @ $5.00	1,500
	Total cost of goods available for sale		$6,450

Under a **perpetual inventory system**, the cost of goods sold under each cost flow method is as follows.

FIFO Method

Date	Purchases	Sales	Balance
March 1			(200 @ $4.00) $ 800
March 10	(500 @ $4.50) $2,250		(200 @ $4.00) (500 @ $4.50) } $3,050
March 15		(200 @ $4.00) (300 @ $4.50) ⎿ $2,150 ⏌	(200 @ $4.50) $ 900
March 20	(400 @ $4.75) $1,900		(200 @ $4.50) (400 @ $4.75) } $2,800
March 25		(200 @ $4.50) (200 @ $4.75) ⎿ $1,850 ⏌	(200 @ $4.75) $ 950
March 30	(300 @ $5.00) $1,500		(200 @ $4.75) (300 @ $5.00) } $2,450
Ending inventory,	$2,450	Cost of goods sold: $6,450 − $2,450 = $4,000	

ACTION PLAN
- Compute the cost of goods sold under the perpetual FIFO method by allocating to the goods sold the **earliest** cost of goods purchased.
- Compute the cost of goods sold under the perpetual LIFO method by allocating to the goods sold the **latest** cost of goods purchased.
- Compute the cost of goods sold under the perpetual average cost method by allocating to the goods sold a **moving-average** cost.

LIFO Method

Date	Purchases		Sales		Balance	
March 1					(200 @ $4.00)	$ 800
March 10	(500 @ $4.50)	$2,250			(200 @ $4.00) (500 @ $4.50) }	$3,050
March 15			(500 @ $4.50)	$2,250	(200 @ $4.00)	$ 800
March 20	(400 @ $4.75)	$1,900			(200 @ $4.00) (400 @ $4.75) }	$2,700
March 25			(400 @ $4.75)	$1,900	(200 @ $4.00)	$ 800
March 30	(300 @ $5.00)	$1,500			(200 @ $4.00) (300 @ $5.00) }	$2,300

Ending inventory, $2,300   Cost of goods sold: $6,450 − $2,300 = $4,150

Moving-Average Cost Method

Date	Purchases		Sales		Balance	
March 1					(200 @ $ 4.00)	$ 800
March 10	(500 @ $4.50)	$2,250			(700 @ $4.357)	$3,050
March 15			(500 @ $4.357)	$2,179	(200 @ $4.357)	$ 871
March 20	(400 @ $4.75)	$1,900			(600 @ $4.618)	$2,771
March 25			(400 @ $4.618)	$1,847	(200 @ $4.618)	$ 924
March 30	(300 @ $5.00)	$1,500			(500 @ $4.848)	$2,424
Ending inventory, $2,424	Cost of goods sold: $6,450 − $2,424 = $4,026					

SUMMARY OF STUDY OBJECTIVE FOR APPENDIX 6C

11. Apply the inventory cost flow methods to perpetual inventory records. Under FIFO, the cost of the earliest goods on hand prior to each sale is charged to cost of goods sold. Under LIFO, the cost of the most recent purchase prior to sale is charged to cost of goods sold. Under the average cost method, a new average cost is computed after each purchase.

*Note: All **asterisked** Questions, Exercises, and Problems relate to material in the appendixes to the chapter.

Chapter 6 Self-Test

SELF-STUDY QUESTIONS

Answers are at the end of the chapter.

(SO 1) **1.** Which of the following should *not* be included in the physical inventory of a company?
   a. Goods held on consignment from another company.
   b. Goods shipped on consignment to another company.
   c. Goods in transit from another company shipped FOB shipping point.
   d. None of the above.

(SO 2) **2.** When goods are purchased for resale by a company using a periodic inventory system:
   a. purchases on account are debited to Merchandise Inventory.
   b. purchases on account are debited to Purchases.
   c. purchase returns are debited to Purchase Returns and Allowances.
   d. freight costs are debited to Purchases.

3. In determining cost of goods sold: (SO 3)
   a. purchase discounts are deducted from net purchases.
   b. freight-out is added to net purchases.
   c. purchase returns and allowances are deducted from net purchases.
   d. freight-in is added to net purchases.

4. If beginning inventory is $60,000, cost of goods purchased (SO 3) is $380,000, and ending inventory is $50,000, cost of goods sold is:
   a. $390,000.   c. $330,000.
   b. $370,000.   d. $420,000.

5. Inventoriable costs consist of two elements: beginning in- (SO 5) ventory and
   a. ending inventory.
   b. cost of goods purchased.
   c. cost of goods sold.
   d. cost of goods available for sale.

(SO 5) **6.** Bullwinkle Company has the following:

	Units	Unit Cost
Inventory, Jan. 1	8,000	$11
Purchase, June 19	13,000	12
Purchase, Nov. 8	5,000	13

If 9,000 units are on hand at December 31, the cost of the ending inventory under FIFO is:
a. $99,000.   c. $113,000.
b. $108,000.   d. $117,000.

(SO 5) **7.** Using the data in (6) above, the cost of the ending inventory under LIFO is:
a. $113,000.   c. $99,000.
b. $108,000.   d. $100,000.

(SO 6) **8.** In periods of rising prices, LIFO will produce:
a. higher net income than FIFO.
b. the same net income as FIFO.
c. lower net income than FIFO.
d. higher net income than average costing.

(SO 6) **9.** Factors that affect the selection of an inventory costing method do *not* include:
a. tax effects.
b. balance sheet effects.
c. income statement effects.
d. perpetual vs. periodic inventory system.

(SO 7) **10.** The lower of cost or market basis may be applied to:
a. categories of inventories.
b. individual items of inventories.
c. total inventory.
d. all of the above.

(SO 8) **11.** Titan A.E. Company's ending inventory is understated $4,000. The effects of this error on the current year's cost

of goods sold and net income, respectively, are:
a. understated, overstated.
b. overstated, understated.
c. overstated, overstated.
d. understated, understated.

(SO 9) **12.** Which of these would cause the inventory turnover ratio to increase the most?
a. Increasing the amount of inventory on hand.
b. Keeping the amount of inventory on hand constant but increasing sales.
c. Keeping the amount of inventory on hand constant but decreasing sales.
d. Decreasing the amount of inventory on hand and increasing sales.

(SO 10) ***13.** Butterfly Company has sales of $150,000 and cost of goods available for sale of $135,000. If the gross profit rate is 30%, the estimated cost of the ending inventory under the gross profit method is:
a. $15,000.
b. $30,000.
c. $45,000.
d. $75,000.

(SO 10) ***14.** In a perpetual inventory system,
a. LIFO cost of goods sold will be the same as in a periodic inventory system.
b. average costs are based entirely on unit cost averages.
c. a new average is computed under the average cost method after each sale.
d. FIFO cost of goods sold will be the same as in a periodic inventory system.

QUESTIONS

1. Goods costing $2,000 are purchased on account on July 15 with credit terms of 2/10, n/30. On July 18 a $200 credit memo is received from the supplier for damaged goods. Give the journal entry on July 24 to record payment of the balance due within the discount period.

2. Identify the accounts that are added to or deducted from Purchases to determine the cost of goods purchased. For each account, indicate (a) whether it is added or deducted and (b) its normal balance.

3. In the following separate mini cases, using a periodic inventory system, identify the item(s) designated by letter.
(a) Purchases − X − Y = Net purchases.
(b) Cost of goods purchased − Net purchases = X.
(c) Beginning inventory + X = Cost of goods available for sale.
(d) Cost of goods available for sale − Cost of goods sold = X.

4. "The key to successful business operations is effective inventory management." Do you agree? Explain.

5. An item must possess two characteristics to be classified as inventory by a merchandiser. What are these two characteristics?

6. Your friend Tom Wetzel has been hired to help take the physical inventory in Kikujiro Hardware Store. Explain to Tom Wetzel what this job will entail.

7. (a) Janine Company ships merchandise to Laura Company on December 30. The merchandise reaches the buyer on January 6. Indicate the terms of sale that will result in the goods being included in (1) Janine's December 31 inventory, and (2) Laura's December 31 inventory.
(b) Under what circumstances should Janine Company include consigned goods in its inventory?

8. Brim Hat Shop received a shipment of hats for which it paid the wholesaler $2,940. The price of the hats was $3,000 but Brim was given a $60 cash discount and required to pay freight charges of $80. In addition, Brim paid $130 to cover the travel expenses of an employee who negotiated the purchase of the hats. What amount will Brim record for inventory? Why?

9. What is the primary basis of accounting for inventories? What is the major objective in accounting for inventories? What accounting principles are involved here?

10. Identify the distinguishing features of an income statement for a merchandiser.

11. Roger Holloway believes that the allocation of inventoriable costs should be based on the actual physical flow of the goods. Explain to Roger why this may be both impractical and inappropriate.

12. What is a major advantage and a major disadvantage of the specific identification method of inventory costing?

13. "The selection of an inventory cost flow method is a decision made by accountants." Do you agree? Explain. Once a method has been selected, what accounting requirement applies?

14. Which assumed inventory cost flow method:
   (a) usually parallels the actual physical flow of merchandise?
   (b) assumes that goods available for sale during an accounting period are identical?
   (c) assumes that the latest units purchased are the first to be sold?

15. In a period of rising prices, the inventory reported in Terry Duffy Company's balance sheet is close to the current cost of the inventory. Greg Hanson Company's inventory is considerably below its current cost. Identify the inventory cost flow method being used by each company. Which company has probably been reporting the higher gross profit?

16. Char Lewis Company has been using the FIFO cost flow method during a prolonged period of rising prices. During the same time period, Char Lewis has been paying out all of its net income as dividends. What adverse effects may result from this policy?

17. Bob Thebeau is studying for the next accounting midterm examination. What should Bob know about (a) departing from the cost basis of accounting for inventories and (b) the meaning of "market" in the lower of cost or market method?

18. Henning Music Center has 5 CD players on hand at the balance sheet date. Each cost $400. The current replacement cost is $320 per unit. Under the lower of cost or market basis of accounting for inventories, what value should be reported for the CD players on the balance sheet? Why?

19. What methods may be used under the lower of cost or market basis of accounting for inventories? Which method will produce the lowest inventory value?

20. Hitachi Company discovers in 2002 that its ending inventory at December 31, 2001, was $5,000 understated. What effect will this error have on (a) 2001 net income, (b) 2002 net income, and (c) the combined net income for the 2 years?

21. Maureen & Nathan Company's balance sheet shows Inventories $162,800. What additional disclosures should be made?

22. Under what circumstances might inventory turnover be too high? That is, what possible negative consequences might occur?

*23. When is it necessary to estimate inventories?

*24. Both the gross profit method and the retail inventory method are based on averages. For each method, indicate the average used, how it is determined, and how it is applied.

*25. Jana Kingston Company has net sales of $400,000 and cost of goods available for sale of $300,000. If the gross profit rate is 30%, what is the estimated cost of the ending inventory? Show computations.

*26. Cavanaugh Shoe Shop had goods available for sale in 2002 with a retail price of $120,000. The cost of these goods was $84,000. If sales during the period were $100,000, what is the ending inventory at cost using the retail inventory method?

*27. "When perpetual inventory records are kept, the results under the FIFO and LIFO methods are the same as they would be in a periodic inventory system." Do you agree? Explain.

*28. How does the average cost method of inventory costing differ between a perpetual inventory system and a periodic inventory system?

BRIEF EXERCISES

BE6-1   Prepare the journal entries to record the following transactions on IMAX Company's books using a periodic inventory system.

Journalize purchases transactions.
(SO 2)

   (a) On March 2, IMAX Company purchased $700,000 of merchandise from Sing Tao Company, terms 2/10, n/30.
   (b) On March 6, IMAX Company returned $130,000 of the merchandise purchased on March 2 because it was defective.
   (c) On March 12, IMAX Company paid the balance due to Sing Tao Company.

Compute net purchases and cost of goods purchased.
(SO 3)

BE6-2 Assume that Mephisto Company uses a periodic inventory system and has the following account balances: Purchases $480,000, Purchase Returns and Allowances $11,000, Purchase Discounts $8,000, and Freight-in $16,000. Determine (a) net purchases and (b) cost of goods purchased.

Compute cost of goods sold and gross profit.
(SO 3)

BE6-3 Assume the same information as in BE6-2, and also that Mephisto Company has beginning inventory of $60,000, ending inventory of $90,000, and net sales of $620,000. Determine the amounts to be reported for cost of goods sold and gross profit.

Identify items to be included in taking a physical inventory.
(SO 1)

BE6-4 Fantasia Press Company identifies the following items for possible inclusion in the taking of a physical inventory. Indicate whether each item should be included or excluded from the inventory taking.

(a) Goods shipped on consignment by Fantasia Press to another company.
(b) Goods in transit from a supplier shipped FOB destination.
(c) Goods sold but being held for customer pickup.
(d) Goods held on consignment from another company.

Identify the components of inventoriable costs.
(SO 5)

BE6-5 The ledger of Shinhan Company includes the following items: (a) Freight-in, (b) Purchase Returns and Allowances, (c) Purchases, (d) Sales Discounts, (e) Purchase Discounts. Identify which items are included in inventoriable costs.

Compute ending inventory using FIFO and LIFO.
(SO 5)

BE6-6 In its first month of operations, Manion Company made three purchases of merchandise in the following sequence: (1) 300 units at $6, (2) 400 units at $7, and (3) 300 units at $8. Assuming there are 450 units on hand, compute the cost of the ending inventory under the (a) FIFO method and (b) LIFO method. Manion uses a periodic inventory system.

Compute the ending inventory using average costs.
(SO 5)

BE6-7 Data for Manion Company are presented in BE6-6. Compute the cost of the ending inventory under the average cost method, assuming there are 450 units on hand.

Determine the LCM valuation using inventory categories.
(SO 7)

BE6-8 Svenska Appliance Center accumulates the following cost and market data at December 31.

Inventory Categories	Cost Data	Market Data
Cameras	$12,000	$11,200
Camcorders	9,000	9,700
VCRs	14,000	12,800

Compute the lower of cost or market valuation using categories.

Compute inventory turnover and days in inventory.
(SO 9)

BE6-9 At December 31, 2002, the following information was available for B. Sherrick Company: ending inventory $80,000, beginning inventory $60,000, cost of goods sold $280,000, and sales revenue $380,000. Calculate inventory turnover and days in inventory for B. Sherrick Company.

Determine correct income statement amounts.
(SO 8)

BE6-10 Rome Company reports net income of $90,000 in 2002. However, ending inventory was understated $5,000. What is the correct net income for 2002? What effect, if any, will this error have on total assets as reported in the balance sheet at December 31, 2002?

Apply the gross profit method.
(SO 10)

*BE6-11 At May 31, Denmark Company has net sales of $350,000 and cost of goods available for sale of $230,000. Compute the estimated cost of the ending inventory, assuming the gross profit rate is 40%.

Apply the retail inventory method.
(SO 10)

*BE6-12 On June 30, Irish Fabrics has the following data pertaining to the retail inventory method: Goods available for sale: at cost $35,000, at retail $50,000; net sales $40,000, and ending inventory at retail $10,000. Compute the estimated cost of the ending inventory using the retail inventory method.

Apply cost flow methods to records.
(SO 11)

*BE6-13 Dodi's Department Store uses a perpetual inventory system. Data for product E2-D2 include the following purchases.

Date	Number of Units	Unit Price
May 7	50	$10
July 28	30	15

On June 1 Dodi's sold 30 units, and on August 27, 35 more units. Prepare the perpetual inventory card for the above transactions using (1) FIFO, (2) LIFO, and (3) average cost.

EXERCISES

Journalize purchases
transactions.
(SO 2)

E6-1 Presented below is the following information related to Argentina Co.

1. On April 5, purchased merchandise from Chile Company for $15,000, terms 2/10, net/30, FOB shipping point.
2. On April 6, paid freight costs of $800 on merchandise purchased from Chile.
3. On April 7, purchased equipment on account from Wayne Higley Mfg. Co. for $26,000.
4. On April 8, returned damaged merchandise to Chile Company and was granted a $3,000 allowance.
5. On April 15, paid the amount due to Chile Company in full.

Instructions

(a) Prepare the journal entries to record these transactions on the books of Argentina Co. using a periodic inventory system.
(b) Assume that Argentina Co. paid the balance due to Chile Company on May 4 instead of April 15. Prepare the journal entry to record this payment.

Prepare cost of goods sold
section.
(SO 3)

E6-2 The trial balance of Peru Company at the end of its fiscal year, August 31, 2002, includes the following accounts: Merchandise Inventory $17,200, Purchases $145,400, Sales $190,000, Freight-in $4,000, Sales Returns and Allowances $3,000, Freight-out $1,000, and Purchase Returns and Allowances $2,000. The ending (August 31, 2002) merchandise inventory is $25,000.

Instructions

Prepare a cost of goods sold section for the year ending August 31 (periodic inventory).

Prepare an income
statement.
(SO 4)

E6-3 Presented is information related to Bolivia Co. for the month of January 2002.

Freight-in	$ 10,000	Rent expense	$ 19,000
Freight-out	5,000	Salary expense	61,000
Insurance expense	12,000	Sales discounts	8,000
Purchases	220,000	Sales returns and allowances	13,000
Purchase discounts	3,000	Sales	325,000
Purchase returns and allowances	6,000		

Beginning merchandise inventory was $42,000. Ending inventory was $63,000.

Instructions

Prepare an income statement using the format presented on page 232. Operating expenses should not be segregated into selling and administrative expenses.

Determine the correct inventory amount.
(SO 1)

E6-4 Rockford Bank and Trust is considering giving Canada Company a loan. Before doing so, they decide that further discussions with Canada's accountant may be desirable. One area of particular concern is the inventory account, which has a year-end balance of $297,000. Discussions with the accountant reveal the following.

1. Canada sold goods costing $38,000 to Cineplex Company, FOB shipping point, on December 28. The goods are not expected to arrive at Cineplex until January 12. The goods were not included in the physical inventory because they were not in the warehouse.
2. The physical count of the inventory did not include goods costing $95,000 that were shipped to Canada FOB destination on December 27 and were still in transit at year-end.
3. Canada received goods costing $20,000 on January 2. The goods were shipped FOB shipping point on December 26 by Gladiator Co. The goods were not included in the physical count.
4. Canada sold goods costing $40,000 to Rochelle Co., FOB destination, on December 30. The goods were received at Rochelle on January 8. They were not included in Canada's physical inventory.
5. Canada received goods costing $44,000 on January 2 that were shipped FOB destination on December 29. The shipment was a rush order that was supposed to arrive December 31. This purchase was included in the ending inventory of $297,000.

Instructions

Determine the correct inventory amount on December 31.

Compute inventory and cost of
goods sold using FIFO and
LIFO.
(SO 5)

E6-5 Spain Co. uses a periodic inventory system. Its records show the following for the month of May, in which 70 units were sold.

			Units	Unit Cost	Total Cost
May	1	Inventory	30	$ 8	$240
	15	Purchases	25	10	250
	24	Purchases	35	13	455
		Totals	90		$945

Instructions

Compute the ending inventory at May 31 using the FIFO and LIFO methods. Prove the amount allocated to cost of goods sold under each method.

Compute inventory and cost of goods sold using FIFO and LIFO.
(SO 5, 6)

E6-6 In June, Naperville Company reports the following for the month of June.

			Units	Unit Cost	Total Cost
June	1	Inventory	200	$5	$1,000
	12	Purchases	300	6	1,800
	23	Purchases	500	7	3,500
	30	Inventory	150		

Instructions

(a) Compute the cost of the ending inventory and the cost of goods sold under (1) FIFO and (2) LIFO.

(b) Which costing method gives the higher ending inventory? Why?

(c) Which method results in the higher cost of goods sold? Why?

Compute inventory and cost of goods sold using average costs.
(SO 5, 6)

E6-7 Inventory data for Naperville Company are presented in E6-6.

Instructions

(a) Compute the cost of the ending inventory and the cost of goods sold using the average cost method.

(b) Will the results in (a) be higher or lower than the results under (1) FIFO and (2) LIFO?

(c) Why is the average unit cost not $6?

Determine ending inventory under lower of cost or market inventory method.
(SO 7)

E6-8 Oriental Camera Shop uses the lower of cost or market basis for its inventory. The following data are available at December 31.

Item	Units	Unit Cost	Market
Cameras:			
Minolta	5	$170	$160
Canon	6	150	152
Light Meters:			
Vivitar	12	125	110
Kodak	11	115	135

Instructions

Determine the amount of the ending inventory by applying the lower of cost or market basis to **(a)** individual items, **(b)** inventory categories, and **(c)** the total inventory.

Determine effects of inventory errors.
(SO 8)

E6-9 Iqbal Hardware reported cost of goods sold as follows.

	2002	2003
Beginning inventory	$ 20,000	$ 30,000
Cost of goods purchased	150,000	175,000
Cost of goods available for sale	170,000	205,000
Ending inventory	30,000	35,000
Cost of goods sold	$140,000	$170,000

Iqbal made two errors: (1) 2002 ending inventory was overstated $5,000, and (2) 2003 ending inventory was understated $4,000.

Instructions

Compute the correct cost of goods sold for each year.

Prepare correct income statements.
(SO 8)

E6-10 Finlandia Watch Company reported the following income statement data for a 2-year period.

	2002	2003
Sales	$210,000	$250,000
Cost of goods sold		
Beginning inventory	32,000	40,000
Cost of goods purchased	173,000	202,000
Cost of goods available for sale	205,000	242,000
Ending inventory	40,000	52,000
Cost of goods sold	165,000	190,000
Gross profit	$ 45,000	$ 60,000

Finlandia uses a periodic inventory system. The inventories at January 1, 2002, and December 31, 2003, are correct. However, the ending inventory at December 31, 2002, was overstated $3,000.

Instructions

(a) Prepare correct income statement data for the 2 years.
(b) What is the cumulative effect of the inventory error on total gross profit for the 2 years?
(c) ▭▭▭▭▭▷ Explain in a letter to the president of Finlandia Company what has happened— i.e., the nature of the error and its effect on the financial statements.

E6-11 This information is available for Wideangle Lens Corporation for 2000, 2001, and 2002.

Compute inventory turnover, days in inventory, and gross profit rate.
(SO 9, 10)

	2000	2001	2002
Beginning inventory	$ 200,000	$ 300,000	$ 400,000
Ending inventory	300,000	400,000	500,000
Cost of goods sold	850,000	1,120,000	1,200,000
Sales	1,200,000	1,600,000	1,900,000

Instructions

Calculate inventory turnover, days in inventory, and gross profit rate (from Chapter 5) for Wideangle Lens Corporation for 2000, 2001, 2002. Comment on any trends.

*E6-12 The inventory of Odeon Company was destroyed by fire on March 1. From an examination of the accounting records, the following data for the first 2 months of the year are obtained: Sales $51,000, Sales Returns and Allowances $1,000, Purchases $28,200, Freight-in $1,200, and Purchase Returns and Allowances $1,400.

Determine merchandise lost using the gross profit method of estimating inventory.
(SO 10)

Instructions

Determine the merchandise lost by fire, assuming:

(a) A beginning inventory of $25,000 and a gross profit rate of 30% on net sales.
(b) A beginning inventory of $30,000 and a gross profit rate of 25% on net sales.

*E6-13 Gucci Shoe Store uses the retail inventory method for its two departments, Women's Shoes and Men's Shoes. The following information for each department is obtained.

Determine ending inventory at cost using retail method.
(SO 10)

Item	Women's Department	Men's Department
Beginning inventory at cost	$ 32,000	$ 46,450
Cost of goods purchased at cost	148,000	137,300
Net sales	177,000	185,000
Beginning inventory at retail	45,000	60,000
Cost of goods purchased at retail	182,000	185,000

Instructions

Compute the estimated cost of the ending inventory for each department under the retail inventory method.

*E6-14 Alpine Appliance uses a perpetual inventory system. For its flat-screen television sets, the January 1 inventory was 4 sets at $600 each. On January 10, Alpine purchased 6 units at $640 each. The company sold 2 units on January 8 and 5 units on January 15.

Apply cost flow methods to perpetual records.
(SO 11)

Instructions

Compute the ending inventory under (1) FIFO, (2) LIFO, and (3) average cost.

PROBLEMS: SET A

Journalize, post, and prepare a trial balance and partial income statement.
(SO 2, 3, 4)

P6-1A Vanessa Williams, a professional tennis star, operates VW's Tennis Shop at the Florida Lake Resort. At the beginning of the current season, the ledger of VW's Tennis Shop showed Cash $2,500, Merchandise Inventory $1,700, and Capital $4,200. The following transactions were completed during April.

Apr.	4	Purchased racquets and balls from Daddy Co. $840 FOB shipping point, terms 3/10, n/30.
	6	Paid freight on Daddy Co. purchase $40.
	8	Sold merchandise to members $900, terms n/30.
	10	Received credit of $40 from Daddy Co. for a damaged racquet that was returned.
	11	Purchased tennis shoes from Niki Sports for cash $300.
	13	Paid Daddy Co. in full.
	14	Purchased tennis shirts and shorts from Martina's Sportswear $900, FOB shipping point, terms 2/10, n/60.
	15	Received cash refund of $50 from Niki Sports for damaged merchandise that was returned.
	17	Paid freight on Martina's Sportswear purchase $30.
	18	Sold merchandise to members $800, terms n/30.
	20	Received $500 in cash from members in settlement of their accounts.
	21	Paid Martina's Sportswear in full.
	27	Granted credit of $30 to members for tennis clothing that did not fit.
	30	Sold merchandise to members $900, terms n/30.
	30	Received cash payments on account from members $500.

The chart of accounts for the tennis shop includes the following: No. 101 Cash, No. 112 Accounts Receivable, No. 120 Merchandise Inventory, No. 201 Accounts Payable, No. 301 Capital, No. 401 Sales, No. 412 Sales Returns and Allowances, No. 510 Purchases, No. 512 Purchase Returns and Allowances, No. 514 Purchase Discounts, No. 516 Freight-in.

Instructions

(a) Journalize the April transactions using a periodic inventory system.
(b) Enter the beginning balances in the ledger accounts and post the April transactions. (Use J1 for the journal reference.)

(c) Total debits $6,932
(d) Gross profit $692

(c) Prepare a trial balance on April 30, 2002.
(d) Prepare an income statement through gross profit, assuming merchandise inventory on hand at April 30 is $1,800.

Prepare an income statement.
(SO 3, 4)

P6-2A Anna Mossity Department Store is located near the Village shopping mall. At the end of the company's fiscal year on December 31, 2002, the following accounts appeared in its adjusted trial balance.

Accounts Payable	$ 89,300
Accounts Receivable	50,300
Accumulated Depreciation—Building	52,500
Accumulated Depreciation—Equipment	42,900
Building	190,000
Cash	23,000
Depreciation Expense—Building	10,400
Depreciation Expense—Equipment	13,300
Equipment	110,000
Freight-in	3,600
Insurance Expense	7,200
Merchandise Inventory	40,500
Mortgage Payable	80,000
Office Salaries Expense	32,000
Prepaid Insurance	2,400
Property Taxes Payable	4,300
Purchases	482,000

Purchase Discounts	12,000
Purchase Returns and Allowances	6,400
Sales Salaries Expense	74,000
Sales	658,000
Sales Commissions Expense	14,500
Sales Commissions Payable	4,000
Sales Returns and Allowances	8,000
A. Mossity, Capital	177,600
A. Mossity, Drawing	28,000
Property Taxes Expense	4,800
Utilities Expense	11,000

Analysis reveals the following additional data.

1. Merchandise inventory on December 31, 2002, is $75,000.
2. Insurance expense and utilities expense are 60% selling and 40% administrative.
3. Depreciation on the building and property tax expense are administrative expenses; depreciation on the equipment is a selling expense.

Instructions
Prepare an income statement for the year ended December 31, 2002.

Net income $50,100

P6-3A   Scott Company had a beginning inventory of 400 units of Product E2-D2 at a cost of $8.00 per unit. During the year, purchases were:

Feb. 20	700 units at $9.00	Aug. 12	300 units at $11.00
May 5	500 units at $10.00	Dec. 8	100 units at $12.00

Scott Company uses a periodic inventory system. Sales totaled 1,500 units.

Determine cost of goods sold and ending inventory, using FIFO, LIFO, and average cost.
(SO 5, 6)

Instructions

(a) Determine the cost of goods available for sale.
(b) Determine (1) the ending inventory, and (2) the cost of goods sold under each of the assumed cost flow methods (FIFO, LIFO, and average). Prove the accuracy of the cost of goods sold under the FIFO and LIFO methods.
(c) Which cost flow method results in (1) the lowest inventory amount for the balance sheet, and (2) the lowest cost of goods sold for the income statement?

P6-4A   The management of Aurora Co. is reevaluating the appropriateness of using its present inventory cost flow method, which is average cost. They request your help in determining the results of operations for 2002 if either the FIFO method or the LIFO method had been used. For 2002, the accounting records show the following data.

Compute ending inventory, prepare income statements, and answer questions using FIFO and LIFO.
(SO 5, 6)

Inventories		Purchases and Sales	
Beginning (15,000 units)	$34,000	Total net sales (225,000 units)	$865,000
Ending (20,000 units)		Total cost of goods purchased	
		(230,000 units)	591,500

Purchases were made quarterly as follows.

Quarter	Units	Unit Cost	Total Cost
1	60,000	$2.40	$144,000
2	50,000	2.50	125,000
3	50,000	2.60	130,000
4	70,000	2.75	192,500
	230,000		$591,500

Operating expenses were $147,000, and the company's income tax rate is 32%.

Instructions

(a) Prepare comparative condensed income statements for 2002 under FIFO and LIFO. (Show computations of ending inventory.)

(a) Net income
FIFO $100,300
LIFO $94,180

(b) (4) $2,880

(b) ▭▭▭▷ Answer the following questions for management in the form of a business letter.

(1) Which cost flow method (FIFO or LIFO) produces the more meaningful inventory amount for the balance sheet? Why?

(2) Which cost flow method (FIFO or LIFO) produces the more meaningful net income? Why?

(3) Which cost flow method (FIFO or LIFO) is more likely to approximate actual physical flow of the goods? Why?

(4) How much additional cash will be available for management under LIFO than under FIFO? Why?

(5) Will gross profit under the average cost method be higher or lower than (a) FIFO and (b) LIFO? (*Note:* It is not necessary to quantify your answer.)

Estimate inventory loss using gross profit method. (SO 10)

*P6-5A   Wayne E. Weather Company lost 80% of its inventory in a fire on March 25, 2002. The accounting records showed the following gross profit data for February and March.

	February	**March (to 3/25)**
Net sales	$300,000	$260,000
Net purchases	200,800	191,000
Freight-in	2,900	4,000
Beginning inventory	16,500	25,200
Ending inventory	25,200	?

Wayne E. Weather Company is fully insured for fire losses but must prepare a report for the insurance company.

Instructions

(a) Compute the gross profit rate for the month of February.

(b) Using the gross profit rate for February, determine both the estimated total inventory and inventory lost in the fire in March.

Compute ending inventory and cost of inventory lost using retail method. (SO 10)

*P6-6A   Korean Department Store uses the retail inventory method to estimate its monthly ending inventories. The following information is available for two of its departments at August 31, 2002.

	Sporting Goods		**Jewelry and Cosmetics**	
	Cost	**Retail**	**Cost**	**Retail**
Net sales		$1,010,000		$1,150,000
Purchases	$670,000	1,066,000	$733,000	1,158,000
Purchase returns	(26,000)	(40,000)	(12,000)	(20,000)
Purchase discounts	(15,360)	—	(9,440)	—
Freight-in	6,000	—	8,000	—
Beginning inventory	47,360	74,000	36,440	62,000

At December 31, Korean Department Store takes a physical inventory at retail. The actual retail values of the inventories in each department are Sporting Goods $85,000, and Jewelry and Cosmetics $54,000.

Instructions

(a) Determine the estimated cost of the ending inventory for each department on **August 31, 2002**, using the retail inventory method.

(b) Compute the ending inventory at cost for each department at **December 31**, assuming the cost-to-retail ratios are 60% for Sporting Goods and 65% for Jewelry and Cosmetics.

Determine ending inventory under a perpetual inventory system. (SO 11)

*P6-7A   Reliable Appliance Mart begins operations on May 1. It uses a perpetual inventory system. During May the company had the following purchases and sales for its Model 25 Sureshot camera.

| | Purchases | | Sales |
Date	Units	Unit Cost	Units
May 1	7	$150	
4			5
8	8	$170	
12			5
15	5	$180	
20			4
25			2

Instructions

(a) Determine the ending inventory under a perpetual inventory system using (1) FIFO, (2) average cost, and (3) LIFO.

(b) Which costing method produces (1) the highest ending inventory valuation and (2) the lowest ending inventory valuation?

(a) FIFO $720
Average $692
LIFO $640

PROBLEMS: SET B

P6-1B Nicklaus Bear, a former professional golf star, operates Nick's Pro Shop at Bay Golf Course. At the beginning of the current season on April 1, 2002, the ledger of Nick's Pro Shop showed Cash $3,000, Merchandise Inventory $3,500, and Capital $6,500. The following transactions were completed during April.

Journalize, post, and prepare trial balance and partial income statement.
(SO 2, 3, 4)

Apr.	5	Purchased golf bags, clubs, and balls on account from Balata Co. $1,900, FOB shipping point, terms 2/10, n/60.
	7	Paid freight on Balata purchase $80.
	9	Received credit from Balata Co. for merchandise returned $100.
	10	Sold merchandise on account to members $900, terms n/30.
	12	Purchased golf shoes, sweaters, and other accessories on account from Westphal Sportswear $860, terms 1/10, n/30.
	14	Paid Balata Co. in full.
	17	Received credit from Westphal Sportswear for merchandise returned $60.
	20	Made sales on account to members $700, terms n/30.
	21	Paid Westphal Sportswear in full.
	27	Granted credit to members for clothing that did not fit $30.
	30	Made cash sales $600.
	30	Received payments on account from members $1,100.

The chart of accounts for the pro shop includes the following: No. 101 Cash, No. 112 Accounts Receivable, No. 120 Merchandise Inventory, No. 201 Accounts Payable, No. 301 Capital, No. 401 Sales, No. 412 Sales Returns and Allowances, No. 510 Purchases, No. 512 Purchase Returns and Allowances, No. 514 Purchase Discounts, No. 516 Freight-in.

Instructions

(a) Journalize the April transactions using a periodic inventory system.

(b) Enter the beginning balances in the ledger accounts and post the April transactions. (Use J1 for the journal reference.)

(c) Prepare a trial balance on April 30, 2002.

(d) Prepare an income statement through gross profit, assuming merchandise inventory on hand at April 30 is $4,200.

(c) Total debits $8,904
(d) Gross profit $234

P6-2B Bedazzle Department Store is located in midtown Metropolis. During the past several years, net income has been declining because of suburban shopping centers. At the end of the company's fiscal year on November 30, 2002, the following accounts appeared in its adjusted trial balance.

Prepare an income statement.
(SO 3, 4)

Accounts Payable	$ 35,310
Accounts Receivable	11,770
Accumulated Depreciation—Delivery Equipment	19,680
Accumulated Depreciation—Store Equipment	41,800
Cash	8,000
Delivery Expense	8,200
Delivery Equipment	57,000
Depreciation Expense—Delivery Equipment	4,000
Depreciation Expense—Store Equipment	9,500
Freight-in	5,060
B. Dazzle, Capital	87,200
B. Dazzle, Drawing	12,000
Insurance Expense	9,000
Merchandise Inventory	34,360
Notes Payable	46,000
Prepaid Insurance	4,500
Property Tax Expense	3,500
Purchases	650,000
Purchase Discounts	7,000
Purchase Returns and Allowances	3,000
Rent Expense	19,000
Salaries Expense	150,000
Sales	910,000
Sales Commissions Expense	12,000
Sales Commissions Payable	8,000
Sales Returns and Allowances	10,000
Store Equipment	125,000
Property Taxes Payable	3,500
Utilities Expense	10,600

Analysis reveals the following additional data.

1. Salaries expense is 70% selling and 30% administrative.
2. Insurance expense is 50% selling and 50% administrative.
3. Merchandise inventory at November 30, 2002, is $36,200.
4. Rent expense, utilities expense, and property tax expense are administrative expenses.

Instructions

Net income $30,980

Prepare an income statement for the year ended November 30, 2002.

Determine cost of goods sold and ending inventory, using FIFO, LIFO, and average cost with analysis.
(SO 5, 6)

P6-3B   John Lewis Company had a beginning inventory on January 1 of 100 units of Product WD-44 at a cost of $20 per unit. During the year, the following purchases were made.

Mar. 15	300 units at $24	Sept. 4	300 units at $28
July 20	200 units at $25	Dec. 2	100 units at $30

750 units were sold. John Lewis Company uses a periodic inventory system.

Instructions

(a) Determine the cost of goods available for sale.
(b) Determine (1) the ending inventory, and (2) the cost of goods sold under each of the assumed cost flow methods (FIFO, LIFO, and average cost). Prove the accuracy of the cost of goods sold under the FIFO and LIFO methods.
(c) Which cost flow method results in (1) the highest inventory amount for the balance sheet, and (2) the highest cost of goods sold for the income statement?

Compute ending inventory, prepare income statements, and answer questions using FIFO and LIFO.
(SO 5, 6)

P6-4B   The management of Congo Co. asks your help in determining the comparative effects of the FIFO and LIFO inventory cost flow methods. For 2002, the accounting records show the following data.

Inventory, January 1 (10,000 units)	$ 35,000
Cost of 110,000 units purchased	478,000
Selling price of 95,000 units sold	665,000
Operating expenses	120,000

Units purchased consisted of 40,000 units at $4.20 on May 10; 50,000 units at $4.40 on August 15; and 20,000 units at $4.50 on November 20. Income taxes are 28%.

Instructions

(a) Prepare comparative condensed income statements for 2002 under FIFO and LIFO. (Show computations of ending inventory.)

(b) ▭▭▭▭▷ Answer the following questions for management in the form of a business letter.

    (1) Which inventory cost flow method produces the most meaningful inventory amount for the balance sheet? Why?

    (2) Which inventory cost flow method produces the most meaningful net income? Why?

    (3) Which inventory cost flow method is most likely to approximate actual physical flow of the goods? Why?

    (4) How much additional cash will be available for management under LIFO than under FIFO? Why?

    (5) How much of the gross profit under FIFO is illusory in comparison with the gross profit under LIFO?

(a) Net income
  FIFO $103,680
  LIFO $93,600
(b) (5) $14,000

*P6-5B   Dutch Company lost all of its inventory in a fire on December 26, 2002. The accounting records showed the following gross profit data for November and December.

Compute gross profit rate and inventory loss using gross profit method.
(SO 10)

	November	December (to 12/26)
Net sales	$500,000	$400,000
Beginning inventory	22,100	31,100
Purchases	314,975	236,000
Purchase returns and allowances	11,800	5,000
Purchase discounts	8,577	6,000
Freight-in	4,402	3,700
Ending inventory	31,100	?

Dutch is fully insured for fire losses but must prepare a report for the insurance company.

Instructions

(a) Compute the gross profit rate for November.

(b) Using the gross profit rate for November, determine the estimated cost of the inventory lost in the fire.

*P6-6B   Enlighten Book Store uses the retail inventory method to estimate its monthly ending inventories. The following information is available for two of its departments at October 31, 2002.

Compute ending inventory using retail method.
(SO 10)

	Hardcovers		Paperbacks	
	Cost	Retail	Cost	Retail
Beginning inventory	$ 260,000	$ 400,000	$ 65,000	$ 90,000
Purchases	1,180,000	1,800,000	266,000	380,000
Freight-in	5,000		2,000	
Purchase discounts	15,000		4,000	
Net sales		1,820,000		368,000

At December 31, Enlighten takes a physical inventory at retail. The actual retail values of the inventories in each department are Hardcovers $400,000 and Paperbacks $95,000.

Instructions

(a) Determine the estimated cost of the ending inventory for each department at **October 31**, 2002, using the retail inventory method.

(b) Compute the ending inventory at cost for each department at **December 31**, assuming the cost-to-retail ratios for the year are 65% for hardcovers and 70% for paperbacks.

*P6-7B   Angelina Jolie Co. began operations on July 1. It uses a perpetual inventory system. During July the company had the following purchases and sales.

Determine ending inventory under a perpetual inventory system.
(SO 11)

| | Purchases | | |
Date	Units	Unit Cost	Sales Units
July 1	5	$ 90	
July 6			3
July 11	4	$ 99	
July 14			3
July 21	3	$106	
July 27			3

Instructions

(a) Determine the ending inventory under a perpetual inventory system using (1) FIFO, (2) average cost, and (3) LIFO.

(b) Which costing method produces the highest ending inventory valuation?

BROADENING YOUR PERSPECTIVE

FINANCIAL REPORTING AND ANALYSIS

FINANCIAL REPORTING PROBLEM: Lands' End, Inc.

BYP6-1   The notes that accompany a company's financial statements provide informative details that would clutter the amounts and descriptions presented in the statements. Refer to the financial statements of **Lands' End, Inc.** and the Notes to Consolidated Financial Statements in Appendix A.

Instructions
Answer the following questions. Complete the requirements in millions of dollars, as shown in Lands' End's annual report.

(a) What did Lands' End report for the amount of inventories in its Consolidated Balance Sheet at January 28, 2000? At January 29, 1999?

(b) Compute the dollar amount of change and the percentage change in inventories between 1999 and 2000. Compute inventory as a percentage of current assets at January 28, 2000.

(c) How does Lands' End value its inventories? Which inventory cost flow method does Lands' End use?

(d) What is the cost of sales (cost of goods sold) reported by Lands' End for 2000, 1999, and 1998? Compute the percentage of cost of sales to net sales in 2000.

COMPARATIVE ANALYSIS PROBLEM: Lands' End vs. Abercrombie & Fitch

BYP6-2   **Lands' End's** financial statements are presented in Appendix A. **Abercrombie & Fitch's** financial statements are presented in Appendix B.

Instructions

(a) Based on the information contained in these financial statements, compute the following 2000 ratios for each company.
   (1) Inventory turnover ratio
   (2) Average days to sell inventory

(b) What conclusions concerning the management of the inventory can be drawn from these data?

INTERPRETING FINANCIAL STATEMENTS: A Global Focus

BYP6-3   **Fuji Photo Film Company** is a Japanese manufacturer of photographic products. Its U.S. counterpart, and arch rival, is **Eastman Kodak**. Together the two dominate the global market for film. The following information was extracted from the financial statements of the two companies.

FUJI PHOTO FILM
Notes to the Financial Statements

Summary of significant accounting policies

The Company and its domestic subsidiaries maintain their records and prepare their financial statements in accordance with accounting practices generally accepted in Japan. . . . Certain reclassifications and adjustments, including those relating to tax effects of temporary differences and the accrual of certain expenses, have been incorporated in the accompanying consolidated financial statements to conform with accounting principles generally accepted in the United States.

Inventories

Inventories are valued at the lower of cost or market, cost being determined generally by the moving-average method, except that the cost of the principal raw materials is determined by the last-in, first-out method.

Note 6. Inventories

Inventories at March 31, 1998 and 1997, consisted of the following:

	(millions of yen)		(thousands of U.S. dollars)
	1998	**1997**	**1998**
Finished goods	¥135,795	¥123,010	$1,028,750
Work in process	51,001	48,867	386,371
Raw materials and supplies	55,525	46,959	420,644
	¥242,321	¥218,836	$1,835,765

EASTMAN KODAK COMPANY
Notes to the Financial Statements

Inventories

Inventories are valued at cost, which is not in excess of market. The cost of most inventories in the U.S. is determined by the "last-in, first-out" (LIFO) method.

Note 3. Inventories

	(in millions)	
	1998	**1997**
At FIFO or average cost (approximates current cost)		
Finished goods	$ 907	$ 788
Work in process	569	538
Raw materials and supplies	439	460
	1,915	1,786
LIFO reserve	(491)	(534)
Total at LIFO	$1,424	$1,252

Inventories valued on the LIFO method are approximately 57% and 56% of total inventories in 1998 and 1997, respectively.

Additional information:

	Fuji Photo Film (yen)	Eastman Kodak (dollars)
1998 Cost of goods sold (millions)	735,953	7,293

Instructions
Answer each of the following questions.

(a) Why do you suppose that Fuji makes adjustments to its accounts so that they conform with U.S. accounting principles when it reports its results?

(b) What are the 1998 inventory turnover ratios and average days in inventory of the two companies (use inventory at FIFO, that is, before the LIFO reserve).

(c) What are the 1998 inventory turnover and average days in inventory of the two companies, adjusting for the LIFO reserve, if given? Do you encounter any problems when making this comparison?

(d) Calculate as a percentage of total inventory the portion that each of the components of 1998 inventory (raw materials, work in process, and finished goods) represents. Comment on your findings. (Use FIFO for Kodak.)

EXPLORING THE WEB

BYP6-4 A company's annual report usually will identify the inventory method used. Knowing that, you can analyze the effects of the inventory method on the income statement and balance sheet.

Address: www.cisco.com *(or go to www.wiley.com/college/weygandt)*

Steps:
1. From Cisco System's homepage, choose **Investor Relations**.
2. Choose **Annual Reports**.
3. Choose **2000 Annual Report**.
4. Choose **Online Report**.
5. Choose **Financial**.

Instructions
Answer the following questions based on the 2000 Annual Report.

(a) At Cisco's fiscal year-end, what was the net inventory on the balance sheet?

(b) How has this changed from the previous fiscal year-end?

(c) How much of the inventory was finished goods?

(d) What inventory method does Cisco use?

*C*RITICAL THINKING

GROUP DECISION CASE

BYP6-5 On April 10, 2001, fire damaged the office and warehouse of Gibson Company. Most of the accounting records were destroyed, but the following account balances were determined as of March 31, 2001: Merchandise Inventory, January 1, 2001, $80,000; Sales (January 1–March 31, 2001), $180,000; Purchases (January 1–March 31, 2001) $94,000.

The company's fiscal year ends on December 31. It uses a periodic inventory system.

From an analysis of the April bank statement, you discover cancelled checks of $4,200 for cash purchases during the period April 1–10. Deposits during the same period totaled $18,500. Of that amount, 60% were collections on accounts receivable, and the balance was cash sales.

Correspondence with the company's principal suppliers revealed $12,400 of purchases on account from April 1 to April 10. Of that amount, $1,800 was for merchandise in transit on April 10 that was shipped FOB destination.

Correspondence with the company's principal customers produced acknowledgments of credit sales totaling $28,000 from April 1 to April 10. It was estimated that $4,600 of credit sales will never be acknowledged or recovered from customers.

Gibson Company reached an agreement with the insurance company that its [...]
should be based on the average of the gross profit rates for the preceding 2 ye[...]
cial statements for 1999 and 2000 showed the following data.

	2000	1999
Net sales	$600,000	$480,000
Cost of goods purchased	416,000	356,000
Beginning inventory	60,000	40,00[...]
Ending inventory	80,000	60,0[...]

Inventory with a cost of $19,000 was salvaged from the fire.

Instructions

With the class divided into groups, answer the following.

(a) Determine the balances in (1) Sales and (2) Purchases at April 10.

*__(b)__ Determine the average profit rate for the years 1999 and 2000. (*Hint:* Find the gross profit rate for each year and divide the sum by 2.)

*__(c)__ Determine the inventory loss as a result of the fire, using the gross profit method.

COMMUNICATION ACTIVITY

BYP6-6   You are the controller of Small Toys Inc. Andy Manion, the president, recently mentioned to you that he found an error in the 2001 financial statements which he believes has corrected itself. He determined, in discussions with the Purchasing Department, that 2001 ending inventory was overstated by $1 million. Andy says that the 2002 ending inventory is correct. Thus he assumes that 2002 income is correct. Andy says to you, "What happened has happened—there's no point in worrying about it anymore."

Instructions

You conclude that Andy is incorrect. Write a brief, tactful memo to Andy, clarifying the situation.

ETHICS CASE

BYP6-7   J.K. Leask Wholesale Corp. uses the LIFO method of inventory costing. In the current year, profit at J.K. Leask is running unusually high. The corporate tax rate is also high this year, but it is scheduled to decline significantly next year. In an effort to lower the current year's net income and to take advantage of the changing income tax rate, the president of J.K. Leask Wholesale instructs the plant accountant to recommend to the purchasing department a large purchase of inventory for delivery 3 days before the end of the year. The price of the inventory to be purchased has doubled during the year, and the purchase will represent a major portion of the ending inventory value.

Instructions

(a) What is the effect of this transaction on this year's and next year's income statement and income tax expense? Why?

(b) If J.K. Leask Wholesale had been using the FIFO method of inventory costing, would the president give the same directive?

(c) Should the plant accountant order the inventory purchase to lower income? What are the ethical implications of this order?

Answers to Self-Study Questions

1. a   **2.** b   **3.** d   **4.** a   **5.** b   **6.** c   **7.** d   **8.** c   **9.** d   **10.** d
11. b   **12.** d   ***13.** b   ***14.** d

Answer to *Lands' End* Review It Question 5, p. 242

Lands' End reported inventories of $162,193,000 at January 28, 2000. Lands' End reports in "Note 1—Summary of significant accounting policies" that it uses the last-in, first-out (LIFO) cost method in applying product costs to inventories and cost of goods sold.

Remember to go back to the Navigator box on the chapter-opening page and check off your completed work.

ACCOUNTING INFORMATION SYSTEMS

THE NAVIGATOR ✓

- Understand *Concepts for Review* ❏
- Read *Feature Story* ❏
- Scan *Study Objectives* ❏
- Read *Preview* ❏
- Read text and answer *Before You Go On*
  p. 281 ❏   p. 294 ❏
- Work *Demonstration Problem* ❏
- Review *Summary of Study Objectives* ❏
- Answer *Self-Study Questions* ❏
- Complete *Assignments* ❏

CONCEPTS FOR REVIEW

Before studying this chapter, you should know or, if necessary, review:

- **a.** How to perform each of the steps in the accounting cycle. (Ch. 4, pp. 146–150)
- **b.** How to record transactions for a merchandiser. (Ch. 5, pp. 184–197)
- **c.** How to prepare financial statements for a merchandiser. (Ch. 5, pp. 197–202)

☑ THE NAVIGATOR

Accidents Happen

How organized are you financially? Take a short quiz.

- Is your wallet jammed full of gas station receipts from places you don't remember ever going?

- Is your wallet such a mess that it is often faster to fish for money in the crack of your car seat than to dig around in your wallet?

- Have you ever been tempted to burn down your house so you don't have to look for the receipts and records that you need to fill out your tax returns?

If you think it is hard to keep track of the many transactions that make up *your* life, imagine what it is like for a major corporation like **Fidelity Investments**. As the largest mutual fund management firm in the world, Fidelity manages more than $400 billion of investments. Millions of individuals have the bulk of their life savings invested in mutual funds. If you had your savings invested at Fidelity, you might be just slightly displeased if, when you called to find out your balance, the representative said, "You know, I kind of remember someone with a name like yours sending us some money— now what did we do with that?"

To ensure the accuracy of your balance and the security of your funds, Fidelity Investments, like all other companies large and small, relies on a sophisticated accounting information system. That's not to say that Fidelity or anybody else is error-free. In fact, if you've ever really messed up your checkbook register, you may take some comfort from one accountant's mistake at Fidelity Investments. The accountant failed to include a minus sign while doing a calculation, making what was actually a $1.3 billion loss look like a $1.3 billion gain! Fortunately, like most accounting errors, it was detected before any real harm was done.

No one expects that kind of mistake at a firm like Fidelity, which has sophisticated computer systems and top investment managers. In explaining the mistake to shareholders, a spokesperson wrote: "Some people have asked how, in this age of technology, such a mistake could be made. While many of our processes are computerized, accounting systems are complex and dictate that some steps must be handled manually by our managers and accountants, and people can make mistakes."

www.fidelity.com

After studying this chapter, you should be able to:

1. Identify the basic principles of accounting information systems.
2. Explain the major phases in the development of an accounting system.
3. Describe the nature and purpose of a subsidiary ledger.
4. Explain how special journals are used in journalizing.
5. Indicate how a multi-column journal is posted.

As you see from the Feature Story, a reliable information system is a necessity for any company. Whether you use pen, pencil, or computers in maintaining accounting records, certain principles and procedures apply. The purpose of this chapter is to explain and illustrate these features.

The content and organization of Chapter 7 are as follows.

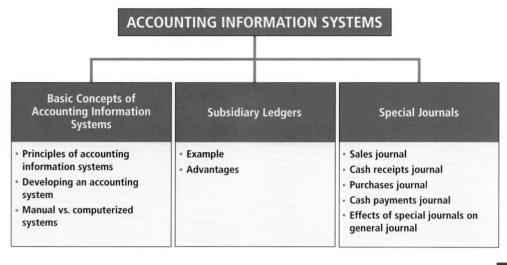

THE NAVIGATOR

BASIC CONCEPTS OF ACCOUNTING INFORMATION SYSTEMS

The system that collects and processes transaction data and disseminates financial information to interested parties is known as the **accounting information system**. It includes each of the steps in the accounting cycle that you have studied in earlier chapters. It also includes the documents that provide evidence of the transactions and events, and the records, trial balances, work sheets, and financial statements that result. An accounting information system may be either manual or electronic (computerized).

In this chapter, we explore the basic concepts that underlie accounting information systems, which from here on we will often refer to simply as **accounting systems**.

PRINCIPLES OF ACCOUNTING INFORMATION SYSTEMS

STUDY OBJECTIVE 1

Identify the basic principles of accounting information systems.

Efficient and effective accounting information systems are based on certain basic principles. These principles are: (1) cost effectiveness, (2) usefulness, and (3) flexibility, as described in Illustration 7-1. If the accounting system is cost effective, provides useful output, and has the flexibility to meet future needs, it can contribute to both individual and organizational goals.

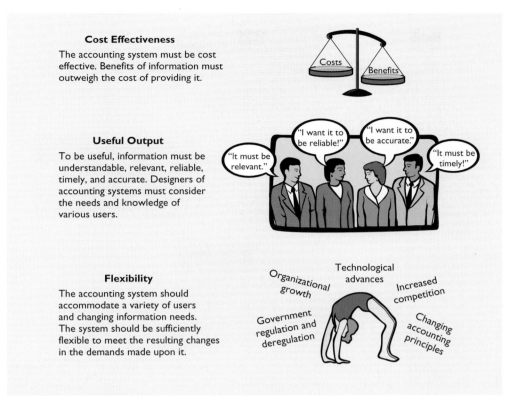

Cost Effectiveness

The accounting system must be cost effective. Benefits of information must outweigh the cost of providing it.

Useful Output

To be useful, information must be understandable, relevant, reliable, timely, and accurate. Designers of accounting systems must consider the needs and knowledge of various users.

Flexibility

The accounting system should accommodate a variety of users and changing information needs. The system should be sufficiently flexible to meet the resulting changes in the demands made upon it.

DEVELOPING AN ACCOUNTING SYSTEM

Good accounting systems do not just happen. They are carefully planned, designed, installed, managed, and refined. Generally, an accounting system is developed in the following four phases.

STUDY OBJECTIVE 2

Explain the major phases in the development of an accounting system.

1. **Analysis.** The starting point is to determine the information needs of internal and external users. The system analyst then identifies the sources of the needed information and the records and procedures for collecting and reporting the data. If an existing system is being analyzed, its strengths and weaknesses must be identified.

2. **Design.** A new system must be built from the ground up: forms and documents designed, methods and procedures selected, job descriptions prepared, controls integrated, reports formatted, and equipment selected. Redesigning an existing system may involve only minor changes or a complete overhaul.

3. **Implementation.** Implementation of new or revised systems requires that documents, procedures, and processing equipment be installed and made operational. Also, personnel must be trained and closely supervised through a start-up period.

4. **Follow-up.** After the system is up and running, it must be monitored for weaknesses or breakdowns. Also, its effectiveness must be compared to design and organizational objectives. Changes in design or implementation may be necessary.

Illustration 7-2 highlights the relationship of these four phases in the life cycle of the accounting system.

Illustration 7-2

Phases in the development of an accounting system

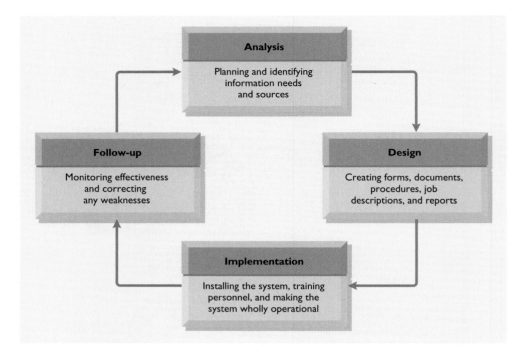

These phases represent the life cycle of an accounting system. They suggest that few systems remain the same forever. As experience and knowledge are obtained, and as technological and organizational changes occur, the accounting system may also have to grow and change.

The accounting system represented in the first six chapters is satisfactory in a company where the volume of transactions is extremely low. However, in most companies, it is necessary to add additional ledgers and journals to the accounting system to record transaction data efficiently.

MANUAL VS. COMPUTERIZED SYSTEMS

In a **manual accounting system**, each of the steps in the accounting cycle is performed by hand. For example, each accounting transaction is entered manually in the journal; each is posted manually to the ledger. Other manual computations must be made to obtain ledger account balances and to prepare a trial balance and financial statements.

In a computerized accounting system, there are programs for performing the steps in the accounting cycle, such as journalizing, posting, and preparing a trial balance. In addition, there is software for business functions such as billing customers, preparing the payroll, and budgeting.

*A*CCOUNTING IN ACTION ℮ *Business Insight*

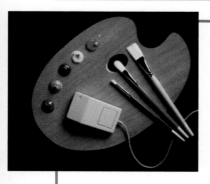

Accounting software companies have recognized the tremendous opportunities that result from making the accounting system an integral part of a comprehensive e-business package. For example, **Great Plains** recently published a story about an online art gallery called Art.com that uses two Great Plains e-business packages, eEnterprise™ and e.Commerce™ to meet the information needs of every aspect of its business. eEnterprise provides financial, distribution, purchasing, and manufacturing applications. e.Commerce provides real-time product information and on-the-fly customer data collection, reducing the need for order-desk staff because the customer keys in the order. This feature eliminates data re-entry errors.

SOURCE: www.greatplains.com/ebusiness

You might be wondering, "Why cover manual accounting systems if the real world uses computerized systems?" First, small businesses still abound. Most of them begin operations with manual accounting systems and convert to computerized systems as the business grows. Second, to understand what computerized accounting systems do, you need to understand how manual accounting systems work.

SUBSIDIARY LEDGERS

STUDY OBJECTIVE 3

Describe the nature and purpose of a subsidiary ledger.

Imagine a business that has several thousand charge (credit) customers and shows the transactions with these customers in only one general ledger account—Accounts Receivable. It would be virtually impossible to determine the balance owed by an individual customer at any specific time. Similarly, the amount payable to one creditor would be difficult to locate quickly from a single Accounts Payable account in the general ledger.

Instead, companies use subsidiary ledgers to keep track of individual balances. A **subsidiary ledger** is a group of accounts with a common characteristic (for example, all accounts receivable). The subsidiary ledger frees the general ledger from the details of individual balances. A subsidiary ledger is an addition to, and an expansion of, the general ledger.

Two common subsidiary ledgers are:

1. The **accounts receivable** (or **customers'**) **subsidiary ledger**, which collects transaction data of individual customers.

2. The **accounts payable** (or **creditors'**) **subsidiary ledger**, which collects transaction data of individual creditors.

In each of these subsidiary ledgers, individual accounts are usually arranged in alphabetical order.

The detailed data from a subsidiary ledger are summarized in a general ledger account. For example, the detailed data from the accounts receivable subsidiary ledger are summarized in Accounts Receivable in the general ledger. The general ledger account that summarizes subsidiary ledger data is called a **control account**. An overview of the relationship of subsidiary ledgers to the general ledger is shown in Illustration 7-3. The general ledger control accounts and subsidiary ledger accounts are shown in green color. Note that cash and owner's capital in this illustration are not control accounts because there are no subsidiary ledger accounts related to these accounts.

Illustration 7-3

Relationship of general ledger and subsidiary ledgers

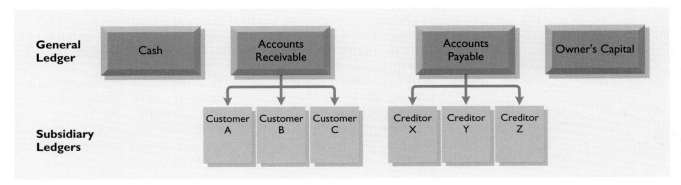

Each general ledger control account balance must equal the composite balance of the individual accounts in the related subsidiary ledger at the end of an accounting period. For example, the balance in Accounts Payable in Illustration 7-3 must equal the total of the subsidiary balances of Creditors X + Y + Z.

EXAMPLE

An example of a control account and subsidiary ledger for Larson Enterprises is provided in Illustration 7-4. (The explanation column in these accounts is not shown in this and subsequent illustrations due to space considerations.)

Illustration 7-4

Relationship between general and subsidiary ledgers

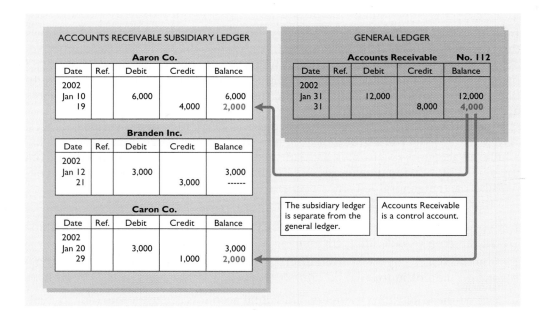

The example is based on the transactions listed below.

Illustration 7-5

Sales and collection transactions

	Credit Sales			Collections on Account	
Jan. 10	Aaron Co.	$ 6,000	Jan. 19	Aaron Co.	$ 4,000
12	Branden Inc.	3,000	21	Branden Inc.	3,000
20	Caron Co.	3,000	29	Caron Co.	1,000
		$12,000			$ 8,000

The total debits ($12,000) and credits ($8,000) in Accounts Receivable in the general ledger are reconcilable to the detailed debits and credits in the subsidiary accounts. Also, the balance of $4,000 in the control account agrees with the total of the balances in the individual accounts (Aaron Co. $2,000 + Branden Inc. $0 + Caron Co. $2,000) in the subsidiary ledger.

As shown, postings are made monthly to the control accounts in the general ledger. This practice allows monthly financial statements to be prepared. Postings to the individual accounts in the subsidiary ledger are made daily. Daily posting ensures that account information is current. This enables the company to monitor credit limits, bill customers, and answer inquiries from customers about their account balances.

ADVANTAGES OF SUBSIDIARY LEDGERS

Subsidiary ledgers have several advantages. They:

1. **Show transactions affecting one customer or one creditor in a single account**, thus providing up-to-date information on specific account balances.

2. **Free the general ledger of excessive details.** As a result, a trial balance of the general ledger does not contain vast numbers of individual account balances.

3. **Help locate errors in individual accounts** by reducing the number of accounts in one ledger and by using control accounts.

4. **Make possible a division of labor** in posting. One employee can post to the general ledger while someone else posts to the subsidiary ledgers.

*T*ECHNOLOGY IN ACTION

Rather than relying on customer or creditor names in a subsidiary ledger, a computerized system expands the account number of the control account in a pre-specified manner. For example, if Accounts Receivable was numbered 10010, the first account in the accounts receivable subsidiary ledger might be numbered 10010-0001. Most systems allow inquiries about specific accounts in the subsidiary ledger (by account number) or about the control account. With the latter, the system would automatically total all the subsidiary accounts whenever an inquiry to the control account was made.

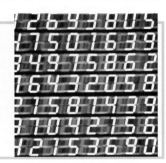

BEFORE YOU GO ON...

▶ *REVIEW IT*

1. What basic principles are followed in designing and developing an effective accounting information system?

2. What are the major phases in the development of an accounting information system?

3. What is a subsidiary ledger, and what purpose does it serve?

▶ *DO IT*

Presented below is information related to Sims Company for its first month of operations. Determine the balances that appear in the accounts payable subsidiary ledger. What Accounts Payable balance appears in the general ledger at the end of January?

Credit Purchases			Cash Paid		
Jan. 5	Devon Co.	$11,000	Jan. 9	Devon Co.	$7,000
11	Shelby Co.	7,000	14	Shelby Co.	2,000
22	Taylor Co.	14,000	27	Taylor Co.	9,000

ACTION PLAN

• Subtract cash paid from credit purchases to determine the balances in the accounts payable subsidiary ledger.

• Sum the individual balances to determine the Accounts Payable balance.

SOLUTION

Subsidiary ledger balances: Devon Co. $4,000 ($11,000 − $7,000); Shelby Co. $5,000 ($7,000 − $2,000); Taylor Co. $5,000 ($14,000 − $9,000). General ledger Accounts Payable balance: $14,000 ($4,000 + $5,000 + $5,000).

Related exercise material: BE7-3, BE7-4, E7-1, E7-2, E7-3, E7-4, E7-5, and E7-9.

☑ THE NAVIGATOR

SPECIAL JOURNALS

STUDY OBJECTIVE 4

Explain how special journals are used in journalizing.

Illustration 7-6

Use of special journals and the general journal

So far you have learned to journalize transactions in a two-column general journal and post each entry to the general ledger. This procedure is satisfactory in only the very smallest companies. To expedite journalizing and posting, most companies use special journals **in addition to the general journal**.

A **special journal** is used to record similar types of transactions. Examples would be all sales of merchandise on account, or all cash receipts. What special journals a company uses depends largely on the types of transactions that occur frequently. Most merchandising enterprises use the journals shown in Illustration 7-6 to record transactions daily.

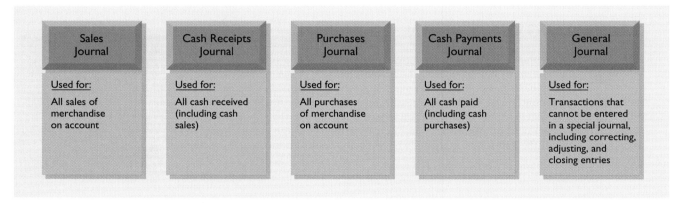

If a transaction cannot be recorded in a special journal, it is recorded in the general journal. For example, if you had special journals only for the four types of transactions listed above, purchase returns and allowances would be recorded in the general journal. So would sales returns and allowances. Similarly, **correcting, adjusting, and closing entries are recorded in the general journal**. Other types of special journals may sometimes be used in some situations. For example, when sales returns and allowances are frequent, special journals may be used to record these transactions.

Special journals **permit greater division of labor** because several people can record entries in different journals at the same time. For example, one employee may journalize all cash receipts, and another may journalize all credit sales. Also, the use of special journals **reduces the time needed to complete the posting process**. With special journals, some accounts may be posted monthly, instead of daily, as will be illustrated later in the chapter.

SALES JOURNAL

The **sales journal** is used to record sales of merchandise on account. Cash sales of merchandise are entered in the cash receipts journal. Credit sales of assets other than merchandise are entered in the general journal.

Journalizing Credit Sales

HELPFUL HINT
Postings are also made daily to individual ledger accounts in the inventory subsidiary ledger to maintain a perpetual inventory.

Karns Wholesale Supply uses a **perpetual inventory** system. Under this system, each entry in the sales journal results in one entry **at selling price** and another entry at cost—a debit to Accounts Receivable (a control account) and a credit of equal amount to Sales. The entry **at cost** is a debit to Cost of Goods Sold and a credit of equal amount to Merchandise Inventory (a control account). A sales journal with two amount columns can show on only one line a sales transaction at both selling price and cost. The two-column sales journal of Karns Wholesale Supply is shown in Illustration 7-7, using assumed credit sales transactions (for sales invoices 101–107).

Karns Wholesale Supply
SALES JOURNAL   S1

Date	Account Debited	Invoice No.	Ref.	Accts. Receivable Dr. Sales Cr.	Cost of Goods Sold Dr. Merchandise Inventory Cr.
2002					
May 3	Abbot Sisters	101		10,600	6,360
7	Babson Co.	102		11,350	7,370
14	Carson Bros.	103		7,800	5,070
19	Deli Co.	104		9,300	6,510
21	Abbot Sisters	105		15,400	10,780
24	Deli Co.	106		21,210	15,900
27	Babson Co.	107		14,570	10,200
				90,230	62,190

Illustration 7-7

Journalizing the sales journal—perpetual inventory system

The reference (Ref.) column is not used in journalizing. It is used in posting the sales journal, as explained in the next section. Also, note that, unlike the general journal, an explanation is not required for each entry in a special journal. Finally, note that each invoice is prenumbered to ensure that all invoices are journalized.

Posting the Sales Journal

Postings from the sales journal are made **daily to the individual accounts receivable** in the subsidiary ledger. Posting **to the general ledger** is made **monthly**. Illustration 7-8 (on page 284) shows both the daily and monthly postings.

A check mark (✓) is inserted in the reference posting column to indicate that the daily posting to the customer's account has been made. A check mark (✓) is used in this illustration because the subsidiary ledger accounts are not numbered. At the end of the month, the column totals of the sales journal are posted to the general ledger. Here, the column totals are a debit of $90,230 to Accounts Receivable (account No. 112), a credit of $90,230 to Sales (account No. 401), a debit of $62,190 to Cost of Goods Sold (account No. 505), and a credit of $62,190 to Merchandise Inventory (account No. 120). Insertion of the account numbers below the column total indicates that the postings have been made. In both the general ledger and subsidiary ledger accounts, the reference **S1** indicates that the posting came from page 1 of the sales journal.

Proving the Ledgers

The next step is to "prove" the ledgers. To do so, we must determine two things: (1) The total of the general ledger debit balances must equal the total of the general ledger credit balances. (2) The sum of the subsidiary ledger balances must equal the balance in the control account. The proof of the postings from the sales journal to the general and subsidiary ledger is shown in Illustration 7-9 (on page 285).

Advantages of the Sales Journal

The use of a special journal to record sales on account has a number of advantages. First, the one-line entry for each sales transaction **saves time**. In the sales journal, it is not necessary to write out the four account titles for each transaction. Second, only totals, rather than individual entries, are posted to the general ledger. This **saves posting time and reduces the possibilities of errors in posting**. Finally, **a division of labor results**, because one individual can take responsibility for the sales journal.

Illustration 7-8

Posting the sales journal

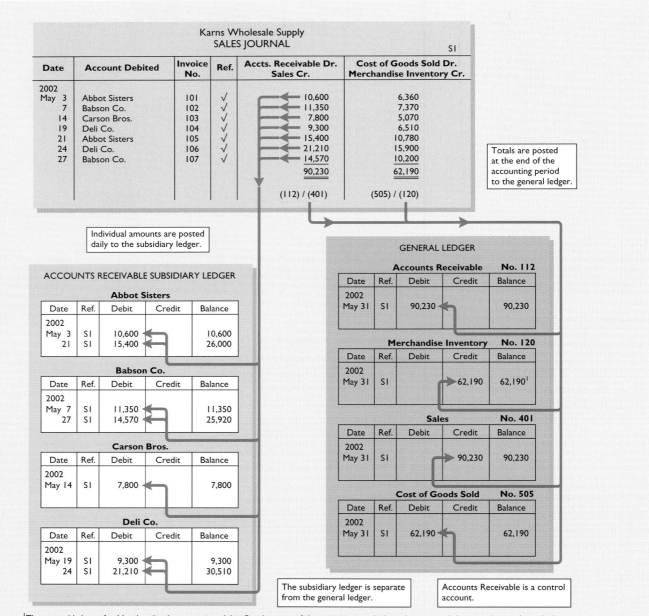

¹The normal balance for Merchandise Inventory is a debit. But, because of the sequence in which we have posted the special journals, with the sales journals first, the credits to Merchandise Inventory are posted before the debits. This posting sequence explains the credit balance, in Merchandise Inventory, which exists only until the other journals are posted.

CASH RECEIPTS JOURNAL

All receipts of cash are recorded in the **cash receipts journal**. The most common types of cash receipts are cash sales of merchandise and collections of accounts receivable. Many other possibilities exist, such as receipt of money from bank loans and cash proceeds from disposal of equipment. A one- or two-column cash receipts journal would not have space enough for all possible cash receipt transactions. Therefore, a multiple-column cash receipts journal is used.

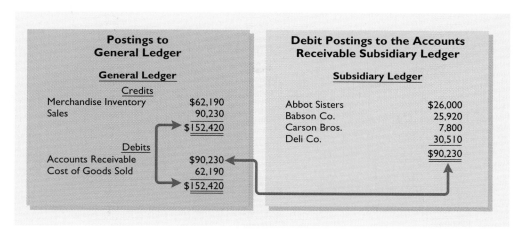

Illustration 7-9

Proving the equality of the postings from the sales journal

Generally, a cash receipts journal includes the following columns: debit columns for cash and sales discounts; and credit columns for accounts receivable, sales, and "other" accounts. The Other Accounts category is used when the cash receipt does not involve a cash sale or a collection of accounts receivable. Under a perpetual inventory system, each sales entry is accompanied by another entry that debits Cost of Goods Sold and credits Merchandise Inventory for the cost of the merchandise sold. This entry may be recorded separately. A six-column cash receipts journal is shown in Illustration 7-10 (on page 286).

Additional credit columns may be used if they significantly reduce postings to a specific account. For example, a loan company, such as **Household International**, receives thousands of cash collections from customers. A significant saving in posting would result from using separate credit columns for Loans Receivable and Interest Revenue, rather than using the Other Accounts credit column. In contrast, a retailer that has only one interest collection a month would not find it useful to have a separate column for Interest Revenue.

Journalizing Cash Receipts Transactions

To illustrate the journalizing of cash receipts transactions, we will continue with the May transactions of Karns Wholesale Supply. Collections from customers relate to the entries recorded in the sales journal in Illustration 7-7. The entries in the cash receipts journal are based on the following cash receipts.

May 1   D. A. Karns makes an investment of $5,000 in the business.
     7   Cash sales of merchandise total $1,900 (cost, $1,240).
    10   A check for $10,388 is received from Abbot Sisters in payment of invoice No. 101 for $10,600 less a 2% discount.
    12   Cash sales of merchandise total $2,600 (cost, $1,690).
    17   A check for $11,123 is received from Babson Co. in payment of invoice No. 102 for $11,350 less a 2% discount.
    22   Cash is received by signing a note for $6,000.
    23   A check for $7,644 is received from Carson Bros. in full for invoice No. 103 for $7,800 less a 2% discount.
    28   A check for $9,114 is received from Deli Co. in full for invoice No. 104 for $9,300 less a 2% discount.

Further information about the columns in the cash receipts journal (see Illustration 7-10) is listed on page 287.

Illustration 7-10

Journalizing and posting the cash receipts journal

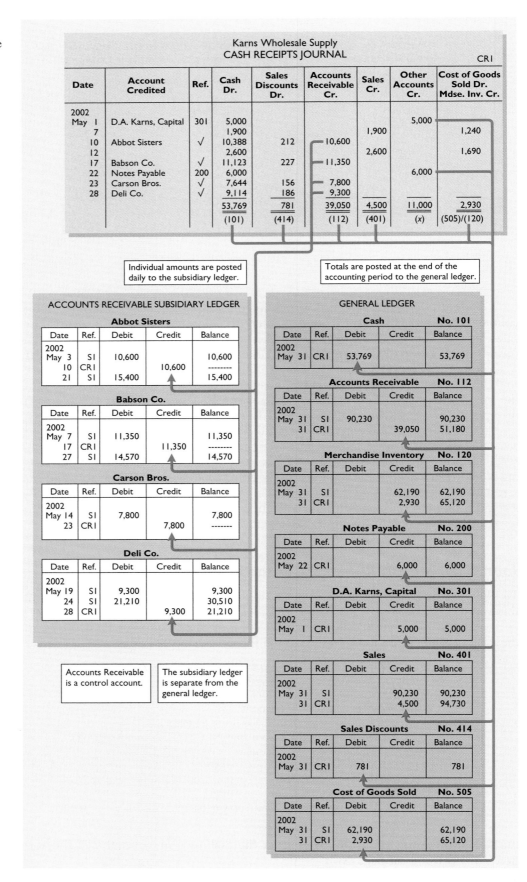

Debit Columns:

1. **Cash.** The amount of cash actually received in each transaction is entered in this column. The column total indicates the total cash receipts for the month.

2. **Sales Discounts.** Karns includes a Sales Discounts column in its cash receipts journal. By doing so, it is not necessary to enter sales discount items in the general journal. As a result, the collection of an account receivable within the discount period is expressed on one line in the appropriate columns of the cash receipts journal.

Credit Columns:

3. **Accounts Receivable.** The Accounts Receivable column is used to record cash collections on account. The amount entered here is the amount to be credited to the individual customer's account.

4. **Sales.** The Sales column records all cash sales of merchandise. Cash sales of other assets (plant assets, for example) are not reported in this column.

5. **Other Accounts.** The Other Accounts column is used whenever the credit is other than to Accounts Receivable or Sales. For example, in the first entry, $5,000 is entered as a credit to D. A. Karns, Capital. This column is often referred to as the **sundry accounts column**.

Debit and Credit Column:

6. **Cost of Goods Sold and Merchandise Inventory.** This column records debits to Cost of Goods Sold and credits to Merchandise Inventory.

> **HELPFUL HINT**
> When is an account title entered in the "Account Credited" column of the cash receipts journal?
> Answer: A *subsidiary ledger* title is entered there whenever the entry involves a collection of accounts receivable. A *general ledger* account title is entered there whenever the entry involves an account that is not the subject of a special column (and an amount must be entered in the Other Accounts column). No account title is entered there if neither of the foregoing applies.

In a multi-column journal, generally only one line is needed for each entry. Debit and credit amounts for each line must be equal. When the collection from Abbot Sisters on May 10 is journalized, for example, three amounts are indicated. Note also that the Account Credited column is used to identify both general ledger and subsidiary ledger account titles. General ledger accounts are illustrated in the May 1 and May 22 entries. A subsidiary account is illustrated in the May 10 entry for the collection from Abbot Sisters.

When the journalizing of a multi-column journal has been completed, the amount columns are totaled, and the totals are compared to prove the equality of debits and credits. The proof of the equality of Karns's cash receipts journal is as follows.

Illustration 7-11

Proving the equality of the cash receipts journal

Debits		Credits	
Cash	$53,769	Accounts Receivable	$39,050
Sales Discounts	781	Sales	4,500
Cost of Goods Sold	2,930	Other Accounts	11,000
	$57,480	Merchandise Inventory	2,930
			$57,480

Totaling the columns of a journal and proving the equality of the totals is called **footing** and **cross-footing** a journal.

Posting the Cash Receipts Journal

Posting a multi-column journal involves the following steps.

STUDY OBJECTIVE 5

Indicate how a multi-column journal is posted.

1. All column totals except for the Other Accounts total are posted **once at the end of the month** to the account title(s) specified in the column heading (such as Cash or Accounts Receivable). Account numbers are entered below the column totals to show that they have been posted. Cash is posted to account No. 101, accounts receivable to account No. 112, merchandise inventory to account No. 120, sales to account No. 401, sales discounts to account No. 414, and cost of goods sold to account No. 505.

2. The **individual amounts comprising the Other Accounts total are posted separately** to the general ledger accounts specified in the Account Credited column. See, for example, the credit posting to D. A. Karns, Capital. The total amount of this column is not posted. The symbol (X) is inserted below the total to this column to indicate that the amount has not been posted.

3. The individual amounts in a column, posted in total to a control account (Accounts Receivable, in this case), are posted **daily to the subsidiary ledger** account specified in the Account Credited column. See, for example, the credit posting of $10,600 to Abbot Sisters.

The symbol **CR** is used in both the subsidiary and general ledgers to identify postings from the cash receipts journal.

Proving the Ledgers

After posting of the cash receipts journal is completed, it is necessary to prove the ledgers. As shown in Illustration 7-12, the general ledger totals are in agreement. Also, the sum of the subsidary ledger balances equals the control account balance.

Illustration 7-12

Proving the ledgers after posting the sales and the cash receipts journals

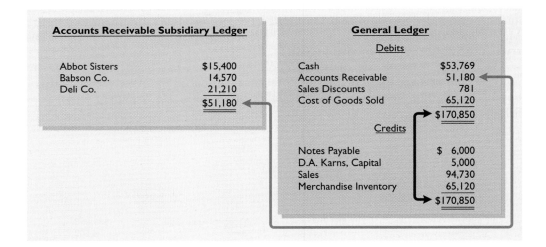

PURCHASES JOURNAL

All purchases of merchandise on account are recorded in the **purchases journal**. Each entry in this journal results in a debit to Merchandise Inventory and a credit to Accounts Payable. When a one-column purchases journal is used (as in Illustration 6-13), other types of purchases on account and cash purchases cannot be journalized in it. For example, credit purchases of equipment or supplies must be recorded in the general journal. Likewise, all cash purchases are entered in the cash payments journal. As illustrated later, where credit purchases for items other than merchandise are numerous, the purchases journal is often expanded to a multi-column format. The purchases journal for Karns Wholesale Supply is shown in Illustration 7-13.

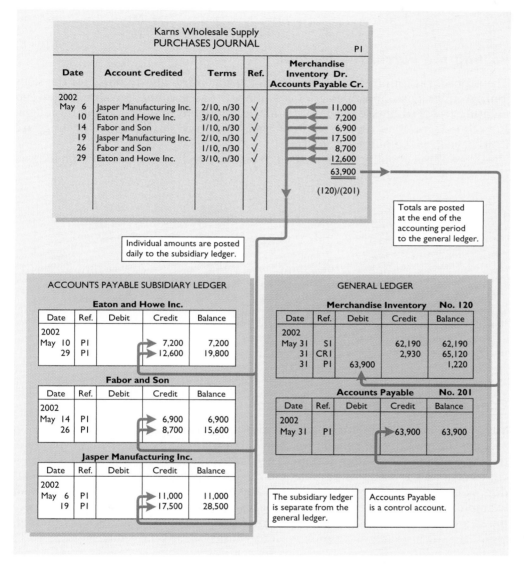

Illustration 7-13

Journalizing and posting the purchases journal

HELPFUL HINT
A single-column purchases journal needs only to be footed to prove the equality of debits and credits.

Journalizing Credit Purchases of Merchandise

Entries in the purchases journal are made from purchase invoices. The journalizing procedure is similar to that for a sales journal. In contrast to the sales journal, the purchases journal may not have an invoice number column, because invoices received from different suppliers will not be in numerical sequence. To assure that all purchase invoices are recorded, some companies consecutively number each invoice upon receipt and then use an internal document number column in the purchases journal.

The entries for Karns Wholesale Supply are based on the following assumed credit purchases.

Illustration 7-14

Credit purchases
transactions

Date	Supplier	Amount
5/6	Jasper Manufacturing Inc.	$11,000
5/10	Eaton and Howe Inc.	7,200
5/14	Fabor and Son	6,900
5/19	Jasper Manufacturing Inc.	17,500
5/26	Fabor and Son	8,700
5/29	Eaton and Howe Inc.	12,600

Posting the Purchases Journal

HELPFUL HINT
Postings to subsidiary ledger accounts are done daily because it is often necessary to know a current balance for the subsidiary accounts.

The procedures for posting the purchases journal are similar to those for the sales journal. In this case, postings are made **daily** to the **accounts payable ledger** and **monthly** to Merchandise Inventory and Accounts Payable in the general ledger. In both ledgers, P1 is used in the reference column to show that the postings are from page 1 of the purchases journal.

Proof of the equality of the postings from the purchases journal to both ledgers is shown by the following.

Illustration 7-15

Proving the equality of the
purchases journal

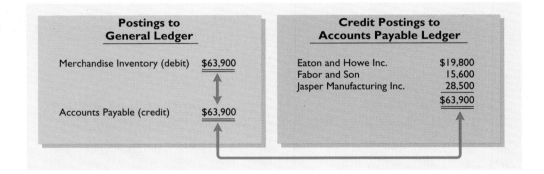

Expanding the Purchases Journal

HELPFUL HINT
A multiple-column purchases journal must be footed and cross-footed to prove the equality of debits and credits.

Some companies expand the purchases journal to include all types of purchases on account. Instead of one column for merchandise inventory and accounts payable, they use a multiple-column format. The multi-column format usually includes a credit column for accounts payable and debit columns for purchases of merchandise, of office supplies, of store supplies, and other accounts. Illustration 7-16 is an example of a multi-column purchases journal for Hanover Co. The posting procedures are similar to those illustrated earlier for posting the cash receipts journal.

Illustration 7-16

Columnar purchases journal

Hanover Co.
PURCHASES JOURNAL **P1**

Date	Account Credited	Ref.	Accounts Payable Cr.	Merchandise Inventory Dr.	Office Supplies Dr.	Store Supplies Dr.	Other Accounts Dr. Account	Ref.	Amount
2002									
June 1	Signe Audio	✓	2,000		2,000				
3	Wright Co.	✓	1,500	1,500					
5	Orange Tree Co.	✓	2,600				Equipment	157	2,600
30	Sue's Business Forms	✓	800			800			
			56,600	43,000	7,500	1,200			4,900

CASH PAYMENTS JOURNAL

All disbursements of cash are entered in a **cash payments journal**. Entries are made from prenumbered checks. Because cash payments are made for various purposes, the cash payments journal has multiple columns. A four-column journal is shown in Illustration 7-17.

ALTERNATIVE TERMINOLOGY
The cash payments journal is sometimes called the *cash disbursements journal.*

Illustration 7-17

Journalizing and posting the cash payments journal

Journalizing Cash Payments Transactions

The procedures for journalizing transactions in this journal are similar to those described earlier for the cash receipts journal. Each transaction is entered on one line, and for each line there must be equal debit and credit amounts. The entries in the cash payments journal in Illustration 7-17 are based on the following transactions for Karns Wholesale Supply.

May 1 Check No. 101 for $1,200 issued for the annual premium on a fire insurance policy.
3 Check No. 102 for $100 issued in payment of freight when terms were FOB shipping point.
8 Check No. 103 for $4,400 issued for the purchase of merchandise.
10 Check No. 104 for $10,780 sent to Jasper Manufacturing Inc. in payment of May 6 invoice for $11,000 less a 2% discount.
19 Check No. 105 for $6,984 mailed to Eaton and Howe Inc. in payment of May 10 invoice for $7,200 less a 3% discount.
23 Check No. 106 for $6,831 sent to Fabor and Son in payment of May 14 invoice for $6,900 less a 1% discount.
28 Check No. 107 for $17,150 sent to Jasper Manufacturing Inc. in payment of May 19 invoice for $17,500 less a 2% discount.
30 Check No. 108 for $500 issued to D. A. Karns as a cash withdrawal for personal use.

Note that whenever an amount is entered in the Other Accounts column, a specific general ledger account must be identified in the Account Debited column. The entries for checks No. 101, 102, and 103 illustrate this situation. Similarly, a subsidiary account must be identified in the Account Debited column whenever an amount is entered in the Accounts Payable column. See, for example, the entry for check No. 104.

After the cash payments journal has been journalized, the columns are totaled. The totals are then balanced to prove the equality of debits and credits.

Posting the Cash Payments Journal

The procedures for posting the cash payments journal are similar to those for the cash receipts journal. The amounts recorded in the Accounts Payable column are posted individually to the subsidiary ledger and in total to the control account. Merchandise Inventory and Cash are posted only in total at the end of the month. Transactions in the Other Accounts column are posted individually to the appropriate account(s) affected. No totals are posted for this column.

The posting of the cash payments journal is shown in Illustration 7-17. Note that the symbol **CP** is used as the posting reference. After postings are completed, the equality of the debit and credit balances in the general ledger should be determined. In addition, the control account balances should agree with the subsidiary ledger total balance. The agreement of these balances is shown in Illustration 7-18.

EFFECTS OF SPECIAL JOURNALS ON GENERAL JOURNAL

Special journals for sales, purchases, and cash substantially reduce the number of entries that are made in the general journal. **Only transactions that cannot be entered in a special journal are recorded in the general journal.** For example, the general journal may be used to record such transactions as granting of credit to a customer for a sales return or allowance, granting of credit from a supplier for purchases returned, acceptance of a note receivable from a customer, and pur-

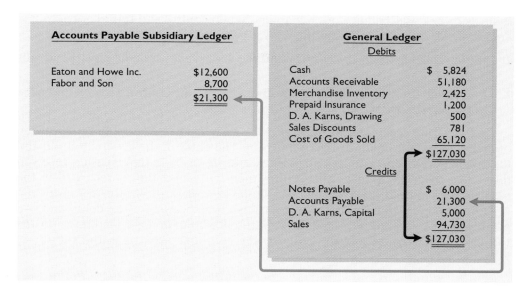

Illustration 7-18

Proving the ledgers after postings from the sales, cash receipts, purchases, and cash payments journals

chase of equipment by issuing a note payable. Also, correcting, adjusting, and closing entries are made in the general journal.

The general journal has columns for date, account title and explanation, reference, and debit and credit amounts. When control and subsidiary accounts are not involved, the procedures for journalizing and posting of transactions are the

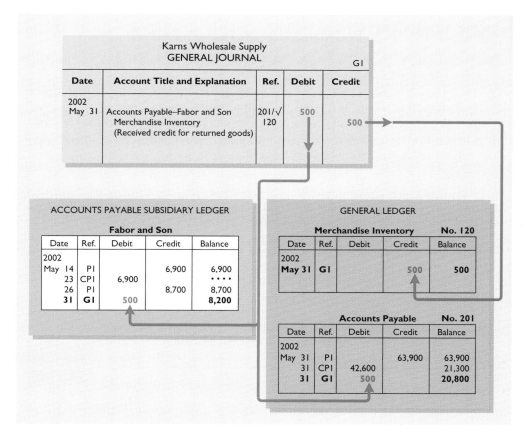

Illustration 7-19

Journalizing and posting the general journal

same as those described in earlier chapters. When control and subsidiary accounts are involved, two changes from the earlier procedures are required:

1. In **journalizing**, both the control and the subsidiary accounts must be identified.

2. In **posting**, there must be a **dual posting**: once to the control account and once to the subsidiary account.

To illustrate, assume that on May 31, Karns Wholesale Supply returns $500 of merchandise for credit to Fabor and Son. The entry in the general journal and the posting of the entry are shown in Illustration 7-19. Note that if cash is received instead of credit granted on this return, then the transaction is recorded in the cash receipts journal.

Observe in the journal that two accounts are indicated for the debit, and two postings ("201/✓") are indicated in the reference column. One amount is posted to the control account and the other to the creditor's account in the subsidiary ledger.

BEFORE YOU GO ON...

▶ *REVIEW IT*

1. What types of special journals are frequently used to record transactions? Why are special journals used?

2. Explain how transactions recorded in the sales journal and the cash receipts journal are posted.

3. Indicate the types of transactions that are recorded in the general journal when special journals are used.

𝓐 LOOK BACK AT OUR FEATURE STORY

Refer back to the Feature Story about Fidelity Investments at the beginning of the chapter, and answer the following questions.

1. How could a highly sophisticated and computerized firm like Fidelity Investments make an embarrassing $1.3 billion accounting error?

2. Is it likely that in the future some businesses will continue to use manual systems?

3. The balance of your account at Fidelity Investments is found in its subsidiary ledger. Why do companies use subsidiary ledgers?

SOLUTION

1. Although Fidelity Investments is highly computerized, some financial information, like the computation of some gains and losses, is generated manually. When people perform such tasks, they occasionally make errors.

2. While the percentage of businesses using manual systems will likely decline, it will probably always make sense for certain businesses to use manual systems. For many start-up businesses, or businesses with few transactions, the advantages of installing a computerized system do not appear to outweigh the costs.

3. Advantages of a subsidiary ledger for a company like Fidelity are: (1) It shows transactions for one customer or creditor in a single account. (2) It frees the general ledger of excessive detail. (3) It helps locate errors in individual accounts. And (4) in manual systems it provides for a division of labor.

☑ THE NAVIGATOR

DEMONSTRATION PROBLEM

Celine Dion Company uses a six-column cash receipts journal with the following columns: Cash (Dr.), Sales Discounts (Dr.), Accounts Receivable (Cr.), Sales (Cr.), Other Accounts (Cr.), and Cost of Goods Sold (Dr.) and Merchandise Inventory (Cr.). Cash receipts transactions for the month of July 2002 are as follows.

July 3 Cash sales total $5,800 (cost, $3,480).
     5 A check for $6,370 is received from Jeltz Company in payment of an invoice dated June 26 for $6,500, terms 2/10, n/30.
     9 An additional investment of $5,000 in cash is made in the business by Celine Dion, the proprietor.
    10 Cash sales total $12,519 (cost, $7,511).
    12 A check for $7,275 is received from R. Eliot & Co. in payment of a $7,500 invoice dated July 3, terms 3/10, n/30.
    15 A customer advance of $700 cash is received for future sales.
    20 Cash sales total $15,472 (cost, $9,283).
    22 A check for $5,880 is received from Beck Company in payment of $6,000 invoice dated July 13, terms 2/10, n/30.
    29 Cash sales total $17,660 (cost, $10,596).
    31 Cash of $200 is received on interest earned for July.

Instructions

(a) Journalize the transactions in the cash receipts journal.
(b) Contrast the posting of the Accounts Receivable and Other Accounts columns.

ACTION PLAN

• Record all cash receipts in the cash receipts journal.
• The "account credited" indicates items posted individually to the subsidiary ledger or general ledger.
• Record cash sales in the cash receipts journal—not in the sales journal.
• The total debits must equal the total credits.

SOLUTION TO DEMONSTRATION PROBLEM

(a)

Celine Dion Company
CASH RECEIPTS JOURNAL   **CR1**

Date	Account Credited	Ref.	Cash Dr.	Sales Discounts Dr.	Accounts Receivable Cr.	Sales Cr.	Other Accounts Cr.	Cost of Goods Sold Dr. Mdse. Inv. Cr.
2002								
7/3			5,800			5,800		3,480
5	Jeltz Company		6,370	130	6,500			
9	Celine Dion, Capital		5,000				5,000	
10			12,519			12,519		7,511
12	R. Eliot & Co.		7,275	225	7,500			
15	Unearned Revenues		700				700	
20			15,472			15,472		9,283
22	Beck Company		5,880	120	6,000			
29			17,660			17,660		10,596
31	Interest Revenue		200				200	
			76,876	475	20,000	51,451	5,900	30,870

(b) The Accounts Receivable column is posted as a credit to Accounts Receivable. The individual amounts are credited to the customers' accounts identified in the Account Credited column, which are maintained in the accounts receivable subsidiary ledger.

The amounts in the Other Accounts column are only posted individually. They are credited to the account titles identified in the Account Credited column.

THE NAVIGATOR

SUMMARY OF STUDY OBJECTIVES

1. Identify the basic principles of accounting information systems. The basic principles in developing an accounting information system are cost effectiveness, useful output, and flexibility.

2. Explain the major phases in the development of an accounting system. The major phases in the development of an accounting system are analysis, design, implementation, and follow-up.

3. Describe the nature and purpose of a subsidiary ledger. A subsidiary ledger is a group of accounts with a common characteristic. It facilitates the recording process by freeing the general ledger from details of individual balances.

4. Explain how special journals are used in journalizing. A special journal is used to group similar types of transactions.

In a special journal, generally only one line is used to record a complete transaction.

5. Indicate how a multi-column journal is posted. In posting a multi-column journal:
(a) All column totals except for the Other Accounts column are posted once at the end of the month to the account title specified in the column heading.
(b) The total of the Other Accounts column is not posted. Instead, the individual amounts comprising the total are posted separately to the general ledger accounts specified in the Account Credited column.
(c) The individual amounts in a column posted in total to a control account are posted daily to the subsidiary ledger accounts specified in the Account Credited column.

Key Term Matching Activity

GLOSSARY

Accounting information system A system that collects and processes transaction data, and disseminates financial information to interested parties. (p. 276).

Accounts payable (creditors') subsidiary ledger A subsidiary ledger that contains accounts of individual creditors. (p. 279).

Accounts receivable (customers') subsidiary ledger A subsidiary ledger that contains individual customer accounts. (p. 279).

Cash payments journal A special journal used to record all cash paid. (p. 291).

Cash receipts journal A special journal used to record all cash received. (p. 284).

Control account An account in the general ledger that controls a subsidiary ledger. (p. 279).

Manual accounting system A system in which each of the steps in the accounting cycle is performed by hand. (p. 278).

Purchases journal A special journal used to record all purchases of merchandise on account. (p. 288).

Sales journal A special journal used to record all sales of merchandise on account. (p. 282).

Special journal A journal that is used to record similar types of transactions, such as all credit sales. (p. 282).

Subsidiary ledger A group of accounts with a common characteristic. (p. 279).

Chapter 7 Self-Test

SELF-STUDY QUESTIONS

Answers are at the end of the chapter.

(SO 1) **1.** The basic principles of an accounting information system include all of the following *except*:
   a. cost effectiveness.
   b. flexibility.
   c. useful output.
   d. periodicity.

(SO 2) **2.** Which of the following is *not* a major phase in the development of an accounting information system?
   a. Design.
   b. Responsiveness.
   c. Implementation.
   d. Follow-up.

(SO 3) **3.** Which of the following is *incorrect* concerning subsidiary ledgers?
   a. The purchases ledger is a common subsidiary ledger for creditor accounts.

   b. The accounts receivable ledger is a subsidiary ledger.
   c. A subsidiary ledger is a group of accounts with a common characteristic.
   d. An advantage of the subsidiary ledger is that it permits a division of labor in posting.

4. A sales journal will be used for: (SO 4)

	Credit Sales	Cash Sales	Sales Discounts
a.	no	yes	yes
b.	yes	no	yes
c.	yes	no	no
d.	yes	yes	no

5. Which of the following statements is correct?   (SO 5)
   a. The sales discount column is included in the cash receipts journal.

b. The purchases journal records all purchases of merchandise whether for cash or on account.

c. The cash receipts journal records sales on account.

d. Merchandise returned by the buyer is recorded by the seller in the purchases journal.

(SO 5) **6.** Which of the following is *incorrect* concerning the posting of the cash receipts journal?

a. The total of the Other Accounts column is not posted.

b. All column totals except the total for the Other Accounts column are posted once at the end of the month to the account title(s) specified in the column heading.

c. The totals of all columns are posted daily to the accounts specified in the column heading.

d. The individual amounts in a column posted in total to a control account are posted daily to the subsidiary ledger account specified in the Account Credited column.

(SO 5) **7.** Postings from the purchases journal to the subsidiary ledger are generally made:

a. yearly.

b. monthly.

c. weekly.

d. daily.

8. Which statement is *incorrect* regarding the general journal? (SO 4)

a. Only transactions that cannot be entered in a special journal are recorded in the general journal.

b. Dual postings are always required in the general journal.

c. The general journal may be used to record acceptance of a note receivable in payment of an account receivable.

d. Correcting, adjusting, and closing entries are made in the general journal.

9. When special journals are used: (SO 4)

a. all purchase transactions are recorded in the purchases journal.

b. all cash received, except from cash sales, is recorded in the cash receipts journal.

c. all cash disbursements are recorded in the cash payments journal.

d. a general journal is not necessary.

10. If a customer returns goods for credit, an entry is nor- (SO 4) mally made in the:

a. cash payments journal.

b. sales journal.

c. general journal.

d. cash receipts journal.

Questions

1. (a) What is an accounting information system? (b) "An accounting information system applies only to a manual system." Do you agree? Explain.

2. Certain principles should be followed in the development of an accounting information system. Identify and explain each of the principles.

3. Hawkeye Company might change its accounting system for accounts receivable billing. At present, the procedure is performed manually by three clerks. A consultant has recommended that a new computer and related software be purchased for $1,000,000. What basic principle of designing and developing an effective accounting system might be violated by this proposal?

4. There are four phases in the life cycle of an accounting system. Identify and briefly explain each phase.

5. What are the advantages of using subsidiary ledgers?

6. (a) When are postings normally made to (1) the subsidiary accounts and (2) the general ledger control accounts? (b) Describe the relationship between a control account and a subsidiary ledger.

7. Identify and explain the four specific journals discussed in the chapter. List an advantage of using each of these journals rather than using only a general journal.

8. A. Mega Company uses special journals. A sale made on account to K. Hansen for $435 was recorded in a sales journal. A few days later, K. Hansen returns $70 worth of merchandise for credit. Where should A. Mega Company record the sales return? Why?

9. A $500 purchase of merchandise on account from Julia Company was properly recorded in the purchases journal. When posted, however, the amount recorded in the subsidiary ledger was $50. How might this error be discovered?

10. Why would special journals used in different businesses not be identical in format? Can you think of a business that would maintain a cash receipts journal but not include a column for accounts receivable?

11. The cash and the accounts receivable columns in the cash receipts journal were mistakenly overadded by $4,000 at the end of the month. (a) Will the customers' ledger agree with the Accounts Receivable control account? (b) Assuming no other errors, will the trial balance totals be equal?

12. One column total of a special journal is posted at month-end to only two general ledger accounts. One of these two accounts is Accounts Receivable. What is the name of this special journal? What is the other general ledger account to which that same month-end total is posted?

13. In what journal would the following transactions be recorded? (Assume that a two-column sales journal and a single-column purchases journal are used.)

(a) Recording of depreciation expense for the year.

(b) Credit given to a customer for merchandise purchased on credit and returned.

(c) Sales of merchandise for cash.

(d) Sales of merchandise on account.

(e) Collection of cash on account from a customer.
(f) Purchase of office supplies on account.

14. In what journal would the following transactions be recorded? (Assume that a two-column sales journal and a single-column purchases journal are used.)
  (a) Cash received from signing a note payable.
  (b) Investment of cash by the owner of the business.
  (c) Closing of the expense accounts at the end of the year.
  (d) Purchase of merchandise on account.
  (e) Credit received for merchandise purchased and returned to supplier.
  (f) Payment of cash on account due a supplier.

15. What transactions might be included in a multiple-column purchases journal that would not be included in a single-column purchases journal?

16. Give an example of a transaction in the general journal that causes an entry to be posted twice (i.e., to two accounts), one in the general ledger, the other in the subsidiary ledger. Does this affect the debit/credit equality of the general ledger?

17. Give some examples of appropriate general journal transactions for an organization using special journals.

BRIEF EXERCISES

Identify basic principles of accounting information system development.
(SO 1)

BE7-1 Indicate whether each of the following statements is true or false.

  1. When designing an accounting system, we need to think about the needs and knowledge of both the top management and various other users.
  2. When the environment changes as a result of technological advances, increased competition, or government regulation, an accounting system does not have to be sufficiently flexible to meet the changes in order to save money.
  3. In developing an accounting system, cost is relevant. The system must be cost-effective. That is, the benefits obtained from the information disseminated must outweigh the cost of providing it.

Identify major phases in accounting system development.
(SO 2)

BE7-2 The development of an accounting system involves four phases: analysis, design, implementation, and follow-up. Identify the statement that best describes each of these four phases.

  1. Determining internal and external information needs, identifying information sources and the needs for controls, and studying alternatives.
  2. Evaluation and monitoring of effectiveness and efficiency, and correction of weaknesses, implementation, and design.
  3. Creation of forms and documents, selection of procedures, and preparation of job descriptions.
  4. Implementing new or revised documents, procedures, reports, and processing equipment; hiring and training personnel through a start-up or transition period.

Identify subsidiary ledger balances.
(SO 3)

BE7-3 Presented below is information related to Bradley Company for its first month of operations. Identify the balances that appear in the accounts receivable subsidiary ledger and the accounts receivable balance that appears in the general ledger at the end of January.

Credit Sales			Cash Collections		
Jan. 7	Avon Co.	$8,000	Jan. 17	Avon Co.	$7,000
15	Barto Co.	6,000	24	Barto Co.	5,000
23	Cecil Co.	9,000	29	Cecil Co.	9,000

Identify subsidiary ledger accounts.
(SO 3)

BE7-4 Identify in what ledger (general or subsidiary) each of the following accounts is shown.

  1. Rent Expense
  2. Accounts Receivable—Olsen
  3. Notes Payable
  4. Accounts Payable—Kerns

Identify special journals.
(SO 4)

BE7-5 Identify the journal in which each of the following transaction is recorded.

  1. Cash sales
  2. Owner withdrawal of cash
  3. Cash purchase of land
  4. Credit sales
  5. Purchase of merchandise on account
  6. Receipt of cash for services performed

Identify entries to cash receipts journal.
(SO 4)

BE7-6 Indicate whether each of the following debits and credits is included in the cash receipts journal. (Use "Yes" or "No" to answer this question.)

  1. Debit to Sales
  2. Credit to Merchandise Inventory
  3. Credit to Accounts Receivable
  4. Debit to Accounts Payable

BE7-7 Steering Computer Components Inc. uses a multi-column cash receipts journal. Indicate which column(s) is/are posted only in total, only daily, or both in total and daily.

1. Accounts Receivable	**3.** Cash
2. Sales Discounts	**4.** Other Accounts

Indicate postings to cash receipts journal.
(SO 5)

BE7-8 Cohen Co. uses special journals and a general journal. Identify the journal in which each of the following transactions is recorded.

(a) Purchased equipment on account.
(b) Purchased merchandise on account.
(c) Paid utility expense in cash.
(d) Sold merchandise on account.

Identify transactions for special journals.
(SO 4)

BE7-9 Identify the special journal(s) in which the following column headings appear.

1. Sales Discounts Dr.	**4.** Sales Cr.
2. Accounts Receivable Cr.	**5.** Merchandise Inventory Dr.
3. Cash Dr.	

Identify transactions for special journals.
(SO 4)

EXERCISES

E7-1 Yan Company uses both special journals and a general journal as described in this chapter. On June 30, after all monthly postings had been completed, the Accounts Receivable control account in the general ledger had a debit balance of $350,000; the Accounts Payable control account had a credit balance of $87,000.

The July transactions recorded in the special journals are summarized below. No entries affecting accounts receivable and accounts payable were recorded in the general journal for July.

Determine control account balances, and explain posting of special journals.
(SO 3, 5)

Sales journal	Total sales $161,400
Purchases journal	Total purchases $54,360
Cash receipts journal	Accounts receivable column total $141,000
Cash payments journal	Accounts payable column total $47,500

Instructions
(a) What is the balance of the Accounts Receivable control account after the monthly postings on July 31?
(b) What is the balance of the Accounts Payable control account after the monthly postings on July 31?
(c) To what account(s) is the column total of $161,400 in the sales journal posted?
(d) To what account(s) is the accounts receivable column total of $144,000 in the cash receipts journal posted?

E7-2 Presented below is the subsidiary accounts receivable account of Warren Moyer.

Explain postings to subsidiary ledger.
(SO 3)

Date	Ref.	Debit	Credit	Balance
2002				
Sept. 2	S31	61,000		61,000
9	G4		14,000	47,000
27	CR8		47,000	—

Instructions
▭▭▷ Write a memo that explains each transaction.

E7-3 On September 1 the balance of the Accounts Receivable control account in the general ledger of Odesto Company was $11,960. The customers' subsidiary ledger contained account balances as follows: Edmonds $2,440, Park $2,640, Roemer $2,060, Schulz $4,820. At the end of September the various journals contained the following information.

Post various journals to control and subsidiary accounts.
(SO 3, 5)

Sales journal: Sales to Schulz $800; to Edmonds $1,350; to Henry $1,030; to Roemer $1,100.

Cash receipts journal: Cash received from Roemer $1,310; from Schulz $2,300; from Henry $410; from Park $1,800; from Edmonds $1,240.

General journal: An allowance is granted to Schulz $220.

Instructions

(a) Set up control and subsidiary accounts and enter the beginning balances. Do not construct the journals.

(b) Post the various journals. Post the items as individual items or as totals, whichever would be the appropriate procedure. (No sales discounts given.)

(c) Prepare a list of customers and prove the agreement of the controlling account with the subsidiary ledger at September 30, 2002.

Record transactions in sales and purchases journal.
(SO 3, 4)

E7-4 Hurley Company uses special journals and a general journal. The following transactions occurred during September 2002.

Sept. 2 Sold merchandise on account to S. Rusch, invoice no. 101, $480, terms n/30. The cost of the merchandise sold was $300.

10 Purchased merchandise on account from L. Dayne $600, terms 2/10, n/30.

12 Purchased office equipment on account from B. Piazza $6,500.

21 Sold merchandise on account to L. Perez, invoice no. 102 for $800, terms 2/10, n/30. The cost of the merchandise sold was $480.

25 Purchased merchandise on account from F. Sage $900, terms n/30.

27 Sold merchandise to M. Deitrich for $700 cash. The cost of the merchandise sold was $420.

Instructions

(a) Draw a sales journal (see Illustration 7-8) and a single-column purchase journal (see Illustration 7-13). (Use page 1 for each journal.)

(b) Record the transaction(s) for September that should be journalized in the sales journal and the purchases journal.

Record transactions in cash receipts and cash payments journal.
(SO 3, 4)

E7-5 Pena Co. uses special journals and a general journal. The following transactions occurred during May 2002.

May 1 R. Pena invested $60,000 cash in the business.

2 Sold merchandise to J. Simon for $6,000 cash. The cost of the merchandise sold was $4,200.

3 Purchased merchandise for $9,000 from L. M. Farr using check no. 101.

14 Paid salary to S. Little $700 by issuing check no. 102.

16 Sold merchandise on account to B. Jones for $900, terms n/30. The cost of the merchandise sold was $630.

22 A check of $9,000 is received from R. Dusto in full for invoice 101; no discount given.

Instructions

(a) Draw a multiple-column cash receipts journal (see Illustration 7-10) and a multiple-column cash payments journal (see Illustration 7-17). (Use page 1 for each journal.)

(b) Record the transaction(s) for May that should be journalized in the cash receipts journal and cash payments journal.

Explain journalizing in cash journals.
(SO 4)

E7-6 Abbott Company uses the columnar cash journals illustrated in the textbook. In April, the following selected cash transactions occurred.

1. Made a refund to a customer for the return of damaged goods.
2. Received collection from customer within the 3% discount period.
3. Purchased merchandise for cash.
4. Paid a creditor within the 3% discount period.
5. Received collection from customer after the 3% discount period had expired.
6. Paid freight on merchandise purchased.
7. Paid cash for office equipment.
8. Received cash refund from supplier for merchandise returned.
9. Withdrew cash for personal use of owner.
10. Made cash sales.

Instructions

Indicate **(a)** the journal, and **(b)** the columns in the journal that should be used in recording each transaction.

E7-7 Santiago Company has the following selected transactions during March.

Journalize transactions in general journal and post.
(SO 3, 4)

Mar. 2 Purchased equipment costing $6,000 from Briggs Company on account.
5 Received credit memorandum for $300 from Sanchez Company for merchandise damaged in shipment to Santiago.
7 Issued a credit memorandum for $400 to Sparks Company for merchandise the customer returned. The returned merchandise had a cost of $260.

Santiago Company uses a one-column purchases journal, a sales journal, the columnar cash journals used in the text, and a general journal.

Instructions

(a) Journalize the transactions in the general journal.
(b) ✏️ In a brief memo to the president of Santiago Company, explain the postings to the control and subsidiary accounts.

E7-8 Below are some typical transactions incurred by Heide Company.

Indicate journalizing in special journals.
(SO 4)

1. Payment of creditors on account.
2. Return of merchandise sold for credit.
3. Collection on account from customers.
4. Sale of land for cash.
5. Sale of merchandise on account.
6. Sale of merchandise for cash.
7. Received credit for merchandise purchased on credit.
8. Sales discount taken on goods sold.
9. Payment of employee wages.
10. Income summary closed to owner's capital.
11. Depreciation on building.
12. Purchase of office supplies for cash.
13. Purchase of merchandise on account.

Instructions

For each transaction, indicate whether it would normally be recorded in a cash receipts journal, cash payments journal, sales journal, single-column purchases journal, or general journal.

E7-9 The general ledger of Williams Company contained the following Accounts Payable control account (in T-account form). Also shown is the related subsidiary ledger.

Explain posting to control account and subsidiary ledger.
(SO 3, 5)

GENERAL LEDGER

Accounts Payable

Feb. 15	General journal	1,400	Feb. 1	Balance	26,025
28	?	?	5	General journal	265
			11	General journal	550
			28	Purchases	13,900
			Feb. 28	Balance	9,840

ACCOUNTS PAYABLE LEDGER

Sealy		Wolcott	
	Feb. 28 Bal. 4,600		Feb. 28 Bal. ?

Gates	
	Feb. 28 Bal. 2,000

Instructions

(a) Indicate the missing posting reference and amount in the control account, and the missing ending balance in the subsidiary ledger.
(b) Indicate the amounts in the control account that were dual-posted (i.e., posted to the control account and the subsidiary accounts).

Prepare purchases and general journals.
(SO 3, 4)

E7-10   Selected accounts from the ledgers of Juan Perez Company at July 31 showed the following.

GENERAL LEDGER

Store Equipment   No. 153

Date	Explanation	Ref.	Debit	Credit	Balance
July 1		G1	3,600		3,600

Accounts Payable   No. 201

Date	Explanation	Ref.	Debit	Credit	Balance
July 1		G1		3,600	3,600
15		G1		400	4,000
18		G1	100		3,900
25		G1	200		3,700
31		P1		8,700	12,400

Merchandise Inventory   No. 120

Date	Explanation	Ref.	Debit	Credit	Balance
July 15		G1	400		400
18		G1		100	300
25		G1		200	100
31		P1	8,400		8,500

ACCOUNTS PAYABLE LEDGER

Alou Equipment Co.

Date	Explanation	Ref.	Debit	Credit	Balance
July 1		G1		3,600	3,600

Dunlap Co.

Date	Explanation	Ref.	Debit	Credit	Balance
July 14		P1		1,100	1,100
25		G1	200		900

Benton Co.

Date	Explanation	Ref.	Debit	Credit	Balance
July 3		P1		2,000	2,000
20		P1		700	2,700

Emerick Co.

Date	Explanation	Ref.	Debit	Credit	Balance
July 12		P1		500	500
21		P1		600	1,100

Comerica Materials

Date	Explanation	Ref.	Debit	Credit	Balance
July 17		P1		1,400	1,400
18		G1	100		1,300
29		P1		2,100	3,400

Galant Transit

Date	Explanation	Ref.	Debit	Credit	Balance
July 15		G1		400	400

Instructions
From the data prepare:

(a) the single-column purchases journal for July.

(b) the general journal entries for July.

Determine correct posting amount to control account.
(SO 5)

E7-11   Valdez Products uses both special journals and a general journal as described in this chapter. Valdez also posts customers' accounts in the accounts receivable subsidiary ledger. The postings for the most recent month are included in the subsidiary T accounts below.

Ellie

Bal.	340	250
	200	

Rambo

Bal.	150	150
	290	

Panos

Bal.	–0–	145
	145	

Tenant

Bal.	120	120
	190	
	170	

Instructions

Determine the correct amount of the end-of-month posting from the sales journal to the Accounts Receivable control account.

PROBLEMS: SET A

P7-1A Lemon Company's chart of accounts includes the following selected accounts.

Journalize transactions in cash receipts journal; post to control account and subsidiary ledger.
(SO 3, 4, 5)

Peachtree

101 Cash	401 Sales
112 Accounts Receivable	414 Sales Discounts
120 Merchandise Inventory	505 Cost of Goods Sold
301 F. Lemon, Capital	

On April 1 the accounts receivable ledger of Lemon Company showed the following balances: Horner $1,550, Harris $1,200, Northeast Co. $2,900, and Smith $1,700. The April transactions involving the receipt of cash were as follows.

Apr. 1 The owner, F. Lemon, invested additional cash in the business $6,000.
    4 Received check for payment of account from Smith less 2% cash discount.
    5 Received check for $620 in payment of invoice no. 307 from Northeast Co.
    8 Made cash sales of merchandise totaling $7,245. The cost of the merchandise sold was $4,347.
   10 Received check for $800 in payment of invoice no. 309 from Horner.
   11 Received cash refund from a supplier for damaged merchandise $550.
   23 Received check for $1,500 in payment of invoice no. 310 from Northeast Co.
   29 Received check for payment of account from Harris.

Instructions

(a) Journalize the transactions above in a six-column cash receipts journal with columns for Cash Dr., Sales Discounts Dr., Accounts Receivable Cr., Sales Cr., Other Accounts Cr., and Cost of Goods Sold Dr./Merchandise Inventory Cr. Foot and crossfoot the journal.
(b) Insert the beginning balances in the Accounts Receivable control and subsidiary accounts, and post the April transactions to these accounts.
(c) Prove the agreement of the control account and subsidiary account balances.

(a) Balancing totals $19,615

(c) Accounts Receivable $1,530

P7-2A Simpson Company's chart of accounts includes the following selected accounts.

Journalize transactions in cash payments journal; post to control account and subsidiary ledgers.
(SO 3, 4, 5)

101 Cash	201 Accounts Payable
120 Merchandise Inventory	306 L. Simpson, Drawing
130 Prepaid Insurance	505 Cost of Goods Sold
157 Equipment	

On October 1 the accounts payable ledger of Simpson Company showed the following balances: Hester Company $1,700, Milo Co. $2,500, Ontario Co. $1,400, and Pagan Company $3,700. The October transactions involving the payment of cash were as follows.

Oct. 1 Purchased merchandise, check no. 63, $700.
    3 Purchased equipment, check no. 64, $800.
    5 Paid Hester Company balance due of $1,700, less 2% discount, check no. 65, $1,666.
   10 Purchased merchandise, check no. 66, $2,250.
   15 Paid Ontario Co. balance due of $1,400, check no. 67.
   16 L. Simpson, the owner, pays his personal insurance premium of $400, check no. 68.
   19 Paid Milo Co. in full for invoice no. 610, $1,400 less 2% cash discount, check no. 69, $1,372.
   29 Paid Pagan Company in full for invoice no. 264, $2,600, check no. 70.

Instructions

(a) Balancing totals $11,250

(a) Journalize the transactions above in a four-column cash payments journal with columns for Other Accounts Dr., Accounts Payable Dr., Merchandise Inventory Cr., and Cash Cr. Foot and crossfoot the journal.

(b) Insert the beginning balances in the Accounts Payable control and subsidiary accounts, and post the October transactions to these accounts.

(c) Accounts Payable $2,200

(c) Prove the agreement of the control account and the subsidiary account balances.

Journalize transactions in multi-column purchases journal; post to the general and subsidiary ledgers.
(SO 3, 4, 5)

Peachtree

P7-3A The chart of accounts of Hernandez Company includes the following selected accounts.

112	Accounts Receivable	401	Sales
120	Merchandise Inventory	412	Sales Returns and Allowances
126	Supplies	505	Cost of Goods Sold
157	Equipment	610	Advertising Expense
201	Accounts Payable		

In July the following selected transactions were completed. All purchases and sales were on account. The cost of all merchandise sold was 70% of the sales price.

July
1 Purchased merchandise from Denton Company $7,000.
2 Received freight bill from Johnson Shipping on Denton purchase $400.
3 Made sales to Lyons Company $1,300, and to Franklin Bros. $1,900.
5 Purchased merchandise from Grant Company $3,200.
8 Received credit on merchandise returned to Grant Company $300.
13 Purchased store supplies from Brent Supply $720.
15 Purchased merchandise from Denton Company $3,600 and from Ruiz Company $2,900.
16 Made sales to Martin Company $3,450 and to Franklin Bros. $1,570.
18 Received bill for advertising from Marlin Advertisements $600.
21 Sales were made to Lyons Company $310 and to Randee Company $2,300.
22 Granted allowance to Lyons Company for merchandise damaged in shipment $40.
24 Purchased merchandise from Grant Company $3,000.
26 Purchased equipment from Brent Supply $600.
28 Received freight bill from Johnson Shipping on Grant purchase of July 24, $380.
30 Sales were made to Martin Company $4,900.

Instructions

(a) Purchases journal—Accounts Payable $22,400
Sales journal $15,730

(a) Journalize the transactions above in a purchases journal, a sales journal, and a general journal. The purchases journal should have the following column headings: Date, Account Credited (Debited), Ref., Other Accounts Dr., and Merchandise Inventory Dr./Accounts Payable Cr.

(b) Post to both the general and subsidiary ledger accounts. (Assume that all accounts have zero beginning balances.)

(c) Accounts Receivable $15,690
Accounts Payable $22,100

(c) Prove the agreement of the control and subsidiary accounts.

Journalize transactions in special journals.
(SO 3, 4, 5)

P7-4A Selected accounts from the chart of accounts of Clark Company are shown below.

101	Cash	401	Sales
112	Accounts Receivable	412	Sales Returns and Allowances
120	Merchandise Inventory	414	Sales Discounts
126	Supplies	505	Cost of Goods Sold
157	Equipment	726	Salaries Expense
201	Accounts Payable		

The cost of all merchandise sold was 60% of the sales price. During January, Clark completed the following transactions.

Jan. 3   Purchased merchandise on account from Bell Co. $10,000.
      4   Purchased supplies for cash $80.
      4   Sold merchandise on account to Gilbert $7,250, invoice no. 371, terms 1/10, n/30.
      5   Issued a debit memorandum to Bell Co. and returned $300 worth of damaged goods.
      6   Made cash sales for the week totaling $3,150.
      8   Purchased merchandise on account from Law Co. $4,500.
      9   Sold merchandise on account to Mays Corp. $5,800, invoice no. 372, terms 1/10, n/30.
     11   Purchased merchandise on account from Hoble Co. $3,700.
     13   Paid in full Bell Co. on account less a 2% discount.
     13   Made cash sales for the week totaling $5,340.
     15   Received payment from Mays Corp. for invoice no. 372.
     15   Paid semi-monthly salaries of $14,300 to employees.
     17   Received payment from Gilbert for invoice no. 371.
     17   Sold merchandise on account to Amber Co. $1,200, invoice no. 373, terms 1/10, n/30.
     19   Purchased equipment on account from Johnson Corp. $5,500.
     20   Cash sales for the week totaled $3,200.
     20   Paid in full Law Co. on account less a 2% discount.
     23   Purchased merchandise on account from Bell Co. $7,800.
     24   Purchased merchandise on account from Levine Corp. $4,690.
     27   Made cash sales for the week totaling $3,730.
     30   Received payment from Amber Co. for invoice no. 373.
     31   Paid semi-monthly salaries of $13,200 to employees.
     31   Sold merchandise on account to Gilbert $9,330, invoice no. 374, terms 1/10, n/30.

Clark Company uses the following journals.

1. Sales journal.
2. Single-column purchases journal.
3. Cash receipts journal with columns for Cash Dr., Sales Discounts Dr., Accounts Receivable Cr., Sales Cr., Other Accounts Cr., and Cost of Goods Sold Dr./Merchandise Inventory Cr.
4. Cash payments journal with columns for Other Accounts Dr., Accounts Payable Dr., Merchandise Inventory Cr., and Cash Cr.
5. General journal.

Instructions

Using the selected accounts provided:

(a) Record the January transactions in the appropriate journal noted.
(b) Foot and crossfoot all special journals.
(c) Show how postings would be made by placing ledger account numbers and checkmarks as needed in the journals. (Actual posting to ledger accounts is not required.)

(a) Sales journal $23,580
    Purchases journal $30,690
    Cash receipts journal
      balancing total $29,670
    Cash payments journal
      balancing total $41,780

P7-5A Presented below are the purchases and cash payments journals for Collins Co. for its first month of operations.

Journalize in sales and cash receipts journals; post; prepare a trial balance; prove control to subsidiary; prepare adjusting entries; prepare an adjusted trial balance.
(SO 3, 4, 5)

Peachtree

Date		Account Credited	Ref.	Merchandise Inventory Dr. Accounts Payable Cr.
July	4	J. Dixon		6,800
	5	W. Engel		7,500
	11	R. Gamble		3,920
	13	M. Hill		15,300
	20	D. Jacob		8,800
				42,320

PURCHASES JOURNAL   **P1**

CASH PAYMENTS JOURNAL   CP1

Date	Account Debited	Ref.	Other Accounts Dr.	Accounts Payable Dr.	Merchandise Inventory Cr.	Cash Cr.
July 4	Store Supplies		600			600
10	W. Engel			7,500	75	7,425
11	Prepaid Rent		6,000			6,000
15	J. Dixon			6,800		6,800
19	Collins, Drawing		2,500			2,500
21	M. Hill			15,300	153	15,147
			9,100	29,600	228	38,472

In addition, the following transactions have not been journalized for July. The cost of all merchandise sold was 65% of the sales price.

July 1 The founder, R. Collins, invests $80,000 in cash.
6 Sell merchandise on account to Hardy Co. $5,400 terms 1/10, n/30.
7 Make cash sales totaling $4,000.
8 Sell merchandise on account to D. Wasburn $3,600, terms 1/10, n/30.
10 Sell merchandise on account to L. Lemansky $4,900, terms 1/10, n/30.
13 Receive payment in full from D. Wasburn.
16 Receive payment in full from L. Lemansky.
20 Receive payment in full from Hardy Co.
21 Sell merchandise on account to S. Kane $4,000, terms 1/10, n/30.
29 Returned damaged goods to J. Dixon and received cash refund of $450.

Instructions

(a) Open the following accounts in the general ledger.

101 Cash	306 Collins, Drawing
112 Accounts Receivable	401 Sales
120 Merchandise Inventory	414 Sales Discounts
127 Store Supplies	505 Cost of Goods Sold
131 Prepaid Rent	631 Supplies Expense
201 Accounts Payable	729 Rent Expense
301 Collins, Capital	

(b) Sales journal total
$17,900
Cash receipts journal
balancing totals $98,350

(e) Totals $114,620
(f) Accounts Receivable $4,000
Accounts Payable $12,720

(h) Totals $114,620

(b) Journalize the transactions that have not been journalized in the sales journal, the cash receipts journal (see Illustration 7-10), and the general journal.
(c) Post to the accounts receivable and accounts payable subsidiary ledgers. Follow the sequence of transactions as shown in the problem.
(d) Post the individual entries and totals to the general ledger.
(e) Prepare a trial balance at July 31, 2002.
(f) Determine whether the subsidiary ledgers agree with the control accounts in the general ledger.
(g) The following adjustments at the end of July are necessary.
(1) A count of supplies indicates that $140 is still on hand.
(2) Recognize rent expense for July, $500.
Prepare the necessary entries in the general journal. Post the entries to the general ledger.
(h) Prepare an adjusted trial balance at July 31, 2002.

P7-6A   The post-closing trial balance for Alomar Co. is as follows.

Journalize in special journals; post; prepare a trial balance.
(SO 3, 4, 5)

ALOMAR CO.
Post-Closing Trial Balance
December 31, 2002

	Debit	Credit
Cash	$ 41,500	
Accounts Receivable	15,000	
Notes Receivable	45,000	
Merchandise Inventory	23,000	
Equipment	6,450	
Accumulated Depreciation—Equipment		$ 1,500
Accounts Payable		43,000
S. Alomar, Capital		86,450
	$130,950	$130,950

The subsidiary ledgers contain the following information: (1) accounts receivable—R. Barton $2,500, B. Cole $7,500, S. Devine $5,000; (2) accounts payable—S. Field $10,000, R. Grilson $18,000, and D. Harms $15,000. The cost of all merchandise sold was 65% of the sales price. The transactions for January 2003 are as follows.

Jan. 3 Sell merchandise to B. Senton $4,000, terms 2/10, n/30.
      5 Purchase merchandise from S. Warren $2,500, terms 2/10, n/30.
      7 Receive a check from S. Devine $3,500.
     11 Pay freight on merchandise purchased $300.
     12 Pay rent of $1,000 for January.
     13 Receive payment in full from B. Senton.
     14 Post all entries to the subsidiary ledgers. Issue a credit memo to acknowledge receipt of damaged merchandise of $700 returned by R. Barton.
     15 Send D. Harms a check for $14,850 in full payment of account, discount $150.
     17 Purchase merchandise from D. Lapeska $1,600, terms 2/10, n/30.
     18 Pay sales salaries of $2,800 and office salaries $1,500.
     20 Give R. Grilson a 60-day note for $18,000 in full payment of account payable.
     23 Total cash sales amount to $8,600.
     24 Post all entries to the subsidiary ledgers. Sell merchandise on account to B. Cole $7,700, terms 1/10, n/30.
     27 Send S. Warren a check for $950.
     29 Receive payment on a note of $40,000 from S. Lava.
     30 Return merchandise of $500 to D. Lapeska for credit. Post all journals to the subsidiary ledger.

Instructions

(a) Open general and subsidiary ledger accounts for the following.

101 Cash	301 S. Alomar, Capital
112 Accounts Receivable	401 Sales
115 Notes Receivable	412 Sales Returns and Allowances
120 Merchandise Inventory	414 Sales Discounts
157 Equipment	505 Cost of Goods Sold
158 Accumulated Depreciation—Equipment	726 Sales Salaries Expense
200 Notes Payable	727 Office Salaries Expense
201 Accounts Payable	729 Rent Expense

(b) Record the January transactions in a sales journal, a single-column purchases journal, a cash receipts journal (see Illustration 7-10), a cash payments journal (see Illustration 7-17), and a general journal.

(c) Post the appropriate amounts to the general ledger.

(d) Prepare a trial balance at January 31, 2003.

(e) Determine whether the subsidiary ledgers agree with controlling accounts in the general ledger.

(b) Sales journal $11,700
Purchases journal $4,100
Cash receipts journal
(balancing) $56,100
Cash payments journal
(balancing) $21,550
(d) Totals $138,900
(e) Accounts Receivable
$18,500
Accounts Payable $12,650

PROBLEMS: SET B

Journalize transactions in cash receipts journal; post to control account and subsidiary ledger.
(SO 3, 4, 5)

P7-1B   Kimball Company's chart of accounts includes the following selected accounts.

101	Cash	401	Sales
112	Accounts Receivable	414	Sales Discounts
120	Merchandise Inventory	505	Cost of Goods Sold
301	J. Kimball, Capital		

On June 1 the accounts receivable ledger of Kimball Company showed the following balances: Block & Son $3,500, Field Co. $1,900, Green Bros. $1,600, and Mastin Co. $1,000. The June transactions involving the receipt of cash were as follows.

June 1 The owner, J. Kimball, invested additional cash in the business $10,000.
      3 Received check in full from Mastin Co. less 2% cash discount.
      6 Received check in full from Field Co. less 2% cash discount.
      7 Made cash sales of merchandise totaling $6,135. The cost of the merchandise sold was $4,090.
      9 Received check in full from Block & Son less 2% cash discount.
     11 Received cash refund from a supplier for damaged merchandise $200.
     15 Made cash sales of merchandise totaling $5,250. The cost of the merchandise sold was $3,500.
     20 Received check in full from Green Bros. $1,600.

Instructions

(a) Balancing totals $29,585

(a) Journalize the transactions above in a six-column cash receipts journal with columns for Cash Dr., Sales Discounts Dr., Accounts Receivable Cr., Sales Cr., Other Accounts Cr., and Cost of Goods Sold Dr./Merchandise Inventory Cr. Foot and crossfoot the journal.
(b) Insert the beginning balances in the Accounts Receivable control and subsidiary accounts, and post the June transactions to these accounts.

(c) Accounts Receivable $0

(c) Prove the agreement of the control account and subsidiary account balances.

Journalize transactions in cash payments journal; post to the general and subsidiary ledgers.
(SO 3, 4, 5)

P7-2B   Creek Company's chart of accounts includes the following selected accounts.

101	Cash	157	Equipment
120	Merchandise Inventory	201	Accounts Payable
130	Prepaid Insurance	306	V. Creek, Drawing

On November 1 the accounts payable ledger of Creek Company showed the following balances: R. Huff & Co. $4,500, G. Paul $2,350, R. Snyder $1,000, and Waldo Bros. $1,900. The November transactions involving the payment of cash were as follows.

Nov. 1 Purchased merchandise, check no. 11, $900.
      3 Purchased store equipment, check no. 12, $1,700.
      5 Paid Waldo Bros. balance due of $1,900, less 1% discount, check no. 13, $1,881.
     11 Purchased merchandise, check no. 14, $2,000.
     15 Paid R. Snyder balance due of $1,000, less 3% discount, check no. 15, $970.
     16 V. Creek, the owner, withdrew $500 cash for own use, check no. 16.
     19 Paid G. Paul in full for invoice no. 1245, $1,300 less 2% discount, check no. 17, $1,274.
     25 Paid premium due on one-year insurance policy, check no. 18, $3,000.
     30 Paid R. Huff & Co. in full for invoice no. 832, $2,500, check no. 19.

Instructions

(a) Balancing totals $14,800

(a) Journalize the transactions above in a four-column cash payments journal with columns for Other Accounts Dr., Accounts Payable Dr., Merchandise Inventory Cr., and Cash Cr. Foot and crossfoot the journal.
(b) Insert the beginning balances in the Accounts Payable control and subsidiary accounts, and post the November transactions to these accounts.

(c) Accounts Payable $3,050

(c) Prove the agreement of the control account and the subsidiary account balances.

P7-3B The chart of accounts of Virginia Company includes the following selected accounts.

Journalize transactions in multi-column purchases journal; post to the general and subsidiary ledgers.
(SO 3, 4, 5)

112	Accounts Receivable	401	Sales
120	Merchandise Inventory	412	Sales Returns and Allowances
126	Supplies	505	Cost of Goods Sold
157	Equipment	610	Advertising Expense
201	Accounts Payable		

In May the following selected transactions were completed. All purchases and sales were on account except as indicated. The cost of all merchandise sold was 70% of the sales price.

May 2 Purchased merchandise from Vons Company $9,500.
  3 Received freight bill from Acme Freight on Vons purchase $400.
  5 Sales were made to Penner Company $1,750, Hendrix Bros. $2,700, and Nelles Company $1,500.
  8 Purchased merchandise from Golden Company $8,000 and Dorn Company $8,700.
  10 Received credit on merchandise returned to Dorn Company $500.
  15 Purchased supplies from Engle Supply $900.
  16 Purchased merchandise from Vons Company $4,500, and Golden Company $6,000.
  17 Returned supplies to Engle Supply, receiving credit $100. (*Hint:* Credit Supplies.)
  18 Received freight bills on May 16 purchases from Acme Freight $500.
  20 Returned merchandise to Vons Company receiving credit $300.
  23 Made sales to Hendrix Bros. $2,400 and to Nelles Company $2,200.
  25 Received bill for advertising from Ball Advertising $900.
  26 Granted allowance to Nelles Company for merchandise damaged in shipment $200.
  28 Purchased equipment from Engle Supply $250.

Instructions

(a) Journalize the transactions above in a purchases journal, a sales journal, and a general journal. The purchases journal should have the following column headings: Date, Accounts Credited (Debited), Ref., Other Accounts Dr., and Merchandise Inventory Dr./Accounts Payable Cr.

(b) Post to both the general and subsidiary ledger accounts. (Assume that all accounts have zero beginning balances.)

(c) Prove the agreement of the control and subsidiary accounts.

(a) Purchases journal—Accounts
  Payable Cr. $39,650
  Sales journal total $10,550

(c) Accounts Receivable
  $10,350
  Accounts Payable $38,750

P7-4B Selected accounts from the chart of accounts of Ramos Company are shown below.

Journalize transactions in special journals.
(SO 3, 4, 5)

101	Cash	201	Accounts Payable
112	Accounts Receivable	401	Sales
120	Merchandise Inventory	414	Sales Discounts
126	Supplies	505	Cost of Goods Sold
140	Land	610	Advertising Expense
145	Buildings		

The cost of all merchandise sold was 60% of the sales price. During October, Ramos Company completed the following transactions.

Oct. 2 Purchased merchandise on account from Mason Company $18,500.
  4 Sold merchandise on account to Parker Co. $9,000. Invoice no. 204, terms 2/10, n/30.
  5 Purchased supplies for cash $80.
  7 Made cash sales for the week totaling $9,160.
  9 Paid in full the amount owed Mason Company less a 2% discount.
  10 Purchased merchandise on account from Quinn Corp. $4,200.
  12 Received payment from Parker Co. for invoice no. 204.
  13 Issued a debit memorandum to Quinn Corp. and returned $250 worth of damaged goods.
  14 Made cash sales for the week totaling $8,180.
  16 Sold a parcel of land for $27,000 cash, the land's book value.

17 Sold merchandise on account to L. Boyton & Co. $5,350, invoice no. 205, terms 2/10, n/30.
18 Purchased merchandise for cash $2,125.
21 Made cash sales for the week totaling $8,465.
23 Paid in full the amount owed Quinn Corp. for the goods kept (no discount).
25 Purchased supplies on account from Frey Co. $260.
25 Sold merchandise on account to Green Corp. $5,220, invoice no. 206, terms 2/10, n/30.
25 Received payment from L. Boyton & Co. for invoice no. 205.
26 Purchased for cash a small parcel of land and a building on the land to use as a storage facility. The total cost of $35,000 was allocated $21,000 to the land and $14,000 to the building.
27 Purchased merchandise on account from Schmid Co. $8,500.
28 Made cash sales for the week totaling $8,540.
30 Purchased merchandise on account from Mason Company $14,000.
30 Paid advertising bill for the month from the *Gazette*, $400.
30 Sold merchandise on account to L. Boyton & Co. $4,600, invoice no. 207, terms 2/10, n/30.

Ramos Company uses the following journals.

(b) Sales journal $24,170
  Purchases journal $45,200
  Cash receipts journal,
    Cash debit $75,408
  Cash payments journal,
    Cash credit $59,685

1. Sales journal.
2. Single-column purchases journal.
3. Cash receipts journal with columns for Cash Dr., Sales Discounts Dr., Accounts Receivable Cr., Sales Cr., Other Accounts Cr., and Cost of Goods Sold Dr./Merchandise Inventory Cr.
4. Cash payments journal with columns for Other Accounts Dr., Accounts Payable Dr., Merchandise Inventory Cr., and Cash Cr.
5. General journal.

Journalize in purchase and cash payments journals; post; prepare a trial balance; prove control to subsidiary; prepare adjusting entries; prepare an adjusted trial balance.
(SO 3, 4, 5)

Instructions

Using the selected accounts provided:

(a) Record the October transactions in the appropriate journals.
(b) Foot and crossfoot all special journals.
(c) Show how postings would be made by placing ledger account numbers and check marks as needed in the journals. (Actual posting to ledger accounts is not required.)

P7-5B Presented below are the sales and cash receipts journals for Toko Co. for its first month of operations.

SALES JOURNAL   S1

Date	Account Debited	Ref.	Accounts Receivable Dr. Sales Cr.	Cost of Goods Sold Dr. Merchandise Inventory Cr.
Feb. 3	D. Adams		5,500	3,630
9	P. Babcock		6,500	4,290
12	D. Chambers		8,000	5,280
26	K. Dawson		6,000	3,960
			26,000	17,160

CASH RECEIPTS JOURNAL   CR1

Date	Account Credited	Ref.	Cash Dr.	Sales Discounts Dr.	Accounts Receivable Cr.	Sales Cr.	Other Accounts Cr.	Cost of Goods Sold Dr. Merchandise Inventory Cr.
Feb. 1	J. Toko, Capital		30,000				30,000	
2			6,500			6,500		4,290
13	D. Adams		5,445	55	5,500			
18	Merchandise Inventory		150				150	
26	P. Babcock		6,500		6,500			
			48,595	55	12,000	6,500	30,150	4,290

In addition, the following transactions have not been journalized for February 2002.

Feb.   2   Purchased merchandise on account from S. Healy for $4,000, terms 1/10, n/30.
         7   Purchased merchandise on account from L. Held for $30,000, terms 1/10, n/30.
         9   Paid cash of $1,000 for purchase of supplies.
        12   Paid $3,960 to S. Healy in payment for $4,000 invoice, less 1% discount.
        15   Purchased equipment for $8,000 cash.
        16   Purchased merchandise on account from R. Landly $2,400, terms 2/10, n/30.
        17   Paid $29,700 to L. Held in payment of $30,000 invoice, less 1% discount.
        20   Withdrew cash of $1,100 from business for personal use.
        21   Purchased merchandise on account from J. Able for $6,500, terms 1/10, n/30.
        28   Paid $2,400 to R. Landly in payment of $2,400 invoice.

Instructions

(a) Open the following accounts in the general ledger.

101 Cash	301 J. Toko, Capital
112 Accounts Receivable	306 J. Toko, Drawing
120 Merchandise Inventory	401 Sales
126 Supplies	414 Sales Discounts
157 Equipment	505 Cost of Goods Sold
158 Accumulated Depreciation—Equipment	631 Supplies Expense
201 Accounts Payable	711 Depreciation Expense

(b) Journalize the transactions that have not been journalized in a one-column purchases journal and the cash payments journal (see Illustration 7-17).

(c) Post to the accounts receivable and accounts payable subsidiary ledgers. Follow the sequence of transactions as shown in the problem.

(d) Post the individual entries and totals to the general ledger.

(e) Prepare a trial balance at February 28, 2002.

(f) Determine that the subsidiary ledgers agree with the control accounts in the general ledger.

(g) The following adjustments at the end of February are necessary.
   (1) A count of supplies indicates that $300 is still on hand.
   (2) Depreciation on equipment for February is $200.
   Prepare the adjusting entries and then post the adjusting entries to the general ledger.

(h) Prepare an adjusted trial balance at February 28, 2002.

(b) Purchases journal total
   $42,900
   Cash payments journal
   Cash, Cr. $46,160

(e) Totals $69,000
(f) Accounts Receivable
   $14,000
   Accounts Payable $6,500

(h) Totals $69,200

COMPREHENSIVE PROBLEM: CHAPTERS 3 TO 7

Hunt Company has the following opening account balances in its general and subsidiary ledgers on January 1. All accounts have normal debit and credit balances.

General Ledger

Account Number	Account Title	January 1 Opening Balance
101	Cash	$35,750
112	Accounts Receivable	13,000
115	Notes Receivable	39,000
120	Merchandise Inventory	18,000
125	Office Supplies	1,000
130	Prepaid Insurance	2,000
157	Equipment	6,450
158	Accumulated Depreciation	1,500
201	Accounts Payable	35,000
301	S. Hunt, Capital	78,700

Accounts Receivable Subsidiary Ledger		Accounts Payable Subsidiary Ledger	
Customer	**January 1 Opening Balance**	**Creditor**	**January 1 Opening Balance**
R. Dansig	$1,500	S. Lee	$ 9,000
B. Jaggar	7,500	R. Mannon	15,000
S. Lowell	4,000	D. Nordin	11,000

Jan. 3 Sell merchandise on credit to B. Sargent $3,100, invoice no. 510, and J. Eaton $1,800, invoice no. 511.
   5 Purchase merchandise from S. Walden $3,000 and D. Landell $2,200.
   7 Receive checks for $4,000 from S. Lowell and $2,000 from B. Jaggar.
   8 Pay freight on merchandise purchased $180.
   9 Send checks to S. Lee for $9,000 and D. Nordin for $11,000.
   9 Issue credit memo for $300 to J. Eaton for merchandise returned.
  10 Summary cash sales total $15,500.
  11 Sell merchandise on credit to R. Dansig for $1,300, invoice no. 512, and to S. Lowell $900, invoice no. 513.
     Post all entries to the subsidiary ledgers.
  12 Pay rent of $1,000 for January.
  13 Receive payment in full from B. Sargent and J. Eaton.
  15 Withdraw $800 cash by S. Hunt for personal use.
  16 Purchase merchandise from D. Nordin for $15,000, from S. Lee for $14,200, and from S. Walden for $1,500.
  17 Pay $400 cash for office supplies.
  18 Return $200 of merchandise to S. Lee and receive credit.
  20 Summary cash sales total $17,500.
  21 Issue $15,000 note to R. Mannon in payment of balance due.
  21 Receive payment in full from S. Lowell.
     Post all entries to the subsidiary ledgers.
  22 Sell merchandise on credit to B. Sargent for $1,700, invoice no. 514, and to R. Dansig for $800, invoice no. 515.
  23 Send checks to D. Nordin and S. Lee in full payment.
  25 Sell merchandise on credit to B. Jaggar for $3,500, invoice no. 516, and to J. Eaton for $6,100, invoice no. 517.
  27 Purchase merchandise from D. Nordin for $14,500, from D. Landell for $1,200, and from S. Walden for $2,800.
  28 Pay $200 cash for office supplies.
  31 Summary cash sales total $21,300.
  31 Pay sales salaries of $4,300 and office salaries of $2,600.

Instructions

(a) Record the January transactions in the appropriate journal—sales, purchases, cash receipts, cash payments, and general.

(b) Post the journals to the general and subsidiary ledgers. New accounts should be added and numbered in an orderly fashion as needed.

(c) Prepare a trial balance at January 31, 2002, using a work sheet. Complete the work sheet using the following additional information.
   (1) Office supplies at January 31 total $500.
   (2) Insurance coverage expires on October 31, 2002.
   (3) Annual depreciation on the equipment is $1,500.
   (4) Interest of $30 has accrued on the note payable.
   (5) Merchandise inventory at January 31 is $16,000.

(d) Prepare a multiple-step income statement and a statement of owner's equity for January and a classified balance sheet at the end of January.

(e) Prepare and post the adjusting and closing entries.

(f) Prepare a post-closing trial balance, and determine whether the subsidiary ledgers agree with the control accounts in the general ledger.

BROADENING YOUR PERSPECTIVE

FINANCIAL REPORTING AND ANALYSIS

FINANCIAL REPORTING PROBLEM—MINI PRACTICE SET

BYP7-1 (The working papers that accompany this textbook are needed in order to work this mini practice set.)

Cheng Co. uses both an accounts receivable and an accounts payable subsidiary ledger. Balances related to both the general ledger and the subsidiary ledger for Cheng are indicated in the working papers. Presented below are a series of transactions for Cheng Co. for the month of January. Credit sales terms are 2/10, n/30. The cost of all merchandise sold was 60% of the sales price.

Jan.	3	Sell merchandise on credit to B. Sanchez $3,200, invoice no. 510, and to J. Egan $1,800, invoice no. 511.
	5	Purchase merchandise from S. Whitfield $3,000 and D. Land $2,200, terms n/30.
	7	Receive checks from S. Levin $4,000 and B. Jiminez $2,000 after discount period has lapsed.
	8	Pay freight on merchandise purchased $180.
	9	Send checks to S. Jin for $9,000 less 2% cash discount, and to D. Northcutt for $11,000 less 1% cash discount.
	9	Issue credit memo for $300 to J. Egan for merchandise returned.
	10	Summary daily cash sales total $15,500.
	11	Sell merchandise on credit to R. Danforth $1,300, invoice no. 512, and to S. Levin $900, invoice no. 513.
	12	Pay rent of $1,000 for January.
	13	Receive payment in full from B. Sanchez and J. Egan less cash discounts.
	15	Withdraw $800 cash by M. Cheng for personal use.
	15	Post all entries to the subsidiary ledgers.
	16	Purchase merchandise from D. Northcutt $16,000, terms 1/10, n/30; S. Jin $14,200, terms 2/10, n/30; and S. Whitfield $1,500, terms n/30.
	17	Pay $400 cash for office supplies.
	18	Return $200 of merchandise to S. Jin and receive credit.
	20	Summary daily cash sales total $17,500.
	21	Issue $15,000 note to R. Manual in payment of balance due.
	21	Receive payment in full from S. Levin less cash discount.
	22	Sell merchandise on credit to B. Sanchez $2,700, invoice no. 514, and to R. Danforth $800, invoice no. 515.
	22	Post all entries to the subsidiary ledger.
	23	Send checks to D. Northcutt and S. Jin in full payment less cash discounts.
	25	Sell merchandise on credit to B. Jiminez $3,500, invoice no. 516, and to J. Egan $6,100, invoice no. 517.
	27	Purchase merchandise from D. Northcutt $14,500, terms 1/10, n/30; D. Land $1,200, terms n/30; and S. Whitfield $4,800, terms n/30.
	27	Post all entries to the subsidiary ledger.
	28	Pay $200 cash for office supplies.
	31	Summary daily cash sales total $21,300.
	31	Pay sales salaries $4,300 and office salaries $2,600.

Instructions

(a) Record the January transactions in a sales journal, a single-column purchases journal, a cash receipts journal as shown on page 286, a cash payments journal as shown on page 291, and a two-column general journal.

(b) Post the journals to the general ledger.

(c) Prepare a trial balance at January 31, 2002, in the trial balance columns of the work sheet. Complete the work sheet using the following additional information.

(1) Office supplies at January 31 total $500.

(2) Insurance coverage expires on October 31, 2002.

(3) Annual depreciation on the equipment is $1,500.

(4) Interest of $60 has accrued on the note payable.

(d) Prepare a multiple-step income statement and an owner's equity statement for January and a classified balance sheet at the end of January.

(e) Prepare and post adjusting and closing entries.

(f) Prepare a post-closing trial balance, and determine whether the subsidiary ledgers agree with the control accounts in the general ledger.

EXPLORING THE WEB

BYP7-2   Great Plains' Accounting is one of the leading accounting software packages. Information related to this package is found at its Web site.

Address: **www.greatplains.com/accounting/productinfo.asp** *(or go to www.wiley.com/college/ weygandt)*

Steps:

1. Go to the site shown above.

2. Choose **General Ledger**. Perform instruction (a) below.

3. Choose **Accounts Payable**. Perform instruction (b) below.

Instructions

(a) What are three key features of the general ledger module highlighted by the company?

(b) What are three key features of the payables management module highlighted by the company?

CRITICAL THINKING

GROUP DECISION CASE

BYP7-3   Ehlert & Ramos is a wholesaler of small appliances and parts. Ehlert & Ramos is operated by two owners, Bill Ehlert and Denise Ramos. In addition, the company has one employee, a repair specialist, who is on a fixed salary. Revenues are earned through the sale of appliances to retailers (approximately 75% of total revenues), appliance parts to do-it-yourselfers (10%), and the repair of appliances brought to the store (15%). Appliance sales are made on both a credit and cash basis. Customers are billed on prenumbered sales invoices. Credit terms are always net/30 days. All parts sales and repair work are cash only.

Merchandise is purchased on account from the manufacturers of both the appliances and the parts. Practically all suppliers offer cash discounts for prompt payments, and it is company policy to take all discounts. Most cash payments are made by check. Checks are most frequently issued to suppliers, to trucking companies for freight on merchandise purchases, and to newspapers, radio, and TV stations for advertising. All advertising bills are paid as received. Bill and Denise each make a monthly drawing in cash for personal living expenses. The salaried repairman is paid twice monthly. Ehlert & Ramos currently has a manual accounting system.

Instructions

With the class divided into groups, answer the following.

(a) Identify the special journals that Ehlert & Ramos should have in its manual system. List the column headings appropriate for each of the special journals.

(b) What control and subsidiary accounts should be included in Ehlert & Ramos's manual system? Why?

COMMUNICATION ACTIVITY

BYP7-4   Sue Marsh, a classmate, has a part-time bookkeeping job. She is concerned about the inefficiencies in journalizing and posting transactions. Raul Hindi is the owner of the company where Sue works. In response to numerous complaints from Sue and others, Raul hired two additional bookkeepers a month ago. However, the inefficiencies have continued at an even higher rate. The accounting information system for the company has only a general journal and a general ledger. Raul refuses to install an electronic accounting system.

Instructions

Now that Sue is an expert in manual accounting information systems, she decides to send a letter to Raul Hindi explaining (1) why the additional personnel did not help and (2) what changes should be made to improve the efficiency of the accounting department. Write the letter that you think Sue should send.

ETHICS CASE

BYP7-5   Tyler Products Company operates three divisions, each with its own manufacturing plant and marketing/sales force. The corporate headquarters and central accounting office are in Tyler, and the plants are in Freeport, Rockport, and Bayport, all within 50 miles of Tyler. Corporate management treats each division as an independent profit center and encourages competition among them. They each have similar but different product lines. As a competitive incentive, bonuses are awarded each year to the employees of the fastest growing and most profitable division.

Don Henke is the manager of Tyler's centralized computer accounting operation that keyboards the sales transactions and maintains the accounts receivable for all three divisions. Don came up in the accounting ranks from the Bayport division where his wife, several relatives, and many friends still work.

As sales documents are keyboarded into the computer, the originating division is identified by code. Most sales documents (95%) are coded, but some (5%) are not coded or are coded incorrectly. As the manager, Don has instructed the keyboard operators to assign the Bayport code to all uncoded and incorrectly coded sales documents. This is done he says, "in order to expedite processing and to keep the computer files current since they are updated daily." All receivables and cash collections for all three divisions are handled by Tyler as one subsidiary accounts receivable ledger.

Instructions

   (a) Who are the stakeholders in this situation?
   (b) What are the ethical issues in this case?
   (c) How might the system be improved to prevent this situation?

Answers to Self-Study Questions

1. d   **2.** b   **3.** a   **4.** c   **5.** a   **6.** c   **7.** d   **8.** b   **9.** c   **10.** c

☑ Remember to go back to the Navigator box on the chapter-opening page and check off your completed work.

INTERNAL CONTROL AND CASH

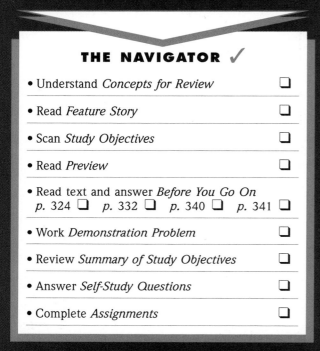

THE NAVIGATOR ✓

- Understand *Concepts for Review* ❑
- Read *Feature Story* ❑
- Scan *Study Objectives* ❑
- Read *Preview* ❑
- Read text and answer *Before You Go On*
  p. 324 ❑   *p.* 332 ❑   *p.* 340 ❑   *p.* 341 ❑
- Work *Demonstration Problem* ❑
- Review *Summary of Study Objectives* ❑
- Answer *Self-Study Questions* ❑
- Complete *Assignments* ❑

CONCEPTS FOR REVIEW

Before studying this chapter, you should know or, if necessary, review:

    a. How cash transactions are recorded. (Ch. 2, pp. 54–63)

    b. How cash is classified on a balance sheet. (Ch. 4, pp. 155–156)

    c. The role ethics plays in proper financial reporting. (Ch.1, pp. 9–10)

THE NAVIGATOR

Minding the Money in Moose Jaw

If you're ever looking for a cappuccino in Moose Jaw, Saskatchewan, stop by **Stephanie's Gourmet Coffee and More**, located on Main Street. Staff there serve, on average, 646 cups of coffee a day—including both regular and specialty coffees—not to mention soups, Italian sandwiches, and a wide assortment of gourmet cheesecakes.

"We've got high school students who come here, and students from the community college," says owner/manager Stephanie Mintenko, who has run the place since opening it in 1995. "We have customers who are retired, and others who are working people and have only 30 minutes for lunch. We have to be pretty quick."

That means that the cashiers have to be efficient. Like most businesses where purchases are low-cost and high-volume, cash control has to be simple.

"We have an electronic cash register, but it's not the fancy new kind where you just punch in the item," explains Ms. Mintenko. "You have to punch in the prices." The machine does keep track of sales in several categories, however. Cashiers punch a button to indicate whether each item is a beverage, a meal, or a charge for the cafe's Internet connections. All transactions are recorded on an internal tape in the machine; the customer receives a receipt only upon request.

There is only one cash register. "Up to three of us might operate it on any given shift, including myself," says Ms. Mintenko.

She and her staff do two "cashouts" each day—one with the shift change at 5:00, and one when the shop closes at 10:00. The cash in the register drawer is counted. That amount, minus the cash change carried forward (the float), should match the shift total on the register tape. If there's a discrepancy, they do another count. Then, if necessary, "we go through the whole tape to find the mistake," she explains. "It usually turns out to be someone who punched in $18 instead of $1.80, or something like that."

Ms. Mintenko sends all the cash tapes and float totals to a bookkeeper, who double checks everything and provides regular reports. "We try to keep the accounting simple, so we can concentrate on making great coffee and food."

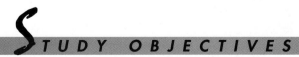

After studying this chapter, you should be able to:

1. Define internal control.
2. Identify the principles of internal control.
3. Explain the applications of internal control principles to cash receipts.
4. Explain the applications of internal control principles to cash disbursements.
5. Describe the operation of a petty cash fund.
6. Indicate the control features of a bank account.
7. Prepare a bank reconciliation.
8. Explain the reporting of cash.

As the story about recording cash sales at **Stephanie's Gourmet Coffee and More** indicates, control of cash is important. Controls are also needed to safeguard other types of assets. For example, Stephanie's undoubtedly has controls to prevent the theft of food and supplies, and controls to prevent the theft of silverware and dishes from its kitchen.

In this chapter, we explain the essential features of an internal control system and then describe how those controls apply to cash. The applications include some controls with which you may be already familiar. Toward the end of the chapter, we describe the use of a bank and explain how cash is reported on the balance sheet.

The content and organization of Chapter 8 are as follows.

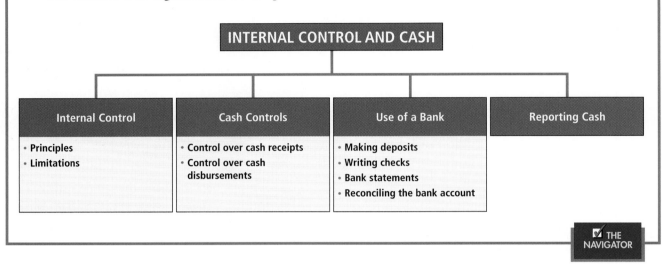

INTERNAL CONTROL

STUDY OBJECTIVE 1

Define internal control.

Could there be dishonest employees where you work? Unfortunately, the answer sometimes is Yes. For example, the financial press recently reported the following.

> A bookkeeper in a small company diverted $750,000 of bill payments to a personal bank account over a 3-year period.

> A shipping clerk with 28 years of service shipped $125,000 of merchandise to himself.

> A computer operator embezzled $21 million from **Wells Fargo Bank** over a 2-year period.

> A church treasurer "borrowed" $150,000 of church funds to finance a friend's business dealings.

These situations emphasize the need for a good system of internal control.

Internal control consists of the plan of organization and all the related methods and measures adopted within a business to:

1. **Safeguard its assets** from employee theft, robbery, and unauthorized use.

2. **Enhance the accuracy and reliability of its accounting records.** This is done by reducing the risk of **errors** (unintentional mistakes) and **irregularities** (intentional mistakes and misrepresentations) in the accounting process.

The Foreign Corrupt Practices Act of 1977 requires all major U.S. corporations to maintain an adequate system of internal control. Companies that fail to comply are subject to fines, and company officers may be imprisoned. Also, the National Commission on Fraudulent Financial Reporting concluded that all companies whose stock is publicly traded should maintain internal controls that can provide reasonable assurance that fraudulent financial reporting will be prevented or subject to early detection.[1]

INTERNATIONAL NOTE

U.S. companies also adopt model business codes that guide their international operations to provide for a safe and healthy workplace, avoid child and forced labor, abstain from bribes, and follow sound environmental practices.

TECHNOLOGY IN ACTION

Good internal control must be designed into computerized systems. The starting point is usually flow charts that graphically depict each component of a firm's operations. The assembled flow charts serve as the basis for writing detailed programs. An example of flow charting is given in this chapter (see Illustration 8-6). When attempts to automate or improve accounting systems fail, it is often due to the absence of such well-documented procedures.

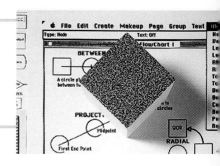

PRINCIPLES OF INTERNAL CONTROL

To safeguard its assets and enhance the accuracy and reliability of its accounting records, a company follows specific control principles. Of course, internal control measures vary with the size and nature of the business and with management's control philosophy. The six principles listed in Illustration 8-1 apply to most enterprises. Each principle is explained in the following sections.

STUDY OBJECTIVE 2

Identify the principles of internal control.

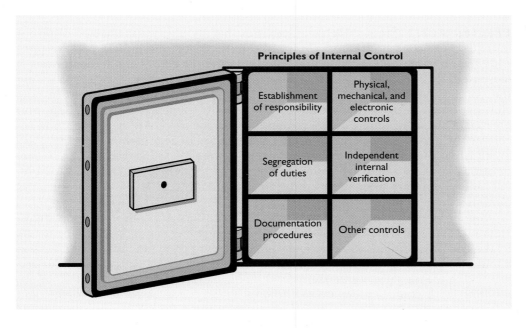

Illustration 8-1

Principles of internal control

[1] Report of the National Commission on Fraudulent Financial Reporting, October 1987, p. 11.

It's your shift now. I'm turning in my cash drawer and heading home.

Transfer of cash drawers

Establishment of Responsibility

An essential characteristic of internal control is the assignment of responsibility to specific employees. **Control is most effective when only one person is responsible for a given task.** To illustrate, assume that the cash on hand at the end of the day in a Safeway supermarket is $10 short of the cash rung up on the cash register. If only one person has operated the register, responsibility for the shortage can be assessed quickly. If two or more individuals have worked the register, it may be impossible to determine who is responsible for the error unless each person is assigned a separate cash drawer and register key. The principle of establishing responsibility does not appear to be strictly applied by Stephanie's (in the Feature Story) since three people operate the cash register on any given shift. To identify any shortages quickly at Stephanie's, two cashouts are performed each day.

Establishing responsibility includes the authorization and approval of transactions. For example, the vice president of sales should have the authority to establish policies for making credit sales. The policies ordinarily will require written credit department approval of credit sales.

Segregation of Duties

Segregation of duties (also called separation of functions or division of work) is indispensable in a system of internal control. There are two common applications of this principle:

1. Related activities should be assigned to different individuals.
2. Establishing the accountability (keeping the records) for an asset should be separate from the physical custody of that asset.

The rationale for segregation of duties is this: **The work of one employee should, without a duplication of effort, provide a reliable basis for evaluating the work of another employee.**

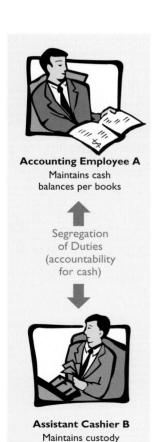

Accounting Employee A
Maintains cash balances per books

Segregation of Duties (accountability for cash)

Assistant Cashier B
Maintains custody of cash on hand

RELATED ACTIVITIES. Related activities that should be assigned to different individuals arise in both purchasing and selling. **When one individual is responsible for all of the related activities, the potential for errors and irregularities is increased.** Related purchasing activities include ordering merchandise, receiving the goods, and paying (or authorizing payment) for the merchandise. In purchasing, for example, orders could be placed with friends or with suppliers who give kickbacks. Or, only a cursory count and inspection could be made upon receiving the goods, which could lead to errors and poor-quality merchandise. Payment might be authorized without a careful review of the invoice. Even worse, fictitious invoices might be approved for payment. When the ordering, receiving, and paying are assigned to different individuals, the risk of such abuses is minimized.

Similarly, related sales activities should be assigned to different individuals. Related selling activities include making a sale, shipping (or delivering) the goods to the customer, billing the customer, and receiving payment. When one person handles related sales transactions, a salesperson could make sales at unauthorized prices to increase sales commissions; a shipping clerk could ship goods to himself; a billing clerk could understate the amount billed for sales made to friends and relatives. These abuses are reduced by dividing the sales tasks: the salespersons make the sale; the shipping department ships the goods on the basis of the sales order; and the billing department prepares the sales invoice after comparing the sales order with the report of goods shipped.

ACCOUNTABILITY FOR ASSETS. To provide a valid basis of accountability for an asset, the accountant should have neither physical custody of the asset nor access to it. Likewise, the custodian of the asset should not maintain or have access to the accounting records. **When one employee maintains the record of the asset that should be on hand, and a different employee has physical custody of the asset, the custodian of the asset is not likely to convert the asset to personal use.** The separation of accounting responsibility from the custody of assets is especially important for cash and inventories because these assets are very vulnerable to unauthorized use or misappropriation.

Accounting in Action *International Insight*

Sumitomo Corporation announced a huge loss, $1.8 billion, due to a single copper trader. Some blamed Sumitomo's poor internal control on Japanese culture because it encourages group harmony over confrontation. For example, good controls require that both parties to a copper trade send a confirmation slip to management to verify the trade. In Japan, the counterparty to the trade often sends the confirmation slip to the trader, who then forwards it to management. Thus, it is possible for the trader to change the confirmation slip. An unethical trader could create fictitious trades to hide losses for an extended period of time or to conceal trades that are larger than allowed limits.

SOURCE: Sheryl Wudunn, "Big New Loss Makes Japan Look Inward," *New York Times,* June 17, 1996, p. D1.

Documentation Procedures

Documents provide evidence that transactions and events have occurred. At **Stephanie's Gourmet Coffee and More**, the cash register tape was the restaurant's documentation for the sale and the amount of cash received. Similarly, the shipping document indicates that the goods have been shipped, and the sales invoice indicates that the customer has been billed for the goods. By adding signatures (or initials) to the documents, the individual(s) responsible for the transaction or event can be identified. Documentation of transactions should be made when the transaction occurs. Documentation of events, such as those leading to adjusting entries, is generally developed when the adjustments are made.

Several procedures should be established for documents. First, whenever possible, **documents should be prenumbered, and all documents should be accounted for**. Prenumbering helps to prevent a transaction from being recorded more than once. It also helps to prevent the transactions from not being recorded. Second, documents that are **source documents for accounting entries should be promptly forwarded to the accounting department. This control measure helps to ensure timely recording of the transaction** and contributes directly to the accuracy and reliability of the accounting records.

Prenumbered invoices

HELPFUL HINT
An important corollary to prenumbering is that voided documents be kept until all documents are accounted for.

Physical, Mechanical, and Electronic Controls

Use of physical, mechanical, and electronic controls is essential. Physical controls relate primarily to the safeguarding of assets. Mechanical and electronic controls also safeguard assets; some enhance the accuracy and reliability of the accounting records. Examples of these controls are shown in Illustration 8-2.

Illustration 8-2

Physical, mechanical, and electronic controls

Physical Controls

Safes, vaults, and safety deposit boxes for cash and business papers

Locked warehouses and storage cabinets for inventories and records

Computer facilities with pass key access

Mechanical and Electronic Controls

Alarms to prevent break-ins

Television monitors and garment sensors to deter theft

Time clocks for recording time worked

ACCOUNTING IN ACTION *Business Insight*

John Patterson, a young Ohio merchant, couldn't understand why his retail business didn't show a profit. There were lots of customers, but the money just seemed to disappear. Patterson suspected pilferage and sloppy bookkeeping by store clerks. Frustrated, he placed an order with a Dayton, Ohio, company for two rudimentary cash registers. A year later, Patterson's store was in the black.

"What is a good thing for this little store is a good thing for every retail store in the world," he observed. A few months later, in 1884, John Patterson and his brother, Frank, bought the tiny cash register maker for $6,500. The word around Dayton was that the Patterson boys got stung.

In the following 37 years, John Patterson built **National Cash Register Co.** into a corporate giant. Patterson died in 1922, the year in which NCR sold its two millionth cash register.

SOURCE: The Wall Street Journal, January 28, 1989.

Independent Internal Verification

Most internal control systems provide for **independent internal verification**. This principle involves the review, comparison, and reconciliation of data prepared by other employees. To obtain maximum benefit from independent internal verification:

1. The verification should be made periodically or on a surprise basis.
2. The verification should be done by someone who is independent of the employee responsible for the information.
3. Discrepancies and exceptions should be reported to a management level that can take appropriate corrective action.

Independent internal verification is especially useful in comparing recorded accountability with existing assets. The reconciliation of the cash register tape with the cash in the register at **Stephanie's Gourmet Coffee and More** is an example of this internal control principle. Another common example is the reconciliation by an independent person of the cash balance per books with the cash balance per bank. The relationship between this principle and the segregation of duties principle is shown graphically in Illustration 8-3.

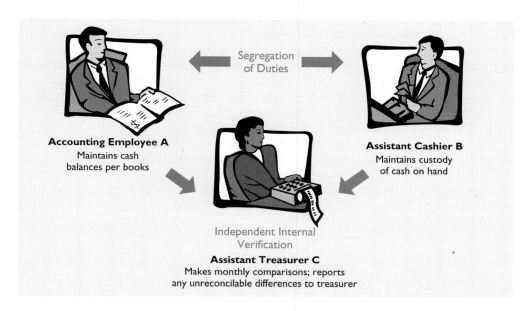

Illustration 8-3

Comparison of segregation of duties principle with independent internal verification principle

In large companies, independent internal verification is often assigned to internal auditors. **Internal auditors** are company employees who evaluate on a continuous basis the effectiveness of the company's system of internal control. They periodically review the activities of departments and individuals to determine whether prescribed internal controls are being followed. They also recommend improvements when needed. The importance of this function is illustrated by the number of internal auditors employed by companies.

Other Controls

Other control measures include the following.

1. **Bonding of employees who handle cash.** Bonding involves obtaining insurance protection against misappropriation of assets by dishonest employees. This measure contributes to the safeguarding of cash in two ways: First, the insurance company carefully screens all individuals before adding them to the policy and may reject risky applicants. Second, bonded employees know that the insurance company will vigorously prosecute all offenders.

2. **Rotating employees' duties and requiring employees to take vacations.** These measures are designed to deter employees from attempting any thefts since they will not be able to permanently conceal their improper actions. Many bank embezzlements, for example, have been discovered when the perpetrator was on vacation or assigned to a new position.

LIMITATIONS OF INTERNAL CONTROL

A company's system of internal control is generally designed to provide **reasonable assurance** that assets are properly safeguarded and that the accounting records are reliable. **The concept of reasonable assurance rests on the premise that the costs of establishing control procedures should not exceed their expected benefit.** To illustrate, consider shoplifting losses in retail stores. Such losses could be eliminated by having a security guard stop and search customers as they leave the store. But, store managers have concluded that the negative effects of adopting such a procedure cannot be justified. Instead, stores have attempted to "control" shoplifting losses by less costly procedures such as: (1) posting signs saying, "We reserve the right to inspect all packages," and "All shoplifters will be prosecuted," (2) using hidden TV cameras and store detectives to monitor customer activity, and (3) using sensoring equipment at exits.

The **human element** is an important factor in every system of internal control. A good system can become ineffective as a result of employee fatigue, carelessness, or indifference. For example, a receiving clerk may not bother to count goods received or may just "fudge" the counts. Occasionally, two or more individuals may work together to get around prescribed controls. Such **collusion** can significantly impair the effectiveness of a system, eliminating the protection offered by segregation of duties. If a supervisor and a cashier collaborate to understate cash receipts, the system of internal control may be negated (at least in the short run). No system of internal control is perfect.

The size of the business also may impose limitations on internal control. In a small company, for example, it may be difficult to segregate duties or to provide for independent internal verification.

TECHNOLOGY IN ACTION

 Unfortunately, computer-related frauds have become a major concern. The average computer fraud loss is $650,000, compared with an average loss of only $19,000 resulting from other types of white-collar crime.

Computer fraud can be perpetrated almost invisibly and done with electronic speed. Psychologically, stealing with impersonal computer tools can seem far less criminal to some people. Therefore, the moral threshold to commit computer fraud is lower than fraud involving person-to-person contact.

Preventing and detecting computer fraud represents a major challenge. One of the best ways for a company to minimize the likelihood of computer fraud is to have a good system of internal control that allows the benefits of computerization to be gained without opening the possibility for rampant fraud.

BEFORE YOU GO ON...

▶ *REVIEW IT*
1. What are the two primary objectives of internal control?
2. Identify and describe the principles of internal control.
3. What are the limitations of internal control?

▶ *DO IT*
Li Song owns a small retail store. Li wants to establish good internal control procedures but is confused about the difference between segregation of duties and independent internal verification. Explain the differences to Li.

ACTION PLAN
• Understand and explain the differences between (1) segregation of duties and (2) independent internal verification.

SOLUTION: Segregation of duties involves assigning responsibility so that the work of one employee evaluates the work of another employee. Segregation of duties occurs daily in executing and recording transactions. In contrast, independent internal verification involves reviewing, comparing, and reconciling data prepared by one or several employees. Independent internal verification occurs after the fact, as in the case of reconciling cash register totals at the end of the day with cash on hand.

Related exercise material: BE8-1, BE8-2, and E8-1.

CASH CONTROLS

Just as cash is the beginning of a company's operating cycle, it is also usually the starting point for a company's system of internal control. Cash is the one asset that is readily convertible into any other type of asset. It is easily concealed and transported, and it is highly desired. Because of these characteristics, **cash is the asset most susceptible to improper diversion and use**. Moreover, because of the large volume of cash transactions, numerous errors may occur in executing and recording them. To safeguard cash and to ensure the accuracy of the accounting records for cash, effective internal control over cash is imperative.

Cash consists of coins, currency (paper money), checks, money orders, and money on hand or on deposit in a bank or similar depository. The general rule is that if the bank will accept it for deposit, it is cash. Items such as postage stamps and postdated checks (checks payable in the future) are not cash. Stamps are a prepaid expense; the postdated checks are accounts receivable. In the following sections we explain the application of internal control principles to cash receipts and cash disbursements.

INTERNATIONAL NOTE

Other countries also have control problems. For example, a judge in France has issued a 36-page "book" detailing many of the scams that are widespread, such as kickbacks in public-works contracts, the skimming of development aid money to Africa, and bribes on arms sales.

INTERNAL CONTROL OVER CASH RECEIPTS

Cash receipts come from a variety of sources: cash sales; collections on account from customers; the receipt of interest, rent, and dividends; investments by owners; bank loans; and proceeds from the sale of noncurrent assets. Illustration 8-4 shows how the internal control principles explained earlier apply to cash receipts transactions.

As might be expected, companies vary considerably in how they apply these principles. To illustrate internal control over cash receipts, we will examine control measures for a retail store with both over-the-counter and mail receipts.

STUDY OBJECTIVE 3

Explain the applications of internal control principles to cash receipts.

Over-the-Counter Receipts

Control of over-the-counter receipts in retail businesses is centered on cash registers that are visible to customers. In supermarkets and in variety stores such as **Kmart**, cash registers are placed in check-out lines near the exit. In stores such as **Sears, Roebuck & Co.** and **J. C. Penney**, each department has its own cash register. A cash sale is "rung up" on a cash register **with the amount clearly visible to the customer**. This measure prevents the cashier from ringing up a lower amount and pocketing the difference. The customer receives an itemized cash register receipt slip and is expected to count the change received. A cash register tape is locked into the register until removed by a supervisor or manager. This tape accumulates the daily transactions and totals. When the tape is removed, the supervisor compares the total with the amount of cash in the register. The tape should show all registered receipts accounted for. The supervisor's findings are reported on a cash count sheet which is signed by both the cashier and supervisor. The cash count sheet used by Alrite Food Mart is shown in Illustration 8-5.

Illustration 8-4

Application of internal control principles to cash receipts

Internal Control over Cash Receipts

Establishment of Responsibility

Only designated personnel are authorized to handle cash receipts (cashiers)

Segregation of Duties

Different individuals receive cash, record cash receipts, and hold the cash

Documentation Procedures

Use remittance advice (mail receipts), cash register tapes, and deposit slips

Physical, Mechanical, and Electronic Controls

Store cash in safes and bank vaults; limit access to storage areas; use cash registers

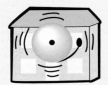

Independent Internal Verification

Supervisors count cash receipts daily; treasurer compares total receipts to bank deposits daily

Other Controls

Bond personnel who handle cash; require employees to take vacations; deposit all cash in bank daily

Illustration 8-5

Cash count sheet

Store No. 8	Date March 8, 2002
1. Opening cash balance	$ 50.00
2. Cash sales per tape (attached)	6,956.20
3. Total cash to be accounted for	7,006.20
4. Cash on hand (see list)	6,996.10
5. Cash (short) or over	$ (10.10)
6. Ending cash balance	$ 50.00
7. Cash for deposit (Line 4 – Line 6)	$6,946.10

Cashier J. Cruse   Supervisor M. Braun

The count sheets, register tapes, and cash are then given to the head cashier. This individual prepares a daily cash summary showing the total cash received and the amount from each source, such as cash sales and collections on account. The head cashier sends one copy of the summary to the accounting department for entry into the cash receipts journal. The other copy goes to the treasurer's office for later comparison with the daily bank deposit.

Next, the head cashier prepares a deposit slip (see Illustration 8-9 on page 333) and makes the bank deposit. The total amount deposited should be equal to the total receipts on the daily cash summary. This will ensure that all receipts have been placed in the custody of the bank. In accepting the bank deposit, the bank stamps (authenticates) the duplicate deposit slip and sends it to the company treasurer, who makes the comparison with the daily cash summary.

These measures for cash sales are graphically presented in Illustration 8-6. The activities of the sales department are shown separately from those of the cashier's department to indicate the segregation of duties in handling cash.

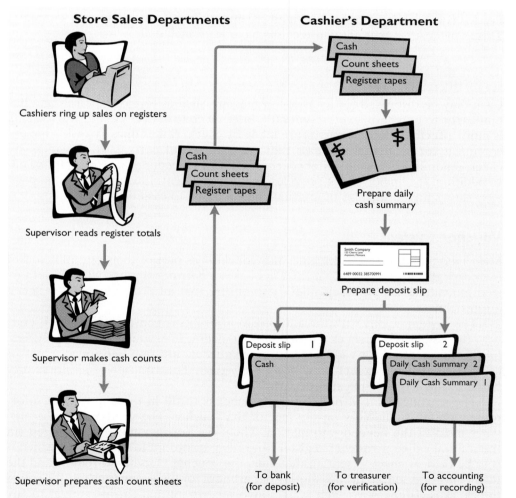

Illustration 8-6

Executing over-the-counter cash sales

HELPFUL HINT
Flowcharts such as this one enhance the understanding of the flow of documents, the processing steps, and the internal control procedures.

Mail Receipts

As an individual customer, you may be more familiar with over-the-counter receipts than with mail receipts. However, mail receipts resulting from billings and credit sales are by far the most common way cash is received by businesses. Think, for example, of the number of checks received through the mail daily by a national retailer such as **Lands' End** or **Abercrombie & Fitch**.

All mail receipts should be opened in the presence of two mail clerks. These receipts are generally in the form of checks or money orders. They frequently are accompanied by a remittance advice stating the purpose of the check (sometimes attached to the check, but often a part of the bill that the customer tears off and returns). Each check should be promptly endorsed "For Deposit Only" by use of a company stamp. This **restrictive endorsement** reduces the likelihood that the check will be diverted to personal use. Banks will not give an individual any cash under this type of endorsement.

A list of the checks received each day should be prepared in duplicate. This list shows the name of the issuer of the check, the purpose of the payment, and the amount of the check. Each mail clerk should sign the list to establish responsibility for the data. The original copy of the list, along with the checks and remittance advices, are then sent to the cashier's department. There they are added to over-the-counter receipts (if any) in preparing the daily cash summary and in making the daily bank deposit. Also, a copy of the list is sent to the treasurer's office for comparison with the total mail receipts shown on the daily cash summary. This copy ensures that all mail receipts have been included.

INTERNAL CONTROL OVER CASH DISBURSEMENTS

STUDY OBJECTIVE **4**

Explain the applications of internal control principles to cash disbursements.

Cash may be disbursed for a variety of reasons, such as to pay expenses and liabilities, or to purchase assets. **Generally, internal control over cash disbursements is more effective when payments are made by check, rather than by cash.** One exception is **for incidental amounts that are paid out of petty cash.**[2] Payment by check generally occurs only after specified control procedures have been followed. In addition, the "paid" check provides proof of payment. Illustration 8-7 (on page 329) shows how principles of internal control apply to cash disbursements.

Voucher System

Most medium and large companies use vouchers as part of their internal control over cash disbursements. A **voucher system** is a network of approvals by authorized individuals acting independently to ensure that all disbursements by check are proper.

The system begins with the authorization to incur a cost or expense. It ends with the issuance of a check for the liability incurred. A **voucher** is an authorization form prepared for each expenditure. Vouchers are required for all types of cash disbursements except those from petty cash. The voucher generally is prepared in the accounts payable department.

The starting point in preparing a voucher is to fill in the appropriate information about the liability on the face of the voucher. The vendor's invoice provides most of the needed information. Then, the voucher must be recorded (in the journal called a **voucher register**) and filed according to the date on which it is to be paid. A check is sent on that date, the voucher is stamped "paid," and the paid voucher is sent to the accounting department for recording (in a journal called the **check register**). A voucher system involves two journal entries, similar to any accounts payable transaction, one to issue the voucher and a second to pay the voucher.

---

[2]The operation of a petty cash fund is explained on pages 330–332.

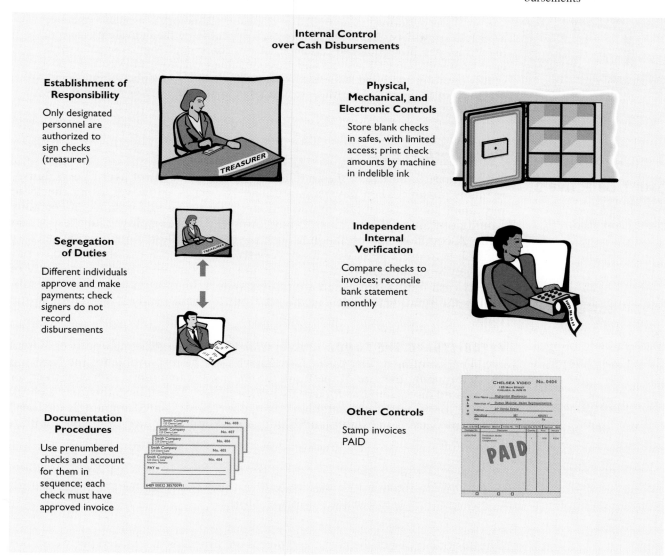

Internal Control
over Cash Disbursements

Establishment of Responsibility

Only designated personnel are authorized to sign checks (treasurer)

Segregation of Duties

Different individuals approve and make payments; check signers do not record disbursements

Documentation Procedures

Use prenumbered checks and account for them in sequence; each check must have approved invoice

Physical, Mechanical, and Electronic Controls

Store blank checks in safes, with limited access; print check amounts by machine in indelible ink

Independent Internal Verification

Compare checks to invoices; reconcile bank statement monthly

Other Controls

Stamp invoices PAID

Electronic Funds Transfer (EFT) System

To account for and control cash is an expensive and time-consuming process. It was estimated recently that the cost to process a check through a bank system ranges from $0.55 to $1.00 and is increasing. It is not surprising that new approaches are being developed to transfer funds among parties without the use of paper (deposit tickets, checks, etc.). Such a procedure is called **electronic funds transfer (EFT)**. This disbursement system uses wire, telephone, telegraph, or computer to transfer cash from one location to another. Use of EFT is quite common. For example, the authors receive no formal payroll checks from their universities, which instead send magnetic tapes to the appropriate banks for deposit. Regular payments such as those for house, car, and utilities are frequently made by EFT.

*T*ECHNOLOGY IN ACTION

The development of EFT will continue. Already it is estimated that over 80 percent of the total volume of bank transactions in the United States is performed using EFT. The computer technology is available to create a "checkless" society. The only major barriers appear to be the individual's concern for privacy and protection and certain legislative constraints. Numerous safeguards have been built into EFT systems and are continuing to improve. However, the possibility of errors and fraud still exists because only a limited number of individuals are involved in the transfers, which may prevent appropriate segregation of duties.

Petty Cash Fund

STUDY OBJECTIVE 5

Describe the operation of a petty cash fund.

As you learned earlier in the chapter, better internal control over cash disbursements is possible when payments are made by check. However, using checks to pay small amounts is both impractical and a nuisance. For instance, a company would not want to write checks to pay for postage due, employee lunches, or taxi fares. A common way of handling such payments, while maintaining satisfactory control, is to use a petty cash fund. A **petty cash fund** is a cash fund used to pay relatively small amounts but still maintain satisfactory control. The operation of a petty cash fund, often called an **imprest system**, involves three steps: (1) establishing the fund, (2) making payments from the fund, and (3) replenishing the fund.[3]

ESTABLISHING THE FUND. Two essential steps in establishing a petty cash fund are (1) appointing a petty cash custodian who will be responsible for the fund and (2) determining the size of the fund. Ordinarily, the amount is expected to cover anticipated disbursements for a 3- to 4-week period. To establish the fund, a check payable to the petty cash custodian is issued for the stipulated amount. If the Laird Company decides to establish a $100 fund on March 1, the entry in general journal form is:

A	=	L	+	OE
+100				
−100				

Mar. 1	Petty Cash		100	
	Cash			100
	(To establish a petty cash fund)			

The custodian cashes the check and places the proceeds in a locked petty cash box or drawer. Most petty cash funds are established on a fixed-amount basis. No additional entries will be made to the Petty Cash account unless management changes the stipulated amount of the fund. For example, if Laird Company decides on July 1 to increase the size of the fund to $250, it would debit Petty Cash $150 and credit Cash $150.

MAKING PAYMENTS FROM THE FUND. The custodian of the petty cash fund has the authority to make payments from the fund that conform to prescribed management policies. Usually, management limits the size of expenditures that may be made. Likewise, it may not permit use of the fund for certain types of transactions (such as making short-term loans to employees). Each payment from the fund must be documented on a prenumbered petty cash receipt (or petty cash voucher), as shown in Illustration 8-8. Note that the signatures of both the custo-

---

[3]The term "imprest" means an advance of money for a designated purpose.

Illustration 8-8

Petty cash receipt

```
No. 7                W. A. LAIRD COMPANY
                        Petty Cash Receipt

                                        Date    3/6/02

    Paid to   Acme Express Agency       Amount  $18.00

    For    Collect Express Charges

    CHARGE TO        Freight-in


    Approved                            Received Payment

    L. A. Bird    Custodian             R. E. Meins
```

dian and the person receiving payment are required on the receipt. If other supporting documents such as a freight bill or invoice are available, they should be attached to the petty cash receipt.

The receipts are kept in the petty cash box until the fund runs low and needs to be replenished. The sum of the petty cash receipts and money in the fund should equal the established total at all times. Surprise counts can be made at any time by an independent person, such as an internal auditor, to determine whether the fund is being maintained intact.

No accounting entry is made to record a payment at the time it is made from petty cash. It is considered unnecessary to do so. Instead, the accounting effects of each payment are recognized when the fund is replenished.

REPLENISHING THE FUND.   When the money in the petty cash fund reaches a minimum level, the fund is replenished. The request for reimbursement is initiated by the petty cash custodian. This individual prepares a schedule (or summary) of the payments that have been made and sends the schedule, supported by petty cash receipts and other documentation, to the treasurer's office. The receipts and supporting documents are examined in the treasurer's office to verify that they were proper payments from the fund. The treasurer then approves the request and a check is prepared to restore the fund to its established amount. At the same time, all supporting documentation is stamped "paid" so that it cannot be submitted again for payment.

To illustrate, assume that on March 15 the petty cash custodian requests a check for $87. The fund contains $13 cash and petty cash receipts for postage $44, freight-out $38, and miscellaneous expenses $5. The general journal entry to record the check is:

Mar. 15	Postage Expense	44	
	Freight-out	38	
	Miscellaneous Expense	5	
	Cash		87
	(To replenish petty cash fund)		

A	=	L	+	OE
−87				−44
				−38
				−5

Note that the Petty Cash account is not affected by the reimbursement entry. Replenishment changes the composition of the fund by replacing the petty cash receipts with cash. It does not change the balance in the fund.

It may be necessary in replenishing a petty cash fund to recognize a cash shortage or overage. This results when the cash plus receipts in the petty cash box do not equal the established amount of the petty cash fund. To illustrate, assume in the example on the preceding page that the custodian had only $12 in cash in the fund plus the receipts as listed. The request for reimbursement would, therefore, have been for $88. The following entry would be made:

HELPFUL HINT

Cash over and short situations result from mathematical errors or from failure to keep accurate records.

A	=	L	+	OE
−88				−44
				−38
				−5
				−1

Mar. 15	Postage Expense	44	
	Freight-out	38	
	Miscellaneous Expense	5	
	Cash Over and Short	1	
	Cash		88
	(To replenish petty cash fund)		

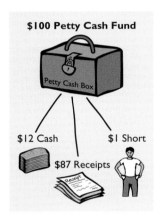

$100 Petty Cash Fund

Petty Cash Box

$12 Cash $1 Short

$87 Receipts

If the custodian had $14 in cash, the reimbursement request would have been for $86 and Cash Over and Short would have been credited for $1 (overage). A debit balance in Cash Over and Short is reported in the income statement as miscellaneous expense. A credit balance in the account is reported as miscellaneous revenue. Cash Over and Short is closed to Income Summary at the end of the year.

A petty cash fund should be replenished at the end of the accounting period regardless of the cash in the fund. Replenishment at this time is necessary in order to recognize the effects of the petty cash payments on the financial statements.

Internal control over a petty cash fund is strengthened by (1) having a supervisor make surprise counts of the fund to ascertain whether the paid vouchers and fund cash equal the imprest amount and (2) canceling or mutilating the paid vouchers so they cannot be resubmitted for reimbursement.

BEFORE YOU GO ON...

▶ *REVIEW IT*

1. How do the principles of internal control apply to cash receipts?
2. How do the principles of internal control apply to cash disbursements?
3. When are entries required in a petty cash system?

▶ *DO IT*

L. R. Cortez is concerned about the control over cash receipts in his fast-food restaurant, Big Cheese. The restaurant has two cash registers. At no time do more than two employees take customer orders and ring up sales. Work shifts for employees range from 4 to 8 hours. Cortez asks your help in installing a good system of internal control over cash receipts.

ACTION PLAN

- Differentiate among the internal control principles of (1) establishing responsibility, (2) using electronic controls, and (3) independent internal verification.
- Design an effective system of internal control over cash receipts.

SOLUTION: Cortez should assign a cash register to each employee at the start of each work shift, with register totals set at zero. Each employee should be instructed to use only the assigned register and to ring up all sales. At the end of each work shift, Cortez or a supervisor/manager should total the register and make a cash count to see whether all cash is accounted for.

Related exercise material: BE8-3, BE8-4, BE8-5, E8-2, E8-3, E8-4, and E8-5.

☑ THE NAVIGATOR

USE OF A BANK

The use of a bank contributes significantly to good internal control over cash. A company can safeguard its cash by using a bank as a depository and as a clearing house for checks received and checks written. Use of a bank minimizes the amount of currency that must be kept on hand. Also, the use of a bank facilitates the control of cash because it creates a double record of all bank transactions—one by the business and the other by the bank. The asset account Cash maintained by the depositor is the reciprocal of the bank's liability account for each depositor. It should be possible to **reconcile these accounts** (make them agree) at any time.

Opening a bank checking account is a relatively simple procedure. Typically, the bank makes a credit check on the new customer and the depositor is required to sign a **signature card**. The card contains the signatures of each person authorized to sign checks on the account. The signature card is used by bank employees to validate signatures on the checks.

Soon after an account is opened, the bank provides the depositor with serially numbered checks and deposit slips imprinted with the depositor's name and address. Each check and deposit slip is imprinted with both a bank and a depositor identification number. This number, printed in magnetic ink, permits computer processing of transactions.

Many companies have more than one bank account. For efficiency of operations and better control, national retailers like **Wal-Mart** and **Kmart** may have regional bank accounts. A company such as **Intel** with more than 70,000 employees may have a payroll bank account, as well as one or more general bank accounts. Also, a company may maintain several bank accounts in order to have more than one source for short-term loans when needed.

STUDY OBJECTIVE 6

Indicate the control features of a bank account.

MAKING BANK DEPOSITS

Bank deposits should be made by an authorized employee, such as the head cashier. Each deposit must be documented by a deposit slip (ticket), as shown in Illustration 8-9.

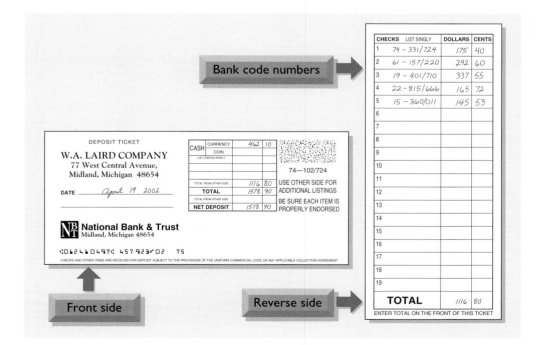

Illustration 8-9

Deposit slip

Deposit slips are prepared in duplicate. The original is retained by the bank; the duplicate, machine-stamped by the bank to establish its authenticity, is retained by the depositor.

WRITING CHECKS

A **check** is a written order signed by the depositor directing the bank to pay a specified sum of money to a designated recipient. There are three parties to a check: (1) the **maker** (or drawer) who issues the check; (2) the **bank** (or payer) on which the check is drawn; and (3) the **payee** to whom the check is payable. A check is a **negotiable instrument** that can be transferred to another party by endorsement. Each check should be accompanied by an explanation of its purposes. In many businesses, this is done by a remittance advice attached to the check, as shown in Illustration 8-10.

Illustration 8-10

Check with remittance advice

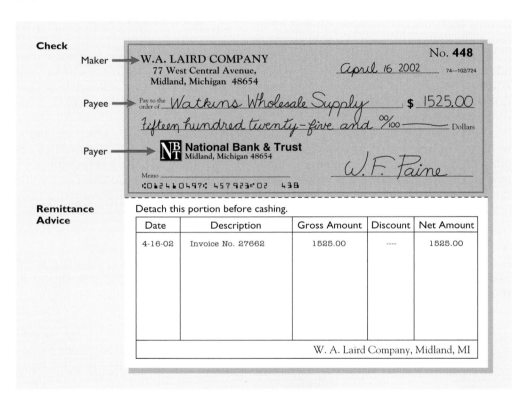

It is important to know the balance in the checking account at all times. To keep the balance current, each deposit and check should be entered on running balance memorandum forms provided by the bank or on the check stubs contained in the checkbook.

*A*CCOUNTING IN ACTION ∧ *Business Insight*

Cash is virtually obsolete. We use debit cards and credit cards to pay for most of our purchases. But debit cards are usable only at specified locations, and credit cards are cumbersome for small transactions. They are no good for transferring cash between individuals or to small companies that don't want to pay credit card fees. Digital cash is the next online wave.

There are many digital-cash companies. One of the most flexible appears to be **PayPal.com**. PayPal has become popular with users of the auction site **eBay**, because it allows them to transfer funds to each other as easily as sending e-mail.

SOURCE: Mathew Ingram, "Will Digital Cash Work This Time?" *The Globe and Mail*, March 18, 2000, p. N4.

BANK STATEMENTS

Each month, the depositor receives a bank statement from the bank. A **bank statement** shows the depositor's bank transactions and balances. A typical statement is presented in Illustration 8-11. It shows (1) checks paid and other debits that reduce the balance in the depositor's account, (2) deposits and other credits that increase the balance in the depositor's account, and (3) the account balance after each day's transactions.

Illustration 8-11

Bank statement

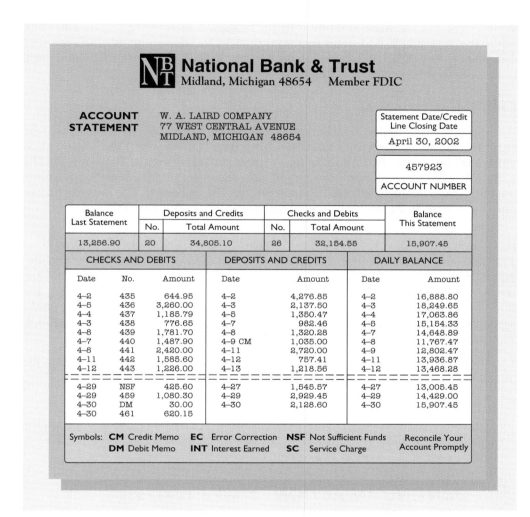

All "paid" checks are listed in numerical sequence on the bank statement along with the date the check was paid and its amount. Upon paying a check, the bank stamps the check "paid"; a paid check is sometimes referred to as a **canceled** check. Most banks offer depositors the option of receiving "paid" checks with their bank statements. For those who decline, the bank keeps a record of each check on microfilm.

The bank also includes on the bank statement memoranda explaining other debits and credits made by the bank to the depositor's account.

Debit Memorandum

Banks charge a monthly fee for their services. Often the fee is charged only when the average monthly balance in a checking account falls below a specified amount.

The fee, called a **bank service charge**, is identified on the bank statement by a code symbol such as SC. A debit memorandum explaining the charge is included with the bank statement and noted on the statement. Separate debit memoranda may also be issued for other bank services such as the cost of printing checks, issuing traveler's checks, and wiring funds to other locations. The symbol DM is often used for such charges.

A debit memorandum is also used by the bank when a deposited check from a customer "bounces" because of insufficient funds. In such a case, the check is marked **NSF** (not sufficient funds) by the customer's bank and is returned to the depositor's bank. The bank then debits the depositor's account, as shown by the symbol NSF on the bank statement in Illustration 8-11 (on page 335). The bank sends the NSF check and debit memorandum to the depositor as notification of the charge. The NSF check creates an account receivable for the depositor and reduces cash in the bank account.

Credit Memorandum

A depositor may ask the bank to collect its notes receivable. In such a case, the bank will credit the depositor's account for the cash proceeds of the note. This is illustrated on the W. A. Laird Company bank statement by the symbol CM. The bank will issue a credit memorandum which is sent with the statement to explain the entry. Many banks also offer interest on checking accounts. The interest earned may be indicated on the bank statement by the symbol CM or INT.

RECONCILING THE BANK ACCOUNT

STUDY OBJECTIVE 7

Prepare a bank reconciliation.

The bank and the depositor maintain independent records of the depositor's checking account. If you've never had a checking account, you might assume that the respective balances will always agree. In fact, the two balances are seldom the same at any given time. It is therefore necessary to make the balance per books agree with the balance per bank—a process called **reconciling the bank account**. The lack of agreement between the two balances is due to:

1. **Time lags** that prevent one of the parties from recording the transaction in the same period.

2. **Errors** by either party in recording transactions.

Time lags occur frequently. For example, several days may elapse between the time a check is mailed to a payee and the date the check is paid by the bank.

ACCOUNTING IN ACTION   Ethics Insight

Some firms have used time lags to their advantage. For example, **E. F. Hutton** managers at one time overdrew their accounts by astronomical amounts—on some days the overdrafts totaled $1 billion. These overdrafts created interest-free loans that the company could invest. The loans lasted as long as it took for the covering checks to be collected. Although not technically illegal at the time, Hutton's actions were wrong because it did not have the bank's permission to do so. The discovery of this practice led to E. F. Hutton's demise.

Similarly, when the depositor uses the bank's night depository to make its deposits, there will be a difference of at least one day between the time the receipts are recorded by the depositor and the time they are recorded by the bank. A time lag also occurs whenever the bank mails a debit or credit memorandum to the depositor.

Also, errors sometimes occur. The incidence of errors depends on the effectiveness of the internal controls of the depositor and the bank. Bank errors are infrequent. However, either party could inadvertently record a $450 check as $45 or $540. In addition, the bank might mistakenly charge a check drawn by C. D. Berg to the account of C. D. Burg.

Reconciliation Procedure

To obtain maximum benefit from a bank reconciliation, the reconciliation should be prepared by an employee who has no other responsibilities pertaining to cash. When the internal control principle of independent internal verification is not followed in preparing the reconciliation, cash embezzlements may go unnoticed. For example, a cashier who prepares the reconciliation can embezzle cash and conceal the embezzlement by misstating the reconciliation. Thus, the bank accounts would reconcile, and the embezzlement would not be detected.

In reconciling the bank account, it is customary to reconcile the balance per books and balance per bank to their adjusted (correct or true) cash balances. The reconciliation schedule is divided into two sections. The starting point in preparing the reconciliation is to enter the balance per bank statement and balance per books on the schedule. Adjustments are then made to each section, as shown in Illustration 8-12. The steps listed on the next page should reveal all the reconciling items that cause the difference between the two balances.

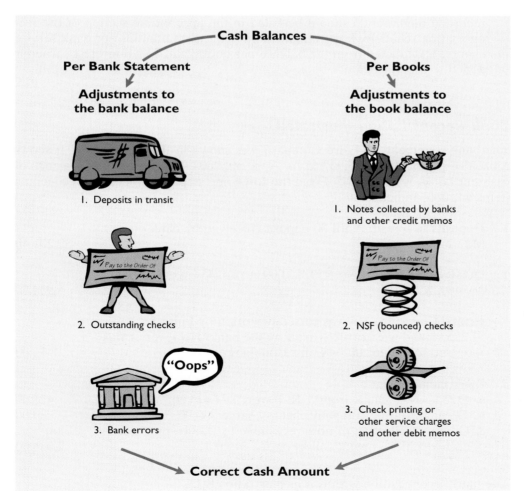

Illustration 8-12

Bank reconciliation procedures

Steps in the Reconciliation Procedure

1. **Deposits in transit.** Compare the individual deposits on the bank statement with deposits in transit from the preceding bank reconciliation and with the deposits per company records or duplicate deposit slips. Deposits recorded by the depositor that have not been recorded by the bank represent **deposits in transit**. They are added to the balance per bank.

2. **Outstanding checks.** Compare the paid checks shown on the bank statement or the paid checks returned with the bank statement with (a) checks outstanding from the preceding bank reconciliation, and (b) checks issued by the company as recorded in the cash payments journal. Issued checks recorded by the company that have not been paid by the bank represent **outstanding checks**. They are deducted from the balance per the bank.

3. **Errors.** Note any **errors** discovered in the foregoing steps. List them in the appropriate section of the reconciliation schedule. For example, if a paid check correctly written by the company for $195 was mistakenly recorded by the company for $159, the error of $36 is deducted from the balance per books. All errors made by the depositor are reconciling items in determining the adjusted cash balance per books. In contrast, all errors made by the bank are reconciling items in determining the adjusted cash balance per the bank.

4. **Bank memoranda.** Trace **bank memoranda** to the depositor's records. Any unrecorded memoranda should be listed in the appropriate section of the reconciliation schedule. For example, a $5 debit memorandum for bank service charges is deducted from the balance per books, and $32 of interest earned is added to the balance per books.

Bank Reconciliation Illustrated

The bank statement for Laird Company was shown in Illustration 8-11. It shows a balance per bank of $15,907.45 on April 30, 2002. On this date the balance of cash per books is $11,589.45. From the foregoing steps, the following reconciling items are determined.

1. **Deposits in transit:** April 30 deposit (received by bank on May 1). $2,201.40

2. **Outstanding checks:** No. 453, $3,000.00; no. 457, $1,401.30; no. 460, $1,502.70.   5,904.00

3. **Errors:** Check no. 443 was correctly written by Laird for $1,226.00 and was correctly paid by the bank. However, it was recorded for $1,262.00 by Laird Company.   36.00

4. **Bank memoranda:**
    a. Debit—NSF check from J. R. Baron for $425.60   425.60
    b. Debit—Printing company checks charge $30.00   30.00
    c. Credit—Collection of note receivable for $1,000 plus interest earned $50, less bank collection fee $15.00   1,035.00

The bank reconciliation is shown in Illustration 8-13.

W. A. LAIRD COMPANY Bank Reconciliation April 30, 2002		
Cash balance per bank statement		$15,907.45
Add: Deposits in transit		2,201.40
		18,108.85
Less: Outstanding checks		
No. 453	$3,000.00	
No. 457	1,401.30	
No. 460	1,502.70	5,904.00
Adjusted cash balance per bank		**$12,204.85**
Cash balance per books		$11,589.45
Add: Collection of note receivable $1,000, plus interest		
earned $50, less collection fee $15	$1,035.00	
Error in recording check no. 443	36.00	1,071.00
		12,660.45
Less: NSF check	425.60	
Bank service charge	30.00	455.60
Adjusted cash balance per books		**$12,204.85**

Illustration 8-13

Bank reconciliation

ALTERNATIVE TERMINOLOGY

The terms *adjusted balance,*
true cash balance, and *correct*
cash balance may be used
interchangeably.

Entries from Bank Reconciliation

Each reconciling item in determining the **adjusted cash balance per books** should be recorded by the depositor. **If these items are not journalized and posted, the Cash account will not show the correct balance.** The entries for W. A. Laird Company on April 30 are as follows.

HELPFUL HINT

The entries that follow are adjusting entries. In prior chapters, Cash was an account that did not require adjustment. That was a simplifying assumption for learning purposes, because a bank reconciliation had not been explained.

COLLECTION OF NOTE RECEIVABLE. This entry involves four accounts. Assuming that the interest of $50 has not been accrued and the collection fee is charged to Miscellaneous Expense, the entry is:

Apr. 30	Cash	1,035.00	
	Miscellaneous Expense	15.00	
	Notes Receivable		1,000.00
	Interest Revenue		50.00
	(To record collection of notes receivable by bank)		

A	=	L	+	OE
+1,035				−15
−1,000				+50

BOOK ERROR. The cash disbursements journal shows that check no. 443 was a payment on account to Andrea Company, a supplier. The correcting entry is:

Apr. 30	Cash	36.00	
	Accounts Payable—Andrea Company		36.00
	(To correct error in recording check no. 443)		

A	=	L	+	OE
+36		+36		

NSF CHECK. As indicated earlier, an NSF check becomes an account receivable to the depositor. The entry is:

Apr. 30	Accounts Receivable—J. R. Baron	425.60	
	Cash		425.60
	(To record NSF check)		

A	=	L	+	OE
+425.60				
−425.60				

BANK SERVICE CHARGES.　Check printing charges (DM) and other bank service charges (SC) are debited to Miscellaneous Expense. They are usually nominal in amount. The entry is:

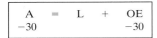

	A	=	L	+	OE
	−30				−30

Apr. 30	Miscellaneous Expense	30.00	
	Cash		30.00
	(To record charge for printing company checks)		

The foregoing four entries could also be combined into one compound entry. After the entries are posted, the cash account will show the following.

Illustration 8-14

Adjusted balance in cash account

		Cash		
Apr. 30　Bal.	11,589.45	Apr. 30	425.60
30	1,035.00	30	30.00
30	36.00		
Apr. 30　Bal.	**12,204.85**		

The adjusted cash balance in the ledger should agree with the adjusted cash balance per books in the bank reconciliation in Illustration 8-13.

What entries does the bank make? If any bank errors are discovered in preparing the reconciliation, the bank should be notified. It then can make the necessary corrections on its records. The bank does not make any entries for deposits in transit or outstanding checks. Only when these items reach the bank will the bank record these items.

BEFORE YOU GO ON...

▶ *REVIEW IT*
1. Why is it necessary to reconcile a bank account?
2. What steps are involved in the reconciliation procedure?
3. What information is included in a bank reconciliation?

▶ *DO IT*

Sally Kist owns Linen Kist Fabrics. Sally asks you to explain how the following reconciling items should be treated in reconciling the bank account: (1) a debit memorandum for an NSF check, (2) a credit memorandum for a note collected by the bank, (3) outstanding checks, and (4) a deposit in transit.

ACTION PLAN
• Understand the purpose of a bank reconciliation.
• Identify time lags and explain how they cause reconciling items.

SOLUTION: In reconciling the bank account, the reconciling items are treated as follows.
　NSF check: Deducted from balance per books.
　Collection of note: Added to balance per books.
　Outstanding checks: Deducted from balance per bank.
　Deposit in transit: Added to balance per bank.

Related exercise material: BE8-6, BE8-7, BE8-8, BE8-9, BE8-10, E8-6, E8-7, E8-8, E8-9, and E8-10.

THE NAVIGATOR

REPORTING CASH

Cash on hand, cash in banks, and petty cash are often combined and reported simply as **Cash**. Because it is the most liquid asset owned by a company, cash is listed first in the current assets section of the balance sheet. Some companies use the term "Cash and cash equivalents" in reporting cash, as illustrated by the following.

STUDY OBJECTIVE 8

Explain the reporting of cash.

Illustration 8-15

Presentation of cash and cash equivalents

EASTMAN KODAK COMPANY Balance Sheets (partial)		
	1999	**1998**
Current assets (in millions)		
Cash and cash equivalents	$373	$457

Cash equivalents are highly liquid investments that can be converted into a specific amount of cash. They typically have maturities of three months or less when purchased. They include money market funds, money market savings certificates, bank certificates of deposit, and U.S. Treasury bills and notes.

A company may have cash that is restricted for a special purpose. An example is a payroll bank account for paying salaries and wages. Another would be a plant expansion cash fund for financing new construction. If the restricted cash is expected to be used **within the next year**, the amount should be reported as a current asset. When the restricted funds will not be used in that time, they should be reported as a noncurrent asset. Since a payroll bank account will be used as early as the next payday, it is reported as a current asset. In contrast, unless the new construction will begin within the next year, plant expansion fund cash is classified as a noncurrent asset (long-term investment).

In making loans to depositors, banks commonly require borrowers to maintain minimum cash balances. These minimum balances, called **compensating balances**, provide the bank with support for the loans. They are a restriction on the use of cash that may affect a company's liquidity. Thus, compensating balances should be disclosed in the financial statements.

BEFORE YOU GO ON...

▶ *REVIEW IT*
1. What is generally reported as cash on a company's balance sheet?
2. What is meant by cash equivalents and compensating balances?
3. At what amount does **Lands' End** report cash and cash equivalents in its 2000 consolidated balance sheet? The answer to this question is provided on page 359.

A LOOK BACK AT OUR FEATURE STORY

Refer back to the Feature Story about **Stephanie's Gourmet Coffee and More** café at the beginning of the chapter, and answer the following questions.

1. Does Stephanie Mintenko have a valid basis for establishing responsibility for overages or shortages? Why or why not?
2. What internal control principles are applicable to reconciling the cash register tape and the amount of cash in the cash drawer at the end of each shift?
3. What internal control principle is violated by not printing a receipt for each customer who purchases beverages, a meal, or uses the café's computers?
4. Do you think cashiers are, or should be, bonded (insured against misappropriation of assets)?
5. What adjusting entry would the bookkeeper likely make to record a cash shortage of $5?

SOLUTION

1. Establishing responsibility for overages or shortages occurs twice a day: at the end of the 5:00 pm shift, and at closing. This procedure provides a valid basis for evaluation only if one person worked an assigned register since the last reconciliation. Since up to three people work a single register during a shift, there is no valid basis for establishing who is responsible for any overage or shortage.
2. Internal control principles are: (a) Authorization—not applicable since cashiers are not assigned to a specific cash register for their shift. (b) Segregation of duties—cashiers (other than the owner/manager) are not involved in performing the reconciliation. (c) Documentation—the cash register tape provides the documentation for total receipts for the shift. (d) Safeguard assets—an electronic cash register is used with an internal tape whose access presumably is restricted. (e) Independent verification—a bookkeeper, in addition to Stephanie Mintenko, performs the reconciliation regularly.
3. The principle of documentation procedures is involved. If a customer making a purchase sees that a sale isn't rung up or if the customer doesn't request a receipt, there is a possibility that the transaction has not been recorded. But the internal control does not reside in the receipt itself. The control is forcing the cashier to ring up each sale so that a receipt is produced. Each receipt is recorded on an internal cash register tape. At the end of the day, the tape is used in determining overages or shortages.
4. It is doubtful that Stephanie's café would bond part-time employees. From the employer's standpoint, bonding is protection against major embezzlements by dishonest employees. The risk of this occurring in a small café, with the active participation of the owner/manager, is relatively low.
5. Cash Over and Short (miscellaneous expense account) | 5 |
        Cash | | 5

☑ THE NAVIGATOR

Additional Demonstration Problem

DEMONSTRATION PROBLEM

Trillo Company's bank statement for May 2002 shows the following data.

Balance 5/1	$12,650	Balance 5/31	$14,280
Debit memorandum:		Credit memorandum:	
NSF check	$175	Collection of note receivable	$505

The cash balance per books at May 31 is $13,319. Your review of the data reveals the following.

1. The NSF check was from Hup Co., a customer.
2. The note collected by the bank was a $500, 3-month, 12% note. The bank charged a $10 collection fee. No interest has been accrued.
3. Outstanding checks at May 31 total $2,410.
4. Deposits in transit at May 31 total $1,752.
5. A Trillo Company check for $352 dated May 10 cleared the bank on May 25. This check, which was a payment on account, was journalized for $325.

Instructions

(a) Prepare a bank reconciliation at May 31.
(b) Journalize the entries required by the reconciliation.

SOLUTION TO DEMONSTRATION PROBLEM

ACTION PLAN
- Follow the four steps in the reconciliation procedure. (p. 338).
- Work carefully to minimize mathematical errors in the reconciliation.
- Prepare adjusting entries from reconciling items per books.
- Make sure the cash ledger balance after posting the reconciling entries agrees with the adjusted cash balance per books.

(a)

TRILLO COMPANY
Bank Reconciliation
May 31, 2002

Cash balance per bank statement		$14,280
Add: Deposits in transit		1,752
		16,032
Less: Outstanding checks		2,410
Adjusted cash balance per bank		$13,622
Cash balance per books		$13,319
Add: Collection of note receivable $500, plus $15 interest, less collection fee $10		505
		13,824
Less: NSF check	$175	
Error in recording check	27	202
Adjusted cash balance per books		$13,622

(b)

May 31	Cash	505	
	Miscellaneous Expense	10	
	Notes Receivable		500
	Interest Revenue		15
	(To record collection of note by bank)		
31	Accounts Receivable—Hup Co.	175	
	Cash		175
	(To record NSF check from Hup Co.)		
31	Accounts Payable	27	
	Cash		27
	(To correct error in recording check)		

THE NAVIGATOR

SUMMARY OF STUDY OBJECTIVES

1. Define internal control. Internal control is the plan of organization and related methods and procedures adopted within a business to safeguard its assets and to enhance the accuracy and reliability of its accounting records.

2. Identify the principles of internal control. The principles of internal control are: establishment of responsibility; segregation of duties; documentation procedures; physical, mechanical, and electronic controls; independent internal verification; and other controls.

3. Explain the applications of internal control principles to cash receipts. Internal controls over cash receipts include: (a) designating only personnel such as cashiers to handle cash; (b) assigning the duties of receiving cash, recording cash, and custody of cash to different individuals; (c) obtaining remittance advices for mail receipts, cash register tapes for over-the-counter receipts, and deposit slips for bank deposits; (d) using company safes and bank vaults to store cash with access limited to authorized personnel, and using cash registers in executing over-the-counter receipts; (e) making independent daily counts of register receipts and daily comparisons of total receipts with total deposits; and (f) bonding personnel that handle cash and requiring them to take vacations.

4. Explain the applications of internal control principles to cash disbursements. Internal controls over cash disbursements include: (a) having only specified individuals such as the treasurer authorized to sign checks; (b) assigning the duties of approving items for payment, paying the items, and recording the payment to different individuals; (c) using prenumbered checks and accounting for all checks, with each check supported by an approved invoice; (d) storing blank checks in a safe or vault with access restricted to authorized personnel, and using a checkwriter to imprint amounts on checks; (e) comparing each check with the approved invoice before issuing the check, and making monthly reconciliations of bank and book balances; and (f) after payment, stamping each approved invoice "paid."

5. Describe the operation of a petty cash fund. In operating a petty cash fund, it is necessary to establish the fund, make payments from the fund, and replenish the fund.

6. Indicate the control features of a bank account. A bank account contributes to good internal control by providing physical controls for the storage of cash. It minimizes the amount of currency that must be kept on hand, and it creates a double record of a depositor's bank transactions.

7. Prepare a bank reconciliation. It is customary to reconcile the balance per books and balance per bank to their adjusted balances. The steps in determining the reconciling items are to ascertain deposits in transit, outstanding checks, errors by the depositor or the bank, and unrecorded bank memoranda.

8. Explain the reporting of cash. Cash is listed first in the current assets section of the balance sheet. In some cases, cash is reported together with cash equivalents. Cash restricted for a special purpose is reported separately as a current asset or as a noncurrent asset, depending on when the cash is expected to be used.

THE NAVIGATOR

Key Term Matching Activity

GLOSSARY

Bank service charge A fee charged by a bank for the use of its services. (p. 336).

Bank statement A statement received monthly from the bank that shows the depositor's bank transactions and balances. (p. 335).

Cash Resources that consist of coins, currency, checks, money orders, and money on hand or on deposit in a bank or similar depository. (p. 325).

Cash equivalents Highly liquid investments, with maturities of three months or less when purchased, that can be converted to a specific amount of cash. (p. 341).

Check A written order signed by the depositor directing the bank to pay a specified sum of money to a designated recipient. (p. 334).

Compensating balances Minimum cash balances required by a bank in support of bank loans. (p. 341).

Deposits in transit Deposits recorded by the depositor that have not been recorded by the bank. (p. 338).

Electronic funds transfer (EFT) A disbursement system that uses wire, telephone, telegraph, or computer to transfer cash from one location to another. (p. 329).

Internal auditors Company employees who evaluate on a continuous basis the effectiveness of the company's system of internal control. (p. 323).

Internal control The plan of organization and all the related methods and measures adopted within a business to safeguard its assets and enhance the accuracy and reliability of its accounting records. (p. 318).

NSF check A check that is not paid by a bank because of insufficient funds in a customer's bank account. (p. 336).

Outstanding checks Checks issued and recorded by a company that have not been paid by the bank. (p. 338).

Petty cash fund A cash fund used to pay relatively small amounts. (p. 330).

Voucher An authorization form prepared for each payment by check in a voucher system. (p. 328).

Voucher system A network of approvals by authorized individuals acting independently to ensure that all disbursements by check are proper. (p. 328).

SELF-STUDY QUESTIONS

Answers are at the end of the chapter.

(SO 1) **1.** Internal control is used in a business to enhance the accuracy and reliability of its accounting records and to:
a. safeguard its assets.
b. prevent fraud.
c. produce correct financial statements.
d. deter employee dishonesty.

(SO 2) **2.** The principles of internal control do not include:
a. establishment of responsibility.
b. documentation procedures.
c. management responsibility.
d. independent internal verification.

(SO 2) **3.** Physical controls do *not* include:
a. safes and vaults to store cash.
b. independent bank reconciliations.
c. locked warehouses for inventories.
d. bank safety deposit boxes for important papers.

(SO 3) **4.** Which of the following items in a cash drawer at November 30 is *not* cash?
a. Money orders.
b. Coins and currency.
c. A customer check dated December 1.
d. A customer check dated November 28.

(SO 3) **5.** Permitting only designated personnel to handle cash receipts is an application of the principle of:
a. segregation of duties.
b. establishment of responsibility.
c. independent check.
d. other controls.

(SO 4) **6.** The use of prenumbered checks in disbursing cash is an application of the principle of:
a. establishment of responsibility.
b. segregation of duties.
c. physical, mechanical, and electronic controls.
d. documentation procedures.

(SO 5) **7.** A check is written to replenish a $100 petty cash fund when the fund contains receipts of $94 and $3 in cash. In recording the check,
a. Cash Over and Short should be debited for $3.
b. Petty Cash should be debited for $94.
c. Cash should be credited for $94.
d. Petty Cash should be credited for $3.

(SO 6) **8.** The control features of a bank account do *not* include:
a. having bank auditors verify the correctness of the bank balance per books.
b. minimizing the amount of cash that must be kept on hand.
c. providing a double record of all bank transactions.
d. safeguarding cash by using a bank as a depository.

(SO 7) **9.** In a bank reconciliation, deposits in transit are:
a. deducted from the book balance.
b. added to the book balance.
c. added to the bank balance.
d. deducted from the bank balance.

(SO 7) **10.** The reconciling item in a bank reconciliation that will result in an adjusting entry by the depositor is:
a. outstanding checks.
b. deposit in transit.
c. a bank error.
d. bank service charges.

(SO 8) **11.** The statement that correctly describes the reporting of cash is:
a. Cash cannot be combined with cash equivalents.
b. Restricted cash funds may be combined with Cash.
c. Cash is listed first in the current assets section.
d. Restricted cash funds cannot be reported as a current asset.

QUESTIONS

1. "Internal control is concerned only with enhancing the accuracy of the accounting records." Do you agree? Explain.

2. What principles of internal control apply to most business enterprises?

3. At the corner grocery store, all sales clerks make change out of one cash register drawer. Is this a violation of internal control? Why?

4. Roger Holloway is reviewing the principle of segregation of duties. What are the two common applications of this principle?

5. How do documentation procedures contribute to good internal control?

6. What internal control objectives are met by physical, mechanical, and electronic controls?

7. (a) Explain the control principle of independent internal verification. (b) What practices are important in applying this principle?

8. The management of Borke Company asks you, as the company accountant, to explain (a) the concept of reasonable assurance in internal control and (b) the importance of the human factor in internal control.

9. Fred's Fertilizer Co. owns the following assets at the balance sheet date.

Cash in bank savings account	$ 6,000
Cash on hand	850
Cash refund due from the IRS	1,000
Checking account balance	12,000
Postdated checks	500

What amount should be reported as cash in the balance sheet?

10. What principle(s) of internal control is (are) involved in making daily cash counts of over-the-counter receipts?

11. Motown Department Stores has just installed new electronic cash registers in its stores. How do cash registers improve internal control over cash receipts?

12. At West Side Wholesale Company, two mail clerks open all mail receipts. How does this strengthen internal control?

13. "To have maximum effective internal control over cash disbursements, all payments should be made by check." Is this true? Explain.

14. Mary Miller Company's internal controls over cash disbursements provide for the treasurer to sign checks imprinted by a checkwriter after comparing the check with the approved invoice. Identify the internal control principles that are present in these controls.

15. How do the principles of (a) physical, mechanical, and electronic controls and (b) other controls apply to cash disbursements?

16. (a) What is a voucher system? (b) What principles of internal control apply to a voucher system?

17. What is the essential feature of an electronic funds transfer (EFT) procedure?

18. (a) Identify the three activities that pertain to a petty cash fund, and indicate an internal control principle that is applicable to each activity. (b) When are journal entries required in the operation of a petty cash fund?

19. "The use of a bank contributes significantly to good internal control over cash." Is this true? Why or why not?

20. Jana Kingston is confused about the lack of agreement between the cash balance per books and the balance per the bank. Explain the causes for the lack of agreement to Jana, and give an example of each cause.

21. What are the four steps involved in finding differences between the balance per books and balance per bank?

22. Candy Mowinski asks your help concerning an NSF check. Explain to Candy (a) what an NSF check is, (b) how it is treated in a bank reconciliation, and (c) whether it will require an adjusting entry per bank.

23. (a) "Cash equivalents are the same as cash." Do you agree? Explain. (b) How should restricted cash funds be reported on the balance sheet?

*B*RIEF EXERCISES

Explain the importance of internal control.
(SO 1)

BE8-1   Sandy Alcorn is the new owner of Galaxy Parking. She has heard about internal control but is not clear about its importance for her business. Explain to Sandy the two purposes of internal control and give her one application of each purpose for Galaxy Parking.

Identify internal control principles.
(SO 2)

BE8-2   The internal control procedures in Energy Company provide that:

(a) Employees who have physical custody of assets do not have access to the accounting records.

(b) Each month the assets on hand are compared to the accounting records by an internal auditor.

(c) A prenumbered shipping document is prepared for each shipment of goods to customers.

Identify the principles of internal control that are being followed.

Identify the internal control principles applicable to cash receipts.
(SO 3)

BE8-3   Endrun Company has the following internal control procedures over cash receipts. Identify the internal control principle that is applicable to each procedure.

1. All over-the-counter receipts are registered on cash registers.
2. All cashiers are bonded.
3. Daily cash counts are made by cashier department supervisors.
4. The duties of receiving cash, recording cash, and custody of cash are assigned to different individuals.
5. Only cashiers may operate cash registers.

Identify the internal control principle applicable to cash disbursements.
(SO 4)

BE8-4   Oswego Company has the following internal control procedures over cash disbursements. Identify the internal control principle that is applicable to each procedure.

1. Company checks are prenumbered.
2. The bank statement is reconciled monthly by an internal auditor.
3. Blank checks are stored in a safe in the treasurer's office.
4. Only the treasurer or assistant treasurer may sign checks.
5. Check signers are not allowed to record cash disbursement transactions.

BE8-5 On March 20, Elgin's petty cash fund of $100 is replenished when the fund contains $11 in cash and receipts for postage $52, freight-out $26, and travel expense $10. Prepare the journal entry to record the replenishment of the petty cash fund.

Prepare entry to replenish a petty cash fund.
(SO 5)

BE8-6 John Gleason is uncertain about the control features of a bank account. Explain the control benefits of **(a)** a signature card, **(b)** a check, and **(c)** a bank statement.

Identify the control features of a bank account.
(SO 6)

BE8-7 The following reconciling items are applicable to the bank reconciliation for St. Charles Company: (1) outstanding checks, (2) bank debit memorandum for service charge, (3) bank credit memorandum for collecting a note for the depositor, (4) deposit in transit. Indicate how each item should be shown on a bank reconciliation.

Indicate location of reconciling items in a bank reconciliation.
(SO 7)

BE8-8 Using the data in BE8-7, indicate **(a)** the items that will result in an adjustment to the depositor's records and **(b)** why the other items do not require adjustment.

Identify reconciling items that require adjusting entries.
(SO 7)

BE8-9 At July 31, Batavia Company has the following bank information: cash balance per bank $7,420, outstanding checks $762, deposits in transit $1,700, and a bank service charge $20. Determine the adjusted cash balance per bank at July 31.

Prepare partial bank reconciliation.
(SO 7)

BE8-10 At August 31, Eola Company has a cash balance per books of $9,200 and the following additional data from the bank statement: charge for printing Eola Company checks $35, interest earned on checking account balance $40, and outstanding checks $800. Determine the adjusted cash balance per books at August 31.

Prepare partial bank reconciliation.
(SO 7)

BE8-11 Naperville Company has the following cash balances: Cash in Bank $15,742, Payroll Bank Account $6,000, and Plant Expansion Fund Cash $25,000. Explain how each balance should be reported on the balance sheet.

Explain the statement presentation of cash balances.
(SO 8)

EXERCISES

E8-1 Jackie Bennett is the owner of Bennett's Pizza. Bennett's is operated strictly on a carry-out basis. Customers pick up their orders at a counter where a clerk exchanges the pizza for cash. While at the counter, the customer can see other employees making the pizzas and the large ovens in which the pizzas are baked.

Identify the principles of internal control.
(SO 2)

Instructions
Identify the six principles of internal control and give an example of each principle that you might observe when picking up your pizza. (*Note:* It may not be possible to observe all the principles.)

E8-2 The following control procedures are used at Sheridan Company for over-the-counter cash receipts.

Identify internal control weaknesses over cash receipts and suggest improvements.
(SO 2, 3)

1. To minimize the risk of robbery, cash in excess of $100 is stored in an unlocked attaché case in the stock room until it is deposited in the bank.
2. All over-the-counter receipts are registered by three clerks who use a cash register with a single cash drawer.
3. The company accountant makes the bank deposit and then records the day's receipts.
4. At the end of each day, the total receipts are counted by the cashier on duty and reconciled to the cash register total.
5. Cashiers are experienced; they are not bonded.

Instructions
   (a) For each procedure, explain the weakness in internal control, and identify the control principle that is violated.
   (b) For each weakness, suggest a change in procedure that will result in good internal control.

E8-3 The following control procedures are used in Erin's Boutique Shoppe for cash disbursements.

Identify internal control weaknesses over cash disbursements and suggest improvements.
(SO 2, 4)

1. The company accountant prepares the bank reconciliation and reports any discrepancies to the owner.
2. The store manager personally approves all payments before signing and issuing checks.
3. Each week, Erin leaves 100 company checks in an unmarked envelope on a shelf behind the cash register.
4. After payment, bills are filed in a paid invoice folder.
5. The company checks are unnumbered.

Instructions

(a) For each procedure, explain the weakness in internal control, and identify the internal control principle that is violated.

(b) For each weakness, suggest a change in the procedure that will result in good internal control.

Identify internal control weaknesses for cash disbursements and suggest improvements.
(SO 4)

E8-4   At Elburn Company, checks are not prenumbered because both the puchasing agent and the treasurer are authorized to issue checks. Each signer has access to unissued checks kept in an unlocked file cabinet. The purchasing agent pays all bills pertaining to goods purchased for resale. Prior to payment, the purchasing agent determines that the goods have been received and verifies the mathematical accuracy of the vendor's invoice. After payment, the invoice is filed by vendor, and the purchasing agent records the payment in the cash disbursements journal. The treasurer pays all other bills following approval by authorized employees. After payment, the treasurer stamps all bills PAID, files them by payment date, and records the checks in the cash disbursements journal. Elburn Company maintains one checking account that is reconciled by the treasurer.

Instructions

(a) List the weaknesses in internal control over cash disbursements.

(b) ⬜▭➤ Write a memo to the company treasurer indicating your recommendations for improvement.

Prepare journal entries for a petty cash fund.
(SO 5)

E8-5   Leland Company uses an imprest petty cash system. The fund was established on March 1 with a balance of $100. During March the following petty cash receipts were found in the petty cash box.

Date	Receipt No.	For	Amount
3/5	1	Stamp Inventory	$35
7	2	Freight-out	19
9	3	Miscellaneous Expense	12
11	4	Travel Expense	24
14	5	Miscellaneous Expense	5

The fund was replenished on March 15 when the fund contained $4 in cash. On March 20, the amount in the fund was increased to $150.

Instructions
Journalize the entries in March that pertain to the operation of the petty cash fund.

Prepare bank reconciliation and adjusting entries.
(SO 7)

E8-6   Cindy Crawford is unable to reconcile the bank balance at January 31. Cindy's reconciliation is as follows.

Cash balance per bank	$3,660.20
Add: NSF check	630.00
Less: Bank service charge	25.00
Adjusted balance per bank	$4,265.20
Cash balance per books	$3,875.20
Less: Deposits in transit	490.00
Add: Outstanding checks	930.00
Adjusted balance per books	$4,315.20

Instructions

(a) Prepare a correct bank reconciliation.

(b) Journalize the entries required by the reconciliation.

Determine outstanding checks.
(SO 7)

E8-7   On April 30, the bank reconciliation of Hinckley Company shows three outstanding checks: no. 254, $650, no. 255, $720, and no. 257, $410. The May bank statement and the May cash payments journal show the following.

Bank Statement			Cash Payments Journal		
Checks Paid			Checks Issued		
Date	Check No.	Amount	Date	Check No.	Amount
5/4	254	650	5/2	258	159
5/2	257	410	5/5	259	275
5/17	258	159	5/10	260	925
5/12	259	275	5/15	261	500
5/20	261	500	5/22	262	750
5/29	263	480	5/24	263	480
5/30	262	750	5/29	264	560

Instructions

Using step 2 in the reconciliation procedure, list the outstanding checks at May 31.

E8-8 The following information pertains to Cody Video Company.

1. Cash balance per bank, July 31, $7,263.
2. July bank service charge not recorded by the depositor $15.
3. Cash balance per books, July 31, $7,190.
4. Deposits in transit, July 31, $1,500.
5. Bank collected $800 note for Cody in July, plus interest $36, less fee $20. The collection has not been recorded by Cody, and no interest has been accrued.
6. Outstanding checks, July 31, $772.

Prepare bank reconciliation and adjusting entries.
(SO 7)

Instructions

(a) Prepare a bank reconciliation at July 31.
(b) Journalize the adjusting entries at July 31 on the books of Cody Video Company.

E8-9 The information below relates to the Cash account in the ledger of Newark Company.
Balance September 1—$17,150; Cash deposited—$64,000.
Balance September 30—$17,404; Checks written—$63,746.

The September bank statement shows a balance of $16,422 on September 30 and the following memoranda.

Prepare bank reconciliation and adjusting entries.
(SO 7)

Credits		Debits	
Collection of $1,500 note plus interest $30	$1,530	NSF check: J.E. Hoover	$410
Interest earned on checking account	$45	Safety deposit box rent	$30

At September 30, deposits in transit were $4,500, and outstanding checks totaled $2,383.

Instructions

(a) Prepare the bank reconciliation at September 30.
(b) Prepare the adjusting entries at September 30, assuming (1) the NSF check was from a customer on account, and (2) no interest had been accrued on the note.

E8-10 The cash records of Ottawa Company show the following four situations.

1. The June 30 bank reconciliation indicated that deposits in transit total $950. During July the general ledger account Cash shows deposits of $15,750, but the bank statement indicates that only $15,600 in deposits were received during the month.
2. The June 30 bank reconciliation also reported outstanding checks of $920. During the month of July, Ottawa Company books show that $17,200 of checks were issued. The bank statement showed that $16,400 of checks cleared the bank in July.
3. In September, deposits per the bank statement totaled $26,700, deposits per books were $25,400, and deposits in transit at September 30 were $2,600.
4. In September, cash disbursements per books were $23,700, checks clearing the bank were $24,000, and outstanding checks at September 30 were $2,100.

There were no bank debit or credit memoranda. No errors were made by either the bank or Ottawa Company.

Compute deposits in transit and outstanding checks for two bank reconciliations.
(SO 7)

Instructions

Answer the following questions.

(a) In situation (1), what were the deposits in transit at July 31?
(b) In situation (2), what were the outstanding checks at July 31?
(c) In situation (3), what were the deposits in transit at August 31?
(d) In situation (4), what were the outstanding checks at August 31?

PROBLEMS: SET A

Identify internal control principles over cash disbursements.
(SO 2, 4)

P8-1A Mexican Office Supply Company recently changed its system of internal control over cash disbursements. The system includes the following features.

Instead of being unnumbered and manually prepared, all checks must now be prenumbered and written by using the new checkwriter purchased by the company. Before a check can be issued, each invoice must have the approval of Norma Hanson, the purchasing agent, and John Countryman, the receiving department supervisor. Checks must be signed by either Linda Anderson, the treasurer, or Bob Skabo, the assistant treasurer. Before signing a check, the signer is expected to compare the amount of the check with the amount on the invoice.

After signing a check, the signer stamps the invoice PAID and inserts within the stamp, the date, check number, and amount of the check. The "paid" invoice is then sent to the accounting department for recording.

Blank checks are stored in a safe in the treasurer's office. The combination to the safe is known only by the treasurer and assistant treasurer. Each month, the bank statement is reconciled with the bank balance per books by the assistant chief accountant.

Instructions

Identify the internal control principles and their application to cash disbursements of Mexican Office Supply Company.

Journalize and post petty cash fund transactions.
(SO 5)

Peachtree

P8-2A Maple Park Company maintains a petty cash fund for small expenditures. The following transactions occurred over a 2-month period.

July	1	Established petty cash fund by writing a check on Cortland Bank for $200.
	15	Replenished the petty cash fund by writing a check for $197.00. On this date the fund consisted of $3.00 in cash and the following petty cash receipts: freight-out $94.00, postage expense $42.40, entertainment expense $46.60, and miscellaneous expense $11.90.
	31	Replenished the petty cash fund by writing a check for $192.00. At this date, the fund consisted of $8.00 in cash and the following petty cash receipts: freight-out $82.10, charitable contributions expense $40.00, postage expense $27.80, and miscellaneous expense $42.10.
Aug.	15	Replenished the petty cash fund by writing a check for $187.00. On this date, the fund consisted of $13.00 in cash and the following petty cash receipts: freight-out $74.60, entertainment expense $43.00, postage expense $33.00, and miscellaneous expense $37.00.
	16	Increased the amount of the petty cash fund to $300 by writing a check for $100.
	31	Replenished petty cash fund by writing a check for $284.00. On this date, the fund consisted of $16 in cash and the following petty cash receipts: postage expense $140.00, travel expense $95.60, and freight-out $46.40.

Instructions

(a) July 15, Cash short $2.10
(b) Aug. 31 balance $300

(a) Journalize the petty cash transactions.
(b) Post to the Petty Cash account.
(c) What internal control features exist in a petty cash fund?

Prepare a bank reconciliation and adjusting entries.
(SO 7)

P8-3A On May 31, 2002, Sosa Company had a cash balance per books of $6,781.50. The bank statement from Sandwich Community Bank on that date showed a balance of $6,804.60. A comparison of the statement with the cash account revealed the following facts.

1. The statement included a debit memo of $40 for the printing of additional company checks.
2. Cash sales of $836.15 on May 12 were deposited in the bank. The cash receipts journal entry and the deposit slip were incorrectly made for $846.15. The bank credited Sosa Company for the correct amount.
3. Outstanding checks at May 31 totaled $276.25. Deposits in transit were $1,936.15.
4. On May 18, the company issued check No. 1181 for $685 to Kap Shin, on account. The check, which cleared the bank in May, was incorrectly journalized and posted by Sosa Company for $658.
5. A $3,000 note receivable was collected by the bank for Sosa Company on May 31 plus $80 interest. The bank charged a collection fee of $20. No interest has been accrued on the note.
6. Included with the cancelled checks was a check issued by Tacamoto Company to Yee Chow for $600 that was incorrectly charged to Sosa Company by the bank.
7. On May 31, the bank statement showed an NSF charge of $700 for a check issued by John Lewis, a customer, to Sosa Company on account.

Instructions

(a) Prepare the bank reconciliation at May 31, 2002.
(b) Prepare the necessary adjusting entries for Sosa Company at May 31, 2002.

(a) Adjusted cash balance per bank $9,064.50

P8-4A　The bank portion of the bank reconciliation for Hilo Company at November 30, 2002, was as follows.

Prepare a bank reconciliation and adjusting entries from detailed data.
(SO 7)

HILO COMPANY
Bank Reconciliation
November 30, 2002

Cash balance per bank		$14,367.90
Add: Deposits in transit		2,530.20
		16,898.10
Less: Outstanding checks		

Check Number	Check Amount	
3451	$2,260.40	
3470	720.10	
3471	844.50	
3472	1,426.80	
3474	1,050.00	6,301.80
Adjusted cash balance per bank		$10,596.30

The adjusted cash balance per bank agreed with the cash balance per books at November 30. The December bank statement showed the following checks and deposits.

Bank Statement

Checks			Deposits	
Date	**Number**	**Amount**	**Date**	**Amount**
12-1	3451	$ 2,260.40	12-1	$ 2,530.20
12-2	3471	844.50	12-4	1,211.60
12-7	3472	1,426.80	12-8	2,365.10
12-4	3475	1,640.70	12-16	2,672.70
12-8	3476	1,300.00	12-21	2,945.00
12-10	3477	2,130.00	12-26	2,567.30
12-15	3479	3,080.00	12-29	2,836.00
12-27	3480	600.00	12-30	1,025.00
12-30	3482	475.50	Total	$18,152.90
12-29	3483	1,140.00		
12-31	3485	540.80		
	Total	$15,438.70		

The cash records per books for December showed the following.

	Cash Payments Journal						Cash Receipts Journal	
Date	Number	Amount	Date	Number	Amount		Date	Amount
12-1	3475	$1,640.70	12-20	3482	$ 475.50		12-3	$ 1,211.60
12-2	3476	1,300.00	12-22	3483	1,140.00		12-7	2,365.10
12-2	3477	2,130.00	12-23	3484	832.00		12-15	2,672.70
12-4	3478	538.20	12-24	3485	450.80		12-20	2,954.00
12-8	3479	3,080.00	12-30	3486	1,889.50		12-25	2,567.30
12-10	3480	600.00	Total		$14,884.10		12-28	2,836.00
12-17	3481	807.40					12-30	1,025.00
							12-31	1,190.40
							Total	$16,822.10

The bank statement contained two memoranda:

1. A credit of $3,645 for the collection of a $3,500 note for Hilo Company plus interest of $160 and less a collection fee of $15.00. Hilo Company has not accrued any interest on the note.
2. A debit of $547.10 for an NSF check written by D. Lu, a customer. At December 31, the check had not been redeposited in the bank.

At December 31 the cash balance per books was $12,534.30, and the cash balance per the bank statement was $20,180.00. The bank did not make any errors, but two errors were made by Hilo Company.

Instructions

(a) Adjusted balance per books $15,533.20

(a) Using the four steps in the reconciliation procedure, prepare a bank reconciliation at December 31.
(b) Prepare the adjusting entries based on the reconciliation. (*Hint*: The correction of any errors pertaining to recording checks should be made to Accounts Payable. The correction of any errors relating to recording cash receipts should be made to Accounts Receivable.)

Prepare a bank reconciliation and adjusting entries.
(SO 7)

Peachtree

P8-5A Videosoft Company maintains a checking account at the Intelex Bank. At July 31, selected data from the ledger balance and the bank statement are as follows.

	Cash in Bank	
	Per Books	Per Bank
Balance, July 1	$17,600	$18,800
July receipts	82,000	
July credits		80,470
July disbursements	76,900	
July debits		74,740
Balance, July 31	$22,700	$24,530

Analysis of the bank data reveals that the credits consist of $79,000 of July deposits and a credit memorandum of $1,470 for the collection of a $1,400 note plus interest revenue of $70. The July debits per bank consist of checks cleared $74,700 and a debit memorandum of $40 for printing additional company checks.

You also discover the following errors involving July checks: (1) A check for $230 to a creditor on account that cleared the bank in July was journalized and posted as $320. (2) A salary check to an employee for $255 was recorded by the bank for $155.

The June 30 bank reconciliation contained only two reconciling items: deposits in transit $5,000 and outstanding checks of $6,200.

Instructions

(a) Adjusted balance per books $24,220

(a) Prepare a bank reconciliation at July 31.
(b) Journalize the adjusting entries to be made by Videosoft Company at July 31, 2002. Assume that the interest on the note has been accrued.

P8-6A   Cedar Grove Middle School wants to raise money for a new sound system for its auditorium. The primary fund-raising event is a dance at which the famous disc jockey Obnoxious Al will play classic and not-so-classic dance tunes. Roger DeMaster, the music and theater instructor, has been given the responsibility for coordinating the fund-raising efforts. This is Roger's first experience with fund-raising. He decides to put the eighth-grade choir in charge of the event; he will be a relatively passive observer.

Identify internal control weaknesses in cash receipts and cash disbursements.
(SO 2, 3, 4, 5, 6)

Roger had 500 unnumbered tickets printed for the dance. He left the tickets in a box on his desk and told the choir students to take as many tickets as they thought they could sell for $5 each. In order to ensure that no extra tickets would be floating around, he told them to dispose of any unsold tickets. When the students received payment for the tickets, they were to bring the cash back to Roger, and he would put it in a locked box in his desk drawer.

Some of the students were responsible for decorating the gymnasium for the dance. Roger gave each of them a key to the money box and told them that if they took money out to purchase materials, they should put a note in the box saying how much they took and what it was used for. After 2 weeks the money box appeared to be getting full, so Roger asked Steve Stevens to count the money, prepare a deposit slip, and deposit the money in a bank account Roger had opened.

The day of the dance, Roger wrote a check from the account to pay the DJ. Obnoxious Al, however, said that he accepted only cash and did not give receipts. So Roger took $200 out of the cash box and gave it to Al. At the dance Roger had Sara Billings working at the entrance to the gymnasium, collecting tickets from students and selling tickets to those who had not prepurchased them. Roger estimated that 400 students attended the dance.

The following day Roger closed out the bank account, which had $250 in it, and gave that amount plus the $180 in the cash box to Principal Skinner. Principal Skinner seemed surprised that, after generating roughly $2,000 in sales, the dance netted only $430 in cash. Roger did not know how to respond.

Instructions
Identify as many internal control weaknesses as you can in this scenario, and suggest how each could be addressed.

PROBLEMS: SET B

P8-1B   Sycamore Theater is located in the Sycamore Mall. A cashier's booth is located near the entrance to the theater. Two cashiers are employed. One works from 1–5 P.M., the other from 5–9 P.M. Each cashier is bonded. The cashiers receive cash from customers and operate a machine that ejects serially numbered tickets. The rolls of tickets are inserted and locked into the machine by the theater manager at the beginning of each cashier's shift.

Identify internal control weaknesses over cash receipts.
(SO 2, 3)

After purchasing a ticket, the customer takes the ticket to an usher stationed at the entrance of the theater lobby some 60 feet from the cashier's booth. The usher tears the ticket in half, admits the customer, and returns the ticket stub to the customer. The other half of the ticket is dropped into a locked box by the usher.

At the end of each cashier's shift, the theater manager removes the ticket rolls from the machine and makes a cash count. The cash count sheet is initialed by the cashier. At the end of the day, the manager deposits the receipts in total in a bank night deposit vault located in the mall. The manager also sends copies of the deposit slip and the initialed cash count sheets to the theater company treasurer for verification and to the company's accounting department. Receipts from the first shift are stored in a safe located in the manager's office.

Instructions
  (a) Identify the internal control principles and their application to the cash receipts transactions of the Sycamore Theater.
  (b) If the usher and cashier decide to collaborate to misappropriate cash, what actions might they take?

Journalize and post petty cash fund transactions.
(SO 5)

P8-2B   DeKalb Company maintains a petty cash fund for small expenditures. The following transactions occurred over a 2-month period.

July   1   Established petty cash fund by writing a check on Corner Bank for $200.
    15   Replenished the petty cash fund by writing a check for $196.30. On this date the fund consisted of $3.70 in cash and the following petty cash receipts: freight-out $94.00, postage expense $42.40, entertainment expense $46.60, and miscellaneous expense $10.70.
    31   Replenished the petty cash fund by writing a check for $192.00. At this date, the fund consisted of $8.00 in cash and the following petty cash receipts: freight-out $82.10, charitable contributions expense $30.00, postage expense $47.80, and miscellaneous expense $32.10.
Aug. 15   Replenished the petty cash fund by writing a check for $188.00. On this date, the fund consisted of $12.00 in cash and the following petty cash receipts: freight-out $74.40, entertainment expense $43.00, postage expense $33.00, and miscellaneous expense $38.00.
    16   Increased the amount of the petty cash fund to $300 by writing a check for $100.
    31   Replenished petty cash fund by writing a check for $283.00. On this date, the fund consisted of $17 in cash and the following petty cash receipts: postage expense $145.00, entertainment expense $90.60, and freight-out $45.40.

Instructions

(a) July 15 Cash short $2.60
(b) Aug. 31 balance $300

(a) Journalize the petty cash transactions.
(b) Post to the Petty Cash account.
(c) What internal control features exist in a petty cash fund?

Prepare a bank reconciliation and adjusting entries.
(SO 7)

P8-3B   Agricultural Genetics Company of Emporia, Kansas, spreads herbicides and applies liquid fertilizer for local farmers. On May 31, 2002, the company's cash account per its general ledger showed the following balance.

	CASH				No. 101
Date	**Explanation**	**Ref.**	**Debit**	**Credit**	**Balance**
May 31	Balance				6,781.50

The bank statement from Emporia State Bank on that date showed the following balance.

EMPORIA STATE BANK

Checks and Debits	Deposits and Credits	Daily Balance
XXX	XXX	5/31 6,804.60

A comparison of the details on the bank statement with the details in the cash account revealed the following facts.

1. The statement included a debit memo of $40 for the printing of additional company checks.
2. Cash sales of $836.15 on May 12 were deposited in the bank. The cash receipts journal entry and the deposit slip were incorrectly made for $846.15. The bank credited Agricultural Genetics Company for the correct amount.
3. Outstanding checks at May 31 totaled $276.25, and deposits in transit were $936.15.
4. On May 18, the company issued check no. 1181 for $685 to L. Kingston, on account. The check, which cleared the bank in May, was incorrectly journalized and posted by Agricultural Genetics Company for $658.
5. A $2,000 note receivable was collected by the bank for Agricultural Genetics Company on May 31 plus $80 interest. The bank charged a collection fee of $20. No interest has been accrued on the note.
6. Included with the cancelled checks was a check issued by Teller Company to Larry Falcetto for $600 that was incorrectly charged to Agricultural Genetics Company by the bank.
7. On May 31, the bank statement showed an NSF charge of $700 for a check issued by Pete Dell, a customer, to Agricultural Genetics Company on account.

Instructions

(a) Adj. cash bal. $8,064.50

(a) Prepare the bank reconciliation at May 31, 2002.
(b) Prepare the necessary adjusting entries for Agricultural Genetics Company at May 31, 2002.

P8-4B The bank portion of the bank reconciliation for Rochelle Company at October 31, 2002 was as follows.

Prepare a bank reconciliation and adjusting entries from detailed data.
(SO 7)

ROCHELLE COMPANY
Bank Reconciliation
October 31, 2002

Cash balance per bank			$12,367.90
Add: Deposits in transit			1,530.20
			13,898.10
Less: Outstanding checks			
	Check Number	Check Amount	
	2451	$1,260.40	
	2470	720.10	
	2471	844.50	
	2472	426.80	
	2474	1,050.00	4,301.80
Adjusted cash balance per bank			$ 9,596.30

The adjusted cash balance per bank agreed with the cash balance per books at October 31. The November bank statement showed the following checks and deposits:

Bank Statement

Checks			Deposits	
Date	**Number**	**Amount**	**Date**	**Amount**
11-1	2470	$ 720.10	11-1	$ 1,530.20
11-2	2471	844.50	11-4	1,211.60
11-5	2474	1,050.00	11-8	990.10
11-4	2475	1,640.70	11-13	2,575.00
11-8	2476	2,830.00	11-18	1,472.70
11-10	2477	600.00	11-21	2,945.00
11-15	2479	1,750.00	11-25	2,567.30
11-18	2480	1,330.00	11-28	1,650.00
11-27	2481	695.40	11-30	1,186.00
11-30	2483	575.50	Total	$16,127.90
11-29	2486	900.00		
	Total	$12,936.20		

The cash records per books for November showed the following.

Cash Payments Journal						Cash Receipts Journal	
Date	**Number**	**Amount**	**Date**	**Number**	**Amount**	**Date**	**Amount**
11-1	2475	$1,640.70	11-20	2483	$ 575.50	11-3	$ 1,211.60
11-2	2476	2,830.00	11-22	2484	829.50	11-7	990.10
11-2	2477	600.00	11-23	2485	974.80	11-12	2,575.00
11-4	2478	538.20	11-24	2486	900.00	11-17	1,472.70
11-8	2479	1,570.00	11-29	2487	398.00	11-20	2,954.00
11-10	2480	1,330.00	11-30	2488	1,200.00	11-24	2,567.30
11-15	2481	695.40	Total		$14,694.10	11-27	1,650.00
11-18	2482	612.00				11-29	1,186.00
						11-30	1,225.00
						Total	$15,831.70

The bank statement contained two bank memoranda:

1. A credit of $1,505.00 for the collection of a $1,400 note for Rochelle Company plus interest of $120 and less a collection fee of $15. Rochelle Company has not accrued any interest on the note.
2. A debit for the printing of additional company checks $50.00.

At November 30, the cash balance per books was $10,733.90, and the cash balance per the bank statement was $17,014.60. The bank did not make any errors, but two errors were made by Rochelle Company.

Instructions

(a) Adjusted cash balance per bank $11,999.90

(a) Using the four steps in the reconciliation procedure described on page 338, prepare a bank reconciliation at November 30.
(b) Prepare the adjusting entries based on the reconciliation. (*Hint*: The correction of any errors pertaining to recording checks should be made to Accounts Payable. The correction of any errors relating to recording cash receipts should be made to Accounts Receivable).

Prepare a bank reconciliation and adjusting entries.
(SO 7)

P8-5B   Bettendorf Company's bank statement from Last National Bank at August 31, 2002, shows the following information.

Balance, August 1	$17,400	Bank credit memoranda:	
August deposits	72,000	Collection of note	
Checks cleared in August	69,660	receivable plus $90	
Balance, August 31	24,850	interest	$5,090
		Interest earned	45
		Bank debit memorandum:	
		Safety deposit box rent	25

A summary of the Cash account in the ledger for August shows: Balance, August 1, $16,900; receipts $77,000; disbursements $73,570; and balance, August 31, $20,330. Analysis reveals that the only reconciling items on the July 31 bank reconciliation were a deposit in transit for $4,000 and outstanding checks of $4,500. The deposit in transit was the first deposit recorded by the bank in August. In addition, you determine that there were two errors involving company checks drawn in August: (1) A check for $400 to a creditor on account that cleared the bank in August was journalized and posted for $420. (2) A salary check to an employee for $275 was recorded by the bank for $285.

Instructions

(a) Adjusted balance per books $25,460

(a) Prepare a bank reconciliation at August 31.
(b) Journalize the adjusting entries to be made by Bettendorf Company at August 31. Assume the interest on the note has been accrued by the company.

Prepare comprehensive bank reconciliation with theft and internal control deficiencies.
(SO 2, 3, 4, 7)

P8-6B   Gigantic Company is a very profitable small business. It has not, however, given much consideration to internal control. For example, in an attempt to keep clerical and office expenses to a minimum, the company has combined the jobs of cashier and bookkeeper. As a result, Jake Stickyfingers handles all cash receipts, keeps the accounting records, and prepares the monthly bank reconciliations.

The balance per the bank statement on October 31, 2002, was $18,280. Outstanding checks were: no. 62 for $326.75, no. 183 for $150, no. 284 for $253.25, no. 862 for $190.71, no. 863 for $226.80, and no. 864 for $165.28. Included with the statement was a credit memorandum of $300 indicating the collection of a note receivable for Gigantic Company by the bank on October 25. This memorandum has not been recorded by Gigantic Company.

The company's ledger showed one cash account with a balance of $21,892.72. The balance included undeposited cash on hand. Because of the lack of internal controls, Stickyfingers took for personal use all of the undeposited receipts in excess of $3,795.51. He then prepared the following bank reconciliation in an effort to conceal his theft of cash.

BANK RECONCILIATION

Cash balance per books, October 31		$21,892.72
Add: Outstanding checks		
No. 862	$190.71	
No. 863	226.80	
No. 864	165.28	482.79
		22,375.51
Less: Undeposited receipts		3,795.51
Unadjusted balance per bank, October 31		18,580.00
Less: Bank credit memorandum		300.00
Cash balance per bank statement, October 31		$18,280.00

Instructions

(a) Prepare a correct bank reconciliation. (*Hint*: Deduct the amount of the theft from the adjusted balance per books.)

(b) Indicate the three ways that Stickyfingers attempted to conceal the theft and the dollar amount pertaining to each method.

(c) What principles of internal control were violated in this case?

(a) Adjusted balance per
books $20,762.72

BROADENING YOUR PERSPECTIVE

*F*INANCIAL REPORTING AND ANALYSIS

FINANCIAL REPORTING PROBLEM: Lands' End, Inc.

BYP8-1 The financial statements of **Lands' End, Inc.** are presented in Appendix A at the end of this textbook.

Instructions

(a) What comments, if any, are made about cash in the report of the independent auditors?

(b) What data about cash and cash equivalents are shown in the consolidated balance sheet (statement of financial condition)?

(c) What activities are identified in the consolidated statement of cash flows as being responsible for the changes in cash during the year ended January 28, 2000?

(d) In management's letter that assumes "Responsibility for Consolidated Financial Statements," what does Lands' End's management say about internal control? (See page 31 of its 2000 Annual Report.)

COMPARATIVE ANALYSIS PROBLEM: Lands' End vs. Abercrombie & Fitch

BYP8-2 **Lands' End's** financial statements are presented in Appendix A. **Abercrombie & Fitch's** financial statements are presented in Appendix B.

Instructions

(a) Based on the information contained in these financial statements, determine each of the following for each company:

(1) Cash and cash equivalents balance at January 28, 2000, for Lands' End and at January 29, 2000, for Abercrombie & Fitch.

(2) Increase (decrease) in cash and cash equivalents from 1999 to 2000.

(3) Cash provided by operating activities during the year ended January 2000 (from Statement of Cash Flows).

(b) What conclusions concerning the management of cash can be drawn from these data?

INTERPRETING FINANCIAL STATEMENTS: A Global Focus

BYP8-3   The July 10, 2000, issue of *The Wall Street Journal* includes an article by Michael M. Phillips entitled "U.S., Major Allies to Urge Bank Scrutiny of 15 Nations' Money-Laundering Curbs."

Instructions
Read the article and answer the following questions.

(a) Countries around the world have worked to improve capital mobility (the ease with which funds can flow from one country to another). What is the potential "dark side" to international capital mobility?

(b) What countries were named in the warning?

(c) What possible actions might be taken against countries on the list?

EXPLORING THE WEB

BYP8-4   All organizations should have systems of internal control. Universities are no exception. This site discusses the basics of internal control in a university setting.

Address: **www.bc.edu/bc_org/fvp/ia/ic/intro.html** *(or go to www.wiley.com/college/weygandt)*

Steps: Go the site shown above.

Instructions
The front page of this site provides links to pages that answer six critical questions. Use these links to answer the following questions.

(a) In a university setting who has responsibility for evaluating the adequacy of the system of internal control?

(b) What do reconciliations ensure in the university setting? Who should review the reconciliation?

(c) What are some examples of physical controls?

(d) What are two ways to accomplish inventory counts?

CRITICAL THINKING

GROUP DECISION CASE

BYP8-5   The board of trustees of a local church is concerned about the internal accounting controls for the offering collections made at weekly services. The trustees ask you to serve on a three-person audit team with the internal auditor of a local college and a CPA who has just joined the church.

At a meeting of the audit team and the board of trustees you learn the following.

1. The church's board of trustees has delegated responsibility for the financial management and audit of the financial records to the finance committee. This group prepares the annual budget and approves major disbursements. It is not involved in collections or record keeping. No audit has been made in recent years because the same trusted employee has kept church records and served as financial secretary for 15 years. The church does not carry any fidelity insurance.

2. The collection at the weekly service is taken by a team of ushers who volunteer to serve one month. The ushers take the collection plates to a basement office at the rear of the church. They hand their plates to the head usher and return to the church service. After all plates have been turned in, the head usher counts the cash received. The head usher then places the cash in the church safe along with a notation of the amount counted. The head usher volunteers to serve for 3 months.

3. The next morning the financial secretary opens the safe and recounts the collection. The secretary withholds $150–$200 in cash, depending on the cash expenditures expected for the week, and deposits the remainder of the collections in the bank. To facilitate the deposit, church members who contribute by check are asked to make their checks payable to "Cash."

4. Each month, the financial secretary reconciles the bank statement and submits a copy of the reconciliation to the board of trustees. The reconciliations have rarely contained any bank errors and have never shown any errors per books.

Instructions

With the class divided into groups, answer the following.

(a) Indicate the weaknesses in internal accounting control over the handling of collections.

(b) List the improvements in internal control procedures that you plan to make at the next meeting of the audit team for (1) the ushers, (2) the head usher, (3) the financial secretary, and (4) the finance committee.

(c) What church policies should be changed to improve internal control?

COMMUNICATION ACTIVITY

BYP8-6 As a new auditor for the CPA firm of Kennedy, Maison, and Davis you have been assigned to review the internal controls over mail cash receipts of Emerik Company. Your review reveals the following: Checks are promptly endorsed "For Deposit Only," but no list of the checks is prepared by the person opening the mail. The mail is opened either by the cashier or by the employee who maintains the accounts receivable records. Mail receipts are deposited in the bank weekly by the cashier.

Instructions

Write a letter to L. S. Croix, owner of the Emerik Company, explaining the weaknesses in internal control and your recommendations for improving the system.

ETHICS CASE

BYP8-7 You are the assistant controller in charge of general ledger accounting at Bad Water Bottling Company. Your company has a large loan from an insurance company. The loan agreement requires that the company's cash account balance be maintained at $200,000 or more, as reported monthly.

At June 30 the cash balance is $80,000, which you report to Marais Thompson, the financial vice president. Marais excitedly instructs you to keep the cash receipts book open for one additional day for purposes of the June 30 report to the insurance company. Marais says, "If we don't get that cash balance over $200,000, we'll default on our loan agreement. They could close us down, put us all out of our jobs!" Marais continues, "I talked to Grochum Distributors (one of Bad Water's largest customers) this morning. They said they sent us a check for $150,000 yesterday. We should receive it tomorrow. If we include just that one check in our cash balance, we'll be in the clear. It's in the mail!"

Instructions

(a) Who will suffer negative effects if you do not comply with Marais Thompson's instructions? Who will suffer if you do comply?

(b) What are the ethical considerations in this case?

(c) What alternatives do you have?

Answers to Self-Study Questions

1. a **2.** c **3.** b **4.** c **5.** b **6.** d **7.** a **8.** a **9.** c **10.** d **11.** c

Answer to *Lands' End* Review It Question 3, p. 341

Lands' End reports cash and cash equivalents on its balance sheet for 2000 of $76.4 million.

Remember to go back to the Navigator box on the chapter-opening page and check off your completed work.

ACCOUNTING FOR RECEIVABLES

9

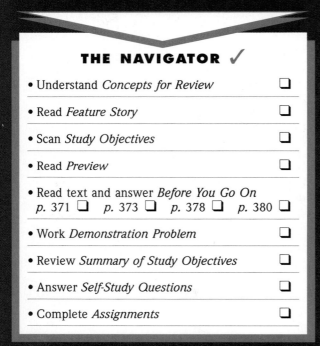

THE NAVIGATOR ✓

- Understand *Concepts for Review* ❑
- Read *Feature Story* ❑
- Scan *Study Objectives* ❑
- Read *Preview* ❑
- Read text and answer *Before You Go On*
  p. 371 ❑   *p.* 373 ❑   *p.* 378 ❑   *p.* 380 ❑
- Work *Demonstration Problem* ❑
- Review *Summary of Study Objectives* ❑
- Answer *Self-Study Questions* ❑
- Complete *Assignments* ❑

*C*ONCEPTS FOR REVIEW

Before studying this chapter, you should know or, if necessary, review:

   a. How to record sales transactions. (Ch. 5, pp. 191–194)

   b. Why adjusting entries are made. (Ch. 3, pp. 91–92)

   c. How to compute interest. (Ch. 3, p. 101)

☑ THE NAVIGATOR

How Do You Spell Relief?

Fred Tarter believes that in every problem lies an opportunity—and sometimes that opportunity can mean a big profit. For example, today fewer people pay cash for their prescriptions. Instead, pharmacies bill a customer's health plan for some or all of the prescription's cost. As a result, pharmacies must spend a lot of time and energy collecting cash from these health plans. This procedure is a headache for pharmacies because there are 4,500 different health plans in the United States. Also, it often leaves pharmacies with too many receivables and not enough cash. Their suppliers want to be paid within 15 days, but their receivables are outstanding for 30 and often 60 days.

Enter Fred Tarter. Having recently sold his advertising agency, Fred had some spare time and money on his hands. While reading a pharmacy trade journal, he learned of the pharmacies' headache. To Fred this problem spelled opportunity.

Fred found out that 56,000 pharmacies are connected by computer to a claims-processing business. Fred's idea was this: Using this network, he would purchase pharmacy receivables, charging a fee of 1.4–2 percent. Pharmacies would be willing to pay this fee because they would get their cash sooner and would be spared the headache of having to collect the accounts. Fred would then use the receivables as backing to raise new money so he could buy more receivables.

Based on this idea, Fred started a company called the **Pharmacy Fund**. Over 500 small pharmacies sell their receivables to his company. By means of a computer link with each pharmacy, the Pharmacy Fund buys the receivables at the end of each day and credits the pharmacy's account immediately. Rather than having to wait weeks to receive its cash from insurance companies, the pharmacy gets its cash the same day as the sale. The Pharmacy Fund's customers say that this has solved their cash-flow problems. It also has reduced their overhead costs and allowed them to automate their billing and record-keeping.

Fred Tarter has already identified his next opportunity—a target some would say is a "natural" for him: dentistry receivables. (Get it? Tarter—dentistry. We'll stick to accounting jokes from now on!)

After studying this chapter, you should be able to:

1. Identify the different types of receivables.
2. Explain how accounts receivable are recognized in the accounts.
3. Distinguish between the methods and bases used to value accounts receivable.
4. Describe the entries to record the disposition of accounts receivable.
5. Compute the maturity date of and interest on notes receivable.
6. Explain how notes receivable are recognized in the accounts.
7. Describe how notes receivable are valued.
8. Describe the entries to record the disposition of notes receivable.
9. Explain the statement presentation and analysis of receivables.

As indicated in the Feature Story, receivables are a significant asset on the books of many pharmacies. Receivables are significant to companies in other industries as well, because a significant portion of sales are done on credit in the United States. As a consequence, companies must pay close attention to their receivables and manage them carefully. In this chapter you will learn what journal entries companies make when products are sold, when cash is collected from those sales, and when accounts that cannot be collected are written off.

The content and organization of the chapter are as follows.

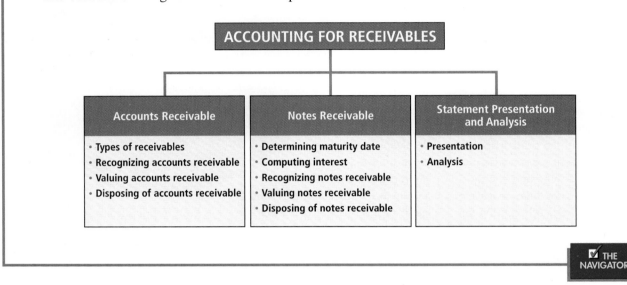

ACCOUNTING FOR RECEIVABLES

Accounts Receivable	Notes Receivable	Statement Presentation and Analysis
• Types of receivables • Recognizing accounts receivable • Valuing accounts receivable • Disposing of accounts receivable	• Determining maturity date • Computing interest • Recognizing notes receivable • Valuing notes receivable • Disposing of notes receivable	• Presentation • Analysis

☑ THE NAVIGATOR

ACCOUNTS RECEIVABLE

TYPES OF RECEIVABLES

STUDY OBJECTIVE 1

Identify the different types of receivables.

The term "receivables" refers to amounts due from individuals and other companies. They are claims that are expected to be collected in cash. Receivables are frequently classified as (1) accounts, (2) notes, and (3) other.

Accounts receivable are amounts owed by customers on account. They result from the sale of goods and services. These receivables generally are expected to be collected within 30 to 60 days. They are the most significant type of claim held by a company.

Notes receivable are claims for which formal instruments of credit are issued as proof of the debt. A note receivable normally extends for time periods of 60–90 days or longer and requires the debtor to pay interest. Notes and accounts receivable that result from sales transactions are often called **trade receivables**.

Other receivables include nontrade receivables. Examples are interest receivable, loans to company officers, advances to employees, and income taxes refundable. These are unusual. Therefore they are generally classified and reported as separate items in the balance sheet.

ETHICS NOTE

Receivables from employees and officers of a company are reported in the financial statements. The reason: Sometimes those assets are valued inappropriately or are not based on an "arm's length" transaction.

Three primary accounting issues are associated with accounts receivable.

1. **Recognizing** accounts receivable.
2. **Valuing** accounts receivable.
3. **Disposing of** accounts receivable.

RECOGNIZING ACCOUNTS RECEIVABLE

Recognizing accounts receivable is relatively straightforward. In Chapter 5 we saw how accounts receivable are affected by the sale of merchandise. To illustrate, assume that Jordache Co. on July 1, 2002, sells merchandise on account to Polo Company for $1,000 terms 2/10, n/30. On July 5, Polo returns merchandise worth $100 to Jordache Co. On July 11, Jordache receives payment from Polo Company for the balance due. The journal entries to record these transactions on the books of Jordache Co. are as follows.

STUDY OBJECTIVE 2

Explain how accounts receivable are recognized in the accounts.

July 1	Accounts Receivable—Polo Company	1,000	
	Sales		1,000
	(To record sales on account)		
July 5	Sales Returns and Allowances	100	
	Accounts Receivable—Polo Company		100
	(To record merchandise returned)		
July 11	Cash ($900 − $18)	882	
	Sales Discounts ($900 × .02)	18	
	Accounts Receivable—Polo Company		900
	(To record collection of accounts receivable)		

```
A   =   L   +   OE
+1,000          +1,000
```

```
A   =   L   +   OE
−100            −100
```

```
A   =   L   +   OE
+882            −18
−900
```

The opportunity to receive a cash discount usually occurs when a manufacturer sells to a wholesaler or a wholesaler sells to a retailer. A discount is given in these situations either to encourage prompt payment or for competitive reasons.

Retailers rarely grant cash discounts to customers. We would be surprised if you ever received a cash discount in purchasing goods from any well-known retailer, such as **Sears**, **Kmart**, or **Wal-Mart**. In fact, when you use a retailer's credit card (Sears, for example), instead of giving a discount, the retailer charges interest on the balance due if not paid within a specified period (usually 25–30 days).

To illustrate, assume that you use your **J. C. Penney Co.** credit card to purchase an outfit with a sales price of $300. J. C. Penney will make the following entry at the date of sale.

HELPFUL HINT
The preceding entries are the same as those described in Chapter 5. For simplicity, inventory and cost of goods sold are omitted from this set of journal entries and from end-of-chapter material.

Accounts Receivable	300	
Sales		300
(To record sale of merchandise)		

```
A   =   L   +   OE
+300            +300
```

J. C. Penney will send you a monthly statement of this transaction and any others that have occurred during the month. If you do not pay in full within 30 days, J. C. Penney adds an interest (financing) charge to the balance due. Although interest rates vary by region and over time, a common rate for retailers is 18% per year (1.5% per month).

When financing charges are added, the seller recognizes interest revenue. Assuming that you owe $300 at the end of the month, and J. C. Penney charges 1.5%

per month on the balance due, the adjusting entry to record interest revenue of $4.50 ($300 × 1.5%) is as follows.

A	=	L	+	OE
+4.50				+4.50

Accounts Receivable	4.50	
Interest Revenue		4.50
(To record interest on amount due)		

Interest revenue is often substantial for many retailers.

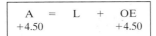

ACCOUNTING IN ACTION　Business Insight

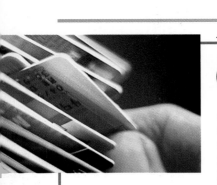

Interest rates on most credit cards are quite high, averaging 18.8 percent. As a result, consumers often look for companies that charge lower rates. Be careful—some companies offer lower interest rates but have eliminated the standard 25-day grace period before finance charges are incurred. Other companies encourage consumers to get more in debt by advertising that only a $1 minimum payment is due on a $1,000 account balance. The less you pay off, the more interest they earn! One bank markets a credit card that allows cardholders to skip a payment twice a year. However, the outstanding balance continues to incur interest. Other credit card companies calculate finance charges initially on two-month, rather than one-month, averages, a practice which often translates into higher interest charges. In short, read the fine print.

VALUING ACCOUNTS RECEIVABLE

STUDY OBJECTIVE 3

Distinguish between the methods and bases used to value accounts receivable.

Once receivables are recorded in the accounts, the next question is: How should receivables be reported in the financial statements? They are reported on the balance sheet as an asset. But determining the **amount** to report is sometimes difficult because some receivables will become uncollectible.

Each customer must satisfy the credit requirements of the seller before the credit sale is approved. Inevitably, though, some accounts receivable become uncollectible. For example, one of your customers may not be able to pay because of a decline in sales due to a downturn in the economy. Similarly, individuals may be laid off from their jobs or be faced with unexpected hospital bills. Credit losses are recorded as debits to **Bad Debts Expense** (or Uncollectible Accounts Expense). Such losses are considered a normal and necessary risk of doing business on a credit basis.

Two methods are used in accounting for uncollectible accounts: (1) the direct write-off method and (2) the allowance method. These methods are explained in the following sections.

Direct Write-off Method for Uncollectible Accounts

Under the **direct write-off method**, when a particular account is determined to be uncollectible, the loss is charged to Bad Debts Expense. Assume, for example, that Warden Co. writes off M. E. Doran's $200 balance as uncollectible on December 12. The entry is:

A	=	L	+	OE
−200				−200

Dec. 12	Bad Debts Expense	200	
	Accounts Receivable—M. E. Doran		200
	(To record write-off of M. E. Doran account)		

When this method is used, bad debts expense will show only **actual losses** from uncollectibles. Accounts receivable will be reported at its gross amount.

Although this method is simple, its use can reduce the usefulness of both the income statement and balance sheet. Consider the following example. Assume that in 2002, Quick Buck Computer Company decided it could increase its revenues by offering computers to college students without requiring any money down and with no credit-approval process. On campuses across the country it distributed 1,000,000 computers with a selling price of $800 each. This increased Quick Buck's revenues and receivables by $800,000,000. The promotion was a huge success! The 2002 balance sheet and income statement looked great. Unfortunately, during 2003, nearly 40 percent of the college student customers defaulted on their loans. This made the 2003 income statement and balance sheet look terrible. Illustration 9-1 shows the effect of these events on the financial statements if the direct write-off method is used.

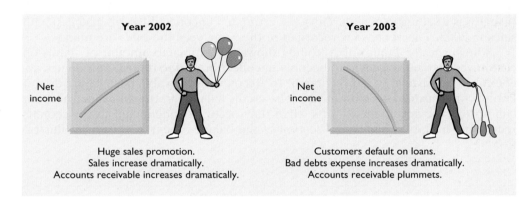

Illustration 9-1

Effects of direct write-off method

Under the direct write-off method, bad debts expense is often recorded in a period different from the period in which the revenue was recorded. No attempt is made to match bad debts expense to sales revenues in the income statement. Nor does the direct write-off method show accounts receivable in the balance sheet at the amount actually expected to be received. **Consequently, unless bad debts losses are insignificant, the direct write-off method is not acceptable for financial reporting purposes.**

Allowance Method for Uncollectible Accounts

The **allowance method** of accounting for bad debts involves estimating uncollectible accounts at the end of each period. This provides better matching on the income statement and ensures that receivables are stated at their cash (net) realizable value on the balance sheet. **Cash (net) realizable value** is the net amount expected to be received in cash. It excludes amounts that the company estimates it will not collect. Receivables are therefore reduced by estimated uncollectible receivables in the balance sheet through use of this method.

The allowance method is required for financial reporting purposes when bad debts are material in amount. It has three essential features:

1. Uncollectible accounts receivable are **estimated**. This estimate is treated as an expense and is **matched against sales** in the same accounting period in which the sales occurred.

2. Estimated uncollectibles are debited to Bad Debts Expense and are credited to Allowance for Doubtful Accounts (a contra asset account) through an adjusting entry at the end of each period.

HELPFUL HINT

In this context, *material* means significant or important to financial statement users.

3. When a specific account is written off, actual uncollectibles are debited to Allowance for Doubtful Accounts and credited to Accounts Receivable.

RECORDING ESTIMATED UNCOLLECTIBLES. To illustrate the allowance method, assume that Hampson Furniture has credit sales of $1,200,000 in 2002. Of this amount, $200,000 remains uncollected at December 31. The credit manager estimates that $12,000 of these sales will be uncollectible. The adjusting entry to record the estimated uncollectibles is:

```
A   =   L   +   OE
-12,000         -12,000
```

Dec. 31	Bad Debts Expense	12,000	
	Allowance for Doubtful Accounts		12,000
	(To record estimate of uncollectible accounts)		

Bad Debts Expense is reported in the income statement as an operating expense (usually as a selling expense). Thus, the estimated uncollectibles are matched with sales in 2002. The expense is recorded in the same year the sales are made.

Allowance for Doubtful Accounts shows the estimated amount of claims on customers that are expected to become uncollectible in the future. This contra account is used instead of a direct credit to Accounts Receivable because we do not know which customers will not pay. The credit balance in the allowance account will absorb the specific write-offs when they occur. It is deducted from accounts receivable in the current assets section of the balance sheet as shown in Illustration 9-2.

Illustration 9-2

Presentation of allowance for doubtful accounts

HAMPSON FURNITURE Balance Sheet (partial)		
Current assets		
Cash		$ 14,800
Accounts receivable	**$200,000**	
Less: Allowance for doubtful accounts	**12,000**	**188,000**
Merchandise inventory		310,000
Prepaid expense		25,000
Total current assets		$537,800

The amount of $188,000 in Illustration 9-2 represents the expected **cash realizable value** of the accounts receivable at the statement date. **Allowance for Doubtful Accounts is not closed at the end of the fiscal year.**

RECORDING THE WRITE-OFF OF AN UNCOLLECTIBLE ACCOUNT. Companies use various methods of collecting past-due accounts, such as letters, calls, and legal action. When all means of collecting a past-due account have been exhausted and collection appears impossible, the account should be written off. In the credit card industry, for example, it is standard practice to write off accounts that are 210 days past due. To prevent premature or unauthorized write-offs, each write-off should be formally approved in writing by management. To maintain good internal control, authorization to write off accounts should not be given to someone who also has daily responsibilities related to cash or receivables.

To illustrate a receivables write-off, assume that the vice-president of finance of Hampson Furniture authorizes a write-off of the $500 balance owed by R. A. Ware on March 1, 2003. The entry to record the write-off is:

Mar. 1	Allowance for Doubtful Accounts	500	
	Accounts Receivable—R. A. Ware		500
	(Write-off of R. A. Ware account)		

A	=	L	+	OE
+500				
−500				

Bad Debts Expense is not increased when the write-off occurs. **Under the allowance method, every bad debt write-off is debited to the allowance account rather than to Bad Debts Expense.** A debit to Bad Debts Expense would be incorrect because the expense has already been recognized when the adjusting entry was made for estimated bad debts. Instead, the entry to record the write-off of an uncollectible account reduces both Accounts Receivable and the Allowance for Doubtful Accounts. After posting, the general ledger accounts will appear as in Illustration 9-3.

Accounts Receivable			
Jan. 1 Bal. 200,000	Mar. 1		500
Mar. 1 Bal. 199,500			

Allowance for Doubtful Accounts			
Mar. 1	500	Jan. 1 Bal.	12,000
		Mar. 1 Bal.	11,500

Illustration 9-3

General ledger balances after write-off

A write-off affects only balance sheet accounts. The write-off of the account reduces both Accounts Receivable and Allowance for Doubtful Accounts. Cash realizable value in the balance sheet, therefore, remains the same, as shown in Illustration 9-4.

	Before Write-off	**After Write-off**
Accounts receivable	$200,000	$199,500
Allowance for doubtful accounts	12,000	11,500
Cash realizable value	$188,000	$188,000

Illustration 9-4

Cash realizable value comparison

RECOVERY OF AN UNCOLLECTIBLE ACCOUNT. Occasionally, a company collects from a customer after the account has been written off. Two entries are required to record the recovery of a bad debt: (1) The entry made in writing off the account is reversed to reinstate the customer's account. (2) The collection is journalized in the usual manner.

To illustrate, assume that on July 1, R. A. Ware pays the $500 amount that had been written off on March 1. These are the entries:

	(1)		
July 1	Accounts Receivable—R. A. Ware	500	
	Allowance for Doubtful Accounts		500
	(To reverse write-off of R. A. Ware account)		

A	=	L	+	OE
+500				
−500				

	(2)		
July 1	Cash	500	
	Accounts Receivable—R. A. Ware		500
	(To record collection from R. A. Ware)		

A	=	L	+	OE
+500				
−500				

Note that the recovery of a bad debt, like the write-off of a bad debt, affects only balance sheet accounts. The net effect of the two entries above is a debit to Cash and a credit to Allowance for Doubtful Accounts for $500. Accounts Receivable is debited and the Allowance for Doubtful Accounts is credited in entry (1) for two reasons: First, the company made an error in judgment when it wrote

HELPFUL HINT

Like the write-off, a recovery does not involve the income statement.

off the account receivable. Second, after R. A. Ware did pay, Accounts Receivable in the general ledger and Ware's account in the subsidiary ledger should show the collection for possible future credit purposes.

BASES USED FOR ALLOWANCE METHOD. To simplify the preceding explanation, we assumed we knew the amount of the expected uncollectibles. In "real life," companies must estimate that amount if they use the allowance method. Two bases are used to determine this amount: **(1) percentage of sales,** and **(2) percentage of receivables**. Both bases are generally accepted. The choice is a management decision. It depends on the relative emphasis that management wishes to give to expenses and revenues on the one hand or to cash realizable value of the accounts receivable on the other. The choice is whether to emphasize income statement or balance sheet relationships. Illustration 9-5 compares the two bases.

Illustration 9-5

Comparison of bases for estimating uncollectibles

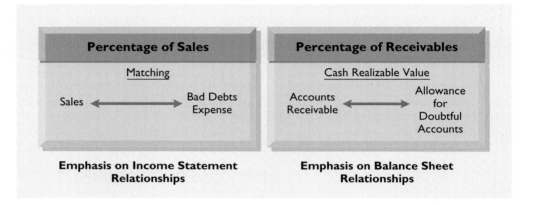

The percentage of sales basis results in a better matching of expenses with revenues—an income statement viewpoint. The percentage of receivables basis produces the better estimate of cash realizable value—a balance sheet viewpoint. Under both bases, it is necessary to determine the company's past experience with bad debt losses.

Percentage of Sales. In the percentage of sales basis, management estimates what percentage of credit sales will be uncollectible. This percentage is based on past experience and anticipated credit policy.

The percentage is applied to either total credit sales or net credit sales of the current year. To illustrate, assume that Gonzalez Company elects to use the percentage of sales basis. It concludes that 1 percent of net credit sales will become uncollectible. If net credit sales for 2002 are $800,000, the estimated bad debts expense is $8,000 (1% × $800,000). The adjusting entry is:

A	=	L	+	OE
−8,000				−8,000

Dec. 31	Bad Debts Expense	8,000	
	Allowance for Doubtful Accounts		8,000
	(To record estimated bad debts for year)		

After the adjusting entry is posted, assuming the allowance account already has a credit balance of $1,723, the accounts of Gonzalez Company will show:

Illustration 9-6

Bad debts accounts after posting

Bad Debts Expense		Allowance for Doubtful Accounts	
Dec. 31 Adj. 8,000		Jan. 1 Bal. 1,723	
		Dec. 31 Adj. 8,000	
		Dec. 31 Bal. 9,723	

This basis of estimating uncollectibles emphasizes the matching of expenses with revenues. As a result, Bad Debts Expense will show a direct percentage relationship to the sales base on which it is computed. **When the adjusting entry is made, the existing balance in Allowance for Doubtful Accounts is disregarded.** The adjusted balance in this account should be a reasonable approximation of the realizable value of the receivables. If actual write-offs differ significantly from the amount estimated, the percentage for future years should be modified.

Percentage of Receivables. Under the percentage of receivables basis, management estimates what percentage of receivables will result in losses from uncollectible accounts. An **aging schedule** is prepared, in which customer balances are classified by the length of time they have been unpaid. Because of its emphasis on time, the analysis is often called aging the accounts receivable.

ACCOUNTING IN ACTION ∧ *Business Insight*

Companies that provide services and bill on a per hour basis often must spend considerable time preparing detailed bills that specify the billable activities performed. A new company, **TimeBills.com**, has an online product that reduces the amount of time it takes to prepare a bill, while increasing the information provided to the customer. To use the service, you create an electronic record that lists the type of project, customer name, project dates, and billing rate. By clicking on the "timer" function, you can automatically track time spent on a particular project as the work is being performed. TimeBills.com will either mail or e-mail invoices to customers, and keep track of collections, including providing an aging schedule.

After the accounts are aged, the expected bad debt losses are determined. This is done by applying percentages based on past experience to the totals in each category. The longer a receivable is past due, the less likely it is to be collected. So, the estimated percentage of uncollectible debts increases as the number of days past due increases. An aging schedule for Dart Company is shown in Illustration 9-7. Note the increasing percentages from 2 to 40 percent.

Illustration 9-7

Aging schedule

Customer	Total	Not Yet Due	Number of Days Past Due			
			1–30	31–60	61–90	Over 90
T. E. Adert	$ 600		$ 300		$ 200	$ 100
R. C. Bortz	300	$ 300				
B. A. Carl	450		200	$ 250		
O. L. Diker	700	500			200	
T. O. Ebbet	600			300		300
Others	36,950	26,200	5,200	2,450	1,600	1,500
	$39,600	$27,000	$5,700	$3,000	$2,000	$1,900
Estimated Percentage Uncollectible		2%	4%	10%	20%	40%
Total Estimated Bad Debts	$ 2,228	$ 540	$ 228	$ 300	$ 400	$ 760

HELPFUL HINT
The higher percentages are used for the older categories because the longer an account is past due, the less likely it is to be collected.

Total estimated bad debts for Dart Company ($2,228) represent the amount of existing customer claims expected to become uncollectible in the future. This amount represents the **required balance** in Allowance for Doubtful Accounts at the balance sheet date. **The amount of the bad debt adjusting entry is the difference between the required balance and the existing balance in the allowance account**. If the trial balance shows Allowance for Doubtful Accounts with a credit balance of $528, an adjusting entry for $1,700 ($2,228 − $528) is necessary, as shown below.

A = L + OE				
−1,700 −1,700	Dec. 31	Bad Debts Expense	1,700	
		Allowance for Doubtful Accounts		1,700
		(To adjust allowance account to total estimated uncollectibles)		

After the adjusting entry is posted, the accounts of the Dart Company will show:

Illustration 9-8

Bad debts accounts after posting

Bad Debts Expense		Allowance for Doubtful Accounts	
Dec. 31 Adj. **1,700**		Bal. 528	
		Dec. 31 Adj. **1,700**	
		Bal. 2,228	

Occasionally the allowance account will have a **debit balance** prior to adjustment. This occurs when write-offs during the year have exceeded previous provisions for bad debts. In such a case **the debit balance is added to the required balance** when the adjusting entry is made. Thus, if there had been a $500 debit balance in the allowance account before adjustment, the adjusting entry would have been for $2,728 ($2,228 + $500) to arrive at a credit balance of $2,228.

The percentage of receivables method will normally result in the better approximation of cash realizable value. But it will not result in the better matching of expenses with revenues if some customers' accounts are more than one year past due. In such a case, bad debts expense for the current period would include amounts related to the sales of a prior year.

ACCOUNTING IN ACTION *Business Insight*

Nearly half of the goods sold by Sears, Roebuck & Co. are purchased with a Sears credit card. This means that how Sears accounts for its uncollectible accounts can have a very significant effect on Sears's net income. In one quarter in a recent year Sears reduced its bad debts expense by 61 percent compared to the same quarter in the previous year. In so doing, Sears was able to report earnings that slightly exceeded analysts' forecasts. Some analysts expressed concern that, because the number of delinquent accounts receivable had actually increased, Sears should probably have *increased* its bad debts expense, rather than reduced it. While Sears management defended its actions, analysts appeared to be unimpressed, and Sears's stock price declined on the news.

BEFORE YOU GO ON...

▶ *REVIEW IT*

1. What is the primary criticism of the direct write-off method?
2. Explain the difference between the percentage of sales and the percentage of receivables methods.
3. **Lands' End** has a generous customer return policy. What accounting treatment does Lands' End use for customer returns? (*Hint:* Review Lands' End's notes.) The answer to this question is provided on page 396.

▶ *DO IT*

Brule Co. has been in business 5 years. The ledger at the end of the current year shows: Accounts Receivable $30,000, Sales $180,000, and Allowance for Doubtful Accounts with a debit balance of $2,000. Bad debts are estimated to be 10% of receivables. Prepare the entry to adjust the Allowance for Doubtful Accounts.

ACTION PLAN

- Report receivables at their cash (net) realizable value.
- Estimate the amount the company does not expect to collect.
- Consider the existing balance in the allowance account when using the percentage of receivables basis.

SOLUTION

The following entry should be made to bring the balance in the Allowance for Doubtful Accounts up to a balance of $3,000 (0.1 × $30,000):

Bad Debts Expense	5,000	
Allowance for Doubtful Accounts		5,000
(To record estimate of uncollectible accounts)		

Related exercise material: BE9-3, BE9-4, BE9-5, BE9-6, BE9-7, E9-2, E9-3, and E9-4.

☑ THE NAVIGATOR

DISPOSING OF ACCOUNTS RECEIVABLE

In the normal course of events, accounts receivable are collected in cash and removed from the books. However, as credit sales and receivables have grown in significance, their "normal course of events" has changed. Companies now frequently sell their receivables to another company for cash, thereby shortening the cash-to-cash operating cycle.

Receivables are sold for two major reasons. First, **receivables may be sold because they may be the only reasonable source of cash**. When money is tight, companies may not be able to borrow money in the usual credit markets. Or, if money is available, the cost of borrowing may be prohibitive.

A second reason for selling receivables is that **billing and collection are often time consuming and costly**. It is often easier for a retailer to sell the receivable to another party with expertise in billing and collection matters. Credit card companies such as **MasterCard**, **VISA**, **American Express**, and **Diners Club** specialize in billing and collecting accounts receivable.

Sale of Receivables

A common sale of receivables is a sale to a factor. A **factor** is a finance company or bank that buys receivables from businesses and then collects the payments directly from the customers. Factoring is a multibillion dollar business. For example, **Sears, Roebuck and Co.** recently sold $14.8 billion of customer accounts receivable to a factor.

Factoring arrangements vary widely. Typically the factor charges a commission to the company that is selling the receivables. This fee ranges from 1–3

STUDY OBJECTIVE 4

Describe the entries to record the disposition of accounts receivable.

HELPFUL HINT

Two common expressions apply here:
1. Time is money. That is, waiting for the normal collection process costs money.
2. A bird in the hand is worth two in the bush. That is, getting cash now is better than getting it later.

percent of the amount of receivables purchased. To illustrate, assume that Hendredon Furniture factors $600,000 of receivables to Federal Factors. Federal Factors assesses a service charge of 2 percent of the amount of receivables sold. The journal entry to record the sale by Hendredon Furniture is as follows.

A = L + OE		
+588,000 −12,000		
−600,000		

Cash	588,000	
Service Charge Expense (2% × $600,000)	12,000	
Accounts Receivable		600,000
(To record the sale of accounts receivable)		

If the company often sells its receivables, the service charge expense (such as that incurred by Hendredon) is recorded as selling expense. If receivables are sold infrequently, this amount may be reported in the "other expenses and losses" section of the income statement.

Credit Card Sales

One billion credit cards were estimated to be in use recently—more than three credit cards for every man, woman, and child in this country. Companies such as VISA, MasterCard, Discover, American Express, and Diners Club offer national credit cards. Three parties are involved when national credit cards are used in making retail sales: (1) the credit card issuer, who is independent of the retailer, (2) the retailer, and (3) the customer. A retailer's acceptance of a national credit card is another form of selling (factoring) the receivable.

The major advantages of these national credit cards to the retailer are shown in Illustration 9–9. In exchange for these advantages, the retailer pays the credit card issuer a fee of 2–6 percent of the invoice price for its services.

Illustration 9-9

Advantages of credit cards to the retailer

Issuer does credit investigation of customer

Credit card issuer   Customer   Retailer

Issuer maintains customer accounts

Issuer undertakes collection process and absorbs any losses

Retailer receives cash more quickly from credit card issuer

CASH SALES: VISA AND MASTERCARD. Sales resulting from the use of VISA and MasterCard are considered cash sales by the retailer. These cards are issued by banks. Upon receipt of credit card sales slips from a retailer, the bank immediately adds the amount to the seller's bank balance, deducting a fee of 2–4 percent of the credit card sales slips for this service. These credit card sales slips are recorded in the same manner as checks deposited from a cash sale.

To illustrate, Anita Ferreri purchases $1,000 of compact discs for her restaurant from Karen Kerr Music Co., using her VISA First Bank Card. The service fee that First Bank charges is 3 percent. The entry to record this transaction by Karen Kerr Music is as follows.

Cash	970		
Service Charge Expense	30		
Sales		1,000	
(To record VISA credit card sales)			

A	=	L	+	OE
+970				−30
				+1,000

CREDIT SALES: AMERICAN EXPRESS AND DINERS CLUB. Sales using American Express and Diners Club cards are reported as credit sales, not cash sales. Conversion into cash does not occur until these companies remit the net amount to the seller. To illustrate, assume that Four Seasons restaurant accepts an American Express card for a $300 bill. The entry for the sale by Four Seasons, assuming a 5 percent service fee, is:

Accounts Receivable—American Express	285		
Service Charge Expense	15		
Sales		300	
(To record American Express credit card sales)			

A	=	L	+	OE
+285				−15
				+300

American Express will subsequently pay the restaurant $285. The restaurant will record this payment as follows.

Cash	285		
Accounts Receivable—American Express		285	
(To record redemption of credit card billings)			

A	=	L	+	OE
+285				
−285				

Service Charge Expense is reported by the restaurant as a selling expense in the income statement.

BEFORE YOU GO ON...

▶ *REVIEW IT*
1. Why do companies sell their receivables?
2. What is the journal entry when a company sells its receivables to a factor?
3. How are sales using a VISA or MasterCard reported? Is a sale using an American Express card recorded differently? Explain.

▶ *DO IT*
Peter M. Dell Wholesalers Co. has been expanding faster than it can raise capital. According to its local banker, the company has reached its debt ceiling. Dell's customers are slow in paying (60–90 days), but its suppliers (creditors) are demanding 30-day payment. Dell has a cash flow problem.

Dell needs $120,000 in cash to safely cover next Friday's employee payroll. Its balance of outstanding receivables totals $750,000. What might Dell do to alleviate this cash crunch? Record the entry that Dell would make when it raises the needed cash.

ACTION PLAN
• To speed up the collection of cash, sell receivables to a factor.

• Calculate service charge expense as a percentage of the factored receivables.

SOLUTION: Assuming that Dell Co. factors $125,000 of its accounts receivable at a 1% service charge, the following entry would be made.

Cash	123,750	
Service Charge Expense	1,250	
Accounts Receivable		125,000
(To record sale of receivables to factor)		

Related exercise material: BE9–10 and E9–5.

☑ THE NAVIGATOR

NOTES RECEIVABLE

Credit may also be granted in exchange for a promissory note. A promissory note is a written promise to pay a specified amount of money on demand or at a definite time. Promissory notes may be used (1) when individuals and companies lend or borrow money; (2) when the amount of the transaction and the credit period exceed normal limits; or (3) in settlement of accounts receivable.

In a promissory note, the party making the promise to pay is called the **maker**. The party to whom payment is to be made is called the **payee**. The payee may be specifically identified by name or may be designated simply as the bearer of the note. In the note shown in Illustration 9-10, Brent Company is the maker, Wilma Company is the payee. To Wilma Company, the promissory note is a note receivable; to Brent Company, it is a note payable.

Illustration 9-10

Promissory note

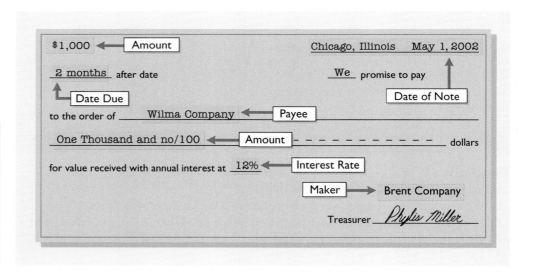

HELPFUL HINT

Who are the two key parties to a note, and what entry does each party make when the note is issued?
Answer:
1. The maker, Brent Company, credits Notes Payable.
2. The payee, Wilma Company, debits Notes Receivable.

Notes receivable give the payee a stronger legal claim to assets than accounts receivable. Like accounts receivable, notes receivable can be readily sold to another party. Promissory notes are negotiable instruments (as are checks), which means that they can be transferred to another party by endorsement.

Notes receivable are frequently accepted from customers who need to extend the payment of an account receivable. They are often required from high-risk customers. In some industries (such as the pleasure boat industry), all credit sales are supported by notes. The majority of notes originate from loans. The basic issues in accounting for notes receivable are the same as those for accounts receivable:

1. **Recognizing** notes receivable.
2. **Valuing** notes receivable.
3. **Disposing of** notes receivable.

On the following pages, we will look at these issues. Before we do, we need to consider two issues that did not apply to accounts receivable: maturity date and computing interest.

DETERMINING THE MATURITY DATE

When the life of a note is expressed in terms of months, the due date when it matures is found by counting the months from the date of issue. For example, the maturity date of a three-month note dated May 1 is August 1. A note drawn on the last day of a month matures on the last day of a subsequent month. That is, a July 31 note due in two months matures on September 30. When the due date is stated in terms of days, you need to count the exact number of days to determine the maturity date. In counting, **the date the note is issued is omitted but the due date is included**. For example, the maturity date of a 60-day note dated July 17 is September 15, computed as follows.

STUDY OBJECTIVE **5**

Compute the maturity date of and interest on notes receivable.

Term of note		60 days
July (31 − 17)	14	
August	31	45
Maturity date: September		15

Illustration 9-11

Computation of maturity date

The due date (maturity date) of a promissory note may be stated in one of three ways, as shown in Illustration 9-12.

Illustration 9-12

Maturity date of different notes

COMPUTING INTEREST

As indicated in Chapter 3, the basic formula for computing interest on an interest-bearing note is:

Illustration 9-13

Formula for computing interest

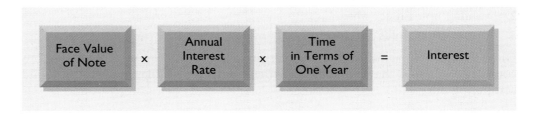

| Face Value of Note | × | Annual Interest Rate | × | Time in Terms of One Year | = | Interest |

HELPFUL HINT
The interest rate specified is the *annual* rate.

The interest rate specified in a note is an **annual** rate of interest. The time factor in the formula above expresses the fraction of a year that the note is outstanding. When the maturity date is stated in days, the time factor is often the number of days divided by 360. When the due date is stated in months, the time factor is the number of months divided by 12. Computation of interest for various time periods is shown in Illustration 9-14.

Illustration 9-14

Computation of interest

Terms of Note	Interest Computation
	Face × Rate × Time = Interest
$ 730, 18%, 120 days	$ 730 × 18% × 120/360 = $ 43.80
$1,000, 15%, 6 months	$1,000 × 15% × 6/12 = $ 75.00
$2,000, 12%, 1 year	$2,000 × 12% × 1/1 = $240.00

There are many different ways to calculate interest. The computation above assumed 360 days for the length of the year. Many financial institutions use 365 days. It is more profitable to use 360 days; the holder of the note receives more interest than if 365 days are used. For homework problems, assume 360 days.

RECOGNIZING NOTES RECEIVABLE

STUDY OBJECTIVE 6

Explain how notes receivable are recognized in the accounts.

To illustrate the basic entry for notes receivable, we will use the $1,000, 2-month, 12% promissory note on page 374. Assuming that the note was written to settle an open account, the entry for the receipt of the note by Wilma Company is:

May 1	Notes Receivable	1,000	
	Accounts Receivable—Brent Company		1,000
	(To record acceptance of Brent Company note)		

A	=	L	+	OE
+1,000				
−1,000				

Observe that the note receivable is recorded at its **face value**, the value shown on the face of the note. No interest revenue is reported when the note is accepted because the revenue recognition principle does not recognize revenue until earned. Interest is earned (accrued) as time passes.

If a note is exchanged for cash, the entry is a debit to Notes Receivable and a credit to Cash in the amount of the loan.

VALUING NOTES RECEIVABLE

STUDY OBJECTIVE 7

Describe how notes receivable are valued.

Valuing short-term notes receivable is the same as valuing accounts receivable. Like accounts receivable, short-term notes receivable are reported at their **cash (net) realizable value**. The notes receivable allowance account is Allowance for Doubtful Accounts. The estimations involved in determining cash realizable value and in recording bad debts expense and related allowance are similar.

*A*CCOUNTING IN ACTION   *International Insight*

Long-term receivables do pose additional estimation problems. For example, banks that loaned money to developing countries have often found it difficult to collect on those receivables. At one time, banks were owed $1.3 trillion by developing countries. (A trillion is a lot of money—-enough to give every man, woman, and child in the world $250 each.) Banks made these loans for various reasons: (1) to provide stability to these governments and increase trade, (2) in the belief that governments would never default on payment, and (3) with the desire to increase banks' income by lending. Determining the proper allowance is understandably difficult for these types of long-term receivables.

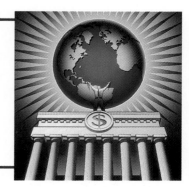

DISPOSING OF NOTES RECEIVABLE

Notes may be held to their maturity date, at which time the face value plus accrued interest is due. Sometimes the maker of the note defaults and an adjustment to the accounts must be made. At other times the holder of the note speeds up the conversion to cash by selling the note. The entries for honoring and dishonoring notes are illustrated below.

STUDY OBJECTIVE 8

Describe the entries to record the disposition of notes receivable.

Honor of Notes Receivable

A note is **honored** when it is paid in full at its maturity date. For an interest-bearing note, the amount due at maturity is the face value of the note plus interest for the length of time specified on the note.

To illustrate, assume that Betty Co. lends Wayne Higley Inc. $10,000 on June 1, accepting a 4-month, 9% interest note. Interest will be $300 ($10,000 × 9% × 4/12). The amount due, the maturity value, will be $10,300. To obtain payment, Betty Co. (the payee) must present the note either to Wayne Higley Inc. (the maker) or to the maker's duly appointed agent, such as a bank. Assuming that Betty Co. presents the note to Wayne Higley Inc. on the maturity date, the entry by Betty Co. to record the collection is:

Oct. 1	Cash	10,300	
	Notes Receivable		10,000
	Interest Revenue		300
	(To record collection of Higley Inc. note)		

A	=	L	+	OE
+10,300				+300
−10,000				

If Betty Co. prepares financial statements as of September 30, it would be necessary to accrue interest. In this case, the adjusting entry by Betty Co. would be to record 4 months' interest ($300), as shown below.

Sept. 30	Interest Receivable	300	
	Interest Revenue		300
	(To accrue 4 months' interest)		

A	=	L	+	OE
+300				+300

When interest has been accrued, at maturity it is necessary to credit Interest Receivable. The entry by Betty Co. to record the honoring of the Wayne Higley Inc. note on October 1 is:

Oct. 1	Cash	10,300	
	Notes Receivable		10,000
	Interest Receivable		300
	(To record collection of note at maturity)		

A	=	L	+	OE
+10,300				
−10,000				
−300				

In this case, Interest Receivable is credited because the receivable was established in the adjusting entry.

Dishonor of Notes Receivable

A **dishonored note** is a note that is not paid in full at maturity. A dishonored note receivable is no longer negotiable. However, the payee still has a claim against the maker of the note. Therefore the Notes Receivable account is usually transferred to an Account Receivable.

To illustrate, assume that Wayne Higley Inc. on October 1 indicates that it cannot pay at the present time. The entry to record the dishonor of the note depends on whether eventual collection is expected. If Betty Co. expects eventual collection, the amount due (face value and interest) on the note is debited to Accounts Receivable. Betty Co. would make the following entry at the time the note is dishonored (assuming no previous accrual of interest).

Oct. 1	Accounts Receivable—Wayne Higley Inc.	10,300	
	Notes Receivable		10,000
	Interest Revenue		300
	(To record the dishonor of Higley Inc. note)		

If there is no hope of collection, the face value of the note would be written off by debiting the Allowance for Doubtful Accounts. No interest revenue would be recorded because collection will not occur.

Sale of Notes Receivable

The accounting for the sales of notes receivable is recorded similarly to the sale of accounts receivable. The accounting entries for the sale of notes receivable are left for a more advanced course.

BEFORE YOU GO ON...

▶ *REVIEW IT*
1. What is the basic formula for computing interest?
2. At what value are notes receivable reported on the balance sheet?
3. Explain the difference between honoring and dishonoring a note receivable.

▶ *DO IT*
Gambit Stores accepts from Leonard Co. a $3,400, 90-day, 12% note dated May 10 in settlement of Leonard's overdue account. What is the maturity date of the note? What is the entry made by Gambit at the maturity date, assuming Leonard pays the note and interest in full at that time?

ACTION PLAN
- Count the exact number of days to determine the maturity date. Omit the date the note is issued, but include the due date.
- Determine whether interest was accrued. The entry here assumes that no interest has been previously accrued on this note.

SOLUTION: The maturity date is August 8, computed as follows.

Term of note:		90 days
May (31 − 10)	21	
June	30	
July	31	82
Maturity date: August		8

The interest payable at maturity date is $102, computed as follows.

$$\text{Face} \times \text{Rate} \times \text{Time} = \text{Interest}$$
$$\$3,400 \times 12\% \times 90/360 = \$102$$

The entry recorded by Gambit Stores at the maturity date is:

Cash	3,502	
Notes Receivable		3,400
Interest Revenue		102
(To record collection of Leonard note)		

Related exercise material: BE9-8, BE9-9, E9-8, E9-9, and E9-10.

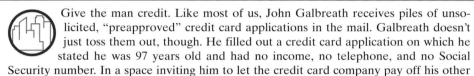

*A*CCOUNTING IN ACTION *Business Insight*

Give the man credit. Like most of us, John Galbreath receives piles of unsolicited, "preapproved" credit card applications in the mail. Galbreath doesn't just toss them out, though. He filled out a credit card application on which he stated he was 97 years old and had no income, no telephone, and no Social Security number. In a space inviting him to let the credit card company pay off his other credit card balances, Galbreath said he owed money to the Mafia.

Back came a credit card and a letter welcoming John to the fold with a $1,500 credit limit. Galbreath had requested the card under a false name, John C. Reath, an alias under which he had received two other credit cards—earning exemplary credit. John C. Reath might be a senior citizen with no means, but it seems he paid his bills on time.

SOURCE: "Forbes Informer," edited by Kate Bohner Lewis, *Forbes*, August 14, 1995, p. 19. Reprinted by permission of FORBES Magazine © Forbes Inc., 1995.

*S*TATEMENT PRESENTATION AND ANALYSIS

PRESENTATION

Each of the major types of receivables should be identified in the balance sheet or in the notes to the financial statements. Short-term receivables are reported in the current assets section of the balance sheet, below short-term investments. Short-term investments appear before receivables, because short-term investments are more liquid (nearer to cash). Both the gross amount of receivables and the allowance for doubtful accounts should be reported.

In a multiple-step income statement, bad debts expense and service charge expense are reported as selling expenses in the operating expenses section. Interest revenue is shown under "other revenues and gains" in the nonoperating activities section of the income statement.

STUDY OBJECTIVE **9**

Explain the statement presentation and analysis of receivables.

ANALYSIS

Financial ratios are frequently computed to evaluate the liquidity of a company's accounts receivable. The **accounts receivable turnover ratio** is used to assess the liquidity of the receivables. This ratio measures the number of times, on average, accounts receivable are collected during the period. It is computed by dividing net credit sales (net sales less cash sales) by the average net accounts receivable during the year. Unless seasonal factors are significant, average net accounts receivable outstanding can be computed from the beginning and ending balances of net accounts receivable.

For example, in 2000 **Lands' End** had net sales of $1,319.8 million for the year. It had a beginning net accounts receivable balance of $21.1 million and an ending net accounts receivable balance of $17.8 million. Assuming that Lands' End's sales were all on credit, its accounts receivable turnover ratio is computed as follows.

Illustration 9-15

Accounts receivable
turnover ratio and
computation

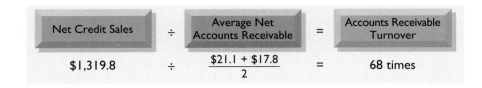

The result indicates an accounts receivable turnover ratio of 68 times per year. The higher the turnover ratio the more liquid the company's receivables.

A variant of the accounts receivable turnover ratio that makes the liquidity even more evident is the conversion of it into an **average collection period** in terms of days. This is done by dividing the turnover ratio into 365 days. For example, Lands' End's turnover of 68 times is divided into 365 days, as follows, to obtain approximately 5.4 days.

Illustration 9-16

Average collection period
for receivables formula and
computation

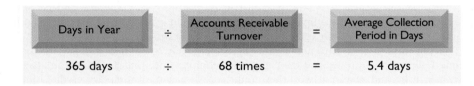

This means that it takes Lands' End about 5.4 days to collect its accounts receivable.

The average collection period is frequently used to assess the effectiveness of a company's credit and collection policies. The general rule is that the collection period should not greatly exceed the credit term period (i.e., the time allowed for payment).[1]

BEFORE YOU GO ON...

▶ *REVIEW IT*
1. Explain where accounts and notes receivable are reported on the balance sheet.
2. Where are bad debts expense, service charge expense, and interest revenue reported on the multiple-step income statement?

A LOOK BACK AT OUR FEATURE STORY

Refer back to the Feature Story about Fred Tarter's **Pharmacy Fund** at the beginning of the chapter, and answer the following questions.
1. Why has the pharmacy business moved from a cash-based business to a receivables-based business?
2. What is the economic motivation for pharmacies to sell their receivables?
3. What is the economic motivation for the Pharmacy Fund to purchase the receivables?

SOLUTION
1. Due to the proliferation of health plans (of which there are more than 4,500 in the U.S.), pharmacists now deal with many small receivables from third-party payers instead of cash payments from customers.

---

[1]One factor that may distort this liquidity analysis is that Lands' End's sales number includes many cash sales. Therefore, the receivables turnover ratio would be high, and the days to collect receivables would be low.

2. Pharmacists must wait between 30 and 60 days to receive their receivables. Selling the receivables provides cash within 24 hours and relieves pharmacists of collection responsibilities. (It is estimated that credit losses equal 3 percent of the $40 billion of prescriptions purchased through health care plans.)

3. The Pharmacy Fund maintains credit files on health plan sponsors. Thus, it can minimize credit losses. The fund receives a 1.4–2 percent fee on receivables purchased. As the volume of business expands, it is expected that this fee will cover expenses and provide a profit.

☑ THE NAVIGATOR

DEMONSTRATION PROBLEM

The following selected transactions relate to Falcetto Company.

Additional Demonstration Problem

Mar. 1 Sold $20,000 of merchandise to Potter Company, terms 2/10, n/30.
 11 Received payment in full from Potter Company for balance due.
 12 Accepted Juno Company's $20,000, 6-month, 12% note for balance due.
 13 Made Falcetto Company credit card sales for $13,200.
 15 Made American Express credit sales totaling $6,700. A 5% service fee is charged by American Express.
 30 Received payment in full from American Express Company.
Apr. 11 Sold accounts receivable of $8,000 to Harcot Factor. Harcot Factor assesses a service charge of 2% of the amount of receivables sold.
 13 Received collections of $8,200 on Falcetto Company credit card sales and added finance charges of 1.5% to the remaining balances.
May 10 Wrote off as uncollectible $16,000 of accounts receivable. Falcetto uses the percentage of sales basis to estimate bad debts.
June 30 Credit sales for the first 6 months total $2,000,000. The bad debt percentage is 1% of credit sales. At June 30, the balance in the allowance account is $3,500.
July 16 One of the accounts receivable written off in May was from J. Simon, who pays the amount due, $4,000, in full.

Instructions
Prepare the journal entries for the transactions.

SOLUTION TO DEMONSTRATION PROBLEM

Mar. 1	Accounts Receivable–Potter	20,000	
	Sales		20,000
	(To record sales on account)		
Mar. 11	Cash	19,600	
	Sales Discounts (2% × $20,000)	400	
	Accounts Receivable—Potter		20,000
	(To record collection of accounts receivable)		
Mar. 12	Notes Receivable	20,000	
	Accounts Receivable—Juno		20,000
	(To record acceptance of Juno Company note)		
Mar. 13	Accounts Receivable	13,200	
	Sales		13,200
	(To record company credit card sales)		
Mar. 15	Accounts Receivable—American Express	6,365	
	Service Charge Expense (5% × $6,700)	335	
	Sales		6,700
	(To record credit card sales)		

ACTION PLAN

• Generally, record accounts receivable at invoice price.

• Recognize that sales returns and allowances and cash discounts reduce the amount received on accounts receivable.

• Record a service charge expense on the seller's books when accounts receivable are sold.

• Prepare an adjusting entry for bad debts expense.

• Ignore any balance in the allowance account under the percentage of sales basis. Recognize the balance in the allowance account under the percentage of receivables basis.

• Record write-offs of accounts receivable only in balance sheet accounts.

Mar. 30	Cash	6,365	
	Accounts Receivable—American Express		6,365
	(To record redemption of credit card billings)		
Apr. 11	Cash	7,840	
	Service Charge Expense (2% × $8,000)	160	
	Accounts Receivable		8,000
	(To record sale of receivables to factor)		
Apr. 13	Cash	8,200	
	Accounts Receivable		8,200
	(To record collection of accounts receivable)		
	Accounts Receivable [($13,200 − $8,200) × 1.5%]	75	
	Interest Revenue		75
	(To record interest on amount due)		
May 10	Allowance for Doubtful Accounts	16,000	
	Accounts Receivable		16,000
	(To record write-off of accounts receivable)		
June 30	Bad Debts Expense ($2,000,000 × 1%)	20,000	
	Allowance for Doubtful Accounts		20,000
	(To record estimate of uncollectible accounts)		
July 16	Accounts Receivable—J. Simon	4,000	
	Allowance for Doubtful Accounts		4,000
	(To reverse write-off of accounts receivable)		
	Cash	4,000	
	Accounts Receivable—J. Simon		4,000
	(To record collection of accounts receivable)		

SUMMARY OF STUDY OBJECTIVES

1. Identify the different types of receivables. Receivables are frequently classified as (1) accounts, (2) notes, and (3) other. Accounts receivable are amounts owed by customers on account. Notes receivable are claims for which formal instruments of credit are issued as proof of the debt. Other receivables include nontrade receivables such as interest receivable, loans to company officers, advances to employees, and income taxes refundable.

2. Explain how accounts receivable are recognized in the accounts. Accounts receivable are recorded at invoice price. They are reduced by Sales Returns and Allowances. Cash discounts reduce the amount received on accounts receivable. When interest is charged on a past due receivable, this interest is added to the accounts receivable balance and is recognized as interest revenue.

3. Distinguish between the methods and bases used to value accounts receivable. There are two methods of accounting for uncollectible accounts: (1) the allowance method and (2) the direct write-off method. Either the percentage of sales or the percentage of receivables basis may be used to estimate uncollectible accounts using the allowance method. The percentage of sales basis emphasizes the matching principle. The percentage of receivables basis emphasizes the cash realizable value of the accounts receivable. An aging schedule is often used with this basis.

4. Describe the entries to record the disposition of accounts receivable. When an account receivable is collected, Accounts Receivable is credited. When an account receivable is sold, a service charge expense is charged which reduces the amount collected.

5. Compute the maturity date of and interest on notes receivable. The maturity date of a note must be computed unless the due date is specified or the note is payable on demand. For a note stated in months, the maturity date is found by counting the months from the date of issue. For a note stated in days, the number of days is counted, omitting the issue date and counting the due date. The formula for computing interest is face value × interest rate × time.

6. Explain how notes receivable are recognized in the accounts. Notes receivable are recorded at face value. In some cases, it is necessary to accrue interest prior to maturity. In this case, Interest Receivable is debited and Interest Revenue is credited.

7. Describe how notes receivable are valued. Like accounts receivable, notes receivable are reported at their cash (net) realizable value. The notes receivable allowance account is the Allowance for Doubtful Accounts. The computation and estimations involved in valuing notes receivable at cash realizable value, and in recording the proper amount of bad debts expense and related allowance are similar to those for accounts receivable.

8. Describe the entries to record the disposition of notes receivable. Notes can be held to maturity. At that time the face value plus accrued interest is due, and the note is removed from the accounts. In many cases, the holder of the note speeds up the conversion by selling the receivable to another party. In some situations, the maker of the note dishonors the note (defaults), and the note is written off.

9. Explain the statement presentation and analysis of receivables. Each major type of receivable should be identified in the balance sheet or in the notes to the financial statements. Short-term receivables are considered current assets. The gross amount of receivables and the allowance for doubtful accounts should be reported. Bad debts and service charge expenses are reported in the multiple-step income statement as operating (selling) expenses; interest revenue is shown as other revenues and gains in the nonoperating activities section of the statement. Accounts receivable may be evaluated for liquidity by computing a turnover ratio and an average collection period.

Key Term Matching Activity

GLOSSARY

Accounts receivable turnover ratio A measure of the liquidity of accounts receivable; computed by dividing net credit sales by average net accounts receivable. (p. 379).

Aging of accounts receivable The analysis of customer balances by the length of time they have been unpaid. (p. 369).

Allowance method A method of accounting for bad debts that involves estimating uncollectible accounts at the end of each period. (p. 365).

Average collection period The average amount of time that a receivable is outstanding; calculated by dividing 365 days by the receivables turnover ratio. (p. 380).

Bad Debts Expense An expense account to record uncollectible receivables. (p. 364).

Cash (net) realizable value The net amount expected to be received in cash. (p. 365).

Direct write-off method A method of accounting for bad debts that involves expensing accounts at the time they are determined to be uncollectible. (p. 364).

Dishonored note A note that is not paid in full at maturity. (p. 378).

Factor A finance company or bank that buys receivables from businesses and then collects the payments directly from the customers. (p. 371).

Maker The party in a promissory note who is making the promise to pay. (p. 374).

Payee The party to whom payment of a promissory note is to be made. (p. 374).

Percentage of receivables basis Management establishes a percentage relationship between the amount of receivables and the expected losses from uncollectible accounts. (p. 369).

Percentage of sales basis Management establishes a percentage relationship between the amount of credit sales and expected losses from uncollectible accounts. (p. 368).

Promissory note A written promise to pay a specified amount of money on demand or at a definite time. (p. 374).

Trade receivables Notes and accounts receivable that result from sales transactions. (p. 362).

Chapter 9 Self-Test

SELF-STUDY QUESTIONS

Answers are at the end of the chapter.

(SO 2) **1.** Remmers Company on June 15 sells merchandise on account to Tucci Co. for $1,000, terms 2/10, n/30. On June 20, Tucci Co. returns merchandise worth $300 to Remmers Company. On June 24, payment is received from Tucci Co. for the balance due. What is the amount of cash received?
  a. $700.
  b. $680.
  c. $686.
  d. None of the above.

(SO 3) **2.** Which of the following approaches for bad debts is best described as a balance sheet method?
  a. Percentage of receivables basis.
  b. Direct write-off method.
  c. Percentage of sales basis.
  d. Both a and b.

(SO 3) **3.** Net sales for the month are $800,000, and bad debts are expected to be 1.5% of net sales. The company uses the percentage of sales basis. If the Allowance for Doubtful Accounts has a credit balance of $15,000 before adjustment, what is the balance after adjustment?
  a. $15,000.
  b. $27,000.
  c. $23,000.
  d. $31,000.

4. In 2002, Roland Carlson Company had net credit sales (SO 3) of $750,000. On January 1, 2002, Allowance for Doubtful Accounts had a credit balance of $18,000. During 2002, $30,000 of uncollectible accounts receivable were written off. Past experience indicates that 3% of net credit sales become uncollectible. What should be the adjusted balance of Allowance for Doubtful Accounts at December 31, 2002?
  a. $10,050.
  b. $10,500.
  c. $22,500.
  d. $40,500.

(SO 3) **5.** An analysis and aging of the accounts receivable of Machiavelli Company at December 31 reveals the following data.

Accounts receivable	$800,000
Allowance for doubtful accounts per books before adjustment	50,000
Amounts expected to become uncollectible	65,000

The cash realizable value of the accounts receivable at December 31, after adjustment, is:
a. $685,000.
b. $750,000.
c. $800,000.
d. $735,000.

(SO 6) **6.** One of the following statements about promissory notes is incorrect. The *incorrect* statement is:
a. The party making the promise to pay is called the maker.
b. The party to whom payment is to be made is called the payee.
c. A promissory note is not a negotiable instrument.
d. A promissory note is more liquid than an account receivable.

(SO 4) **7.** Which of the following statements about VISA credit card sales is *incorrect*?
a. The credit card issuer makes the credit investigation of the customer.
b. The retailer is not involved in the collection process.
c. Two parties are involved.
d. The retailer receives cash more quickly than it would from individual customers on account.

(SO 4) **8.** Morgan Retailers accepted $50,000 of Citibank VISA credit card charges for merchandise sold on July 1. Citibank charges 4% for its credit card use. The entry to record this transaction by Morgan Retailers will include a credit to Sales of $50,000 and a debit(s) to:

a. Cash	$48,000
and Service Charge Expense	2,000
b. Accounts Receivable	$48,000
and Service Charge Expense	$2,000
c. Cash	$50,000
d. Accounts Receivable	$50,000

9. Bickner Co. accepts a $1,000, 3-month, 12% promissory (SO 6) note in settlement of an account with Streisand Co. The entry to record this transaction is as follows.

a. Notes Receivable	1,030	
Accounts Receivable		1,030
b. Notes Receivable	1,000	
Accounts Receivable		1,000
c. Notes Receivable	1,000	
Sales		1,000
d. Notes Receivable	1,020	
Accounts Receivable		1,020

10. Schlicht Co. holds Osgrove Inc.'s $10,000, 120-day, 9% note. (SO 8) The entry made by Schlicht Co. when the note is collected, assuming no interest has been previously accrued, is:

a. Cash	10,300	
Notes Receivable		10,300
b. Cash	10,000	
Notes Receivable		10,000
c. Accounts Receivable	10,300	
Notes Receivable		10,000
Interest Revenue		300
d. Cash	10,300	
Notes Receivable		10,000
Interest Revenue		300

✓ THE NAVIGATOR

QUESTIONS

1. What is the difference between an account receivable and a note receivable?

2. What are some common types of receivables other than accounts receivable and notes receivable?

3. Texaco Oil Company issues its own credit cards. Assume that Texaco charges you $40 on an unpaid balance. Prepare the journal entry that Texaco makes to record this revenue.

4. What are the essential features of the allowance method of accounting for bad debts?

5. Soo Eng cannot understand why cash realizable value does not decrease when an uncollectible account is written off under the allowance method. Clarify this point for Soo Eng.

6. Distinguish between the two bases that may be used in estimating uncollectible accounts.

7. Hersee Company has a credit balance of $3,500 in Allowance for Doubtful Accounts. The estimated bad debts expense under the percentage of sales basis is $4,100. The total estimated uncollectibles under the percentage of receivables basis is $5,800. Prepare the adjusting entry under each basis.

8. How are bad debts accounted for under the direct write-off method? What are the disadvantages of this method?

9. Hope Company accepts both its own credit cards and national credit cards. What are the advantages of accepting both types of cards?

10. An article recently appeared in *The Wall Street Journal* indicating that companies are selling their receivables at a record rate. Why are companies selling their receivables?

11. Eastern Textiles decides to sell $800,000 of its accounts receivable to First Factors Inc. First Factors assesses a service charge of 2% of the amount of receivables sold. Prepare the journal entry that Eastern Textiles makes to record this sale.

12. Your roommate is uncertain about the advantages of a promissory note. Compare the advantages of a note receivable with those of an account receivable.

13. How may the maturity date of a promissory note be stated?

14. Indicate the maturity date of each of the following promissory notes:

Date of Note	Terms
(a) March 13	one year after date of note
(b) May 4	3 months after date
(c) June 20	30 days after date
(d) July 1	60 days after date

15. Compute the missing amounts for each of the following notes.

	Principal	Annual Interest Rate	Time	Total Interest
(a)	?	9%	120 days	$ 450
(b)	$30,000	10%	3 years	?
(c)	$60,000	?	5 months	$3,000
(d)	$50,000	11%	?	$1,375

16. In determining interest revenue, some financial institutions use 365 days per year and others use 360 days. Why might a financial institution use 360 days?

17. May Company dishonors a note at maturity. What actions by May may occur with the dishonoring of the note?

18. **General Motors Corporation** has accounts receivable and notes receivable. How should the receivables be reported on the balance sheet?

19. The accounts receivable turnover ratio is 8.25, and average net receivables during the period are $300,000. What is the amount of net credit sales for the period?

BRIEF EXERCISES

BE9-1   Presented below are three receivables transactions. Indicate whether these receivables are reported as accounts receivable, notes receivable, or other receivables on a balance sheet.

Identify different types of receivables.
(SO 1)

(a) Sold merchandise on account for $70,000 to a customer.
(b) Received a promissory note of $57,000 for services performed.
(c) Advanced $10,000 to an employee.

BE9-2   Record the following transactions on the books of Essex Co.

Record basic accounts receivable transactions.
(SO 2)

(a) On July 1, Essex Co. sold merchandise on account to Harrard Inc. for $16,000, terms 2/10, n/30.
(b) On July 8, Harrard Inc. returned merchandise worth $3,800 to Essex Co.
(c) On July 11, Harrard Inc. paid for the merchandise.

BE9-3   During its first year of operations, Jose Company had credit sales of $3,000,000; $600,000 remained uncollected at year-end. The credit manager estimates that $36,000 of these receivables will become uncollectible.

Prepare entries for allowance method and classifications.
(SO 3, 9)

(a) Prepare the journal entry to record the estimated uncollectibles.
(b) Prepare the current assets section of the balance sheet for Jose Company. Assume that in addition to the receivables it has cash of $90,000, merchandise inventory of $130,000, and prepaid expenses of $13,000.

BE9-4   At the end of 2002, Searcy Co. has accounts receivable of $700,000 and an allowance for doubtful accounts of $54,000. On January 24, 2003, the company learns that its receivable from Hunt Inc. is not collectible, and management authorizes a write-off of $7,000.

Prepare entries for write-off; determine cash realizable value.
(SO 3)

(a) Prepare the journal entry to record the write-off.
(b) What is the cash realizable value of the accounts receivable (1) before the write-off and (2) after the write-off?

BE9-5   Assume the same information as BE9-4. On March 4, 2003, Searcy Co. receives payment of $7,000 in full from Hunt Inc. Prepare the journal entries to record this transaction.

Prepare entries for collection of bad debts write-off.
(SO 3)

BE9-6   Massey Co. elects to use the percentage of sales basis in 2002 to record bad debts expense. It estimates that 2% of net credit sales will become uncollectible. Sales are $800,000 for 2002, sales returns and allowances are $40,000, and the allowance for doubtful accounts has a credit balance of $12,000. Prepare the adjusting entry to record bad debts expense in 2002.

Prepare entry using percentage of sales method.
(SO 3)

Prepare entry using percentage of receivables method.
(SO 3)

BE9-7 St. Pierre Co. uses the percentage of accounts receivable basis to record bad debts expense. It estimates that 2% of accounts receivable will become uncollectible. Accounts receivable are $400,000 at the end of the year, and the allowance for doubtful accounts has a credit balance of $3,000.

(a) Prepare the adjusting journal entry to record bad debts expense for the year.
(b) If the allowance for doubtful accounts had a debit balance of $800 instead of a credit balance of $3,000, determine the amount to be reported for bad debts expense.

Compute interest and determine maturity dates on notes.
(SO 5)

BE9-8 Compute interest and find the maturity date for the following notes.

	Date of Note	Principal	Interest Rate (%)	Terms
(a)	June 10	$100,000	9%	60 days
(b)	July 14	$ 50,000	7½%	90 days
(c)	April 27	$ 12,000	8%	75 days

Determine maturity dates and compute interest and rates on notes.
(SO 5)

BE9-9 Presented below are data on three promissory notes. Determine the missing amounts.

	Date of Note	Terms	Maturity Date	Principal	Annual Interest Rate	Total Interest
(a)	April 1	60 days	?	$900,000	9%	?
(b)	July 2	30 days	?	90,000	?	$600
(c)	March 7	6 months	?	120,000	12%	?

Prepare entries to dispose of accounts receivable.
(SO 4)

BE9-10 Presented below are two independent transactions.

(a) Raja Restaurant accepted a VISA card in payment of a $200 lunch bill. The bank charges a 3% fee. What entry should Raja make?
(b) Wendy Company sold its accounts receivable of $80,000. What entry should Wendy make, given a service charge of 3% on the amount of receivables sold?

Prepare entry for notes receivable exchanged for account receivable.
(SO 6)

BE9-11 On January 10, 2002, Opal Co. sold merchandise on account to Fernando Alvarez for $12,000, n/30. On February 9, Fernando Alvarez gave Opal Co. a 10% promissory note in settlement of this account. Prepare the journal entry to record the sale and the settlement of the account receivable.

Compute ratios to analyze receivables.
(SO 9)

BE9-12 The financial statements of **Minnesota Mining and Manufacturing Company (3M)** report net sales of $15.0 billion. Accounts receivable are $2.5 billion at the beginning of the year and $2.8 billion at the end of the year. Compute 3M's receivables turnover ratio. Compute 3M's average collection period for accounts receivable in days.

*E*XERCISES

Journalize entries for recognizing accounts receivable.
(SO 2)

E9-1 Presented below are two independent situations.

(a) On January 6, Whitney Co. sells merchandise on account to Julio, Inc. for $5,000, terms 2/10, n/30. On January 16, Julio, Inc. pays the amount due. Prepare the entries on Whitney's books to record the sale and related collection.
(b) On January 10, Sue Ernesto uses her Oregon Co. credit card to purchase merchandise from Oregon Co. for $11,000. On February 10, Ernesto is billed for the amount due of $11,000. On February 12, Ernesto pays $6,000 on the balance due. On March 10, Ernesto is billed for the amount due, including interest at 2% per month on the unpaid balance as of February 12. Prepare the entries on Oregon Co.'s books related to the transactions that occurred on January 10, February 12, and March 10.

Journalize entries to record allowance for doubtful accounts using two different bases.
(SO 3)

E9-2 The ledger of Salizar Company at the end of the current year shows Accounts Receivable $110,000, Sales $840,000, and Sales Returns and Allowances $40,000.

Instructions

(a) If Allowance for Doubtful Accounts has a credit balance of $2,500 in the trial balance, journalize the adjusting entry at December 31, assuming bad debts are expected to be (1) 1% of net sales, and (2) 10% of accounts receivable.
(b) If Allowance for Doubtful Accounts has a debit balance of $500 in the trial balance, journalize the adjusting entry at December 31, assuming bad debts are expected to be (1) 0.75% of net sales and (2) 6% of accounts receivable.

E9-3 Patillo Company has accounts receivable of $97,500 at March 31. An analysis of the accounts shows the following.

Determine bad debts expense; prepare the adjusting entry for bad debts expense.
(SO 3)

Month of Sale	Balance, March 31
March	$65,000
February	17,600
January	8,500
Prior to January	6,400
	$97,500

Credit terms are 2/10, n/30. At March 31, Allowance for Doubtful Accounts has a credit balance of $1,600 prior to adjustment. The company uses the percentage of receivables basis for estimating uncollectible accounts. The company's estimate of bad debts is as follows.

Age of Accounts	Estimated Percentage Uncollectible
1–30 days past due	2.0%
30–60 days past due	5.0%
60–90 days past due	30.0%
Over 90 days	50.0%

Instructions

(a) Determine the total estimated uncollectibles.

(b) Prepare the adjusting entry at March 31 to record bad debts expense.

E9-4 On December 31, 2002, Garcia Co. estimates that 2% of its net sales of $400,000 will become uncollectible. The company records this amount as an addition to Allowance for Doubtful Accounts. On May 11, 2003, Garcia Co. determined that Ray William's account was uncollectible and wrote off $1,100. On June 12, 2003, William paid the amount previously written off.

Journalize percentage of sales basis, write-off, recovery.
(SO 3)

Instructions

Prepare the journal entries on December 31, 2002, May 11, 2003, and June 12, 2003.

E9-5 Presented below are two independent situations.

Journalize entries for the sale of accounts receivable.
(SO 4)

(a) On March 3, Lisa Ceja Appliances sells $700,000 of its receivables to Horatio Factors Inc. Horatio Factors assesses a finance charge of 3% of the amount of receivables sold. Prepare the entry on Lisa Ceja Appliances' books to record the sale of the receivables.

(b) On May 10, Worthy Company sold merchandise for $4,000 and accepted the customer's Firstar Bank MasterCard. At the end of the day, the Firstar Bank MasterCard receipts were deposited in the company's bank account. Firstar Bank charges a 4% service charge for credit card sales. Prepare the entry on Worthy Company's books to record the sale of merchandise.

E9-6 Presented below are two independent situations.

Journalize entries for credit card sales.
(SO 4)

(a) On April 2, Sue Moat uses her J. C. Penney Company credit card to purchase merchandise from a J.C. Penney store for $1,300. On May 1, Moat is billed for the $1,300 amount due. Moat pays $700 on the balance due on May 3. On June 1, Moat receives a bill for the amount due, including interest at 1.0% per month on the unpaid balance as of May 3. Prepare the entries on J. C. Penney Co.'s books related to the transactions that occurred on April 2, May 3, and June 1.

(b) On July 4, Healy's Restaurant accepts an American Express card for a $300 dinner bill. American Express charges a 4% service fee. On July 10, American Express pays Healy $288. Prepare the entries on Healy's books related to the transactions.

E9-7 Satter Stores accepts both its own and national credit cards. During the year the following selected summary transactions occurred.

Journalize credit card sales, and indicate the statement presentation of financing charges and service charge expense.
(SO 4)

Jan. 15   Made Satter credit card sales totaling $15,000. (There were no balances prior to January 15.)

     20   Made American Express credit card sales (service charge fee 5%) totaling $4,500.

30   Received payment in full from American Express less a 5% service charge.
Feb. 10   Collected $12,000 on Satter credit card sales.
15   Added finance charges of 1.5% to Satter credit card balance.

Instructions

(a) Journalize the transactions for Satter Stores.
(b) Indicate the statement presentation of the financing charges and the credit card service expense for Satter Stores.

Journalize entries for notes receivable transactions.
(SO 5, 6)

E9-8   Gore Supply Co. has the following transactions related to notes receivable during the last 2 months of the year.

Nov. 1   Loaned $18,000 cash to Sally Morgan on a 1-year, 10% note.
Dec. 11   Sold goods to Sue Adams, Inc., receiving a $6,000, 90-day, 12% note.
16   Received a $4,000, 6-month, 12% note on account from Prentice Berge.
31   Accrued interest revenue on all notes receivable.

Instructions

Journalize the transactions for Gore Supply Co.

Journalize entries for notes receivable.
(SO 5, 6)

E9-9   Record the following transactions for Icke Co. in the general journal.

2002

May 1   Received a $10,500, 1-year, 10% note on account from Paul Warfield
Dec. 31   Accrued interest on the Warfield note.
Dec. 31   Closed the interest revenue account.

2003

May 1   Received principal plus interest on the Warfield note. (No interest has been accrued in 2003.)

Journalize entries for dishonor of notes receivable.
(SO 5, 8)

E9-10   On May 2, Chung Company lends $7,000 to Ann Johnson, Inc., issuing a 6-month, 10% note. At the maturity date, November 2, Johnson indicates that it cannot pay.

Instructions

(a) Prepare the entry to record the dishonor of the note, assuming that Chung Company expects collection will occur.
(b) Prepare the entry to record the dishonor of the note, assuming that Chung Company does not expect collection in the future.

Determine missing amounts related to sales and accounts receivable.
(SO 2, 4, 9)

E9-11 The following information pertains to Moosa Merchandising Company.

Merchandise inventory at end of year	$33,000
Accounts receivable at beginning of year	24,000
Cash sales made during the year	15,000
Gross profit on sales	27,000
Accounts receivable written off during the year	1,000
Purchases made during the year	60,000
Accounts receivable collected during the year	78,000
Merchandise inventory at beginning of year	36,000

Instructions

(a) Calculate the amount of credit sales made during the year. (*Hint:* You will need to use income statement relationships—introduced in Chapter 5—in order to determine this.)
(b) Calculate the balance of accounts receivable at the end of the year.

PROBLEMS: SET A

Prepare journal entries related to bad debts expense.
(SO 2, 3, 4)

P9-1A   At December 31, 2002, Cellular Ten Co. reported the following information on its balance sheet.

Accounts receivable	$960,000
Less: Allowance for doubtful accounts	70,000

During 2003, the company had the following transactions related to receivables.

1.	Sales on account	$3,300,000
2.	Sales returns and allowances	50,000
3.	Collections of accounts receivable	2,800,000
4.	Write-offs of accounts receivable deemed uncollectible	90,000
5.	Recovery of bad debts previously written off as uncollectible	25,000

Instructions

(a) Prepare the journal entries to record each of these five transactions. Assume that no cash discounts were taken on the collections of accounts receivable.

(b) Enter the January 1, 2003, balances in Accounts Receivable and Allowance for Doubtful Accounts, post the entries to the two accounts (use T accounts), and determine the balances.

(b) Accounts receivable
$1,320,000
ADA $5,000

(c) Prepare the journal entry to record bad debts expense for 2003, assuming that an aging of accounts receivable indicates that expected bad debts are $125,000.

(c) Bad debts expense
$120,000

(d) Compute the accounts receivable turnover ratio for 2003.

P9-2A Information related to Holland Company for 2002 is summarized below.

Compute bad debts amounts.
(SO 3)

Total credit sales	$2,100,000
Accounts receivable at December 31	840,000
Bad debts written off	38,000

Instructions

(a) What amount of bad debts expense will Holland Company report if it uses the direct write-off method of accounting for bad debts?

(b) Assume that Holland Company estimates its bad debts expense to be 3% of credit sales. What amount of bad debts expense will Holland record if it has an Allowance for Doubtful Accounts credit balance of $4,000?

(c) Assume that Holland Company estimates its bad debts expense based on 6% of accounts receivable. What amount of bad debts expense will Holland record if it has an Allowance for Doubtful Accounts credit balance of $3,000?

(d) Assume the same facts as in (c), except that there is a $3,000 debit balance in Allowance for Doubtful Accounts. What amount of bad debts expense will Holland record?

(e) What is the weakness of the direct write-off method of reporting bad debts expense?

P9-3A Presented below is an aging schedule for Sandy Grifton Company.

Journalize entries to record transactions related to bad debts.
(SO 2, 3)

Customer	Total	Not Yet Due	Number of Days Past Due			
			1–30	31–60	61–90	Over 90
Anita	$ 22,000		$10,000	$12,000		
Barry	40,000	$ 40,000				
Chagnon	57,000	16,000	6,000		$35,000	
David	34,000					$34,000
Others	132,000	96,000	16,000	14,000		6,000
	$285,000	$152,000	$32,000	$26,000	$35,000	$40,000
Estimated Percentage Uncollectible		4%	7%	13%	25%	50%
Total Estimated Bad Debts	$ 40,450	$ 6,080	$ 2,240	$ 3,380	$ 8,750	$20,000

At December 31, 2002, the unadjusted balance in Allowance for Doubtful Accounts is a credit of $12,000.

Instructions

(a) Journalize and post the adjusting entry for bad debts at December 31, 2002.

(a) Bad debts expense
$28,450

(b) Journalize and post to the allowance account the following events and transactions in the year 2003.

　(1) On March 31, a $1,000 customer balance originating in 2002 is judged uncollectible.

　(2) On May 31, a check for $1,000 is received from the customer whose account was written off as uncollectible on March 31.

(c) Bad debts expense $31,100

(c) Journalize the adjusting entry for bad debts on December 31, 2003, assuming that the unadjusted balance in Allowance for Doubtful Accounts is a debit of $800 and the aging schedule indicates that total estimated bad debts will be $30,300.

Journalize entries to record transactions related to bad debts.
(SO 3)

P9-4A At December 31, 2002, the trial balance of Lexington Company contained the following amounts before adjustment.

	Debits	Credits
Accounts Receivable	$400,000	
Allowance for Doubtful Accounts		$ 800
Sales		930,000

Instructions

(a) Based on the information given, which method of accounting for bad debts is Lexington Company using—the direct write-off method or the allowance method? How can you tell?

(b) (2) $9,300

(b) Prepare the adjusting entry at December 31, 2002, for bad debts expense under each of the following independent assumptions.

　(1) An aging schedule indicates that $11,750 of accounts receivable will be uncollectible.

　(2) The company estimates that 1% of sales will be uncollectible.

(c) Repeat part (b) assuming that instead of a credit balance there is an $800 debit balance in Allowance for Doubtful Accounts.

(d) During the next month, January 2003, a $5,000 account receivable is written off as uncollectible. Prepare the journal entry to record the write-off.

(e) Repeat part (d) assuming that Lexington uses the direct write-off method instead of the allowance method in accounting for uncollectible accounts receivable.

(f) ✏️ What type of account is the Allowance for Doubtful Accounts? How does it affect how accounts receivable is reported on the balance sheet at the end of the accounting period?

Prepare entries for various notes receivable transactions.
(SO 2, 4, 5, 8, 9)

Peachtree

P9-5A Melanie Griffith Company closes its books monthly. On September 30, selected ledger account balances are:

Notes Receivable	$28,000
Interest Receivable	$ 216

Notes Receivable include the following.

Date	Maker	Face	Term	Interest
Aug. 16	Foran Inc.	$ 8,000	60 days	12%
Aug. 25	Drexler Co.	8,000	60 days	12%
Sept. 30	Sego Corp.	12,000	6 months	9%

Interest is computed using a 360-day year. During October, the following transactions were completed.

Oct.　7　Made sales of $6,900 on Melanie Griffith credit cards.
　　　12　Made sales of $750 on MasterCard credit cards. The credit card service charge is 4%.
　　　15　Added $485 to Melanie Griffith customer balance for finance charges on unpaid balances.
　　　15　Received payment in full from Foran Inc. on the amount due.
　　　24　Received notice that Drexler note has been dishonored. (Assume that Drexler is expected to pay in the future.)

Instructions

(a) Journalize the October transactions and the October 31 adjusting entry for accrued interest receivable.

(b) Enter the balances at October 1 in the receivable accounts. Post the entries to all of the receivable accounts.

(c) Show the balance sheet presentation of the receivable accounts at October 31.

(b) Accounts receivable
$15,545
(c) Total receivables $27,635

P9-6A On January 1, 2002, John Diego Company had Accounts Receivable $146,000, Notes Receivable $15,000, and Allowance for Doubtful Accounts $13,200. The note receivable is from Trudy Borke Company. It is a 4-month, 12% note dated December 31, 2001. John Diego Company prepares financial statements annually. During the year the following selected transactions occurred.

Prepare entries for various receivable transactions.
(SO 2, 4, 5, 6, 7, 8)

Jan.	5	Sold $18,000 of merchandise to Jones Company, terms n/15.
	20	Accepted Jones Company's $18,000, 3-month, 9% note for balance due.
Feb.	18	Sold $8,000 of merchandise to Swan Company and accepted Swan's $8,000, 6-month, 10% note for the amount due.
Apr.	20	Collected Jones Company note in full.
	30	Received payment in full from Trudy Borke Company on the amount due.
May	25	Accepted Avita Inc.'s $6,000, 3-month, 8% note in settlement of a past-due balance on account.
Aug.	18	Received payment in full from Swan Company on note due.
	25	The Avita Inc. note was dishonored. Avita Inc. is not bankrupt; future payment is anticipated.
Sept.	1	Sold $12,000 of merchandise to Jose Trevino Company and accepted a $12,000, 6-month, 10% note for the amount due.

Instructions

Journalize the transactions.

PROBLEMS: SET B

P9-1B At December 31, 2002, Murlow Imports reported the following information on its balance sheet.

Prepare journal entries related to bad debts expense.
(SO 2, 3, 4)

Accounts receivable	$1,000,000
Less: Allowance for doubtful accounts	60,000

During 2003, the company had the following transactions related to receivables.

1.	Sales on account	$2,700,000
2.	Sales returns and allowances	40,000
3.	Collections of accounts receivable	2,300,000
4.	Write-offs of accounts receivable deemed uncollectible	65,000
5.	Recovery of bad debts previously written off as uncollectible	25,000

Instructions

(a) Prepare the journal entries to record each of these five transactions. Assume that no cash discounts were taken on the collections of accounts receivable.

(b) Enter the January 1, 2003, balances in Accounts Receivable and Allowance for Doubtful Accounts. Post the entries to the two accounts (use T accounts), and determine the balances.

(c) Prepare the journal entry to record bad debts expense for 2003, assuming that an aging of accounts receivable indicates that estimated bad debts are $95,000.

(d) Compute the accounts receivable turnover ratio for the year 2003.

(b) Accounts receivable
$1,295,000
ADA $20,000
(c) Bad debts expense $75,000

P9-2B Information related to Cain Company for 2002 is summarized below.

Compute bad debts amounts.
(SO 3)

Total credit sales	$1,600,000
Accounts receivable at December 31	640,000
Bad debts written off	26,000

Instructions

(a) What amount of bad debts expense will Cain Company report if it uses the direct write-off method of accounting for bad debts?

(b) Assume that Cain Company decides to estimate its bad debts expense to be 3% of credit sales. What amount of bad debts expense will Cain record if Allowance for Doubtful Accounts has a credit balance of $3,000?

(c) Assume that Cain Company decides to estimate its bad debts expense based on 5% of accounts receivable. What amount of bad debts expense will Cain Company record if Allowance for Doubtful Accounts has a credit balance of $4,000?

(d) Assume the same facts as in (c), except that there is a $2,000 debit balance in Allowance for Doubtful Accounts. What amount of bad debts expense will Cain record?

(e) ▭▰▰▰▰▰▶ What is the weakness of the direct write-off method of reporting bad debts expense?

Journalize entries to record transactions related to bad debts.
(SO 2, 3)

P9-3B This is an aging schedule for Timban Company.

Customer	Total	Not Yet Due	Number of Days Past Due			
			1–30	**31–60**	**61–90**	**Over 90**
Aber	$ 20,000		$ 9,000	$11,000		
Bohr	30,000	$ 30,000				
Case	50,000	15,000	5,000		$30,000	
Datz	38,000					$38,000
Others	126,000	92,000	15,000	13,000		6,000
	$264,000	$137,000	$29,000	$24,000	$30,000	$44,000
Estimated Percentage Uncollectible			3%	6%	12%	24%	50%
Total Estimated Bad Debts	$ 37,930	$ 4,110	$ 1,740	$ 2,880	$ 7,200	$22,000

At December 31, 2002, the unadjusted balance in Allowance for Doubtful Accounts is a credit of $10,000.

Instructions

(a) Bad debts expense $27,930

(a) Journalize and post the adjusting entry for bad debts at December 31, 2002.

(b) Journalize and post to the allowance account the following events and transactions in the year 2003.

    (1) March 1, an $1,100 customer balance originating in 2002 is judged uncollectible.

    (2) May 1, a check for $1,100 is received from the customer whose account was written off as uncollectible on March 1.

(c) Bad debts expense $30,300

(c) Journalize the adjusting entry for bad debts on December 31, 2003. Assume that the unadjusted balance in Allowance for Doubtful Accounts is a debit of $1,200, and the aging schedule indicates that total estimated bad debts will be $29,100.

Journalize entries to record transactions related to bad debts.
(SO 3)

P9-4B At December 31, 2002, the trial balance of Mario Tizani Company contained the following amounts before adjustment.

	Debits	**Credits**
Accounts Receivable	$350,000	
Allowance for Doubtful Accounts		$ 1,300
Sales		860,000

Instructions

(a) (2) $17,200

(a) Prepare the adjusting entry at December 31, 2002, to record bad debts expense under each of the following independent assumptions.

    (1) An aging schedule indicates that $16,750 of accounts receivable will be uncollectible.

    (2) The company estimates that 2% of sales will be uncollectible.

(b) Repeat part (a) assuming that instead of a credit balance, there is a $1,300 debit balance in Allowance for Doubtful Accounts.

(c) During the next month, January 2003, a $4,500 account receivable is written off as uncollectible. Prepare the journal entry to record the write-off.

(d) Repeat part (c) assuming that Mario Tizani Company uses the direct write-off method instead of the allowance method in accounting for uncollectible accounts receivable.

(e) ⬜▭▭▭➤ What are the advantages of using the allowance method in accounting for uncollectible accounts as compared to the direct write-off method?

P9-5B John Gleason Co. closes its books monthly. On June 30, selected ledger account balances are:

Prepare entries for various notes receivable transactions.
(SO 2, 4, 5, 8, 9)

Notes Receivable	$31,000
Interest Receivable	$ 245

Notes Receivable include the following.

Date	Maker	Face	Term	Interest
May 21	Alder Inc.	$ 6,000	60 days	12%
May 25	Dorn Co.	15,000	60 days	11%
June 30	MJH Corp.	10,000	6 months	9%

During July, the following transactions were completed.

July 5 Made sales of $6,200 on John Gleason Co. credit cards.
    14 Made sales of $700 on VISA credit cards. The credit card service charge is 3%.
    16 Added $440 to John Gleason Co. credit card customer balances for finance charges on unpaid balances.
    20 Received payment in full from Alder Inc. on the amount due.
    25 Received notice that Dorn Co. note has been dishonored. (Assume that Dorn Co. is expected to pay in the future.)

Instructions

(a) Journalize the July transactions and the July 31 adjusting entry for accrued interest receivable. (Interest is computed using 360 days.)

(b) Enter the balances at July 1 in the receivable accounts. Post the entries to all of the receivable accounts.

(c) Show the balance sheet presentation of the receivable accounts at July 31.

(b) Accounts receivable $21,915

(c) Total receivables $31,990

P9-6B On January 1, 2002, Case Western Company had Accounts Receivable $54,200 and Allowance for Doubtful Accounts $4,700. Case Western Company prepares financial statements annually. During the year the following selected transactions occurred.

Prepare entries for various receivables transactions.
(SO 2, 4, 5, 6, 7, 8)

Jan. 5 Sold $7,000 of merchandise to Garth Brooks Company, terms n/30.
Feb. 2 Accepted a $7,000, 4-month, 12% promissory note from Garth Brooks Company for balance due.
    12 Sold $7,800 of merchandise to Gage Company and accepted Gage's $7,800, 2-month, 10% note for the balance due.
    26 Sold $4,000 of merchandise to Mathias Co., terms n/10.
Apr. 5 Accepted a $4,000, 3-month, 8% note from Mathias Co. for balance due.
    12 Collected Gage Company note in full.
June 2 Collected Garth Brooks Company note in full.
July 5 Mathias Co. dishonors its note of April 5. It is expected that Mathias will eventually pay the amount owed.
    15 Sold $5,000 of merchandise to Tritt Co. and accepted Tritt's $5,000, 3-month, 12% note for the amount due.
Oct. 15 Tritt Co.'s note was dishonored. Tritt Co. is bankrupt, and there is no hope of future settlement.

Instructions
Journalize the transactions.

BROADENING YOUR PERSPECTIVE

Financial REPORTING AND ANALYSIS

FINANCIAL REPORTING PROBLEM: SCH Company

BYP9-1 SCH Company sells office equipment and supplies to many organizations in the city and surrounding area on contract terms of 2/10, n/30. In the past, over 75% of the credit customers have taken advantage of the discount by paying within 10 days of the invoice date.

The number of customers taking the full 30 days to pay has increased within the last year. Current indications are that less than 60% of the customers are now taking the discount. Bad debts as a percentage of gross credit sales have risen from the 1.5% provided in past years to about 4% in the current year.

The company's Finance Committee has requested more information on the collections of accounts receivable. The controller responded to this request with the report reproduced below.

SCH COMPANY
Accounts Receivable Collections
May 31, 2002

The fact that some credit accounts will prove uncollectible is normal. Annual bad debts write-offs have been 1.5% of gross credit sales over the past 5 years. During the last fiscal year, this percentage increased to slightly less than 4%. The current Accounts Receivable balance is $1,400,000. The condition of this balance in terms of age and probability of collection is as follows.

Proportion of Total	Age Categories	Probability of Collection
60%	not yet due	98%
22%	less than 30 days past due	95$\frac{1}{2}$%
9%	30 to 60 days past due	94%
5%	61 to 120 days past due	91%
2$\frac{1}{2}$%	121 to 180 days past due	75%
1$\frac{1}{2}$%	over 180 days past due	30%

The Allowance for Doubtful Accounts had a credit balance of $29,500 on June 1, 2001. SCH has provided for a monthly bad debts expense accrual during the current fiscal year based on the assumption that 4% of gross credit sales will be uncollectible. Total gross credit sales for the 2001–02 fiscal year amounted to $2,800,000. Write-offs of bad accounts during the year totaled $96,000.

Instructions

(a) Prepare an accounts receivable aging schedule for SCH Company using the age categories identified in the controller's report to the Finance Committee showing the following.
  (1) The amount of accounts receivable outstanding for each age category and in total.
  (2) The estimated amount that is uncollectible for each category and in total.
(b) Compute the amount of the year-end adjustment necessary to bring Allowance for Doubtful Accounts to the balance indicated by the age analysis. Then prepare the necessary journal entry to adjust the accounting records.
(c) In a recessionary environment with tight credit and high interest rates:
  (1) Identify steps SCH Company might consider to improve the accounts receivable situation.
  (2) Then evaluate each step identified in terms of the risks and costs involved.

COMPARATIVE ANALYSIS PROBLEM: Lands' End vs. Abercrombie & Fitch

BYP9-2 Lands' End's financial statements are presented in Appendix A. Abercrombie & Fitch's financial statements are presented in Appendix B.

Instructions

   (a) Based on the information contained in these financial statements, compute the following 2000 ratios for each company. (Assume all sales are credit sales.)
     (1) Accounts receivable turnover ratio.
     (2) Average collection period for receivables.
   (b) What conclusions concerning the management of accounts receivable can be drawn from these data?

INTERPRETING FINANCIAL STATEMENTS: A Global Focus

BYP9-3   **Art World Industries, Inc.** was incorporated in 1986 in Delaware, and is located in Los Angeles. The company prints, publishes, and sells limited-edition graphics and reproductive prints in the wholesale market.

    The company's balance sheet at the end of a recent year showed an allowance for doubtful accounts of $175,477. The allowance was set up against certain Japanese accounts receivable that average more than one year in age. The Japanese acknowledge the amount due, but with the slow economy in Japan lack the resources to pay at this time.

Instructions

   (a) Which method of accounting for uncollectible accounts does Art World Industries use?
   (b) Explain the difference between the direct write-off and percentage of receivables methods. Based on Art World's disclosure above, what important factor would you have to consider in arriving at appropriate percentages to apply for the percentage of receivables method?
   (c) What are the implications for a company's receivables management of selling its products internationally?

EXPLORING THE WEB

BYP9-4   *Purpose:* The Security Exchange Act of 1934 requires any firm that is listed on one of the national exchanges to file annual reports (form 10-K), financial statements, and quarterly reports (form 10-Q) with the SEC. This exercise demonstrates how to search and access available SEC filings through the Internet.

Address: biz.yahoo.com/i *(or go to www.wiley.com/college/weygandt)*

Steps:

  1. Type in a company's name, or use index to find a company name.
  2. Choose **Profile**.
  3. Choose **Raw SEC Filings**.

Instructions
Answer the following questions.

   (a) Which SEC filings were available for the company you selected?
   (b) In the company's quarterly report (SEC form 10-Q), what was one key point discussed in the "Management's Discussion and Analysis of Results of Operations and Financial Condition"?
   (c) What was the net income for the period selected?

CRITICAL THINKING

GROUP DECISION CASE

BYP9-5   Johanna and Jake Berkvom own Campus Fashions. From its inception Campus Fashions has sold merchandise on either a cash or credit basis, but no credit cards have been accepted. During the past several months, the Berkvoms have begun to question their sales policies. First, they have lost some sales because of refusing to accept credit cards. Second, representatives of two metropolitan banks have been persuasive in almost convincing them to accept their national credit cards. One bank, City National Bank, has stated that (1) its credit card fee is 4%, and (2) it pays the retailer 96 cents on each $1 of sales within 3 days of receiving the credit card billings.

The Berkvoms decide that they should determine the cost of carrying their own credit sales. From the accounting records of the past 3 years they accumulate the following data.

	2002	2001	2000
Net credit sales	$500,000	$600,000	$400,000
Collection agency fees for slow-paying customers	2,450	2,500	2,400
Salary of part-time accounts receivable clerk	3,800	3,800	3,800

Credit and collection expenses as a percentage of net credit sales are: uncollectible accounts 1.6%, billing and mailing costs 0.5%, and credit investigation fee on new customers 0.15%.

Johanna and Jake also determine that the average accounts receivable balance outstanding during the year is 5% of net credit sales. The Berkvoms estimate that they could earn an average of 10% annually on cash invested in other business opportunities.

Instructions
With the class divided into groups, answer the following.
(a) Prepare a table showing, for each year, total credit and collection expenses in dollars and as a percentage of net credit sales.
(b) Determine the net credit and collection expense in dollars and as a percentage of sales after considering the revenue not earned from other investment opportunities. (*Note:* The income lost on the cash held by the bank for 3 days is considered to be immaterial.)
(c) Discuss both the financial and nonfinancial factors that are relevant to the decision.

COMMUNICATION ACTIVITY

BYP9-6 Jackie Henning, a friend of yours, overheard a discussion at work about changes her employer wants to make in accounting for uncollectible accounts. Jackie knows little about accounting, and she asks you to help make sense of what she heard. Specifically, she asks you to explain the differences between the percentage of sales, percentage of receivables, and the direct write-off methods for uncollectible accounts.

Instructions
In a letter of one page (or less), explain to Jackie the three methods of accounting for uncollectibles. Be sure to discuss differences among these methods.

ETHICS CASE

BYP 9-7 The controller of Shirt Co. believes that the yearly allowance for doubtful accounts for Shirt Co. should be 2% of net credit sales. The president of Shirt Co., nervous that the stockholders might expect the company to sustain its 10% growth rate, suggests that the controller increase the allowance for doubtful accounts to 4%. The president thinks that the lower net income, which reflects a 6% growth rate, will be a more sustainable rate for Shirt Co.

Instructions
(a) Who are the stakeholders in this case?
(b) Does the president's request pose an ethical dilemma for the controller?
(c) Should the controller be concerned with Shirt Co.'s growth rate in estimating the allowance? Explain your answer.

Answers to Self-Study Questions
1. c **2.** a **3.** b **4.** b **5.** d **6.** c **7.** c **8.** a **9.** b **10.** d

Answer to Lands' End Review It Question 3, p. 371

At the time of sale, the company provides a reserve equal to the gross profit on projected merchandise returns, based on its prior return experience.

Remember to go back to the Navigator box on the chapter-opening page and check off your completed work.

PLANT ASSETS, NATURAL RESOURCES, AND INTANGIBLE ASSETS

10

*C*ONCEPTS FOR REVIEW

Before studying this chapter, you should know or, if necessary, review:

    a. The time period assumption. (Ch. 3, p. 89)

    b. The cost principle (Ch. 1, p. 10) and the matching principle. (Ch. 3, pp. 90–91)

    c. What is depreciation? (Ch. 3, p. 95)

    d. How to make adjustments for depreciation. (Ch. 3, pp. 95–97)

☑ THE NAVIGATOR

How Much Must I Pay for a Ride to the Beach?

It's spring break. Your plane has landed, you've finally found your bags, and you're dying to hit the beach—but first you need a "vehicular unit" to get you there. As you turn away from baggage claim you see a long row of rental agency booths. Many are names you are familiar with—Hertz, Avis, and Budget. But a booth at the far end catches your eye—**Rent-A-Wreck**. Now there's a company making a clear statement!

Any company that relies on equipment to generate revenues must make decisions about what kind of equipment to buy, how long to keep it, and how vigorously to maintain it. Rent-A-Wreck has decided to rent used rather than new cars and trucks. It rents these vehicles across the United States, Europe, and Asia. While the big-name agencies push vehicles with that "new car smell,"

Rent-A-Wreck competes on price. The message is simple: Rent a used car and save some cash. It's not a message that appeals to everyone. If you're a marketing executive wanting to impress a big client, you probably don't want to pull up in a Rent-A-Wreck car. But if you want to get from point A to point B for the minimum cash per mile, then they are playing your tune. The company's message seems to be getting across to the right clientele. Revenues have increased from $29.9 million in 1996 to $51.7 million in 2000.

When you rent a car from Rent-A-Wreck, you are renting from an independent business person who has paid a "franchise fee" for the right to use the Rent-A-Wreck name. In order to gain a franchise, he or she must meet financial and other criteria, and must agree to run the

rental agency according to rules prescribed by Rent-A-Wreck. Some of these rules require that each franchise maintain its cars in a reasonable fashion. This ensures that, though you might not be flying down Daytona Beach's Atlantic Avenue in a Mercedes convertible, you can be reasonably assured that you won't be calling a tow-truck.

THE NAVIGATOR

www.rent-a-wreck.com

STUDY OBJECTIVES

After studying this chapter, you should be able to:

1. Describe the application of the cost principle to plant assets.
2. Explain the concept of depreciation.
3. Compute periodic depreciation using different methods.
4. Describe the procedure for revising periodic depreciation.
5. Distinguish between revenue and capital expenditures, and explain the entries for these expenditures.
6. Explain how to account for the disposal of a plant asset through retirement, sale, or exchange.
7. Compute periodic depletion of natural resources.
8. Contrast the accounting for intangible assets with the accounting for plant assets.
9. Indicate how plant assets, natural resources, and intangible assets are reported and analyzed.

THE NAVIGATOR

The accounting for long-term assets has important implications for a company's reported results. In this chapter, we explain the application of the cost principle of accounting to property, plant, and equipment, such as **Rent-A-Wreck** vehicles, as well as to natural resources and intangible assets such as the "Rent-A-Wreck" trademark. We also describe the methods that may be used to allocate an asset's cost over its useful life. In addition, the accounting for expenditures incurred during the useful life of assets, such as the cost of replacing tires and brake pads on rental cars, is discussed.

The content and organization of Chapter 10 are as follows.

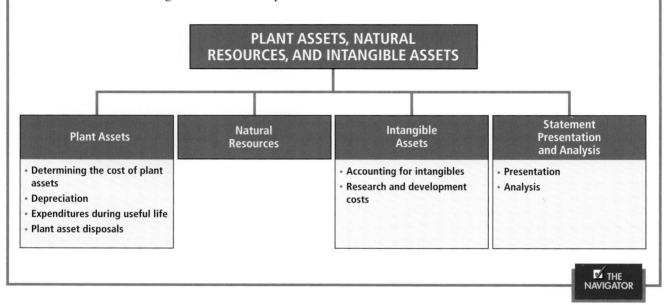

PLANT ASSETS, NATURAL RESOURCES, AND INTANGIBLE ASSETS

Plant Assets	Natural Resources	Intangible Assets	Statement Presentation and Analysis
• Determining the cost of plant assets • Depreciation • Expenditures during useful life • Plant asset disposals		• Accounting for intangibles • Research and development costs	• Presentation • Analysis

☑ THE NAVIGATOR

SECTION 1 *Plant Assets*

Plant assets are tangible resources that are used in the operations of a business and are not intended for sale to customers. They are also called **property**, **plant**, **and equipment**; **plant and equipment**; or **fixed assets**. These assets are generally long-lived. They are expected to provide services to the company for a number of years. Except for land, plant assets decline in service potential over their useful lives. Many companies have substantial investments in plant assets. Illustration 10-1 shows the percentages of plant assets in relation to total assets of companies in a number of industries.

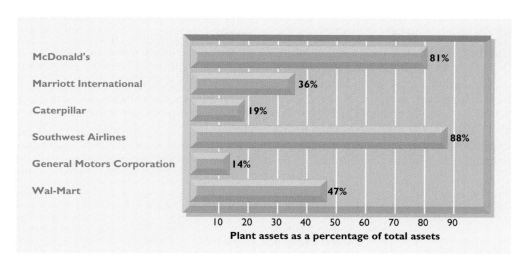

Illustration 10-1

Percentages of plant assets in relation to total assets

Plant assets are often subdivided into four classes:

1. **Land**, such as a building site.
2. **Land improvements**, such as driveways, parking lots, fences, and underground sprinkler systems.
3. **Buildings**, such as stores, offices, factories, and warehouses.
4. **Equipment**, such as store check-out counters, cash registers, coolers, office furniture, factory machinery, and delivery equipment.

Like the purchase of a home by an individual, the acquisition of plant assets is an important decision for a business. It is also important for a business to (1) keep assets in good operating condition, (2) replace worn-out or outdated assets, and (3) expand its productive resources as needed. The decline of rail travel in the United States can be traced in part to the failure of railroad companies to meet the first two conditions. The growth of U.S. air travel is due in part to airlines having generally met these conditions.

DETERMINING THE COST OF PLANT ASSETS

Plant assets are recorded **at cost** in accordance with the **cost principle** of accounting. Thus the vehicles at **Rent-A-Wreck** are recorded at cost. Cost consists of **all expenditures necessary to acquire the asset and make it ready for its intended use**. For example, the cost of factory machinery includes the purchase price, freight costs paid by the purchaser, and installation costs. Once cost is established, it becomes the basis of accounting for the plant asset over its useful life. Current market or replacement values are not used after acquisition.

The application of the cost principle to each of the major classes of plant assets is explained in the following sections.

LAND

The cost of land includes the cash purchase price plus other related costs. These costs might include closing costs such as title and attorney's fees, real estate brokers' commissions, and accrued property taxes and other liens on the land assumed by the purchaser. For example, if the cash price is $50,000 and the purchaser agrees to pay accrued taxes of $5,000, the cost of the land is $55,000.

STUDY OBJECTIVE 1

Describe the application of the cost principle to plant assets.

INTERNATIONAL NOTE

The United Kingdom (UK) is more flexible than the U.S. about asset valuation. Most companies in the UK make revaluations to fair value when they believe fair value is more relevant. Other countries that permit revaluations are Switzerland and the Netherlands.

HELPFUL HINT

Management's intended use is important in applying the cost principle.

All necessary costs incurred to make land **ready for its intended use** are debited to the Land account. For vacant land, these costs include expenditures for clearing, draining, filling, and grading. Sometimes the land has a building on it that must be removed before construction of a new building. In this case, all demolition and removal costs, less any proceeds from salvaged materials, are debited to the Land account. To illustrate, assume that Hayes Manufacturing Company acquires land for $100,000. An old warehouse on the property is razed at a net cost of $6,000 ($7,500 in costs less $1,500 proceeds from salvaged materials). Other expenditures are the attorney's fee, $1,000, and the real estate broker's commission, $8,000. The cost of the land is $115,000, computed as follows.

Illustration 10-2

Computation of cost of land

Land	
Cash price of property	$100,000
Net removal cost of warehouse	6,000
Attorney's fee	1,000
Real estate broker's commission	8,000
Cost of land	**$115,000**

In recording the acquisition, Land is debited for $115,000 and Cash is credited for $115,000.

LAND IMPROVEMENTS

The cost of land improvements includes all expenditures needed to make the improvements ready for their intended use. For example, the cost of a new company parking lot will include the amount paid for paving, fencing, and lighting. Thus, these costs are debited to Land Improvements. Because these improvements have limited useful lives and their maintenance and replacement are the responsibility of the company, **they are depreciated over their useful lives**.

BUILDINGS

All necessary costs related to the purchase or construction of a building are debited to the Buildings account. When a building is purchased, such costs include the purchase price, closing costs (attorney's fees, title insurance, etc.) and broker's commission. Costs to make the building ready for its intended use include expenditures for remodeling and replacing or repairing the roof, floors, electrical wiring, and plumbing.

When a new building is constructed, cost consists of the contract price plus payments for architects' fees, building permits, and excavation costs. Also, interest costs incurred to finance the project are included when a significant period of time is required to get the building ready for use. These interest costs are considered as necessary as materials and labor. The inclusion of interest costs is **limited to the construction period**, however. When construction has been completed, subsequent interest payments on funds borrowed to finance the construction are debited to Interest Expense.

EQUIPMENT

HELPFUL HINT

Two criteria apply in determining cost here: (1) the frequency of the cost—one-time or recurring, and (2) the benefit period—life of asset or one year.

The cost of equipment, such as **Rent-A-Wreck** vehicles, consists of the **cash purchase price plus certain related costs**. These costs include **sales taxes, freight charges, and insurance during transit paid by the purchaser**. They also include **expenditures required in assembling, installing, and testing the unit**. However, motor vehicle licenses and accident insurance on company trucks and cars are not included in the cost of equipment. They are treated as expenses as they are incurred. They represent annual recurring expenditures and do not benefit future periods.

To illustrate, assume Merten Company purchases factory machinery at a cash price of $50,000. Related expenditures consist of sales taxes $3,000, insurance during shipping $500, and installation and testing $1,000. The cost of the factory machinery is $54,500, computed as follows.

Illustration 10-3

Computation of cost of factory machinery

Factory Machinery	
Cash price	$50,000
Sales taxes	3,000
Insurance during shipping	500
Installation and testing	1,000
Cost of factory machinery	**$54,500**

The summary entry to record the purchase and related expenditures is:

Factory Machinery	54,500	
Cash		54,500
(To record purchase of factory machine)		

A	=	L	+	OE
+54,500				
−54,500				

For another example, assume that Lenard Company purchases a delivery truck at a cash price of $22,000. Related expenditures consist of sales taxes $1,320, painting and lettering $500, motor vehicle license $80, and a 3-year accident insurance policy $1,600. The cost of the delivery truck is $23,820, computed as follows.

Illustration 10-4

Computation of cost of delivery truck

Delivery Truck	
Cash price	$22,000
Sales taxes	1,320
Painting and lettering	500
Cost of delivery truck	**$23,820**

The motor vehicle license is expensed when incurred; the insurance policy is a prepaid asset. The summary entry to record the purchase of the truck and related expenditures is:

Delivery Truck	23,820	
License Expense	80	
Prepaid Insurance	1,600	
Cash		25,500
(To record purchase of delivery truck and related		
expenditures)		

A	=	L	+	OE
+23,820				−80
+1,600				
−25,500				

BEFORE YOU GO ON...

▶ *REVIEW IT*

1. What are plant assets? What are the major classes of plant assets? How is the cost principle applied to accounting for plant assets?

2. What classifications and amounts does **Lands' End** report on its balance sheet under the heading "Property, plant and equipment, at cost"? The answer to this question is provided on p. 443.

▶ *DO IT*

Assume that a delivery truck is purchased for $15,000 cash, plus sales taxes of $900 and delivery costs to the dealer of $500. The buyer also pays $200 for painting and lettering, $600 for an annual insurance policy, and $80 for a motor vehicle license. Explain how each of these costs would be accounted for.

ACTION PLAN

• Identify expenditures made in order to get delivery equipment ready for its intended use.

• Expense operating costs incurred during the useful life of the equipment.

SOLUTION: The first four payments ($15,000, $900, $500, and $200) are considered to be expenditures necessary to make the truck ready for its intended use. Thus, the cost of the truck is $16,600. The payments for insurance and the license are considered to be operating expenses incurred during the useful life of the asset.

Related exercise material: BE10-1, BE10-2, E10-1, and E10-2.

*D*EPRECIATION

STUDY OBJECTIVE **2**

Explain the concept of depreciation.

As explained in Chapter 3, **depreciation is the allocation of the cost of a plant asset to expense over its useful (service) life in a rational and systematic manner**. Cost allocation provides for the proper matching of expenses with revenues in accordance with the matching principle (see Illustration 10-5).

Illustration 10-5

Depreciation as an allocation concept

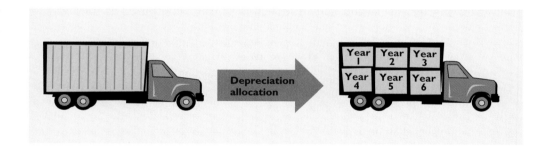

HELPFUL HINT

Remember that depreciation is the allocation of cost over the useful life of an asset. It is not a measure of value.

Depreciation is a process of cost allocation, not a process of asset valuation. The change in an asset's market value is not measured during ownership because plant assets are not held for resale. So, the **book value** (cost less accumulated depreciation) of a plant asset may be quite different from its market value.

Depreciation applies to three classes of plant assets: land improvements, buildings, and equipment. Each asset in these classes is considered to be a **depreciable asset**. Why? Because the usefulness to the company and revenue-producing ability of each asset will decline over the asset's useful life. Depreciation does not apply to land because its usefulness and revenue-producing ability generally remain intact over time. In fact, in many cases, the usefulness of land is greater over time because of the scarcity of good land sites. Thus, **land is not a depreciable asset**.

HELPFUL HINT

Land does not depreciate because it does not wear out.

During a depreciable asset's useful life its revenue-producing ability will decline because of **wear and tear**. A delivery truck that has been driven 100,000 miles will be less useful to a company than one driven only 800 miles. Trucks and planes exposed to snow and salt will deteriorate faster than equipment that is not exposed to these elements.

Revenue-producing ability may also decline because of **obsolescence**. Obsolescence is the process of becoming out of date before the asset physically wears out. Major airlines were re-routed from Chicago's Midway Airport to Chicago-

O'Hare International Airport because Midway's runways were too short for jumbo jets, for example.

It is important to understand that **recognizing depreciation on an asset does not result in an accumulation of cash for replacement of the asset**. The balance in Accumulated Depreciation represents the total cost that has been charged to expense. It is not a cash fund.

FACTORS IN COMPUTING DEPRECIATION

Three factors affect the computation of depreciation:

1. **Cost.** Issues affecting the cost of a depreciable asset were explained earlier in this chapter. Recall that plant assets are recorded at cost, in accordance with the cost principle.

2. **Useful life.** Useful life is an estimate of the expected productive life, also called service life, of the asset. Useful life may be expressed in terms of time, units of activity (such as machine hours), or units of output. Useful life is an estimate. In making the estimate, management considers such factors as the intended use of the asset, its expected repair and maintenance, and its vulnerability to obsolescence. Past experience with similar assets is often helpful in deciding on expected useful life. We might reasonably expect the estimated useful life used by **Rent-A-Wreck** to differ from that used by **Avis**.

3. **Salvage value.** Salvage value is an estimate of the asset's value at the end of its useful life. This value may be based on the asset's worth as scrap or on its expected trade-in value. Like useful life, salvage value is an estimate. In making the estimate, management considers how it plans to dispose of the asset and its experience with similar assets.

ALTERNATIVE TERMINOLOGY
Another term sometimes used for salvage value is *residual value*.

Illustration 10-6 summarizes the three factors used in computing depreciation.

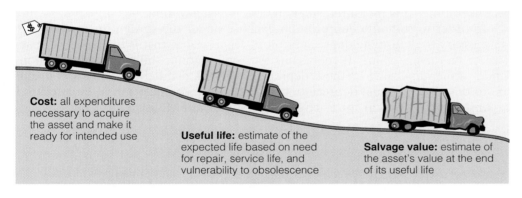

Cost: all expenditures necessary to acquire the asset and make it ready for intended use

Useful life: estimate of the expected life based on need for repair, service life, and vulnerability to obsolescence

Salvage value: estimate of the asset's value at the end of its useful life

Illustration 10-6

Three factors in computing depreciation

HELPFUL HINT
Depreciation expense is reported on the income statement, and accumulated depreciation is reported as a deduction from plant assets on the balance sheet.

ACCOUNTING IN ACTION *Business Insight*

Willamette Industries, Inc., of Portland, Oregon, said in March 1999 that it would change its accounting estimates relating to depreciation of certain assets, beginning with the first quarter of 1999. The vertically integrated forest products company said the changes were due to advances in technology that have increased the service life on its equipment an extra five years. Willamette expected the accounting changes to increase its 1999 full-year earnings by about $57 milion, or $0.52 a share. Its 1998 earnings were $89 million, or $0.80 a share. Imagine a 65 percent improvement in earnings per share from a mere change in the estimated life of equipment!

DEPRECIATION METHODS

STUDY OBJECTIVE 3

Compute periodic depreciation using different methods.

Depreciation is generally computed using one of the following methods:

1. Straight-line
2. Units-of-activity
3. Declining-balance

Each method is acceptable under generally accepted accounting principles. Management selects the method(s) it believes to be appropriate. The objective is to select the method that best measures an asset's contribution to revenue over its useful life. Once a method is chosen, it should be applied consistently over the useful life of the asset. Consistency enhances the comparability of financial statements.

We will compare the three depreciation methods using the following data for a small delivery truck purchased by Barb's Florists on January 1, 2002.

Illustration 10-7

Delivery truck data

Cost	$13,000
Expected salvage value	$ 1,000
Estimated useful life in years	5
Estimated useful life in miles	100,000

Depreciation affects the balance sheet through accumulated depreciation and the income statement through depreciation expense. Illustration 10-8 (in the margin) shows the use of the different depreciation methods in 600 of the largest companies in the United States.

Straight-Line

Under the **straight-line method**, depreciation is the same for each year of the asset's useful life. It is measured solely by the passage of time.

In order to compute depreciation expense under the straight-line method, it is necessary to determine depreciable cost. **Depreciable cost** is the cost of the asset less its salvage value. It represents the total amount subject to depreciation. Under the straight-line method, depreciable cost is divided by the asset's useful life to determine annual depreciation expense. The computation of depreciation expense in the first year for Barb's Florists is shown in Illustration 10-9.

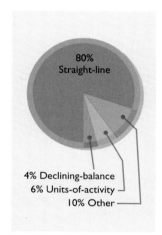

Illustration 10-8

Use of depreciation methods in 600 large U.S. companies

80% Straight-line

4% Declining-balance
6% Units-of-activity
10% Other

Illustration 10-9

Formula for straight-line method

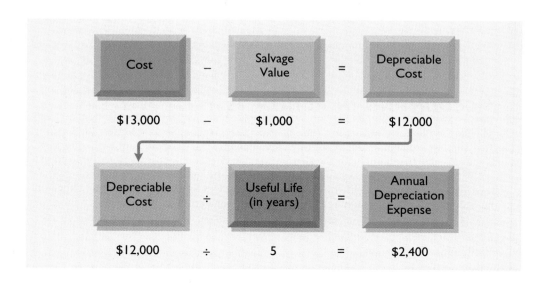

Alternatively, we also can compute an **annual rate of depreciation**. In this case, the rate is 20% (100% ÷ 5 years). When an annual straight-line rate is used, the percentage rate is applied to the depreciable cost of the asset. The use of an annual rate is shown in the following **depreciation schedule**.

	BARB'S FLORISTS					
	Computation			**Annual**	**End of Year**	
Year	**Depreciable Cost**	×	**Depreciation Rate**	= **Depreciation Expense**	**Accumulated Depreciation**	**Book Value**
2002	$12,000		20%	$2,400	$ 2,400	$10,600*
2003	12,000		20	2,400	4,800	8,200
2004	12,000		20	2,400	7,200	5,800
2005	12,000		20	2,400	9,600	3,400
2006	12,000		20	2,400	12,000	1,000

*($13,000 − $2,400).

Illustration 10-10

Straight-line depreciation schedule

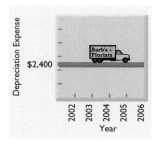

Note that the depreciation expense of $2,400 is the same each year. The book value at the end of the useful life is equal to the estimated $1,000 salvage value.

What happens when an asset is purchased **during** the year, rather than on January 1, as in our example? In that case, it is necessary to **prorate the annual depreciation** on a time basis. If Barb's Florists had purchased the delivery truck on April 1, 2002, the depreciation for 2002 would be $1,800 ($12,000 × 20% × 9/12 of a year).

The straight-line method predominates in practice. Such large companies as **Campbell Soup**, **Marriott Corporation**, and **General Mills** use the straight-line method. It is simple to apply, and it matches expenses with revenues when the use of the asset is reasonably uniform throughout the service life. In the Feature Story, for simplicity **Rent-A-Wreck** is probably using the straight-line method of depreciation for its vehicles.

Units-of-Activity

Under the **units-of-activity method**, useful life is expressed in terms of the total units of production or use expected from the asset, rather than as a time period. The units-of-activity method is ideally suited to factory machinery. Production can be measured in units of output or in machine hours. This method can also be used for such assets as delivery equipment (miles driven) and airplanes (hours in use). The units-of-activity method is generally not suitable for buildings or furniture, because depreciation for these assets is more a function of time than of use.

ALTERNATIVE TERMINOLOGY
Another term often used is the *units-of-production method.*

To use this method, the total units of activity for the entire useful life are estimated, and these units are divided into depreciable cost. The resulting number represents the depreciation cost per unit. The depreciation cost per unit is then applied to the units of activity during the year to determine the annual depreciation expense.

To illustrate, assume that Barb's Florists' delivery truck is driven 15,000 miles in the first year. The computation of depreciation expense in the first year is:

HELPFUL HINT
Under any method, depreciation stops when the asset's book value equals expected salvage value.

Illustration 10-11

Formula for units-of-activity method

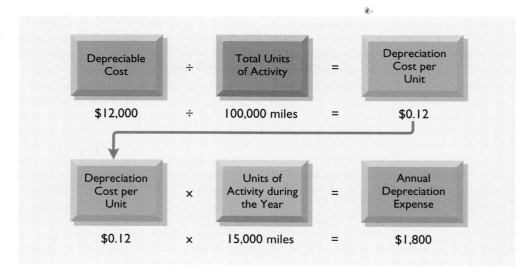

The units-of-activity depreciation schedule, using assumed mileage, is as follows.

Illustration 10-12

Units-of-activity depreciation schedule

	Computation			Annual	End of Year	
Year	**Units of Activity**	×	**Depreciation Cost/Unit**	= **Depreciation Expense**	**Accumulated Depreciation**	**Book Value**
2002	15,000		$0.12	**$1,800**	$ 1,800	$11,200*
2003	30,000		0.12	**3,600**	5,400	7,600
2004	20,000		0.12	**2,400**	7,800	5,200
2005	25,000		0.12	**3,000**	10,800	2,200
2006	10,000		0.12	**1,200**	12,000	**1,000**

*($13,000 − $1,800).

BARB'S FLORISTS

This method is easy to apply when assets are purchased during the year. In such a case, the productivity of the asset for the partial year is used in computing the depreciation.

The units-of-activity method is not nearly as popular as the straight-line method (see Illustration 10-8), primarily because it is often difficult to make a reasonable estimate of total activity. However, this method is used by some very large companies, such as **Chevron Oil** and **Boise Cascade Corporation** (a forestry company). When the productivity of an asset varies significantly from one period to another, the units-of-activity method results in the best matching of expenses with revenues.

Declining-Balance

The **declining-balance method** produces a decreasing annual depreciation expense over the asset's useful life. The method is so named because the periodic depreciation is based on a **declining book value** (cost less accumulated depreciation) of the asset. Annual depreciation expense is computed by multiplying the book value at the beginning of the year by the declining-balance depreciation rate. **The depreciation rate remains constant from year to year, but the book value to which the rate is applied declines each year.**

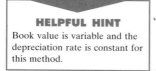

HELPFUL HINT

Book value is variable and the depreciation rate is constant for this method.

Book value at the beginning of the first year is the cost of the asset. This is so because the balance in accumulated depreciation at the beginning of the asset's useful life is zero. In subsequent years, book value is the difference between cost and accumulated depreciation to date. Unlike the other depreciation methods, the declining-balance method does not use depreciable cost. That is, **salvage value is ignored in determining the amount to which the declining-balance rate is applied**. Salvage value, however, does limit the total depreciation that can be taken. Depreciation stops when the asset's book value equals expected salvage value.

A common declining-balance rate is double the straight-line rate. As a result, the method is often referred to as the **double-declining-balance method**. If Barb's Florists uses the double-declining-balance method, the depreciation rate is 40% (2 × the straight-line rate of 20%). The computation of depreciation for the first year on the delivery truck is:

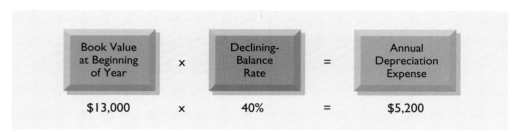

Illustration 10-13

Formula for declining-balance method

The depreciation schedule under this method is as follows.

Illustration 10-14

Double-declining-balance depreciation schedule

| | Computation | | | | End of Year | |
| | Book Value | × | Depreciation | = | Annual Depreciation | Accumulated | Book |
Year	Beginning of Year		Rate		Expense	Depreciation	Value
2002	$13,000		40%		**$5,200**	$ 5,200	$7,800
2003	7,800		40		**3,120**	8,320	4,680
2004	4,680		40		**1,872**	10,192	2,808
2005	2,808		40		**1,123**	11,315	1,685
2006	1,685		40		685*	12,000	**1,000**

BARB'S FLORISTS

*Computation of $674 ($1,685 × 40%) is adjusted to $685 in order for book value to equal salvage value.

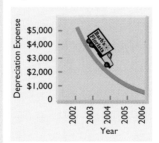

You can see that the delivery equipment is 69% depreciated ($8,320 ÷ $12,000) at the end of the second year. Under the straight-line method it would be depreciated 40% ($4,800 ÷ $12,000) at that time. Because the declining-balance method produces higher depreciation expense in the early years than in the later years, it is considered an **accelerated-depreciation method**. The declining-balance method is compatible with the matching principle. The higher depreciation expense in early years is matched with the higher benefits received in these years. On the other hand, lower depreciation expense is recognized in later years when the asset's contribution to revenue is less. Also, some assets lose usefulness rapidly because of obsolescence. In these cases, the declining-balance method provides a more appropriate depreciation amount.

When an asset is purchased during the year, the first year's declining-balance depreciation must be prorated on a time basis. For example, if Barb's Florists had purchased the truck on April 1, 2002, depreciation for 2002 would become $3,900

HELPFUL HINT
The method to be used for an asset that is expected to be more productive in the first half of its useful life is the declining-balance method.

($13,000 × 40% × 9/12). The book value at the beginning of 2003 is then $9,100 ($13,000 − $3,900), and the 2003 depreciation is $3,640 ($9,100 × 40%). Subsequent computations would follow from those amounts.

Comparison of Methods

A comparison of annual and total depreciation expense under each of the three methods is shown for Barb's Florists in Illustration 10-15.

Illustration 10-15

Comparison of depreciation methods

Year	Straight-Line	Units-of-Activity	Declining-Balance
2002	$ 2,400	$ 1,800	$ 5,200
2003	2,400	3,600	3,120
2004	2,400	2,400	1,872
2005	2,400	3,000	1,123
2006	2,400	1,200	685
	$12,000	$12,000	$12,000

Observe that annual depreciation varies considerably among the methods. But total depreciation is the same for the 5-year period under all three methods. Each method is acceptable in accounting, because each recognizes the decline in service potential of the asset in a rational and systematic manner. The depreciation expense pattern under each method is presented graphically in Illustration 10-16.

Illustration 10-16

Patterns of depreciation

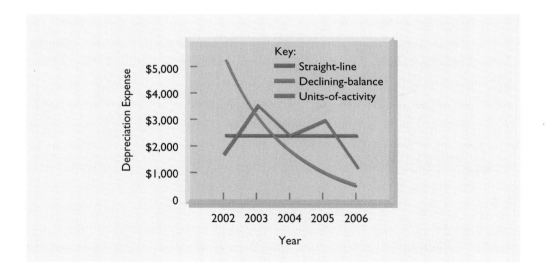

DEPRECIATION AND INCOME TAXES

The Internal Revenue Service (IRS) allows corporate taxpayers to deduct depreciation expense when they compute taxable income. However, the IRS does not require the taxpayer to use the same depreciation method on the tax return that is used in preparing financial statements. Many corporations use straight-line in their financial statements to maximize net income. At the same time, they use a special accelerated-depreciation method on their tax returns to minimize their income taxes. Taxpayers must use on their tax returns either the straight-line method or a special accelerated-depreciation method called the **Modified Accelerated Cost Recovery System** (MACRS).

*T*ECHNOLOGY IN ACTION

 Software packages to account for plant assets exist for both large and small computer systems. Even the least sophisticated packages can maintain a control and subsidiary ledger for plant assets and make the necessary depreciation computations and adjusting entries. Many packages also maintain separate depreciation schedules for both financial statement and income tax purposes, with reconciliations made for any differences.

REVISING PERIODIC DEPRECIATION

Depreciation is one example of the use of estimation in the accounting process. Annual depreciation expense should be reviewed periodically by management. If wear and tear or obsolescence indicate that annual depreciation estimates are inadequate or excessive, a change should be made.

When a change in an estimate is required, the change is made in **current and future years**. It is not made retroactively **to prior periods**. Thus, there is no correction of previously recorded depreciation expense. Instead, depreciation expense for current and future years is revised. The rationale is that continual restatement of prior periods would adversely affect confidence in financial statements.

To determine the new annual depreciation expense, we first compute the asset's depreciable cost at the time of the revision. We then allocate the revised depreciable cost to the remaining useful life. To illustrate, assume that Barb's Florists decides on January 1, 2005, to extend the useful life of the truck one year because of its excellent condition. The company has used the straight-line method to depreciate the asset to date, and book value is $5,800 ($13,000 − $7,200). The new annual depreciation is $1,600, computed as follows.

STUDY OBJECTIVE **4**

Describe the procedure for revising periodic depreciation.

Book value, 1/1/05	$5,800
Less: Salvage value	1,000
Depreciable cost	$4,800
Remaining useful life	3 years (2005–2007)
Revised annual depreciation ($4,800 ÷ 3)	**$1,600**

Illustration 10-17

Revised depreciation computation

Barb's Florists makes no entry for the change in estimate. On December 31, 2005, during the preparation of adjusting entries, it would record depreciation expense of $1,600. Significant changes in estimates must be described in the financial statements.

HELPFUL HINT
Use a step-by-step approach: (1) determine new depreciable cost; (2) divide by remaining useful life.

BEFORE YOU GO ON...

▶ *REVIEW IT*
1. What is the relationship, if any, of depreciation to (a) cost allocation, (b) asset valuation, and (c) cash accumulation?
2. Explain the factors that affect the computation of depreciation.

3. What are the formulas for computing annual depreciation under each of the depreciation methods?

4. How do the methods differ in terms of their effects on annual depreciation over the useful life of the asset?

5. Are revisions of periodic depreciation made to prior periods? Explain.

▶ *DO IT*

On January 1, 2002, Iron Mountain Ski Corporation purchased a new snow-grooming machine for $50,000. The machine is estimated to have a 10-year life with a $2,000 salvage value. What journal entry would Iron Mountain Ski Corporation make at December 31, 2002, if it uses the straight-line method of depreciation?

ACTION PLAN
• Calculate depreciable cost (Cost − Salvage value).
• Divide the depreciable cost by the estimated useful life.

SOLUTION

$$\text{Depreciation expense} = \frac{\text{Cost} - \text{Salvage value}}{\text{Useful life}} = \frac{\$50,000 - \$2,000}{10} = \$4,800$$

The entry to record the first year's depreciation would be:

Dec. 31	Depreciation Expense	4,800	
	Accumulated Depreciation		4,800
	(To record annual depreciation on snow-grooming machine)		

Related exercise material: BE10-3, BE10-4, BE10-5, BE10-6, E10-3, and E10-4.

 THE NAVIGATOR

EXPENDITURES DURING USEFUL LIFE

STUDY OBJECTIVE 5

Distinguish between revenue and capital expenditures, and explain the entries for these expenditures.

During the useful life of a plant asset a company may incur costs for ordinary repairs, additions, or improvements. **Ordinary repairs** are expenditures to maintain the operating efficiency and productive life of the unit. They usually are fairly small amounts that occur frequently. Motor tune-ups and oil changes, the painting of buildings, and the replacing of worn-out gears on machinery are examples. Such repairs are debited to Repair (or Maintenance) Expense as they are incurred. Because they are immediately charged as an expense against revenues, these costs are often referred to as **revenue expenditures**.

Additions and improvements are costs incurred to increase the operating efficiency, productive capacity, or useful life of a plant asset. They are usually material in amount and occur infrequently. Additions and improvements increase the company's investment in productive facilities and are generally debited to the plant asset affected. They are often referred to as **capital expenditures**. Most major U.S. corporations disclose annual capital expenditures. In a recent year, both IBM and General Motors reported capital expenditures slightly in excess of $6 billion.

PLANT ASSET DISPOSALS

STUDY OBJECTIVE 6

Explain how to account for the disposal of a plant asset through retirement, sale, or exchange.

Plant assets may be disposed of in three ways—retirement, sale, or exchange—as shown in Illustration 10-18. Whatever the method, at the time of disposal it is necessary to determine the book value of the plant asset. As noted earlier, book value is the difference between the cost of a plant asset and the accumulated depreciation to date.

Retirement
Equipment is scrapped
or discarded.

Sale
Equipment is sold
to another party.

Exchange
Existing equipment is traded
for new equipment.

Illustration 10-18

Methods of plant asset
disposal

At the time of disposal, depreciation for the fraction of the year to the date of disposal must be recorded. The book value is then eliminated by debiting (decreasing) Accumulated Depreciation for the total depreciation to date and crediting (decreasing) the asset account for the cost of the asset. In this section we will examine the accounting for each of the three methods of plant asset disposal.

RETIREMENT OF PLANT ASSETS

To illustrate the retirement of plant assets, assume that Hobart Enterprises retires its computer printers, which cost $32,000. The accumulated depreciation on these printers is $32,000. The equipment, therefore, is fully depreciated (zero book value). The entry to record this retirement is as follows.

Accumulated Depreciation—Printing Equipment	32,000	
Printing Equipment		32,000
(To record retirement of fully depreciated equipment)		

A	=	L	+	OE
+32,000				
−32,000				

What happens if a fully depreciated plant asset is still useful to the company? In this case, the asset and its accumulated depreciation continue to be reported on the balance sheet without further depreciation adjustment until the asset is retired. Reporting the asset and related accumulated depreciation on the balance sheet informs the financial statement reader that the asset is still in use. However, once an asset is fully depreciated, even if it is still being used, no additional depreciation should be taken. In no situation can the accumulated depreciation on a plant asset exceed its cost.

If a plant asset is retired before it is fully depreciated, and no scrap or salvage value is received, a loss on disposal occurs. For example, assume that Sunset Company discards delivery equipment that cost $18,000 and has accumulated depreciation of $14,000. The entry is as follows.

> **HELPFUL HINT**
> When a plant asset is disposed of, all amounts related to the asset must be removed from the accounts. This includes the original cost in the asset account and the total depreciation to date in the accumulated depreciation account.

Accumulated Depreciation—Delivery Equipment	14,000	
Loss on Disposal	4,000	
Delivery Equipment		18,000
(To record retirement of delivery equipment at a loss)		

A	=	L	+	OE
+14,000				−4,000
−18,000				

The loss on disposal is reported in the "other expenses and losses" section of the income statement.

SALE OF PLANT ASSETS

In a disposal by sale, the book value of the asset is compared with the proceeds received from the sale. **If the proceeds of the sale exceed the book value of the plant asset, a gain on disposal occurs. If the proceeds of the sale are less than the book value of the plant asset sold, a loss on disposal occurs.**

Only by coincidence will the book value and the fair market value of the asset be the same when the asset is sold. Gains and losses on sales of plant assets are therefore quite common. For example, **Delta Airlines** reported a $94,343,000 gain on the sale of five **Boeing** B-727-200 aircraft and five **Lockheed** L-1011-1 aircraft.

Gain on Disposal

To illustrate a gain, assume that on July 1, 2002, Wright Company sells office furniture for $16,000 cash. The office furniture originally cost $60,000. As of January 1, 2002, it had accumulated depreciation of $41,000. Depreciation for the first 6 months of 2002 is $8,000. The entry to record depreciation expense and update accumulated depreciation to July 1 is as follows.

A	=	L	+	OE
−8,000				−8,000

July 1	Depreciation Expense	8,000	
	Accumulated Depreciation—Office Furniture		8,000
	(To record depreciation expense for the first 6 months of 2002)		

After the accumulated depreciation balance is updated, a gain on disposal of $5,000 is computed:

Illustration 10-19

Computation of gain on disposal

Cost of office furniture	$60,000
Less: Accumulated depreciation ($41,000 + $8,000)	49,000
Book value at date of disposal	11,000
Proceeds from sale	16,000
Gain on disposal	**$ 5,000**

The entry to record the sale and the gain on disposal is as follows.

A	=	L	+	OE
+16,000				+5,000
+49,000				
−60,000				

July 1	Cash	16,000	
	Accumulated Depreciation—Office Furniture	49,000	
	Office Furniture		60,000
	Gain on Disposal		5,000
	(To record sale of office furniture at a gain)		

The gain on disposal is reported in the "other revenues and gains" section of the income statement.

Loss on Disposal

Assume that instead of selling the office furniture for $16,000, Wright sells it for $9,000. In this case, a loss of $2,000 is computed:

Illustration 10-20

Computation of loss on disposal

Cost of office furniture	$60,000
Less: Accumulated depreciation	49,000
Book value at date of disposal	11,000
Proceeds from sale	9,000
Loss on disposal	**$ 2,000**

The entry to record the sale and the loss on disposal is as follows.

July 1	Cash	9,000	
	Accumulated Depreciation—Office Furniture	49,000	
	Loss on Disposal	2,000	
	Office Furniture		60,000
	(To record sale of office furniture at a loss)		

A	=	L	+	OE
+9,000				−2,000
+49,000				
−60,000				

The loss on disposal is reported in the "other expenses and losses" section of the income statement.

EXCHANGE OF PLANT ASSETS

Plant assets may also be disposed of through exchange. Exchanges can be for either similar or dissimilar assets. Because exchanges of similar assets are more common, they are discussed here. An exchange of similar assets occurs, for example, when old office furniture is exchanged for new office furniture. In an exchange of similar assets, the new asset performs the **same function** as the old asset.

In exchanges of similar plant assets, it is necessary to determine two things: (1) the cost of the asset acquired, and (2) the gain or loss on the asset given up. Because a noncash asset is given up in the exchange, cost is the **cash equivalent price** paid. That is, cost is the fair market value of the asset given up plus the cash paid. The gain or loss on disposal is the **difference between the fair market value and the book value of the asset given up**. These determinations are explained and illustrated below.

> **HELPFUL HINT**
> A building costing $200,000 was destroyed by fire. At the date of the fire, accumulated depreciation was $150,000. Insurance proceeds were $325,000. Prepare the entry to record the insurance proceeds and disposition of building. Answer: Debit Cash $325,000; debit Accumulated Depreciation $150,000; credit Building $200,000; and credit Gain on Disposal $275,000.

Loss Treatment

A loss on the exchange of similar assets is recognized immediately. To illustrate, assume that Roland Company exchanged old office equipment for new office equipment. The book value of the old equipment is $26,000 (cost $70,000 less accumulated depreciation $44,000). Its fair market value is $10,000, and cash of $81,000 is paid. The cost of the new office equipment, $91,000, is computed as follows.

Fair market value of old office equipment	$10,000
Cash	81,000
Cost of new office equipment	**$91,000**

Illustration 10-21

Computation of cost of new office equipment

A loss on disposal of $16,000 on this exchange is incurred. The reason is that the book value is greater than the fair market value of the asset given up. The computation is as follows.

Book value of old office equipment ($70,000 − $44,000)	$26,000
Fair market value of old office equipment	10,000
Loss on disposal	**$16,000**

Illustration 10-22

Computation of loss on disposal

In recording an exchange at a loss, three steps are required: (1) Eliminate the book value of the asset given up, (2) record the cost of the asset acquired, and (3) recognize the loss on disposal. The entry for Roland Company is as follows.

A	=	L	+	OE
+91,000				−16,000
+44,000				
−70,000				
−81,000				

Office Equipment (new)	91,000	
Accumulated Depreciation—Office Equipment (old)	44,000	
Loss on Disposal	16,000	
Office Equipment (old)		70,000
Cash		81,000
(To record exchange of old office equipment for similar new equipment)		

Gain Treatment

A gain on the exchange of similar assets is not recognized immediately but, instead, is deferred. This is done by reducing the cost basis of the new asset. In determining the cost of the new asset, compute the **cost before deferral of the gain** and then the **cost after deferral of the gain**.

To illustrate, assume that Mark's Express Delivery decides to exchange its old delivery equipment plus cash of $3,000 for new delivery equipment. The book value of the old delivery equipment is $12,000 (cost $40,000 less accumulated depreciation $28,000). The fair market value of the old delivery equipment is $19,000.

The cost of the new asset (before deferral of the gain) is the **fair market value of the old asset exchanged plus any cash (or other consideration given up)**. The cost of the new delivery equipment (before deferral of the gain) is $22,000, computed as follows.

HELPFUL HINT

Why aren't gains on the exchange of similar assets recognized? Because the earnings process is not considered completed. To be conservative, however, losses are recognized.

Illustration 10-23

Cost of new equipment (before deferral of gain)

Fair market value of old delivery equipment	$19,000
Cash	3,000
Cost of new delivery equipment (before deferral of gain)	**$22,000**

A gain results when the fair market value is greater than the book value of the asset given up. For Mark's Express, there is a gain of $7,000, computed as follows, on the disposal.

Illustration 10-24

Computation of gain on disposal

Fair market value of old delivery equipment	$19,000
Book value of old delivery equipment ($40,000 − $28,000)	12,000
Gain on disposal	**$ 7,000**

The $7,000 gain on disposal is then offset against the $22,000 cost of the new delivery equipment. The result is a $15,000 cost of the new delivery equipment, after deferral of the gain, as shown in Illustration 10-25.

Illustration 10-25

Cost of new equipment (after deferral of gain)

Cost of new delivery equipment (before deferral of gain)	$22,000
Less: Gain on disposal	7,000
Cost of new delivery equipment (after deferral of gain)	**$15,000**

The entry to record the exchange is as follows.

Delivery Equipment (new)	15,000		
Accumulated Depreciation—Delivery Equipment (old)	28,000		
Delivery Equipment (old)		40,000	
Cash		3,000	
(To record exchange of old delivery equipment for			
similar new delivery equipment)			

A	=	L	+	OE
+15,000				
+28,000				
−40,000				
−3,000				

This entry does not eliminate the gain; it just postpones or defers it to future periods. The deferred gain of $7,000 reduces the $22,000 cost to $15,000. As a result, net income in future periods increases because depreciation expense on the newly acquired delivery equipment is less by $7,000.

Summarizing, the rules for accounting for exchanges of similar assets are as follows.

Illustration 10-26

Accounting rules for plant asset exchanges

Type of Event	Recognition
Loss	Recognize immediately by debiting Loss on Disposal
Gain	Defer and reduce cost of new asset

BEFORE YOU GO ON...

▶ *REVIEW IT*

1. How does a capital expenditure differ from a revenue expenditure?
2. What is the proper accounting for the retirement and sale of plant assets?
3. What is the proper accounting for the exchange of similar plant assets?

▶ *DO IT*

Overland Trucking has an old truck that cost $30,000. The truck has accumulated depreciation of $16,000 and a fair value of $17,000. Overland has a choice of either selling the truck for $17,000 cash or exchanging the old truck and $3,000 cash for a new truck. What is the entry that Overland Trucking would record under each option?

ACTION PLAN
- Compare the asset's book value and fair value to determine whether a gain or loss has occurred.
- Defer gains on the exchange of similar assets by reducing the recorded value of the new asset.

SOLUTION
Sale of truck for cash:

Cash	17,000		
Accumulated Depreciation—Truck (old)	16,000		
Truck (old)		30,000	
Gain on Disposal [$17,000 − ($30,000 − $16,000)]		3,000	
(To record sale of truck at a gain)			

Exchange of old truck and cash for new truck:

Truck (new)	17,000*		
Accumulated Depreciation—Truck (old)	16,000		
Truck (old)		30,000	
Cash		3,000	
(To record exchange of old truck for similar new truck)			
*($20,000 − $3,000)			

If the old truck is exchanged for the new truck, the $3,000 gain is deferred, and the recorded cost of the new truck is reduced by $3,000.

Related exercise material: BE10-8, BE10-9, BE10-10, BE10-11, E10-6, E10-7, E10-8, and E10-9.

THE NAVIGATOR

SECTION 2 *Natural Resources*

STUDY OBJECTIVE 7

Compute periodic depletion of natural resources.

Natural resources consist of standing timber and underground deposits of oil, gas, and minerals. These long-lived productive assets have two distinguishing characteristics: (1) They are physically extracted in operations (such as mining, cutting, or pumping), and (2) they are replaceable only by an act of nature. The acquisition cost of a natural resource is the price needed to acquire the resource and prepare it for its intended use. For an already discovered resource, such as an existing coal mine, cost is the price paid for the property.

The allocation of the cost of natural resources to expense in a rational and systematic manner over the resource's useful life is called **depletion**. **The units-of-activity method** (learned earlier in the chapter) **is generally used to compute depletion**. The reason it is used is that **depletion generally is a function of the units extracted during the year**.

Under the units-of-activity method, the total cost of the natural resource minus salvage value is divided by the number of units estimated to be in the resource. The result is a depletion cost per unit of product. The depletion cost per unit is then multiplied by the number of units extracted and sold. The result is the annual depletion expense. The formula is as follows.

Illustration 10-27

Formula to compute depletion expense

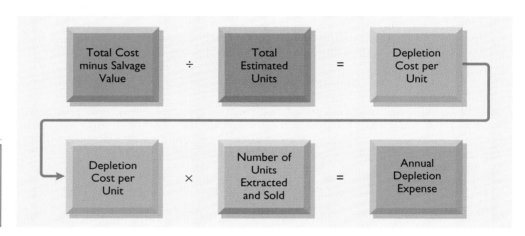

To illustrate, assume that Lane Coal Company invests $5 million in a mine estimated to have 10 million tons of coal and no salvage value. In the first year, 800,000 tons of coal are extracted and sold. Using the formulas above, the computations are as follows:

$$\$5,000,000 \div 10,000,000 = \$0.50 \text{ depletion cost per ton}$$

$$\$0.50 \times 800,000 = \$400,000 \text{ annual depletion expense}$$

The entry to record depletion expense for the first year of operation is as follows.

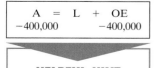

A	=	L	+	OE
−400,000				−400,000

Dec. 31	Depletion Expense	400,000	
	Accumulated Depletion		400,000
	(To record depletion expense on coal		
	deposits)		

The account Depletion Expense is reported as a part of the cost of producing the product. Accumulated Depletion is a contra asset account similar to accumulated depreciation. It is deducted from the cost of the natural resource in the balance sheet, as shown in Illustration 10-28.

LANE COAL COMPANY Balance Sheet (partial)		
Coal mine	$5,000,000	
Less: Accumulated depletion	400,000	$4,600,000

Illustration 10-28

Statement presentation of accumulated depletion

However, in many companies an Accumulated Depletion account is not used. In such cases, the amount of depletion is credited directly to the natural resources account.

Sometimes, natural resources extracted in one accounting period will not be sold until a later period. In this case, depletion is not expensed until the resource is sold. The amount not sold is reported in the current assets section as inventory.

► SECTION 3 *Intangible Assets*

Intangible assets are rights, privileges, and competitive advantages that result from the ownership of long-lived assets that do not possess physical substance. Evidence of intangibles may exist in the form of contracts or licenses. Intangibles may arise from:

1. Government grants, such as patents, copyrights, and trademarks.
2. Acquisition of another business, in which the purchase price includes a payment for the company's favorable attributes (called goodwill).
3. Private monopolistic arrangements arising from contractual agreements, such as franchises and leases.

Some widely known intangibles are the patents of **Polaroid**, the franchises of **McDonald's**, the trade name of Col. Sander's **Kentucky Fried Chicken**, and the trademark **Rent-A-Wreck** in the Feature Story.

*A*CCOUNTING *FOR INTANGIBLE ASSETS*

In general, accounting for intangible assets parallels the accounting for plant assets. That is, **intangible assets are recorded at cost**, and this cost is expensed **over the useful life of the intangible asset in a rational and systematic manner**. At disposal, the book value of the intangible asset is eliminated, and a gain or loss, if any, is recorded.

There are several differences between accounting for intangible assets and accounting for plant assets. First, the term used to describe the allocation of the cost of an intangible asset to expense is **amortization**, rather than depreciation. Also, to record amortization of an intangible, an amortization expense is debited and the specific intangible asset is credited (rather than crediting a contra account). An alternative is to credit an accumulated amortization account, similar to accumulated depreciation.

There is also a difference in determining cost. For plant assets, cost includes both the purchase price of the asset and the costs incurred in designing and constructing the asset. In contrast, cost for an intangible asset includes only the purchase price. Any costs incurred in developing an intangible asset are expensed as incurred.

STUDY OBJECTIVE 8

Contrast the accounting for intangible assets with the accounting for plant assets.

A final difference is that **the amortization period of an intangible asset cannot be longer than 40 years**. Even if the useful life of an intangible asset is 60 years, it must be written off over 40 years. If the useful life is less than 40 years, the useful life is used. This rule ensures that all intangibles, especially those with indeterminable lives, will be written off in a reasonable period of time.

Intangible assets are typically amortized on a straight-line basis. The widespread use of this method adds comparability in accounting for intangible assets.

PATENTS

A **patent** is an exclusive right issued by the U.S. Patent Office that enables the recipient to manufacture, sell, or otherwise control an invention for a period of 20 years from the date of the grant. A patent is nonrenewable. But the legal life of a patent may be extended by obtaining new patents for improvements or other changes in the basic design.

The initial cost of a patent is the cash or cash equivalent price paid to acquire the patent. The saying, "A patent is only as good as the money you're prepared to spend defending it" is very true. Many patents are subject to some type of litigation. For example, **Polaroid** won a patent infringement suit against **Eastman Kodak** in protecting its patent on instant cameras. Legal costs an owner incurs in successfully defending a patent in an infringement suit are considered necessary to establish the validity of the patent. **They are added to the Patent account and amortized over the remaining life of the patent**.

The cost of a patent should be amortized over its 20-year legal life or its useful life, whichever is shorter. Obsolescence and inadequacy should be considered in determining useful life. These factors may cause a patent to become economically ineffective before the end of its legal life.

To illustrate the computation of patent expense, assume that National Labs purchases a patent at a cost of $60,000. If the useful life of the patent is 8 years, the annual amortization expense is $7,500 ($60,000 ÷ 8). The entry to record the annual amortization is:

A	=	L	+	OE			
−7,500				−7,500			

Dec. 31	Amortization Expense—Patents	7,500	
	Patents		7,500
	(To record patent amortization)		

Amortization Expense—Patents is classified as an **operating expense** in the income statement.

COPYRIGHTS

Copyrights are grants from the federal government, giving the owner the exclusive right to reproduce and sell an artistic or published work. Copyrights extend for the life of the creator plus 50 years. The cost of a copyright is the **cost of acquiring and defending it**. The cost may be only the $10 fee paid to the U.S. Copyright Office. Or it may amount to a great deal more if a copyright infringement suit is involved.

Similar to other intangible assets, the maximum write-off is 40 years. The useful life of a copyright generally is significantly shorter than its legal life, though. Therefore, copyrights usually are amortized over a relatively short period of time.

TRADEMARKS AND TRADE NAMES

A **trademark** or **trade name** is a word, phrase, jingle, or symbol that identifies a particular enterprise or product. Trade names like Wheaties, Game Boy, Sunkist, Kleenex, Windows, Coca-Cola, Big Mac, and Jeep create immediate product identification. They also generally enhance the sale of the product. The creator or original user may obtain exclusive legal right to the trademark or trade name by registering it with the U.S. Patent Office. Such registration provides 20 years' protection. The registration may be renewed indefinitely as long as the trademark or trade name is in use.

If the trademark or trade name is **purchased** by the company that will sell the product, its cost is the purchase price. If the trademark or trade name is **developed** by the company itself, the cost includes attorney's fees, registration fees, design costs, successful legal defense costs, and other expenditures directly related to securing it.

As with other intangibles, the cost of trademarks and trade names must be amortized over the shorter of 40 years or the useful life. Because of the uncertainty involved in estimating the useful life, the cost is frequently amortized over a much shorter period.

FRANCHISES AND LICENSES

When you drive down the street in your RAV4 purchased from a **Toyota** dealer, fill up your tank at the corner **Shell** station, eat lunch at **Taco Bell**, or rent a car from **Rent-A-Wreck**, you are dealing with franchises. A **franchise** is a contractual arrangement under which the franchisor grants the franchisee the right to sell certain products, render specific services, or use certain trademarks or trade names. The franchise is usually restricted to a designated geographical area.

Another type of franchise is that entered into between a governmental body (commonly municipalities) and a business enterprise. This franchise permits the enterprise to use public property in performing its services. Examples are the use of city streets for a bus line or taxi service, use of public land for telephone and electric lines, and the use of airwaves for radio or TV broadcasting. Such operating rights are referred to as **licenses**.

When costs can be identified with the acquisition of a franchise or license, an intangible asset should be recognized. Franchises and licenses may be granted for a definite period of time, an indefinite period, or perpetual. The cost of a limited-life franchise (or license) should be amortized over the useful life. If the life is indefinite or perpetual, the cost may be amortized over a reasonable period not to exceed 40 years. Annual payments made under a franchise agreement are recorded as **operating expenses** in the period in which they are incurred.

> ETHICS NOTE
>
> A pharmaceutical company was growing rapidly by buying unwanted drug licensing rights. These licensing rights, reported as intangible assets, represented over 70% of the company's total assets. The company experienced a 50% drop in value when the market realized the rights were being amortized over 40 years. If a more reasonable life had been used to amortize the rights, the company's reported profits would, instead, have been huge losses.

ACCOUNTING IN ACTION *Business Insight*

King World's most valuable asset is the right to license television shows such as "Wheel of Fortune," "Jeopardy," "The Oprah Winfrey Show," and "Inside Edition." Almost 88 percent of its $683.8 million in 1998 came from the fees associated with the rights to licenses on these intangible assets.

GOODWILL

Usually, the largest intangible asset that appears on a company's balance sheet is goodwill. **Goodwill** is the value of all favorable attributes that relate to a business enterprise. These include exceptional management, desirable location, good customer relations, skilled employees, high-quality products, and harmonious relations with labor unions. Some view goodwill as expected earnings in excess of normal earnings. Goodwill is therefore unusual: Unlike other assets such as investments and plant assets, which can be sold individually in the marketplace, goodwill can be identified only with the business as a whole.

HELPFUL HINT
Goodwill is recorded only when it has been purchased along with tangible and identifiable intangible assets of a business.

If goodwill can be identified only with the business as a whole, how can it be determined? One could try to put a dollar value on the factors listed above (exceptional management, desirable location, and so on), but the results would be very subjective. Such subjective valuations would not contribute to the reliability of financial statements. **Therefore, goodwill is recorded only when there is a transaction that involves the purchase of an entire business. In that case, goodwill is the excess of cost over the fair market value of the net assets (assets less liabilities) acquired.**

In recording the purchase of a business, the net assets are debited at their fair market values, cash is credited for the purchase price, and goodwill is debited for the difference. Subsequently, goodwill is written off over its useful life, not to exceed 40 years. The amortization entry generally results in a debit to Amortization Expense—Goodwill and a credit to Goodwill. Goodwill is reported in the balance sheet under intangible assets.

ACCOUNTING IN ACTION *International Insight*

Does the amortization requirement for goodwill create a disadvantage for U.S. companies? British companies do not have to amortize goodwill against earnings. Rather, they bypass the income statement completely and charge goodwill directly to stockholders' equity. For example, **Pillsbury** was purchased by **Grand Met**, a British firm. Many complained that U.S. companies were reluctant to bid for Pillsbury because it would mean that they would have to record a large amount of goodwill, which would substantially depress income in the future.

What can or should be done when accounting practices are different among countries and perhaps give one country a competitive edge?

RESEARCH AND DEVELOPMENT COSTS

HELPFUL HINT
Research and development (R&D) costs are not intangible assets. But because they may ̣to patents and copyrights, ̣̣hem in this section.

Research and development costs are expenditures that may lead to patents, copyrights, new processes, and new products. Many companies spend considerable sums of money on research and development (R&D). For example, in a recent year **IBM** spent over $2.5 billion on R&D, an amount greater than the total expenditure budget of some state governments.

Research and development costs present accounting problems. For one thing, it is sometimes difficult to assign the costs to specific projects. Also, there are uncertainties in identifying the extent and timing of future benefits. As a result, R&D ̣costs are **usually recorded as an expense when incurred**, whether the research and ̣̣̣opment is successful or not.

̣̣̣̣rate, assume that Laser Scanner Company spent $3 million on research ̣̣̣̣ment. This expenditure resulted in the development of two highly successful ̣̣̣nts. The R&D costs, however, cannot be included in the cost of the ̣̣̣ther, they are recorded as an expense when incurred.

̣̣̣y disagree with this accounting approach. They argue that expensing R&D ̣̣ds to understated assets and net income. Others, however, argue that cap- ̣̣g these costs will lead to highly speculative assets on the balance sheet. It ̣̣icult to determine who is right. The controversy illustrates how difficult it is ̣̣tablish proper guidelines for financial reporting.

STATEMENT PRESENTATION AND ANALYSIS

PRESENTATION

Usually plant assets and natural resources are combined under "property, plant, and equipment" in the balance sheet. Intangibles are shown separately under intangible assets. The balances of the major classes of assets, such as land, buildings, and equipment, and accumulated depreciation by major classes or in total should be disclosed in the balance sheet or notes. In addition, the depreciation and amortization methods that were used should be described. Finally, the amount of depreciation and amortization expense for the period should be disclosed.

The financial statement presentation of property, plant, and equipment and intangibles by **Lands' End** in its 2000 balance sheet is shown in Illustration 10-29.

STUDY OBJECTIVE 9

Indicate how plant assets, natural resources, and intangible assets are reported and analyzed.

LANDS' END
DIRECT MERCHANTS

LANDS' END, INC. **Balance Sheet (partial)** **(in thousands)**		
	January 28, 2000	**January 29, 1999**
Property, plant and equipment, at cost		
Land and buildings	$102,776	$102,018
Fixtures and equipment	175,910	154,663
Leasehold improvements	4,453	5,475
Total property, plant and equipment	283,139	262,156
Less: Accumulated depreciation and amortization	117,317	101,570
Property, plant and equipment, net	165,822	160,586
Intangibles, net	966	1,030

Illustration 10-29

Lands' End's presentation of property, plant, and equipment, and intangible assets

The notes to Lands' End's financial statements present greater details, namely, that the intangibles section contains goodwill and trademarks.

Another comprehensive presentation of property, plant, and equipment, excerpted from the balance sheet of **Owens-Illinois**, is shown in Illustration 10-30.

OWENS-ILLINOIS, INC. **Balance Sheet (partial)** **(in millions)**		
Property, plant, and equipment		
Timberlands, at cost, less accumulated depletion		$ 95.4
Buildings and equipment, at cost	$2,207.1	
Less: Accumulated depreciation	1,229.0	978.1
Total property, plant, and equipment		$1,073.5
Intangibles		
Patents		410.0
Total		$1,483.5

Illustration 10-30

Owens-Illinois' presentation of property, plant, and equipment, and intangible assets

The notes to the financial statements of Owens-Illinois identify the major classes of property, plant, and equipment. They also indicate that depreciation is by the straight-line method, depletion is by the units-of-activity method, and amortization is by the straight-line method.

ANALYSIS

We can analyze how efficiently a company uses its assets to generate sales. The **asset turnover ratio** analyzes the productivity of a company's assets. It is computed by dividing net sales by average total assets for the period, as shown in the formula in Illustration 10-31. The computation is for **Lands' End**. Its net sales for 2000 were $1,320 million; its total ending assets were $456 million, and beginning assets also were $456 million.

Illustration 10-31

Asset turnover formula and computation

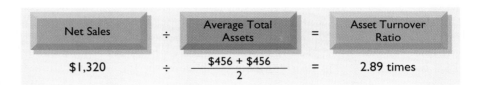

Net Sales	÷	Average Total Assets	=	Asset Turnover Ratio
$1,320	÷	$\dfrac{\$456 + \$456}{2}$	=	2.89 times

This ratio shows the dollars of sales produced for each dollar invested in average total assets. Each dollar invested in assets produced $2.89 in sales for Lands' End. If a company is using its assets efficiently, each dollar of assets will create a high amount of sales. This ratio varies greatly among different industries—from those that are asset intensive (utilities) to those that are not (services).

▶ BEFORE YOU GO ON...

▶ *REVIEW IT*
1. How is depletion expense computed?
2. What are the main differences between accounting for intangible assets and for plant assets?
3. Identify the major types of intangibles and the proper accounting for them.
4. Explain the accounting for research and development costs.
5. What ratio may be computed to analyze property, plant, and equipment?

A *LOOK BACK AT OUR FEATURE STORY*

Refer back to the Feature Story about **Rent-A-Wreck** at the beginning of the chapter, and answer the following questions.
1. Why should Rent-A-Wreck depreciate its vehicles?
2. How could Rent-A-Wreck have an asset with a zero book value but a substantial market value?
3. Give some examples of intangibles other than a trademark that you might find on your college campus.
4. Give some examples of company or product trademarks or trade names. Are trade names and trademarks reported on a company's balance sheet? Explain.

SOLUTION
1. Rent-A-Wreck depreciates its vehicles in order to allocate the cost of the vehicles to the periods in which they are used.
2. An asset can have a zero book value if it has no salvage value and it is fully depreciated—that is, if it has been used for a period longer than its expected life. Because depreciation is used to allocate cost rather than to reflect actual value, it is not at all unlikely that an asset could have a low or zero book value, but a positive market value.

3. Examples of other intangibles that might be found on a college campus are franchise of a bookstore chain or a fast-food outlet, license to operate a radio station, patents developed by professors, and a permit to operate a bus service.

4. Typical company or product trade names are:
   Clothes—Gap, Gitano, Dockers, Calvin Klein, Chaus, Guess.
   Perfume—Passion, Ruffles, Chanel No. 5, Diamonds.
   Cars—TransAm, Nova, Prelude, Cherokee, Outback.
   Shoes—Nike, Florsheim, L.A. Gear, Adidas.
   Breakfast cereals—Cheerios, Wheaties, Frosted Mini-Wheats, Rice Krispies.

Trade names and trademarks are reported on a balance sheet if there is a cost attached to them. If the trade name or trademark has been purchased, the cost is the purchase price. If it has been developed by the enterprise, the cost includes attorney's fees, registration fees, design costs, successful legal defense costs, and other expenditures directly related to securing the trade name or trademark.

☑ THE NAVIGATOR

DEMONSTRATION PROBLEM 1

DuPage Company purchases a factory machine at a cost of $18,000 on January 1, 2002. The machine is expected to have a salvage value of $2,000 at the end of its 4-year useful life.

During its useful life, the machine is expected to be used 160,000 hours. Actual annual hourly use was: 2002, 40,000; 2003, 60,000; 2004, 35,000; and 2005, 25,000.

Additional Demonstration Problem

Instructions
Prepare depreciation schedules for the following methods: (a) the straight-line, (b) units-of-activity, and (c) declining-balance using double the straight-line rate.

SOLUTION TO DEMONSTRATION PROBLEM 1

(a)

Straight-Line Method

| | Computation | | | | End of Year | |
Year	Depreciable Cost	× Depreciation Rate	=	Annual Depreciation Expense	Accumulated Depreciation	Book Value
2002	$16,000	25%		$4,000	$ 4,000	$14,000*
2003	16,000	25%		4,000	8,000	10,000
2004	16,000	25%		4,000	12,000	6,000
2005	16,000	25%		4,000	16,000	2,000

*$18,000 − $4,000.

(b)

Units-of-Activity Method

| | Computation | | | | End of Year | |
Year	Units of Activity	× Depreciation Cost/Unit	=	Annual Depreciation Expense	Accumulated Depreciation	Book Value
2002	40,000	$0.10		$4,000	$ 4,000	$14,000
2003	60,000	0.10		6,000	10,000	8,000
2004	35,000	0.10		3,500	13,500	4,500
2005	25,000	0.10		2,500	16,000	2,000

ACTION PLAN
- Under the straight-line method, apply the depreciation rate to depreciable cost.
- Under the units-of-activity method, compute the depreciation cost per unit by dividing depreciable cost by total units of activity.
- Under the declining-balance method, apply the depreciation rate to **book value** at the beginning of the year.

(c)

Declining-Balance Method

	Computation				End of Year	
Year	Book Value Beginning of Year	× Depreciation Rate	=	Annual Depreciation Expense	Accumulated Depreciation	Book Value
2002	$18,000	50%		$9,000	$ 9,000	$9,000
2003	9,000	50%		4,500	13,500	4,500
2004	4,500	50%		2,250	15,750	2,250
2005	2,250	50%		250*	16,000	2,000

*Adjusted to $250 because ending book value should not be less than expected salvage value.

Additional Demonstration Problem

DEMONSTRATION PROBLEM 2

On January 1, 2000, Skyline Limousine Co. purchased a limo at an acquisition cost of $28,000. The vehicle has been depreciated by the straight-line method using a 4-year service life and a $4,000 salvage value. The company's fiscal year ends on December 31.

Instructions
Prepare the journal entry or entries to record the disposal of the limousine assuming that it was:

(a) Retired and scrapped with no salvage value on January 1, 2004.
(b) Sold for $5,000 on July 1, 2003.
(c) Traded in on a new limousine on January 1, 2003. The fair market value of the old vehicle was $9,000, and $22,000 was paid in cash.
(d) Traded in on a new limousine on January 1, 2003. The fair market value of the old vehicle was $11,000, and $2,000 was paid in cash.

SOLUTION TO DEMONSTRATION PROBLEM 2

ACTION PLAN

- At the time of disposal, determine the book value of the asset.
- Recognize any gain or loss from disposal of the asset.
- Remove the book value of the asset from the records by debiting Accumulated Depreciation for the total depreciation to date of disposal and crediting the asset account for the cost of the asset.

(a)	1/1/04	Accumulated Depreciation—Limousine	24,000	
		Loss on Disposal	4,000	
		Limousine		28,000
		(To record retirement of limousine)		
(b)	7/1/03	Depreciation Expense	3,000	
		Accumulated Depreciation—Limousine		3,000
		(To record depreciation to date of disposal)		
		Cash	5,000	
		Accumulated Depreciation—Limousine	21,000	
		Loss on Disposal	2,000	
		Limousine		28,000
		(To record sale of limousine)		
(c)	1/1/03	Limousine (new)	31,000	
		Accumulated Depreciation—Limousine (old)	18,000	
		Loss on Disposal	1,000	
		Limousine (old)		28,000
		Cash		22,000
		(To record exchange of limousines)		
(d)	1/1/03	Limousine (new)*	12,000	
		Accumulated Depreciation—Limousine (old)	18,000	
		Limousine (old)		28,000
		Cash		2,000
		(To record exchange of limousines)		
		*($11,000 + $2,000 − $1,000)		

SUMMARY OF STUDY OBJECTIVES

1. Describe the application of the cost principle to plant assets. The cost of plant assets includes all expenditures necessary to acquire the asset and make it ready for its intended use. Cost is measured by the cash or cash equivalent price paid.

2. Explain the concept of depreciation. Depreciation is the allocation of the cost of a plant asset to expense over its useful (service) life in a rational and systematic manner. Depreciation is not a process of valuation. Nor is it a process that results in an accumulation of cash. Depreciation is caused by wear and tear or by obsolescence.

3. Compute periodic depreciation using different methods. There are three depreciation methods:

Method	Effect on Annual Depreciation	Formula
Straight-line	Constant amount	Depreciable cost ÷ Useful life (in years)
Units-of-activity	Varying amount	Depreciation cost per unit × Units of activity during the year
Declining-balance	Decreasing amount	Book value at beginning of year × Declining-balance rate

4. Describe the procedure for revising periodic depreciation. Revisions of periodic depreciation are made in present and future periods, not retroactively. The new annual depreciation is found by dividing the depreciable cost at the time of the revision by the remaining useful life.

5. Distinguish between revenue and capital expenditures, and explain the entries for these expenditures. Revenue expenditures are incurred to maintain the operating efficiency and expected productive life of the asset. These expenditures are debited to Repair Expense as incurred. Capital expenditures increase the operating efficiency, productive capacity, or expected useful life of the asset. These expenditures are generally debited to the plant asset affected.

6. Explain how to account for the disposal of a plant asset through retirement, sale, or exchange. The accounting for disposal of a plant asset through retirement or sale is as follows:
(a) Eliminate the book value of the plant asset at the date of disposal.
(b) Record cash proceeds, if any.
(c) Account for the difference between the book value and the cash proceeds as a gain or loss on disposal.

In accounting for exchanges of similar assets:
(a) Eliminate the book value of the old asset at the date of the exchange.
(b) Record the acquisition cost of the new asset.
(c) Account for the loss or gain, if any, on the old asset:
   (1) If a loss, recognize it immediately.
   (2) If a gain, defer and reduce the cost of the new asset.

7. Compute periodic depletion of natural resources. Compute depletion cost per unit by dividing the total cost of the natural resource minus salvage value by the number of units estimated to be in the resource. Then multiply the depletion cost per unit by the number of units extracted and sold.

8. Contrast the accounting for intangible assets with the accounting for plant assets. The accounting for intangible assets and plant assets is much the same. One difference is that the term used to describe the write-off of an intangible asset is amortization, rather than depreciation. Also, the amortization of an intangible asset cannot be longer than 40 years. The straight-line method is normally used for amortizing intangible assets.

9. Indicate how plant assets, natural resources, and intangible assets are reported and analyzed. Usually plant assets and natural resources are combined under property, plant, and equipment; intangibles are shown separately under intangible assets. Either within the balance sheet or in the notes, the balances of the major classes of assets, such as land, buildings, and equipment, and accumulated depreciation by major classes or in total, should be disclosed. Also, the depreciation and amortization methods used should be described, and the amount of depreciation and amortization expense for the period should be disclosed. The asset turnover ratio measures the productivity of a company's assets in generating sales.

Key Term Matching Activity

GLOSSARY

Accelerated-depreciation method Depreciation method that produces higher depreciation expense in the early years than in the later years. (p. 409).

Additions and improvements Costs incurred to increase the operating efficiency, productive capacity, or useful life of a plant asset. (p. 412).

Amortization The allocation of the cost of an intangible asset to expense over its useful life in a systematic and rational manner. (p. 419).

Asset turnover ratio A measure of how efficiently a company uses its assets to generate sales; calculated as net sales divided by average total assets. (p. 424).

Capital expenditures Expenditures that increase the company's investment in productive facilities. (p. 412).

Copyright Exclusive grant from the federal government that allows the owner to reproduce and sell an artistic or published work. (p. 420).

Declining-balance method Depreciation method that applies a constant rate to the declining book value of the asset and produces a decreasing annual depreciation expense over the useful life of the asset. (p. 408).

Depletion The allocation of the cost of a natural resource to expense in a rational and systematic manner over the resource's useful life. (p. 418).

Depreciable cost   The cost of a plant asset less its salvage value. (p. 406).

Franchise (license)   A contractual arrangement under which the franchisor grants the franchisee the right to sell certain products, render specific services, or use certain trademarks or trade names, usually within a designated geographical area. (p. 421).

Goodwill   The value of all favorable attributes that relate to a business enterprise. (p. 421).

Intangible assets   Rights, privileges, and competitive advantages that result from the ownership of long-lived assets that do not possess physical substance. (p. 419).

Licenses   Operating rights to use public property, granted to a business enterprise by a governmental agency. (p. 421).

Natural resources   Assets that consist of standing timber and underground deposits of oil, gas, or minerals. (p. 418).

Ordinary repairs   Expenditures to maintain the operating efficiency and productive life of the unit. (p. 412).

Patent   An exclusive right issued by the U.S. Patent Office that enables the recipient to manufacture, sell, or otherwise control an invention for a period of 20 years from the date of the grant. (p. 420).

Plant assets   Tangible resources that are used in the operations of the business and are not intended for sale to customers. (p. 400).

Research and development (R&D) costs   Expenditures that may lead to patents, copyrights, new processes, or new products. (p. 422).

Revenue expenditures   Expenditures that are immediately charged against revenues as an expense. (p. 412).

Salvage value   An estimate of an asset's value at the end of its useful life. (p. 405).

Straight-line method   Depreciation method in which periodic depreciation is the same for each year of the asset's useful life. (p. 406).

Trademark (trade name)   A word, phrase, jingle, or symbol that identifies a particular enterprise or product. (p. 420).

Units-of-activity method   Depreciation method in which useful life is expressed in terms of the total units of production or use expected from an asset. (p. 407).

Useful life   An estimate of the expected productive life, also called service life, of an asset. (p. 405).

Chapter 10 Self-Test

SELF-STUDY QUESTIONS

Answers are at the end of the chapter.

(SO 1) **1.** Erin Danielle Company purchased equipment and incurred the following costs.

Cash price	$24,000
Sales taxes	1,200
Insurance during transit	200
Installation and testing	400
Total costs	$25,800

What amount should be recorded as the cost of the equipment?
a. $24,000.
b. $25,200.
c. $25,400.
d. $25,800.

(SO 2) **2.** Depreciation is a process of:
a. valuation.
b. cost allocation.
c. cash accumulation.
d. appraisal.

(SO 3) **3.** Micah Bartlett Company purchased equipment on January 1, 2001, at a total invoice cost of $400,000. The equipment has an estimated salvage value of $10,000 and an estimated useful life of 5 years. The amount of accumulated depreciation at December 31, 2002, if the straight-line method of depreciation is used, is:
a. $80,000.
b. $160,000.
c. $78,000.
d. $156,000.

(SO 3) **4.** Ann Torbert purchased a truck for $11,000 on January 1, 2001. The truck will have an estimated salvage value of $1,000 at the end of 5 years. Using the units-of-activity method, the balance in accumulated depreciation at December 31, 2002, can be computed by the following formula:
a. ($11,000 ÷ Total estimated activity) × Units of activity for 2002.
b. ($10,000 ÷ Total estimated activity) × Units of activity for 2002.
c. ($11,000 ÷ Total estimated activity) × Units of activity for 2001 and 2002.
d. ($10,000 ÷ Total estimated activity) × Units of activity for 2001 and 2002.

(SO 4) **5.** When there is a change in estimated depreciation:
a. previous depreciation should be corrected.
b. current and future years' depreciation should be revised.
c. only future years' depreciation should be revised.
d. None of the above.

(SO 5) **6.** Additions to plant assets are:
a. revenue expenditures.
b. debited to a Repair Expense account.
c. debited to a Purchases account.
d. capital expenditures.

(SO 6) **7.** Schopenhauer Company exchanged an old machine, with a book value of $39,000 and a fair market value of $35,000, and paid $10,000 cash for a similar new machine. At what amount should the machine acquired in the exchange be recorded on Schopenhauer's books?
a. $45,000.
b. $46,000.
c. $49,000.
d. $50,000.

(SO 6) **8.** In exchanges of similar assets:
    a. neither gains nor losses are recognized immediately.
    b. gains, but not losses, are recognized immediately.
    c. losses, but not gains, are recognized immediately.
    d. both gains and losses are recognized immediately.

(SO 7) **9.** Maggie Sharrer Company expects to extract 20 million tons of coal from a mine that cost $12 million. If no salvage value is expected, and 2 million tons are mined and sold in the first year, the entry to record depletion will include a:
    a. debit to Accumulated Depletion of $2,000,000.
    b. credit to Depletion Expense of $1,200,000.
    c. debit to Depletion Expense of $1,200,000.
    d. credit to Accumulated Depletion of $2,000,000.

(SO 8, 9) **10.** Martha Beyerlein Company incurred $150,000 of research and development costs in its laboratory to develop a patent granted on January 2, 2002. On July 31, 2002, Beyerlein paid $35,000 for legal fees in a successful defense of the patent. The total amount debited to Patents through July 31, 2002, should be:
    a. $150,000.
    b. $35,000.
    c. $185,000.
    d. some other amount.

11. Indicate which of the following statements is *true*. (SO 9)
    a. Since intangible assets lack physical substance, they need be disclosed only in the notes to the financial statements.
    b. Goodwill should be reported as a contra-account in the owner's equity section.
    c. Totals of major classes of assets can be shown in the balance sheet, with asset details disclosed in the notes to the financial statements.
    d. Intangible assets are typically combined with plant assets and natural resources and shown in the property, plant, and equipment section.

☑ THE NAVIGATOR

QUESTIONS

1. Joe Barone is uncertain about the applicability of the cost principle to plant assets. Explain the principle to Joe.

2. What are some examples of land improvements?

3. Sam-Ho Company acquires the land and building owned by Corrs Company. What types of costs may be incurred to make the asset ready for its intended use if Sam-Ho Company wants to use (a) only the land, and (b) both the land and the building?

4. In a recent newspaper release, the president of Smashing Pumpkins Company asserted that something has to be done about depreciation. The president said, "Depreciation does not come close to accumulating the cash needed to replace the asset at the end of its useful life." What is your response to the president?

5. Thomas is studying for the next accounting examination. He asks your help on two questions: (a) What is salvage value? (b) Is salvage value used in determining depreciable cost under each depreciation method? Answer Thomas's questions.

6. Contrast the straight-line method and the units-of-activity method as to (a) useful life, and (b) the pattern of periodic depreciation over useful life.

7. Contrast the effects of the three depreciation methods on annual depreciation expense.

8. In the fourth year of an asset's 5-year useful life, the company decides that the asset will have a 6-year service life. How should the revision of depreciation be recorded? Why?

9. Distinguish between revenue expenditures and capital expenditures during useful life.

10. How is a gain or loss on the sale of a plant asset computed?

11. Lopez Corporation owns a machine that is fully depreciated but is still being used. How should Lopez account for this asset and report it in the financial statements?

12. When similar assets are exchanged, how is the gain or loss on disposal computed?

13. Lim Refrigeration Company trades in an old machine on a new model when the fair market value of the old machine is greater than its book value. Should Lim recognize a gain on disposal? If the fair market value of the old machine is less than its book value, should Lim recognize a loss on disposal?

14. Moon Company experienced a gain on disposal when exchanging similar machines. In accordance with generally accepted accounting principles, the gain was not recognized. How will Moon's future financial statements be affected by not recognizing the gain?

15. What are natural resources, and what are their distinguishing characteristics?

16. Explain what depletion is and how it is computed.

17. What are the similarities and differences between the terms depreciation, depletion, and amortization?

18. Guen Company hires an accounting intern who says that intangible assets should always be amortized over their legal lives. Is the intern correct? Explain.

19. Goodwill has been defined as the value of all favorable attributes that relate to a business enterprise. What types of attributes could result in goodwill?

20. Clint Eastwood, a business major, is working on a case problem for one of his classes. In the case problem, the company needs to raise cash to market a new product it developed. Jack Gleason, an engineering major, takes one look at the company's balance sheet and says, "This company has an awful lot of goodwill. Why don't you recommend that they sell some of it to raise cash?" How should Clint respond to Jack?

21. Under what conditions is goodwill recorded?

22. Often research and development costs provide companies with benefits that last a number of years. (For example, these costs can lead to the development of a patent that will increase the company's income for many years.) However, generally accepted accounting principles require that such costs be recorded as an expense when incurred. Why?

23. **McDonald's Corporation** reports total average assets of $14.5 billion and net sales of $9.8 billion. What is the company's asset turnover ratio?

24. Overheu Corporation and Orlow Corporation operate in the same industry. Overheu uses the straight-line method to account for depreciation; Orlow uses an accelerated method. Explain what complications might arise in trying to compare the results of these two companies.

25. Lucille Corporation uses straight-line depreciation for financial reporting purposes but an accelerated method for tax purposes. Is it acceptable to use different methods for the two purposes? What is Lucille's motivation for doing this?

26. You are comparing two companies in the same industry. You have determined that Wow Corp. depreciates its plant assets over a 40-year life, whereas Wooster Corp. depreciates its plant assets over a 20-year life. Discuss the implications this has for comparing the results of the two companies.

27. Pizner Company is doing significant work to revitalize its warehouses. It is not sure whether it should capitalize these costs or expense them. What are the implications for current-year net income and future net income of expensing versus capitalizing these costs?

BRIEF EXERCISES

Determine the cost of land.
(SO 1)

BE10-1   The following expenditures were incurred by Gene Shumway Company in purchasing land: cash price $50,000, accrued taxes $3,000, attorneys' fees $2,500, real estate broker's commission $2,000, and clearing and grading $3,500. What is the cost of the land?

Determine the cost of a truck.
(SO 1)

BE10-2   Shirley Basler Company incurs the following expenditures in purchasing a truck: cash price $25,000, accident insurance $2,000, sales taxes $900, motor vehicle license $100, and painting and lettering $400. What is the cost of the truck?

Compute straight-line depreciation.
(SO 3)

BE10-3   Graig Mabasa Company acquires a delivery truck at a cost of $30,000. The truck is expected to have a salvage value of $2,000 at the end of its 4-year useful life. Compute annual depreciation for the first and second years using the straight-line method.

Compute depreciation and evaluate treatment.
(SO 3)

BE10-4   Olympic Company purchased land and a building on January 1, 2002. Management's best estimate of the value of the land was $100,000 and of the building $200,000. But management told the accounting department to record the land at $220,000 and the building at $80,000. The building is being depreciated on a straight-line basis over 20 years with no salvage value. Why do you suppose management requested this accounting treatment? Is it ethical?

Compute declining-balance depreciation.
(SO 3)

BE10-5   Depreciation information for Graig Mabasa Company is given in BE10-3. Assuming the declining-balance depreciation rate is double the straight-line rate, compute annual depreciation for the first and second years under the declining-balance method.

Compute depreciation using the units-of-activity method.
(SO 3)

BE10-6   Jerry Englehart Taxi Service uses the units-of-activity method in computing depreciation on its taxicabs. Each cab is expected to be driven 150,000 miles. Taxi no. 10 cost $36,500 and is expected to have a salvage value of $500. Taxi no. 10 is driven 30,000 miles in year 1 and 20,000 miles in year 2. Compute the depreciation for each year.

Compute revised depreciation.
(SO 4)

BE10-7   On January 1, 2002, the Jose Villaluz Company ledger shows Equipment $32,000 and Accumulated Depreciation $9,000. The depreciation resulted from using the straight-line method with a useful life of 10 years and salvage value of $2,000. On this date, the company concludes that the equipment has a remaining useful life of only 5 years with the same salvage value. Compute the revised annual depreciation.

Prepare entries for disposal by retirement.
(SO 6)

BE10-8   Prepare journal entries to record the following.

(a) Ruiz Company retires its delivery equipment, which cost $41,000. Accumulated depreciation is also $41,000 on this delivery equipment. No salvage value is received.

(b) Assume the same information as (a), except that accumulated depreciation for Ruiz Company is $39,000, instead of $41,000.

Prepare entries for disposal by sale.
(SO 6)

BE10-9   Welch Company sells office equipment on September 30, 2002, for $20,000 cash. The office equipment originally cost $72,000 and as of January 1, 2002, had accumulated depreciation of $42,000. Depreciation for the first 9 months of 2002 is $6,000. Prepare the journal entries to (a) update depreciation to September 30, 2002, and (b) record the sale of the equipment.

BE10-10 Concord Company exchanges old delivery equipment for similar new delivery equipment. The book value of the old delivery equipment is $31,000 (cost $61,000 less accumulated depreciation $30,000). Its fair market value is $21,000, and cash of $5,000 is paid. Prepare the entry to record the exchange.

Prepare entry for disposal by exchange.
(SO 6)

BE10-11 Assume the same information as BE10-10, except that the fair market value of the old delivery equipment is $40,000. Prepare the entry to record the exchange.

Prepare entry for disposal by exchange.
(SO 6)

BE10-12 Cuono Mining Co. purchased for $7 million a mine that is estimated to have 28 million tons of ore and no salvage value. In the first year, 4 million tons of ore are extracted and sold.

Prepare depletion expense entry and balance sheet presentation for natural resources.
(SO 7)

(a) Prepare the journal entry to record depletion expense for the first year.
(b) Show how this mine is reported on the balance sheet at the end of the first year.

BE10-13 Popper Company purchases a patent for $180,000 on January 2, 2002. Its estimated useful life is 10 years.

Prepare patent expense entry and balance sheet presentation for intangibles.
(SO 8)

(a) Prepare the journal entry to record patent expense for the first year.
(b) Show how this patent is reported on the balance sheet at the end of the first year.

BE10-14 Information related to plant assets, natural resources, and intangibles at the end of 2002 for Joker Company is as follows: buildings $900,000; accumulated depreciation—buildings $650,000; goodwill $410,000; coal mine $300,000; accumulated depletion—coal mine $108,000. Prepare a partial balance sheet of Joker Company for these items.

Classify long-lived assets on balance sheet.
(SO 9)

BE10-15 In its 1998 annual report **McDonald's Corporation** reported beginning total assets of $18.2 billion; ending total assets of $19.8 billion; property, plant, and equipment (at cost) of $20.1 billion; and net sales of $12.4 billion. Compute McDonald's asset turnover ratio.

Analyze long-lived assets.
(SO 9)

EXERCISES

E10-1 The following expenditures relating to plant assets were made by John Kosinski Company during the first 2 months of 2002.

Determine cost of plant acquisitions.
(SO 1)

1. Paid $5,000 of accrued taxes at time plant site was acquired.
2. Paid $200 insurance to cover possible accident loss on new factory machinery while the machinery was in transit.
3. Paid $850 sales taxes on new delivery truck.
4. Paid $17,500 for parking lots and driveways on new plant site.
5. Paid $250 to have company name and advertising slogan painted on new delivery truck.
6. Paid $8,000 for installation of new factory machinery.
7. Paid $900 for one-year accident insurance policy on new delivery truck.
8. Paid $75 motor vehicle license fee on the new truck.

Instructions

(a) ◻▦▦➤ Explain the application of the cost principle in determining the acquisition cost of plant assets.
(b) List the numbers of the foregoing transactions, and opposite each indicate the account title to which each expenditure should be debited.

E10-2 On March 1, 2002, Roy Orbis Company acquired real estate on which it planned to construct a small office building. The company paid $80,000 in cash. An old warehouse on the property was razed at a cost of $6,600; the salvaged materials were sold for $1,700. Additional expenditures before construction began included $1,100 attorney's fee for work concerning the land purchase, $4,000 real estate broker's fee, $7,800 architect's fee, and $14,000 to put in driveways and a parking lot.

Determine acquisition costs on land.
(SO 1)

Instructions

(a) Determine the amount to be reported as the cost of the land.
(b) For each cost not used in part (a), indicate the account to be debited.

Compute depreciation under units-of-activity method.
(SO 3)

E10-3 Always-Late Bus Lines uses the units-of-activity method in depreciating its buses. One bus was purchased on January 1, 2002, at a cost of $128,000. Over its 4-year useful life, the bus is expected to be driven 100,000 miles. Salvage value is expected to be $8,000.

Instructions

(a) Compute the depreciation cost per unit.
(b) Prepare a depreciation schedule assuming actual mileage was: 2002, 26,000; 2003, 32,000; 2004, 25,000; and 2005, 17,000.

Determine depreciation for partial periods.
(SO 3)

E10-4 Elvis Costello Company purchased a new machine on October 1, 2002, at a cost of $89,000. The company estimated that the machine will have a salvage value of $12,000. The machine is expected to be used for 70,000 working hours during its 5-year life.

Instructions

Compute the depreciation expense under the following methods for the year indicated.
(a) Straight-line for 2002.
(b) Units-of-activity for 2002, assuming machine usage was 1,700 hours.
(c) Declining-balance using double the straight-line rate for 2002 and 2003.

Compute revised annual depreciation.
(SO 3, 4)

E10-5 Lindy Rig, the new controller of Bellingham Company, has reviewed the expected useful lives and salvage values of selected depreciable assets at the beginning of 2002. Her findings are as follows.

Type of Asset	Date Acquired	Cost	Accumulated Depreciation 1/1/02	Useful Life in Years		Salvage Value	
				Old	Proposed	Old	Proposed
Building	1/1/96	$800,000	$114,000	40	50	$40,000	$70,000
Warehouse	1/1/99	100,000	11,400	25	20	5,000	3,600

All assets are depreciated by the straight-line method. Bellingham Company uses a calendar year in preparing annual financial statements. After discussion, management has agreed to accept Lindy's proposed changes.

Instructions

(a) Compute the revised annual depreciation on each asset in 2002. (Show computations.)
(b) Prepare the entry (or entries) to record depreciation on the building in 2002.

Journalize entries for disposal of plant assets.
(SO 6)

E10-6 Presented below are selected transactions at Beck Company for 2002.

Jan.   1   Retired a piece of machinery that was purchased on January 1, 1992. The machine cost $62,000 on that date. It had a useful life of 10 years with no salvage value.
June 30   Sold a computer that was purchased on January 1, 1999. The computer cost $35,000. It had a useful life of 7 years with no salvage value. The computer was sold for $22,000.
Dec. 31   Discarded a delivery truck that was purchased on January 1, 1998. The truck cost $30,000. It was depreciated based on a 6-year useful life with a $3,000 salvage value.

Instructions

Journalize all entries required on the above dates, including entries to update depreciation, where applicable, on assets disposed of. Beck Company uses straight-line depreciation. (Assume depreciation is up to date as of December 31, 2001.)

Journalize entries for exchange of similar assets.
(SO 6)

E10-7 Presented below are two independent transactions.

1. Noyes Co. exchanged old trucks (cost $64,000 less $22,000 accumulated depreciation) plus cash of $17,000 for new trucks. The old trucks had a fair market value of $40,000.
2. Salzer Inc. trades its used machine (cost $10,000 less $5,000 accumulated depreciation) for a new machine. In addition to exchanging the old machine (which had a fair market value of $9,000), Salzer also paid cash of $2,000.

Instructions

(a) Prepare the entry to record the exchange of similar assets by Noyes Co.

(b) Prepare the entry to record the exchange of similar assets by Salzer Inc.

E10-8   Mueller Company exchanges similar equipment with Logan Company. Also Sun Company exchanges similar equipment with Moon Company. The following information pertains to these two exchanges.

Journalize entries for the exchange of similar plant assets.
(SO 6)

	Mueller Co.	**Sun Co.**
Equipment (cost)	$28,000	$22,000
Accumulated depreciation	21,000	5,000
Fair market value of equipment	12,000	13,000
Cash paid	2,000	–0–

Instructions

Prepare the journal entries to record the exchange on the books of Mueller Company and Sun Company.

E10-9   Abner's Delivery Company and Wainwrights' Express Delivery exchanged similar delivery trucks on January 1, 2002. Abner's truck cost $20,000. It has accumulated depreciation of $13,000 and a fair market value of $4,000. Wainwrights' truck cost $10,000. It has accumulated depreciation of $8,000 and a fair market value of $4,000.

Journalize entries for the exchange of similar plant assets.
(SO 6)

Instructions

(a) Journalize the exchange for Abner's Delivery Company.

(b) Journalize the exchange for Wainwright's Express Delivery.

E10-10   On July 1, 2002, Phillips Inc. invested $320,000 in a mine estimated to have 800,000 tons of ore of uniform grade. During the last 6 months of 2002, 100,000 tons of ore were mined and sold.

Journalize entries for natural resources depletion.
(SO 7)

Instructions

(a) Prepare the journal entry to record depletion expense.

(b) Assume that the 100,000 tons of ore were mined, but only 80,000 units were sold. How are the costs applicable to the 20,000 unsold units reported?

E10-11   The following are selected 2002 transactions of Graf Corporation.

Prepare adjusting entries for amortization.
(SO 8)

Jan. 1   Purchased a small company and recorded goodwill of $180,000. The goodwill has a useful life of 55 years.

May 1   Purchased for $45,000 a patent with an estimated useful life of 5 years and a legal life of 20 years.

Instructions

Prepare all adjusting entries at December 31 to record amortization required by the events above.

E10-12   Collins Company, organized in 2002, has the following transactions related to intangible assets.

Prepare entries to set up appropriate accounts for different intangibles; amortize intangible assets.
(SO 8)

1/2/02	Purchased patent (7-year life)	$490,000
4/1/02	Goodwill purchased (indefinite life)	360,000
7/1/02	10-year franchise; expiration date 7/1/2012	420,000
9/1/02	Research and development costs	185,000

Instructions

Prepare the necessary entries to record these intangibles. All costs incurred were for cash. Make the entries as of December 31, 2002, recording any necessary amortization and reflecting all balances accurately as of that date.

E10-13   During 2001 Onyinke Corporation reported net sales of $3,500,000 and net income of $1,500,000. Its balance sheet reported total assets of $1,400,000.

Calculate asset turnover ratio.
(SO 9)

Instructions

Calculate the asset turnover ratio.

PROBLEMS: SET A

Determine acquisition costs of land and building.
(SO 1)

P10-1A Mendoza Company was organized on January 1. During the first year of operations, the following plant asset expenditures and receipts were recorded in random order.

Debits

1.	Cost of filling and grading the land	$ 4,000
2.	Full payment to building contractor	700,000
3.	Real estate taxes on land paid for the current year	5,000
4.	Cost of real estate purchased as a plant site (land $100,000 and building $45,000)	145,000
5.	Excavation costs for new building	20,000
6.	Architect's fees on building plans	10,000
7.	Accrued real estate taxes paid at time of purchase of real estate	2,000
8.	Cost of parking lots and driveways	14,000
9.	Cost of demolishing building to make land suitable for construction of new building	15,000
		$915,000

Credits

10.	Proceeds from salvage of demolished building	$ 3,500

Instructions

Totals
Land $162,500
Building $730,000

Analyze the foregoing transactions using the following column headings. Insert the number of each transaction in the Item space, and insert the amounts in the appropriate columns. For amounts entered in the Other Accounts column, also indicate the account titles.

Item	**Land**	**Building**	**Other Accounts**

Compute depreciation under different methods.
(SO 3)

P10-2A In recent years, Waterfront Transportation purchased three used buses. Because of frequent turnover in the accounting department, a different accountant selected the depreciation method for each bus, and various methods were selected. Information concerning the buses is summarized below.

Bus	Acquired	Cost	Salvage Value	Useful Life in Years	Depreciation Method
1	1/1/00	$ 86,000	$ 6,000	4	Straight-line
2	1/1/00	140,000	10,000	5	Declining-balance
3	1/1/01	80,000	8,000	5	Units-of-activity

For the declining-balance method, the company uses the double-declining rate. For the units-of-activity method, total miles are expected to be 120,000. Actual miles of use in the first 3 years were: 2001, 24,000; 2002, 34,000; and 2003, 30,000.

Instructions

(a) Compute the amount of accumulated depreciation on each bus at December 31, 2002.

(b) If bus no. 2 was purchased on April 1 instead of January 1, what is the depreciation expense for this bus in (1) 2000 and (2) 2001?

Compute depreciation under different methods.
(SO 3)

P10-3A On January 1, 2002, Khan Company purchased the following two machines for use in its production process.

Machine A: The cash price of this machine was $30,000. Related expenditures included: sales tax $1,500, shipping costs $150, insurance during shipping $80, installation and testing costs $70, and $100 of oil and lubricants to be used with the machinery during its first year of operations. Khan estimates that the useful life of the machine is 5 years with a $5,000 salvage value remaining at the end of that time period. Assume that the straight-line method of depreciation is used.

Machine B: The recorded cost of this machine was $60,000. Khan estimates that the useful life of the machine is 4 years with a $5,000 salvage value remaining at the end of that time period.

Instructions

(a) Prepare the following for Machine A.
  (1) The journal entry to record its purchase on January 1, 2002.
  (2) The journal entry to record annual depreciation at December 31, 2002.
(b) Calculate the amount of depreciation expense that Khan should record for machine B each year of its useful life under the following assumptions.
  (1) Khan uses the straight-line method of depreciation.
  (2) Khan uses the declining-balance method. The rate used is twice the straight-line rate.
  (3) Khan uses the units-of-activity method and estimates that the useful life of the machine is 125,000 units. Actual usage is as follows: 2002, 45,000 units; 2003, 35,000 units; 2004, 25,000 units; 2005, 20,000 units.
(c) Which method used to calculate depreciation on machine B reports the highest amount of depreciation expense in year 1 (2002)? The highest amount in year 4 (2005)? The highest total amount over the 4-year period?

P10-4A At the beginning of 2000, Duncan Company acquired equipment costing $60,000. It was estimated that this equipment would have a useful life of 6 years and a residual value of $6,000 at that time. The straight-line method of depreciation was considered the most appropriate to use with this type of equipment. Depreciation is to be recorded at the end of each year. *Calculate revisions to depreciation expense.* (SO 3, 4)

During 2002 (the third year of the equipment's life), the company's engineers reconsidered their expectations, and estimated that the equipment's useful life would probably be 7 years (in total) instead of 6 years. The estimated residual value was not changed at that time. However, during 2005 the estimated residual value was reduced to $4,400.

Instructions

Indicate how much depreciation expense should be recorded each year for this equipment, by completing the following table.

Year	Depreciation Expense	Accumulated Depreciation
2000		
2001		
2002		
2003		
2004		
2005		
2006		

P10-5A At December 31, 2002, Santa Fe Company reported the following as plant assets. *Journalize a series of equipment transactions related to purchase, sale, retirement, and depreciation.* (SO 6, 9)

Land		$ 4,000,000
Buildings	$28,500,000	
Less: Accumulated depreciation—buildings	12,100,000	16,400,000
Equipment	48,000,000	
Less: Accumulated depreciation—equipment	5,000,000	43,000,000
Total plant assets		$63,400,000

During 2003, the following selected cash transactions occurred.

April 1   Purchased land for $2,630,000.
May 1   Sold equipment that cost $570,000 when purchased on January 1, 1999. The equipment was sold for $350,000.
June 1   Sold land purchased on June 1, 1993, for $1,800,000. The land cost $200,000.
July 1   Purchased equipment for $2,000,000.
Dec. 31   Retired equipment that cost $500,000 when purchased on December 31, 1993. No salvage value was received.

Instructions

(a) Journalize the above transactions. The company uses straight-line depreciation for buildings and equipment. The buildings are estimated to have a 50-year life and no salvage value. The equipment is estimated to have a 10-year useful life and no salvage value. Update depreciation on assets disposed of at the time of sale or retirement.
(b) Record adjusting entries for depreciation for 2003.
(c) Prepare the plant assets section of Santa Fe's balance sheet at December 31, 2003.

(b) Depreciation Expense—
building $570,000;
equipment $4,793,000
(c) Total plant assets
$62,075,000

Record disposals.
(SO 6)

P10-6A   Elliot Co. has office furniture that cost $75,000 and that has been depreciated $48,000. Record the disposal under the following assumptions.

(a) It was scrapped as having no value.
(b) It was sold for $21,000.
(c) It was sold for $61,000.
(d) It was exchanged for similar office furniture. The old office furniture has a fair market value of $46,000, and $8,000 was paid.
(e) It was exchanged for similar office furniture. The old office furniture has a fair market value of $25,000, and $29,000 was paid.

Prepare entries to record trans-
actions related to acquisition
and amortization of intangi-
bles; prepare the intangible
assets section.
(SO 8, 9)

P10-7A   The intangible assets section of Toribio Company at December 31, 2002, is presented below.

Patent ($70,000 cost less $7,000 amortization)	$63,000
Copyright ($48,000 cost less $19,200 amortization)	28,800
Total	$91,800

The patent was acquired in January 2002 and has a useful life of 10 years. The copyright was acquired in January 1999 and also has a useful life of 10 years. The following cash transactions may have affected intangible assets during 2000.

Jan. 2   Paid $27,000 legal costs to successfully defend the patent against infringement by another company.

Jan.–June   Developed a new product, incurring $140,000 in research and development costs. A patent was granted for the product on July 1. Its useful life is equal to its legal life.

Sept. 1   Paid $80,000 to an extremely large defensive lineman to appear in commercials advertising the company's products. The commercials will air in September and October.

Oct. 1   Acquired a copyright for $120,000. The copyright has a useful life of 50 years.

(b) Amortization Expense—
Patents $10,000
Amortization Expense—
Copyrights $5,550
(c) Total intangible assets
$223,250

Instructions

(a) Prepare journal entries to record the transactions above.
(b) Prepare journal entries to record the 2003 amortization expense.
(c) Prepare the intangible assets section of the balance sheet at December 31, 2003.

Prepare entries to correct for
errors made in recording and
amortizing intangible assets.
(SO 8)

P10-8A   Due to rapid turnover in the accounting department, a number of transactions involving intangible assets were improperly recorded by the Henry Company in 2002.

1. Henry developed a new manufacturing process, incurring research and development costs of $186,900. The company also purchased a patent for $39,100. In early January, Henry capitalized $226,000 as the cost of the patents. Patent amortization expense of $11,300 was recorded based on a 20-year useful life.

2. On July 1, 2002, Henry purchased a small company and as a result acquired goodwill of $92,000. Henry recorded a half-year's amortization in 2002, based on a 50-year life ($920 amortization).

1. R&D $186,900
2. Amortization Expense—
Goodwill $230

Instructions

Prepare all journal entries necessary to correct any errors made during 2002. Assume the books have not yet been closed for 2002.

Calculate and comment on
asset turnover ratio.
(SO 9)

P10-9A   Samone Company and Baxter Corporation, two corporations of roughly the same size, are both involved in the manufacture of in-line skates. Each company depreciates its plant assets using the straight-line approach. An investigation of their financial statements reveals the following information.

	Samone Co.	**Baxter Corp.**
Net income	$ 700,000	$1,000,000
Sales	1,400,000	1,300,000
Total assets	2,500,000	2,000,000
Plant assets	1,800,000	1,000,000

Instructions

(a) For each company, calculate the asset turnover ratio.
(b) ▭▭▭▭▷ Based on your calculations in part (a), comment on the relative effectiveness of the two companies in using their assets to generate sales and produce net income.

PROBLEMS: SET B

P10-1B Leno Company was organized on January 1. During the first year of operations, the following plant asset expenditures and receipts were recorded in random order.

Determine acquisition costs of land and building.
(SO 1)

Debits

1.	Accrued real estate taxes paid at time of purchase of real estate	$ 2,000
2.	Real estate taxes on land paid for the current year	3,000
3.	Full payment to building contractor	600,000
4.	Excavation costs for new building	20,000
5.	Cost of real estate purchased as a plant site (land $100,000 and building $25,000)	125,000
6.	Cost of parking lots and driveways	15,000
7.	Architect's fees on building plans	10,000
8.	Installation cost of fences around property	4,000
9.	Cost of demolishing building to make land suitable for construction of new building	13,000
		$792,000

Credit

10.	Proceeds from salvage of demolished building	$ 2,500

Instructions

Analyze the foregoing tranactions using the following column headings. Insert the number of each transaction in the Item space, and insert the amounts in the appropriate columns. For amounts entered in the Other Accounts column, also indicate the account title.

Item	Land	Building	Other Accounts

Totals

Land $137,500

Building $630,000

P10-2B In recent years, Letterman Company purchased three machines. Because of heavy turnover in the accounting department, a different accountant was in charge of selecting the depreciation method for each machine, and various methods were selected. Information concerning the machines is summarized below.

Compute depreciation under different methods.
(SO 3)

Machine	Acquired	Cost	Salvage Value	Useful Life in Years	Depreciation Method
1	1/1/99	$96,000	$ 6,000	10	Straight-line
2	1/1/00	60,000	10,000	8	Declining-balance
3	11/1/02	66,000	6,000	6	Units-of-activity

For the declining-balance method, the company uses the double-declining rate. For the units-of-activity method, total machine hours are expected to be 24,000. Actual hours of use in the first 3 years were: 2002, 1,000; 2003, 4,500; and 2004, 5,000.

Instructions

(a) Compute the amount of accumulated depreciation on each machine at December 31, 2002.

(b) If machine 2 had been purchased on April 1 instead of January 1, what would be the depreciation expense for this machine in (1) 2000 and (2) 2001?

P10-3B On January 1, 2002, Gaudinez Company purchased the following two machines for use in its production process.

Compute depreciation under different methods.
(SO 3)

Machine A: The cash price of this machine was $35,000. Related expenditures included: sales tax $1,800, shipping costs $175, insurance during shipping $75, installation and testing costs $50, and $90 of oil and lubricants to be used with the machinery during its first year of operation. Gaudinez estimates that the useful life of the machine is 4 years with a $5,000 salvage value remaining at the end of that time period.

Machine B: The recorded cost of this machine was $80,000. Gaudinez estimates that the useful life of the machine is 4 years with a $5,000 salvage value remaining at the end of that time period.

Instructions

(a) Prepare the following for Machine A.

(a) (2) $8,025

  (1) The journal entry to record its purchase on January 1, 2002.
  (2) The journal entry to record annual depreciation at December 31, 2002, assuming the straight-line method of depreciation is used.

(b) Calculate the amount of depreciation expense that Gaudinez should record for machine B each year of its useful life under the following assumption.

  (1) Gaudinez uses the straight-line method of depreciation.
  (2) Gaudinez uses the declining-balance method. The rate used is twice the straight-line rate.
  (3) Gaudinez uses the units-of-activity method and estimates the useful life of the machine is 25,000 units. Actual usage is as follows: 2002, 6,500 units; 2003, 7,500 units; 2004, 6,000 units; 2005, 5,000 units.

(c) Which method used to calculate depreciation on machine B reports the lowest amount of depreciation expense in year 1 (2002)? The lowest amount in year 4 (2005)? The lowest total amount over the 4-year period?

Calculate revisions to depreciation expense.
(SO 3, 4)

P10-4B   At the beginning of 2000, Boenes Company acquired equipment costing $40,000. It was estimated that this equipment would have a useful life of 6 years and a residual value of $4,000 at that time. The straight-line method of depreciation was considered the most appropriate to use with this type of equipment. Depreciation is to be recorded at the end of each year.

During 2002 (the third year of the equipment's life), the company's engineers reconsidered their expectations, and estimated that the equipment's useful life would probably be 7 years (in total) instead of 6 years. The estimated residual value was not changed at that time. However, during 2005 the estimated residual value was reduced to $2,400.

Instructions

Indicate how much depreciation expense should be recorded for this equipment each year by completing the following table.

Year	Depreciation Expense	Accumulated Depreciation
2000		
2001		
2002		
2003		
2004		
2005		
2006		

2006 depreciation expense, $5,600

Journalize a series of equipment transactions related to purchase, sale, retirement, and depreciation.
(SO 6, 9)

P10-5B   At December 31, 2002, Hamsmith Company reported the following as plant assets.

Land		$ 3,000,000
Buildings	$26,500,000	
Less: Accumulated depreciation—buildings	12,100,000	14,400,000
Equipment	40,000,000	
Less: Accumulated depreciation—equipment	5,000,000	35,000,000
Total plant assets		$52,400,000

During 2003, the following selected cash transactions occurred.

April 1 Purchased land for $2,200,000.
May 1 Sold equipment that cost $540,000 when purchased on January 1, 1999. The equipment was sold for $360,000.
June 1 Sold land purchased on June 1, 1993, for $1,800,000. The land cost $500,000.
July 1 Purchased equipment for $1,400,000.
Dec. 31 Retired equipment that cost $500,000 when purchased on December 31, 1993. No salvage value was received.

Instructions

(a) Journalize the above transactions. Hamsmith uses straight-line depreciation for buildings and equipment. The buildings are estimated to have a 50-year useful life and no salvage value. The equipment is estimated to have a 10-year useful life and no salvage value. Update depreciation on assets disposed of at the time of sale or retirement.

(b) Record adjusting entries for depreciation for 2003.

(c) Prepare the plant assets section of Hamsmith's balance sheet at December 31, 2003.

(b) Depreciation Expense—
    Building $530,000;
    Equipment $3,966,000
(c) Total plant assets
    $50,630,000

P10-6B Express Co. has delivery equipment that cost $45,000 and that has been depreciated $20,000. Record the disposal under the following assumptions.

(a) It was scrapped as having no value.

(b) It was sold for $31,000.

(c) It was sold for $18,000.

(d) It was exchanged for similar delivery equipment. The old delivery equipment has a fair market value of $12,000, and $32,000 was paid.

(e) It was exchanged for similar delivery equipment. The old delivery equipment has a fair market value of $35,000, and $9,000 was paid.

Record disposals.
(SO 6)

P10-7B The intangible assets section of Zevon Company at December 31, 2002, is presented below.

Patent ($60,000 cost less $6,000 amortization)	$54,000
Copyright ($36,000 cost less $14,400 amortization)	21,600
Total	$75,600

Prepare entries to record transactions related to acquisition and amortization of intangibles; prepare the intangible assets section.
(SO 8, 9)

The patent was acquired in January 2002 and has a useful life of 10 years. The copyright was acquired in January 1999 and also has a useful life of 10 years. The following cash transactions may have affected intangible assets during 2003.

Jan. 2   Paid $27,000 legal costs to successfully defend the patent against infringement by another company.

Jan.–June   Developed a new product, incurring $140,000 in research and development costs. A patent was granted for the product on July 1. Its useful life is equal to its legal life.

Sept. 1   Paid $60,000 to a quarterback to appear in commercials advertising the company's products. The commercials will air in September and October.

Oct. 1   Acquired a copyright for $40,000. The copyright has a useful life of 50 years.

Instructions

(a) Prepare journal entries to record the transactions above.

(b) Prepare journal entries to record the 2003 amortization expense for intangible assets.

(c) Prepare the intangible assets section of the balance sheet at December 31, 2003.

(d) ▭▭▭▷ Prepare the note to the financials on Zevon's intangibles as of December 31, 2003.

(b) Amortization Expense—
    Patents $9,000;
    Amortization Expense—
    Copyrights $3,850
(c) Total intangible assets,
    $129,750

P10-8B Due to rapid turnover in the accounting department, a number of transactions involving intangible assets were improperly recorded by Lee Company in 2002.

1. Lee developed a new manufacturing process, incurring research and development costs of $85,000. The company also purchased a patent for $37,000. In early January, Lee capitalized $122,000 as the cost of the patents. Patent amortization expense of $6,100 was recorded based on a 20-year useful life.

2. On July 1, 2002, Lee purchased a small company and as a result acquired goodwill of $80,000. Lee recorded a half-year's amortization in 2002, based on a 50-year life ($800 amortization).

Prepare entries to correct errors made in recording and amortizing intangible assets.
(SO 8)

Instructions

Prepare all journal entries necessary to correct any errors made during 2002. Assume the books have not yet been closed for 2002.

R&D $85,000
Amortization Expense—
Goodwill $200

Calculate and comment on asset turnover ratio.
(SO 9)

P10-9B Croix Corporation and Marais Corporation, two corporations of roughly the same size, are both involved in the manufacture of canoes and sea kayaks. Each company depreciates its plant assets using the straight-line approach. An investigation of their financial statements reveals the following information.

	Croix Corp.	**Marais Corp.**
Net income	$ 400,000	$ 600,000
Sales	1,600,000	1,350,000
Total assets	2,000,000	1,500,000
Plant assets	1,500,000	800,000

Instructions

(a) Croix Corp. .80 times

(a) For each company, calculate the asset turnover ratio.

(b) ▭▭▭▶ Based on your calculations in part (a), comment on the relative effectiveness of the two companies in using their assets to generate sales and produce net income.

BROADENING YOUR PERSPECTIVE

FINANCIAL REPORTING AND ANALYSIS

FINANCIAL REPORTING AND ANALYSIS: Lands' End, Inc.

BYP10-1 The financial statements and the Notes to Consolidated Financial Statements of **Lands' End, Inc.** are presented in Appendix A.

Instructions

Refer to Lands' End's financial statements and answer the following questions.

(a) What was the total cost and book value of property, plant, and equipment at January 28, 2000?

(b) What method or methods of depreciation are used by the company for financial reporting purposes?

(c) What was the amount of depreciation and amortization expense for each of the three years 1998–2000?

(d) Using the statement of cash flows, what is the amount of additions to properties (capital additions) in 2000 and 1999?

(e) Where does the company disclose its intangible assets, and what types of intangibles did it have at January 28, 2000?

COMPARATIVE ANALYSIS PROBLEM: Lands' End vs. Abercrombie & Fitch

BYP10-2 Lands' End's financial statements are presented in Appendix A. **Abercrombie & Fitch's** financial statements are presented in Appendix B.

Instructions

(a) Compute the asset turnover ratio for each company for 2000.

(b) What conclusions concerning the efficiency of assets can be drawn from these data?

INTERPRETING FINANCIAL STATEMENTS: A Global Focus

BYP10-3 As noted in the chapter, the accounting for goodwill differs in countries around the world. The following discussion of a change in goodwill accounting practices was taken from the notes to the financial statements of **J Sainsbury Plc**, one of the world's leading retailers. Headquartered in the United Kingdom, it serves 15 million customers a week.

J Sainsbury plc	**J SAINSBURY PLC** **Notes to the Financial Statements**

Accounting Policies

Goodwill arising in connection with the acquisition of shares in subsidiaries and associated undertakings is calculated as the excess of the purchase price over the fair value of the net tangible assets acquired. In prior years goodwill has been deducted from reserves in the period of acquisition. FRS 10 is applicable in the currect financial year, and in accordance with the standard acquired goodwill is now shown as an asset on the Group's Balance Sheet. As permitted by FRS 10, goodwill written off to reserves in prior periods has not been restated as an asset.

Goodwill is treated as having an indefinite economic life where it is considered that the acquired business has strong customer loyalty built up over a long period of time, based on advantageous store locations and a commitment to maintain the marketing advantage of the retail brand. The carrying value of the goodwill will be reviewed annually for impairment and adjusted to its recoverable amount if required. Where goodwill is considered to have a finite life, amortisation will be applied over that period.

For amounts stated as goodwill which are considered to have indefinite life, no amortisation is charged to the Profit and Loss Account.

Instructions

(a) How does the initial determination and recording of goodwill compare with that in the United States? That is, is goodwill initially recorded in the same circumstances, and is the calculation of the initial amount the same in both the United Kingdom and the United States?

(b) Prior to adoption of the new accounting standard (FRS 10), how did the company account for goodwill? What were the implications for the income statement?

(c) Under the new accounting standard, how does the company account for its goodwill? Is it possible, under the new standard, for a company to avoid charging goodwill amortization to net income?

(d) In what ways is the new standard similar to U.S. standards, and in what ways is it different?

EXPLORING THE WEB

BYP10-4   A company's annual report identifies the amount of its plant assets and the depreciation method used.

Address: www.reportgallery.com *(or go to www.wiley.com/college/weygandt)*

Steps:

1. From Report Gallery Homepage, choose **Library of Annual Reports**.
2. Select a particular company.
3. Choose **Annual Report**.
4. Follow instructions below.

Instructions

(a) What is the name of the company?
(b) At fiscal year-end, what is the net amount of its plant assets?
(c) What is the accumulated depreciation?
(d) Which method of depreciation does the company use?

CRITICAL THINKING

GROUP DECISION CASE

BYP10-5   Fresno Company and Auburn Company are two proprietorships that are similar in many respects. One difference is that Fresno Company uses the straight-line method and Auburn

Company uses the declining-balance method at double the straight-line rate. On January 2, 2000, both companies acquired the following depreciable assets.

Asset	Cost	Salvage Value	Useful Life
Building	$320,000	$20,000	50 years
Equipment	110,000	10,000	10 years

Including the appropriate depreciation charges, annual net income for the companies in the years 2000, 2001, and 2002 and total income for the 3 years were as follows.

	2000	2001	2002	Total
Fresno Company	$84,000	$88,400	$90,000	$262,400
Auburn Company	68,000	76,000	85,000	229,000

At December 31, 2002, the balance sheets of the two companies are similar except that Auburn Company has more cash than Fresno Company.

Mary Flaherty is interested in buying one of the companies. She comes to you for advice.

Instructions

With the class divided into groups, answer the following.

(a) Determine the annual and total depreciation recorded by each company during the 3 years.

(b) Assuming that Auburn Company also uses the straight-line method of depreciation instead of the declining-balance method as in (a), prepare comparative income data for the 3 years.

(c) Which company should Mary Flaherty buy? Why?

COMMUNICATION ACTIVITY

BYP10-6 The following was published with the financial statements to American Exploration Company.

AMERICAN EXPLORATION COMPANY
Notes to the Financial Statements

Property, Plant, and Equipment—The Company accounts for its oil and gas exploration and production activities using the successful efforts method of accounting. Under this method, acquisition costs for proved and unproved properties are capitalized when incurred.... The costs of drilling exploratory wells are capitalized pending determination of whether each well has discovered proved reserves. If proved reserves are not discovered, such drilling costs are charged to expense.... Depletion of the cost of producing oil and gas properties is computed on the units-of-activity method.

Instructions

Write a brief memo to your instructor discussing American Exploration Company's note regarding property, plant, and equipment. Your memo should address what is meant by the "successful efforts method" and "units-of-activity method."

ETHICS CASE

BYP10-7 Finney Container Company is suffering declining sales of its principal product, non-biodegradeable plastic cartons. The president, Philip Shapeero, instructs his controller, Sharon Fetters, to lengthen asset lives to reduce depreciation expense. A processing line of automated plastic extruding equipment, purchased for $2.7 million in January 2002, was originally estimated to have a useful life of 8 years and a salvage value of $300,000. Depreciation has been recorded for 2 years on that basis. Philip wants the estimated life changed to 12 years total, and the straight-line method continued. Sharon is hesitant to make the change, believing it is unethical to increase net income in this manner. Philip says, "Hey, the life is only an estimate, and I've heard that our competition uses a 12-year life on their production equipment."

Instructions

(a) Who are the stakeholders in this situation?

(b) Is the change in asset life unethical, or is it simply a good business practice by an astute president?

(c) What is the effect of Philip Shapeero's proposed change on income before taxes in the year of change?

Answers to Self-Study Questions

1. d   **2.** b   **3.** d   **4.** d   **5.** b   **6.** d   **7.** a   **8.** c   **9.** c   **10.** b   **11.** c

Answer to *Lands' End* Review It Question 2, p. 403

Lands' End reports the following categories and amounts under the heading "Property, plant and equipment, at cost": Land and buildings $102,776,000; Fixtures and equipment $175,910,000; and Leasehold improvements $4,453,000.

Remember to go back to the Navigator box on the chapter-opening page and check off your completed work.

CURRENT LIABILITIES AND PAYROLL ACCOUNTING

11

THE NAVIGATOR ✓

- Understand *Concepts for Review* ❑
- Read *Feature Story* ❑
- Scan *Study Objectives* ❑
- Read *Preview* ❑
- Read text and answer *Before You Go On*
  p. 453 ❑   *p.* 463 ❑   *p.* 467 ❑   *p.* 469 ❑
- Work *Demonstration Problem* ❑
- Review *Summary of Study Objectives* ❑
- Answer *Self-Study Questions* ❑
- Complete *Assignments* ❑

*C*ONCEPTS FOR REVIEW

Before studying this chapter, you should know or, if necessary, review:

a. The importance of liquidity in evaluating the financial position of a company. (Ch. 4, p. 154)

b. How to make adjusting entries related to unearned revenue (Ch. 3, pp. 97–98) and accrued expenses. (Ch. 3, pp. 101–103)

c. The principles of internal control. (Ch. 8, p. 319)

☑ THE NAVIGATOR

Financing His Dreams

What would you do if you had a great idea for a new product, but couldn't come up with the cash to get the business off the ground? Small businesses often can't attract investors, nor can they obtain traditional debt financing through bank loans or bond issuances. Instead, they often resort to unusual, and costly, forms of nontraditional financing.

Such was the case for Wilbert Murdock. Murdock grew up in a New York housing project, and always had great ambitions. This ambitious spirit led him into some business ventures that failed: a medical diagnostic tool, a device to eliminate carpal-tunnel syndrome, custom sneakers, and a device to keep people from falling asleep while driving.

His latest idea was computerized golf clubs that analyze a golfer's swing and provide immediate feedback. Murdock saw great potential in the idea: Many golfers are willing to shell out considerable sums of

money for devices that might improve their game. But Murdock had no cash to develop his product, and banks and other lenders had shied away. Rather than give up, Murdock resorted to credit cards—in a big way. He quickly owed $25,000 to credit card companies.

While funding a business with credit cards might sound unusual, it isn't. A recent study found that one-third of businesses with fewer than 20 employees financed at least part of their operations with credit cards. As Murdock explained, credit cards are an appealing way to finance a start-up because "credit-card companies don't care how the money is spent." But they do care how they are paid. And so Murdock faced high interest charges and a barrage of credit card collection letters.

Murdock's debt forced him to sacrifice nearly everything in order

to keep his business afloat. His car stopped running, he barely has enough money to buy food, and he lives and works out of a dimly lit apartment in his mother's basement. Through it all he tries to maintain a positive spirit, joking that, if he becomes successful, he might some day get to appear in an American Express commercial.

Source: Rodney Ho, "Banking on Plastic: To Finance a Dream, Many Entrepreneurs Binge on Credit Cards," *The Wall Street Journal,* March 9, 1998, p. A1.

☑ THE NAVIGATOR

After studying this chapter, you should be able to:

1. Explain a current liability, and identify the major types of current liabilities.
2. Describe the accounting for notes payable.
3. Explain the accounting for other current liabilities.
4. Explain the financial statement presentation and analysis of current liabilities.
5. Describe the accounting and disclosure requirements for contingent liabilities.
6. Discuss the objectives of internal control for payroll.
7. Compute and record the payroll for a pay period.
8. Describe and record employer payroll taxes.
9. Identify additional fringe benefits associated with employee compensation.

☑ THE NAVIGATOR

Inventor-entrepreneur Wilbert Murdock, as you can tell from the Feature Story, has had to use multiple credit cards to finance his business ventures. Murdock's credit card debts would be classified as *current liabilities* because they are due every month. Yet by making minimal payments and paying high interest each month, Murdock uses this credit source long-term. Some credit card balances remain outstanding for years as they accumulate interest.

In Chapter 4, we defined liabilities as creditors' claims on total assets and as existing debts and obligations. These claims, debts, and obligations must be settled or paid at some time **in the future** by the transfer of assets or services. The future date on which they are due or payable (maturity date) is a significant feature of liabilities. This "future date" feature gives rise to two basic classifications of liabilities: (1) current liabilities and (2) long-term liabilities. We will explain current liabilities, along with payroll accounting, in this chapter. We will explain long-term liabilities in Chapter 16.

The content and organization of Chapter 11 are as follows.

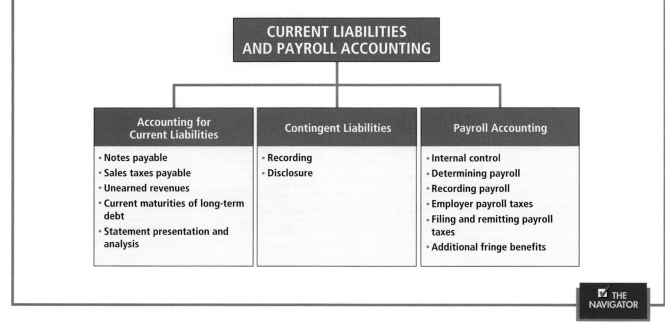

THE NAVIGATOR

ACCOUNTING FOR CURRENT LIABILITIES

STUDY OBJECTIVE 1

Explain a current liability, and identify the major types of current liabilities.

As explained in Chapter 4, a **current liability** is a debt with two key features: (1) It can reasonably be expected to be paid from existing current assets or through the creation of other current liabilities. And (2) it will be paid within one year or the operating cycle, whichever is longer. Debts that do not meet **both criteria** are classified as long-term liabilities. Most companies pay current liabilities within one year out of current assets, rather than by creating other liabilities.

Companies must carefully monitor the relationship of current liabilities to current assets. This relationship is critical in evaluating a company's short-term debt-paying ability. A company that has more current liabilities than current assets is usually the subject of some concern because the company may not be able to meet its current obligations when they become due.

Current liabilities include notes payable, accounts payable, and unearned revenues. They also include accrued liabilities such as taxes, salaries and wages, and interest payable. The entries for accounts payable and adjusting entries for some

HELPFUL HINT

The current liabilities section of the balance sheet gives creditors a good idea of what obligations are coming due.

current liabilities have been explained in previous chapters. Other types of current liabilities that are often encountered are discussed in the following sections.

NOTES PAYABLE

Obligations in the form of written promissory notes are recorded as **notes payable**. Notes payable are often used instead of accounts payable. Doing so gives the lender formal proof of the obligation in case legal remedies are needed to collect the debt. Notes payable usually require the borrower to pay interest and frequently are issued to meet short-term financing needs.

STUDY OBJECTIVE 2

Describe the accounting for notes payable.

Notes are issued for varying periods. **Those due for payment within one year of the balance sheet date are usually classified as current liabilities.** Most notes are interest bearing.

To illustrate the accounting for notes payable, assume that First National Bank agrees to lend $100,000 on March 1, 2002, if Cole Williams Co. signs a $100,000, 12%, 4-month note. With an interest-bearing promissory note, the amount of assets received upon issuance of the note generally equals the note's face value. Cole Williams Co. therefore will receive $100,000 cash and will make the following journal entry.

Mar. 1	Cash	100,000	
	Notes Payable		100,000
	(To record issuance of 12%, 4-month note to First National Bank)		

A	=	L	+	OE
+100,000		+100,000		

Interest accrues over the life of the note and must be recorded periodically. If Cole Williams Co. prepares financial statements semiannually, an adjusting entry is required at June 30 to recognize interest expense and interest payable of $4,000 ($100,000 × 12% × 4/12). The formula for computing interest and its application to Cole Williams Co.'s note are shown in Illustration 11-1.

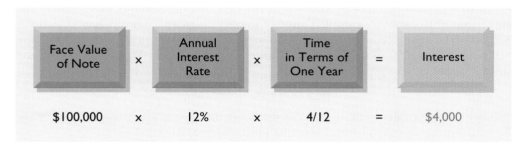

Illustration 11-1

Formula for computing interest

The adjusting entry is:

June 30	Interest Expense	4,000	
	Interest Payable		4,000
	(To accrue interest for 4 months on First National Bank note)		

A	=	L	+	OE
		+4,000		−4,000

In the June 30 financial statements, the current liabilities section of the balance sheet will show notes payable $100,000 and interest payable $4,000. In addition, interest expense of $4,000 will be reported under "other expenses and losses" in the income statement. If Cole Williams Co. prepared financial statements monthly, the adjusting entry at the end of each month would have been $1,000 ($100,000 × 12% × 1/12).

At maturity (July 1, 2002), Cole Williams Co. must pay the face value of the note ($100,000) plus $4,000 interest ($100,000 × 12% × 4/12). The entry to record payment of the note and accrued interest is as follows.

A = L + OE
−104,000 −100,000
−4,000

July 1	Notes Payable	100,000	
	Interest Payable	4,000	
	Cash		104,000
	(To record payment of First National Bank interest-bearing note and accrued interest at maturity)		

SALES TAXES PAYABLE

STUDY OBJECTIVE 3

Explain the accounting for other current liabilities.

As a consumer, you know that many of the products you purchase at retail stores are subject to sales taxes. The tax is expressed as a stated percentage of the sales price. The retailer collects the tax from the customer when the sale occurs. Periodically (usually monthly), the retailer remits the collections to the state's department of revenue.

Under most state sales tax laws, the amount of the sale and the amount of the sales tax collected must be rung up separately on the cash register. (Gasoline sales are a major exception.) The cash register readings are then used to credit Sales and Sales Taxes Payable. For example, if the March 25 cash register reading for Cooley Grocery shows sales of $10,000 and sales taxes of $600 (sales tax rate of 6%), the entry is:

A = L + OE
+10,600 +600 +10,000

Mar. 25	Cash	10,600	
	Sales		10,000
	Sales Taxes Payable		600
	(To record daily sales and sales taxes)		

When the taxes are remitted to the taxing agency, Sales Taxes Payable is debited and Cash is credited. The company does not report sales taxes as an expense. It simply forwards to the government the amount paid by the customers. Thus, Cooley Grocery serves only as a **collection agent** for the taxing authority.

When sales taxes are not rung up separately on the cash register, they must be extracted from the total receipts. To determine the amount of sales in such cases, divide total receipts by 100% plus the sales tax percentage. To illustrate, assume that in the above example Cooley Grocery rings up total receipts, which are $10,600. The receipts from the sales are equal to the sales price (100%) plus the tax percentage (6% of sales), or 1.06 times the sales total. We can compute the sales amount as follows.

$$\$10,600 \div 1.06 = \$10,000$$

Thus, Cooley Grocery could find the sales tax amount it must remit to the state by subtracting sales from total receipts ($10,600 − $10,000).

HELPFUL HINT

Alternatively, Cooley could find the tax by multiplying sales by the sales tax rate ($10,000 × 6%).

*A*CCOUNTING IN ACTION ∧ *Business Insight*

If you buy a book at a bookstore, you pay sales tax. If you buy the same book over the Internet, you don't pay a sales tax (in most cases). This is one reason why e-commerce, as it has come to be called, is growing exponentially and why "dot-com" businesses like **Amazon.com** have become so popular. A recent study suggested that Internet sales would fall by 30 percent if sales tax were applied. Partly as a result of this study, the Clinton administration and Congress agreed to a three-year moratorium on Internet taxation. Most people in Washington expect that after the moratorium runs out in 2001, some kind of sales tax will be imposed on e-commerce. The idea is that by then the e-commerce model will have "matured" and can serve as a veritable gold mine for federal, state, and local taxation.

SOURCE: John Ellis. "The Tax Consequences of Commerce on the Internet," *Boston Globe*, April 10, 1999, p. A23.

UNEARNED REVENUES

A magazine publisher, such as **Sports Illustrated**, receives a customer's check when magazines are ordered. An airline company, such as **American Airlines**, receives cash when it sells tickets for future flights. Through these transactions, both companies have incurred unearned revenues—revenues that are received before goods are delivered or services are rendered. How do companies account for unearned revenues?

1. When the advance payment is received, Cash is debited, and a current liability account identifying the source of the unearned revenue is credited.
2. When the revenue is earned, the Unearned Revenue account is debited, and an earned revenue account is credited.

To illustrate, assume that Superior University sells 10,000 season football tickets at $50 each for its five-game home schedule. The entry for the sale of season tickets is:

Aug. 6	Cash	500,000	
	Unearned Football Ticket Revenue		500,000
	(To record sale of 10,000 season tickets)		

A = L + OE
+500,000 +500,000

As each game is completed, the following entry is made:

Sept. 7	Unearned Football Ticket Revenue	100,000	
	Football Ticket Revenue		100,000
	(To record football ticket revenues earned)		

A = L + OE
−100,000 +100,000

Any balance in an unearned revenue account (in Unearned Football Ticket Revenue, for example) is reported as a current liability in the balance sheet. As revenue is earned, a transfer from unearned revenue to earned revenue occurs. Unearned revenue is material for some companies: In the airline industry, for example, tickets sold for future flights represent almost 50% of total current liabilities. At **United Air Lines**, unearned ticket revenue is the largest current liability, recently amounting to over $1 billion.

Illustration 11-2 shows specific unearned and earned revenue accounts used in selected types of businesses.

Type of Business	Account Title	
	Unearned Revenue	**Earned Revenue**
Airline	Unearned Passenger Ticket Revenue	Passenger Revenue
Magazine publisher	Unearned Subscription Revenue	Subscription Revenue
Hotel	Unearned Rental Revenue	Rental Revenue
Insurance company	Unearned Premium Revenue	Premium Revenue

Illustration 11-2

Unearned and earned revenue accounts

CURRENT MATURITIES OF LONG-TERM DEBT

Companies often have a portion of long-term debt that comes due in the current year. That amount would be considered a current liability. For example, assume that Wendy Construction issues a 5-year interest-bearing $25,000 note on January 1, 2002. Each January 1, starting January 1, 2003, $5,000 of the note is due to be paid. When financial statements are prepared on December 31, 2002, $5,000 should be reported as a current liability. The remaining $20,000 on the note would be reported as a long-term liability. Current maturities of long-term debt are often termed **long-term debt due within one year**.

It is not necessary to prepare an adjusting entry to recognize the current maturity of long-term debt. The proper statement classification of each balance sheet account is recognized when the balance sheet is prepared.

STATEMENT PRESENTATION AND ANALYSIS

STUDY OBJECTIVE **4**

Explain the financial statement presentation and analysis of current liabilities.

Presentation

As indicated in Chapter 4, current liabilities are the first category under liabilities on the balance sheet. Each of the principal types of current liabilities is listed separately. In addition, the terms of notes payable and other key information about the individual items are disclosed in the notes to the financial statements.

Current liabilities are seldom listed in the order of maturity. The reason is that varying maturity dates may exist for specific obligations such as notes payable. A more common method of presenting current liabilities is to list them by **order of magnitude**, with the largest ones first. Or, many companies, as a matter of custom, show notes payable and accounts payable first, regardless of amount. The following adapted excerpt from the balance sheet of **Lands' End, Inc.** illustrates its order of presentation.

Illustration 11-3

Balance sheet presentation of current liabilities

LANDS' END, INC.
Balance Sheet
January 28, 2000
(in millions)

Assets

Current assets	$289.4
Property, plant and equipment (net)	165.8
Intangibles, net	1.0
Total assets	$456.2

Liabilities and Stockholders' Equity

Current liabilities	
Lines of credit	$ 11.7
Accounts payable	74.5
Reserve for returns	7.9
Accrued liabilities	43.8
Accrued profit sharing	2.7
Income taxes payable	10.3
Total current liabilities	150.9
Noncurrent liabilities	9.1
Total liabilities	160.0
Shareholders' equity	296.2
Total liabilities and stockholders' equity	$456.2

HELPFUL HINT

For another example of a current liabilities section, refer to the **Abercrombie & Fitch** balance sheet in Appendix B.

Analysis

Use of current and noncurrent classifications makes it possible to analyze a company's liquidity. **Liquidity** refers to the ability to pay maturing obligations and meet unexpected needs for cash. The relationship of current assets to current liabilities is critical in analyzing liquidity. This relationship can be expressed as a dollar amount (called working capital) and as a ratio (called the current ratio).

The excess of current assets over current liabilities is **working capital**. The formula for the computation of Lands' End's working capital is shown in Illustration 11-4 (dollar amounts in millions).

Illustration 11-4

Working capital formula and computation

As an absolute dollar amount, working capital is limited in its informational value. For example, $1 million of working capital may be far more than needed for a small company but be inadequate for a large corporation. And, $1 million of working capital may be adequate for a company at one time but be inadequate at another time.

The **current ratio** permits us to compare the liquidity of different sized companies and of a single company at different times. The current ratio is current assets divided by current liabilities. The formula for this ratio is illustrated below, along with its computation using Lands' End's current asset and current liability data (dollar amounts in millions).

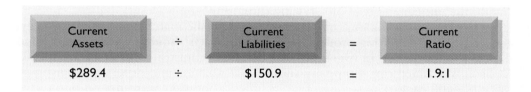

Illustration 11-5

Current ratio formula and computation

Historically, a ratio of 2:1 was considered to be the standard for a good credit rating. In recent years, however, many healthy companies have maintained ratios well below 2:1. Lands' End's ratio of 1.9:1 is comparable to the standard of 2:1.

CONTINGENT LIABILITIES

With notes payable, interest payable, accounts payable, and sales taxes payable, we know that an obligation to make payment exists. But suppose that your company is involved in a dispute with the Internal Revenue Service (IRS) over the amount of its income tax liability. Should you report the disputed amount as a liability on the balance sheet? Or suppose your company is involved in a lawsuit which, if you lose, might result in bankruptcy. How should this major contingency be reported? The answers to these questions are difficult, because these liabilities are dependent—contingent—upon some future event. In other words, a **contingent liability** is a potential liability that may become an actual liability in the future.

How should contingent liabilities be reported? Guidelines have been adopted that help resolve these problems. The guidelines require that:

1. If the contingency is **probable** (if it is likely to occur) **and** the amount can be **reasonably estimated**, the liability should be recorded in the accounts.

2. If the contingency is only **reasonably possible** (if it could happen), then it need be disclosed only in the notes that accompany the financial statements.

3. If the contingency is **remote** (if it is unlikely to occur), it need not be recorded or disclosed.

STUDY OBJECTIVE 5

Describe the accounting and disclosure requirements for contingent liabilities.

HELPFUL HINT
Another example of a contingency is toxic waste cleanup costs. Some companies expect that insurance will cover these costs, but insurance companies are arguing that general liability policies were never meant to cover this type of situation.

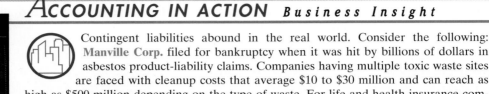

ACCOUNTING IN ACTION *Business Insight*

Contingent liabilities abound in the real world. Consider the following: **Manville Corp.** filed for bankruptcy when it was hit by billions of dollars in asbestos product-liability claims. Companies having multiple toxic waste sites are faced with cleanup costs that average $10 to $30 million and can reach as high as $500 million depending on the type of waste. For life and health insurance companies and their stockholders, the cost of AIDS is like an iceberg: Everyone wonders how big it really is and what damage it might do in the future; according to the U.S. Centers for Disease Control treatment costs could be $8 billion to $16 billion. And frequent-flyer programs are so popular that airlines at one time owed participants more than 3 million round-trip domestic tickets. That's enough to fly at least 5.4 billion miles—free for the passengers, but at what future cost to the airlines?

RECORDING A CONTINGENT LIABILITY

INTERNATIONAL NOTE

International accounting standards basically use criteria similar to those in the U.S. in determining how to account for contingencies.

Product warranties are an example of a contingent liability that should be recorded in the accounts. Warranty contracts result in future costs that may be incurred in replacing defective units or repairing malfunctioning units. Generally, a manufacturer, such as **Black & Decker**, knows that some warranty costs will be incurred. From prior experience with the product, the company usually can reasonably estimate the anticipated cost of servicing (honoring) the warranty.

The accounting for warranty costs is based on the matching principle. **The estimated cost of honoring product warranty contracts should be recognized as an expense in the period in which the sale occurs.** To illustrate, assume that in 2002 Denson Manufacturing Company sells 10,000 washers and dryers at an average price of $600 each. The selling price includes a one-year warranty on parts. It is expected that 500 units (5%) will be defective and that warranty repair costs will average $80 per unit. In 2002, warranty contracts are honored on 300 units at a total cost of $24,000.

At December 31, it is necessary to accrue the estimated warranty costs on the 2002 sales. The computation is as follows.

Illustration 11-6

Computation of estimated product warranty liability

Number of units sold	10,000
Estimated rate of defective units	× 5%
Total estimated defective units	500
Average warranty repair cost	× $80
Estimated product warranty liability	**$40,000**

The adjusting entry, therefore, is:

A = L + OE
+40,000 −40,000

Dec. 31	Warranty Expense	40,000	
	Estimated Warranty Liability		40,000
	(To accrue estimated warranty costs)		

The entry to record those repair costs incurred in 2002 to honor warranty contracts on 2002 sales is shown below.

A = L + OE
−24,000 −24,000

Jan. 1– Dec. 31	Estimated Warranty Liability	24,000	
	Repair Parts		24,000
	(To record honoring of 300 warranty contracts on 2002 sales)		

Warranty expense of $40,000 is reported under selling expenses in the income statement. Estimated warranty liability of $16,000 ($40,000 − $24,000) is classified as a current liability on the balance sheet.

In the following year, all expenses incurred in honoring warranty contracts on 2002 sales should be debited to Estimated Warranty Liability. To illustrate, assume that 20 defective units are replaced in January 2003, at an average cost of $80 in parts and labor. The summary entry for the month of January 2003 is:

Jan. 31	Estimated Warranty Liability	1,600	
	Repair Parts		1,600
	(To record honoring of 20 warranty		
	contracts on 2002 sales)		

A	=	L	+	OE
−1,600		−1,600		

DISCLOSURE OF CONTINGENT LIABILITIES

When it is probable that a contingent liability will be incurred but the amount cannot be reasonably estimated, or when the contingent liability is only reasonably possible, only disclosure of the contingency is required. Examples of contingencies that may require disclosure are pending or threatened lawsuits and assessment of additional income taxes pending an IRS audit of the tax return.

The disclosure should identify the nature of the item and, if known, the amount of the contingency and the expected outcome of the future event. Disclosure is usually accomplished through a note to the financial statements, as illustrated by the following.

USAIR
Notes to the Financial Statements
Legal Proceedings
The Company and various subsidiaries have been named as defendants in various suits and proceedings which involve, among other things, environmental concerns about noise and air pollution and employment matters. These suits and proceedings are in various stages of litigation, and the status of the law with respect to several of the issues involved is unsettled. For these reasons the outcome of these suits and proceedings is difficult to predict. In the Company's opinion, however, the disposition of these matters is not likely to have a material adverse effect on its financial condition.

Illustration 11-7

Disclosure of contingent liability

BEFORE YOU GO ON...

▶ *REVIEW IT*

1. What are the two criteria for classifying a debt as a current liability?
2. Identify three liabilities classified as current by **Lands' End**. The answer to this question is provided on page 485.
3. What entries are made for an interest-bearing note payable?
4. How are sales taxes recorded by a retailer? Identify three unearned revenues.
5. How may the liquidity of a company be analyzed?
6. What are the accounting guidelines for contingent liabilities?

▶ *DO IT*

You and several classmates are studying for the next accounting examination. They ask you to answer the following questions: (1) How is the sales tax amount determined when the cash register total includes sales taxes? (2) When should a contingency be recorded in the accounts?

ACTION PLAN
- Remove the sales tax from the total sales.
- Identify the criteria for recording and disclosing contingent liabilities.

SOLUTION
(1) First, divide the total proceeds by 100% plus the sales tax percentage to find the sales amount. Second, subtract the sales amount from the total proceeds to determine the sales taxes.
(2) A contingency should be recorded when it is *probable* that a liability will be incurred *and* the amount can be *reasonably* estimated.

Related exercise material: BE11-3, BE11-4, BE11-5, E11-2, E11-3, E11-4, and E11-5.

Payroll Accounting

Payroll and related fringe benefits often make up a large percentage of current liabilities. Employee compensation is often the most significant expense that a company incurs. For example, **General Motors** recently reported total employees of 516,000 and labor costs of $31.3 billion. Add to labor costs such fringe benefits as health insurance, life insurance, disability insurance, and so on, and you can see why proper accounting and control of payroll are so important.

Payroll accounting involves more than paying employees' wages. Companies are required by law to maintain payroll records for each employee, file and pay payroll taxes, and comply with numerous state and federal tax laws related to employee compensation. Accounting for payroll has become much more complex due to these regulations.

The term "payroll" pertains to both salaries and wages. Managerial, administrative, and sales personnel are generally paid **salaries**. Salaries are often expressed in terms of a specified amount per month or per year rather than an hourly rate. For example, the faculty and administrative personnel at the college or university you are attending are paid salaries. In contrast, store clerks, factory employees, and manual laborers are normally paid **wages**. Wages are based on a rate per hour or on a piecework basis (such as per unit of product). Frequently, the terms "salaries" and "wages" are used interchangeably.

The term "payroll" does not apply to payments made for services of professionals such as certified public accountants, attorneys, and architects. Such professionals are independent contractors rather than salaried employees. Payments to them are called **fees**, rather than salaries or wages. This distinction is important because government regulations relating to the payment and reporting of payroll taxes apply only to employees.

INTERNAL CONTROL

STUDY OBJECTIVE 6

Discuss the objectives of internal control for payroll.

Internal control was introduced in Chapter 8. As applied to payrolls, the objectives of internal control are (1) to safeguard company assets against unauthorized payments of payrolls, and (2) to ensure the accuracy and reliability of the accounting records pertaining to payrolls.

Irregularities often result if internal control is lax. Overstating hours, using unauthorized pay rates, adding fictitious employees to the payroll, continuing terminated employees on the payroll, and distributing duplicate payroll checks are all methods of stealing from a company. Moreover, inaccurate records will result in incorrect paychecks, financial statements, and payroll tax returns.

TECHNOLOGY IN ACTION

A Senate hearing revealed that the U.S. Army spent $8 million on unauthorized pay, including payments to deserters and "ghost" soldiers. The underlying cause was a computer system so lax that it was possible to create new pay records and destroy old ones without leaving an audit trail.

Payroll activities involve four functions: hiring employees, timekeeping, preparing the payroll, and paying the payroll. For effective internal control, these four functions should be assigned to different departments or individuals. To illustrate these functions, we will examine the case of Academy Company and one of its employees, Michael Jordan.

Hiring Employees

The human resources (personnel) department is responsible for posting job openings, screening and interviewing applicants, and hiring employees. From a control standpoint, this department provides significant documentation and authorization. When an employee is hired, the human resources department prepares an authorization form. The one used by Academy Company for Michael Jordan is shown in Illustration 11-8.

The authorization form is sent to the payroll department, where it is used to place the new employee on the payroll. A chief concern of the human resources department is ensuring the accuracy of this form. The reason is quite simple: one of the most common types of payroll frauds is adding fictitious employees to the payroll.

The human resources department is also responsible for authorizing changes in employment status. Specifically, they must authorize (1) changes in pay rates

Hiring Employees

Human Resources department documents and authorizes employment.

Illustration 11-8

Authorization form prepared by the human resources department

---

ACADEMY COMPANY

Employee Name: Jordan, (LAST)   Michael (FIRST)   (MI)   Starting Date: 9/01/98

Classification: Skilled-Level 10   Social Security No.: 329-36-9547

Department: Shipping   Division: Entertainment

NEW HIRE	Classification: Clerk Salary Grade: Level 10 Trans. from Temp. ☐ Rate $10.00 per hour Bonus: N/A Non-exempt ☒ Exempt ☐
RATE CHANGE	New Rate $12.00 Effective Date: 9/1/00 Present Rate $10.00 Merit ☒ Promotion ☐ Decrease ☐ Other _____ Previous Increase Date: None Amount $_____ per_____ Type_____
SEPARATION	Resignation ☐ Discharge ☐ Retirement ☐ Reason _____ _____ Leave of absence ☐ From_____ to_____ Type_____ Last Day Worked_____
APPROVALS	BEW 9/1/00 EMW 9-1-00 BRANCH OR DEPT. MANAGER DATE DIVISION V.P. DATE James E. Speer PERSONNEL DEPARTMENT

Timekeeping

Supervisors monitor hours worked through time cards and time reports.

and (2) terminations of employment. Every authorization should be in writing, and a copy of the change in status should be sent to the payroll department. Notice in Illustration 11-8 that Jordan received a pay increase of $2 per hour.

Timekeeping

Another area in which internal control is important is timekeeping. Hourly employees are usually required to record time worked by "punching" a time clock. Times of arrival and departure are automatically recorded by the employee by inserting a time card into the clock. Michael Jordan's time card is shown in Illustration 11-9.

Illustration 11-9

Time card

			PAY PERIOD ENDING
No. 17			1/14/02

NAME Michael Jordan

EXTRA TIME		REGULAR TIME
	1st Day	A.M. IN 8:58
		NOON OUT 12:00
		IN 1:00
		P.M. OUT 5:01
	2nd Day	A.M. IN 9:00
		NOON OUT 11:59
		IN 12:59
		P.M. OUT 5:00
	3rd Day	A.M. IN 8:59
		NOON OUT 12:01
		IN 1:01
		P.M. OUT 5:00
5:00	4th Day	A.M. IN 9:00
9:00		NOON OUT 12:00
		IN 1:00
		P.M. OUT 5:00
	5th Day	A.M. IN 8:57
		NOON OUT 11:58
		IN 1:00
		P.M. OUT 5:01
	6th Day	A.M. IN 8:00
		NOON OUT 1:00
		IN
		P.M. OUT
	7th Day	A.M. IN
		NOON OUT
		IN
		P.M. OUT
TOTAL 4		TOTAL 40

THIS SIDE OUT

In large companies, time clock procedures are often monitored by a supervisor or security guard to make sure an employee punches only one card. At the end of the pay period, each employee's supervisor approves the hours shown by signing the time card. When overtime hours are involved, approval by a supervisor is usually mandatory. This guards against unauthorized overtime. The approved time cards are then sent to the payroll department. For salaried employees, a manually prepared weekly or monthly time report kept by a supervisor may be used to record time worked.

Preparing the Payroll

Two (or more) employees verify payroll amounts; supervisor approves.

Preparing the Payroll

The payroll is prepared in the payroll department on the basis of two inputs: (1) human resources department authorizations and (2) approved time cards. Numerous calculations are involved in determining gross wages and payroll deductions. Therefore, a second payroll department employee, working independently, verifies all calculated amounts, and a payroll department supervisor then approves the payroll. The payroll department is also responsible for preparing (but not signing) payroll checks, maintaining payroll records, and preparing payroll tax returns.

Paying the Payroll

The payroll is paid by the treasurer's department. **Payment by check minimizes the risk of loss from theft, and the endorsed check provides proof of payment.** For good internal control, payroll checks should be prenumbered, and all checks should be accounted for. All checks must be signed by the treasurer (or a designated agent). Distribution of the payroll checks to employees should be controlled by the treasurer's department. Checks may be distributed by the treasurer or paymaster.

Occasionally the payroll is paid in currency. In such cases it is customary to have a second person count the cash in each pay envelope. The paymaster should obtain a signed receipt from the employee upon payment. If alleged discrepancies arise, adequate safeguards have been established to protect each party involved.

DETERMINING THE PAYROLL

Determining the payroll involves computing three amounts: (1) gross earnings, (2) payroll deductions, and (3) net pay.

Gross Earnings

Gross earnings is the total compensation earned by an employee. It consists of wages or salaries, plus any bonuses and commissions.

Total **wages** for an employee are determined by multiplying the hours worked by the hourly rate of pay. In addition to the hourly pay rate, most companies are required by law to pay hourly workers a minimum of $1\frac{1}{2}$ times the regular hourly rate for overtime work in excess of 8 hours per day or 40 hours per week. In addition, many employers pay overtime rates for work done at night, on weekends, and on holidays.

Michael Jordan's time card shows that he worked 44 hours for the weekly pay period ending January 14. The computation of his gross earnings (total wages) is as follows.

Type of Pay	Hours	×	Rate	=	Gross Earnings
Regular	40	×	$12.00	=	$480.00
Overtime	4	×	18.00	=	72.00
Total wages					**$552.00**

This computation assumes that Jordan receives $1\frac{1}{2}$ times his regular hourly rate ($12.00 × 1.5) for his overtime hours. Union contracts often require that overtime rates be as much as twice the regular rates.

The **salary** for an employee is generally based on a monthly or yearly rate. These rates are then prorated to the payroll periods used by the company. Most executive and administrative positions are salaried. Federal law does not require overtime pay for employees in such positions.

Many companies have **bonus** agreements for management personnel and other employees. A recent survey found that over 94% of the largest U.S. manufacturing companies offer annual bonuses to their key executives. Bonus arrangements may be based on such factors as increased sales or net income. Bonuses may be paid in cash and/or by granting executives and employees the opportunity to acquire shares of company stock at favorable prices (called stock option plans).

Payroll Deductions

As anyone who has received a paycheck knows, gross earnings are usually very different from the amount actually received. The difference is due to **payroll deductions**. Such deductions do not result in payroll tax expense to the employer.

Paying the Payroll

Treasurer signs and distributes checks.

STUDY OBJECTIVE 7

Compute and record the payroll for a pay period.

HELPFUL HINT
The law that governs pay rates is the Federal Fair Labor Standards Act. It applies to all companies involved in interstate commerce.

Illustration 11-10

Computation of total wages

ETHICS NOTE

Bonuses often reward outstanding individual performance; but successful corporations also need considerable teamwork. A challenge is to motivate individuals while preventing an unethical employee from taking another's idea for his or her own advantage.

The employer is merely a collection agent, and subsequently transfers the amounts deducted to the government and designated recipients. Payroll deductions may be mandatory or voluntary. Mandatory deductions are required by law and consist of FICA taxes and income taxes. Voluntary deductions are at the option of the employee. Illustration 11-11 summarizes the types of payroll deductions.

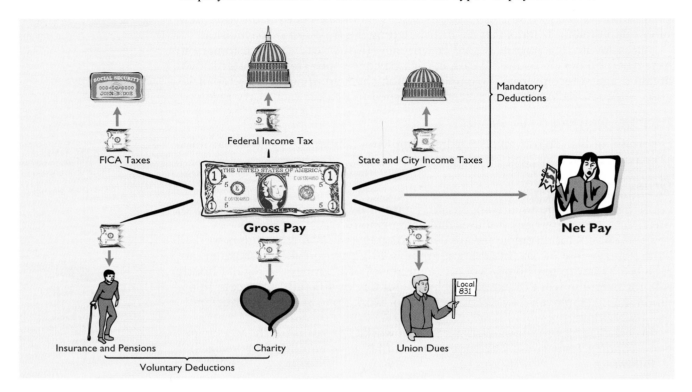

Illustration 11-11

Payroll deductions

FICA TAXES. In 1937 Congress enacted the Federal Insurance Contribution Act (FICA). **FICA taxes are designed to provide workers with supplemental retirement, employment disability, and medical benefits.** In 1965, benefits were expanded to include Medicare for individuals over 65 years of age. The benefits are financed by a tax levied on employees' earnings. FICA taxes are commonly referred to as **Social Security taxes**.

The tax rate and the tax base for FICA taxes are set by Congress. When FICA taxes were first imposed, the rate was 1% on the first $3,000 of gross earnings, or a maximum of $30 per year. The rate and base have changed dramatically since that time! In 2000, the rate was 7.65% (6.2% Social Security plus 1.45% Medicare) on the first $80,400 of gross earnings for each employee.[1] For purpose of illustration in this chapter, we will assume a rate of 8% on the first $65,000 of gross earnings, or a maximum of $5,200. Using the 8% rate, the FICA withholding for Jordan for the weekly pay period ending January 14 is $44.16 ($552 × 8%).

INCOME TAXES. Under the U.S. pay-as-you-go system of federal income taxes, employers are required to withhold income taxes from employees each pay period. The amount to be withheld is determined by three variables: (1) the employee's gross earnings; (2) the number of allowances claimed by the employee; and (3) the length of the pay period. The number of allowances claimed typically includes the employee, his or her spouse, and other dependents. **To indicate to**

---

[1]The Medicare provision also includes a tax of 1.45% on gross earnings in excess of $80,400. In the interest of simplification, we ignore this 1.45% charge in our end-of-chapter assignment material. We assume zero FICA withholdings on gross earnings above $65,000.

the Internal Revenue Service the number of allowances claimed, the employee must complete an Employee's Withholding Allowance Certificate (Form W-4). As shown in Illustration 11-12, Michael Jordan claims two allowances on his W-4.

Withholding tables furnished by the Internal Revenue Service indicate the

Illustration 11-12

W-4 form

amount of income tax to be withheld. Withholding amounts are based on gross wages and the number of allowances claimed. Separate tables are provided for weekly, bi-weekly, semimonthly, and monthly pay periods. The withholding tax table for Michael Jordan (assuming he earns $552 per week) is shown in Illustration 11-13. For a weekly salary of $552 with two allowances, the income tax to be withheld is $49.

Most states (and some cities) also require employers to withhold income taxes

Illustration 11-13

Withholding tax table

MARRIED Persons — WEEKLY Payroll Period
(For Wages Paid in 2002)

If the wages are –		And the number of withholding allowances claimed is –										
At least	But less than	0	1	2	3	4	5	6	7	8	9	10
		The amount of income tax to be withheld is –										
490	500	56	48	40	32	24	17	9	1	0	0	0
500	510	57	49	42	34	26	18	10	3	0	0	0
510	520	59	51	43	35	27	20	12	4	0	0	0
520	530	60	52	45	37	29	21	13	6	0	0	0
530	540	62	54	46	38	30	23	15	7	0	0	0
540	550	63	55	48	40	32	24	16	9	1	0	0
550	560	65	57	49	41	33	26	18	10	2	0	0
560	570	66	58	51	43	35	27	19	12	4	0	0
570	580	68	60	52	44	36	29	21	13	5	0	0
580	590	69	61	54	46	38	30	22	15	7	0	0
590	600	71	63	55	47	39	32	24	16	8	1	0
600	610	72	64	57	49	41	33	25	18	10	2	0
610	620	74	66	58	50	42	35	27	19	11	4	0
620	630	75	67	60	52	44	36	28	21	13	5	0
630	640	77	69	61	53	45	38	30	22	14	7	0
640	650	78	70	63	55	47	39	31	24	16	8	0
650	660	80	72	64	56	48	41	33	25	17	10	2
660	670	81	73	66	58	50	42	34	27	19	11	3
670	680	83	75	67	59	51	44	36	28	20	13	5
680	690	84	76	69	61	53	45	37	30	22	14	6

from employees' earnings. As a rule, the amounts withheld are a percentage (specified in the state revenue code) of the amount withheld for the federal income tax. Or they may be a specified percentage of the employee's earnings. For the sake of simplicity, we have assumed that Jordan's wages are subject to state income taxes of 2%, or $11.04 (2% × $552) per week.

There is no limit on the amount of gross earnings subject to income tax withholdings. In fact, the higher the earnings, the higher the amount of taxes withheld.

OTHER DEDUCTIONS. Employees may voluntarily authorize withholdings for charitable, retirement, and other purposes. All voluntary deductions from gross earnings should be authorized in writing by the employee. The authorization(s) may be made individually or as part of a group plan. Deductions for charitable organizations, such as the United Fund, or for financial arrangements, such as U.S. savings bonds and repayment of loans from company credit unions, are made individually. Deductions for union dues, health and life insurance, and pension plans are often made on a group basis. We will assume that Jordan has weekly voluntary deductions of $10 for the United Fund and $5 for union dues.

Net Pay

ALTERNATIVE TERMINOLOGY
Net pay is also called *take-home pay.*

Net pay is determined by subtracting payroll deductions from gross earnings. For Michael Jordan, net pay for the pay period is $432.80, computed as follows.
Assuming that Michael Jordan's wages for each week during the year are $552,

Illustration 11-14

Computation of net pay

Gross earnings		$552.00
Payroll deductions:		
FICA taxes	$44.16	
Federal income taxes	49.00	
State income taxes	11.04	
United Fund	10.00	
Union dues	5.00	119.20
Net pay		**$432.80**

total wages for the year are $28,704 (52 × $552). Thus, all of Jordan's wages are subject to FICA tax during the year. Let's assume that Jordan's department head earns $1,350 per week, or $70,200 for the year. Since only the first $65,000 is subject to FICA taxes, the maximum FICA withholdings on the department head's earnings would be $5,200 ($65,000 × 8%).

RECORDING THE PAYROLL

Recording the payroll involves maintaining payroll department records, recognizing payroll expenses and liabilities, and recording payment of the payroll.

Maintaining Payroll Department Records

To comply with state and federal laws, an employer must keep a cumulative record of each employee's gross earnings, deductions, and net pay during the year. The record that provides this information is the **employee earnings record**. Michael

Illustration 11-15

Employee earnings record

ACADEMY COMPANY
Employee Earnings Record
For the Year 2002

Name	Michael Jordan	Address	2345 Mifflin Ave.
Social Security Number	329-36-9547		Hampton, Michigan 48292
Date of Birth	December 24, 1962	Telephone	555-238-9051
Date Employed	September 1, 1998	Date Employment Ended	
Sex	Male	Exemptions	2
Single		Married	x

2002 Period Ending	Total Hours	Gross Earnings				Deductions						Payment	
		Regular	Overtime	Total	Cumulative	FICA	Fed. Inc. Tax	State Inc. Tax	United Fund	Union Dues	Total	Net Amount	Check No.
1/7	42	480.00	36.00	516.00	516.00	41.28	43.00	10.32	10.00	5.00	109.60	406.40	974
1/14	44	480.00	72.00	552.00	1,068.00	44.16	49.00	11.04	10.00	5.00	119.20	432.80	1028
1/21	43	480.00	54.00	534.00	1,602.00	42.72	46.00	10.68	10.00	5.00	114.40	419.60	1077
1/28	42	480.00	36.00	516.00	2,118.00	41.28	43.00	10.32	10.00	5.00	109.60	406.40	1133
Jan. Total		1,920.00	198.00	2,118.00		169.44	181.00	42.36	40.00	20.00	452.80	1,665.20	

Jordan's employee earnings record is shown in Illustration 11-15.

A separate earnings record is kept for each employee. It is updated after each pay period. The cumulative payroll data on the earnings record are used by the employer to: (1) determine when an employee has earned the maximum earnings subject to FICA taxes, (2) file state and federal payroll tax returns (as explained later in the chapter), and (3) provide each employee with a statement of gross earnings and tax withholdings for the year. Illustration 11-19 on page 466 shows this statement.

In addition to employee earnings records, many companies find it useful to prepare a **payroll register**. This record accumulates the gross earnings, deductions, and net pay by employee for each pay period. It provides the documentation for preparing a paycheck for each employee. Academy Company's payroll register is presented in Illustration 11-16. It shows the data for Michael Jordan in the wages section. In this example, Academy Company's total weekly payroll is $17,210, as shown in the gross earnings column.

Note that this record is a listing of each employee's payroll data for the pay period. In some companies, a payroll register is a journal or book of original entry. Postings are made from it directly to ledger accounts. In other companies, the payroll register is a memorandum record that provides the data for a general journal entry and subsequent posting to the ledger accounts. At Academy Company, the latter procedure is followed.

Illustration 11-16

Payroll register

		Earnings			Deductions						Paid		Accounts Debited	
						Federal	State						Office	
	Total		Over-			Income	Income	United	Union			Check	Salaries	Wages
Employee	Hours	Regular	time	Gross	FICA	Tax	Tax	Fund	Dues	Total	Net Pay	No.	Expense	Expense
Office Salaries														
Arnold, Patricia	40	580.00		580.00	46.40	61.00	11.60	15.00		134.00	446.00	998	580.00	
Canton, Matthew	40	590.00		590.00	47.20	63.00	11.80	20.00		142.00	448.00	999	590.00	
Mueller, William	40	530.00		530.00	42.40	54.00	10.60	11.00		118.00	412.0	1000	530.00	
Subtotal		5,200.00		5,200.00	416.00	1,090.00	104.00	120.00		1,730.00	3,470.00		5,200.00	
Wages														
Bennett, Robin	42	480.00	36.00	516.00	41.28	43.00	10.32	18.00	5.00	117.60	398.40	1025		516.00
Jordan, Michael	44	480.00	72.00	552.00	44.16	49.00	11.04	10.00	5.00	119.20	432.80	1028		552.00
Milroy, Lee	43	480.00	54.00	534.00	42.72	46.00	10.68	10.00	5.00	114.40	419.60	1029		534.00
Subtotal		11,000.00	1,010.00	12,010.00	960.80	2,400.00	240.20	301.50	115.00	4,017.50	7,992.50			12,010.00
Total		16,200.00	1,010.00	17,210.00	1,376.80	3,490.00	344.20	421.50	115.00	5,747.50	11,462.50		5,200.00	12,010.00

ACADEMY COMPANY
Payroll Register
For the Week Ending January 14, 2002

Recognizing Payroll Expenses and Liabilities

From the payroll register in Illustration 11-16, a journal entry is made to record the payroll. For the week ending January 14 the entry is:

Jan. 14	Office Salaries Expense	5,200.00	
	Wages Expense	12,010.00	
	FICA Taxes Payable		1,376.80
	Federal Income Taxes Payable		3,490.00
	State Income Taxes Payable		344.20
	United Fund Payable		421.50
	Union Dues Payable		115.00
	Salaries and Wages Payable		11,462.50
	(To record payroll for the week ending January 14)		

```
A  =  L   +   OE
   +1,376.80  −5,200.00
   +3,490.00  −12,010.00
   +344.20
   +421.50
   +115.00
   +11,462.50
```

Specific liability accounts are credited for the mandatory and voluntary deductions made during the pay period. In the example, debits to Office Salaries and Wages Expense are used for gross earnings because office workers are on a salary and other employees are paid on an hourly rate. In other companies, there may be debits to other accounts such as Store Salaries or Sales Salaries. The amount credited to Salaries and Wages Payable is the sum of the individual checks the employees will receive.

Recording Payment of the Payroll

Payment by check is made either from the employer's regular bank account or a payroll bank account. Each paycheck is usually accompanied by a detachable **statement of earnings** document. This shows the employee's gross earnings, payroll deductions, and net pay for the period and for the year-to-date. The Academy Company uses its regular bank account for payroll checks. The paycheck and statement of earnings for Michael Jordan are shown in Illustration 11-17.

Illustration 11-17

Paycheck and statement of earnings

AC	ACADEMY COMPANY 19 Center St. Hampton, MI 48291	No. 1028

January 14, 20 *02* $\frac{62-1113}{610}$

Pay to the
order of *Michael Jordan* $ *432.80*

Four Hundred Thirty-two and $\frac{80}{100}$ —————————— Dollars

City Bank & Trust
P.O. Box 3000
Hampton, MI 48291

For *Payroll*   *Randall E. Barnes*

⑈003244 77⑈ 7⑆60

- -

DETACH AND RETAIN THIS PORTION FOR YOUR RECORDS

NAME						SOC. SEC. NO.	EMPL. NUMBER	NO. EXEMP	PAY PERIOD ENDING
Michael Jordan						329-36-9547		2	1/14/02

REG. HRS.	O.T. HRS.	OTH. HRS. (1)	OTH. HRS. (2)	REG. EARNINGS	O.T. EARNINGS	OTH. EARNINGS (1)	OTH. EARNINGS (2)	GROSS
40	4			480.00	72.00			$552.00

FED. W/H TAX	FICA	STATE TAX	LOCAL TAX	OTHER DEDUCTIONS				NET PAY
49.00	44.16	11.04		(1) 10.00	(2) 5.00	(3)	(4)	432.80

YEAR TO DATE								
FED. W/H TAX	FICA	STATE TAX	LOCAL TAX	OTHER DEDUCTIONS				NET PAY
92.00	85.44	21.36		(1) 20.00	(2) 10.00	(3)	(4)	$839.20

Following payment of the payroll, the check numbers are entered in the payroll register. The entry to record payment of the payroll for Academy Company is as follows.

Jan. 14	Salaries and Wages Payable	11,462.50	
	Cash		11,462.50
	(To record payment of payroll)		

A	=	L	+	OE
−11,462.50		−11,462.50		

When currency is used in payment, one check is prepared for the payroll's total amount of net pay. This check is then cashed, and the coins and currency are inserted in individual pay envelopes for disbursement to individual employees.

*T*ECHNOLOGY IN ACTION

In addition to supplying the entry to record the payroll, the output for a computerized payroll system would include (1) payroll checks, (2) a payroll check register sorted by check and department, and (3) updated employee earnings records. Those employee records become the source for monthly, quarterly, and annual reporting of wages to taxing agencies.

BEFORE YOU GO ON...

▶ *REVIEW IT*
1. Identify two internal control procedures that apply to each payroll function.
2. What are the primary sources of gross earnings?
3. What payroll deductions are (a) mandatory and (b) voluntary?
4. What account titles are used in recording a payroll, assuming only mandatory payroll deductions are involved?

▶ *DO IT*

Your cousin Stan is establishing a house-cleaning business and will have a number of employees working for him. He is aware that documentation procedures are an important part of internal control. But he is confused about the difference between an employee earnings record and a payroll register. He asks you to explain the principal differences, because he wants to be sure that he sets up the proper payroll procedures.

ACTION PLAN
- Determine the earnings and deductions data that must be recorded and reported for each employee.
- Design a record that will accumulate earnings and deductions data and will serve as a basis for journal entries to be prepared and posted to the general ledger accounts.
- Explain the difference between the employee earnings record and the payroll register.

SOLUTION: An employee earnings record is kept for *each* employee. It shows gross earnings, payroll deductions, and net pay for each pay period. It provides cumulative payroll data for that employee. In contrast, a payroll register is a listing of *all* employees' gross earnings, payroll deductions, and net pay for each pay period. It is the documentation for preparing paychecks and for recording the payroll. Of course, Stan will need to keep both documents.

Related exercise material: BE11-7, BE11-8, BE11-9, E11-8, E11-9, E11-10, and E11-11.

EMPLOYER PAYROLL TAXES

STUDY OBJECTIVE 8

Describe and record employer payroll taxes.

Payroll tax expense for businesses results from three taxes **levied on employers** by governmental agencies. These taxes are: (1) FICA, (2) federal unemployment tax, and (3) state unemployment tax. These taxes plus such items as paid vacations and pensions are collectively referred to as **fringe benefits**. As indicated earlier, the cost of fringe benefits in many companies is substantial.

FICA Taxes

We have seen that each employee must pay FICA taxes. An employer must match each employee's FICA contribution. The matching contribution results in **payroll tax expense** to the employer. The employer's tax is subject to the same rate and maximum earnings applicable to the employee. The account, FICA Taxes Payable, is used for both the employee's and the employer's FICA contributions. For the January 14 payroll, Academy Company's FICA tax contribution is $1,376.80 ($17,210.00 × 8%).

Federal Unemployment Taxes

HELPFUL HINT
FICA taxes are paid by both the employer and employee. Federal unemployment taxes and (in most states) the state unemployment taxes are borne entirely by the employer.

The Federal Unemployment Tax Act (FUTA) is another feature of the federal Social Security program. **Federal unemployment taxes** provide benefits for a limited period of time to employees who lose their jobs through no fault of their own. Under provisions of the Act, the employer is required to pay a tax of 6.2% on the first $7,000 of gross wages paid to each employee during a calendar year. The law allows the employer a maximum credit of 5.4% on the federal rate for contributions to state unemployment taxes. Because of this provision, state unemployment tax laws generally provide for a 5.4% rate. The effective federal unemployment tax rate thus becomes 0.8% (6.2% − 5.4%). This tax is borne **entirely by the employer**. There is no deduction or withholding from employees.

The account Federal Unemployment Taxes Payable is used to recognize this liability. The federal unemployment tax for Academy Company for the January 14 payroll is $137.68 ($17,210.00 × 0.8%).

State Unemployment Taxes

All states have unemployment compensation programs under state unemployment tax acts (SUTA). Like federal unemployment taxes, **state unemployment taxes** provide benefits to employees who lose their jobs. These taxes are levied on employers.[2] The basic rate is usually 5.4% on the first $7,000 of wages paid to an employee during the year. The basic rate is adjusted according to the employer's experience rating: Companies with a history of unstable employment may pay more than the basic rate. Companies with a history of stable employment may pay less than 5.4%. Regardless of the rate paid, the credit on the federal unemployment tax is still 5.4%.

The account State Unemployment Taxes Payable is used for this liability. The state unemployment tax for Academy Company for the January 14 payroll is $929.34 ($17,210.00 × 5.4%).

Illustration 11-18 summarizes the types of employer payroll taxes.

Illustration 11-18

Employer payroll taxes

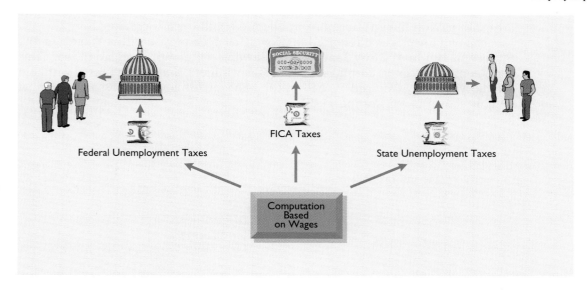

Recording Employer Payroll Taxes

Employer payroll taxes are usually recorded at the same time the payroll is journalized. The entire amount of gross pay ($17,210.00) shown in the payroll register in Illustration 11-16 is subject to each of the three taxes mentioned above. Accordingly, the entry to record the payroll tax expense associated with the January 14 payroll is:

Jan. 14	Payroll Tax Expense	2,443.82		
	FICA Taxes Payable		1,376.80	
	Federal Unemployment Taxes Payable		137.68	
	State Unemployment Taxes Payable		929.34	
	(To record employer's payroll taxes on			
	January 14 payroll)			

A = L + OE
+1,376.80 −2,443.82
+137.68
+929.34

---

[2] In a few states, the employee is also required to make a contribution. In this textbook, including the homework, we will assume that the tax is only on the employer.

Separate liability accounts are used instead of a single credit to Payroll Taxes Payable. Why? Because these liabilities are payable to different taxing authorities at different dates. The liability accounts are classified in the balance sheet as current liabilities since they will be paid within the next year. Payroll Tax Expense is classified on the income statement as an operating expense.

FILING AND REMITTING PAYROLL TAXES

Preparation of payroll tax returns is the responsibility of the payroll department. Payment of the taxes is made by the treasurer's department. Much of the information for the returns is obtained from employee earnings records.

For purposes of reporting and remitting to the IRS, FICA taxes and federal income taxes that were withheld are combined. **The taxes must be reported quarterly**, no later than one month following the close of each quarter. The remitting requirements depend on the amount of taxes withheld and the length of the pay period. Remittances are made through deposits in either a Federal Reserve bank or an authorized commercial bank.

Federal unemployment taxes are generally filed and remitted **annually** on or before January 31 of the subsequent year. Earlier payments are required when the tax exceeds a specified amount. State unemployment taxes usually must be filed and paid by the **end of the month following each quarter**. When payroll taxes are paid, payroll liability accounts are debited, and Cash is credited.

The employer is also required to provide each employee with a **Wage and Tax Statement (Form W-2)** by January 31 following the end of a calendar year. This statement shows gross earnings, FICA taxes withheld, and income taxes withheld for the year. The required W-2 form for Michael Jordan, using assumed annual data, is shown in Illustration 11-19.

Illustration 11-19

W-2 form

Form **W-2 Wage and Tax Statement** Calendar Year **2002**

1 Control number	OMB No. 1545-0008		
2 Employer's name, address and ZIP code Academy Company 19 Center St. Hampton, MI 48291		3 Employer's identification number 36-2167852	4 Employer's State number
		5 Stat. employee ☐ Deceased ☐ Legal rep. ☐ 942 emp. ☐ Subtotal ☐ Void ☐	
		6 Allocated tips	7 Advance EIC payment
8 Employee's social security number 329-36-9547	9 Federal income tax withheld $2,248.00	10 Wages, tips, other compensation $26,300.00	11 Social security tax withheld $2,104.00
12 Employee's name, address, and ZIP code Michael Jordan 2345 Mifflin Ave. Hampton, MI 48292		13 Social security wages $26,300.00	14 Social security tips
		16	
		17 State income tax $526.00 · 18 State wages, tips, etc.	19 Name of State Michigan
		20 Local income tax · 21 Local wages, tips, etc.	22 Name of locality

The employer must send a copy of each employee's Wage and Tax Statement (Form W-2) to the Social Security Administration. This agency subsequently furnishes the Internal Revenue Service with the income data required.

B E F O R E   Y O U   G O   O N . . .

▶ *REVIEW IT*

1. What payroll taxes are levied on employers?
2. What accounts are involved in accruing employer payroll taxes?

▶ *DO IT*

In January, the payroll supervisor determines that gross earnings in Halo Company are $70,000. All earnings are subject to 8% FICA taxes, 5.4% state unemployment taxes, and 0.8% federal unemployment taxes. You are asked to record the employer's payroll taxes.

ACTION PLAN
- Compute the employer's payroll taxes on the period's gross earnings.
- Identify the expense account(s) to be debited.
- Identify the liability account(s) to be credited.

SOLUTION: The entry to record the employer's payroll taxes is:

Payroll Tax Expense	9,940	
FICA Taxes Payable ($70,000 × 8%)		5,600
Federal Unemployment Taxes Payable ($70,000 × 0.8%)		560
State Unemployment Taxes Payable ($70,000 × 5.4%)		3,780
(To record employer's payroll taxes on January payroll)		

Related exercise material: BE11-10, E11-10, and E11-12.

☑ THE NAVIGATOR

ADDITIONAL FRINGE BENEFITS

In addition to the three payroll tax fringe benefits, employers incur other substantial fringe benefit costs. Two of the most important are paid absences and postretirement benefits.

STUDY OBJECTIVE 9

Identify additional fringe benefits associated with employee compensation.

Paid Absences

Employees often are given rights to receive compensation for absences when certain conditions of employment are met. The compensation may be for paid vacations, sick pay benefits, and paid holidays. When the payment for such absences is **probable** and the amount can be **reasonably estimated**, a liability should be accrued for paid future absences. When the amount cannot be reasonably estimated, the potential liability should be disclosed. Ordinarily, vacation pay is the only paid absence that is accrued. The other types of paid absences are only disclosed.[3]

To illustrate, assume that Academy Company employees are entitled to one day's vacation for each month worked. If 30 employees earn an average of $110 per day in a given month, the accrual for vacation benefits in one month is $3,300. The liability is recognized at the end of the month by the following adjusting entry.

Jan. 31	Vacation Benefits Expense	3,300	
	Vacation Benefits Payable		3,300
	(To accrue vacation benefits expense)		

A	=	L	+	OE
		+3,300		−3,300

This accrual is required by the matching principle. Vacation Benefits Expense is reported as an operating expense in the income statement, and Vacation Benefits Payable is reported as a current liability in the balance sheet.

---

[3]The typical U.S. company provides an average of 12 days of paid vacations for its employees, at an average cost of 5% of gross earnings.

Later, when vacation benefits are paid, Vacation Benefits Payable is debited and Cash is credited. For example, if the above benefits for 10 employees are paid in July, the entry is:

A	=	L	+	OE
−1,100		−1,100		

July 31	Vacation Benefits Payable	1,100	
	Cash		1,100
	(To record payment of vacation benefits)		

The magnitude of unpaid absences has gained employers' attention. Consider the case of an assistant superintendent of schools who worked for 20 years and rarely took a vacation or sick day. A month or so before she retired, the school district discovered that she was due nearly $30,000 in accrued benefits. Yet the liability had never been accrued.

Postretirement Benefits

Postretirement benefits are benefits provided by employers to retired employees for (1) health care and life insurance and (2) pensions. For many years the accounting for postretirement benefits was on a cash basis. Now, both types of postretirement benefits are accounted for on the accrual basis.

POSTRETIREMENT HEALTH CARE AND LIFE INSURANCE BENEFITS.
Providing medical and related health care benefits for retirees was at one time an inexpensive and highly effective way of generating employee goodwill. This practice has now turned into one of corporate America's most worrisome financial problems. Runaway medical costs, early retirement, and increased longevity are sending the liability for retiree health plans through the roof.

Many companies began offering retiree health care coverage in the form of Medicare supplements in the 1960s. Almost all plans operated on a pay-as-you-go basis. The companies simply paid for the bills as they came in, rather than setting aside funds to meet the cost of future benefits. These plans were accounted for on the cash basis. But, the FASB concluded that shareholders and creditors should know the amount of the employer's obligations. As a result, employers must now use the **accrual basis** in accounting for postretirement health care and life insurance benefits.

ACCOUNTING IN ACTION $B u s i n e s s$ $I n s i g h t$

The battle over fringe benefits has increased as benefits outpace wages and salaries. Growing faster than pay, benefits equaled 38% of wages and salaries in a recent year. While vacations and other forms of paid leave still take the biggest bite of the benefits pie, medical costs are the fastest-growing item.

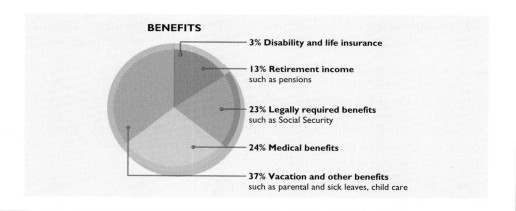

BENEFITS

- 3% Disability and life insurance
- 13% Retirement income such as pensions
- 23% Legally required benefits such as Social Security
- 24% Medical benefits
- 37% Vacation and other benefits such as parental and sick leaves, child care

PENSION PLANS. A **pension plan** is an agreement whereby an employer provides benefits (payments) to employees after they retire. Over 50 million workers currently participate in pension plans in the United States. The need for good accounting for pension plans becomes apparent when one appreciates the size of existing pension funds. Most pension plans are subject to the provisions of ERISA (Employee Retirement Income Security Act), a law enacted to curb abuses in the administration and funding of such plans.

Three parties are generally involved in a pension plan. The **employer** (company) sponsors the pension plan. The **plan administrator** receives the contributions from the employer, invests the pension assets, and makes the benefit payments to the **pension recipients** (retired employees). Illustration 11-20 indicates the flow of cash among the three parties involved in a pension plan.

> **HELPFUL HINT**
> With more than $4 trillion in assets overall, both public and private pension funds comprise over one-fifth of the total financial assets in the United States today—and these amounts are growing.

Illustration 11-20

Parties in a pension plan

An employer-financed pension is part of the employees' compensation. ERISA establishes the minimum contribution that a company must make each year toward employee pensions. The company records the pension costs as an expense while the employees are working because that is when the company receives benefits from the employees' services. Generally the pension expense is reported as an operating expense in the company's income statement.

Frequently, the amount contributed by the company to the pension plan is different from the amount of the pension expense. A **liability** is recognized when the pension expense to date is **more than** the company's contributions to date. An **asset** is recognized when the pension expense to date is **less than** the company's contributions to date. Further consideration of the accounting for pension plans is left for more advanced courses.

BEFORE YOU GO ON...

▶ *REVIEW IT*
1. What accounts are involved in accruing and paying vacation benefits?
2. What basis should be used in accounting for postretirement benefits?

A LOOK BACK AT OUR FEATURE STORY

Refer back to the Feature Story about Wilbert Murdock at the beginning of the chapter, and answer the following questions.
1. Why do entrepreneurs like Wilbert Murdock and other small businesses have difficulty obtaining traditional debt financing?
2. What type of financing did Wilbert Murdock resort to, as did one-third of businesses with fewer than 20 employees? Why is Murdock's method of financing at all appealing?
3. What are the disadvantages of using credit cards as a means of debt financing?

SOLUTION

1. Traditional debt financing is generally not available to entrepreneurs and other small businesses because bank loans and bond issuances require established credit ratings, earnings records, positive cash flow, and collateral—none of which are usually possessed by new, emerging small businesses.

2. Wilbert Murdock resorted to using credit cards to finance his business ventures. Credit cards are appealing because they are readily available (new card applications appear in mailboxes weekly) and because credit card companies don't monitor how the money is spent.

3. Credit card financing is generally expensive, with interest ranging between 14% and 21% (except for special introductory offers, which are temporary in nature), and the amounts per individual credit card are generally small ($2,000–$10,000).

Additional Demonstration Problem

DEMONSTRATION PROBLEM

Indiana Jones Company had the following selected transactions.

Feb. 1	Signs a $50,000, 6-month, 9%-interest-bearing note payable to CitiBank and receives $50,000 in cash.	
10	Cash register sales total $43,200, which includes an 8% sales tax.	
28	The payroll for the month consists of Sales Salaries $32,000 and Office Salaries $18,000. All wages are subject to 8% FICA taxes. A total of $8,900 federal income taxes are withheld. The salaries are paid on March 1.	
28	The following adjustment data are developed.	

1. Interest expense of $375 has been incurred on the note.
2. Employer payroll taxes include 8% FICA taxes, a 5.4% state unemployment tax, and a 0.8% federal unemployment tax.
3. Some sales were made under warranty. Of the units sold under warranty, 350 are expected to become defective. Repair costs are estimated to be $40 per unit.

Instructions

(a) Journalize the February transactions.

(b) Journalize the adjusting entries at February 28.

ACTION PLAN

- To determine sales, divide the cash register total by 100% plus the sales tax percentage.
- Base payroll taxes on gross earnings.
- Expense warranty costs in the period in which the sale occurs.

SOLUTION TO DEMONSTRATION PROBLEM

(a) Feb. 1	Cash		50,000	
	Notes Payable			50,000
	(Issued 6-month, 9%-interest-bearing note to CitiBank)			
10	Cash		43,200	
	Sales ($43,200 ÷ 1.08)			40,000
	Sales Taxes Payable ($40,000 × 8%)			3,200
	(To record sales and sales taxes payable)			
28	Sales Salaries Expense		32,000	
	Office Salaries Expense		18,000	
	FICA Taxes Payable (8% × $50,000)			4,000
	Federal Income Taxes Payable			8,900
	Salaries Payable			37,100
	(To record February salaries)			
(b) Feb. 28	Interest Expense		375	
	Interest Payable			375
	(To record accrued interest for February)			

28	Payroll Tax Expense	7,100	
	FICA Taxes Payable		4,000
	Federal Unemployment Taxes Payable		400
	(0.8% × $50,000)		
	State Unemployment Taxes Payable		2,700
	(5.4% × $50,000)		
	(To record employer's payroll taxes on February payroll)		
28	Warranty Expense (350 × $40)	14,000	
	Estimated Warranty Liability		14,000
	(To record estimated product warranty liability)		

SUMMARY OF STUDY OBJECTIVES

1. *Explain a current liability, and identify the major types of current liabilities.* A current liability is a debt that can reasonably be expected to be paid (1) from existing current assets or through the creation of other current liabilities, and (2) within one year or the operating cycle, whichever is longer. The major types of current liabilities are notes payable, accounts payable, sales taxes payable, unearned revenues, and accrued liabilities such as taxes, salaries and wages, and interest payable.

2. *Describe the accounting for notes payable.* When a promissory note is interest-bearing, the amount of assets received upon the issuance of the note is generally equal to the face value of the note. Interest expense is accrued over the life of the note. At maturity, the amount paid is equal to the face value of the note plus accrued interest.

3. *Explain the accounting for other current liabilities.* Sales taxes payable are recorded at the time the related sales occur. The company serves as a collection agent for the taxing authority. Sales taxes are not an expense to the company. Unearned revenues are initially recorded in an unearned revenue account. As the revenue is earned, a transfer from unearned revenue to earned revenue occurs. The current maturities of long-term debt are reported as a current liability in the balance sheet.

4. *Explain the financial statement presentation and analysis of current liabilities.* The nature and amount of each current liability should be reported in the balance sheet or in schedules in the notes accompanying the statements. The liquidity of a company may be analyzed by computing working capital and the current ratio.

5. *Describe the accounting and disclosure requirements for contingent liabilities.* If the contingency is probable (likely to occur) and the amount is reasonably estimable, the liability should be recorded in the accounts. If the contingency is only reasonably possible (it could happen), then it should be disclosed only in the notes to the financial statements. If the possibility that the contingency will happen is remote (unlikely to occur), it need not be recorded or disclosed.

6. *Discuss the objectives of internal control for payroll.* The objectives of internal control for payroll are (1) to safeguard company assets against unauthorized payments of payrolls, and (2) to ensure the accuracy of the accounting records pertaining to payrolls.

7. *Compute and record the payroll for a pay period.* The computation of the payroll involves gross earnings, payroll deductions, and net pay. In recording the payroll, salaries (or wages) expense is debited for gross earnings, individual tax and other liability accounts are credited for payroll deductions, and salaries (wages) payable is credited for net pay. When the payroll is paid, Salaries and Wages Payable is debited, and Cash is credited.

8. *Describe and record employer payroll taxes.* Employer payroll taxes consist of FICA, federal unemployment taxes, and state unemployment taxes. The taxes are usually accrued at the time the payroll is recorded by debiting Payroll Tax Expense and crediting separate liability accounts for each type of tax.

9. *Identify additional fringe benefits associated with employee compensation.* Additional fringe benefits associated with wages are paid absences (paid vacations, sick pay benefits, and paid holidays), and postretirement benefits (health care and life insurance and pensions). Both types of benefits should be accounted for on the accrual basis.

Key Term Matching Activity

GLOSSARY

Bonus Compensation to management and other personnel, based on factors such as increased sales or the amount of net income. (p. 457).

Contingent liability A potential liability that may become an actual liability in the future. (p. 451).

Current ratio A measure of a company's liquidity; computed as current assets divided by current liabilities. (p. 451).

Employee earnings record A cumulative record of each employee's gross earnings, deductions, and net pay during the year. (p. 461).

Employee's Withholding Allowance Certificate (Form W-4) An Internal Revenue Service form on which the employee indicates the number of allowances claimed for withholding federal income taxes. (p. 459).

Federal unemployment taxes Taxes imposed on the employer by the federal government that provide benefits for a limited time period to employees who lose their jobs through no fault of their own. (p. 464).

FICA taxes Taxes designed to provide workers with supplemental retirement, employment disability, and medical benefits. (p. 458).

Gross earnings Total compensation earned by an employee. (p. 457).

Net pay Gross earnings less payroll deductions. (p. 460).

Notes payable Obligations in the form of written promissory notes. (p. 447).

Payroll deductions Deductions from gross earnings to determine the amount of a paycheck. (p. 457).

Payroll register A payroll record that accumulates the gross earnings, deductions, and net pay by employee for each pay period. (p. 461).

Pension plan An agreement whereby an employer provides benefits to employees after they retire. (p. 469).

Postretirement benefits Payments by employers to retired employees for health care, life insurance, and pensions. (p. 468).

Salaries Employee pay based on a fixed amount rather than an hourly rate. (p. 454).

Statement of earnings A document attached to a paycheck that indicates the employee's gross earnings, payroll deductions, and net pay. (p. 462).

State unemployment taxes Taxes imposed on the employer by states that provide benefits to employees who lose their jobs. (p. 465).

Wage and Tax Statement (Form W-2) A form showing gross earnings, FICA taxes withheld, and income taxes withheld, prepared annually by an employer for each employee. (p. 466).

Wages Amounts paid to employees based on a rate per hour or on a piece-work basis. (p. 454).

Working capital A measure of a company's liquidity; computed as current assets minus current liabilities. (p. 450).

Chapter 11 Self-Test

$ELF-STUDY QUESTIONS
Answers are at the end of the chapter.

(SO 1) **1.** The time period for classifying a liability as current is one year or the operating cycle, whichever is:
   a. longer.
   b. shorter.
   c. probable.
   d. possible.

(SO 1) **2.** To be classified as a current liability, a debt must be expected to be paid:
   a. out of existing current assets.
   b. by creating other current liabilities.
   c. within 2 years.
   d. both (a) and (b).

(SO 2) **3.** Maggie Sharrer Company borrows $88,500 on September 1, 2002, from Sandwich State Bank by signing an $88,500, 12%, one-year note. What is the accrued interest at December 31, 2002?
   a. $2,655.
   b. $3,540.
   c. $4,425.
   d. $10,620.

(SO 3) **4.** Rhodes Company has total proceeds from sales of $4,515. If the proceeds include sales taxes of 5%, the amount to be credited to Sales is:
   a. $4,000.
   b. $4,300.
   c. $4,289.25.
   d. No correct answer given.

(SO 4) **5.** Working capital is calculated as:
   a. current assets minus current liabilities.
   b. total assets minus total liabilities.
   c. long-term liabilities minus current liabilities.
   d. both (b) and (c).

(SO 5) **6.** A contingent liability should be recorded in the accounts when:
   a. it is probable the contingency will happen, but the amount cannot be reasonably estimated.

   b. it is reasonably possible the contingency will happen, and the amount can be reasonably estimated.
   c. it is probable the contingency will happen, and the amount can be reasonably estimated.
   d. it is reasonably possible the contingency will happen, but the amount cannot be reasonably estimated.

7. At December 31, Hanes Company prepares an adjusting (SO 5) entry for a product warranty contract. Which of the following accounts is/are included in the entry?
   a. Miscellaneous Expense.
   b. Estimated Warranty Liability.
   c. Repair Parts/Wages Payable.
   d. Both (a) and (b).

8. The department that should pay the payroll is the: (SO 6)
   a. timekeeping department.
   b. human resources department.
   c. payroll department.
   d. treasurer's department.

9. J. Barr earns $14 per hour for a 40-hour week and $21 (SO 7) per hour for any overtime work. If Barr works 45 hours in a week, gross earnings are:
   a. $560.
   b. $630.
   c. $650.
   d. $665.

10. Employer payroll taxes do not include: (SO 8)
   a. federal unemployment taxes.
   b. state unemployment taxes.
   c. federal income taxes.
   d. FICA taxes.

11. Which of the following is *not* an additional fringe (SO 9) benefit?
   a. Postretirement pensions.
   b. Paid absences.
   c. Paid vacations.
   d. Salaries.

QUESTIONS

1. Jeff Baumgartner believes a current liability is a debt that can be expected to be paid in one year. Is Jeff correct? Explain.

2. Mesa Verde Company obtains $25,000 in cash by signing a 9%, 6-month, $25,000 note payable to First Bank on July 1. Mesa Verde's fiscal year ends on September 30. What information should be reported for the note payable in the annual financial statements?

3. (a) Your roommate says, "Sales taxes are reported as an expense in the income statement." Do you agree? Explain.
   (b) Planet Hollywood has cash proceeds from sales of $10,400. This amount includes $400 of sales taxes. Give the entry to record the proceeds.

4. Aurora University sold 10,000 season football tickets at $80 each for its five-game home schedule. What entries should be made (a) when the tickets were sold, and (b) after each game?

5. What is liquidity? What are two measures of liquidity?

6. What is a contingent liability? Give an example of a contingent liability that is usually recorded in the accounts.

7. Under what circumstances is a contingent liability disclosed only in the notes to the financial statements? Under what circumstances is a contingent liability not recorded in the accounts nor disclosed in the notes to the financial statements?

8. You are a newly hired accountant with Spartan Company. On your first day, the controller asks you to identify the main internal control objectives related to payroll accounting. How would you respond?

9. What are the four functions associated with payroll activities?

10. What is the difference between gross pay and net pay? Which amount should a company record as wages or salaries expense?

11. Which payroll tax is levied on both employers and employees?

12. Are the federal and state income taxes withheld from employee paychecks a payroll tax expense for the employer? Explain your answer.

13. What do the following acronyms stand for: FICA, FUTA, and SUTA?

14. What information is shown in a W-4 statement? In a W-2 statement?

15. Distinguish between the two types of payroll deductions and give examples of each.

16. What are the primary uses of the employee earnings record?

17. (a) Identify the three types of employer payroll taxes.
   (b) How are tax liability accounts and payroll tax expense classified in the financial statements?

18. Identify three additional types of fringe benefits associated with employees' compensation.

19. Often during job interviews, the candidate asks the potential employer about the firm's paid absences policy. What are paid absences? How are they accounted for?

20. What are two types of postretirement benefits? During what years does the FASB advocate expensing the employer's costs of these postretirement benefits?

21. What basis of accounting for the employer's cost of postretirement health care and life insurance benefits has been used by most companies, and what basis does the FASB now require? Explain the basic difference between these methods in accounting for postretirement benefit costs.

22. Identify the three parties in a pension plan. What role does each party have in the plan?

BRIEF EXERCISES

BE11-1 Compagna Company has the following obligations at December 31: (a) a note payable for $100,000 due in 2 years, (b) a 10-year mortgage payable of $400,000 payable in ten $40,000 annual payments, (c) interest payable of $15,000 on the mortgage, and (d) accounts payable of $60,000. For each obligation, indicate whether it should be classified as a current liability. (Assume an operating cycle of less than one year.)

Identify whether obligations are current liabilities.
(SO 1)

BE11-2 Borke Company borrows $90,000 on July 1 from the bank by signing a $90,000, 10%, one-year note payable.

(a) Prepare the journal entry to record the proceeds of the note.
(b) Prepare the journal entry to record accrued interest at December 31, assuming adjusting entries are made only at the end of the year.

Prepare entries for an interest-bearing note payable.
(SO 2)

BE11-3 Brotcke Auto Supply does not segregate sales and sales taxes at the time of sale. The register total for March 16 is $11,970. All sales are subject to a 5% sales tax. Compute sales taxes payable, and make the entry to record sales taxes payable and sales.

Compute and record sales taxes payable.
(SO 3)

BE11-4 Illinois State University sells 4,000 season basketball tickets at $96 each for its 12-game home schedule. Give the entry to record (a) the sale of the season tickets and (b) the revenue earned by playing the first home game.

Prepare entries for unearned revenues.
(SO 3)

Analyze liquidity.
(SO 4)

BE11-5 Yahoo! Inc.'s 1998 financial statements contain the following selected data (in thousands).

Current assets	$467,239
Total assets	621,884
Current liabilities	79,983
Total liabilities	85,674

Compute the following ratios.

(a) Working capital.

(b) Current ratio.

Prepare adjusting entry for warranty costs.
(SO 5)

BE11-6 On December 1, Gonzalez Company introduces a new product that includes a one-year warranty on parts. In December, 1,000 units are sold. Management believes that 5% of the units will be defective and that the average warranty costs will be $75 per unit. Prepare the adjusting entry at December 31 to accrue the estimated warranty cost.

Identify payroll functions.
(SO 6)

BE11-7 Gutierrez Company has the following payroll procedures.

(a) Supervisor approves overtime work.

(b) The human resources department prepares hiring authorization forms for new hires.

(c) A second payroll department employee verifies payroll calculations.

(d) The treasurer's department pays employees.

Identify the payroll function to which each procedure pertains.

Compute gross earnings and net pay.
(SO 7)

BE11-8 Becky Sherrick's regular hourly wage rate is $14, and she receives an hourly rate of $21 for work in excess of 40 hours. During a January pay period, Becky works 45 hours. Becky's federal income tax withholding is $95, and she has no voluntary deductions. Compute Becky Sherrick's gross earnings and net pay for the pay period.

Record a payroll and the payment of wages.
(SO 7)

BE11-9 Data for Becky Sherrick are presented in BE11-8. Prepare the journal entries to record (a) Becky's pay for the period and (b) the payment of Becky's wages. Use January 15 for the end of the pay period and the payment date.

Record employer payroll taxes.
(SO 8)

BE11-10 In January, gross earnings in Bri Company totaled $70,000. All earnings are subject to 8% FICA taxes, 5.4% state unemployment taxes, and 0.8% federal unemployment taxes. Prepare the entry to record January payroll tax expense.

Record estimated vacation benefits.
(SO 9)

BE11-11 At Sublette.com Company employees are entitled to one day's vacation for each month worked. In January, 50 employees worked the full month. Record the vacation pay liability for January assuming the average daily pay for each employee is $150.

EXERCISES

Prepare entries for interest-bearing notes.
(SO 2)

E11-1 On June 1, Eddy Microchip Company borrows $70,000 from First Bank on a 6-month, $70,000, 12% note.

Instructions

(a) Prepare the entry on June 1.

(b) Prepare the adjusting entry on June 30.

(c) Prepare the entry at maturity (December 1), assuming monthly adjusting entries have been made through November 30.

(d) What was the total financing cost (interest expense)?

Journalize sales and related taxes.
(SO 3)

E11-2 In providing accounting services to small businesses, you encounter the following situations pertaining to cash sales.

1. Valarie Flynn Company rings up sales and sales taxes separately on its cash register. On April 10, the register totals are sales $25,000 and sales taxes $1,500.

2. Fleury Company does not segregate sales and sales taxes. Its register total for April 15 is $18,404, which includes a 7% sales tax.

Instructions

Prepare the entry to record the sales transactions and related taxes for each client.

E11-3 Etheredge Company publishes a monthly sports magazine, *Fishing Preview*. Subscriptions to the magazine cost $30 per year. During November 2002, Etheredge sells 8,000 subscriptions beginning with the December issue. Etheredge prepares financial statements quarterly and recognizes subscription revenue earned at the end of the quarter. The company uses the accounts Unearned Subscriptions and Subscription Revenue.

Journalize unearned subscription revenue.
(SO 3)

Instructions

(a) Prepare the entry in November for the receipt of the subscriptions.

(b) Prepare the adjusting entry at December 31, 2002, to record subscription revenue earned in December 2002.

(c) Prepare the adjusting entry at March 31, 2003, to record subscription revenue earned in the first quarter of 2003.

E11-4 Zareena Company sells automatic can openers under a 75-day warranty for defective merchandise. Based on past experience, Zareena estimates that 4% of the units sold will become defective during the warranty period. Management estimates that the average cost of replacing or repairing a defective unit is $15. The units sold and units defective that occurred during the last 2 months of 2002 are as follows.

Record estimated liability and expense for warranties.
(SO 5)

Month	Units Sold	Units Defective Prior to December 31
November	30,000	700
December	32,000	500

Instructions

(a) Determine the estimated warranty liability at December 31 for the units sold in November and December.

(b) Prepare the journal entries to record the estimated liability for warranties and the costs incurred in honoring 1,200 warranty claims. (Assume actual costs of $18,000.)

(c) Give the entry to record the honoring of 550 warranty contracts in January at an average cost of $15.

E11-5 Leask Online Company has the following liability accounts after posting adjusting entries: Accounts Payable $66,000, Unearned Ticket Revenue $24,000, Estimated Warranty Liability $18,000, Interest Payable $8,000, Mortgage Payable $120,000, Notes Payable $80,000, and Sales Taxes Payable $10,000. Assume the company's operating cycle is less than 1 year, ticket revenue will be earned within 1 year, warranty costs are expected to be incurred within 1 year, and the notes mature in 3 years.

Prepare the current liability section of the balance sheet.
(SO 1, 2, 3, 4, 5)

Instructions

(a) Prepare the current liabilities section of the balance sheet, assuming $30,000 of the mortgage is payable next year.

(b) Comment on Leask Online Company's liquidity, assuming total current assets are $300,000.

E11-6 **Kroger Co.'s** 2000 financial statements contained the following selected data (in millions).

Calculate liquidity ratios.
(SO 4)

Current assets	$ 5,531	Accounts receivable	$622
Total assets	17,966	Interest expense	652
Current liabilities	5,728	Income taxes	491
Total liabilities	15,283	Net income	628
Cash	281		

Instructions
Compute these values:

(a) Working capital.

(b) Current ratio.

E11-7 The following financial data were reported by **Polaroid Corporation** for 1998 and 1999 ($ in millions).

Calculate current ratio and working capital before and after paying accounts payable.
(SO 4)

◆**Polaroid**

POLAROID CORPORATION
Balance Sheets (partial)

	1998	1999
Current assets		
Cash and cash equivalents	$ 105.0	$ 92.0
Accounts receivable, net	459.6	489.7
Inventories	533.3	395.6
Prepaid expenses and other assets	195.5	139.6
Total current assets	$1,293.4	$1,116.9
Current liabilities	$ 933.0	$ 750.2

Instructions
(a) Calculate the current ratio and working capital for Polaroid for 1998 and 1999.
(b) Suppose that at the end of 1999 Polaroid management used $85 million cash to pay off $85 million of accounts payable. How would its current ratio and working capital have changed?

Compute net pay and record pay for one employee.
(SO 7)

E11-8   Linda O'Neill's regular hourly wage rate is $16.00, and she receives a wage of $1\frac{1}{2}$ times the regular hourly rate for work in excess of 40 hours. During a March weekly pay period Linda worked 42 hours. Her gross earnings prior to the current week were $19,000. Linda is married and claims three withholding allowances. Her only voluntary deduction is for group hospitalization insurance at $15.00 per week.

Instructions
(a) Compute the following amounts for Linda's wages for the current week.
   (1) Gross earnings.
   (2) FICA taxes. (Assume an 8% rate on maximum of $65,000.)
   (3) Federal income taxes withheld. (Use the withholding table in the text, page 459.)
   (4) State income taxes withheld. (Assume a 2.0% rate.)
   (5) Net pay.
(b) Record Linda's pay, assuming she is an office computer operator.

Compute maximum FICA deductions.
(SO 7)

E11-9   Employee earnings records for Borelias Company reveal the following gross earnings for four employees through the pay period of December 15.

C. Mull	$62,500	D. Chambers	$64,300
L. Church	$64,600	T. Olejnik	$65,000

For the pay period ending December 31, each employee's gross earnings is $2,000. The FICA tax rate is 8% on gross earnings of $65,000.

Instructions
Compute the FICA withholdings that should be made for each employee for the December 31 pay period. (Show computations.)

Prepare payroll register and record payroll and payroll tax expense.
(SO 7, 8)

E11-10   Martinez Company has the following data for the weekly payroll ending January 31.

| | Hours | | | | | | Hourly | Federal Income Tax | Health |
Employee	M	T	W	T	F	S	Rate	Withholding	Insurance
M. Miller	8	8	9	8	10	3	$10	$34	$10
E. Neupert	8	8	8	8	8	2	12	37	15
K. Mann	9	10	8	8	9	0	13	58	15

Employees are paid $1\frac{1}{2}$ times the regular hourly rate for all hours worked in excess of 40 hours per week. FICA taxes are 8% on the first $65,000 of gross earnings. Martinez Company is subject to 5.4% state unemployment taxes and 0.8% federal unemployment taxes on the first $7,000 of gross earnings.

Instructions

(a) Prepare the payroll register for the weekly payroll.

(b) Prepare the journal entries to record the payroll and Martinez's payroll tax expense.

E11-11   Selected data from a February payroll register for Andrew Manion Company are presented below. Some amounts are intentionally omitted.

Compute missing payroll amounts and record payroll.
(SO 7)

Gross earnings:			
Regular	$8,900	State income taxes	$ (3)
Overtime	(1)	Union dues	100
Total	(2)	Total deductions	(4)
Deductions:		Net pay	$ 7,660
FICA taxes	$ 800	Accounts debited:	
Federal income taxes	1,140	Warehouse wages	(5)
		Store wages	$ 4,000

FICA taxes are 8%. State income taxes are 3% of gross earnings.

Instructions

(a) Fill in the missing amounts.

(b) Journalize the February payroll and the payment of the payroll.

E11-12   According to a payroll register summary of Parolini Company, the amount of employees' gross pay in December was $800,000, of which $70,000 was not subject to FICA tax and $760,000 was not subject to state and federal unemployment taxes.

Determine employer's payroll taxes; record payroll tax expense.
(SO 8)

Instructions

(a) Determine the employer's payroll tax expense for the month, using the following rates: FICA 8%, state unemployment 5.4%, federal unemployment 0.8%.

(b) Prepare the journal entry to record December payroll tax expense.

E11-13   Sawdey Company has two fringe benefit plans for its employees:

Prepare adjusting entries for fringe benefits.
(SO 9)

1. It grants employees 2 days' vacation for each month worked. Ten employees worked the entire month of March at an average daily wage of $100 per employee.

2. In its pension plan the company recognizes 10% of gross earnings as an expense. Gross earnings in March were $40,000. No contribution has been made to the pension fund.

Instructions

Prepare the adjusting entries at March 31.

PROBLEMS: SET A

P11-1A   On January 1, 2002, the ledger of Twyla Company contains the following liability accounts.

Prepare current liability entries, adjusting entries, and current liabilities section.
(SO 1, 2, 3, 4, 5)

Accounts Payable	$52,000
Sales Taxes Payable	7,700
Unearned Service Revenue	16,000

During January the following selected transactions occurred.

Jan. 5   Sold merchandise for cash totaling $16,632, which includes 8% sales taxes.

12   Provided services for customers who had made advance payments of $10,000. (Credit Service Revenue.)

14   Paid state revenue department for sales taxes collected in December 2001 ($7,700).

20   Sold 500 units of a new product on credit at $50 per unit, plus 8% sales tax. This new product is subject to a 1-year warranty.

21   Borrowed $18,000 from UCLA Bank on a 3-month, 10%, $18,000 note.

25   Sold merchandise for cash totaling $11,340, which includes 8% sales taxes.

Instructions

(a) Journalize the January transactions.

(b) Journalize the adjusting entries at January 31 for (1) the outstanding notes payable, and (2) estimated warranty liability, assuming warranty costs are expected to equal 7% of sales of the new product. (*Hint:* Use one-third of a month for the UCLA Bank note.)

(c) Current liability total $81,872

(c) Prepare the current liabilities section of the balance sheet at January 31, 2002. Assume no change in accounts payable.

Prepare payroll register and payroll entries.
(SO 7, 8)

P11-2A Happy Hardware has four employees who are paid on an hourly basis plus time-and-a half for all hours worked in excess of 40 a week. Payroll data for the week ended March 15, 2002, are presented below.

Employee	Hours Worked	Hourly Rate	Federal Income Tax Withholdings	United Fund
Joe McKane	40	$14.00	$?	$5.00
Mary Miller	42	13.00	?	5.00
Andy Manion	44	13.00	60	8.00
Kim Cheng	46	13.00	51	5.00

McKane and Miller are married. They claim 0 and 4 withholding allowances, respectively. The following tax rates are applicable: FICA 8%, state income taxes 3%, state unemployment taxes 5.4%, and federal unemployment 0.8%. The first three employees are sales clerks (store wages expense). The fourth employee performs administrative duties (office wages expense).

Instructions

(a) Net pay $1,862.06; Store wages expense $1,717

(b) Payroll tax expense $334.27

(d) Cash paid $586.64

(a) Prepare a payroll register for the weekly payroll. (Use the wage-bracket withholding table in the text for federal income tax withholdings.)

(b) Journalize the payroll on March 15, 2002, and the accrual of employer payroll taxes.

(c) Journalize the payment of the payroll on March 16, 2002.

(d) Journalize the deposit in a Federal Reserve bank on March 31, 2002, of the FICA and federal income taxes payable to the government.

Identify internal control weaknesses and make recommendations for improvement.
(SO 6)

P11-3A Selected payroll procedures of Palmcopiolet Company are described below.

1. Department managers interview applicants and on the basis of the interview either hire or reject the applicants. When an applicant is hired, the applicant fills out a W-4 form (Employer's Withholding Exemption Certificate). One copy of the form is sent to the human resources department, and one copy is sent to the payroll department as notice that the individual has been hired. On the copy of the W-4 sent to payroll, the managers manually indicate the hourly pay rate for the new hire.

2. The payroll checks are manually signed by the chief accountant and given to the department managers for distribution to employees in their department. The managers are responsible for seeing that any absent employees receive their checks.

3. There are two clerks in the payroll department. The payroll is divided alphabetically; one clerk has employees A to L and the other has employees M to Z. Each clerk computes the gross earnings, deductions, and net pay for employees in the section and posts the data to the employee earning records.

Instructions

(a) Indicate the weaknesses in internal control.

(b) For each weakness, describe the control procedures that will provide effective internal control. Use the following format for your answer:

(a) Weaknesses	**(b) Recommended Procedures**

Journalize payroll transactions and adjusting entries.
(SO 7, 8, 9)

 Peachtree

P11-4A The following payroll liability accounts are included in the ledger of Nam Viet Company on January 1, 2002.

FICA Taxes Payable	$ 760.00
Federal Income Taxes Payable	1,004.60
State Income Taxes Payable	108.95
Federal Unemployment Taxes Payable	288.95
State Unemployment Taxes Payable	1,954.40
Union Dues Payable	870.00
U.S. Savings Bonds Payable	360.00

In January, the following transactions occurred.

Jan. 10 Sent check for $870.00 to union treasurer for union dues.
12 Deposited check for $1,764.60 in Federal Reserve bank for FICA taxes and federal income taxes withheld.
15 Purchased U.S. Savings Bonds for employees by writing check for $360.00.
17 Paid state income taxes withheld from employees.
20 Paid federal and state unemployment taxes.
31 Completed monthly payroll register, which shows office salaries $14,600, store wages $28,400, FICA taxes withheld $3,440, federal income taxes payable $1,684, state income taxes payable $360, union dues payable $400, United Fund contributions payable $1,888, and net pay $35,228.
31 Prepared payroll checks for the net pay and distributed checks to employees.

At January 31, the company also makes the following accrued adjustments pertaining to employee compensation.

1. Employer payroll taxes: FICA taxes 8%, federal unemployment taxes 0.8%, and state unemployment taxes 5.4%.
2. Vacation pay: 6% of gross earnings.

Instructions
(a) Journalize the January transactions.
(b) Journalize the adjustments pertaining to employee compensation at January 31.

(b) Payroll tax expense $6,106.00; Vacation benefits expense $2,580

P11-5A For the year ended December 31, 2002, Malaysia Electrical Repair Company reports the following summary payroll data.

Prepare entries for payroll and payroll taxes; prepare W-2 data.
(SO 7, 8, 9)

Gross earnings:	
Administrative salaries	$180,000
Electricians' wages	470,000
Total	$650,000

Deductions:	
FICA taxes	$ 45,200
Federal income taxes withheld	188,000
State income taxes withheld (2.6%)	16,900
United Fund contributions payable	32,500
Hospital insurance premiums	20,300
Total	$302,900

Malaysia Company's payroll taxes are: FICA 8%, state unemployment 2.5% (due to a stable employment record), and 0.8% federal unemployment. Gross earnings subject to FICA taxes total $565,000, and unemployment taxes total $145,000.

Instructions
(a) Prepare a summary journal entry at December 31 for the full year's payroll.
(b) Journalize the adjusting entry at December 31 to record the employer's payroll taxes.
(c) The W-2 Wage and Tax Statement requires the following dollar data.

(a) Wages payable $347,100
(b) Payroll tax expense $49,985

Wages, Tips, Other Compensation	Federal Income Tax Withheld	State Income Tax Withheld	FICA Wages	FICA Tax Withheld

Complete the required data for the following employees.

Employee	Gross Earnings	Federal Income Tax Withheld
Anna Makarov	$59,000	$28,500
Sharon Livingston	28,000	10,800

P11-6A The following are selected transactions of Cosky Company. Cosky prepares financial statements *quarterly*.

Journalize and post note transactions; show balance sheet presentation.
(SO 2)

Jan. 2 Purchased merchandise on account from Alicea Company, $15,000, terms 2/10, n/30.
Feb. 1 Issued a 10%, 2-month, $15,000 note to Alicea in payment of account.

Mar. 31 Accrued interest for 2 months on Alicea note.
Apr. 1 Paid face value and interest on Alicea note.
July 1 Purchased equipment from Vincent Equipment paying $11,000 in cash and signing a 10%, 3-month, $25,000 note.
Sept. 30 Accrued interest for 3 months on Vincent note.
Oct. 1 Paid face value and interest on Vincent note.
Dec. 1 Borrowed $20,000 from the Otago Bank by issuing a 3-month, 12%-interest-bearing note with a face value of $20,000.
Dec. 31 Recognized interest expense for 1 month on Otago Bank note.

Instructions
(a) Prepare journal entries for the above transactions and events.
(b) Post to the accounts Notes Payable, Interest Payable, and Interest Expense.
(c) Show the balance sheet presentation of notes payable at December 31.

(d) $1,075
(d) What is total interest expense for the year?

PROBLEMS: SET B

Prepare current liability entries, adjusting entries, and current liabilities section.
(SO 1, 2, 3, 4, 5)

P11-1B On January 1, 2002, the ledger of Malaga Software Company contains the following liability accounts.

Accounts Payable	$42,500
Sales Taxes Payable	5,800
Unearned Service Revenue	15,000

During January the following selected transactions occurred.

Jan. 1 Borrowed $15,000 in cash from Amsterdam Bank on a 4-month, 12%, $15,000 note.
5 Sold merchandise for cash totaling $7,800, which includes 4% sales taxes.
12 Provided services for customers who had made advance payments of $9,000. (Credit Service Revenue.)
14 Paid state treasurer's department for sales taxes collected in December 2001, $5,800.
20 Sold 500 units of a new product on credit at $52 per unit, plus 4% sales tax. This new product is subject to a 1-year warranty.
25 Sold merchandise for cash totaling $11,440, which includes 4% sales taxes.

Instructions
(a) Journalize the January transactions.
(b) Journalize the adjusting entries at January 31 for (1) the outstanding notes payable, and (2) estimated warranty liability, assuming warranty costs are expected to equal 8% of sales of the new product.

(c) Current liability total $67,510
(c) Prepare the current liabilities section of the balance sheet at January 31, 2002. Assume no change in accounts payable.

Prepare payroll register and payroll entries.
(SO 7, 8)

P11-2B Paris Drug Store has four employees who are paid on an hourly basis plus time-and-a-half for all hours worked in excess of 40 a week. Payroll data for the week ended February 15, 2002, are presented below.

Employees	Hours Worked	Hourly Rate	Federal Income Tax Withholdings	United Fund
L. Scott	39	$13.00	$?	$–0–
S. Stahl	42	12.00	?	5.00
M. Rasheed	44	12.00	61	7.50
L. Quick	46	12.00	49	5.00

Scott and Stahl are married. They claim 2 and 4 withholding allowances, respectively. The following tax rates are applicable: FICA 8%, state income taxes 3%, state unemployment taxes 5.4%, and federal unemployment 0.8%. The first three employees are sales clerks (store wages expense). The fourth employee performs administrative duties (office wages expense).

Instructions

(a) Prepare a payroll register for the weekly payroll. (Use the wage-bracket withholding table in the text for federal income tax withholdings.)

(b) Journalize the payroll on February 15, 2002, and the accrual of employer payroll taxes.

(c) Journalize the payment of the payroll on February 16, 2002.

(d) Journalize the deposit in a Federal Reserve bank on February 28, 2002, of the FICA and federal income taxes payable to the government.

(a) Net pay $1,728.57; Store wages expense $1,575.00

(b) Payroll tax expense $307.14

(d) Cash paid $525.08

P11-3B   The payroll procedures used by three different companies are described below.

1. In Ecom Company each employee is required to mark on a clock card the hours worked. At the end of each pay period, the employee must have this clock card approved by the department manager. The approved card is then given to the payroll department by the employee. Subsequently, the treasurer's department pays the employee by check.

2. In Yerkes Computer Company clock cards and time clocks are used. At the end of each pay period, the department manager initials the cards, indicates the rates of pay, and sends them to payroll. A payroll register is prepared from the cards by the payroll department. Cash equal to the total net pay in each department is given to the department manager, who pays the employees in cash.

3. In Min Wu Company employees are required to record hours worked by "punching" clock cards in a time clock. At the end of each pay period, the clock cards are collected by the department manager. The manager prepares a payroll register in duplicate and forwards the original to payroll. In payroll, the summaries are checked for mathematical accuracy, and a payroll supervisor pays each employee by check.

Identify internal control weaknesses and make recommendations for improvement. (SO 6)

Instructions

(a) ⬛▭▭▷ Indicate the weakness(es) in internal control in each company.

(b) For each weakness, describe the control procedure(s) that will provide effective internal control. Use the following format for your answer:

<u>**(a) Weaknesses**</u>   <u>**(b) Recommended Procedures**</u>

P11-4B   The following payroll liability accounts are included in the ledger of Nathan Microscanner Company on January 1, 2002.

Journalize payroll transactions and adjusting entries. (SO 7, 8, 9)

FICA Taxes Payable	$ 662.20
Federal Income Taxes Payable	1,054.60
State Income Taxes Payable	102.15
Federal Unemployment Taxes Payable	2,400.00
State Unemployment Taxes Payable	1,954.40
Union Dues Payable	250.00
U.S. Savings Bonds Payable	350.00

In January, the following transactions occurred.

Jan. 10   Sent check for $250.00 to union treasurer for union dues.

   12   Deposited check for $1,716.80 in Federal Reserve bank for FICA taxes and federal income taxes withheld.

   15   Purchased U.S. Savings Bonds for employees by writing check for $350.00.

   17   Paid state income taxes withheld from employees.

   20   Paid federal and state unemployment taxes.

   31   Completed monthly payroll register, which shows office salaries $14,600, store wages $27,400, FICA taxes withheld $3,360, federal income taxes payable $1,654, state income taxes payable $360, union dues payable $400, United Fund contributions payable $1,688, and net pay $34,538.

   31   Prepared payroll checks for the net pay and distributed checks to employees.

At January 31, the company also makes the following accruals pertaining to employee compensation.

1. Employer payroll taxes: FICA taxes 8%, state unemployment taxes 5.4%, and federal unemployment taxes 0.8%.

2. Vacation pay: 5% of gross earnings.

(b) Payroll tax expense
$5,964.00; Vacation benefits
expense $2,100

Prepare entries for payroll and payroll taxes; prepare W-2 data.
(SO 7, 8, 9)

Instructions

(a) Journalize the January transactions.

(b) Journalize the adjustments pertaining to employee compensation at January 31.

P11-5B   For the year ended December 31, 2002, R. Westphal Company reports the following summary payroll data.

Gross earnings:	
Administrative salaries	$180,000
Electricians' wages	370,000
Total	$550,000

Deductions:	
FICA taxes	$ 38,800
Federal income taxes withheld	168,000
State income taxes withheld (2.6%)	14,300
United Fund contributions payable	27,500
Hospital insurance premiums	17,200
Total	265,800

R. Westphal Company's payroll taxes are: FICA 8%, state unemployment 2.5% (due to a stable employment record), and 0.8% federal unemployment. Gross earnings subject to FICA taxes total $485,000, and unemployment taxes total $120,000.

Instructions

(a) Wages Payable $284,200
(b) Payroll tax expense $42,760

(a) Prepare a summary journal entry at December 31 for the full year's payroll.

(b) Journalize the adjusting entry at December 31 to record the employer's payroll taxes.

(c) The W-2 Wage and Tax Statement requires the following dollar data.

Wages, Tips, Other Compensation	Federal Income Tax Withheld	State Income Tax Withheld	FICA Wages	FICA Tax Withheld

Complete the required data for the following employees.

Employee	Gross Earnings	Federal Income Tax Withheld
R. Cheng	$60,000	$27,500
K. McNeil	25,000	10,200

BROADENING YOUR PERSPECTIVE

*F*INANCIAL REPORTING AND ANALYSIS

FINANCIAL REPORTING PROBLEM: Lands' End, Inc.

BYP11-1   The financial statements of **Lands' End, Inc.** and the Notes to Consolidated Financial Statements appear in Appendix A.

Instructions

Refer to Lands' End's financial statements and answer the following questions about current and contingent liabilities and payroll costs.

(a) What were Lands' End's total current liabilities at January 28, 2000? What was the increase/decrease in Lands' End's total current liabilities from the prior year?

(b) What is the nature (composition) of the "Reserve for returns" at January 28, 2000? (See Lands' End's Note 1 for a discussion of "Reserve for losses on customer returns.")

(c) What were the components of total current liabilities on January 28, 2000 (other than "Reserve for returns" already discussed in (b) above)?

COMPARATIVE ANALYSIS PROBLEM: Lands' End vs. Abercrombie & Fitch

BYP11-2   **Lands' End**'s financial statements are presented in Appendix A. **Abercrombie & Fitch**'s financial statements are presented in Appendix B.

Instructions
(a) At January 28, 2000, what was Lands' End's largest current liability account? What were its total current liabilities? At January 29, 2000, what was Abercrombie & Fitch's largest current liability account? What were its total current liabilities?
(b) Based on information contained in those financial statements, compute the following 2000 values for each company.
 (1) Working capital.
 (2) Current ratio.
(c) What conclusions concerning the relative liquidity of these companies can be drawn from these data?

INTERPRETING FINANCIAL STATEMENTS: A Global Focus

BYP11-3   Many multinational companies find it beneficial to have their shares listed on stock exchanges in foreign countries. In order to do this, they must comply with the securities laws of those countries. Some of these laws relate to the form of financial disclosure the company must provide, including disclosures related to contingent liabilities. This exercise investigates the **Tokyo Stock Exchange**, the largest stock exchange in Japan.

Address: www.tse.or.jp/eindex.html *(or go to www.wiley.com/college/weygandt)*

Steps:
1. Choose **K-square**. Answer questions (a) and (b).
2. Choose **Investor Info**.
3. Choose **Listing guide for foreign corporations**.
4. Choose **Disclosure after listing**. Answer questions (c) and (d).

Instructions
Answer the following questions.

(a) When was the first stock exchange opened in Japan? How many exchanges does Japan have today?
(b) What event caused trading to stop for a period of time in Japan?
(c) What are four examples of decisions by corporations that must be disclosed at the time of their occurrence?
(d) What are four examples of "occurrence of material fact" that must be disclosed at the time of their occurrence?

EXPLORING THE WEB

BYP11-4   The Internal Revenue Service provides considerable information over the Internet. The following demonstrates how useful one of its sites is in answering payroll tax questions faced by employers.

Address: www.irs.ustreas.gov/prod/forms_pubs/index.html
         (or go to www.wiley.com/college/weygandt)

Steps:
1. Go to the site shown above.
2. Choose **Publications Online**.
3. Choose **Circular E, Employer's Tax Guide**.

Instructions
Answer each of the following questions.

(a) How does the government define "employees"?
(b) What are the special rules for Social Security and Medicare regarding children who are employed by their parents?

(c) How can an employee obtain a Social Security card if he or she doesn't have one?
(d) Must employees report to their employer tips received from customers? If so, what is the process?
(e) Where should the employer deposit Social Security taxes withheld or contributed?

CRITICAL THINKING

GROUP DECISION CASE

BYP11-5 Kishwaukee Processing Company provides word-processing services for business clients and students in a university community. The work for business clients is fairly steady throughout the year. The work for students peaks significantly in December and May as a result of term papers, research project reports, and dissertations.

Two years ago, the company attempted to meet the peak demand by hiring part-time help. However, this led to numerous errors and considerable customer dissatisfaction. A year ago, the company hired four experienced employees on a permanent basis instead of using part-time help. This proved to be much better in terms of productivity and customer satisfaction. But, it has caused an increase in annual payroll costs and a significant decline in annual net income.

Recently, Valarie Flynn, a sales representative of Harrington Services Inc., has made a proposal to the company. Under her plan, Harrington Services will provide up to four experienced workers at a daily rate of $110 per person for an 8-hour workday. Harrington workers are not available on an hourly basis. Kishwaukee Processing would have to pay only the daily rate for the workers used.

The owner of Kishwaukee Processing, Martha Bell, asks you, as the company's accountant, to prepare a report on the expenses that are pertinent to the decision. If the Harrington plan is adopted, Martha will terminate the employment of two permanent employees and will keep two permanent employees. At the moment, each employee earns an annual income of $30,000. Kishwaukee Processing pays 8% FICA taxes, 0.8% federal unemployment taxes, and 5.4% state unemployment taxes. The unemployment taxes apply to only the first $7,000 of gross earnings. In addition, Kishwaukee Processing pays $40 per month for each employee for medical and dental insurance.

Martha indicates that if the Harrington Services plan is accepted, her needs for workers will be as follows.

Months	Number	Working Days per Month
January–March	2	20
April–May	3	25
June–October	2	18
November–December	3	23

Instructions
With the class divided into groups, answer the following.

(a) Prepare a report showing the comparative payroll expense of continuing to employ permanent workers compared to adopting the Harrington Services Inc. plan.
(b) What other factors should Martha consider before finalizing her decision?

COMMUNICATION ACTIVITY

BYP11-6 Emil Korenewych, president of the Low Cloud Company, has recently hired a number of additional employees. He recognizes that additional payroll taxes will be due as a result of this hiring, and that the company will serve as the collection agent for other taxes.

Instructions
In a memorandum to Emil Korenewych, explain each of the taxes, and identify the taxes that result in payroll tax expense to Low Cloud Company.

ETHICS CASE

BYP11-7 Harry Smith owns and manages Harry's Restaurant, a 24-hour restaurant near the city's medical complex. Harry employs 9 full-time employees and 16 part-time employees. He pays all of the full-time employees by check, the amounts of which are determined by Harry's public accountant, Pam Web. Harry pays all of his part-time employees in currency. He computes their wages and withdraws the cash directly from his cash register.

Pam has repeatedly urged Harry to pay all employees by check. But as Harry has told his competitor and friend, Steve Hill, who owns the Greasy Diner, "First of all, my part-time employees prefer the currency over a check, and secondly I don't withhold or pay any taxes or workmen's compensation insurance on those wages because they go totally unrecorded and unnoticed."

Instructions

(a) Who are the stakeholders in this situation?

(b) What are the legal and ethical considerations regarding Harry's handling of his payroll?

(c) Pam Web is aware of Harry's payment of the part-time payroll in currency. What are her ethical responsibilities in this case?

(d) What internal control principle is violated in this payroll process?

Answers to Self-Study Questions

1. a **2.** d **3.** b **4.** b **5.** a **6.** c **7.** b **8.** d **9.** d **10.** c **11.** d

Answer to *Lands' End* Review It Question 2, p. 453

Under the heading of current liabilities, Lands' End has listed lines of credit, accounts payable, reserve for returns, accrued liabilities, accrued profit sharing, and income taxes payable.

ACCOUNTING PRINCIPLES

12

THE NAVIGATOR ✓

- Understand *Concepts for Review* ❑
- Read *Feature Story* ❑
- Scan *Study Objectives* ❑
- Read *Preview* ❑
- Read text and answer *Before You Go On*
  p. 492 ❑   p. 503 ❑
- Work *Demonstration Problems* ❑
- Review *Summary of Study Objectives* ❑
- Answer *Self-Study Questions* ❑
- Complete *Assignments* ❑

*C*ONCEPTS FOR REVIEW

Before studying this chapter, you should know or, if necessary, review:

a. The two organizations primarily responsible for setting accounting standards. (Ch. 1, p. 10)

b. The monetary unit assumption, the economic entity assumption, and the time period assumption. (Chs. 1 and 3, pp. 11 and 89)

c. The cost principle, the revenue recognition principle, and the matching principle. (Chs. 1 and 3, pp. 10 and 90–91)

☑ THE NAVIGATOR

Certainly Worth Investigating!

It is often difficult to determine in what period some revenues and expenses should be reported. There are rules that give guidance, but occasionally these rules are overlooked, misinterpreted, or even intentionally ignored. Consider the following examples.

• **Policy Management Systems**, which makes insurance software, said that it reported some sales before contracts were signed or products delivered.

• **Sunbeam Corporation**, while under the control of the (in)famous "Chainsaw" Al Dunlap, prematurely booked revenues and recorded overly large restructuring charges. Ultimately the company was forced to restate its net income figures, and Mr. Dunlap lost his job.

• **Rent-Way Inc.**, which owns a large chain of rent-to-own stores,

saw its share price plummet from $23.44 down to $5 within a week after it disclosed what the company termed "fictitious" accounting entries on its books. These entries included improper accounting for fixed-asset write-offs, and understating the amount of damaged or missing merchandise.

Often in cases such as these, the company's shareholders sue the company because of the decline in the stock price due to the disclosure of the misinformation. In light of this eventuality, why might management want to report revenues or expenses in the wrong period? Company managers are under intense pressure to report higher earnings every year. If actual performance falls

short of expectations, management might be tempted to bend the rules.

One analyst suggests that investors and auditors should be suspicious of sharp increases in monthly sales at the end of each quarter or big jumps in fourth-quarter sales. Such events don't always mean management is cheating, but they are certainly worth investigating.

THE NAVIGATOR

After studying this chapter, you should be able to:

1. Explain the meaning of generally accepted accounting principles and identify the key items of the conceptual framework.
2. Describe the basic objectives of financial reporting.
3. Discuss the qualitative characteristics of accounting information and elements of financial statements.
4. Identify the basic assumptions used by accountants.
5. Identify the basic principles of accounting.
6. Identify the two constraints in accounting.
7. Explain the accounting principles used in international operations.

THE NAVIGATOR

As indicated in the Feature Story, it is important that general guidelines be available to resolve accounting issues. Without these basic guidelines, each enterprise would have to develop its own set of accounting practices. If this happened, we would have to become familiar with every company's peculiar accounting and reporting rules in order to understand their financial statements. It would be difficult, if not impossible, to compare the financial statements of different companies. This chapter explores the basic accounting principles that are followed in developing specific accounting guidelines.

The content and organization of Chapter 12 are as follows.

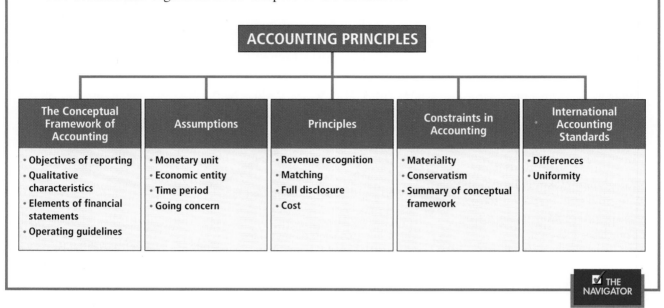

ACCOUNTING PRINCIPLES				
The Conceptual Framework of Accounting	**Assumptions**	**Principles**	**Constraints in Accounting**	**International Accounting Standards**
• Objectives of reporting • Qualitative characteristics • Elements of financial statements • Operating guidelines	• Monetary unit • Economic entity • Time period • Going concern	• Revenue recognition • Matching • Full disclosure • Cost	• Materiality • Conservatism • Summary of conceptual framework	• Differences • Uniformity

☑ THE NAVIGATOR

THE CONCEPTUAL FRAMEWORK OF ACCOUNTING

STUDY OBJECTIVE 1

Explain the meaning of generally accepted accounting principles and identify the key items of the conceptual framework.

What you have learned up to this point in the book is a process that leads to the preparation of financial reports about a company. These are the company's financial statements. This area of accounting is called **financial accounting**. The accounting profession has established a set of standards and rules that are recognized as a general guide for financial reporting. This recognized set of standards is called **generally accepted accounting principles (GAAP)**. "Generally accepted" means that these principles must have "substantial authoritative support." Such support usually comes from two standard-setting bodies: the Financial Accounting Standards Board (FASB) and the Securities and Exchange Commission (SEC).[1]

Since the early 1970s the business and governmental communities have given the FASB the responsibility for developing accounting principles in this country.

---

[1]The SEC is an agency of the U.S. government that was established in 1933 to administer laws and regulations relating to the exchange of securities and the publication of financial information by U.S. businesses. The agency has the authority to mandate generally accepted accounting principles for companies under its jurisdiction. However, throughout its history, the SEC has been willing to accept the principles set forth by the FASB and similar bodies.

This is an ongoing process; accounting principles change to reflect changes in the business environment and in the needs of users of accounting information.

Prior to the establishment of the FASB, accounting principles were developed on a problem-by-problem basis. Rule-making bodies developed accounting rules and methods to solve specific problems. Critics charged that the problem-by-problem approach led over time to inconsistent rules and practices. No clearly developed conceptual framework of accounting existed to refer to in solving new problems.

In response to these criticisms, the FASB developed a **conceptual framework**. It serves as the basis for resolving accounting and reporting problems. The FASB spent considerable time and effort on this project. The Board views its conceptual framework as ". . . a constitution, a coherent system of interrelated objectives and fundamentals."[2]

The FASB's conceptual framework consists of the following four items:

1. Objectives of financial reporting.
2. Qualitative characteristics of accounting information.
3. Elements of financial statements.
4. Operating guidelines (assumptions, principles, and constraints).

We will discuss these items on the following pages.

> **HELPFUL HINT**
> Accounting principles are affected by economic and political conditions which change over time. As a result, accounting principles are not cut into stone like the periodic table in chemistry or a formula in math.

*A*CCOUNTING IN ACTION   *International Insight*

 You should recognize that different political and cultural influences affect the accounting that occurs in foreign countries. For example, in Sweden, accounting is considered an instrument to be used to shape fiscal policy. In Europe generally, more emphasis is given to social reporting (more information on employment statistics, health of workers, and so on) than it is in the United States. European labor organizations are strong and demand that type of information from management.

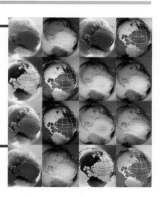

OBJECTIVES OF FINANCIAL REPORTING

The FASB began to work on the conceptual framework by looking at the objectives of financial reporting. Determining these objectives required answers to such basic questions as: Who uses financial statements? Why? What information do they need? How knowledgeable about business and accounting are financial statement users? How should financial information be reported so that it is best understood?

In answering these questions, the FASB concluded that the objectives of financial reporting are to provide information that:

1. Is useful to those making investment and credit decisions.
2. Is helpful in assessing future cash flows.
3. Identifies the economic resources (assets), the claims to those resources (liabilities), and the changes in those resources and claims.

The FASB then undertook to describe the characteristics that make accounting information useful.

STUDY OBJECTIVE **2**

Describe the basic objectives of financial reporting.

---

[2]"Conceptual Framework for Financial Accounting and Reporting: Elements of Financial Statements and Their Measurement," *FASB Discussion Memorandum* (Stamford, Conn.: 1976), p. 1.

QUALITATIVE CHARACTERISTICS OF ACCOUNTING INFORMATION

STUDY OBJECTIVE 3

Discuss the qualitative characteristics of accounting information and elements of financial statements.

How does a company like **Microsoft** decide on the amount of financial information to disclose? In what format should its financial information be presented? How should assets, liabilities, revenues, and expenses be measured? The FASB concluded that the overriding criterion for such accounting choices is **decision usefulness**. The accounting practice selected should be the one that generates the most useful financial information for making a decision. To be useful, information should possess the following qualitative characteristics: relevance, reliability, comparability, and consistency.

Relevance

Accounting information has **relevance** if it makes a difference in a decision. Relevant information has either predictive or feedback value or both. **Predictive value** helps users forecast future events. For example, when **ExxonMobil** issues financial statements, the information in them is considered relevant because it provides a basis for predicting future earnings. **Feedback value** confirms or corrects prior expectations. When ExxonMobil issues financial statements, it confirms or corrects prior expectations about the financial health of the company.

In addition, accounting information has relevance if it is **timely**. It must be available to decision makers before it loses its capacity to influence decisions. If ExxonMobil reported its financial information only every five years, the information would be of limited use in decision-making.

HELPFUL HINT

What makes accounting information relevant? Answer: Relevant accounting information provides feedback, serves as a basis for predictions, and is timely (current).

Reliability

Reliability of information means that the information is free of error and bias. In short, it can be depended on. To be reliable, accounting information must be **verifiable**: We must be able to prove that it is free of error and bias. It also must be a **faithful representation** of what it purports to be: It must be factual. If **Sears, Roebuck's** income statement reports sales of $100 billion when it had sales of $51 billion, then the statement is not a faithful representation. Finally, accounting information must be **neutral**: It cannot be selected, prepared, or presented to favor one set of interested users over another. To ensure reliability, certified public accountants audit financial statements.

HELPFUL HINT

What makes accounting information reliable? Answer: Reliable accounting information is free of error and bias, is factual, verifiable, and neutral.

Comparability

Accounting information about an enterprise is most useful when it can be compared with accounting information about other enterprises. **Comparability** results when different companies use the same accounting principles. For example, **Lands' End**, **L. L. Bean**, and **The Limited** all use the cost principle in reporting plant assets on the balance sheet. Also, each company uses the revenue recognition and matching principles in determining its net income.

Conceptually, comparability should also extend to the methods used by companies in complying with an accounting principle. Accounting methods include the FIFO and LIFO methods of inventory costing, and various depreciation methods. At this point, comparability of methods is not required, even for companies in the same industry. Thus, **Ford**, **General Motors**, and **DaimlerChrysler** may use different inventory costing and depreciation methods in their financial statements. The only accounting requirement is that each company **must disclose** the accounting methods used. From the disclosures, the external user can determine whether the financial information is comparable.

Consistency

Consistency means that a company uses the same accounting principles and methods from year to year. If a company selects FIFO as the inventory costing method in the first year of operations, it is expected to use FIFO in succeeding years. When financial information has been reported on a consistent basis, the financial statements permit meaningful analysis of trends within a company.

A company *can* change to a new method of accounting. To do so, management must justify that the new method results in more meaningful financial information. In the year in which the change occurs, the change must be disclosed in the notes to the financial statements. Such disclosure makes users of the financial statements aware of the lack of consistency.

ACCOUNTING IN ACTION *Business Insight*

There is a classic story that professors often tell students about a company looking for an accountant. The company approached the first accountant and asked: "What do you believe our net income will be this year?" The accountant said "4 million dollars." The company asked the second accountant the same question, and the answer was "What would you like it to be?" Guess who got the job?

The reason we tell the story here is that, because accounting principles offer flexibility, it is important that a consistent treatment be provided from period to period. Otherwise it would be very difficult to interpret financial statements. Perhaps *no* alternative methods should be permitted in accounting. What do you think?

The qualitative characteristics of accounting information are summarized in Illustration 12-1.

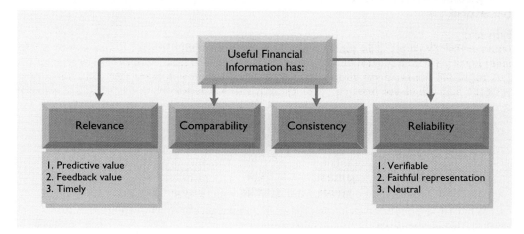

Illustration 12-1

Qualitative characteristics of accounting information

ELEMENTS OF FINANCIAL STATEMENTS

An important part of the accounting conceptual framework is a set of definitions that describe the basic terms used in accounting. The FASB refers to this set of definitions as the **elements of financial statements**. They include such terms as assets, liabilities, equity, revenues, and expenses.

Because these elements are so important, it is crucial that they be precisely defined and universally applied. Finding the appropriate definition for many of these elements is not easy. For example, should the value of a company's employees be reported as an asset on a balance sheet? Should the death of the company's president be reported as a loss? A good set of definitions should provide answers to these types of questions. Because you have already encountered most of these definitions in earlier chapters, they are not repeated here.

OPERATING GUIDELINES

The objectives of financial reporting, the qualitative characteristics of accounting information, and the elements of financial statements are very broad. Because practicing accountants must solve practical problems, more detailed guidelines are needed. In its conceptual framework, the FASB recognized the need for operating guidelines. We classify these guidelines as assumptions, principles, and constraints. These guidelines are well-established and accepted in accounting.

Assumptions provide a foundation for the accounting process. **Principles** are specific rules that indicate how economic events should be reported in the accounting process. **Constraints** on the accounting process allow for a relaxation of the principles under certain circumstances. Illustration 12-2 provides a roadmap of the operating guidelines of accounting. These guidelines (some of which you know from earlier chapters) are discussed in more detail in the following sections.

Illustration 12-2

The operating guidelines of accounting

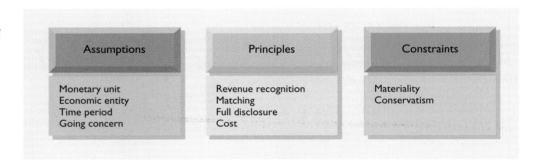

Assumptions	Principles	Constraints
Monetary unit	Revenue recognition	Materiality
Economic entity	Matching	Conservatism
Time period	Full disclosure	
Going concern	Cost	

BEFORE YOU GO ON...

▶ *REVIEW IT*

1. What are generally accepted accounting principles?
2. What is stated about generally accepted accounting principles in the Report of Independent Public Accountants for **Lands' End**? The answer to this question appears on page 517.
3. What are the basic objectives of financial information?
4. What are the qualitative characteristics that make accounting information useful? Identify two elements of the financial statements.

☑ THE NAVIGATOR

*A*SSUMPTIONS

STUDY OBJECTIVE 4

Identify the basic assumptions used by accountants.

As noted above, assumptions provide a foundation for the accounting process. You already know three of the major assumptions—the monetary unit, economic entity, and time period assumptions. The fourth is the going concern assumption.

MONETARY UNIT ASSUMPTION

The **monetary unit assumption** states that only transaction data that can be expressed in terms of money be included in the accounting records. For example, the value of a company president is not reported in a company's financial records because it cannot be expressed easily in dollars.

An important corollary to the monetary unit assumption is the assumption that the unit of measure remains relatively constant over time. This point will be discussed in more detail later in this chapter.

ECONOMIC ENTITY ASSUMPTION

The **economic entity assumption** states that the activities of the entity be kept separate and distinct from the activities of the owner and of all other economic entities. For example, it is assumed that the activities of **IBM** can be distinguished from those of other computer companies such as **Apple**, **Compaq**, and **Hewlett-Packard**.

***I*NTERNATIONAL NOTE**

In an action that sent shock waves through the French business community, the CEO of Alcatel-Alsthom was taken into custody for an apparent violation of the economic entity assumption. Allegedly, the executive improperly used company funds to install an expensive security system in his home.

TIME PERIOD ASSUMPTION

The **time period assumption** states that the economic life of a business can be divided into artificial time periods. Thus, it is assumed that the activities of business enterprises such as **General Electric**, **America Online**, **ExxonMobil**, or any enterprise can be subdivided into months, quarters, or a year for meaningful financial reporting purposes.

GOING CONCERN ASSUMPTION

The **going concern assumption** assumes that the enterprise will continue in operation long enough to carry out its existing objectives. In spite of numerous business failures, companies have a fairly high continuance rate. It has proved useful to adopt a going concern assumption for accounting purposes.

The accounting implications of this assumption are critical. If a going concern assumption is not used, then plant assets should be stated at their liquidation value (selling price less cost of disposal)—not at their cost. In that case, depreciation and amortization of these assets would not be needed. Each period, these assets would simply be reported at their liquidation value. Also, without this assumption, the current–noncurrent classification of assets and liabilities would not matter. Labeling anything as long-term would be difficult to justify.

Acceptance of the going concern assumption gives credibility to the cost principle. Only when liquidation appears imminent is the going concern assumption inapplicable. In that case, assets would be better stated at liquidation value than at cost.

These basic accounting assumptions are illustrated graphically in Illustration 12-3 on the next page.

HELPFUL HINT
(1) Which accounting assumption assumes that an enterprise will remain in business long enough to recover the cost of its assets? (2) Which accounting assumption is justification for the cost principle? Answers: (1) and (2) Going concern assumption.

*P*RINCIPLES

On the basis of the fundamental assumptions of accounting, the accounting profession has developed principles that dictate how economic events should be recorded and reported. In earlier chapters we discussed the cost principle (Chapter 1) and the revenue recognition and matching principles (Chapter 3). Here we now examine a number of reporting issues related to these principles. In addition, we introduce another principle, the full disclosure principle.

STUDY **OBJECTIVE 5**

Identify the basic principles of accounting.

Illustration 12-3

Assumptions used in accounting

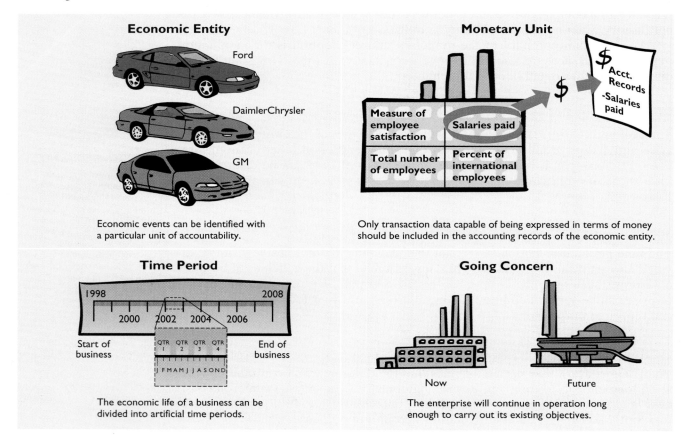

Economic Entity

Ford

DaimlerChrysler

GM

Economic events can be identified with a particular unit of accountability.

Monetary Unit

Measure of employee satisfaction   Salaries paid

Total number of employees   Percent of international employees

$ Acct. Records -Salaries paid

Only transaction data capable of being expressed in terms of money should be included in the accounting records of the economic entity.

Time Period

1998   2008

2000   2002   2004   2006

QTR 1   QTR 2   QTR 3   QTR 4

J F M A M J J A S O N D

Start of business   End of business

The economic life of a business can be divided into artificial time periods.

Going Concern

Now   Future

The enterprise will continue in operation long enough to carry out its existing objectives.

REVENUE RECOGNITION PRINCIPLE

The **revenue recognition principle** dictates that revenue should be recognized in the accounting period in which it is earned. But applying this general principle in practice can be difficult. For example, some companies improperly recognize revenue on goods that have not been shipped to customers. Similarly, until recently, financial institutions immediately recorded a large portion of their fees for granting a loan as revenue rather than spreading those fees over the life of the loan.

When a sale is involved, revenue is recognized at the point of sale. This **sales basis** involves an exchange transaction between the seller and buyer. The sales price is an objective measure of the amount of revenue realized. However, there are two exceptions to the sales basis for revenue recognition that have become generally accepted. They are the percentage-of-completion method and the installment method.

Percentage-of-Completion Method

In long-term construction contracts, revenue recognition is usually required before the contract is completed. For example, assume that Warrior Construction Co. had a contract to build a dam for the U.S. Department of the Interior for $400 million. Construction is estimated to take 3 years (starting in 2000) at a cost of

$360 million. If Warrior applies the point-of-sale basis, it will report no revenues and no profit in the first two years. In 2002, when completion and sale take place, Warrior will report $400 million in revenues, costs of $360 million, and the entire profit of $40 million. Was Warrior really producing no revenues and earning no profit in 2000 and 2001? Obviously not. Instead, the earning process can be considered substantially completed at various stages. Therefore revenue should be recognized as construction progresses.

In recognizing revenue, Warrior can apply the **percentage-of-completion method**. This method recognizes revenue on a long-term project on the basis of reasonable estimates of progress toward completion. Progress toward completion is measured by comparing the costs incurred in a year to the total estimated costs for the entire project. That percentage is multiplied by the total revenue for the project. The result is then recognized as revenue for the period. The formulas for this method are as follows.

HELPFUL HINT

For long-term construction contracts, it is appropriate to use the percentage-of-completion method of revenue recognition. The critical event in the earning process is making progress toward completion. The ultimate sale and selling price are assured by the contract.

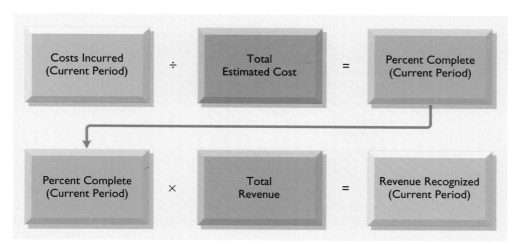

Illustration 12-4

Formula to recognize revenue in the percentage-of-completion method

The costs incurred in the current period are then subtracted from the revenue recognized during the current period to arrive at the gross profit for the current period. This formula is shown in Illustration 12-5.

Illustration 12-5

Formula to compute gross profit in current period

Let's look at an illustration of the percentage-of-completion method. Assume that Warrior Construction Co. incurs costs of $54 million in 2000, $180 million in 2001, and $126 million in 2002 on the dam project. The portion of the $400 million of revenue recognized in each of the three years is shown in Illustration 12-6.

Year	Costs Incurred (Current Period)	÷	Total Estimated Cost	=	Percent Complete (Current Period)	×	Total Revenue	=	Revenue Recognized (Current Period)
2000	$ 54,000,000		$360,000,000		15%		$400,000,000		$ 60,000,000
2001	180,000,000		360,000,000		50%		400,000,000		200,000,000
2002	126,000,000		Balance required to complete the contract						140,000,000
Totals	$360,000,000								$400,000,000

Illustration 12-6

Revenue recognized—percentage-of-completion method

No estimate is made of the percentage of work completed during the final period. In the final period, all remaining revenue is recognized. In this example, the company's cost estimates have been very accurate. The costs incurred in the third year were 35% of the total estimated cost ($126,000 ÷ $360,000).

The gross profit recognized each period is as follows.

Illustration 12-7

Gross profit recognized—percentage-of-completion method

Year	Revenue Recognized (Current Period)	−	Actual Cost Incurred (Current Period)	=	Gross Profit Recognized (Current Period)
2000	$ 60,000,000		$ 54,000,000		$ 6,000,000
2001	200,000,000		180,000,000		20,000,000
2002	140,000,000		126,000,000		14,000,000
Totals	$400,000,000		$360,000,000		$40,000,000

Use of the percentage-of-completion method involves some subjectivity. As a result, errors are possible in determining the amount of revenue recognized and gross profit recognized. Yet to wait until completion would seriously distort each period's financial statements. Naturally, **if it is not possible to obtain dependable estimates of costs and progress, then the revenue should be recognized at the completion date** and not by the percentage-of-completion method.

Installment Method

Another basis for revenue recognition is the receipt of cash. The **cash basis** is generally used only when it is difficult to determine the revenue amount at the time of a credit sale because collection is uncertain. One popular revenue recognition approach using the cash basis is the installment method.

Under the installment method, each cash collection from a customer consists of (1) a partial recovery of the cost of the goods sold, and (2) partial gross profit from the sale. For example, if the gross profit rate at the date of sale is 40%, each receipt of cash consists of 60% recovery of cost of goods sold and 40% gross profit. The formula to recognize gross profit is as follows.

Illustration 12-8

Gross profit formula—installment method

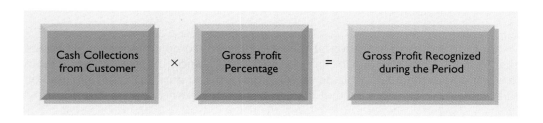

To illustrate, assume that an Iowa farm machinery dealer in the first year of operations had installment sales of $600,000. Its cost of goods sold on installment was $420,000. Total gross profit is therefore $180,000 ($600,000 − $420,000), and the gross profit percentage is 30% ($180,000 ÷ $600,000). Collections on the installment sales were as follows: first year $280,000 (down payment plus monthly payments), second year $200,000, and third year $120,000. The computation of gross profit recognized is shown in Illustration 12-9. (Interest charges are ignored in this illustration.)

Year	Cash Collected	×	Gross Profit Percentage	=	Gross Profit Recognized
2000	$280,000		30%		$ 84,000
2001	200,000		30%		60,000
2002	120,000		30%		36,000
Total	$600,000				$180,000

Illustration 12-9

Gross profit recognized—installment method

Under the installment method of accounting, gross profit is therefore recognized **in the period in which the cash is collected**.

As indicated earlier, the installment method is used when there is risk of not collecting an account receivable. In that case, the sale itself is not sufficient evidence for revenue to be recognized.

ACCOUNTING IN ACTION   Business Insight

Datapoint Corp. encouraged its customers to load up with large shipments at the end of the year. This strategy allowed Datapoint to report these shipments as revenues, even though payment hadn't been collected. Unfortunately, some of the customers either went broke or quit before paying for the equipment received. The company had to record substantial bad debts or in some cases reverse previously recorded sales. If Datapoint had used the installment method, this revenue would not have been reported. As a result, revenue recognition practices that are cash-basis oriented, such as the installment method, are becoming more acceptable as it becomes difficult to tell when a sale is a sale.

MATCHING PRINCIPLE (EXPENSE RECOGNITION)

Expense recognition is traditionally tied to revenue recognition: "Let the expense follow the revenue." As you learned in Chapter 3, this practice is referred to as the **matching principle**. It dictates that expenses be matched with revenues in the period in which efforts are made to generate revenues. Expenses are not recognized when cash is paid, or when the work is performed, or when the product is produced. Rather, they are recognized when the labor (service) or the product actually makes its contribution to revenue.

But, it is sometimes difficult to determine the accounting period in which the expense contributed to revenues. Several approaches have therefore been devised for matching expenses and revenues on the income statement.

To understand these approaches, you need to understand the nature of expenses. Costs are the source of expenses. Costs that will generate revenues only in the current accounting period are expensed immediately. They are reported as **operating expenses** in the income statement. Examples include costs for advertising, sales salaries, and repairs. These expenses are often called **expired costs**.

HELPFUL HINT
Costs become expenses when they are charged against revenue.

Costs that will generate revenues in future accounting periods are recognized as assets. Examples include merchandise inventory, prepaid expenses, and plant assets. These costs represent **unexpired costs**. Unexpired costs become expenses in two ways:

1. **Cost of goods sold.** Costs carried as merchandise inventory become expenses when the inventory is sold. They are expensed as cost of goods sold in the period when the sale occurs. Thus, there is a direct matching of expenses with revenues.

2. **Operating expenses.** Other unexpired costs become operating expenses through use or consumption (as in the case of store supplies) or through the passage of time (as in the case of prepaid insurance). The costs of plant assets and other long-lived resources are expensed through rational and systematic allocation methods—periodic depreciation or amortization. Operating expenses contribute to the revenues for the period, but their association with revenues is less direct than for cost of goods sold.

These points about expense recognition are illustrated in Illustration 12-10.

Illustration 12-10

Expense recognition pattern

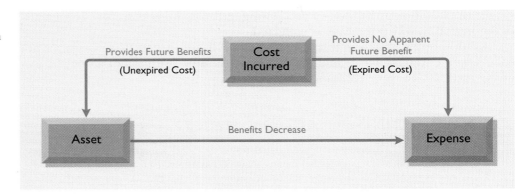

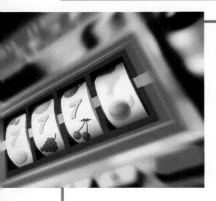

*A*CCOUNTING IN ACTION   *Business Insight*

Implementing expense recognition guidelines can be difficult. Consider, for example, **Harold's Club** (a gambling casino) in Reno, Nevada. How should it report expenses related to the payoff of its progressive slot machines? Progressive slot machines, which generally have no ceiling on their jackpots, provide a lucky winner with all the money that many losers had previously put in. Payoffs tend to be huge, but infrequent. At Harold's, the progressive slots pay off on average every 4½ months.

The basic accounting question is: Can Harold's deduct the millions of dollars sitting in its progressive slot machines from the revenue recognized at the end of the accounting period? One might argue that no, you cannot deduct the money until the "winning handle pull." However, a winning handle pull might not occur for many months or even years. Although an estimate would have to be used, the better answer is to match these costs with the revenue recognized, assuming that an average 4½ months' payout is well documented. Obviously, the matching principle can be difficult to apply in practice.

FULL DISCLOSURE PRINCIPLE

The **full disclosure principle** requires that circumstances and events that make a difference to financial statement users be disclosed. For example, most accountants would agree that **Manville Corporation** should have disclosed the 52,000 asbestos liability suits (totaling $2 billion) pending against it. Interested parties would want to be made aware of this contingent loss. Similarly, it is generally agreed that companies should disclose the major provisions of employee pension plans and long-term lease contracts.

Compliance with the full disclosure principle occurs through the data in the financial statements and the information in the notes that accompany the statements. The first note in most cases is a **summary of significant accounting policies**. It includes, among others, the methods used for inventory costing, depreciation of plant assets, and amortization of intangible assets.

Deciding how much disclosure is enough can be difficult. Accountants could disclose every financial event that occurs and every contingency that exists. But the benefits of providing additional information in some cases may be less than the costs of doing so. Many companies complain of an accounting standards overload. They also object to requirements that force them to disclose confidential information. Determining where to draw the line on disclosure is not easy.

One thing is certain: financial statements were much simpler years ago. In 1930, **General Electric** had no notes to its financial statements. Today it has over 20 pages of notes! Why this change? A major reason is that the objectives of financial statements have changed. In the past, information was generally presented on what the business had done. Today, the objectives of financial reporting are more future-oriented. The goal is to provide information that makes it possible to predict the amounts, timing, and uncertainty of future cash flows.

ACCOUNTING IN ACTION ∧ Business Insight

Some accountants are reconsidering the current means of financial reporting. They propose a database concept of financial reporting. In such a system, all the information from transactions would be stored in a computerized database to be accessed by various user groups. The main benefit of such a system is the ability to tailor the information requested to the needs of each user.

What makes this idea controversial? Discussion currently revolves around access and aggregation issues. Questions abound: "Who should be allowed to make inquiries of the system?" "What is the lowest/smallest level of information to be provided?" "Will such a system necessarily improve on the current means of disclosure?" Such questions must be answered before database financial accounting can be implemented on a large scale.

COST PRINCIPLE

As you know, the **cost principle** dictates that assets be recorded at their cost. Cost is used because it is both relevant and reliable. Cost is **relevant** because it represents the price paid, the assets sacrificed, or the commitment made at date of acquisition. Cost is **reliable** because it is objectively measurable, factual, and verifiable. It is the result of an exchange transaction. Cost is the basis used in preparing financial statements.

The cost principle, however, has come under criticism. Some criticize it as irrelevant. After acquisition, the argument goes, the cost of an asset is not equivalent to market value or current value. Also, as the purchasing power of the dollar changes, so does the meaning associated with the dollar used as the basis of measurement. Consider the classic story about the individual who went to sleep and woke up 10 years later. Hurrying to a telephone, he called his broker and asked what his formerly modest stock portfolio was worth. He was told that he was a multi-millionaire. His **General Motors** stock was worth $5 million, and his **Microsoft** stock was up to $10 million. Elated, he was about to inquire about his other holdings, when the telephone operator cut in with "Your time is up. Please deposit $100,000 for the next three minutes."[3]

Despite the inevitability of changing prices due to inflation, the accounting profession still follows the stable monetary unit assumption in preparing the primary financial statements. While admitting that some changes in prices do occur, the profession believes the unit of measure—the dollar—has remained sufficiently constant over time to provide meaningful financial information. Sometimes, the **disclosure of price-level adjusted data is in the form of supplemental information** that accompanies the financial statements.

The basic principles of accounting are summarized in Illustration 12-11.

Illustration 12-11

Basic principles used in accounting

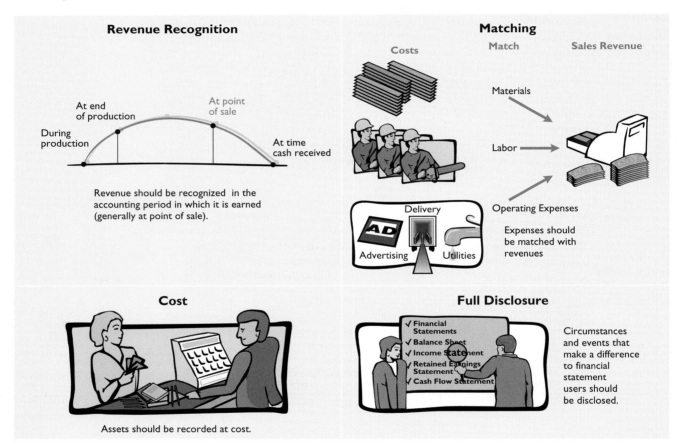

CONSTRAINTS IN ACCOUNTING

STUDY OBJECTIVE 6

Identify the two constraints in accounting.

Constraints permit a company to modify generally accepted accounting principles without reducing the usefulness of the reported information. The constraints are materiality and conservatism.

MATERIALITY

Materiality relates to an item's impact on a firm's overall financial condition and operations. An item is **material** when it is likely to influence the decision of a reasonably prudent investor or creditor. It is immaterial if its inclusion or omission

---

[3]Adapted from *Barron's*, January 28, 1980, p. 27.

has no impact on a decision maker. In short, if the item does not make a difference in decision making, GAAP does not have to be followed. To determine the materiality of an amount, the accountant usually compares it with such items as total assets, total liabilities, and net income.

To illustrate how the materiality constraint is applied, assume that Rodriguez Co. purchases a number of low-cost plant assets, such as wastepaper baskets. Although the proper accounting would appear to be to depreciate these wastepaper baskets over their useful life, they are usually expensed immediately. This practice is justified because these costs are considered immaterial. Establishing depreciation schedules for these assets is costly and time-consuming and will not make a material difference on total assets and net income. Another application of the materiality constraint would be the expensing of small tools. Some companies expense any plant assets under a specified dollar amount.

CONSERVATISM

The **conservatism** constraint dictates that when in doubt, choose the method that will be least likely to overstate assets and income. It does **not** mean **understating** assets or income. Conservatism provides a reasonable guide in difficult situations: Do not overstate assets and income.

A common application of the conservatism constraint is the use of the lower of cost or market method for inventories. As indicated in Chapter 6, inventories are reported at market value if market value is below cost. This practice results in a higher cost of goods sold and lower net income. In addition, inventory on the balance sheet is stated at a lower amount.

Other examples of conservatism in accounting are the use of the LIFO method for inventory valuation when prices are rising and the use of accelerated depreciation methods for plant assets. Both these methods result in lower asset carrying values and lower net income than alternative methods.

The two constraints in accounting are graphically depicted in Illustration 12-12.

> **HELPFUL HINT**
> In other words, if two methods are otherwise equally appropriate, choose the one that will least likely overstate assets and income.

Materiality	Conservatism
For small amounts, GAAP does not have to be followed.	When in doubt, choose the solution that will be least likely to overstate assets and income.

Illustration 12-12

Constraints in accounting

SUMMARY OF CONCEPTUAL FRAMEWORK

As we have seen, the conceptual framework for developing sound reporting practices starts with a set of objectives for financial reporting. It follows with the description of qualities that make information useful. In addition, elements of financial statements are defined. More detailed operating guidelines are then provided. These guidelines take the form of assumptions and principles.

The conceptual framework also recognizes that constraints exist on the reporting environment. The conceptual framework is illustrated graphically in Illustration 12-13.

Illustration 12-13

Conceptual framework

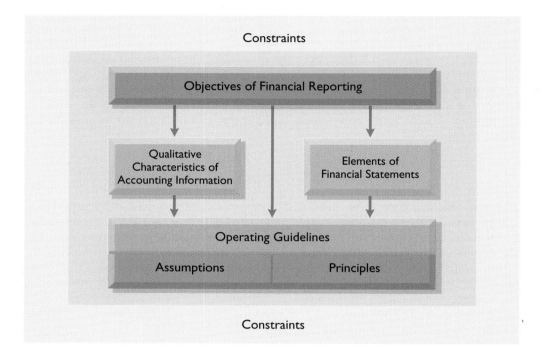

INTERNATIONAL ACCOUNTING STANDARDS

STUDY OBJECTIVE 7

Explain the accounting principles used in international operations.

World markets are becoming increasingly intertwined. Foreigners use American computers, eat American breakfast cereals, read American magazines, listen to American rock music, watch American movies and TV shows, and drink American soda. Americans drive Japanese cars, wear Italian shoes and Scottish woolens, drink Brazilian coffee and Indian tea, eat Swiss chocolate bars, sit on Danish furniture, and use Arabian oil. The variety and volume of exported and imported goods indicates the extensive involvement of U.S. business in international trade. Many U.S. companies consider the world their market.

Firms that conduct operations in more than one country through subsidiaries, divisions, or branches in foreign countries are referred to as **multinational corporations**. The accounting for such corporations is complicated because foreign currencies are involved. These international transactions must be translated into U.S. dollars.

DIFFERENCES IN STANDARDS

In the new global economy many investment and credit decisions require the analysis of foreign financial statements. Unfortunately, accounting standards are not uniform from country to country. This lack of uniformity results from differences in legal systems, in processes for developing accounting standards, in governmental requirements, and in economic environments.

ACCOUNTING IN ACTION   *International Insight*

Research and development costs are an example of different international accounting standards. Compare how four countries account for research and development (R&D):

Country	Accounting Treatment
United States	Expenditures are expensed.
United Kingdom	Certain expenditures may be capitalized.
Germany	Expenditures are expensed.
Japan	Expenditures may be capitalized and amortized over 5 years.

Thus, an R&D expenditure of $100 million is charged totally to expense in the current period in the United States and Germany. This same expense could range from zero to $100 million in the United Kingdom and from $20 million to $100 million in Japan! Do you believe that accounting principles should be comparable across countries?

UNIFORMITY IN STANDARDS

Efforts to obtain uniformity in international accounting practices are taking place. In 1973 the **International Accounting Standards Committee (IASC)** was formed by agreement of accounting organizations in the United States, the United Kingdom, Canada, Australia, France, Germany, Japan, Mexico, and the Netherlands. Its purpose is to formulate international accounting standards and to promote their acceptance worldwide.

To date, numerous standards have been issued for IASC members to introduce to their respective countries. But, the IASC has no enforcement powers, so these standards are by no means universally applied. They are, though, generally followed by the multinational companies that are audited by international public accounting firms. The foundation has been laid for progress toward greater uniformity in international accounting.

BEFORE YOU GO ON...

▶ *REVIEW IT*
1. What are the monetary unit assumption, the economic entity assumption, the time period assumption, and the going concern assumption?
2. What are the revenue recognition principle, the matching principle, the full disclosure principle, and the cost principle?
3. What are the materiality constraint and the conservatism constraint?
4. What is the purpose of the International Accounting Standards Committee?

A *LOOK BACK AT OUR FEATURE STORY*

Refer back to the Feature Story at the beginning of the chapter, and answer the following questions.
1. **Policy Management Systems Corp.** produces insurance software. It reported some sales before contracts were signed or products delivered. Is the concept of revenue recognition violated in this situation? Explain.

2. Sunbeam Corporation prematurely booked revenues and recorded overly large restructuring charges.

SOLUTION

1. The revenue recognition principle dictates that revenue should be recognized in the accounting period in which it is earned. Revenue is generally recognized at the point of sale. Policy Management violated the revenue recognition principle because the sale had not yet occurred.
2. Many companies feel intense pressure to report higher earnings every year. If actual performance falls short of expectations, management might be tempted to bend the rules to prevent its stock price from falling. Although high-tech firms are particularly susceptible to earnings declines, many companies attempt to manage their net income from period to period, as Sunbeam Corporation appears to have done.

☑ THE NAVIGATOR

Additional Demonstration Problem

DEMONSTRATION PROBLEM 1

Carver Construction Company is under contract to build a condominium at a contract price of $2,000,000. The building will take 18 months to complete at an estimated cost of $1,400,000. Construction began in November 2001, and was finished in April 2003. Actual construction costs incurred in each year were: 2001, $140,000; 2002, $910,000; and 2003, $350,000.

Instructions
Compute the gross profit to be recognized in each year.

ACTION PLAN

- Determine percent complete by dividing costs incurred by total estimated costs.
- Find revenue recognized by multiplying percent complete by contract price.
- Calculate gross profit: revenue recognized less actual costs incurred.
- Under percentage-of-completion method, recognize revenue as the construction occurs. (Revenue is viewed as a series of sales.)

☑ THE NAVIGATOR

SOLUTION TO DEMONSTRATION PROBLEM 1

Year	Costs Incurred (Current Period)	÷ Total Estimated Cost =	Percent Complete (Current Period)	× Total Revenue =	Revenue Recognized (Current Period)
2001	$ 140,000	$1,400,000	10%	$2,000,000	$ 200,000
2002	910,000	1,400,000	65%	2,000,000	1,300,000
2003	350,000	Balance to complete contract			500,000
	$1,400,000				$2,000,000

Year	Revenue Recognized (Current Period)	− Actual Costs Incurred (Current Period)	= Gross Profit Recognized (Current Period)
2001	$ 200,000	$ 140,000	$ 60,000
2002	1,300,000	910,000	390,000
2003	500,000	350,000	150,000
	$2,000,000	$1,400,000	$600,000

DEMONSTRATION PROBLEM 2

Additional Demonstration Problem

Valdes Inc. uses the installment method in accounting for its sales. In 2000, its first year of operations, it had installment sales of $900,000 and a cost of goods sold on installments of $600,000. The collections on installment sales were as follows: 2000, $330,000; 2001, $420,000; and 2002, $150,000.

Instructions
Compute the amount of gross profit to be recognized each year.

SOLUTION TO DEMONSTRATION PROBLEM 2

Year	Cash Collected	×	Gross Profit Percentage*	=	Gross Profit Recognized
2000	$330,000		33⅓%		$110,000
2001	420,000		33⅓%		140,000
2002	150,000		33⅓%		50,000
	$900,000				$300,000

*$900,000 − $600,000 = $300,000; $300,000 ÷ $900,000 = 33⅓%

ACTION PLAN

- Use the installment method when cash collection is uncertain.
- Always find gross profit percentage.
- Recognize gross profit each period by multiplying cash collected times gross profit percentage.

SUMMARY OF STUDY OBJECTIVES

1. Explain the meaning of generally accepted accounting principles and identify the key items of the conceptual framework. Generally accepted accounting principles are a set of rules and practices that are recognized as a general guide for financial reporting purposes. Generally accepted means that these principles must have "substantial authoritative support." The key items of the conceptual framework are: (1) objectives of financial reporting; (2) qualitative characteristics of accounting information; (3) elements of financial statements; and (4) operating guidelines (assumptions, principles, and constraints).

2. Describe the basic objectives of financial reporting. The basic objectives of financial reporting are to provide information that is (1) useful to those making investment and credit decisions; (2) helpful in assessing future cash flows; and (3) helpful in identifying economic resources (assets), the claims to those resources (liabilities), and the changes in those resources and claims.

3. Discuss the qualitative characteristics of accounting information and elements of financial statements. To be judged useful, information should possess the following qualitative characteristics: relevance, reliability, comparability, and consistency. The elements of financial statements are a set of definitions that can be used to describe the basic terms used in accounting.

4. Identify the basic assumptions used by accountants. The major assumptions are: monetary unit, economic entity, time period, and going concern.

5. Identify the basic principles of accounting. The major principles are revenue recognition, matching, full disclosure, and cost.

6. Identify the two constraints in accounting. The major constraints are materiality and conservatism.

7. Explain the accounting principles used in international operations. There are few recognized worldwide accounting standards. The International Accounting Standards Committee (IASC) is working to obtain conformity in international accounting practices.

Key Term Matching Activity

GLOSSARY

Comparability Ability to compare accounting information of different companies because they use the same accounting principles. (p. 490).

Conceptual framework A coherent system of interrelated objectives and fundamentals that can lead to consistent standards. (p. 489).

Conservatism The constraint of choosing an accounting method, when in doubt, that will least likely overstate assets and net income. (p. 501).

Consistency Use of the same accounting principles and methods from year to year within a company. (p. 491).

Cost principle The principle that assets should be recorded at their historical cost. (p. 499).

Economic entity assumption The assumption that the activities of an economic entity be kept separate from the activities of the owner and of all other entities. (p. 493).

Elements of financial statements Definitions of basic terms used in accounting. (p. 491).

Full disclosure principle The principle that circumstances and events that make a difference to financial statement users should be disclosed. (p. 498).

Generally accepted accounting principles (GAAP) A set of rules and practices, having substantial authoritative support, that are recognized as a general guide for financial reporting purposes. (p. 488).

Going concern assumption The assumption that the enterprise will continue in operation long enough to carry out its existing objectives and commitments. (p. 493).

Installment method A method of recognizing revenue using the cash basis; each cash collection consists of a partial recovery of cost of goods sold and partial gross profit from the sale. (p. 496).

International Accounting Standards Committee (IASC) An accounting organization whose purpose is to formulate and publish international accounting standards and to promote their acceptance worldwide. (p. 503).

Matching principle The principle that expenses should be matched with revenues in the period when efforts are expended to generate revenues. (p. 497).

Materiality The constraint of determining if an item is important enough to likely influence the decision of a reasonably prudent investor or creditor. (p. 500).

Monetary unit assumption The assumption that only transaction data capable of being expressed in monetary terms should be included in accounting records. (p. 493).

Percentage-of-completion method A method of recognizing revenue and income on a construction project on the basis of costs incurred during the period to the total estimated costs for the entire project. (p. 495).

Relevance The quality of information that indicates the information makes a difference in a decision. (p. 490).

Reliability The quality of information that gives assurance that information is free of error and bias. (p. 490).

Revenue recognition principle The principle that revenue should be recognized in the accounting period in which it is earned (generally at the point of sale). (p. 494).

Time period assumption The assumption that the economic life of a business can be divided into artificial time periods. (p. 493).

Chapter 12 Self-Test

SELF-STUDY QUESTIONS

Answers are at the end of the chapter.

(SO 1) **1.** Generally accepted accounting principles are:
- a. a set of standards and rules that are recognized as a general guide for financial reporting.
- b. usually established by the Internal Revenue Service.
- c. the guidelines used to resolve ethical dilemmas.
- d. fundamental truths that can be derived from the laws of nature.

(SO 2) **2.** Which of the following is *not* an objective of financial reporting?
- a. Provide information that is useful in investment and credit decisions.
- b. Provide information about economic resources, claims to those resources, and changes in them.
- c. Provide information that is useful in assessing future cash flows.
- d. Provide information on the liquidation value of a business.

(SO 3) **3.** The primary criterion by which accounting information can be judged is:
- a. consistency.
- b. predictive value.
- c. decision-usefulness.
- d. comparability.

(SO 3) **4.** Verifiability is an ingredient of:

	Reliability	Relevance
a.	Yes	Yes
b.	No	No
c.	Yes	No
d.	No	Yes

(SO 4, 5, 6) **5.** Valuing assets at their liquidation value rather than their cost is *inconsistent* with the:
- a. time period assumption.
- b. matching principle.
- c. going concern assumption.
- d. materiality constraint.

(SO 5) **6.** Gonzalez's Construction Company began a long-term construction contract on January 1, 2002. The contract is expected to be completed in 2003 at a total cost of $20,000,000. Gonzalez's revenue for the project is $24,000,000. Gonzalez incurred contract costs of $4,000,000 in 2002. What gross profit should be recognized in 2002?
- a. $800,000.
- b. $1,000,000.
- c. $2,000,000.
- d. $4,000,000.

(SO 5) **7.** Dunlop Company had installment sales of $1,000,000 in its first year of operations. The cost of goods sold on installment was $650,000. Dunlop collected a total of $500,000 on the installment sales. Using the installment method, how much gross profit should be recognized in the first year?
- a. $140,000.
- b. $175,000.
- c. $350,000.
- d. $500,000.

(SO 5) **8.** The full disclosure principle dictates that:
- a. financial statements should disclose all assets at their cost.
- b. financial statements should disclose only those events that can be measured in dollars.
- c. financial statements should disclose all events and circumstances that would matter to users of financial statements.
- d. financial statements should not be relied on unless an auditor has expressed an unqualified opinion on them.

(SO 6) **9.** The accounting constraint that means that when in doubt the accountant should choose the method that will be least likely to overstate assets and income is called:
- a. the matching principle.
- b. materiality.
- c. conservatism.
- d. the monetary unit assumption.

(SO 7) **10.** The organization that issues international accounting standards is the:
- a. Financial Accounting Standards Board.
- b. International Accounting Standards Committee.
- c. International Auditing Standards Committee.
- d. None of the above.

QUESTIONS

1. (a) What are generally accepted accounting principles (GAAP)? (b) What bodies provide authoritative support for GAAP?

2. What elements comprise the FASB's conceptual framework?

3. (a) What are the objectives of financial reporting? (b) Identify the qualitative characteristics of accounting information.

4. Mark McGwire, the president of Cardinal Company, is pleased. Cardinal substantially increased its net income in 2002 while keeping its unit inventory relatively the same. Sammy Sosa, chief accountant, cautions McGwire that since Cardinal changed from the LIFO to the FIFO method of inventory valuation, there is a consistency problem. It would be difficult to determine if Cardinal is better off. Is Sosa correct? Why or why not?

5. What is the distinction between comparability and consistency?

6. Why is it necessary for accountants to assume that an economic entity will remain a going concern?

7. When should revenue be recognized? Why has the date of sale been chosen as the point at which to recognize the revenue resulting from the entire producing and selling process?

8. Goodwin Construction Company has a $210 million contract to build a bridge. Its total estimated cost for the project is $170 million. Costs incurred in the first year of the project were $34 million. Goodwin appropriately uses the percentage-of-completion method. How much revenue and gross profit should Goodwin recognize in the first year of the project?

9. Merchandise with a cost of $80,000 was sold during the year for $100,000. Cash collected for the year amounted to $45,000. How much gross profit should be recognized during the year if the company uses the installment method?

10. Distinguish between expired costs and unexpired costs.

11. (a) Where does the accountant disclose information about an entity's financial position, operations, and cash flows? (b) The full disclosure principle recognizes that the nature and amount of information included in financial reports reflect a series of judgmental trade-offs. What are the objectives of these trade-offs?

12. Mark Lofton is the president of Mystery Books. He has no accounting background. Lofton cannot understand why current cost is not used as the basis for accounting measurement and reporting. Explain what basis is used and why.

13. Describe the two constraints inherent in the presentation of accounting information.

14. Your roommate believes that international accounting standards are uniform throughout the world. Is your roommate correct? Explain.

15. What organization establishes international accounting standards?

BRIEF EXERCISES

BE12-1 Indicate whether each of the following statements is true or false.

(a) ____ "Generally accepted" means that these principles must have "substantial authoritative support."

(b) ____ GAAP is a set of rules and practices established by the accounting profession to serve as a general guide for financial reporting purposes.

(c) ____ Substantial authoritative support for GAAP usually comes from two standard-setting bodies: the FASB and the IRS.

Identify generally accepted accounting principles.
(SO 1)

BE12-2 Indicate which of the following items is(are) included in the FASB's conceptual framework. (Use "Yes" or "No" to answer this question.)

(a) ____ Qualitative characteristics of accounting information.

(b) ____ Analysis of financial statement ratios.

(c) ____ Objectives of financial reporting.

Identify items included in conceptual framework.
(SO 1)

BE12-3 According to the FASB's conceptual framework, which of the following are objectives of financial reporting? (Use "Yes" or "No" to answer this question.)

(a) ____ Provide information that identifies the economic resources (assets), the claims to those resources (liabilities), and the changes in those resources and claims.

(b) ____ Provide information that is helpful in assessing past cash flows and stock prices.

(c) ____ Provide information that is useful to those making investment and credit decisions.

Identify objectives of financial reporting.
(SO 2)

BE12-4 Presented on page 508 is a chart of the qualitative characteristics of accounting information. Fill in the blanks from (a) to (e).

Identify qualitative characteristics.
(SO 3)

```
                              ┌─────────────────┐
                              │   Usefulness    │
                              └─────────────────┘
        ┌──────────────────────────┼──────────────────────────┐
        ▼                          ▼            ▼              ▼
┌─────────────────┐      ┌─────────────┐  ┌─────────┐  ┌─────────────────┐
│   Relevance     │      │Comparability│  │   (c)   │  │   Reliability   │
│   ─────────     │      └─────────────┘  └─────────┘  │   ─────────     │
│      (a)        │                                    │      (d)        │
│   ─────────     │                                    │   ─────────     │
│      (b)        │                                    │    Neutral      │
│   ─────────     │                                    │   ─────────     │
│     Timely      │                                    │      (e)        │
└─────────────────┘                                    └─────────────────┘
```

Identify qualitative characteristics.
(SO 3)

BE12-5   Given the *qualitative characteristics* of accounting established by the FASB's conceptual framework, complete each of the following statements.

(a) _____ is the quality of information that gives assurance that it is free of error and bias; it can be depended on.

(b) _____ means using the same accounting principles and methods from year to year within a company.

(c) For information to be _____, it should have predictive or feedback value, and it must be presented on a timely basis.

Identify qualitative characteristics.
(SO 3)

BE12-6   Presented below is a set of qualitative characteristics of accounting information.

1. Predictive value   **3.** Verifiable
2. Neutral   **4.** Timely

Match these qualitative characteristics to the following statements, using numbers 1 through 4.

(a) _____Accounting information should help users make predictions about the outcome of past, present, and future events.

(b) _____Accounting information cannot be selected, prepared, or presented to favor one set of interested users over another.

(c) _____Accounting information must be proved to be free of error and bias.

(d) _____Accounting information must be available to decision makers before it loses its capacity to influence their decisions.

Identify operating guidelines.
(SO 4, 5, 6)

BE12-7   Presented below are four concepts discussed in this chapter.

1. Time period assumption   **3.** Full disclosure principle
2. Cost principle   **4.** Conservatism

Match these concepts to the following accounting practices. Each number can be used only once.

(a) _____Recording inventory at its purchase price.

(b) _____Using notes and supplementary schedules in the financial statements.

(c) _____Preparing financial statements on an annual basis.

(d) _____Using the lower of cost or market method for inventory valuation.

Compute revenue—percentage-of-completion.
(SO 5)

BE12-8   Yoon Construction Company is under contract to build a commercial building at a price of $3,800,000. Construction began in January 2001 and was finished in December 2003. Total estimated construction costs are $2,800,000. Actual construction costs incurred in each year were: 2001, $560,000; 2002, $1,820,000; 2003, $420,000. Compute the revenue to be recognized in each year using the percentage-of-completion method.

Compute gross profit—installment method.
(SO 5)

BE12-9   Padillio Co. uses the installment method to determine its net income. In 2002, its first year of operations, it had installment sales of $800,000 and a cost of goods sold of $480,000. The collections on installment sales were as follows: 2002, $360,000; 2003, $440,000. Determine the gross profit recognized for 2002 and 2003.

Identify the constraints that have been violated.
(SO 6)

BE12-10   Alomar Company uses the following accounting practices.

(a) Small tools are recorded as plant assets and depreciated.

(b) Inventory is reported at cost when market value is lower.

(c) The income statement shows paper clips expense of $10.

(d) Revenue on installment sales is recognized at the time of sale.

Indicate the accounting constraint, if any, that has been violated by each practice.

EXERCISES

E12-1   A number of accounting reporting situations are described below.

 1. Person Company is in its fifth year of operation and has yet to issue financial statements. (Do not use full disclosure principle.)
 2. Nevin Company has inventory on hand that cost $400,000. Nevin reports inventory on its balance sheet at its current market value of $425,000.
 3. Sue Jackson, president of Always Music Company, bought a computer for her personal use. She paid for the computer by using company funds and debited the "computers" account.
 4. Boone Company recognizes revenue at the end of the production cycle, but before sale. The price of the product, as well as the amount that can be sold, is not certain.
 5. In preparing its financial statements, Rupe Company omitted information concerning its method of accounting for inventories.
 6. Larkin Company uses the direct write-off method of accounting for uncollectible accounts.
 7. Brantley Hospital Supply Corporation reports only current assets and current liabilities on its balance sheet. Property, plant, and equipment are reported as current assets. Bonds payable are reported as current liabilities. Liquidation of the company is unlikely.

Identify the assumption, principle, or constraint that has been violated.
(SO 4, 5, 6)

Instructions
For each of the above, list the assumption, principle, or constraint that has been violated, if any. List only one term for each case.

E12-2   Presented below are some business transactions that occurred during 2002 for Cleveland Co.

 1. An account receivable has been deemed to be a bad debt. The following entry was made.

Allowance for Doubtful Accounts	10,000	
Accounts Receivable		10,000

Identify the assumption, principle, or constraint that has been violated; prepare correct entries.
(SO 4, 5, 6)

 2. The president of Cleveland Co., Ben Williams, purchased a truck for personal use and charged it to his expense account. The following entry was made.

Travel Expense	18,000	
Cash		18,000

 3. An electric pencil sharpener costing $40 is being depreciated over 5 years. The following entry was made.

Depreciation Expense—Pencil Sharpener	8	
Accumulated Depreciation—Pencil Sharpener		8

 4. Equipment worth $80,000 was acquired at a cost of $60,000 from a company that had water damage in a flood. The following entry was made.

Equipment	80,000	
Cash		60,000
Gain		20,000

 5. Merchandise inventory with a cost of $208,000 is reported at its market value of $260,000. The following entry was made.

Merchandise Inventory	52,000	
Gain		52,000

Instructions
In each of the situations above, identify the assumption, principle, or constraint that has been violated, if any. Discuss the appropriateness of the journal entries, and give the correct journal entry, if necessary.

E12-3   Presented below are the assumptions, principles, and constraints discussed in this chapter:

 1. Economic entity assumption
 2. Going concern assumption
 3. Monetary unit assumption
 4. Time period assumption
 5. Cost principle
 6. Matching principle
 7. Full disclosure principle
 8. Revenue recognition principle
 9. Materiality
 10. Conservatism

Identify accounting assumptions, principles, and constraints.
(SO 4, 5, 6)

Instructions

Identify by number the accounting assumption, principle, or constraint that describes each situation below. Do not use a number more than once.

(a) Requires recognition of expenses in the same period as related revenues.
(b) Indicates that market value changes subsequent to purchase are not recorded in the accounts.
(c) Is the rationale for why plant assets are not reported at liquidation value. (Do not use historical cost principle.)
(d) Indicates that personal and business record keeping should be separately maintained.
(e) Ensures that all relevant financial information is reported.
(f) Assumes that the dollar is the "measuring stick" used to report on financial performance.
(g) Requires that the operational guidelines be followed for all significant items.
(h) Separates financial information into time periods for reporting purposes.

Determine the amount of revenue to be recognized.
(SO 5)

E12-4 Consider the following transactions of Hacking Group Company for 2002.

1. Leased office space to Easley Supplies for a 1-year period beginning September 1. The rent of $18,000 was paid in advance.
2. Sold a 6-month insurance policy to Orosco Corporation for $8,000 on March 1.
3. Received a sales order for merchandise costing $9,000 and a sales price of $12,000 on December 28 from Warren Company. The goods were shipped FOB shipping point on December 31. Warren received them on January 3, 2003.
4. Signed a long-term contract to construct a building at a total price of $1,800,000. Total estimated cost of construction is $1,200,000. During 2002, the company incurred $300,000 of costs and collected $330,000 in cash. The percentage-of-completion method is used to recognize revenue.
5. Had merchandise inventory on hand at year-end that amounted to $160,000. Hacking Group expects to sell the inventory in 2003 for $190,000.

Instructions

For each item above, indicate the amount of revenue Hacking Group should recognize in calendar year 2002. Explain.

Determine gross profit for construction projects.
(SO 5)

E12-5 Ortiz Construction Company currently has one long-term construction project. The project has a contract price of $120,000,000, with total estimated costs of $100,000,000. Ortiz appropriately uses the percentage-of-completion method. After 2 years of construction, the following costs have been accumulated.

Actual cost incurred, Year 1	$30,000,000
Total estimated cost remaining after Year 1	70,000,000
Actual cost incurred, Year 2	50,000,000
Total estimated cost remaining after Year 2	20,000,000

Instructions

Determine the gross profit for each of the first 2 years of the construction contract.

Determine gross profit using installment sales and point-of-sale bases.
(SO 5)

E12-6 Buford Company sold equipment for $300,000 in 2001. Collections on the sale were as follows: 2001, $70,000; 2002, $190,000; 2003, $40,000. Buford's cost of goods sold is typically 60% of sales.

Instructions

(a) Determine Buford's gross profit for 2001, 2002, and 2003, assuming that Buford recognizes revenue under the installment method.
(b) Determine Buford's gross profit for 2001, 2002, and 2003, assuming that Buford recognizes revenue under the point-of-sale basis.

PROBLEMS: SET A

Analyze transactions to identify accounting principle or assumption violated, and prepare correct entries.
(SO 4, 5)

P12-1A Jeter and Yu are accountants for Landmark Printers. They disagree over the following transactions that occurred during the year.

1. Land costing $41,000 was appraised at $49,000. Jeter suggests the following journal entry.

Land	8,000	
Gain on Appreciation of Land		8,000

2. Landmark bought equipment for $40,000, including installation costs. The equipment has a useful life of 5 years. Landmark depreciates equipment using the straight-line method. "Since the equipment as installed into our system cannot be removed without considerable damage, it will have no resale value. Therefore, it should not be depreciated, but instead should be expensed immediately," argues Jeter. "Besides, it lowers net income."

3. Depreciation for the year was $26,000. Since net income is expected to be lower this year, Jeter suggests deferring depreciation to a year when there is more net income.

4. Landmark purchased equipment at a fire sale for $20,000. The equipment was worth $26,000. Jeter believes that the following entry should be made.

Equipment	26,000	
Cash		20,000
Gain		6,000

5. Jeter suggests that Landmark should carry equipment on the balance sheet at its liquidation value, which is $20,000 less than its cost.

6. Landmark rented office space for 1 year starting October 1, 2002. The total amount of $20,000 was paid in advance. Jeter believes that the following entry should be made on October 1.

Rent Expense	20,000	
Cash		20,000

Yu disagrees with Jeter on each of the situations above.

Instructions

For each transaction, indicate why Yu disagrees. Identify the accounting principle or assumption that Jeter would be violating if his suggestions were used. Prepare the correct journal entry for each transaction, if any.

P12-2A   Presented below are a number of business transactions that occurred during the current year for Delgado, Inc.

Determine the appropriateness of journal entries in terms of generally accepted accounting principles or assumptions.
(SO 4, 5)

1. Because the general level of prices increased during the current year, Delgado, Inc. determined that there was a $40,000 understatement of depreciation expense on its equipment and decided to record it in its accounts. The following entry was made.

Depreciation Expense	40,000	
Accumulated Depreciation		40,000

2. Because of a "flood sale," equipment obviously worth $300,000 was acquired at a cost of $240,000. The following entry was made.

Equipment	300,000	
Cash		240,000
Gain on Purchase of Equipment		60,000

3. An order for $60,000 has been received from a customer for products on hand. This order is to be shipped on January 9 next year. The following entry was made.

Accounts Receivable	60,000	
Sales		60,000

4. Land was purchased on April 30 for $200,000. This amount was entered in the Land account. On December 31, the land would have cost $230,000, so the following entry was made.

Land	30,000	
Gain on Land		30,000

5. The president of Delgado, Inc. used his expense account to purchase a pre-owned Mercedes-Benz E420 solely for personal use. The following entry was made.

Miscellaneous Expense	54,000	
Cash		54,000

Instructions

⬛▭▭▭▷ In each situation, discuss the appropriateness of the journal entries in terms of generally accepted accounting principles.

Recognize gross profit using the percentage-of-completion method.
(SO 5)

P12-3A Cruz Construction Company is involved in a long-term construction contract to build a shopping center with a total estimated cost of $20 million, and a contract price of $26 million. Additional information follows.

	Shopping Center	
	Cash Collections	Actual Costs Incurred
2001	$ 4,500,000	$3,000,000
2002	10,000,000	9,000,000
2003	7,000,000	5,000,000
2004	4,500,000	3,000,000

The project was completed in 2004, and all cash collections related to the contract have been received.

Instructions
Prepare a schedule to determine the gross profit for each year for the long-term construction contract, using the percentage-of-completion method.

Recognize gross profit using the installment method.
(SO 5)

P12-4A Bunill sold to Lee Management Company condominiums it had constructed. The sales price was $6 million. Bunill's cost to construct the condominiums was $3.9 million. Bunill appropriately uses the installment method. Additional information follows.

	Cash Collected
2001	$ 900,000
2002	3,800,000
2003	1,300,000

Instructions
(a) Prepare a schedule to determine the gross profit for each year using the installment method.
(b) Repeat (a) assuming construction costs were $4.2 million.

Identify accounting assumptions, principles, and constraints.
(SO 4, 5, 6)

P12-5A Presented below are assumptions, principles, and constraints.

1. Economic entity assumption
2. Going concern assumption
3. Monetary unit assumption
4. Time period assumption
5. Full disclosure principle
6. Revenue recognition principle
7. Matching principle
8. Cost principle
9. Materiality
10. Conservatism

Instructions
Identify by number the accounting assumption, principle, or constraint that describes each situation below. Do not use a number more than once.

(a) All important information related to inventories is presented in the financial statements or in the footnotes.
(b) Assets are not stated at their liquidation value. (Do not use the cost principle.)
(c) The death of the president is not recorded in the accounts.
(d) Pencil sharpeners are expensed when purchased.
(e) An allowance for doubtful accounts is established. (Do not use conservatism.)
(f) Each entity is kept as a unit distinct from its owner or owners.
(g) Reporting must be done at defined intervals.
(h) Revenue is recorded at the point of sale.
(i) When in doubt, it is better to understate rather than overstate net income.

PROBLEMS: SET B

Analyze transactions to identify accounting principle or assumption violated, and prepare correct entries.
(SO 4, 5)

P12-1B Dye and Zaur are accountants for Desktop Computers. They disagree over the following transactions that occurred during the calendar year 2002.

1. Dye suggests that equipment should be reported on the balance sheet at its liquidation value, which is $15,000 less than its cost.

2. Desktop bought a custom-made piece of equipment for $24,000. This equipment has a use-ful life of 6 years. Desktop depreciates equipment using the straight-line method. "Since the equipment is custom-made, it will have no resale value. Therefore, it shouldn't be de-preciated but instead should be expensed immediately," argues Dye. "Besides, it provides for lower net income."

3. Depreciation for the year was $18,000. Since net income is expected to be lower this year, Dye suggests deferring depreciation to a year when there is more net income.

4. Land costing $60,000 was appraised at $90,000. Dye suggests the following journal entry.

Land	30,000	
Gain on Appreciation of Land		30,000

5. Desktop purchased equipment for $30,000 at a going-out-of-business sale. The equipment was worth $45,000. Dye believes that the following entry should be made.

Equipment	45,000	
Cash		30,000
Gain		15,000

Zaur disagrees with Dye on each of the above situations.

Instructions

For each transaction, indicate why Zaur disagrees. Identify the accounting principle or as-sumption that Dye would be violating if his suggestions were used. Prepare the correct journal entry for each transaction, if any.

P12-2B   Presented below are a number of business transactions that occurred during the cur-rent year for Chavez, Inc.

Determine the appropriateness of journal entries in terms of generally accepted accounting principles or assumptions.
(SO 4, 5)

1. Because the general level of prices increased during the current year, Chavez, Inc. deter-mined that there was a $10,000 understatement of depreciation expense on its equipment and decided to record it in its accounts. The following entry was made.

Depreciation Expense	10,000	
Accumulated Depreciation		10,000

2. Because of a "flood sale," equipment obviously worth $250,000 was acquired at a cost of $150,000. The following entry was made.

Equipment	250,000	
Cash		150,000
Gain on Purchase of Equipment		100,000

3. The president of Chavez, Inc. used his expense account to purchase a new Saab 9000 solely for personal use. The following entry was made.

Miscellaneous Expense	34,000	
Cash		34,000

4. An order for $30,000 has been received from a customer for products on hand. This order is to be shipped on January 9 next year. The following entry was made.

Accounts Receivable	30,000	
Sales		30,000

5. Materials were purchased on March 31 for $65,000. This amount was entered in the In-ventory account. On December 31, the materials would have cost $85,000, so the follow-ing entry was made.

Inventory	20,000	
Gain on Inventories		20,000

Instructions

In each situation, discuss the appropriateness of the journal entries in terms of gen-erally accepted accounting principles.

*Recognize gross profit using
percentage-of-completion.*
(SO 5)

P12-3B Wallace Construction Company is involved in a long-term construction contract to build an office building. The estimated cost is $30 million, and the contract price is $36 million. Additional information follows.

	Office Building	
	Cash Collections	**Actual Costs Incurred**
2001	$ 6,000,000	$ 4,500,000
2002	8,000,000	6,000,000
2003	12,500,000	12,000,000
2004	9,500,000	7,500,000

The project is completed in 2004, and all cash to be received from the contract has been received.

Instructions

Prepare a schedule to determine the gross profit in each year for the long-term construction contract using the percentage-of-completion method.

*Recognize gross profit using
the installment method.*
(SO 5)

P12-4B Coomer Construction sold to Walker Management Company apartments it had constructed. The sales price was $2.5 million. Coomer's cost to construct the apartments was $1.4 million. Coomer appropriately uses the installment method. Additional information follows.

	Cash Collected
2001	$ 800,000
2002	1,200,000
2003	500,000

(a) Determine the gross profit for each year using the installment method.
(b) Repeat (a) assuming the construction costs were $1.5 million.

*Identify accounting assumptions, principles, and
constraints.*
(SO 4, 5, 6)

P12-5B Presented below are the assumptions, principles, and constraints used in this chapter.

1. Economic entity assumption
2. Going concern assumption
3. Monetary unit assumption
4. Time period assumption
5. Full disclosure principle
6. Revenue recognition principle
7. Matching principle
8. Cost principle
9. Materiality
10. Conservatism

Identify by number the accounting assumption, principle, or constraint that describes each situation below. Do not use a number more than once.

(a) Repair tools are expensed when purchased. These repair tools have a useful life of more than one accounting period. (Do not use conservatism.)
(b) Expenses should be allocated to revenues in proper period.
(c) The dollar is the measuring stick used to report financial information.
(d) Financial information is separated into time periods for reporting purposes.
(e) Market value changes subsequent to purchase are not recorded in the accounts. (Do not use the revenue recognition principle.)
(f) Personal and business record keeping should be separately maintained.
(g) All relevant financial information should be reported.
(h) Lower of cost or market is used to value inventories.

COMPREHENSIVE PROBLEM: CHAPTERS 9 TO 12

Nahas Company and Nordlund Company are competing businesses. Both began operations 6 years ago and are quite similar in most respects. The current balance sheet data for the two companies are as follows.

	Nahas Company	Nordlund Company
Cash	$ 50,300	$ 48,400
Accounts receivable	309,700	312,500
Allowance for doubtful accounts	(13,600)	-0-
Merchandise inventory	463,900	520,200
Plant and equipment	245,300	257,300
Accumulated depreciation, plant and equipment	(107,650)	(189,850)
Total assets	$947,950	$948,550
Current liabilities	$440,200	$436,500
Long-term liabilities	78,000	80,000
Total liabilities	518,200	516,500
Owner's equity	429,750	432,050
Total liabilities and owner's equity	$947,950	$948,550

You have been engaged as a consultant to conduct a review of the two companies. Your goal is to determine which of them is in the stronger financial position.

Your review of their financial statements quickly reveals that the two companies have not followed the same accounting practices. The differences and your conclusions regarding them are summarized below.

1. Nahas Company has used the allowance method of accounting for bad debts. A review shows that the amount of its write-offs each year has been quite close to the allowances that have been provided. It therefore seems reasonable to have confidence in its current estimate of bad debts.

   Nordlund Company has used the direct write-off method for bad debts, and it has been somewhat slow to write off its uncollectible accounts. Based upon an aging analysis and review of its accounts receivable, it is estimated that $24,000 of its existing accounts will probably prove to be uncollectible.

2. Nahas Company has determined the cost of its merchandise inventory on a LIFO basis. The result is that its inventory appears on the balance sheet at an amount that is below its current replacement cost. Based upon a detailed physical examination of its merchandise on hand, the current replacement cost of its inventory is estimated at $517,000.

   Nordlund Company has used the FIFO method of valuing its merchandise inventory. Its ending inventory appears on the balance sheet at an amount that quite closely approximates its current replacement cost.

3. Nahas Company estimated a useful life of 12 years and a salvage value of $30,000 for its plant and equipment. It has been depreciating them on a straight-line basis.

   Nordlund Company has the same type of plant and equipment. However, it estimated a useful life of 10 years and a salvage value of $10,000. It has been depreciating its plant and equipment using the double-declining-balance method.

   Based upon engineering studies of these types of plant and equipment, you conclude that Nordlund's estimates and method for calculating depreciation are the more appropriate.

4. Among its current liabilities, Nahas has included the portions of long-term liabilities that become due within the next year. Nordlund has not done so.

   You find that $20,000 of Nordlund's $80,000 of long-term liabilities are due to be repaid in the current year.

Instructions

(a) Revise the balance sheets presented above so that the data are comparable and reflect the current financial position for each of the two companies.

(b) ▭▭▭▷ Prepare a brief report to your client stating your conclusions.

(a) Total assets:
Nahas $847,604
Nordlund $924,550

BROADENING YOUR PERSPECTIVE

*F*INANCIAL REPORTING AND ANALYSIS

FINANCIAL REPORTING PROBLEM

BYP12-1   Becky Bishop successfully completed her first accounting course during the spring semester. She is now working as a management trainee for First Arizona Bank during the summer. One of her fellow management trainees, Lance Jones, is taking the same accounting course this summer and has been having a "lot of trouble." On the second exam, for example, Lance became confused about inventory valuation methods. He completely missed all the points on a problem involving LIFO and FIFO.

Lance's instructor recently indicated that the third exam will probably have a number of essay questions dealing with accounting principle issues. Lance is quite concerned about the third exam for two reasons. First, he has never taken an accounting exam in which essay answers were required. Second, Lance feels he must do well on this exam to get an acceptable grade in the course.

Lance has asked Becky to help him prepare for the next exam. She agrees, and suggests that Lance develop a set of possible questions on the accounting principles material that they might discuss.

Instructions
Answer the following questions that were developed by Lance.

- **(a)** What is a conceptual framework?
- **(b)** Why is there a need for a conceptual framework?
- **(c)** What are the objectives of financial reporting?
- **(d)** If you had to explain generally accepted accounting principles to a nonaccountant, what essential characteristics would you include in your explanation?
- **(e)** What are the qualitative characteristics of accounting? Explain each one.
- **(f)** Identify the basic assumptions used in accounting.
- **(g)** What are two major constraints involved in financial reporting? Explain both of them.

EXPLORING THE WEB

BYP12-2   The **Financial Accounting Standards Board (FASB)** is a private organization established to improve accounting standards and financial reporting. The FASB conducts extensive research before issuing a "Statement of Financial Accounting Standards," which represents an authoritative expression of generally accepted accounting principles.

Address: www.rutgers.edu/accounting/raw *(or go to www.wiley.com/college/weygandt)*

Steps:
1. Choose **FASB**.
2. Choose **FASB Facts**.

Instructions
Answer the following questions.

- **(a)** What is the mission of the FASB?
- **(b)** How are topics added to the FASB technical agenda?
- **(c)** What characteristics make the FASB's procedures an "open" decision-making process?

*C*RITICAL THINKING

GROUP DECISION CASE

BYP12-3   Margo Industries has two operating divisions—Talley Construction Division and Shumway Securities Division. Each division maintains its own accounting system and method of revenue recognition.

Talley Construction Division

During the fiscal year ended November 30, 2002, Talley Construction Division had one construction project in process. A $30,000,000 contract for construction of a civic center was granted on June 19, 2002, and construction began on August 1, 2002. Estimated costs of completion at the contract date were $26,000,000 over a 2-year time period from the date of the contract. On November 30, 2002, construction costs of $9,000,000 had been incurred. The construction costs to complete the remainder of the project were reviewed on November 30, 2002, and were estimated to amount to only $16,000,000 because of an expected decline in raw materials costs. Revenue recognition is based upon a percentage-of-completion method.

Shumway Securities Division

Shumway Securities Division works through manufacturers' agents in various cities. Orders for alarm systems and down payments are forwarded from agents, and the division ships the goods f.o.b. factory directly to customers (usually police departments and security guard companies). Customers are billed directly for the balance due plus actual shipping costs. The firm received orders for $6,000,000 of goods during the fiscal year ended November 30, 2002. Down payments of $600,000 were received and goods with a selling price of $5,500,000 were billed and shipped. Actual freight costs of $100,000 were also billed. Commissions of 10% on product price are paid manufacturing agents after goods are shipped to customers. Such goods are covered under warranty for 90 days after shipment, and warranty returns have been about 1% of sales. Revenue is recognized at the point of sale by this division.

Instructions

With the class divided into groups, answer the following.

(a) There are a variety of methods of revenue recognition. Define and describe each of the following methods of revenue recognition, and indicate whether each is in accordance with generally accepted accounting principles.
  (1) Point of sale.
  (2) Percentage-of-completion.
  (3) Installment contract.

(b) Compute the revenue to be recognized in fiscal year 2002 for both operating divisions of Margo Industries in accordance with generally accepted accounting principles.

ETHICS CASE

BYP12-4 When the Financial Accounting Standards Board issues new standards, the required implementation date is usually 12 months or more from the date of issuance, with early implementation encouraged. Sarah Lane, accountant at Mintur Corporation, discusses with her financial vice president the need for early implementation of a recently issued standard that would result in a much fairer presentation of the company's financial condition and earnings. When the financial vice president determines that early implementation of the standard will adversely affect reported net income for the year, he strongly discourages Sarah from implementing the standard until it is required.

Instructions

(a) Who are the stakeholders in this situation?

(b) What, if any, are the ethical considerations in this situation?

(c) What does Sarah have to gain by advocating early implementation? Who might be affected by the decision against early implementation?

Answers to Self-Study Questions

1. a **2.** d **3.** c **4.** c **5.** c **6.** a **7.** b **8.** c **9.** c **10.** b

Answer to Lands' End *Review It Question 2, p. 492*

The Report of Independent Public Accountants indicates that Lands' End's financial statements (balance sheet, income statement, shareholders' equity, and cash flows) are presented fairly, in accordance with generally accepted accounting principles.

> ✓ *Remember to go back to the Navigator box on the chapter-opening page and check off your completed work.*

ACCOUNTING FOR PARTNERSHIPS

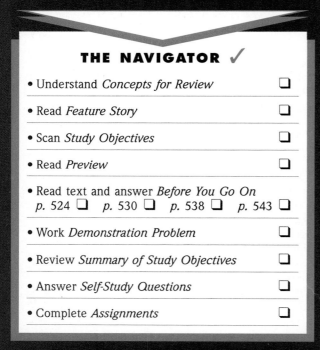

THE NAVIGATOR ✓

- Understand *Concepts for Review* ❑
- Read *Feature Story* ❑
- Scan *Study Objectives* ❑
- Read *Preview* ❑
- Read text and answer *Before You Go On*
  p. 524 ❑   p. 530 ❑   p. 538 ❑   p. 543 ❑
- Work *Demonstration Problem* ❑
- Review *Summary of Study Objectives* ❑
- Answer *Self-Study Questions* ❑
- Complete *Assignments* ❑

CONCEPTS FOR REVIEW

Before studying this chapter, you should know or, if necessary, review:

   a. The cost principle of accounting. (Ch. 1, p. 10)

   b. The owner's equity statement. (Ch. 1, pp. 22–24)

   c. How to make closing entries and prepare the post-closing trial balance.
(Ch. 4, pp. 140–145)

   d. The steps in the accounting cycle. (Ch. 4, p. 148)

   e. The format of classified financial statements. (Ch. 4, pp. 151–156)

THE NAVIGATOR

From Trials to the Top Ten

In 1990 Cliff Chenfield and Craig Balsam gave up the razors, ties, and six-figure salaries they had become accustomed to as New York lawyers. Instead, they set up a partnership, **Razor & Tie Music**, in Cliff's living room. Ten years later the label is the only record company in the country that has achieved success by selling music both on television and in the stores. Razor & Tie's entertaining and effective TV commercials have yielded unprecedented sales for multi-artist music compilations. At the same time, its hot young retail label has been behind some of the most recent original, progressive releases.

Razor & Tie's first TV release, *Those Fabulous '70s* (100,000 copies sold), was followed by *Disco Fever* (over 300,000 sold). These albums generated so much publicity that partners Cliff and Craig were guests on dozens of TV interview shows.

After restoring the respectability of the oft-maligned 1970s, the part-

ners forged into the musical '80s with the same zeal that elicited success with their first releases. In July 1993, Razor & Tie released *Totally '80s*, a collection of Top-10 singles from the 1980s that has sold over 450,000 units since its release. Featuring the tag line, "The greatest hits from the decade when communism died and music videos were born," *Totally '80s* was the best-selling direct-response album in the country in 1993.

In 1995, Razor & Tie broke into the contemporary music world with *Living In The '90s*, the most successful record in the history of the company. Featuring a number of songs that were still recurrent hits on the radio at the time the package initially aired, *Living In The '90s* was a blockbuster. It received Gold certification in less than nine months and rewrote the rules on direct-response albums. For the first time,

contemporary music was available through an album offered only through direct-response spots.

How has Razor & Tie carved out its sizable piece of the market? Through the complementary talents of the two partners. Their imagination and savvy, along with exciting new releases planned for the coming years, ensure Razor & Tie such continued growth that the partnership form of organization may be challenged to its limits.

www.razorandtie.com

S T U D Y   O B J E C T I V E S

After studying this chapter, you should be able to:

1. Identify the characteristics of the partnership form of business organization.
2. Explain the accounting entries for the formation of a partnership.
3. Identify the bases for dividing net income or net loss.
4. Describe the form and content of partnership financial statements.
5. Explain the effects of the entries when a new partner is admitted.
6. Describe the effects of the entries when a partner withdraws from the firm.
7. Explain the effects of the entries to record the liquidation of a partnership.

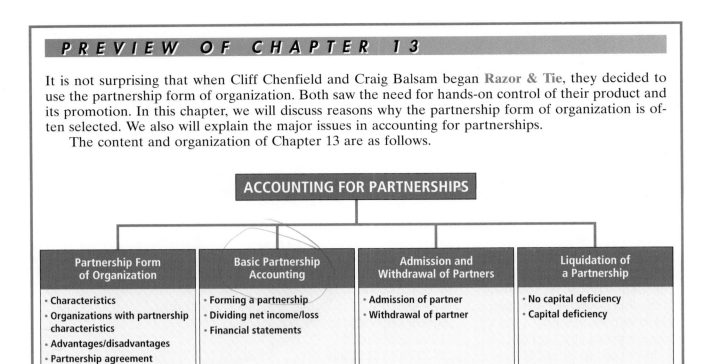

It is not surprising that when Cliff Chenfield and Craig Balsam began **Razor & Tie**, they decided to use the partnership form of organization. Both saw the need for hands-on control of their product and its promotion. In this chapter, we will discuss reasons why the partnership form of organization is often selected. We also will explain the major issues in accounting for partnerships.

The content and organization of Chapter 13 are as follows.

PARTNERSHIP FORM OF ORGANIZATION

The Uniform Partnership Act provides the basic rules for the formation and operation of partnerships in more than 90 percent of the states. This act defines a **partnership** as an association of two or more persons to carry on as co-owners of a business for profit. Partnerships are common in retail establishments and in small manufacturing companies. Also, accountants, lawyers, and doctors find it desirable to form partnerships with other professionals in their field. Professional partnerships vary in size from a medical partnership of 3 to 5 doctors, to 150 to 200 partners in a large law firm, to more than 2,000 partners in an international accounting firm.

CHARACTERISTICS OF PARTNERSHIPS

STUDY OBJECTIVE 1

Identify the characteristics of the partnership form of business organization.

Partnerships are fairly easy to form. They can be formed simply by a verbal agreement or, more formally, by putting in writing the rights and obligations of the partners. Partners who have not put their agreement in writing sometimes have found that the characteristics of partnerships can lead to later difficulties. The principal characteristics of the partnership form of business organization are shown in Illustration 13-1 and explained in the following sections.

Illustration 13-1
Partnership characteristics

Association of Individuals

The voluntary association of two or more individuals in a partnership may be based on as simple an act as a handshake. However, it is preferable to state the agreement in writing. Under the Uniform Partnership Act, a partnership is a legal entity for certain purposes. For instance, property (land, buildings, equipment) can be owned in the name of the partnership, and the firm can sue or be sued. **A partnership also is an accounting entity for financial reporting purposes.** Thus, the purely personal assets, liabilities, and transactions of the partners are excluded from the accounting records of the partnership, just as they are in a proprietorship.

The net income of a partnership is not taxed as a separate entity. But, a partnership must file an information tax return showing partnership net income and each partner's share of that net income. Each partner's share is taxable at personal tax rates, regardless of the amount of net income withdrawn from the business during the year.

Mutual Agency

Mutual agency means that each partner acts on behalf of the partnership when engaging in partnership business. The act of any partner is binding on all other partners. This is true even when partners act beyond the scope of their authority, so long as the act appears to be appropriate for the partnership. For example, a partner of a grocery store who purchases a delivery truck creates a binding contract in the name of the partnership, even if the partnership agreement denies this authority. On the other hand, if a partner in a law firm purchased a snowmobile for the partnership, such an act would not be binding on the partnership. The purchase is clearly outside the scope of partnership business.

Limited Life

A partnership does not have unlimited life. It may be ended voluntarily at any time through the acceptance of a new partner or the withdrawal of a partner. A partnership may be ended involuntarily by the death or incapacity of a partner. Thus the life of a partnership is indefinite. **Partnership dissolution** occurs whenever a

HELPFUL HINT
Because of mutual agency, an individual should be extremely cautious in selecting partners.

partner withdraws or a new partner is admitted. Dissolution of a partnership does not necessarily mean that the business ends. If the continuing partners agree, operations can continue without interruption by forming a new partnership.

Unlimited Liability

Each partner is **personally and individually liable** for all partnership liabilities. Creditors' claims attach first to partnership assets. If these are insufficient, the claims then attach to the personal resources of any partner, irrespective of that partner's equity in the partnership. Because each partner is responsible for all the debts of the partnership, each partner is said to have **unlimited liability**.

ACCOUNTING IN ACTION Business Insight

The prestigious New York law firm of **Kaye, Scholer, Fierman, Hays, & Handler**, accused of withholding damaging information during a federal investigation of its client **Lincoln Savings & Loan**, settled out of court for $41 million. The firm's liability insurance covered only $25 million of the total. Its 109 partners had to pay the remaining $16 million out of their own pockets.

In a recent year, court damage awards in malpractice suits against U.S. accountants and attorneys was close to $1 billion.

Co-Ownership of Property

Partnership assets are owned jointly by the partners. If the partnership is dissolved, the assets do not legally revert to the original contributor. Each partner has a claim on total assets equal to the balance in his or her respective capital account. This claim does not attach to specific assets that an individual partner contributed to the firm. Similarly, if a partner invests a building in the partnership valued at $100,000 and the building is later sold at a gain of $20,000, that partner does not personally receive the entire gain.

Partnership net income (or net loss) is also co-owned. **If the partnership contract does not specify to the contrary, all net income or net loss is shared equally by the partners.** As you will see later, though, partners may agree to unequal sharing of net income or net loss.

ORGANIZATIONS WITH PARTNERSHIP CHARACTERISTICS

With surprising speed, states are creating special forms of business organizations that have partnership characteristics. These new organizations are being adopted by many small companies. These special forms are: limited partnerships, limited liability partnerships, limited liability companies, and "S" corporations.

Limited Partnerships

In a limited partnership, one or more partners have **unlimited liability** and one or more partners have **limited liability** for the debts of the firm. Those with unlimited liability are called general partners. Those with limited liability are called limited partners. Limited partners are responsible for the debts of the partnership up to the limit of their investment in the firm. This organization is identified in its name with the words "Limited Partnership," or "Ltd.," or "LP." For the privilege of limited liability, the limited partner usually accepts less compensation than a general partner and exercises less influence in the affairs of the firm.

Limited Liability Partnership

Most states allow professionals such as lawyers, doctors, and accountants to form a **limited liability partnership** or "LLP." The LLP is designed to protect innocent partners from malpractice or negligence claims resulting from the acts of another partner. LLPs generally carry large insurance policies in case the partnership is guilty of malpractice.

Limited Liability Companies

A new, hybrid form of business organization with certain features like a corporation and others like a limited partnership is the **limited liability company**, or "LLC" (or "LC"). An LLC usually has a limited life. The owners, called **members**, have limited liability like owners of a corporation. Whereas limited partners do not actively participate in the management of a limited partnership (LP), the members of a limited liability company (LLC) can assume an active management role. For income tax purposes, the IRS usually classifies an LLC as a partnership.

"S" Corporations

An **"S" corporation** is a corporation that is taxed in the same way that a partnership is taxed. To qualify as an "S" corporation, the company must have 75 or fewer stockholders, all of whom must be citizens or residents of the United States. The advantage of an "S" corporation (also called a Sub-Chapter "S" corporation) is that, like a partnership and unlike a corporation, it does not pay income taxes.

ADVANTAGES AND DISADVANTAGES OF PARTNERSHIPS

Why do people choose partnerships? One major advantage of a partnership is that the **skills and resources of two or more individuals can be combined**. For example, a large public accounting firm such as **Ernst & Young** must have expertise in auditing, taxation, and management consulting. In addition, a partnership is **easily formed and is relatively free from governmental regulations and restrictions**. A partnership does not have to contend with the "red tape" that a corporation must face. Also, decisions can be made quickly on substantive matters affecting the firm; there is no board of directors that must be consulted.

On the other hand, partnerships also have some major disadvantages: **mutual agency**, **limited life**, and **unlimited liability**. Unlimited liability is particularly troublesome. Many individuals fear they may lose not only their initial investment but also their personal assets, if those assets are needed to pay partnership creditors. As a result, partnerships often find it difficult to obtain large amounts of investment capital. That is one reason why the largest business enterprises in the United States are corporations, not partnerships.

The advantages and disadvantages of the partnership form of business organization are summarized in Illustration 13-2.

Advantages	Disadvantages
Combining skills and resources of two or more individuals	Mutual agency
Ease of formation	Limited life
Freedom from governmental regulations and restrictions	Unlimited liability
Ease of decision making	

Illustration 13-2

Advantages and disadvantages of a partnership

THE PARTNERSHIP AGREEMENT

Ideally, the agreement of two or more individuals to form a partnership should be expressed in writing. This written contract is often called the **partnership agreement** or **articles of co-partnership**. The partnership agreement contains such basic information as the name and principal location of the firm, the purpose of the business, and date of inception. In addition, relationships among the partners should be specified, such as:

1. Names and capital contributions of partners.
2. Rights and duties of partners.
3. Basis for sharing net income or net loss.
4. Provision for withdrawals of assets.
5. Procedures for submitting disputes to arbitration.
6. Procedures for the withdrawal or addition of a partner.
7. Rights and duties of surviving partners in the event of a partner's death.

We cannot overemphasize the importance of a written contract. The agreement should be drawn with care and should attempt to anticipate all possible situations, contingencies, and disagreements. The help of a lawyer is highly desirable in preparing the agreement.

ACCOUNTING IN ACTION   Business Insight

Accounting firms generally use the limited liability (LLP) form. As a consequence, they do not have publicly traded shares of stock. During the dot-com stock market craze of the late 1990s, this proved to be somewhat of a disadvantage for partnerships. The reason: Many dot-com firms lured top high-tech employees to their companies by offering shares of stock. As dot-com stock prices soared, many of these people became very rich—at least for a while. However, when many of these same dot-com companies started to falter and fail, their stock prices plummeted, and they laid off many employees.

BEFORE YOU GO ON...

▶ *REVIEW IT*

1. What are the distinguishing characteristics of a partnership?
2. What are the principal advantages and disadvantages of a partnership? Why is Land's End, Inc. not a partnership? The answer to this question is provided on page 556.
3. What are the major items in a partnership agreement?

THE NAVIGATOR

BASIC PARTNERSHIP ACCOUNTING

We now turn to the basic accounting for partnerships. The major accounting issues relate to forming the partnership, dividing income or loss, and preparing financial statements.

STUDY OBJECTIVE 2

Explain the accounting entries for the formation of a partnership.

FORMING A PARTNERSHIP

Each partner's initial investment in a partnership is entered in the partnership records. These investments should be recorded at the **fair market value of the assets at the date of their transfer to the partnership**. The values assigned must be agreed to by all of the partners.

To illustrate, assume that A. Rolfe and T. Shea combine their proprietorships to start a partnership named U.S. Software. The firm will specialize in developing financial modeling software packages. Rolfe and Shea have the following assets prior to the formation of the partnership.

	Book Value		Market Value	
	A. Rolfe	**T. Shea**	**A. Rolfe**	**T. Shea**
Cash	$ 8,000	$ 9,000	$ 8,000	$ 9,000
Office equipment	5,000		4,000	
Accumulated depreciation	(2,000)			
Accounts receivable		4,000		4,000
Allowance for doubtful accounts		(700)		(1,000)
	$11,000	$12,300	$12,000	$12,000

Illustration 13-3

Book and market values of assets invested

The entries to record the investments are:

Investment of A. Rolfe

Cash	8,000	
Office Equipment	4,000	
A. Rolfe, Capital		12,000
(To record investment of Rolfe)		

A	=	L	+	OE
+8,000				+12,000
+4,000				

Investment of T. Shea

Cash	9,000	
Accounts Receivable	4,000	
Allowance for Doubtful Accounts		1,000
T. Shea, Capital		12,000
(To record investment of Shea)		

A	=	L	+	OE
+9,000				+12,000
+4,000				
−1,000				

Note that neither the original cost of the office equipment ($5,000) nor its book value ($5,000 − $2,000) is recorded by the partnership. The equipment is recorded at its fair market value, $4,000. Because the equipment has not been used by the partnership, there is no accumulated depreciation.

In contrast, the gross claims on customers ($4,000) are carried forward to the partnership. The allowance for doubtful accounts is adjusted to $1,000 to arrive at a cash (net) realizable value of $3,000. A partnership may start with an allowance for doubtful accounts because it will continue to collect existing accounts receivable, some of which are expected to be uncollectible. In addition, this procedure maintains the control and subsidiary relationship between Accounts Receivable and the accounts receivable subsidiary ledger.

After the partnership has been formed, the accounting for transactions is similar to any other type of business organization. For example, all transactions with outside parties, such as the purchase or sale of merchandise inventory and the payment or receipt of cash, should be recorded the same for a partnership as for a proprietorship.

The steps in the accounting cycle described in Chapter 4 for a proprietorship also apply to a partnership. For example, the partnership prepares a trial balance and journalizes and posts adjusting entries. A work sheet may be used. There are minor differences in journalizing and posting closing entries and in preparing financial statements, as explained in the following sections. The differences occur because there is more than one owner.

DIVIDING NET INCOME OR NET LOSS

Partnership net income or net loss is shared equally unless the partnership contract indicates otherwise. The same basis of division usually applies to both net income and net loss. It is customary to refer to this basis as the **income ratio**, the

income and loss ratio, or the **profit and loss (P&L) ratio**. Because of its wide acceptance, we will use the term income ratio to identify the basis for dividing net income and net loss. A partner's share of net income or net loss is recognized in the accounts through closing entries.

Closing Entries

As in the case of a proprietorship, four entries are required in preparing closing entries for a partnership. The entries are:

1. Debit each revenue account for its balance, and credit Income Summary for total revenues.
2. Debit Income Summary for total expenses, and credit each expense account for its balance.
3. Debit Income Summary for its balance, and credit each partner's capital account for his or her share of net income. Or, credit Income Summary, and debit each partner's capital account for his or her share of net loss.
4. Debit each partner's capital account for the balance in that partner's drawing account, and credit each partner's drawing account for the same amount.

The first two entries are the same as in a proprietorship. The last two entries are different because (1) there are two or more owners' capital and drawing accounts, and (2) it is necessary to divide net income (or net loss) among the partners.

To illustrate the last two closing entries, assume that AB Company has net income of $32,000 for 2002. The partners, L. Arbor and D. Barnett, share net income and net loss equally. Drawings for the year were Arbor $8,000 and Barnett $6,000. The last two closing entries are:

Illustration 13-4

Closing net income and drawing accounts

Dec. 31	Income Summary		32,000	
	L. Arbor, Capital ($32,000 × 50%)			16,000
	D. Barnett, Capital ($32,000 × 50%)			16,000
	(To transfer net income to partners' capital accounts)			
31	L. Arbor, Capital		8,000	
	D. Barnett, Capital		6,000	
	L. Arbor, Drawing			8,000
	D. Barnett, Drawing			6,000
	(To close drawing accounts to capital accounts)			

Assume that the beginning capital balance is $47,000 for Arbor and $36,000 for Barnett. The capital and drawing accounts will show the following after posting the closing entries.

Illustration 13-5

Partners' capital and drawing accounts after closing

L. Arbor, Capital						D. Barnett, Capital				
12/31 **Clos.**	**8,000**	1/1	Bal.	47,000		12/31 **Clos.**	**6,000**	1/1	Bal.	36,000
		12/31	**Clos.**	**16,000**				12/31	**Clos.**	**16,000**
		12/31	Bal.	55,000				12/31	Bal.	46,000

L. Arbor, Drawing					D. Barnett, Drawing			
12/31 Bal.	8,000	12/31 **Clos.**	**8,000**		12/31 Bal.	6,000	12/31 **Clos.**	**6,000**

As in a proprietorship, the partners' capital accounts are permanent accounts; their drawing accounts are temporary accounts. Normally, the capital accounts will have credit balances and the drawing accounts will have debit balances. Drawing accounts are debited when partners withdraw cash or other assets from the partnership for personal use.

Income Ratios

As noted earlier, the partnership agreement should specify the basis for sharing net income or net loss. The following are typical income ratios.

STUDY OBJECTIVE 3

Identify the bases for dividing net income or net loss.

1. A fixed ratio, expressed as a proportion (6:4), a percentage (70% and 30%), or a fraction (2/3 and 1/3).
2. A ratio based either on capital balances at the beginning of the year or on average capital balances during the year.
3. Salaries to partners and the remainder on a fixed ratio.
4. Interest on partners' capital balances and the remainder on a fixed ratio.
5. Salaries to partners, interest on partners' capital, and the remainder on a fixed ratio.

The objective is to settle on a basis that will equitably reflect the partners' capital investment and service to the partnership.

A fixed ratio is easy to apply, and it may be an equitable basis in some circumstances. Assume, for example, that Hughes and Lane are partners. Each contributes the same amount of capital, but Hughes expects to work full-time in the partnership and Lane expects to work only half-time. Accordingly, the partners agree to a fixed ratio of 2/3 to Hughes and 1/3 to Lane.

A ratio based on capital balances may be appropriate when the funds invested in the partnership are considered the critical factor. Capital ratios may also be equitable when a manager is hired to run the business and the partners do not plan to take an active role in daily operations.

The three remaining ratios (items 3, 4, and 5) give specific recognition to differences among partners. These ratios provide salary allowances for time worked and interest allowances for capital invested. Then, any remaining net income or net loss is allocated on a fixed ratio. Some caution needs to be exercised in working with these types of income ratios. These ratios pertain exclusively to **the computations that are required in dividing net income or net loss** among the partners.

Salaries to partners and interest on partners' capital are not expenses of the partnership. Therefore, these items do not enter into the matching of expenses with revenues and the determination of net income or net loss. For a partnership, as for other entities, salaries expense pertains to the cost of services performed by employees. Likewise, interest expense relates to the cost of borrowing from creditors. But partners, as owners, are not considered either **employees** or **creditors**. Therefore, when the income ratio includes a salary allowance for partners, some partnership agreements permit the partner to make monthly withdrawals of cash based on their "salary." Such withdrawals are debited to the partner's drawing account.

HELPFUL HINT
Use one relationship for all; that is, proportion—3:1 percentage—75% and 25% fraction— 3/4 and 1/4

ACCOUNTING IN ACTION *Business Insight*

Partners in professional firms can make substantial incomes. In one international public accounting firm, the average earnings of all partners in a recent year was over $600,000. Note, though, that the compensation of partners in most large partnerships differs in both form and substance from the compensation of a corporate executive. Partners are not guaranteed an annual salary. Compensation depends entirely on each year's operating results. Also, substantial investment is required of each partner. This capital is at risk for the partner's entire career—often 25–30 years—without an established return. Upon leaving, it is repayable without adjustment for inflation or appreciation in value.

Salaries, Interest, and Remainder on a Fixed Ratio

Under income ratio (5) in the list above, the provisions for salaries and interest must be applied **before** the remainder is allocated on the specified fixed ratio. **This is true even if the provisions exceed net income. It is also true even if the partnership has suffered a net loss for the year.** Detailed information concerning the division of net income or net loss should be shown below net income on the income statement.

To illustrate this income ratio, assume that Sara King and Ray Lee are co-partners in the Kingslee Company. The partnership agreement provides for: (1) salary allowances of $8,400 to King and $6,000 to Lee, (2) interest allowances of 10% on capital balances at the beginning of the year, and (3) the remainder equally. Capital balances on January 1 were King $28,000, and Lee $24,000. In 2002, partnership net income is $22,000. The division of net income is as follows.

Illustration 13-6

Income statement with division of net income

KINGSLEE COMPANY Income Statement (partial) For the Year Ended December 31, 2002			
Sales			$200,000
Net income			$ 22,000

Division of Net Income	Sara King	Ray Lee	Total
Salary allowance	$ 8,400	$6,000	$14,400
Interest allowance on partners' capital			
Sara King ($28,000 × 10%)	2,800		
Ray Lee ($24,000 × 10%)		2,400	
Total interest allowance			5,200
Total salaries and interest	11,200	8,400	19,600
Remaining income, $2,400			
($22,000 − $19,600)			
Sara King ($2,400 × 50%)	1,200		
Ray Lee ($2,400 × 50%)		1,200	
Total remainder			2,400
Total division of net income	$12,400	$9,600	$22,000

The entry to record the division of net income is:

Dec. 31	Income Summary	22,000		A = L + OE
	Sara King, Capital		12,400	−22,000
	Ray Lee, Capital		9,600	+12,400
	(To close net income to partners' capital)			+9,600

Now let's look at a situation in which the salary and interest allowances exceed net income. Assume that Kingslee Company's net income is only $18,000. In this case, the salary and interest allowances will create a deficiency of $1,600 ($19,600 − $18,000). The computations of the allowances are the same as those in the preceding example. Beginning with total salaries and interest, we complete the division of net income as follows.

	Sara King	Ray Lee	Total
Total salaries and interest	$11,200	$8,400	$19,600
Remaining deficiency ($1,600)			
($18,000 − $19,600)			
Sara King ($1,600 × 50%)	(800)		
Ray Lee ($1,600 × 50%)		(800)	
Total remainder			(1,600)
Total division	**$10,400**	**$7,600**	**$18,000**

Illustration 13-7

Division of net income—income deficiency

PARTNERSHIP FINANCIAL STATEMENTS

The financial statements of a partnership are similar to those of a proprietorship. The differences are due to the number of owners involved. The income statement for a partnership is identical to the income statement for a proprietorship except for the division of net income, as shown earlier.

The owners' equity statement for a partnership is called the **partners' capital statement**. Its function is to explain the changes in each partner's capital account and in total partnership capital during the year. The partners' capital statement for Kingslee Company is shown below. It is based on the division of $22,000 of net income in Illustration 13-6. The statement includes assumed data for the additional investment and drawings.

STUDY OBJECTIVE 4

Describe the form and content of partnership financial statements.

Illustration 13-8

Partners' capital statement

KINGSLEE COMPANY Partners' Capital Statement For the Year Ended December 31, 2002			
	Sara King	Ray Lee	Total
Capital, January 1	$28,000	$24,000	$52,000
Add: Additional investment	2,000		2,000
Net income	12,400	9,600	22,000
	42,400	33,600	76,000
Less: Drawings	7,000	5,000	12,000
Capital, December 31	**$35,400**	**$28,600**	**$64,000**

HELPFUL HINT

As in a proprietorship, partners' capital may change due to (1) additional investment, (2) drawings, and (3) net income or net loss.

The partners' capital statement is prepared from the income statement and the partners' capital and drawing accounts.

The balance sheet for a partnership is the same as for a proprietorship except for the owner's equity section. In a partnership, the capital balances of each partner are shown in the balance sheet. The owners' equity section for Kingslee Company would show the following.

Illustration 13-9

Owners' equity section of a partnership balance sheet

KINGSLEE COMPANY Balance Sheet (partial) December 31, 2002		
Total liabilities (assumed amount)		$115,000
Owners' equity		
Sara King, Capital	$35,400	
Ray Lee, Capital	28,600	
Total owners' equity		64,000
Total liabilities and owners' equity		$179,000

BEFORE YOU GO ON...

▶ *REVIEW IT*

1. How should a partner's initial investment of assets be valued?
2. What are the closing entries for a partnership?
3. What income ratios may be used in a partnership?
4. How do partnership financial statements differ from proprietorship financial statements?

▶ *DO IT*

LeeMay Company reports net income of $57,000. The partnership agreement provides for salaries of $15,000 to L. Lee and $12,000 to R. May. The remainder is to be shared on a 60:40 basis (60% to Lee). L. Lee asks your help to divide the net income between the partners and to prepare the closing entry.

ACTION PLAN

- Compute net income exclusive of any salaries to partners and interest on partners' capital.
- Deduct salaries to partners from net income.
- Apply the partners' income ratios to the remaining net income.
- Prepare the closing entry distributing net income or net loss among the partners' capital accounts.

SOLUTION: The division of net income is as follows.

	L. Lee	R. May	Total
Salary allowance	$15,000	$12,000	$27,000
Remaining income ($57,000 − $27,000)			
L. Lee (60% × $30,000)	18,000		
R. May (40% × $30,000)		12,000	
Total remaining income			30,000
Total division of net income	$33,000	$24,000	$57,000

The closing entry for net income therefore is:

Income Summary	57,000	
L. Lee, Capital		33,000
R. May, Capital		24,000
(To close net income to partners' capital accounts)		

Related exercise material: BE13-3, BE13-4, BE13-5, and E13-2.

THE NAVIGATOR

ADMISSION AND WITHDRAWAL OF PARTNERS

We have seen how the basic accounting for a partnership works. We now look at how to account for a common occurrence in partnerships—the addition or withdrawal of a partner.

ADMISSION OF A PARTNER

The admission of a new partner results in the **legal dissolution of the existing partnership** and **the beginning of a new one**. From an economic standpoint, the admission of a new partner (or partners) may be of minor significance in the continuity of the business. For example, in large public accounting or law firms, partners are admitted annually without any change in operating policies. **To recognize the economic effects, it is necessary only to open a capital account for each new partner.** In the entries illustrated below, we assume that the accounting records of the predecessor firm will continue to be used by the new partnership.

A new partner may be admitted either by (1) purchasing the interest of an existing partner or (2) investing assets in the partnership, as shown in Illustration 13-10. The former affects only the capital accounts of the partners who are parties to the transaction. The latter increases both net assets and total capital of the partnership.

STUDY OBJECTIVE 5

Explain the effects of the entries when a new partner is admitted.

Admission of Partner through:

1. Purchase of a Partner's Interest

2. Investment of Assets in Partnership

Illustration 13-10

Procedures in adding partners

Purchase of a Partner's Interest

The admission of a partner by purchase of an interest is a personal transaction between one or more existing partners and the new partner. Each party acts as an individual separate from the partnership entity. The price paid is negotiated by the individuals involved. It may be equal to or different from the capital equity acquired. The purchase price passes directly from the new partner to the partners who are giving up part or all of their ownership claims.

Any money or other consideration exchanged is the personal property of the participants and **not** the property of the partnership. Upon purchase of an interest, the new partner acquires each selling partner's capital interest and income ratio.

HELPFUL HINT

In a purchase of an interest, the partnership is **not** a participant in the transaction. No cash is contributed to the partnership.

Accounting for the purchase of an interest is straightforward. In the partnership records, only the realignment of partners' capital is recorded. **Each partner's capital account is debited for the ownership claims that have been relinquished, and the new partner's capital account is credited with the capital equity purchased.** Total assets, total liabilities, and total capital remain unchanged, as do all individual asset and liability accounts.

To illustrate, assume that L. Carson agrees to pay $10,000 each to C. Ames and D. Barker for $33\frac{1}{3}\%$ (one-third) of their interest in the Ames–Barker partnership. At the time of the admission of Carson, each partner has a $30,000 capital balance. Both partners, therefore, give up $10,000 of their capital equity. The entry to record the admission of Carson is:

C. Ames, Capital	10,000	
D. Barker, Capital	10,000	
L. Carson, Capital		20,000
(To record admission of Carson by purchase)		

Illustration 13-11

Ledger balances after purchase of a partner's interest

The effect of this transaction on net assets and partners' capital is shown below.

Net Assets		C. Ames, Capital		D. Barker, Capital		L. Carson, Capital
60,000		10,000 30,000		10,000 30,000		20,000
		Bal. 20,000		Bal. 20,000		

Note that net assets remain unchanged at $60,000, and each partner has a $20,000 capital balance. Ames and Barker continue as partners in the firm, but the capital interest of each has changed. The cash paid by Carson goes directly to the individual partners and not to the partnership.

Regardless of the amount paid by Carson for the one-third interest, the entry above would be exactly the same. If Carson pays $12,000 each to Ames and Barker for $33\frac{1}{3}\%$ of the partnership, the foregoing entry is still made.

Investment of Assets in a Partnership

The admission of a partner by an investment of assets is a transaction between the new partner and the partnership. Often referred to simply as **admission by investment**, the transaction **increases both the net assets and total capital of the partnership**. Assume that instead of purchasing an interest, Carson invests $30,000 in cash in the Ames–Barker partnership for a $33\frac{1}{3}\%$ capital interest. In such a case, the entry is:

Cash	30,000	
L. Carson, Capital		30,000
(To record admission of Carson by investment)		

Illustration 13-12

Ledger balances after investment of assets

The effects of this transaction on the partnership accounts would be:

Net Assets		C. Ames, Capital		D. Barker, Capital		L. Carson, Capital
60,000			30,000		30,000	30,000
30,000						
Bal. 90,000						

Note that both net assets and total capital have increased by $30,000.

Remember that Carson's one-third capital interest might not result in a one-third income ratio. Carson's income ratio should be specified in the new partnership agreement, and it may or may not be equal to the one-third capital interest.

The different effects of the purchase of an interest and admission by investment are shown in the comparison of the net assets and capital balances in Illustration 13-13.

Purchase of an Interest		Admission by Investment	
Net Assets	$60,000	Net Assets	$90,000
Capital		Capital	
C. Ames	$20,000	C. Ames	$30,000
D. Barker	20,000	D. Barker	30,000
L. Carson	20,000	L. Carson	30,000
Total capital	$60,000	Total capital	$90,000

Illustration 13-13

Comparison of purchase of an interest and admission by investment

When an interest is purchased, the total net assets and total capital of the partnership do not change. When a partner is admitted by investment, both the total net assets and the total capital change.

In the case of admission by investment, further complications occur when the new partner's investment differs from the capital equity acquired. When those amounts are not the same, the difference is considered a bonus either to (1) the existing (old) partners or (2) the new partner.

BONUS TO OLD PARTNERS. For both personal and business reasons, the existing partners may be unwilling to admit a new partner without receiving a bonus. In an established firm, existing partners may insist on a bonus as compensation for the work they have put into the company over the years. Two accounting factors underlie the business reason: First, total partners' capital equals the **book value** of the recorded net assets of the partnership. When the new partner is admitted, the fair market values of assets such as land and buildings may be higher than their book values. The bonus will help make up the difference between fair market value and book value. Second, when the partnership has been profitable, goodwill may exist. But, the goodwill will not be recorded or included in total partners' capital. In such cases the new partner is usually willing to pay the bonus to become a partner.

A bonus to old partners results when the new partner's investment in the firm is greater than the capital credit on the date of admittance. The bonus results in **an increase in the capital balances of the old partners. It is allocated to them on the basis of their income ratios before the admission of the new partner.**

To illustrate, assume that the Bart–Cohen partnership, owned by Sam Bart and Tom Cohen, has total capital of $120,000. Lea Eden acquires a 25% ownership (capital) interest in the partnership by making a cash investment of $80,000. The procedure for determining Eden's capital credit and the bonus to the old partners is as follows.

1. **Determine the total capital of the new partnership:** Add the new partner's investment to the total capital of the old partnership. In this case the total capital of the new firm is $200,000, computed as follows.

Total capital of existing partnership	$120,000
Investment by new partner, Eden	80,000
Total capital of new partnership	$200,000

2. **Determine the new partner's capital credit:** Multiply the total capital of the new partnership by the new partner's ownership interest. Eden's capital credit is $50,000 ($200,000 × 25%).

3. **Determine the amount of bonus:** Subtract the new partner's capital credit from the new partner's investment. The bonus in this case is $30,000 ($80,000 − $50,000).

4. **Allocate the bonus to the old partners on the basis of their income ratios:** Assuming the ratios are Bart 60%, and Cohen 40%, the allocation is: Bart $18,000 ($30,000 × 60%) and Cohen $12,000 ($30,000 × 40%).

The entry to record the admission of Eden is:

A	=	L	+	OE
+80,000				+18,000
				+12,000
				+50,000

Cash	80,000	
Sam Bart, Capital		18,000
Tom Cohen, Capital		12,000
Lea Eden, Capital		50,000
(To record admission of Eden and bonus to old partners)		

BONUS TO NEW PARTNER. A bonus to a new partner results when the new partner's investment in the firm is less than his or her capital credit. This may occur when the new partner possesses resources or special attributes that are desired by the partnership. For example, the new partner may be able to supply cash that is urgently needed for expansion or to meet maturing debts. Or the new partner may be a recognized expert or authority in a relevant field. Thus, an engineering firm may be willing to give a renowned engineer a bonus to join the firm. The partners of a restaurant may offer a bonus to a sports celebrity in order to add the athlete's name to the partnership. A bonus to a new partner may also result when recorded book values on the partnership books are higher than their market values.

A bonus to a new partner results in a **decrease in the capital balances of the old partners. The amount of the decrease for each partner is based on their income ratios before the admission of the new partner.** To illustrate, assume that Lea Eden invests $20,000 in cash for a 25% ownership interest in the Bart–Cohen partnership. Using the four procedures described in the preceding section, the computations for Eden's capital credit and the bonus are as follows.

Illustration 13-14

Computation of capital credit and bonus to new partner

1. Total capital of Bart–Cohen partnership		$120,000
Investment by new partner, Eden		20,000
Total capital of new partnership		$140,000
2. **Eden's capital credit** (25% × $140,000)		**$ 35,000**
3. **Bonus to Eden** ($35,000 − $20,000)		**$ 15,000**
4. Allocation of bonus to old partners:		
Bart ($15,000 × 60%)	$9,000	
Cohen ($15,000 × 40%)	6,000	$ 15,000

The entry to record the admission of Eden is as follows:

A	=	L	+	OE
+20,000				−9,000
				−6,000
				+35,000

Cash	20,000	
Sam Bart, Capital	9,000	
Tom Cohen, Capital	6,000	
Lea Eden, Capital		35,000
(To record Eden's admission and bonus)		

WITHDRAWAL OF A PARTNER

Now let's look at the opposite situation—the withdrawal of a partner. A partner may withdraw from a partnership **voluntarily**, by selling his or her equity in the firm. Or he or she may withdraw **involuntarily**, by reaching mandatory retirement age or by dying. The withdrawal of a partner, like the admission of a partner, legally dissolves the partnership. The legal effects may be recognized by dissolving the firm. However, it is customary to record only the economic effects of the partner's withdrawal, while the firm continues to operate and reorganizes itself legally.

As indicated earlier, the partnership agreement should specify the terms of withdrawal. The withdrawal of a partner may be accomplished by (1) payment from partners' personal assets or (2) payment from partnership assets, as shown in Illustration 13-15. The former affects only the partners' capital accounts. The latter decreases total net assets and total capital of the partnership.

Study OBJECTIVE 6

Describe the effects of the entries when a partner withdraws from the firm.

Withdrawal of Partner through:

1. Payment from Partners' Personal Assets

2. Payment from Partnership Assets

Illustration 13-15

Procedures in partnership withdrawal

Payment from Partners' Personal Assets

Withdrawal by payment from partners' personal assets is a personal transaction between the partners. **It is the direct opposite of admitting a new partner who purchases a partner's interest.** Payment to the retiring partner is made directly from the remaining partners' personal assets. **Partnership assets are not involved in any way, and total capital does not change.** The effect on the partnership is limited to a realignment of the partners' capital balances.

To illustrate, assume that Anne Morz, Mary Nead, and Jill Odom have capital balances of $25,000, $15,000, and $10,000, respectively. Morz and Nead agree to buy out Odom's interest. Each of them agrees to pay Odom $8,000 in exchange for one-half of Odom's total interest of $10,000. The entry to record the withdrawal is:

Jill Odom, Capital	10,000	
Anne Morz, Capital		5,000
Mary Nead, Capital		5,000
(To record purchase of Odom's interest)		

A	=	L	+	OE
				−10,000
				+5,000
				+5,000

The effect of this entry on the partnership accounts is shown below.

Net Assets		Anne Morz, Capital		Mary Nead, Capital		Jill Odom, Capital	
50,000			25,000		15,000	**10,000**	10,000
			5,000		**5,000**		
							Bal. –0–
		Bal. 30,000		Bal. 20,000			

Illustration 13-16

Ledger balances after payment from partners' personal assets

Note that net assets and total capital remain the same at $50,000.

What about the $16,000 paid to Odom? You've probably noted that it is not recorded. Odom's capital is debited only for $10,000, not for the $16,000 that she received. Similarly, both Morz and Nead credit their capital accounts for only $5,000, not for the $8,000 they each paid.

After Odom's withdrawal, Morz and Nead will share net income or net loss equally unless they specifically indicate another income ratio in the partnership agreement.

Payment from Partnership Assets

Withdrawal by payment from partnership assets is a transaction that involves the partnership. **Both partnership net assets and total capital are decreased.** Using partnership assets to pay for a withdrawing partner's interest is the **reverse** of admitting a partner through the investment of assets in the partnership.

Many partnership agreements provide that the amount paid should be based on the fair market value of the assets at the time of the partner's withdrawal. When this basis is required, some maintain that any differences between recorded asset balances and their fair market values should be (1) recorded by an adjusting entry and (2) allocated to all partners on the basis of their income ratios. This position has serious flaws. Recording the revaluations violates the cost principle, which requires that assets be stated at original cost. It also is a departure from the going-concern assumption, which assumes the entity will continue indefinitely. The terms of the partnership contract should not dictate the accounting for this event.

In accounting for a withdrawal by payment from partnership assets, asset revaluations should not be recorded. Any difference between the amount paid and the withdrawing partner's capital balance should be considered a bonus to the retiring partner or a bonus to the remaining partners.

BONUS TO RETIRING PARTNER. A bonus may be paid to a retiring partner when:

1. The fair market value of partnership assets is more than their book value,
2. There is unrecorded goodwill resulting from the partnership's superior earnings record, or
3. The remaining partners are anxious to remove the partner from the firm.

The bonus is deducted from the remaining partners' capital balances on the basis of their income ratios at the time of the withdrawal.

To illustrate, assume that the following capital balances exist in the RST partnership: Fred Roman $50,000, Dee Sand $30,000, and Betty Terk $20,000. The partners share income in the ratio of 3:2:1, respectively. Terk retires from the partnership and receives a cash payment of $25,000 from the firm. The procedure for determining the bonus to the retiring partner and the allocation of the bonus to the remaining partners is as follows.

1. **Determine the amount of the bonus:** Subtract the retiring partner's capital balance from the cash paid by the partnership. The bonus in this case is $5,000 ($25,000 − $20,000).

2. **Allocate the bonus to the remaining partners on the basis of their income ratios:** The ratios of Roman and Sand are 3:2. Thus, the allocation of the $5,000 bonus is: Roman $3,000 ($5,000 × 3/5) and Sand $2,000 ($5,000 × 2/5).

The entry to record the withdrawal of Terk is:

Betty Terk, Capital	20,000	
Fred Roman, Capital	3,000	
Dee Sand, Capital	2,000	
Cash		25,000
(To record withdrawal of and bonus to Terk)		

$$A = L + OE$$
$$-25,000 \quad\quad -20,000$$
$$-3,000$$
$$-2,000$$

The remaining partners, Roman and Sand, will recover the bonus given to Terk as the undervalued assets are sold or used.

BONUS TO REMAINING PARTNERS.   The retiring partner may give a bonus to the remaining partners when:

1. Recorded assets are overvalued,
2. The partnership has a poor earnings record, or
3. The partner is anxious to leave the partnership.

In such cases, the cash paid to the retiring partner will be less than the retiring partner's capital balance. **The bonus is allocated (credited) to the capital accounts of the remaining partners on the basis of their income ratios.**

To illustrate, assume (instead of the example above) that Terk is paid only $16,000 for her $20,000 equity when she withdraws from the partnership. In that case:

1. The bonus to remaining partners is $4,000 ($20,000 − $16,000).
2. The allocation of the $4,000 bonus is: Roman $2,400 ($4,000 × 3/5) and Sand $1,600 ($4,000 × 2/5).

The entry to record the withdrawal is:

Betty Terk, Capital	20,000	
Fred Roman, Capital		2,400
Dee Sand, Capital		1,600
Cash		16,000
(To record withdrawal of Terk and bonus to remaining partners)		

$$A = L + OE$$
$$-16,000 \quad\quad -20,000$$
$$+2,400$$
$$+1,600$$

Note that if Sand had withdrawn from the partnership, any bonus would be divided between Roman and Terk on the basis of their income ratio, which is 3:1 or 75% and 25%.

> **HELPFUL HINT**
> Compare this entry to the one at the top of page 534.

> **HELPFUL HINT**
> Compare this entry to the one at the top of page 534.

Death of a Partner

The death of a partner dissolves the partnership. But provision generally is made for the surviving partners to continue operations. When a partner dies, it usually is necessary to determine the partner's equity at the date of death. This is done by (1) determining the net income or loss for the year to date, (2) closing the books, and (3) preparing financial statements. The partnership agreement may also require an independent audit of the financial statements and a revaluation of assets by an appraisal firm.

The surviving partners may agree to purchase the deceased partner's equity from their personal assets. Or it may use partnership assets to settle with the deceased partner's estate. In both instances, the entries to record the withdrawal of the partner are similar to those presented earlier.

To facilitate payment from partnership assets, some partnerships obtain life insurance policies on each partner. The partnership is named as the beneficiary. The proceeds from the insurance policy on the deceased partner are then used to settle with the estate.

BEFORE YOU GO ON...

▶ *REVIEW IT*

1. How does the accounting for admission by purchase of an interest differ from admission by investing assets in the partnership?
2. Contrast the accounting effects of the withdrawal of a partner by payment from (a) personal assets and (b) partnership assets.

▶ *DO IT*

Curly, Moe, and Larry have a partnership. Each partner has a $40,000 balance in his capital account. Record journal entries for each of the independent events listed below.

1. Curly, Moe, and Larry agree to admit Stan as a new one-quarter-interest partner. Stan pays $10,000 in cash directly to each partner.
2. Curly, Moe, and Larry agree to admit Stan as a new one-quarter-interest partner. Stan contributes $40,000 into the partnership.
3. Curly and Moe agree to let Larry withdraw from the partnership; $30,000 of partnership cash is distributed to Larry. Curly and Moe share income and losses equally.
4. Curly and Moe agree to let Larry withdraw from the partnership. Each pays Larry $25,000 out of his personal assets. Curly and Moe share income and losses equally.

ACTION PLAN

• Recognize that the admission (withdrawal) by purchase (sale) of a partnership interest is a personal transaction between one or more existing partners and the new (withdrawing) partner.
• Recognize that the admission (withdrawal) by investment (distribution) of partnership assets is a transaction between the new (withdrawing) partner and the partnership.

SOLUTION

1.	Curly, Capital	10,000	
	Moe, Capital	10,000	
	Larry, Capital	10,000	
	Stan, Capital		30,000
	(To record admission of Stan by purchase)		
2.	Cash	40,000	
	Stan, Capital		40,000
	(To record admission of Stan by investment)		
3.	Larry, Capital	40,000	
	Cash		30,000
	Curly, Capital		5,000
	Moe, Capital		5,000
	(To record withdrawal of Larry and bonus to remaining partners)		

4.	Larry, Capital	40,000	
	Curly, Capital		20,000
	Moe, Capital		20,000
	(To record purchase of Larry's interest)		

Related exercise material: BE13-6, BE13-7, BE13-8, BE13-9, E13-4, E13-5, E13-6, and E13-7.

LIQUIDATION OF A PARTNERSHIP

The liquidation of a partnership terminates the business. It involves selling the assets of the firm, paying liabilities, and distributing any remaining assets to the partners. Liquidation may result from the sale of the business by mutual agreement of the partners, from the death of a partner, or from bankruptcy. In contrast to partnership dissolution, partnership liquidation ends both the legal and economic life of the entity.

From an accounting standpoint, liquidation should be preceded by completing the accounting cycle for the final operating period. This includes preparing adjusting entries and financial statements. It also involves preparing closing entries and a post-closing trial balance. Thus, only balance sheet accounts should be open as the liquidation process begins.

In liquidation, the sale of noncash assets for cash is called **realization**. Any difference between book value and the cash proceeds is called the **gain or loss on realization**. To liquidate a partnership, it is necessary to:

1. Sell noncash assets for cash and recognize a gain or loss on realization.
2. Allocate gain/loss on realization to the partners based on their income ratios.
3. Pay partnership liabilities in cash.
4. Distribute remaining cash to partners on the basis of their **capital balances**.

Each of the steps must be performed in sequence. Creditors must be paid **before** partners receive any cash distributions. Each step also must be recorded by an accounting entry.

When a partnership is liquidated, all partners may have credit balances in their capital accounts. This situation is called no capital deficiency. Or, at least one partner's capital account may have a debit balance. This situation is termed a capital deficiency. To illustrate each of these conditions, assume that the Ace Company is liquidated when its ledger shows the following assets, liabilities, and owners' equity accounts.

STUDY OBJECTIVE 7

Explain the effects of the entries to record the liquidation of a partnership.

Illustration 13-17

Account balances prior to liquidation

Assets		Liabilities and Owners' Equity	
Cash	$ 5,000	Notes payable	$15,000
Accounts receivable	15,000	Accounts payable	16,000
Inventory	18,000	R. Arnet, Capital	15,000
Equipment	35,000	P. Carey, Capital	17,800
Accum. depr.—equipment	(8,000)	W. Eaton, Capital	1,200
	$65,000		$65,000

NO CAPITAL DEFICIENCY

The partners of Ace Company agree to liquidate the partnership on the following terms: (1) The noncash assets of the partnership will be sold to Jackson Enterprises for $75,000 cash. And (2) the partnership will pay its partnership liabilities. The income ratios of the partners are 3 : 2 : 1, respectively. The steps in the liquidation process are as follows.

1. The noncash assets (accounts receivable, inventory, and equipment) are sold for $75,000. The book value of these assets is $60,000 ($15,000 + $18,000 + $35,000 − $8,000). Thus a gain of $15,000 is realized on the sale. The entry is:

	A	=	L	+	OE
+75,000					+15,000
+8,000					
−15,000					
−18,000					
−35,000					

(1)

Cash	75,000	
Accumulated Depreciation–Equipment	8,000	
Accounts Receivable		15,000
Inventory		18,000
Equipment		35,000
Gain on Realization		15,000
(To record realization of noncash assets)		

2. The gain on realization of $15,000 is allocated to the partners on their income ratios, which are 3 : 2 : 1. The entry is:

A	=	L	+	OE
				−15,000
				+7,500
				+5,000
				+2,500

(2)

Gain on Realization	15,000	
R. Arnet, Capital ($15,000 × 3/6)		7,500
P. Carey, Capital ($15,000 × 2/6)		5,000
W. Eaton, Capital ($15,000 × 1/6)		2,500
(To allocate gain to partners' capital accounts)		

3. Partnership liabilities consist of Notes Payable $15,000 and Accounts Payable $16,000. Creditors are paid in full by a cash payment of $31,000. The entry is:

	A	=	L	+	OE
−31,000			−15,000		
			−16,000		

(3)

Notes Payable	15,000	
Accounts Payable	16,000	
Cash		31,000
(To record payment of partnership liabilities)		

4. The remaining cash is distributed to the partners on the basis of **their capital balances**. After the entries in the first three steps are posted, all partnership accounts, including Gain on Realization, will have zero balances except for four accounts: Cash $49,000; R. Arnet, Capital $22,500; P. Carey, Capital $22,800; and W. Eaton, Capital $3,700, as shown below.

Illustration 13-18

Ledger balances before distribution of cash

Cash		R. Arnet, Capital		P. Carey, Capital		W. Eaton, Capital	
Bal. 5,000 (3) 31,000		Bal. 15,000		Bal. 17,800		Bal. 1,200	
(1) 75,000		(2) 7,500		(2) 5,000		(2) 2,500	
Bal. 49,000		**Bal. 22,500**		**Bal. 22,800**		**Bal. 3,700**	

The entry to record the distribution of cash is as follows.

	A	=	L	+	OE
−49,000					−22,500
					−22,800
					−3,700

(4)

R. Arnet, Capital	22,500	
P. Carey, Capital	22,800	
W. Eaton, Capital	3,700	
Cash		49,000
(To record distribution of cash to partners)		

HELPFUL HINT

Zero balances after posting is a quick proof of the accuracy of the cash distribution entry.

After this entry is posted, all partnership accounts will have zero balances.

A word of caution: **Cash should not be distributed to partners on the basis of their income-sharing ratios.** On this basis, Arnet would receive three-sixths, or $24,500, which would produce an erroneous debit balance of $2,000. The income ratio is the proper basis for allocating net income or loss. **It is not a proper basis for making the final distribution of cash to the partners**.

Schedule of Cash Payments

Some accountants prepare a cash payments schedule to determine the distribution of cash to the partners in the liquidation of a partnership. The **schedule of cash payments** is organized around the basic accounting equation. The schedule for the Ace Company is shown in Illustration 13-19. The numbers in parentheses refer to the four required steps in the liquidation of a partnership. They also identify the accounting entries that must be made. The cash payments schedule is especially useful when the liquidation process extends over a period of time.

ALTERNATIVE TERMINOLOGY
The schedule of cash payments is sometimes called a *safe cash payments schedule*.

Illustration 13-19
Schedule of cash payments, no capital deficiency

Item		Cash	+	Noncash Assets	=	Liabilities	+	R. Arnet Capital	+	P. Carey Capital	+	W. Eaton Capital
Balances before liquidation		5,000	+	60,000	=	31,000	+	15,000	+	17,800	+	1,200
Sales of noncash assets and allocation of gain	(1)&(2)	75,000	+	(60,000)	=			7,500	+	5,000	+	2,500
New balances		80,000	+	–0–	=	31,000	+	22,500	+	22,800	+	3,700
Pay liabilities	(3)	(31,000)			=	(31,000)						
New balances		49,000	+	–0–	=	–0–	+	22,500	+	22,800	+	3,700
Cash distribution to partners	(4)	(49,000)			=			(22,500)	+	(22,800)	+	(3,700)
Final balances		–0–		–0–		–0–		–0–		–0–		–0–

CAPITAL DEFICIENCY

A capital deficiency may be caused by recurring net losses, excessive drawings, or losses from realization suffered during liquidation. To illustrate, assume that Ace Company is on the brink of bankruptcy. The partners decide to liquidate by having a "going-out-of-business" sale. Merchandise is sold at substantial discounts, and the equipment is sold at auction. Cash proceeds from these sales and collections from customers total only $42,000. Thus, the loss from liquidation is $18,000 ($60,000 − $42,000). The steps in the liquidation process are as follows.

1. The entry for the realization of noncash assets is:

(1)

Cash	42,000	
Accumulated Depreciation—Equipment	8,000	
Loss on Realization	18,000	
Accounts Receivable		15,000
Inventory		18,000
Equipment		35,000
(To record realization of noncash assets)		

A	=	L	+	OE
+42,000				−18,000
+8,000				
−15,000				
−18,000				
−35,000				

2. The loss on realization is allocated to the partners on the basis of their income ratios. The entry is:

(2)

R. Arnet, Capital ($18,000 × 3/6)	9,000	
P. Carey, Capital ($18,000 × 2/6)	6,000	
W. Eaton, Capital ($18,000 × 1/6)	3,000	
Loss on Realization		18,000
(To allocate loss on realization to partners)		

A	=	L	+	OE
				−9,000
				−6,000
				−3,000
				+18,000

3. Partnership liabilities are paid. This entry is the same as in the previous example.

(3)

Notes Payable	15,000	
Accounts Payable	16,000	
Cash		31,000
(To record payment of partnership liabilities)		

A = L + OE
−31,000 −15,000
  −16,000

Illustration 13-20

Ledger balances before distribution of cash

4. After posting the three entries, two accounts will have debit balances—Cash $16,000, and W. Eaton, Capital $1,800. Two accounts will have credit balances—R. Arnet, Capital $6,000, and P. Carey, Capital $11,800. All four accounts are shown below.

Cash				R. Arnet, Capital				P. Carey, Capital				W. Eaton, Capital			
Bal.	5,000	(3)	31,000	(2)	9,000	Bal.	15,000	(2)	6,000	Bal.	17,800	(2)	3,000	Bal.	1,200
(1)	42,000					Bal.	6,000			Bal.	11,800			Bal.	1,800
Bal.	16,000														

Eaton has a capital deficiency of $1,800, and so owes the partnership $1,800. Arnet and Carey have a legally enforceable claim for that amount against Eaton's personal assets. The distribution of cash is still made on the basis of capital balances. But the amount will vary depending on how Eaton's deficiency is settled. Two alternatives are presented below.

Payment of Deficiency

If the partner with the capital deficiency pays the amount owed the partnership, the deficiency is eliminated. To illustrate, assume that Eaton pays $1,800 to the partnership. The entry is:

(a)

A = L + OE
+1,800   +1,800

Cash	1,800	
W. Eaton, Capital		1,800
(To record payment of capital deficiency by Eaton)		

After posting this entry, account balances are as follows.

Cash				R. Arnet, Capital				P. Carey, Capital				W. Eaton, Capital			
Bal.	5,000	(3)	31,000	(2)	9,000	Bal.	15,000	(2)	6,000	Bal.	17,800	(2)	3,000	Bal.	1,200
(1)	42,000					Bal.	6,000			Bal.	11,800			(a)	1,800
(a)	1,800													Bal.	−0−
Bal.	17,800														

Illustration 13-21

Ledger balances after paying capital deficiency

A = L + OE
−17,800   −6,000
    −11,800

The cash balance of $17,800 is now equal to the credit balances in the capital accounts (Arnet $6,000 + Carey $11,800). Cash now is distributed on the basis of these balances. The entry is:

R. Arnet, Capital	6,000	
P. Carey, Capital	11,800	
Cash		17,800
(To record distribution of cash to the partners)		

After this entry is posted, all accounts will have zero balances.

Nonpayment of Deficiency

If a partner with a capital deficiency is unable to pay the amount owed to the partnership, the partners with credit balances must absorb the loss. The loss is allocated on the basis of the income ratios that exist between the partners with credit balances.

For example, the income ratios of Arnet and Carey are 3:2, or 3/5 and 2/5, respectively. Thus, the following entry would be made to remove Eaton's capital deficiency.

<table>
<tr><td>(a)</td><td></td><td></td></tr>
<tr><td>R. Arnet, Capital ($1,800 × 3/5)</td><td>1,080</td><td></td></tr>
<tr><td>P. Carey, Capital ($1,800 × 2/5)</td><td>720</td><td></td></tr>
<tr><td>   W. Eaton, Capital</td><td></td><td>1,800</td></tr>
<tr><td>   (To record write-off of capital deficiency)</td><td></td><td></td></tr>
</table>

A	=	L	+	OE
				−1,080
				−720
				+1,800

Illustration 13-22

Ledger balances after nonpayment of capital deficiency

After posting this entry, the cash and capital accounts will have the following balances.

Cash		R. Arnet, Capital		P. Carey, Capital		W. Eaton, Capital	
Bal. 5,000 | (3) 31,000		(2) 9,000 | Bal. 15,000		(2) 6,000 | Bal. 17,800		(2) 3,000 | Bal. 1,200	
(1) 42,000 |		(a) 1,080 |		(a) 720 |		| (a) 1,800	
Bal. 16,000 |		| Bal. 4,920		| Bal. 11,080		| Bal. –0–	

The cash balance of $16,000 now equals the sum of the credit balances in the capital accounts (Arnet $4,920 + Carey $11,080). The entry to record the distribution of cash is:

<table>
<tr><td>R. Arnet, Capital</td><td>4,920</td><td></td></tr>
<tr><td>P. Carey, Capital</td><td>11,080</td><td></td></tr>
<tr><td>   Cash</td><td></td><td>16,000</td></tr>
<tr><td>   (To record distribution of cash to the partners)</td><td></td><td></td></tr>
</table>

A	=	L	+	OE
−16,000				−4,920
				−11,080

After this entry is posted, all accounts will have zero balances.

BEFORE YOU GO ON...

▶ *REVIEW IT*
1. What are the steps in liquidating a partnership?
2. What basis is used in making the final distribution of cash to the partners?

A LOOK BACK AT OUR FEATURE STORY

Refer back to the Feature Story about Razor & Tie Music at the beginning of the chapter, and answer the following questions.
1. Speculate as to why Razor & Tie selected the partnership form of organization for its business.
2. What might be some of the major items written into the partnership agreement for Razor & Tie?
3. How is net income or loss divided if the partnership is silent regarding the percentage allocation?

SOLUTION

1. Cliff Chenfield and Craig Balsam may have chosen to form a partnership, rather than a corporation, for a number of reasons. First, the partnership is much quicker and easier to form, with little of the red tape a corporation faces. Second, the partnership form has distinct tax advantages relative to a corporation. Third, since the two partners knew each other well, they may have had fewer concerns about the risk of unlimited liabilities that might be incurred by the other partner.

2. The partnership agreement of Razor & Tie should specify the capital contributed by both partners, and the basis for sharing income and losses and for withdrawing funds. Also, it might specify mechanisms for resolving disputes, adding or removing a partner, or what to do in the event of the death of one of the partners. A well-written partnership agreement can significantly reduce conflicts as the firm grows.

3. In this case, income and losses are shared equally.

☑ THE NAVIGATOR

Additional Demonstration Problem

DEMONSTRATION PROBLEM

On January 1, 2002, the capital balances in Hollingsworth Company are Lois Holly $26,000, and Jim Worth $24,000. In 2002 the partnership reports net income of $30,000. The income ratio provides for salary allowances of $12,000 for Holly and $10,000 to Worth and the remainder equally. Neither partner had any drawings in 2002.

Assume that the following independent transactions occur on January 1, 2003.

1. Donna Reichenbacher purchases one-half of Holly's capital interest for $25,000.

2. Marsha Mears is admitted with a 25% capital interest by a cash investment of $40,000.

3. Stan Wells is admitted with a 35% capital interest by a cash investment of $40,000.

Instructions
(a) Prepare a schedule showing the distribution of net income in 2002.

(b) Journalize the division of 2002 net income to the partners.

(c) Journalize each of the independent transactions that occurred on January 1, 2003.

SOLUTION TO DEMONSTRATION PROBLEM

ACTION PLAN

- Compute the net income of the partnership.
- Allocate the partners' salaries.
- Divide the remaining net income among the partners, applying the income/loss ratio.
- Journalize the division of net income in a closing entry.
- Recognize the admission by purchase of a partnership interest as a personal transaction between an existing partner and the new partner.
- Recognize the admission by investment of partnership assets as a transaction between the new partner and the partnership.

(a) Net income — $30,000

Division of Net Income

	Lois Holly	Jim Worth	Total
Salary allowance	$12,000	$10,000	$22,000
Remaining income $8,000 ($30,000 − $22,000)			
Lois Holly ($8,000 × 50%)	4,000		
Jim Worth ($8,000 × 50%)		4,000	
Total remainder			8,000
Total division of net income	$16,000	$14,000	$30,000

(b) 12/31/02	Income Summary	30,000	
	Lois Holly, Capital		16,000
	Jim Worth, Capital		14,000
	(To close net income to partners' capital)		

(1)

(c) 1/1/03	Lois Holly, Capital [($26,000 + $16,000) × ½]	21,000	
	Donna Reichenbacher, Capital		21,000
	(To record purchase of one-half of Holly's interest)		

(2)

1/1/03	Cash		40,000	
	Lois Holly, Capital			5,000
	Jim Worth, Capital			5,000
	Marsha Mears, Capital			30,000
	(To record admission of Mears and bonus to			
	old partners)			

Total capital after investment: $120,000
  (Holly, $42,000, Worth $38,000, Mears
  investment $40,000)

Mears' capital credit (25% × $120,000) $30,000

Bonus to old partners ($40,000 − $30,000) $10,000

Allocation of bonus:
  Holly ($10,000 × 50%) $ 5,000
  Worth ($10,000 × 50%)   5,000 $10,000

(3)

1/1/03	Cash		40,000	
	Lois Holly, Capital		1,000	
	Jim Worth, Capital		1,000	
	Stan Wells, Capital			42,000
	(To record Wells's admission and bonus)			

Wells's capital credit (35% × $120,000) $42,000

Bonus to Wells ($42,000 − $40,000) $ 2,000

Allocation of bonus:
  Holly ($2,000 × 50%) $1,000
  Worth ($2,000 × 50%)   1,000 $ 2,000

SUMMARY OF STUDY OBJECTIVES

1. Identify the characteristics of the partnership form of business organization. The principal characteristics of a partnership are: (a) association of individuals, (b) mutual agency, (c) limited life, (d) unlimited liability, and (e) co-ownership of property.

2. Explain the accounting entries for the formation of a partnership. When a partnership is formed, each partner's initial investment should be recorded at the fair market value of the assets at the date of their transfer to the partnership.

3. Identify the bases for dividing net income or net loss. Net income or net loss is divided on the basis of the income ratio, which may be (a) a fixed ratio, (b) a ratio based on beginning or average capital balances, (c) salaries to partners and the remainder on a fixed ratio, (d) interest on partners' capital and the remainder on a fixed ratio, and (e) salaries to partners, interest on partners' capital, and the remainder on a fixed ratio.

4. Describe the form and content of partnership financial statements. The financial statements of a partnership are similar to those of a proprietorship. The principal differences are: (a) the division of net income is shown on the income statement, (b) the owners' equity statement is called a partners' capital statement, and (c) each partner's capital is reported on the balance sheet.

5. Explain the effects of the entries when a new partner is admitted. The entry to record the admittance of a new partner by purchase of a partner's interest affects only partners' capital accounts. The entries to record the admittance by investment of assets in the partnership (a) increase both net assets and total capital and (b) may result in recognition of a bonus to either the old partners or the new partner.

6. Describe the effects of the entries when a partner withdraws from the firm. The entry to record a withdrawal from the firm when payment is made from partners' personal assets affects only partners' capital accounts. The entry to record a withdrawal when payment is made from partnership assets (a) decreases net assets and total capital and (b) may result in recognizing a bonus either to the retiring partner or the remaining partners.

7. Explain the effects of the entries to record the liquidation of a partnership. When a partnership is liquidated, it is necessary to record the (a) sale of noncash assets, (b) allocation of the gain or loss on realization, (c) payment of partnership liabilities, and (d) distribution of cash to the partners on the basis of their capital balances.

GLOSSARY

Admission by investment Admission of a partner by investing assets in the partnership, causing both partnership net assets and total capital to increase. (p. 532).

Admission by purchase of an interest Admission of a partner in a personal transaction between one or more existing partners and the new partner; does not change total partnership assets or total capital. (p. 531).

Capital deficiency A debit balance in a partner's capital account after allocation of gain or loss. (p. 539).

General partner A partner who has unlimited liability for the debts of the firm. (p. 522).

Income ratio The basis for dividing net income and net loss in a partnership. (p. 526).

Limited liability company A form of business organization, usually classified as a partnership and usually with limited life, in which partners, who are called *members*, have limited liability. (p. 523).

Limited liability partnership A partnership of professionals in which partners are given limited liability and the public is protected from malpractice by insurance carried by the partnership. (p. 523).

Limited partner A partner who has limited liability for the debts of the firm. (p. 522).

Limited partnership A partnership in which one or more general partners have unlimited liability and one or more partners have limited liability for the obligations of the firm. (p. 522).

No capital deficiency All partners have credit balances after allocation of gain or loss. (p. 539).

Partners' capital statement The owners' equity statement for a partnership which shows the changes in each partner's capital balance and in total partnership capital during the year. (p. 529).

Partnership An association of two or more persons to carry on as co-owners of a business for profit. (p. 520).

Partnership agreement A written contract expressing the voluntary agreement of two or more individuals in a partnership. (p. 524).

Partnership dissolution A change in partners due to withdrawal or admission, which does not necessarily terminate the business. (p. 521).

Partnership liquidation An event that ends both the legal and economic life of a partnership. (p. 539).

"S" corporation Corporation, with 75 or fewer stockholders, that is taxed like a partnership. (p. 523).

Schedule of cash payments A schedule showing the distribution of cash to the partners in a partnership liquidation. (p. 541).

Withdrawal by payment from partners' personal assets Withdrawal of a partner in a personal transaction between partners; does not change total partnership assets or total capital. (p. 535).

Withdrawal by payment from partnership assets Withdrawal of a partner in a transaction involving the partnership, causing both partnership net assets and total capital to decrease. (p. 536).

SELF-STUDY QUESTIONS

Answers are at the end of the chapter.

(SO 1) **1.** Which of the following is *not* a characteristic of a partnership?
    a. Taxable entity
    b. Co-ownership of property
    c. Mutual agency
    d. Limited life

(SO 1) **2.** The advantages of a partnership do *not* include:
    a. ease of formation.
    b. unlimited liability.
    c. freedom from government regulation.
    d. ease of decision making.

(SO 2) **3.** Upon formation of a partnership, each partner's initial investment of assets should be recorded at their:
    a. book values.
    b. cost.
    c. market values.
    d. appraised values.

(SO 3) **4.** The NBC Company reports net income of $60,000. If partners N, B, and C have an income ratio of 50%, 30%, and 20%, respectively, C's share of the net income is:
    a. $30,000.

    b. $12,000.
    c. $18,000.
    d. No correct answer is given.

(SO 3) **5.** Using the data in (4) above, what is B's share of net income if the percentages are applicable after each partner receives a $10,000 salary allowance?
    a. $12,000
    b. $20,000
    c. $19,000
    d. $21,000

(SO 4) **6.** Which of the following statements about partnership financial statements is true?
    a. Details of the distribution of net income are shown in the owners' equity statement.
    b. The distribution of net income is shown on the balance sheet.
    c. Only the total of all partner capital balances is shown in the balance sheet.
    d. The owners' equity statement is called the partners' capital statement.

(SO 5) **7.** Maria Taxco purchases 50% of Louie Lime's capital interest in the K & L partnership for $22,000. If the capital balance of Kim Kanary and Louie Lime are $40,000

and $30,000, respectively, Taxco's capital balance following the purchase is:
a. $22,000.
b. $35,000.
c. $20,000.
d. $15,000.

(SO 5) **8.** Capital balances in the DEA partnership are Don Capital $60,000, Ed Capital $50,000, and Amy Capital $40,000, and income ratios are 5:3:2, respectively. The DEAR partnership is formed by admitting Ray to the firm with a cash investment of $60,000 for a 25% capital interest. The bonus to be credited to Amy Capital in admitting Ray is:
a. $10,000.
b. $7,500.
c. $3,750.
d. $1,500.

(SO 6) **9.** Capital balances in the TERM partnership are Terry Capital $50,000, Enid Capital $40,000, Rob Capital

$30,000, and Mary Capital $20,000, and income ratios are 4:3:2:1, respectively. Mary withdraws from the firm following payment of $29,000 in cash from the partnership. Enid's capital balance after recording the withdrawal of Mary is:
a. $36,000.
b. $37,000.
c. $38,000.
d. $40,000.

10. In the liquidation of a partnership it is necessary to (1) (SO 7) distribute cash to the partners, (2) sell noncash assets, (3) allocate any gain or loss on realization to the partners, and (4) pay liabilities. These steps should be performed in the following order:
a. (2), (3), (4), (1).
b. (2), (3), (1), (4).
c. (3), (2), (1), (4).
d. (3), (2), (4), (1).

THE NAVIGATOR

QUESTIONS

1. The characteristics of a partnership include the following: (a) association of individuals, (b) limited life, and (c) co-ownership of property. Explain each of these terms.

2. Vera Cruz is confused about the partnership characteristics of (a) mutual agency and (b) unlimited liability. Explain these two characteristics for Vera.

3. Swen Varberg and Egor Karlstad are considering a business venture. They ask you to explain the advantages and disadvantages of the partnership form of organization.

4. Ginny Brown and Dorothy Fleming form a partnership. Brown contributes land with a book value of $50,000 and a fair market value of $75,000. Brown also contributes equipment with a book value of $52,000 and a fair market value of $57,000. The partnership assumes a $20,000 mortgage on the land. What should be the balance in Brown's capital account upon formation of the partnership?

5. Roy Orbison, S. Innis, and David Bowie have a partnership called Depeche Mode. A dispute has arisen among the partners. Orbison has invested twice as much in assets as the other two partners, and he believes net income and net losses should be shared in accordance with the capital ratios. The partnership agreement does not specify the division of profits and losses. How will net income and net loss be divided?

6. Leon Redbone and Elvis Costello are discussing how income and losses should be divided in a partnership they plan to form. What factors should be considered in determining the division of net income or net loss?

7. Doreen Shaffer and Quincy Jones have partnership capital balances of $40,000 and $80,000, respectively. The partnership agreement indicates that net income or net loss should be shared equally. If net income for the partnership is $24,000, how should the net income be divided?

8. Robben Ford and Gregg Allman share net income and net loss equally. (a) Which account(s) is (are) debited and credited to record the division of net income between the partners? (b) If Robben Ford withdraws $30,000 in cash for personal use in lieu of salary, which account is debited and which is credited?

9. Partners Reba McEntire and B. Zander are provided salary allowances of $30,000 and $25,000, respectively. They divide the remainder of the partnership income in a ratio of 60:40. If partnership net income is $50,000, how much is allocated to McEntire and Zander?

10. Are the financial statements of a partnership similar to those of a proprietorship? Discuss.

11. Patty Loveless decides to pay $50,000 for a one-third interest in an existing partnership. What effect does this transaction have on partnership net assets?

12. Billy Joel decides to invest $25,000 in a new partnership for a one-sixth capital interest. How much do the partnership's net assets increase? Does Joel also acquire a one-sixth income ratio through this investment?

13. Pia Zadora purchases for $72,000 Cole's interest in the Morgan-Cole partnership. Assuming that Cole has a $63,000 capital balance in the partnership, what journal entry is made by the partnership to record this transaction?

14. Won Jang has a $37,000 capital balance in a partnership. She sells her interest to Carla Cardosa for $45,000 cash. What entry is made by the partnership for this transaction?

15. Natalie Cole retires from the partnership of Suarez, Tanks, and Cole. She receives $89,000 of partnership assets in settlement of her capital balance of $77,000. Assuming that the income-sharing ratios are 5:3:2, respectively, how much of Cole's bonus is debited to Tanks' capital account?

16. Your roommate argues that partnership assets should be revalued in situations like those in question 15. Why is this generally not done?

17. How is a deceased partner's equity determined?

18. How does the liquidation of a partnership differ from the dissolution of a partnership?

19. Phil Collins and Herb Alpert are discussing the liquidation of a partnership. Phil maintains that all cash should be distributed to partners on the basis of their income ratios. Is he correct? Explain.

20. In continuing their discussion, Herb says that even in the case of a capital deficiency, all cash should still be distributed on the basis of capital balances. Is Herb correct? Explain.

21. Erin, Cole, and Morgan have income ratios of 5:3:2 and capital balances of $34,000, $31,000, and $28,000, respectively. Noncash assets are sold at a gain. After creditors are paid, $119,000 of cash is available for distribution to the partners. How much cash should be paid to Cole?

22. Before the final distribution of cash, account balances are: Cash $25,000; B. Springsteen, Capital $19,000 (Cr.); L. Hamilton, Capital $12,000 (Cr.); and T. Zaret, Capital $6,000 (Dr.). Zaret is unable to pay any of the capital deficiency. If the income-sharing ratios are 5:3:2, respectively, how much cash should be paid to L. Hamilton?

BRIEF EXERCISES

Journalize entries in forming a partnership.
(SO 2)

BE13-1 Britney Spears and Pablo Cruise decide to organize the ALL-Star partnership. Britney Spears invests $15,000 cash, and Cruise contributes $10,000 cash and equipment having a book value of $3,500. Prepare the entry to record Cruise's investment in the partnership, assuming the equipment has a fair market value of $7,000

Prepare portion of opening balance sheet for partnership.
(SO 2)

BE13-2 H. Tylo and R. Moss decide to merge their proprietorships into a partnership called Tylomoss Company. The balance sheet of Moss Co. shows:

Accounts receivable	$16,000	
Less: Allowance for doubtful accounts	1,200	$14,800
Equipment	20,000	
Less: Accumulated depreciation	8,000	12,000

The partners agree that the net realizable value of the receivables is $12,500 and that the fair market value of the equipment is $10,000. Indicate how the four accounts should appear in the opening balance sheet of the partnership.

Journalize the division of net income using fixed income ratios.
(SO 3)

BE13-3 Led Zeppelin Co. reports net income of $70,000. The income ratios are Led 60% and Zeppelin 40%. Indicate the division of net income to each partner, and prepare the entry to distribute the net income.

Compute division of net income with a salary allowance and fixed ratios.
(SO 3)

BE13-4 MET Co. reports net income of $65,000. Partner salary allowances are Moses $20,000, Evelyn $5,000, and Tom $5,000. Indicate the division of net income to each partner, assuming the income ratio is 50:30:20, respectively.

Show division of net income when allowances exceed net income.
(SO 3)

BE13-5 Bill&Til Co. reports net income of $24,000. Interest allowances are Bill $6,000 and Til $5,000; salary allowances are Bill $15,000 and Til $10,000; the remainder is shared equally. Show the distribution of income on the income statement.

Journalize admission by purchase of an interest.
(SO 5)

BE13-6 In Kansas Co. capital balances are: Ali $30,000, Babson $25,000, and Curtis $22,000. The partners share income equally. Daniel is admitted to the firm by purchasing one-half of Curtis's interest for $14,000. Journalize the admission of Daniel to the partnership.

Journalize admission by investment.
(SO 5)

BE13-7 In Nebraska Co., capital balances are Evelynn $40,000 and Zane $30,000. The partners share income equally. Kerns is admitted to the firm with a 45% interest by an investment of cash of $42,000. Journalize the admission of Kerns.

Journalize withdrawal paid by personal assets.
(SO 6)

BE13-8 Capital balances in DEB Co. are Ditka $40,000, Elbert $30,000, and Bob $30,000. Ditka and Elbert each agree to pay Bob $12,000 from their personal assets. Ditka and Elbert each receive 50% of Bob's equity. The partners share income equally. Journalize the withdrawal of Bob.

Journalize withdrawal paid by partnership assets.
(SO 6)

BE13-9 Data pertaining to DEB Co. are presented in BE13-8. Instead of payment from personal assets, assume that Bob receives $32,000 from partnership assets in withdrawing from the firm. Journalize the withdrawal of Bob.

Journalize final cash distribution in liquidation.
(SO 7)

BE13-10 After liquidating noncash assets and paying creditors, account balances in the Missouri Co. are Cash $21,000, A Capital (Cr.) $9,000, R Capital (Cr.) $7,000, and B Capital (Cr.) $5,000. The partners share income equally. Journalize the final distribution of cash to the partners.

EXERCISES

E13-1 Frank Voris has owned and operated a proprietorship for several years. On January 1, he decides to terminate this business and become a partner in the firm of Payne and Voris. Voris's investment in the partnership consists of $15,000 in cash, and the following assets of the proprietorship: accounts receivable $14,000 less allowance for doubtful accounts of $2,000, and equipment $20,000 less accumulated depreciation of $4,000. It is agreed that the allowance for doubtful accounts should be $3,000 for the partnership. The fair market value of the equipment is $17,500.

Journalize entry for formation of a partnership.
(SO 2)

Instructions
Journalize Voris's admission to the firm of Payne and Voris.

E13-2 B. Manilow and O. Newton have capital balances on January 1 of $50,000 and $40,000, respectively. The partnership income-sharing agreement provides for (1) annual salaries of $20,000 for Manilow and $12,000 for Newton, (2) interest at 10% on beginning capital balances, and (3) remaining income or loss to be shared 70% by Manilow and 30% by Newton.

Prepare schedule showing distribution of net income and closing entry.
(SO 3)

Instructions
(a) Prepare a schedule showing the distribution of net income, assuming net income is (1) $55,000 and (2) $30,000.
(b) Journalize the allocation of net income in each of the situations above.

E13-3 In Fleetwood Mac Co., beginning capital balances on January 1, 2002, are Ken Tucki $20,000 and Chris Cross $18,000. During the year, drawings were Tucki $8,000 and Cross $3,000. Net income was $32,000, and the partners share income equally.

Prepare partners' capital statement and partial balance sheet.
(SO 4)

Instructions
(a) Prepare the partners' capital statement for the year.
(b) Prepare the owners' equity section of the balance sheet at December 31, 2002.

E13-4 T. Halo, K. Rose, and J. Lamp share income on a 5:3:2 basis. They have capital balances of $32,000, $26,000, and $18,000, respectively, when Dave Matthews is admitted to the partnership.

Journalize admission of a new partner by purchase of an interest.
(SO 5)

Instructions
Prepare the journal entry to record the admission of Dave Matthews under each of the following assumptions.

(a) Purchase of 50% of Halo's equity for $19,000.
(b) Purchase of 50% of Rose's equity for $10,000.
(c) Purchase of 33⅓% of Lamp's equity for $9,000.

E13-5 Joe Keho and Mike McLain share income on a 6:4 basis. They have capital balances of $90,000 and $70,000, respectively, when Liz Hurley is admitted to the partnership.

Journalize admission of a new partner by investment.
(SO 5)

Instructions
Prepare the journal entry to record the admission of Liz Hurley under each of the following assumptions.

(a) Investment of $100,000 cash for a 30% ownership interest with bonuses to the existing partners.
(b) Investment of $36,000 cash for a 30% ownership interest with a bonus to the new partner.

E13-6 Mary Toshiba, Vera Miles, and Barb Eden have capital balances of $50,000, $40,000, and $25,000, respectively. Their income ratios are 5:3:2. Eden withdraws from the partnership under each of the following independent conditions.

Journalize withdrawal of a partner with payment from partners' personal assets.
(SO 6)

1. Toshiba and Miles agree to purchase Eden's equity by paying $15,000 each from their personal assets. Each purchaser receives 50% of Eden's equity.
2. Miles agrees to purchase all of Eden's equity by paying $22,000 cash from her personal assets.
3. Toshiba agrees to purchase all of Eden's equity by paying $26,000 cash from her personal assets.

Instructions
Journalize the withdrawal of Eden under each of the assumptions above.

E13-7 Dale Nagel, Rocky Rim, and Todd Rundgren have capital balances of $95,000, $75,000, and $60,000, respectively. They share income or loss on a 5:3:2 basis. Rim withdraws from the partnership under each of the following conditions.

Journalize withdrawal of a partner with payment from partnership assets.
(SO 6)

1. Rim is paid $85,500 in cash from partnership assets, and a bonus is granted to the retiring partner.
2. Rim is paid $68,000 in cash from partnership assets, and bonuses are granted to the remaining partners.

Instructions
Journalize the withdrawal of Rim under each of the assumptions above.

Prepare cash distribution schedule.
(SO 7)

E13-8 The Pips Company at December 31 has cash $20,000, noncash assets $100,000, liabilities $55,000, and the following capital balances: Agnes $45,000 and Mildred $20,000. The firm is liquidated, and $120,000 in cash is received for the noncash assets. Agnes and Mildred income ratios are 55% and 45%, respectively.

Instructions
Prepare a cash distribution schedule.

Journalize transactions in a liquidation.
(SO 7)

E13-9 Data for The Pips partnership are presented in E13-8.

Instructions
Prepare the entries to record:

(a) The sale of noncash assets.
(b) The allocation of the gain or loss on liquidation to the partners.
(c) Payment of creditors.
(d) Distribution of cash to the partners.

Journalize transactions with a capital deficiency.
(SO 7)

E13-10 Prior to the distribution of cash to the partners, the accounts in the MEL Company are: Cash $30,000, Maureen Capital (Cr.) $18,000, Ellen Capital (Cr.) $14,000, and Lou Capital (Dr.) $2000. The income ratios are 5:3:2, respectively.

Instructions
(a) Prepare the entry to record (1) Lou's payment of $2,000 in cash to the partnership and (2) the distribution of cash to the partners with credit balances.
(b) Prepare the entry to record (1) the absorption of Lou's capital deficiency by the other partners and (2) the distribution of cash to the partners with credit balances.

PROBLEMS: SET A

Prepare entries for formation of a partnership and a balance sheet.
(SO 2, 4)

P13-1A The post-closing trial balances of two proprietorships on January 1, 2002, are presented below.

	Mel Company		Gibson Company	
	Dr.	**Cr.**	**Dr.**	**Cr.**
Cash	$ 14,000		$ 13,000	
Accounts receivable	17,500		26,000	
Allowance for doubtful accounts		$ 3,000		$ 4,400
Merchandise inventory	26,500		18,400	
Equipment	45,000		28,000	
Accumulated depreciation—equipment		24,000		12,000
Notes payable		20,000		15,000
Accounts payable		20,000		31,000
Mel, Capital		36,000		
Gibson, Capital				23,000
	$103,000	$103,000	$ 85,400	$85,400

Mel and Gibson decide to form a partnership, Mel Gibson Company, with the following agreed upon valuations for noncash assets.

	Mel Company	Gibson Company
Accounts receivable	$17,500	$26,000
Allowance for doubtful accounts	4,500	4,000
Merchandise inventory	30,000	20,000
Equipment	25,000	18,000

All cash will be transferred to the partnership, and the partnership will assume all the liabilities of the two proprietorships. Further, it is agreed that Mel will invest $3,000 in cash, and Gibson will invest $18,000 in cash.

Instructions

(a) Prepare separate journal entries to record the transfer of each proprietorship's assets and liabilities to the partnership.

(b) Journalize the additional cash investment by each partner.

(c) Prepare a balance sheet for the partnership on January 1, 2002.

(a) Mel, Capital $42,000
Gibson, Capital $27,000

(c) Total assets $176,000

P13-2A At the end of its first year of operations on December 31, 2002, MTC Company's accounts show the following.

Journalize divisions of net income and prepare a partners' capital statement.
(SO 3, 4)

Partner	Drawings	Capital
Teena Marie	$23,000	$48,000
Robin Tower	14,000	30,000
George Clinton	10,000	25,000

The capital balance represents each partner's initial capital investment. Therefore, net income or net loss for 2002 has not been closed to the partners' capital accounts.

Instructions

(a) Journalize the entry to record the division of net income for the year 2002 under each of the following independent assumptions.

(1) Net income is $28,000. Income is shared 6:3:1.

(2) Net income is $34,000. Marie and Tower are given salary allowances of $18,000 and $10,000, respectively. The remainder is shared equally.

(3) Net income is $22,000. Each partner is allowed interest of 10% on beginning capital balances. Marie is given a $15,000 salary allowance. The remainder is shared equally.

(b) Prepare a schedule showing the division of net income under assumption (3) above.

(c) Prepare a partners' capital statement for the year under assumption (3) above.

(a) (1) Marie $16,800
(2) Marie $20,000
(3) Marie $18,700

(c) Marie $43,700

P13-3A At April 30, partners' capital balances in NTW Company are: A. Nolan $62,000, T. Tritt $36,000, and T. Wuhan $12,000. The income sharing ratios are 5:4:1, respectively. On May 1, the NTWO Company is formed by admitting M. Otton to the firm as a partner.

Journalize admission of a partner under different assumptions.
(SO 5)

Instructions

(a) Journalize the admission of Otton under each of the following independent assumptions.

(1) Otton purchases 50% of Wuhan's ownership interest by paying Wuhan $16,000 in cash.

(2) Otton purchases 33⅓% of Tritt's ownership interest by paying Tritt $15,000 in cash.

(3) Otton invests $70,000 for a 30% ownership interest, and bonuses are given to the old partners.

(4) Otton invests $40,000 for a 30% ownership interest, which includes a bonus to the new partner.

(a) (1) Otton, Capital $6,000
(2) Otton $12,000
(3) Otton $54,000
(4) Otton $45,000

(b) Tritt's capital balance is $30,000 after admitting Otton to the partnership by investment. If Tritt's ownership interest is 20% of total partnership capital, what were (1) Otton's cash investment and (2) the bonus to the new partner?

P13-4A On December 31, the capital balances and income ratios in BAG Company are as follows.

Journalize withdrawal of a partner under different assumptions.
(SO 6)

Partner	Capital Balance	Income Ratio
Lois Hamilton	$60,000	50%
Mary McGovern	40,000	30%
Donna Guehler	34,000	20%

Instructions

(a) Journalize the withdrawal of Guehler under each of the following assumptions.

(1) Each of the continuing partners agrees to pay $18,000 in cash from personal funds to purchase Guehler's ownership equity. Each receives 50% of Guehler's equity.

(2) McGovern agrees to purchase Guehler's ownership interest for $30,000 cash.

(a) (1) McGovern, Capital $17,000
(2) McGovern, Capital $34,000

(3) Bonus $4,000

(4) Bonus $6,000

(3) Guehler is paid $38,000 from partnership assets, which includes a bonus to the retiring partner.

(4) Guehler is paid $28,000 from partnership assets, and bonuses to the remaining partners are recognized.

(b) If McGovern's capital balance after Guehler's withdrawal is $43,000 what were (1) the total bonus to the remaining partners and (2) the cash paid by the partnership to Guehler?

Prepare entries with a capital deficiency in liquidation of a partnership.
(SO 7)

Peachtree

P13-5A The partners in Wilkowski Company decide to liquidate the firm when the balance sheet shows the following.

WILKOWSKI COMPANY
Balance Sheet
May 31, 2002

Assets		Liabilities and Owners' Equity	
Cash	$ 27,500	Notes payable	$ 13,500
Accounts receivable	25,000	Accounts payable	27,000
Allowance for doubtful accounts	(1,000)	Wages payable	3,800
Merchandise inventory	34,500	S. Wilkowski, Capital	36,000
Equipment	21,000	J. Harkins, Capital	20,000
Accumulated depreciation—equipment	(5,500)	Mick Jagger, Capital	1,200
Total	$101,500	Total	$101,500

The partners share income and loss 5:3:2. During the process of liquidation, the following transactions were completed in the following sequence.

1. A total of $53,000 was received from converting noncash assets into cash.
2. Liabilities were paid in full.
3. Mick Jagger paid his capital deficiency.
4. Cash was paid to the partners with credit balances.

Instructions
(a) Prepare the entries to record the transactions.
(b) Post to the cash and capital accounts.
(c) Assume that Jagger is unable to pay the capital deficiency.

   (1) Prepare the entry to allocate Jagger's debit balance to Wilkowski and Harkins.
   (2) Prepare the entry to record the final distribution of cash.

PROBLEMS: SET B

Prepare entries for formation of a partnership and a balance sheet.
(SO 2, 4)

P13-1B The post-closing trial balances of two proprietorships on January 1, 2002, are presented below.

	Randy Company		Travis Company	
	Dr.	**Cr.**	**Dr.**	**Cr.**
Cash	$ 7,500		$ 6,000	
Accounts receivable	15,000		23,000	
Allowance for doubtful accounts		$ 2,500		$ 4,000
Merchandise inventory	28,000		17,000	
Equipment	52,000		30,000	
Accumulated depreciation—equipment		24,000		13,000
Notes payable		20,000		
Accounts payable		25,000		37,000
Randy, Capital		31,000		
Travis, Capital				22,000
	$102,500	$102,500	$76,000	$76,000

Randy and Travis decide to form a partnership, Randy Travis Company, with the following agreed upon valuations for noncash assets.

	Randy Company	Travis Company
Accounts receivable	$15,000	$23,000
Allowance for doubtful accounts	3,500	5,000
Merchandise inventory	32,000	21,000
Equipment	31,000	18,000

All cash will be transferred to the partnership, and the partnership will assume all the liabilities of the two proprietorships. Further, it is agreed that Randy will invest $3,000 in cash, and Travis will invest $14,000 in cash.

Instructions

(a) Prepare separate journal entries to record the transfer of each proprietorship's assets and liabilities to the partnership.

(b) Journalize the additional cash investment by each partner.

(c) Prepare a balance sheet for the partnership on January 1, 2002.

(a) Randy, Capital $37,000
Travis, Capital $26,000

(c) Total assets $162,000

P13-2B   At the end of its first year of operations on December 31, 2002, the KMC Company's accounts show the following.

Journalize divisions of net income and prepare a partners' capital statement.
(SO 3, 4)

Partner	Drawings	Capital
Jana Kingston	$12,000	$33,000
Mary Mio	9,000	20,000
Kim Casey	6,000	10,000

The capital balance represents each partner's initial capital investment. Therefore, net income or net loss for 2002 has not been closed to the partners' capital accounts.

Instructions

(a) Journalize the entry to record the division of net income for 2002 under each of the following independent assumptions.

(1) Net income is $32,600. Income is shared 5:3:2.

(2) Net income is $30,000. Kingston and Mio are given salary allowances of $13,000 and $8,000, respectively. The remainder is shared equally.

(3) Net income is $25,200. Each partner is allowed interest of 10% on beginning capital balances. Kingston is given a $15,000 salary allowance. The remainder is shared equally.

(b) Prepare a schedule showing the division of net income under assumption (3) above.

(c) Prepare a partner's capital statement for the year under assumption (3) above.

(a) (1) Kingston $16,300
(2) Kingston $16,000
(3) Kingston $19,600

(c) Kingston $40,600

P13-3B   At April 30, partners' capital balances in ELM Company are: V. Easi $49,000, K. Lester $24,000, and W. Matt $22,000. The income-sharing ratios are 5:3:2, respectively. On May 1, the ELMO Company is formed by admitting N. Ortiz to the firm as a partner.

Journalize admission of a partner under different assumptions.
(SO 5)

Instructions

(a) Journalize the admission of Ortiz under each of the following independent assumptions.

(1) Ortiz purchases 50% of Matt's ownership interest by paying Matt $9,000 in cash.

(2) Ortiz purchases 50% of Lester's ownership interest by paying Lester $16,000 in cash.

(3) Ortiz invests $35,000 cash in the partnership for a 40% ownership interest that includes a bonus to the new partner.

(4) Ortiz invests $30,000 in the partnership for a 15% ownership interest, and bonuses are given to the old partners.

(a) (1) Ortiz, Capital $11,000
(2) Ortiz $12,000
(3) Ortiz $52,000
(4) Ortiz $18,750

(b) Matt's capital balance is $24,000 after admitting Ortiz to the partnership by investment. If Matt's ownership interest is 15% of total partnership capital, what were (1) Ortiz's cash investment and (2) the total bonus to the old partners?

P13-4B   On December 31, the capital balances and income ratios in the Blue Man Company are as follows.

Journalize withdrawal of a partner under different assumptions.
(SO 6)

Partner	Capital Balance	Income Ratio
Pat Schoen	$70,000	60%
Natalie Striegl	30,000	30
Malou Nelson	21,500	10

(a) (1) Striegl, Capital $10,750
   (2) Striegl, Capital $21,500
   (3) Bonus $7,500
   (4) Bonus $4,500

Instructions

(a) Journalize the withdrawal of Nelson under each of the following independent assumptions.

   (1) Each of the remaining partners agrees to pay $12,000 in cash from personal funds to purchase Nelson's ownership equity. Each receives 50% of Nelson's equity.

   (2) Striegl agrees to purchase Nelson's ownership interest for $18,000 in cash.

   (3) From partnership assets, Nelson is paid $29,000, which includes a bonus to the retiring partner.

   (4) Nelson is paid $17,000 from partnership assets. Bonuses to the remaining partners are recognized.

(b) If Striegl's capital balance after Nelson's withdrawal is $33,000, what were (1) the total bonus to the remaining partners and (2) the cash paid by the partnership to Nelson?

Prepare entries and schedule of cash payments in liquidation of a partnership
(SO 7)

P13-5B The partners in Holiday Company decide to liquidate the firm when the balance sheet shows the following.

HOLIDAY COMPANY
Balance Sheet
April 30, 2002

Assets		**Liabilities and Owners' Equity**	
Cash	$24,000	Notes payable	$14,000
Accounts receivable	19,000	Accounts payable	24,000
Allowance for doubtful accounts	(1,000)	Wages payable	2,000
Merchandise inventory	30,000	Gert Robson, Capital	25,000
Equipment	17,000	Dottie Olson, Capital	12,800
Accumulated depreciation—equipment	(8,000)	Debbie Bailey, Capital	3,200
Total	$81,000	Total	$81,000

The partners share income and loss 5:3:2. During the process of liquidation, the transactions below were completed in the following sequence.

1. A total of $48,000 was received from converting noncash assets into cash.
2. Liabilities were paid in full.
3. Cash was paid to the partners with credit balances.

Instructions

(a) Prepare a cash distribution schedule.

(b) Prepare the entries to record the transactions.

(c) Post to the cash and capital accounts.

BROADENING YOUR PERSPECTIVE

FINANCIAL REPORTING AND ANALYSIS

EXPLORING THE WEB

BYP13-1 This exercise is an introduction to the Big Five Accounting firms, all of which are partnerships.

Addresses:

Arthur Andersen	www.arthurandersen.com/
Deloitte & Touche	www.dttus.com/
Ernst & Young	www.ey.com/
KPMG Peat Marwick	www.us.kpmg.com/
PricewaterhouseCoopers	www.pw.com/

(or go to www.wiley.com/college/weygandt)

Steps:

1. Select a firm that is of interest to you.
2. Go to the firm's homepage.

Instructions

(a) Name two services provided by the firm.
(b) What is the firm's total annual revenue?
(c) How many clients does it service?
(d) How many people are employed by the firm?
(e) How many partners are there in the firm?

CRITICAL THINKING

GROUP DECISION CASE

BYP13-2 Doug Stahl and Joy Sommers, two professionals in the finance area, have worked for Pimpernel Leasing for a number of years. Pimpernel Leasing is a company that leases high-tech medical equipment to hospitals. Doug and Joy have decided that, with their financial expertise, they might start their own company to provide consulting services to individuals interested in leasing equipment. One form of organization they are considering is a partnership.

If they start a partnership, each individual plans to contribute $50,000 in cash. In addition, Doug has a used IBM microcomputer that originally cost $3,700, which he intends to invest in the partnership. The computer has a present market value of $1,500.

Although both Doug and Joy are financial wizards, they do not know a great deal about how a partnership operates. As a result, they have come to you for advice.

Instructions
With the class divided into groups, answer the following.

(a) What are the major disadvantages of starting a partnership?
(b) What type of document is needed for a partnership, and what should this document contain?
(c) Both Doug and Joy plan to work full-time in the new partnership. They believe that net income or net loss should be shared equally. However, they are wondering how they can provide compensation to Doug Stahl for his additional investment of the microcomputer. What would you tell them?
(d) Doug is not sure how the computer equipment should be reported on his tax return. What would you tell him?
(e) As indicated above, Doug and Joy have worked together for a number of years. Doug's skills complement Joy's and vice versa. If one of them dies, it will be very difficult for the other to maintain the business, not to mention the difficulty of paying the deceased partner's estate for his or her partnership interest. What would you advise them to do?

COMMUNICATION ACTIVITY

BYP13-3 You are an expert in the field of forming partnerships. George Clooney and Enid Halsingborg want to establish a partnership to start "Enid's Pasta Shop," and they are going to meet with you to discuss their plans. Prior to the meeting you will send them a memo discussing the issues they need to consider before their visit.

Instructions
Write a memo in good form to be sent to Clooney and Halsingborg.

ETHICS CASE

BYP13-4 Morgan and Erin operate a beauty salon as partners who share profits and losses equally. The success of their business has exceeded their expectations; the salon is operating quite profitably. Erin is anxious to maximize profits and schedules appointments from 8 a.m. to 6 p.m. daily, even sacrificing some lunch hours to accommodate regular customers. Morgan schedules her appointments from 9 a.m. to 5 p.m. and takes long lunch hours. Morgan regularly makes significantly larger withdrawals of cash than Erin does, but, she says, "Erin, you

n't worry, I never make a withdrawal without you knowing about it, so it is properly
·ded in my drawing account and charged against my capital at the end of the year." Mor-
 withdrawals to date are double Erin's.

uctions

Who are the stakeholders in this situation?
Identify the problems with Morgan's actions and discuss the ethical considerations of her
actions.
How might the partnership agreement be revised to accommodate the differences in Morgan's and Erin's work and withdrawal habits?

Answers to Self-Study Questions

1. a   **2.** b   **3.** c   **4.** b   **5.** c   **6.** d   **7.** d   **8.** d   **9.** b   **10.** a

Answer to Lands' End Review It Question 2, p. 524

Mutual agency, limited life, unlimited liability, and co-ownership of property are major
characteristics of a partnership. As a company like Lands' End becomes very large, it becomes difficult to remain as a partnership because of these factors. Unlimited liability is
particularly troublesome because owners may lose not only their initial investment but also
their personal assets, if those assets are needed to pay partnership creditors.

CORPORATIONS: ORGANIZATION AND CAPITAL STOCK TRANSACTIONS

14

THE NAVIGATOR ✓

- Understand *Concepts for Review* ❑
- Read *Feature Story* ❑
- Scan *Study Objectives* ❑
- Read *Preview* ❑
- Read text and answer *Before You Go On*
  p. 566 ❑   p. 570 ❑   p. 573 ❑   p. 577 ❑
  p. 584 ❑
- Work *Demonstration Problem* ❑
- Review *Summary of Study Objectives* ❑
- Answer *Self-Study Questions* ❑
- Complete *Assignments* ❑

*C*ONCEPTS FOR REVIEW

Before studying this chapter, you should know or, if necessary, review:

   a. The content of the owner's equity section of the balance sheet for a
   proprietorship (Ch. 1, pp. 22–24, Ch. 4, pp. 154–156) and for a
   partnership. (Ch. 13, pp. 531–532)

   b. How to prepare closing entries for a proprietorship (Ch. 4,
   pp. 140–144) and for a partnership. (Ch. 13, pp. 528–529)

☑ THE NAVIGATOR

"Have You Driven a Ford Lately?"

A company that has produced such renowned successes as the Model T and the Mustang, and such a dismal failure as the Edsel, would have some interesting tales to tell. Henry Ford was a defiant visionary from the day **Ford Motor Company** was formed in 1903. His goal from day one was to design a car he could mass-produce and sell at a price that was affordable to the masses. In short order he accomplished this goal. By 1920, 60 percent of all vehicles on U.S. roads were Fords.

Henry Ford was intolerant of anything that stood between him and success. In the early years Ford had issued shares to the public in order to finance the company's exponential growth. In 1916 he decided to retain funds to finance expansion, rather than pay funds out to stockholders in the form of a dividend. The shareholders sued. Henry Ford's reaction was swift and direct: If the shareholders didn't see things his way, he would get rid of them. In 1919 the Ford family purchased 100 percent of the outstanding shares of Ford, eliminating any outside "interference." It was over 35 years before shares were again issued to the public.

Ford Motor Company has continued to evolve and grow over the years into one of the largest international corporations. Today there are nearly a billion shares of publicly traded Ford stock outstanding, and the president and chief executive of the company is not a member of the Ford family. But the Ford family still retains a significant stake in Ford Motor Company. In a move Henry Ford might have supported, top management recently decided to centralize decision making—that is, to have more key decisions made by top management, rather than by division managers. And, reminiscent of Henry Ford's most famous car, the company is attempting to make a "global car"—a mass-produced car that can be sold around the world with only minor changes.

www.ford.com

After studying this chapter, you should be able to:

1. Identify the major characteristics of a corporation.
2. Differentiate between paid-in capital and retained earnings.
3. Record the issuance of common stock.
4. Explain the accounting for treasury stock.
5. Differentiate preferred stock from common stock.
6. Prepare a stockholders' equity section.
7. Compute book value per share.

Corporations like **Ford Motor Company** have substantial resources. In fact, the corporation is the dominant form of business organization in the United States in terms of dollar volume of sales and earnings, and number of employees. All of the 500 largest companies in the United States are corporations. In this chapter we will explain the essential features of a corporation and the accounting for a corporation's capital stock transactions. In Chapter 15 we will look at other issues related to accounting for corporations.

The content and organization of Chapter 14 are as follows.

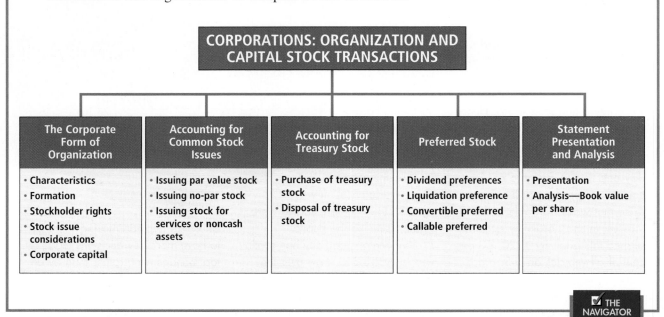

*T*HE CORPORATE FORM OF ORGANIZATION

In 1819, Chief Justice John Marshall defined a corporation as "an artificial being, invisible, intangible, and existing only in contemplation of law." This definition is the foundation for the prevailing legal interpretation that a **corporation** is an **entity separate and distinct from its owners**.

A corporation is created by law, and its continued existence depends upon the statutes of the state in which it is incorporated. As a legal entity, a corporation has most of the rights and privileges of a person. The major exceptions relate to privileges that only a living person can exercise, such as the right to vote or to hold public office. A corporation is subject to the same duties and responsibilities as a person. For example, it must abide by the laws and it must pay taxes.

Corporations may be classified in a variety of ways. Two common bases are by purpose and by ownership. A corporation may be organized for the purpose of making a **profit**, or it may be **nonprofit**. Corporations for profit include such well-known companies as **McDonald's**, **General Motors**, **Lands' End**, and **Apple Computer**. Nonprofit corporations are organized for charitable, medical, or educational purposes. Examples are the **Salvation Army**, the **American Cancer Society**, and the **Ford Foundation**.

Classification by **ownership** distinguishes between publicly held and privately held corporations. A **publicly held corporation** may have thousands of stockholders. Its stock is regularly traded on a national securities exchange such as the

New York Stock Exchange. Most of the largest U.S. corporations are publicly held. Examples of publicly held corporations are **Intel**, **IBM**, **Caterpillar Inc.**, and **General Electric**. In contrast, a **privately held corporation**, often referred to as a closely held corporation, usually has only a few stockholders, and does not offer its stock for sale to the general public. Privately held companies are generally much smaller than publicly held companies, although some notable exceptions exist. **Cargill Inc.**, a private corporation that trades in grain and other commodities, is one of the largest companies in the United States.

CHARACTERISTICS OF A CORPORATION

A number of characteristics distinguish a corporation from proprietorships and partnerships. The most important of these characteristics are explained below.

Separate Legal Existence

As an entity separate and distinct from its owners, the corporation acts under its own name rather than in the name of its stockholders. **Ford Motor Company** may buy, own, and sell property. It may borrow money, and may enter into legally binding contracts in its own name. It may also sue or be sued, and it pays its own taxes.

Remember that in a partnership the acts of the owners (partners) bind the partnership. In contrast, the acts of its owners (stockholders) do not bind the corporation unless such owners are duly appointed agents of the corporation. For example, if you owned shares of Ford Motor Company stock, you would not have the right to purchase automobile parts for the company unless you were appointed as an agent of the corporation.

Limited Liability of Stockholders

Since a corporation is a separate legal entity, creditors have recourse only to corporate assets to satisfy their claims. The liability of stockholders is normally limited to their investment in the corporation. Creditors have no legal claim on the personal assets of the owners unless fraud has occurred. Even in the event of bankruptcy, stockholders' losses are generally limited to their capital investment in the corporation.

Transferable Ownership Rights

Ownership of a corporation is held in shares of capital stock. These are transferable units. Stockholders may dispose of part or all of their interest in a corporation simply by selling their stock. Remember that the transfer of an ownership interest in a partnership requires the consent of each owner. In contrast, the transfer of stock is entirely at the discretion of the stockholder. It does not require the approval of either the corporation or other stockholders.

The transfer of ownership rights between stockholders normally has no effect on the operating activities of the corporation. Nor does it affect the corporation's assets, liabilities, and total ownership equity. The transfer of these ownership rights is a transaction between individual owners. The enterprise does not participate in such transfers after it issues the capital stock.

Ability to Acquire Capital

It is relatively easy for a corporation to obtain capital through the issuance of stock. Buying stock in a corporation is often attractive to an investor because a stockholder has limited liability and shares of stock are readily transferable. Also, numerous individuals can become stockholders by investing small amounts of money. In sum, the ability of a successful corporation to obtain capital is virtually unlimited.

STUDY OBJECTIVE 1

Identify the major characteristics of a corporation.

Legal existence separate from owners

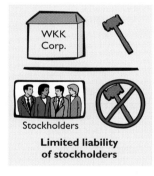

Limited liability of stockholders

Transferable ownership rights

Ability to acquire capital

Continuous life

Continuous Life

The life of a corporation is stated in its charter. The life may be perpetual or it may be limited to a specific number of years. If it is limited, the life can be extended through renewal of the charter. Since a corporation is a separate legal entity, its continuance as a going concern is not affected by the withdrawal, death, or incapacity of a stockholder, employee, or officer. As a result, a successful enterprise can have a continuous and perpetual life.

Corporation Management

As in **Ford Motor Company**, stockholders legally own the corporation. But they manage the corporation indirectly through a board of directors they elect. The board, in turn, formulates the operating policies for the company. The board also selects officers, such as a president and one or more vice presidents, to execute policy and to perform daily management functions.

A typical organization chart showing the delegation of responsibility is shown in Illustration 14-1.

Illustration 14-1

Corporation organization chart

*E*THICS NOTE

Managers who are not owners are often compensated based upon the performance of the firm. They thus may be tempted to exaggerate firm performance by inflating income figures.

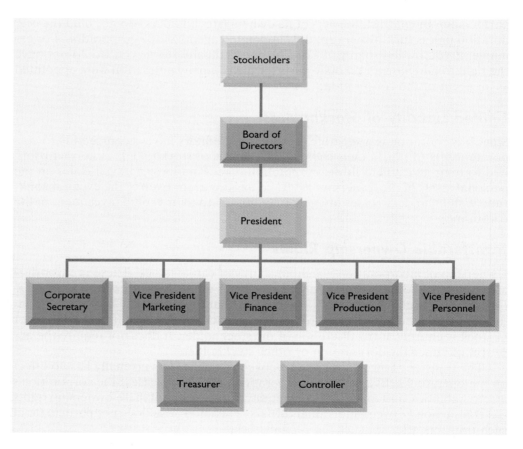

The **president** is the chief executive officer. This individual has direct responsibility for managing the business. As the organization chart shows, the president delegates responsibility to other officers. The chief accounting officer is the **controller**. The controller's responsibilities include (1) maintaining the accounting records, (2) maintaining an adequate system of internal control, and (3) preparing financial statements, tax returns, and internal reports. The **treasurer** has custody of the corporation's funds and is responsible for maintaining the company's cash position.

The organizational structure of a corporation enables a company to hire professional managers to run the business. On the other hand, the separation of ownership and management prevents owners from having an active role in managing the company, which some owners like to have.

ACCOUNTING IN ACTION ∧ *Business Insight*

When a group of investors in a company is unhappy with a company's performance, it sometimes tries to elect new members to the board of directors at the company's annual stockholder meeting. This is referred to as a proxy fight. Usually these efforts fail because it has been very expensive to get in contact with all of the company's shareholders to try to convince them to vote for your group of nominees.

But the Internet has changed that, says James Heard, chief executive of **Proxy Monitor**, a New York firm that consults institutional shareholders on how to vote on corporate governance issues. "Increasingly the Internet is being used as a tool of communication among shareholders to pressure managements," he said. One recent case involved an effort by a shareholder at **Luby's** to get four new people elected to that company's board of directors. He attracted considerable support from other Luby's shareholders by posting messages on a **Yahoo!** message board.

SOURCE: Aaron Elstein, "Online Grousing Over Luby's Escalates to Proxy Solicitation," *The Wall Street Journal*, October 25, 2000.

Government Regulations

A corporation is subject to numerous state and federal regulations. State laws usually prescribe the requirements for issuing stock, the distributions of earnings permitted to stockholders, and the effects of retiring stock. Federal securities laws govern the sale of capital stock to the general public. Also, most publicly held corporations are required to make extensive disclosure of their financial affairs to the Securities and Exchange Commission through quarterly and annual reports. In addition, when a corporate stock is traded on organized securities exchanges, the corporation must comply with the reporting requirements of these exchanges. Government regulations are designed to protect the owners of the corporation. Such protection is needed because most stockholders do not participate in the day-to-day management of the company.

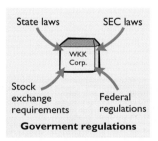

Government regulations

Additional Taxes

Neither proprietorships nor partnerships pay income taxes. The owner's share of earnings from these organizations is reported on his or her personal income tax return. Taxes are then paid by the individual on this amount. Corporations, on the other hand, must pay federal and state income taxes as a separate legal entity. These taxes are substantial: They can amount to more than 40 percent of taxable income.

In addition, stockholders are required to pay taxes on cash dividends (pro rata distributions of net income). Thus, many argue that corporate income is **taxed twice (double taxation)**, once at the corporate level, and again at the individual level.

From the foregoing, we can identify the following advantages and disadvantages of a corporation compared to a proprietorship and partnership.

Additional taxes

Illustration 14-2

Advantages and disadvantages of a corporation

Advantages	Disadvantages
Separate legal existence	Corporation management—separation of
Limited liability of stockholders	ownership and management
Transferable ownership rights	Government regulations
Ability to acquire capital	Additional taxes
Continuous life	
Corporation management—professional	
managers	

FORMING A CORPORATION

The initial step in forming a corporation is to file an application with the Secretary of State in the state in which incorporation is desired. The application contains such information as: (1) the name and purpose of the proposed corporation; (2) amounts, kinds, and number of shares of capital stock to be authorized; (3) the names of the incorporators; and (4) the shares of stock to which each has subscribed.

ALTERNATIVE TERMINOLOGY

The charter is often referred to as the *articles of incorporation.*

After the application is approved, a **charter** is granted. The charter may be an approved copy of the application form or it may be a separate document containing the same basic data. The issuance of the charter creates the corporation. Upon receipt of the charter, the corporation develops its by-laws. The **by-laws** establish the internal rules and procedures for conducting the affairs of the corporation. They also indicate the powers of the stockholders, directors, and officers of the enterprise.[1]

Regardless of the number of states in which a corporation has operating divisions, it is incorporated in only one state. It is to the company's advantage to incorporate in a state whose laws are favorable to the corporate form of business organization. **General Motors**, for example, is incorporated in Delaware, whereas **QUALCOMM** is a New Jersey corporation. Many corporations choose to incorporate in states with rules favorable to existing management. For example, **Gulf Oil** at one time changed its state of incorporation to Delaware to thwart possible unfriendly takeovers. There, certain defensive tactics against takeovers can be approved by the board of directors alone, without a vote by shareholders.

ACCOUNTING IN ACTION Business Insight

It is not necessary for a corporation to have an office in the state in which it incorporates. In fact, more than 50 percent of the Fortune 500 corporations are incorporated in Delaware. A primary reason is the Delaware courts' longstanding "business judgment rule." The rule provides that as long as directors exercise "due care" in the interests of stockholders, their actions will not be second-guessed by the courts. The rule has enabled directors to reject hostile takeover offers and to spurn takeovers simply because they did not want to sell the company. However, new interpretations are emerging. In a recent case, the state court ruled for a company that made a hostile takeover bid. On appeal, the Delaware Supreme Court ruled for the directors but gave the following guideline to the state courts: "Was the board's response reasonable in the light of the threat posed?"

---

[1]Following approval by two-thirds of the stockholders, the by-laws become binding upon all stockholders, directors, and officers. Legally, a corporation is regulated first by the laws of the state, second by its charter, and third by its by-laws. Care must be exercised to ensure that the provisions of the by-laws are not in conflict with either state laws or the charter.

Corporations engaged in interstate commerce must also obtain a license from each state in which they do business. The license subjects the corporation's operating activities to the corporation laws of the state.

Costs incurred in the formation of a corporation are called **organization costs**. These costs include legal and state fees, and promotional expenditures involved in the organization of the business. **Organization costs are expensed as incurred.** To determine the amount and timing of future benefits is so difficult that a conservative approach of expensing these costs immediately is followed.

OWNERSHIP RIGHTS OF STOCKHOLDERS

When chartered, the corporation may begin selling ownership rights in the form of shares of stock. When a corporation has only one class of stock, it is identified as **common stock**. Each share of common stock gives the stockholder the ownership rights pictured in Illustration 14-3. The ownership rights of a share of stock are stated in the articles of incorporation or in the by-laws.

*I*NTERNATIONAL NOTE

U.S. corporations are identified by *Inc.*, which stands for Incorporated. In Italy the letters used are *SpA* (Societa per Azioni); in Sweden *AB* (Aktiebolag); in France *SA* (Sociedad Anonima); and in the Netherlands *NV* (Naamloze Vennootschap).

In the United Kingdom public limited corporations are identified by *PLC*, and private corporations are denoted by *LTD*. The parallel designations in Germany are *AG* for public corporations and *GmbH* for private corporations.

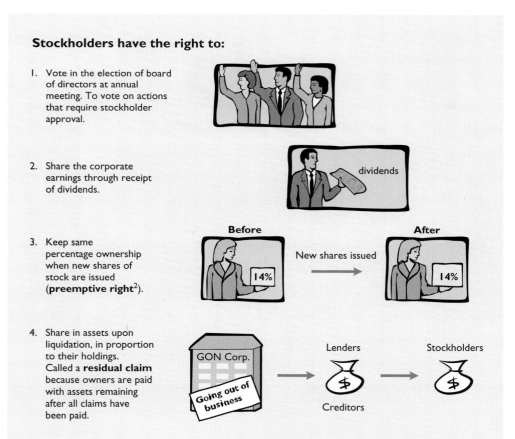

Stockholders have the right to:

1. Vote in the election of board of directors at annual meeting. To vote on actions that require stockholder approval.

2. Share the corporate earnings through receipt of dividends.

3. Keep same percentage ownership when new shares of stock are issued (**preemptive right**[2]).

4. Share in assets upon liquidation, in proportion to their holdings. Called a **residual claim** because owners are paid with assets remaining after all claims have been paid.

Illustration 14-3

Ownership rights of stockholders

---

[2] A number of companies have eliminated the preemptive right, because they believe it makes an unnecessary and cumbersome demand on management. For example, by stockholder approval, **IBM** has dropped its preemptive right for stockholders.

ACCOUNTING IN ACTION *International Insight*

In Japan, stockholders are considered to be far less important to a corporation than employees, customers, and suppliers. There, stockholders are rarely asked to vote on an issue, and the notion of bending corporate policy to favor stockholders borders on the heretical. This attitude toward stockholders appears to be slowly changing, however, as influential Japanese are advocating listening to investors, raising the extremely low dividends paid by Japanese corporations, and improving disclosure of financial information.

Proof of stock ownership is evidenced by a form known as a **stock certificate**. As shown in Illustration 14-4, the face of the certificate shows the name of the corporation, the stockholder's name, the class and special features of the stock, the number of shares owned, and the signatures of duly authorized corporate officials. Certificates are prenumbered to facilitate accountability. They may be issued for any quantity of shares.

Illustration 14-4

A stock certificate

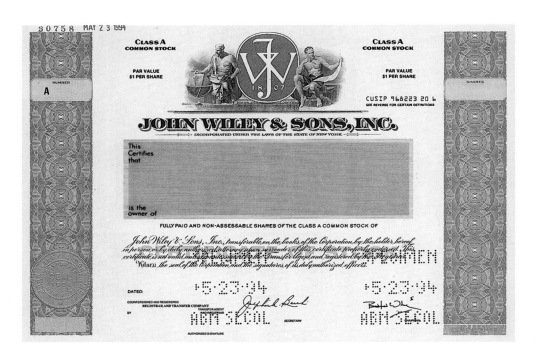

BEFORE YOU GO ON...

▶ *REVIEW IT*
1. What are the advantages and disadvantages of a corporation compared to a proprietorship and a partnership?
2. Identify the principal steps in forming a corporation.
3. What rights are inherent in owning a share of stock in a corporation?

THE NAVIGATOR

STOCK ISSUE CONSIDERATIONS

In considering the issuance of stock, a corporation must resolve a number of basic questions: How many shares should be authorized for sale? How should the stock be issued? At what price should the shares be issued? What value should be assigned to the stock? These questions are answered in the following sections.

Authorized Stock

The amount of stock that a corporation is **authorized** to sell is indicated in its charter. The total amount of authorized stock at the time of incorporation normally anticipates both initial and subsequent capital needs. As a result, the number of shares authorized generally exceeds the number initially sold. If all authorized stock is sold, a corporation must obtain consent of the state to amend its charter before it can issue additional shares.

The authorization of capital stock does not result in a formal accounting entry. This event has no immediate effect on either corporate assets or stockholders' equity. But, disclosure of the number of authorized shares is often reported in the stockholders' equity section. It is then simple to determine the number of unissued shares that can be issued without amending the charter: subtract the total shares issued from the total authorized. For example, if Advanced Micro was authorized to sell 100,000 shares of common stock and issued 80,000 shares, 20,000 shares would remain unissued.

Issuance of Stock

A corporation can issue common stock **directly** to investors. Or it can issue the stock **indirectly** through an investment banking firm (brokerage house) that specializes in bringing securities to the attention of prospective investors. Direct issue is typical in closely held companies. Indirect issue is customary for a publicly held corporation.

In an indirect issue, the investment banking firm may agree to **underwrite** the entire stock issue. In this arrangement, the investment banker buys the stock from the corporation at a stipulated price and resells the shares to investors. The corporation thus avoids any risk of being unable to sell the shares. Also, it obtains immediate use of the cash received from the underwriter. The investment banking firm, in turn, assumes the risk of reselling the shares in return for an underwriting fee.[3] For example, Kolff Medical, maker of the Jarvik artificial heart, used an underwriter to help it issue common stock to the public. The underwriter charged a 6.6 percent underwriting fee on Kolff Medical's approximately $20 million public offering.

How does a corporation set the price for a new issue of stock? Among the factors to be considered are (1) the company's anticipated future earnings, (2) its expected dividend rate per share, (3) its current financial position, (4) the current state of the economy, and (5) the current state of the securities market. The calculation can be complex and is properly the subject of a finance course.

Indirect Issuance

Market Value of Stock

The stock of publicly held companies is traded on organized exchanges. The dollar prices per share are established by the interaction between buyers and sellers.

---

[3]Alternatively, the investment banking firm may agree only to enter into a **best efforts** contract with the corporation. In such cases, the banker agrees to sell as many shares as possible at a specified price. The corporation bears the risk of unsold stock. Under a best efforts arrangement, the banking firm is paid a fee or commission for its services.

In general, the prices set by the marketplace tend to follow the trend of a company's earnings and dividends. But, factors beyond a company's control, such as an oil embargo, changes in interest rates, and the outcome of a presidential election, may cause day-to-day fluctuations in market prices.

*A*CCOUNTING IN ACTION *Business Insight*

The volume of trading on national and international exchanges is heavy. Shares in excess of 800 million are often traded daily on the New York Stock Exchange alone. For each listed stock, the financial press reports the total volume of stock traded for a given day, the high and low price for the day (now in decimals), the closing market price, and the net change for the day. A recent listing for **Lands' End** is shown below.

Stock	Volume	High	Low	Close	Net Change
LandsEnd	3478	28^{38}	26^{63}	26^{94}	-1^{19}

These numbers indicate that Lands' End's trading volume was 347,800 shares. The high, low, and closing prices for that date were $28.38, $26.63, and $26.94, respectively. The net change for the day was a decrease of $1.19 per share.

The trading of capital stock on securities exchanges involves the transfer of **already issued shares** from an existing stockholder to another investor. These transactions have no impact on a corporation's stockholders' equity.

*T*ECHNOLOGY IN ACTION

Giant, publicly held corporations could not exist without the organized stock markets, and the stock markets could not exist without massive computerization. Not too many years ago, the NYSE "ticker" would run behind, or trading would even be halted, when sales exceeded 30 million shares or so. Now, with sales sometimes in excess of 800 million shares, the NYSE and its companion exchanges throughout the country operate efficiently with computer technology. Technology has also made possible extended trading hours. An investor in New York can trade electronically at 3:30 A.M., which is the time in New York when the London Stock Exchange opens. Some predict that 24-hour trading is not far off.

Par and No-Par Value Stocks

Par value stock is capital stock that has been assigned a value per share in the corporate charter. The par value may be any amount selected by the corporation. Generally, the par value is quite low, because states often levy a tax on the corporation based on par value. For example, **Eastman Kodak** has a par of $2.50, **Ford Motor Company** has a $1 par, **PepsiCo** has a $1\frac{2}{3}$ cents par, and **America Online** has a 1 cent par.

Par value does not indicate the worth or market value of the stock. **IBM** has a par value of $1.25, but its recent market price was $120 per share. **Par**

value has legal significance. It represents the legal capital per share that must be retained in the business for the protection of corporate creditors. That amount is not available for withdrawal by stockholders. Thus, most states require the corporation to sell its shares at par or above.

No-par value stock is capital stock that has not been assigned a value in the corporate charter. It is often issued because some confusion still exists concerning par value and fair market value. If shares are not assigned a par value, the questionable use of par value as a basis for fair market value never arises. The major disadvantage of no-par value stock is that some states levy a high tax on such shares.

No-par value stock is quite common today. For example, **Procter & Gamble** and **North American Van Lines** both have no-par stock. In many states the board of directors is permitted to assign a stated value to the no-par shares. This value becomes the legal capital per share. The stated value of no-par stock may be changed at any time by action of the directors. Stated value, like par value, does not indicate the market value of the stock. When there is no assigned stated value, the entire proceeds received upon issuance of the stock is considered to be legal capital.

The relationship of par and no-par value to legal capital is shown below.

Stock	Legal Capital per Share
Par value ————————————→	Par value
No-par value with stated value ———→	Stated value
No-par value without stated value ——→	Entire proceeds

Illustration 14-5

Relationship of par and no-par value stock to legal capital

CORPORATE CAPITAL

Owners' equity is identified as **stockholders' equity**, **shareholders' equity**, or **corporate capital**. The stockholders' equity section of a corporation's balance sheet consists of: (1) paid-in (contributed) capital and (2) retained earnings (earned capital). The distinction between paid-in capital and retained earnings is important from both a legal and a financial point of view. Legally, distributions of earnings (dividends) can be declared out of retained earnings in all states, but in many states they cannot be declared out of paid-in capital. Financially, management, stockholders, and others look to earnings for the continued existence and growth of the corporation.

STUDY OBJECTIVE 2

Differentiate between paid-in capital and retained earnings.

Paid-in Capital

Paid-in capital is the total amount of cash and other assets paid in to the corporation by stockholders in exchange for capital stock. As noted earlier, when a corporation has only one class of stock, it is identified as **common stock**.

Retained Earnings

Retained earnings is net income that is retained in a corporation. Net income is recorded in Retained Earnings by a closing entry in which Income Summary is debited and Retained Earnings is credited. For example, assuming that net income for Delta Robotics in its first year of operations is $130,000, the closing entry is:

Income Summary	130,000	
Retained Earnings		130,000
(To close income summary and transfer net income to retained earnings)		

A	=	L	+	SE
				−130,000
				+130,000

If Delta Robotics has a balance of $800,000 in common stock at the end of its first year, its stockholders' equity section is as follows.

Illustration 14-6

Stockholders' equity section

DELTA ROBOTICS Balance Sheet (partial)		
Stockholders' equity		
Paid-in-capital		
Common stock	$800,000	
Retained earnings	130,000	
Total stockholders' equity		**$930,000**

The following illustration compares the owners' equity (stockholders' equity) accounts reported on a balance sheet for a proprietorship, a partnership, and a corporation.

Illustration 14-7

Comparison of owners' equity accounts

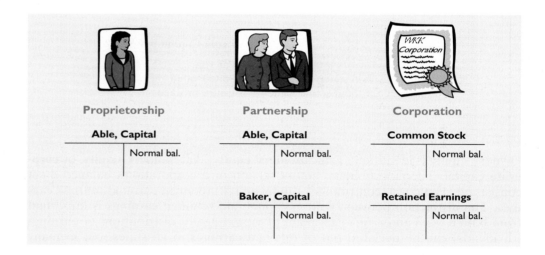

BEFORE YOU GO ON...

▶ *REVIEW IT*

1. Of what significance to a corporation is the amount of authorized stock?
2. What alternative approaches may a corporation use in issuing stock?
3. Distinguish between par value and fair market value.

▶ *DO IT*

At the end of its first year of operation, Doral Corporation has $750,000 of common stock and net income of $122,000. Prepare (a) the closing entry for net income and (b) the stockholders' equity section at year-end.

ACTION PLAN

- Record net income in Retained Earnings by a closing entry in which Income Summary is debited and Retained Earnings is credited.
- In the stockholders' equity section, show (1) paid-in capital and (2) retained earnings.

SOLUTION

(a) Income Summary | 122,000 |
      Retained Earnings | | 122,000
        (To close income summary and transfer net
        income to retained earnings)

(b) Stockholders' equity
      Paid-in capital
        Common stock | $750,000
      Retained earnings | 122,000
        Total stockholders' equity | | $872,000

Related exercise material: BE14-2, BE14-8, E14-5, and E14-9.

✓ THE NAVIGATOR

ACCOUNTING FOR COMMON STOCK ISSUES

Let's now look at how to account for issues of common stock. The primary objectives in accounting for the issuance of common stock are: (1) to identify the specific sources of paid-in capital and (2) to maintain the distinction between paid-in capital and retained earnings. **The issuance of common stock affects only paid-in capital accounts.**

STUDY OBJECTIVE 3

Record the issuance of common stock.

ISSUING PAR VALUE COMMON STOCK FOR CASH

As discussed earlier, par value does not indicate a stock's market value. Therefore, the cash proceeds from issuing par value stock may be equal to, greater than, or less than par value. When the issuance of common stock for cash is recorded, the par value of the shares is credited to Common Stock. The portion of the proceeds that is above or below par value is recorded in a separate paid-in capital account.

To illustrate, assume that Hydro-Slide, Inc. issues 1,000 shares of $1 par value common stock at par for cash. The entry to record this transaction is:

Cash | 1,000 |
    Common Stock | | 1,000
      (To record issuance of 1,000 shares of $1 par common
      stock at par)

$$A = L + SE$$
$$+1,000 \qquad +1,000$$

If Hydro-Slide issues an additional 1,000 shares of the $1 par value common stock for cash at $5 per share, the entry is:

ALTERNATIVE TERMINOLOGY
Paid-in Capital in Excess of Par is also called *Premium on Stock.*

Cash | 5,000 |
    Common Stock | | 1,000
    Paid-in Capital in Excess of Par Value | | 4,000
      (To record issuance of 1,000 shares of common stock in
      excess of par)

$$A = L + SE$$
$$+5,000 \qquad +1,000$$
$$+4,000$$

The total paid-in capital from these two transactions is $6,000, and the legal capital is $2,000. If Hydro-Slide, Inc. has retained earnings of $27,000, the stockholders' equity section is shown in Illustration 14-8.

Illustration 14-8

Stockholders' equity—
paid-in capital in excess of
par value

HYDRO-SLIDE, INC. Balance Sheet (partial)		
Stockholders' equity		
Paid-in-capital		
Common stock	$ 2,000	
Paid-in capital in excess of par value	4,000	
Total paid-in capital	6,000	
Retained earnings	27,000	
Total stockholders' equity	$33,000	

When stock is issued for less than par value, the account Paid-in Capital in Excess of Par Value is debited, if a credit balance exists in this account. If a credit balance does not exist, then the amount less than par is debited to Retained Earnings. This situation occurs only rarely: The sale of common stock below par value is not permitted in most states, because stockholders may be held personally liable for the difference between the price paid upon original sale and par value.

ISSUING NO-PAR COMMON STOCK FOR CASH

When no-par common stock has a stated value, the entries are similar to those illustrated for par value stock. The stated value represents legal capital. Therefore it is credited to Common Stock. Also, when the selling price of no-par stock exceeds stated value, the excess is credited to Paid-in Capital in Excess of Stated Value. For example, assume that instead of $1 par value stock, Hydro-Slide, Inc. has $5 stated value no-par stock and the company issues 5,000 shares at $8 per share for cash. The entry is:

A	=	L	+	SE
+40,000				+25,000
				+15,000

Cash	40,000	
Common Stock		25,000
Paid-in Capital in Excess of Stated Value		15,000
(To record issue of 5,000 shares of $5 stated value no- par stock)		

Paid-in Capital in Excess of Stated Value is reported as part of paid-in capital in the stockholders' equity section.

What happens when no-par stock does not have a stated value? In that case, the entire proceeds from the issue become legal capital and are credited to Common Stock. Thus, if Hydro-Slide does not assign a stated value to its no-par stock, the issuance of the 5,000 shares at $8 per share for cash is recorded as follows.

A	=	L	+	SE
+40,000				+40,000

Cash	40,000	
Common Stock		40,000
(To record issue of 5,000 shares of no-par stock)		

The amount of legal capital for Hydro-Slide stock with a $5 stated value is $25,000. Without a stated value, it is $40,000.

ISSUING COMMON STOCK FOR SERVICES OR NONCASH ASSETS

Stock may also be issued for services (compensation to attorneys or consultants) or for noncash assets (land, buildings, and equipment). In such cases, what cost should be recognized in the exchange transaction? To comply with the **cost prin-**

ciple, in a noncash transaction **cost is the cash equivalent price**. Thus, **cost is either the fair market value of the consideration given up**, or the fair market value of the consideration received, whichever is more clearly determinable.

To illustrate, assume that attorneys have helped Jordan Company incorporate. They have billed the company $5,000 for their services. They agree to accept 4,000 shares of $1 par value common stock in payment of their bill. At the time of the exchange, there is no established market price for the stock. In this case, the market value of the consideration received, $5,000, is more clearly evident. Accordingly, the entry is:

Organization Expense	5,000	
Common Stock		4,000
Paid-in Capital in Excess of Par Value		1,000
(To record issuance of 4,000 shares of $1 par value		
stock to attorneys)		

```
A   =   L   +   SE
              -5,000
              +4,000
              +1,000
```

As explained on page 565, organization costs are expensed as incurred.

In contrast, assume that Athletic Research Inc. is an existing publicly held corporation. Its $5 par value stock is actively traded at $8 per share. The company issues 10,000 shares of stock to acquire land recently advertised for sale at $90,000. The most clearly evident value in this noncash transaction is the market price of the consideration given, $80,000. The transaction is recorded as follows.

Land	80,000	
Common Stock		50,000
Paid-in Capital in Excess of Par Value		30,000
(To record issuance of 10,000 shares of $5 par value		
stock for land)		

```
A        =   L   +   SE
+80,000            +50,000
                   +30,000
```

As illustrated in these examples, **the par value of the stock is never a factor in determining the cost of the assets received**. This is also true of the stated value of no-par stock.

BEFORE YOU GO ON...

▶ *REVIEW IT*
1. Explain the accounting for par and no-par common stock issued for cash.
2. Explain the accounting for the issuance of stock for services or noncash assets.
3. What is the par or stated value per share of **Lands' End's** common stock? How many shares has Lands' End issued at January 28, 2000? The answers to these questions are provided on page 598.

▶ *DO IT*
Cayman Corporation begins operations on March 1 by issuing 100,000 shares of $10 par value common stock for cash at $12 per share. On March 15 it issues 5,000 shares of common stock to attorneys in settlement of their bill of $50,000 for organization costs. Journalize the issuance of the shares, assuming the stock is not publicly traded.

ACTION PLAN
- In issuing shares for cash, credit Common Stock for par value per share.
- Credit any additional proceeds in excess of par value to a separate paid-in capital account.
- When stock is issued for services, use the cash equivalent price.
- For the cash equivalent price use either the fair market value of what is given up or the fair market value of what is received, whichever is more clearly determinable.

SOLUTION

Mar. 1	Cash		1,200,000	
	Common Stock			1,000,000
	Paid-in Capital in Excess of Par Value			200,000
	(To record issuance of 100,000 shares at $12 per share)			
Mar. 15	Organization Expense		50,000	
	Common Stock			50,000
	(To record issuance of 5,000 shares for attorneys' fees)			

Related exercise material: BE14-3, BE14-4, BE14-5, E14-1, E14-2, E14-3, E14-7, and E14-8.

☑ THE NAVIGATOR

Accounting for Treasury Stock

STUDY OBJECTIVE 4

Explain the accounting for treasury stock.

HELPFUL HINT

Treasury stock is so named because the company often holds the shares in its treasury for safekeeping.

HELPFUL HINT

Treasury shares do not have dividend rights or voting rights.

Treasury stock is a corporation's own stock that has been issued, fully paid for, and reacquired by the corporation but not retired. A corporation may acquire treasury stock for various reasons:

1. To reissue the shares to officers and employees under bonus and stock compensation plans.
2. To increase trading of the company's stock in the securities market in the hopes of enhancing its market value.
3. To have additional shares available for use in the acquisition of other companies.
4. To reduce the number of shares outstanding and thereby increase earnings per share.
5. To rid the company of disgruntled investors, perhaps to avoid a takeover, as illustrated in the **Ford Motor Company** Feature Story.

Many corporations have treasury stock. One survey of 600 companies in the United States found that 65 percent have treasury stock.[4] Specifically, **The Gillette Company** recently reported 299 million treasury shares, **The Coca-Cola Company** 994.7 million shares, and **United Airlines** 14.9 million shares.

PURCHASE OF TREASURY STOCK

Treasury stock is generally accounted for by **the cost method**. This method uses the cost of the shares purchased to value the treasury stock. Under the cost method, **Treasury Stock is debited for the price paid to reacquire the shares**. **The same amount is credited to Treasury Stock when the shares are disposed of.** To illustrate, assume that on January 1, 2002, the stockholders' equity section of Mead, Inc. has 100,000 shares of $5 par value common stock outstanding (all

---

[4]*Accounting Trends & Techniques 2000* (New York: American Institute of Certified Public Accountants).

ACCOUNTING IN ACTION   *Business Insight*

In a bold (and some would say risky) move in late 1996, **Reebok** bought back nearly a *third* of its shares. This repurchase of shares dramatically reduced Reebok's available cash. In fact, the company borrowed significant funds to accomplish the repurchase. In a press release, management stated that it was repurchasing the shares because it believed its stock was severely underpriced. The repurchase of so many shares was meant to signal management's belief in good future earnings.

Skeptics, however, suggested that Reebok's management was repurchasing shares to make it less likely that the company would be acquired by another company (in which case Reebok's top managers would likely lose their jobs). By depleting its cash, Reebok became a less likely acquisition target. Acquiring companies like to purchase companies with large cash reserves so they can pay off debt used in the acquisition.

issued at par value) and Retained Earnings of $200,000. The stockholders' equity section before purchase of treasury stock is as follows.

MEAD, INC. Balance Sheet (partial)	
Stockholders' equity	
Paid-in capital	
Common stock, $5 par value, 100,000 shares	
issued and outstanding	$500,000
Retained earnings	200,000
Total stockholders' equity	$700,000

Illustration 14-9

Stockholders' equity with no treasury stock

On February 1, 2002, Mead acquires 4,000 shares of its stock at $8 per share. The entry is:

Feb. 1	Treasury Stock	32,000	
	Cash		32,000
	(To record purchase of 4,000 shares		
	of treasury stock at $8 per share)		

A	=	L	+	SE
−32,000				−32,000

Note that Treasury Stock is debited for the cost of the shares purchased. Is the original paid-in capital account, Common Stock, affected? No, because the number of issued shares does not change. In the stockholders' equity section of the balance sheet, treasury stock is deducted from total paid-in capital and retained earnings. Treasury Stock is a contra stockholders' equity account.

The stockholders' equity section of Mead, Inc. after purchase of treasury stock is as follows.

Illustration 14-10

Stockholders' equity with
treasury stock

MEAD, INC. **Balance Sheet (partial)**	
Stockholders' equity	
Paid-in capital	
Common stock, $5 par value, 100,000 shares issued	
and 96,000 shares outstanding	$500,000
Retained earnings	200,000
Total paid-in capital and retained earnings	700,000
Less: Treasury stock (4,000 shares)	32,000
Total stockholders' equity	$668,000

Thus, the acquisition of treasury stock reduces stockholders' equity.

In the balance sheet, both the number of shares issued (100,000) and the number in the treasury (4,000) are disclosed. The difference between these two amounts is the number of shares of stock outstanding (96,000). The term **outstanding stock** means the number of shares of issued stock that are being held by stockholders.

Some maintain that treasury stock should be reported as an asset because it can be sold for cash. Under this reasoning, unissued stock should also be shown as an asset, clearly an erroneous conclusion. Rather than being an asset, treasury stock reduces stockholder claims on corporate assets. This effect is correctly shown by reporting treasury stock as a deduction from total paid-in capital and retained earnings.

DISPOSAL OF TREASURY STOCK

Treasury stock is usually sold or retired. The accounting for its sale is different when treasury stock is sold above cost than when it is sold below cost.

Sale of Treasury Stock above Cost

If the selling price of the treasury shares is equal to cost, the sale of the shares is recorded by a debit to Cash and a credit to Treasury Stock. When the selling price of the shares is greater than cost, the difference is credited to Paid-in Capital from Treasury Stock.

To illustrate, assume that 1,000 shares of treasury stock of Mead, Inc., previously acquired at $8 per share, are sold at $10 per share on July 1. The entry is as follows.

A	=	L	+	SE
+10,000				+8,000
				+2,000

July 1	Cash	10,000	
	Treasury Stock		8,000
	Paid-in Capital from Treasury Stock		2,000
	(To record sale of 1,000 shares of treasury stock above cost)		

The $2,000 credit in the entry would not be considered a gain on sale of treasury stock for two reasons: (1) Gains on sales occur when **assets** are sold, and treasury stock is not an asset. (2) A corporation does not realize a gain or suffer a loss from stock transactions with its own stockholders. Thus, paid-in capital arising from the sale of treasury stock should not be included in the measurement of net income. Paid-in Capital from Treasury Stock is listed separately on the balance sheet as a part of paid-in capital.

Sale of Treasury Stock below Cost

When treasury stock is sold below its cost, the excess of cost over selling price is usually debited to Paid-in Capital from Treasury Stock. Thus, if Mead, Inc. sells an additional 800 shares of treasury stock on October 1 at $7 per share, the entry is as follows.

Oct. 1	Cash		5,600	
	Paid-in Capital from Treasury Stock		800	
	Treasury Stock			6,400
	(To record sale of 800 shares of treasury			
	stock below cost)			

A	=	L	+	SE
+5,600				−800
				+6,400

Observe the following from the two sales entries: (1) Treasury Stock is credited at cost in each entry. (2) Paid-in Capital from Treasury Stock is used for the difference between cost and the resale price of the shares. And (3) the original paid-in capital account, Common Stock, is not affected. **The sale of treasury stock increases both total assets and total stockholders' equity.**

After posting the foregoing entries, the treasury stock accounts will show the following balances on October 1.

Treasury Stock					**Paid-in Capital from Treasury Stock**			
Feb. 1	32,000	July 1	8,000		Oct. 1	800	July 1	2,000
		Oct. 1	6,400					
							Oct. 1 Bal.	1,200
Oct. 1 Bal. 17,600								

Illustration 14-11

Treasury stock accounts

When the credit balance in Paid-in Capital from Treasury Stock is eliminated, any additional excess of cost over selling price is debited to Retained Earnings. To illustrate, assume that Mead, Inc. sells its remaining 2,200 shares at $7 per share on December 1. The excess of cost over selling price is $2,200 [2,200 × ($8 − $7)]. In this case, $1,200 of the excess is debited to Paid-in Capital from Treasury Stock. The remainder is debited to Retained Earnings. The entry is:

Dec. 1	Cash		15,400	
	Paid-in Capital from Treasury Stock		1,200	
	Retained Earning		1,000	
	Treasury Stock			17,600
	(To record sale of 2,200 shares of treasury			
	stock at $7 per share)			

A	=	L	+	SE
+15,400				−1,200
				−1,000
				+17,600

BEFORE YOU GO ON...

▶ *REVIEW IT*

1. What is treasury stock, and why do companies acquire it?
2. How is treasury stock recorded?
3. Where is treasury stock reported in the financial statements? Does a company record gains and losses on treasury stock transactions? Explain.
4. How many shares of treasury stock did **Lands' End** have at January 28, 2000 and at January 29, 1999? What caused the change between 1999 and 2000? The answers to these questions are provided on page 598.

▶ *DO IT*

Santa Anita Inc. purchases 3,000 shares of its $50 par value common stock for $180,000 cash on July 1. The shares are to be held in the treasury until resold. On November 1, the corporation sells 1,000 shares of treasury stock for cash at $70 per share. Journalize the treasury stock transactions.

ACTION PLAN
- Record the purchase of treasury stock at cost.
- When treasury stock is sold above its cost, credit the excess of the selling price over cost to Paid-in Capital from Treasury Stock.
- When treasury stock is sold below its cost, debit the excess of cost over selling price to Paid-in Capital from Treasury Stock.

SOLUTION

July 1	Treasury Stock	180,000	
	Cash		180,000
	(To record the purchase of 3,000 shares at $60 per share)		
Nov. 1	Cash	70,000	
	Treasury Stock		60,000
	Paid-in Capital from Treasury Stock		10,000
	(To record the sale of 1,000 shares at $70 per share)		

Related exercise material: BE14-6, E14-2, E14-4, E14-7, and E14-8.

☑ THE NAVIGATOR

PREFERRED STOCK

STUDY OBJECTIVE 5

Differentiate preferred stock from common stock.

To appeal to more potential investors, a corporation may issue an additional class of stock, called preferred stock. **Preferred stock** has contractual provisions that give it a preference or priority over common stock in certain areas. Typically, preferred stockholders have a priority as to (1) distributions of earnings (dividends) and (2) assets in the event of liquidation. However, they generally do not have voting rights.

Like common stock, preferred stock may be issued for cash or for noncash assets. The entries for these transactions are similar to the entries for common stock. When a corporation has more than one class of stock, each paid-in capital account title should identify the stock to which it relates. For example, a company might have the following accounts: Preferred Stock, Common Stock, Paid-in Capital in Excess of Par Value—Preferred Stock, and Paid-in Capital in Excess of Par Value—Common Stock. Assume that Stine Corporation issues 10,000 shares of $10 par value preferred stock for $12 cash per share. The entry to record the issuance is:

A = L + SE
+120,000   +100,000
+20,000

Cash	120,000	
Preferred Stock		100,000
Paid-in Capital in Excess of Par Value–Preferred Stock		20,000
(To record the issuance of 10,000 shares of $10 par value preferred stock)		

Preferred stock may have either a par value or no-par value. In the stockholders' equity section of the balance sheet, preferred stock is shown first because of its dividend and liquidation preferences over common stock.

Various features associated with the issuance of preferred stock, including dividend preferences, liquidation preferences, convertibility, and callability, are discussed on the following pages.

DIVIDEND PREFERENCES

As noted earlier, **preferred stockholders have the right to share in the distribution of corporate income before common stockholders**. For example, if the dividend rate on preferred stock is $5 per share, common shareholders will not receive any dividends in the current year until preferred stockholders have received $5 per share. The first claim to dividends does not, however, guarantee the payment of dividends. Dividends depend on many factors, such as adequate retained earnings and availability of cash.

The per share dividend amount is stated as a percentage of the preferred stock's par value or as a specified amount. For example, Crane Company specifies a 3¾ percent dividend on its $100 par value preferred ($100 × 3¾% = $3.75 per share). DuPont has both a $4.50 and a $3.50 series of no-par preferred stock.

I hope there is some money left when it's my turn.

Preferred   Common
stockholders   stockholders

Dividend Preference

Cumulative Dividend

Preferred stock often contains a cumulative dividend feature. This means that preferred stockholders must be paid both current-year dividends and any unpaid prior-year dividends before common stockholders receive dividends. When preferred stock is cumulative, preferred dividends not declared in a given period are called **dividends in arrears**.

To illustrate, assume that Scientific-Leasing has 5,000 shares of 7 percent, $100 par value, cumulative preferred stock outstanding. The annual dividend is $35,000 (5,000 × $7 per share), but dividends are two years in arrears. In this case preferred stockholders are entitled to receive the following dividends in the current year.

Dividends in arrears ($35,000 × 2)	$ 70,000
Current-year dividends	35,000
Total preferred dividends	**$105,000**

Illustration 14-12

Computation of total dividends to preferred stock

No distribution can be made to common stockholders until this entire preferred dividend is paid. In other words, dividends cannot be paid to common stockholders while any preferred stock is in arrears.

ACCOUNTING IN ACTION *Business Insight*

Dividends in arrears can extend for fairly long periods of time. Long Island Lighting Company's directors voted at one time to make up some $390 million in preferred dividends that had been in arrears for nearly ten years and to resume normal quarterly preferred payments. The announcement resulted from an agreement between the company and New York State. The company agreed to abandon a nuclear power plant in exchange for sizable rate increases over the next ten years.

Dividends in arrears are not considered a liability. No payment obligation exists until a dividend is declared by the board of directors. However, the amount of dividends in arrears should be disclosed in the notes to the financial statements. Doing so enables investors to assess the potential impact of this commitment on the corporation's financial position.

Companies that are unable to meet their dividend obligations are not looked upon favorably by the investment community. As a financial officer noted in discussing one company's failure to pay its cumulative preferred dividend for a

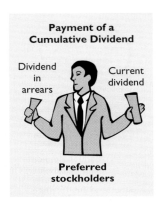

**Payment of a
Cumulative Dividend**

Dividend in arrears — Current dividend

**Preferred
stockholders**

period of time, "Not meeting your obligations on something like that is a major black mark on your record." The accounting entries for preferred stock dividends are explained in Chapter 15.

LIQUIDATION PREFERENCE

Most preferred stocks also have a preference on corporate assets if the corporation fails. This feature provides security for the preferred stockholder. The preference to assets may be for the par value of the shares or for a specified liquidating value. **Commonwealth Edison's** preferred stock entitles the holders to receive $31.80 per share, plus accrued and unpaid dividends, in the event of involuntary liquidation. The liquidation preference establishes the respective claims of creditors and preferred stockholders.

CONVERTIBLE PREFERRED STOCK

Preferred stock is enhanced as an investment by adding a conversion privilege. **Convertible preferred stock** provides for the exchange of preferred stock into common stock, at a specified ratio, at the stockholder's option.

Convertible preferred stock is purchased by investors who want the greater security of a preferred stock, but who also want to be able to capture the market value of the common stock if it increases significantly. To illustrate, assume that Ross Industries issues, at par value, 1,000 shares of $100 par value convertible preferred stock. One share of preferred is convertible into 10 shares of $5 par value common (current price $9 per share). At this point, holders of the preferred would not want to convert. Their preferred stock is worth $100,000 (1,000 × $100), and the common stock is worth only $90,000 (10,000 × $9). However, if the price of the common stock increases above $10 per share, conversion would be advantageous for the preferred holders.

In recording the conversion, it is customary to transfer the amount paid in on the preferred stock to appropriate common stock accounts. To illustrate, assume that the 1,000 shares of Ross Industries $100 par preferred are issued at $105 and are converted into 10,000 shares of common stock ($5 par) when the market values per share of the two classes of stock are $101 and $12, respectively. The entry to record the conversion is:

A = L + SE		
−100,000		
−5,000		
+50,000		
+55,000		

Preferred Stock	100,000	
Paid-in Capital in Excess of Par Value—Preferred Stock	5,000	
Common Stock		50,000
Paid-in Capital in Excess of Par Value—Common Stock		55,000
(To record conversion of 1,000 shares of preferred stock into 10,000 shares of $5 par value common stock)		

The market values of the shares at the time of the transaction are not considered in recording the transaction. The reason is that the exchange of shares is made directly through the corporation, and the corporation has not received any assets equal to fair market value. **Therefore, the conversion of preferred stock does not result in either gain or loss to the corporation.** If the preferred stock was issued for more than its par value, the paid-in capital in excess of the par value on the preferred stock should be eliminated.

CALLABLE PREFERRED STOCK

Many preferred stocks are issued with a call feature. A **callable preferred stock** grants the issuing corporation the right to purchase the stock from stockholders at specified future dates and prices. The call feature enables a corporation to eliminate the preferred stock when it is advantageous to do so. The **call (or redemption) price** is frequently slightly above the par or stated value of the shares. Often shares that are callable are also convertible. Sometimes companies will call their preferred shares to induce investors to convert those preferred shares into common stock.

STATEMENT PRESENTATION AND ANALYSIS

In the stockholders' equity section of the balance sheet, paid-in capital and retained earnings are reported. The specific sources of paid-in capital are identified. Within paid-in capital, two classifications are recognized:

1. **Capital stock.** This category consists of preferred and common stock. Preferred stock is shown before common stock because of its preferential rights. Par value, shares authorized, shares issued, and shares outstanding are reported for each class of stock.

2. **Additional paid-in capital.** This includes the excess of amounts paid in over par or stated value and paid-in capital from treasury stock.

STUDY OBJECTIVE 6

Prepare a stockholders' equity section.

PRESENTATION

The stockholders' equity section of Connally Inc. in Illustration 14-13 includes most of the accounts discussed in this chapter. The disclosures pertaining to Connally's common stock indicate that: 400,000 shares are issued; 100,000 shares are unissued (500,000 authorized less 400,000 issued); and 390,000 shares are outstanding (400,000 issued less 10,000 shares in treasury).

ALTERNATIVE TERMINOLOGY
Paid-in capital is sometimes called *contributed capital.*

Illustration 14-13
Stockholders' equity section

CONNALLY INC. Balance Sheet (partial)		
Stockholders' equity		
Paid-in capital		
Capital stock		
9% preferred stock, $100 par value, callable at $120, cumulative, 10,000 shares authorized, 6,000 shares issued and outstanding		$ 600,000
Common stock, no par, $5 stated value, 500,000 shares authorized, 400,000 shares issued, and 390,000 outstanding		2,000,000
Total capital stock		2,600,000
Additional paid-in capital		
In excess of par value—preferred stock	$ 30,000	
In excess of stated value—common stock	860,000	
From treasury stock	140,000	
Total additional paid-in capital		1,030,000
Total paid-in capital		3,630,000
Retained earnings		1,058,000
Total paid-in capital and retained earnings		4,688,000
Less: Treasury stock—common (10,000 shares) (at cost)		(80,000)
Total stockholders' equity		$4,608,000

In published annual reports, the individual sources of additional paid-in capital are often combined and reported as a single amount, as shown in Illustration 14-14. In addition, authorized shares are sometimes not reported.

Illustration 14-14

Published stockholders' equity section

KELLOGG COMPANY Balance Sheet (partial) (in millions)	
Stockholders' equity	
Common stock, $0.25 par value, 500,000,000 shares authorized	
Issued: 415,343 shares	$ 103.8
Capital in excess of par value	105.0
Retained earnings	1,367.7
Treasury stock, at cost	
10,346,524 shares	(394.3)
Accumulated other comprehensive income	(292.4)
Total stockholders' equity	$ 889.8

In practice, the term "capital surplus" is sometimes used in place of additional paid-in capital and "earned surplus" in place of retained earnings. The use of the term "surplus" suggests that an excess amount of funds is available. Such is not necessarily the case. Therefore, **the term "surplus" should not be employed in accounting**. Unfortunately, a number of financial statements still do use it.

ANALYSIS—BOOK VALUE PER SHARE

STUDY OBJECTIVE 7

Compute book value per share.

You have learned about a number of per share amounts in this chapter. Another per share amount of some importance is book value per share. It represents **the equity a common stockholder has in the net assets of the corporation** from owning one share of stock. Remember that the net assets of a corporation must be equal to total stockholders' equity. Therefore, the formula for computing book value per share when a company has only one class of stock outstanding is:

Illustration 14-15

Book value per share formula

Thus, if Marlo Corporation has total stockholders' equity of $1,500,000 (common stock $1,000,000 and retained earnings $500,000) and 50,000 shares of common stock outstanding, book value per share is $30 ($1,500,000 ÷ 50,000).

When a company has both preferred and common stock, the computation of book value is a bit more complex. Since preferred stockholders have a prior claim on net assets over common stockholders, their equity must be deducted from total stockholders' equity. Then we can determine the stockholders' equity that applies to the common stock. The computation of book value per share involves the following steps.

1. **Compute the preferred stock equity.** This equity is equal to the sum of the call price of preferred stock plus any cumulative dividends in arrears. If the preferred stock does not have a call price, the par value of the stock is used.

2. **Determine the common stock equity.** Subtract the preferred stock equity from total stockholders' equity.

3. **Determine book value per share.** Divide common stock equity by shares of common stock outstanding.

Illustration

We will use the stockholders' equity section of Connally Inc. shown in Illustration 14-13. Connally's preferred stock is callable at $120 per share and cumulative. Assume that dividends on Connally's preferred stock were in arrears for one year, $54,000 (6,000 × $9). The computation of preferred stock equity (Step 1) is:

Call price (6,000 shares × $120)	$720,000
Dividends in arrears (6,000 shares × $9)	54,000
Preferred stock equity	**$774,000**

Illustration 14-16

Computation of preferred stock equity—Step 1

The computation of book value (Steps 2 and 3) is as follows.

Total stockholders' equity	$4,608,000
Less: Preferred stock equity	774,000
Common stock equity	**$3,834,000**
Shares of common stock outstanding	390,000
Book value per share ($3,834,000 ÷ 390,000)	**$9.83**

Illustration 14-17

Computation of book value per share with preferred stock—Steps 2 and 3

Note that we used the call price of $120 instead of the par value of $100. Note also that the paid-in capital in excess of par value of preferred stock, $30,000, **is not assigned to the preferred stock equity.** Preferred stockholders ordinarily do not have a right to amounts paid-in in excess of par value. Therefore, such amounts are assigned to the common stock equity in computing book value.

Book Value versus Market Value

Be sure you understand that **book value per share may not equal market value per share**. Book value generally is based on recorded costs. Market value reflects the subjective judgments of thousands of stockholders and prospective investors about a company's potential for future earnings and dividends. Market value per share may exceed book value per share, but that fact does not necessarily mean that the stock is overpriced. The correlation between book value and the annual range of a company's market value per share is often remote, as indicated by the following recent data.

Company	Book Value (year-end)	Market Range (for year)
Limited, Inc.	$9.99	$30.50–$50.13
H. J. Heinz Company	$5.02	$44.56–$61.75
Cisco Systems	$3.57	$21.94–$67.06
Lands' End	$9.82	$28.00–$83.50

Illustration 14-18

Book and market values compared

Book value per share **is useful** in determining the trend of a stockholder's per share equity in a corporation. It is also significant in many contracts and in court cases where the rights of individual parties are based on cost information.

BEFORE YOU GO ON...

▶ *REVIEW IT*

1. Identify the classifications within the paid-in capital section and the totals that are stated in the stockholders' equity section of a balance sheet.

2. What is the method for computing book value per share when there is (a) only one class of stock and (b) both preferred and common stock?

A LOOK BACK AT OUR FEATURE STORY

Refer back to the Feature Story about **Ford Motor Company** at the beginning of the chapter, and answer the following questions.

1. Why did Henry Ford originally choose to form a corporation rather than a sole proprietorship?

2. Why did Ford Motor Company repurchase all of its shares?

3. What advantages and disadvantages of being organized as a corporation are illustrated by Ford?

SOLUTION

1. Henry Ford wanted to take full advantage of mass-production. This would require large factories and many employees, which would in turn require considerable funds. The most efficient way to raise these funds was to issue stock.

2. Ford Motor Company initiated a massive treasury stock purchase when Henry Ford's vision was not consistent with the wishes of the shareholders.

3. The history of Ford Motor Company illustrates a number of the strengths and weaknesses of being formed as a corporation. Forming a corporation allowed for more efficient access to funds, and thus more rapid expansion. This was critical because in the early 1900s, many companies were trying to build cars for the U.S. market.

   However, by issuing shares, Henry Ford relinquished control over the firm. This led to a collision in 1916 when he believed that it was in the company's best interest to retain funds in the firm rather than to pay dividends. To the extent that outside shareholders are not as well-informed as a corporation's managers, the shareholders may force management to do things that hinder the firm's success.

☑ THE NAVIGATOR

Additional Demonstration Problem

DEMONSTRATION PROBLEM

The Rolman Corporation is authorized to issue 1,000,000 shares of $5 par value common stock. In its first year, the company has the following stock transactions.

Jan. 10   Issued 400,000 shares of stock at $8 per share.

July 1   Issued 100,000 shares of stock for land. The land had an asking price of $900,000. The stock is currently selling on a national exchange at $8.25 per share.

Sept. 1   Purchased 10,000 shares of common stock for the treasury at $9 per share.

Dec. 1   Sold 4,000 shares of the treasury stock at $10 per share.

Instructions

(a) Journalize the transactions.

(b) Prepare the stockholders' equity section assuming the company had retained earnings of $200,000 at December 31.

SOLUTION TO DEMONSTRATION PROBLEM

(a)	Jan. 10	Cash	3,200,000	
		Common Stock		2,000,000
		Paid-in Capital in Excess of Par Value		1,200,000
		(To record issuance of 400,000 shares of $5 par value stock)		
	July 1	Land	825,000	
		Common Stock		500,000
		Paid-in Capital in Excess of Par Value		325,000
		(To record issuance of 100,000 shares of $5 par value stock for land)		
	Sept. 1	Treasury Stock	90,000	
		Cash		90,000
		(To record purchase of 10,000 shares of treasury stock at cost)		
	Dec. 1	Cash	40,000	
		Treasury Stock		36,000
		Paid-in Capital from Treasury Stock		4,000
		(To record sale of 4,000 shares of treasury stock above cost)		

ACTION PLAN

- When common stock has a par value, credit Common Stock for par value.
- Use fair market value in a noncash transaction.
- Debit and credit the Treasury Stock account at cost.
- Record differences between the cost and selling price of treasury stock in stockholders' equity accounts, not as gains or losses.

(b)

ROLMAN CORPORATION
Balance Sheet (partial)

Stockholders' equity		
Paid-in capital		
Capital stock		
Common stock, $5 par value, 1,000,000 shares authorized, 500,000 shares issued, 494,000 shares outstanding		$2,500,000
Additional paid-in capital		
In excess of par value	$1,525,000	
From treasury stock	4,000	
Total additional paid-in capital		1,529,000
Total paid-in capital		4,029,000
Retained earnings		200,000
Total paid-in capital and retained earnings		4,229,000
Less: Treasury stock (6,000 shares)		(54,000)
Total stockholders' equity		$4,175,000

☑ THE NAVIGATOR

SUMMARY OF STUDY OBJECTIVES

1. Identify the major characteristics of a corporation. The major characteristics of a corporation are separate legal existence, limited liability of stockholders, transferable ownership rights, ability to acquire capital, continuous life, corporation management, government regulations, and additional taxes.

2. Differentiate between paid-in capital and retained earnings. Paid-in capital is the total amount paid in on capital stock. It is often referred to as contributed capital. Retained earnings is net income retained in a corporation. It is often referred to as earned capital.

3. Record the issuance of common stock. When the issuance of common stock for cash is recorded, the par value of the shares is credited to Common Stock. The portion of the proceeds that is above or below par value is recorded in a separate paid-in capital account. When no-par common stock has a stated value, the entries are similar to those for par value stock. When no-par stock does not have a stated value, the entire proceeds from the issue become legal capital and are credited to Common Stock.

4. *Explain the accounting for treasury stock.* The cost method is generally used in accounting for treasury stock. Under this approach, Treasury Stock is debited at the price paid to reacquire the shares. The same amount is credited to Treasury Stock when the shares are sold. The difference between the sales price and cost is recorded in stockholders' equity accounts, not in income statement accounts.

5. *Differentiate preferred stock from common stock.* Preferred stock has contractual provisions that give it priority over common stock in certain areas. Typically, preferred stockholders have a preference (1) to dividends and (2) to assets in liquidation. They usually do not have voting rights. Also, preferred stock may be convertible and/or callable. A convertible preferred stock entitles the holder to convert those shares to common stock in a specified ratio. The callable feature grants to the issuing corporation the right to purchase the stock from stockholders at specified future dates and prices.

6. *Prepare a stockholders' equity section.* In the stockholders' equity section, paid-in capital and retained earnings are reported and specific sources of paid-in capital are identified. Within paid-in capital, two classifications are shown: capital stock and additional paid-in capital. If a corporation has treasury stock, the cost of treasury stock is deducted from total paid-in capital and retained earnings to obtain total stockholders' equity.

7. *Compute book value per share.* Book value per share represents the equity a common stockholder has in the net assets of a corporation from owning one share of stock. When there is only common stock outstanding, the formula for computing book value is: Total stockholders' equity ÷ Number of common shares outstanding = Book value per share.

Key Term Matching Activity

GLOSSARY

Authorized stock   The amount of stock that a corporation is authorized to sell as indicated in its charter. (p. 567).

Book value per share   The equity a common stockholder has in the net assets of the corporation from owning one share of stock. (p. 582).

By-laws   The internal rules and procedures for conducting the affairs of a corporation. (p. 564).

Callable preferred stock   Preferred stock that grants the issuer the right to purchase the stock from stockholders at specified future dates and prices. (p. 580).

Charter   A document that creates a corporation. (p. 564).

Convertible preferred stock   Preferred stock that provides for the exchange of preferred stock into common stock, at a specified ratio, at the stockholder's option. (p. 580).

Corporation   A business organized as a legal entity separate and distinct from its owners under state corporation law. (p. 560).

Cumulative dividend   A feature of preferred stock entitling the stockholder to receive current and unpaid prior-year dividends before common stockholders receive dividends. (p. 579).

Legal capital   The amount per share of stock that must be retained in the business for the protection of corporate creditors. (p. 569).

No-par value stock   Capital stock that has not been assigned a value in the corporate charter. (p. 569).

Organization costs   Costs incurred in the formation of a corporation. (p. 565).

Outstanding stock   Capital stock that has been issued and is being held by stockholders. (p. 576).

Paid-in capital   Total amount of cash and other assets paid in to the corporation by stockholders in exchange for capital stock. (p. 569).

Par value stock   Capital stock that has been assigned a value per share in the corporate charter. (p. 568).

Preferred stock   Capital stock that has contractual preferences over common stock in certain areas. (p. 578).

Privately held corporation   A corporation that has only a few stockholders and whose stock is not available for sale to the general public. (p. 561).

Publicly held corporation   A corporation that may have thousands of stockholders and whose stock is regularly traded on a national securities exchange. (p. 560).

Retained earnings   Net income that is retained in the corporation. (p. 569).

Stated value   The amount per share assigned by the board of directors to no-par stock that becomes legal capital per share. (p. 569).

Treasury stock   A corporation's own stock that has been issued, fully paid for, and reacquired by the corporation but not retired. (p. 574).

Chapter 14 Self-Test

SELF-STUDY QUESTIONS

Answers are at the end of the chapter.

(SO 1) **1.** Which of the following is *not* a major advantage of a corporation?
   a. Separate legal existence.
   b. Continuous life.
   c. Government regulations.
   d. Transferable ownership rights.

2. A major disadvantage of a corporation is: (SO 1)
   a. limited liability of stockholders.
   b. additional taxes.
   c. transferable ownership rights.
   d. none of the above.

3. Which of the following statements is *false*?   (SO 2)
   a. Ownership of common stock gives the owner a voting right.

b. The stockholders' equity section begins with paid-in capital.

c. The authorization of capital stock does not result in a formal accounting entry.

d. Legal capital per share applies to par value stock but not to no-par value stock.

(SO 2) **4.** The account Retained Earnings is:

a. a subdivision of paid-in capital.

b. net income retained in the corporation.

c. reported as an expense in the income statement.

d. closed to capital stock.

(SO 3) **5.** ABC Corporation issues 1,000 shares of $10 par value common stock at $12 per share. In recording the transaction, credits are made to:

a. Common Stock $10,000 and Paid-in Capital in Excess of Stated Value $2,000.

b. Common Stock $12,000.

c. Common Stock $10,000 and Paid-in Capital in Excess of Par Value $2,000.

d. Common Stock $10,000 and Retained Earnings $2,000.

(SO 4) **6.** XYZ, Inc. sells 100 shares of $5 par value treasury stock at $13 per share. If the cost of acquiring the shares was $10 per share, the entry for the sale should include credits to:

a. Treasury Stock $1,000 and Paid-in Capital from Treasury Stock $300.

b. Treasury Stock $500 and Paid-in Capital from Treasury Stock $800.

c. Treasury Stock $1,000 and Retained Earnings $300.

d. Treasury Stock $500 and Paid-in Capital in Excess of Par Value $800.

7. In the stockholders' equity section, the cost of treasury (SO 4) stock is deducted from:

a. total paid-in capital and retained earnings.

b. retained earnings.

c. total stockholders' equity.

d. common stock in paid-in capital.

8. Preferred stock may have priority over common stock (SO 5) *except* in:

a. dividends.

b. assets in the event of liquidation.

c. conversion.

d. voting.

9. Which of the following is *not* reported under additional (SO 6) paid-in capital?

a. Paid-in capital in excess of par value.

b. Common stock.

c. Paid-in capital in excess of stated value.

d. Paid-in capital from treasury stock.

10. The ledger of JFK, Inc. shows common stock, common (SO 7) treasury stock, and no preferred stock. For this company, the formula for computing book value per share is:

a. Total paid-in capital and retained earnings divided by the number of shares of common stock issued.

b. Common stock divided by the number of shares of common stock issued.

c. Total stockholders' equity divided by the number of shares of common stock outstanding.

d. Total stockholders' equity divided by the number of shares of common stock issued.

QUESTIONS

1. Lil Carmen, a student, asks your help in understanding the following characteristics of a corporation: (a) separate legal existence, (b) limited liability of stockholders, and (c) transferable ownership rights. Explain these characteristics to Lil.

2. (a) Your friend Mark Federia cannot understand how the characteristic of corporation management is both an advantage and a disadvantage. Clarify this problem for Mark.

(b) Identify and explain two other disadvantages of a corporation.

3. (a) The following terms pertain to the forming of a corporation: (1) charter, (2) by-laws, and (3) organization costs. Explain the terms.

(b) Sally Fields believes a corporation must be incorporated in the state in which its headquarters office is located. Is Sally correct? Explain.

4. What are the basic ownership rights of common stockholders in the absence of restrictive provisions?

5. (a) What are the two principal components of stockholders' equity?

(b) What is paid-in capital? Give three examples.

6. How do the financial statements for a corporation differ from the statements for a proprietorship?

7. The corporate charter of Letterman Corporation allows the issuance of a maximum of 100,000 shares of common stock. During its first two years of operations, Letterman sold 70,000 shares to shareholders and reacquired 7,000 of these shares. After these transactions, how many shares are authorized, issued, and outstanding?

8. Which is the better investment—common stock with a par value of $5 per share, or common stock with a par value of $20 per share? Why?

9. What factors help determine the market value of stock?

10. What effect does the issuance of stock at a price above par value have on the issuer's net income? Explain.

11. Why is common stock usually not issued at a price that is less than par value?

12. Land appraised at $80,000 is purchased by issuing 1,000 shares of $20 par value common stock. The market price of the shares at the time of the exchange, based on active trading in the securities market, is $95 per share. Should the land be recorded at $20,000, $80,000, or $95,000? Explain.

13. For what reasons might a company like **IBM** repurchase some of its stock (treasury stock)?

14. Cederno, Inc. purchases 1,000 shares of its own previously issued $5 par common stock for $12,000. Assuming the shares are held in the treasury, what effect does this transaction have on (a) net income, (b) total assets, (c) total paid-in capital, and (d) total stockholders' equity?

15. The treasury stock purchased in question 14 is resold by Cederno, Inc. for $14,500. What effect does this transaction have on (a) net income, (b) total assets, (c) total paid-in capital, and (d) total stockholders' equity?

16. (a) What are the principal differences between common stock and preferred stock?
    (b) Preferred stock may be cumulative. Discuss this feature.
    (c) How are dividends in arrears presented in the financial statements?

17. A preferred stockholder exercises her right to convert her convertible preferred stock into common stock. What effect does this have on the corporation's (a) total assets, (b) total liabilities, and (c) total stockholders' equity?

18. What is the formula for computing book value per share when a corporation has only common stock?

19. MCE Inc.'s common stock has a par value of $1, a book value of $29, and a current market value of $15. Explain why these amounts are all different.

20. Indicate how each of the following accounts should be classified in the stockholders' equity section.
    (a) Common stock
    (b) Paid-in capital in excess of par value
    (c) Retained earnings
    (d) Treasury stock
    (e) Paid-in capital from treasury stock
    (f) Paid-in capital in excess of stated value
    (g) Preferred stock

*B*RIEF EXERCISES

List the advantages and disadvantages of a corporation.
(SO 1)

BE14-1 Ron Weiland is studying for his accounting midterm examination. Identify for Ron the advantages and disadvantages of the corporate form of business organization.

Prepare closing entries for a corporation.
(SO 2)

BE14-2 At December 31, Chavez Corporation reports net income of $575,000. Prepare the entry to close net income.

Prepare entries for issuance of par value common stock.
(SO 3)

BE14-3 On May 10, Walters Corporation issues 1,000 shares of $10 par value common stock for cash at $16 per share. Journalize the issuance of the stock.

Prepare entries for issuance of no-par value common stock.
(SO 3)

BE14-4 On June 1, Rickey Martin Inc. issues 2,000 shares of no-par common stock at a cash price of $7 per share. Journalize the issuance of the shares assuming the stock has a stated value of $1 per share.

Prepare entries for issuance of stock in a noncash transaction.
(SO 3)

BE14-5 Henning Inc.'s $10 par value common stock is actively traded at a market value of $15 per share. Henning issues 5,000 shares to purchase land advertised for sale at $85,000. Journalize the issuance of the stock in acquiring the land.

Prepare entries for treasury stock transactions.
(SO 4)

BE14-6 On July 1, Iron Mountain Corporation purchases 500 shares of its $5 par value common stock for the treasury at a cash price of $8 per share. On September 1, it sells 300 shares of the treasury stock for cash at $11 per share. Journalize the two treasury stock transactions.

Prepare entries for issuance of preferred stock.
(SO 5)

BE14-7 Omar Inc. issues 5,000 shares of $100 par value preferred stock for cash at $112 per share. Journalize the issuance of the preferred stock.

Prepare stockholders' equity section.
(SO 6)

BE14-8 Alzado Corporation has the following accounts at December 31: Common Stock, $10 par, 5,000 shares issued, $50,000; Paid-in Capital in Excess of Par Value $10,000; Retained Earnings $39,000; and Treasury Stock—Common, 500 shares, $11,000. Prepare the stockholders' equity section of the balance sheet.

Compute book value per share.
(SO 7)

BE14-9 The balance sheet for Tanner Inc. shows the following: total paid-in capital and retained earnings $870,000, total stockholders' equity $830,000, common stock issued 44,000 shares, and common stock outstanding 40,000 shares. Compute the book value per share.

*E*XERCISES

Journalize issuance of common stock.
(SO 3)

E14-1 During its first year of operations, Bono Corporation had the following transactions pertaining to its common stock.

Jan. 10 Issued 70,000 shares for cash at $5 per share.
July 1 Issued 40,000 shares for cash at $7 per share.

Instructions

(a) Journalize the transactions, assuming that the common stock has a par value of $5 per share.

(b) Journalize the transactions, assuming that the common stock is no-par with a stated value of $1 per share.

E14-2 Armada Co. had the following transactions during the current period.

Mar. 2   Issued 5,000 shares of $1 par value common stock to attorneys in payment of a bill for $26,000 for services rendered in helping the company to incorporate.

June 12   Issued 60,000 shares of $1 par value common stock for cash of $375,000.

July 11   Issued 1,000 shares of $100 par value preferred stock for cash at $108 per share.

Nov. 28   Purchased 2,000 shares of treasury stock for $80,000.

Journalize issuance of common and preferred stock and purchase of treasury stock. (SO 3, 4, 5)

Instructions

Journalize the transactions.

E14-3 As an auditor for the CPA firm of Arnez and Ball, you encounter the following situations in auditing different clients.

1. Desi Corporation is a closely held corporation whose stock is not publicly traded. On December 5, the corporation acquired land by issuing 5,000 shares of its $20 par value common stock. The owners' asking price for the land was $120,000, and the fair market value of the land was $113,000.

2. Lucille Corporation is a publicly held corporation whose common stock is traded on the securities markets. On June 1, it acquired land by issuing 20,000 shares of its $10 par value stock. At the time of the exchange, the land was advertised for sale at $250,000, The stock was selling at $12 per share.

Journalize noncash common stock transactions. (SO 3)

Instructions

Prepare the journal entries for each of the situations above.

E14-4 On January 1, 2002, the stockholders' equity section of Anita Corporation shows: Common stock ($5 par value) $1,500,000; paid-in capital in excess of par value $1,000,000; and retained earnings $1,200,000. During the year, the following treasury stock transactions occurred.

Mar. 1   Purchased 50,000 shares for cash at $15 per share.

July 1   Sold 10,000 treasury shares for cash at $17 per share.

Sept. 1   Sold 8,000 treasury shares for cash at $14 per share.

Journalize treasury stock transactions. (SO 4)

Instructions

(a) Journalize the treasury stock transactions.

(b) Restate the entry for September 1, assuming the treasury shares were sold at $11 per share.

E14-5 Abdella Corporation is authorized to issue both preferred and common stock. The par value of the preferred is $50. During the first year of operations, the company had the following events and transactions pertaining to its preferred stock.

Feb. 1   Issued 30,000 shares for cash at $51 per share.

July 1   Issued 12,000 shares for cash at $57 per share.

Journalize preferred stock transactions and indicate statement presentation. (SO 5, 6)

Instructions

(a) Journalize the transactions.

(b) Post to the stockholders' equity accounts.

(c) Indicate the financial statement presentation of the related accounts.

E14-6 Omar Corporation has 10,000 shares of $100 par value preferred stock outstanding. Each share is convertible into 5 shares of $15 par value common stock. When the market values of the two classes of stock are $110 and $25, respectively, 2,200 shares of preferred stock are converted into common stock. The preferred stock was issued at par.

Journalize conversion of preferred stock (SO 5)

Instructions

(a) Journalize the conversion of the 2,200 shares.

(b) Repeat (a) assuming that market values at conversion are $105 and $25, respectively.

(c) Repeat (a) assuming each share is convertible into 8 shares of $10 par value common stock.

Prepare correct entries for capital stock transactions.
(SO 3, 4, 5)

E14-7 Swartz Corporation recently hired a new accountant with extensive experience in accounting for partnerships. Because of the pressure of the new job, the accountant was unable to review his textbooks on the topic of corporation accounting. During the first month, the accountant made the following entries for the corporation's capital stock.

May 2	Cash	120,000	
	Capital Stock		120,000
	(Issued 10,000 shares of $5 par value common		
	stock at $12 per share)		
10	Cash	600,000	
	Capital Stock		600,000
	(Issued 10,000 shares of $50 par value preferred		
	stock at $60 per share)		
15	Capital Stock	14,000	
	Cash		14,000
	(Purchased 1,000 shares of common stock for the		
	treasury at $14 per share)		
31	Cash	7,500	
	Capital Stock		2,500
	Gain on Sale of Stock		5,000
	(Sold 500 shares of treasury stock at $15 per share)		

Instructions

On the basis of the explanation for each entry, prepare the entry that should have been made for the capital stock transactions.

Answer questions about stockholders' equity section.
(SO 3, 4, 5, 6)

E14-8 The stockholders' equity section of Chile Corporation at December 31 is as follows.

CHILE CORPORATION
Balance Sheet (partial)

Paid-in capital	
Preferred stock, cumulative, 10,000 shares authorized, 6,000 shares issued	
and outstanding	$ 600,000
Common stock, no par, 750,000 shares authorized, 600,000 shares issued	1,800,000
Total paid-in capital	2,400,000
Retained earnings	1,258,000
Total paid-in capital and retained earnings	3,658,000
Less: Treasury stock (15,000 common shares)	(64,000)
Total stockholders' equity	$3,594,000

Instructions

▭▭▭▭▷ From a review of the stockholders' equity section, as chief accountant, write a memo to the president of the company answering the following questions.

(a) How many shares of common stock are outstanding?
(b) Assuming there is a stated value, what is the stated value of the common stock?
(c) What is the par value of the preferred stock?
(d) If the annual dividend on preferred stock is $36,000, what is the dividend rate on preferred stock?
(e) If dividends of $72,000 were in arrears on preferred stock, what would be the balance in Retained Earnings?

Prepare a stockholders' equity section and compute book value.
(SO 6, 7)

E14-9 In a recent year, the stockholders' equity section of the **Aluminum Company of America (Alcoa)** showed the following (in alphabetical order): additional (paid-in) capital $680.5, common stock $88.3, preferred stock $66.0, and retained earnings $3,750.2. All dollar data are in millions.

The preferred stock has 660,000 shares authorized, with a par value of $100 and an annual $3.75 per share cumulative dividend preference. At December 31, all authorized preferred stock is issued and outstanding. There are 300 million shares of $1 par value common stock authorized, of which 88.3 million are outstanding at December 31.

Instructions

(a) Prepare the stockholders' equity section, including disclosure of all relevant data.

(b) Compute the book value per share of common stock, assuming there are no preferred dividends in arrears. (Round to two decimals.)

E14-10   The ledger of Springer Corporation contains the following accounts: Common Stock, Preferred Stock, Treasury Stock—Common, Paid-in Capital in Excess of Par Value—Preferred Stock, Paid-in Capital in Excess of Stated Value—Common Stock, Paid-in Capital from Treasury Stock, and Retained Earnings.

Classify stockholders' equity accounts.
(SO 6)

Instructions

Classify each account using the following table headings.

	Paid-in Capital			
Account	**Capital Stock**	**Additional**	**Retained Earnings**	**Other**

E14-11   At December 31, Castle Corporation has total stockholders' equity of $4,000,000. Included in this total are preferred stock $500,000 and paid-in capital in excess of par value—preferred stock $50,000. There are 10,000 shares of $50 par value 10% cumulative preferred stock outstanding. At year-end, 250,000 shares of common stock are outstanding.

Compute book value per share with preferred stock.
(SO 7)

Instructions

Compute the book value per share of common stock, under each of the following assumptions.

(a) There are no preferred dividends in arrears, and the preferred stock does not have a call price.

(b) Preferred dividends are 1 year in arrears, and the preferred stock has a call price of $60 per share.

PROBLEMS: SET A

P14-1A   Tiger Corporation was organized on January 1, 2002. It is authorized to issue 10,000 shares of 8%, $100 par value preferred stock, and 500,000 shares of no-par common stock with a stated value of $2 per share. The following stock transactions were completed during the first year.

Journalize stock transactions, post, and prepare paid-in capital section.
(SO 3, 5, 6)

Peachtree

Jan. 10	Issued 80,000 shares of common stock for cash at $3 per share.
Mar. 1	Issued 5,000 shares of preferred stock for cash at $105 per share.
Apr. 1	Issued 24,000 shares of common stock for land. The asking price of the land was $90,000. The fair market value of the land was $80,000.
May 1	Issued 80,000 shares of common stock for cash at $4 per share.
Aug. 1	Issued 10,000 shares of common stock to attorneys in payment of their bill of $50,000 for services rendered in helping the company organize.
Sept. 1	Issued 10,000 shares of common stock for cash at $5 per share.
Nov. 1	Issued 1,000 shares of preferred stock for cash at $109 per share.

Instructions

(a) Journalize the transactions.

(b) Post to the stockholders' equity accounts. (Use J5 as the posting reference.)

(c) Prepare the paid-in capital section of stockholders' equity at December 31, 2002.

(c) Total paid-in capital
     $1,374,000

P14-2A   Gore Corporation had the following stockholders' equity accounts on January 1, 2002: Common Stock ($5 par) $500,000, Paid-in Capital in Excess of Par Value $200,000, and Retained Earnings $100,000. In 2002, the company had the following treasury stock transactions.

Journalize and post treasury stock transactions, and prepare stockholders' equity section.
(SO 4, 6)

Mar. 1	Purchased 5,000 shares at $7 per share.
June 1	Sold 1,000 shares at $12 per share.
Sept. 1	Sold 2,000 shares at $9 per share.
Dec. 1	Sold 1,000 shares at $6 per share.

Gore Corporation uses the cost method of accounting for treasury stock. In 2002, the company reported net income of $50,000.

Instructions

(a) Journalize the treasury stock transactions, and prepare the closing entry at December 31, 2002, for net income.

(b) Open accounts for (1) Paid-in Capital from Treasury Stock, (2) Treasury Stock, and (3) Retained Earnings. Post to these accounts using J10 as the posting reference.

(c) Prepare the stockholders' equity section for Gore Corporation at December 31, 2002.

(b) Treasury Stock $7,000
(c) Total stockholders' equity
     $851,000

Journalize and post transactions, prepare stockholders' equity section, and compute book value.
(SO 2, 3, 4, 5, 6, 7)

P14-3A   The stockholders' equity accounts of Notah Begay Corporation on January 1, 2002, were as follows.

Preferred Stock (12%, $50 par cumulative, 10,000 shares authorized)	$ 400,000
Common Stock ($1 stated value, 2,000,000 shares authorized)	1,000,000
Paid-in Capital in Excess of Par Value—Preferred Stock	100,000
Paid-in Capital in Excess of Stated Value—Common Stock	1,450,000
Retained Earnings	1,816,000
Treasury Stock—Common (10,000 shares)	40,000

During 2002, the corporation had the following transactions and events pertaining to its stockholders' equity.

Feb. 1   Issued 20,000 shares of common stock for $100,000.

Apr. 14   Sold 6,000 shares of treasury stock—common for $28,000.

Sept. 3   Issued 5,000 shares of common stock for a patent valued at $25,000.

Nov. 10   Purchased 1,000 shares of common stock for the treasury at a cost of $6,000.

Dec. 31   Determined that net income for the year was $402,000.

The preferred stock has a call price of $55 per share. No dividends were declared during the year.

Instructions

(a) Journalize the transactions and the closing entry for net income.

(b) Enter the beginning balances in the accounts, and post the journal entries to the stockholders' equity accounts. (Use J5 for the posting reference.)

(c) Total stockholders' equity
     $5,275,000

(c) Prepare a stockholders' equity section at December 31, 2002, including the disclosure of the preferred dividends in arrears.

(d) Compute the book value per share of common stock at December 31, 2002. (Round to two decimals.)

Journalize and post preferred stock transactions, and prepare stockholders' equity section.
(SO 2, 5, 6)

Peachtree

P14-4A   Roberto Moreno Corporation is authorized to issue 10,000 shares of $100 par value, 10% convertible preferred stock and 125,000 shares of $5 par value common stock. On January 1, 2002, the ledger contained the following stockholders' equity balances.

Preferred Stock (5,000 shares)	$500,000
Paid-in Capital in Excess of Par Value—Preferred	75,000
Common Stock (70,000 shares)	350,000
Paid-in Capital in Excess of Par Value—Common	700,000
Retained Earnings	300,000

During 2002, the following transactions occurred.

Feb. 1   Issued 1,000 shares of preferred stock for land having a fair market value of $125,000.

Mar. 1   Issued 1,000 shares of preferred stock for cash at $125 per share.

July 1   Holders of 2,000 shares of preferred stock, purchased at $110 per share, converted the shares into common stock. Each share of preferred was convertible into 8 shares of common stock. Market values were preferred stock $122 and common stock $17.

Sept. 1   Issued 400 shares of preferred stock for a patent. The asking price of the patent was $60,000. Market values were preferred stock $125 and patent indeterminable.

Dec. 1   Holders of 1,000 shares of preferred stock, purchased at $130 per share, converted the shares into common stock. Each share of preferred was convertible into 8 shares of common stock. Market values were preferred stock $134 and common stock $16.

Dec. 31   Net income for the year was $260,000. No dividends were declared.

Instructions

(a) Journalize the transactions and the closing entry for net income.

(b) Enter the beginning balances in the accounts, and post the journal entries to the stock-holders' equity accounts. (Use J2 for the posting reference.)

(c) Prepare a stockholders' equity section at December 31, 2002.

(c) Total stockholders' equity
  $2,485,000

P14-5A   The following stockholders' equity accounts arranged alphabetically are in the ledger of Servia Corporation at December 31, 2002.

Prepare stockholders' equity section and compute book value.
(SO 6, 7)

Common Stock ($5 stated value)	$2,500,000
Paid-in Capital from Treasury Stock	10,000
Paid-in Capital in Excess of Stated Value—Common Stock	1,600,000
Paid-in Capital in Excess of Par Value—Preferred Stock	739,000
Preferred Stock (8%, $50 par, noncumulative)	800,000
Retained Earnings	2,448,000
Treasury Stock—Common (10,000 shares)	130,000

Instructions

(a) Prepare a stockholders' equity section at December 31, 2002.

(b) Compute the book value per share of the common stock, assuming the preferred stock has a call price of $60 per share.

(a) Total stockholders' equity
  $7,967,000
(b) $14.30

P14-6A   Bush Corporation has been authorized to issue 20,000 shares of $100 par value, 10%, noncumulative preferred stock and 1,000,000 shares of no-par common stock. The corporation assigned a $2.50 stated value to the common stock. At December 31, 2002, the ledger contained the following balances pertaining to stockholders' equity.

Prepare entries for stock trans-actions and stockholders' equity section.
(SO 3, 4, 5, 6)

Preferred Stock	$ 120,000
Paid-in Capital in Excess of Par Value—Preferred	28,000
Common Stock	1,000,000
Paid-in Capital in Excess of Stated Value—Common	2,850,000
Treasury Stock—Common (1,000 shares)	11,000
Paid-in Capital from Treasury Stock	1,500
Retained Earnings	82,000

The preferred stock was issued for land having a fair market value of $148,000. All common stock issued was for cash. In November, 1,500 shares of common stock were purchased for the treasury at a per share cost of $11. In December, 500 shares of treasury stock were sold for $14 per share. No dividends were declared in 2002.

Instructions

(a) Prepare the journal entries for the:
  (1) Issuance of preferred stock for land.
  (2) Issuance of common stock for cash.
  (3) Purchase of common treasury stock for cash.
  (4) Sale of treasury stock for cash.

(b) Prepare the stockholders' equity section at December 31, 2002.

(b) Total stockholders' equity
  $4,070,500

*P*ROBLEMS: *SET B*

P14-1B   Argentina Corporation was organized on January 1, 2002. It is authorized to issue 20,000 shares of 6%, $50 par value preferred stock, and 500,000 shares of no-par common stock with a stated value of $1 per share. The following stock transactions were completed during the first year.

Journalize stock transactions, post, and prepare paid-in capital section.
(SO 3, 5, 6)

Jan. 10	Issued 100,000 shares of common stock for cash at $3 per share.
Mar. 1	Issued 10,000 shares of preferred stock for cash at $52 per share.
Apr. 1	Issued 25,000 shares of common stock for land. The asking price of the land was $90,000. The company's estimate of fair market value of the land was $85,000.
May 1	Issued 75,000 shares of common stock for cash at $4 per share.

Aug. 1 Issued 10,000 shares of common stock to attorneys in payment of their bill for $50,000 for services provided in helping the company organize.
Sept. 1 Issued 5,000 shares of common stock for cash at $6 per share.
Nov. 1 Issued 2,000 shares of preferred stock for cash at $54 per share.

Instructions
(a) Journalize the transactions.
(b) Post to the stockholders' equity accounts. (Use J1 as the posting reference.)
(c) Prepare the paid-in capital section of stockholders' equity at December 31, 2002.

(c) Total paid-in capital $1,393,000

Journalize and post treasury stock transactions, and prepare stockholders' equity section. (SO 4, 6)

P14-2B Hassan Corporation had the following stockholders' equity accounts on January 1, 2002: Common Stock ($1 par) $400,000, Paid-in Capital in Excess of Par Value $500,000, and Retained Earnings $100,000. In 2002, the company had the following treasury stock transactions.

Mar. 1 Purchased 5,000 shares at $6 per share.
June 1 Sold 1,000 shares at $10 per share.
Sept. 1 Sold 2,000 shares at $8 per share.
Dec. 1 Sold 1,000 shares at $5 per share.

Hassan Corporation uses the cost method of accounting for treasury stock. In 2002, the company reported net income of $50,000.

Instructions
(a) Journalize the treasury stock transactions, and prepare the closing entry at December 31, 2002, for net income.
(b) Open accounts for (1) Paid-in Capital from Treasury Stock, (2) Treasury Stock, and (3) Retained Earnings. Post to these accounts using J12 as the posting reference.
(c) Prepare the stockholders' equity section for Hassan Corporation at December 31, 2002.

(b) Treasury-Stock $6,000
(c) Total stockholders' equity $1,051,000

Journalize and post transactions, prepare stockholders' equity section, and compute book value. (SO 2, 3, 4, 5, 6, 7)

P14-3B The stockholders' equity accounts of Chen Corporation on January 1, 2002, were as follows.

Preferred Stock (10%, $100 par noncumulative, 5,000 shares authorized)	$ 300,000
Common Stock ($5 stated value, 300,000 shares authorized)	1,000,000
Paid-in Capital in Excess of Par Value—Preferred Stock	20,000
Paid-in Capital in Excess of Stated Value—Common Stock	425,000
Retained Earnings	488,000
Treasury Stock—Common (5,000 shares)	40,000

During 2002, the corporation had the following transactions and events pertaining to its stockholders' equity.

Feb. 1 Issued 4,000 shares of common stock for $25,000.
Mar. 20 Purchased 1,000 additional shares of common treasury stock at $8 per share.
June 14 Sold 4,000 shares of treasury stock—common for $34,000.
Sept. 3 Issued 2,000 shares of common stock for a patent valued at $13,000.
Dec. 31 Determined that net income for the year was $240,000.

Instructions
(a) Journalize the transactions and the closing entry for net income.
(b) Enter the beginning balances in the accounts and post the journal entries to the stockholders' equity accounts. (Use J1 as the posting reference.)
(c) Prepare a stockholders' equity section at December 31, 2002.
(d) Compute the book value per share of common stock at December 31, 2002, assuming the preferred stock does not have a call price.

(c) Total stockholders' equity $2,497,000

Journalize and post preferred stock transactions, and prepare stockholders' equity section. (SO 2, 5, 6)

P14-4B Clinton Corporation is authorized to issue 10,000 shares of $100 par value, 10%, convertible preferred stock and 200,000 shares of $5 par value common stock. On January 1, 2002, the ledger contained the following stockholders' equity balances.

Preferred Stock (4,000 shares)	$400,000
Paid-in Capital in Excess of Par Value—Preferred	60,000
Common Stock (70,000 shares)	350,000
Paid-in Capital in Excess of Par Value—Common	700,000
Retained Earnings	300,000

During 2002, the following transactions occurred.

Feb. 1 Issued 1,000 shares of preferred stock for land having a fair market value of $125,000.

Mar. 1 Issued 1,000 shares of preferred stock for cash at $120 per share.

July 1 Holders of 2,000 shares of preferred stock purchased at $115 per share converted the shares into common stock. Each share of preferred was convertible into 10 shares of common stock. Market values were preferred stock $122 and common stock $15.

Sept. 1 Issued 400 shares of preferred stock for a patent. The asking price of the patent was $60,000. Market values were preferred stock $125 and patent, indeterminable.

Dec. 1 Holders of 1,000 shares of preferred stock purchased at $120 per share converted the shares into common stock. Each share of preferred was convertible into 10 shares of common stock. Market values were preferred stock $125 and common stock $16.

Dec. 31 Net income for the year was $210,000. No dividends were declared.

Instructions
(a) Journalize the transactions and the closing entry for net income.
(b) Enter the beginning balances in the accounts, and post the journal entries to the stockholders' equity accounts. (Use J2 as the posting reference.)
(c) Prepare a stockholders' equity section at December 31, 2002.

(c) Total stockholders' equity $2,315,000

P14-5B The following stockholders' equity accounts arranged alphabetically are in the ledger of Iceland Corporation at December 31, 2002.

Prepare stockholders' equity section and compute book value.
(SO 6, 7)

Common Stock ($10 stated value)	$1,500,000
Paid-in Capital from Treasury Stock	6,000
Paid-in Capital in Excess of Stated Value—Common Stock	920,000
Paid-in Capital in Excess of Par Value—Preferred Stock	288,400
Preferred Stock (8%, $100 par, noncumulative)	400,000
Retained Earnings	1,276,000
Treasury Stock—Common (8,000 shares)	88,000

Instructions
(a) Prepare a stockholders' equity section at December 31, 2002.
(b) Compute the book value per share of the common stock, assuming the preferred stock has a call price of $110 per share.

(a) Total stockholders' equity $4,302,400

BROADENING YOUR PERSPECTIVE

*F*INANCIAL REPORTING AND ANALYSIS

FINANCIAL REPORTING PROBLEM: Lands' End, Inc.

BYP14-1 The stockholders' equity section for **Lands' End, Inc.** is shown in Appendix A. You will also find data relative to this problem on other pages of the appendix.

Instructions
(a) What is the par or stated value per share of Lands' End's common stock?
(b) What percentage of Lands' End's authorized common stock was issued at January 28, 2000? (Round to the nearest full percentage.)
(c) How many shares of common stock were outstanding at January 28, 2000, and at January 29, 1999?
(d) What was book value per share at January 28, 2000, and at January 29, 1999?
(e) What was the high and low market price per share in the fourth quarter of fiscal 2000, as reported under Note 14?

COMPARATIVE ANALYSIS PROBLEM: Lands' End vs. Abercrombie & Fitch

BYP14-2 **Lands' End's** financial statements are presented in Appendix A. **Abercrombie & Fitch's** financial statements are presented in Appendix B.

Instructions
(a) Based on the information contained in these financial statements, compute the 2000 book value per share for each company.
(b) Compare the market value per share for each company to the book value per share at year-end 2000. Assume that the market value of Abercrombie & Fitch's stock was $32.25 at year-end 2000.
(c) Why are book value and market value per share different?

INTERPRETING FINANCIAL STATEMENTS: A Global Focus

BYP14-3 Investors with less than a controlling interest in a company are considered minority stockholders. The September 13, 1999, issue of *The Wall Street Journal* included an article by Namju Cho entitled "Minority Shareholders Lag in Emerging Markets."

Instructions
Read the article and answer the following questions.
(a) What are three weaknesses of many companies in emerging markets that contribute to those companies' lack of response to stockholders?
(b) What approach is Edward Schneider taking to try to improve the treatment of stockholders in Latin America?
(c) Why is it in the interest of emerging markets to react to stockholder concerns?

EXPLORING THE WEB

BYP 14-4 SEC filings of publicly traded companies are available to view online.

Address: http//biz.yahoo.com/i *(or go to www.wiley.com/college/weygandt)*

Steps:
1. Pick a company and type in the company's name.
2. Choose **Quote**.

Instructions
Answer the following questions.
(a) What company did you select?
(b) What is its stock symbol?
(c) What was the stock's trading range today?
(d) What was the stock's trading range for the year?

CRITICAL THINKING

GROUP DECISION CASE

BYP14-5 The stockholders' meeting for Chow Corporation has been in progress for some time. The chief financial officer for Chow is presently reviewing the company's financial statements and is explaining the items that comprise the stockholders' equity section of the balance sheet for the current year. The stockholders' equity section of Chow Corporation at December 31, 2002, is as follows.

CHOW CORPORATION
Balance Sheet (partial)
December 31, 2002

Paid in capital
  Capital stock
    Preferred stock, authorized 1,000,000 shares
      cumulative, $100 par value, $8 per share, 6,000

shares issued and outstanding			$ 600,000
Common stock, authorized 5,000,000 shares, $1 par value, 3,000,000 shares issued, and 2,700,000 outstanding			3,000,000
Total capital stock			3,600,000
Additional paid-in capital			
In excess of par value—preferred stock		$ 50,000	
In excess of par value—common stock		25,000,000	
Total additional paid-in capital			25,050,000
Total paid-in capital			28,650,000
Retained earnings			900,000
Total paid-in capital and retained earnings			29,550,000
Less: Common treasury stock (300,000 shares)			9,300,000
Total stockholders' equity			$20,250,000

At the meeting, stockholders have raised a number of questions regarding the stockholders' equity section.

Instructions

With the class divided into groups, answer the following questions as if you were the chief financial officer for Chow Corporation.

(a) "What does the cumulative provision related to the preferred stock mean?"

(b) "I thought the common stock was presently selling at $29.75, but the company has the stock stated at $1 per share. How can that be?"

(c) "Why is the company buying back its common stock? Furthermore, the treasury stock has a debit balance because it is subtracted from stockholders' equity. Why is treasury stock not reported as an asset if it has a debit balance?"

(d) "Why is it necessary to show additional paid-in capital? Why not just show common stock at the total amount paid in?"

COMMUNICATION ACTIVITY

BYP14-6 Paul Tracey, your uncle, is an inventor who has decided to incorporate. Uncle Paul knows that you are an accounting major at U.N.O. In a recent letter to you, he ends with the question, "I'm filling out a state incorporation application. Can you tell me the difference in the following terms: (1) authorized stock, (2) issued stock, (3) outstanding stock, (4) preferred stock?"

Instructions

In a brief note, differentiate for Uncle Paul among the four different stock terms. Write the letter to be friendly, yet professional.

ETHICS CASE

BYP14-7 The R&D division of Nakona Chemical Corp. has just developed a chemical for sterilizing the vicious Brazilian "killer bees" which are invading Mexico and the southern states of the United States. The president of Nakona is anxious to get the chemical on the market to boost Nakona's profits. He believes his job is in jeopardy because of decreasing sales and profits. Nakona has an opportunity to sell this chemical in Central American countries, where the laws are much more relaxed than in the United States.

The director of Nakona's R&D division strongly recommends further testing in the laboratory for side-effects of this chemical on other insects, birds, animals, plants, and even humans. He cautions the president, "We could be sued from all sides if the chemical has tragic side-effects that we didn't even test for in the labs." The president answers, "We can't wait an additional year for your lab tests. We can avoid losses from such lawsuits by establishing a separate wholly owned corporation to shield Nakona Corp. from such lawsuits. We can't lose any more than our investment in the new corporation, and we'll invest just the patent covering this chemical. We'll reap the benefits if the chemical works and is safe, and avoid the losses from lawsuits if it's a disaster." The following week Nakona creates a new wholly owned corporation called Marques Inc., sells the chemical patent to it for $10, and watches the spraying begin.

Instructions

(a) Who are the stakeholders in this situation?
(b) Are the president's motives and actions ethical?
(c) Can Nakona shield itself against losses of Marques Inc.?

Answers to Self-Study Questions

1. c **2.** b **3.** d **4.** b **5.** c **6.** a **7.** a **8.** d **9.** b **10.** c

---

Answers to Lands' End Review It Question 3, p. 573 and Question 4, p. 577

3. The par value of Lands' End's common stock is $0.001 per share. On January 28, 2000, Lands' End had issued 40,221,000 shares.

4. Treasury shares held at Lands' End on January 28, 2000, were 10,070,868, and on January 29, 1999, were 10,317,118, as shown in "Note 2. Shareholders' Investment."

Remember to go back to the Navigator box on the chapter-opening page and check off your completed work.

CORPORATIONS: DIVIDENDS, RETAINED EARNINGS, AND INCOME REPORTING

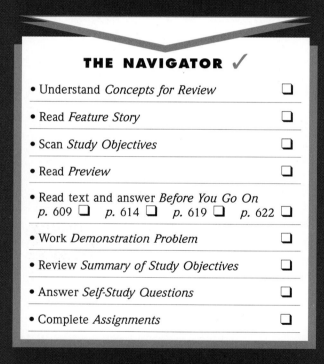

THE NAVIGATOR ✓

- Understand *Concepts for Review* ❑
- Read *Feature Story* ❑
- Scan *Study Objectives* ❑
- Read *Preview* ❑
- Read text and answer *Before You Go On*
  p. 609 ❑   p. 614 ❑   p. 619 ❑   p. 622 ❑
- Work *Demonstration Problem* ❑
- Review *Summary of Study Objectives* ❑
- Answer *Self-Study Questions* ❑
- Complete *Assignments* ❑

CONCEPTS FOR REVIEW

Before studying this chapter, you should know or, if necessary, review:

  a. Why it is important to distinguish between paid-in capital and retained earnings. (Ch. 14, p. 569)

  b. The significance of legal capital in accounting for capital stock transactions. (Ch. 14, pp. 568–569)

  c. The form and content of the stockholders' equity section of the balance sheet. (Ch. 14, pp. 581–582)

  d. The rights of cumulative preferred stockholders to dividends. (Ch. 14, pp. 579–580)

THE NAVIGATOR

*F*EATURE STORY

What's Cooking?

What major U.S. corporation got its start almost 30 years ago with a waffle iron? Hint: It doesn't sell food. Another hint: Swoosh. Another hint: "Just do it." That's right, **Nike**. In 1971 Nike cofounder Bill Bowerman put a piece of rubber into a kitchen waffle iron, and the trademark waffle sole was born.

Nike was cofounded by Bowerman and Phil Knight, a member of Bowerman's University of Oregon track team. Each began in the shoe business independently during the early 1960s. Bowerman got his start by making hand-crafted running shoes for his university track team. Knight, after completing graduate school, started a small business importing low-cost, high-quality shoes from Japan. In 1964 the two joined forces. Each contributed $500, and formed Blue Ribbon Sports, a partnership. At first they marketed Japanese shoes. It wasn't until 1971 that the company began manufacturing its own line of shoes. With the new shoes came a new corporate name—Nike—the Greek goddess of victory. It is hard to

imagine that the company that now enlists promoters such as Tiger Woods, Mia Hamm, and Michael Jordan at one time had part-time employees selling shoes out of car trunks.

By 1980 Nike was sufficiently established that it was able to issue its first stock to the public. In that same year it also created a stock ownership program that allowed its employees to share in the company's success. Since then Nike has enjoyed phenomenal growth. Sales in 1999 were $8.8 billion. Its dividend per share to shareholders has increased every year for the last 11 years.

Nike is not alone in its quest for the top of the sport shoe world. Reebok pushes Nike every step of the way. It's a race to see who will dominate the sports shoe industry. Currently Nike is outpacing Reebok. But is the race over? Probably not. The shoe market is fickle, with new

styles becoming popular almost daily. Reebok's unwillingness to give up the race was boldly stated in its recent ad campaign, "This is my planet." Whether one of these two giants does eventually take control of the planet remains to be seen. Meanwhile the shareholders sit anxiously in the stands as this Olympic-size drama unfolds.

THE NAVIGATOR

www.nike.com
www.reebok.com

*S*TUDY OBJECTIVES

After studying this chapter, you should be able to:

1. Prepare the entries for cash dividends and stock dividends.
2. Identify the items that are reported in a retained earnings statement.
3. Prepare and analyze a comprehensive stockholders' equity section.
4. Describe the form and content of corporation income statements.
5. Indicate the statement presentation of material items not typical of regular operations.
6. Compute earnings per share.

THE NAVIGATOR

As indicated in the Feature Story, a profitable corporation like **Nike** often distributes substantial portions of corporate income to owners (stockholders), in the form of dividends. In addition, it often reinvests a portion of its earnings in the business. This chapter discusses dividends, retained earnings, corporation income statements, and earnings per share.

The content and organization of Chapter 15 are as follows.

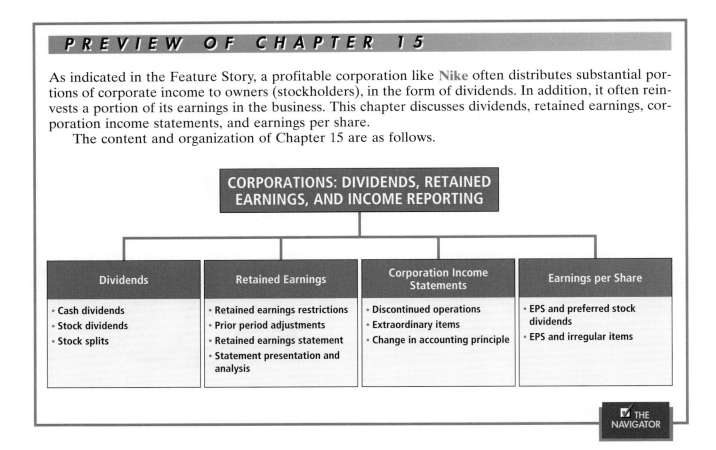

CORPORATIONS: DIVIDENDS, RETAINED EARNINGS, AND INCOME REPORTING			
Dividends	**Retained Earnings**	**Corporation Income Statements**	**Earnings per Share**
• Cash dividends • Stock dividends • Stock splits	• Retained earnings restrictions • Prior period adjustments • Retained earnings statement • Statement presentation and analysis	• Discontinued operations • Extraordinary items • Change in accounting principle	• EPS and preferred stock dividends • EPS and irregular items

☑ THE NAVIGATOR

*D*IVIDENDS

STUDY OBJECTIVE 1

Prepare the entries for cash dividends and stock dividends.

A **dividend** is a distribution by a corporation to its stockholders on a pro rata (proportional) basis. Potential buyers and sellers of stock are very interested in a company's dividend policies and practices. Dividends can take four forms: cash, property, scrip (a promissory note to pay cash), or stock. Cash dividends predominate in practice. Also, stock dividends are declared with some frequency. These two forms of dividends will be the focus of discussion in this chapter.

Dividends may be expressed in two ways: (1) as a percentage of the par or stated value of the stock, or (2) as a dollar amount per share. In the financial press, **dividends are generally reported quarterly as a dollar amount per share.** For example, **Boeing Company's** quarterly dividend rate is 14 cents a share, **Ford Motor Company's** is 50 cents, and **Nike's** is 12 cents.

CASH DIVIDENDS

A **cash dividend** is a pro rata distribution of cash to stockholders. For a corporation to pay a cash dividend, it must have:

1. **Retained earnings.** The legality of a cash dividend depends on the laws of the state in which the company is incorporated. Payment of cash dividends from retained earnings is legal in all states. In general, cash dividend distributions based only on common stock (legal capital) are illegal. Statutes vary considerably with respect to cash dividends based on paid-in capital in excess of par or stated value. Many states permit such dividends. A dividend declared out of paid-in capital is termed a **liquidating dividend.** The amount originally paid in by stockholders is being reduced or "liquidated" by such a dividend.

2. **Adequate cash.** The legality of a dividend and the ability to pay a dividend are two different things. For example, **Nike**, with retained earnings of $3,067 million, could legally declare a dividend of $3,067 million. But Nike's cash balance is only $198 million. In order to pay a $3,067 million dividend, Nike would need to raise additional cash through the sale of other assets or through additional financing.

   Before declaring a cash dividend, a company's board of directors must carefully consider both current and future demands on the company's cash resources. In some cases, current liabilities may make a cash dividend inappropriate. In other cases, a major plant expansion program may warrant only a relatively small dividend.

3. **A declaration of dividends.** A company does not pay dividends unless its board of directors decides to do so, at which point the board "declares" the dividend. The board of directors has full authority to determine the amount of income to be distributed in the form of a dividend and the amount to be retained in the business. Dividends do not accrue like interest on a note payable, and they are not a liability until declared.

The amount and timing of a dividend are important issues. The payment of a large cash dividend could lead to liquidity problems for the enterprise. On the other hand, a small dividend or a missed dividend may cause unhappiness among stockholders. Many of them expect to receive a reasonable cash payment from the company on a periodic basis. Many companies declare and pay cash dividends quarterly.

ACCOUNTING IN ACTION   *Business Insight*

In order to remain in business, companies must honor their interest payments to creditors, bankers, and bondholders. The payment of dividends to stockholders is another matter. Many companies can survive, even thrive, without such payouts. In fact, some managements consider dividend payments unnecessary, or even harmful. Pay your creditors, by all means. But, fork over perfectly good cash to stockholders? "Why give money to those strangers?" is the response of one company president.

Investors must keep an eye on the company's dividend policy and understand what it may signal. For most companies, regular boosts in the face of irregular earnings can be a warning signal of financial trouble. Companies with high dividends and rising debt may be borrowing money to pay shareholders. Low dividends sometimes indicate an expectation by management of low future earnings. Or, they may indicate a policy of retaining earnings for corporate expansion that will result in a higher stock price in the future.

Entries for Cash Dividends

Three dates are important in connection with dividends: (1) the declaration date, (2) the record date, and (3) the payment date. Normally, there are two to four weeks between each date. Accounting entries are required on two of the dates—the declaration date and the payment date.

On the **declaration date**, the board of directors formally declares (authorizes) the cash dividend and announces it to stockholders. Declaration of a cash dividend **commits the corporation to a legal obligation.** The obligation is binding and cannot be rescinded. An entry is required to recognize the decrease in retained earnings and the increase in the liability Dividends Payable. To illustrate, assume

> **HELPFUL HINT**
> What is the effect of the *declaration* of a cash dividend on (1) total stockholders' equity, (2) total liabilities, (3) total assets? Answer: (1) Decrease, (2) increase, (3) no effect.

that on December 1, 2002, the directors of Media General declare a 50¢ per share cash dividend on 100,000 shares of $10 par value common stock. The dividend is $50,000 (100,000 × 50¢). The entry to record the declaration is:

Declaration Date

A = L + SE	Dec. 1	Retained Earnings	50,000	
+50,000 −50,000		Dividends Payable		50,000
		(To record declaration of cash dividend)		

Dividends Payable is a current liability: it will normally be paid within the next several months.

Instead of debiting Retained Earnings, the account Dividends may be debited. This account provides additional information in the ledger. Also, a company may have separate dividend accounts for each class of stock. When a dividend account is used, its balance is transferred to Retained Earnings at the end of the year by a closing entry. Whichever account is used for the dividend declaration, the effect is the same: retained earnings is decreased and a current liability is increased. For homework problems, you should use the Retained Earnings account for recording dividend declarations.

At the **record date**, ownership of the outstanding shares is determined for dividend purposes. The records maintained by the corporation supply this information. In the interval between the declaration date and the record date, the corporation updates its stock ownership records. For Media General, the record date is December 22. No entry is required on this date because the corporation's liability recognized on the declaration date is unchanged.

HELPFUL HINT

Between the declaration date and record date, the number of shares outstanding should remain the same. The purpose of the record date is to identify the persons or entities that will receive the dividend, not to determine the amount of the dividend liability.

Record Date

Dec. 22	No entry necessary	

On the **payment date**, dividend checks are mailed to the stockholders and the payment of the dividend is recorded. Assuming that the payment date is January 20 for Media General, the entry on that date is:

Payment Date

A = L + SE	Jan. 20	Dividends Payable	50,000	
−50,000 −50,000		Cash		50,000
		(To record payment of cash dividend)		

Note that payment of the dividend reduces both current assets and current liabilities. It has no effect on stockholders' equity. The **cumulative effect** of the **declaration and payment** of a cash dividend is to **decrease both stockholders' equity and total assets**. Illustration 15-1 (on the next page) summarizes the three important dates associated with dividends.

Allocating Cash Dividends between Preferred and Common Stock

As explained in Chapter 14, preferred stock has priority over common stock in regard to dividends. Preferred stockholders must be paid any unpaid prior-year dividends before common stockholders receive dividends.

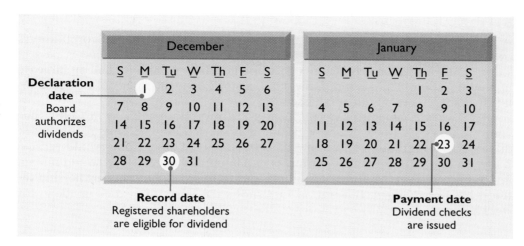

Illustration 15-1

Key dividend dates

To illustrate, assume that at December 31, 2002, IBR Inc. has 1,000 shares of 8%, $100 par value cumulative preferred stock. It also has 50,000 shares of $10 par value common stock outstanding. The dividend per share for preferred stock is $8 ($100 par value × 8%). The required annual dividend for preferred stock is therefore $8,000 (1,000 × $8). At December 31, 2002, the directors declare a $6,000 cash dividend. In this case, the entire dividend amount goes to preferred stockholders because of their dividend preference. The entry to record the declaration of the dividend is:

Dec. 31	Retained Earnings	6,000	
	Dividends Payable		6,000
	(To record $6 per share cash dividend to preferred stockholders)		

A	=	L	+	SE
		+6,000		−6,000

Because of the cumulative feature, dividends of $2 per share are in arrears on preferred stock for 2002. These dividends must be paid to preferred stockholders before any future dividends can be paid to common stockholders. Dividends in arrears should be disclosed in the financial statements.

At December 31, 2003, IBR declares a $50,000 cash dividend. The allocation of the dividend to the two classes of stock is as follows.

Total dividend		$50,000
Allocated to preferred stock		
Dividends in arrears, 2002 (1,000 × $2)	$2,000	
2003 dividend (1,000 × $8)	8,000	10,000
Remainder allocated to common stock		$40,000

Illustration 15-2

Allocating dividends to preferred and common stock

The entry to record the declaration of the dividend is:

Dec. 31	Retained Earnings	50,000	
	Dividends Payable		50,000
	(To record declaration of cash dividends of $10,000 to preferred stock and $40,000 to common stock)		

A	=	L	+	SE
		+50,000		−50,000

What if IBR's preferred stock were not cumulative? In that case preferred stockholders would have received only $8,000 in dividends in 2003. Common stockholders would have received $42,000.

STOCK DIVIDENDS

A **stock dividend** is a pro rata distribution to stockholders of the corporation's own stock. Whereas a cash dividend is paid in cash, a stock dividend is paid in stock. **A stock dividend results in a decrease in retained earnings and an increase in paid-in capital.** Unlike a cash dividend, a stock dividend does not decrease total stockholders' equity or total assets.

To illustrate, assume that you have a 2% ownership interest in Cetus Inc.; you own 20 of its 1,000 shares of common stock. If Cetus declares a 10% stock dividend, it would issue 100 shares (1,000 × 10%) of stock. You would receive 2 shares (2% × 100). Would your ownership interest change? No, it would remain at 2% (22 ÷ 1,100). **You now own more shares of stock, but your ownership interest has not changed.** Illustration 15-3 shows the effect of a stock dividend for stockholders.

Illustration 15-3

Effect of stock dividend for stockholders

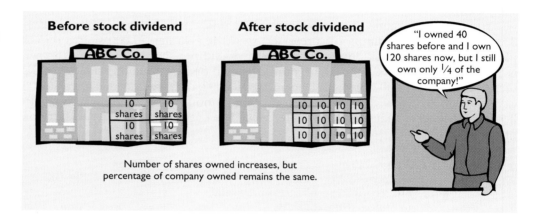

From the company's point of view, no cash has been disbursed, and no liabilities have been assumed by the corporation. What are the purposes and benefits of a stock dividend? Corporations issue stock dividends generally for one or more of the following reasons.

1. To satisfy stockholders' dividend expectations without spending cash.

2. To increase the marketability of the corporation's stock. When the number of shares outstanding increases, the market price per share decreases. Decreasing the market price of the stock makes it easier for smaller investors to purchase the shares.

3. To emphasize that a portion of stockholders' equity has been permanently reinvested in the business (and is unavailable for cash dividends).

The size of the stock dividend and the value to be assigned to each dividend share are determined by the board of directors when the dividend is declared. The per share amount must be at least equal to the par or stated value in order to meet legal requirements.

The accounting profession distinguishes between a **small stock dividend** (less than 20–25% of the corporation's issued stock) and a **large stock dividend** (greater than 20–25%). For small stock dividends, it recommends that the directors assign the **fair market value per share**. This treatment is based on the assumption that a small stock dividend will have little effect on the market price of the outstanding shares. Many stockholders consider small stock dividends to be distributions of earnings equal to the fair market value of the shares distributed. The amount to be assigned for a large stock dividend is not specified by the accounting profession. **Par or stated value per share** is normally assigned. Small stock dividends predominate in practice. Thus, we will illustrate only the entries for small stock dividends.

Entries for Stock Dividends

To illustrate the accounting for small stock dividends, assume that Medland Corporation has a balance of $300,000 in retained earnings. It declares a 10% stock dividend on its 50,000 shares of $10 par value common stock. The current fair market value of its stock is $15 per share. The number of shares to be issued is 5,000 (10% × 50,000). Therefore the total amount to be debited to Retained Earnings is $75,000 (5,000 × $15). The entry to record the declaration of the stock dividend is as follows.

Retained Earnings	75,000	
Common Stock Dividends Distributable		50,000
Paid-in Capital in Excess of Par Value		25,000
(To record declaration of 10% stock dividend)		

$$A \;=\; L \;+\; SE$$
$$-75{,}000$$
$$+50{,}000$$
$$+25{,}000$$

Note that Retained Earnings is debited for the fair market value of the stock issued ($15 × 5,000). Common Stock Dividends Distributable is credited for the par value of the dividend shares ($10 × 5,000), and the excess over par ($5 × 5,000) is credited to Paid-in Capital in Excess of Par Value.

Common Stock Dividends Distributable is a **stockholders' equity account**. It is not a liability because assets will not be used to pay the dividend. If a balance sheet is prepared before the dividend shares are issued, the distributable account is reported under Paid-in capital, as an addition to common stock issued:

Paid-in capital		
Common stock	$500,000	
Common stock dividends distributable	50,000	$550,000

Illustration 15-4

Statement presentation of common stock dividends distributable

When the dividend shares are issued, Common Stock Dividends Distributable is debited, and Common Stock is credited as follows.

Common Stock Dividends Distributable	50,000	
Common Stock		50,000
(To record issuance of 5,000 shares in a stock dividend)		

$$A \;=\; L \;+\; SE$$
$$-50{,}000$$
$$+50{,}000$$

Effects of Stock Dividends

How do stock dividends affect stockholders' equity? They **change the composition of stockholders' equity**, because a portion of retained earnings is transferred to paid-in capital. However, **total stockholders' equity remains the same**. Stock dividends also have no effect on the par or stated value per share. But the number of shares outstanding increases, and the book value per share decreases. These effects are shown for Medland Corporation in Illustration 15-5.

Illustration 15-5

Stock dividend effects

	Before Dividend	After Dividend
Stockholders' equity		
Paid-in capital		
Common stock, $10 par	$500,000	$550,000
Paid-in capital in excess of par value	—	25,000
Total paid-in capital	500,000	575,000
Retained earnings	300,000	225,000
Total stockholders' equity	$800,000	$800,000
Outstanding shares	50,000	55,000
Book value per share	$ 16.00	$ 14.55

In this example, total paid-in capital is increased by $75,000, and retained earnings is decreased by the same amount. Note also that total stockholders' equity remains unchanged at $800,000.

STOCK SPLITS

A **stock split**, like a stock dividend, involves the issuance of additional shares to stockholders according to their percentage ownership. **A stock split results in a reduction in the par or stated value per share.** The purpose of a stock split is to increase the marketability of the stock by lowering its market value per share. A lower market value also makes it easier for the corporation to issue additional stock.

The effect of a split on market value is generally inversely proportional to the size of the split. For example, after a recent 2-for-1 stock split, the market value of **Nike's** stock fell from $111 to approximately $55. The lower market value stimulated market activity, and within one year the stock was trading above $100 again.

In a stock split, the number of shares is increased in the same proportion that par or stated value per share is decreased. For example, in a 2-for-1 split, one share of $10 par value stock is exchanged for two shares of $5 par value stock. **A stock split does not have any effect on total paid-in capital, retained earnings, or total stockholders' equity.** But the number of shares outstanding increases and book value per share decreases. These effects are shown in Illustration 15-6 for Medland Corporation, assuming that it splits its 50,000 shares of common stock on a 2-for-1 basis.

> **HELPFUL HINT**
> A stock split changes the par value per share but does not affect any balances in stockholders' equity.

Illustration 15-6

Stock split effects

	Before Stock Split	After Stock Split
Stockholders' equity		
Paid-in capital		
Common stock	$500,000	$500,000
Paid-in capital in excess of par value	–0–	–0–
Total paid-in capital	500,000	500,000
Retained earnings	300,000	300,000
Total stockholders' equity	$800,000	$800,000
Outstanding shares	50,000	100,000
Book value per share	$16.00	$8.00

A stock split does not affect the balances in any stockholders' equity accounts. Therefore **it is not necessary to journalize a stock split**.

The significant differences between stock splits and stock dividends are shown in Illustration 15-7.

Item	Stock Split	Stock Dividend
Total paid-in capital	No change	Increase
Total retained earnings	No change	Decrease
Total par value (common stock)	No change	Increase
Par value per share	Decrease	No change

Illustration 15-7

Differences between the effects of stock splits and stock dividends

ACCOUNTING IN ACTION *Business Insight*

A handful of U.S. companies have no intention of keeping their stock trading in a range accessible to mere mortals. These companies never split their stock, no matter how high their stock price gets. The king is investment company **Berkshire Hathaway's** Class A stock, which sells for a pricey $53,400—per share! The company's Class B stock is a relative bargain at roughly $1,700 per share. Other "premium" stocks are **A. D. Makepeace** at $9,000 and **Mechanics Bank** of Richmond, California, at $11,000.

BEFORE YOU GO ON...

▶ *REVIEW IT*

1. What entries are made for cash dividends on (a) the declaration date, (b) the record date, and (c) the payment date?
2. Distinguish between a small and large stock dividend, and indicate the basis for valuing each kind of dividend.
3. Contrast the effects of a small stock dividend and a 2-for-1 stock split on (a) stockholders' equity, (b) outstanding shares, and (c) book value per share.

▶ *DO IT*

Sing CD Company has had 5 years of record earnings. Due to this success, the market price of its 500,000 shares of $2 par value common stock has tripled from $15 per share to $45. During this period, paid-in capital remained the same at $2,000,000. Retained earnings increased from $1,500,000 to $10,000,000. President Joan Elbert is considering either (1) a 10% stock dividend or (2) a 2-for-1 stock split. She asks you to show the before-and-after effects of each option on (a) retained earnings and (b) book value per share.

ACTION PLAN

* Calculate the stock dividend's effect on retained earnings by multiplying the number of new shares times the market price of the stock (or par value for a large stock dividend).
* Recall that a stock dividend increases the number of shares without affecting total equity, thus decreasing the book value per share.
* Recall that a stock split only increases the number of shares outstanding and decreases the par value per share.

SOLUTION

(a) **(1)** The stock dividend amount is $2,250,000 [(500,000 × 10%) × $45]. The new balance in retained earnings is $7,750,000 ($10,000,000 − $2,250,000).

(2) The retained earnings balance after the stock split would be the same as it was before the split: $10,000,000.

(b) The book value effects are as follows:

	Original Balances	After Dividend	After Split
Paid-in capital	$ 2,000,000	$ 4,250,000	$ 2,000,000
Retained earnings	10,000,000	7,750,000	10,000,000
Total stockholders' equity	$12,000,000	$12,000,000	$12,000,000
Shares outstanding	500,000	550,000	1,000,000
Book value per share	$24	$21.82	$12

Related exercise material: BE15-2, BE15-3, E15-3, E15-4, E15-5, E15-6, and E15-7.

RETAINED EARNINGS

STUDY OBJECTIVE 2

Identify the items that are reported in a retained earnings statement.

As you learned in Chapter 14, **retained earnings** is net income that is retained in the business. The balance in retained earnings is part of the stockholders' claim on the total assets of the corporation. It does not, though, represent a claim on any specific asset. Nor can the amount of retained earnings be associated with the balance of any asset account. For example, a $100,000 balance in retained earnings does not mean that there should be $100,000 in cash. The reason is that the cash resulting from the excess of revenues over expenses may have been used to purchase buildings, equipment, and other assets. To illustrate that retained earnings and cash may be quite different, Illustration 15-8 shows recent amounts of retained earnings and cash in selected companies.

Illustration 15-8

Retained earnings and cash balances

Company	(in millions) Retained Earnings	Cash
Walt Disney Co.	$12,281	$414
Sears, Roebuck and Co.	5,952	729
The Home Depot	7,941	168
Amazon.com	(882)	117

HELPFUL HINT

Remember that Retained Earnings is a stockholders' equity account, whose normal balance is a credit.

Remember from Chapter 14 that when a company has net profit, the net income that is retained in the business is recorded in retained earnings by means of a closing entry. This entry debits Income Summary and credits Retained Earnings.

However, when expenses exceed revenues, a **net loss** results. A net loss is debited to Retained Earnings in a closing entry. This is done even if it results in a debit balance in Retained Earnings. **Net losses are not debited to paid-in capital accounts.** To do so would destroy the distinction between paid-in and earned capital. A debit balance in Retained Earnings is identified as a **deficit**. It is reported as a deduction in the stockholders' equity section, as shown below.

Illustration 15-9

Stockholders' equity with deficit

Balance Sheet (partial)

Stockholders' equity	
Paid-in capital	
Common stock	$800,000
Retained earnings (deficit)	(50,000)
Total stockholders' equity	$750,000

RETAINED EARNINGS RESTRICTIONS

The balance in retained earnings is generally available for dividend declarations. Some companies state this fact. For example, in the notes to its financial statements, **Lockheed Martin Corporation** states:

> **LOCKHEED MARTIN CORPORATION**
> **Notes to the Financial Statements**
>
> At December 31, retained earnings were unrestricted and available for dividend payments.

Illustration 15-10

Disclosure of unrestricted retained earnings

In some cases, there may be **retained earnings restrictions**. These make a portion of the retained earnings balance currently unavailable for dividends. Restrictions result from one or more of the following causes: legal, contractual, or voluntary.

1. **Legal restrictions.** Many states require a corporation to restrict retained earnings for the cost of treasury stock purchased. The restriction keeps intact the corporation's legal capital that is being temporarily held as treasury stock. When the treasury stock is sold, the restriction is lifted.

2. **Contractual restrictions.** Long-term debt contracts may restrict retained earnings as a condition for the loan. The restriction limits the use of corporate assets for payment of dividends. Thus, it increases the likelihood that the corporation will be able to meet required loan payments.

3. **Voluntary restrictions.** The board of directors may voluntarily create retained earnings restrictions for specific purposes. For example, the board may authorize a restriction for future plant expansion. By reducing the amount of retained earnings available for dividends, more cash may be available for the planned expansion.

Retained earnings restrictions are generally disclosed in the notes to the financial statements. For example, **Pratt & Lambert**, a leading producer of paint, had the following note in a recent financial statement.

> **PRATT & LAMBERT**
> **Notes to the Financial Statements**
>
> **Note D: Long-term Debt and Retained Earnings**   Loan agreements contain, among other covenants, a restriction on the payment of dividends, which limits future dividend payments to $20,565,000 plus 75% of future net income.

Illustration 15-11

Disclosure of restriction

PRIOR PERIOD ADJUSTMENTS

Suppose that a corporation's books have been closed and the financial statements have been issued. The corporation then discovers that a material error has been made in reporting net income of a prior year. How should this situation be recorded in the accounts and reported in the financial statements?

The correction of an error in previously issued financial statements is known as a **prior period adjustment**. The correction is made directly to Retained Earnings because the effect of the error is now in this account: The net income for the prior period has been recorded in retained earnings through the journalizing and posting of closing entries.

To illustrate, assume that General Microwave discovers in 2002 that it understated depreciation expense in 2001 by $300,000 due to computational errors. These errors overstated both net income for 2001 and the current balance in retained earnings. The entry for the prior period adjustment, assuming all tax effects are ignored, is as follows.

A = L + SE		
-300,000 -300,000		

Retained Earnings	300,000	
Accumulated Depreciation		300,000
(To adjust for understatement of depreciation in a		
prior period)		

A debit to an income statement account in 2002 would be incorrect because the error pertains to a prior year.

Prior period adjustments are reported in the retained earnings statement.[1] They are added (or deducted, as the case may be) from the beginning retained earnings balance. This results in an adjusted beginning balance. Assuming General Microwave has a beginning balance of $800,000 in retained earnings, the prior period adjustment is reported as follows.

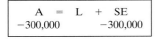

Illustration 15-12

Statement presentation of prior period adjustments

GENERAL MICROWAVE Retained Earnings Statement (partial)	
Balance, January 1, as reported	$800,000
Correction for overstatement of net income	
in prior period (depreciation error)	(300,000)
Balance, January 1, as adjusted	$500,000

Again, reporting the correction in the current year's income statement would be incorrect because it applies to a prior year's income statement.

RETAINED EARNINGS STATEMENT

The **retained earnings statement** shows the changes in retained earnings during the year. The statement is prepared from the Retained Earnings account. Transactions and events that affect retained earnings are tabulated in account form as shown in Illustration 15-13.

Illustration 15-13

Debits and credits to retained earnings

Retained Earnings	
1. Net loss	1. Net income
2. Prior period adjustments for overstatement of net income	2. Prior period adjustments for understatement of net income
3. Cash dividends and stock dividends	
4. Some disposals of treasury stock	

As indicated, net income increases retained earnings, and a net loss decreases retained earnings. Prior period adjustments may either increase or decrease retained earnings. Both cash dividends and stock dividends decrease retained earnings.

---

[1]A complete retained earnings statement is shown in Illustration 15-14 on the next page.

The circumstances under which treasury stock transactions decrease retained earnings are explained in Chapter 14, pages 576–579.

A complete retained earnings statement for Graber Inc., based on assumed data, is as follows.

Illustration 15-14

Retained earnings statement

GRABER INC. Retained Earnings Statement For the Year Ended December 31, 2002		
Balance, January 1, as reported		$1,050,000
Correction for understatement of net income in prior period (inventory error)		50,000
Balance, January 1, as adjusted		1,100,000
Add: Net income		360,000
		1,460,000
Less: Cash dividends	$100,000	
Stock dividends	200,000	300,000
Balance, December 31		$1,160,000

STATEMENT PRESENTATION AND ANALYSIS

Presentation

The stockholders' equity section of Graber Inc.'s balance sheet is presented in Illustration 15-15. Note the following: (1) "Common stock dividends distributable" is shown under "Capital stock," in "Paid-in capital." (2) A retained earnings restriction is disclosed in the notes.

Illustration 15-15

Comprehensive stockholders' equity section

GRABER INC. Balance Sheet (partial)		
Stockholders' equity		
Paid-in capital		
Capital stock		

9% Preferred stock, $100 par value, cumulative,
  callable at $120, 10,000 shares authorized,
  6,000 shares issued and outstanding
		$ 600,000

Common stock, no par, $5 stated value,
  500,000 shares authorized, 400,000 shares issued
  and 390,000 outstanding
	$2,000,000	

Common stock dividends distributable	50,000	2,050,000
Total capital stock		2,650,000
Additional paid-in capital		
In excess of par value—preferred stock	30,000	
In excess of stated value—common stock	1,050,000	
Total additional paid-in capital		1,080,000
Total paid-in capital		3,730,000
Retained earnings (see Note R)		1,160,000
Total paid-in capital and retained earnings		4,890,000
Less: Treasury stock—common (10,000 shares)		80,000
Total stockholders' equity		$4,810,000
Note R: Retained earnings is restricted for the cost of treasury stock, $80,000.		

INTERNATIONAL NOTE

In Switzerland, there are no specific disclosure requirements for stockholders' equity. But Swiss companies typically disclose separate categories of capital on the balance sheet.

Instead of presenting a detailed stockholders' equity section in the balance sheet and a retained earnings statement, many companies prepare a **stockholders' equity statement**. This statement shows the changes in each stockholders' equity account and in total that have occurred during the year. An example of a stockholders' equity statement is illustrated in **Lands' End's** financial statements in Appendix A.

Analysis

Profitability from the viewpoint of the common stockholder can be measured by the **return on common stockholders' equity**. This ratio shows how many dollars of net income were earned for each dollar invested by the stockholders. It is computed by dividing net income available to common stockholders (which is net income minus preferred stock dividends) by average common stockholders' equity. To illustrate, **Lands' End's** beginning-of-the-year and end-of-the-year common stockholders' equity were $242.5 and $296.2 million respectively. Its net income was $48.0 million, and no preferred stock was outstanding. The return on common stockholders' equity ratio is computed as follows.

Illustration 15-16

Return on common stockholders' equity ratio and computation

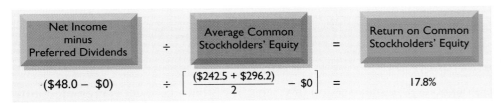

As shown above, if a company has preferred stock, the amount of **preferred dividends** is deducted from net income to compute income available to common stockholders. Also, the par value of preferred stock is deducted from total average stockholders' equity to arrive at the amount of common stockholders' equity.

B E F O R E   Y O U   G O   O N . . .

▶ *REVIEW IT*
1. How are retained earnings restrictions generally reported?
2. What is a prior period adjustment, and how is it reported?
3. What are the principal sources of debits and credits to Retained Earnings?
4. How are stock dividends distributable reported in the stockholders' equity section?
5. Explain the return on common stockholders' equity ratio.

▶ *DO IT*
Vega Corporation has retained earnings of $5,130,000 on January 1, 2002. During the year, Vega earns $2,000,000 of net income. It declares and pays a $250,000 cash dividend. In 2002, Vega records an adjustment of $180,000 due to the understatement of 2001 depreciation expense from a mathematical error. Prepare a retained earnings statement for 2002.

ACTION PLAN
• Recall that a retained earnings statement begins with retained earnings, as reported at the end of the previous year.
• Add or subtract any prior period adjustments to arrive at the adjusted beginning figure.
• Add net income and subtract dividends declared to arrive at the ending balance in retained earnings.

SOLUTION

VEGA CORPORATION Retained Earnings Statement For the Year Ended December 31, 2002	
Balance, January 1, as reported	$5,130,000
Correction for overstatement of net income in prior period (depreciation error)	(180,000)
Balance, January 1, as adjusted	4,950,000
Add: Net income	2,000,000
	6,950,000
Less: Cash dividends	250,000
Balance, December 31	$6,700,000

Related exercise material: BE15-4 and E15-8.

CORPORATION INCOME STATEMENTS

Income statements for **corporations are the same as the statements for proprietorships or partnerships except for one thing: the reporting of income taxes**. For income tax purposes, corporations are a separate legal entity. As a result, **income tax expense** is reported in a separate section of the corporation income statement before net income. The condensed income statement for Leads Inc. in Illustration 15-17 shows a typical presentation. Note that the corporation reports income before income taxes as one line item and income tax expense as another.

STUDY OBJECTIVE 4

Describe the form and content of corporation income statements.

LEADS INC. Income Statement For the Year Ended December 31, 2002	
Sales	$800,000
Cost of goods sold	600,000
Gross profit	200,000
Operating expenses	50,000
Income from operations	150,000
Other revenues and gains	10,000
Other expenses and losses	(4,000)
Income before income taxes	156,000
Income tax expense	46,800
Net income	$109,200

Illustration 15-17

Income statement with income taxes

HELPFUL HINT
Corporations may also use the single-step form of income statement discussed in Chapter 5.

Income tax expense and the related liability for income taxes payable are recorded as part of the adjusting process. Using the data above for Leads Inc., the adjusting entry for income tax expense at December 31, 2002, would be:

Income Tax Expense	46,800	
Income Taxes Payable		46,800
(To record income taxes for 2002)		

A = L + SE
+46,800 −46,800

Another illustration of income taxes is presented in the income statement of **Lands' End** in Appendix A.

The income statements we have studied so far provide insight into a company's income-related activities. In studying such statements, the user may ask: (1) Are the results typical for this company? (2) Are the results a reasonable indicator of the company's future earnings?

To provide answers to these questions, accountants have concluded that **material items not typical of regular operations** should also be reported. These items are reported in the income statement immediately before net income. The non-typical items include (1) discontinued operations, (2) extraordinary items, and (3) changes in accounting principle. These "irregular" items are reported net of income taxes. Thus, the income tax expense (or tax savings) is shown for income before income taxes and for each of the listed irregular items. The general concept is "let the tax follow income or loss."

DISCONTINUED OPERATIONS

STUDY OBJECTIVE 5

Indicate the statement presentation of material items not typical of regular operations.

Discontinued operations refers to the disposal of a **significant segment** of a business. Examples are the cessation of an entire activity and the elimination of a major class of customers. **Kmart's** decision to terminate its interest in four business activities, including **PACE Membership Warehouse** and **PayLess Drug Stores Northwest**, was reported as discontinued operations. On the other hand, the phasing out of a model such as the **GM** Chevette or part of a line of business is not considered to be a disposal of a segment.

Following the disposal of a significant segment, the income statement should report both income from continuing operations and income (or loss) from discontinued operations. **The income (loss) from discontinued operations consists of two parts: the income (loss) from operations and the gain (loss) on disposal of the segment.**

To illustrate, assume that during 2002 Acro Energy Inc. has income before income taxes of $800,000. During 2002 Acro discontinued and sold its unprofitable chemical division. The loss in 2002 from chemical operations (net of $60,000 taxes) was $140,000. The loss on disposal of the chemical division (net of $30,000 taxes) was $70,000. Assuming a 30% tax rate on income, the income statement presentation is shown below.

Illustration 15-18

Statement presentation of discontinued operations

ACRO ENERGY INC. Income Statement (partial) For the Year Ended December 31, 2002		
Income before income taxes		$800,000
Income tax expense		240,000
Income from continuing operations		560,000
Discontinued operations		
Loss from operations of chemical division, net of $60,000 income tax saving	$140,000	
Loss from disposal of chemical division, net of $30,000 income tax saving	70,000	210,000
Net income		$350,000

HELPFUL HINT
Observe the dual disclosures: (1) The results of operations of the discontinued division must be eliminated from the results of continuing operations. (2) The disposal of the operation must also be reported.

Note that the caption "Income from continuing operations" is used and that a new section "Discontinued operations" is added. **Within the new section, both the operating loss and the loss on disposal are reported net of applicable income taxes.** This presentation clearly indicates the separate effects of continuing operations and discontinued operations on net income.

EXTRAORDINARY ITEMS

Extraordinary items are events and transactions that meet two conditions: They are (1) **unusual in nature and** (2) **infrequent in occurrence**. To be "unusual," the item should be abnormal and only incidentally related to the company's customary activities. To be "infrequent," the item should not be reasonably expected to recur in the foreseeable future. Both criteria must be evaluated in terms of the company's operating environment. Thus, **Weyerhaeuser Co.** reported the $36 million in damages to its timberland caused by the volcanic eruption of Mount St. Helens as an extraordinary item. The eruption was both unusual and infrequent. In contrast, Florida-Citrus Company does not report frost damage to its citrus crop as an extraordinary item. Frost damage is not viewed as infrequent. Illustration 15-19 shows the classification of extraordinary and ordinary items.

Illustration 15-19

Examples of extraordinary and ordinary items

Extraordinary items

1. Effects of major casualties (acts of God), if rare in the area.

2. Expropriation (takeover) of property by a foreign government.

3. Effects of a newly enacted law or regulation, such as a condemnation action.

4. Destruction of property by fire or explosion.

Ordinary items

1. Effects of major casualties (acts of God), frequent in the area.

2. Write-down of inventories or write-off of receivables.

3. Losses attributable to labor strikes.

4. Gains or losses from sales of property, plant, or equipment.

ACCOUNTING IN ACTION *Business Insight*

In the recession of the early 1990s, many companies closed plants and reduced their work forces. The costs incurred in these activities are called plant restructuring costs. Such costs are reported as other expenses and losses in the income statement. They are not considered an extraordinary item because plant closings are neither unusual nor infrequent in many industries.

Plant restructuring costs often have a significant effect on net income. For example, **Union Pacific Corp.** had a $585 million after-tax charge, of which $492 million applied to the disposal of 7,100 miles of the Union Pacific Railroad.

Extraordinary items are reported net of taxes in a separate section of the income statement immediately below discontinued operations. To illustrate, assume that in 2002 a foreign government expropriated property held as an investment by Acro Energy Inc. If the loss is $70,000 before applicable income taxes of $21,000, the income statement will report a deduction of $49,000 as shown in Illustration 15-20.

Illustration 15-20

Statement presentation of extraordinary items

ACRO ENERGY INC. Income Statement (partial) For the Year Ended December 31, 2002		
Income before income taxes		$800,000
Income tax expense		240,000
Income from continuing operations		560,000
Discontinued operations		
Loss from operations of chemical division, net of $60,000 income tax saving	$140,000	
Loss from disposal of chemical division, net of $30,000 income tax saving	70,000	210,000
Income before extraordinary item		350,000
Extraordinary item		
Expropriation of investment, net of $21,000 income tax saving		**49,000**
Net income		$301,000

When there is an extraordinary item to report, the caption "Income before extraordinary item" is added immediately before the section for the extraordinary item. This presentation clearly indicates the effect of the extraordinary item on net income.

What if a transaction or event meets one (but not both) of the criteria for an extraordinary item? In that case it is reported under either "Other revenues and gains" or "Other expenses and losses" at its gross amount (not net of tax). This is true, for example, of gains (losses) resulting from the sale of property, plant, and equipment, as explained in Chapter 10. It has become quite common for companies to use the label "Non-recurring charges" for losses that do not meet the extraordinary item criteria.

CHANGE IN ACCOUNTING PRINCIPLE

For ease of comparison, financial statements are expected to be prepared on a basis **consistent** with the preceding period. Where a choice of accounting principles is available, the principle initially chosen should be consistently applied from period to period. A **change in accounting principle** occurs when the principle used in the current year is different from the one used in the preceding year. Examples include a change in depreciation methods (declining-balance to straight-line) and a change in inventory costing methods (FIFO to average cost). When is a change in accounting principle permitted? When two conditions are met: (1) Management can show that the new principle is preferable to the old principle, and (2) the effects of the change are clearly disclosed in the income statement.

When a change in accounting principle has occurred:

1. The new principle should be used in reporting the results of operations of the current year.

2. The cumulative effect of the change on all prior year income statements should be disclosed net of applicable taxes in a special section immediately preceding net income.

To illustrate, assume that at the beginning of 2002, Acro Energy Inc. changes from the straight-line method of depreciation to the declining-balance method for equipment purchased on January 1, 1999. The cumulative effect on prior year income statements (statements for 1999–2001) is to increase depreciation expense and decrease income before income taxes by $24,000. Assuming a 30 percent tax rate, the net-of-tax effect of the change is $16,800 ($24,000 × 70%). The income statement presentation for the change in accounting principle is shown in Illustration 15-21.

Illustration 15-21

Statement presentation of cumulative effect of change in accounting principle

ACRO ENERGY INC. Income Statement (partial) For the Year Ended December 31, 2002		
Income before income taxes		$800,000
Income tax expense		240,000
Income from continuing operations		560,000
Discontinued operations		
Loss from operations of chemical division,		
net of $60,000 income tax saving	$140,000	
Loss from disposal of chemical division,		
net of $30,000 income tax saving	70,000	210,000
Income before extraordinary item and cumulative		
effect of change in accounting principle		350,000
Extraordinary item		
Expropriation of investment, net of $21,000		
income tax saving		49,000
Cumulative effect of change in accounting principle		
Effect on prior years of change in depreciation		
method, net of $7,200 income tax saving		16,800
Net income		$284,200

HELPFUL HINT
If a company does not have either discontinued operations or extraordinary items, the label "Income before cumulative effect of change in accounting principle" is used in place of "Income from continuing operations."

The income statement for Acro Energy will also show depreciation expense for the current year. The amount is based on the new depreciation method. The caption "Income before extraordinary item and cumulative effect of change in accounting principle" is inserted immediately following the effects of discontinued operations. This presentation clearly indicates the cumulative effect of the change on prior years' income.

A complete income statement showing all material items not typical of regular operations is illustrated in the Demonstration Problem (pages 622–623).

*E*THICS NOTE
Changes in accounting principle should result in financial statements that are more informative for statement users. They should not be used to artificially improve the reported performance or financial position of the corporation.

BEFORE YOU GO ON . . .

▶ *REVIEW IT*

1. What is the unique feature of a corporation income statement?
2. What are the similarities and differences in reporting material items not typical of regular operations?
3. Did **Lands' End** report any of the three types of irregular items in its 2000 income statement? The answer to this question is provided on page 637.

▶ *DO IT*

In its proposed 2002 income statement, AIR Corporation reports income before income taxes $400,000, extraordinary loss from fire $100,000, income taxes (30%) $90,000, and net income $210,000. Prepare a correct income statement, beginning with income before income taxes.

ACTION PLAN
- Recall that a fire loss is unusual because it meets the criteria of being both unusual and infrequent.
- Disclose the income tax effect of each component of income, beginning with income before any irregular items.
- Report irregular items net of any income tax effect.

SOLUTION

AIR CORPORATION **Income Statement (partial)**	
Income before income taxes	$400,000
Income tax expense (30%)	120,000
Income before extraordinary item	280,000
Extraordinary loss from fire, net of $30,000 income tax saving	70,000
Net income	$210,000

Related exercise material: BE15-6, BE15-7, BE15-8, E15-12, and E15-13.

☑ THE NAVIGATOR

EARNINGS PER SHARE

STUDY OBJECTIVE 6

Compute earnings per share.

Earnings data are frequently reported in the financial press. They are widely used by stockholders and potential investors in evaluating the profitability of a company. A convenient measure of earnings is **earnings per share (EPS)**, which indicates the net income earned by each share of outstanding **common stock**.

EPS AND PREFERRED DIVIDENDS

When a corporation has both preferred and common stock, the current year's dividend declared on preferred stock is subtracted from net income to arrive at **income available to common stockholders**. The formula for computing EPS is:

Illustration 15-22

Earnings per share

To illustrate, assume that Rally Inc. reports net income of $211,000 on its 102,500 weighted average common shares.[2] During the year it also declares a $6,000 dividend on its preferred stock. Therefore, the amount Rally has available

---

[2]The calculation of the weighted average of common shares outstanding is discussed in advanced accounting courses.

for common stock dividends is \$205,000 (\$211,000 − \$6,000). Earnings per share is \$2 (\$205,000 ÷ 102,500). If the preferred stock is cumulative, the dividend for the current year is deducted whether or not it is declared. Remember that **earnings per share is reported only for common stock**.

Investors often attempt to link earnings per share to the market price per share of a company's stock.[3] Because of the importance of earnings per share, most companies are required to report it on the face of the income statement. Generally this amount is simply reported below net income on the statement. For Rally Inc. the presentation would be:

RALLY INC. Income Statement (partial)	
Net income	\$211,000
Earnings per share	\$2.00

Illustration 15-23

Basic earnings per share disclosure

${A}$CCOUNTING IN ACTION   *Business Insight*

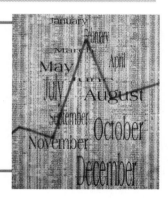

When a company publicly announces its latest earnings per share figure, a change in the company's stock price will often result. The change in stock price will be most pronounced if the company's net income figure differs from what investors were expecting. When **Yahoo!** recently announced earnings per share that exceeded investor expectations, its stock price jumped 14 percent in a single day. When retail giant **Costco Wholesale Corporation** announced earnings per share only 1 cent below analysts' expectations, its stock price fell 22 percent in a single day. To avoid "earnings surprises" and the resultant wide swings in share prices, companies continually try to keep investors informed.

EPS AND IRREGULAR ITEMS

When the income statement contains any of the irregular items described earlier, EPS should be disclosed for each component. Assuming that Acro Energy had 100,000 shares of common stock outstanding during the year, the additional EPS disclosures for the income statement in Illustration 15-21 would be as shown below.

ACRO ENERGY INC. Income Statement (partial) For the Year Ended December 31, 2002	
Net income	\$284,200
Earnings per share	
Income from continuing operations	\$5.60
Loss from discontinued operations	(2.10)
Income before extraordinary item and cumulative effect of change in accounting principle	3.50
Extraordinary loss	(.49)
Cumulative effect of change in accounting principle	(.17)
Net income	\$2.84

Illustration 15-24

Additional earnings per share disclosures

---

[3]The ratio of the market price per share to the earnings per share is referred to as the *price-earnings (P-E) ratio*. This ratio is reported in *The Wall Street Journal* and in other newspapers for common stocks listed on major stock exchanges.

These disclosures enable decision makers to recognize the effects on EPS of income from continuing operations, as separate from income (or loss) from irregular items. **Earnings per share from continuing operations is generally the most useful per share amount.** It represents the results of continuing and ordinary business activity. Thus, it provides the best basis for predicting future operating results.

BEFORE YOU GO ON...

▶ *REVIEW IT*

1. Explain the components of the formula for computing earnings per share when there is only common stock and outstanding shares are unchanged during the year.
2. What effects may preferred stock have on the formula for computing earnings per share?

A LOOK BACK AT OUR FEATURE STORY

Refer back to the Feature Story about Nike at the beginning of the chapter, and answer the following questions.

1. Nike's stock has split numerous times in recent years. What is the likely reason for these splits?
2. Prepare the quarterly journal entry (accounts and amount) recorded by a Nike shareholder when he or she receives a dividend of $1,000 from Nike.
3. Nike has increased its cash dividend per share every year for the past 11 years. What issues must it consider when deciding the level of the dividend payment?

SOLUTION

1. Nike's stock experienced a rapid increase in value. To keep the stock in an affordable price range for the average investor, management has split the stock a number of times.
2. The entry to record receipt of a dividend each quarter is:

Cash	1,000	
Dividend Revenue		1,000
(To record quarterly dividend revenue)		

3. Nike should consider the adequacy of its cash, the adequacy of its retained earnings, the level of its future earnings, and its ability to maintain the dividend level in the future.

☑ THE NAVIGATOR

DEMONSTRATION PROBLEM

Additional Demonstration Problem

The events and transactions of Dever Corporation for the year ending December 31, 2002, resulted in the following data.

Cost of goods sold	$2,600,000
Net sales	4,400,000
Other expenses and losses	9,600
Other revenues and gains	5,600
Selling and administrative expenses	1,100,000
Income from operations of plastics division	70,000
Gain from disposal of plastics division	500,000
Loss from tornado disaster (extraordinary loss)	600,000
Cumulative effect of changing from straight-line depreciation to double-declining-balance (increase in depreciation expense)	300,000

Analysis reveals that:

1. All items are before the applicable income tax rate of 30%.

2. The plastics division was sold on July 1.

3. All operating data for the plastics division have been segregated.

4. There were 100,000 shares of common stock outstanding during the year.

Instructions
Prepare an income statement for the year, including the presentation of earnings per share data.

SOLUTION TO DEMONSTRATION PROBLEM

DEVER CORPORATION
Income Statement
For the Year Ended December 31, 2002

Net sales		$4,400,000
Cost of goods sold		2,600,000
Gross profit		1,800,000
Selling and administrative expenses		1,100,000
Income from operations		700,000
Other revenues and gains	$ 5,600	
Other expenses and losses	9,600	4,000
Income before income taxes		696,000
Income tax expense ($696,000 × 30%)		208,800
Income from continuing operations		487,200
Discontinued operations		
Income from operations of plastics division, net of		
$21,000 income taxes ($70,000 × 30%)	49,000	
Gain from disposal of plastics division, net of $150,000		
income taxes ($500,000 × 30%)	350,000	399,000
Income before extraordinary item and cumulative effect of		
change in accounting principle		886,200
Extraordinary item		
Tornado loss, net of $180,000 income tax saving		
($600,000 × 30%)		420,000
Cumulative effect of change in accounting principle		
Effect on prior years of change in depreciation method,		
net of $90,000 income tax saving ($300,000 × 30%)		210,000
Net income		$256,200
Earnings per share		
Income from continuing operations		$4.87
Gain from discontinued operations		3.99
Income before extraordinary item and cumulative effect		
of change in accounting principle		8.86
Extraordinary loss		(4.20)
Cumulative effect of change in accounting principle		(2.10)
Net income		$2.56

ACTION PLAN

• Report material items not typical of operations in separate sections, net of taxes.

• Associate income taxes with the item that affects the taxes.

• Apply the corporate tax rate to income before income taxes to determine tax expense.

• Recall that all data presented in determining income before income taxes are the same as for unincorporated companies.

☑ THE NAVIGATOR

SUMMARY OF STUDY OBJECTIVES

1. Prepare the entries for cash dividends and stock dividends. Entries for both cash and stock dividends are required at the declaration date and at the payment date. At the declaration date the entries are: cash dividend—debit Retained Earnings, and credit Dividends Payable; small stock dividend—debit Retained Earnings, credit Paid-in Capital in Excess of Par (or Stated) Value, and credit Common Stock Dividends Distributable. At the payment date, the entries for cash and stock dividends are: cash dividend—debit Dividends Payable and credit Cash; small stock dividend—debit Common Stock Dividends Distributable and credit Common Stock.

2. *Identify the items that are reported in a retained earnings statement.* Each of the individual debits and credits to retained earnings should be reported in the retained earnings statement. Additions consist of net income and prior period adjustments to correct understatements of prior years' net income. Deductions consist of net loss, adjustments to correct overstatements of prior years' net income, cash and stock dividends, and some disposals of treasury stock.

3. *Prepare and analyze a comprehensive stockholders' equity section.* A comprehensive stockholders' equity section includes all stockholders' equity accounts. It consists of two sections: paid-in capital and retained earnings. It should also include notes to the financial statements that explain any restrictions on retained earnings and any dividends in arrears. One measure of profitability is the return on common stockholders' equity. It is calculated by dividing net income minus preferred stock dividends by average common stockholders' equity.

4. *Describe the form and content of corporation income statements.* The form and content of corporation income statements are similar to the statements of proprietorships and partnerships with one exception: Income taxes or income tax expense must be reported in a separate section before net income in the corporation's income statement.

5. *Indicate the statement presentation of material items not typical of regular operations.* Material items not typical of regular operations are reported net of taxes in sections on the income statement immediately before net income. These items include (a) discontinued operations, (b) extraordinary items, and (c) changes in accounting principle.

6. *Compute earnings per share.* Earnings per share is computed by dividing net income by the weighted average number of common shares outstanding during the period. When preferred stock dividends exist, they must be deducted from net income in order to calculate EPS.

✓ THE
NAVIGATOR

Key Term Matching Activity

GLOSSARY

Cash dividend A pro rata distribution of cash to stockholders. (p. 602).

Change in accounting principle The use of a principle in the current year that is different from the one used in the preceding year. (p. 618).

Declaration date The date the board of directors formally declares a dividend and announces it to stockholders. (p. 603).

Deficit A debit balance in retained earnings. (p. 610).

Discontinued operations The disposal of a significant segment of a business. (p. 616).

Dividend A distribution by a corporation to its stockholders on a pro rata (proportional) basis. (p. 602).

Earnings per share The net income earned by each share of outstanding common stock. (p. 620).

Extraordinary items Events and transactions that are unusual in nature and infrequent in occurrence. (p. 617).

Liquidating dividend A dividend declared out of paid-in capital. (p. 602).

Payment date The date dividend checks are mailed to stockholders. (p. 604).

Prior period adjustment The correction of an error in previously issued financial statements. (p. 611).

Record date The date when ownership of outstanding shares is determined for dividend purposes. (p. 604).

Retained earnings Net income that is retained in the business. (p. 610).

Retained earnings restrictions Circumstances that make a portion of retained earnings currently unavailable for dividends. (p. 611).

Retained earnings statement A financial statement that shows the changes in retained earnings during the year. (p. 612).

Return on common stockholders' equity A measure of profitability that shows how many dollars of net income were earned for each dollar invested by the owners; computed as net income minus preferred dividends divided by average common stockholders' equity. (p. 614).

Stock dividend A pro rata distribution to stockholders of the corporation's own stock. (p. 606).

Stockholders' equity statement A statement that shows the changes in each stockholders' equity account and in total stockholders' equity during the year. (p. 614).

Stock split The issuance of additional shares of stock to stockholders according to their percentage ownership; is accompanied by a reduction in the par or stated value per share. (p. 608).

Chapter 15 Self-Test

SELF-STUDY QUESTIONS

Answers are at the end of the chapter.

(SO 1) **1.** Entries for cash dividends are required on the:
   a. declaration date and the payment date.
   b. record date and the payment date.
   c. declaration date, record date, and payment date.
   d. declaration date and the record date.

(SO 1) **2.** Which of the following statements about small stock dividends is true?

   a. A debit to Retained Earnings for the par value of the shares issued should be made.

   b. A small stock dividend decreases total stockholders' equity.

   c. Market value per share should be assigned to the dividend shares.

   d. A small stock dividend ordinarily will have no effect on book value per share of stock.

(SO 2) **3.** All *but one* of the following is reported in a retained earnings statement. The exception is:
a. cash and stock dividends.
b. net income and net loss.
c. some disposals of treasury stock below cost.
d. sales of treasury stock above cost.

(SO 2) **4.** A prior period adjustment is:
a. reported in the income statement as a nontypical item.
b. a correction of an error that is made directly to retained earnings.
c. reported directly in the stockholders' equity section.
d. reported in the retained earnings statement as an adjustment of the ending balance of retained earnings.

(SO 3) **5.** In the stockholders' equity section, Common Stock Dividends Distributable is reported as a(n):
a. deduction from total paid-in capital and retained earnings.
b. addition to additional paid-in capital.
c. deduction from retained earnings.
d. addition to capital stock.

(SO 4) **6.** Corporation income statements may be the same as the income statements for unincorporated companies *except* for:
a. gross profit.
b. income tax expense.
c. operating income.
d. net sales.

(SO 3) **7.** The return on common stockholders' equity is defined as:
a. Net income divided by total assets.
b. Cash dividends divided by average common stockholders' equity.

c. Income available to common stockholders divided by average common stockholders' equity.
d. None of these is correct.

8. In reporting discontinued operations, the income state- (SO 5) ment should show in a special section:
a. gains and losses on the disposal of the discontinued segment.
b. gains and losses from operations of the discontinued segment.
c. Both (a) and (b).
d. Neither (a) nor (b).

9. The Rand Corporation has income before taxes of (SO 5) $400,000 and an extraordinary loss of $100,000. If the income tax rate is 25% on all items, the income statement should show income before extraordinary items and extraordinary items, respectively, of:
a. $325,000 and $100,000.
b. $325,000 and $75,000.
c. $300,000 and $100,000.
d. $300,000 and $75,000.

10. The income statement for Nadeen, Inc. shows income (SO 6) before income taxes $700,000, income tax expense $210,000, and net income $490,000. If Nadeen has 100,000 shares of common stock outstanding throughout the year, earnings per share is:
a. $7.00.
b. $4.90.
c. $2.10.
d. No correct answer is given.

QUESTIONS

1. (a) What is a dividend? (b) "Dividends must be paid in cash." Do you agree? Explain.

2. Mike Horn maintains that adequate cash is the only requirement for the declaration of a cash dividend. Is Mike correct? Explain.

3. (a) Three dates are important in connection with cash dividends. Identify these dates, and explain their significance to the corporation and its stockholders.
(b) Identify the accounting entries that are made for a cash dividend and the date of each entry.

4. De Masi Inc. declares a $40,000 cash dividend on December 31, 2002. The required annual dividend on preferred stock is $12,000. Determine the allocation of the dividend to preferred and common stockholders assuming the preferred stock is cumulative and dividends are 1 year in arrears.

5. Contrast the effects of a cash dividend and a stock dividend on a corporation's balance sheet.

6. Veena Gall asks, "Since stock dividends don't change anything, why declare them?" What is your answer to Veena?

7. Noriega Corporation has 20,000 shares of $10 par value common stock outstanding when it announces a 2-for-1

split. Before the split, the stock had a market price of $140 per share. After the split, how many shares of stock will be outstanding? What will be the approximate market price per share?

8. The board of directors is considering either a stock split or a stock dividend. They understand that total stockholders' equity will remain the same under either action. However, they are not sure of the different effects of the two types of actions on other aspects of stockholders' equity. Explain the differences to the directors.

9. What is a prior period adjustment, and how is it reported in the financial statements?

10. ABC Corporation has a retained earnings balance of $210,000 on January 1. During the year, a prior period adjustment of $90,000 is recorded because of the understatement of depreciation in the prior period. Show the retained earnings statement presentation of these data.

11. What is the purpose of a retained earnings restriction? Identify the possible causes of retained earnings restrictions.

12. How are retained earnings restrictions generally reported in the financial statements?

13. Identify the events that result in credits and debits to retained earnings.

14. Shwu Chen believes that both the beginning and ending balances in retained earnings are shown in the stockholders' equity section. Is Shwu correct? Discuss.

15. David Sokol, who owns many investments in common stock, says, "I don't care what a company's net income is. The balance sheet tells me everything I need to know!" How do you respond to David?

16. What is the unique feature of a corporation income statement? Illustrate this feature, using assumed data.

17. Why is it important to report discontinued operations separately from income from continuing operations?

18. You are considering investing in Alou Transportation. The company reports 2002 earnings per share of $6.50 on income before extraordinary items and $4.75 on net income. Which EPS figure would you consider more relevant to your investment decision? Why?

19. Leeds Inc. reported 2001 earnings per share of $3.20 and had no extraordinary items. In 2002, EPS on income before extraordinary items was $2.99, and EPS on net income was $3.49. Is this a favorable trend?

20. Indicate which of the following items would be reported as an extraordinary item in Childs Corporation's income statement.
   (a) Loss from damages caused by volcano eruption.
   (b) Loss from sale of temporary investments.
   (c) Loss attributable to a labor strike.
   (d) Loss caused when manufacture of a product was prohibited by the Food and Drug Administration.
   (e) Loss from flood damage. (The nearby Black River floods every 2 to 3 years.)
   (f) Write-down of obsolete inventory.
   (g) Expropriation of a factory by a foreign government.

21. When studying for an accounting test, a fellow student says, "Changes in accounting principle are reported in the retained earnings statement." Is your friend correct, or should he study harder?

22. Why must preferred stock dividends be subtracted from net income in computing earnings per share?

BRIEF EXERCISES

Prepare entries for a cash dividend.
(SO 1)

BE15-1 Weaner Corporation has 50,000 shares of common stock outstanding. It declares a $2 per share cash dividend on November 1 to stockholders of record on December 1. The dividend is paid on December 31. Prepare the entries on the appropriate dates to record the declaration and payment of the cash dividend.

Prepare entries for a stock dividend.
(SO 1)

BE15-2 Romano Corporation has 80,000 shares of $10 par value common stock outstanding. It declares a 10% stock dividend on December 1 when the market value per share is $16. The dividend shares are issued on December 31. Prepare the entries for the declaration and payment of the stock dividend.

Show before and after effects of a stock dividend.
(SO 1)

BE15-3 The stockholders' equity section of Herrera Corporation consists of common stock ($10 par) $1,000,000 and retained earnings $300,000. A 10% stock dividend (10,000 shares) is declared when the market value per share is $14. Show the before and after effects of the dividend on the following.

(a) The components of stockholders' equity.
(b) Shares outstanding.
(c) Book value per share.

Prepare a retained earnings statement.
(SO 2)

BE15-4 For the year ending December 31, 2002, Fritz Inc. reports net income $150,000 and dividends $85,000. Prepare the retained earnings statement for the year assuming the balance in retained earnings on January 1, 2002, was $220,000.

Compute return on common stockholders' equity.
(SO 3)

BE15-5 Tara Corporation reported net income of $170,000, declared dividends on common stock of $50,000, and had an ending balance in retained earnings of $360,000. Stockholders' equity was $700,000 at the beginning of the year and $820,000 at the end of the year. Compute the return on common stockholders' equity.

Prepare income statement including extraordinary items.
(SO 5)

BE15-6 An inexperienced accountant for Ervay Corporation showed the following in the income statement: income before income taxes and extraordinary item $300,000, and extraordinary loss from flood (before taxes) $70,000. The extraordinary loss and taxable income are both subject to a 25% tax rate. Prepare a correct income statement.

Prepare discontinued operations section of income statement.
(SO 5)

BE15-7 On June 30, Ingram Corporation discontinued its operations in Mexico. During the year, the operating loss was $300,000 before taxes. On September 1, Ingram disposed of the Mexico facility at a pretax loss of $160,000. The applicable tax rate is 35%. Show the discontinued operations section of the income statement.

BE15-8 On January 1, 2002, Jimenez Inc. changed from the straight-line method of depreciation to the declining-balance method. The cumulative effect of the change was to increase prior years' depreciation by $70,000 and 2002 depreciation by $8,000. Show the change in accounting principle section of the 2002 income statement, assuming the tax rate is 30%.

Prepare change in accounting principle section of income statement.
(SO 5)

BE15-9 Klumpe Corporation's income statement shows the following: income from continuing operations $580,000, loss from discontinued operations $200,000, extraordinary loss $90,000 (both net of taxes), and cumulative effect of a change in accounting principle that increases net income $30,000. Show the earnings per share data in the income statement assuming that there are 200,000 shares of common stock outstanding at December 31.

Show earnings per share data in income statement.
(SO 6)

BE15-10 Lumley Corporation reports net income of $370,000 and a weighted average of 200,000 shares of common stock outstanding for the year. Compute the earnings per share of common stock.

Compute earnings per share.
(SO 6)

BE15-11 Income and common stock data for Lumley Corporation are presented in BE15-10. Assume also that Lumley has cumulative preferred stock dividends for the current year of $20,000 that were declared and paid. Compute the earnings per share of common stock.

Compute earnings per share with cumulative preferred stock.
(SO 6)

EXERCISES

E15-1 On January 1, Garza Corporation had 75,000 shares of no-par common stock issued and outstanding. The stock has a stated value of $5 per share. During the year, the following occurred.

Journalize cash dividends; indicate statement presentation.
(SO 1)

Apr.	1	Issued 15,000 additional shares of common stock for $17 per share.
June	15	Declared a cash dividend of $1 per share to stockholders of record on June 30.
July	10	Paid the $1 cash dividend.
Dec.	1	Issued 2,000 additional shares of common stock for $19 per share.
	15	Declared a cash dividend on outstanding shares of $1.30 per share to stockholders of record on December 31.

Instructions
(a) Prepare the entries, if any, on each of the three dividend dates.
(b) How are dividends and dividends payable reported in the financial statements prepared at December 31?

E15-2 Romano Corporation was organized on January 1, 2001. During its first year, the corporation issued 2,000 shares of $50 par value preferred stock and 100,000 shares of $10 par value common stock. At December 31, the company declared the following cash dividends: 2001, $6,000, 2002, $12,000, and 2003, $28,000.

Allocate cash dividends to preferred and common stock.
(SO 1)

Instructions
(a) Show the allocation of dividends to each class of stock, assuming the preferred stock dividend is 9% and not cumulative.
(b) Show the allocation of dividends to each class of stock, assuming the preferred stock dividend is 10% and cumulative.
(c) Journalize the declaration of the cash dividend at December 31, 2003, under part (b).

E15-3 On January 1, 2002, Tinker Corporation had $1,000,000 of common stock outstanding that was issued at par. It also had retained earnings of $750,000. The company issued 50,000 shares of common stock at par on July 1 and earned net income of $400,000 for the year.

Journalize stock dividends.
(SO 1)

Instructions
Journalize the declaration of a 15% stock dividend on December 10, 2002, for the following independent assumptions.

1. Par value is $10, and market value is $16.
2. Par value is $5, and market value is $20.

E15-4 On October 31, the stockholders' equity section of Salita Company consists of common stock $800,000 and retained earnings $1,000,000. Salita is considering the following two courses of action: (1) declaring a 5% stock dividend on the 80,000, $10 par value shares outstanding, or

Compare effects of a stock dividend and a stock split.
(SO 1)

(2) effecting a 2-for-1 stock split that will reduce par value to $5 per share. The current market price is $14 per share.

Instructions

Prepare a tabular summary of the effects of the alternative actions on the components of stockholders' equity, outstanding shares, and book value per share. Use the following column headings: Before Action, After Stock Dividend, and After Stock Split.

Compute book value per share; indicate account balances after a stock dividend.
(SO 1, 3)

E15-5 On October 1, Sipio Corporation's stockholders' equity is as follows.

Common stock, $10 par value	$200,000
Paid-in capital in excess of par value	25,000
Retained earnings	75,000
Total stockholders' equity	$300,000

On October 1, Sipio declares and distributes a 10% stock dividend when the market value of the stock is $17 per share.

Instructions

(a) Compute the book value per share (1) before the stock dividend and (2) after the stock dividend. (Round to two decimals.)

(b) Indicate the balances in the three stockholders' equity accounts after the stock dividend shares have been distributed.

Indicate the effects on stockholders' equity components.
(SO 1, 2, 3)

E15-6 During 2002, Flores Corporation had the following transactions and events.

1. Declared a cash dividend.
2. Issued par value common stock for cash at par value.
3. Completed a 3-for-1 stock split in which $15 par value stock was changed to $5 par value stock.
4. Declared a small stock dividend when the market value was higher than par value.
5. Made a prior period adjustment for overstatement of net income.
6. Issued the shares of common stock required by the stock dividend declaration in item no. 4 above.
7. Paid the cash dividend in item no. 1 above.
8. Issued par value common stock for cash above par value.

Instructions

Indicate the effect(s) of each of the foregoing items on the subdivisions of stockholders' equity. Present your answer in tabular form with the following columns. Use (I) for increase, (D) for decrease, and (NE) for no effect. Item no. 1 is given as an example.

	Paid-in Capital		
Item	**Capital Stock**	**Additional**	**Retained Earnings**
1	NE	NE	D

Prepare correcting entries for dividends and a stock split.
(SO 1)

E15-7 Before preparing financial statements for the current year, the chief accountant for O'Dell Company discovered the following errors in the accounts.

1. The declaration and payment of $30,000 cash dividend was recorded as a debit to Interest Expense $30,000 and a credit to Cash $30,000.
2. A 10% stock dividend (1,000 shares) was declared on the $10 par value stock when the market value per share was $14. The only entry made was: Retained Earnings (Dr.) $10,000 and Dividend Payable (Cr.) $10,000. The shares have not been issued.
3. A 4-for-1 stock split involving the issue of 400,000 shares of $5 par value common stock for 100,000 shares of $20 par value common stock was recorded as a debit to Retained Earnings $2,000,000 and a credit to Common Stock $2,000,000.

Instructions

Prepare the correcting entries at December 31.

Prepare a retained earnings statement.
(SO 2)

E15-8 On January 1, 2002, Mayes Corporation had retained earnings of $550,000. During the year, Mayes had the following selected transactions.

1. Declared cash dividends $120,000.
2. Corrected overstatement of 2001 net income because of depreciation error $20,000.

3. Earned net income $350,000.
4. Declared stock dividends $60,000.

Instructions
Prepare a retained earnings statement for the year.

E15-9   The following accounts appear in the ledger of Byung-Kee Inc. after the books are closed at December 31.

Prepare a stockholders' equity section.
(SO 3)

Common Stock, no par, $1 stated value, 400,000 shares authorized;	
300,000 shares issued	$ 300,000
Common Stock Dividends Distributable	75,000
Paid-in Capital in Excess of Stated Value—Common Stock	1,200,000
Preferred Stock, $5 par value, 8%, 40,000 shares authorized;	
30,000 shares issued	150,000
Retained Earnings	700,000
Treasury Stock (10,000 common shares)	74,000
Paid-in Capital in Excess of Par Value—Preferred Stock	244,000

Instructions
Prepare the stockholders' equity section at December 31, assuming retained earnings is restricted for plant expansion in the amount of $100,000.

E15-10   The following financial information is available for Goldberg Corporation.

Calculate ratios to evaluate earnings performance.
(SO 3, 6)

	2002	**2001**
Average common stockholders' equity	$1,200,000	$900,000
Dividends paid to common stockholders	50,000	30,000
Dividends paid to preferred stockholders	20,000	20,000
Net income	200,000	140,000
Market price of common stock	20	15

The weighted average number of shares of common stock outstanding was 80,000 for 2001 and 100,000 for 2002.

Instructions
Calculate earnings per share and return on common stockholders' equity for 2002 and 2001.

E15-11   This financial information is available for Port City Corporation.

Calculate ratios to evaluate earnings performance.
(SO 3, 6)

	2002	**2001**
Average common stockholders' equity	$1,800,000	$1,900,000
Dividends paid to common stockholders	90,000	70,000
Dividends paid to preferred stockholders	20,000	20,000
Net income	230,000	180,000
Market price of common stock	20	25

The weighted number of shares of common stock outstanding was 180,000 for 2001 and 150,000 for 2002.

Instructions
Calculate earnings per share and return on common stockholders' equity for 2002 and 2001.

E15-12   For its fiscal year ending October 31, 2002, Sass Corporation reports the following partial data.

Prepare a correct income statement.
(SO 4, 5)

Income before income taxes	$640,000
Income tax expense (30% × $540,000)	162,000
Income before extraordinary items	478,000
Extraordinary loss from fire	100,000
Net income	$378,000

The fire loss is considered an extraordinary item. The income tax rate is 30% on all items.

Instructions

(a) Prepare a correct income statement, beginning with income before income taxes.

(b) ▭▭▭▭▷ Explain in memo form why the income statement data are misleading.

Prepare income statement.
(SO 4, 5)

E15-13 Rizzo Corporation has income from continuing operations of $240,000 for the year ended December 31, 2002. It also has the following items (before considering income taxes).

1. An extraordinary fire loss of $80,000.
2. A gain of $50,000 on the discontinuance of a division.
3. A cumulative change in an accounting principle that resulted in an increase in prior years' depreciation of $35,000.
4. A correction of an error in last year's financial statements that resulted in a $20,000 understatement of 2001 net income.

Assume all items are subject to income taxes at a 30% tax rate.

Instructions

(a) Prepare an income statement, beginning with income from continuing operations.

(b) Indicate the statement presentation of any item not included in (a) above.

Compute earnings per share
under different assumptions.
(SO 6)

E15-14 At December 31, 2002, Shields Corporation has 2,000 shares of $100 par value, 8%, preferred stock outstanding and 100,000 shares of $10 par value common stock issued. Shields's net income for the year is $547,000.

Instructions

Compute the earnings per share of common stock under the following independent situations. (Round to two decimals.)

(a) The dividend to preferred stockholders was declared. There has been no change in the number of shares of common stock outstanding during the year.

(b) The dividend to preferred stockholders was not declared. The preferred stock is cumulative. Shields held 10,000 shares of common treasury stock throughout the year.

*P*ROBLEMS: SET A

Prepare dividend entries and
stockholders' equity section.
(SO 1, 3)

Peachtree

P15-1A On Janury 1, 2002, Hayslett Corporation had the following stockholders' equity accounts.

Common Stock ($20 par value, 65,000 shares issued and outstanding)	$1,300,000
Paid-in Capital in Excess of Par Value	200,000
Retained Earnings	600,000

During the year, the following transactions occurred.

Feb.	1	Declared a $1 cash dividend per share to stockholders of record on February 15, payable March 1.
Mar.	1	Paid the dividend declared in February.
Apr.	1	Announced a 4-for-1 stock split. Prior to the split, the market price per share was $36.
July	1	Declared a 5% stock dividend to stockholders of record on July 15, distributable July 31. On July 1, the market price of the stock was $13 per share.
	31	Issued the shares for the stock dividend.
Dec.	1	Declared a $0.50 per share dividend to stockholders of record on December 15, payable January 5, 2003.
	31	Determined that net income for the year was $350,000.

Instructions

(a) Journalize the transactions and the closing entry for net income.

(b) Enter the beginning balances, and post the entries to the stockholders' equity accounts. (*Note:* Open additional stockholders' equity accounts as needed.)

(c) Total stockholders' equity
$2,248,500

(c) Prepare a stockholders' equity section at December 31.

P15-2A   The stockholders' equity accounts of Greene Company at January 1, 2002, are as follows.

Journalize and post transactions; prepare retained earnings statement and stockholders' equity section.
(SO 1, 2, 3)

Peachtree

Preferred Stock, 9%, $50 par	$600,000
Common Stock, $2 par	500,000
Paid-in Capital in Excess of Par Value—Preferred Stock	200,000
Paid-in Capital in Excess of Par Value—Common Stock	300,000
Retained Earnings	800,000

There were no dividends in arrears on preferred stock. During 2002, the company had the following transactions and events.

July 1	Declared a $0.50 cash dividend on common stock.
Aug. 1	Discovered $45,000 understatement of 2001 depreciation. Ignore income taxes.
Sept. 1	Paid the cash dividend declared on July 1.
Dec. 1	Declared 10% stock dividend on common stock when the market value of the stock was $18 per share.
15	Declared a 9% cash dividend on preferred stock payable January 15, 2003.
31	Determined that net income for the year was $385,000.
31	Recognized a $200,000 restriction of retained earnings for plant expansion.

Instructions

(a) Journalize the transactions, events, and closing entries.

(b) Enter the beginning balances in the accounts, and post to the stockholders' equity accounts. (*Note:* Open additional stockholders' equity accounts as needed.)

(c) Prepare a retained earnings statement for the year.

(d) Prepare a stockholders' equity section at December 31, 2002.

(c) Ending balance $511,000
(d) Total stockholders' equity $2,561,000

P15-3A   The post-closing trial balance of Jajoo Corporation at December 31, 2002, contains the following stockholders' equity accounts.

Prepare retained earnings statement and stockholders' equity section, and compute earnings per share.
(SO 1, 2, 3, 6)

Preferred Stock (15,000 shares issued)	$ 750,000
Common Stock (250,000 shares issued)	2,500,000
Paid-in Capital in Excess of Par Value—Preferred	250,000
Paid-in Capital in Excess of Par Value—Common	400,000
Common Stock Dividends Distributable	200,000
Retained Earnings	1,053,000

A review of the accounting records reveals the following.

1. No errors have been made in recording 2002 transactions or in preparing the closing entry for net income.

2. Preferred stock is $50 par, 10%, and cumulative; 15,000 shares have been outstanding since January 1, 2001.

3. Authorized stock is 20,000 shares of preferred, 500,000 shares of common with a $10 par value.

4. The January 1 balance in Retained Earnings was $1,170,000.

5. On July 1, 20,000 shares of common stock were sold for cash at $16 per share.

6. On September 1, the company discovered an understatement error of $60,000 in computing depreciation in 2001. The net of tax effect of $42,000 was properly debited directly to Retained Earnings.

7. A cash dividend of $250,000 was declared and properly allocated to preferred and common stock on October 1. No dividends were paid to preferred stockholders in 2001.

8. On December 31, an 8% common stock dividend was declared out of retained earnings on common stock when the market price per share was $16.

9. Net income for the year was $495,000.

10. On December 31, 2002, the directors authorized disclosure of a $200,000 restriction of retained earnings for plant expansion. (Use Note X.)

Instructions

(a) Reproduce the Retained Earnings account for the year.

(b) Prepare a retained earnings statement for the year.

(c) Prepare a stockholders' equity section at December 31.

(b) Retained earnings:
    $1,053,000
(c) Total stockholders' equity,
    $5,153,000

(d) Compute the earnings per share of common stock using 240,000 as the weighted average shares outstanding for the year.

(e) Compute the allocation of the cash dividend to preferred and common stock.

Prepare income statement with discontinued operations and extraordinary loss, and compute earnings per share.
(SO 4, 5, 6)

P15-4A   Knight Corporation owns a number of cruise ships and a chain of hotels. The hotels, which have not been profitable, were discontinued on September 1, 2002. The 2002 operating results for the company were as follows.

Operating revenues	$12,850,000
Operating expenses	8,700,000
Operating income	$ 4,150,000

Analysis discloses that these data include the operating results of the hotel chain, which were: operating revenues $3,000,000 and operating expenses $4,000,000. The hotels were sold at a gain of $500,000 before taxes. This gain is not included in the operating results. During the year, Knight suffered an extraordinary fire loss of $800,000 before taxes, which is not included in the operating results. In 2002, the company had other revenues and gains of $100,000, which are not included in the operating results. The corporation is in the 30% income tax bracket.

Instructions

(a) Net income $2,765,000

(a) Prepare a condensed income statement.

(b) Compute the earnings per share data that should appear in the income statement. Assume weighted average shares of stock equaled 440,000. (Round to two decimals.)

Prepare income statement with nontypical items, and compute earnings per share data.
(SO 4, 5, 6)

P15-5A   The ledger of McGrath Corporation at December 31, 2002, contains the following summary data.

Net sales	$1,700,000	Cost of goods sold	$1,000,000
Selling expenses	120,000	Administrative expenses	130,000
Other revenues and gains	20,000	Other expenses and losses	28,000

Your analysis reveals the following additional information that is not included in the above data.

1. The entire puzzles division was discontinued on August 31. The income from operations for this division before income taxes was $50,000. The puzzles division was sold at a loss of $70,000 before income taxes.

2. On May 15, company property was expropriated for an interstate highway. The settlement resulted in an extraordinary gain of $90,000 before income taxes.

3. During the year, McGrath changed its depreciation method from double-declining balance to straight-line. The cumulative effect of the change on prior years' net income was an increase of $60,000 before taxes. (Assume that depreciation under the new method is correctly included in the ledger data.)

4. The income tax rate on all items is 30%.

Instructions ·

(a) Net income: $400,400

(a) Prepare an income statement for the year ended December 31, 2002. Use the format illustrated in the Demonstration Problem (p. 623).

(b) Prepare the earnings per share data that should appear in the income statement. Assume there were 100,000 shares of common stock outstanding throughout the year.

PROBLEMS: SET B

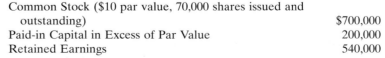

Prepare dividend entries and stockholders' equity section.
(SO 1, 3)

P15-1B   On January 1, 2002, Harris Corporation had the following stockholders' equity accounts.

Common Stock ($10 par value, 70,000 shares issued and outstanding)	$700,000
Paid-in Capital in Excess of Par Value	200,000
Retained Earnings	540,000

During the year, the following transactions occurred.

Jan. 15   Declared a $1 cash dividend per share to stockholders of record on January 31, payable February 15.

Feb. 15   Paid the dividend declared in January.

Apr. 15   Declared a 10% stock dividend to stockholders of record on April 30, distributable May 15. On April 15, the market price of the stock was $13 per share.

May 15   Issued the shares for the stock dividend.

July   1   Announced a 2-for-1 stock split. The market price per share prior to the announcement was $15. (The new par value is $5.)

Dec. 1   Declared a $0.50 per share cash dividend to stockholders of record on December 15, payable January 10, 2003.

      31   Determined that net income for the year was $250,000.

Instructions

(a) Journalize the transactions and the closing entry for net income.

(b) Enter the beginning balances, and post the entries to the stockholders' equity accounts. (*Note:* Open additional stockholders' equity accounts as needed.)

(c) Prepare a stockholders' equity section at December 31.

(c) Total stockholders' equity $1,543,000

P15-2B   The stockholders' equity accounts of Greco Inc., at January 1, 2002, are as follows.

Preferred Stock, $100 par, 9%	$500,000
Common Stock, $5 par	900,000
Paid-in Capital in Excess of Par Value—Preferred Stock	100,000
Paid-in Capital in Excess of Par Value—Common Stock	200,000
Retained Earnings	500,000

Journalize and post transactions, and prepare retained earnings statement and stockholders' equity section.
(SO 1, 2, 3)

There were no dividends in arrears on preferred stock. During 2002, the company had the following transactions and events.

July   1   Declared a $0.50 cash dividend on common stock.

Aug. 1   Discovered a $72,000 overstatement of 2001 depreciation. Ignore income taxes.

Sept. 1   Paid the cash dividend declared on July 1.

Dec. 1   Declared a 10% stock dividend on common stock when the market value of the stock was $12 per share.

      15   Declared a 9% cash dividend on preferred stock payable January 31, 2003.

      31   Determined that net income for the year was $380,000.

Instructions

(a) Journalize the transactions and the closing entry for net income.

(b) Enter the beginning balances in the accounts and post to the stockholders' equity accounts. (*Note:* Open additional stockholders' equity accounts as needed.)

(c) Prepare a retained earnings statement for the year.

(d) Prepare a stockholders' equity section at December 31, 2002.

(c) Ending balance $601,000
(d) Total stockholders' equity $2,517,000

P15-3B   The ledger of Healy Corporation at December 31, 2002, after the books have been closed, contains the following stockholders' equity accounts.

Preferred Stock (10,000 shares issued)	$1,000,000
Common Stock (400,000 shares issued)	2,000,000
Paid-in Capital in Excess of Par Value—Preferred	200,000
Paid-in Capital in Excess of Stated Value—Common	1,100,000
Common Stock Dividends Distributable	100,000
Retained Earnings	2,590,000

Prepare retained earnings statement and stockholders' equity section, and compute earnings per share.
(SO 1, 2, 3, 6)

A review of the accounting records reveals the following.

1. No errors have been made in recording 2002 transactions or in preparing the closing entry for net income.

2. Preferred stock is 10%, $100 par value, noncumulative, and callable at $125. Since January 1, 2001, 10,000 shares have been outstanding; 20,000 shares are authorized.

3. Common stock is no-par with a stated value of $5 per share; 600,000 shares are authorized.

4. The January 1 balance in Retained Earnings was $2,450,000.

5. On October 1, 100,000 shares of common stock were sold for cash at $8 per share.

6. A cash dividend of $600,000 was declared and properly allocated to preferred and common stock on November 1. No dividends were paid to preferred stockholders in 2001.

7. On December 31, a 5% common stock dividend was declared out of retained earnings on common stock when the market price per share was $7.

8. Net income for the year was $880,000.

9. On December 31, 2002, the directors authorized disclosure of a $100,000 restriction of retained earnings for plant expansion. (Use Note A.)

Instructions

(a) Reproduce the Retained Earnings account (T-account) for the year.

(b) Prepare a retained earnings statement for the year.

(c) Prepare a stockholders' equity section at December 31.

(d) Compute the earnings per share of common stock using 325,000 as the weighted average shares outstanding for the year.

(e) Compute the allocation of the cash dividend to preferred and common stock.

(b) Retained earnings: $2,590,000
(c) Total stockholders' equity: $6,990,000

Prepare income statement with discontinued operations and an extraordinary loss; compute earnings per share.
(SO 4, 5, 6)

P15-4B Kee Hau Corporation owns a number of travel agencies and a chain of motels in the Northwest. Its condensed operating results for 2002 show the following.

Operating revenues	$14,800,000
Operating expenses	10,700,000
Income from operations	$ 4,100,000

An additional analysis of the data indicate that the travel agencies are very profitable, but the motel chain has been unprofitable. Through September 30, the motels lost $500,000 from operating revenues of $4,200,000 and operating expenses of $4,700,000. On October 1, the motel operation was discontinued and sold at a loss of $1,000,000 before taxes. The motel operating results are included in income from operations, but the loss on disposal is not included in the operating results shown above.

During the year, the corporation had other expenses and losses of $80,000, which are not included in the operating results. In November, a condemnation action was taken against the company to obtain property for a new national park. As a result, the corporation suffered an extraordinary loss of $800,000 before taxes. That loss is not included in the operating results. The corporation is in a 30% tax bracket.

Instructions

(a) Prepare a condensed income statement for the year.

(b) Compute all of the earnings per share amounts that should appear on the income statement. Assume weighted average shares of stock equaled 400,000. (Round to two decimals.)

(a) Net income $1,554,000

Prepare expanded income statement; compute earnings per share data.
(SO 4, 5, 6)

P15-5B The ledger of Haak Corporation at December 31, 2002, contains the following summary data.

Net sales	$1,400,000	Cost of goods sold	$800,000
Selling expenses	110,000	Administrative expenses	140,000
Other revenues and gains	40,000	Other expenses and losses	30,000

Your analysis reveals the following additional information that is not included in the above data.

1. The entire ceramics division was discontinued on August 31. The loss from operations for this division before income taxes was $150,000. The ceramics division was sold at a gain of $60,000 before income taxes.

2. On July 12, a fire occurred in one plant. The fire resulted in an extraordinary loss of $90,000 before income taxes.

3. During the year, Haak changed its depreciation method from straight-line to declining balance. The cumulative effect of the change on prior years' net income was a decrease of $30,000 before taxes. (Assume that depreciation under the new method is correctly included in the ledger data.)

4. The income tax rate on all items is 30%.

Instructions

(a) Prepare an income statement for the year ended December 31, 2002. Use the format illustrated in the Demonstration Problem (page 623).

(b) Prepare the earnings per share data that should appear in the income statement. Assume there were 100,000 shares of common stock outstanding throughout the year.

(a) Net income: $105,000

BROADENING YOUR PERSPECTIVE

*F*INANCIAL REPORTING AND ANALYSIS

FINANCIAL REPORTING PROBLEM: Lands' End, Inc.

BYP15-1 The financial statements of Lands' End, Inc. are presented in Appendix A.

Instructions

Refer to Lands' End's financial statements and answer the following questions.

(a) What amount did Lands' End pay in dividends in the year ended January 28, 2000? What is the company's dividend policy? (*Hint:* Read the section entitled "Liquidity and capital resources" in Management's Discussion and Analysis.)

(b) Lands' End reported nonrecurring charges or credits in its income statement. What was the nature of these nonrecurring charges and credits? How did these items differ from discontinued operations?

COMPARATIVE ANALYSIS PROBLEM: Lands' End vs. Abercrombie & Fitch

BYP15-2 Lands' End's financial statements are presented in Appendix A. Abercrombie & Fitch's financial statements are presented in Appendix B.

Instructions

(a) Compute earnings per share and return on common stockholders' equity for both companies for the year ending in January 2000. Assume Lands' End's weighted average shares were 30,085,000 and Abercrombie & Fitch's weighted average shares were 103,175,170. Can these measures be used to compare the profitability of the two companies? Why or why not?

(b) What was the total amount of dividends paid by each company in 2000?

(c) Did either company report one of the three types of irregular items on its income statement? If so, what was the nature of the irregular item?

INTERPRETING FINANCIAL STATEMENTS: A Global Focus

BYP15-3 BFGoodrich Company is a worldwide diversified manufacturer of tires, vinyl products, specialty chemicals, and aerospace products. Selected financial data, in millions of dollars, for a recent 2-year period were as follows.

	Current Year	Prior Year
Sales	$2,416.7	$2,023.5
Total operating income	298.0	200.7
Income from continuing operations	209.9	83.6
Income (loss) from discontinued operations (net of taxes)	(16.9)	(4.4)
Extraordinary items (net of taxes)		25.8
Cumulative effect of change in method of accounting for taxes	2.7	
Net income	195.7	105.0
Dividends on preferred stock	8.8	9.8
Dividends on common stock	43.3	37.0
Income retained in the business at end of year	548.9	405.3

The notes to the company's financial statements indicate that the weighted average number of common shares outstanding (in thousands of shares) was 25,179 for the current year and 23,651 for the prior year. In addition, the stockholders' equity section of the balance sheet shows that at December 31 of the current year there were 25,554,627 shares of common stock issued and 352,396 shares of common stock held in the treasury.

Instructions

(a) Present the earnings per share data for the company for each year.

(b) Comment on the relative importance of material nontypical items in each year.

(c) Discuss how you would factor these nontypical items into your prediction of next year's net income for BFGoodrich.

(d) Prepare a retained earnings statement for the current year.

(e) What was the total dividend per share of common stock for the current year?

EXPLORING THE WEB

BYP15-4 Use the stockholders' equity section of an annual report and identify the major components.

Address: **www.reportgallery.com** *(or go to www.wiley.com/college/weygandt)*

Steps:

1. From Report Gallery Homepage, choose **Library of Annual Reports**.
2. Select a particular company.
3. Choose **Annual Report**.
4. Follow instructions below.

Instructions

Answer the following questions.

(a) What is the company's name?

(b) What classes of capital stock has the company issued?

(c) For each class of stock:
   (1) How many shares are authorized, issued, and/or outstanding?
   (2) What is the par value?

(d) What are the company's retained earnings?

(e) Has the company acquired treasury stock? How many shares?

CRITICAL THINKING

GROUP DECISION CASE

BYP15-5 General Dynamics develops, produces, and supports innovative, reliable, and highly sophisticated military and commercial products. In July of a recent year, the corporation announced that its Quincy Shipbuilding Division (Quincy) will be closed following the completion of the Maritime Prepositioning Ship construction program.

Prior to discontinuance, the operating results of Quincy were net sales $246.8 million, income from operations before income taxes $28.3 million, and income taxes $12.5 million. The corporation's loss on disposition of Quincy was $5.0 million, net of $4.3 million income tax benefits.

From its other operating activities, General Dynamics' financial results were net sales $8,163.8 million, cost of goods sold $6,958.8 million, and selling and administrative expenses $537.0 million. In addition, the corporation had interest expense of $17.2 million and interest revenue of $3.6 million. Income taxes were $282.9 million.

General Dynamics had an average of 42.3 million shares of common stock outstanding during the year.

Instructions

With the class divided into groups, answer the following.

(a) Prepare the income statement for the year, assuming that the year ended on December 31, 2002. Show earnings per share data on the income statement. All dollars should be stated in millions, except for per share amounts. (For example, $8 million would be shown as $8.0.)

(b) In the preceding year, Quincy's earnings were $51.6 million before income taxes of $22.8 million. For comparative purposes, General Dynamics reported earnings per share of $0.61 from discontinued operations for Quincy in the preceding year.

(1) What was the average number of common shares outstanding during the preceding year?

(2) If earnings per share from continuing operations was $7.47, what was income from continuing operations during the preceding year? (Round to two decimals.)

COMMUNICATION ACTIVITY

BYP15-6 In the past year, Alameda Corporation declared a 10% stock dividend, and Butte, Inc. announced a 2-for-1 stock split. Your parents own 100 shares of each company's $50 par value common stock. During a recent phone call, your parents ask you, as an accounting student, to explain the difference between the two events.

Instructions

Write a letter to your parents that explains the effects of the two events to them as stockholders and the effects of each event on the financial statements of each corporation.

ETHICS CASE

BYP15-7 Flambeau Corporation has paid 60 consecutive quarterly cash dividends (15 years). The last 6 months, however, have been a cash drain on the company, as profit margins have been greatly narrowed by increasing competition. With a cash balance sufficient to meet only day-to-day operating needs, the president, Vince Ramsey, has decided that a stock dividend instead of a cash dividend should be declared. He tells Flambeau's financial vice president, Janice Rahn, to issue a press release stating that the company is extending its consecutive dividend record with the issuance of a 5% stock dividend. "Write the press release convincing the stockholders that the stock dividend is just as good as a cash dividend," he orders. "Just watch our stock rise when we announce the stock dividend; it must be a good thing if that happens."

Instructions

(a) Who are the stakeholders in this situation?

(b) Is there anything unethical about Ramsey's intentions or actions?

(c) What is the effect of a stock dividend on a corporation's stockholders' equity accounts? Which would you rather receive as a stockholder—a cash dividend or a stock dividend? Why?

Answers to Self-Study Questions

1. a **2.** c **3.** d **4.** b **5.** d **6.** b **7.** c **8.** c **9.** d **10.** b

Answers to *Lands' End* Review It Question 3, p. 619

In its 2000 income statement Lands' End did not report any of the three types of irregular items. It did, however, report "Non-recurring charges and credits."

Remember to go back to the Navigator box on the chapter-opening page and check off your completed work.

LONG-TERM LIABILITIES

16

THE NAVIGATOR ✓

- Understand *Concepts for Review* ❑
- Read *Feature Story* ❑
- Scan *Study Objectives* ❑
- Read *Preview* ❑
- Read text and answer *Before You Go On*
  p. 645 ❑ *p. 652* ❑ *p. 655* ❑ *p. 659* ❑
- Work *Demonstration Problems* ❑
- Review *Summary of Study Objectives* ❑
- Answer *Self-Study Questions* ❑
- Complete *Assignments* ❑

CONCEPTS FOR REVIEW

Before studying this chapter, you should know or, if necessary, review:

a. What is a long-term liability? What is a current liability? (Ch. 4, pp. 153–154 and Ch. 11, p. 446)

b. How to record adjusting entries for interest expense and interest payable. (Ch. 3, p. 101)

c. How to record entries for the issuance of notes payable and related interest expense. (Ch. 11, p. 447)

☑ THE NAVIGATOR

UK Builds with Bonds

Every year, hundreds of colleges construct new buildings. Where do most schools get the money for these expensive projects? From long-term bonds, which are obligations in which the issuer of the bond promises to repay the loan amount plus interest on or before a specified date.

The **University of Kentucky** (UK) has issued "revenue" bonds to build buildings on the 23,000-student Lexington campus, and on 14 community college campuses throughout the state. These bonds pledge the school's revenues as collateral to guarantee payment of the bonds. At one time the outstanding debt on the Lexington campus buildings was $137 million. The total debt on the community college buildings equaled $121 million. The bonds generally have maturities ranging from ten to twenty years.

Additional "guarantees" for bond purchasers are the ratings given the bonds by professional rating agencies. "Our bonds are rated AA— by Standard & Poor's Corp.," says Henry Clay Owen, UK's treasurer. "That's well above investment grade," he says. "We always have a very good market for our bonds. People in Kentucky identify very closely with the university. Even though the bonds are rated AA—, they trade at AAA [the top bond rating] because they're so easy to sell."

One advantage for investors: the bonds' interest revenue is exempt

from federal income tax and from state tax for in-state investors. So, an issue offering 6 percent is the equivalent of 10 percent to individuals in the top tax bracket. "I would feel very comfortable buying UK bonds because it's inconceivable to me that there would ever be a default," says Owen.

☑ THE NAVIGATOR

After studying this chapter, you should be able to:

1. Explain why bonds are issued.
2. Prepare the entries for the issuance of bonds and interest expense.
3. Describe the entries when bonds are redeemed or converted.
4. Describe a bond sinking fund.
5. Describe the accounting for long-term notes payable.
6. Contrast the accounting for operating and capital leases.
7. Identify the methods for the presentation and analysis of long-term liabilities.

☑ THE NAVIGATOR

As you can see from the Feature Story, the **University of Kentucky** has chosen to issue long-term bonds to fund its building projects. The UK bonds are classified as **long-term liabilities** because they are obligations that are expected to be paid after one year. In this chapter we will explain the accounting for the major types of long-term liabilities reported on the balance sheet. These liabilities may be bonds, long-term notes, or lease obligations.

The content and organization of Chapter 16 are as follows.

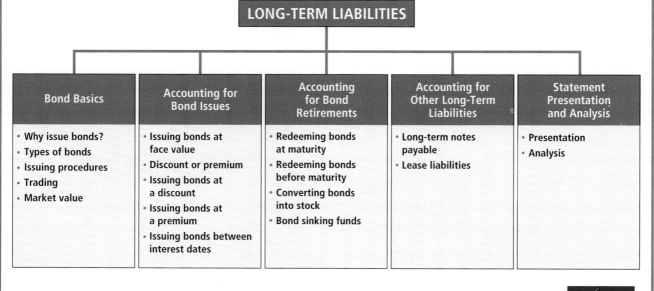

LONG-TERM LIABILITIES

Bond Basics	Accounting for Bond Issues	Accounting for Bond Retirements	Accounting for Other Long-Term Liabilities	Statement Presentation and Analysis
• Why issue bonds? • Types of bonds • Issuing procedures • Trading • Market value	• Issuing bonds at face value • Discount or premium • Issuing bonds at a discount • Issuing bonds at a premium • Issuing bonds between interest dates	• Redeeming bonds at maturity • Redeeming bonds before maturity • Converting bonds into stock • Bond sinking funds	• Long-term notes payable • Lease liabilities	• Presentation • Analysis

☑ THE NAVIGATOR

*B*OND BASICS

Bonds are a form of interest-bearing notes payable. They are issued by corporations, universities, and governmental agencies. Bonds, like common stock, are sold in small denominations (usually a thousand dollars or thousand-dollar multiples). As a result, bonds attract many investors.

WHY ISSUE BONDS?

STUDY OBJECTIVE 1

Explain why bonds are issued.

A corporation may use long-term financing other than bonds, such as notes payable and leasing. These other forms of financing involve finding an individual, a company, or a financial institution willing to supply the needed funds. Notes payable and leasing are therefore seldom sufficient to furnish the funds needed for plant expansion and major projects like new buildings. To obtain **large amounts of long-term capital**, corporate management usually must decide whether to issue common stock (equity financing) or bonds.

From the standpoint of the corporation seeking long-term financing, bonds offer the following advantages over common stock:

Bond Financing	Advantages
	1. **Stockholder control is not affected.** Bondholders do not have voting rights, so current owners (stockholders) retain full control of the company.
	2. **Tax savings result.** Bond interest is deductible for tax purposes; dividends on stock are not.
	3. **Earnings per share may be higher.** Although bond interest expense reduces net income, earnings per share on common stock often is higher under bond financing because no additional shares of common stock are issued.

Illustration 16-1

Advantages of bond financing over common stock

To illustrate the potential effect on earnings per share, assume that Microsystems, Inc. is considering two plans for financing the construction of a new $5 million plant. Plan A involves issuance of 200,000 shares of common stock at the current market price of $25 per share. Plan B involves issuance of $5 million, 12% bonds at face value. Income before interest and taxes on the new plant will be $1.5 million. Income taxes are expected to be 30%. Microsystems currently has 100,000 shares of common stock outstanding. The alternative effects on earnings per share are shown in Illustration 16-2.

	Plan A Issue Stock	Plan B Issue Bonds
Income before interest and taxes	$1,500,000	$1,500,000
Interest (12% × $5,000,000)	—	600,000
Income before income taxes	1,500,000	900,000
Income tax expense (30%)	450,000	270,000
Net income	$1,050,000	$ 630,000
Outstanding shares	300,000	100,000
Earnings per share	**$3.50**	**$6.30**

Illustration 16-2

Effects on earnings per share—stocks vs. bonds

Note that net income is $420,000 less ($1,050,000 − $630,000) with long-term debt financing (bonds). However, earnings per share is higher because there are 200,000 fewer shares of common stock outstanding.

The major disadvantages resulting from the use of bonds are that interest must be paid on a periodic basis and the principal (face value) of the bonds must be paid at maturity. A company with fluctuating earnings and a relatively weak cash position may have great difficulty making interest payments when earnings are low.

TYPES OF BONDS

Bonds may have many different features. Types of bonds commonly issued are described on the next page.

*I*NTERNATIONAL NOTE

The priority of bondholders' versus stockholders' rights varies across countries. In Japan, Germany, and France stockholders and employees are given priority, with liquidation of the firm to pay creditors seen as a last resort. In Britain creditors' interests are put first—the courts are quick to give control of the firm to creditors.

ACCOUNTING IN ACTION *Business Insight*

Although bonds are generally secured by solid, substantial assets like land, buildings, and equipment, exceptions occur. **Trans World Airlines Inc.** (TWA) at one time decided to issue $300 million of high-yielding 5-year bonds. TWA's bonds would be secured by a grab bag of assets, including some durable spare parts, but also a lot of disposable items that TWA had in its warehouses, such as light bulbs and gaskets. Some called the planned TWA bonds "light bulb bonds." As one financial expert noted: "You've got to admit that some security is better than none." Another noted, "They're digging pretty far down the barrel."

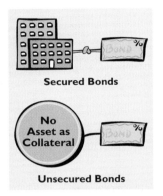

Secured Bonds

Unsecured Bonds

Secured and Unsecured Bonds

Secured bonds have specific assets of the issuer pledged as collateral for the bonds. A bond secured by real estate, for example, is called a **mortgage bond**. A bond secured by specific assets set aside to retire the bonds is called a **sinking fund bond**. (This type of bond is discussed later in the chapter). **Unsecured bonds** are issued against the general credit of the borrower. These bonds, called **debenture bonds**, are used extensively by large corporations with good credit ratings. For example, in a recent annual report, **DuPont** reported over $2 billion of debenture bonds outstanding.

Term and Serial Bonds

Bonds that mature (are due for payment) at a single specified future date are called **term bonds**. In contrast, bonds that mature in installments are called **serial bonds**. For example, **Caterpillar Inc.** debentures due in 2007 are term bonds. Caterpillar's debentures due between 2001 and 2007 are serial bonds (maturing annually).

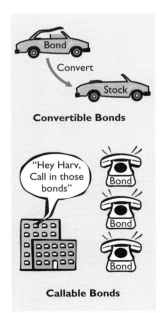

Convertible Bonds

Callable Bonds

Registered and Bearer Bonds

Bonds issued in the name of the owner are called **registered bonds**. Interest payments on registered bonds are made by check to bondholders of record. Bonds not registered are called **bearer** (or **coupon**) **bonds**. Holders of bearer bonds must send in coupons to receive interest payments. Coupon bonds may be transferred directly to another party. In contrast, the transfer of registered bonds requires cancellation of the bonds by the corporation and the issuance of new bonds. Most bonds issued today are registered bonds.

Convertible and Callable Bonds

Bonds that can be converted into common stock at the bondholder's option are called **convertible bonds**. Bonds subject to retirement at a stated dollar amount prior to maturity at the option of the issuer are known as **callable bonds**.

ISSUING PROCEDURES

State laws grant corporations the power to issue bonds. Within the corporation, approval by both the board of directors and stockholders is usually required. **In authorizing the bond issue, the board of directors must stipulate the number of bonds to be authorized, total face value, and contractual interest rate.** The total bond authorization often exceeds the number of bonds originally issued. This gives the corporation the flexibility it needs to meet future cash requirements.

The **face value** is the amount of principal the issuer must pay at the maturity date. The **contractual interest rate**, often referred to as the **stated rate**, is the rate used to determine the amount of cash interest the borrower pays and the investor receives. Usually the contractual rate is stated as an annual rate. Interest is generally paid semiannually.

The terms of the bond issue are set forth in a legal document called a **bond indenture**. In addition to the terms, the indenture summarizes the rights of the bondholders and their trustees, as well as the obligations of the issuing company. The **trustee** (usually a financial institution) keeps records of each bondholder, maintains custody of unissued bonds, and holds conditional title to pledged property.

After the bond indenture is prepared, **bond certificates** are printed. The indenture and the certificate are separate documents. As shown in Illustration 16-3, a bond certificate provides information such as the following: name of the issuer, face value, contractual interest rate, and maturity date. Bonds are generally sold through an investment company that specializes in selling securities.

Illustration 16-3

Bond certificate

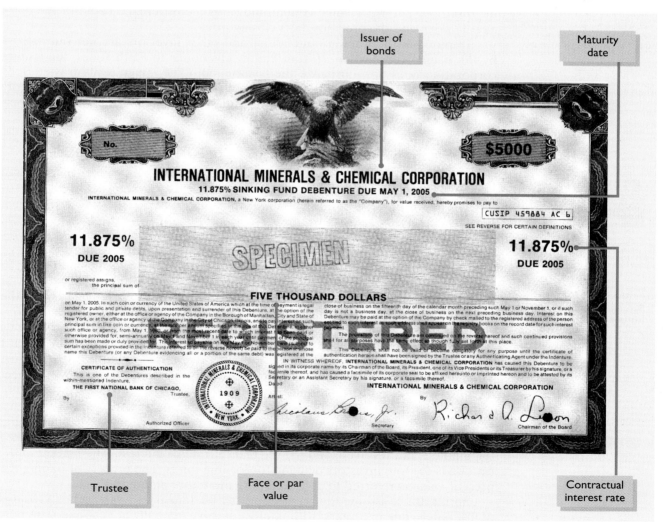

BOND TRADING

Corporate bonds, like capital stock, are traded on national securities exchanges. Thus, bondholders have the opportunity to convert their holdings into cash at any time by selling the bonds at the current market price.

Bond prices are quoted as a percentage of the face value of the bond, which is usually $1,000. A $1,000 bond with a quoted price of 97 means that the selling price of the bond is 97% of face value, or $970. Bond prices and trading activity are published daily in newspapers and the financial press, as illustrated by the following.

Illustration 16-4

Market information for bonds

Bonds	Current Yield	Volume	Close	Net Change
Kmart $8^{3}/8$ 17	8.4	35	$100^{1}/4$	$+^{7}/8$

This bond listing indicates that **Kmart Corporation** has outstanding $8^{3}/8$%, $1,000 bonds that mature in 2017. They currently yield an 8.4% return. On this day, 35 bonds were traded. At the close of trading, the price was $100^{1}/4$% of face value, or $1,002.50. The net change column indicates the difference between the day's closing price and the previous day's closing price.

Transactions between a bondholder and other investors **are not journalized by the issuing corporation.** If Tom Smith sells bonds to Faith Jones, the issuing corporation does not journalize the transaction. (The issuer or its trustee does keep records of the names of bondholders in the case of registered bonds.) A corporation makes journal entries **only when it issues or buys back bonds**, and when bondholders convert bonds into common stock.

DETERMINING THE MARKET VALUE OF BONDS

If you were an investor wanting to purchase a bond, how would you determine how much to pay? To be more specific, assume that Coronet, Inc. issues a zero-interest bond (pays no interest) with a face value of $1,000,000 due in 20 years. For this bond, the only cash you receive is a million dollars at the end of 20 years. Would you pay a million dollars for this bond? We hope not! A million dollars received 20 years from now is not the same as a million dollars received today.

Same dollars at different times are not equal.

The reason you should not pay a million dollars for Coronet's bond relates to what is called the **time value of money**. If you had a million dollars today, you would invest it. From that investment, you would earn interest such that at the end of 20 years, you would have much more than a million dollars. If someone is going to pay you a million dollars 20 years from now, you would want to find its equivalent today. In other words, you would want to determine how much must be invested today at current interest rates to have a million dollars in 20 years. That amount, that must be invested today at a given rate of interest over a specified time, is called **present value**.

The present value of a bond is the value at which it should sell in the marketplace. Market value therefore is a function of the three factors that determine present value: (1) the dollar amounts to be received, (2) the length of time until the amounts are received, and (3) the market rate of interest. The **market interest rate** is the rate investors demand for loaning funds. The process of finding the present value is referred to as **discounting** the future amounts.

To illustrate, assume that Kell Company on January 1, 2002, issues $100,000 of 9% bonds, due in 5 years, with interest payable annually at year-end. The purchaser of the bonds would receive two types of cash inflows: (1) **principal** of

$100,000 to be paid at maturity, and (2) five $9,000 **interest payments** ($100,000 × 9%) over the term of the bonds. The time diagram depicting both cash flows is shown below.

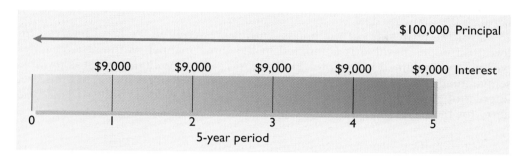

Illustration 16-5

Time diagram depicting cash flows

The present values of these amounts are as shown in Illustration 16-6.

Present value of $100,000 received in 5 years	$ 64,993
Present value of $9,000 received annually for 5 years	35,007
Market price of bonds	**$100,000**

Illustration 16-6

Computing the market price of bonds

Tables are available to find the present value numbers to be used, or these values can be determined mathematically.[1] Further discussion of time value of money computations is provided in Appendix C near the end of the book.

BEFORE YOU GO ON...

▶ *REVIEW IT*

1. What are the advantages of bond versus stock financing?
2. What are secured versus unsecured bonds, term versus serial bonds, registered versus bearer bonds, and callable versus convertible bonds?
3. Explain the terms face value, contractual interest rate, and bond indenture.
4. Explain why you would prefer to receive $1 million today rather than 5 years from now.

☑ THE NAVIGATOR

Accounting for Bond Issues

Bonds may be issued at face value, below face value (at a discount), or above face value (at a premium). They also are sometimes issued between interest dates.

ISSUING BONDS AT FACE VALUE

To illustrate the accounting for bonds, assume that on January 1, 2002, Devor Corporation issues 1,000, 10-year, 9%, $1,000 bonds at 100 (100% of face value). The entry to record the sale is:

STUDY OBJECTIVE 2

Prepare the entries for the issuance of bonds and interest expense.

---

[1]For those knowledgeable in the use of present value tables, the computations in this example are: $100,000 × .64993 = $64,993, and $9,000 × 3.88965 = $35,007 (rounded).

A = L + SE	Jan. 1	Cash	1,000,000	
+1,000,000 +1,000,000		Bonds Payable		1,000,000
		(To record sale of bonds at face value)		

Bonds payable are reported in the long-term liabilities section of the balance sheet because the maturity date is more than one year away.

Over the term (life) of the bonds, entries are required for bond interest. Interest on bonds payable is computed in the same manner as interest on notes payable, as explained in Chapter 11 (page 447). Assume that interest is payable semiannually on January 1 and July 1 on the bonds described above. In that case, interest of $45,000 ($1,000,000 × 9% × 6/12) must be paid on July 1, 2002. The entry for the payment, assuming no previous accrual of interest, is:

A = L + SE	July 1	Bond Interest Expense	45,000	
−45,000 −45,000		Cash		45,000
		(To record payment of bond interest)		

At December 31, an adjusting entry is required to recognize the $45,000 of interest expense incurred since July 1. The entry is:

A = L + SE	Dec. 31	Bond Interest Expense	45,000	
+45,000 −45,000		Bond Interest Payable		45,000
		(To accrue bond interest)		

Bond interest payable is classified as a current liability, because it is scheduled for payment within the next year. When the interest is paid on January 1, 2003, Bond Interest Payable is debited and Cash is credited for $45,000.

DISCOUNT OR PREMIUM ON BONDS

In the previous illustrations, we assumed that the contractual (stated) interest rate paid on bonds and the market (effective) interest rate were the same. The contractual interest rate is the rate applied to the face (par) value to arrive at the interest paid in a year. The market interest rate is the rate investors demand for loaning funds to the corporation. When the contractual interest rate and the market interest rate are the same, bonds sell at face value, as shown above.

However, market interest rates change daily. They are influenced by the type of bond issued, the state of the economy, current industry conditions, and the company's performance. The contractual and market interest rates often differ. As a result, bonds sell below or above face value.

To illustrate, suppose that investors have one of two options: (1) purchase bonds that have a market interest rate of 10%, or (2) purchase bonds that have a contractual interest rate of 8%. If the bonds are of equal risk, investors will select the 10% investment. To make the investments equal, investors will demand a rate of interest higher than the 8% contractual interest rate. But investors cannot change the contractual interest rate. What they can do is to pay less than the face value for the bonds. By paying less for the bonds, investors can obtain the market rate of interest. In these cases, **bonds sell at a discount**.

On the other hand, the market interest rate may be **lower** than the contractual interest rate. In that case investors will have to pay more than face value for the bonds. That is, if the market interest rate is 8% and the contractual interest rate is 9%, the issuer will require more funds from the investor. In these cases, **bonds sell at a premium**. These relationships are shown graphically in Illustration 16-7 (on the next page).

Issuing bonds at an amount different from face value is quite common. By the time a company prints the bond certificates and markets the bonds, it will be a coincidence if the market rate and the contractual rate are the same. Thus, the sale of bonds at a discount does not mean that the issuer's financial strength is suspect. Nor does the sale of bonds at a premium indicate exceptional financial strength.

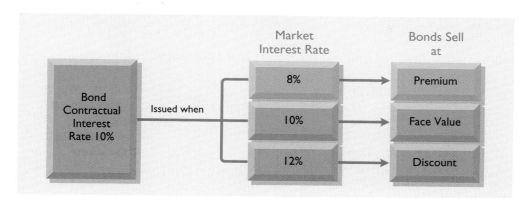

Illustration 16-7

Interest rates and bond prices

ISSUING BONDS AT A DISCOUNT

To illustrate the issuance of bonds at a discount, assume that on January 1, 2002, Candlestick, Inc. sells $100,000, 5-year, 10% bonds for $92,639 (92.639% of face value). Interest is payable on July 1 and January 1. The entry to record the issuance is:

HELPFUL HINT
Discount on Bonds Payable

Increase	Decrease
Debit	Credit
↓	
Normal	
Balance	

Jan. 1	Cash		92,639	
	Discount on Bonds Payable		7,361	
	Bonds Payable			100,000
	(To record sale of bonds at a discount)			

Although Discount on Bonds Payable has a debit balance, **it is not an asset**. Rather, it is a **contra account**. This account is **deducted from bonds payable** on the balance sheet, as illustrated below.

CANDLESTICK, INC.		
Balance Sheet (partial)		
Long-term liabilities		
Bonds payable	$100,000	
Less: Discount on bonds payable	**7,361**	$92,639

Illustration 16-8

Statement presentation of discount on bonds payable

The $92,639 represents the **carrying (or book) value** of the bonds. On the date of issue this amount equals the market price of the bonds.

The issuance of bonds below face value, at a discount, causes the total cost of borrowing to differ from the bond interest paid. That is, at maturity the issuing corporation must pay not only the contractual interest rate over the term of the bonds, but also the face value (rather than the issuance price). Therefore, the difference between the issuance price and face value of the bonds—the discount— is an **additional cost of borrowing. This additional cost should be recorded as bond interest expense over the life of the bonds.** The total cost of borrowing $92,639 for Candlestick, Inc. is $57,361, computed as follows.

HELPFUL HINT
Carrying value (book value) of bonds issued at a discount is determined by subtracting the balance of the discount account from the balance of the Bonds Payable account.

Illustration 16-9

Total cost of borrowing—bonds issued at a discount

Bonds Issued at a Discount	
Semiannual interest payments	
($100,000 × 10% × ½ = $5,000; $5,000 × 10)	$50,000
Add: Bond discount ($100,000 − $92,639)	7,361
Total cost of borrowing	**$57,361**

Alternatively, the total cost of borrowing can be computed as follows.

Illustration 16-10

Alternative computation of total cost of borrowing—bonds issued at a discount

Bonds Issued at a Discount	
Principal at maturity	$100,000
Semiannual interest payments ($5,000 × 10)	50,000
Cash to be paid to bondholders	150,000
Cash received from bondholders	92,639
Total cost of borrowing	**$ 57,361**

Amortizing Bond Discount

To comply with the matching principle, bond discount should be allocated systematically to each accounting period that benefits from the use of the cash proceeds.

One method is the **straight-line method of amortization**. It allocates the same amount to interest expense in each interest period.[2] The formula for determining bond discount amortization is shown in Illustration 16-11.

Illustration 16-11

Formula for straight-line method of bond discount amortization

In this example, the bond discount amortization is $736 ($7,361 ÷ 10). The entry to record the payment of bond interest and the amortization of bond discount on the first interest date (July 1, 2002) is:

A	=	L	+	SE
−5,000		+736		−5,736

July 1	Bond Interest Expense	5,736	
	Discount on Bonds Payable		736
	Cash		5,000
	(To record payment of bond interest and amortization of bond discount)		

At December 31, the adjusting entry is:

A	=	L	+	SE
		+736		−5,736
		+5,000		

Dec. 31	Bond Interest Expense	5,736	
	Discount on Bonds Payable		736
	Bond Interest Payable		5,000
	(To record accrued bond interest and amortization of bond discount)		

---

[2]Another method, the effective-interest method, is discussed in the appendix at the end of this chapter.

Over the term of the bonds, the balance in Discount on Bonds Payable will decrease annually by the same amount until it has a zero balance at maturity. Thus, the carrying value of the bonds at maturity will be equal to the face value.

Preparing a bond discount amortization schedule as shown in Illustration 16-12 is useful. The schedule shows interest expense, discount amortization, and the carrying value of the bond for each interest period. The interest expense recorded each period for the Candlestick bond is $5,736. Also note that the carrying value of the bond increases $736 each period until it reaches its face value $100,000 at the end of period 10.

ALTERNATIVE TERMINOLOGY
The amount in the Discount on Bonds Payable account is often referred to as *Unamortized Discount on Bonds Payable.*

Illustration 16-12
Bond discount amortization schedule

CANDLESTICK, INC.
Bond Discount Amortization
Straight-Line Method—Semiannual Interest Payments

Semiannual Interest Periods	(A) Interest to Be Paid (5% × $100,000)	(B) Interest Expense to Be Recorded (A) + (C)	(C) Discount Amortization ($7,361 ÷ 10)	(D) Unamortized Discount (D) − (C)	(E) Bond Carrying Value ($100,000 − D)
Issue date				$7,361	$ 92,639
1	$ 5,000	$ 5,736	$ 736	6,625	93,375
2	5,000	5,736	736	5,889	94,111
3	5,000	5,736	736	5,153	94,847
4	5,000	5,736	736	4,417	95,583
5	5,000	5,736	736	3,681	96,319
6	5,000	5,736	736	2,945	97,055
7	5,000	5,736	736	2,209	97,791
8	5,000	5,736	736	1,473	98,527
9	5,000	5,736	736	737	99,263
10	5,000	5,737*	737*	–0–	100,000
	$50,000	$57,361	$7,361		

Column **(A)** remains constant because the face value of the bonds ($100,000) is multiplied by the semiannual contractual interest rate (5%) each period.
Column **(B)** is computed as the interest paid (Column A) plus the discount amortization (Column C).
Column **(C)** indicates the discount amortization each period.
Column **(D)** decreases each period by the same amount until it reaches zero at maturity.
Column **(E)** increases each period by the amount of discount amortization until it equals the face value at maturity.

*One dollar difference due to rounding.

We have highlighted columns (A), (B), and (C) in the amortization schedule to emphasize their importance. These three columns provide the numbers for each period's journal entries. They are the primary reason for preparing the schedule. Column (A) provides the amount of the credit to Cash. Column (B) shows the debit to Bond Interest Expense. And column (C) is the credit to Discount on Bonds Payable.

ISSUING BONDS AT A PREMIUM

To illustrate the issuance of bonds at a premium, we now assume the Candlestick, Inc. bonds described above are sold for $108,111 (108.111% of face value) rather than for $92,639.

The entry to record the sale is:

Jan. 1	Cash		108,111	
	Bonds Payable			100,000
	Premium on Bonds Payable			8,111
	(To record sale of bonds at a premium)			

A = L + SE
+108,111 +100,000
+8,111

Premium on bonds payable is **added to bonds payable** on the balance sheet, as shown below.

Illustration 16-13

Statement presentation of bond premium

CANDLESTICK, INC. Balance Sheet (partial)		
Long-term liabilities		
Bonds payable	$100,000	
Add: Premium on bonds payable	8,111	$108,111

HELPFUL HINT

Premium on Bonds Payable

Decrease Debit	Increase Credit ↓ Normal Balance

The sale of bonds above face value causes the total cost of borrowing to be **less than the bond interest paid**. The bond premium is considered to be **a reduction in the cost of borrowing**. It should be credited to Bond Interest Expense over the life of the bonds. The total cost of borrowing $108,111 for Candlestick, Inc. is computed as follows.

Illustration 16-14

Total cost of borrowing— bonds issued at a premium

Bonds Issued at a Premium	
Semiannual interest payments	
($100,000 × 10% × ½ = $5,000; $5,000 × 10)	$50,000
Less: Bond premium ($108,111 − $100,000)	8,111
Total cost of borrowing	**$41,889**

Alternatively, the cost of borrowing can be computed as follows.

Illustration 16-15

Alternative computation of total cost of borrowing— bonds issued at a premium

Bonds Issued at a Premium	
Principal at maturity	$100,000
Semiannual interest payments ($5,000 × 10)	50,000
Cash to be paid to bondholders	150,000
Cash received from bondholders	108,111
Total cost of borrowing	**$ 41,889**

Amortizing Bond Premium

The formula for determining bond premium amortization under the straight-line method is presented in Illustration 16-16.

Illustration 16-16

Formula for straight-line method of bond premium amortization

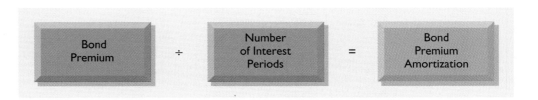

Bond Premium ÷ Number of Interest Periods = Bond Premium Amortization

In our example, the premium amortization for each interest period is $811 ($8,111 ÷ 10). The entry to record the first payment of interest on July 1 is:

July 1	Bond Interest Expense	4,189	
	Premium on Bonds Payable	811	
	Cash		5,000
	(To record payment of bond interest and amortization of bond premium)		

$$\begin{array}{ccccc} A & = & L & + & SE \\ -5,000 & & -811 & & -4,189 \end{array}$$

At December 31, the adjusting entry is:

Dec. 31	Bond Interest Expense	4,189	
	Premium on Bonds Payable	811	
	Bond Interest Payable		5,000
	(To record accrued bond interest and amortization of bond premium)		

$$\begin{array}{ccccc} A & = & L & + & SE \\ & & -811 & & -4,189 \\ & & +5,000 & & \end{array}$$

Over the term of the bonds, the balance in Premium on Bonds Payable will decrease annually by the same amount until it has a zero balance at maturity.

Preparing a bond premium amortization schedule as shown in Illustration 16-17 is useful. It shows interest expense, premium amortization, and the carrying value of the bond. The interest expense recorded each period for the Candlestick bond is $4,189. Also note that the carrying value of the bond decreases $811 each period until it reaches its face value $100,000 at the end of period 10.

Illustration 16-17

Bond premium amortization schedule

CANDLESTICK, INC.
Bond Premium Amortization
Straight-Line Method—Semiannual Interest Payments

Semiannual Interest Periods	(A) Interest to Be Paid (5% × $100,000)	(B) Interest Expense to Be Recorded (A) − (C)	(C) Premium Amortization ($8,111 ÷ 10)	(D) Unamortized Premium (D) − (C)	(E) Bond Carrying Value ($100,000 + D)
Issue date				$8,111	$108,111
1	$ 5,000	$ 4,189	$ 811	7,300	107,300
2	5,000	4,189	811	6,489	106,489
3	5,000	4,189	811	5,678	105,678
4	5,000	4,189	811	4,867	104,867
5	5,000	4,189	811	4,056	104,056
6	5,000	4,189	811	3,245	103,245
7	5,000	4,189	811	2,434	102,434
8	5,000	4,189	811	1,623	101,623
9	5,000	4,189	811	812	100,812
10	5,000	4,188*	812*	–0–	100,000
	$ 50,000	$41,889	$8,111		

Column **(A)** remains constant because the face value of the bonds ($100,000) is multiplied by the semiannual contractual interest rate (5%) each period.
Column **(B)** is computed as the interest paid (Column A) less the premium amortization (Column C).
Column **(C)** indicates the premium amortization each period.
Column **(D)** decreases each period by the same amount until it reaches zero at maturity.
Column **(E)** decreases each period by the amount of premium amortization until it equals the face value at maturity.

*One dollar difference due to rounding.

Similar to Illustration 16-12, page 649, columns (A), (B), and (C) provide information for the required journal entries.

ISSUING BONDS BETWEEN INTEREST DATES

Bonds are often issued between interest payment dates. **When this occurs, the issuer requires the investor to pay the market price for the bonds plus accrued interest since the last interest date.** At the next interest date, the corporation will return the accrued interest to the investor by paying the full amount of interest due on outstanding bonds.

To illustrate, assume that Deer Corporation sells $1,000,000, 9% bonds at face value plus accrued interest on March 1. Interest is payable semiannually on July 1 and January 1. The accrued interest is $15,000 ($1,000,000 × 9% × 2/12). The total proceeds on the sale of the bonds, therefore, are $1,015,000. The entry to record the sale is:

```
 A      =    L     +   SE
+1,015,000  +1,000,000
             +15,000
```

Mar. 1	Cash	1,015,000	
	Bonds Payable		1,000,000
	Bond Interest Payable		15,000
	(To record sale of bonds at face value plus accrued interest)		

At the first interest date, it is necessary to do two things with regard to bond interest: (1) Eliminate the bond interest payable balance. And (2) recognize interest expense for the 4 months (March 1–June 30) the bonds have been outstanding. Interest expense in this example is $30,000 ($1,000,000 × 9% × 4/12): The entry on July 1 for the $45,000 interest payment is:

```
 A     =    L     +    SE
-45,000   -15,000    -30,000
```

July 1	Bond Interest Payable	15,000	
	Bond Interest Expense	30,000	
	Cash		45,000
	(To record payment of bond interest)		

Why does the issuer, Deer Corporation, collect interest at the time of issuance and then return it at the time of payment? The rationale: Collection of accrued interest at the issuance date allows the company to pay a full period's (6 months') interest to all bondholders at the next interest payment date. Deer Corporation as the issuer does not have to determine the individual amount of interest due each holder based on the time each bond has been outstanding. If bonds are not sold "with accrued interest," the issuer would have to keep track of the purchaser and the date of purchase to ensure that each bondholder received the correct amount of interest. It is both simpler and less expensive for the issuer to sell the bonds "with accrued interest."

BEFORE YOU GO ON...

▶ *REVIEW IT*

1. What entry is made to record the issuance of bonds payable of $1 million at 100? At 96? At 102?
2. Why do bonds sell at a discount? At a premium? At face value?
3. Explain the accounting for bonds sold between interest dates.

▶ *DO IT*

A bond amortization table shows (a) interest to be paid $50,000, (b) interest expense to be recorded $52,000, and (c) amortization $2,000. Answer the following questions: (1) Were the bonds sold at a premium or a discount? (2) After recording the interest expense, will the bond carrying value increase or decrease?

ACTION PLAN

- Understand the effects that the amortization of bond discount and bond premium have on bond interest expense and on the carrying value of the bonds.
- Remember that bond discount amortization increases both bond interest expense and the carrying value of the bond.
- Remember that bond premium amortization decreases both bond interest expense and the carrying value of the bond.

SOLUTION: The bond amortization table indicates that interest expense is $2,000 greater than the interest paid. This difference is equal to the amortization amount. Thus, (1) the bonds were sold at a discount. (2) The interest entry will decrease Discount on Bonds Payable and increase the carrying value of the bonds.

Related exercise material: BE16-2, BE16-3, BE16-4, BE16-5, E16-2, E16-3, E16-4, and E16-5.

ACCOUNTING FOR BOND RETIREMENTS

Bonds may be retired either when they are redeemed by the issuing corporation or when they are converted into common stock by bondholders. The appropriate entries for these transactions are explained in the following sections.

STUDY OBJECTIVE 3

Describe the entries when bonds are redeemed or converted.

REDEEMING BONDS AT MATURITY

Regardless of the issue price of bonds, the book value of the bonds at maturity will equal their face value. This can be seen in Illustrations 16-12 and 16-17: The carrying value of the bonds at the end of their 5-year life ($100,000) is equal to the face value of the bonds.

Assuming that the interest for the last interest period is paid and recorded separately, the entry to record the redemption of the Candlestick bonds at maturity is:

Bonds Payable	100,000	
Cash		100,000
(To record redemption of bonds at maturity)		

A	=	L	+	SE
−100,000		−100,000		

REDEEMING BONDS BEFORE MATURITY

Bonds may be redeemed before maturity. A company may decide to retire bonds before maturity to reduce interest cost and remove debt from its balance sheet. A company should retire debt early only if it has sufficient cash resources.

When bonds are retired before maturity, it is necessary to: (1) Eliminate the carrying value of the bonds at the redemption date. (2) Record the cash paid. (3) Recognize the gain or loss on redemption. The carrying value of the bonds is the face value of the bonds less unamortized bond discount or plus unamortized bond premium at the redemption date.

To illustrate, assume that Candlestick, Inc. has sold its bonds at a premium, per Illustration 16-17. At the end of the eighth period Candlestick retires these bonds at 103 after paying the semiannual interest. The carrying value of the bonds at the redemption date is $101,623. (See the bond premium amortization schedule in Illustration 16-17.) The entry to record the redemption at the end of the eighth interest period (January 1, 2006) is:

> **HELPFUL HINT**
> Question: A bond is redeemed prior to its maturity date. Its carrying value exceeds its redemption price. Will the retirement result in a gain or a loss on redemption?
> Answer: Gain.

Jan. 1	Bonds Payable	100,000	
	Premium on Bonds Payable	1,623	
	Loss on Bond Redemption	1,377	
	Cash		103,000
	(To record redemption of bonds at 103)		

A	=	L	+	SE
−103,000		−100,000		−1,377
		−1,623		

Note that the loss of $1,377 is the difference between the cash paid of $103,000 and the carrying value of the bonds of $101,623. Losses (gains) on bond redemption are reported in the income statement as extraordinary items.

CONVERTING BONDS INTO COMMON STOCK

Convertible bonds have features that are attractive both to bondholders and to the issuer. The conversion often gives bondholders an opportunity to benefit if the market price of the common stock increases substantially. Until conversion, though, the bondholder receives interest on the bond. For the issuer, the bonds sell at a higher price and pay a lower rate of interest than comparable debt securities without the conversion option. Many corporations, such as **USAir**, **USX Corp.**, and **DaimlerChrysler Corporation**, have convertible bonds outstanding.

When bonds are converted into common stock and the conversion is recorded, the current market prices of the bonds and the stock are ignored. Instead, the **carrying value** of the bonds is transferred to paid-in capital accounts. **No gain or loss is recognized**. To illustrate, assume that on July 1 Saunders Associates converts $100,000 bonds sold at face value into 2,000 shares of $10 par value common stock. Both the bonds and the common stock have a market value of $130,000. The entry to record the conversion is:

> **HELPFUL HINT**
> The method of recording this conversion of bonds to stock is called the **book value method**. The book value of the bonds is removed from the liability accounts and recorded as common stock and related paid-in capital.

A	=	L	+	SE
		−100,000		+20,000
				+80,000

July 1	Bonds Payable	100,000	
	Common Stock		20,000
	Paid-in Capital in Excess of Par Value		80,000
	(To record bond conversion)		

Note that the current market price of the bonds and stock ($130,000) is not considered in making the entry. This method of recording the bond conversion is often referred to as the **carrying (or book) value method**.

BOND SINKING FUNDS

> **STUDY OBJECTIVE 4**
> Describe a bond sinking fund.

Many bond issues require the borrower to make periodic cash contributions to a sinking (redemption) fund over the life of the bonds. A sinking fund is cash or other assets set aside to retire debt. In other words, it is like a savings account that is used to pay back bondholders. **A sinking fund makes the bonds more attractive to investors, because it enhances the likelihood that the bonds will be redeemed at maturity.** For example, Texaco and Alcoa have sinking funds for their bonds. Such bonds are often referred to as **sinking fund bonds**.

Sinking funds are usually under the control of a trustee, such as a bank or a trust company. The trustee may be permitted to invest the periodic deposits in high-quality income-producing securities. **It is expected that the deposits plus the earnings from the investments will equal the face value of the bonds at maturity.** Shortly before the maturity date, the trustee sells the securities and uses the total cash in the fund to redeem the bonds. Any excess cash in the fund is returned to the bond issuer.

The bond sinking fund is reported as a single amount in the investments section of the balance sheet. Bond sinking fund revenue is classified as "other revenues and gains" in the income statement.

The bond contract may also require the corporation to establish a restriction on its retained earnings. As explained in Chapter 15, this restriction is reported as a note in the financial statements.

▶ *REVIEW IT*

1. Explain the accounting for redemption of bonds at maturity, before maturity by payment in cash, and by conversion into common stock.

2. Did **Lands' End** redeem any of its debt during the fiscal year ended January 28, 2000? (*Hint:* To find information related to this question, examine Lands' End's statement of cash flows. The answer to this question is provided on page 679.)

(*Hint:* To find information related to this question, examine Lands' End's statement of cash flows. The answer to this question is provided on page 679.)

3. What is the purpose of the bond sinking fund? Where is a bond sinking fund reported in the financial statements?

▶ *DO IT*

R & B Inc. issued $500,000, 10-year bonds at a premium. Prior to maturity, when the carrying value of the bonds is $508,000, the company retires the bonds at 102. Prepare the entry to record the redemption of the bonds.

ACTION PLAN
- Determine and eliminate the carrying value of the bonds.
- Record the cash paid.
- Compute and record the gain or loss (which is the difference between the first two items).

SOLUTION: There is a loss on redemption: The cash paid, $510,000 ($500,000 × 102%), is greater than the carrying value of $508,000. The entry is:

Bonds Payable	500,000	
Premium on Bonds Payable	8,000	
Loss on Bond Redemption	2,000	
Cash		510,000
(To record redemption of bonds at 102)		

Related exercise material: BE16-6, E16-3, E16-4, and E16-6.

☑ **THE NAVIGATOR**

ACCOUNTING FOR OTHER LONG-TERM LIABILITIES

Other common types of long-term obligations are notes payable and lease liabilities. The accounting for these liabilities is explained in the following sections.

LONG-TERM NOTES PAYABLE

The use of notes payable in long-term debt financing is quite common. Long-term notes payable are similar to short-term interest-bearing notes payable except that the terms of the notes exceed one year. In periods of unstable interest rates, the interest rate on long-term notes may be tied to changes in the market rate. Examples are the 8.03% adjustable-rate notes issued by **General Motors** and the floating-rate notes issued by **American Express Company**.

A long-term note may be secured by a **mortgage** that pledges title to specific assets as security for a loan. **Mortgage notes payable** are widely used by individuals to purchase homes and by many small and some large companies to acquire plant assets. Approximately 18 percent of **McDonald's** long-term debt relates to mortgage notes on land, buildings, and improvements. Mortgage loan terms may stipulate either a fixed or an adjustable interest rate. Typically, the terms require the borrower to make installment payments over the term of the loan. Each payment consists of (1) interest on the unpaid balance of the loan and (2) a reduction of loan principal. The interest decreases each period, while the portion applied to the loan principal increases.

STUDY OBJECTIVE 5

Describe the accounting for long-term notes payable.

Mortgage notes payable are recorded initially at face value. Subsequent entries are required for each installment payment. To illustrate, assume that Porter Technology Inc. issues a $500,000, 12%, 20-year mortgage note on December 31, 2002, to obtain needed financing for a new research laboratory. The terms provide for semiannual installment payments of $33,231 (not including real estate taxes and insurance). The installment payment schedule for the first 2 years is as follows.

Illustration 16-18

Mortgage installment payment schedule

Semiannual Interest Period	(A) Cash Payment	(B) Interest Expense (D) × 6%	(C) Reduction of Principal (A) − (B)	(D) Principal Balance (D) − (C)
Issue date				$500,000
1	$33,231	$30,000	$3,231	496,769
2	33,231	29,806	3,425	493,344
3	33,231	29,601	3,630	489,714
4	33,231	29,383	3,848	485,866

> **HELPFUL HINT**
> Electronic spreadsheets can create a schedule of installment loan payments. You can put in the data for your own mortgage loan and get information that really hits home.

A	=	L	+	SE
+500,000		+500,000		

A	=	L	+	SE
−33,231		−3,231		−30,000

The entries to record the mortgage loan and first installment payment are as follows.

Dec. 31	Cash	500,000	
	Mortgage Notes Payable		500,000
	(To record mortgage loan)		
June 30	Interest Expense	30,000	
	Mortgage Notes Payable	3,231	
	Cash		33,231
	(To record semiannual payment on mortgage)		

In the balance sheet, the reduction in principal for the next year is reported as a current liability. The remaining unpaid principal balance is classified as a long-term liability. At December 31, 2003, the total liability is $493,344. Of that amount, $7,478 ($3,630 + $3,848) is current, and $485,866 ($493,344 − $7,478) is long-term.

ACCOUNTING IN ACTION   *Business Insight*

Mortgage.com, a pioneer in one of the Web's more promising ideas, recently exited the online home-lending business and laid off most of its 618 employees. A study of Internet consumers showed that only 4 percent of them have applied online for a mortgage, and fewer than 1 percent have closed a loan. "The fact is, there is still a lot about getting a mortgage that can't be done online," says Dianne Glossman, an analyst with UBS Marburg. Although a recent change in federal law allows people to send their signatures electronically, "in most cases, you still need to sign paper documents, someone to visit the property and appraise it, and these loans still usually need to be closed in person."

SOURCE: Excerpts from Aaron Elstein, "Mortgage.com Plans to Cease Its Lending and Pare Its Staff," *The Wall Street Journal*, November 1, 2000. Reprinted by permission of the Wall Street Journal. © 2000 Dow Jones & Co, Inc. All Rights Reserved Worldwide.

LEASE LIABILITIES

STUDY OBJECTIVE 6

Contrast the accounting for operating and capital leases.

As indicated in Chapter 10, a lease is a contractual arrangement between a lessor (owner of the property) and a lessee (renter of the property). It grants the right to use specific property for a period of time in return for cash payments. Leasing is big business. An estimated $125 billion of capital equipment was leased in a recent year. This represents approximately one-third of equipment financed that year. The two most common types of leases are operating leases and capital leases.

Operating Leases

The renting of an apartment and the rental of a car at an airport are examples of **operating leases**. **In an operating lease the intent is temporary use of the property by the lessee. The lessor continues to own the property.** The lease (or rental) payments are recorded as an expense by the lessee and as revenue by the lessor. For example, assume that a sales representative for Western Inc. leases a car from Hertz Car Rental at the Los Angeles airport and that Hertz charges a total of $275. The entry by the lessee, Western Inc., is:

Car Rental Expense	275	
Cash		275
(To record payment of lease rental charge)		

A	=	L	+	SE
−275				−275

The lessee may incur other costs during the lease period. For example, in the case above, the lessee may pay for gas and oil. These costs are also reported as an expense.

Capital Leases

In most lease contracts, a periodic payment is made by the lessee and is recorded as rent expense in the income statement. But, in some cases, the lease contract transfers substantially all the benefits and risks of ownership to the lessee. Such a lease is in effect a purchase of the property. This type of lease is called a **capital lease**. Its name comes from the fact that the present value of the cash payments for the lease are capitalized and recorded as an asset. Illustration 16-19 indicates the major difference between an operating and a capital lease.

> **HELPFUL HINT**
> A capital lease situation is one that, although legally a rental case, is *in substance* an installment purchase by the lessee. Accounting standards require that substance over form be used in such a situation.

Illustration 16-19

Types of leases

Operating lease	Capital lease
"Have it back by 6:00 Sunday." "OK!" U-Drive Corp.	"Only 3 more payments and this baby is ours!"
Lessor has substantially all of the benefits and risks of ownership	Lessee has substantially all of the benefits and risks of ownership

The lessee must record a lease **as an asset**—that is, as a capital lease—if **any one** of the following conditions exists:

1. **The lease transfers ownership of the property to the lessee.** *Rationale:* If during the lease term the lessee receives ownership of the asset, the leased asset should be reported as an asset on the lessee's books.

2. **The lease contains a bargain purchase option.** *Rationale:* If during the term of the lease the lessee can purchase the asset at a price substantially below its fair market value, the lessee will exercise this option. Thus, the lease should be reported as a leased asset on the lessee's books.

3. **The lease term is equal to 75% or more of the economic life of the leased property.** *Rationale:* If the lease term is for much of the asset's useful life, the asset should be recorded by the lessee.

4. **The present value of the lease payments equals or exceeds 90% of the fair market value of the leased property.** *Rationale:* If the present value of the lease payments is equal to or almost equal to the fair market value of the asset, the lessee has essentially purchased the asset. As a result, the leased asset should be recorded on the books of the lessee.

To illustrate, assume that Gonzalez Company decides to lease new equipment. The lease period is 4 years; the economic life of the leased equipment is estimated to be 5 years. The present value of the lease payments is $190,000, which is equal to the fair market value of the equipment. There is no transfer of ownership during the lease term, nor is there any bargain purchase option.

In this example, Gonzalez has essentially purchased the equipment. Conditions 3 and 4 have been met. First, the lease term is 75% or more of the economic life of the asset. Second, the present value of cash payments is equal to the equipment's fair market value. The entry to record the transaction is as follows.

A = L + SE
+190,000 +190,000

Leased Asset—Equipment	190,000	
Lease Liability		190,000
(To record leased asset and lease liability)		

The leased asset is reported on the balance sheet under plant assets. The lease liability is reported on the balance sheet as a liability. **The portion of the lease liability expected to be paid in the next year is reported as a current liability. The remainder is classified as a long-term liability.**

Most lessees do not like to report leases on their balance sheets. Why? Because the lease liability increases the company's total liabilities. This, in turn, may make it more difficult for the company to obtain needed funds from lenders. As a result, companies attempt to keep leased assets and lease liabilities off the balance sheet by not meeting any of the four conditions mentioned above. The practice of keeping liabilities off the balance sheet is referred to as **off-balance sheet financing.**

*S*TATEMENT PRESENTATION AND ANALYSIS

STUDY OBJECTIVE **7**

Identify the methods for the presentation and analysis of long-term liabilities.

PRESENTATION

Long-term liabilities are reported in a separate section of the balance sheet immediately following current liabilities, as shown in Illustration 16-20.

Illustration 16-20

Balance sheet presentation of long-term liabilities

LAX CORPORATION Balance Sheet (partial)		
Long-term liabilities		
Bonds payable 10% due in 2009	$1,000,000	
Less: Discount on bonds payable	80,000	$ 920,000
Mortgage notes payable, 11%, due in 2015		
and secured by plant assets		500,000
Lease liability		540,000
Total long-term liabilities		$1,960,000

Alternatively, summary data may be presented in the balance sheet with detailed data (interest rates, maturity dates, conversion privileges, and assets pledged as collateral) shown in a supporting schedule. The current maturities of long-term debt should be reported under current liabilities if they are to be paid from current assets.

ANALYSIS

Long-term creditors and stockholders are interested in a company's long-run solvency. Of particular interest is the company's ability to pay interest as it comes due and to repay the face value of the debt at maturity. Debt to total assets and times interest earned are two ratios that provide information about debt-paying ability and long-run solvency.

The **debt to total assets ratio** measures the percentage of the total assets provided by creditors. It is computed, as shown in the formula below, by dividing total debt (both current and long-term liabilities) by total assets. The higher the percentage of debt to total assets, the greater the risk that the company may be unable to meet its maturing obligations.

The **times interest earned ratio** indicates the company's ability to meet interest payments as they come due. It is computed by dividing income before income taxes and interest expense by interest expense.

To illustrate these ratios, we will use data from **Lands' End's** 2000 annual report. The company had total liabilities of $160 million, total assets of $456 million, interest expense of $1.9 million, income taxes of $28.2 million, and net income of $48 million. Lands' End's debt to total assets ratio and times interest earned ratio are shown graphically below, along with their computations.

Illustration 16-21

Debt to total assets and times interest earned ratios, with computations

Total Debt	÷	Total Assets	=	Debt to Total Assets
$160	÷	$456	=	35%
Income before Income Taxes and Interest Expense	÷	Interest Expense	=	Times Interest Earned
$48 + $28.2 + $1.9	÷	$1.9	=	41.1 times

Lands' End has a relatively low debt to total assets percentage of 35%; its interest coverage of 41.1 times appears extremely safe.

BEFORE YOU GO ON...

▶ *REVIEW IT*
1. Explain the accounting for long-term mortgage notes payable.
2. What is the difference in accounting for an operating lease versus a capital lease? Explain the four conditions used to determine whether the lease contract transfers substantially all the benefits and risks of ownership.
3. What ratios may be computed to analyze a company's long-run solvency?

A LOOK BACK AT OUR FEATURE STORY

Refer back to the Feature Story about the University of Kentucky at the beginning of the chapter, and answer the following questions.

1. The University of Kentucky's bonds are rated AA− by Standard & Poor's and A1 by Moody's Investor Service. Why is it important to the University of Kentucky that its bonds have a high bond rating?

2. Explain the meaning of the tax-exempt status of the University of Kentucky bonds. What does it mean to say that "a recent issue offering 6% is the equivalent of 10% to those individuals in the top tax bracket"?

3. Why does the state use bonds to finance the buildings rather than taking the funds out of general revenues?

SOLUTION

1. Having a high (good) bond rating is as important to a university as it is to a business corporation. A high bond rating indicates that the bonds are less risky. They are thus more attractive to purchasers. A lower interest rate results, and the cost to the issuer of the bonds is less.

2. Because the University of Kentucky bonds are tax exempt, bondholders do not have to pay federal or state (in-state residents only) income tax on the interest received. To earn an after-tax return of 6%, a person in the maximum tax bracket would have to receive interest equal to approximately 10% on taxable bonds [10% − (40% × 10%)].

3. Financing the buildings through the issuance of bonds spreads the cost of the buildings over many years and more equitably distributes the costs to a broader base of taxpayers. Future taxpayers pay for the buildings as they are used, rather than the taxpayers of one year absorbing the cost out of general revenues in the year of construction.

☑ THE NAVIGATOR

Additional Demonstration Problem

DEMONSTRATION PROBLEM

Snyder Software Inc. has successfully developed a new spreadsheet program. To produce and market the program, the company needed $2.0 million of additional financing. On December 31, 2002, Snyder borrowed money as follows.

1. Snyder issued $500,000, 11%, 10-year convertible bonds. The bonds sold at face value and pay semiannual interest on January 1 and July 1. Each $1,000 bond is convertible into 30 shares of Snyder's $20 par value common stock.

2. Snyder issued $1.0 million, 10%, 10-year bonds for $885,301. Interest is payable semiannually on January 1 and July 1. Snyder uses the straight-line method of amortization.

3. Snyder also issued a $500,000, 12%, 15-year mortgage note payable. The terms provide for semiannual installment payments of $36,324 on June 30 and December 31.

Instructions

1. For the convertible bonds, prepare journal entries for:
   (a) The issuance of the bonds on January 1, 2003.
   (b) Interest expense on July 1 and December 31, 2003.
   (c) The payment of interest on January 1, 2004.
   (d) The conversion of all bonds into common stock on January 1, 2004, when the market value of the common stock was $67 per share.

2. For the 10-year, 10% bonds:
   (a) Journalize the issuance of the bonds on January 1, 2003.
   (b) Prepare a bond discount amortization schedule for the first six interest periods.
   (c) Prepare the journal entries for interest expense and amortization of bond discount in 2003.

(d) Prepare the entry for the redemption of the bonds at 101 on January 1, 2006, after paying the interest due on this date.

3. For the mortgage note payable:
   (a) Prepare the entry for the issuance of the note on December 31, 2002.
   (b) Prepare a payment schedule for the first four installment payments.
   (c) Indicate the current and noncurrent amounts for the mortgage note payable at December 31, 2003.

SOLUTION TO DEMONSTRATION PROBLEM

1. (a) 2003

Jan. 1	Cash		500,000	
	Bonds Payable			500,000
	(To record issue of 11%, 10-year convertible bonds at face value)			

(b) 2003

July 1	Bond Interest Expense		27,500	
	Cash ($500,000 × 0.055)			27,500
	(To record payment of semiannual interest)			
Dec. 31	Bond Interest Expense		27,500	
	Bond Interest Payable			27,500
	(To record accrual of semiannual bond interest)			

(c) 2004

Jan. 1	Bond Interest Payable		27,500	
	Cash			27,500
	(To record payment of accrued interest)			

(d) Jan. 1

	Bonds Payable		500,000	
	Common Stock			300,000*
	Paid-in Capital in Excess of Par Value			200,000
	(To record conversion of bonds into common stock)			
	*($500,000 ÷ $1,000 = 500 bonds; 500 × 30 = 15,000 shares; 15,000 × $20 = $300,000)			

ACTION PLAN

- Compute interest semiannually (six months).
- Record the accrual and payment of interest on appropriate dates.
- Record the conversion of the bonds into common stock by removing the book (carrying) value of the bonds from the liability account.

2. (a) 2003

Jan. 1	Cash		885,301	
	Discount on Bonds Payable		114,699	
	Bonds Payable			1,000,000
	(To record issuance of bonds at a discount			

(b)

Semiannual Interest Period	Interest to Be Paid	Interest Expense to Be Recorded	Discount Amortization	Unamortized Discount	Bond Carrying Value
Issue date				$114,699	$885,301
1	$50,000	$55,735	$5,735	108,964	891,036
2	50,000	55,735	5,735	103,229	896,771
3	50,000	55,735	5,735	97,494	902,506
4	50,000	55,735	5,735	91,759	908,241
5	50,000	55,735	5,735	86,024	913,976
6	50,000	55,735	5,735	80,289	919,711

ACTION PLAN

- Record the discount on bonds issued as a contra liability account.
- Compute interest expense and bond discount amortization using the straight-line method.
- Record the amortization of bond discount as an increase in interest expense.
- Compute the loss on bond redemption as the excess of the cash paid over the carrying value of the redeemed bonds.

(c) 2003

July 1	Bond Interest Expense		55,735	
	Discount on Bonds Payable			5,735
	Cash			50,000
	(To record payment of semiannual interest and amortization of bond discount)			
Dec. 31	Bond Interest Expense		55,735	
	Discount on Bonds Payable			5,735
	Bond Interest Payable			50,000
	(To record accrual of semiannual interest and amortization of bond discount)			

(d) 2006

Jan. 1	Bonds Payable		1,000,000	
	Loss on Bond Redemption		90,289*	
	Discount on Bonds Payable			80,289
	Cash			1,010,000
	(To record redemption of bonds at 101)			
	*($1,010,000 − $919,711)			

3. (a) 2002

Dec. 31	Cash		500,000	
	Mortgage Notes Payable			500,000
	(To record issuance of mortgage note payable)			

(b)

Semiannual Interest Period	Cash Payment	Interest Expense	Reduction of Principal	Principal Balance
Issue date				$500,000
1	$36,324	$30,000	$6,324	493,676
2	36,324	29,621	6,703	486,973
3	36,324	29,218	7,106	479,867
4	36,324	28,792	7,532	472,335

(c) Current liability $14,638 ($7,106 + $7,532)
    Long-term liability $472,335

ACTION PLAN

- Compute periodic interest expense on a mortgage note, recognizing that as the principal amount decreases, so does the interest expense.
- Record mortgage payments, recognizing that each payment consists of (1) interest on the unpaid loan balance and (2) a reduction of the loan principal.

SUMMARY OF STUDY OBJECTIVES

1. Explain why bonds are issued. Bonds may be sold to many investors, and they offer the following advantages over common stock: (a) stockholder control is not affected, (b) tax savings result, (c) earnings per share of common stock may be higher.

2. Prepare the entries for the issuance of bonds and interest expense. When bonds are issued, Cash is debited for the cash proceeds, and Bonds Payable is credited for the face value of the bonds. Also, Bond Interest Payable is credited if there is accrued interest. The accounts Premium on Bonds Payable or Discount on Bonds Payable are used to show the bond pre-

mium or bond discount. Bond discount and bond premium are amortized by the straight-line method.

3. Describe the entries when bonds are redeemed or converted. When bonds are redeemed at maturity, Cash is credited and Bonds Payable is debited for the face value of the bonds. When bonds are redeemed before maturity, it is necessary to (a) eliminate the carrying value of the bonds at the redemption date, (b) record the cash paid, and (c) recognize the gain or loss on redemption. When bonds are converted to common stock, the carrying (or book) value of the bonds is transferred to appropriate paid-in capital accounts; no gain or loss is recognized.

4. Describe a bond sinking fund. A bond sinking fund is cash or other assets set aside to retire the bonds.

5. Describe the accounting for long-term notes payable. Each payment consists of (1) interest on the unpaid balance of the loan and (2) a reduction of loan principal. The interest decreases each period, while the portion applied to the loan principal increases.

6. Contrast the accounting for operating and capital leases. For an operating lease, lease (rental) payments are recorded as an expense by the lessee (renter). For a capital lease, the lessee records the asset and related obligation at the present value of the future lease payments.

7. Identify the methods for the presentation and analysis of long-term liabilities. The nature and amount of each long-term debt should be reported in the balance sheet or in the notes accompanying the financial statements. Stockholders and long-term creditors are interested in a company's long-run solvency. Debt to total assets and times interest earned are two ratios that provide information about debt-paying ability and long-run solvency.

GLOSSARY

Key Term Matching Activity

Bearer (coupon) bonds Bonds not registered. (p. 642).

Bond certificate A legal document that indicates the name of the issuer, the face value of the bonds, and such other data as the contractual interest rate and maturity date of the bonds. (p. 643).

Bond indenture A legal document that sets forth the terms of the bond issue. (p. 643).

Bonds A form of interest-bearing notes payable issued by corporations, universities, and governmental entities. (p. 640).

Callable bonds Bonds that are subject to retirement at a stated dollar amount prior to maturity at the option of the issuer. (p. 642).

Capital lease A contractual arrangement that transfers substantially all the benefits and risks of ownership to the lessee so that the lease is in effect a purchase of the property. (p. 657).

Contractual interest rate Rate used to determine the amount of interest the borrower pays and the investor receives. (p. 643).

Convertible bonds Bonds that permit bondholders to convert them into common stock at their option. (p. 642).

Debenture bonds Bonds issued against the general credit of the borrower. Also called unsecured bonds. (p. 642).

Debt to total assets ratio A solvency measure that indicates the percentage of total assets provided by creditors; computed as total debt divided by total assets. (p. 659).

Face value Amount of principal the issuer must pay at the maturity date of the bond. (p. 643).

Long-term liabilities Obligations expected to be paid after one year. (p. 640).

Market interest rate The rate investors demand for loaning funds to the corporation. (p. 644).

Mortgage bond A bond secured by real estate. (p. 642).

Mortgage note payable A long-term note secured by a mortgage that pledges title to specific assets as security for a loan. (p. 655).

Operating lease A contractual arrangement giving the lessee temporary use of the property, with continued ownership of the property by the lessor. (p. 657).

Registered bonds Bonds issued in the name of the owner. (p. 642).

Secured bonds Bonds that have specific assets of the issuer pledged as collateral. (p. 642).

Serial bonds Bonds that mature in installments. (p. 642).

Sinking fund Cash or other assets set aside to retire debt. (p. 654).

Sinking fund bonds Bonds secured by specific assets set aside to retire them. (p. 642).

Straight-line method of amortization A method of amortizing bond discount or bond premium that allocates the same amount to interest expense in each period. (p. 648).

Term bonds Bonds that mature at a single specified future date. (p. 642).

Times interest earned ratio A solvency measure that indicates a company's ability to meet interest payments; computed by dividing income before income taxes and interest expense by interest expense. (p. 659).

Unsecured bonds Bonds issued against the general credit of the borrower. Also called debenture bonds. (p. 642).

▶ APPENDIX *Effective-Interest Amortization*

The straight-line method of amortization presented in the chapter has a conceptual deficiency: It does not completely satisfy the matching principle. Under the straight-line method, interest expense as a percentage of the carrying value of the bonds varies each interest period. We can see this by looking at data from four of the interest periods of the bond amortization schedule shown in Illustration 16-12.

Illustration 16A-1

Interest percentage rates under straight-line method

Semiannual Interest Period	Interest Expense to Be Recorded (A)	Bond Carrying Value (B)	Interest Expense as a Percentage of Carrying Value (A) ÷ (B)
1	$5,736	$92,639	6.19%
2	5,736	93,375	6.14%
3	5,736	94,111	6.09%
10	5,736	99,263	5.78%

STUDY OBJECTIVE 8

Contrast the effects of the straight-line and effective-interest methods of amortizing bond discount and bond premium.

Note that interest expense as a percentage of carrying value declines in each interest period. To comply with the matching principle, interest expense as a percentage of carrying value should not change over the life of the bonds. This percentage is referred to as the **effective-interest rate**. It is established when the bonds are issued and remains constant in each interest period.

The effective-interest method of amortization better satisfies the matching principle. Under the **effective-interest method**, the amortization of bond discount or bond premium results in periodic interest expense equal to a constant percentage of the carrying value of the bonds. The effective-interest method results in varying amounts of amortization and interest expense per period but **a constant percentage rate**. The straight-line method results in **constant amounts of amortization and interest expense** per period but a varying percentage rate.

The following steps are required under the effective-interest method.

1. Compute the **bond interest expense**. To do so, multiply the carrying value of the bonds at the beginning of the interest period by the effective-interest rate.

2. Compute the **bond interest paid** (or accrued). To do so, multiply the face value of the bonds by the contractual interest rate.

3. Compute the **amortization amount**. To do so, determine the difference between the amounts computed in steps (1) and (2).

These steps are graphically depicted in Illustration 16A-2.

Illustration 16A-2

Computation of amortization—effective-interest method

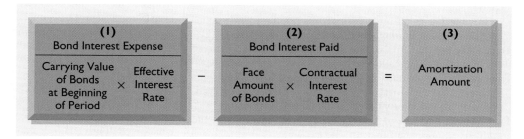

The straight-line and effective-interest methods result in the same total amount of interest expense over the term of the bonds. Also, interest expense each period is generally comparable in amount. However, **when the amounts are materially different, the effective-interest method is required under generally accepted accounting principles (GAAP)**.

AMORTIZING BOND DISCOUNT

To illustrate the effective-interest method of bond discount amortization, assume that Candlestick, Inc. (as per this chapter pages 647–648) issues $100,000 of 10%, 5-year bonds on January 1, 2002, with interest payable each July 1 and January 1. The bonds sell for $92,639 (92.639% of face value). This sales price results in bond discount of $7,361 ($100,000 − $92,639) and an effective-interest rate of 12%. (Note that the $92,639 can be proven by time value of money techniques as shown in Appendix C at the end of this book.) A bond discount amortization schedule as shown in Illustration 16A-3 facilitates the recording of interest expense and the discount amortization. Note that interest expense as a percentage of carrying value remains constant at 6%. Illustration 16A-3 may be compared with Illustration 16-12 (page 649) to see the differences between the straight-line and the effective-interest amortization methods on a bond discount.

Illustration 16A-3

Bond discount amortization schedule

		(B) Interest Expense to Be Recorded (6% × Preceding Bond Carrying Value)		(C) Discount Amortization (B) − (A)	(D) Unamortized Discount (D) − (C)	(E) Bond Carrying Value ($100,000 − D)
Semiannual Interest Periods	**(A) Interest to Be Paid (5% × $100,000)**					
Issue date					$7,361	$ 92,639
1	$ 5,000	$ 5,558	(6% × $92,639)	$ 558	6,803	93,197
2	5,000	5,592	(6% × $93,197)	592	6,211	93,789
3	5,000	5,627	(6% × $93,789)	627	5,584	94,416
4	5,000	5,665	(6% × $94,416)	665	4,919	95,081
5	5,000	5,705	(6% × $95,081)	705	4,214	95,786
6	5,000	5,747	(6% × $95,786)	747	3,467	96,533
7	5,000	5,792	(6% × $96,533)	792	2,675	97,325
8	5,000	5,840	(6% × $97,325)	840	1,835	98,165
9	5,000	5,890	(6% × $98,165)	890	945	99,055
10	5,000	5,945*	(6% × $99,055)	945	–0–	100,000
	$50,000	$57,361		$7,361		

CANDLESTICK, INC.
Bond Discount Amortization
Effective-Interest Method—Semiannual Interest Payments
10% Bonds Issued at 12%

Column (A) remains constant because the face value of the bonds ($100,000) is multiplied by the semiannual contractual interest rate (5%) each period.
Column (B) is computed as the preceding bond carrying value times the semiannual effective-interest rate (6%).
Column (C) indicates the discount amortization each period.
Column (D) decreases each period until it reaches zero at maturity.
Column (E) increases each period until it equals face value at maturity.
*$2 difference due to rounding.

For the first interest period, the computations of bond interest expense and the bond discount amortization are:

Illustration 16A-4

Computation of bond discount amortization

Bond interest expense ($92,639 × 6%)	$5,558
Contractual interest ($100,000 × 5%)	5,000
Bond discount amortization	**$ 558**

The entry to record the payment of interest and amortization of bond discount by Candlestick, Inc. on July 1, 2002, is:

July 1	Bond Interest Expense	5,558	
	Discount on Bonds Payable		558
	Cash		5,000
	(To record payment of bond interest and amortization of bond discount)		

A	=	L	+	SE
−5,000		+558		−5,558

For the second interest period, bond interest expense will be $5,592 ($93,197 × 6%), and the discount amortization will be $592. At December 31, the following adjusting entry is made.

A	=	L	+	SE
		+592		−5,592
		+5,000		

Dec. 31	Bond Interest Expense		5,592	
	Discount on Bonds Payable			592
	Bond Interest Payable			5,000
	(To record accrued interest and			
	amortization of bond discount)			

Total bond interest expense for 2002 is $11,150 ($5,558 + $5,592). On January 1, payment of the interest is recorded by a debit to Bond Interest Payable and a credit to Cash.

AMORTIZING BOND PREMIUM

The amortization of bond premium by the effective-interest method is similar to the procedures described for bond discount. For example, assume that Candlestick, Inc. issues $100,000, 10%, 5-year bonds on January 1, 2002, with interest payable on July 1 and January 1. In this case, the bonds sell for $108,111. This sales price results in bond premium of $8,111 and an effective-interest rate of 8%. The bond premium amortization schedule is shown in Illustration 16A-5.

Illustration 16A-5 may be compared with Illustration 16-17 (page 651) to see the difference between the straight-line and the effective-interest amortization methods on a bond premium.

Illustration 16A-5

Bond premium amortization schedule

CANDLESTICK, INC.					
Bond Premium Amortization					
Effective-Interest Method—Semiannual Interest Payments					
10% Bonds Issued at 8%					
Semiannual Interest Periods	**(A)** Interest to Be Paid (5% × $100,000)	**(B)** Interest Expense to Be Recorded (4% × Preceding Bond Carrying Value)	**(C)** Premium Amortization (A) − (B)	**(D)** Unamortized Premium (D) − (C)	**(E)** Bond Carrying Value ($100,000 + D)
Issue date				$8,111	$108,111
1	$ 5,000	$ 4,324 (4% × $108,111)	$ 676	7,435	107,435
2	5,000	4,297 (4% × $107,435)	703	6,732	106,732
3	5,000	4,269 (4% × $106,732)	731	6,001	106,001
4	5,000	4,240 (4% × $106,001)	760	5,241	105,241
5	5,000	4,210 (4% × $105,241)	790	4,451	104,451
6	5,000	4,178 (4% × $104,451)	822	3,629	103,629
7	5,000	4,145 (4% × $103,629)	855	2,774	102,774
8	5,000	4,111 (4% × $102,774)	889	1,885	101,885
9	5,000	4,075 (4% × $101,885)	925	960	100,960
10	5,000	4,040* (4% × $100,960)	960	–0–	100,000
	$50,000	$41,889	$8,111		

Column **(A)** remains constant because the face value of the bonds ($100,000) is multiplied by the semiannual contractual interest rate (5%) each period.
Column **(B)** is computed as the carrying value of the bonds times the semiannual effective-interest rate (4%).
Column **(C)** indicates the premium amortization each period.
Column **(D)** decreases each period until it reaches zero at maturity.
Column **(E)** decreases each period until it equals face value at maturity.

*$2 difference due to rounding.

For the first interest period, the computations of bond interest expense and the bond premium amortization are:

Bond interest expense ($108,111 × 4%)	$4,324
Contractual interest ($100,000 × 5%)	5,000
Bond premium amortization	**$ 676**

Illustration 16A-6

Computation of bond premium amortization

The entry on the first interest date is:

July 1	Bond Interest Expense	4,324	
	Premium on Bonds Payable	676	
	Cash		5,000
	(To record payment of bond interest and		
	amortization of bond premium)		

A	=	L	+	SE
−5,000		−676		−4,324

For the second interest period, interest expense will be $4,297, and the premium amortization will be $703. Total bond interest expense for 2002 is $8,621 ($4,324 + $4,297).

*T*ECHNOLOGY IN ACTION

The amortization schedule is an excellent example of an accounting computation efficiently and effectively performed by an electronic spreadsheet. Once the selling price, face amount, contractual rate of interest, effective rate of interest, and number of interest periods are determined and entered into the spreadsheet, all of the computations until maturity can be performed by the computer. Remember that all the data needed for the adjusting entries can be taken directly from the amortization schedule.

*D*EMONSTRATION PROBLEM

Gardner Corporation issues $1,750,000, 10-year, 12% bonds on January 1, 2002, at $1,820,000 to yield 10%. The bonds pay semiannual interest July 1 and January 1. Gardner uses the effective-interest method of amortization.

Instructions
(a) Prepare the journal entry to record the issuance of the bonds.
(b) Prepare the journal entry to record the payment of interest on July 1, 2002.

SOLUTION TO DEMONSTRATION PROBLEM

(a) 2002

Jan. 1	Cash	1,820,000	
	Bonds Payable		1,750,000
	Premium on Bonds Payable		70,000
	(To record issuance of bonds at a premium)		

(b) 2002

July 1	Bond Interest Expense	91,000*	
	Premium on Bonds Payable	14,000**	
	Cash		105,000
	(To record payment of semiannual interest		
	and amortization of bond premium)		
	*($1,820,000 × 5%)		
	**($105,000 − $91,000)		

Additional Demonstration Problem

ACTION PLAN

- Compute interest expense by multiplying bond carrying value at the beginning of the period by the effective-interest rate.
- Compute credit to cash (or bond interest payable) by multiplying the face value of the bonds by the contractual interest rate.
- Compute bond premium or discount amortization, which is the difference between (1) and (2).
- Interest expense increases when the effective-interest method is used for bonds issued at a discount. The reason is that a constant percentage is applied to an increasing book value to compute interest expense.

SUMMARY OF STUDY OBJECTIVE FOR APPENDIX

8. Contrast the effects of the straight-line and effective-interest methods of amortizing bond discount and bond premium. The straight-line method of amortization results in a constant amount of amortization and interest expense per period but a varying percentage rate. In contrast, the effective-interest method results in varying amounts of amor- tization and interest expense per period but a constant per- centage rate of interest. The effective-interest method gener- ally results in a better matching of expenses with revenues. When the difference between the straight-line and effective- interest method is material, the use of the effective-interest method is required under GAAP.

GLOSSARY FOR APPENDIX

Effective-interest method of amortization A method of amortizing bond discount or bond premium that results in periodic interest expense equal to a constant percentage of the carrying value of the bonds. (p. 664).

Effective-interest rate Rate established when bonds are is- sued that remains constant in each interest period. (p. 664).

*Note: All asterisked Questions, Exercises, and Problems relate to material in the appendix to the chapter.

Chapter 16 Self-Test

SELF-STUDY QUESTIONS

Answers are at the end of the chapter.

(SO 1) **1.** The term used for bonds that are unsecured is:
   a. callable bonds.
   b. indenture bonds.
   c. debenture bonds.
   d. bearer bonds.

(SO 2) **2.** Karson Inc. issues 10-year bonds with a maturity value of $200,000. If the bonds are issued at a premium, this indi- cates that:
   a. the contractual interest rate exceeds the market in- terest rate.
   b. the market interest rate exceeds the contractual in- terest rate.
   c. the contractual interest rate and the market interest rate are the same.
   d. no relationship exists between the two rates.

(SO 2) **3.** On January 1, Hurley Corporation issues $500,000, 5- year, 12% bonds at 96 with interest payable on July 1 and January 1. The entry on July 1 to record payment of bond interest and the amortization of bond discount using the straight-line method will include a:
   a. debit to Interest Expense $30,000.
   b. debit to Interest Expense $60,000.
   c. credit to Discount on Bonds Payable $4,000.
   d. credit to Discount on Bonds Payable $2,000.

(SO 2) **4.** For the bonds issued in question 3, above, what is the car- rying value of the bonds at the end of the third interest period?
   a. $486,000.
   b. $488,000.
   c. $472,000.
   d. $464,000.

(SO 2) **5.** When the interest payment dates of a bond are May 1 and November 1, and a bond issue is sold on June 1, the amount of cash received by the issuer will be:

   a. decreased by accrued interest from June 1 to Novem- ber 1.
   b. decreased by accrued interest from May 1 to June 1.
   c. increased by accrued interest from May 1 to June 1.
   d. increased by accrued interest from June 1 to Novem- ber 1.

6. Gester Corporation retires its $100,000 face value bonds (SO 3) at 105 on January 1, following the payment of semian- nual interest. The carrying value of the bonds at the re- demption date is $103,745. The entry to record the re- demption will include a:
   a. credit of $3,745 to Loss on Bond Redemption.
   b. debit of $3,745 to Premium on Bonds Payable.
   c. credit of $1,255 to Gain on Bond Redemption.
   d. debit of $5,000 to Premium on Bonds Payable.

7. Colson Inc. converts $600,000 of bonds sold at face value (SO 3) into 10,000 shares of common stock, par value $1. Both the bonds and the stock have a market value of $760,000. What amount should be credited to Paid-in Capital in Ex- cess of Par as a result of the conversion?
   a. $10,000.
   b. $160,000.
   c. $600,000.
   d. $590,000.

8. Sanger Company has a bond sinking fund in the amount (SO 4) of $400,000. Where should this amount be reported on the balance sheet?
   a. Investments section.
   b. Current assets section.
   c. Current liabilities section.
   d. Long-term liabilities section.

9. Andrews Inc. issues a $497,000, 10% 3-year mortgage (SO 5) note on January 1. The note will be paid in three an- nual installments of $200,000, each payable at the end of the year. What is the amount of interest expense that should be recognized by Andrews Inc. in the second year?

a. $16,567.
b. $49,740.
c. $34,670.
d. $347,600.

(SO 6) **10.** Lease A does not contain a bargain purchase option, but the lease term is equal to 90 percent of the estimated economic life of the leased property. Lease B does not transfer ownership of the property to the lessee by the end of the lease term, but the lease term is equal to 75 percent of the estimated economic life of the leased property. How should the lessee classify these leases?

Lease A	Lease B
a. Operating lease	Capital lease
b. Operating lease	Operating lease
c. Capital lease	Operating lease
d. Capital lease	Capital lease

*11. On January 1, Besalius Inc. issued $1,000,000, 9% bonds (SO 8) for $939,000. The market rate of interest for these bonds is 10%. Interest is payable annually on December 31. Besalius uses the effective-interest method of amortizing bond discount. At the end of the first year, Besalius should report unamortized bond discount of:

a. $54,900.
b. $57,100.
c. $51,610.
d. $51,000.

*12. On January 1, Dias Corporation issued $1,000,000, 14%, (SO 8) 5-year bonds with interest payable on July 1 and January 1. The bonds sold for $1,098,540. The market rate of interest for these bonds was 12%. On the first interest date, using the effective-interest method, the debit entry to Bond Interest Expense is for:

a. $60,000.
b. $76,898.
c. $65,912.
d. $131,825.

QUESTIONS

1. (a) What are long-term liabilities? Give three examples. (b) What is a bond?

2. (a) As a source of long-term financing, what are the major advantages of bonds over common stock? (b) What are the major disadvantages in using bonds for long-term financing?

3. Contrast the following types of bonds: (a) secured and unsecured, (b) term and serial, (c) registered and bearer, and (d) convertible and callable.

4. The following terms are important in issuing bonds: (a) face value, (b) contractual interest rate, (c) bond indenture, and (d) bond certificate. Explain each of these terms.

5. Describe the two major obligations incurred by a company when bonds are issued.

6. Assume that Bedazzled Inc. sold bonds with a par value of $100,000 for $104,000. Was the market interest rate equal to, less than, or greater than the bonds' contractual interest rate? Explain.

7. Elizabeth Hurley and Brendan Fraser are discussing how the market price of a bond is determined. Elizabeth believes that the market price of a bond is solely a function of the amount of the principal payment at the end of the term of a bond. Is she right? Discuss.

8. If a 10%, 10-year, $800,000 bond is issued at par and interest is paid semiannually, what is the amount of the interest payment at the end of the first semiannual period?

9. If the Bonds Payable account has a balance of $900,000 and the Discount on Bonds Payable account has a balance of $60,000, what is the carrying value of the bonds?

10. Explain the straight-line method of amortizing discount and premium on bonds payable.

11. Genji Corporation issues $300,000 of 8%, 5-year bonds on January 1, 2002, at 104. Assuming that the straight-line method is used to amortize the premium, what is the total amount of interest expense for 2002?

12. Which accounts are debited and which are credited if a bond issue originally sold at a premium is redeemed before maturity at 97 immediately following the payment of interest?

13. Kishwaukee Corporation is considering issuing a convertible bond. What is a convertible bond? Discuss the advantages of a convertible bond from the standpoint of (a) the bondholders and (b) the issuing corporation.

14. The financial statements of Macon Inc. disclose that it has a bond sinking fund. What is a bond sinking fund? What is its purpose?

15. Dan Dial, a friend of yours, has recently purchased a home for $125,000, paying $25,000 down and the remainder financed by a 10.5%, 20-year mortgage, payable at $998.38 per month. At the end of the first month, Dan receives a statement from the bank indicating that only $123.38 of principal was paid during the month. At this rate, he calculates that it will take over 67 years to pay off the mortgage. Is he right? Discuss.

16. (a) What is a lease agreement? (b) What are the two most common types of leases? (c) Distinguish between the two types of leases.

17. Waubonsee Company rents a warehouse on a month-to-month basis for the storage of its excess inventory. The company periodically must rent space when its production greatly exceeds actual sales. What is the nature of this type of lease agreement, and what accounting treatment should be used?

18. Alvarez Company entered into an agreement to lease 12 computers from Estes Electronics Inc. The present value of the lease payments is $186,300. Assuming that this is a capital lease, what entry would Alvarez Company make on the date of the lease agreement?

19. In general, what are the requirements for the financial statement presentation of long-term liabilities?

*20. Diane Leto is discussing the advantages of the effective-interest method of bond amortization with her accounting staff. What do you think Diane is saying?

*21. Graham Corporation issues $500,000 of 9%, 5-year bonds on January 1, 2002, at 104. If Graham uses the effective-interest method in amortizing the premium, will the annual interest expense increase or decrease over the life of the bonds? Explain.

BRIEF EXERCISES

Compare bond versus stock financing
(SO 1)

BE16-1   Grambling Inc. is considering two alternatives to finance its construction of a new $2 million plant.

(a) Issuance of 200,000 shares of common stock at the market price of $10 per share.
(b) Issuance of $2 million, 8% bonds at par.

Complete the following table, and indicate which alternative is preferable.

	Issue Stock	Issue Bond
Income before interest and taxes	$800,000	$800,000
Interest expense from bonds	_____	_____
Income before income taxes	$	$
Income tax expense (30%)	_____	_____
Net income	$_____	$_____
Outstanding shares		500,000
Earnings per share	_____	_____

Prepare entries for bonds issued at face value.
(SO 2)

BE16-2   Existenz Corporation issued 2,000, 8%, 5-year, $1,000 bonds dated January 1, 2002, at 100.

(a) Prepare the journal entry to record the sale of these bonds on January 1, 2002.
(b) Prepare the journal entry to record the first interest payment on July 1, 2002 (interest payable semiannually), assuming no previous accrual of interest.
(c) Prepare the adjusting journal entry on December 31, 2002, to record interest expense.

Prepare entries for bonds issued at a discount.
(SO 2)

BE16-3   Verdi Company issues $2 million, 10-year, 9% bonds at 96, with interest payable on July 1 and January 1. The straight-line method is used to amortize bond discount.

(a) Prepare the journal entry to record the sale of these bonds on January 1, 2002.
(b) Prepare the journal entry to record interest expense and bond discount amortization on July 1, 2002, assuming no previous accrual of interest.

Prepare entries for bonds issued at a premium.
(SO 2)

BE16-4   Puccini Inc. issues $3 million, 5-year, 10% bonds at 102, with interest payable on July 1 and January 1. The straight-line method is used to amortize bond premium.

(a) Prepare the journal entry to record the sale of these bonds on January 1, 2002.
(b) Prepare the journal entry to record interest expense and bond premium amortization on July 1, 2002, assuming no previous accrual of interest.

Prepare entries for bonds issued between interest dates.
(SO 2)

BE16-5   Bizet Inc. has outstanding $2 million, 10-year, 9% bonds with interest payable on July 1 and January 1. The bonds were dated January 1, 2002, but were issued on May 1, 2002, at face value plus accrued interest.

(a) Prepare the journal entry to record the sale of the bonds on May 1, 2002.
(b) Prepare the journal entry to record the interest payment on July 1, 2002.

Prepare entry for redemption of bonds.
(SO 3)

BE16-6   The balance sheet for Bravo Company reports the following information on July 1, 2002.

Long-term liabilities		
Bonds payable	$1,000,000	
Less: Discount on bonds payable	60,000	$940,000

Bravo decides to redeem these bonds at 102 after paying semiannual interest. Prepare the journal entry to record the redemption on July 1, 2002.

BE16-7 Fleckstones Inc. issues a $600,000, 10%, 10-year mortgage note on December 31, 2002, to obtain financing for a new building. The terms provide for semiannual installment payments of $48,146. Prepare the entry to record the mortgage loan on December 31, 2002, and the first installment payment.

Prepare entries for long-term notes payable.
(SO 5)

BE16-8 Prepare the journal entries that the lessee should make to record the following transactions.

1. The lessee makes a lease payment of $80,000 to the lessor in an operating lease transaction.
2. Yoakam Company leases a new building from Chang Construction, Inc. The present value of the lease payments is $600,000. The lease qualifies as a capital lease.

Contrast accounting for operating and capital lease.
(SO 6)

BE16-9 Presented below are long-term liability items for Ravinia Company at December 31, 2002. Prepare the long-term liabilities section of the balance sheet for Ravinia Company.

Prepare statement presentation of long-term liabilities.
(SO 7)

Bonds payable, due 2004	$600,000
Lease liability	50,000
Notes payable, due 2007	80,000
Discount on bonds payable	45,000

*BE16-10 Presented below is the partial bond discount amortization schedule for Savion Glover Corp. Savion Glover uses the effective-interest method of amortization.

Use effective-interest method of bond amortization.
(SO 8)

Semiannual Interest Periods	Interest to Be Paid	Interest Expense to Be Recorded	Discount Amortization	Unamortized Discount	Bond Carrying Value
Issue date				$62,311	$937,689
1	$45,000	$46,884	$1,884	60,427	939,573
2	45,000	46,979	1,979	58,448	941,552

Instructions

(a) Prepare the journal entry to record the payment of interest and the discount amortization at the end of period 1.
(b) ▭▱▱▱▱➤ Explain why interest expense is greater than interest paid.
(c) Explain why interest expense will increase each period.

Exercises

E16-1 Flypaper Airlines is considering two alternatives for the financing of a purchase of a fleet of airplanes. These two alternatives are:

Compare two alternatives of financing—issuance of common stock vs. issuance of bonds.
(SO 1)

1. Issue 60,000 shares of common stock at $45 per share. (Cash dividends have not been paid nor is the payment of any contemplated).
2. Issue 13%, 10-year bonds at par for $2,700,000.

It is estimated that the company will earn $500,000 before interest and taxes as a result of this purchase. The company has an estimated tax rate of 30% and has 90,000 shares of common stock outstanding prior to the new financing.

Instructions
Determine the effect on net income and earnings per share for these two methods of financing.

E16-2 On January 1, Anyswing Company issued $100,000, 10%, 10-year bonds at par. Interest is payable semiannually on July 1 and January 1.

Prepare entries for issuance of bonds, and payment and accrual of bond interest.
(SO 2)

Instructions
Present journal entries to record the following.

(a) The issuance of the bonds.
(b) The payment of interest on July 1, assuming that interest was not accrued on June 30.
(c) The accrual of interest on December 31.

E16-3 Pimpernel Company issued $400,000, 9%, 20-year bonds on January 1, 2002, at 103. Interest is payable semiannually on July 1 and January 1. Pimpernel uses straight-line amortization for bond premium or discount.

Prepare entries to record issuance of bonds, payment of interest, amortization of premium, and redemption at maturity.
(SO 2, 3)

Instructions

Prepare the journal entries to record the following.

(a) The issuance of the bonds.

(b) The payment of interest and the premium amortization on July 1, 2002, assuming that interest was not accrued on June 30.

(c) The accrual of interest and the premium amortization on December 31, 2002.

(d) The redemption of the bonds at maturity, assuming interest for the last interest period has been paid and recorded.

Prepare entries to record issuance of bonds, payment of interest, amortization of discount, and redemption at maturity.
(SO 2, 3)

E16-4 Jim Brickman Company issued $300,000, 11%, 10-year bonds on December 31, 2001, for $280,000. Interest is payable semiannually on June 30 and December 31. Jim Brickman Company uses the straight-line method to amortize bond premium or discount.

Instructions

Prepare the journal entries to record the following.

(a) The issuance of the bonds.

(b) The payment of interest and the discount amortization on June 30, 2002.

(c) The payment of interest and the discount amortization on December 31, 2002.

(d) The redemption of the bonds at maturity, assuming interest for the last interest period has been paid and recorded.

Prepare entries to record issuance of bonds between interest dates, and payment and accrual of interest.
(SO 2)

E16-5 On April 1, Blue Man Company issued $120,000, 10%, 10-year bonds dated January 1 at par plus accrued interest. Interest is payable semiannually on July 1 and January 1.

Instructions

Present journal entries to record the following.

(a) The issuance of the bonds.

(b) The payment of interest on July 1, assuming that interest was not accrued on June 30.

(c) The accrual of interest on December 31.

Prepare entries for redemption of bonds and conversion of bonds into common stock.
(SO 3)

E16-6 Presented below are three independent situations.

1. Apollo Corporation retired $130,000 face value, 12% bonds on June 30, 2002, at 101. The carrying value of the bonds at the redemption date was $107,500. The bonds pay semiannual interest, and the interest payment due on June 30, 2002, has been made and recorded.

2. Buju Inc. retired $150,000 face value, 12.5% bonds on June 30, 2002, at 96. The carrying value of the bonds at the redemption date was $151,000. The bonds pay semiannual interest, and the interest payment due on June 30, 2002, has been made and recorded.

3. Eden Company has $80,000, 8%, 12-year convertible bonds outstanding. These bonds were sold at face value and pay semiannual interest on June 30 and December 31 of each year. The bonds are convertible into 30 shares of Eden $5 par value common stock for each $1,000 worth of bonds. On December 31, 2002, after the bond interest has been paid, $20,000 face value bonds were converted. The market value of Eden common stock was $44 per share on December 31, 2002.

Instructions

For each independent situation above, prepare the appropriate journal entry for the redemption or conversion of the bonds.

Prepare entries to record mortgage note and installment payments.
(SO 5)

E16-7 J. Lopez Co. receives $150,000 when it issues a $150,000, 10%, mortgage note payable to finance the construction of a building at December 31, 2002. The terms provide for semiannual installment payments of $10,000 on June 30 and December 31.

Instructions

Prepare the journal entries to record the mortgage loan and the first two installment payments.

E16-8 Presented below are two independent situations.

Prepare entries for operating lease and capital lease.
(SO 6)

1. Speedy Car Rental leased a car to D'Onofrio Company for one year. Terms of the operating lease agreement call for monthly payments of $500.

2. On January 1, 2002, Knapp Inc. entered into an agreement to lease 20 computers from Guinn Electronics. The terms of the lease agreement require three annual rental payments of $60,000 (including 10% interest) beginning December 31, 2002. The present value of the three rental payments is $149,211. Knapp considers this a capital lease.

Instructions

(a) Prepare the appropriate journal entry to be made by D'Onofrio Company for the first lease payment.

(b) Prepare the journal entry to record the lease agreement on the books of Knapp Inc. on January 1, 2002.

E16-9   The adjusted trial balance for Wesley Snipes Corporation at the end of the current year contained the following accounts.

Prepare long-term liabilities section.
(SO 7)

Bond Interest Payable	$ 9,000
Lease Liability	59,500
Bonds Payable, due 2010	150,000
Premium on Bonds Payable	32,000
Bond Sinking Fund	241,600

Instructions

(a) Prepare the long-term liabilities section of the balance sheet.

(b) Indicate the proper balance sheet classification for the account(s) listed above that do not belong in the long-term liabilities section.

*E16-10   Tagawa Corporation issued $650,000, 9%, 10-year bonds on January 1, 2002, for $609,497. This price resulted in an effective interest rate of 10% on the bonds. Interest is payable semiannually on July 1 and January 1. Tagawa uses the effective-interest method to amortize bond premium or discount.

Prepare entries for issuance of bonds, payment of interest, and amortization of discount using effective-interest method
(SO 8)

Instructions

Prepare the journal entries to record the following. (Round to the nearest dollar.)

(a) The issuance of the bonds.

(b) The payment of interest and the discount amortization on July 1, 2002, assuming that interest was not accrued on June 30.

(c) The accrual of interest and the discount amortization on December 31, 2002.

*E16-11   Matiko Company issued $600,000, 11%, 10-year bonds on January 1, 2002, for $637,387. This price resulted in an effective interest rate of 10% on the bonds. Interest is payable semiannually on July 1 and January 1. Matiko uses the effective-interest method to amortize bond premium or discount.

Prepare entries for issuance of bonds, payment of interest, and amortization of premium using effective-interest method.
(SO 8)

Instructions

Prepare the journal entries to record the following. (Round to the nearest dollar).

(a) The issuance of the bonds.

(b) The payment of interest and the premium amortization on July 1, 2002, assuming that interest was not accrued on June 30.

(c) The accrual of interest and the premium amortization on December 31, 2002.

PROBLEMS: SET A

P16-1A   Sherrick Electric sold $4,000,000, 10%, 10-year bonds on January 1, 2002. The bonds were dated January 1 and pay interest July 1 and January 1. Sherrick Electric uses the straight-line method to amortize bond premium or discount. The bonds were sold at 104. Assume no interest is accrued on June 30.

Prepare entries to record issuance of bonds, interest accrual, and amortization for 2 years.
(SO 2, 7)

Instructions

(a) Prepare the journal entry to record the issuance of the bonds on January 1, 2002.

(b) Prepare a bond premium amortization schedule for the first 4 interest periods.

(c) Prepare the journal entries for interest and the amortization of the premium in 2002 and 2003.

(d) Show the balance sheet presentation of the bond liability at December 31, 2003.

(b) Amortization $8,000
(d) Premium on bonds payable
    $128,000

P16-2A   Perabo Company sold $2,500,000, 12%, 10-year bonds on July 1, 2002. The bonds were dated July 1, 2002, and pay interest July 1 and January 1. Perabo Company uses the straight-line method to amortize bond premium or discount. Assume no interest is accrued on June 30.

Prepare entries to record issuance of bonds, interest, and amortization of bond premium and discount.
(SO 2, 7)

(a) Amortization $5,000
(b) Amortization $2,500
(c) Premium on bonds payable
$95,000
Discount on bonds payable
$47,500

Prepare entries to record interest payments, premium amortization, and redemption of bonds.
(SO 2, 3)

Instructions

(a) Prepare all the necessary journal entries to record the issuance of the bonds and bond interest expense for 2002, assuming that the bonds sold at 104.

(b) Prepare journal entries as in part (a) assuming that the bonds sold at 98.

(c) Show balance sheet presentation for each bond issue at December 31, 2002.

P16-3A The following is taken from the Mike Sondgeroth Company balance sheet.

MIKE SONDGEROTH COMPANY
Balance Sheet (partial)
December 31, 2002

Current liabilities		
Bond interest payable (for 6 months		
from July 1 to December 31)		$ 180,000
Long-term liabilities		
Bonds payable, 12% due January 1, 2013	$3,000,000	
Add: Premium on bonds payable	200,000	$3,200,000

Interest is payable semiannually on January 1 and July 1. The bonds are callable on any semiannual interest date. Sondgeroth uses straight-line amortization for any bond premium or discount. From December 31, 2002, the bonds will be outstanding for an additional 10 years (120 months).

Instructions

(a) Journalize the payment of bond interest on January 1, 2003

(b) Amortization $10,000

(b) Prepare the entry to amortize bond premium and to pay the interest due on July 1, 2003, assuming no accrual of interest on June 30.

(c) Gain $64,000

(c) Assume that on July 1, 2003, after paying interest, Mike Sondgeroth Company calls bonds having a face value of $1,200,000. The call price is 101. Record the redemption of the bonds.

(d) Amortization $6,000

(d) Prepare the adjusting entry at December 31, 2003, to amortize bond premium and to accrue interest on the remaining bonds.

Prepare installment schedule and journal entries for a mortgage note payable.
(SO 5)

P16-4A Carol Dunn Electronics issues an $800,000, 12%, 10-year mortgage note on December 31, 2001. The proceeds from the note are to be used in financing a new research laboratory. The terms of the note provide for semiannual installment payments, exclusive of real estate taxes and insurance, of $69,748. Payments are due June 30 and December 31.

Instructions

(a) Prepare an installment payment schedule for the first 2 years.

(b) June 30 Mortgage Notes
Payable $21,748
(c) Current liability—2002:
$50,338

(b) Prepare the entries for (1) the loan and (2) the first two installment payments.

(c) Show how the total mortgage liability should be reported on the balance sheet at December 31, 2002.

Analyze three different lease situations and prepare journal entries.
(SO 6)

P16-5A Presented below are three different lease transactions that occurred for Choi Inc. in 2002. Assume that all lease contracts start on January 1, 2002. In no case does Choi receive title to the properties leased during or at the end of the lease term.

	Lessor		
	Shirley Delivery	**Mall Co.**	**Snipes Auto**
Type of property	Computer	Delivery equipment	Automobile
Yearly rental	$ 6,000	$ 4,200	$ 3,700
Lease term	6 years	4 years	2 years
Estimated economic life	7 years	7 years	5 years
Fair market value of lease asset	$33,000	$19,000	$11,000
Present value of the lease rental payments	$31,000	$13,000	$ 6,400
Bargain purchase option	None	None	None

Instructions

(a) Which of the leases above are operating leases and which are capital leases? Explain.

(b) How should the lease transaction for Mall Co. be recorded in 2002?

(c) How should the lease transaction for Shirley Delivery be recorded on January 1, 2002?

*P16-6A   On July 1, 2002, Edmonds Corporation issued $5,000,000 face value, 12%, 10-year bonds at $5,623,112. This price resulted in an effective-interest rate of 10% on the bonds. Edmonds uses the effective-interest method to amortize bond premium or discount. The bonds pay semiannual interest July 1 and January 1.

Prepare entries to record issuance of bonds, payment of interest, and amortization of bond premium using effective-interest method.
(SO 2)

Instructions
(Round all computations to the nearest dollar.)

(a) Prepare the journal entry to record the issuance of the bonds on July 1, 2002.
(b) Prepare the journal entry to record the accrual of interest and the amortization of the premium on December 31, 2002.

(b) Amortization $18,844

(c) Prepare the journal entry to record the payment of interest and the amortization of the premium on July 1, 2003, assuming no accrual of interest on June 30.

(c) Amortization $19,787

(d) Prepare the journal entry to record the accrual of interest and the amortization of the premium on December 31, 2003.

(d) Amortization $20,776

(e) Prepare an amortization table through December 31, 2003 (3 interest periods) for this bond issue.

*P16-7A   On July 1, 2002, Algonquin Company issued $3,000,000 face value, 10%, 10-year bonds at $2,655,888. This price resulted in an effective-interest rate of 12% on the bonds. Algonquin uses the effective-interest method to amortize bond premium or discount. The bonds pay semiannual interest July 1 and January 1.

Prepare entries to record issuance of bonds, payment of interest, and amortization of discount using effective-interest method. In addition, answer questions.
(SO 2, 8)

Instructions
(Round all computations to the nearest dollar.)

(a) Prepare the journal entries to record the following transactions.
   (1) The issuance of the bonds on July 1, 2002.
   (2) The accrual of interest and the amortization of the discount on December 31, 2002.
   (3) The payment of interest and the amortization of the discount on July 1, 2003, assuming no accrual of interest on June 30.

(a) (3) Amortization $9,914

   (4) The accrual of interest and the amortization of the discount on December 31, 2003.

(a) (4) Amortization $10,509

(b) Show the proper balance sheet presentation for the liability for bonds payable on the December 31, 2003, balance sheet.

(b) $2,685,664

(c) ▭▬▭▶ Provide the answers to the following questions in letter form.
   (1) What amount of interest expense is reported for 2003?
   (2) Would the bond interest expense reported in 2003 be the same as, greater than, or less than the amount that would be reported if the straight-line method of amortization were used?
   (3) Determine the total cost of borrowing over the life of the bond.
   (4) Would the total bond interest expense be greater than, the same as, or less than the total interest expense that would be reported if the straight-line method of amortization were used?

PROBLEMS: SET B

P16-1B   Closet Company sold $3,000,000, 9%, 20-year bonds on January 1, 2002. The bonds were dated January 1, 2002, and pay interest on January 1 and July 1. Closet Company uses the straight-line method to amortize bond premium or discount. The bonds were sold at 98. Assume no interest is accrued on June 30.

Prepare entries to record issuance of bonds, interest accrual, and amortization for 2 years.
(SO 2, 7)

Instructions
(a) Prepare the journal entry to record the issuance of the bonds on January 1, 2002.
(b) Prepare a bond discount amortization schedule for the first 4 interest periods.

(b) Amortization $1,500

(c) Prepare the journal entries for interest and the amortization of the discount in 2002 and 2003.
(d) Show the balance sheet presentation of the bond liability at December 31, 2003.

(d) Discount on bonds payable $54,000

P16-2B   Nathan K. Corporation sold $2,500,000, 8%, 10-year bonds on January 1, 2002. The bonds were dated January 1, 2002, and pay interest on July 1 and January 1. Nathan K. Corporation uses the straight-line method to amortize bond premium or discount. Assume no interest is accrued on June 30.

Prepare entries to record issuance of bonds, interest, and amortization of bond premium and discount.
(SO 2, 7)

Instructions
(a) Prepare all the necessary journal entries to record the issuance of the bonds and bond interest expense for 2002, assuming that the bonds sold at 103.

(a) Amortization $3,750

(b) Prepare journal entries as in part (a) assuming that the bonds sold at 96.

(b) Amortization $5,000

(c) Premium on bonds payable
$67,500
Discount on bonds payable
$90,000

Prepare entries to record inter-est payments, discount amorti-zation, and redemption of bonds.
(SO 2, 3)

(c) Show balance sheet presentation for each bond issue at December 31, 2002.

P16-3B The following is taken from the Becky Corp. balance sheet.

BECKY CORPORATION
Balance Sheet (partial)
December 31, 2002

Current liabilities		
Bond interest payable (for 6 months		
from July 1 to December 31)		$ 120,000
Long-term liabilities		
Bonds payable, 10%, due		
January 1, 2013	$2,400,000	
Less: Discount on bonds payable	90,000	$2,310,000

Interest is payable semiannually on January 1 and July 1. The bonds are callable on any semi-annual interest date. Becky uses straight-line amortization for any bond premium or discount. From December 31, 2002, the bonds will be outstanding for an additional 10 years (120 months).

Instructions
(Round all computations to the nearest dollar).

(b) Amortization $4,500

(a) Journalize the payment of bond interest on January 1, 2003.
(b) Prepare the entry to amortize bond discount and to pay the interest due on July 1, 2003, assuming that interest was not accrued on June 30.

(c) Loss $33,375

(c) Assume that on July 1, 2003, after paying interest, Becky Corp. calls bonds having a face value of $600,000. The call price is 102. Record the redemption of the bonds.

(d) Amortization $3,375

(d) Prepare the adjusting entry at December 31, 2003, to amortize bond discount and to ac-crue interest on the remaining bonds.

Prepare installment payments schedule and journal entries for a mortgage note payable.
(SO 5)

P16-4B Gere Electronics issues an $800,000, 10%, 10-year mortgage note on December 31, 2002, to help finance a plant expansion program. The terms provide for semiannual installment payments, not including real estate taxes and insurance, of $64,193. Payments are due June 30 and December 31.

Instructions
(a) Prepare an installment payment schedule for the first 2 years.

(b) June 30 Mortgage Notes
Payable $24,193
(c) Current liability—2003:
$54,679

(b) Prepare the entries for (1) the mortgage loan and (2) the first two installment payments.
(c) Show how the total mortgage liability should be reported on the balance sheet at De-cember 31, 2003.

Analyze three different lease situations and prepare journal entries.
(SO 6)

P16-5B Presented below are three different lease transactions in which Coyote Enterprises engaged in 2002. Assume that all lease transactions start on January 1, 2002. In no case does Coyote receive title to the properties leased during or at the end of the lease term.

	Lessor		
	Winona Co.	**Ryder Co.**	**Wiley Inc.**
Type of property	Bulldozer	Truck	Furniture
Bargain purchase option	None	None	None
Lease term	4 years	6 years	3 years
Estimated economic life	8 years	7 years	5 years
Yearly rental	$13,000	$12,000	$ 4,000
Fair market value of leased asset	$80,000	$58,000	$27,500
Present value of the lease rental payments	$48,000	$50,000	$12,000

Instructions
(a) Identify the leases above as operating or capital leases. Explain.
(b) How should the lease transaction for Ryder Co. be recorded on January 1, 2002?
(c) How should the lease transaction for Wiley Inc. be recorded in 2002?

Prepare entries to record is-suance of bonds, payment of interest, and amortization of bond discount using effective-interest method.
(SO 8)

*P16-6B On July 1, 2002, Godzilla Satellites issued $2,700,000 face value, 9%, 10-year bonds at $2,531,760. This price resulted in an effective-interest rate of 10% on the bonds. Godzilla uses the effective-interest method to amortize bond premium or discount. The bonds pay semi-annual interest July 1 and January 1.

Instructions
(Round all computations to the nearest dollar.)
  (a) Prepare the journal entry to record the issuance of the bonds on July 1, 2002.
  (b) Prepare the journal entry to record the accrual of interest and the amortization of the discount on December 31, 2002.

(b) Amortization $5,088

  (c) Prepare the journal entry to record the payment of interest and the amortization of the discount on July 1, 2003, assuming that interest was not accrued on June 30.

(c) Amortization $5,342

  (d) Prepare the journal entry to record the accrual of interest and the amortization of the discount on December 31, 2003.

(d) Amortization $5,610

  (e) Prepare an amortization table through December 31, 2003 (3 interest periods) for this bond issue.

*P16-7B On July 1, 2002, Michelle Pfeiffer Chemical Company issued $2,000,000 face value, 12%, 10-year bonds at $2,249,245. This price resulted in a 10% effective-interest rate on the bonds. Pfeiffer uses the effective-interest method to amortize bond premium or discount. The bonds pay semiannual interest on each July 1 and January 1.

Prepare entries to record issuance of bonds, payment of interest, and amortization of premium using effective-interest method. In addition, answer questions.
(SO 8)

Instructions
(Round all computations to the nearest dollar.)
  (a) Prepare the journal entries to record the following transactions.
    (1) The issuance of the bonds on July 1, 2002.
    (2) The accrual of interest and the amortization of the premium on December 31, 2002.
    (3) The payment of interest and the amortization of the premium on July 1, 2003, assuming no accrual of interest on June 30.
    (4) The accrual of interest and the amortization of the premium on December 31, 2003.
  (b) Show the proper balance sheet presentation for the liability for bonds payable on the December 31, 2003, balance sheet.
  (c) ▭▭▭▷ Provide the answers to the following questions in letter form.
    (1) What amount of interest expense is reported for 2003?
    (2) Would the bond interest expense reported in 2003 be the same as, greater than, or less than the amount that would be reported if the straight-line method of amortization were used?
    (3) Determine the total cost of borrowing over the life of the bond.
    (4) Would the total bond interest expense be greater than, the same as, or less than the total interest expense if the straight-line method of amortization were used?

(a) (2) Amortization $7,538
(a) (3) Amortization $7,915

(a) (4) Amortization $8,310
(b) $2,225,482

BROADENING YOUR PERSPECTIVE

*F*INANCIAL REPORTING AND ANALYSIS

FINANCIAL REPORTING PROBLEM: *Lands' End, Inc.*

BYP16-1 Refer to the financial statements of **Lands' End, Inc.** and the Notes to Consolidated Financial Statements in Appendix A.

Instructions
  (a) What was Lands' End's total long-term debt (excluding deferred income taxes) at January 28, 2000? What was the increase/decrease in total long-term debt (excluding deferred income taxes) from the prior year? What does Note 5 to the financial statements say about long-term debt?
  (b) What does Lands' End lease (see Note 6)? How does Lands' End classify and account for its leases?
  (c) What was the total rent expense under leases for the year ended January 28, 2000? Do the assets under these leases appear on the balance sheet? What is the total "future fiscal year commitments under these leases as of January 28, 2000"?

COMPARATIVE ANALYSIS PROBLEM: *Lands' End vs. Abercrombie & Fitch*

BYP16-2 **Lands' End's** financial statements are presented in Appendix A. **Abercrombie & Fitch's** financial statements are presented in Appendix B.

Instructions

(a) Based on the information contained in these financial statements, compute the following 2000 ratios for each company.

    (1) Debt (excluding "deferred income taxes" and "other long-term liabilities") to total assets.

    (2) Times interest earned.

(b) What conclusions concerning the companies' long-run solvency can be drawn from these ratios?

(c) Which company has reported the greater amount of future minimum rental commitments? (Abercrombie & Fitch reported a total of $520,342.)

INTERPRETING FINANCIAL STATEMENTS: A Global Focus

BYP16-3 **Apache Corporation** is an international, independent energy enterprise engaged in the exploration, development, production, gathering, processing, and marketing of natural gas and crude oil. Its corporate headquarters are located in Houston, Texas, and it has operations in North America, Australia, Egypt, Poland and the People's Republic of China.

    The 1994 annual report of Apache Corporation disclosed the following information in its management discussion section.

APACHE CORPORATION
Management Discussion

In May 1994, Apache issued 9.25% bonds due 2002 in the principal amount of $100 million. The proceeds of $99 million from the offering were used to reduce bank debt, to pay off the 9.5% convertible debentures due 1996, and for general corporate purposes. In December 1994, the company privately placed 3.93% convertible notes due 1997 in the principal amount of $75 million. The notes are not redeemable before maturity and are convertible into Apache common stock at the option of the holders at any time prior to maturity, at a conversion price of $27 per share. Proceeds from the sale of the notes were used for the repayment of bank debt.

Instructions

(a) Identify the face amount, contractual interest rate, and selling price of the newly issued bonds due in 2002. Explain whether the bonds sold at a premium or a discount.

(b) For what purposes has Apache Corporation been incurring more debt?

EXPLORING THE WEB

BYP16-4 Bond or debt securities pay a stated rate of interest. This rate of interest is dependent on the risk associated with the investment. **Moody's Investment Service** provides rating for companies that issue debt securities.

Address: **www.moodys.com** *(or go to www.wiley.com/college/weygandt)*

Steps: From Moody's homepage, (1) choose **SiteMap**, (2) choose **About Moody's**.

Instructions

(a) What year did Moody's introduce the first bond rating?

(b) List three basic principles Moody's uses in rating bonds.

(c) What is the definition of Moody's Aaa rating on long-term taxable debt?

CRITICAL THINKING

GROUP DECISION CASE

BYP16-5 On January 1, 2001, Remmers Corporation issued $3,000,000 of 5-year, 8% bonds at 96; the bonds pay interest semiannually on July 1 and January 1. By January 1, 2003, the market rate of interest for bonds of risk similar to those of Remmers Corporation had risen. As a result the market value of these bonds was $2,500,000 on January 1, 2003—below their carrying value. Jackie Remmers, president of the company, suggests repurchasing all of these bonds in the open market at the $2,500,000 price. To do so the company will have to issue $2,500,000 (face value) of new 10-year, 12% bonds at par. The president asks you, as controller, "What is the feasibility of my proposed repurchase plan?"

Instructions

With the class divided into groups, answer the following.

(a) What is the carrying value of the outstanding Remmers Corporation 5-year bonds on January 1, 2003? (Assume straight-line amortization.)

(b) Prepare the journal entry to retire the 5-year bonds on January 1, 2003. Prepare the journal entry to issue the new 10-year bonds.

(c) Prepare a short memo to the president in response to her request for advice. List the economic factors that you believe should be considered for her repurchase proposal.

COMMUNICATION ACTIVITY

BYP16-6 Hal Adelman, president of the Adelman Corporation, is considering the issuance of bonds to finance an expansion of his business. He has asked you to (1) discuss the advantages of bonds over common stock financing, (2) indicate the type of bonds he might issue, and (3) explain the issuing procedures used in bond transactions.

Instructions

Write a memo to the president, answering his request.

ETHICS CASE

BYP16-7 Ron Gant is the president, founder, and majority owner of Newman Medical Corporation, an emerging medical technology products company. Newman is in dire need of additional capital to keep operating and to bring several promising products to final development, testing, and production. Ron, as owner of 51% of the outstanding stock, manages the company's operations. He places heavy emphasis on research and development and on long-term growth. The other principal stockholder is Judy Costello who, as a nonemployee investor, owns 40% of the stock. Judy would like to deemphasize the R&D functions and emphasize the marketing function, to maximize short-run sales and profits from existing products. She believes this strategy would raise the market price of Newman's stock.

All of Ron's personal capital and borrowing power is tied up in his 51% stock ownership. He knows that any offering of additional shares of stock will dilute his controlling interest because he won't be able to participate in such an issuance. But, Judy has money and would likely buy enough shares to gain control of Newman. She then would dictate the company's future direction, even if it meant replacing Ron as president and CEO.

The company already has considerable debt. Raising additional debt will be costly, will adversely affect Newman's credit rating, and will increase the company's reported losses due to the growth in interest expense. Judy and the other minority stockholders express opposition to the assumption of additional debt, fearing the company will be pushed to the brink of bankruptcy. Wanting to maintain his control and to preserve the direction of "his" company, Ron is doing everything to avoid a stock issuance. He is contemplating a large issuance of bonds, even if it means the bonds are issued with a high effective-interest rate.

Instructions

(a) Who are the stakeholders in this situation?

(b) What are the ethical issues in this case?

(c) What would you do if you were Ron?

Answers to Self-Study Questions

1. c **2.** a **3.** d **4.** a **5.** c **6.** b **7.** d **8.** a **9.** c **10.** d
*11. b ***12.** c

Answer to *Lands' End* Review It Question 2, p. 655

An examination of Lands' End's statement of cash flows indicates the following reduction of debt: payment of short-term debt, $27.2 million.

☑ *Remember to go back to the Navigator box on the chapter-opening page and check off your completed work.*

INVESTMENTS

17

THE NAVIGATOR ✓

- Understand *Concepts for Review*   ❑

- Read *Feature Story*   ❑

- Scan *Study Objectives*   ❑

- Read *Preview*   ❑

- Read text and answer *Before You Go On*
  p. 686 ❑   p. 691 ❑   p. 696 ❑

- Work *Demonstration Problem*   ❑

- Review *Summary of Study Objectives*   ❑

- Answer *Self-Study Questions*   ❑

- Complete *Assignments*   ❑

CONCEPTS FOR REVIEW

Before studying this chapter, you should know or, if necessary, review:

   a. How to record the issuance of bonds. (Ch. 16, pp. 645–652)

   b. How to compute and record interest. (Ch. 3, p. 101, Ch. 9, p 376, and Ch. 16, pp. 645–646)

   c. How to record amortization of bond discount and bond premium using the straight-line method. (Ch. 16, pp. 648–651)

   d. Where short-term and long-term investments are classified on a balance sheet. (Ch. 4, pp. 151–152)

☑ THE NAVIGATOR

Is There Anything Else We Can Buy?

In a rapidly changing world you must change rapidly or suffer the consequences. In business, change requires investment.

A case in point is found in the entertainment industry. Technology is bringing about innovations so quickly that it is nearly impossible to guess which technologies will last and which will soon fade away. For example, will both satellite TV and cable TV survive, or will just one succeed, or will both be replaced by something else? Or consider the publishing industry. Will paper newspapers and magazines be replaced by online news via the World Wide Web? If you are a publisher, you have to make your best guess about what the future holds and invest accordingly.

Time Warner Corporation lives at the center of this arena. It is not an environment for the timid, and Time Warner's philosophy is anything but timid. It might be characterized as, "If we can't beat you, we will buy you." Its mantra is "invest, invest, invest." A list of Time Warner's holdings gives an idea of its reach. Magazines: *People, Time, Life, Sports Illustrated, Fortune.* Book publishers: Time-Life Books, Book-of-the-Month Club, Little, Brown & Co, Sunset Books. Music: Warner Bros. Records, Reprise, Atlantic, Rhino, Elektra, and Asylum, representing such artists as Hootie and the Blowfish, Tori Amos, Eric Clapton, and Madonna. Television and movies: Warner Bros. ("ER" and "Friends"), HBO, and movies like *Austin Powers* and *The Matrix.* And, in 1996 Time Warner merged with Turner Broadcasting, so it now owns TNT, CNN, and Turner's library of thousands of classic movies. Even before the Turner merger, Time Warner owned more information and entertainment copyrights and brands than any other company in the world.

So what has Time Warner's aggressive acquisition spree meant for the bottom line? It has left Time Warner with huge debt and massive interest costs. Also, some of the acquisitions have not come cheap, resulting in large amounts of reported goodwill and goodwill amortization. At the time this book went to press, Time Warner was involved in its largest deal to date—a merger with **America Online (AOL)**. Although it is being billed as a merger of equals, it is AOL's phenomenal growth and astronomical stock price that made this merger possible. This demonstrates that, in the corporate acquisition food chain, no company is too large to be devoured.

www.timewarner.com

☑ THE
NAVIGATOR

After studying this chapter, you should be able to:

1. Discuss why corporations invest in debt and stock securities.
2. Explain the accounting for debt investments.
3. Explain the accounting for stock investments.
4. Describe the use of consolidated financial statements.
5. Indicate how debt and stock investments are valued and reported on the financial statements.
6. Distinguish between short-term and long-term investments.

☑ THE
NAVIGATOR

Time Warner's management believes in aggressive growth through investing in the stock of existing companies. Besides purchasing stock, companies also purchase other securities such as bonds issued by corporations or by governments. Investments can be purchased for a short or long period of time, as a passive investment, or with the intent to control another company. As you will see in this chapter, the way in which a company accounts for its investments is determined by a number of factors.

The content and organization of Chapter 17 are as follows.

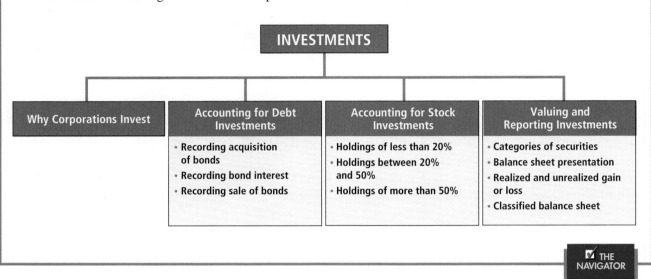

WHY CORPORATIONS INVEST

STUDY OBJECTIVE 1

Discuss why corporations invest in debt and stock securities.

Corporations purchase investments in debt or stock securities generally for one of three reasons. First, a corporation may **have excess cash** that it does not need for the immediate purchase of operating assets. For example, many companies experience seasonal fluctuations in sales. A Cape Cod marina has more sales in the spring and summer than in the fall and winter. The reverse is true for an Aspen ski shop. At the end of an operating cycle, many companies have cash on hand that is temporarily idle until the start of another operating cycle. These companies may invest the excess funds to earn a greater return than they would get by just holding the funds in the bank. The role that such temporary investments play in the operating cycle is depicted in Illustration 17-1.

Excess cash may also result from economic cycles. For example, when the economy is booming, General Motors generates considerable excess cash. It uses some of this cash to purchase new plant and equipment and pays out some of the cash in dividends. But it may also invest excess cash in liquid assets in anticipation of a future downturn in the economy. It can then liquidate these investments during a recession, when sales slow down and cash is scarce.

When investing excess cash for short periods of time, corporations invest in low-risk, highly liquid securities—most often short-term government securities. It is generally not wise to invest short-term excess cash in shares of common stock because stock investments can experience rapid price changes. If you did invest

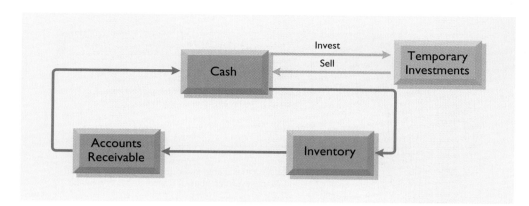

Illustration 17-1

Temporary investments and
the operating cycle

your short-term excess cash in stock and the price of the stock declined significantly just before you needed cash again, you would be forced to sell your stock
investment at a loss.

A second reason some companies such as banks purchase investments is to
generate **earnings from investment income**. Although banks make most of their
earnings by lending money, they also generate earnings by investing in debt and
equity securities. But loan demand varies both seasonally and with changes in the
economic climate. Thus, when loan demand is low, a bank must find other uses
for its cash. Bank regulators severely limit the ability of banks to invest in common stock because of the risk involved. Therefore, most investments held by banks
are debt securities.

Pension funds and mutual funds are corporations that also regularly invest to
generate earnings. However, they do so for **speculative reasons**. They are specu-
lating that the investment will increase in value and thus result in positive returns.
Therefore, they invest primarily in the common stock of other corporations. These
investments are passive in nature. The pension fund or mutual fund does not usually take an active role in controlling the affairs of the companies in which they
invest.

Companies also invest for **strategic reasons**. A company may purchase a non-
controlling interest in another company in a related industry in which it wishes to
establish a presence. For example, Time Warner initially purchased an interest of
less than 20 percent in Turner Broadcasting to have a stake in Turner's expanding business opportunities. Similarly, Canadian giant Seagram purchased a significant interest in Time Warner. (Not even a huge corporation like Time Warner is
at the top of the corporate "food-chain.") Or, a company can exercise some influence over a customer or supplier by purchasing a significant, but not controlling, interest in that company.

A corporation may also choose to purchase a controlling interest in another
company. This might be done to enter a new industry without incurring the tremendous costs and risks associated with starting from scratch. Or a company might
purchase another company in its same industry. The purchase of a company that
is in your industry, but involved in a different activity, is called a **vertical acquisition**. For example, Nike might purchase a chain of athletic shoe stores, such as
The Athlete's Foot. In a **horizontal acquisition** you purchase a company that does
the same activity as your company. For example, Nike might purchase Reebok.

In summary, businesses invest in other companies for the reasons shown in Illustration 17-2.

Illustration 17-2

Why corporations invest

Reason	Typical Investment
To house excess cash until needed	Low-risk, high-liquidity, short-term securities such as government-issued securities
To generate earnings *I need 1,000 Treasury bills by tonight*	Debt securities (banks and other financial institutions); and stock securities (mutual funds and pension funds)
To meet strategic goals	Stocks of companies in a related industry or in an unrelated industry that the company wishes to enter

ACCOUNTING IN ACTION *Business Insight*

In the two months prior to approval by the federal government of the **Time Warner/Turner** deal, as approval appeared more certain, Time Warner's stock price increased by 30 percent. Although investors were applauding the strength of the combined entity, many analysts were very concerned about the mega-corporation's ability to control costs. The Time Warner deal and other acquisitions resulted in a $17.5 billion mountain of debt on Time Warner's balance sheet.

Observers were also interested to see how the two corporate cultures would merge. Ted Turner had been openly critical of Time Warner's management for running a loose ship, with far too much being spent on unnecessary extravagances such as corporate jets. Time Warner executives privately responded that if Mr. Turner was really concerned, he might consider taking a cut in his salary of $10 million a year.

ACCOUNTING FOR DEBT INVESTMENTS

STUDY OBJECTIVE 2

Explain the accounting for debt investments.

Debt investments are investments in government and corporation bonds. In accounting for debt investments, entries are required to record (1) the acquisition, (2) the interest revenue, and (3) the sale.

RECORDING ACQUISITION OF BONDS

At acquisition, the cost principle applies. Cost includes all expenditures necessary to acquire these investments, such as the price paid plus brokerage fees (commissions), if any. Assume, for example, that Kuhl Corporation acquires 50 Doan Inc. 12%, 10-year, $1,000 bonds on January 1, 2002, for $54,000, including brokerage fees of $1,000. The entry to record the investment is:

A	=	L	+	SE
+54,000				
−54,000				

Jan. 1	Debt Investments		54,000	
	Cash			54,000
	(To record purchase of 50 Doan Inc. bonds)			

RECORDING BOND INTEREST

The bonds pay interest of $3,000 semiannually on July 1 and January 1 ($50,000 $\times$ 12% $\times$ ½). The entry for the receipt of interest on July 1 is:

July 1	Cash	3,000	
	Interest Revenue		3,000
	(To record receipt of interest on Doan Inc. bonds		

A	=	L	+	SE
+3,000				+3,000

If Kuhl Corporation's fiscal year ends on December 31, it is necessary to accrue the interest of $3,000 earned since July 1. The adjusting entry is:

Dec. 31	Interest Receivable	3,000	
	Interest Revenue		3,000
	(To accrue interest on Doan Inc. bonds)		

A	=	L	+	SE
+3,000				+3,000

Interest Receivable is reported as a current asset in the balance sheet; Interest Revenue is reported under "other revenues and gains" in the income statement.

When the interest is received on January 1, the entry is:

Jan. 1	Cash	3,000	
	Interest Receivable		3,000
	(To record receipt of accrued interest)		

A	=	L	+	SE
+3,000				
−3,000				

A credit to Interest Revenue at this time would be incorrect. Why? Because the interest revenue was earned and accrued in the preceding accounting period.

RECORDING SALE OF BONDS

When the bonds are sold, it is necessary to credit the investment account for the cost of the bonds. Any difference between the net proceeds from the sale (sales price less brokerage fees) and the cost of the bonds is recorded as a gain or loss.

Assume, for example, that Kuhl Corporation receives net proceeds of $58,000 on the sale of the Doan Inc. bonds on January 1, 2003, after receiving the interest due. Since the securities cost $54,000, a gain of $4,000 has been realized. The entry to record the sale is:

Jan. 1	Cash	58,000	
	Debt Investments		54,000
	Gain on Sale of Debt Investments		4,000
	(To record sale of Doan Inc. bonds)		

A	=	L	+	SE
+58,000				+4,000
−54,000				

The gain on sale of debt investments is reported under "other revenues and gains" in the income statement.

The accounting for short-term debt investments and for long-term debt investments is similar. The major exception is when bonds are purchased at a premium or discount. For short-term investments, the bond premium or discount is not amortized to interest revenue because the bonds are held for a short period of time. A misstatement of interest revenue for such a period is not considered material. For long-term investments, any bond premium or discount is amortized to interest revenue over the remaining term of the bonds. Like the issuer of the bonds, the investor uses either the straight-line or the effective-interest method of amortization. The effective-interest method is required under GAAP when the annual amounts of the two methods are materially different.

BEFORE YOU GO ON...

▶ *REVIEW IT*

1. Why might a company make investments in debt or stock securities?
2. What entries are required in accounting for debt investments?
3. How does the accounting for a short-term debt investment differ from that for a long-term debt investment?

▶ *DO IT*

Waldo Corporation had the following transactions pertaining to debt investments.

Jan. 1   Purchased 30 10%, $1,000 Hillary Co. bonds for $30,000, plus brokerage fees of $900. Interest is payable semiannually on July 1 and January 1.
July 1   Received semiannual interest on Hillary Co. bonds.
July 1   Sold 15 Hillary Co. bonds for $15,000, less $400 brokerage fees.

(a) Journalize the transactions, and (b) prepare the adjusting entry for the accrual of interest on December 31.

ACTION PLAN
- Record bond investments at cost.
- Record interest when received and/or accrued.
- When bonds are sold, credit the investment account for the cost of the bonds.
- Record any difference between the cost and the net proceeds as a gain or loss.

SOLUTION

(a) Jan. 1	Debt Investments		30,900	
	Cash			30,900
	(To record purchase of 30 Hillary Co. bonds)			
July 1	Cash		1,500	
	Interest Revenue ($30,000 × .10 × 6/12)			1,500
	(To record receipt of interest on Hillary Co. bonds)			
July 1	Cash		14,600	
	Loss on Sale of Debt Investments		850	
	Debt Investments ($30,900 × 15/30)			15,450
	(To record sale of 15 Hillary Co. bonds)			
(b) Dec. 31	Interest Receivable		750	
	Interest Revenue ($15,000 × .10 × 6/12)			750
	(To accrue interest on Hillary Co. bonds)			

Related exercise material: BE17-1 and E17-1.

☑ THE NAVIGATOR

ACCOUNTING IN ACTION ∧ *Business Insight*

Amazon.com's Web site receives many "hits" each day. Because of this Amazon earns significant revenue by allowing other companies to advertise there. Many of them pay with stock in their company (since dot-coms often have very little cash). When Amazon receives the stock, it debits Investment in XYZ Company and credits Unearned Revenue for the market value of the shares on the day they are received. It then recognizes revenue over the life of the advertising agreement. In the future, Amazon hopes to do more cash deals and fewer stock deals.

ACCOUNTING FOR STOCK INVESTMENTS

Stock investments are investments in the capital stock of corporations. When a company holds stock (and/or debt) of several different corporations, the group of securities is identified as an **investment portfolio**.

The accounting for investments in common stock is based on the extent of the investor's influence over the operating and financial affairs of the issuing corporation (commonly called the **investee**). Illustration 17-3 shows the guidelines for three levels of influence.

Illustration 17-3

Accounting guidelines for stock investments

Investor's Ownership Interest in Investee's Common Stock	Presumed Influence on Investee	Accounting Guidelines
Less than 20%	Insignificant	Cost method
Between 20% and 50%	Significant	Equity method
More than 50%	Controlling	Consolidated financial statements

The presumed influence may be negated by extenuating circumstances. For example, a company that acquires a 25% interest in another company in a "hostile" takeover may not have significant influence over the investee. Companies are required to use judgment instead of blindly following the guidelines.[1] On the following pages we will explain the application of each guideline.

HOLDINGS OF LESS THAN 20%

In accounting for stock investments of less than 20%, the cost method is used. Under the **cost method**, the investment is recorded at cost, and revenue is recognized only when cash dividends are received.

Recording Acquisition of Stock Investments

At acquisition, the cost principle applies. Cost includes all expenditures necessary to acquire these investments such as the price paid plus any brokerage fees (commissions). Assume, for example, that on July 1, 2002, Sanchez Corporation acquires 1,000 shares (10% ownership) of Beal Corporation common stock. Sanchez pays $40 per share plus brokerage fees of $500. The entry for the purchase is:

July 1	Stock Investments	40,500	
	Cash		40,500
	(To record purchase of 1,000 shares of Beal		
	Corporation common stock)		

```
A   =   L   +   SE
+40,500
-40,500
```

---

[1]Among the questions that are considered in determining an investor's influence are these: (1) Does the investor have representation on the investee's board? (2) Does the investor participate in the investee's policy-making process? (3) Are there material transactions between the investor and investee? (4) Is the common stock held by other stockholders concentrated or dispersed?

Recording Dividends

During the time the stock is held, entries are required for any cash dividends received. If a $2.00 per share dividend is received by Sanchez Corporation on December 31, the entry is:

Dec. 31	Cash (1,000 × $2)	2,000	
	Dividend Revenue		2,000
	(To record receipt of a cash dividend)		

Dividend Revenue is reported under "other revenues and gains" in the income statement. Unlike interest on notes and bonds, dividends do not accrue. Therefore, adjusting entries are not made to accrue dividends.

Recording Sale of Stock

When stock is sold, the difference between the net proceeds from the sale (sales price less brokerage fees) and the cost of the stock is recognized as a gain or a loss. Assume that Sanchez Corporation receives net proceeds of $39,500 on the sale of its Beal stock on February 10, 2003. Because the stock cost $40,500, a loss of $1,000 has been incurred. The entry to record the sale is:

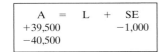

Feb. 10	Cash	39,500	
	Loss on Sale of Stock Investments	1,000	
	Stock Investments		40,500
	(To record sale of Beal common stock)		

The loss account is reported under "other expenses and losses" in the income statement. A gain on sale is shown under "other revenues and gains."

HELPFUL HINT
The entries for investments in common stock also apply to investments in preferred stock.

HOLDINGS BETWEEN 20% AND 50%

When an investor company owns only a small portion of the shares of stock of another company, the investor cannot exercise control over the investee. But, when an investor owns between 20% and 50% of the common stock of a corporation, it is presumed that the investor has significant influence over the financial and operating activities of the investee. The investor probably has a representative on the investee's board of directors. Through that representative, the investor begins to exercise some control over the investee. The investee company in some sense becomes part of the investor company. For example, even prior to purchasing all of Turner Broadcasting, **Time Warner** owned 20% of Turner and could exercise significant control over major decisions made by Turner.

Companies with stock holdings between 20% and 50% in an investee use an approach called the equity method. Under the **equity method**, **the investor records its share of the net income of the investee in the year when it is earned**. An alternative might be to delay recognizing the investor's share of net income until a cash dividend is declared. But that approach would ignore the fact that the investor and investee are, in some sense, one company, making the investor better off by the investee's earned income.

Under the equity method, the investment in common stock is initially recorded at cost. After that, the investment account is **adjusted annually** to show the investor's equity in the investee. Each year, the investor does the following: (1) It increases (debits) the investment account and increases (credits) revenue for its share of the investee's net income.[2] (2) The investor also decreases (credits) the

---

[2]Or, the investor increases (debits) a loss account and decreases (credits) the investment account for its share of the investee's net loss.

investment account for the amount of dividends received. The investment account is reduced for dividends received because the net assets of the investee are decreased when a dividend is paid.

HELPFUL HINT
Under the equity method revenue is recognized on the accrual basis—i.e., when it is earned by the investee.

Recording Acquisition of Stock Investments

Assume that Milar Corporation acquires 30% of the common stock of Beck Company for $120,000 on January 1, 2002. The entry to record this transaction is:

Jan. 1	Stock Investments	120,000	
	Cash		120,000
	(To record purchase of Beck common stock)		

```
A    =   L   +   SE
+120,000
-120,000
```

Recording Revenue and Dividends

For 2002, Beck reports net income of $100,000. It declares and pays a $40,000 cash dividend. Milar is required to record (1) its share of Beck's income, $30,000 (30% × $100,000) and (2) the reduction in the investment account for the dividends received, $12,000 ($40,000 × 30%). The entries are:

(1)

Dec. 31	Stock Investments	30,000	
	Revenue from Investment in Beck Company		30,000
	(To record 30% equity in Beck's 2002 net income)		

```
A    =   L   +   SE
+30,000          +30,000
```

(2)

Dec. 31	Cash	12,000	
	Stock Investments		12,000
	(To record dividends received)		

```
A    =   L   +   SE
+12,000
-12,000
```

After posting the transactions for the year, the investment and revenue accounts will show the following.

Stock Investments				Revenue from Investment in Beck Company	
Jan. 1	120,000	Dec. 31	12,000	Dec. 31	30,000
Dec. 31	30,000				
Dec. 31 Bal.	138,000				

Illustration 17-4

Investment and revenue accounts after posting

During the year, the investment account has increased by $18,000. This $18,000 is Milar's 30% equity in the $60,000 increase in Beck's retained earnings ($100,000 − $40,000). In addition, Milar will report $30,000 of revenue from its investment, which is 30% of Beck's net income of $100,000. Note that the difference between reported revenue under the cost method and reported revenue under the equity method can be significant. For example, Milar would report only $12,000 of dividend revenue (30% × $40,000) if the cost method were used.

HOLDINGS OF MORE THAN 50%

A company that owns more than 50% of the common stock of another entity is known as the **parent company**. The entity whose stock is owned by the parent company is called the **subsidiary (affiliated) company**. Because of its stock ownership, the parent company has a **controlling interest** in the subsidiary.

When a company owns more than 50% of the common stock of another company, **consolidated financial statements** are usually prepared. Consolidated financial statements present the total assets and liabilities controlled by the

STUDY OBJECTIVE 4

Describe the use of consolidated financial statements.

HELPFUL HINT

If parent (A) has three wholly owned subsidiaries (B, C, & D), there are four separate legal entities. But, from the viewpoint of the shareholders of the parent company, there is only one economic entity.

parent company. They also present the total revenues and expenses of the subsidiary companies. Consolidated statements are prepared **in addition to** the financial statements for the parent and individual subsidiary companies. When Time Warner had a 20% investment in Turner, this investment was reported in a single line item—Other Investments—in Time-Warner's balance sheet. After the merger, Time Warner instead consolidated Turner's results with its own. Under this approach, the individual assets and liabilities of Turner are included with those of Time Warner: its plant and equipment are added to Time Warner's plant and equipment, its receivables are added to Time Warner's receivables, and so on.

*A*CCOUNTING IN ACTION *Business Insight*

Time Warner, Inc. owns 100% of the common stock of **Home Box Office (HBO) Corporation**. The common stockholders of Time Warner elect the board of directors of the company, who, in turn, select the officers and managers of the company. Time Warner's board of directors controls the property owned by the corporation, which includes the common stock of HBO. Thus, they are in a position to elect the board of directors of HBO and, in effect, control its operations. These relationships are graphically illustrated here.

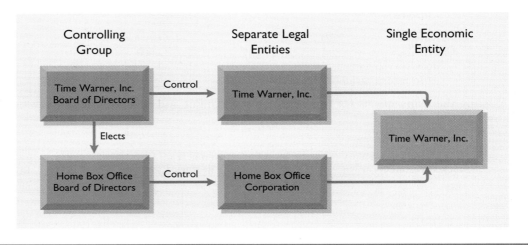

Consolidated statements are useful because they indicate the magnitude and scope of operations of the companies under common control. For example, regulators and the courts undoubtedly used the consolidated statements of **AT&T** to determine whether a breakup of AT&T was in the public interest. Listed below are three companies that prepare consolidated statements and some of the companies they have owned. Note that one, **Walt Disney**, is Time Warner's arch rival.

Beatrice Foods	American Brands, Inc.	The Walt Disney Company
Tropicana Frozen Juices	American Tobacco Company	Capital Cities/ABC, Inc.
Switzer Candy Company	Master Lock Company	Disneyland, Disney World
Samsonite Corporation	Pinkerton's Security Service	Mighty Ducks
Dannon Yogurt Company	Titleist Golf Company	Anaheim Angels
		ESPN

BEFORE YOU GO ON...

▶ *REVIEW IT*

1. What are the accounting entries for stock investments of less than 20%?
2. What entries are made under the equity method when (a) the investor receives a cash dividend from the investee and (b) the investee reports net income for the year?
3. What is the purpose of consolidated financial statements?
4. What does **Lands' End** state regarding its accounting policy involving consolidated financial statements? The answer to this question is provided on page 713.

▶ *DO IT*

Presented below are two independent situations.

1. Rho Jean Inc. acquired 5% of the 400,000 shares of common stock of Stillwater Corp. at a total cost of $6 per share on May 18, 2002. On August 30, Stillwater declared and paid a $75,000 dividend. On December 31, Stillwater reported net income of $244,000 for the year.
2. Debbie, Inc. obtained significant influence over North Sails by buying 40% of North Sails' 60,000 outstanding shares of common stock at a cost of $12 per share on January 1, 2002. On April 15, North Sails declared and paid a cash dividend of $45,000. On December 31, North Sails reported net income of $120,000 for the year.

Prepare all necessary journal entries for 2002 for (1) Rho Jean Inc. and (2) Debbie, Inc.

ACTION PLAN

- Presume that the investor has relatively little influence over the investee when an investor owns less than 20% of the common stock of another corporation. In this case, net income earned by the investee is not considered a proper basis for recognizing income from the investment by the investor.
- Presume significant influence for investments of 20%–50%. Therefore, record the investor's share of the net income of the investee.

SOLUTION

(1) May 18	Stock Investments (20,000 × $6)	120,000	
	Cash		120,000
	(To record purchase of 20,000 shares of Stillwater Co. stock)		
Aug. 30	Cash	3,750	
	Dividend Revenue ($75,000 × 5%)		3,750
	(To record receipt of cash dividend)		
(2) Jan. 1	Stock Investments (60,000 × 40% × $12)	288,000	
	Cash		288,000
	(To record purchase of 24,000 shares of North Sails' stock)		
Apr. 15	Cash	18,000	
	Stock Investments ($45,000 × 40%)		18,000
	(To record receipt of cash dividend)		
Dec. 31	Stock Investments ($120,000 × 40%)	48,000	
	Revenue from Investment in North Sails		48,000
	(To record 40% equity in North Sails' net income)		

Related exercise material: BE17-2, BE17-3, E17-1, E17-2, E17-3, E17-4, and E17-5.

THE NAVIGATOR

VALUING AND REPORTING INVESTMENTS

STUDY OBJECTIVE 5

Indicate how debt and stock investments are valued and reported on the financial statements.

The value of debt and stock investments may fluctuate greatly during the time they are held. For example, in one 12-month peroid, the stock price of **Digital Equipment Corporation** hit a high of $76.50 and a low of $28.37. In light of such price fluctuations, how should investments be valued at the balance sheet date? Valuation could be at cost, at fair value (market value), or at the lower of cost or market value. Many people argue that fair value offers the best approach because it represents the expected cash realizable value of securities. **Fair value** is the amount for which a security could be sold in a normal market. Others counter that, unless a security is going to be sold soon, the fair value is not relevant because the price of the security will likely change again.

CATEGORIES OF SECURITIES

For purposes of valuation and reporting at a financial statement date, debt and stock investments are classified into three categories of securities:

1. **Trading securities** are securities bought and held primarily for sale in the near term to generate income on short-term price differences.

2. **Available-for-sale securities** are securities that may be sold in the future.

3. **Held-to-maturity securities** are debt securities that the investor has the intent and ability to hold to maturity.

The valuation guidelines for these securities are shown in Illustration 17-5. **These guidelines apply to all debt securities and all stock investments in which the holdings are less than 20%.**

Illustration 17-5

Valuation guidelines

Trading	Available-for-sale	Held-to-maturity
"We'll sell within ten days."	"We'll hold the stock for a while to see how it performs."	"We intend to hold these bonds until maturity."
At fair value with changes reported in net income	At fair value with changes reported in the stockholders' equity section	At amortized cost[3]

Trading Securities

Trading securities are held with the intention of selling them in a short period (generally less than a month). Trading means frequent buying and selling. Trading securities are reported at fair value, and changes from cost are reported as part of net income. The changes are reported as **unrealized gains or losses** because the securities have not been sold. The unrealized gain or loss is the difference between the **total cost** of trading securities and their **total fair value.**

---

[3]This category is provided for completeness. The accounting and valuation issues related to held-to-maturity securities are discussed in more advanced accounting courses.

Illustration 17-6 shows the cost and fair values for investments classified as trading securities for Pace Corporation on December 31, 2002. Pace has an unrealized gain of $7,000 because total fair value ($147,000) is $7,000 greater than total cost ($140,000).

Trading Securities, December 31, 2002			
Investments	**Cost**	**Fair Value**	**Unrealized Gain (Loss)**
Yorkville Company bonds	$ 50,000	$ 48,000	$(2,000)
Kodak Company stock	90,000	99,000	9,000
Total	$140,000	$147,000	$ 7,000

Illustration 17-6

Valuation of trading securities

Fair value and unrealized gain or loss are recorded through an adjusting entry at the time financial statements are prepared. In the entry, a valuation allowance account, Market Adjustment—Trading, is used to record the difference between the total cost and the total fair value of the securities. The adjusting entry for Pace Corporation is:

Dec. 31	Market Adjustment—Trading	7,000	
	Unrealized Gain—Income		7,000
	(To record unrealized gain on trading securities)		

> **HELPFUL HINT**
> The fact that trading securities are short-term investments increases the likelihood that they will be sold at fair value (the company may not be able to time their sale) and the likelihood that there will be realized gains or losses.

> A   =   L   +   SE
> +7,000   +7,000

The use of a Market Adjustment—Trading account enables the company to maintain a record of the investment cost. Actual cost is needed to determine the gain or loss realized when the securities are sold. The Market Adjustment—Trading balance is added to the cost of the investments to arrive at a fair value for the trading securities.

The fair value of the securities is the amount reported on the balance sheet. The unrealized gain is reported in the income statement in the "other revenues and gains" section. The term "Income" is used in the account title to indicate that the gain affects net income.

When the total cost of the trading securities is greater than total fair value, an unrealized loss has occurred. In such a case, the adjusting entry is a debit to Unrealized Loss—Income and a credit to Market Adjustment—Trading. The unrealized loss is reported under "other expenses and losses" in the income statement.

The market adjustment account is carried forward into future accounting periods. No entries are made to this account during the period. At the end of each reporting period, the balance in the account is adjusted to the difference between cost and fair value. For trading securities, the Unrealized Gain (Loss)—Income account is closed at the end of the reporting period.

> **HELPFUL HINT**
> An unrealized gain or loss is reported in the income statement because of the likelihood that the securities will be sold at fair value since they are short-term investments.

Available-for-Sale Securities

As indicated earlier, available-for-sale securities are held with the intent of selling them sometime in the future. If the intent is to sell the securities within the next year or operating cycle, the securities are classified as current assets in the balance sheet. Otherwise, they are classified as long-term assets in the investments section of the balance sheet.

Available-for-sale securities are also reported at fair value. The procedure for determining fair value and the unrealized gain or loss for these securities is the same as for trading securities. To illustrate, assume that Elbert Corporation has two securities that are classified as available-for-sale. Illustration 17-7 provides information on their valuation. There is an unrealized loss of $9,537 because total cost ($293,537) is $9,537 more than total fair value ($284,000).

> **ETHICS NOTE**
> Some managers appear to hold their available-for-sale securities that have experienced losses, while selling those that have gains, thus increasing income. Do you think this is ethical?

Illustration 17-7

Valuation of available-for-sale securities

Available-for-Sale Securities, December 31, 2002			
Investments	Cost	Fair Value	Unrealized Gain (Loss)
Campbell Soup Corporation 8% bonds	$ 93,537	$103,600	$10,063
Hershey Corporation stock	200,000	180,400	(19,600)
Total	$293,537	$284,000	$(9,537)

Both the adjusting entry and the reporting of the unrealized gain or loss for available-for-sale securities differ from those illustrated for trading securities. The differences result because these securities are not going to be sold in the near term. Thus, prior to actual sale it is more likely that changes in fair value may reverse either unrealized gains or losses. Therefore, an unrealized gain or loss is not reported in the income statement. Instead, it is reported as a **separate component of stockholders' equity**. In the adjusting entry, the market adjustment account is identified with available-for-sale securities; the unrealized gain or loss account is identified with stockholders' equity. The adjusting entry to record the unrealized loss of $9,537 for Elbert Corporation is as follows:

$$
\begin{array}{ccc}
A & = & L & + & SE \\
-9{,}537 & & & & -9{,}537
\end{array}
$$

Dec. 31	Unrealized Loss—Equity	9,537	
	Market Adjustment—Available-for-Sale		9,537
	(To record unrealized loss on available-for-sale securities)		

If total fair value exceeds total cost, the adjusting entry would have a debit to the market adjustment account and a credit to an unrealized gain or loss account.

For available-for-sale securities, the unrealized gain or loss account is carried forward to future periods. At each future balance sheet date, it is adjusted with the market adjustment account to show the difference between cost and fair value at that time.

BALANCE SHEET PRESENTATION

In the balance sheet, investments are classified as either short-term or long-term.

Short-Term Investments

STUDY OBJECTIVE 6

Distinguish between short-term and long-term investments.

HELPFUL HINT
Trading securities are always classified as short-term. Available-for-sale securities can be either short-term or long-term.

Short-term investments are securities held by a company that are (1) **readily marketable** and (2) **intended to be converted into cash** within the next year or operating cycle, whichever is longer. Investments that do not meet **both criteria** are classified as **long-term investments**.

READILY MARKETABLE. An investment is readily marketable when it can be sold easily whenever the need for cash arises. Short-term paper[4] meets this criterion. It can be readily sold to other investors. Stocks and bonds traded on organized securities exchanges, such as the New York Stock Exchange, are readily marketable. They can be bought and sold daily. In contrast, there may be only a limited market for the securities issued by small corporations, and no market for the securities of a privately held company.

INTENT TO CONVERT. Intent to convert means that management intends to sell the investment within the next year or operating cycle, whichever is longer. Generally, this criterion is satisfied when the investment is considered a resource that will be used whenever the need for cash arises. For example, a ski resort may invest idle cash during the summer months with the intent to sell the securities to

---

[4]Short-term paper includes (1) certificates of deposit (CDs) issued by banks, (2) money market certificates issued by banks and savings and loan associations, (3) Treasury bills issued by the U.S. government, and (4) commercial paper issued by corporations with good credit ratings.

buy supplies and equipment shortly before the next winter season. This investment is considered short-term even if lack of snow cancels the next ski season and eliminates the need to convert the securities into cash as intended.

Because of their high liquidity, short-term investments are listed immediately below cash in the current assets section of the balance sheet. They are reported at fair value. For example, Pace Corporation would report its trading securities as shown in Illustration 17-8.

PACE CORPORATION Balance Sheet (partial)	
Current assets	
Cash	$ 21,000
Short-term investments, at fair value	147,000

Illustration 17-8
Presentation of short-term investments

HELPFUL HINT
In a recent survey of 600 large U.S. companies, over 400 reported short-term investments.

Long-Term Investments

Long-term investments are generally reported in a separate section of the balance sheet immediately below current assets, as shown later in Illustration 17-11. Long-term investments in available-for-sale securities are reported at fair value. Investments in common stock accounted for under the equity method are reported at equity.

PRESENTATION OF REALIZED AND UNREALIZED GAIN OR LOSS

Gains and losses on investments, whether realized or unrealized, must be presented in the financial statements. In the income statement, gains and losses are reported in the nonoperating activities section under the categories listed in Illustration 17-9. Interest and dividend revenue are also reported in that section.

Other Revenue and Gains	Other Expenses and Losses
Interest Revenue	Loss on Sale of Investments
Dividend Revenue	Unrealized Loss—Income
Gain on Sale of Investments	
Unrealized Gain—Income	

Illustration 17-9
Nonoperating items related to investments

As indicated earlier, an unrealized gain or loss on available-for-sale securities is reported as a separate component of stockholders' equity. To illustrate, assume that Dawson Inc. has common stock of $3,000,000, retained earnings of $1,500,000, and an unrealized loss on available-for-sale securities of $100,000. The statement presentation of the unrealized loss is shown in Illustration 17-10.

DAWSON INC. Balance Sheet (partial)	
Stockholders' equity	
Common stock	$3,000,000
Retained earnings	1,500,000
Total paid-in capital and retained earnings	4,500,000
Less: Unrealized loss on available-for-sale securities	(100,000)
Total stockholders' equity	$4,400,000

Illustration 17-10
Unrealized loss in stockholders' equity section

Note that the loss decreases stockholders' equity. The cost of treasury stock is presented in the same way. An unrealized gain would be added to stockholders' equity. Reporting the unrealized gain or loss in the stockholders' equity section serves two important purposes: (1) It reduces the volatility of net income due to fluctuations in fair value. (2) It informs the financial statement user of the gain or loss that would occur if the securities were sold at fair value.

A recent accounting standard requires that items such as this, which affect stockholders' equity but are not included in the calculation of net income, must be reported as part of a more inclusive measure called *comprehensive income*. Comprehensive income is discussed in more advanced courses.

CLASSIFIED BALANCE SHEET

Many sections of classified balance sheets have been presented in this and preceding chapters. The classified balance sheet in Illustration 17-11 on page 697 includes, in one place, key topics from previous chapters: the issuance of par value common stock, restrictions of retained earnings, issuance of long-term bonds, and bond sinking funds. From this chapter, the statement includes (highlighted in red) short-term and long-term investments. The investments in short-term securities are considered trading securities. The long-term investments in stock of less than 20% owned companies are considered available-for-sale securities. Illustration 17-11 also includes a long-term investment reported at equity and descriptive notations within the statement, such as the basis for valuing merchandise and two notes to the statement.

BEFORE YOU GO ON...

▶ *REVIEW IT*

1. What is the proper valuation and reporting of trading and available-for-sale securities on a balance sheet?
2. Explain how the unrealized gain or loss for both trading and available-for-sale securities is reported.
3. Explain where short-term and long-term investments are reported on a balance sheet.

A LOOK BACK AT OUR FEATURE STORY

Refer back to the Feature Story about **Time Warner Corporation** at the beginning of the chapter, and answer the following questions.

1. For what reason(s) is Time Warner investing in equity securities (stocks)?
2. Would you expect Time Warner to prepare consolidated financial statements for the many companies it owns? Explain your answer.
3. What has Time Warner's aggressive acquisition spree meant for its bottom line?

SOLUTION

1. Time Warner is investing for strategic reasons. As indicated in the Feature Story, the company's attitude is, "If we can't beat you, we will buy you." Time Warner is diversifying because it is not sure what industries will be successful in the future. As a result, Time Warner now owns more information and entertainment copyrights and brands than any other company in the world.
2. When a company owns more than 50% of the common stock of another company, consolidated financial statements are usually prepared. Because Time Warner owns over 50% of the companies mentioned in the Feature Story, Time Warner would consolidate these subsidiary companies with its own.
3. To date, Time Warner's acquisition spree has left it with huge debt and massive interest costs. In addition, some of the acquisitions have not come cheap, resulting in large amounts of reported goodwill and goodwill amortization.

THE NAVIGATOR

Illustration 17-11

Classified balance sheet

PACE CORPORATION
Balance Sheet
December 31, 2002

Assets

Current assets
Cash		$ 21,000
Short-term investments, at fair value		147,000
Accounts receivable	$ 84,000	
Less: Allowance for doubtful accounts	4,000	80,000
Merchandise inventory, at FIFO cost		43,000
Prepaid insurance		23,000
Total current assets		314,000

Investments
Bond sinking fund	100,000	
Investments in stock of less than 20% owned companies, at fair value	50,000	
Investment in stock of 20–50% owned company, at equity	150,000	
Total investments		300,000

Property, plant, and equipment
Land		200,000	
Buildings	$800,000		
Less: Accumulated depreciation	200,000	600,000	
Equipment	180,000		
Less: Accumulated depreciation	54,000	126,000	
Total property, plant, and equipment		926,000	

Intangible assets
Goodwill (Note 1)		170,000
Total assets		$1,710,000

Liabilities and Stockholders' Equity

Current liabilities
Accounts payable		$185,000
Bond interest payable		10,000
Federal income taxes payable		60,000
Total current liabilities		255,000

Long-term liabilities
Bonds payable, 10%, due 2013	$ 300,000	
Less: Discount on bonds	10,000	
Total long-term liabilities		290,000
Total liabilities		545,000

Stockholders' equity
Paid-in capital
Common stock, $10 par value, 200,000 shares authorized, 80,000 shares issued and outstanding	800,000	
Paid-in capital in excess of par value	100,000	
Total paid-in capital	900,000	
Retained earnings (Note 2)	255,000	
Total paid-in capital and retained earnings	1,155,000	
Add: Unrealized gain on available-for-sale securities	10,000	
Total stockholders' equity		1,165,000
Total liabilities and stockholders' equity		$1,710,000

Note 1. Goodwill is amortized by the straight-line method over 40 years.

Note 2. Retained earnings of $100,000 is restricted for plant expansion.

Additional Demonstration Problem

DEMONSTRATION PROBLEM

In its first year of operations, DeMarco Company had the following selected transactions in stock investments that are considered trading securities.

June 1 Purchased for cash 600 shares of Sanburg common stock at $24 per share, plus $300 brokerage fees.

July 1 Purchased for cash 800 shares of Cey common stock at $33 per share, plus $600 brokerage fees.

Sept. 1 Received a $1 per share cash dividend from Cey Corporation.

Nov. 1 Sold 200 shares of Sanburg common stock for cash at $27 per share, less $150 brokerage fees.

Dec. 15 Received a $0.50 per share cash dividend on Sanburg common stock.

At December 31, the fair values per share were: Sanburg $25 and Cey $30.

Instructions

(a) Journalize the transactions.

(b) Prepare the adjusting entry at December 31 to report the securities at fair value.

ACTION PLAN

- Include the price paid plus brokerage fees in the cost of the investment.
- Compute the gain or loss on sales as the difference between net selling price and the cost of the securities.
- Base the adjustment to fair value on the total difference between the cost and the fair value of the securities.

SOLUTION TO DEMONSTRATION PROBLEM

(a) June	1	Stock Investments	14,700	
		Cash		14,700
		(To record purchase of 600 shares of Sanburg common stock)		
	July	1	Stock Investments	27,000	
		Cash		27,000
		(To record purchase of 800 shares of Cey common stock)		
	Sept.	1	Cash	800	
		Dividend Revenue		800
		(To record receipt of $1 per share cash dividend from Cey Corporation)		
	Nov.	1	Cash	5,250	
		Stock Investments		4,900
		Gain on Sale of Stock Investments		350
		(To record sale of 200 shares of Sanburg common stock)		
	Dec.	15	Cash	200	
		Dividend Revenue		200
		(To record receipt of $0.50 per share dividend from Sanburg Corporation)		
(b) Dec.	31	Unrealized Loss—Income	2,800	
		Market Adjustment—Trading		2,800
		(To record unrealized loss on trading securities)		

Investment	Cost	Fair Value	Unrealized Gain (Loss)
Sanburg common stock	$ 9,800	$10,000	$ 200
Cey common stock	27,000	24,000	(3,000)
Totals	$36,800	$34,000	$(2,800)

THE NAVIGATOR

SUMMARY OF STUDY OBJECTIVES

1. Discuss why corporations invest in debt and stock securities. Corporations invest for three primary reasons: (a) They have excess cash. (b) They view investments as a significant revenue source. (c) They have strategic goals such as gaining control of a competitor or moving into a new line of business.

2. Explain the accounting for debt investments. Entries for investments in debt securities are required when the bonds are purchased, interest is received or accrued, and the bonds are sold. The accounting for long-term investments in bonds is the same as for temporary investments in bonds, except that bond premium and bond discount must be amortized.

3. Explain the accounting for stock investments. Entries for investments in common stock are required when the stock is purchased, dividends are received, and stock is sold. When ownership is less than 20%, the cost method is used. When ownership is between 20% and 50%, the equity method should be used. When ownership is more than 50%, consolidated financial statements should be prepared.

4. Describe the use of consolidated financial statements. When a company owns more than 50% of the common stock of another company, consolidated financial statements are usually prepared. These statements are useful because they indicate the magnitude and scope of operations of the companies under common control.

5. Indicate how debt and stock investments are valued and reported on the financial statements. Investments in debt and stock securities are classified as trading, available-for-sale, or held-to-maturity securities for valuation and reporting purposes. Trading securities are reported in current assets at fair value, with changes from cost reported in net income. Available-for-sale securities are also reported at fair value, with the changes from cost reported in stockholders' equity. Available-for-sale securities are classified as short-term or long-term depending on their expected realization.

6. Distinguish between short-term and long-term investments. Short-term investments are securities, held by a company, that are (a) readily marketable and (b) intended to be converted to cash within the next year or operating cycle, whichever is longer. Investments that do not meet both criteria are classified as long-term investments.

GLOSSARY

Key Term Matching Activity

Available-for-sale securities   Securities that may be sold in the future. (p. 692).

Consolidated financial statements   Financial statements that present the assets and liabilities controlled by the parent company and the aggregate profitability of the affiliated companies. (p. 689).

Controlling interest   Ownership of more than 50% of the common stock of another entity. (p. 689).

Cost method   An accounting method in which the investment in common stock is recorded at cost, and revenue is recognized only when cash dividends are received. (p. 687).

Debt investments   Investments in government and corporation bonds. (p. 684).

Equity method   An accounting method in which the investment in common stock is initially recorded at cost, and the investment account is then adjusted annually to show the investor's equity in the investee. (p. 688).

Fair value   Amount for which a security could be sold in a normal market. (p. 692).

Held-to-maturity securities   Debt securities that the investor has the intent and ability to hold to their maturity date. (p. 692).

Investment portfolio   A group of stocks in different corporations held for investment purposes. (p. 687).

Long-term investments   Investments that are not readily marketable and that management does not intend to convert into cash within the next year or operating cycle, whichever is longer. (p. 694).

Parent company   A company that owns more than 50% of the common stock of another entity. (p. 689).

Short-term investments   Investments that are readily marketable and intended to be converted into cash within the next year or operating cycle, whichever is longer. (p. 694).

Stock investments   Investments in the capital stock of corporations. (p. 687).

Subsidiary (affiliated) company   A company in which more than 50% of its stock is owned by another company. (p. 689).

Trading securities   Securities bought and held primarily for sale in the near term to generate income on short-term price differences. (p. 692).

SELF-STUDY QUESTIONS

Chapter 17 Self-Test

Answers are at the end of the chapter.

(SO 2) **1.** Debt investments are initially recorded at:
   a. cost.
   b. cost plus accrued interest.
   c. fair value.
   d. None of the above.

2. Hanes Company sells debt investments costing $26,000 (SO 2) for $28,000, plus accrued interest that has been recorded. In journalizing the sale, credits are to:
   a. Debt Investments and Loss on Sale of Debt Investments.
   b. Debt Investments, Gain on Sale of Debt Investments, and Bond Interest Receivable.

c. Stock Investments and Bond Interest Receivable.
d. No correct answer given.

(SO 3) 3. Pryor Company receives net proceeds of $42,000 on the sale of stock investments that cost $39,500. This transaction will result in reporting in the income statement a:
a. loss of $2,500 under "other expenses and losses."
b. loss of $2,500 under "operating expenses."
c. gain of $2,500 under "other revenues and gains."
d. gain of $2,500 under "operating revenues."

(SO 3) 4. The equity method of accounting for long-term investments in stock should be used when the investor has significant influence over an investee and owns:
a. between 20% and 50% of the investee's common stock.
b. 20% or more of the investee's common stock.
c. more than 50% of the investee's common stock.
d. less than 20% of the investee's common stock.

(SO 4) 5. Which of the following statements is *not true*? Consolidated financial statements are useful to:
a. determine the profitability of specific subsidiaries.
b. determine the total profitability of enterprises under common control.
c. determine the breadth of a parent company's operations.
d. determine the full extent of total obligations of enterprises under common control.

(SO 5) 6. At the end of the first year of operations, the total cost of the trading securities portfolio is $120,000. Total fair value is $115,000. The financial statements should show:
a. a reduction of an asset of $5,000 and a realized loss of $5,000.
b. a reduction of an asset of $5,000 and an unrealized loss of $5,000 in the stockholders' equity section.
c. a reduction of an asset of $5,000 in the current assets section and an unrealized loss of $5,000 in "other expenses and losses."
d. a reduction of an asset of $5,000 in the current assets section and a realized loss of $5,000 in "other expenses and losses."

7. In the balance sheet, Unrealized Loss—Equity is reported as a: **(SO 5)**
a. contra asset account.
b. contra stockholders' equity account.
c. loss in the income statement.
d. loss in the retained earnings statement.

8. Short-term debt investments must be readily marketable and be expected to be sold within: **(SO 6)**
a. 3 months from the date of purchase.
b. the next year or operating cycle, whichever is shorter.
c. the next year or operating cycle, whichever is longer.
d. the operating cycle.

QUESTIONS

1. What are the reasons that corporations invest in securities?

2. (a) What is the cost of an investment in bonds?
(b) When is interest on bonds recorded?

3. Juan Ortiz is confused about losses and gains on the sale of debt investments. Explain to Juan (a) how the gain or loss is computed, and (b) the statement presentation of the gains and losses.

4. Wendall Company sells Hurley's bonds costing $40,000 for $45,000, including $2,000 of accrued interest. In recording the sale, Wendall books a $5,000 gain. Is this correct? Explain.

5. What is the cost of an investment in stock?

6. To acquire Parin Corporation stock, R. Scope pays $60,000 in cash, plus $1,500 broker's fees. What entry should be made for this investment, assuming the stock is readily marketable?

7. (a) When should a long-term investment in common stock be accounted for by the equity method? (b) When is revenue recognized under this method?

8. Maxwell Corporation uses the equity method to account for its ownership of 30% of the common stock of Warren Packing. During 2002 Warren reported a net income of $80,000 and declares and pays cash dividends of $10,000. What recognition should Maxwell Corporation give to these events?

9. What constitutes "significant influence" when an investor's financial interest is below the 50% level?

10. Distinguish between the cost and equity methods of accounting for investments in stocks.

11. What are consolidated financial statements?

12. What are the valuation guidelines for investments at a balance sheet date?

13. Mary Carne is the controller of Nakoma Inc. At December 31, the company's investments in trading securities cost $74,000. They have a fair value of $70,000. Indicate how Mary would report these data in the financial statements prepared on December 31.

14. Using the data in question 13, how would Mary report the data if the investment were long-term and the securities were classified as available-for-sale?

15. Kaston Company's investments in available-for-sale securities at December 31 show total cost of $195,000 and total fair value of $205,000. Prepare the adjusting entry.

16. Using the data in question 15, prepare the adjusting entry assuming the securities are classified as trading securities.

17. What is the proper statement presentation of the account Unrealized Loss—Equity (Available-for-Sale Security)?

18. What purposes are served by reporting Unrealized Gains (Losses)—Equity in the stockholders' equity section?

19. Francis Wholesale Supply owns stock in Chen Corporation. Francis intends to hold the stock indefinitely because of some negative tax consequences if sold. Should the investment in Chen be classified as a short-term investment? Why or why not?

BRIEF EXERCISES

BE17-1 Phelps Corporation purchased debt investments for $49,800 on January 1, 2002. On July 1, 2002, Phelps received cash interest of $2,490. Journalize the purchase and the receipt of interest. Assume that no interest has been accrued.

Journalize entries for debt investments.
(SO 2)

BE17-2 On August 1, McClain Company buys 1,000 shares of Morgan common stock for $35,000 cash, plus brokerage fees of $600. On December 1, McClain sells the stock investments for $38,000 in cash. Journalize the purchase and sale of the common stock.

Journalize entries for stock investments.
(SO 3)

BE17-3 Harmon Company owns 25% of Hook Company. For the current year Hook reports net income of $180,000 and declares and pays a $50,000 cash dividend. Record Harmon's equity in Hook's net income and the receipt of dividends from Hook.

Record transactions under the equity method of accounting.
(SO 3)

BE17-4 The cost of the trading securities of Michelle Company at December 31, 2002, is $64,000. At December 31, 2002, the fair value of the securities is $61,000. Prepare the adjusting entry to record the securities at fair value.

Prepare adjusting entry using fair value.
(SO 5)

BE17-5 For the data presented in BE17-4, show the financial statement presentation of the trading securities and related accounts.

Indicate statement presentation using fair value.
(SO 5, 6)

BE17-6 Duggan Corporation holds as a long-term investment available-for-sale stock securities costing $72,000. At December 31, 2002, the fair value of the securities is $66,000. Prepare the adjusting entry to record the securities at fair value.

Prepare adjusting entry using fair value.
(SO 5)

BE17-7 For the data presented in BE17-6, show the financial statement presentation of the available-for-sale securities and related accounts. Assume the available-for-sale securities are noncurrent.

Indicate statements presentation using fair value.
(SO 5, 6)

BE17-8 Saber Corporation has the following long-term investments: (1) Common stock of Kubek Co. (10% ownership) held as available-for-sale securities, cost $108,000, fair value $120,000. (2) Common stock of Ely Inc. (30% ownership), cost $210,000, equity $250,000. (3) A bond sinking fund of $150,000. Prepare the investments section of the balance sheet.

Prepare investments section of balance sheet.
(SO 5, 6)

EXERCISES

E17-1 Jorge Corporation had the following transactions pertaining to debt investments.

Journalize debt investment transactions and accrue interest.
(SO 2)

Jan. 1	Purchased 60 10%, $1,000 Weston Co. bonds for $60,000 cash plus brokerage fees of $900. Interest is payable semiannually on July 1 and January 1.
July 1	Received semiannual interest on Weston Co. bonds.
July 1	Sold 30 Weston Co. bonds for $32,000 less $400 brokerage fees.

Instructions
(a) Journalize the transactions.
(b) Prepare the adjusting entry for the accrual of interest at December 31.

E17-2 Puff Daddy Company had the following transactions pertaining to stock investments.

Journalize stock investment transactions.
(SO 3)

Feb. 1	Purchased 600 shares of GET common stock (2%) for $7,000 cash, plus brokerage fees of $200.
July 1	Received cash dividends of $1 per share on GET common stock.
Sept. 1	Sold 300 shares of GET common stock for $4,000, less brokerage fees of $100.
Dec. 1	Received cash dividends of $1 per share on GET common stock.

Instructions
(a) Journalize the transactions.
(b) Explain how dividend revenue and the gain (loss) on sale should be reported in the income statement.

E17-3 Torre Inc. had the following transactions pertaining to investments in common stock.

Journalize transactions for investments in stocks.
(SO 3)

Jan. 1	Purchased 1,500 shares of Parker Corporation common stock (5%) for $105,000 cash plus $2,100 broker's commission.
July 1	Received a cash dividend of $9 per share.
Dec. 1	Sold 500 shares of Parker Corporation common stock for $37,000 cash, less $800 broker's commission.
Dec. 31	Received a cash dividend of $9 per share.

Journalize and post transactions, and contrast cost and equity method results.
(SO 3)

Instructions
Journalize the transactions.

E17-4 On January 1 Lionel Corporation purchased a 25% equity in Bellingham Corporation for $150,000. At December 31 Bellingham declared and paid a $60,000 cash dividend and reported net income of $200,000.

Instructions
(a) Journalize the transactions.
(b) Determine the amount to be reported as an investment in Bellingham stock at December 31.

Journalize entries under cost and equity methods.
(SO 3)

E17-5 Presented below are two independent situations.

1. Roscoe Cosmetics acquired 10% of the 200,000 shares of common stock of Ling Fashion at a total cost of $13 per share on March 18, 2002. On June 30, Ling declared and paid a $75,000 dividend. On December 31, Ling reported net income of $122,000 for the year. At December 31, the market price of Ling Fashion was $14 per share. The stock is classified as available-for-sale.

2. Juan, Inc., obtained significant influence over Orlando Corporation by buying 30% of Orlando's 30,000 outstanding shares of common stock at a total cost of $9 per share on January 1, 2002. On June 15, Orlando declared and paid a cash dividend of $35,000. On December 31, Orlando reported a net income of $80,000 for the year.

Instructions
Prepare all the necessary journal entries for 2002 for (a) Roscoe Cosmetics and (b) Juan, Inc.

Prepare adjusting entry to record fair value, and indicate statement presentation.
(SO 5, 6)

E17-6 At December 31, 2002, the trading securities for Yanu, Inc. are as follows.

Security	Cost	Fair Value
A	$17,500	$16,000
B	12,500	14,000
C	23,000	19,000
	$53,000	$49,000

Instructions
(a) Prepare the adjusting entry at December 31, 2002, to report the securities at fair value.
(b) Show the balance sheet and income statement presentation at December 31, 2002, after adjustment to fair value.

Prepare adjusting entry to record fair value, and indicate statement presentation.
(SO 5, 6)

E17-7 Data for investments in stock classified as trading securities are presented in E17-6. Assume instead that the investments are classified as available-for-sale securities. They have the same cost and fair value. The securities are considered to be a long-term investment.

Instructions
(a) Prepare the adjusting entry at December 31, 2002, to report the securities at fair value.
(b) Show the statement presentation at December 31, 2002, after adjustment to fair value.
(c) ▭▭▭▷ M. Lieberman, a member of the board of directors, does not understand the reporting of the unrealized gains or losses. Write a letter to Mr. Lieberman explaining the reporting and the purposes that it serves.

Prepare adjusting entries for fair value, and indicate statement presentation for two classes of securities.
(SO 5, 6)

E17-8 Chaney Company has the following data at December 31, 2002.

Securities	Cost	Fair Value
Trading	$120,000	$124,000
Available-for-sale	100,000	94,000

The available-for-sale securities are held as a long-term investment.

Instructions
(a) Prepare the adjusting entries to report each class of securities at fair value.
(b) Indicate the statement presentation of each class of securities and the related unrealized gain (loss) accounts.

PROBLEMS: SET A

P17-1A Willow Carecenters Inc. provides financing and capital to the health-care industry, with a particular focus on nursing homes for the elderly. The following selected transactions relate to bonds acquired as an investment by Willow, whose fiscal year ends on December 31.

Journalize debt investment transactions and show financial statement presentation.
(SO 2, 5, 6)

2002

Jan. 1   Purchased at par $5,000,000 of Friendship Nursing Centers, Inc., 10-year, 10% bonds dated January 1, 2002, directly from Friendship.
July 1   Received the semiannual interest on the Friendship bonds.
Dec. 31   Accrual of interest at year-end on the Friendship bonds.

(Assume that all intervening transactions and adjustments have been properly recorded and that the number of bonds owned has not changed from December 31, 2002, to December 31, 2004.)

2005

Jan. 1   Received the semiannual interest on the Friendship bonds.
Jan. 1   Sold $2,500,000 Friendship bonds at 106. The broker deducted $10,000 for commissions and fees on the sale.
July 1   Received the semiannual interest on the Friendship bonds.
Dec. 31   Accrual of interest at year-end on the Friendship bonds.

Instructions

(a) Journalize the listed transactions for the years 2002 and 2005.

(a) Gain on sale of debt investment $140,000

(b) Assume that the fair value of the bonds at December 31, 2002, was $5,500,000. These bonds are classified as available-for-sale securities. Prepare the adjusting entry to record these bonds at fair value.

(c) Show the balance sheet presentation of the bonds and interest receivable at December 31, 2002. Assume the investments are considered long-term. Indicate where any unrealized gain or loss is reported in the financial statements.

P17-2A In January 2002, the management of Harris Company concludes that it has sufficient cash to permit some short-term investments in debt and stock securities. During the year, the following transactions occurred.

Journalize investment transactions, prepare adjusting entry, and show statement presentation.
(SO 2, 3, 5, 6)

Peachtree

Feb. 1   Purchased 400 shares of Alpha common stock for $21,800, plus brokerage fees of $600.
Mar. 1   Purchased 800 shares of Omega common stock for $20,000, plus brokerage fees of $400.
Apr. 1   Purchased 40 $1,000, 12% Pep bonds for $40,000, plus $1,000 brokerage fees. Interest is payable semiannually on April 1 and October 1.
July 1   Received a cash dividend of $0.60 per share on the Alpha common stock.
Aug. 1   Sold 200 shares of Alpha common stock at $58 per share less brokerage fees of $200.
Sept. 1   Received a $1 per share cash dividend on the Omega common stock.
Oct. 1   Received the semiannual interest on the Pep bonds.
Oct. 1   Sold the Pep bonds for $41,000 less $1,000 brokerage fees.

At December 31, the fair value of the Alpha common stock was $55 per share. The fair value of the Omega common stock was $23 per share.

Instructions

(a) Journalize the transactions and post to the accounts Debt Investments and Stock Investments. (Use the T-account form.)

(a) Gain on stock sale $200

(b) Prepare the adjusting entry at December 31, 2002, to report the investment securities at fair value. All securities are considered to be trading securities.

(c) Show the balance sheet presentation of investment securities at December 31, 2002.

(d) Identify the income statement accounts and give the statement classification of each account.

P17-3A On December 31, 2002, Melanie Associates owned the following securities, held as a long-term investment. The securities are not held for influence or control of the investee.

Journalize transactions and adjusting entry for stock investments.
(SO 3, 5, 6)

Common Stock	Shares	Cost
Carson Co.	6,000	$90,000
Pirie Co.	5,000	45,000
Scott Co.	1,500	30,000

On this date, the total fair value of the securities was equal to its cost. In 2003, the following transactions occurred.

July	1	Received $1 per share semiannual cash dividend on Pirie Co. common stock.
Aug.	1	Received $0.50 per share cash dividend on Carson Co. common stock.
Sept.	1	Sold 1,000 shares of Pirie Co. common stock for cash at $8 per share, less brokerage fees of $200.
Oct.	1	Sold 800 shares of Carson Co. common stock for cash at $17 per share, less brokerage fees of $500.
Nov.	1	Received $1 per share cash dividend on Scott Co. common stock.
Dec.	15	Received $0.50 per share cash dividend on Carson Co. common stock.
	31	Received $1 per share semiannual cash dividend on Pirie Co. common stock.

At December 31, the fair values per share of the common stocks were: Carson Co. $16, Pirie Co. $8, and Scott Co. $18.

Instructions
(a) Journalize the 2003 transactions and post to the account Stock Investments. (Use the T-account form.)

(b) Unrealized loss $1,800

(b) Prepare the adjusting entry at December 31, 2003, to show the securities at fair value. The stock should be classified as available-for-sale securities.
(c) Show the balance sheet presentation of the investments at December 31, 2003. At this date, Melanie Associates has common stock $1,500,000 and retained earnings $1,000,000.

Prepare entries under the cost and equity methods, and tabulate differences.
(SO 3)

P17-4A Handy Services acquired 25% of the outstanding common stock of Quarles Company on January 1, 2002, by paying $800,000 for the 40,000 shares. Quarles declared and paid $0.50 per share cash dividends on March 15, June 15, September 15, and December 15, 2002. Quarles reported net income of $360,000 for the year. At December 31, 2002, the market price of Quarles common stock was $28 per share.

Instructions
(a) Prepare the journal entries for Handy Services for 2002 assuming Handy cannot exercise significant influence over Quarles. (Use the cost method and assume that Quarles' common stock should be classified as a trading security.)
(b) Prepare the journal entries for Handy Services for 2002, assuming Handy can exercise significant influence over Quarles. Use the equity method.
(c) In tabular form, indicate the investment and income statement account balances at December 31, 2002, under each method of accounting.

Journalize stock investment transactions and show statement presentation.
(SO 3, 5, 6)

P17-5A The following securities are in Hi-Tech Company's portfolio of long-term available-for-sale securities at December 31, 2002.

	Cost
1,000 shares of Awixa Corporation common stock	$52,000
1,400 shares of HAL Corporation common stock	84,000
800 shares of Renda Corporation preferred stock	33,600

On December 31, 2002, the total cost of the portfolio equaled total fair value. Hi-Tech had the following transactions related to the securities during 2003.

Jan.	20	Sold 1,000 shares of Awixa Corporation common stock at $56 per share less brokerage fees of $600.
	28	Purchased 400 shares of $70 par value common stock of Mintor Corporation at $78 per share, plus brokerage fees of $480.
	30	Received a cash dividend of $1.15 per share on HAL Corp. common stock.

Feb. 8   Received cash dividends of $0.40 per share on Renda Corp. preferred stock.

18   Sold all 800 shares of Renda Corp. preferred stock at $30.00 per share less brokerage fees of $360.

July 30   Received a cash dividend of $1.00 per share on HAL Corp. common stock.

Sept. 6   Purchased an additional 800 shares of $10 par value common stock of Mintor Corporation at $82 per share, plus brokerage fees of $800.

Dec. 1   Received a cash dividend of $1.50 per share on Mintor Corporation common stock.

At December 31, 2003, the fair values of the securities were:

HAL Corporation common stock	$64 per share
Mintor Corporation common stock	$72 per share

Hi-Tech Company uses separate account titles for each investment, such as "Investment in HAL Corporation Common Stock."

Instructions
(a) Prepare journal entries to record the transactions.
(b) Post to the investment accounts. (Use T accounts.)
(c) Prepare the adjusting entry at December 31, 2003, to report the portfolio at fair value.
(d) Show the balance sheet presentation at December 31, 2003.

(a) Loss on sale $9,960

(c) Unrealized loss $6,080

P17-6A   The following data, presented in alphabetical order, are taken from the records of Scheer Corporation.

Prepare a balance sheet.
(SO 5, 6)

Accounts payable	$ 250,000
Accounts receivable	140,000
Accumulated depreciation—building	180,000
Accumulated depreciation—equipment	52,000
Allowance for doubtful accounts	6,000
Bonds payable (10%, due 2013)	500,000
Bond sinking fund	150,000
Buildings	950,000
Cash	72,000
Common stock ($10 par value; 500,000 shares authorized, 150,000 shares issued)	1,500,000
Dividends payable	80,000
Equipment	275,000
Goodwill	200,000
Income taxes payable	120,000
Investment in Lotto common stock (10% ownership), at cost	278,000
Investment in Portico common stock (30% ownership), at equity	230,000
Land	500,000
Market adjustment—available-for-sale securities (Dr)	8,000
Merchandise inventory	170,000
Notes payable (due 2003)	70,000
Paid-in capital in excess of par value	200,000
Premium on bonds payable	40,000
Prepaid insurance	16,000
Retained earnings	163,000
Short-term stock investment, at fair value (and cost)	180,000
Unrealized gain—available-for-sale securities	8,000

The investment in Lotto common stock is considered to be a long-term available-for-sale security.

Instructions

Prepare a balance sheet at December 31, 2002.

Total assets $2,931,000

PROBLEMS: SET B

Journalize debt investment transactions and show financial statement presentation.
(SO 2, 5, 6)

P17-1B Marvel Davis Farms is a grower of hybrid seed corn for DeKalb Genetics Corporation. It has had two exceptionally good years and has elected to invest its excess funds in bonds. The following selected transactions relate to bonds acquired as an investment by Marvel Davis Farms, whose fiscal year ends on December 31.

2002

Jan.	1	Purchased at par $1,000,000 of Sycamore Corporation 10-year, 9% bonds dated January 1, 2002, directly from the issuing corporation.
July	1	Received the semiannual interest on the Sycamore bonds.
Dec. 31		Accrual of interest at year-end on the Sycamore bonds.

(Assume that all intervening transactions and adjustments have been properly recorded and the number of bonds owned has not changed from December 31, 2002, to December 31, 2004.)

2005

Jan.	1	Received the semiannual interest on the Sycamore bonds.
Jan.	1	Sold $500,000 Sycamore bonds at 114. The broker deducted $7,000 for commissions and fees on the sale.
July	1	Received the semiannual interest on the Sycamore bonds.
Dec. 31		Accrual of interest at year-end on the Sycamore bonds.

Instructions

(a) Gain on sale of debt investments $63,000

(a) Journalize the listed transactions for the years 2002 and 2005.
(b) Assume that the fair value of the bonds at December 31, 2002, was $960,000. These bonds are classified as available-for-sale securities. Prepare the adjusting entry to record these bonds at fair value.
(c) Show the balance sheet presentation of the bonds and interest receivable at December 31, 2002. Assume the investments are considered long-term. Indicate where any unrealized gain or loss is reported in the financial statements.

Journalize investment transactions, prepare adjusting entry, and show statement presentation.
(SO 2, 3, 5, 6)

P17-2B In January 2002, the management of Wolfe Company concludes that it has sufficient cash to purchase some short-term investments in debt and stock securities. During the year, the following transactions occurred.

Feb.	1	Purchased 800 shares of LRT common stock for $32,000, plus brokerage fees of $800.
Mar.	1	Purchased 500 shares of IMA common stock for $15,000, plus brokerage fees of $300.
Apr.	1	Purchased 40 $1,000, 12% CAL bonds for $40,000, plus $1,200 brokerage fees. Interest is payable semiannually on April 1 and October 1.
July	1	Received a cash dividend of $0.60 per share on the LRT common stock.
Aug.	1	Sold 300 shares of LRT common stock at $42 per share, less brokerage fees of $350.
Sept.	1	Received a $1 per share cash dividend on the IMA common stock.
Oct.	1	Received the semiannual interest on the CAL bonds.
Oct.	1	Sold the CAL bonds for $44,000, less $1,000 brokerage fees.

At December 31, the fair value of the LRT common stock was $39 per share. The fair value of the IMA common stock was $30 per share.

Instructions

(a) Journalize the transactions and post to the accounts Debt Investments and Stock Investments. (Use the T-account form.)

(b) Unrealized loss $1,300

(b) Prepare the adjusting entry at December 31, 2002, to report the investments at fair value. All securities are considered to be trading securities.
(c) Show the balance sheet presentation of investment securities at December 31, 2002.
(d) Identify the income statement accounts and give the statement classification of each account.

Journalize transactions and adjusting entry for stock investments.
(SO 3, 5, 6)

P17-3B On December 31, 2002, Appolo Associates owned the following securities, held as long-term investments.

Common Stock	Shares	Cost
Abbot Co.	1,000	$50,000
Burns Co.	6,000	36,000
Costello Co.	1,200	24,000

On this date, the total fair value of the securities was equal to its cost. The securities are not held for influence or control over the investees. In 2003, the following transactions occurred.

July 1   Received $1 per share semiannual cash dividend on Burns Co. common stock.

Aug. 1   Received $0.50 per share cash dividend on Abbot Co. common stock.

Sept. 1   Sold 1,000 shares of Burns Co. common stock for cash at $7 per share, less brokerage fees of $100.

Oct. 1   Sold 600 shares of Abbot Co. common stock for cash at $56 per share, less brokerage fees of $600.

Nov. 1   Received $1 per share cash dividend on Costello Co. common stock.

Dec. 15   Received $0.50 per share cash dividend on Abbot Co. common stock.

31   Received $1 per share semiannual cash dividend on Burns Co. common stock.

At December 31, the fair values per share of the common stocks were: Abbot Co. $47, Burns Co. $6, and Costello Co. $19.

Instructions

(a) Journalize the 2003 transactions and post to the account Stock Investments. (Use the T-account form.)

(b) Prepare the adjusting entry at December 31, 2003, to show the securities at fair value. The stock should be classified as available-for-sale securities.

(c) Show the balance sheet presentation of the investments at December 31, 2003. At this date, Appolo Associates has common stock $2,000,000 and retained earnings $1,200,000.

(a) Gain on sale, $900 and $3,000

P17-4B   Wet Concrete acquired 25% of the outstanding common stock of Hawkins, Inc. on January 1, 2002, by paying $1,200,000 for 50,000 shares. Hawkins declared and paid an $0.80 per share cash dividend on June 30 and again on December 31, 2002. Hawkins reported net income of $800,000 for the year. At December 31, 2002, the market price of Hawkins' common stock was $30 per share.

Prepare entries under the cost and equity methods and tabulate differences.
(SO 3)

Instructions

(a) Prepare the journal entries for Wet Concrete for 2002 assuming Wet cannot exercise significant influence over Hawkins. (Use the cost method and assume Hawkins' common stock should be classified as available-for-sale.)

(b) Prepare the journal entries for Wet Concrete for 2002, assuming Wet can exercise significant influence over Hawkins. (Use the equity method.)

(c) In tabular form, indicate the investment and income account balances at December 31, 2002, under each method of accounting.

(a) Total dividend revenue $80,000

(b) Revenue from investments $200,000

P17-5B   The following are in Sammy Sosa Company's portfolio of long-term available-for-sale securities at December 31, 2002.

Journalize stock transactions and show statement presentation.
(SO 3, 5, 6)

	Cost
500 shares of McGwire Corporation common stock	$26,000
700 shares of B. Ruth Corporation common stock	42,000
400 shares H. Aaron Corporation preferred stock	16,800

On December 31, the total cost of the portfolio equaled total fair value. Sammy Sosa Company had the following transactions related to the securities during 2003.

Jan. 7   Sold 500 shares of McGwire Corporation common stock at $56 per share, less brokerage fees of $700.

Jan. 10   Purchased 200 shares, $70 par value common stock of Mantle Corporation at $78 per share, plus brokerage fees of $240.

26   Received a cash dividend of $1.15 per share on B. Ruth Corporation common stock.

Feb. 2 Received cash dividends of $0.40 per share on H. Aaron Corporation preferred stock.

10 Sold all 400 shares of H. Aaron Corporation preferred stock at $35.00 per share less brokerage fees of $180.

July 1 Received a cash dividend of $1.00 per share on B. Ruth Corporation common stock.

Sept. 1 Purchased an additional 400 shares of the $70 par value common stock of Mantle Corporation at $75 per share, plus brokerage fees of $400.

Dec. 15 Received a cash dividend of $1.50 per share on Mantle Corporation common stock.

At December 31, 2003, the fair values of the securities were:

B. Ruth Corporation common stock	$63 per share
Mantle Corporation common stock	$72 per share

Sosa uses separate account titles for each investment, such as Investment in B. Ruth Corporation Common Stock.

Instructions

(a) Loss on sale $2,980

(a) Prepare journal entries to record the transactions.
(b) Post to the investment accounts. (Use T accounts.)

(c) Unrealized loss $940

(c) Prepare the adjusting entry at December 31, 2003, to report the portfolio at fair value.
(d) Show the balance sheet presentation at December 31, 2003.

Prepare a balance sheet.
(SO, 5, 6)

P17-6B The following data, presented in alphabetical order, are taken from the records of Webb Corporation.

Accounts payable	$ 240,000
Accounts receivable	90,000
Accumulated depreciation—building	180,000
Accumulated depreciation—equipment	52,000
Allowance for doubtful accounts	6,000
Bonds payable (10%, due 2015)	400,000
Bond sinking fund	360,000
Buildings	900,000
Cash	112,000
Common stock ($5 par value; 500,000 shares authorized, 300,000 shares issued)	1,500,000
Discount on bonds payable	20,000
Dividends payable	50,000
Equipment	275,000
Goodwill	200,000
Income taxes payable	120,000
Investment in Saratoga Inc. stock (30% ownership), at equity	240,000
Land	500,000
Merchandise inventory	170,000
Notes payable (due 2003)	70,000
Paid-in capital in excess of par value	200,000
Prepaid insurance	16,000
Retained earnings	250,000
Short-term stock investment, at fair value (and cost)	185,000

Instructions

Total assets $2,810,000

Prepare a balance sheet at December 31, 2002.

COMPREHENSIVE PROBLEM: CHAPTERS 13 TO 17

PART I

Monique Bergeron and her two colleagues Jared Nimitz and Rosaline Soileau are personal trainers at an upscale health spa/resort in Tampa, Florida. They want to start a health club that specializes in health plans for people in the 50+ age range. The growing population in this age range and strong consumer interest in the health benefits of physical activity have convinced them they can profitably operate their own club. In addition to many other decisions, they need to determine what type of business organization they want. Jared believes there are more advantages to the corporate form than a partnership, but he hasn't yet convinced Monique and Rosaline. They have come to you, a small business consulting specialist, seeking information and advice regarding the choice of starting a partnership versus a corporation.

Instructions

(a) ▭▭▭▷ Prepare a memo (dated May 26, 2000) that describes the advantages and disadvantages of both partnerships and corporations. Advise Monique, Jared, and Rosaline regarding which organizational form you believe would better serve their purposes. Make sure to include reasons supporting your advice.

PART II

After deciding to incorporate, each of the three investors receives 20,000 shares of $1 par common stock on June 12, 2000, in exchange for their co-owned building ($180,000 market value) and $120,000 total cash they contributed to the business. The next decision that Monique, Jared, and Rosaline need to make is how to obtain financing for renovation and equipment. They understand the difference between equity securities and debt securities, but do not understand the tax, net income, and earnings per share consequences of equity versus debt financing on the future of their business.

Instructions

(b) Prepare notes for a discussion with the three entrepreneurs in which you will compare the consequences of using equity versus debt financing. As part of your notes, show the differences in interest and tax expense assuming $1,400,000 is financed with common stock, and then alternatively with debt. Assume that when common stock is used, 140,000 shares will be issued. When debt is used, assume the interest rate on debt is 9%, the tax rate is 32%, and income before interest and taxes is $160,000. (You may want to use an electronic spreadsheet.)

PART III

During the discussion about financing, Rosaline mentions that one of her clients, Antonio Sandoval, has approached her about buying a significant interest in the new club. Having an interested investor sways the three to issue equity securities to provide the financing they need. On July 21, 2000, Mr. Sandoval buys 140,000 shares at a price of $10 per share.

The club, LifePath Fitness, opens on January 12, 2001, and after a slow start, begins to produce the revenue desired by the owners. The owners decide to pay themselves a stock dividend, since cash has been less than abundant since they opened their doors. The 5% stock dividend is declared by the owners on July 27, 2001. The market value of the stock is $1.50 on the declaration date. The date of record is July 31, 2001 (there have been no changes in stock ownership since the initial issuance), and the issue date is August 15, 2001. By the middle of the fourth quarter of 2001, the cash flow of LifePath Fitness has improved to the point that the owners feel ready to pay themselves a cash dividend. They declare a $0.01 cash dividend on December 4, 2001. The record date is December 14, 2001, and the payment date is December 24, 2001.

Instructions

(c) (1) Record all of the transactions related to the common stock of LifePath Fitness during the years 2000 and 2001. (2) Indicate how many shares are issued and outstanding after the stock dividend is issued.

PART IV

Since the club opened, a major concern has been the pool facilities. Although the existing pool is adequate, Monique, Jared, and Rosaline all desire to make LifePath a cutting-edge facility. Until the end of 2001, financing concerns prevented this improvement. However, because there has been steady growth in clientele, revenue, and income since the fourth quarter of 2001, the owners have explored possible financing options. They are hesitant to issue stock and change the ownership mix because they have been able to work together as a team with great effectiveness. They have formulated a plan to issue secured term bonds to raise the needed $500,000 for the pool facilities. By the end of April 2002 everything was in place for the bond issue to go ahead. On June 1, 2002, the bonds were issued for $463,200. The bonds pay semiannual interest of $3\frac{1}{2}$% (7% annual) on December 1 and June 1 of each year. The bonds mature in 10 years, and amortization is computed using the straight-line method.

Instructions

(d) Record (1) the issuance of the secured bonds, (2) the interest payment made on December 1, 2002, (3) the adjusting entry required at December 31, 2002, and (4) the interest payment made on June 1, 2003.

PART V

Mr. Sandoval's purchase of LifePath Fitness was done through his business. The investment has always been accounted for using the cost method on his firm's books. However, early in 2003 he decided to take his company public. He is preparing an IPO (initial public offering), and he needs to have the firm's financial statements audited. One of the issues to be resolved is to restate the investment in LifePath Fitness using the equity method, since Mr. Sandoval's ownership percentage is greater than 20%.

Instructions

(e) (1) Give the entries that would have been made on Sandoval's books if the equity method of accounting for investments had been used since the initial investment. Assume the following data for LifePath.

	2000	2001	2002
Net income	$19,000	$70,000	$105,000
Total cash dividends	$ 2,100	$25,000	$ 50,000

(2) Compute the balance in the LifePath Investment account at the end of 2003.

BROADENING YOUR PERSPECTIVE

*F*INANCIAL REPORTING AND ANALYSIS

FINANCIAL REPORTING PROBLEM: Lands' End, Inc.

BYP17-1 The annual report of Lands' End, Inc. is presented in Appendix A.

Instructions

(a) See Note 1 to the financial statements and indicate what the consolidated financial statements include.

(b) Using Lands' End's consolidated statement of cash flows, determine how much was spent for capital acquisitions during the current year.

COMPARATIVE ANALYSIS PROBLEM: Lands' End vs. Abercrombie & Fitch

BYP17-2 Lands' End's financial statements are presented in Appendix A. Abercrombie & Fitch's financial statements are presented in Appendix B.

Instructions

(a) Based on the information contained in these financial statements, determine each of the following for each company.

   (1) Cash used for investing (investment) activities for the current year (from the statement of cash flows).

   (2) Cash used for capital expenditures during the current year.

(b) Each of Lands' End's financial statements is labeled "consolidated." What has been consolidated? That is, from the contents of Lands' End's annual report, identify by name the corporations that have been consolidated (parent and subsidiaries).

INTERPRETING FINANCIAL STATEMENTS: A Global Focus

BYP17-3 Xerox Corporation has a 50% investment interest in a joint venture with the Japanese corporation Fuji, called Fuji Xerox. Xerox accounts for this investment using the equity method. The following additional information regarding this investment was taken from Xerox's 1998 annual report (in millions).

Investment in Fuji Xerox per balance sheet	$ 1,354
Fuji Xerox net income	108
Xerox total assets	30,024
Xerox total liabilities	25,167
Fuji Xerox total assets	6,279
Fuji Xerox total liabilities	3,757

Instructions

(a) What alternative approaches are available for accounting for long-term investments in stock? Discuss whether Xerox is correct in using the equity method to account for this investment.

(b) Under the equity method, how does Xerox reports its investment in Fuji Xerox? If Xerox owned a majority of Fuji Xerox, it then would have to consolidate Fuji Xerox instead of using the equity method. Discuss how this would change Xerox's financial statements. That is, in what way and by how much would assets and liabilities change?

(c) The use of 50% joint ventures is becoming a fairly common practice. Why might companies like Xerox prefer to participate in a joint venture rather than own a majority share?

EXPLORING THE WEB

BYP17-4 The Securities and Exchange Commission (SEC) is the primary regulatory agency of U.S. financial markets. Its job is to ensure that the markets remain fair for all investors. The following SEC site provides useful information for investors.

Address: www.sec.gov/consumer/weisktc.htm *(or go to www.wiley.com/college/weygandt)*

Steps:

1. Go to the site shown above.
2. Choose **Glossary**.

Instructions

Using the glossary, find the definition of the following terms.
(a) Ask price.
(b) Margin account.
(c) Prospectus.
(d) Yield.

BYP17-5 Most publicly traded companies are analyzed by numerous analysts. These analysts often don't agree about a company's future prospects. In this exercise you will find analysts' ratings about companies and make comparisons over time and across companies in the same industry. You will also see to what extent the analysts experienced "earnings surprises." Earnings surprises can cause changes in stock prices.

Address: biz.yahoo.com/i *(or go to www.wiley.com/college/weygandt)*

Steps:

1. Choose a company.
2. Use the index to find the company's name.
2. Choose **Research**.

Instructions

(a) How many brokers rated the company?
(b) What percentage rated it a strong buy?
(c) What was the average rating for the week?
(d) Did the average rating improve or decline relative to the previous week?
(e) How do the brokers rank this company among all the companies in its industry?
(f) What was the amount of the earnings surprise during the last quarter?

CRITICAL THINKING

GROUP DECISION CASE

BYP17-6 At the beginning of the question and answer portion of the annual stockholders' meeting of Purdy Corporation, stockholder Manor Newby asks, "Why did management sell the holdings in Pepco Company at a loss when this company has been very profitable during the period its stock was held by Purdy?"

Since president Tony Garcia has just concluded his speech on the recent success and bright future of Purdy, he is taken aback by this question and responds, "I remember we paid $1,100,000 for that stock some years ago, and I am sure we sold that stock at a much higher price. You must be mistaken."

Newby retorts, "Well, right here in footnote number 7 to the annual report it shows that 240,000 shares, a 30% interest in Pepco, were sold on the last day of the year. Also, it states that Pepco earned $550,000 this year and paid out $150,000 in cash dividends. Further, a summary statement indicates that in past years, while Purdy held Pepco stock, Pepco earned $1,240,000 and paid out $440,000 in dividends. Finally, the income statement for this year shows a loss on the sale of Pepco stock of $180,000. So, I doubt that I am mistaken."

Red-faced, president Garcia turns to you.

Instructions
With the class divided into groups, answer the following.
(a) What dollar amount did Purdy receive upon the sale of the Pepco stock?
(b) Explain why both stockholder Newby and president Garcia are correct.

COMMUNICATION ACTIVITY

BYP17-7 Ramon Corporation has purchased two securities for its portfolio. The first is a stock investment in Tierney Corporation, one of its suppliers. Ramon purchased 10% of Tierney with the intention of holding it for a number of years, but has no intention of purchasing more shares. The second investment was a purchase of debt securities. Ramon purchased the debt securities because its analysts believe that changes in market interest rates will cause these securities to increase in value in a short period of time. Ramon intends to sell the securities as soon as they have increased in value.

Instructions
Write a memo to Deno Constantine, the chief financial officer, explaining how to account for each of these investments. Explain what the implications for reported income are from this accounting treatment.

ETHICS CASE

BYP17-8 Cartwright Financial Services Company holds a large portfolio of debt and stock securities as an investment. The total fair value of the portfolio at December 31, 2002, is greater than total cost. Some securities have increased in value and others have decreased. Ann Dearing, the financial vice president, and Sue Kelso, the controller, are in the process of classifying for the first time the securities in the portfolio.

Dearing suggests classifying the securities that have increased in value as trading securities in order to increase net income for the year. She wants to classify the securities that have decreased in value as long-term available-for-sale securities, so that the decreases in value will not affect 2002 net income.

Kelso disagrees. She recommends classifying the securities that have decreased in value as trading securities and those that have increased in value as long-term available-for-sale securities. Kelso argues that the company is having a good earnings year and that recognizing the losses now will help to smooth income for this year. Moreover, for future years, when the company may not be as profitable, the company will have built-in gains.

Instructions
(a) Will classifying the securities as Dearing and Kelso suggest actually affect earnings as each says it will?

(b) Is there anything unethical in what Dearing and Kelso propose? Who are the stakeholders affected by their proposals?

(c) Assume that Dearing and Kelso properly classify the portfolio. Assume, at year-end, that Dearing proposes to sell the securities that will increase 2002 net income, and that Kelso proposes to sell the securities that will decrease 2002 net income. Is this unethical?

Answers to Self-Study Questions

1. a   **2.** b   **3.** c   **4.** a   **5.** a   **6.** c   **7.** b   **8.** c

Answer to *Lands' End* Review It Question 4, page 691

In Note 1, the following statement is made regarding the consolidation policy of Land's End: "The consolidated financial statements include the accounts of the company and its subsidiaries after elimination of intercompany accounts and transactions."

Remember to go back to the Navigator box on the chapter-opening page and check off your completed work.

THE STATEMENT
OF CASH FLOWS

18

CONCEPTS FOR REVIEW

Before studying this chapter, you should know or, if necessary, review:

a. The difference between the accrual basis and the cash basis of accounting. (Ch. 3, pp. 89–90)

b. The major items included in a corporation's balance sheet. (Ch. 17, pp. 694–697)

c. The major items included in a corporation's income statement. (Ch. 15, pp. 615–622)

"Cash Is Cash, and Everything Else Is Accounting"

For Gerald Biby, vice president and chief financial officer of **Kilian Community College** in Sioux Falls, South Dakota, the statement of cash flows was the difference between being able to refinance a mortgage and being turned down by six local banks. "We recently wanted to refinance a $125,000 mortgage on a piece of property that we own," he says. "It was the statement of cash flows that finally showed our lender that we had the cash flow to service the debt."

As he explains, the traditional statement of cash flows for a not-for-profit, educational institution shows revenues and all expenditures, even the capital expenditures. According to this format, which the banks focused on initially, Kilian Community College was just break-ing even. "In the business world, if we had spent $250,000 on a computer system, then we would have put that on a depreciation schedule. But in the non-profit arena, it's typical that the entire $250,000 is written off as an expense against the general fund." The statement of cash flows showed the bankers that one of the uses of funds was really the purchase of computer equipment that had several years of life.

The college's statement of cash flows has over 30 classifications including tuition, fees, bookstore revenues, and so on. The school has 250 students, charges $70 a credit hour (12 hours is a full-time schedule), and has five terms each year.

The bankers granted the refinancing when they saw that the college's sources of funds exceeded the loan repayments, including principal and interest, by a ratio of 3-to-1. Not only did the school get the loan, but it did so at a favorable rate. "We were able to cut the mortgage rate to prime plus 1 percent from prime plus 3 percent."

☑ THE NAVIGATOR

After studying this chapter, you should be able to:

1. Indicate the primary purpose of the statement of cash flows.
2. Distinguish among operating, investing, and financing activities.
3. Prepare a statement of cash flows using the indirect method.
4. Prepare a statement of cash flows using the direct method.
5. Analyze the statement of cash flows.

☑ THE NAVIGATOR

As the story about **Kilian Community College** indicates, the balance sheet, income statement, and retained earnings statement do not always show the whole picture of the financial condition of a company or institution. In fact, looking at the three traditional financial statements of some well-known companies, a thoughtful investor might have questions like the following: How did **Eastman Kodak** finance cash dividends of $649 million in a year in which it earned only $17 million? How could **Delta Airlines** purchase new planes costing $900 million in a year in which it reported a net loss of $86 million? How did the companies that spent a fantastic $3.4 trillion on merger deals in 1999 (over 36 percent more than the 1998 total) finance those deals? Answers to these and similar questions can be found in this chapter, which presents the **statement of cash flows**.

The content and organization of Chapter 18 are as follows.

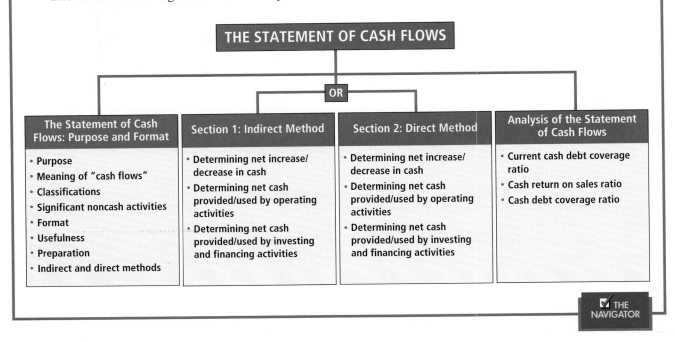

THE STATEMENT OF CASH FLOWS

OR

The Statement of Cash Flows: Purpose and Format	Section 1: Indirect Method	Section 2: Direct Method	Analysis of the Statement of Cash Flows
• Purpose • Meaning of "cash flows" • Classifications • Significant noncash activities • Format • Usefulness • Preparation • Indirect and direct methods	• Determining net increase/decrease in cash • Determining net cash provided/used by operating activities • Determining net cash provided/used by investing and financing activities	• Determining net increase/decrease in cash • Determining net cash provided/used by operating activities • Determining net cash provided/used by investing and financing activities	• Current cash debt coverage ratio • Cash return on sales ratio • Cash debt coverage ratio

☑ THE NAVIGATOR

THE STATEMENT OF CASH FLOWS: PURPOSE AND FORMAT

The three basic financial statements we've studied so far present only fragmentary information about a company's cash flows (cash receipts and cash payments). For example, **comparative balance sheets** show the increase in property, plant, and equipment during the year. But they do not show how the additions were financed or paid for. The **income statement** shows net income. But it does not indicate the amount of cash generated by operating activities. Similarly, the **retained earnings statement** shows cash dividends declared but not the cash dividends paid during the year. None of these statements presents a detailed summary of the net change in cash as a result of operating, investing, and financing activities during the period.

STUDY OBJECTIVE 1

Indicate the primary purpose of the statement of cash flows.

PURPOSE OF THE STATEMENT OF CASH FLOWS

The primary purpose of the statement of cash flows is to provide information about an entity's cash receipts and cash payments during a period. A secondary objective is to provide information about its operating, investing, and financing activities.[1] The **statement of cash flows** reports the cash receipts, cash payments, and net change in cash resulting from operating, investing, and financing activities during a period. It does so in a format that reconciles the beginning and ending cash balances.

Reporting the causes of changes in cash helps investors, creditors, and other interested parties understand what is happening to a company's most liquid resource—its cash. As the opening story about Kilian Community College demonstrates, a statement of cash flows helps us understand what is happening. It provides answers to the following simple, but important, questions about an enterprise.

1. Where did the cash come from during the period?
2. What was the cash used for during the period?
3. What was the change in the cash balance during the period?

MEANING OF "CASH FLOWS"

The statement of cash flows is generally prepared using "**cash and cash equivalents**" as its basis. Cash equivalents are short-term, highly liquid investments that are both:

1. Readily convertible to known amounts of cash, and
2. So near their maturity that their market value is relatively insensitive to changes in interest rates.

Generally, only investments with original maturities of three months or less qualify under this definition. Examples of cash equivalents are Treasury bills, commercial paper (short-term corporate notes), and money market funds. All typically are purchased with cash that is in excess of immediate needs.

Note that since cash and cash equivalents are viewed as the same, transfers between cash and cash equivalents are not treated as cash receipts and cash payments. That is, such transfers are not reported in the statement of cash flows. The term "cash" when used in this chapter includes cash and cash equivalents.

CLASSIFICATION OF CASH FLOWS

The statement of cash flows classifies cash receipts and cash payments as operating, investing, and financing activities. Transactions and other events characteristic of each kind of activity are described in the list below.

STUDY OBJECTIVE 2

Distinguish among operating, investing, and financing activities.

1. **Operating activities** include the cash effects of transactions that create revenues and expenses. They thus enter into the determination of net income.
2. **Investing activities** include (a) acquiring and disposing of investments and productive long-lived assets, and (b) lending money and collecting the loans.
3. **Financing activities** include (a) obtaining cash from issuing debt and repaying the amounts borrowed, and (b) obtaining cash from stockholders and providing them with a return on their investment.

The category of operating activities is the most important. As noted above, it shows the cash provided by company operations. This source of cash is generally considered to be the best measure of a company's ability to generate sufficient cash to continue as a going concern.

---

[1] "Statement of Cash Flows," *Statement of Financial Accounting Standards No. 95* (Stamford, Conn.: FASB, 1987).

Illustration 18-1 below lists typical cash receipts and cash payments within each of the three classifications. **Study the list carefully**. It will prove very useful in solving homework exercises and problems.

Illustration 18-1

Typical receipts and payments classified by business activity and shown in the statement of cash flows

HELPFUL HINT

Operating activities generally relate to changes in current assets and current liabilities. Investing activities generally relate to changes in noncurrent assets. Financing activities relate to changes in long-term liabilities and stockholders' equity accounts.

Types of Cash Inflows and Outflows

Operating activities
Cash inflows:
    From sale of goods or services.
    From returns on loans (interest received) and on equity
      securities (dividends received).
Cash outflows:
    To suppliers for inventory.
    To employees for services.
    To government for taxes.
    To lenders for interest.
    To others for expenses.

Investing activities
Cash inflows:
    From sale of property, plant, and equipment.
    From sale of debt or equity securities of other entities.
    From collection of principal on loans to other entities.
Cash outflows:
    To purchase property, plant, and equipment.
    To purchase debt or equity securities of other entities.
    To make loans to other entities.

Financing activities
Cash inflows:
    From sale of equity securities (company's own stock).
    From issuance of debt (bonds and notes).
Cash outflows:
    To stockholders as dividends.
    To redeem long-term debt or reacquire capital stock.

As you can see, some cash flows related to investing or financing activities are classified as operating activities. For example, receipts of investment revenue (interest and dividends) are classified as operating activities. So are payments of interest to lenders. Why are these considered operating activities? **Because these items are reported in the income statement, where results of operations are shown.**

Note the following general guidelines: (1) Operating activities involve income determination (income statement) items. (2) Investing activities involve cash flows resulting from changes in investments and long-term asset items. (3) Financing activities involve cash flows resulting from changes in long-term liability and stockholders' equity items.

SIGNIFICANT NONCASH ACTIVITIES

Not all of a company's significant activities involve cash. Examples of significant noncash activities are:

1. Issuance of common stock to purchase assets.
2. Conversion of bonds into common stock.
3. Issuance of debt to purchase assets.
4. Exchanges of plant assets.

Significant financing and investing activities that do not affect cash are not reported in the body of the statement of cash flows. However, these activities are reported in either a **separate schedule** at the bottom of the statement of cash flows or in a **separate note or supplementary schedule** to the financial statements.

The reporting of these noncash activities in a separate schedule satisfies the **full disclosure principle**. In solving homework assignments you should present significant noncash investing and financing activities in a separate schedule at the bottom of the statement of cash flows. (See lower section of Illustration 18-2, at the bottom of this page, for an example.)

ACCOUNTING IN ACTION   *Business Insight*

Net income is not the same as net cash provided by operating activities. The differences are illustrated by the following results from recent annual reports for the same fiscal year (all data are in millions of dollars).

Company	Net Income	Net Cash from Operations
Kmart Corporation	$ 518	$1,237
Wal-Mart Stores, Inc.	4,430	7,580
Gap Inc.	1,127	1,478
J.C. Penney Company, Inc.	594	1,058
Sears, Roebuck & Co.	1,048	3,090
The May Department Stores Company	849	1,505

Note the disparity among the companies that engaged in similar types of retail merchandising.

FORMAT OF THE STATEMENT OF CASH FLOWS

The general format of the statement of cash flows is the three activities discussed previously—operating, investing, and financing—plus the significant noncash investing and financing activities. A widely used form of the statement of cash flows is shown in Illustration 18-2.

COMPANY NAME **Statement of Cash Flows** **Period Covered**		
Cash flows from operating activities		
(List of individual items)	XX	
Net cash provided (used) by operating activities		XXX
Cash flows from investing activities		
(List of individual inflows and outflows)	XX	
Net cash provided (used) by investing activities		XXX
Cash flows from financing activities		
(List of individual inflows and outflows)	XX	
Net cash provided (used) by financing activities		XXX
Net increase (decrease) in cash		XXX
Cash at beginning of period		XXX
Cash at end of period		XXX
Noncash investing and financing activities		
(List of individual noncash transactions)		XXX

Illustration 18-2

Format of statement of cash flows

As illustrated, the cash flows from operating activities section always appears first. It is followed by the investing activities and the financing activities sections.

Note also that **the individual inflows and outflows from investing and financing activities are reported separately**. Thus, cash outflow for the purchase of property, plant, and equipment is reported separately from the cash inflow from the sale of property, plant, and equipment. Similarly, the cash inflow from the issuance of debt securities is reported separately from the cash outflow for the retirement of debt. If a company did not report the inflows and outflows separately, it would obscure the investing and financing activities of the enterprise. This would make it more difficult to assess future cash flows.

The reported operating, investing, and financing activities result in either net cash **provided or used** by each activity. The amounts of net cash provided or used by each activity then are totaled. The result is the net increase (decrease) in cash for the period. This amount is then added to or subtracted from the beginning-of-period cash balance. This gives the end-of-period cash balance. Finally, any significant noncash investing and financing activities are reported in a separate schedule, usually at the bottom of the statement.

USEFULNESS OF THE STATEMENT OF CASH FLOWS

The information in a statement of cash flows should help investors, creditors, and others assess the following aspects of the firm's financial position.

1. **The entity's ability to generate future cash flows.** By examining relationships between items in the statement of cash flows, investors and others can make predictions of the amounts, timing, and uncertainty of future cash flows better than they can from accrual basis data.

2. **The entity's ability to pay dividends and meet obligations.** If a company does not have adequate cash, employees cannot be paid, debts settled, or dividends paid. Employees, creditors, and stockholders should be particularly interested in this statement, because it alone shows the flows of cash in a business.

3. **The reasons for the difference between net income and net cash provided (used) by operating activities.** Net income provides information on the success or failure of a business enterprise. However, some are critical of accrual basis net income because it requires many estimates. As a result, the reliability of the number is often challenged. Such is not the case with cash. Many readers of the statement of cash flows want to know the reasons for the difference between net income and net cash provided by operating activities. Then they can assess for themselves the reliability of the income number.

4. **The cash investing and financing transactions during the period.** By examining a company's investing and financing transactions, a financial statement reader can better understand why assets and liabilities changed during the period.

In summary, the information in the statement of cash flows is useful in answering the following questions.

How did cash increase when there was a net loss for the period?

How were the proceeds of the bond issue used?

How was the expansion in the plant and equipment financed?

Why were dividends not increased?

How was the retirement of debt accomplished?

How much money was borrowed during the year?

Is cash flow greater or less than net income?

*E*THICS NOTE

Many investors believe that "Cash is cash and everything else is accounting." That is, they feel that cash flow is less susceptible to management manipulation than traditional accounting measures such as net income. Though we would discourage reliance on cash flows to the exclusion of accrual accounting, comparing cash from operations to net income can reveal important information about the "quality" of reported net income. Such a comparison can reveal the extent to which net income provides a good measure of actual performance.

HELPFUL HINT

Income from operations and cash flow from operating activities are different. Income from operations is based on accrual accounting; cash flow from operating activities is prepared on a cash basis.

PREPARING THE STATEMENT OF CASH FLOWS

The statement of cash flows is prepared differently from the three other basic financial statements. First, it is not prepared from an adjusted trial balance. The statement requires detailed information concerning the changes in account balances that occurred between two periods of time. An adjusted trial balance will not provide the necessary data. Second, the statement of cash flows deals with cash receipts and payments. As a result, **the accrual concept is not used in the preparation of a statement of cash flows**.

The information to prepare this statement usually comes from three sources:

- **Comparative balance sheets.** Information in the comparative balance sheets indicates the amount of the changes in assets, liabilities, and stockholders' equities from the beginning to the end of the period.

- **Current income statement.** Information in this statement helps determine the amount of cash provided or used by operations during the period.

- **Additional information.** Such information includes transaction data that are needed to determine how cash was provided or used during the period.

Preparing the statement of cash flows from these data sources involves three major steps, explained in Illustration 18-3.

Illustration 18-3

Three major steps in preparing the statement of cash flows

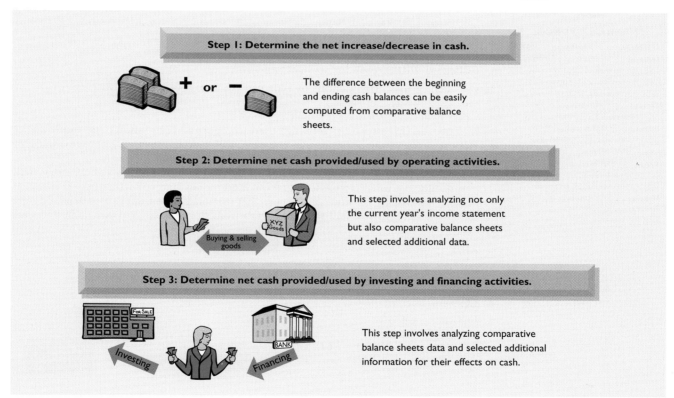

Step 1: Determine the net increase/decrease in cash.

The difference between the beginning and ending cash balances can be easily computed from comparative balance sheets.

Step 2: Determine net cash provided/used by operating activities.

This step involves analyzing not only the current year's income statement but also comparative balance sheets and selected additional data.

Buying & selling goods

Step 3: Determine net cash provided/used by investing and financing activities.

This step involves analyzing comparative balance sheets data and selected additional information for their effects on cash.

Investing   Financing

INDIRECT AND DIRECT METHODS

In order to perform step 2, **the operating activities section must be converted from an accrual basis to a cash basis**. This conversion may be done by either of two methods: (1) the indirect method or (2) the direct method. **Both methods arrive at the same total amount** for "Net cash provided by operating activities." They differ in disclosing the items that comprise the total amount.

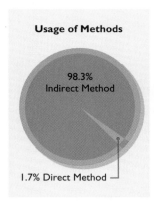

Usage of Methods

98.3%
Indirect Method

1.7% Direct Method

The indirect method is used extensively in practice, as shown in the nearby chart.[2] Companies (98%) favor the indirect method for two reasons: (1) It is easier to prepare, and (2) it focuses on the differences between net income and net cash flow from operating activities.

A minority of companies favor the direct method. This method shows operating cash receipts and payments, and so it is more consistent with the objective of a statement of cash flows. The FASB has expressed a preference for the direct method, but allows the use of either method. When the direct method is used, the net cash flow from operating activities as computed using the indirect method must also be reported in a separate schedule.

BEFORE YOU GO ON...

▶ *REVIEW IT*

1. What is the primary purpose of a statement of cash flows?
2. What are the major classifications of cash flows on the statement of cash flows?
3. Why is the statement of cash flows useful? What key information does it convey?
4. What are the three major steps in preparing a statement of cash flows?

▶ *DO IT*

During its first week of existence, Plano Molding Company had the following transactions.

1. Issued 100,000 shares of $5 par value common stock for $800,000 cash.
2. Borrowed $200,000 from Sandwich State Bank, signing a 5-year note bearing 8% interest.
3. Purchased two semi-trailer trucks for $170,000 cash.
4. Paid employees $12,000 for salaries and wages.
5. Collected $20,000 cash for services rendered.

Classify each of these transactions by type of cash flow activity.

ACTION PLAN

- Identify the three types of activities used to report all cash inflows and outflows.
- Report as operating activities the cash effects of transactions that create revenues and expenses and enter into the determination of net income.
- Report as investing activities transactions that (a) acquire and dispose of investments and productive long-lived assets, and (b) lend money and collect loans.
- Report as financing activities transactions that (a) obtain cash from issuing debt and repay the amounts borrowed, and (b) obtain cash from stockholders and pay them dividends.

SOLUTION

1. Financing activity.
2. Financing activity.
3. Investing activity.
4. Operating activity.
5. Operating activity.

Related exercise material: BE18-3, BE18-5, E18-1, and E18-6.

On the following pages, in two separate sections, we describe the use of the two methods. Section 1 illustrates the indirect method. Section 2 illustrates the direct method. These sections are independent of each other. *Only one or the other* **needs to be covered in order to understand and prepare the statement of cash flows. When you have finished the section assigned by your instructor, turn to the next topic—"Analysis of the Statement of Cash Flows" (on page 748).**

---

[2]*Accounting Trends and Techniques* survey of 600 companies indicated that 590 use the indirect method and 10 use the direct method.

SECTION 1 *Statement of Cash Flows— Indirect Method*

To explain and illustrate the indirect method, we will use the transactions of the Computer Services Company for two years, 2002 and 2003, to prepare annual statements of cash flows. We will show basic transactions in the first year, with additional transactions added in the second year.

STUDY OBJECTIVE 3

Prepare a statement of cash flows using the indirect method.

FIRST YEAR OF OPERATIONS—2002

Computer Services Company started on January 1, 2002. At that time it issued 50,000 shares of $1.00 par value common stock for $50,000 cash. The company rented its office space and furniture and performed consulting services throughout the first year. The comparative balance sheets at the beginning and end of 2002, showing changes in each account, appear in Illustration 18-4. The income statement and additional information for Computer Services Company are shown in Illustration 18-5.

COMPUTER SERVICES COMPANY Comparative Balance Sheets			
Assets	**Dec. 31, 2002**	**Jan. 1, 2002**	**Change Increase/Decrease**
Cash	$34,000	$ –0–	$34,000 Increase
Accounts receivable	30,000	–0–	30,000 Increase
Equipment	10,000	–0–	10,000 Increase
Total	$74,000	$ –0–	
Liabilities and Stockholders' Equity			
Accounts payable	$ 4,000	$ –0–	$ 4,000 Increase
Common stock	50,000	–0–	50,000 Increase
Retained earnings	20,000	–0–	20,000 Increase
Total	$74,000	$ –0–	

Illustration 18-4

Comparative balance sheets, 2002, with increases and decreases

HELPFUL HINT
Although each of the balance sheet items increased, their individual effects are not the same. Some of these increases are cash inflows, and some are cash outflows.

COMPUTER SERVICES COMPANY Income Statement For the Year Ended December 31, 2002	
Revenues	$85,000
Operating expenses	40,000
Income before income taxes	45,000
Income tax expense	10,000
Net income	$35,000

Additional information:
1. A dividend of $15,000 was declared and paid during the year.
2. The equipment was purchased at the end of 2002. No depreciation was taken in 2002.

Illustration 18-5

Income statement and additional information, 2002

STEP 1: DETERMINE THE NET INCREASE/DECREASE IN CASH

To prepare a statement of cash flows, the first step is to **determine the net increase or decrease in cash**. This is a simple computation. For example, Computer Services Company had no cash on hand at the beginning of 2002. It had $34,000 on hand at the end of 2002. Thus, the change in cash for 2002 was an increase of $34,000.

STEP 2: DETERMINE NET CASH PROVIDED/USED BY OPERATING ACTIVITIES

To determine net cash provided by operating activities under the indirect method, **net income is adjusted for items that did not affect cash**. A useful starting point is to understand **why** net income must be converted. Under generally accepted accounting principles, most companies use the accrual basis of accounting. As you have learned, this basis requires that revenue be recorded when earned and that expenses be recorded when incurred. Earned revenues may include credit sales that have not been collected in cash. Expenses incurred may not have been paid in cash. Thus, under the accrual basis of accounting, net income is not the same as net cash provided by operating activities. Therefore, under the indirect method, net income must be adjusted to convert certain items to the cash basis.

The **indirect method** (or reconciliation method) starts with net income and converts it to net cash provided by operating activities. In other words, **the indirect method adjusts net income for items that affected reported net income but did not affect cash**. Illustration 18-6 shows this adjustment. That is, noncash charges in the income statement are added back to net income. Likewise, noncash credits are deducted. The result is net cash provided by operating activities.

Illustration 18-6

Net income versus net cash provided by operating activities

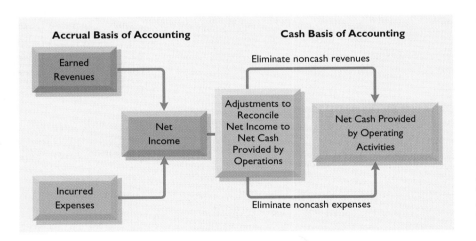

A useful starting point in identifying the adjustments to net income is the current asset and current liability accounts other than cash. Those accounts—receivables, payables, prepayments, and inventories—should be analyzed for their effects on cash.

Increase in Accounts Receivable

When accounts receivable increase during the year, revenues on an accrual basis are higher than revenues on a cash basis. In other words, operations of the period led to revenues, **but not all of these revenues resulted in an increase in cash**. Some of the revenues resulted in an increase in accounts receivable.

Illustration 18-7 shows that Computer Services Company had $85,000 in revenues, but it collected only $55,000 in cash. To convert net income to net cash provided by operating activities, the increase of $30,000 in accounts receivable must be deducted from net income.

Accounts Receivable				
1/1/02 Balance	–0–	**Receipts from customers**	**55,000**
Revenues	**85,000**		
12/31/02 Balance	30,000		

Illustration 18-7

Analysis of accounts receivable

Increase in Accounts Payable

In the first year, operating expenses incurred on account were credited to Accounts Payable. When accounts payable increase during the year, operating expenses on an accrual basis are higher than they are on a cash basis. For Computer Services, operating expenses reported in the income statement were $40,000. But, since Accounts Payable increased $4,000, only $36,000 ($40,000 − $4,000) of the expenses were paid in cash. To adjust net income to net cash provided by operating activities, the increase of $4,000 in accounts payable must be added to net income. A T-account analysis indicates that payments to creditors are less than operating expenses.

Accounts Payable				
Payments to creditors	**36,000**	1/1/02 Balances	–0–
		Operating expenses	**40,000**
		12/31/02 Balance	4,000

Illustration 18-8

Analysis of accounts payable

For Computer Services, the changes in accounts receivable and accounts payable were the only changes in current asset and current liability accounts. This means that any other revenues or expenses reported in the income statement were received or paid in cash. Thus, the income tax expense of $10,000 was paid in cash, and no adjustment of net income is necessary.

The operating activities section of the statement of cash flows for Computer Services Company is shown in Illustration 18-9.

COMPUTER SERVICES COMPANY **Statement of Cash Flows—Indirect Method (partial)** **For the Year Ended December 31, 2002**		
Cash flows from operating activities		
Net income		$35,000
Adjustments to reconcile net income to net cash		
provided by operating activities:		
Increase in accounts receivable	$(30,000)	
Increase in accounts payable	4,000	(26,000)
Net cash provided by operating activities		**$ 9,000**

Illustration 18-9

Presentation of net cash provided by operating activities, 2002—indirect method

STEP 3: DETERMINE NET CASH PROVIDED/USED BY INVESTING AND FINANCING ACTIVITIES

The third and final step in preparing the statement of cash flows begins with a study of the balance sheet. We look at it to determine changes in noncurrent accounts. The change in each noncurrent account is then analyzed to determine the effect, if any, the change had on cash.

In Computer Services Company, the three noncurrent accounts are Equipment, Common Stock, and Retained Earnings. All three have increased during the year. What caused these increases? No transaction data are given in the balance sheet for the increases in Equipment of $10,000 and Common Stock of $50,000. In solving your homework, you should assume that **any unexplained differences in noncurrent accounts involve cash**. Thus, the increase in Equipment is assumed to be a purchase of equipment for $10,000 cash. This purchase of equipment is reported as a cash outflow in the investing activities section of the statement of cash flows. The increase in Common Stock is assumed to result from the issuance of common stock for $50,000 cash. The issuance of common stock is reported as an inflow of cash in the financing activities section.

What caused the net increase of $20,000 in the Retained Earnings account? First, net income increased retained earnings by $35,000. Second, the additional information provided below the income statement in Illustration 18-5 indicates that a cash dividend of $15,000 was declared and paid.

This analysis can also be made directly from the Retained Earnings account in the ledger of Computer Services Company, as shown in Illustration 18-10.

Illustration 18-10

Analysis of retained earnings

	Retained Earnings	
12/31/02 Cash dividend 15,000	1/1/02 Balance	–0–
	12/31/02 Net income	35,000
	12/31/02 Balance	20,000

The $20,000 increase in Retained Earnings in 2002 is a **net** change. When a net change in a noncurrent balance sheet account has occurred during the year, it generally is necessary to report the individual items that cause the net change. Therefore, the $35,000 increase due to net income is reported in the operating activities section. The cash dividend paid is reported in the financing activities section.

STATEMENT OF CASH FLOWS—2002

We now can prepare the statement of cash flows. The statement starts with the operating activities, followed by the investing activities, and then the financing activities. The 2002 statement of cash flows for Computer Services is shown in Illustration 18-11.

Computer Services' statement of cash flows for 2002 shows the following: Operating activities **provided** $9,000 cash. Investing activities **used** $10,000 cash. Financing activities **provided** $35,000 cash. The increase in cash of $34,000 reported in the statement of cash flows agrees with the increase of $34,000 shown as the change in the cash account in the comparative balance sheets.

COMPUTER SERVICES COMPANY
Statement of Cash Flows—Indirect Method
For the Year Ended December 31, 2002

Cash flows from operating activities		
Net income		$35,000
Adjustments to reconcile net income to net cash provided by operating activities:		
Increase in accounts receivable	$(30,000)	
Increase in accounts payable	4,000	(26,000)
Net cash provided by operating activities		9,000
Cash flows from investing activities		
Purchase of equipment	(10,000)	
Net cash used by investing activities		(10,000)
Cash flows from financing activities		
Issuance of common stock	50,000	
Payment of cash dividends	(15,000)	
Net cash provided by financing activities		35,000
Net increase in cash		34,000
Cash at beginning of period		–0–
Cash at end of period		$34,000

Illustration 18-11

Statement of cash flows, 2002—indirect method

SECOND YEAR OF OPERATIONS—2003

Illustrations 18-12 and 18-13 present information related to the second year of operations for Computer Services Company.

COMPUTER SERVICES COMPANY
Comparative Balance Sheets
December 31

Assets	2003	2002	Change Increase/Decrease
Cash	$ 56,000	$34,000	$ 22,000 Increase
Accounts receivable	20,000	30,000	10,000 Decrease
Prepaid expenses	4,000	–0–	4,000 Increase
Land	130,000	–0–	130,000 Increase
Building	160,000	–0–	160,000 Increase
Accumulated depreciation—building	(11,000)	–0–	11,000 Increase
Equipment	27,000	10,000	17,000 Increase
Accumulated depreciation—equipment	(3,000)	–0–	3,000 Increase
Total	$383,000	$74,000	
Liabilities and Stockholders' Equity			
Accounts payable	$ 59,000	$ 4,000	$ 55,000 Increase
Bonds payable	130,000	–0–	130,000 Increase
Common stock	50,000	50,000	–0–
Retained earnings	144,000	20,000	124,000 Increase
Total	$383,000	$74,000	

Illustration 18-12

Comparative balance sheets, 2003, with increases and decreases

Illustration 18-13
Income statement and additional information, 2003

COMPUTER SERVICES COMPANY Income Statement For the Year Ended December 31, 2003		
Revenues		$507,000
Operating expenses (excluding depreciation)	$261,000	
Depreciation expense	15,000	
Loss on sale of equipment	3,000	279,000
Income from operations		228,000
Income tax expense		89,000
Net income		$139,000

Additional information:
1. In 2003, the company declared and paid a $15,000 cash dividend.
2. The company obtained land through the issuance of $130,000 of long-term bonds.
3. A building costing $160,000 was purchased for cash. Equipment costing $25,000 was also purchased for cash.
4. During 2003, the company sold equipment with a book value of $7,000 (cost $8,000, less accumulated depreciation $1,000) for $4,000 cash.

STEP 1: DETERMINE THE NET INCREASE/ DECREASE IN CASH

To prepare a statement of cash flows from this information, the first step is to **determine the net increase or decrease in cash**. As indicated from the information presented, cash increased $22,000 ($56,000 − $34,000).

STEP 2: DETERMINE NET CASH PROVIDED/USED BY OPERATING ACTIVITIES

As in step 2 in 2002, net income on an accrual basis must be adjusted to arrive at net cash provided/used by operating activities. Explanations for the adjustments to net income for Computer Services in 2003 follow.

Decrease in Accounts Receivable

Accounts receivable decreases during the period because cash receipts are higher than revenues reported on the accrual basis. To adjust net income to net cash provided by operating activities, the decrease of $10,000 in accounts receivable must be added to net income.

Increase in Prepaid Expenses

Prepaid expenses increase during a period because cash paid for expenses is higher than expenses reported on the accrual basis. Cash payments have been made in the current period, but expenses (as charges to the income statement) have been deferred to future periods. To adjust net income to net cash provided by operating activities, the $4,000 increase in prepaid expenses must be deducted from net income. An increase in prepaid expenses results in a decrease in cash during the period.

Increase in Accounts Payable

Like the increase in 2002, the 2003 increase of $55,000 in accounts payable must be added to net income to convert to net cash provided by operating activities.

Depreciation Expense

During 2003, the company reported depreciation expense of $15,000. Of this amount, $11,000 related to the building and $4,000 to the equipment. These two amounts were determined by analyzing the accumulated depreciation accounts in the balance sheets.

INCREASE IN ACCUMULATED DEPRECIATION—BUILDING. The Accumulated Depreciation—Building account increased $11,000. This change represents the depreciation expense on the building for the year. **Depreciation expense is a noncash charge. So it is added back to net income** in order to arrive at net cash provided by operating activities.

INCREASE IN ACCUMULATED DEPRECIATION—EQUIPMENT. The Accumulated Depreciation—Equipment account increased $3,000. But this change does not represent depreciation expense for the year. The additional information at the bottom of the income statement indicates why not: This account was decreased (debited $1,000) as a result of the sale of some equipment. Thus depreciation expense for 2003 was $4,000 ($3,000 + $1,000). That amount is added to net income to determine net cash provided by operating activities. The T-account below provides information about the changes that occurred in this account in 2003.

Accumulated Depreciation—Equipment				
Accumulated depreciation on equipment sold	1,000	1/1/03	Balance	–0–
			Depreciation expense	**4,000**
		12/31/03	Balance	3,000

Illustration 18-14

Analysis of accumulated depreciation—equipment

Depreciation expense on the building ($11,000) plus depreciation expense on the equipment ($4,000) equals the depreciation expense of $15,000 reported in the income statement.

Other charges to expense that do not require the use of cash, such as the amortization of intangible assets and depletion expense, are treated in the same way as depreciation. Depreciation and similar noncash charges are frequently listed in the statement of cash flows as the first adjustments to net income.

Loss on Sale of Equipment

In the income statement, Computer Services Company reported a $3,000 loss on the sale of equipment (book value $7,000, less cash proceeds $4,000). The loss reduced net income but **did not reduce cash.** So the loss is **added to net income** in determining net cash provided by operating activities.[3]

As a result of the previous adjustments, net cash provided by operating activities is $218,000, as computed in Illustration 18-15.

---

[3]If a gain on sale occurs, a different situation results. To allow a gain to flow through to net cash provided by operating activities would be double-counting the gain—once in net income and again in the investing activities section as part of the cash proceeds from sale. As a result, a gain is deducted from net income in reporting net cash provided by operating activities.

COMPUTER SERVICES COMPANY Statement of Cash Flows—Indirect Method (partial) For the Year Ended December 31, 2003		
Cash flows from operating activities		
Net income		$139,000
Adjustments to reconcile net income to net cash provided by operating activities:		
Depreciation expense	$15,000	
Loss on sale of equipment	3,000	
Decrease in accounts receivable	10,000	
Increase in prepaid expenses	(4,000)	
Increase in accounts payable	55,000	79,000
Net cash provided by operating activities		**$218,000**

STEP 3: DETERMINE NET CASH PROVIDED/USED BY INVESTING AND FINANCING ACTIVITIES

The next step involves analyzing the remaining changes in balance sheet accounts to determine net cash provided (used) by investing and financing activities.

Increase in Land

As indicated from the change in the Land account and the additional information, land of $130,000 was purchased through the issuance of long-term bonds. The issuance of bonds payable for land has no effect on cash. But it is a significant non-cash investing and financing activity that merits disclosure in a separate schedule.

Increase in Building

As the additional data indicate, an office building was acquired for $160,000 cash. This is a cash outflow reported in the investing section.

Increase in Equipment

The Equipment account increased $17,000. The additional information explains that this was a net increase that resulted from two transactions: (1) a purchase of equipment of $25,000 and (2) the sale for $4,000 of equipment costing $8,000. These transactions are classified as investing activities. Each transaction should be reported separately. Thus the purchase of equipment should be reported as an outflow of cash for $25,000. The sale should be reported as an inflow of cash for $4,000. The T-account below shows the reasons for the change in this account during the year.

Illustration 18-16

Analysis of equipment

Equipment					
1/1/03	Balance	10,000		Cost of equipment sold	8,000
	Purchase of equipment	**25,000**			
12/31/03	Balance	27,000			

The following entry shows the details of the equipment sale transaction.

A	=	L	+	OE
+4,000				−3,000
+1,000				
−8,000				

Cash	4,000	
Accumulated Depreciation	1,000	
Loss on Sale of Equipment	3,000	
Equipment		8,000

Increase in Bonds Payable

The Bonds Payable account increased $130,000. As indicated in the additional information, land was acquired from the issuance of these bonds. This noncash transaction is reported in a separate schedule at the bottom of the statement.

Increase in Retained Earnings

Retained earnings increased $124,000 during the year. This increase can be explained by two factors: (1) Net income of $139,000 increased retained earnings. (2) Dividends of $15,000 decreased retained earnings. Net income is adjusted to net cash provided by operating activities in the operating activities section. Payment of the dividends is a **cash outflow that is reported as a financing activity**.

STATEMENT OF CASH FLOWS—2003

Combining the previous items, we obtain a statement of cash flows for 2003 for Computer Services Company as presented in Illustration 18-17.

HELPFUL HINT
When stocks or bonds are issued for cash, the actual proceeds will appear in the statement of cash flows as a financing inflow (rather than the par value of the stocks or face value of bonds).

HELPFUL HINT
It is the **payment** of dividends, not the declaration, that appears in the cash flow statement.

Illustration 18-17

Statement of cash flows, 2003—indirect method

COMPUTER SERVICES COMPANY Statement of Cash Flows—Indirect Method For the Year Ended December 31, 2003		
Cash flows from operating activities		
Net income		$139,000
Adjustments to reconcile net income to net cash provided by operating activities:		
Depreciation expense	$ 15,000	
Loss on sale of equipment	3,000	
Decrease in accounts receivable	10,000	
Increase in prepaid expenses	(4,000)	
Increase in accounts payable	55,000	79,000
Net cash provided by operating activities		218,000
Cash flows from investing activities		
Purchase of building	(160,000)	
Purchase of equipment	(25,000)	
Sale of equipment	4,000	
Net cash used by investing activities		(181,000)
Cash flows from financing activities		
Payment of cash dividends	(15,000)	
Net cash used by financing activities		(15,000)
Net increase in cash		22,000
Cash at beginning of period		34,000
Cash at end of period		$ 56,000
Noncash investing and financing activities		
Issuance of bonds payable to purchase land		$130,000

HELPFUL HINT
Note that in the investing and financing activities sections, positive numbers indicate cash inflows (receipts), and negative numbers indicate cash outflows (payments).

SUMMARY OF CONVERSION TO NET CASH PROVIDED BY OPERATING ACTIVITIES—INDIRECT METHOD

As shown in the previous illustrations, the statement of cash flows prepared by the indirect method starts with net income. It then adds (or deducts) items not affecting cash, to arrive at net cash provided by operating activities. The additions and deductions consist of (1) changes in specific current assets and current liabilities and (2) noncash charges reported in the income statement. A summary of the adjustments for current assets and current liabilities is provided in Illustration 18-18.

Illustration 18-18

Adjustments for current assets and current liabilities

Current Assets and Current Liabilities	Adjustments to Convert Net Income to Net Cash Provided by Operating Activities	
	Add to Net Income a(n):	Deduct from Net Income a(n):
Accounts receivable	Decrease	Increase
Inventory	Decrease	Increase
Prepaid expenses	Decrease	Increase
Accounts payable	Increase	Decrease
Accrued expenses payable	Increase	Decrease

Adjustments for the noncash charges reported in the income statement are made as shown in Illustration 18-19.

Illustration 18-19

Adjustments for noncash charges

Noncash Charges	Adjustments to Convert Net Income to Net Cash Provided by Operating Activities
Depreciation expense	Add
Patent amortization expense	Add
Depletion expense	Add
Loss on sale of asset	Add

B E F O R E   Y O U   G O   O N . . .

▶ *REVIEW IT*

1. What is the format of the operating activities section of the statement of cash flows using the indirect method?
2. Where is depreciation expense shown on a statement of cash flows using the indirect method?
3. Where are significant noncash investing and financing activities shown in a statement of cash flows? Give some examples.
4. Which method of computing net cash provided by operating activities does **Lands' End** use? What single item used the largest amount of cash outflow for Lands' End in the fiscal year ended January 28, 2000? The answers to these questions are provided on page 777.

▶ *DO IT*

Presented below is information related to Reynolds Company. Use it to prepare a statement of cash flows using the indirect method.

REYNOLDS COMPANY
Comparative Balance Sheets
December 31

Assets	2003	2002	Change Increase/Decrease
Cash	$ 54,000	$ 37,000	$ 17,000 Increase
Accounts receivable	68,000	26,000	42,000 Increase
Inventories	54,000	–0–	54,000 Increase
Prepaid expenses	4,000	6,000	2,000 Decrease
Land	45,000	70,000	25,000 Decrease
Buildings	200,000	200,000	–0–
Accumulated depreciation—buildings	(21,000)	(11,000)	10,000 Increase
Equipment	193,000	68,000	125,000 Increase
Accumulated depreciation—equipment	(28,000)	(10,000)	18,000 Increase
Totals	$569,000	$386,000	

Liabilities and Stockholders' Equity			
Accounts payable	$ 23,000	$ 40,000	$ 17,000 Decrease
Accrued expenses payable	10,000	–0–	10,000 Increase
Bonds payable	110,000	150,000	40,000 Decrease
Common stock ($1 par)	220,000	60,000	160,000 Increase
Retained earnings	206,000	136,000	70,000 Increase
Totals	$569,000	$386,000	

REYNOLDS COMPANY
Income Statement
For the Year Ended December 31, 2003

Revenues		$890,000
Cost of goods sold	$465,000	
Operating expenses	221,000	
Interest expense	12,000	
Loss on sale of equipment	2,000	700,000
Income from operations		190,000
Income tax expense		65,000
Net income		$125,000

Additional information:
1. Operating expenses include depreciation expense of $33,000 and charges from prepaid expenses of $2,000.
2. Land was sold at its book value for cash.
3. Cash dividends of $55,000 were declared and paid in 2003.
4. Interest expense of $12,000 was paid in cash.
5. Equipment with a cost of $166,000 was purchased for cash. Equipment with a cost of $41,000 and a book value of $36,000 was sold for $34,000 cash.
6. Bonds of $10,000 were redeemed at their book value for cash. Bonds of $30,000 were converted into common stock.
7. Common stock ($1 par) of $130,000 was issued for cash.
8. Accounts payable pertain to merchandise suppliers.

ACTION PLAN

- Determine the net increase/decrease in cash.
- Determine net cash provided/used by operating activities by adjusting net income for items that did not affect cash.
- Determine net cash provided/used by investing activities.
- Determine net cash provided/used by financing activities.

SOLUTION

HELPFUL HINT

1. Determine net cash provided/used by operating activities, recognizing that operating activities generally relate to changes in current assets and current liabilities.
2. Determine net cash provided/used by investing activities, recognizing that investing activities generally relate to changes in noncurrent assets.
3. Determine net cash provided/used by financing activities, recognizing that financing activities generally relate to changes in long-term liabilities and stockholders' equity accounts.

REYNOLDS COMPANY
Statement of Cash Flows—Indirect Method
For the Year Ended December 31, 2003

Cash flows from operating activities		
Net income		$125,000
Adjustments to reconcile net income to net cash provided by operating activities:		
Depreciation expense	$ 33,000	
Increase in accounts receivable	(42,000)	
Increase in inventories	(54,000)	
Decrease in prepaid expenses	2,000	
Decrease in accounts payable	(17,000)	
Increase in accrued expenses payable	10,000	
Loss on sale of equipment	2,000	(66,000)
Net cash provided by operating activities		59,000
Cash flows from investing activities		
Sale of land	25,000	
Sale of equipment	34,000	
Purchase of equipment	(166,000)	
Net cash used by investing activities		(107,000)
Cash flows from financing activities		
Redemption of bonds	(10,000)	
Sale of common stock	130,000	
Payment of dividends	(55,000)	
Net cash provided by financing activities		65,000
Net increase in cash		17,000
Cash at beginning of period		37,000
Cash at end of period		$ 54,000
Noncash investing and financing activities		
Conversion of bonds into common stock		$ 30,000

Related exercise material: BE18-1, BE18-2, BE18-4, E18-2, E18-3, E18-4, and E18-5.

☑ THE NAVIGATOR

Note: This concludes Section 1 on preparation of the statement of cash flows using the indirect method. Unless your instructor assigns Section 2, you should turn to the concluding section of the chapter, "Analysis of the Statement of Cash Flows," on page 748.

> ## SECTION 2 *Statement of Cash Flows—Direct Method*

To explain and illustrate the direct method, we will use the transactions of Juarez Company for two years, 2002 and 2003, to prepare annual statements of cash flow. We will show basic transactions in the first year, with additional transactions added in the second year.

STUDY OBJECTIVE 4

Prepare a statement of cash flows using the direct method.

*F*IRST YEAR OF OPERATIONS—2002

Juarez Company began business on January 1, 2002. At that time it issued 300,000 shares of $1 par value common stock for $300,000 cash. The company rented office and sales space along with equipment. The comparative balance sheets at the beginning and end of 2002, showing changes in each account, appear in Illustration 18-20. The income statement and additional information for Juarez Company are shown in Illustration 18-21.

JUAREZ COMPANY			
Comparative Balance Sheet			
Assets	**Dec. 31, 2002**	**Jan. 1, 2002**	**Change Increase/Decrease**
Cash	$159,000	$–0–	$159,000 Increase
Accounts receivable	15,000	–0–	15,000 Increase
Inventory	160,000	–0–	160,000 Increase
Prepaid expenses	8,000	–0–	8,000 Increase
Land	80,000	–0–	80,000 Increase
Total	$422,000	$–0–	
Liabilities and Stockholders' Equity			
Accounts payable	$ 60,000	$–0–	$ 60,000 Increase
Accrued expenses payable	20,000	–0–	20,000 Increase
Common stock	300,000	–0–	300,000 Increase
Retained earnings	42,000	–0–	42,000 Increase
Total	$422,000	$–0–	

Illustration 18-20

Comparative balance sheet, 2002, with increases and decreases

JUAREZ COMPANY	
Income Statement	
For the Year Ended December 31, 2002	
Revenues	$780,000
Cost of goods sold	450,000
Gross profit	330,000
Operating expenses	170,000
Income before income taxes	160,000
Income tax expense	48,000
Net income	$112,000

Additional information:
1. Dividends of $70,000 were declared and paid in cash.
2. The accounts payable increase resulted from the purchase of merchandise.

Illustration 18-21

Income statement and additional information, 2002

The three steps cited on page 721 for preparing the statement of cash flows are used in the direct method.

STEP 1: DETERMINE THE NET INCREASE/ DECREASE IN CASH

The comparative balance sheets for Juarez Company show a zero cash balance at January 1, 2002, and a cash balance of $159,000 at December 31, 2002. Thus, the change in cash for 2002 was a net increase of $159,000.

STEP 2: DETERMINE NET CASH PROVIDED/USED BY OPERATING ACTIVITIES

Under the **direct method**, net cash provided by operating activities is computed by **adjusting each item in the income statement** from the accrual basis to the cash basis. To simplify and condense the operating activities section, **only major classes of operating cash receipts and cash payments are reported**. For these major classes, the difference between cash receipts and cash payments is the net cash provided by operating activities. These relationships are as shown in Illustration 18-22.

Illustration 18-22

Major classes of cash receipts and payments

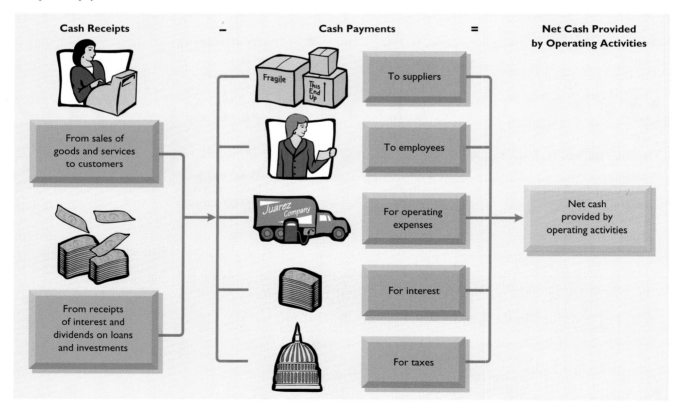

An efficient way to apply the direct method is to analyze the items reported in the income statement in the order in which they are listed. Cash receipts and cash payments related to these revenues and expenses are then determined. The direct method adjustments for Juarez Company in 2002 to determine net cash provided by operating activities are presented on the following pages.

Cash Receipts from Customers

The income statement for Juarez Company reported revenues from customers of $780,000. How much of that was cash receipts? To answer that, it is necessary to consider the change in accounts receivable during the year. When accounts receivable increase during the year, revenues on an accrual basis are higher than cash receipts from customers. Operations led to revenues, but not all of these revenues resulted in cash receipts. To determine the amount of cash receipts, the increase in accounts receivable is deducted from sales revenues. On the other hand, there may be a decrease in accounts receivable. That would occur if cash receipts from customers exceeded sales revenues. In that case, the decrease in accounts receivable is added to sales revenues.

For Juarez Company, accounts receivable increased $15,000. Thus, cash receipts from customers were $765,000, computed as follows.

Revenues from sales	$780,000
Deduct: Increase in accounts receivable	15,000
Cash receipts from customers	**$765,000**

Illustration 18-23

Computation of cash receipts from customers

Cash receipts from customers may also be determined from an analysis of the Accounts Receivable account, as shown in Illustration 18-24.

Accounts Receivable					
1/1/02	Balance	–0–	**Receipts from customers**		**765,000**
	Revenues from sales	780,000			
12/31/02	Balance	15,000			

Illustration 18-24

Analysis of accounts receivable

> **HELPFUL HINT**
> The T-account shows that revenue less increase in receivables equals cash receipts.

The relationships among cash receipts from customers, revenues from sales, and changes in accounts receivable are shown in Illustration 18-25.

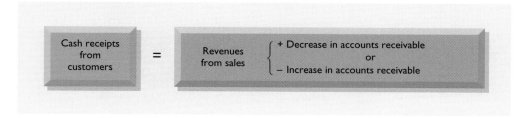

Illustration 18-25

Formula to compute cash receipts from customers—direct method

Cash Payments to Suppliers

Juarez Company reported cost of goods sold of $450,000 on its income statement. How much of that was cash payments to suppliers? To answer that, it is first necessary to find purchases for the year. To find purchases, cost of goods sold is adjusted for the change in inventory. When inventory increases during the year, purchases for the year have exceeded cost of goods sold. As a result, to determine the amount of purchases, the increase in inventory is added to cost of goods sold.

In 2002, Juarez Company's inventory increased $160,000. Purchases are computed as follows.

Illustration 18-26

Computation of purchases

Cost of goods sold	$450,000
Add: Increase in inventory	160,000
Purchases	**$610,000**

After purchases are computed, cash payments to suppliers can be determined. This is done by adjusting purchases for the change in accounts payable. When accounts payable increase during the year, purchases on an accrual basis are higher than they are on a cash basis. As a result, to determine cash payments to suppliers, an increase in accounts payable is deducted from purchases. On the other hand, there may be a decrease in accounts payable. That would occur if cash payments to suppliers exceed purchases. In that case, the decrease in accounts payable is added to purchases.

For Juarez Company, cash payments to suppliers were $550,000, computed as follows.

Illustration 18-27

Computation of cash payments to suppliers

Purchases	$610,000
Deduct: Increase in accounts payable	60,000
Cash payments to suppliers	**$550,000**

Cash payments to suppliers may also be determined from an analysis of the Accounts Payable account as shown in Illustration 18-28.

Illustration 18-28

Analysis of accounts payable

Accounts Payable			
Payments to suppliers **550,000**	1/1/02 Balance		–0–
		Purchases	610,000
	12/31/02 Balance		60,000

Illustration 18-29

Formula to compute cash payments to suppliers—direct method

The relationships among cash payments to suppliers, cost of goods sold, changes in inventory, and changes in accounts payable are shown in the following formula.

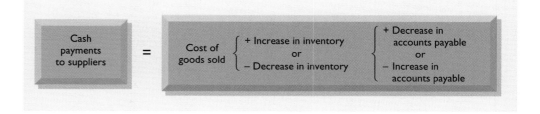

Cash Payments for Operating Expenses

Operating expenses of $170,000 were reported on Juarez's income statement. How much of that amount was cash paid for operating expenses? To answer that, we need to adjust this amount for any changes in prepaid expenses and accrued expenses payable. For example, when prepaid expenses increased $8,000 during the year, cash paid for operating expenses was $8,000 higher than operating expenses reported on the income statement. To convert operating expenses to cash payments for operating expenses, the increase must be added to operating expenses.

On the other hand, if prepaid expenses decrease during the year, the decrease must be deducted from operating expenses.

Operating expenses must also be adjusted for changes in accrued expenses payable. When accrued expenses payable increase during the year, operating expenses on an accrual basis are higher than they are in a cash basis. As a result, to determine cash payments for operating expenses, an increase in accrued expenses payable is deducted from operating expenses. On the other hand, a decrease in accrued expenses payable is added to operating expenses because cash payments exceed operating expenses.

Juarez Company's cash payments for operating expenses were $158,000, computed as follows.

> **Increase in prepaid expenses** indicates that the amount paid for the prepayments exceeded the amount that was recorded as an expense.
> **Decrease in prepaid expenses** indicates that the amount recorded as an expense exceeded the amount of cash paid for the prepayments.
> **Increase in accounts payable** indicates that expenses incurred exceed the cash paid for expenses that period.

Operating expenses	$170,000
Add: Increase in prepaid expenses	8,000
Deduct: Increase in accrued expenses payable	(20,000)
Cash payments for operating expenses	**$158,000**

Illustration 18-30

Computation of cash payments for operating expenses

The relationships among cash payments for operating expenses, changes in prepaid expenses, and changes in accrued expenses payable are shown in the following formula.

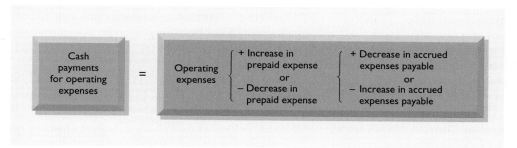

Illustration 18-31

Formula to compute cash payments for operating expenses—direct method

Cash Payments for Income Taxes

The income statement for Juarez shows income tax expense of $48,000. This amount equals the cash paid. The comparative balance sheets indicated no income taxes payable at either the beginning or end of the year.

All of the revenues and expenses in the 2002 income statement have now been adjusted to a cash basis. The operating activities section of the statement of cash flows is as follows.

Illustration 18-32

Operating activities section—direct method

JUAREZ COMPANY Statement of Cash Flows—Direct Method (partial) For the Year Ended December 31, 2002		
Cash flows from operating activities		
Cash receipts from customers		$765,000
Cash payments:		
To suppliers	$550,000	
For operating expenses	158,000	
For income taxes	48,000	756,000
Net cash provided by operating activities		**$ 9,000**

STEP 3: DETERMINE NET CASH PROVIDED/USED BY INVESTING AND FINANCING ACTIVITIES

Preparing the investing and financing activities sections of the statement of cash flows begins by determining the changes in noncurrent accounts reported in the comparative balance sheets. The change in each account is then analyzed to determine the effect, if any, the change had on cash.

Increase in Land

No additional information is given for the increase in land. In such case, you should assume that the increase affected cash. In solving homework problems, you should assume that **any unexplained differences in noncurrent accounts involve cash**. The purchase of land is an investing activity. Thus, an outflow of cash of $80,000 for the purchase of land should be reported in the investing activities section.

Increase in Common Stock

As indicated earlier, 300,000 shares of $1 par value stock were sold for $300,000 cash. The issuance of common stock is a financing activity. Thus, a cash inflow of $300,000 from the issuance of common stock is reported in the financing activities section.

Increase in Retained Earnings

What caused the net increase of $42,000 in the Retained Earnings account? First, net income increased retained earnings by $112,000. Second, the additional information section indicates that a cash dividend of $70,000 was declared and paid. The adjustment of revenues and expenses to arrive at net cash provided by operations was done in step 2 above. The cash dividend paid is reported as an outflow of cash in the financing activities section.

This analysis can also be made directly from the Retained Earnings account in the ledger of Juarez Company as shown in Illustration 18-33.

Illustration 18-33

Analysis of retained earnings

Retained Earnings				
12/31/02	Cash dividend	70,000	1/1/02 Balance	–0–
			12/31/02 Net income	112,000
			12/31/02 Balance	42,000

The $42,000 increase in Retained Earnings in 2002 is a net change. When a net change in a noncurrent balance sheet account has occurred during the year, it generally is necessary to report the individual items that cause the net change.

STATEMENT OF CASH FLOWS—2002

We can now prepare the statement of cash flows. The operating activities section is reported first, followed by the investing and financing activities sections. The statement of cash flows for Juarez Company for 2002 is shown in Illustration 18-34.

The statement of cash flows shows the following: Operating activities **provided** $9,000 of the net increase in cash. Investing activities **used** $80,000 of cash. Financing activities **provided** $230,000 of cash. The $159,000 net increase in cash for the year agrees with the increase in cash of $159,000 reported in the comparative balance sheets.

JUAREZ COMPANY Statement of Cash Flows—Direct Method For the Year Ended December 31, 2002			
Cash flows from operating activities			
Cash receipts from customers			$765,000
Cash payments:			
To suppliers		$550,000	
For operating expenses		158,000	
For income taxes		48,000	756,000
Net cash provided by operating activities			9,000
Cash flows from investing activities			
Purchase of land		(80,000)	
Net cash used by investing activities			(80,000)
Cash flows from financing activities			
Issuance of common stock		300,000	
Payment of cash dividend		(70,000)	
Net cash provided by financing activities			230,000
Net increase in cash			159,000
Cash at beginning of period			–0–
Cash at end of period			$159,000

Illustration 18-34

Statement of cash flows, 2002—direct method

HELPFUL HINT

Note that in the investing and financing activities sections, positive numbers indicate cash inflows (receipts), and negative numbers indicate cash outflows (payments).

SECOND YEAR OF OPERATIONS—2003

Illustrations 18-35 and 18-36 present information related to the second year of operations for Juarez Company.

JUAREZ COMPANY Comparative Balance Sheets December 31			
Assets	**2003**	**2002**	**Change Increase/Decrease**
Cash	$191,000	$159,000	$ 32,000 Increase
Accounts receivable	12,000	15,000	3,000 Decrease
Inventory	130,000	160,000	30,000 Decrease
Prepaid expenses	6,000	8,000	2,000 Decrease
Land	180,000	80,000	100,000 Increase
Equipment	160,000	–0–	160,000 Increase
Accumulated depreciation—equipment	(16,000)	–0–	16,000 Increase
Total	$663,000	$422,000	
Liabilities and Stockholders' Equity			
Accounts payable	$ 52,000	$ 60,000	$ 8,000 Decrease
Accrued expenses payable	15,000	20,000	5,000 Decrease
Income taxes payable	12,000	–0–	12,000 Increase
Bonds payable	90,000	–0–	90,000 Increase
Common stock	400,000	300,000	100,000 Increase
Retained earnings	94,000	42,000	52,000 Increase
Total	$663,000	$422,000	

Illustration 18-35

Comparative balance sheets, 2003, with increases and decreases

Illustration 18-36

Income statement and additional information, 2003

JUAREZ COMPANY		
Income Statement		
For the Year Ended December 31, 2003		
Revenues		$975,000
Cost of goods sold	$660,000	
Operating expenses (excluding depreciation)	176,000	
Depreciation expense	18,000	
Loss on sale of store equipment	1,000	855,000
Income before income taxes		120,000
Income tax expense		36,000
Net income		$ 84,000

Additional information:
1. In 2003, the company declared and paid a $32,000 cash dividend.
2. Bonds were issued at face value for $90,000 in cash.
3. Equipment costing $180,000 was purchased for cash.
4. Equipment costing $20,000 was sold for $17,000 cash when the book value of the equipment was $18,000.
5. Common stock of $100,000 was issued to acquire land.

STEP 1: DETERMINE THE NET INCREASE/ DECREASE IN CASH

The comparative balance sheets show a beginning cash balance of $159,000 and an ending cash balance of $191,000. Thus, there was a net increase in cash in 2003 of $32,000.

STEP 2: DETERMINE NET CASH PROVIDED/USED BY OPERATING ACTIVITIES

Cash Receipts from Customers

Revenues from sales were $975,000. Since accounts receivable decreased $3,000, cash receipts from customers were greater than sales revenues. Cash receipts from customers were $978,000, computed as follows.

Illustration 18-37

Computation of cash receipts from customers

Revenues from sales	$975,000
Add: Decrease in accounts receivable	3,000
Cash receipts from customers	**$978,000**

Cash Payments to Suppliers

The conversion of cost of goods sold to purchases and purchases to cash payments to suppliers is similar to the computations made in 2002. For 2003, purchases are computed using cost of goods sold of $660,000 from the income statement and the decrease in inventory of $30,000 from the comparative balance sheets. Purchases are then adjusted by the decrease in accounts payable of $8,000. Cash payments to suppliers were $638,000, computed as follows.

Illustration 18-38

Computation of cash payments to suppliers

Cost of goods sold	$660,000
Deduct: Decrease in inventory	30,000
Purchases	630,000
Add: Decrease in accounts payable	8,000
Cash payments to suppliers	**$638,000**

Cash Payments for Operating Expenses

Operating expenses (exclusive of depreciation expense) for 2003 were reported at $176,000. This amount is then adjusted for changes in prepaid expenses and accrued expenses payable to determine cash payments for operating expenses.

As shown in the comparative balance sheets, prepaid expenses decreased $2,000 during the year. This means that $2,000 was allocated to operating expenses (thereby increasing operating expenses), but cash payments did not increase by that $2,000. To determine cash payments for operating expenses, the decrease in prepaid expenses is deducted from operating expenses.

Accrued operating expenses decreased $5,000 during the period. As a result, cash payments were higher by $5,000 than the amount reported for operating expenses. The decrease in accrued expenses payable is added to operating expenses. Cash payments for operating expenses were $179,000, computed as follows.

		Illustration 18-39
Operating expenses, exclusive of depreciation	$176,000	Computation of cash payments for operating expenses
Deduct: Decrease in prepaid expenses	(2,000)	
Add: Decrease in accrued expenses payable	5,000	
Cash payments for operating expenses	**$179,000**	

Depreciation Expense and Loss on Sale of Equipment

Operating expenses are shown exclusive of depreciation. Depreciation expense in 2003 was $18,000. Depreciation expense is not shown on a statement of cash flows because it is a noncash charge. If the amount for operating expenses includes depreciation expense, operating expenses must be reduced by the amount of depreciation to determine cash payments for operating expenses.

The loss on sale of equipment of $1,000 is also a noncash charge. The loss on sale of equipment reduces net income, but it does not reduce cash. Thus, the loss on sale of equipment is not reported on a statement of cash flows.

Other charges to expense that do not require the use of cash, such as the amortization of intangible assets and depletion expense, are treated in the same manner as depreciation.

Cash Payments for Income Taxes

Income tax expense reported on the income statement was $36,000. Income taxes payable, however, increased $12,000. This increase means that $12,000 of the income taxes have not been paid. As a result, income taxes paid were less than income taxes reported in the income statement. Cash payments for income taxes were, therefore, $24,000 as shown below.

		Illustration 18-40
Income tax expense	$36,000	Computation of cash payments for income taxes
Deduct: Increase in income taxes payable	12,000	
Cash payments for income taxes	**$24,000**	

The relationships among cash payments for income taxes, income tax expense, and changes in income taxes payable are shown in the following formula.

Illustration 18-41

Formula to compute cash payments for income taxes—direct method

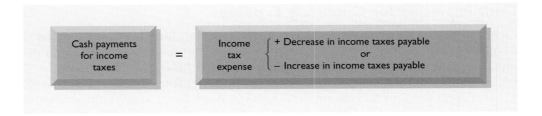

STEP 3: DETERMINE NET CASH PROVIDED/USED BY INVESTING AND FINANCING ACTIVITIES

Increase in Land

Land increased $100,000. The additional information section indicates that common stock was issued to purchase the land. The issuance of common stock for land has no effect on cash. But it is a **significant noncash investing and financing transaction**. This transaction requires disclosure in a separate schedule at the bottom of the statement of cash flows.

Increase in Equipment

The comparative balance sheets show that equipment increased $160,000 in 2003. The additional information in Illustration 18-36 indicates that the increase resulted from two investing transactions: (1) Equipment costing $180,000 was purchased for cash. And (2) equipment costing $20,000 was sold for $17,000 cash when its book value was $18,000. The relevant data for the statement of cash flows is the cash paid for the purchase and the cash proceeds from the sale. For Juarez Company, the investing activities section will show the following: The $180,000 purchase of equipment as an outflow of cash, and the $17,000 sale of equipment also as an inflow of cash. The two amounts **should not be netted**. **Both individual outflows and inflows of cash should be shown.**

The analysis of the changes in equipment should include the related Accumulated Depreciation account. These two accounts for Juarez Company are shown in Illustration 18-42.

Illustration 18-42

Analysis of equipment and related accumulated depreciation

Equipment				
1/1/03 Balance	–0–	Cost of equipment sold	20,000
Cash purchase	**180,000**		
12/31/03 Balance	160,000		

Accumulated Depreciation—Equipment				
Sale of equipment	2,000	1/1/03 Balance	–0–
		Depreciation expense	18,000
		12/31/03 Balance	16,000

Increase in Bonds Payable

Bonds Payable increased $90,000. The additional information in Illustration 18-36 indicated that bonds with a face value of $90,000 were issued for $90,000 cash. The issuance of bonds is a financing activity. For Juarez Company, there is an inflow of cash of $90,000 from the issuance of bonds.

Increase in Common Stock

The Common Stock account increased $100,000. The additional information indicated that land was acquired from the issuance of common stock. This transaction is a **significant noncash investing and financing transaction** that should be reported separately at the bottom of the statement.

Increase in Retained Earnings

The $52,000 net increase in Retained Earnings resulted from net income of $84,000 and the declaration and payment of a cash dividend of $32,000. **Net income is not reported in the statement of cash flows under the direct method.** Cash dividends paid of $32,000 are reported in the financing activities section as an outflow of cash.

STATEMENT OF CASH FLOWS—2003

The statement of cash flows for Juarez Company is shown in Illustration 18-43.

Illustration 18-43

Statement of cash flows, 2003—direct method

JUAREZ COMPANY Statement of Cash Flows—Direct Method For the Year Ended December 31, 2003		
Cash flows from operating activities		
Cash receipts from customers		$978,000
Cash payments:		
To suppliers	$638,000	
For operating expenses	179,000	
For income taxes	24,000	841,000
Net cash provided by operating activities		137,000
Cash flows from investing activities		
Purchase of equipment	(180,000)	
Sale of equipment	17,000	
Net cash used by investing activities		(163,000)
Cash flows from financing activities		
Issuance of bonds payable	90,000	
Payment of cash dividends	(32,000)	
Net cash provided by financing activities		58,000
Net increase in cash		32,000
Cash at beginning of period		159,000
Cash at end of period		$191,000
Noncash investing and financing activities		
Issuance of common stock to purchase land		$100,000

BEFORE YOU GO ON...

▶ REVIEW IT

1. What is the format of the operating activities section of the statement of cash flows using the direct method?
2. Where is depreciation expense shown on a statement of cash flows using the direct method?
3. Where are significant noncash investing and financing activities shown on a statement of cash flows? Give some examples.

DO IT

Presented below is information related to Reynolds Company. Use it to prepare a statement of cash flows using the direct method.

				REYNOLDS COMPANY
				Comparative Balance Sheets
				December 31

Assets	2003	2002	Change Increase/Decrease
Cash	$ 54,000	$ 37,000	$ 17,000 Increase
Accounts receivable	68,000	26,000	42,000 Increase
Inventories	54,000	–0–	54,000 Increase
Prepaid expenses	4,000	6,000	2,000 Decrease
Land	45,000	70,000	25,000 Decrease
Buildings	200,000	200,000	–0–
Accumulated depreciation—buildings	(21,000)	(11,000)	10,000 Increase
Equipment	193,000	68,000	125,000 Increase
Accumulated depreciation—equipment	(28,000)	(10,000)	18,000 Increase
Totals	$569,000	$386,000	
Liabilities and Stockholders' Equity			
Accounts payable	$ 23,000	$ 40,000	$ 17,000 Decrease
Accrued expenses payable	10,000	–0–	10,000 Increase
Bonds payable	110,000	150,000	40,000 Decrease
Common stock ($1 par)	220,000	60,000	160,000 Increase
Retained earnings	206,000	136,000	70,000 Increase
Totals	$569,000	$386,000	

	REYNOLDS COMPANY	
	Income Statement	
	For the Year Ended December 31, 2003	
Revenues		$890,000
Cost of goods sold	$465,000	
Operating expenses	221,000	
Interest expense	12,000	
Loss on sale of equipment	2,000	700,000
Income from operations		190,000
Income tax expense		65,000
Net income		$125,000

Additional information:

1. Operating expenses include depreciation expense of $33,000 and charges from prepaid expenses of $2,000.
2. Land was sold at its book value for cash.
3. Cash dividends of $55,000 were declared and paid in 2003.
4. Interest expense of $12,000 was paid in cash.
5. Equipment with a cost of $166,000 was purchased for cash. Equipment with a cost of $41,000 and a book value of $36,000 was sold for $34,000 cash.
6. Bonds of $10,000 were redeemed at their book value for cash. Bonds of $30,000 were converted into common stock.
7. Common stock ($1 par) of $130,000 was issued for cash.
8. Accounts payable pertain to merchandise suppliers.

ACTION PLAN

- Determine the net increase/decrease in cash.
- Determine net cash provided/used by operating activities by adjusting each item in the income statement from the accrual basis to the cash basis.
- Determine net cash provided/used by investing activities.
- Determine net cash provided/used by financing activities.

SOLUTION

REYNOLDS COMPANY
Statement of Cash Flows—Direct Method
For the Year Ended December 31, 2003

Cash flows from operating activities		
Cash receipts from customers		$848,000[a]
Cash payments:		
To suppliers	$536,000[b]	
For operating expenses	176,000[c]	
For interest expense	12,000	
For income taxes	65,000	789,000
Net cash provided by operating activities		59,000
Cash flows from investing activities		
Sale of land	25,000	
Sale of equipment	34,000	
Purchase of equipment	(166,000)	
Net cash used by investing activities		(107,000)
Cash flows from financing activities		
Redemption of bonds	(10,000)	
Sale of common stock	130,000	
Payment of dividends	(55,000)	
Net cash provided by financing activities		65,000
Net increase in cash		17,000
Cash at beginning of period		37,000
Cash at end of period		$ 54,000
Noncash investing and financing activities		
Conversion of bonds into common stock		$ 30,000

Computations:

[a]$848,000 = $890,000 − $42,000

[b]$536,000 = $465,000 + $54,000 + $17,000

[c]$176,000 = $221,000 − $33,000 − $2,000 − $10,000

Technically, an additional schedule reconciling net income to net cash provided by operating activities should be presented as part of the statement of cash flows when using the direct method.

HELPFUL HINT

1. Determine net cash provided/used by operating activities, recognizing that each item in the income statement must be adjusted to the cash basis.
2. Determine net cash provided/used by investing activities, recognizing that investing activities generally relate to changes in noncurrent assets.
3. Determine net cash provided/used by financing activities, recognizing that financing activities generally relate to changes in long-term liabilities and stockholders' equity accounts.

Related exercise material: BE18-6, BE18-7, BE18-8, E18-7, E18-8, E18-9, and E18-10.

☑ THE NAVIGATOR

Note: This concludes Section 2 on preparation of the statement of cash flows using the direct method. You should now proceed to the concluding section of the chapter, "Analysis of the Statement of Cash Flows."

ANALYSIS OF THE STATEMENT OF CASH FLOWS

STUDY OBJECTIVE 5

Analyze the statement of cash flows.

The statement of cash flows provides information about a company's financial health that is not evident from the balance sheet or the income statement. Bankers, creditors, and other users of the statement of cash flows are as concerned with cash flow from operations as they are with net income because they are interested in a company's ability to pay its bills. Does accrual accounting conceal cash flow problems? What can be learned about a company and its management from the statement of cash flows?

In the following discussion of cash flow analysis, we use financial information from the fiscal 2000 annual report of **Gap Inc.** (manufacturer and retailer of Gap, Banana Republic, and Old Navy brands). Gap Inc. reported the following relevant information:

Illustration 18-44

Gap Inc. data used in cash flow analysis

GAP INC.		
($ in millions)	**Fiscal 2000**	**Fiscal 1999**
Current liabilities	$ 1,753	$1,553
Total liabilities	2,956	2,390
Net sales	11,635	9,054
Net cash provided by operating activities	1,478	1,394

As with the balance sheet and the income statement, ratio analysis of the statement of cash flows can evaluate Gap Inc.'s liquidity, profitability, and solvency. Three cash flow ratios that contribute to these evaluations are (a) the current cash debt coverage ratio, (b) the cash return on sales ratio, and (c) the cash debt coverage ratio. Each of these ratios uses net cash provided by operating activities as the numerator.

CURRENT CASH DEBT COVERAGE RATIO

A disadvantage of the current ratio is that it employs year-end balances of current asset and current liability accounts. These year-end balances may not be representative of what the company's current position was during most of the year. A ratio that partially corrects for this problem is the ratio of net cash provided by operating activities to average current liabilities, referred to as the **current cash debt coverage ratio**. Because it uses net cash provided by operating activities during the period, rather than a balance at a point in time, it may provide a better representation of **liquidity**. Using Gap Inc.'s financial data, the current cash debt coverage ratio is computed as follows.

Illustration 18-45

Current cash debt coverage ratio

$$\text{Net Cash Provided by Operating Activities} \div \text{Average Current Liabilities} = \text{Current Cash Debt Coverage Ratio}$$

$$\$1,478 \div \frac{\$1,753 + \$1,553}{2} = .89{:}1$$

This ratio indicates that for every dollar of debt due during the year, $0.89 of cash was generated from operations to pay that debt.

CASH RETURN ON SALES RATIO

One measure of profitability under accrual accounting is the profit margin ratio. This ratio is defined as net income divided by net sales and measures net income generated by each dollar of sales. The cash-based ratio that is the counterpart of the profit margin ratio is the **cash return on sales ratio**. It is computed by dividing net cash provided by operating activities by net sales. For Gap Inc., this ratio is computed as follows.

ALTERNATIVE TERMINOLOGY
The cash return on sales ratio is sometimes referred to as *cash flow margin*.

Illustration 18-46

Cash return on sales ratio

Net Cash Provided by Operating Activities	÷	Net Sales	=	Cash Return on Sales
$1,478	÷	$11,635	=	13%

Some difference is to be expected between similar cash and accrual accounting ratios. But significant differences should be investigated. When Gap Inc.'s cash return on sales of 13% is compared with its profit margin of 9.7%, it appears that Gap Inc. is efficient at turning sales into cash—since its cash flow margin is greater than its profit margin (accrual basis).

CASH DEBT COVERAGE RATIO

One measure of long-term **solvency** is the debt to total assets ratio. The cash basis measure of solvency is the **cash debt coverage ratio**. It is the ratio of net cash provided by operating activities to average total liabilities. This ratio demonstrates a company's ability to repay its liabilities from net cash provided by operating activities, without having to liquidate the assets employed in its operations. Gap Inc.'s cash debt coverage ratio is computed as follows.

Illustration 18-47

Cash debt coverage ratio

Net Cash Provided by Operating Activities	÷	Average Total Liabilities	=	Cash Debt Coverage Ratio
$1,478	÷	$\dfrac{\$2,956 + \$2,390}{2}$	=	.55:1

This ratio indicates that for every dollar of total debt, $0.55 of cash was generated from operations to pay that debt.

The three cash-based ratios presented here show that **Gap Inc.** is efficiently generating cash. Its cash flow coverage ratios are in line with industry averages. These ratios indicate that the company is liquid, profitable, and solvent.

BEFORE YOU GO ON...

▶ *REVIEW IT*

1. Why might an analyst want to supplement accrual-based ratios with cash-based ratios?
2. What cash-basis ratios may be prepared to evaluate liquidity, profitability, and solvency?

A LOOK BACK AT OUR FEATURE STORY

Refer back to the Feature Story at the beginning of the chapter about Gerald Biby's attempt to refinance **Kilian Community College's** mortgage, and answer the following questions.

1. How was the purchase of the $250,000 computer system presented on the "traditional educational institution financial statement" so that it negatively affected Biby's ability to refinance the mortgage?
2. How was the purchase of the $250,000 computer system presented on the statement of cash flows? How did the preparation of the statement of cash flows aid Biby in securing the refinancing of the mortgage?

SOLUTION

1. A traditional financial statement for a not-for-profit, educational institution reports receipts as revenues. It expenses all expenditures, even capital expenditures such as the $250,000 computer system. The traditional financial statement reported the entire $250,000 as an expense in one year, making it look like the college was just breaking even.
2. The statement of cash flows classified the computer purchase as an investing activity. It therefore showed the bankers that one of the uses of funds was the purchase of computer equipment that had several years of life. In addition, the bankers noted from the statement of cash flows that the college's cash flows from operating activities exceeded the cash outflows for financing activities (the loan repayments, including principal and interest) by a ratio of 3-to-1.

Additional Demonstration Problem

DEMONSTRATION PROBLEM

The income statement for the year ended December 31, 2002, for John Kosinski Manufacturing Company contains the following condensed information.

JOHN KOSINSKI MANUFACTURING COMPANY
Income Statement

Revenues		$6,583,000
Operating expenses (excluding depreciation)	$4,920,000	
Depreciation expense	880,000	5,800,000
Income before income taxes		783,000
Income tax expense		353,000
Net income		$ 430,000

Included in operating expenses is a $24,000 loss resulting from the sale of machinery for $270,000 cash. Machinery was purchased at a cost of $750,000.

The following balances are reported on Kosinski's comparative balance sheets at December 31.

JOHN KOSINSKI MANUFACTURING COMPANY
Comparative Balance Sheets (partial)

	2002	2001
Cash	$672,000	$130,000
Accounts receivable	775,000	610,000
Inventories	834,000	867,000
Accounts payable	521,000	501,000

Income tax expense of $353,000 represents the amount paid in 2002. Dividends declared and paid in 2002 totaled $200,000.

Instructions

(a) Prepare the statement of cash flows using the indirect method.

OR

(b) Prepare the statement of cash flows using the direct method.

SOLUTION TO DEMONSTRATION PROBLEM

(a)
JOHN KOSINSKI MANUFACTURING COMPANY
Statement of Cash Flows—Indirect Method
For the Year Ended December 31, 2002

Cash flows from operating activities		
Net income		$ 430,000
Adjustments to reconcile net income to net cash provided by operating activities:		
Depreciation expense	$880,000	
Loss on sale of machinery	24,000	
Increase in accounts receivable	(165,000)	
Decrease in inventories	33,000	
Increase in accounts payable	20,000	792,000
Net cash provided by operating activities		1,222,000
Cash flows from investing activities		
Sale of machinery	270,000	
Purchase of machinery	(750,000)	
Net cash used by investing activities		(480,000)
Cash flows from financing activities		
Payment of cash dividends		(200,000)
Net increase in cash		542,000
Cash at beginning of period		130,000
Cash at end of period		$ 672,000

(b)
JOHN KOSINSKI MANUFACTURING COMPANY
Statement of Cash Flows—Direct Method
For the Year Ended December 31, 2002

Cash flows from operating activities		
Cash receipts from customers		$6,418,000*
Cash payments:		
For operating expenses	$4,843,000**	
For income taxes	353,000	5,196,000
Net cash provided by operating activities		1,222,000
Cash flows from investing activities		
Sale of machinery	270,000	
Purchase of machinery	(750,000)	

ACTION PLAN

• Apply the same data to the preparation of a statement of cash flows under both the indirect and direct methods.

• Note the similarities of the two methods: Both methods report the same information in the investing and financing sections.

• Note the differences between the two methods: The cash flows from operating activities sections report different information (but the amount of net cash provided by operating activities is the same for both methods).

Net cash used by investing activities	(480,000)
Cash flows from financing activities	
Payment of cash dividends	(200,000)
Net increase in cash	542,000
Cash at beginning of period	130,000
Cash at end of period	$ 672,000

Direct Method Computations:

* Computation of cash receipts from customers:

Revenues per the income statement	$6,583,000
Less increase in accounts receivable	165,000
Cash receipts from customers	$6,418,000

** Computation of cash payments for operating expenses:

Operating expenses per the income statement	$4,920,000
Deduct loss from sale of machinery	(24,000)
Deduct decrease in inventories	(33,000)
Deduct increase in accounts payable	(20,000)
Cash payments for operating expenses	$4,843,000

SUMMARY OF STUDY OBJECTIVES

1. Indicate the primary purpose of the statement of cash flows. The primary purpose of the statement of cash flows is to provide information about the cash receipts and cash payments during a period. A secondary objective is to provide information about the operating, investing, and financing activities during the period.

2. Distinguish among operating, investing, and financing activities. Operating activities include the cash effects of transactions that enter into the determination of net income. Investing activities involve cash flows resulting from changes in investments and long-term asset items. Financing activities involve cash flows resulting from changes in long-term liability and stockholders' equity items.

3. Prepare a statement of cash flows using the indirect method. The preparation of a statement of cash flows involves three major steps: (1) Determine the net increase or decrease in cash. (2) Determine net cash provided (used) by operating activities. (3) Determine net cash flows provided (used) by investing and financing activities. Under the indirect method, accrual basis net income is adjusted to net cash provided by operating activities.

4. Prepare a statement of cash flows using the direct method. The preparation of the statement of cash flows involves three major steps: (1) Determine the net increase or decrease in cash. (2) Determine net cash provided (used) by operating activities. (3) Determine net cash flows provided (used) by investing and financing activities. To determine net cash provided by operating activities, the direct method reports cash receipts less cash payments.

5. Analyze the statement of cash flows. The statement of cash flows can be used for cash-based ratio analysis. The current cash debt coverage ratio measures liquidity. The cash return on sales ratio measures profitability. The cash debt coverage ratio measures solvency.

Key Term Matching Activity

GLOSSARY

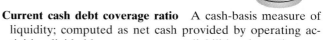

Cash debt coverage ratio A cash-basis measure of solvency; computed as net cash provided by operating activities divided by average total liabilities. (p. 749).

Cash return on sales ratio A cash-basis measure of profitability; computed as net cash provided by operating activities divided by net sales. Also called *cash flow margin.* (p. 749).

Current cash debt coverage ratio A cash-basis measure of liquidity; computed as net cash provided by operating activities divided by average current liabilities. (p. 748).

Direct method A method of determining the net cash provided by operating activities by adjusting each item in the income statement from the accrual basis to the cash basis. (p. 736).

Financing activities   Cash flow activities that include (a) obtaining cash from issuing debt and repaying the amounts borrowed and (b) obtaining cash from stockholders and providing them with a return on their investment. (p. 717).

Indirect method   A method of preparing a statement of cash flows in which net income is adjusted for items that did not affect cash, to determine net cash provided by operating activities. (p. 724).

Investing activities   Cash flow activities that include (a) acquiring and disposing of investments and productive long-lived assets and (b) lending money and collecting on those loans. (p. 717).

Operating activities   Cash flow activities that include the cash effects of transactions that create revenues and expenses and thus enter into the determination of net income. (p. 717).

Statement of cash flows   A financial statement that provides information about the cash receipts and cash payments of an entity during a period, classified as operating, investing, and financing activities, in a format that reconciles the beginning and ending cash balances. (p. 717).

> **APPENDIX** *Using a Work Sheet to Prepare the Statement of Cash Flows—Indirect Method*

When preparing a statement of cash flows, numerous adjustments of net income may be necessary. In such cases, **a work sheet is often used to assemble and classify the data that will appear on the statement**. The work sheet is merely an aid in the preparation of the statement. Its use is optional. The skeleton format of the work sheet for preparation of the statement of cash flows is shown in Illustration 18A-1.

STUDY OBJECTIVE 6

Explain the guidelines and procedural steps in using a work sheet to prepare the statement of cash flows using the indirect method.

Illustration 18A-1

Format of work sheet

XYZ COMPANY
Work Sheet
Statement of Cash Flows
For the Year Ended . . .

Balance Sheet Accounts	End of Last Year Balances	Reconciling Items Debits	Reconciling Items Credits	End of Current Year Balances
Debit balance accounts	XX	XX	XX	XX
	XX	XX	XX	XX
Totals	XXX			XXX
Credit balance accounts	XX	XX	XX	XX
	XX	XX	XX	XX
Totals	XXX			XXX

Statement of Cash Flows Effects

Operating activities				
Net income		XX		
Adjustments to net income		XX	XX	
Investing activities				
Receipts and payments		XX	XX	
Financing activities				
Receipts and payments		XX	XX	
Totals		XXX	XXX	
Increase (decrease) in cash		(XX)	XX	
Totals		XXX	XXX	

The following guidelines are important in using a work sheet.

1. In the balance sheet accounts section, **accounts with debit balances are listed separately from those with credit balances.** This means, for example, that Accumulated Depreciation is listed under credit balances and not as a contra account under debit balances. The beginning and ending balances of each account are entered in the appropriate columns. The transactions that caused the change in the account balance during the year are entered as reconciling items in the two middle columns.

   After all reconciling items have been entered, each line pertaining to a balance sheet account should "foot across." That is, the beginning balance plus or minus the reconciling item(s) must equal the ending balance. When this agreement exists for all balance sheet accounts, all changes in account balances have been reconciled.

2. The bottom portion of the work sheet consists of the operating, investing, and financing activities sections. It provides the information necessary to prepare the formal statement of cash flows. **Inflows of cash are entered as debits in the reconciling columns. Outflows of cash are entered as credits in the reconciling columns.** Thus, in this section, the sale of equipment for cash at book value is entered as a debit under investing activities. Similarly, the purchase of land for cash is entered as a credit under investing activities.

3. **The reconciling items shown in the work sheet are not entered in any journal or posted to any account.** They do not represent either adjustments or corrections of the balance sheet accounts. They are used only to facilitate the preparation of the statement of cash flows.

*P*REPARING THE WORK SHEET

As in the case of work sheets illustrated in earlier chapters, the preparation of a work sheet involves a series of prescribed steps. The steps in this case are:

1. Enter in the balance sheet accounts section the balance sheet accounts and their beginning and ending balances.

2. Enter in the reconciling columns of the work sheet the data that explain the changes in the balance sheet accounts other than cash and their effects on the statement of cash flows.

3. Enter on the cash line and at the bottom of the work sheet the increase or decrease in cash. This entry should enable the totals of the reconciling columns to be in agreement.

To illustrate the preparation of a work sheet, we will use the 2003 data for Computer Services Company. Your familiarity with these data should help you understand the use of a work sheet. For ease of reference, the comparative balance sheets, income statement, and selected data for 2003 are presented in Illustrations 18A-2 and 18A-3.

COMPUTER SERVICES COMPANY
Comparative Balance Sheets
December 31

Assets	2003	2002	Change Increase/Decrease
Cash	$ 56,000	$34,000	$ 22,000 Increase
Accounts receivable	20,000	30,000	10,000 Decrease
Prepaid expenses	4,000	–0–	4,000 Increase
Land	130,000	–0–	130,000 Increase
Building	160,000	–0–	160,000 Increase
Accumulated depreciation—building	(11,000)	–0–	11,000 Increase
Equipment	27,000	10,000	17,000 Increase
Accumulated depreciation—equipment	(3,000)	–0–	3,000 Increase
Totals	$383,000	$74,000	
Liabilities and Stockholders' Equity			
Accounts payable	$ 59,000	$ 4,000	55,000 Increase
Bonds payable	130,000	–0–	130,000 Increase
Common stock	50,000	50,000	–0–
Retained earnings	144,000	20,000	124,000 Increase
Totals	$383,000	$74,000	

Illustration 18A-2

Comparative balance sheets, 2003, with increases and decreases

COMPUTER SERVICES COMPANY
Income Statement
For the Year Ended December 31, 2003

Revenues		$507,000
Operating expenses (excluding depreciation)	$261,000	
Depreciation expense	15,000	
Loss on sale of equipment	3,000	279,000
Income from operations		228,000
Income tax expense		89,000
Net income		$139,000

Additional information:
1. In 2003, the company declared and paid a $15,000 cash dividend.
2. The company obtained land through the issuance of $130,000 of long-term bonds.
3. A building costing $160,000 was purchased for cash. Equipment costing $25,000 was also purchased for cash.
4. During 2003, the company sold equipment with a book value of $7,000 (cost $8,000, less accumulated depreciation $1,000) for $4,000 cash.

Illustration 18A-3

Income statement and additional information, 2003

DETERMINING THE RECONCILING ITEMS

Several approaches may be used to determine the reconciling items. For example, the changes affecting net cash provided by operating activities can be completed first, and then the effects of financing and investing transactions can be determined. Or, the balance sheet accounts can be analyzed in the order in which they are listed on the work sheet. We will follow this latter approach for Computer Services, except for cash. As indicated above, **cash is handled last**.

Accounts Receivable

The decrease of $10,000 in accounts receivable means that cash collections from revenues are higher than the revenues reported in the income statement. To convert net income to net cash provided by operating activities, the decrease of $10,000 is added to net income. The entry in the reconciling columns of the work sheet is:

(a)	Operating—Decrease in Accounts Receivable	10,000	
	Accounts Receivable		10,000

Prepaid Expenses

An increase of $4,000 in prepaid expenses means that expenses deducted in determining net income are less than expenses that were paid in cash. The increase of $4,000 must be deducted from net income in determining net cash provided by operating activities. The work sheet entry is:

(b)	Prepaid Expenses	4,000	
	Operating—Increase in Prepaid Expenses		4,000

HELPFUL HINT
These amounts are asterisked in the work sheet to indicate that they result from a significant noncash transaction.

Land

The increase in land of $130,000 resulted from a purchase through the issuance of long-term bonds. This transaction should be reported as a significant noncash investing and financing activity. The work sheet entry is:

(c)	Land	130,000	
	Bonds Payable		130,000

Building

The cash purchase of a building for $160,000 is an investing activity cash outflow. The entry in the reconciling columns of the work sheet is:

(d)	Building	160,000	
	Investing—Purchase of Building		160,000

Equipment

The increase in equipment of $17,000 resulted from a cash purchase of $25,000 and the sale of equipment costing $8,000. The book value of the equipment was $7,000, the cash proceeds were $4,000, and a loss of $3,000 was recorded. The work sheet entries are:

(e)	Equipment	25,000	
	Investing—Purchase of Equipment		25,000

(f)	Investing—Sale of Equipment	4,000	
	Operating—Loss on Sale of Equipment	3,000	
	Accumulated Depreciation—Equipment	1,000	
	Equipment		8,000

Accounts Payable

The increase of $55,000 in accounts payable must be added to net income to determine net cash provided by operating activities. The following work sheet entry is made.

(g)	Operating—Increase in Accounts Payable	55,000	
	Accounts Payable		55,000

Bonds Payable

The increase of $130,000 in this account resulted from the issuance of bonds for land. This is a significant noncash investing and financing activity. Work sheet entry (c) above is the only entry necessary.

Accumulated Depreciation—Building, and Accumulated Depreciation—Equipment

The increases in these accounts of $11,000 and $4,000, respectively, resulted from depreciation expense. Depreciation expense is a **noncash charge that must be added to net income** to determine net cash provided by operating activities. The work sheet entries are:

(h)	Operating—Depreciation Expense—Building	11,000	
	Accumulated Depreciation—Building		11,000

(i)	Operating—Depreciation Expense—Equipment	4,000	
	Accumulated Depreciation—Equipment		4,000

Retained Earnings

The $124,000 increase in retained earnings resulted from net income of $139,000 and the declaration and payment of a $15,000 cash dividend. Net income is included in net cash provided by operating activities, and the dividends are a financing activity cash outflow. The entries in the reconciling columns of the work sheet are:

(j)	Operating—Net Income	139,000	
	Retained Earnings		139,000

(k)	Retained Earnings	15,000	
	Financing—Payment of Dividends		15,000

Disposition of Change in Cash

The firm's cash increased $22,000 in 2003. The final entry on the work sheet, therefore, is:

(l)	Cash	22,000	
	Increase in Cash		22,000

As shown in the work sheet, the increase in cash is entered in the reconciling credit column as a **balancing** amount. This entry should complete the reconciliation of the changes in the balance sheet accounts. Also, it should permit the totals of the reconciling columns to be in agreement. When all changes have been explained and the reconciling columns are in agreement, the reconciling columns are ruled to complete the work sheet. The completed work sheet for Computer Services Company is shown in Illustration 18A-4.

Illustration 18A-4

Completed work sheet—
indirect method

			COMPUTER SERVICES COMPANY			
			Work Sheet			
			Statement of Cash Flows			
			For the Year Ended December 31, 2003			

Balance Sheet Accounts	Balance 12/31/02	Reconciling Items Debit		Reconciling Items Credit		Balance 12/31/03
Debits						
Cash	34,000	(l)	22,000			56,000
Accounts receivable	30,000			(a)	10,000	20,000
Prepaid expenses	–0–	(b)	4,000			4,000
Land	–0–	(c)	130,000*			130,000
Building	–0–	(d)	160,000			160,000
Equipment	10,000	(e)	25,000	(f)	8,000	27,000
Total	74,000					397,000
Credits						
Accounts payable	4,000			(g)	55,000	59,000
Bonds payable	–0–			(c)	130,000*	130,000
Accumulated depreciation—building	–0–			(h)	11,000	11,000
Accumulated depreciation—equipment	–0–	(f)	1,000	(i)	4,000	3,000
Common stock	50,000					50,000
Retained earnings	20,000	(k)	15,000	(j)	139,000	144,000
Total	74,000					397,000

Statement of Cash Flows Effects

		Debit		Credit	
Operating activities					
Net income		(j)	139,000		
Decrease in accounts receivable		(a)	10,000		
Increase in prepaid expenses				(b)	4,000
Increase in accounts payable		(g)	55,000		
Depreciation expense—building		(h)	11,000		
Depreciation expense—equipment		(i)	4,000		
Loss on sale of equipment		(f)	3,000		
Investing activities					
Purchase of building				(d)	160,000
Purchase of equipment				(e)	25,000
Sale of equipment		(f)	4,000		
Financing activities					
Payment of dividends				(k)	15,000
Totals			583,000		561,000
Increase in cash				(l)	22,000
Totals			583,000		583,000

*Significant noncash investing and financing activity.

PREPARING THE STATEMENT

The statement of cash flows is prepared primarily from the data that appear in the work sheet under "Statement of Cash Flows Effects." The reconciling columns should also be scanned for any asterisked items that designate significant noncash activities. The formal statement was shown in Illustration 18-17.

SUMMARY OF STUDY OBJECTIVE FOR APPENDIX

6. Explain the guidelines and procedural steps in using a work sheet to prepare the statement of cash flows using the indirect method. When there are numerous adjustments, a work sheet can be a helpful tool in preparing the statement of cash flows. Key guidelines for using a work sheet are: (1) List accounts with debit balances separately from those with credit balances. (2) In the reconciling columns in the bottom portion of the work sheet, show cash inflows as debits and cash outflows as credits. (3) Do not enter reconciling items in any journal or account, but use them only to help prepare the statement of cash flows.

The steps in preparing the work sheet are: (1) Enter beginning and ending balances of balance sheet accounts. (2) Enter debits and credits in reconciling columns. (3) Enter the increase or decrease in cash in two places as a balancing amount.

*Note: All **asterisked** Questions, Exercises, and Problems relate to material in the appendix to the chapter.

SELF-STUDY QUESTIONS

Chapter 18 Self-Test

Answers are at the end of the chapter.

(SO 1) **1.** Which of the following is *incorrect* about the statement of cash flows?
  a. It is a fourth basic financial statement.
  b. It provides information about cash receipts and cash payments of an entity during a period.
  c. It reconciles the ending cash account balance to the balance per the bank statement.
  d. It provides information about the operating, investing, and financing activities of the business.

(SO 2) **2.** The statement of cash flows classifies cash receipts and cash payments by the following activities:
  a. operating and nonoperating.
  b. investing, financing, and operating.
  c. financing, operating, and nonoperating.
  d. investing, financing, and nonoperating.

(SO 2) **3.** An example of a cash flow from an operating activity is:
  a. payment of cash to lenders for interest.
  b. receipt of cash from the sale of capital stock.
  c. payment of cash dividends to the company's stockholders.
  d. None of the above.

(SO 2) **4.** An example of a cash flow from an investing activity is:
  a. receipt of cash from the issuance of bonds payable.
  b. payment of cash to repurchase outstanding capital stock.
  c. receipt of cash from the sale of equipment.
  d. payment of cash to suppliers for inventory.

(SO 2) **5.** Cash dividends paid to stockholders are classified on the statement of cash flows as:
  a. operating activities.
  b. investing activities.
  c. a combination of the above.
  d. financing activities.

6. An example of a cash flow from a financing activity is: (SO 2)
  a. receipt of cash from sale of land.
  b. issuance of debt for cash.
  c. purchase of equipment for cash.
  d. None of the above.

7. Which of the following about the statement of cash flows (SO 2) is *incorrect?*
  a. The direct method may be used to report cash provided by operations.
  b. The statement shows the cash provided (used) for three categories of activity.
  c. The operating section is the last section of the statement.
  d. The indirect method may be used to report cash provided by operations.

Questions 8 and 9 apply only to the indirect method.

8. Net income is $132,000. During the year, accounts (SO 3) payable increased $10,000, inventory decreased $6,000, and accounts receivable increased $12,000. Under the indirect method, net cash provided by operations is:
  a. $102,000.
  b. $112,000.
  c. $124,000.
  d. $136,000.

9. Noncash charges that are added back to net income in (SO 3) determining cash provided by operations under the indirect method do *not* include:
  a. depreciation expense.

b. an increase in inventory.
c. amortization expense.
d. loss on sale of equipment.

Questions 10 and 11 apply only to the direct method.

(SO 4) **10.** The beginning balance in accounts receivable is $44,000. The ending balance is $42,000. Sales during the period are $129,000. Cash receipts from customers are:
  a. $127,000.
  b. $129,000.
  c. $131,000.
  d. $141,000.

(SO 4) **11.** Which of the following items is reported on a cash flow statement prepared by the direct method?
  a. Loss on sale of building.
  b. Increase in accounts receivable.

c. Depreciation expense.
d. Cash payments to suppliers.

12. The statement of cash flows should *not* be used to eval- (SO 3) uate an entity's ability to:
  a. earn net income.
  b. generate future cash flows.
  c. pay dividends.
  d. meet obligations.

*13. In a work sheet for the statement of cash flows, a de- (SO 5) crease in accounts receivable is entered in the reconciling columns as a credit to Accounts Receivable and a debit in the:
  a. investing activities section.
  b. operating activities section.
  c. financing activities section.
  d. None of the above.

QUESTIONS

1. (a) What is the statement of cash flows? (b) Alice Weiseman maintains that the statement of cash flows is an optional financial statement. Do you agree? Explain.

2. What questions about cash are answered by the statement of cash flows?

3. What are "cash equivalents"? How do cash equivalents affect the statement of cash flows?

4. Distinguish among the three types of activities reported in the statement of cash flows.

5. What are the major sources (inflows) of cash in a statement of cash flows? What are the major uses (outflows) of cash?

6. Why is it important to disclose certain noncash transactions? How should they be disclosed?

7. Wilma Flintstone and Barny Rublestone were discussing the presentation format of the statement of cash flows of Rock Candy Co. At the bottom of Rock Candy's statement of cash flows was a separate section entitled "Noncash investing and financing activities." Give three examples of significant noncash transactions that would be reported in this section.

8. Why is it necessary to use comparative balance sheets, a current income statement, and certain transaction data in preparing a statement of cash flows?

9. Contrast the advantages and disadvantages of the direct and indirect methods. Are both methods acceptable? Which method is preferred by the FASB? Which method is more popular?

10. When the total cash inflows exceed the total cash outflows in the statement of cash flows, how and where is this excess identified?

11. Describe the indirect method for determining net cash provided by operating activities.

12. Why is it necessary to convert accrual-based net income to cash-basis income when preparing a statement of cash flows?

13. The president of Styx Company is puzzled. During the year, the company experienced a net loss of $800,000, yet its cash increased $300,000 during the same period. Explain to the president how this situation could occur.

14. Identify five items that are adjustments to reconcile net income to net cash provided by operating activities under the indirect method.

15. Why and how is depreciation expense reported in a statement prepared using the indirect method?

16. Why is the statement of cash flows useful?

17. During 2002, Joe Pesci Company converted $1,600,000 of its total $2,000,000 of bonds payable into common stock. Indicate how the transaction would be reported on a statement of cash flows, if at all.

18. Describe the direct method for determining net cash provided by operating activities.

19. Give the formulas under the direct method for computing (a) cash receipts from customers and (b) cash payments to suppliers.

20. Kim Bassinger Inc. reported sales of $2 million for 2002. Accounts receivable decreased $200,000 and accounts payable increased $325,000. Compute cash receipts from customers, assuming that the receivable and payable transactions related to operations.

21. Why is depreciation expense not reported in the direct-method cash flow from operating activities section?

22. Give an example of one accrual-based ratio and one cash-based ratio to measure these characteristics of a company: (a) liquidity, (b) solvency, and (c) profitability.

*23. Why is it advantageous to use a work sheet when preparing a statement of cash flows? Is a work sheet required to prepare a statement of cash flows?

BRIEF EXERCISES

BE18-1 Titanic Co. reported net income of $2.5 million in 2002. Depreciation for the year was $260,000, accounts receivable decreased $350,000, and accounts payable decreased $310,000. Compute net cash provided by operating activities using the indirect approach.

Compute cash provided by operating activities—indirect method.
(SO 3)

BE18-2 The net income for Robin Williams Co. for 2002 was $250,000. For 2002, depreciation on plant assets was $60,000, and the company incurred a loss on sale of plant assets of $10,000. Compute net cash provided by operating activities under the indirect method.

Compute cash provided by operating activities—indirect method.
(SO 3)

BE18-3 Each of the following items must be considered in preparing a statement of cash flows for Rudy Boesch Co. for the year ended December 31, 2002. For each item, state how it should be shown in the statement of cash flows for 2002.
- **(a)** Issued bonds for $200,000 cash.
- **(b)** Purchased equipment for $180,000 cash.
- **(c)** Sold land costing $20,000 for $20,000 cash.
- **(d)** Declared and paid a $50,000 cash dividend.

Indicate statement presentation of selected transactions.
(SO 2)

BE18-4 The comparative balance sheets for Survivor Company show the following changes in noncash current asset accounts: accounts receivable decrease $75,000, prepaid expenses increase $12,000, and inventories increase $30,000. Compute net cash provided by operating activities using the indirect method, assuming that net income is $220,000.

Compute net cash provided by operating activities using indirect method.
(SO 3)

BE18-5 Classify the following items as an operating, investing, or financing activity. Assume all items involve cash unless there is information to the contrary.
- **(a)** Purchase of equipment.
- **(d)** Depreciation.
- **(b)** Sale of building.
- **(e)** Payment of dividends.
- **(c)** Redemption of bonds.
- **(f)** Issuance of capital stock.

Classify items by activities.
(SO 2)

BE18-6 Kate Winslet Co. has accounts receivable of $14,000 at January 1, 2002, and $24,000 at December 31, 2002. Sales revenues for 2002 were $470,000. What is the amount of cash receipts from customers in 2002?

Compute receipts from customers using direct method.
(SO 4)

BE18-7 Amistad Company reported income taxes of $90,000 in its 2002 income statement and income taxes payable of $14,000 at December 31, 2001 and $9,000 at December 31, 2002. What amount of cash payments was made for income taxes during 2002?

Compute cash payments for income taxes using direct method.
(SO 4)

BE18-8 DiCaprio Company reports operating expenses of $100,000 excluding depreciation expense of $15,000 for 2002. During the year prepaid expenses decreased $6,600, and accrued expenses payable increased $2,400. Compute the cash payments for operating expenses in 2002.

Compute cash payments for operating expenses using direct method.
(SO 4)

BE18-9 The T accounts for Equipment and the related Accumulated Depreciation for Sharon Stone Company at the end of 2002 are as follows.

Determine cash received in sale of equipment.
(SO 3, 4)

Equipment					Accumulated Depreciation				
Beg. bal.	80,000	Disposals	22,000		Disposals	5,500	Beg. bal.	44,500
Acquisitions	41,600						Depr.	12,000
End. bal.	99,600						End. bal.	51,000

Sharon Stone Company's income statement reported a loss on the sale of equipment of $4,900. What amount was reported on the statement of cash flows as "cash flow from sale of equipment"?

BE18-10 The following T account is a summary of the cash account of Amy Company.

Identify financing activity transactions.
(SO 2)

Cash (Summary Form)

Balance, 1/1/02	8,000		
Receipts from customers	364,000	Payments for goods	200,000
Dividends on stock investments	6,000	Payments for operating expenses	140,000
Proceeds from sale of equipment	36,000	Interest paid	10,000
Proceeds from issuance of bonds payable	200,000	Taxes paid	8,000
		Dividends paid	45,000
Balance, 12/31/02	211,000		

For Amy Company what amount of net cash provided (used) by financing activities should be reported in the statement of cash flows?

Calculate cash-based ratios.
(SO 5)

BE18-11 Matt Damon Company reported cash from operations of $450,000, net sales $1,500,000, average current liabilities of $150,000, and average total liabilities of $225,000. Calculate these ratios.

(a) Current cash debt coverage ratio.
(b) Cash debt coverage ratio.
(c) Cash return on sales ratio.

Indicate entries in work sheet.
(SO 6)

*BE18-12   Using the data in BE18-8, indicate how the changes in prepaid expenses and accrued expenses payable should be entered in the reconciling columns of a work sheet. Assume that beginning balances were: prepaid expenses $18,600 and accrued expenses payable $8,200.

EXERCISES

Classify transactions by type of activity.
(SO 2)

E18-1   Barbara Eden Corporation had the following transactions during 2002.

1. Issued $50,000 par value common stock for cash.
2. Collected $16,000 of accounts receivable.
3. Declared and paid a cash dividend of $25,000.
4. Sold a long-term investment with a cost of $15,000 for $15,000 cash.
5. Issued $200,000 par value common stock upon conversion of bonds having a face value of $200,000.
6. Paid $18,000 on accounts payable.
7. Purchased a machine for $30,000, giving a long-term note in exchange.

Instructions
Analyze the transactions above and indicate whether each transaction resulted in a cash flow from **(a)** operating activities, **(b)** investing activities, **(c)** financing activities, or **(d)** noncash investing and financing activities.

Prepare the operating activities section—indirect method.
(SO 3)

E18-2   Porky Company reported net income of $195,000 for 2002. Porky also reported depreciation expense of $35,000, and a loss of $5,000 on the sale of equipment. The comparative balance sheets show an increase in accounts receivable of $15,000 for the year, an $8,000 increase in accounts payable, and a decrease in prepaid expenses $4,000.

Instructions
Prepare the operating activities section of the statement of cash flows for 2002 using the indirect method.

Prepare the operating activities section—indirect method.
(SO 3)

E18-3   The current sections of Depeche Mode Co. balance sheets at December 31, 2001 and 2002, are presented below.

DEPECHE MODE CO.
Comparative Balance Sheets (partial)
December 31

	2002	2001
Current assets		
Cash	$105,000	$ 99,000
Accounts receivable	110,000	89,000
Inventory	171,000	186,000
Prepaid expenses	27,000	32,000
Total current assets	$413,000	$406,000
Current liabilities		
Accrued expenses payable	$ 15,000	$ 5,000
Accounts payable	$ 85,000	$ 92,000
Total current liabilities	$100,000	$ 97,000

Depeche Mode's net income for 2002 was $163,000. Depreciation expense was $30,000.

Instructions

Prepare the net cash provided by operating activities section of Depeche Mode's statement of cash flows for the year ended December 31, 2002, using the indirect method.

E18-4 Presented below are three accounts that appear in the general ledger of Wesley Snipes Co. during 2002.

Prepare a partial statement of cash flows—indirect method.
(SO 3)

Equipment

Date		Debit	Credit	Balance
Jan. 1	Balance			160,000
July 31	Purchase of equipment	70,000		230,000
Sept. 2	Cost of equipment constructed	53,000		283,000
Nov. 10	Cost of equipment sold		45,000	238,000

Accumulated Depreciation—Equipment

Date		Debit	Credit	Balance
Jan. 1	Balance			71,000
Nov. 10	Accumulated depreciation on equipment sold	30,000		41,000
Dec. 31	Depreciation for year		24,000	65,000

Retained Earnings

Date		Debit	Credit	Balance
Jan. 1	Balance			105,000
Aug. 23	Dividends (cash)	14,000		91,000
Dec. 31	Net income		57,000	148,000

Instructions

From the postings in the accounts above, indicate how the information is reported on a statement of cash flows by preparing a partial statement of cash flows using the indirect method. The loss on sale of equipment was $4,000.

E18-5 Comparative balance sheets for Eddie Murphy Company are presented below.

Prepare a statement of cash flows—indirect method.
(SO 3, 5)

EDDIE MURPHY COMPANY
Comparative Balance Sheets
December 31

Assets	2002	2001
Cash	$ 63,000	$ 22,000
Accounts receivable	85,000	76,000
Inventories	180,000	189,000
Land	75,000	100,000
Equipment	260,000	200,000
Accumulated depreciation	(66,000)	(42,000)
Total	$597,000	$545,000

Liabilities and Stockholders' Equity	2002	2001
Accounts payable	$ 34,000	$ 47,000
Bonds payable	150,000	200,000
Common stock ($1 par)	214,000	164,000
Retained earnings	199,000	134,000
Total	$597,000	$545,000

Additional information:

1. Net income for 2002 was $125,000.
2. Cash dividends of $60,000 were declared and paid.
3. Bonds payable amounting to $50,000 were redeemed for cash $50,000.
4. Common stock was issued for $50,000 cash.

5. Depreciation expense was $24,000.
6. Sales for the year were $978,000.

Instructions

(a) Prepare a statement of cash flows for 2002 using the indirect method.
(b) Compute the following cash-basis ratios.
    (1) Current cash debt coverage ratio.
    (2) Cash return on sales ratio.
    (3) Cash debt coverage ratio.

Classify transactions by type of activity.
(SO 2)

E18-6 An analysis of comparative balance sheets, the current year's income statement, and the general ledger accounts of Oprah Winfrey Corp. uncovered the following items. Assume all items involve cash unless there is information to the contrary.

1. Issuance of capital stock.	8. Purchase of land.
2. Amortization of patent.	9. Payment of dividends.
3. Issuance of bonds for land.	10. Sale of building at book value.
4. Payment of interest on notes payable.	11. Exchange of land for patent.
5. Conversion of bonds into common stock.	12. Depreciation.
6. Sale of land at a loss.	13. Redemption of bonds.
7. Receipt of dividends on investment in stock.	14. Receipt of interest on notes receivable.

Instructions

Indicate how the above items should be classified in the statement of cash flows using the following four major classifications: operating activity (indirect method), investing activity, financing activity, and significant noncash investing and financing activity.

Compute cash provided by operating activities—direct method.
(SO 4)

E18-7 Satchmo Company has just completed its first year of operations on December 31, 2002. Its initial income statement showed that Satchmo had revenues of $137,000 and operating expenses of $88,000. Accounts receivable at year-end were $42,000. Accounts payable at year-end were $33,000. Assume that accounts payable related to operating expenses. Ignore income taxes.

Instructions

Compute net cash provided by operating activities using the direct method.

Compute cash payments—direct method.
(SO 4)

E18-8 The income statement for Mel Gibson Company shows cost of goods sold $325,000 and operating expenses (exclusive of depreciation) $250,000. The comparative balance sheets for the year show that inventory increased $6,000, prepaid expenses decreased $6,000, accounts payable (merchandise suppliers) decreased $8,000, and accrued expenses payable increased $4,000.

Instructions

Using the direct method, compute (a) cash payments to suppliers and (b) cash payments for operating expenses.

Compute cash flow from operating activities—direct method.
(SO 2, 4)

E18-9 The 2002 accounting records of Winona Ryder Co. reveal the following transactions and events.

Payment of interest	$ 6,000	Collection of accounts receivable	$180,000
Cash sales	38,000	Payment of salaries and wages	65,000
Receipt of dividend revenue	14,000	Depreciation expense	18,000
Payment of income taxes	15,000	Proceeds from sale of aircraft	812,000
Net income	38,000	Purchase of equipment for cash	22,000
Payment of accounts payable		Loss on sale of aircraft	3,000
for merchandise	90,000	Payment of dividends	14,000
Payment for land	74,000	Payment of operating expenses	20,000

Instructions

Prepare the cash flows from operating activities section using the direct method. (Not all of the above items will be used.)

Calculate cash flows—direct method.
(SO 4)

E18-10 The following information is taken from the 2002 general ledger of Richard Gere Company.

Rent	Rent expense	$ 33,000
	Prepaid rent, January 1	7,900
	Prepaid rent, December 31	3,000
Salaries	Salaries expense	$ 54,000
	Salaries payable, January 1	5,000
	Salaries payable, December 31	8,000

Sales	Revenue from sales	$180,000
	Accounts receivable, January 1	12,000
	Accounts receivable, December 31	7,000

Instructions

In each of the above cases, compute the amount that should be reported in the operating activities section of the statement of cash flows using the direct method.

E18-11   Presented here is information for two companies in the same industry: Morgan Corporation and Erin Corporation.

Compare two companies by using cash-based ratios. (SO 5)

	Morgan Corporation	Erin Corporation
Cash provided by operations	$300,000	$300,000
Average current liabilities	50,000	100,000
Average total liabilities	200,000	250,000
Net income	200,000	200,000
Sales	400,000	800,000

Instructions

Using the cash-based ratios presented in this chapter, compare the (a) liquidity, (b) solvency, and (c) profitability of the two companies.

*E18-12   Information for Eddie Murphy Company is presented in E18-5.

Prepare a work sheet. (SO 6)

Instructions

Use the data in E18-5 to prepare a work sheet for a statement of cash flows for 2002. Enter the reconciling items directly on the work sheet, presenting the entries alphabetically.

*P*ROBLEMS: SET A

P18-1A   The income statement of Rebecca Sherrick Company is shown below.

Prepare the operating activities section—indirect method. (SO 3)

REBECCA SHERRICK COMPANY
Income Statement
For the Year Ended December 31, 2002

Sales		$7,100,000
Cost of goods sold		
Beginning inventory	$1,700,000	
Purchases	5,430,000	
Goods available for sale	7,130,000	
Ending inventory	1,920,000	
Cost of goods sold		5,210,000
Gross profit		1,890,000
Operating expenses		
Selling expenses	380,000	
Administrative expense	525,000	
Depreciation expense	75,000	
Amortization expense	30,000	1,010,000
Net income		$ 880,000

Additional information:

1. Accounts receivable increased $490,000 during the year.
2. Prepaid expenses increased $170,000 during the year.
3. Accounts payable to merchandise suppliers increased $40,000 during the year.
4. Accrued expenses payable decreased $180,000 during the year.

Instructions

Prepare the operating activities section of the statement of cash flows for the year ended December 31, 2002, for Rebecca Sherrick Company using the indirect method.

Net cash used $35,000

Prepare the operating activities section—direct method.
(SO 4)

Net cash used $35,000

P18-2A Data for Rebecca Sherrick Company are presented in P18-1A.

Instructions
Prepare the operating activities section of the statement of cash flows using the direct method.

Prepare the operating activities section—direct method.
(SO 4)

P18-3A The income statement of Dreamworks International Co. for the year ended December 31, 2002, reported the following condensed information.

Revenue from fees	$470,000
Operating expenses	280,000
Income from operations	190,000
Income tax expense	47,000
Net income	$143,000

Dreamworks' balance sheet contained the following comparative data at December 31.

	2002	**2001**
Accounts receivable	$55,000	$40,000
Accounts payable	32,000	41,000
Income taxes payable	6,000	4,000

Dreamworks has no depreciable assets. (Accounts payable pertains to operating expenses.)

Instructions

Net cash provided $121,000

Prepare the operating activities section of the statement of cash flows using the direct method.

Prepare the operating activities section—indirect method.
(SO 3)
Net cash provided $121,000

P18-4A Data for Dreamworks International Co. are presented in P18-3A.

Instructions
Prepare the operating activities section of the statement of cash flows using the indirect method.

Prepare a statement of cash flows—indirect method.
(SO 3, 5)

P18-5A The financial statements of Jim Carrey Company appear below.

JIM CARREY COMPANY
Comparative Balance Sheets
December 31

Assets		2002		2001
Cash		$ 24,000		$ 13,000
Accounts receivable		20,000		14,000
Merchandise inventory		38,000		35,000
Property, plant, and equipment	$70,000		$78,000	
Less: Accumulated depreciation	(30,000)	40,000	(24,000)	54,000
Total		$122,000		$116,000

Liabilities and Stockholders' Equity		2002		2001
Accounts payable		$ 26,000		$ 33,000
Income taxes payable		15,000		20,000
Bonds payable		20,000		10,000
Common stock		25,000		25,000
Retained earnings		36,000		28,000
Total		$122,000		$116,000

JIM CARREY COMPANY
Income Statement
For the Year Ended December 31, 2002

Sales		$240,000
Cost of goods sold		180,000
Gross profit		60,000
Selling expenses	$24,000	
Administrative expenses	10,000	34,000
Income from operations		26,000
Interest expense		2,000
Income before income taxes		24,000
Income tax expense		7,000
Net income		$ 17,000

Additional information:

1. Dividends of $9,000 were declared and paid.
2. During the year equipment was sold for $10,000 cash. This equipment cost $15,000 originally and had a book value of $10,000 at the time of sale.
3. All depreciation expense, $11,000, is in the selling expense category.
4. All sales and purchases are on account.
5. Additional equipment was purchased for $7,000 cash.

Instructions

(a) Prepare a statement of cash flows using the indirect method.
(b) Compute the following cash-basis ratios.
  (1) Current cash debt coverage ratio.
  (2) Cash return on sales ratio.
  (3) Cash debt coverage ratio.

(a) Net cash provided by operating activities $7,000

P18-6A Data for the Jim Carrey Company are presented in P18-5A. Further analysis reveals the following.

Prepare a statement of cash flows—direct method (SO 4, 5)

1. Accounts payable pertains to merchandise creditors.
2. All operating expenses except for depreciation are paid in cash.

Instructions

(a) Prepare a statement of cash flows using the direct method.
(b) Compute the following cash-basis ratios.
  (1) Current cash debt coverage ratio.
  (2) Cash return on sales ratio.
  (3) Cash debt coverage ratio.

(a) Net cash provided by operating activities $7,000

P18-7A Condensed financial data of Tom Cruise Company appear below.

Prepare a statement of cash flows—indirect method. (SO 3)

TOM CRUISE COMPANY
Comparative Balance Sheets
December 31

Assets	2002	2001
Cash	$ 92,700	$ 47,250
Accounts receivable	90,800	57,000
Inventories	121,900	102,650
Investments	84,500	87,000
Plant assets	250,000	205,000
Accumulated depreciation	(49,500)	(40,000)
	$590,400	$458,900

Liabilities and Stockholders' Equity	2002	2001
Accounts payable	$ 57,700	$ 48,280
Accrued expenses payable	12,100	18,830
Bonds payable	100,000	70,000
Common stock	250,000	200,000
Retained earnings	170,600	121,790
	$590,400	$458,900

TOM CRUISE COMPANY
Income Statement Data
For the Year Ended December 31, 2002

Sales		$297,500
Gain on sale of plant assets		8,750
		306,250
Less:		
Cost of goods sold	$99,460	
Operating expenses (excluding depreciation expense)	14,670	
Depreciation expense	49,700	
Income taxes	7,270	
Interest expense	2,940	174,040
Net income		$132,210

Additional information:

1. New plant assets costing $92,000 were purchased for cash during the year.
2. Investments were sold at cost.
3. Plant assets costing $47,000 were sold for $15,550, resulting in a gain of $8,750.
4. A cash dividend of $83,400 was declared and paid during the year.

Net cash provided by operating activities $122,800
Investing activities used $73,950

Instructions
Prepare a statement of cash flows using the indirect method.

Prepare a statement of cash flows—direct method.
(SO 4)
Cash receipts from customers $263,700
Investing activities used $73,950

P18-8A   Data for Tom Cruise Company are presented in P18-7A. Further analysis reveals that accounts payable pertains to merchandise creditors.

Instructions
Prepare a statement of cash flows for Tom Cruise Company using the direct method.

Prepare a statement of cash flows—indirect method.
(SO 3, 5)

P18-9A   Presented below are the comparative balance sheets for Nicolas Cage Company at December 31.

NICOLAS CAGE COMPANY
Comparative Balance Sheets
December 31

Assets	2002	2001
Cash	$ 45,000	$ 57,000
Accounts receivable	72,000	64,000
Inventory	132,000	140,000
Prepaid expenses	12,140	16,540
Land	125,000	150,000
Equipment	200,000	175,000
Accumulated depreciation—equipment	(60,000)	(42,000)
Building	250,000	250,000
Accumulated depreciation—building	(75,000)	(50,000)
	$701,140	$760,540

Liabilities and Stockholders' Equity	2002	2001
Accounts payable	$ 38,000	$ 45,000
Bonds payable	235,000	265,000
Common stock, $1 par	280,000	250,000
Retained earnings	148,140	200,540
	$701,140	$760,540

Additional information:

1. Operating expenses include depreciation expense of $70,000 and charges from prepaid expenses of $4,400.
2. Land was sold for cash at cost.
3. Cash dividends of $79,290 were paid.
4. Net income for 2002 was $26,890.
5. Equipment was purchased for $65,000 cash. In addition, equipment costing $40,000 with a book value of $13,000 was sold for $14,000 cash.
6. Bonds were converted at face value by issuing 30,000 shares of $1 par value common stock.
7. Net sales in 2002 were $367,000.

Instructions
(a) Prepare a statement of cash flows for 2002 using the indirect method.
(b) Compute the following cash-basis ratios for 2002.
  (1) Current cash debt coverage ratio.
  (2) Cash return on sales ratio.
  (3) Cash debt coverage ratio.

(a) Net cash provided by operating activities $93,290

*P18-10A   Data for Tom Cruise Company are presented in P18-7A.

Instructions
Prepare a work sheet for a statement of cash flows. Enter the reconciling items directly in the work sheet columns, identifying the debit and credit amounts alphabetically.

Prepare a work sheet (SO 6)

Total reconciling columns $610,210

PROBLEMS: SET B

P18-1B   The income statement of Barbara Streisand Company is shown below.

Prepare the operating activities section—indirect method. (SO 3)

BARBARA STREISAND COMPANY
Income Statement
For the Year Ended November 30, 2002

Sales		$6,900,000
Cost of goods sold		
Beginning inventory	$2,000,000	
Purchases	4,300,000	
Goods available for sale	6,300,000	
Ending inventory	1,600,000	
Cost of goods sold		4,700,000
Gross profit		2,200,000
Operating expenses		
Selling expenses	450,000	
Administrative expenses	700,000	1,150,000
Net income		$1,050,000

Additional information:

1. Accounts receivable decreased $280,000 during the year.
2. Prepaid expenses increased $150,000 during the year.
3. Accounts payable to suppliers of merchandise decreased $200,000 during the year.
4. Accrued expenses payable decreased $100,000 during the year.
5. Administrative expenses include depreciation expense of $70,000.

Net cash provided $1,350,000

Instructions

Prepare the operating activities section of the statement of cash flows for the year ended November 30, 2002, for Barbara Streisand Company using the indirect method.

Prepare the operating activities section—direct method.
(SO 4)
Net cash provided $1,350,000

P18-2B   Data for Barbara Streisand Company are presented in P18-1B.

Instructions

Prepare the operating activities section of the statement of cash flows using the direct method.

Prepare the operating activities section—direct method.
(SO 4)

P18-3B   George Clooney Company's income statement for the year ended December 31, 2002, contained the following condensed information.

Revenue from fees		$900,000
Operating expenses (excluding depreciation)	$624,000	
Depreciation expense	60,000	
Loss on sale of equipment	26,000	710,000
Income before income taxes		190,000
Income tax expense		40,000
Net income		$150,000

Clooney's balance sheet contained the following comparative data at December 31.

	2002	2001
Accounts receivable	$47,000	$57,000
Accounts payable	41,000	36,000
Income taxes payable	4,000	9,000

(Accounts payable pertains to operating expenses.)

Instructions

Net cash provided $246,000

Prepare the operating activities section of the statement of cash flows using the direct method.

Prepare the operating activities section—indirect method.
(SO 3)
Net cash provided $246,000

P18-4B   Data for George Clooney Company are presented in P18-3B.

Instructions

Prepare the operating activities section of the statement of cash flows for George Clooney Company using the indirect method.

Prepare a statement of cash flows—indirect method.
(SO 3, 5)

P18-5B   The financial statements of Frank B. Robinson Company appear below:

FRANK B. ROBINSON COMPANY
Comparative Balance Sheets
December 31

Assets	2002	2001
Cash	$ 29,000	$ 13,000
Accounts receivable	28,000	14,000
Merchandise inventory	25,000	35,000
Property, plant, and equipment	60,000	78,000
Accumulated depreciation	(20,000)	(24,000)
Total	$122,000	$116,000

Liabilities and Stockholders' Equity		
Accounts payable	$ 27,000	$ 23,000
Income taxes payable	5,000	8,000
Bonds payable	27,000	33,000
Common stock	18,000	14,000
Retained earnings	45,000	38,000
Total	$122,000	$116,000

FRANK B. ROBINSON COMPANY
Income Statement
For the Year Ended December 31, 2002

Sales		$220,000
Cost of goods sold		180,000
Gross profit		40,000
Selling expenses	$14,000	
Administrative expenses	10,000	24,000
Income from operations		16,000
Interest expense		2,000
Income before income taxes		14,000
Income tax expense		4,000
Net income		$ 10,000

Additional information:

1. Dividends declared and paid were $3,000.
2. During the year equipment was sold for $8,500 cash. This equipment cost $18,000 originally and had a book value of $8,500 at the time of sale.
3. All depreciation expense is in the selling expense category.
4. All sales and purchases are on account.

Instructions

(a) Prepare a statement of cash flows using the indirect method.
(b) Compute the following cash-basis ratios.
   (1) Current cash debt coverage ratio.
   (2) Cash return on sales ratio.
   (3) Cash debt coverage ratio.

(a) Net cash provided by operating activities $12,500

P18-6B Data for the Frank B. Robinson Company are presented in P18-5B. Further analysis reveals the following.

Prepare a statement of cash flows—direct method.
(SO 4, 5)

1. Accounts payable pertain to merchandise suppliers.
2. All operating expenses except for depreciation were paid in cash.

Instructions

(a) Prepare a statement of cash flows for Frank B. Robinson Company using the direct method.
(b) Compute the following cash-basis ratios.
   (1) Current cash debt coverage ratio.
   (2) Cash return on sales ratio.
   (3) Cash debt coverage ratio.

(a) Cash receipts from customers $206,000

P18-7B The financial statements of Bruce Willis Company appear below.

Prepare a statement of cash flows—indirect method.
(SO 3)

BRUCE WILLIS COMPANY
Comparative Balance Sheets
December 31

Assets	2002	2001
Cash	$ 23,000	$ 11,000
Accounts receivable	24,000	33,000
Merchandise inventory	20,000	29,000
Prepaid expenses	15,000	13,000
Land	40,000	40,000
Property, plant, and equipment	210,000	225,000
Less: Accumulated depreciation	(55,000)	(67,500)
Total	$277,000	$283,500

Liabilities and Stockholders' Equity	2002	2001
Accounts payable	$ 9,000	$ 18,500
Accrued expenses payable	9,500	7,500
Interest payable	1,000	1,500
Income taxes payable	3,000	2,000
Bonds payable	50,000	80,000
Common stock	125,000	105,000
Retained earnings	79,500	69,000
Total	$277,000	$283,500

BRUCE WILLIS COMPANY
Income Statement
For the Year Ended December 31, 2002

Revenues		
Sales	$600,000	
Gain on sale of plant assets	2,500	$602,500
Less: Expenses		
Cost of goods sold	500,000	
Operating expenses (excluding depreciation)	60,000	
Depreciation expense	7,500	
Interest expense	5,000	
Income tax expense	9,000	581,500
Net income		$ 21,000

Additional information:

1. Plant assets were sold at a sales price of $37,500.
2. Additional equipment was purchased at a cost of $40,000.
3. Dividends of $10,500 were paid.
4. All sales and purchases were on account.
5. Bonds were redeemed at face value.
6. Additional shares of stock were issued for cash.

Net cash provided by operating activities $35,000
Investing activities used $2,500

Prepare a statement of cash flows—direct method.
(SO 4)

Instructions
Prepare a statement of cash flows for Bruce Willis Company for the year ended December 31, 2002, using the indirect method.

P18-8B Data for Bruce Willis Company is presented in P18-7B. Further analysis reveals the following.

1. Accounts payable relates to merchandise creditors.
2. All operating expenses, except depreciation expense, were paid in cash.

Net cash provided by operating activities $35,000. Investing activities used $2,500

Prepare a statement of cash flows—indirect method.
(SO 3, 5)

Instructions
Prepare a statement of cash flows for Bruce Willis Company for the year ended December 31, 2002, using the direct method.

P18-9B Presented below are the comparative balance sheets for Dennis Weigle Company as of December 31.

DENNIS WEIGLE COMPANY
Comparative Balance Sheets
December 31

Assets	2002	2001
Cash	$ 39,000	$ 45,000
Accounts receivable	49,500	52,000
Inventory	151,450	142,000
Prepaid expenses	16,780	21,000
Land	100,000	130,000
Equipment	228,000	155,000
Accumulated depreciation—equipment	(45,000)	(35,000)
Building	200,000	200,000
Accumulated depreciation—building	(60,000)	(40,000)
	$679,730	$670,000

Liabilities and Stockholders' Equity		
Accounts payable	$ 38,730	$ 40,000
Bonds payable	250,000	300,000
Common stock, $1 par	200,000	150,000
Retained earnings	191,000	180,000
	$679,730	$670,000

Additional information:

1. Operating expenses include depreciation expense of $42,000.
2. Land was sold for cash at book value.
3. Cash dividends of $27,000 were paid.
4. Net income for 2002 was $38,000.
5. Equipment was purchased for $95,000 cash. In addition, equipment costing $22,000 with a book value of $10,000 was sold for $8,100 cash.
6. Bonds were converted at face value by issuing 50,000 shares of $1 par value common stock.
7. Net sales for 2002 totaled $420,000.

Instructions

(a) Prepare a statement of cash flows for the year ended December 31, 2002, using the indirect method.

(b) Compute the following cash-basis ratios for 2002.
   (1) Current cash debt coverage ratio.
   (2) Cash return on sales ratio.
   (3) Cash debt coverage ratio.

(a) Net cash from operating activities $77,900

*P18-10B   Data for Bruce Willis Company are presented in P18-7B.

Instructions

Prepare a work sheet for a statement of cash flows for 2002. Enter the reconciling entries directly on the work sheet, presenting the entries alphabetically.

Prepare a work sheet.
(SO 6)

Total reconciling items $231,500

BROADENING YOUR PERSPECTIVE

*F*INANCIAL REPORTING AND ANALYSIS

FINANCIAL REPORTING PROBLEM: Lands' End, Inc.

BYP18-1   Refer to the financial statements of Lands' End, Inc. presented in Appendix A, and answer the following questions.
  (a) What was the amount of net cash provided by operating activities for the year ended January 28, 2000? For the year ended January 29, 1999?
  (b) What was the amount of increase or decrease in cash and cash equivalents for the year ended January 28, 2000? For the year ended January 29, 1999?
  (c) Which method of computing net cash provided by operating activities does Lands' End use?
  (d) From your analysis of the 2000 statement of cash flows, did the change in accounts receivable require or provide cash? Did the change in inventories require or provide cash? Did the change in accounts payable require or provide cash?
  (e) What was the net outflow or inflow of cash from investing activities for the year ended January 28, 2000?
  (f) What was the amount of interest paid in the year ended January 28, 2000? What was the amount of income taxes paid in the year ended January 28, 2000?

COMPARATIVE ANALYSIS PROBLEM: Lands' End vs. Abercrombie & Fitch

BYP18-2   Lands' End's financial statements are presented in Appendix A. Abercrombie & Fitch's financial statements are presented in Appendix B.

Instructions
  (a) Based on the information contained in these financial statements, compute the following 2000 ratios for each company.
    (1) Current cash debt coverage ratio.
    (2) Cash return on sales ratio.
    (3) Cash debt coverage ratio.
  (b) What conclusions concerning the management of cash can be drawn from these data?

INTERPRETING FINANCIAL STATEMENTS: A Global Focus

BYP18-3   The statement of cash flows has become a commonly provided financial statement by companies throughout the world. It is interesting to note, however, that its format does vary across countries. The following statement of cash flows is from the 1998 financial statements of Saint-Gobain (Paris, France). Saint-Gobain, one of the top 100 industrial companies in the world, is a leading producer of flat glass, reinforcements, glass packaging, insulation, building materials, pipe, abrasives, high-performance plastics, and industrial ceramics.

Instructions
  (a) What similarities to U.S. cash flow statements do you notice in terms of general format, as well as terminology?
  (b) What differences do you notice in terms of general format, as well as terminology?

SAINT-GOBAIN GROUP
Consolidated Statements of Cash Flows

(in millions of euro)	1998	1997
Cash flow from operating activities		
Net operating income	1,096	920
Profit on sale of non-current assets	(394)	(307)
Depreciation and amortization (note 14)	1,136	1,037
Dividends from associated companies	74	43
Sources from operations	**1,912**	**1,693**
(Increase) decrease in stocks	(174)	(41)
(Increase) decrease in trade accounts receivable	(59)	(241)
Increase (decrease) in trade accounts payable	79	79
Changes in income taxes payable and deferred taxes	14	3
Change in provisions	(48)	4
Cash provided by operating activities	**1,724**	**1,497**
Cash flow from investing activities		
Acquisition of fixed assets	(1,288)	(1,353)
Investments in consolidated companies (note 2)	(1,349)	(850)
Investments in unconsolidated companies	(382)	(244)
Total expenditure on fixed assets and investments	**(3,019)**	**(2,447)**
Cash (debt) acquired (note 2)	(19)	(17)
Acquisition of treasury stock	(344)	(3)
Disposal of fixed and intangible assets	25	55
Disposal of investments	1,107	814
(Cash) debt disposed of (note 2)	3	(125)
(Increase) decrease in deferred charges and other intangible assets	(68)	(48)
(Increase) decrease in deposits, long term receivables	9	31
(Increase) decrease in receivables related to investing activities	(124)	37
Cash used for investing activities	**(2,430)**	**(1,703)**
Cash flow from financing activities		
Issue of share capital	105	265
Minority interests in share capital increases of subsidiaries	4	4
(Decrease) increase in long term debt	132	541
Dividends paid	(248)	(221)
Dividends paid to minority shareholders of consolidated subsidiaries	(44)	(82)
Cash provided by (used for) financing activities	**(51)**	**507**
Net effect of exchange rate fluctuations on cash and cash equivalents	(9)	(39)
Increase (decrease) in cash and cash equivalents (net)	**(766)**	**262**
Net cash and cash equivalents at the beginning of the year	(92)	(354)
Net cash and cash equivalents at the end of the year	**(858)**	**(92)**

EXPLORING THE WEB

BYP18-4   *Purpose:* Learn about the SEC.

Address: **www.sec.gov/index.html** *(or go to www.wiley.com/college/weygandt)*

Steps:

1. From the SEC homepage, choose **About the SEC**.

Instructions

Answer the following questions.

   (a) How many enforcement actions does the SEC take each year against securities law violators? What are typical infractions?

   (b) After the Depression, Congress passed the Securities Acts of 1933 and 1934 to improve investor confidence in the markets. What two "common sense" notions are these laws based on?

   (c) Who was the President of the United States at the time of the creation of the SEC? Who was the first SEC Chairperson?

BYP18-5 *Purpose:* Use the Internet to view SEC filings.

Address: biz.yahoo.com/i *(or go to www.wiley.com/college/weygandt)*

Steps:

   1. Type in a company name.
   2. Choose **SEC filings** (this will take you to Yahoo-Edgar Online).

Instructions

Answer the following questions.

   (a) What company did you select?
   (b) What other recent SEC filings are available for your viewing?
   (c) Which filing is the most recent? What is the date?

CRITICAL THINKING

GROUP DECISION CASE

BYP18-6 Greg Rhoda and Debra Sondgeroth are examining the following statement of cash flows for K.K. Bean Trading Company for the year ended January 31, 2001.

K.K. BEAN TRADING COMPANY
Statement of Cash Flows
For the Year Ended January 31, 2001

Sources of cash	
From sales of merchandise	$390,000
From sale of capital stock	420,000
From sale of investment (purchased below)	80,000
From depreciation	55,000
From issuance of note for truck	20,000
From interest on investments	6,000
Total sources of cash	971,000
Uses of cash	
For purchase of fixtures and equipment	340,000
For merchandise purchased for resale (all sold)	258,000
For operating expenses (including depreciation)	160,000
For purchase of investment	75,000
For purchase of truck by issuance of note	20,000
For purchase of treasury stock	10,000
For interest on note payable	3,000
Total uses of cash	866,000
Net increase in cash	$105,000

Greg claims that K.K. Bean's statement of cash flows is an excellent example of a superb first year, with cash increasing $105,000. Debra replies that it was not a superb first year—but rather, that the year was an operating failure. She says that the statement was incorrectly presented and that $105,000 is not the actual increase in cash. The cash balance at the beginning of the year was $140,000.

Instructions

With the class divided into groups, answer the following.

(a) With whom do you agree, Greg or Debra? Explain your position.

(b) Using the data provided, prepare a statement of cash flows in proper form using the indirect method. The only noncash items in the income statement are depreciation and the gain from the sale of the investment.

COMMUNICATION ACTIVITY

BYP18-7 Arnold Byte, the owner-president of Computer Services Company, is unfamiliar with the statement of cash flows which you, as his accountant, prepared. He asks for further explanation.

Instructions

Write him a brief memo explaining the form and content of the statement of cash flows as shown in Illustration 18-17 on page 731.

ETHICS CASE

BYP18-8 Puebla Corporation is a medium-sized wholesaler of automotive parts. It has ten stockholders, who have been paid a total of $1 million in cash dividends for eight consecutive years. The policy of the Board of Directors requires that in order for this dividend to be declared, net cash provided by operating activities as reported in Puebla's current year's statement of cash flows must be in excess of $1 million. President and CEO Phil Monat's job is secure so long as he produces annual operating cash flows to support the usual dividend.

At the end of the current year, controller Rick Rodgers presents president Monat with some disappointing news: The net cash provided by operating activities is calculated, by the indirect method, to be only $970,000. The president says to Rick, "We must get that amount above $1 million. Isn't there some way to increase operating cash flow by another $30,000?" Rick answers, "These figures were prepared by my assistant. I'll go back to my office and see what I can do." The president replies, "I know you won't let me down, Rick."

Upon close scrutiny of the statement of cash flows, Rick concludes that he can get the operating cash flows above $1 million by reclassifying a $60,000, 2-year note payable listed in the financing activities section as "Proceeds from bank loan—$60,000." He will report the note instead as "Increase in payables—$60,000" and treat it as an adjustment of net income in the operating activities section. He returns to the president saying, "You can tell the Board to declare their usual dividend. Our net cash flow provided by operating activities is $1,030,000." "Good man, Rick! I knew I could count on you," exults the president.

Instructions

(a) Who are the stakeholders in this situation?

(b) Was there anything unethical about the president's actions? Was there anything unethical about the controller's actions?

(c) Are the Board members or anyone else likely to discover the misclassification?

Answers to Self-Study Questions

1. c **2.** b **3.** a **4.** c **5.** d **6.** b **7.** c **8.** d **9.** b **10.** c
11. d **12.** a **13.** b

Answer to *Lands' End* Review It Question 4, p. 732

Lands' End uses the indirect method of computing net cash provided by operating activities. The largest single item of cash outflow for Lands' End in the fiscal year ended January 28, 2000, is "Cash paid for capital additions" $28.013 million.

Remember to go back to the Navigator box on the chapter-opening page and check off your completed work.

FINANCIAL
STATEMENT
ANALYSIS

THE NAVIGATOR ✓

- Understand *Concepts for Review* ❑
- Read *Feature Story* ❑
- Scan *Study Objectives* ❑
- Read *Preview* ❑
- Read text and answer *Before You Go On*
  p. 787 ❑ *p.* 804 ❑ *p.* 805 ❑
- Work *Demonstration Problem* ❑
- Review *Summary of Study Objectives* ❑
- Answer *Self-Study Questions* ❑
- Complete *Assignments* ❑

*C*ONCEPTS FOR REVIEW

Before studying this chapter, you should know or, if necessary, review:

  a. The contents and classification of a corporate balance sheet. (Ch. 4, pp. 151–156)

  b. The contents and classification of a corporate income statement. (Ch. 5, pp. 197–202)

  c. Who are the various users of financial statement information. (Ch. 1, pp. 3–5)

  d. How to compute earnings per share (EPS). (Ch. 15, pp. 620–622)

  e. How the liquidity of a company is determined. (Ch. 4, p. 154)

☑ THE
NAVIGATOR

"Follow that Stock!"

If you thought cab drivers with cell phones were scary, how about a cab driver with a trading desk in the front seat?

When a stoplight turns red or traffic backs up, New York City cabby Carlos Rubino morphs into a day trader, scanning real-time quotes of his favorite stocks as they spew across a PalmPilot mounted next to the steering wheel. "It's kind of stressful," he says. "But I like it."

Itching to know how a particular stock is doing? Mr. Rubino is happy to look up quotes for passengers. **Yahoo!, Amazon.com**, and **America Online** are the most requested ones. He even lets customers use his **Hitachi** Traveler laptop to send urgent e-mails from the back seat. Aware of a new local law prohibiting cabbies from using cell phones while they're driving, Mr. Rubino extends that rule to his trading. "I stop the cab at the side of the road if I have to make a trade," he says. "Safety first."

Originally from São Paulo, Brazil, Mr. Rubino has been driving his cab since 1987, and started trading stocks a few years ago. His curiosity grew as he began to educate himself by reading business publications. The Wall Street brokers he picks up are usually impressed with his knowledge, he says. But the feeling generally isn't mutual. Some of them "don't know much," he says. "They buy what people tell them to buy—they're like a toll collector."

Mr. Rubino is an enigma to his fellow cab drivers. A lot of his colleagues say they want to trade too. "But cab drivers are a little cheap," he says. "The [real-time] quotes cost $100 a month. The wireless Internet access is $54 a month."

Will he give up his brokerage firm on wheels for a stationary job?

Not likely. Though he claims a 70 percent return on his investments in recent months, he says he makes $1,300 and up a week driving his cab—more than he does trading. Besides, he adds, "Why go somewhere and have a boss?"

Source: Excerpted from Barbara Boydston, "With this Cab, People Jump in and Shout, 'Follow that Stock!'," *The Wall Street Journal*, August 18, 1999, p. C1. Reprinted by permission of the Wall Street Journal © 1999 Dow Jones & Company, Inc. All Rights Reserved Worldwide.

☑ THE NAVIGATOR

STUDY OBJECTIVES

After studying this chapter, you should be able to:

1. Discuss the need for comparative analysis.
2. Identify the tools of financial statement analysis.
3. Explain and apply horizontal analysis.
4. Describe and apply vertical analysis.
5. Identify and compute ratios, and describe their purpose and use in analyzing a firm's liquidity, profitability, and solvency.
6. Recognize the limitations of financial statement analysis.

An important lesson can be learned from the Feature Story: Experience is the best teacher. By now you have learned a significant amount about financial reporting by U.S. corporations. Using some of the basic decision tools presented in this book, you can perform a rudimentary analysis on any U.S. company and draw basic conclusions about its financial health. Although it would not be wise for you to bet your life savings on a company's stock relying solely on your current level of knowledge, we strongly encourage you to practice your new skills wherever possible. Only with practice will you improve your ability to interpret financial numbers.

Before unleashing you on the world of high finance, we will present a few more important concepts and techniques, as well as provide you with one more comprehensive review of corporate financial statements. We use all of the decision tools presented in this text to analyze a single company—**Sears, Roebuck and Co.,** one of the country's oldest and largest retail store chains.

The content and organization of Chapter 19 are as follows.

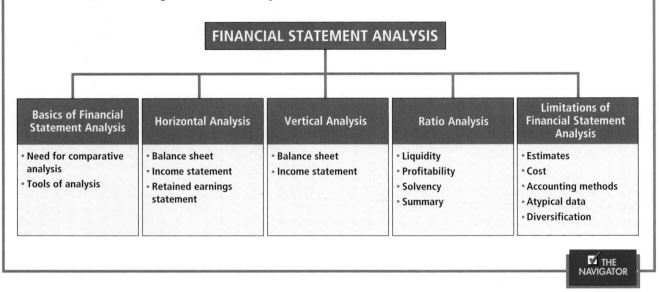

BASICS OF FINANCIAL STATEMENT ANALYSIS

Analyzing financial statements involves evaluating three characteristics of a company: its liquidity, its profitability, and its solvency. A **short-term creditor**, such as a bank, is primarily interested in the ability of the borrower to pay obligations when they come due. The liquidity of the borrower is extremely important in evaluating the safety of a loan. A **long-term creditor**, such as a bondholder, however, looks to profitability and solvency measures that indicate the company's ability to survive over a long period of time. Long-term creditors consider such measures as the amount of debt in the company's capital structure and its ability to meet interest payments. Similarly, **stockholders** are interested in the profitability and solvency of the company. They want to assess the likelihood of dividends and the growth potential of the stock.

STUDY OBJECTIVE 1

Discuss the need for comparative analysis.

NEED FOR COMPARATIVE ANALYSIS

Every item reported in a financial statement has significance. When **Sears, Roebuck and Co.** reports cash of $729 million on its balance sheet, we know the company had that amount of cash on the balance sheet date. But, we do not know whether the amount represents an increase over prior years, or whether it is adequate in relation to the company's need for cash. To obtain such information, it is necessary to compare the amount of cash with other financial statement data.

Comparisons can be made on a number of different bases. Three are illustrated in this chapter.

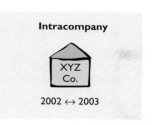

Intracompany

2002 ↔ 2003

1. **Intracompany basis.** This basis compares an item or financial relationship **within a company** in the current year with the same item or relationship in one or more prior years. For example, Sears, Roebuck and Co. can compare its cash balance at the end of the current year with last year's balance to find the amount of the increase or decrease. Likewise, Sears can compare the percentage of cash to current assets at the end of the current year with the percentage in one or more prior years. Intracompany comparisons are useful in detecting changes in financial relationships and significant trends.

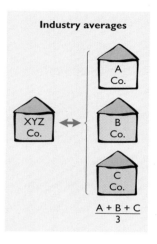

Industry averages

$\frac{A + B + C}{3}$

2. **Industry averages.** This basis compares an item or financial relationship of a company with **industry averages** (or **norms**) published by financial ratings organizations such as **Dun & Bradstreet**, **Moody's**, and **Standard & Poor's**. For example, Sears's net income can be compared with the average net income of all companies in the retail chain-store industry. Comparisons with industry averages provide information as to a company's relative performance within the industry.

3. **Intercompany basis.** This basis compares an item or financial relationship of one company with the same item or relationship in **one or more competing companies**. The comparisons are made on the basis of the published financial statements of the individual companies. For example, Sears's total sales for the year can be compared with the total sales of its major competitors such as **Kmart** and **Wal-Mart**. Intercompany comparisons are useful in determining a company's competitive position.

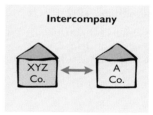

Intercompany

TOOLS OF FINANCIAL STATEMENT ANALYSIS

Various tools are used to evaluate the significance of financial statement data. Three commonly used tools are these:

- **Horizontal analysis** evaluates a series of financial statement data over a period of time.

- **Vertical analysis** evaluates financial statement data by expressing each item in a financial statement as a percent of a base amount.

- **Ratio analysis** expresses the relationship among selected items of financial statement data.

Horizontal analysis is used primarily in intracompany comparisons. Two features in published financial statements facilitate this type of comparison: First, each of the basic financial statements is presented on a comparative basis for a minimum of two years. Second, a summary of selected financial data is presented for a series of five to ten years or more. Vertical analysis is used in both intra- and intercompany comparisons. Ratio analysis is used in all three types of comparisons. In the following sections, we will explain and illustrate each of the three types of analysis.

STUDY OBJECTIVE 2

Identify the tools of financial statement analysis.

*H*ORIZONTAL ANALYSIS

STUDY OBJECTIVE 3

Explain and apply horizontal analysis.

Horizontal analysis, also called **trend analysis**, is a technique for evaluating a series of financial statement data over a period of time. Its purpose is to determine the increase or decrease that has taken place. This change may be expressed as either an amount or a percentage. For example, the recent net sales figures of **Sears, Roebuck and Co.** are as follows. (Yes, that's $41 **billion** 71 million in 1999.)

Illustration 19-1

Sears, Roebuck and Co.'s net sales

SEARS

SEARS, ROEBUCK AND CO. Net Sales (in millions)				
1999	**1998**	**1997**	**1996**	**1995**
$41,071	$41,575	$41,574	$38,064	$34,835

If we assume that 1995 is the base year, we can measure all percentage increases or decreases from this base period amount as follows.

Illustration 19-2

Formula for horizontal analysis of changes since base period

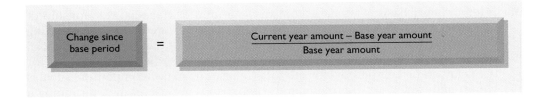

$$\text{Change since base period} = \frac{\text{Current year amount} - \text{Base year amount}}{\text{Base year amount}}$$

For example, we can determine that net sales for Sears increased from 1995 to 1996 approximately 9.3% [($38,064 − $34,835) ÷ $34,835]. Similarly, we can determine that net sales increased from 1995 to 1999 more than 17.9% [($41,071 − $34,835) ÷ $34,835].

Alternatively, we can express current year sales as a percentage of the base period. This is done by dividing the current year amount by the base year amount, as shown below.

Illustration 19-3

Formula for horizontal analysis of current year in relation to base year

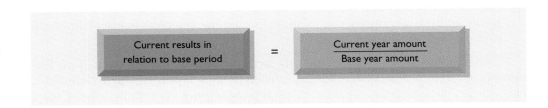

$$\text{Current results in relation to base period} = \frac{\text{Current year amount}}{\text{Base year amount}}$$

Illustration 19-4 presents this analysis for Sears for a five-year period using 1995 as the base period.

SEARS

SEARS, ROEBUCK AND CO. Net Sales (in millions) in relation to base period 1995				
1999	**1998**	**1997**	**1996**	**1995**
$41,071	$41,575	$41,574	$38,064	$34,835
117.9%	119.3%	119.3%	109.3%	100%

Illustration 19-4

Horizontal analysis of Sears, Roebuck and Co.'s net sales in relation to base period

BALANCE SHEET

To further illustrate horizontal analysis, we will use the financial statements of Quality Department Store Inc. It is a downtown, full-line department store in a southeastern city of 55,000 people. A horizontal analysis of its two-year condensed balance sheets, showing dollar and percentage changes, is presented in Illustration 19-5.

QUALITY DEPARTMENT STORE INC. Condensed Balance Sheets December 31				
			Increase or (Decrease) during 1999	
	1999	**1998**	**Amount**	**Percent**
Assets				
Current assets	$1,020,000	$ 945,000	$ 75,000	7.9%
Plant assets (net)	800,000	632,500	167,500	26.5%
Intangible assets	15,000	17,500	(2,500)	(14.3%)
Total assets	$1,835,000	$1,595,000	$240,000	15.0%
Liabilities				
Current liabilities	$ 344,500	$ 303,000	$ 41,500	13.7%
Long-term liabilities	487,500	497,000	(9,500)	(1.9%)
Total liabilities	832,000	800,000	32,000	4.0%
Stockholders' Equity				
Common stock, $1 par	275,400	270,000	5,400	2.0%
Retained earnings	727,600	525,000	202,600	38.6%
Total stockholders' equity	1,003,000	795,000	208,000	26.2%
Total liabilities and stockholders' equity	$1,835,000	$1,595,000	$240,000	15.0%

Illustration 19-5

Horizontal analysis of balance sheets

HELPFUL HINT
It is difficult to comprehend the significance of a change when only the dollar amount of change is examined. When the change is expressed in percentage form, it is easier to grasp the true magnitude of the change.

The comparative balance sheets in Illustration 19-5 show that a number of significant changes have occurred in Quality Department Store's financial structure from 1998 to 1999. In the assets section, plant assets (net) increased $167,500, or 26.5%. In the liabilities section, current liabilities increased $41,500, or 13.7%. In the stockholders' equity section, retained earnings increased $202,600, or 38.6%. This suggests that the company expanded its asset base during 1999 and **financed this expansion primarily by retaining income** rather than assuming additional long-term debt.

INCOME STATEMENT

Presented in Illustration 19-6 is a horizontal analysis of the two-year condensed income statements of Quality Department Store Inc. for the years 1999 and 1998.

Illustration 19-6

Horizontal analysis of income statements

QUALITY DEPARTMENT STORE INC. Condensed Income Statements For the Years Ended December 31				
			Increase or (Decrease) during 1999	
	1999	1998	Amount	Percent
Sales	$2,195,000	$1,960,000	$235,000	12.0%
Sales returns and allowances	98,000	123,000	(25,000)	(20.3%)
Net sales	2,097,000	1,837,000	260,000	14.2%
Cost of goods sold	1,281,000	1,140,000	141,000	12.4%
Gross profit	816,000	697,000	119,000	17.1%
Selling expenses	253,000	211,500	41,500	19.6%
Administrative expenses	104,000	108,500	(4,500)	(4.1%)
Total operating expenses	357,000	320,000	37,000	11.6%
Income from operations	459,000	377,000	82,000	21.8%
Other revenues and gains				
Interest and dividends	9,000	11,000	(2,000)	(18.2%)
Other expenses and losses				
Interest expense	36,000	40,500	(4,500)	(11.1%)
Income before income taxes	432,000	347,500	84,500	24.3%
Income tax expense	168,200	139,000	29,200	21.0%
Net income	$ 263,800	$ 208,500	$ 55,300	26.5%

HELPFUL HINT

Note that though the amount column is additive (the total is $55,300), the percentage column is not additive (26.5% is not the total). A separate percentage has been calculated for each item.

Horizontal analysis of the income statements shows the following changes:

1. Net sales increased $260,000, or 14.2% ($260,000 ÷ $1,837,000).

2. Cost of goods sold increased $141,000, or 12.4% ($141,000 ÷ $1,140,000).

3. Total operating expenses increased $37,000, or 11.6% ($37,000 ÷ $320,000).

Overall, gross profit and net income were up substantially. Gross profit increased 17.1%, and net income, 26.5%. Quality's profit trend appears favorable.

RETAINED EARNINGS STATEMENT

A horizontal analysis of Quality Department Store's comparative retained earnings statements is presented in Illustration 19-7. Analyzed horizontally, net income increased $55,300, or 26.5%, whereas dividends on the common stock increased only $1,200, or 2%. We saw in the horizontal analysis of the balance sheet that ending retained earnings increased 38.6%. As indicated earlier, the company retained a significant portion of net income to finance additional plant facilities.

QUALITY DEPARTMENT STORE INC. Retained Earnings Statements For the Years Ended December 31				
			Increase or (Decrease) during 1999	
	1999	**1998**	**Amount**	**Percent**
Retained earnings, Jan. 1	$525,000	$376,500	$148,500	39.4%
Add: Net income	263,800	208,500	55,300	26.5%
	788,800	585,000	203,800	
Deduct: Dividends	61,200	60,000	1,200	2.0%
Retained earnings, Dec. 31	$727,600	$525,000	$202,600	38.6%

Illustration 19-7

Horizontal analysis of retained earnings statements

Horizontal analysis of changes from period to period is relatively straightforward and is quite useful. But complications can occur in making the computations. If an item has no value in a base year or preceding year and a value in the next year, no percentage change can be computed. Similarly, if a negative amount appears in the base or preceding period and a positive amount exists the following year (or vice versa), no percentage change can be computed.

VERTICAL ANALYSIS

Vertical analysis, also called **common size analysis**, is a technique for evaluating financial statement data that expresses each item within a financial statement as a percent of a base amount. On a balance sheet we might say that current assets are 22% of total assets (total assets being the base amount). Or on an income statement, we might say that selling expenses are 16% of net sales (net sales being the base amount).

STUDY OBJECTIVE 4

Describe and apply vertical analysis.

BALANCE SHEET

Presented in Illustration 19-8 on page 786 is the vertical analysis of Quality Department Store Inc.'s comparative balance sheets. The base for the asset items is **total assets**. The base for the liability and stockholders' equity items is **total liabilities and stockholders' equity**.

Vertical analysis shows the relative size of each category in the balance sheet. It also can show the **percentage change** in the individual asset, liability, and stockholders' equity items. For example, we can see that current assets decreased from 59.2% of total assets in 1998 to 55.6% in 1999 (even though the absolute dollar amount increased $75,000 in that time). Plant assets (net) have increased from 39.7% to 43.6% of total assets. Retained earnings have increased from 32.9% to 39.7% of total liabilities and stockholders' equity. These results reinforce the earlier observations that **Quality is choosing to finance its growth through retention of earnings rather than through issuing additional debt.**

INCOME STATEMENT

Vertical analysis of Quality's income statements is shown in Illustration 19-9. We see that cost of goods sold as a percentage of net sales declined 1% (62.1% vs.

Illustration 19-8

Vertical analysis of balance sheets

QUALITY DEPARTMENT STORE INC.
Condensed Balance Sheets
December 31

	1999 Amount	1999 Percent	1998 Amount	1998 Percent
Assets				
Current assets	$1,020,000	55.6%	$ 945,000	59.2%
Plant assets (net)	800,000	43.6%	632,500	39.7%
Intangible assets	15,000	0.8%	17,500	1.1%
Total assets	$1,835,000	100.0%	$1,595,000	100.0%
Liabilities				
Current liabilities	$ 344,500	18.8%	$ 303,000	19.0%
Long-term liabilities	487,500	26.5%	497,000	31.2%
Total liabilities	832,000	45.3%	800,000	50.2%
Stockholders' Equity				
Common stock, $1 par	275,400	15.0%	270,000	16.9%
Retained earnings	727,600	39.7%	525,000	32.9%
Total stockholders' equity	1,003,000	54.7%	795,000	49.8%
Total liabilities and stockholders' equity	$1,835,000	100.0%	$1,595,000	100.0%

HELPFUL HINT
The formula for calculating these balance sheet percentages is:

$$\frac{\text{Each item on B/S}}{\text{Total assets}} = \%$$

61.1%) and total operating expenses declined 0.4% (17.4% vs. 17.0%). As a result, it is not surprising to see net income as a percent of net sales increase from 11.4% to 12.6%. Quality appears to be a profitable enterprise that is becoming even more successful.

Illustration 19-9

Vertical analysis of income statements

QUALITY DEPARTMENT STORE INC.
Condensed Income Statements
For the Years Ended December 31

	1999 Amount	1999 Percent	1998 Amount	1998 Percent
Sales	$2,195,000	104.7%	$1,960,000	106.7%
Sales returns and allowances	98,000	4.7%	123,000	6.7%
Net sales	2,097,000	100.0%	1,837,000	100.0%
Cost of goods sold	1,281,000	61.1%	1,140,000	62.1%
Gross profit	816,000	38.9%	697,000	37.9%
Selling expenses	253,000	12.0%	211,500	11.5%
Administrative expenses	104,000	5.0%	108,500	5.9%
Total operating expenses	357,000	17.0%	320,000	17.4%
Income from operations	459,000	21.9%	377,000	20.5%
Other revenues and gains				
Interest and dividends	9,000	0.4%	11,000	0.6%
Other expenses and losses				
Interest expense	36,000	1.7%	40,500	2.2%
Income before income taxes	432,000	20.6%	347,500	18.9%
Income tax expense	168,200	8.0%	139,000	7.5%
Net income	$ 263,800	12.6%	$ 208,500	11.4%

HELPFUL HINT
The formula for calculating these income statement percentages is:

$$\frac{\text{Each item on I/S}}{\text{Net sales}} = \%$$

An associated benefit of vertical analysis is that it enables you to compare companies of different sizes. For example, Quality's main competitor is a Sears store in a nearby town. Using vertical analysis, the condensed income statements of the small local retail enterprise, Quality Department Store Inc., can be more meaningfully compared with the 1999 income statement of the giant international retailer, **Sears, Roebuck and Co.**, as shown in Illustration 19-10.

CONDENSED INCOME STATEMENTS (in thousands)				
	Quality Department Store Inc.		Sears, Roebuck and Co.[1]	
	Dollars	Percent	Dollars	Percent
Net sales	$2,097	100.0%	$41,071,000	100.0%
Cost of goods sold	1,281	61.1%	27,212,000	66.3%
Gross profit	816	38.9%	13,859,000	33.7%
Selling and administrative expenses	357	17.0%	10,137,000	24.7%
Income from operations	459	21.9%	3,722,000	9.0%
Other expenses and revenues (including income taxes)	195	9.3%	2,269,000	5.5%
Net income	$ 264	12.6%	$ 1,453,000	3.5%

Illustration 19-10

Intercompany income statement comparison

Sears' net sales are 19,585 times greater than the net sales of relatively tiny Quality Department Store. But vertical analysis eliminates this difference in size. The percentages show that Quality's and Sears's gross profit rates were somewhat comparable at 38.9% and 33.7%. However, the percentages related to income from operations were significantly different at 21.9% and 9.0%. This disparity can be attributed to Quality's selling and administrative expense percentage (17%) which is much lower than Sears's (24.7%). Although Sears earned net income more than 5,500 times larger than Quality's, Sears's net income as a **percent of each sales dollar** (3.5%) is only 28% of Quality's (12.6%).

BEFORE YOU GO ON...

▶ *REVIEW IT*

1. What are the different tools that might be used to compare financial information?
2. What is horizontal analysis?
3. What is vertical analysis?
4. Identify the specific sections in **Lands' End's** 1999 Annual Report where horizontal and vertical analysis of financial data is presented. The answer to this question is provided on page 824.

▶ *DO IT*

Summary financial information for Rosepatch Company is as follows.

	December 31, 2002	December 31, 2001
Current assets	$234,000	$180,000
Plant assets (net)	756,000	420,000
Total assets	$990,000	$600,000

---

[1]Sears, Roebuck and Co., *1999 Annual Report* (Hoffman Estates, Illinois).

Compute the amount and percentage changes in 2002 using horizontal analysis, assuming 2001 is the base year.

ACTION PLAN
- Find the percentage change by dividing the amount of the increase by the 2001 amount (base year).

SOLUTION

	Increase in 2002	
	Amount	**Percent**
Current assets	$ 54,000	30% [($234,000 − $180,000) ÷ $180,000]
Plant assets (net)	336,000	80% [($756,000 − $420,000) ÷ $420,000]
Total assets	$390,000	65% [($990,000 − $600,000) ÷ $600,000]

Related exercise material: BE19-1, BE19-3, BE19-4, BE19-6, E19-1, E19-3, and E19-4.

RATIO ANALYSIS

STUDY OBJECTIVE 5

Identify and compute ratios, and describe their purpose and use in analyzing a firm's liquidity, profitability, and solvency.

Ratio analysis expresses the relationship among selected items of financial statement data. A **ratio** expresses the mathematical relationship between one quantity and another. The relationship is expressed in terms of either a percentage, a rate, or a simple proportion. To illustrate, in 1999 **Nike, Inc.**, had current assets of $3,265 million and current liabilities of $1,446 million. The relationship is determined by dividing current assets by current liabilities. The alternative means of expression are:

Percentage: Current assets are 226% of current liabilities.
Rate: Current assets are 2.26 times greater than current liabilities.
Proportion: The relationship of current assets to liabilities is 2.26:1.

HELPFUL HINT
Each of these is illustrated in the following sections.

TECHNOLOGY IN ACTION

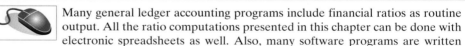

Many general ledger accounting programs include financial ratios as routine output. All the ratio computations presented in this chapter can be done with electronic spreadsheets as well. Also, many software programs are written specifically for financial statement analysis. These are written for both general purpose use and for use in specific industries. For example, financial institutions routinely use over 60 ratios geared specifically to the banking industry.

For analysis of the primary financial statements, ratios can be used to evaluate liquidity, profitability, and solvency. These classifications are described and pictured in Illustration 19-11.

Ratios can provide clues to underlying conditions that may not be apparent from individual financial statement components. However, a single ratio by itself is not very meaningful. Accordingly, in the discussion of ratios we will use the following types of comparisons.

1. **Intracompany comparisons** for two years for Quality Department Store.
2. **Industry average comparisons** based on median ratios for department stores.

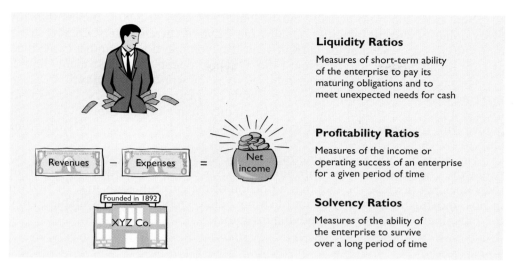

Illustration 19-11

Financial ratio classifications

3. **Intercompany comparisons** based on **Sears, Roebuck and Co.** as Quality Department Store's principal competitor.

LIQUIDITY RATIOS

Liquidity ratios measure the short-term ability of the enterprise to pay its maturing obligations and to meet unexpected needs for cash. Short-term creditors such as bankers and suppliers are particularly interested in assessing liquidity. The ratios that can be used to determine the enterprise's short-term debt-paying ability are the current ratio, the acid-test ratio, the current cash debt coverage ratio, receivables turnover, and inventory turnover.

1. Current Ratio

The **current ratio** is a widely used measure for evaluating a company's liquidity and short-term debt-paying ability. The ratio is computed by dividing current assets by current liabilities.

The 1999 and 1998 current ratios for Quality Department Store and comparative data are shown in Illustration 19-12.

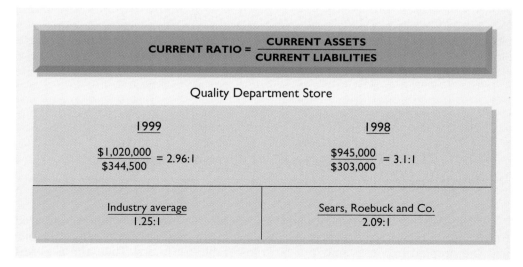

Illustration 19-12

Current ratio

HELPFUL HINT
Can any corporation operate successfully without working capital? Yes, if it has very predictable cash flows and solid earnings. A surprising number of companies, including **Whirlpool, American Standard**, and **Campbell's Soup**, are pursuing this goal. The rationale: Less money tied up in working capital means more money to invest in the business.

What does the ratio actually mean? The 1999 ratio of 2.96:1 means that for every dollar of current liabilities, Quality has $2.96 of current assets. Quality's current ratio has decreased in the current year. But, compared to the industry average of 1.25:1, and Sears's 2.09:1 current ratio, Quality appears to be reasonably liquid.

The current ratio is sometimes referred to as the **working capital ratio** because **working capital** is the excess of current assets over current liabilities. The current ratio is a more dependable indicator of liquidity than working capital. Two companies with the same amount of working capital may have significantly different current ratios.

The current ratio is only one measure of liquidity. It does not take into account the composition of the current assets. For example, a satisfactory current ratio does not disclose the fact that a portion of the current assets may be tied up in slow-moving inventory. A dollar of cash would be more readily available to pay the bills than a dollar of slow-moving inventory.

ACCOUNTING IN ACTION *Business Insight*

The apparent simplicity of the current ratio can have real-world limitations. An addition of equal amounts to both the numerator and the denominator causes the ratio to decrease. Assume, for example, that a company has $2,000,000 of current assets and $1,000,000 of current liabilities. Its current ratio is 2:1. If it purchases $1,000,000 of inventory on account, it will have $3,000,000 of current assets and $2,000,000 of current liabilities. Its current ratio will decrease to 1.5:1. If, instead, the company pays off $500,000 of its current liabilities, it will have $1,500,000 of current assets and $500,000 of current liabilities, and its current ratio will increase to 3:1. Any trend analysis should be done with care, since the ratio is susceptible to quick changes and is easily influenced by management.

2. Acid-Test Ratio

ALTERNATIVE TERMINOLOGY
The acid-test ratio is also called the *quick ratio.*

The **acid-test (quick) ratio** is a measure of a company's immediate short-term liquidity. It is computed by dividing the sum of cash, short-term investments, and net receivables by current liabilities. Thus, it is an important complement to the current ratio. For example, assume that the current assets of Quality Department Store for 1999 and 1998 consist of the following items.

Illustration 19-13

Current assets of Quality Department Store

QUALITY DEPARTMENT STORE INC. Balance Sheet (partial)		
	1999	**1998**
Current assets		
Cash	$ 100,000	$155,000
Short-term investments	20,000	70,000
Receivables (net)	230,000	180,000
Inventory	620,000	500,000
Prepaid expenses	50,000	40,000
Total current assets	$1,020,000	$945,000

Cash, short-term investments, and receivables (net) are highly liquid compared to inventory and prepaid expenses. The inventory may not be readily saleable, and the prepaid expenses may not be transferable to others. Thus, the acid-test ratio measures **immediate** liquidity. The 1999 and 1998 acid-test ratios for Quality Department Store and comparative data are as follows.

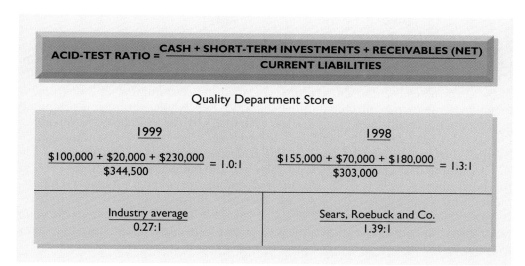

Illustration 19-14

Acid-test ratio

The ratio has declined in 1999. Is an acid-test ratio of 1.0:1 adequate? When compared with the industry average of 0.27:1 and Sears's of 1.39:1, Quality's acid-test ratio seems adequate.

3. Current Cash Debt Coverage Ratio

A disadvantage of the current and acid-test ratios is that they use year-end balances of current asset and current liability accounts. These balances may not represent the company's current position during most of the year. A ratio that partially corrects for this problem is the **current cash debt coverage ratio**. It is calculated by dividing net cash provided by operating activities by average current liabilities. Because it uses net cash provided by operating activities rather than a balance at a point in time, it may provide a better idea of a company's liquidity.

Assume that Quality Department Store's statement of cash flows shows net cash flows provided by operating activities of $404,000 in 1999 and $340,000 in 1998. Current liabilities at January 1, 1998, are $290,000. The current cash debt coverage ratio for Quality Department Store and comparative data are as follows.

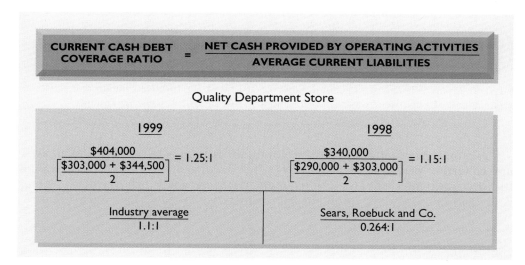

Illustration 19-15

Current cash debt coverage ratio

The ratio increased in 1999. Is the coverage adequate? Probably so. Quality's operating cash flow coverage of average current liabilities is slightly greater than the industry average. Sears's current cash debt coverage ratio in 1999 was 0.264:1.

4. Receivables Turnover

Liquidity may be measured by how quickly certain assets can be converted to cash. How liquid, for example, are the receivables? The ratio used to assess the liquidity of the receivables is **receivables turnover**. It measures the number of times, on average, receivables are collected during the period. Receivables turnover is computed by dividing net credit sales (net sales less cash sales) by the average net receivables. Unless seasonal factors are significant, average net receivables outstanding can be computed from the beginning and ending balances of the net receivables.[2]

Assuming that all sales are credit sales and the balance of receivables (net) at the beginning of 1998 is $200,000, the receivables turnover for Quality Department Store and comparative data are shown in Illustration 19-16. Quality's receivables turnover improved in 1999. The turnover of 10.2 times compares quite favorably with Sears's 2.39 times but is inferior to the department store industry's average of 13.7 times.

Illustration 19-16

Receivables turnover

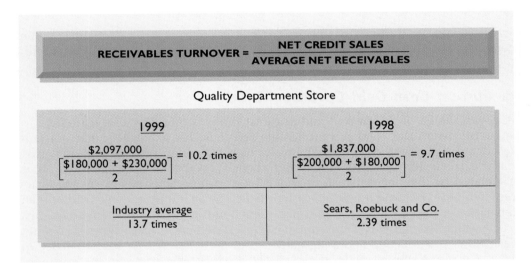

ACCOUNTING IN ACTION *Business Insight*

In some cases, receivables turnover may be misleading. Some companies, especially large retail chains, encourage credit and revolving charge sales. They may even slow collections in order to earn a healthy return on the outstanding receivables at interest rates of 18% to 22%. This may explain why **Sears's** turnover is only 2.39 times. In general, however, the faster the turnover, the greater the reliance that can be placed on the current and acid-test ratios for assessing liquidity.

A popular variant of the receivables turnover ratio is to convert it to an **average collection period** in terms of days. This is done by dividing the receivables turnover ratio into 365 days. For example, the receivables turnover of 10.2 times is divided into 365 days to obtain approximately 35.8 days. This means that re-

---

[2]If seasonal factors are significant, the average receivables balance might be determined by using monthly amounts.

ceivables are collected on average every 36 days, or about every 5 weeks. The average collection period is frequently used to assess the effectiveness of a company's credit and collection policies. The general rule is that the collection period should not greatly exceed the credit term period (the time allowed for payment).

5. Inventory Turnover

Inventory turnover measures the number of times on average the inventory is sold during the period. Its purpose is to measure the liquidity of the inventory. The inventory turnover is computed by dividing cost of goods sold by the average inventory. Unless seasonal factors are significant, average inventory can be computed from the beginning and ending inventory balances.

Assuming that the inventory balance for Quality Department Store at the beginning of 1998 was $450,000, its inventory turnover and comparative data are as shown in Illustration 19-17. Quality's inventory turnover declined slightly in 1999. The turnover of 2.3 times is relatively low compared with the industry average of 6.2 and Sears's 5.14. Generally, the faster the inventory turnover, the less cash that is tied up in inventory and the less the chance of inventory obsolescence.

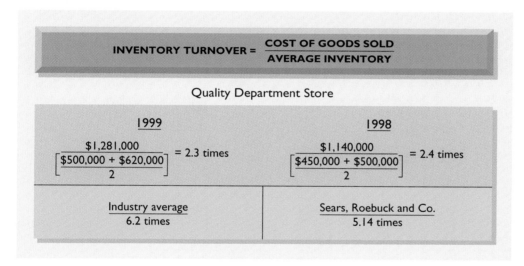

Illustration 19-17

Inventory turnover

A variant of inventory turnover is the **average days to sell the inventory**. It is calculated by dividing the inventory turnover into 365. For example, Quality's 1999 inventory turnover of 2.3 times divided into 365 is approximately 159 days. An average selling time of 159 days is also relatively high compared with the industry average of 59 days (365 ÷ 6.2) and Sears's 71 days (365 ÷ 5.14).

ACCOUNTING IN ACTION *Business Insight*

Inventory turnover ratios vary considerably among industries. For example, grocery store chains have a turnover of 10 times and an average selling period of 37 days. In contrast, jewelry stores have an average turnover of 1.3 times and an average selling period of 281 days. Even within a company there may be significant differences in inventory turnover among different types of products. Thus, in a grocery store the turnover of perishable items such as produce, meats, and dairy products will be faster than the turnover of soaps and detergents.

PROFITABILITY RATIOS

Profitability ratios measure the income or operating success of an enterprise for a given period of time. Income, or the lack of it, affects the company's ability to obtain debt and equity financing. It also affects the company's liquidity position and the company's ability to grow. As a consequence, both creditors and investors are interested in evaluating earning power—profitability. Profitability is frequently used as the ultimate test of management's operating effectiveness.

6. Profit Margin

ALTERNATIVE TERMINOLOGY
Profit margin is also called the *rate of return on sales.*

Profit margin is a measure of the percentage of each dollar of sales that results in net income. It is computed by dividing net income by net sales. Quality Department Store's profit margin and comparative data are shown in Illustration 19-18.

Illustration 19-18

Profit margin

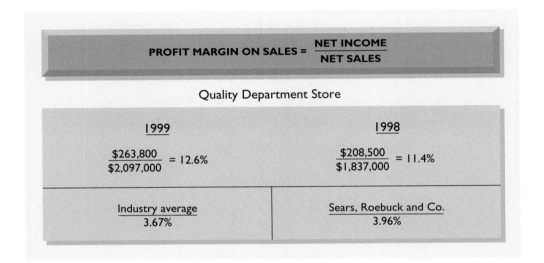

Quality experienced an increase in its profit margin from 1998 to 1999. Its profit margin is unusually high in comparison with the industry average of 3.67% and Sears's 3.96%.

High-volume (high inventory turnover) enterprises such as grocery stores (**Safeway** or **Kroger**) and discount stores (**Kmart** or **Wal-Mart**) generally experience low profit margins. In contrast, low-volume enterprises such as jewelry stores (**Tiffany & Co.**) or airplane manufacturers (**Boeing Co.**) have high profit margins.

7. Cash Return on Sales

Profit margin, discussed above, is an accrual-based ratio, using net income as the numerator. The cash-basis counterpart is the **cash return on sales**. It uses net cash provided by operating activities as the numerator and net sales as the denominator. The difference between these two ratios relates to differences between accrual-basis accounting and cash-basis accounting, that is, differences in the timing of revenue and expense recognition. Using net cash provided by operating activities of $404,000 in 1999 and $340,000 in 1998, Quality Department Store's cash return on sales is computed as shown in Illustration 19-19.

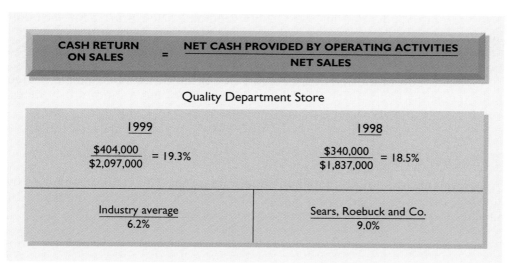

Illustration 19-19

Cash return on sales

Quality's cash return on sales is considerably higher than its profit margin on sales. The difference of 6.7% in 1999 (19.3% − 12.6%) is due to more noncash charges than noncash credits in the income statement. Quality appears to have a very healthy cash return on sales.

8. Asset Turnover

Asset turnover measures how efficiently a company uses its assets to generate sales. It is determined by dividing net sales by average assets. The resulting number shows the dollars of sales produced by each dollar invested in assets. Unless seasonal factors are significant, average total assets can be computed from the beginning and ending balance of total assets. Assuming that total assets at the beginning of 1998 were $1,446,000, the 1999 and 1998 asset turnover for Quality Department Store and comparative data are as follows.

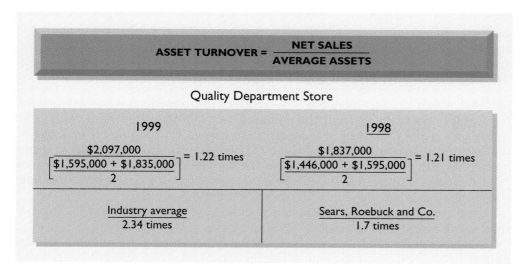

Illustration 19-20

Asset turnover

Asset turnover shows that in 1999 Quality generated sales of $1.22 for each dollar it had invested in assets. The ratio changed little from 1998 to 1999. Quality's asset turnover is below the industry average of 2.34 times and also below Sears's ratio of 1.7 times.

Asset turnover ratios vary considerably among industries. For example, a large utility company like **Consolidated Edison** (New York) has a ratio of 0.49 times, and the large grocery chain **Kroger Stores** has a ratio of 4.34 times.

9. Return on Assets

An overall measure of profitability is **return on assets**. This ratio is computed by dividing net income by average assets. The 1999 and 1998 return on assets for Quality Department Store and comparative data are shown below.

Illustration 19-21

Return on assets

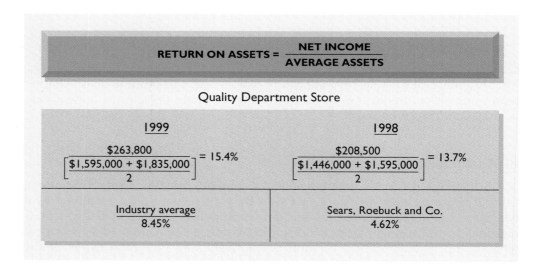

$$\text{RETURN ON ASSETS} = \frac{\text{NET INCOME}}{\text{AVERAGE ASSETS}}$$

Quality Department Store

1999	1998
$\dfrac{\$263,800}{\left[\dfrac{\$1,595,000 + \$1,835,000}{2}\right]} = 15.4\%$	$\dfrac{\$208,500}{\left[\dfrac{\$1,446,000 + \$1,595,000}{2}\right]} = 13.7\%$
Industry average 8.45%	Sears, Roebuck and Co. 4.62%

Quality's return on assets improved from 1998 to 1999. Its return of 15.4% is very high, compared with the department store industry average of 8.45% and Sears's 4.62%.

10. Return on Common Stockholders' Equity

Another widely used profitability ratio is **return on common stockholders equity**. It measures profitability from the common stockholders' viewpoint. This ratio shows how many dollars of net income were earned for each dollar invested by the owners. It is computed by dividing net income by average common stockholders' equity. Assuming that common stockholders' equity at the beginning of 1998 was $667,000, the 1999 and 1998 ratios for Quality Department Store and comparative data are shown in Illustration 19-22 on page 797.

Quality's rate of return on common stockholders' equity is high at 29.3%, considering an industry average of 22.4% and a rate of 24.6% for Sears.

When preferred stock is present, **preferred dividend** requirements are deducted from net income to compute income available to common stockholders.

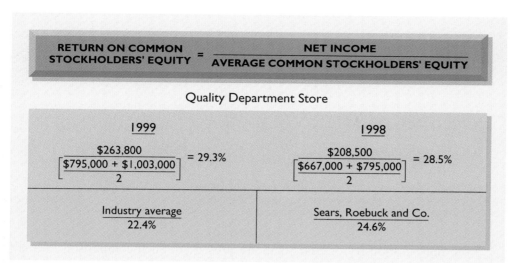

Illustration 19-22

Return on common stock-
holders' equity

Similarly, the par value of preferred stock (or call price, if applicable) must be deducted from total stockholders' equity to determine the amount of common stock
equity used in this ratio. The ratio then appears as follows.

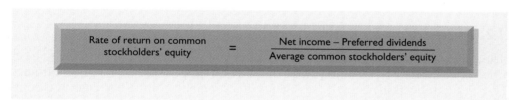

Illustration 19-23

Return on common stock-
holders' equity with pre-
ferred stock

Note that Quality's rate of return on stockholders' equity (29.3%) is substantially higher than its rate of return on assets (15.4%). The reason is that Quality
has made effective use of **leverage** or **trading on the equity** at a gain. Trading on
the equity at a gain means that the company has borrowed money at a lower rate
of interest than it is able to earn by using the borrowed money. Leverage enables
Quality Department Store to use money supplied by nonowners to increase the
return to the owners. A comparison of the rate of return on total assets with the
rate of interest paid for borrowed money indicates the profitability of trading on
the equity. Quality Department Store earns more on its borrowed funds than it
has to pay in the form of interest. Thus the return to stockholders exceeds the return on the assets, benefiting from the positive leveraging.

11. Earnings per Share (EPS)

Earnings per share (EPS) is a measure of the net income earned on each share
of common stock. It is computed by dividing net income by the number of weighted
average common shares outstanding during the year. A measure of net income
earned on a per share basis provides a useful perspective for determining profitability. Assuming that there is no change in the number of outstanding shares
during 1998 and that the 1999 increase occurred midyear, the net income per share
for Quality Department Store for 1999 and 1998 is computed as shown in Illustration 19-24 on page 798.

Illustration 19-24

Earnings per share

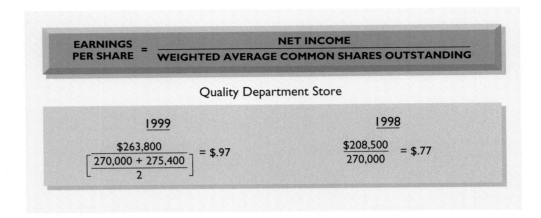

Note that no industry or Sears data are presented. Such comparisons are not meaningful because of the wide variations in the number of shares of outstanding stock among companies. The only meaningful EPS comparison is an intracompany trend comparison: Quality's earnings per share increased 20 cents per share in 1999. This represents a 26% increase over the 1998 earnings per share of 77 cents.

The terms "earnings per share" and "net income per share" refer to the amount of net income applicable to each share of **common stock**. Therefore, in computing EPS, if there are preferred dividends declared for the period, they must be deducted from net income to determine income available to the common stockholders.

12. Price-Earnings Ratio

The **price-earnings (P-E) ratio** is an oft-quoted measure of the ratio of the market price of each share of common stock to the earnings per share. The price-earnings (P-E) ratio reflects investors' assessments of a company's future earnings. It is computed by dividing the market price per share of the stock by earnings per share. Assuming that the market price of Quality Department Store Inc. stock is $8 in 1998 and $12 in 1999, the price-earnings ratio is computed as follows.

Illustration 19-25

Price-earnings ratio

In 1999 each share of Quality's stock sold for 12.4 times the amount that was earned on each share. Quality's price-earnings ratio is lower than the industry average of 18 times, but it is higher than the ratio of 8 times for Sears. The average price-earnings ratio for the stocks that constitute the Dow-Jones industrial average on the New York Stock Exchange in December 2000 was an unusually high 20 times.

ACCOUNTING IN ACTION *Business Insight*

For the stock of some companies, investors are willing to pay over 20 times the current per share earnings. They feel the company's future growth in earnings will provide an adequate (or superior) return on the investment. Examples of companies with price-earnings ratios over 20 are **Oracle** (37), **Microsoft** (38), **Coca-Cola** (77), and **Gillette Co.** (38). Examples of companies with low price-earnings ratios are **Ford Motor** (7), **General Motors** (8), and **United Airlines** (6).

13. Payout Ratio

The **payout ratio** measures the percentage of earnings distributed in the form of cash dividends. It is computed by dividing cash dividends by net income. Companies that have high growth rates generally have low payout ratios because they reinvest most of their net income into the business. The 1999 and 1998 payout ratios for Quality Department Store are computed as follows.

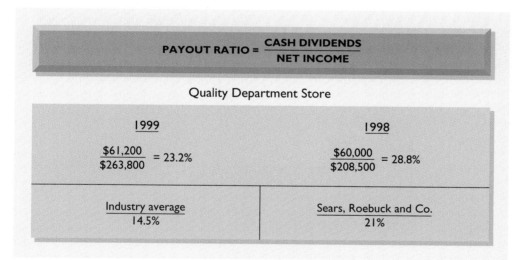

Illustration 19-26

Payout ratio

$$\text{PAYOUT RATIO} = \frac{\text{CASH DIVIDENDS}}{\text{NET INCOME}}$$

Quality Department Store

1999	1998
$\dfrac{\$61,200}{\$263,800} = 23.2\%$	$\dfrac{\$60,000}{\$208,500} = 28.8\%$
Industry average 14.5%	Sears, Roebuck and Co. 21%

Quality's payout ratio is comparable to Sears's payout ratio of 21%. As indicated earlier (page 783), Quality apparently has decided to fund its purchase of plant assets through retention of earnings.

ACCOUNTING IN ACTION *Business Insight*

Many companies with stable earnings have high payout ratios. For example, **Baltimore Gas and Electric** had an 84% payout ratio over a recent five-year period. **Omega Healthcare's** dividends exceeded net income over the same period. Conversely, companies that are expanding rapidly, such as **Toys "R" Us**, **Microsoft**, and **Tellabs Inc.** have never paid a cash dividend.

SOLVENCY RATIOS

Solvency ratios measure the ability of the company to survive over a long period of time. Long-term creditors and stockholders are particularly interested in a company's ability to pay interest as it comes due and to repay the face value of debt at maturity. Debt to total assets, times interest earned, and cash debt coverage are three ratios that provide information about debt-paying ability.

14. Debt to Total Assets Ratio

The **debt to total assets ratio** measures the percentage of the total assets provided by creditors. It is computed by dividing total debt (both current and long-term liabilities) by total assets. This ratio indicates the company's degree of leverage. It also provides some indication of the company's ability to withstand losses without impairing the interests of creditors. The higher the percentage of debt to total assets, the greater the risk that the company may be unable to meet its maturing obligations. The 1999 and 1998 ratios for Quality Department Store and comparative data are as follows.

Illustration 19-27

Debt to total assets ratio

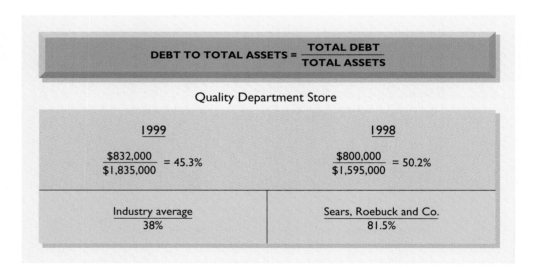

A ratio of 45.3% means that creditors have provided 45.3% of Quality Department Store's total assets. Quality's 45.3% is above the industry average of 38%. But it is considerably below the high 81.5% ratio of Sears. The lower the ratio, the more equity "buffer" there is available to the creditors. Thus, from the creditors' point of view, a low ratio of debt to total assets is usually desirable.

The adequacy of this ratio is often judged in the light of the company's earnings. Generally, companies with relatively stable earnings (such as public utilities) have higher debt to total assets ratios than cyclical companies with widely fluctuating earnings (such as many high-tech companies).

ACCOUNTING IN ACTION *Business Insight*

Examples of total debt to total assets ratios for selected companies are:

	Total Debt to Total Assets as a Percent
Toys "R" Us	56%
The Coca-Cola Company	56%
Merck & Co.	63%
Kellogg Company	83%
Bob Evans Farms	31%
Eastman Kodak	72%

Another means used in practice to measure leverage is the **debt to equity ratio**. It is computed by dividing total liabilities by total stockholders' equity. It shows the relative use of borrowed funds (total liabilities) as compared to resources invested by the owners. This ratio may be computed in several ways. Debt may be defined to include only the noncurrent portion of the liabilities. Also, intangible assets may be excluded from owners' equity (resulting in tangible net worth). Therefore, care should be taken when making comparisons using this ratio.

15. Times Interest Earned

Times interest earned provides an indication of the company's ability to meet interest payments as they come due. It is computed by dividing income before interest expense and income taxes by interest expense. The 1999 and 1998 ratios for Quality Department Store and comparative data are shown in Illustration 19-28. Note that times interest earned uses income before income taxes and interest expense. This represents the amount available to cover interest. For Quality Department Store the 1999 amount of $468,000 is computed by taking the income before income taxes of $432,000 and adding back the $36,000 of interest expense.

ALTERNATIVE TERMINOLOGY
Times interest earned is also called *interest coverage.*

Illustration 19-28
Times interest earned

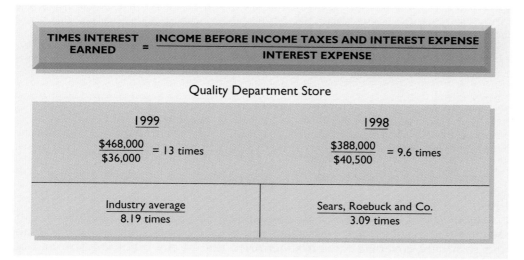

Quality's interest expense is well covered at 13 times, compared with the industry average of 8.19 times and Sears's 3.09 times.

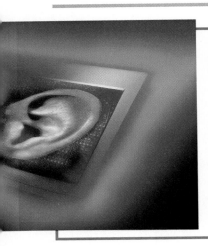

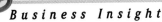

ACCOUNTING IN ACTION ∧ *Business Insight*

Today, investors have access to information provided by corporate managers that used to be available only to professional analysts. Corporate managers have always made themselves available to security analysts for questions at the end of every quarter. Now, because of a combination of new corporate disclosure requirements by the Securities and Exchange Commission and technologies that make communication to large numbers of people possible at a very low price, the average investor can listen in on these discussions. For example, one individual investor, Matthew Johnson, a **Nortel Networks** local area network engineer in Belfast, Northern Ireland, "stayed up past midnight to listen to **Apple Computer's** recent Internet conference call. Hearing the company's news 'from the dog's mouth,' he says 'gave me better information' than hunting through chat-rooms."

SOURCE: Jeff D. Opdyke, "Individuals Pick Up on Conference Calls," *The Wall Street Journal*, November 20, 2000.

16. Cash Debt Coverage Ratio

The ratio of net cash provided by operating activities to average total liabilities is the **cash debt coverage ratio**. This ratio is a cash-basis measure of **solvency**. It demonstrates a company's ability to repay its liabilities from cash generated by operating activities, without having to liquidate assets. Using Quality's net cash provided by operating activities of $404,000 in 1999 and $340,000 in 1998 and assuming total liabilities of $740,000 on January 1, 1998, the cash debt coverage ratios are as follows.

Illustration 19-29

Cash debt coverage ratio

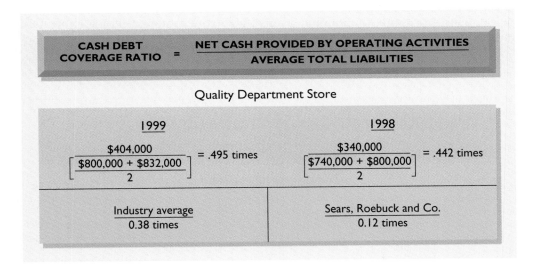

Based on net cash generated from operations in 1999, it would take Quality approximately two years to generate enough cash to pay off all its liabilities. This assumes that all of the net cash generated is used for that purpose only. Quality's cash debt coverage ratio is superior to that of the retail industry and of Sears.

SUMMARY OF RATIOS

A summary of the ratios discussed in the chapter is presented in Illustration 19-30. The summary includes the formula and purpose or use of each ratio.

Illustration 19-30
Summary of liquidity, profitability, and solvency ratios

Ratio	Formula	Purpose or Use
Liquidity Ratios		
1. Current ratio	$\dfrac{\text{Current assets}}{\text{Current liabilities}}$	Measures short-term debt-paying ability.
2. Acid-test (quick) ratio	$\dfrac{\text{Cash} + \text{Short-term investments} + \text{Receivables (net)}}{\text{Current liabilities}}$	Measures immediate short-term liquidity.
3. Current cash debt coverage ratio	$\dfrac{\text{Net cash provided by operating activities}}{\text{Average current liabilities}}$	Measures short-term debt-paying ability (cash basis).
4. Receivables turnover	$\dfrac{\text{Net credit sales}}{\text{Average net receivables}}$	Measures liquidity of receivables.
5. Inventory turnover	$\dfrac{\text{Cost of goods sold}}{\text{Average inventory}}$	Measures liquidity of inventory.
Profitability Ratios		
6. Profit margin	$\dfrac{\text{Net income}}{\text{Net sales}}$	Measures net income generated by each dollar of sales.
7. Cash return on sales	$\dfrac{\text{Net cash provided by operating activities}}{\text{Net sales}}$	Measures net cash flow generated by each dollar of sales.
8. Asset turnover	$\dfrac{\text{Net sales}}{\text{Average assets}}$	Measures how efficiently assets are used to generate sales.
9. Return on assets	$\dfrac{\text{Net income}}{\text{Average assets}}$	Measures overall profitability of assets.
10. Return on common stockholders' equity	$\dfrac{\text{Net income}}{\text{Average common stockholders' equity}}$	Measures profitability of owners' investment.
11. Earnings per share (EPS)	$\dfrac{\text{Net income}}{\text{Weighted average common shares outstanding}}$	Measures net income earned on each share of common stock.
12. Price-earnings (P-E) ratio	$\dfrac{\text{Market price per share of stock}}{\text{Earnings per share}}$	Measures the ratio of the market price per share to earnings per share.
13. Payout ratio	$\dfrac{\text{Cash dividends}}{\text{Net income}}$	Measures percentage of earnings distributed in the form of cash dividends.
Solvency Ratios		
14. Debt to total assets ratio	$\dfrac{\text{Total debt}}{\text{Total assets}}$	Measures the percentage of total assets provided by creditors.
15. Times interest earned	$\dfrac{\text{Income before income taxes and interest expense}}{\text{Interest expense}}$	Measures ability to meet interest payments as they come due.
16. Cash debt coverage ratio	$\dfrac{\text{Net cash provided by operating activities}}{\text{Average total liabilities}}$	Measures the long-term debt-paying ability (cash basis).

B E F O R E   Y O U   G O   O N . . .

▶ *REVIEW IT*

1. What are liquidity ratios? Explain the current ratio, acid-test ratio, current cash debt coverage ratio, receivables turnover, and inventory turnover.

2. What are profitability ratios? Explain the profit margin, cash return on sales, asset turnover ratio, return on assets, return on common stockholders' equity, earnings per share, price-earnings ratio, and payout ratio.

3. What are solvency ratios? Explain the debt to total assets ratio, times interest earned, and cash debt coverage ratio.

▶ *DO IT*

Selected financial data for Drummond Company at December 31, 2002, are as follows: cash $60,000; receivables (net) $80,000; inventory $70,000; current liabilities $140,000. Compute the current and acid-test ratios.

ACTION PLAN

• Use the formula for the current ratio: Current assets ÷ Current liabilities.
• Use the formula for the acid-test ratio: Cash + Short-term investments + Receivables (net) ÷ Current liabilities.

SOLUTION: The current ratio is 1.5:1 ($210,000 ÷ $140,000). The acid-test ratio is 1:1 ($140,000 ÷ $140,000).

Related exercise material: BE19-7, BE19-8, BE19-9, BE19-10, BE19-11, E19-5, E19-6, and E19-7.

LIMITATIONS OF FINANCIAL STATEMENT ANALYSIS

STUDY OBJECTIVE 6

Recognize the limitations of financial statement analysis.

Significant business decisions are frequently made using one or more of the analytical tools illustrated in this chapter. But, you should be aware of the limitations of these tools and of the financial statements on which they are based.

ESTIMATES

Financial statements contain numerous estimates. Estimates are used in determining the allowance for uncollectible receivables, periodic depreciation, the costs of warranties, and contingent losses. To the extent that these estimates are inaccurate, the financial ratios and percentages are inaccurate.

COST

Traditional financial statements are based on cost. They are not adjusted for price-level changes. Comparisons of unadjusted financial data from different periods may be rendered invalid by significant inflation or deflation. For example, a five-year comparison of Sears's revenues might show a growth of 36%. But this growth trend would be misleading if the general price level had increased significantly during the same period.

ALTERNATIVE ACCOUNTING METHODS

Companies vary in the generally accepted accounting principles they use. Such variations may hamper comparability. For example, one company may use the FIFO method of inventory costing; another company in the same industry may use LIFO. If inventory is a significant asset to both companies, it is unlikely that their current ratios are comparable. For example, if **General Motors Corporation** had used FIFO instead of LIFO in valuing its inventories, its inventories would have been 26% higher. This difference would significantly affect the current ratio (and other ratios as well). In addition to differences in inventory costing methods, differences also exist in reporting such items as depreciation, depletion, and amortization. These differences in accounting methods might be detectable from reading the notes to the financial statements. But, adjusting the financial data to compensate for the different methods is difficult, if not impossible in some cases.

> ***I*NTERNATIONAL NOTE**
>
> In many industries competition is global. To evaluate a firm's standing, an investor or analyst must make comparisons to firms from other countries. But, given the many differences in accounting practices, these comparisons can be both difficult and misleading.

ATYPICAL DATA

Fiscal year-end data may not be typical of the financial condition during the year. Firms frequently establish a fiscal year-end that coincides with the low point in operating activity or in inventory levels. Therefore, certain account balances (cash, receivables, payables, and inventories) may not be representative of the balances in the accounts during the year.

DIVERSIFICATION OF FIRMS

Diversification in U.S. industry also limits the usefulness of financial analysis. Many firms today are so diversified that they cannot be classified by a single industry—they are true conglomerates. Others appear to be comparable but are not.

> ***E*THICS NOTE**
>
> When investigating diversified firms, investors are often most interested to learn about the results of particular divisions. Firms are required to disclose the results of distinct lines of business separately if they are a material part of operations. Unfortunately, shifting revenues and expenses across divisions to achieve desired results reduces the usefulness of this information for financial statement analysis.

B E F O R E   Y O U   G O   O N . . .

▶ *REVIEW IT*

1. What are some limitations of financial statement analysis?
2. Give examples of alternative accounting methods that hamper comparability.
3. In what way does diversification limit the usefulness of financial statement analysis?

A LOOK BACK AT OUR FEATURE STORY

Refer back to the Feature Story about cabby Carlos Rubino at the beginning of the chapter, and answer the following questions.

1. In what ways has cabby Carlos Rubino joined the technological revolution?
2. What extra service does Rubino provide his passengers?
3. What is the monthly cost of Rubino's quotes and Internet access?

SOLUTION

1. Cabby Rubino carries in his cab an Hitachi Traveler laptop computer and a wireless cell phone.
2. Rubino provides real-time stock quotes using his wireless Internet access to **Yahoo!**, **Amazon.com**, and **America Online**. He also gladly provides his own stock tips and investment advice.
3. Rubino pays $100 a month for access to real-time quotes and $54 a month for wireless Internet access (plus he has the investment cost in his laptop computer and his cell phone).

☑ THE NAVIGATOR

DEMONSTRATION PROBLEM

The condensed financial statements ot The Estée Lauder Companies, Inc., for the years ended June 30, 1998 and 1997, are presented below.

THE ESTÉE LAUDER COMPANIES, INC.
Balance Sheets
June 30

	(in millions)	
Assets	**1998**	**1997**
Current assets		
Cash and cash equivalents	$ 277.5	$ 255.6
Accounts receivable (net)	497.8	471.7
Inventories	513.2	440.6
Prepaid expenses and other current assets	166.1	143.2
Total current assets	1,454.6	1,311.1
Property, plant, and equipment (net)	335.8	265.0
Investments	27.7	25.9
Intangibles and other assets	694.7	271.1
Total assets	$2,512.8	$1,873.1
Liabilities and Stockholders' Equity		
Current liabilities	$ 837.4	$ 759.5
Long-term liabilities	619.0	565.9
Stockholders' equity—common	1,056.4	547.7
Total liabilities and stockholders' equity	$2,512.8	$1,873.1

THE ESTÉE LAUDER COMPANIES, INC.
Income Statements
For the Year Ended June 30

	(in millions)	
	1998	**1997**
Revenues	$3,618.0	$3,381.6
Costs and expenses		
Cost of goods sold	819.5	765.1
Selling and administrative expenses	2,357.6	2,224.6
Interest expense	38.1	52.4
Total costs and expenses	3,215.2	3,042.1
Income before income taxes	402.8	339.5
Income tax expense	166.0	165.3
Net income	$ 236.8	$ 174.2

Instructions

Compute the following ratios for 1998 and 1997.

(a) Current ratio.
(b) Inventory turnover. (Inventory on 6/30/96 was $452.8.)
(c) Profit margin ratio.
(d) Return on assets. (Assets on 6/30/96 were $1,779.4.)
(e) Return on common stockholders' equity. (Equity on 6/30/96 was $394.2.)
(f) Debt to total assets ratio.
(g) Times interest earned.

SOLUTION TO DEMONSTRATION PROBLEM

	1998	1997
(a) Current ratio:		
$1,454.6 ÷ $837.4 =	1.7:1	
$1,311.1 ÷ $759.5 =		1.7:1
(b) Inventory turnover:		
$819.5 ÷ [($513.2 + $440.6) ÷ 2] =	1.7 times	
$765.1 ÷ [($440.6 + $452.8) ÷ 2] =		1.7 times
(c) Profit margin:		
$236.8 ÷ $3,618.0 =	6.5%	
$174.2 ÷ $3,381.6 =		5.2%
(d) Return on assets:		
$236.8 ÷ [($2,512.8 + $1,873.1) ÷ 2] =	10.8%	
$174.2 ÷ [($1,873.1 + $1,779.4) ÷ 2] =		9.5%
(e) Return on common stockholders' equity:		
$236.8 ÷ [($1,056.4 + $547.7) ÷ 2] =	30%	
$174.2 ÷ [($547.7 + $394.2) ÷ 2] =		37%
(f) Debt to total assets ratio:		
($837.4 + $619.0) ÷ $2,512.8 =	58%	
($795.5 + $565.9) ÷ $1,873.1 =		71%
(g) Times interest earned:		
($236.8 + $166.0 + $38.1) ÷ $38.1 =	11.6 times	
($174.2 + $165.3 + $52.4) ÷ $52.4 =		7.5 times

ACTION PLAN

- Remember that the current ratio includes all current assets. The acid-test ratio uses only cash, temporary investments, and net receivables.
- Use average balances for turnover ratios like inventory, receivables, and assets.
- Remember that return on assets is greater or smaller than return on common stockholders' equity depending on cost of debt.

SUMMARY OF STUDY OBJECTIVES

1. Discuss the need for comparative analysis. There are three bases of comparison: (1) Intracompany, which compares an item or financial relationship with other data within a company. (2) Industry, which compares company data with industry averages. (3) Intercompany, which compares an item or financial relationship of a company with data of one or more competing companies.

2. Identify the tools of financial statement analysis. Financial statements can be analyzed horizontally, vertically, and with ratios.

3. Explain and apply horizontal (trend) analysis. Horizontal analysis is a technique for evaluating a series of data over a period of time to determine the increase or decrease that has taken place, expressed as either an amount or a percentage.

4. Describe and apply vertical analysis. Vertical analysis is a technique that expresses each item within a financial statement in terms of a percentage of a relevant total or a base amount.

5. Identify and compute ratios, and describe their purpose and use in analyzing a firm's liquidity, profitability, and solvency. The formula and purpose of each ratio was presented in Illustration 19-30.

6. Recognize the limitations of financial statement analysis. The usefulness of analytical tools is limited by the use of estimates, the cost basis, the application of alternative accounting methods, atypical data at year-end, and the diversification of firms.

Key Term Matching Activity

GLOSSARY

Acid-test (quick) ratio   A measure of a company's immediate short-term liquidity; computed by dividing the sum of cash, short-term investments, and (net) receivables by current liabilities. (p. 790).

Asset turnover   A measure of how efficiently a company uses its assets to generate sales; computed by dividing net sales by average assets. (p. 795).

Cash debt coverage ratio   A cash-basis measure of long-term debt-paying ability; computed as net cash provided by operating activities divided by average total liabilities. (p. 802).

Cash return on sales   A measure of the cash generated by each dollar of sales; computed as net cash provided by operating activities divided by net sales. (p. 794).

Current cash debt coverage ratio   A cash-basis measure of short-term debt-paying ability; computed as net cash provided by operating activities divided by average current liabilities. (p. 791).

Current ratio   A measure used to evaluate a company's liquidity and short-term debt-paying ability; computed by dividing current assets by current liabilities. (p. 789).

Debt to total assets ratio   Measures the percentage of total assets provided by creditors; computed by dividing total debt by total assets. (p. 800).

Earnings per share (EPS)   The net income earned by each share of common stock; computed by dividing net income by the weighted average common shares outstanding. (p. 797).

Horizontal analysis A technique for evaluating a series of financial statement data over a period of time, to determine the increase (decrease) that has taken place, expressed as either an amount or a percentage. (p. 782).

Inventory turnover A measure of the liquidity of inventory; computed by dividing cost of goods sold by average inventory. (p. 793).

Leverage See Trading on the equity.

Liquidity ratios Measures of the short-term ability of the enterprise to pay its maturing obligations and to meet unexpected needs for cash. (p. 789).

Payout ratio Measures the percentage of earnings distributed in the form of cash dividends; computed by dividing cash dividends by net income. (p. 799).

Price-earnings (P-E) ratio Measures the ratio of the market price of each share of common stock to the earnings per share; computed by dividing the market price of the stock by earnings per share. (p. 798).

Profit margin Measures the percentage of each dollar of sales that results in net income; computed by dividing net income by net sales. (p. 794).

Profitability ratios Measures of the income or operating success of an enterprise for a given period of time. (p. 794).

Ratio An expression of the mathematical relationship between one quantity and another. The relationship may be expressed either as a percentage, a rate, or a simple proportion. (p. 788).

Ratio analysis A technique for evaluating financial statements that expresses the relationship between selected financial statement data. (p. 788).

Receivables turnover A measure of the liquidity of receivables; computed by dividing net credit sales by average net receivables. (p. 792).

Return on assets An overall measure of profitability; computed by dividing net income by average assets. (p. 796).

Return on common stockholders' equity Measures the dollars of net income earned for each dollar invested by the owners; computed by dividing net income by average common stockholders' equity. (p. 796).

Solvency ratios Measures of the ability of the enterprise to survive over a long period of time. (p. 800).

Times interest earned Measures a company's ability to meet interest payments as they come due; computed by dividing income before interest expense and income taxes by interest expense. (p. 801).

Trading on the equity (leverage) Borrowing money at a lower rate of interest than can be earned by using the borrowed money. (p. 797).

Vertical analysis A technique for evaluating financial statement data that expresses each item within a financial statement as a percent of a base amount. (p. 785).

Chapter 19 Self-Test

SELF-STUDY QUESTIONS

Answers are at the end of the chapter.

(SO 1) **1.** Comparisons of data within a company are an example of the following comparative basis:
   a. Industry averages.
   b. Intracompany.
   c. Intercompany.
   d. Both (b) and (c).

(SO 2) **2.** In horizontal analysis, each item is expressed as a percentage of the:
   a. net income amount.
   b. stockholders' equity amount.
   c. total assets amount.
   d. base year amount.

(SO 4) **3.** In vertical analysis, the base amount for depreciation expense is generally:
   a. net sales.
   b. depreciation expense in a previous year.
   c. gross profit.
   d. fixed assets.

(SO 4) **4.** The following schedule is a display of what type of analysis?

	Amount	Percent
Current assets	$200,000	25%
Property, plant, and equipment	600,000	75%
Total assets	$800,000	

   a. Horizontal analysis.
   b. Differential analysis.
   c. Vertical analysis.
   d. Ratio analysis.

(SO 3) **5.** Earlville Corporation reported net sales of $300,000, $330,000, and $360,000 in the years, 2000, 2001, and 2002, respectively. If 2000 is the base year, what is the trend percentage for 2002?
   a. 77%.
   b. 108%.
   c. 120%.
   d. 130%.

(SO 5) **6.** Which of the following measures is an evaluation of a firm's ability to pay current liabilities?
   a. Acid-test ratio.
   b. Current ratio.
   c. Both (a) and (b).
   d. None of the above.

(SO 5) **7.** A measure useful in evaluating the efficiency in managing inventories is:
   a. inventory turnover.
   b. average days to sell inventory.
   c. Both (a) and (b).
   d. None of the above.

(SO 5) **8.** Which of the following is *not* a liquidity ratio?
   a. Current ratio.
   b. Asset turnover.
   c. Inventory turnover.
   d. Receivables turnover.

(SO 5)   **9.** Yorkville Corporation reported net income $24,000, net sales $400,000, and average assets $600,000 for 2002. The 2002 profit margin was:
a. 6%.
b. 12%.
c. 40%.
d. 200%.

10. Which of the following is generally *not* considered to be (SO 6) a limitation of financial analysis?
a. Use of estimates.
b. Use of ratio analysis.
c. Use of cost.
d. Use of alternative accounting methods.

QUESTIONS

1. (a) Tom Truemper believes that the analysis of financial statements is directed at two characteristics of a company: liquidity and profitability. Is Tom correct? Explain.
(b) Are short-term creditors, long-term creditors, and stockholders interested primarily in the same characteristics of a company? Explain.

2. (a) Distinguish among the following bases of comparison: (1) intracompany, (2) industry averages, and (3) intercompany.
(b) Give the principal value of using each of the three bases of comparison.

3. Two popular methods of financial statement analysis are horizontal analysis and vertical analysis. Explain the difference between these two methods.

4. (a) If DeKalb Company had net income of $480,000 in 2002 and it experienced a 24.5% increase in net income for 2003, what is its net income for 2003?
(b) If six cents of every dollar of DeKalb's revenue is net income in 2002, what is the dollar amount of 2002 revenue?

5. What is a ratio? What are the different ways of expressing the relationship of two amounts? What information does a ratio provide?

6. Name the major ratios useful in assessing (a) liquidity and (b) solvency.

7. Roger Holloway is puzzled. His company had a profit margin of 10% in 2002. He feels that this is an indication that the company is doing well. Loren Foelske, his accountant, says that more information is needed to determine the firm's financial well-being. Who is correct? Why?

8. What do the following classes of ratios measure? (a) Liquidity ratios. (b) Profitability ratios. (c) Solvency ratios.

9. What is the difference between the current ratio and the acid-test ratio?

10. Seneca Company, a retail store, has a receivables turnover of 4.5 times. The industry average is 12.5 times. Does Seneca have a collection problem with its receivables?

11. Which ratios should be used to help answer the following questions?
(a) How efficient is a company in using its assets to produce sales?
(b) How near to sale is the inventory on hand?
(c) How many dollars of net income were earned for each dollar invested by the owners?
(d) How able is a company to meet interest charges as they fall due?

12. The price-earnings ratio of **General Motors** (automobile builder) was 8, and the price-earnings ratio of **Microsoft** (computer software) was 38. Which company did the stock market favor? Explain.

13. What is the formula for computing the payout ratio? Would you expect this ratio to be high or low for a growth company?

14. Holding all other factors constant, indicate whether each of the following changes generally signals good or bad news about a company.
(a) Increase in profit margin.
(b) Decrease in inventory turnover.
(c) Increase in the current ratio.
(d) Decrease in earnings per share.
(e) Increase in price-earnings ratio.
(f) Increase in debt to total assets ratio.
(g) Decrease in times interest earned.

15. The return on total assets for Matson Corporation is 7.6%. During the same year Matson's return on common stockholders' equity is 12.8%. What is the explanation for the difference in the two rates?

16. Which two ratios do you think should be of greatest interest to:
(a) A pension fund considering the purchase of 20-year bonds?
(b) A bank contemplating a short-term loan?
(c) A common stockholder?

17. (a) What is meant by trading on the equity?
(b) How would you determine the profitability of trading on the equity?

18. Downing Inc. has net income of $210,000, weighted average shares of common stock outstanding of 50,000, and preferred dividends for the period of $40,000. What is Downing's earnings per share of common stock? Downing Sherrick, the president of Downing Inc., believes the computed EPS of the company is high. Comment.

19. Identify and briefly explain five limitations of financial analysis.

20. Explain how the choice of one of the following accounting methods over the other raises or lowers a company's net income during a period of continuing inflation.
(a) Use of FIFO instead of LIFO for inventory costing.
(b) Use of a 6-year life for machinery instead of a 9-year life.
(c) Use of straight-line depreciation instead of accelerated declining-balance depreciation.

21. What three ratios are dependent on cash-basis data? That is, what ratios use data from the statement of cash flows?

BRIEF EXERCISES*

Prepare horizontal analysis.
(SO 3)

BE19-1 Using the following data from the comparative balance sheet of Hal Adelman Company, illustrate horizontal analysis.

	December 31, 2003	**December 31, 2002**
Accounts receivable	$ 520,000	$ 400,000
Inventory	$ 840,000	$ 600,000
Total assets	$3,500,000	$2,800,000

Prepare vertical analysis.
(SO 4)

BE19-2 Using the same data presented above in BE19-1 for Hal Adelman Company, illustrate vertical analysis.

Calculate percentage of change.
(SO 3)

BE19-3 Net income was $500,000 in 2001, $400,000 in 2002, and $504,000 in 2003. What is the percentage of change from **(a)** 2001 to 2002 and **(b)** 2002 to 2003? Is the change an increase or a decrease?

Calculate net income.
(SO 3)

BE19-4 If Domingo Company had net income of $700,000 in 2003 and it experienced a 25% increase in net income over 2002, what was its 2002 net income?

Calculate change in net income.
(SO 4)

BE19-5 Vertical analysis (common size) percentages for Veronica Company's sales, cost of goods sold, and expenses are shown below.

Vertical Analysis	**2003**	**2002**	**2001**
Sales	100.0	100.0	100.0
Cost of goods sold	58.2	62.4	64.5
Expenses	25.0	26.6	28.5

Did Veronica's net income as a percent of sales increase, decrease, or remain unchanged over the 3-year period? Provide numerical support for your answer.

Calculate change in net income.
(SO 3)

BE19-6 Horizontal analysis (trend analysis) percentages for Flatt Company's sales, cost of goods sold, and expenses are shown below.

Horizontal Analysis	**2003**	**2002**	**2001**
Sales	96.2	106.8	100.0
Cost of goods sold	102.0	97.0	100.0
Expenses	110.6	95.4	100.0

Did Flatt's net income increase, decrease, or remain unchanged over the 3-year period?

Calculate liquidity ratios.
(SO 5)

BE19-7 Selected condensed data taken from a recent balance sheet of Becky Farms are as follows.

BECKY FARMS
Balance Sheet (partial)

Cash	$ 8,241,000
Marketable securities	1,947,000
Accounts receivable	12,545,000
Inventories	14,814,000
Other current assets	5,371,000
Total current assets	$42,918,000
Total current liabilities	$40,844,000

What are the **(a)** working capital, **(b)** current, and **(c)** acid-test ratios?

Calculate profitability ratios.
(SO 5)

BE19-8 Crear Corporation has net income of $13.5 million and net revenue of $90 million in 2002. Its assets were $12 million at the beginning of the year and $18 million at the end of the year. What are **(a)** Crear's asset turnover and **(b)** profit margin?

---

*Follow the rounding procedures used in the chapter.

BE19-9 The following data are taken from the financial statements of Geiss Company.

Evaluate collection of accounts receivable.
(SO 5)

	2003	2002
Accounts receivable (net), end of year	$ 560,000	$ 540,000
Net sales on account	3,850,000	3,100,000
Terms for all sales are 1/10, n/60.		

(a) Compute for each year (1) the receivables turnover and (2) the average collection period.
(b) What conclusions about the management of accounts receivable can be drawn from these data? At the end of 2001, accounts receivable (net) was $490,000.

BE19-10 The following data are from the income statements of Shirley Denson Company.

Evaluate management of inventory.
(SO 5)

	2003	2002
Sales	$6,420,000	$6,240,000
Beginning inventory	980,000	860,000
Purchases	4,540,000	4,661,000
Ending inventory	1,020,000	980,000

(a) Compute for each year (1) the inventory turnover and (2) the average days to sell the inventory. **(b)** What conclusions concerning the management of the inventory can be drawn from these data?

BE19-11 Nofftz Company has owners' equity of $400,000 and net income of $50,000. It has a payout ratio of 20% and a rate of return on assets of 16%. How much did Nofftz pay in cash dividends, and what were its average assets?

Calculate profitability ratios.
(SO 5)

BE19-12 Selected data taken from the 2002 financial statements of Lester Fredrick Manufacturing Company are as follows.

Calculate cash-basis liquidity, profitability, and solvency ratios.
(SO 5)

Net sales for 2002	$6,860,000
Current liabilities, January 1, 2002	180,000
Current liabilities, December 31, 2002	240,000
Net cash provided by operating activities	720,000
Total liabilities, January 1, 2002	1,500,000
Total liabilities, December 31, 2002	1,300,000

Compute the following ratios at December 31, 2002: **(a)** current cash debt coverage ratio, **(b)** cash return on sales, and **(c)** the cash debt coverage ratio.

E*XERCISES**

E19-1 Financial information for Merlynn Inc. is presented below.

Prepare horizontal analysis.
(SO 3)

	December 31, 2003	**December 31, 2002**
Current assets	$125,000	$100,000
Plant assets (net)	400,000	330,000
Current liabilities	91,000	70,000
Long-term liabilities	144,000	95,000
Common stock, $1 par	155,000	115,000
Retained earnings	135,000	150,000

Instructions
Prepare a schedule showing a horizontal analysis for 2003 using 2002 as the base year.

---

*Follow the rounding procedures used in the chapter.

Prepare vertical analysis.
(SO 4)

E19-2 Operating data for Enid Corporation are presented below.

	2003	2002
Sales	$800,000	$600,000
Cost of goods sold	472,000	390,000
Selling expenses	120,000	72,000
Administrative expenses	80,000	54,000
Income tax expense	38,400	25,200
Net income	89,600	58,800

Instructions
Prepare a schedule showing a vertical analysis for 2003 and 2002.

Prepare horizontal and vertical analyses.
(SO 3, 4)

E19-3 The comparative balance sheets of Ricky Corporation are presented below.

RICKY CORPORATION
Comparative Balance Sheets
December 31

	2003	2002
Assets		
Current assets	$ 76,000	$ 80,000
Property, plant, and equipment (net)	99,000	90,000
Intangibles	20,000	40,000
Total assets	$195,000	$210,000
Liabilities and stockholders' equity		
Current liabilities	$ 40,800	$ 48,000
Long-term liabilities	138,000	150,000
Stockholders' equity	16,200	12,000
Total liabilities and stockholders' equity	$195,000	$210,000

Instructions
(a) Prepare a horizontal analysis of the balance sheet data for Ricky Corporation using 2002 as a base. (Show the amount of increase or decrease as well.)
(b) Prepare a vertical analysis of the balance sheet data for Ricky Corporation in columnar form for 2003.

Prepare horizontal and vertical analyses.
(SO 3, 4)

E19-4 The comparative income statements of Sondgeroth Corporation are shown below.

SONDGEROTH CORPORATION
Comparative Income Statements
For the Years Ended December 31

	2003	2002
Net sales	$600,000	$500,000
Cost of goods sold	450,000	420,000
Gross profit	150,000	80,000
Operating expenses	57,200	44,000
Net income	$ 92,800	$ 36,000

Instructions
(a) Prepare a horizontal analysis of the income statement data for Sondgeroth Corporation using 2002 as a base. (Show the amounts of increase or decrease.)
(b) Prepare a vertical analysis of the income statement data for Sondgeroth Corporation in columnar form for both years.

E19-5   Nordstrom, Inc. operates department stores in numerous states. Selected financial statement data for the year ending January 31, 2000, are as follows.

Compute liquidity ratios and compare results.
(SO 5)

NORDSTROM

NORDSTROM, INC. Balance Sheet (partial)		
(in millions)	End-of-Year	Beginning-of-Year
Cash and cash equivalents	$ 27	$ 242
Short-term investments	26	–0–
Receivables (net)	617	587
Merchandise inventory	798	750
Prepaid expenses	97	74
Total current assets	$1,565	$1,659
Total current liabilities	$807	$779

For the year, net sales were $5,124, and cost of goods sold was $3,360. Net cash provided by operating activities was $378.

Instructions

(a) Compute the five liquidity ratios at the end of the current year.

(b) Using the data in the chapter, compare Nordstrom's liquidity with (1) that of **Sears, Roebuck and Co.**, and (2) the industry averages for department stores.

E19-6   Sycamore Incorporated had the following transactions occur involving current assets and current liabilities during February 2002.

Perform current and acid-test ratio analysis.
(SO 5)

Feb. 3   Accounts receivable of $15,000 are collected.
     7   Equipment is purchased for $25,000 cash.
    11   Paid $3,000 for a 3-year insurance policy.
    14   Accounts payable of $12,000 are paid.
    18   Cash dividends of $6,000 are declared.

Additional information:

1. As of February 1, 2002, current assets were $140,000, and current liabilities were $50,000.
2. As of February 1, 2002, current assets included $15,000 of inventory and $5,000 of prepaid expenses.

Instructions

(a) Compute the current ratio as of the beginning of the month and after each transaction.
(b) Compute the acid-test ratio as of the beginning of the month and after each transaction.

E19-7   Bobbette Company has the following comparative balance sheet data.

Compute selected ratios.
(SO 5)

BOBBETTE COMPANY Balance Sheets December 31		
	2002	2001
Cash	$ 15,000	$ 30,000
Receivables (net)	65,000	60,000
Inventories	60,000	50,000
Plant assets (net)	205,000	180,000
	$345,000	$320,000
Accounts payable	$ 50,000	$ 60,000
Mortgage payable (15%)	100,000	100,000
Common stock, $10 par	140,000	120,000
Retained earnings	55,000	40,000
	$345,000	$320,000

Additional information for 2002:

1. Net income was $25,000.
2. Sales on account were $420,000. Sales returns and allowances were $20,000.
3. Cost of goods sold was $198,000.
4. Net cash provided by operating activities was $33,000.

Instructions
Compute the following ratios at December 31, 2002.

(a) Current.   (e) Cash return on sales.
(b) Acid-test.   (f) Cash debt coverage.
(c) Receivables turnover.   (g) Current cash debt coverage.
(d) Inventory turnover.

Compute selected ratios.
(SO 5)

E19-8   Selected comparative statement data for Li Na Products Company are presented below. All balance sheet data are as of December 31.

	2003	2002
Net sales	$800,000	$720,000
Cost of goods sold	480,000	40,000
Interest expense	7,000	5,000
Net income	56,000	42,000
Accounts receivable	120,000	100,000
Inventory	85,000	75,000
Total assets	600,000	500,000
Total common stockholders' equity	450,000	325,000

Instructions
Compute the following ratios for 2003.

(a) Profit margin.
(b) Asset turnover.
(c) Return on assets.
(d) Return on common stockholders' equity.

Compute selected ratios.
(SO 5)

E19-9   The income statement for Laura Wilkinson, Inc., appears below.

LAURA WILKINSON, INC.
Income Statement
For the Year Ended December 31, 2002

Sales	$400,000
Cost of goods sold	230,000
Gross profit	170,000
Expenses (including $20,000 interest and $24,000 income taxes)	100,000
Net income	$ 70,000

Additional information:

1. Common stock outstanding January 1, 2002, was 30,000 shares.
2. The market price of Laura Wilkinson, Inc. stock was $15 in 2002.
3. Cash dividends of $21,000 were paid, $5,000 of which were to preferred stockholders.
4. Net cash provided by operating activities was $92,000.

Instructions
Compute the following ratios for 2002.

(a) Earnings per share.   (d) Times interest earned.
(b) Price-earnings.   (e) Cash return on sales.
(c) Payout.

E19-10 Alverez Corporation experienced a fire on December 31, 2003, in which its financial records were partially destroyed. It has been able to salvage some of the records and has ascertained the following balances.

Compute amounts from ratios.
(SO 5)

	December 31, 2003	December 31, 2002
Cash	$ 30,000	$ 10,000
Receivables (net)	72,500	126,000
Inventory	200,000	180,000
Accounts payable	50,000	90,000
Notes payable	30,000	60,000
Common stock, $100 par	400,000	400,000
Retained earnings	113,500	101,000

Additional information:

1. The inventory turnover is 3.6 times.
2. The return on common stockholders' equity is 22%. The company had no additional paid-in capital.
3. The receivables turnover is 9.4 times.
4. The return on assets is 20%.
5. Total assets at December 31, 2002, were $605,000.

Instructions

Compute the following for Alverez Corporation.

(a) Cost of goods sold for 2003.
(b) Net sales (credit) for 2003.
(c) Net income for 2003.
(d) Total assets at December 31, 2003.

PROBLEMS*

P19-1 Comparative statement data for Sara Company and Reiling Company, two competitors, appear below. All balance sheet data are as of December 31, 2003, and December 31, 2002.

Prepare vertical analysis and comment on profitability.
(SO 4, 5)

	Sara Company		Reiling Company	
	2003	**2002**	**2003**	**2002**
Net sales	$1,549,035		$339,038	
Cost of goods sold	1,080,490		238,006	
Operating expenses	292,275		79,000	
Interest expense	6,800		2,252	
Income tax expense	41,230		6,650	
Current assets	325,975	$312,410	83,336	$ 79,467
Plant assets (net)	521,310	500,000	139,728	125,812
Current liabilities	66,325	75,815	35,348	30,281
Long-term liabilities	108,500	90,000	29,620	25,000
Common stock, $10 par	500,000	500,000	120,000	120,000
Retained earnings	172,460	146,595	38,096	29,998

Instructions

(a) Prepare a vertical analysis of the 2003 income statement data for Sara Company and Reiling Company in columnar form.
(b) ▭▭▭▷ Comment on the relative profitability of the companies by computing the return on assets and the return on common stockholders' equity ratios for both companies.

---

*Follow the rounding procedures used in the chapter.

Compute ratios from balance sheet and income statement.
(SO 5)

P19-2   The comparative statements of Westphal Tool Company are presented below.

WESTPHAL TOOL COMPANY
Income Statement
For the Year Ended December 31

	2002	2001
Net sales	$1,818,500	$1,750,500
Cost of goods sold	1,005,500	996,000
Gross profit	813,000	754,500
Selling and administrative expense	506,000	479,000
Income from operations	307,000	275,500
Other expenses and losses		
Interest expense	27,000	19,000
Income before income taxes	280,000	256,500
Income tax expense	84,000	77,000
Net income	$ 196,000	$ 179,500

WESTPHAL TOOL COMPANY
Balance Sheets
December 31

Assets	2002	2001
Current assets		
Cash	$ 60,100	$ 64,200
Marketable securities	54,000	50,000
Accounts receivable (net)	107,800	102,800
Inventory	123,000	115,500
Total current assets	344,900	332,500
Plant assets (net)	625,300	520,300
Total assets	$970,200	$852,800

Liabilities and Stockholders' Equity		
Current liabilities		
Accounts payable	$160,000	$145,400
Income taxes payable	43,500	42,000
Total current liabilities	203,500	187,400
Bonds payable	200,000	200,000
Total liabilities	403,500	387,400
Stockholders' equity		
Common stock ($5 par)	280,000	300,000
Retained earnings	286,700	165,400
Total stockholders' equity	566,700	465,400
Total liabilities and stockholders' equity	$970,200	$852,800

On April 1, 2002, 4,000 shares were repurchased and canceled. All sales were on account. Net cash provided by operating activities for 2002 was $270,000.

Instructions
Compute the following ratios for 2002. (Weighted average common shares in 2002 were 57,000.)

(a) Earnings per share.

(b) Return on common stockholders' equity.

(c) Return on assets.

(d) Current.

(e) Acid-test.

(f) Receivables turnover.

(g) Inventory turnover.

(h) Times interest earned.

(i) Asset turnover.

(j) Debt to total assets.

(k) Current cash debt coverage.

(l) Cash return on sales.

(m) Cash debt coverage.

P19-3   Condensed balance sheet and income statement data for Terry Duffy Corporation appear below.

Perform ratio analysis, and evaluate financial position and operating results.
(SO 5)

TERRY DUFFY CORPORATION
Balance Sheets
December 31

	2003	2002	2001
Cash	$ 25,000	$ 20,000	$ 18,000
Receivables (net)	50,000	45,000	48,000
Other current assets	90,000	85,000	64,000
Investments	75,000	70,000	45,000
Plant and equipment (net)	400,000	370,000	358,000
	$640,000	$590,000	$533,000
Current liabilities	$ 75,000	$ 80,000	$ 70,000
Long-term debt	80,000	85,000	50,000
Common stock, $10 par	340,000	300,000	300,000
Retained earnings	145,000	125,000	113,000
	$640,000	$590,000	$533,000

TERRY DUFFY CORPORATION
Income Statement
For the Year Ended December 31

	2003	2002
Sales	$740,000	$700,000
Less: Sales returns and allowances	40,000	50,000
Net sales	700,000	650,000
Cost of goods sold	420,000	400,000
Gross profit	280,000	250,000
Operating expenses (including income taxes)	236,000	218,000
Net income	$ 44,000	$ 32,000

Additional information:

1. The market price of Duffy's common stock was $4.00, $5.00, and $7.95 for 2001, 2002, and 2003, respectively.
2. All dividends were paid in cash.
3. On July 1, 2003, 4,000 shares of common stock were issued.

Instructions

(a) Compute the following ratios for 2002 and 2003.
   (1) Profit margin.
   (2) Asset turnover.
   (3) Earnings per share. (Weighted average common shares in 2003 were 32,000.)
   (4) Price-earnings.
   (5) Payout.
   (6) Debt to total assets.

(b) ▭▭▭▭▷ Based on the ratios calculated, discuss briefly the improvement or lack thereof in financial position and operating results from 2002 to 2003 of Terry Duffy Corporation.

Compute ratios, and comment on overall liquidity and profitability.
(SO 5)

P19-4   Financial information for Mexicalli Company is presented below.

MEXICALLI COMPANY
Balance Sheets
December 31

Assets	2003	2002
Cash	$ 70,000	$ 65,000
Short-term investments	45,000	40,000
Receivables (net)	94,000	90,000
Inventories	130,000	125,000
Prepaid expenses	25,000	23,000
Land	130,000	130,000
Building and equipment (net)	190,000	175,000
	$684,000	$648,000

Liabilities and Stockholders' Equity		
Notes payable	$100,000	$100,000
Accounts payable	45,000	42,000
Accrued liabilities	40,000	40,000
Bonds payable, due 2006	150,000	150,000
Common stock, $10 par	200,000	200,000
Retained earnings	149,000	116,000
	$684,000	$648,000

MEXICALLI COMPANY
Income Statement
For the Years Ended December 31

	2003	2002
Sales	$850,000	$790,000
Cost of goods sold	620,000	575,000
Gross profit	230,000	215,000
Operating expenses	194,000	180,000
Net income	$ 36,000	$ 35,000

Additional information:

1. Inventory at the beginning of 2002 was $115,000.
2. Receivables at the beginning of 2002 were $88,000.
3. Total assets at the beginning of 2002 were $630,000.
4. No common stock transactions occurred during 2002 or 2003.
5. All sales were on account.

Instructions

(a) Indicate, by using ratios, the change in liquidity and profitability of Mexicalli Company from 2002 to 2003. (*Note:* Not all profitability ratios can be computed.)

(b) Given below are three independent situations and a ratio that may be affected. For each situation, compute the affected ratio (1) as of December 31, 2003, and (2) as of December 31, 2004, after giving effect to the situation. Net income for 2004 was $40,000. Total assets on December 31, 2004, were $700,000.

Situation	Ratio
(1) 18,000 shares of common stock were sold at par on July 1, 2004.	Return on common stockholders' equity
(2) All of the notes payable were paid in 2004. The only change in liabilities was that the notes payable were paid.	Debt to total assets
(3) Market price of common stock was $9 on December 31, 2003, and $12.80 on December 31, 2004.	Price-earnings ratio

P19-5 Selected financial data of two intense competitors in a recent year are presented below.

Compute selected ratios, and compare liquidity, profitability, and solvency for two companies.
(SO 5)

	Kmart Corporation	Wal-Mart Stores, Inc.
(in millions)		
Income Statement Data for Year		
Net sales	$34,025	$82,494
Cost of goods sold	25,992	65,586
Selling and administrative expenses	7,701	12,858
Interest expense	494	706
Other income (net)	572	918
Income taxes	114	1,581
Net income	$ 296	$ 2,681
Balance Sheet Data (End-of-Year)		
Current assets	$ 9,187	$15,338
Property, plant, and equipment (net)	7,842	17,481
Total assets	$17,029	$32,819
Current liabilities	$ 5,626	$ 9,973
Long-term debt	5,371	10,120
Total stockholders' equity	6,032	12,726
Total liabilities and stockholders' equity	$17,029	$32,819
Beginning-of-Year Balances		
Total assets	$17,504	$26,441
Total stockholders' equity	6,093	10,753
Other Data		
Average net receivables	$ 1,570	$ 695
Average inventory	7,317	12,539
Net cash provided by operating activities	351	3,106
Average current liabilities	5,720	10,110
Average total liabilities	11,230	20,160

Instructions

(a) For each company, compute the following ratios.

(1) Current.
(2) Receivables turnover.
(3) Inventory turnover.
(4) Profit margin.
(5) Asset turnover.
(6) Return on assets.
(7) Return on common stockholders' equity.
(8) Debt to total assets.
(9) Times interest earned.
(10) Current cash debt coverage.
(11) Cash return on sales.
(12) Cash debt coverage.

(b) Compare the liquidity, profitability, and solvency of the two companies.

Compute numerous ratios.
(SO 5)

P19-6 The comparative statements of Johansen Company are presented below.

JOHANSEN COMPANY
Income Statement
For Year Ended December 31

	2003	2002
Net sales (all on account)	$600,000	$520,000
Expenses		
Cost of goods sold	415,000	354,000
Selling and administrative	120,800	114,800
Interest expense	7,200	6,000
Income tax expense	18,000	14,000
Total expenses	561,000	488,800
Net income	$ 39,000	$ 31,200

JOHANSEN COMPANY
Balance Sheets
December 31

Assets	2003	2002
Current assets		
Cash	$ 21,000	$ 18,000
Marketable securities	18,000	15,000
Accounts receivable (net)	92,000	74,000
Inventory	84,000	70,000
Total current assets	215,000	177,000
Plant assets (net)	423,000	383,000
Total assets	$638,000	$560,000

Liabilities and Stockholders' Equity	2003	2002
Current liabilities		
Accounts payable	$112,000	$110,000
Income taxes payable	23,000	20,000
Total current liabilities	135,000	130,000
Long-term liabilities		
Bonds payable	130,000	80,000
Total liabilities	265,000	210,000
Stockholders' equity		
Common stock ($5 par)	150,000	150,000
Retained earnings	223,000	200,000
Total stockholders' equity	373,000	350,000
Total liabilities and stockholders' equity	$638,000	$560,000

Additional data:
The common stock recently sold at $19.50 per share.

Instructions
Compute the following ratios for 2003.

(a) Current.
(b) Acid-test.
(c) Receivables turnover.
(d) Inventory turnover.
(e) Profit margin.
(f) Asset turnover.
(g) Return on assets.

(h) Return on common stockholders' equity.
(i) Earnings per share.
(j) Price-earnings.
(k) Payout.
(l) Debt to total assets.
(m) Times interest earned.

P19-7   Presented below is an incomplete income statement and an incomplete comparative balance sheet of Windsor Corporation.

Compute missing information given a set of ratios.
(SO 5)

WINDSOR CORPORATION
Income Statement
For the Year Ended December 31, 2003

Sales	$11,000,000
Cost of goods sold	?
Gross profit	?
Operating expenses	1,665,000
Income from operations	?
Other expenses and losses	
Interest expense	?
Income before income taxes	?
Income tax expense	560,000
Net income	$?

WINDSOR CORPORATION
Balance Sheets
December 31

Assets	2003	2002
Current assets		
Cash	$ 450,000	$ 375,000
Accounts receivable (net)	?	950,000
Inventory	?	1,720,000
Total current assets	?	3,045,000
Plant assets (net)	4,620,000	3,955,000
Total assets	$?	$7,000,000

Liabilities and Stockholders' Equity	2003	2002
Current liabilities	$?	$ 825,000
Long-term notes payable	?	2,800,000
Total liabilities	?	3,625,000
Common stock, $1 par	3,000,000	3,000,000
Retained earnings	400,000	375,000
Total stockholders' equity	3,400,000	3,375,000
Total liabilities and stockholders' equity	$?	$7,000,000

Additional information:

1. The receivables turnover for 2003 is 10 times.
2. All sales are on account.
3. The profit margin for 2003 is 14.5%.
4. Return on assets is 22% for 2003.
5. The current ratio on December 31, 2003, is 3.2.
6. The inventory turnover for 2003 is 4.8 times.

Instructions

Compute the missing information given the ratios above. Show computations. (*Note*: Start with one ratio and derive as much information as possible from it before trying another ratio. List all missing amounts under the ratio used to find the information.)

BROADENING YOUR PERSPECTIVE

FINANCIAL REPORTING AND ANALYSIS

FINANCIAL REPORTING PROBLEM: Lands' End, Inc.

BYP19-1 Your parents are considering investing in Lands' End, Inc., common stock. They ask you, as an accounting expert, to make an analysis of the company for them. Fortunately, excerpts from a current annual report of Lands' End are presented in Appendix A of this textbook. Note that all amounts omit 000's (i.e., all dollar amounts are in thousands).

Instructions
(Follow the approach in the chapter for rounding numbers.)

(a) Make a 5-year trend analysis, using 1996 as the base year, of (1) net sales and (2) net income. Comment on the significance of the trend results.

(b) Compute for 2000 and 1999 the (1) profit margin, (2) asset turnover, (3) return on assets, and (4) return on common stockholders' equity. How would you evaluate Lands' End's profitability? Total assets at December 31, 1998, were $4,334.7, and total stockholders' equity at December 31, 1998, was $2,427.1.

(c) Compute for 2000 and 1999 the (1) debt to total assets and (2) times interest earned ratio. How would you evaluate Lands' End's long-term solvency?

(d) What information outside the annual report may also be useful to your parents in making a decision about Lands' End, Inc.?

COMPARATIVE ANALYSIS PROBLEM: Lands' End vs. Abercrombie & Fitch

BYP19-2 Lands' End's financial statements are presented in Appendix A. Abercrombie & Fitch's financial statements are presented in Appendix B.

Instructions
(a) Based on the information contained in these financial statements, determine each of the following for each company.
   (1) The percentage increase (decrease) in (i) net sales and (ii) net income from 1999 to 2000.
   (2) The percentage increase in (i) total assets and (ii) total stockholders' (shareholders') equity from 1999 to 2000.
   (3) The earnings per share and price-earnings ratio for 2000. Abercrombie & Fitch's common stock had a market price of $29.62 at the end of fiscal-year 2000.
(b) What conclusions concerning the two companies can be drawn from these data?

INTERPRETING FINANCIAL STATEMENTS: A Global Focus

BYP19-3 In England, the railroads were run by the government until recently. Five years ago, Railtrack Group PLC became a publicly traded company. The largest railroad company in the United States is Burlington Northern Railroad Company. The following data were taken from the 1998 financial statements of each company.

Financial Highlights	Railtrack Group (pounds in millions)		Burlington Northern (dollars in millions)	
	1998	**1997**	**1998**	**1997**
Cash and short-term investments	£ 380	£ 26	$ 95	$ –0–
Accounts receivable	434	402	676	632
Total current assets	909	521	1,357	1,197
Total assets	7,095	5,760	22,725	21,199
Current liabilities	1,128	1,209	2,175	2,089
Total liabilities	3,882	2,888	14,497	14,176
Total stockholders' equity	3,213	2,872	8,228	7,023
Sales	2,573		8,936	
Operating costs	2,102		6,781	

Financial Highlights	Railtrack Group (pounds in millions)		Burlington Northern (dollars in millions)	
	1998	1997	1998	1997
Interest expense	£ 93		$ 293	
Income tax expense	3		733	
Net income	425		1,206	
Cash provided by operations	988		2,107	

Instructions

(a) Calculate the following 1998 liquidity ratios and discuss the relative liquidity of the two companies.

   (1) Current ratio.   **(3)** Current cash debt coverage.

   (2) Acid-test.   **(4)** Receivables turnover.

(b) Calculate the following 1998 solvency ratios and discuss the relative solvency of the two companies.

   (1) Debt to total assets.   **(3)** Cash debt coverage.

   (2) Times interest earned.

(c) Calculate the following 1998 profitability ratios and discuss the relative profitability of the two companies.

   (1) Asset turnover.   **(3)** Return on assets.

   (2) Profit margin.   **(4)** Return on common stockholders' equity.

(d) What other issues must you consider when comparing these two companies?

EXPLORING THE WEB

BYP19-4 The Management Discussion and Analysis section of an annual report addresses corporate performance for the year, and sometimes uses financial ratios to support its claims.

Address: **www.ibm.com/financialguide** *(or go to www.wiley.com/college/weygandt)*

Steps:

1. From IBM's Financial Guide, choose **Guides Contents**.
2. Choose **Anatomy of an Annual Report**.

Instructions

Using the information from the above site, answer the following questions.

(a) What are the optional elements that are often included in an annual report?

(b) What are the elements of an annual report that are required by the SEC?

(c) Describe the contents of the Management Discussion.

(d) Describe the contents of the Auditors' Report.

(e) Describe the contents of the Selected Financial Data.

CRITICAL THINKING

GROUP DECISION CASE

BYP19-5 As the CPA for Latino Manufacturing Inc., you have been asked to develop some key ratios from the comparative financial statements. This information is to be used to convince creditors that the company is solvent and will continue as a going concern. The data requested and the computations developed from the financial statements follow.

	2000	1999
Current ratio	3.1 times	2.1 times
Acid-test ratio	.8 times	1.4 times
Asset turnover	2.8 times	2.2 times
Sales to stockholders' equity	2.3 times	2.7 times
Net income	Up 32%	Down 8%
Earnings per share	$3.30	$2.50
Book value per share	Up 8%	Up 11%

Instructions

With the class divided into groups, answer the following.

(a) Latino Manufacturing Inc. asks you to prepare a list of brief comments stating how each of these items supports the solvency and going-concern potential of the business. The company wishes to use these comments to support its presentation of data to its creditors. You are to prepare the comments as requested, giving the implications and the limitations of each item separately. Then prepare a collective inference that may be drawn from the individual items about Latino's solvency and going-concern potential.

(b) What warnings should you offer these creditors about the limitations of ratio analysis for the purpose stated here?

COMMUNICATION ACTIVITY

BYP19-6   Carol Dunn is the CEO of Midwest Electronics. Dunn is an expert engineer but a novice in accounting. She asks you to explain (1) the bases for comparison in analyzing Midwest's financial statements, and (2) the limitations, if any, in financial statement analysis.

Instructions

Write a letter to Carol Dunn that explains the bases for comparison and the limitations of financial statement analysis.

ETHICS CASE

BYP19-7   Andy Manion, president of Manion Industries, wishes to issue a press release to bolster his company's image and maybe even its stock price, which has been gradually falling. As controller, you have been asked to provide a list of twenty financial ratios along with some other operating statistics relative to Manion Industries' first quarter financials and operations.

Two days after you provide the ratios and data requested, Manny Alomar, the public relations director of Manion, asks you to prove the accuracy of the financial and operating data contained in the press release written by the president and edited by Manny. In the news release, the president highlights the sales increase of 25% over last year's first quarter and the positive change in the current ratio from 1.5:1 last year to 3:1 this year. He also emphasizes that production was up 50% over the prior year's first quarter.

You note that the press release contains only positive or improved ratios and none of the negative or deteriorated ratios. For instance, no mention is made that the debt to total assets ratio has increased from 35% to 55%, that inventories are up 89%, and that while the current ratio improved, the acid-test ratio fell from 1:1 to .5:1. Nor is there any mention that the reported profit for the quarter would have been a loss had not the estimated lives of Manion's plant and machinery been increased by 30%. Manny emphasized, "The prez wants this release by early this afternoon."

Instructions

(a) Who are the stakeholders in this situation?

(b) Is there anything unethical in president Manion's actions?

(c) Should you as controller remain silent? Does Manny have any responsibility?

Answers to Self Study Questions

1. b   2. d   3. a   4. c   5. c   6. c   7. c   8. b   9. a   10. b

---

Answer to *Lands' End* Review It Question 4, p. 787

Lands' End presents horizontal analyses in its "Financial Highlights" section and its Management's Discussion and Analysis section. Vertical analysis is used in schedules presented in the Management's Discussion and Analysis section (page A10 especially).

✓ *Remember to go back to the Navigator box on the chapter-opening page and check off your completed work.*

Appendixes A–D

SPECIMEN FINANCIAL STATEMENTS: Lands' End, Inc.

*T*HE ANNUAL REPORT

Once each year a corporation communicates to its stockholders and other interested parties by issuing a complete set of audited financial statements. The **annual report**, as this communication is called, summarizes the financial results of its operations for the year and its plans for the future. Many annual reports have become attractive, multicolored, glossy public relations pieces containing pictures of corporate officers and directors as well as photos and descriptions of new products and new buildings. Yet the basic function of every annual report is to report **financial information**, almost all of which is a product of the corporation's accounting system.

The content and organization of corporate annual reports have become fairly standardized. Excluding the public relations part of the report (pictures and products), the following items are the traditional financial portions of the annual report:

Financial Highlights
Letter to the Stockholders
Auditor's Report
Management Discussion and Analysis
Financial Statements and Accompanying Notes
Five- or Ten-Year Summary

In this appendix we illustrate current financial reporting with a comprehensive set of corporate financial statements. They have been prepared in accordance with generally accepted accounting principles and audited by an international independent certified public accounting firm. We are grateful for permission to use the actual financial statements and other accompanying financial information from the annual report of a large, publicly held company, **Lands' End, Inc.**

FINANCIAL HIGHLIGHTS

The financial highlights section is usually presented inside the front cover or on the first two pages of the annual report. This section generally reports the total or per share amounts for five to ten financial items for the current year and one or more previous years. Financial items from the income statement and the balance sheet that typically are presented are sales, income from continuing operations, net income, net income per share, dividends per common share, and the amount of capital expenditures. The financial highlights section from Lands' End's Annual Report is shown below.

Financial Highlights

LANDS' END
DIRECT MERCHANTS

Lands' End, Inc. & Subsidiaries

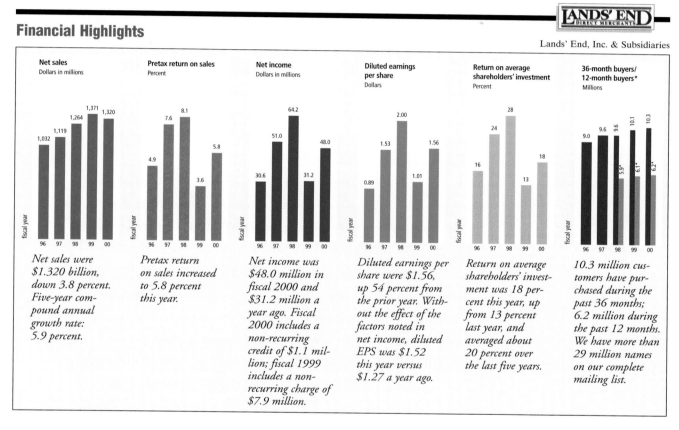

Net sales
Dollars in millions

Net sales were $1.320 billion, down 3.8 percent. Five-year compound annual growth rate: 5.9 percent.

Pretax return on sales
Percent

Pretax return on sales increased to 5.8 percent this year.

Net income
Dollars in millions

Net income was $48.0 million in fiscal 2000 and $31.2 million a year ago. Fiscal 2000 includes a non-recurring credit of $1.1 million; fiscal 1999 includes a non-recurring charge of $7.9 million.

Diluted earnings per share
Dollars

Diluted earnings per share were $1.56, up 54 percent from the prior year. Without the effect of the factors noted in net income, diluted EPS was $1.52 this year versus $1.27 a year ago.

Return on average shareholders' investment
Percent

Return on average shareholders' investment was 18 percent this year, up from 13 percent last year, and averaged about 20 percent over the last five years.

36-month buyers/ 12-month buyers*
Millions

10.3 million customers have purchased during the past 36 months; 6.2 million during the past 12 months. We have more than 29 million names on our complete mailing list.

As shown above, Lands' End chose to present its financial highlights using bar graphs accompanied with narrative describing current-year results and comparisons.

LETTER TO THE STOCKHOLDERS

Nearly every annual report contains a letter to the stockholders from the Chairman of the Board or the President (or both). This letter typically discusses the company's accomplishments during the past year. It also highlights significant events

Lands' End has completed a challenging year of planned transition. While net sales for fiscal 2000 were down about 4 percent to $1.320 billion, we are pleased with our earnings of $48 million. Before non-recurring items, our earnings per diluted share improved by almost 20 percent. The year is explained in full in the Management's Discussion and Analysis section of this annual report.

Last year in my letter to shareholders, I outlined the steps that we would take to put our company on the right track for long-term growth and improved profitability. These steps included reinvigorating our merchandise offering and creative presentation, a more disciplined approach to inventory and SKU management, reduction of unprofitable circulation, improved sourcing and gross profit margins, and an energetic focus on growing our e-commerce business.

In terms of these goals, the year overall was most satisfactory. The company transformed itself from a U.S. catalog company to a global direct merchant selling through multiple channels of distribution. We were recognized by FORTUNE® magazine as one of the

Dear Shareholder   top 10 companies that "get it" when it comes to e-commerce, and we have built the largest, most successful, acclaimed and profitable apparel Web site. We managed our inventory masterfully through the transition, clearing out the old merchandise without excessive markdowns and bringing in the new merchandise, all while maintaining our high standard for initial fulfillment – our measure of outstanding customer service. We made great strides in resourcing our products and, as a result, expect strong margin performance this coming year. We have rationalized our circulation plans and now have a profitable platform on which to build. We augmented our existing talented staff with new, strong and talented executives who together have reinvigorated our company. And for the third year in a row, we were recognized as one of the "100 Best Companies to Work For" in the United States – and we have done all of this while increasing profitability.

Inventory at year-end was down to $162 million, 26 percent below last year, and SKUs were down from 110,000 to 92,000 at year-end. Throughout the year, our initial fulfillment rate was at the very high level that we require for excellent customer service.

This pivotal year is now behind us. We accomplished a lot and learned a lot, and necessary course corrections have been made for this coming year. While it's too early to know with absolute certainty, our early spring business indications are indeed promising.

We have a number of terrific growth opportunities in the year ahead. We believe that we can advance all of our businesses, including the core catalog. But especially noteworthy such as mergers and acquisitions, new products, operating achievements, business philosophy, changes in officers or directors, financing commitments, expansion plans, and future prospects. The letter to the stockholders signed by David F. Dyer, President and Chief Executive Officer of Lands' End, is shown on pages A4 to A6.

are the prospects for our Internet and Corporate Sales business-to-business divisions.

To begin with, Internet sales last year were $138 million, more than double the $61 million of the previous year. From all reports we have seen to date, Lands' End remains the world's largest apparel Web site. Even after full expense allocation, Internet sales in the past year were more profitable than our catalog sales.

Based on results from fall 1999, circulation tests to Internet buyers confirmed the synergistic relationship of our catalog to the Web. We know that withholding catalogs from Internet buyers does not generate online sales. We believe that a smaller catalog (fewer pages) with sufficient mailing frequency may produce the best results over time. Still, we will continue to refine our tests to determine the optimum frequency and pages for keeping our Internet customers apprised of Lands' End's exciting new products.

The Internet was the fastest growing source of new customer names to our file last year. It is less costly to bring these customers to the Lands' End file through e-commerce than through printed media. About 20 percent of our Internet buyers are totally new to Lands' End.

As for our Corporate Sales business-to-business division, it should continue its double-digit growth increases this coming year. Nine out of 10 Fortune 500 companies have purchased business apparel from the Lands' End Corporate Sales division. Last year we achieved about $140 million in sales, and we just announced plans to develop an additional facility in Stevens Point, Wisconsin, in anticipation of the future planned growth. The new site will be fully operational in time for the 2001 peak season.

David F. Dyer

Corporate Sales is one of our most profitable businesses. We are uniquely positioned to provide a respected brand and a high-quality embroidery product featuring very rapid turnaround even for larger orders. We are exploring the possibility of broadening our product line beyond apparel.

Earlier this year, we launched a transaction-enabled Corporate Sales Web site. For large customers, we can now create online custom company stores. We currently have seven custom company stores online and expect to have about 30 more by year-end. For example, we just announced an agreement with Saturn to provide their dealers, employees and customers with logo apparel.

In addition to our Internet and Corporate Sales business, our other specialty businesses – kids' apparel and home furnishings – are planned for nice growth this year. Finally, we believe that our reinvigorated merchandise and creative presentation will also revitalize our core business.

As for our FY 2001 plans and goals, we seek a balance of top line sales growth and bottom line profit. Circulation is planned up 6 percent for the year and sales somewhat higher, which will occur largely in the fourth quarter when we cut back circulation too aggressively last year. In the fourth quarter of this year, we will add back a post-Thanksgiving mailing and reinstate the January catalog.

Gross profit is planned to improve by about 225 basis points due to better sourcing and more normalized liquidations.

We have cleared the deck of old merchandise. We have negotiated more effectively with our vendors for lower costs.

We plan to invest about a third of our gross profit improvement in Internet advertising and national advertising. Our capital expenditures are planned at about $50 million, the large majority of which is focused on systems for our call centers, the Internet and Corporate Sales. Our goal is to achieve about a 7.5 percent pretax profit on net sales.

These are exciting times for our company. We believe that Lands' End possesses the necessary key attributes to position us for success in the digital age.

Lands' End is a trusted, nationally recognized brand with a very loyal customer base. We are dedicated to provide outstanding customer service. We have very high standards for product quality. We control the distribution of our product, and our primary categories of apparel and home textiles offer sufficient margin to produce good profit. We have a leading direct-to-consumer infrastructure that positions us perfectly for future e-commerce growth.

And, most important of all, we at Lands' End are passionate about our company and our customers, and we'll work hard to create our future success.

Thanks for being a shareholder.

David F. Dyer
President and Chief Executive Officer

> *"We have a leading direct-to-consumer infrastructure that positions us perfectly for future e-commerce growth."*

AUDITOR'S REPORT

All publicly held corporations, as well as many other enterprises and organizations (both profit and not-for-profit, large and small) engage the services of independent certified public accountants who will provide an objective, expert report on their financial statements. Based on a comprehensive examination of the company's accounting system and records, and of the financial statements, the outside CPA issues the auditor's report.

The standard auditor's report consists of three pieces of information, expressed in separate sentences or paragraphs: (1) a responsibilities statement, (2) a scope statement, and (3) the opinion. In the **responsibilities statement**, the auditor identifies who and what was audited and indicates the responsibilities of management and the auditor relative to the financial statements. In the **scope statement**, the auditor states that the audit was conducted in accordance with generally accepted auditing standards and discusses the nature and limitations of the audit. In the **opinion statement**, the auditor expresses an informed opinion as to (1) the fairness of the financial statements and (2) their conformity with generally accepted accounting principles. The **Report of Arthur Andersen, Independent Public Accountants**, appearing in Lands' End's Annual Report is shown below.

To the Board of Directors and Shareholders of Lands' End, Inc.:

We have audited the accompanying consolidated balance sheets of Lands' End, Inc. (a Delaware corporation) and its subsidiaries as of January 28, 2000, and January 29, 1999, and the related consolidated statements of operations, shareholders' investment and cash flows for each of the three years in the period ended January 28, 2000. These financial statements are the responsibility of the company's management. Our responsibility is to express an opinion on these financial statements based on our audits.

We conducted our audits in accordance with generally accepted auditing standards. Those standards require that we plan and perform the audit to obtain reasonable assurance about whether the financial statements are free of material misstatement. An audit includes examining, on a test basis, evidence supporting the amounts and disclosures in the financial statements. An audit also includes assessing the accounting principles used and significant estimates made by management, as well as evaluating the overall financial statement presentation. We believe that our audits provide a reasonable basis for our opinion.

In our opinion, the financial statements referred to above present fairly, in all material respects, the financial position of Lands' End, Inc. and subsidiaries as of January 28, 2000, and January 29, 1999, and the results of their operations and their cash flows for each of the three years in the period ended January 28, 2000, in conformity with generally accepted accounting principles.

Arthur Andersen LLP

Arthur Andersen LLP

Milwaukee, Wisconsin
March 3, 2000

The auditor's report issued on Lands' End's financial statements is **unqualified** or "clean." That is, it contains no qualifications or exceptions. The auditor conformed completely with generally accepted auditing standards in performing the audit, and the financial statements conformed in all material respects with generally accepted accounting principles.

When the financial statements do not conform with generally accepted accounting principles, the auditor must issue a **qualified** opinion and describe the exception. If the lack of conformity with GAAP is sufficiently material, the auditor is compelled to issue an **adverse** or negative opinion. An adverse opinion means that the financial statements do not present fairly the company's financial condition and/or the results of the company's operations at the dates and for the periods reported.

In circumstances where the auditor is unable to perform all the auditing procedures necessary to reach a conclusion as to the fairness of the financial statements, a **disclaimer** must be issued. In these rare instances, the auditor must report the reason for failure to reach a conclusion on the fairness of the financial statements.

Companies strive to obtain an unqualified auditor's report. Hence, only infrequently are you likely to encounter anything other than this type of opinion on the financial statements.

MANAGEMENT'S REPORT

A relatively recent addition to corporate annual reports is the statement made by management about its role in and responsibility for the accuracy and integrity of the financial statements. Lands' End's management letter is entitled **Management's Responsibility for Financial Statements**. In it the Chief Executive Officer along with the Chief Financial Officer, on behalf of management, do the following: They (1) assume primary responsibility for the financial statements and the related notes, (2) outline and assess the company's internal control system, (3) declare the financial statements in conformity with generally accepted accounting principles, and (4) comment on the audit by the certified public accountant and the composition and role of the Audit Committee of the Board of Directors. Lands' End's management report is presented below.

Management's Responsibility for Financial Statements

The management of Lands' End, Inc. and its subsidiaries has the responsibility for preparing the accompanying financial statements and for their integrity and objectivity. The statements were prepared in accordance with generally accepted accounting principles applied on a consistent basis. The consolidated financial statements include amounts that are based on management's best estimates and judgments. Management also prepared the other information in the annual report and is responsible for its accuracy and consistency with the consolidated financial statements.

The company's consolidated financial statements have been audited by Arthur Andersen LLP, independent certified public accountants. Management has made available to Arthur Andersen LLP all the company's financial records and related data, as well as the minutes of shareholders' and directors' meetings. Furthermore, management believes that all representations made to Arthur Andersen LLP during its audit were valid and appropriate.

Management of the company has established and maintains a system of internal control that provides for appropriate division of responsibility, reasonable assurance as to the integrity and reliability of the consolidated financial statements, the protection of assets from unauthorized use or disposition, the prevention and detection of fraudulent financial reporting, and the maintenance of an active program of internal audits. Management believes that, as of January 28, 2000, the company's system of internal control is adequate to accomplish the objectives discussed herein.

Two directors of the company, not members of management, serve as the audit committee of the board of directors and are the principal means through which the board supervises the performance of the financial reporting duties of management. The audit committee meets with management, the internal audit staff and the company's independent auditors to review the results of the audits of the company and to discuss plans for future audits. At these meetings, the audit committee also meets privately with the internal audit staff and the independent auditors to assure its free access to them.

David F. Dyer
Chief Executive Officer

Stephen A. Orum
Executive Vice President and Chief Financial Officer

MANAGEMENT'S DISCUSSION AND ANALYSIS

The **management's discussion and analysis (MD&A)** section covers three financial aspects of a company: its results of operations, its ability to pay near-term obligations, and its ability to fund operations and expansion. Management must highlight favorable or unfavorable trends and identify significant events and uncertainties that affect these three factors. This discussion obviously involves a number of subjective estimates and opinions. The MD&A section of Lands' End's annual report is presented on the following pages.

LANDS' END
DIRECT MERCHANTS

Management's Discussion and Analysis

Lands' End, Inc. & Subsidiaries

The company planned fiscal year 2000 as a transition year in which it reduced unprofitable mailings, reduced expenses and liquidated excess inventory to prepare for a reinvigorated and new merchandise offering.

For fiscal 2000, sales declined 3.8 percent. The decrease in net sales was primarily from the company's core business segment, offset in part by growth in the specialty business. Net income increased 54 percent to $48 million in fiscal 2000. Net income includes an after-tax non-recurring credit of $1.1 million for fiscal 2000, compared with an after-tax non-recurring charge of $7.9 million in fiscal 1999.

Consolidated statements of operations presented as a percentage of net sales

For the period ended	January 28, 2000	January 29, 1999	January 30, 1998
Net sales	100.0%	100.0%	100.0%
Cost of sales	55.1	55.0	53.4
Gross profit	44.9	45.0	46.6
Selling, general and administrative expenses	39.0	39.7	38.8
Non-recurring charge (credit)	(0.1)	0.9	–
Income from operations	6.0	4.4	7.8
Interest income (expense), net	(0.1)	(0.6)	–
Gain on sale of subsidiary	–	–	0.6
Other	(0.1)	(0.2)	(0.3)
Income before income taxes	5.8	3.6	8.1
Income tax provision	2.2	1.3	3.0
Net income	3.6%	2.3%	5.1%

Segment net sales

(Amounts in millions)	January 28, 2000		January 29, 1999		January 30, 1998	
	Amount	% of Net Sales	Amount	% of Net Sales	Amount	% of Net Sales
Core	$ 780	59%	$ 861	63%	$ 825	66%
Specialty	397	30%	364	27%	307	24%
International	143	11%	146	10%	132	10%
Total net sales	$1,320	100%	$1,371	100%	$1,264	100%

Segment income (loss) before income taxes

(Amounts in millions)	January 28, 2000		January 29, 1999		January 30, 1998	
	Amount	% of Net Sales	Amount	% of Net Sales	Amount	% of Net Sales
Core	$ 33	2.5 %	$ 27	2.0 %	$ 59	4.7%
Specialty	43	3.3 %	23	1.7 %	30	2.4%
International	2	0.2 %	5	0.3 %	8	0.6%
Other	(2)	(0.2)%	(5)	(0.4)%	5	0.4%
Income before income taxes	$ 76	5.8 %	$ 50	3.6 %	$ 102	8.1%

Results of operations for fiscal 2000, compared with fiscal 1999

Net sales decreased by 3.8 percent

Net sales for the year just ended totaled $1.320 billion, compared with $1.371 billion in the prior year, a decrease of 3.8 percent. This decrease was greater than anticipated, even with the planned reduction in catalog pages mailed during the year. The specialty business segment had the strongest performance for fiscal 2000, with sales up about 9 percent to $396.3 million, due in large part to another successful year for our Corporate Sales business-to-business division, which now accounts for about $140 million in sales. Sales for the core business segment were $780.3 million, down 9 percent from the prior year, due largely to an 18 percent page circulation reduction. Sales for the international business segment were $143.2 million, slightly down from $146 million last year. Lower inventory levels throughout the year resulted in a first-time fulfillment of about 88 percent.

Sales for November and December, the two most important months of our critical holiday season, were down almost 15 percent from the prior year. This was due principally to the planned strategy of mailing fewer catalog pages to reduce unprofitable mailings, the elimination of a full-size catalog at Thanksgiving time, and a lower level of liquidation sales compared with the prior year when catalog mailings and promotional pricing were aggressively increased to clear excess inventory. In January, the company traditionally mails its January full-price primary catalog, as well as an end-of-season clearance catalog. This year these two mailings were combined into one book, with only a small presentation devoted to full-price merchandise, resulting in a 30 percent page reduction and a 24 percent decline in sales for the month of January.

Our Internet sales at *www.landsend.com* more than doubled in fiscal 2000, with sales of $138 million, compared with $61 million in fiscal 1999. We continue to find that more than 20 percent of our Internet buyers are new to Lands' End, and believe this channel will continue to be an important growth opportunity for us.

Gross profit margin

Gross profit for the year just ended was $593 million, or 44.9 percent of net sales, compared with $617 million, or 45.0 percent of net sales, for the prior year. During the first nine months of fiscal 2000, gross profit margin was running well below the prior year, due primarily to a higher level of liquidated merchandise sales at steeper markdowns. However, in the fourth quarter, gross profit margin was strong due to higher initial margins as a result of improved sourcing and the lower level of liquidations. Liquidations were about 12 percent of total net sales in fiscal 2000, compared with 10 percent in the prior year.

In fiscal 2000, the cost of inventory purchases was down 2.7 percent, compared with inflation of 0.5 percent in fiscal 1999. This reduction was a result of deflation, as well as more efficient negotiations with our suppliers. As a result, the LIFO reserve was reduced by $5.9 million in fiscal 2000.

Selling, general and administrative expenses

Selling, general and administrative (SG&A) expenses decreased 5.3 percent to $515 million in fiscal 2000, compared with $544 million in the prior year. The decrease was due to a reduction in the number of catalog pages mailed, somewhat offset by relatively higher fulfillment costs. As a percentage of sales, SG&A was 39.0 percent in fiscal 2000 and 39.7 percent in the prior year. The decrease in the SG&A ratio was primarily the result of the reduction in the number of pages mailed and greater overall catalog productivity (sales per page). The number of full-price catalogs mailed totaled 236 million in fiscal 2000, down 9 percent from the prior year, while the total number of pages mailed decreased by about 17 percent.

The cost of producing and mailing catalogs represented about 37 percent and 43 percent of total SG&A in fiscal 2000 and 1999, respectively.

Depreciation and amortization expense was $20.7 million, up 10.6 percent from the prior year, related primarily to additional computer hardware and software, and buildings. Rental expense was $15.5 million, down 0.8 percent from fiscal 1999, as a result of three store closings.

Utilization of credit lines decreased

Inventory decreased to $162 million in fiscal 2000, down 26 percent from $220 million in the prior year. As a result of lower inventory levels and reduced purchases of treasury stock, borrowing decreased under our short-term lines of credit. Interest expense decreased to $1.9 million in fiscal 2000, compared to $7.7 million in fiscal 1999. We spent $28 million in capital expenditures and purchased about $4.5 million in treasury stock. Our lines of credit peaked at $53 million in fiscal 2000, compared with a peak of $257 million in the prior year. At January 28, 2000, the company's foreign subsidiaries had short-term debt outstanding of $11.7 million and domestic operations had no outstanding borrowings. No long-term debt was outstanding at fiscal year-end 2000.

Net income increased

Net income for fiscal 2000 was $48.0 million, up 54 percent from the $31.2 million earned in fiscal 1999. Diluted earnings per share for the year just ended were $1.56, compared with $1.01 per share for the prior year. In the third and fourth quarters of fiscal 1999, the company had after-tax non-recurring charges of $0.9 million and $7.0 million, respectively, or $0.26 per share for the entire fiscal year. Fiscal 2000 includes an addition to after-tax net income of $1.1 million, or $0.04

per share, from the reversal of a portion of that non-recurring charge. Before the effect of these adjustments, net income for the year just ended was $46.9 million, or $1.52 per diluted share, compared with fiscal 1999 net income of $39.1 million, or $1.27 per share. The diluted weighted average number of common shares outstanding was 30.9 million for fiscal 2000 and 30.8 million for fiscal 1999.

Segment results

The company has three business segments consisting of Core (regular monthly and prospecting catalogs, First Person, and Beyond Buttondowns), Specialty (Kids, Corporate Sales, and Coming Home catalogs) and International (foreign-based operations in Japan, United Kingdom and Germany). "Other" includes corporate expenses, intercompany eliminations, other income and deduction items that are not allocated to segments. (See Note 12.)

The core segment's net sales were $780.3 million or 59 percent of total net sales in fiscal 2000, which represents a decrease of $80.6 million from the prior year. Within the core operating segment, sales from the monthly and prospecting full-price catalogs were down from the prior year due principally to a planned reduction in circulation and pages mailed. Total pages circulated were down 18 percent in the core segment.

The specialty segment's net sales were $396.3 million or 30 percent of total net sales in fiscal 2000, which represents an increase of $31.8 million from the prior year. This sales increase was mainly from our Corporate Sales business-to-business division.

The international segment's net sales were $143.2 million or 11 percent of total net sales in fiscal 2000, which represents a decrease of $2.7 million from the prior year. The decrease was due mainly to lower sales for the United Kingdom and Japan.

Income (loss) before income taxes for the segments were: core increased by $5.4 million to $32.7 million in fiscal 2000 from $27.3 million in the prior year; specialty increased by $20.1 million to $43.1 million in fiscal 2000 from $23.0 million in the prior year; and international decreased by $2.4 million to $2.3 million in fiscal 2000 from $4.7 million last year. The core and specialty segments' increase in income before income taxes was primarily the result of the company's strategy to reduce circulation and focus on catalog productivity. In addition, both core and specialty segments incurred non-recurring credits of $0.5 million and $1.3 million, respectively. This compares to fiscal 1999 non-recurring charges of $7.6 million and $5.0 million allocated to core and specialty, respectively. International's decrease in income before income taxes was attributed mainly to its sales decrease in the United Kingdom and Japan.

Management's Discussion and Analysis   Lands' End, Inc. & Subsidiaries

Adoption of SFAS 133

The company adopted SFAS 133 at the beginning of the third quarter of fiscal 2000. For the company's cash flow hedges, changes in fair value are recognized in shareholders' investment as other comprehensive income to the extent determined to be effective until the hedged item is recognized in earnings. For fiscal 2000, $0.6 million of gains were included in other comprehensive income. Prior to the adoption of SFAS 133 for fiscal 2000, $0.7 million of losses were recognized in other expenses. For fiscal 2000, $0.8 million of losses were recognized in other expenses compared to $1.9 million of losses in fiscal 1999. Pursuant to this standard, the ineffective portion of cash flow hedges, as well as certain changes related to the company's option contracts, are reflected in earnings as the changes occur. These changes resulted in a $0.1 million non-cash charge for fiscal 2000. Results of operations will continue to be affected by changes in fair value for these contracts, the amount and timing of which cannot be predicted.

Results of operations for fiscal 1999, compared with fiscal 1998

Net sales grew by 8.5 percent

Net sales for fiscal 1999 totaled $1.371 billion, compared with $1.264 billion in the prior year, an increase of 8.5 percent. The increase in sales was due primarily to additional catalogs and pages mailed to customers. The growth in sales came from all of the company's operating segments. In fiscal 1999, our company expanded the number of reported operating segments to three: core, specialty and international. Prior to this, only domestic and foreign segments were disclosed. (See Note 12.)

Within the core operating segment, sales from the monthly and prospecting full-price catalogs were down from the prior year despite an increase in pages circulated. The specialty segment has a higher operating profit compared with the core and international segments, due principally to higher gross profit margins and relatively lower costs of catalog advertising.

Fiscal 1999 inventory was $220 million, down 9 percent from $241 million in fiscal 1998. Inventory throughout most of the year was higher as we experienced softening sales, especially in the third quarter. To correct this, we instituted price rollbacks, price reductions and some promotional pricing in the fourth quarter. This helped increase sales, but also had a negative effect on the gross profit margin. Higher inventory levels throughout the year allowed the company to achieve a first-time fulfillment of 91 percent.

Gross profit margin decreased

Gross profit for fiscal 1999 was $617 million, or 45.0 percent of net sales, compared with $588 million, or 46.6 percent of net sales, for the prior year. The decrease in gross profit margin was due primarily to more steep markdowns on higher sales of liquidated merchandise, especially in the fourth quarter when we aggressively addressed our overstock situation, as well as from lower initial markups. Liquidations were about 10 percent of total net sales in fiscal 1999, compared with 8 percent in the prior year.

In fiscal 1999, inflationary pressure was low, and costs of inventory purchases increased 0.5 percent, compared with 1.2 percent in fiscal 1998.

Selling, general and administrative expenses

Selling, general and administrative (SG&A) expenses rose 11.1 percent to $544 million in fiscal 1999, compared with $490 million in the prior year. As a percentage of sales, SG&A was 39.7 percent in fiscal 1999 and 38.8 percent in fiscal 1998. The increase in the SG&A percentage was mainly the result of lower productivity in the catalogs due to an increase in pages and catalogs mailed and a weaker response from customers. Additional factors increasing the SG&A percentage were relatively higher salaries and benefits, higher Year 2000 expenses, and increased investment in the Internet site. This was partially offset by lower bonus and profit-sharing expense due to lower profitability. The number of full-price catalogs mailed totaled 259 million in fiscal 1999, up 12 percent from the prior year, while the total number of pages mailed increased by about 10 percent.

Over the past two years, catalog circulation had increased 22 percent and page circulation by 38 percent. This level of circulation was due in part to our efforts to clear excess inventory in the fourth quarter. Starting with fall of 1999, we will circulate fewer catalogs and pages to reduce less profitable mailings. This will have a negative effect on sales growth, but is expected to have a positive impact on operating profit margins by increasing catalog productivity, or sales per page.

The cost of producing and mailing catalogs represented about 43 percent and 41 percent of total SG&A in fiscal 1999 and 1998, respectively.

Depreciation and amortization expense was $18.7 million, up 23.8 percent from the prior year, primarily because of additional equipment, computer hardware and software, and buildings. Rental expense was $15.6 million, up 15.7 percent, due mainly to increased computer-related rentals.

In fiscal 1999, we recorded a non-recurring charge of $12.6 million. This charge includes costs associated with severance payments due to organizational changes, liquidation of the Willis & Geiger division, closing of three outlet stores and the termination of a licensing agreement with MontBell Co. Ltd.

Utilization of credit lines increased

Because of higher inventory levels and lower profits throughout the year, there was additional borrowing under our short-term lines of credit, increasing our interest expense to $7.7 million in fiscal 1999. In addition, we spent $47 million in capital expenditures and purchased about $36 million in treasury stock. Our lines of credit peaked at $257 million in October 1998, compared with a peak of $118 million in the prior year. At January 29, 1999, the company's foreign subsidiaries had short-term debt outstanding of $17.1 million and domestic operations had borrowings of $21.8 million. No long-term debt was outstanding at January 29, 1999.

Net income decreased

Net income for fiscal 1999 was $31.2 million, down 51 percent from the $64.2 million earned in fiscal 1998. Diluted earnings per share for fiscal 1999 were $1.01, compared with $2.00 per share for the prior year. The diluted weighted average number of common shares outstanding was 30.8 million for fiscal 1999 and 32.1 million for fiscal 1998.

The fiscal 1999 results include an after-tax non-recurring charge of $7.9 million, or $0.26 per share. In the first quarter of fiscal 1998 the company had an after-tax gain of $4.9 million, or $0.15 per share, from the sale of its majority interest in The Territory Ahead. Before the effect of these adjustments, net income for fiscal 1999 was $39.1 million, or $1.27 per share, compared with $59.2 million, or $1.85 per share, in fiscal 1998.

Segment results

The core segment's net sales were $860.9 million or 63 percent of total net sales in fiscal year 1999, which represents an increase of $36.0 million from the prior year. Within the core operating segment, sales from the monthly and prospecting full-price catalogs were down from the prior year despite an increase in pages circulated.

The specialty segment's net sales were $364.6 million or 27 percent of total net sales in fiscal year 1999, which represents an increase of $57.6 million from the prior year. The specialty segment has a higher operating profit, compared with the core and international segments, due principally to higher gross profit margins and relatively lower catalog advertising costs.

The international segment's net sales were $145.9 million or 10 percent of total net sales in fiscal year 1999, which represents an increase of $14.1 million from the prior year.

Income before income taxes for the segments was: core decreased by $32.1 million to $27.3 million in fiscal year 1999 from $59.4 million in the prior year; specialty decreased by $7.2 million to $23.0 million in fiscal year 1999 from $30.2 million in the prior year; and international decreased by $3.0 million to $4.7 million in fiscal year 1999 from $7.7 million in the prior year. The decreases in the segments' income before

income taxes were the result of steep markdowns on a higher portion of liquidated merchandise, and higher expenses resulting from lower productivity of the catalogs. In fiscal 1999, both the core and specialty segments incurred non-recurring charges of $7.6 million and $5.0 million, respectively.

The Christmas season is our busiest

Our business is highly seasonal. The fall/winter season is a five-month period ending in December. In the longer spring/summer season, orders are fewer and the merchandise offered generally has lower unit selling prices than products offered in the fall/winter season. As a result, net sales are usually substantially greater in the fall/winter season, and SG&A as a percentage of net sales is usually higher in the spring/summer season. Additionally, as we continue to refine our marketing efforts by experimenting with the timing of our catalog mailings, quarterly results may fluctuate.

Nearly 34 percent of our annual sales came in the fourth quarter of fiscal 2000, compared with about 40 percent in fiscal 1999. Approximately 59 percent and 82 percent of before-tax profit was realized in the same quarter of fiscal 2000 and 1999, respectively.

Liquidity and capital resources

To date, the bulk of our working capital needs have been met through funds generated from operations and from short-term bank loans. Our principal need for working capital has been to meet peak inventory requirements associated with our seasonal sales pattern. In addition, our resources have been used to make asset additions and purchase treasury stock. During fiscal 2000 we entered into a new domestic credit facility providing unsecured credit totaling $200 million. As of January 28, 2000, the only reduction of this facility was $28.7 million of outstanding letters of credit. The company also maintains foreign credit lines for use in foreign operations totaling the equivalent of approximately $54 million, of which $11.7 million was used at January 28, 2000.

Since fiscal 1990, the company's board of directors has authorized the purchase of a total of 12.7 million shares of the company's common stock. A total of 0.1 million, 1.1 million and 1.5 million shares have been purchased in the fiscal years ended January 28, 2000, January 29, 1999 and January 30, 1998, respectively. As of January 28, 2000, 11.6 million shares have been purchased, and there is a balance of 1.1 million shares authorized to be purchased by the company.

The board of directors from time to time evaluates its dividend practice. Given our current authorization to buy back additional shares, the payment of cash dividends is not planned for the foreseeable future.

Management's Discussion and Analysis Lands' End, Inc. & Subsidiaries

Capital investment

Capital investment was about $28 million in fiscal 2000. Major projects included computer hardware and software and distribution center equipment.

In the coming year, we plan to invest about $50 million in capital expenditures, investing primarily in our information technology. We believe that our cash flow from operations and borrowings under our current credit facilities will provide adequate resources to meet our capital requirements and operational needs for the foreseeable future.

Other matters

Year 2000

We began to address the Year 2000 issue (possibility that some date-sensitive computer software will not correctly process two-digit year references and other date-related functions) in 1996, and established a Year 2000 project office in 1997. The project office worked with our information systems department and outside consultants to identify and assess the Year 2000 readiness of our internal computer systems and microprocessors and, where appropriate, to remediate and test them. The project office also worked with our buyers, quality assurance and other personnel to assess the readiness of our suppliers.

We completed substantially all the identification, assessment, remediation and testing of significant internal systems (mainframe, mid-range and personal computers, and embedded hardware and software in our warehouses and other operations) by the fourth quarter of 1999, and have encountered no material Year 2000-related problems in those systems. We have also encountered no material problems in the ability of our product vendor and supply base to deliver goods and services. Although we believe no further significant Year 2000 contingencies exist, contingency plans developed throughout 1999 remain available for implementation in the event such problems were to develop.

Cost: The total cost of our Year 2000 efforts is expected to be approximately $21 million, which is being expensed as incurred except for $1.2 million of hardware replacement costs that has been capitalized. About $3.4 million of the total amount was incurred through the end of fiscal 1998. An additional $8.9 million was spent in fiscal 1999, and $8.7 million was incurred in fiscal 2000. We currently expect total expenditures of less than $100,000 in fiscal 2001. The timing and amount of these future expenditures are forward-looking and subject to uncertainties relating to our ongoing assessment of

the Year 2000 issue, as well as the occurrence and response to any problem that may arise. Our Year 2000 expenses have been part of our annual budgets for information services. Accordingly, other technology development projects have been delayed to the extent that resources have been devoted to the Year 2000 project.

Market risk disclosure

The company uses derivative instruments to hedge, and therefore attempts to reduce its exposure to the effects of currency fluctuations on cash flows. The company is subject to foreign currency risk related to its transactions with operations in the United Kingdom, Japan, Germany and with foreign third-party vendors. The company's foreign currency risk management policy is to hedge the majority of merchandise purchases by foreign operations and from foreign third-party vendors, which includes forecasted transactions, through the use of foreign exchange forward contracts and options to minimize this risk. The company's policy is not to speculate in derivative instruments for profit on the exchange rate price fluctuation, trade in currencies for which there are no underlying exposures, or enter into trades for any currency to intentionally increase the underlying exposure. Derivative instruments used as hedges must be effective at reducing the risk associated with the exposure being hedged and must be designated as a hedge at the inception of the contract.

As of January 28, 2000, the company had net outstanding foreign currency forward contracts totaling about $46 million and options totaling $4 million. Based on the anticipated cash flows and outflows for the next 12 months and the foreign currency derivative instruments in place at January 28, 2000, a hypothetical 10 percent strengthening of the U.S. dollar relative to all other currencies would adversely affect the expected fiscal 2001 cash flows by $2.1 million.

The company is subject to the risk of fluctuating interest rates in the normal course of business, primarily as a result of its short-term borrowing and investment activities at variable interest rates. As of January 28, 2000, the company had no outstanding financial instruments related to its debt or investments. At January 28, 2000, a sensitivity analysis was performed for its short-term debt and investments that have interest rate risk. The company has determined that a 10 percent change in the company's weighted average interest rates would have no material effect on the consolidated financial statements.

Possible future changes

A 1992 Supreme Court decision confirmed that the Commerce Clause of the United States Constitution prevents a state from requiring the collection of its use tax by a mail order company unless the company has a physical presence in the state. However, there continues to be uncertainty due to inconsistent application of the Supreme Court decision by state and federal courts. The company attempts to conduct its operations in compliance with its interpretation of the applicable legal standard, but there can be no assurance that such compliance will not be challenged.

In recent challenges, various states have sought to require companies to begin collection of use taxes and/or pay taxes from previous sales. The company has not received assessments from any state.

The Supreme Court decision also established that Congress has the power to enact legislation that would permit states to require collection of use taxes by mail order companies. Congress has from time to time considered proposals for such legislation. The company anticipates that any legislative change, if adopted, would be applied only on a prospective basis.

In October 1998, The Internet Tax Freedom Act was signed into law. Among the provisions of this Act is a three-year moratorium on multiple and discriminatory taxes on electronic commerce. An Advisory Commission on Electronic Commerce has been appointed to study and report back to Congress on whether, and if so, how, electronic commerce should be taxed. We are monitoring the activities of the Commission, as well as any proposed changes in the sales and use tax laws and policies in general.

Business outlook

In the year just ended, one of the company's major initiatives had been to revamp its merchandise line. Beginning with the spring line this year, more new and enhanced products are being offered to customers than ever before. Due to changes in sourcing and more successful negotiations with its vendors, the company expects an improvement in gross profit margin of about 225 basis points for fiscal 2001. About one-third of the increased margin dollars will be invested in additional Internet and national advertising.

Another major initiative for the year just ended was to reduce unprofitable mailings, and as the company anniversaries these significant cuts, beginning with this year's second quarter, it will focus on growth from a more productive base. Our circulation strategy for fiscal 2001 will include an increase of about 6 percent in page circulation for the year, most of which will take place in the fourth quarter. Due to improved merchandise offerings and more compelling creative presentations, the company expects sales to improve somewhat more than the 6 percent increase in page circulation. Based on these expectations, the company's goal is to achieve about a 7.5 percent pretax profit on net sales. Because of circulation changes currently planned, the company anticipates fluctuating quarterly comparisons with the prior year for both sales and earnings.

For the first half of fiscal 2001, the company anticipates a sales increase in the mid-single digits, together with a strong increase in earnings. The first quarter is expected to show flat sales on 5 percent fewer pages mailed, with somewhat weaker earnings. The sales comparison trend excludes the impact of the discontinued Willis & Geiger business, which accounted for $11 million in sales in the first quarter of fiscal 2000. In the second quarter of fiscal 2001, the company plans to increase circulation and anticipates strong sales for that period.

The company anticipates that the fourth quarter will represent the largest improvement over the prior year in both sales and earnings, in light of the planned merchandise introductions and the current circulation strategy for the last half of fiscal 2001.

Statement regarding forward-looking information

Statements in this report (including, but not limited to, the president's letter and Management's Discussion and Analysis) that are not historical, including, without limitation, statements regarding our goals for fiscal 2001 sales, gross profit margin, pretax profit and earnings, as well as anticipated sales trends and future development of our business strategy, are considered forward-looking in this report. As such, these statements are subject to a number of risks and uncertainties. Future results may be materially different from those expressed or implied by these statements due to a number of factors. Currently, we believe that the principal factors that create uncertainty about our future results are the following: customer response to our new merchandise introductions, circulation changes and other initiatives; general economic or business conditions, both domestic and foreign; effects of shifting patterns of e-commerce versus catalog purchases; costs associated with printing and mailing catalogs; dependence on consumer seasonal buying patterns; and fluctuations in foreign currency exchange rates. Our future results could, of course, be affected by other factors as well.

The company does not undertake to publicly update or revise its forward-looking statements even if experience or future changes make it clear that any projected results expressed or implied therein will not be realized.

Lands' End *Direct Merchants*

As a leading global direct merchant, we are dedicated to offering exceptional quality products at prices that represent honest value, backed by the best customer service in the industry. *Guaranteed. Period.*®

Our **core business** segment is composed of adult apparel offered through our regular monthly and prospecting catalogs and our two catalogs of classic clothing for the workplace – *First Person* for women and *Beyond Buttondowns* for men. Sales in our core business segment were $780 million in fiscal 2000 and $861 million in fiscal 1999.

Our **specialty business** segment contains three catalogs – *Kids*, a collection of comfortable casual clothing for children; *Corporate Sales*, our business-to-business catalog offering the Lands' End brand as an option for company incentives, rewards, gifts and group apparel; and *Coming Home*, featuring products for the home. Sales in this segment were $397 million in fiscal 2000 and $364 million in fiscal 1999.

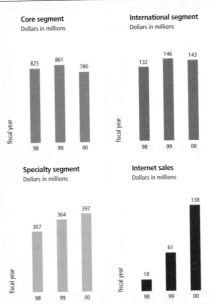

Our **international business** segment includes operations in Japan, Germany and the United Kingdom. These catalogs are written in local languages and denominated in local currencies. International segment sales were $143 million in fiscal 2000 and $146 million in fiscal 1999.

landsend.com is our Lands' End Web site, where we have expanded our Direct Merchant concept for the growing number of customers who prefer cybershopping. All of our products are available on the Web. Internet sales were $138 million in fiscal 2000 and $61 million in fiscal 1999. All Internet, export and liquidation sales are included in the respective business segment figures.

FINANCIAL STATEMENTS AND ACCOMPANYING NOTES

The standard set of financial statements consists of: (1) a comparative income statement (statement of operations) for three years, (2) a comparative balance sheet for two years, (3) a comparative statement of cash flows for three years, (4) a statement of stockholders' equity (or shareholders' investment) for three years, and (5) a set of accompanying notes that are considered an integral part of the financial statements. The auditor's report, unless stated otherwise, covers the financial statements and the accompanying notes. The financial statements and accompanying notes plus some supplementary data for Lands' End, Inc. appear on the following pages.

Consolidated Statements of Operations

Lands' End, Inc. & Subsidiaries

	For the period ended		
(In thousands, except per share data)	January 28, 2000	January 29, 1999	January 30, 1998
Net sales	$1,319,823	$1,371,375	$1,263,629
Cost of sales	727,291	754,661	675,138
Gross profit	592,532	616,714	588,491
Selling, general and administrative expenses	515,375	544,446	489,923
Non-recurring charge (credit)	(1,774)	12,600	–
Income from operations	78,931	59,668	98,568
Other income (expense):			
Interest expense	(1,890)	(7,734)	(1,995)
Interest income	882	16	1,725
Gain on sale of subsidiary	–	–	7,805
Other	(1,679)	(2,450)	(4,278)
Total other income (expense), net	(2,687)	(10,168)	3,257
Income before income taxes	76,244	49,500	101,825
Income tax provision	28,210	18,315	37,675
Net income	$ 48,034	$ 31,185	$ 64,150
Basic earnings per share	$ 1.60	$ 1.02	$ 2.01
Diluted earnings per share	$ 1.56	$ 1.01	$ 2.00
Basic weighted average shares outstanding	30,085	30,471	31,851
Diluted weighted average shares outstanding	30,854	30,763	32,132

Consolidated Balance Sheets

Lands' End, Inc. & Subsidiaries

(In thousands)	January 28, 2000	January 29, 1999
Assets		
Current assets:		
Cash and cash equivalents	$ 76,413	$ 6,641
Receivables, net	17,753	21,083
Inventory	162,193	219,686
Prepaid advertising	16,572	21,357
Other prepaid expenses	5,816	7,589
Deferred income tax benefits	10,661	17,947
Total current assets	289,408	294,303
Property, plant and equipment, at cost:		
Land and buildings	102,776	102,018
Fixtures and equipment	175,910	154,663
Leasehold improvements	4,453	5,475
Total property, plant and equipment	283,139	262,156
Less – accumulated depreciation and amortization	117,317	101,570
Property, plant and equipment, net	165,822	160,586
Intangibles, net	966	1,030
Total assets	$ 456,196	$ 455,919
Liabilities and shareholders' investment		
Current liabilities:		
Lines of credit	$ 11,724	$ 38,942
Accounts payable	74,510	87,922
Reserve for returns	7,869	7,193
Accrued liabilities	43,754	54,392
Accrued profit sharing	2,760	2,256
Income taxes payable	10,255	14,578
Total current liabilities	150,872	205,283
Deferred income taxes	9,117	8,133
Shareholders' investment:		
Common stock, 40,221 shares issued	402	402
Donated capital	8,400	8,400
Additional paid-in capital	29,709	26,994
Deferred compensation	(236)	(394)
Accumulated other comprehensive income	2,675	2,003
Retained earnings	454,430	406,396
Treasury stock, 10,071 and 10,317 shares at cost, respectively	(199,173)	(201,298)
Total shareholders' investment	296,207	242,503
Total liabilities and shareholders' investment	$ 456,196	$ 455,919

The accompanying notes to consolidated financial statements are an integral part of these consolidated balance sheets.

Consolidated Statements of Shareholders' Investments

Lands' End, Inc. & Subsidiaries

(Dollars in thousands)	Comprehensive Income	Common Stock	Donated Capital	Additional Paid-in Capital	Deferred Compensation	Accumulated Other Comprehensive Income	Retained Earnings	Treasury Stock	Total
Balance, Jan. 31, 1997		$402	$8,400	$26,230	$(1,370)	$ 378	$311,061	$(122,096)	$223,005
Purchase of treasury stock		–	–	–	–	–	–	(45,899)	(45,899)
Issuance of treasury stock		–	–	–	–	–	–	409	409
Tax benefit of stock options exercised		–	–	227	–	–	–	–	227
Deferred compensation expense		–	–	–	323	–	–	–	323
Comprehensive income:									
Net income	$64,150	–	–	–	–	–	64,150	–	64,150
Other comprehensive income:									
Foreign currency translation adjustments	497	–	–	–	–	497	–	–	497
Comprehensive income	$64,647								
Balance, Jan. 30, 1998		$402	$8,400	$26,457	$(1,047)	$ 875	$375,211	$(167,586)	$242,712
Purchase of treasury stock		–	–	–	–	–	–	(35,557)	(35,557)
Issuance of treasury stock		–	–	–	–	–	–	1,845	1,845
Tax benefit of stock options exercised		–	–	537	–	–	–	–	537
Deferred compensation expense		–	–	–	653	–	–	–	653
Comprehensive income:									
Net income	$31,185	–	–	–	–	–	31,185	–	31,185
Other comprehensive income:									
Foreign currency translation adjustments	1,128	–	–	–	–	1,128	–	–	1,128
Comprehensive income	$32,313								
Balance, Jan. 29, 1999		$402	$8,400	$26,994	$ (394)	$2,003	$406,396	$(201,298)	$242,503
Purchase of treasury stock		–	–	–	–	–	–	(4,516)	(4,516)
Issuance of treasury stock		–	–	–	–	–	–	6,641	6,641
Tax benefit of stock options exercised		–	–	2,715	–	–	–	–	2,715
Deferred compensation expense		–	–	–	158	–	–	–	158
Comprehensive income:									
Net income	$48,034	–	–	–	–	–	48,034	–	48,034
Other comprehensive income:									
Foreign currency translation adjustments	92	–	–	–	–	92	–	–	92
Unrealized gain on forward contracts and options	580	–	–	–	–	580	–	–	580
Comprehensive income	$48,706								
Balance, Jan. 28, 2000		$402	$8,400	$29,709	$ (236)	$2,675	$454,430	$(199,173)	$296,207

The accompanying notes to consolidated financial statements are an integral part of these consolidated statements.

Consolidated Statements of Cash Flows

Lands' End, Inc. & Subsidiaries

	For the period ended		
(In thousands)	January 28, 2000	January 29, 1999	January 30, 1998
Cash flows from (used for) operating activities:			
Net income	$ 48,034	$ 31,185	$ 64,150
Adjustments to reconcile net income to net cash flows from operating activities –			
Non-recurring charge (credit)	(1,774)	12,600	–
Depreciation and amortization	20,715	18,731	15,127
Deferred compensation expense	158	653	323
Deferred income taxes	8,270	(5,948)	(1,158)
Pre-tax gain on sale of subsidiary	–	–	(7,805)
Loss on disposal of fixed assets	926	586	1,127
Changes in assets and liabilities excluding the effects of divestitures:			
Receivables, net	3,330	(5,640)	(7,019)
Inventory	57,493	21,468	(104,545)
Prepaid advertising	4,785	(2,844)	(7,447)
Other prepaid expenses	1,773	(2,504)	(1,366)
Accounts payable	(13,412)	4,179	11,616
Reserve for returns	676	1,065	944
Accrued liabilities	(7,664)	6,993	8,755
Accrued profit sharing	504	(2,030)	1,349
Income taxes payable	(4,323)	(5,899)	(1,047)
Other	3,387	1,665	64
Net cash flows from (used for) operating activities	122,878	74,260	(26,932)
Cash flows from (used for) investing activities:			
Cash paid for capital additions	(28,013)	(46,750)	(47,659)
Proceeds from sale of subsidiary	–	–	12,350
Net cash flows used for investing activities	(28,013)	(46,750)	(35,309)
Cash flows from (used for) financing activities:			
Proceeds from (payment of) short-term debt	(27,218)	6,505	21,242
Purchases of treasury stock	(4,516)	(35,557)	(45,899)
Issuance of treasury stock	6,641	1,845	409
Net cash flows used for financing activities	(25,093)	(27,207)	(24,248)
Net increase (decrease) in cash and cash equivalents	69,772	303	(86,489)
Beginning cash and cash equivalents	6,641	6,338	92,827
Ending cash and cash equivalents	$ 76,413	$ 6,641	$ 6,338
Supplemental cash flow disclosures:			
Interest paid	$ 1,890	$ 7,693	$ 1,995
Income taxes paid	21,078	27,857	39,337

The accompanying notes to consolidated financial statements are an integral part of these consolidated statements.

Notes to Consolidated Financial Statements

Note 1. Summary of significant accounting policies

Nature of business

Lands' End, Inc. (the company) is a direct marketer of traditionally styled apparel, domestics (primarily bedding and bath items), soft luggage and other products. The company manages its business in three operating segments consisting of core, specialty and international, based principally on type of catalog focusing on customer needs and markets served. The company's primary market is the United States, and other markets include Europe, the Pacific Basin area and Canada.

Principles of consolidation

The consolidated financial statements include the accounts of the company and its subsidiaries after elimination of intercompany accounts and transactions.

Year-end

The company's fiscal year is comprised of 52-53 weeks ending on the Friday closest to January 31. Fiscal 2000 ended on January 28, 2000, fiscal 1999 ended on January 29, 1999, and fiscal 1998 ended on January 30, 1998. All three years were comprised of 52 weeks.

Use of estimates

The preparation of financial statements in conformity with generally accepted accounting principles requires management to make estimates and assumptions that affect the reported amounts of assets and liabilities and disclosure of contingent assets and liabilities at the date of the financial statements and the reported amounts of revenues and expenses during the reporting periods. Actual results could differ from those estimates.

Inventory

Inventory, primarily merchandise held for sale, is stated at last-in, first-out (LIFO) cost, which is lower than market. If the first-in, first-out (FIFO) method of accounting for inventory had been used, inventory would have been approximately $21.0 million and $26.9 million higher than reported at January 28, 2000 and January 29, 1999, respectively.

Advertising

The company expenses the costs of advertising for magazines, television, radio and other media the first time the advertising takes place, except for direct-response advertising, which is capitalized and amortized over its expected period of future benefits.

Direct-response advertising consists primarily of catalog production and mailing costs that are generally amortized within three months from the date catalogs are mailed. Advertising costs reported as prepaid assets were $16.6 million and $21.4 million as of January 28, 2000 and January 29, 1999, respectively. Advertising expense was $225.0 million, $262.9 million and $226.7 million for fiscal years ended January 28, 2000, January 29, 1999 and January 30, 1998, respectively.

Depreciation

Depreciation expense is calculated using the straight-line method over the estimated useful lives of the assets, which are 20 to 30 years for buildings and land improvements and five to 10 years for leasehold improvements and furniture, fixtures, equipment and software. The company provides one-half year of depreciation in the year of addition and retirement.

Intangibles

Intangible assets consist primarily of trademarks, as well as their associated goodwill that is being amortized over 15 years on a straight-line basis.

Reserve for losses on customer returns

At the time of sale, the company provides a reserve equal to the gross profit on projected merchandise returns, based on its prior returns experience.

Financial instruments with off-balance-sheet risk

The company uses import letters of credit to purchase foreign-sourced merchandise. The letters of credit are primarily U.S. dollar-denominated and are issued through third-party financial institutions to guarantee payment for such merchandise within agreed-upon time periods. At January 28, 2000, the company had outstanding letters of credit of approximately $28.7 million, all of which had expiration dates of less than one year.

The counterparties to the financial instruments discussed above are primarily large financial institutions; management believes the risk of counterparty nonperformance on these financial instruments is not significant.

Foreign currency translations and transactions

Financial statements of the foreign subsidiaries are translated into U.S. dollars in accordance with the provisions of Statement of Financial Accounting Standards (SFAS) No. 52. Translation adjustments are recorded in accumulated other comprehensive income, which is a component of stockholders' equity. Foreign currency transaction gains and losses, recorded as other income and expense on the consolidated statements of operations, included losses of $0.8 million, $1.9 million and $3.8 million in fiscal 2000, 1999 and 1998, respectively.

Fair values of financial instruments

The fair value of financial instruments does not materially differ from their carrying values.

Reclassifications

Certain financial statement amounts have been reclassified to be consistent with the fiscal 2000 presentation.

Notes to Consolidated Financial Statements

Note 2. Shareholders' investment

Capital stock

The company currently has 160 million shares of $0.01 par value common stock. The company is authorized to issue 5 million shares of preferred stock, $0.01 par value. The company's board of directors has the authority to issue shares and to fix dividend, voting and conversion rights, redemption provisions, liquidation preferences, and other rights and restrictions of the preferred stock. No preferred shares have been issued.

Treasury stock

The company's board of directors has authorized the purchase of a total of 12.7 million shares of the company's common stock. A total of 11.6 million, 11.4 million and 10.3 million shares had been purchased as of January 28, 2000, January 29, 1999 and January 30, 1998, respectively.

Treasury stock activity in terms of shares was as follows:

For the period ended	January 28, 2000	January 29, 1999	January 30, 1998
Beginning balance	10,317,118	9,281,138	7,778,258
Purchase of stock	122,400	1,144,460	1,533,880
Issuance of stock	(368,650)	(108,480)	(31,000)
Ending balance	10,070,868	10,317,118	9,281,138

Earnings per share

A reconciliation of the basic and diluted per share computations is as follows:

(In thousands, except per share data)	January 28, 2000	January 29, 1999	January 30, 1998
Net income	$48,034	$31,185	$64,150
Basic weighted average shares of common stock outstanding	30,085	30,471	31,851
Incremental shares from assumed exercise of stock options	769	292	281
Diluted weighted average shares of common stock outstanding	30,854	30,763	32,132
Basic earnings per share	$ 1.60	$ 1.02	$ 2.01
Diluted earnings per share	$ 1.56	$ 1.01	$ 2.00

As of January 28, 2000, 130,000 shares of common stock with exercise prices ranging from $46.56 to $66.13 per share were not included in the computation of diluted EPS, because the options' exercise prices were greater than the average market price of the common shares during fiscal 2000.

Stock awards and grants

The company has a restricted stock award plan. Under the provisions of the plan, a committee of the company's board of directors may award shares of the company's common stock to its officers and key employees. Such shares vest over a five- or 10-year period on a straight-line basis from the date of the award.

The granting of these awards and grants has been recorded as deferred compensation based on the fair market value of the shares at the date of grant. Compensation expense under these plans is recorded as shares vest. The balance of the awards and grants totaled 17,960 shares, 31,000 shares and 77,000 shares for the period ended January 28, 2000, January 29, 1999 and January 30, 1998, respectively.

Stock options

The company has 5.5 million shares of common stock and 0.4 million shares of treasury shares that may be issued pursuant to the exercise of options granted under the company's Stock Option Plan (for employees) and the Non-Employee Director Stock Option Plan, respectively.

Under the company's stock option plans, options are granted at the discretion of a committee of the company's board of directors to officers, key employees of the company, and members of the board of directors of the company who are not also employed by the company. No option may have an exercise price less than the fair market value per share of the common stock at the date of the grant.

Activity under the stock option plans was as follows:

	Options	Average Exercise Price	Exercisable Options
Balance at January 31, 1997	1,150,400	$18.49	193,140
Granted	347,917	$33.45	
Exercised	(31,000)	$13.21	
Forfeited	–	–	
Balance at January 30, 1998	1,467,317	$21.42	350,107
Granted	1,874,000	$23.73	
Exercised	(108,480)	$17.01	
Forfeited	(541,330)	$22.35	
Balance at January 29, 1999	2,691,507	$23.41	473,597
Granted	591,000	$38.64	
Exercised	(368,650)	$18.02	
Forfeited	(137,840)	$32.17	
Balance at January 28, 2000	**2,776,017**	**$26.94**	**1,371,397**

Notes to Consolidated Financial Statements

The range of options outstanding as of January 28, 2000 is as follows:

Price Range Per Share	Number of Options Shares Outstanding/Exercisable	Weighted Average Exercise Price Outstanding/Exercisable	Weighted Average Remaining Contractual Life (In years)
$15.00–$29.99	1,490,600/1,237,230	$19.58/$19.36	8.2
$30.00–$44.99	1,155,417/ 129,167	33.16/ 32.48	9.0
Over $45.00	130,000/ 5,000	56.01/ 57.56	9.5
	2,776,017/1,371,397	$26.94/$20.73	8.6

The options above generally have a 10-year term. Options granted under the company's Stock Option Plan generally vest from six months to five years; options granted under the Non-Employee Director Stock Option Plan vest over a period from zero to two years.

Stock-based compensation

As permitted by SFAS No. 123, "Accounting for Stock-Based Compensation," the company accounts for its stock-based compensation plans as presented by APB Opinion No. 25 and related interpretations. Accordingly, compensation costs related to the stock awards and grants were $0.2 million, $0.7 million and $0.3 million in fiscal 2000, 1999 and 1998, respectively. These compensation costs are recorded in Deferred Compensation in the Shareholders' investment section of the Consolidated Balance Sheet.

Had compensation cost for the company's options granted after January 27, 1995 been determined consistent with the provisions of SFAS No. 123, the company's net income and earnings per share would have been reduced to the following pro forma amounts:

(In thousands, except per share data)	January 28, 2000	January 29, 1999	January 30, 1998
Net income			
As reported	$48,034	$31,185	$64,150
Pro forma	$42,378	$26,429	$62,511
Basic earnings per share			
As reported	$ 1.60	$ 1.02	$ 2.01
Pro forma	$ 1.41	$ 0.87	$ 1.96
Diluted earnings per share			
As reported	$ 1.56	$ 1.01	$ 2.00
Pro forma	$ 1.38	$ 0.86	$ 1.95

The fair value of each option grant was estimated as of the date of grant using the Black-Scholes pricing model. The resulting compensation cost was amortized over the vesting period.

The option grant fair values and assumptions used to determine such value are as follows:

Options granted during	2000	1999	1998
Weighted average grant-date fair value	$19.74	$11.21	$17.02
Assumptions:			
Risk-free interest rate	5.58%	4.74%	6.10%
Expected volatility	38.55%	35.86%	37.30%
Expected term (in years)	7.0	7.0	7.0

Note 3. Income taxes

Earnings before income taxes consisted of the following :

(In thousands)	2000	1999	1998
United States	$ 78,050	$ 44,499	$ 95,909
Foreign	(1,806)	5,001	5,916
Total	$ 76,244	$ 49,500	$101,825

The components of the provision for income taxes for each of the periods presented are as follows (in thousands):

Period ended	January 28, 2000	January 29, 1999	January 30, 1998
Current:			
Federal	$19,984	$21,026	$31,335
State	473	1,752	4,449
Foreign	(517)	1,485	3,049
Deferred	8,270	(5,948)	(1,158)
	$28,210	$18,315	$37,675

The difference between income taxes at the statutory federal income tax rate of 35 percent and income tax reported in the statements of operations is as follows (in thousands):

Period ended	January 28, 2000		January 29, 1999		January 30, 1998	
	Amount	%	Amount	%	Amount	%
Tax at statutory federal tax rate	$26,685	35%	$17,325	35%	$35,640	35%
Foreign taxes (excess over statutory rate)	22	–	263	–	1,130	1
State income taxes, net of federal benefit	907	1	1,306	3	3,999	4
Tax credits and other	596	1	(579)	(1)	(3,094)	(3)
	$28,210	37%	$18,315	37%	$37,675	37%

Under the liability method prescribed by SFAS No. 109, "Accounting for Income Taxes," deferred taxes are provided based upon enacted tax laws and rates applicable to the periods in which taxes become payable.

Notes to Consolidated Financial Statements

Temporary differences that give rise to deferred tax assets and liabilities as of January 28, 2000 and January 29, 1999 are as follows (in thousands):

Period ended	January 28, 2000	January 29, 1999
Deferred tax assets:		
Catalog advertising	$ (4,968)	$ (3,914)
Inventory	8,233	9,198
Employee benefits	4,231	7,937
Reserve for returns	2,912	2,661
Foreign operating loss carryforwards	124	686
Valuation allowance	(124)	(686)
Other	253	2,065
Total	$10,661	$17,947
Deferred tax liabilities:		
Depreciation	$ 8,581	$ 8,141
Other	536	(8)
Total	$ 9,117	$ 8,133

The valuation allowance required under SFAS No. 109 has been established for the deferred income tax benefits related to certain subsidiary loss carryforwards, which management currently estimates may not be realized. These carryforwards do not expire.

Note 4. Lines of credit

During fiscal 2000, the company entered into a new domestic credit facility providing unsecured credit totaling $200 million. There were no short-term borrowings as of January 28, 2000, compared to $21.8 million outstanding at January 29, 1999.

In addition, the company has unsecured lines of credit with various foreign banks totaling the equivalent of approximately $54 million for its wholly owned subsidiaries. There was $11.7 million outstanding at January 28, 2000, compared with $17.1 million as of January 29, 1999.

The following table summarizes certain information regarding these short-term borrowings:

(Dollars in millions)	2000	1999	1998
Maximum amount of borrowings	$53	$257	$118
Average amount of borrowings	$33	$134	$ 38
Weighted average interest rate during year	4.96%	5.77%	5.25%
Weighted average interest rate at year-end	3.43%	5.42%	5.27%

Note 5. Long-term debt

There was no long-term debt as of January 28, 2000 and January 29, 1999.

Note 6. Leases

The company leases store and office space and equipment under various leasing arrangements. The leases are accounted for as operating leases. Total rental expense under these leases was $15.5 million, $15.6 million and $13.5 million for the years ended January 28, 2000, January 29, 1999 and January 30, 1998, respectively.

Total future fiscal year commitments under these leases as of January 28, 2000 are as follows (in thousands):

2001	$ 7,900
2002	5,702
2003	3,568
2004	1,960
2005	1,473
Thereafter	6,337
	$26,940

Note 7. Retirement plan

The company has a retirement plan, which covers most regular employees and provides for annual contributions at the discretion of the board of directors. Also included in the plan is a 401(k) feature that allows employees to make contributions, and the company matches a portion of those contributions. Total expense provided under this plan was $5.2 million, $4.8 million and $6.6 million for the years ended January 28, 2000, January 29, 1999 and January 30, 1998, respectively.

Note 8. Postretirement benefits

In January 1998, the company implemented a plan to provide health insurance benefits for eligible retired employees. These insurance benefits will be funded through insurance contracts, a group benefit trust or general assets of the company. The assets were contributed to the plan in January 2000 and January 1999. The cost of these insurance benefits is recognized as the eligible employees render service.

Notes to Consolidated Financial Statements

Lands' End, Inc. & Subsidiaries

The following table presents the change in the benefit obligation and plan assets in fiscal years 2000 and 1999:

(In thousands)	2000	1999
Change in benefit obligation:		
Benefit obligation at beginning of year	$ 5,731	$ 4,419
Service cost	767	630
Interest cost	385	308
Plan participants' contributions	16	13
Actuarial (gain)/loss	(1,448)	376
Benefits paid	(57)	(15)
Implementation of plan	–	–
Benefit obligation at end of year	$ 5,394	$ 5,731
Change in plan assets:		
Fair value of plan assets at beginning of year	$ 1,978	$ –
Actual return on plan assets	58	–
Employer contributions	1,970	1,980
Plan participants' contributions	16	13
Benefits paid	(57)	(15)
Fair value of plan assets at end of year	$ 3,965	$ 1,978
Net amount recognized:		
Funded status	$(1,429)	$(3,753)
Unrecognized net actuarial (gain)/loss	(985)	373
Unrecognized prior service cost	3,783	4,052
Prepaid benefit cost	$ 1,369	$ 672
Weighted-average assumptions at end of year:		
Discount rate	8.00%	6.75%
Expected return on plan assets	7.50%	7.50%

The components of net periodic benefit cost for the years ended January 28, 2000 and January 29, 1999 were as follows:

(In thousands)	2000	1999
Service cost	$ 767	$ 630
Interest cost	385	308
Expected return on plan assets	(148)	–
Amortization of prior service cost	269	270
Postretirement benefit cost	$1,273	$1,208

For measurement purposes, a 6.5 percent annual rate of increase in the per capita cost of covered health care benefits was assumed for fiscal year 2001. The rate was assumed to decrease gradually to 5 percent for fiscal year 2004 and remain at that level thereafter.

Assumed health care cost trend rates have a significant effect on the amounts reported for the health care plan. A 1 percentage point change in assumed health care cost trend rates would have the following effects:

(In thousands)	Service and Interest Costs	Postretirement Benefit Obligation
1 percent increase	$ 66	$ 252
1 percent decrease	(56)	(216)

Note 9. Non-recurring charge and related reversal

During fiscal year 1999, in connection with changes in executive management, the company announced a Plan designed to reduce administrative and operational costs stemming from duplicative responsibilities and certain non-profitable operations. This Plan included the reduction of staff positions, the closing of three outlet stores, the liquidation of the Willis & Geiger operations and the termination of a licensing agreement with MontBell Co. Ltd. A non-recurring charge of $12.6 million was recorded in fiscal 1999 related to these matters.

Below is a summary of related costs for the periods ended January 28, 2000:

(In thousands)	Balance January 29, 1999	Cost Incurred	Charges Reversed	Balance January 28, 2000
Severance costs	$ 6,700	$(5,693)	$ –	$1,007
Asset impairments	3,199	(2,057)	(1,111)	31
Facility exit costs and other	2,590	(1,820)	(663)	107
Total	$12,489	$(9,570)	$ (1,774)	$1,145

For the year ended January 28, 2000, the company executed the Plan and incurred costs totaling $9.6 million. In addition, there was a reversal of $1.8 million of the reserves recorded in fiscal 1999. Those included $0.7 million for better than expected lease termination settlements related to fiscal 2000 store closings, and $1.1 million for better than anticipated sell-through of Willis & Geiger inventory liquidations. Based on these two factors, there was an addition to net income of $1.1 million, or $0.04 per share, in the year ended January 28, 2000. The balance of $1.1 million, predominantly severance, will be paid in fiscal 2001.

Note 10. Divestitures

Willis & Geiger
During fiscal 2000, the company completed the liquidation of its Willis & Geiger inventory and fixed assets. The company retains the Willis & Geiger tradename.

The Territory Ahead
During the first quarter of fiscal 1998, the company sold its majority interest in The Territory Ahead to The International Cornerstone Group, Inc. of Boston, Massachusetts, resulting in an after-tax gain of $4.9 million. The after-tax gain was recorded in the first quarter of fiscal 1998.

Sales and results of operations of The Territory Ahead and Willis & Geiger were not material to the consolidated financial statements.

Notes to Consolidated Financial Statements   Lands' End, Inc. & Subsidiaries

Note 11. Sales and use tax

A 1992 Supreme Court decision confirmed that the Commerce Clause of the United States Constitution prevents a state from requiring the collection of its use tax by a mail order company unless the company has a physical presence in the state. However, there continues to be uncertainty due to inconsistent application of the Supreme Court decision by state and federal courts. The company attempts to conduct its operations in compliance with its interpretation of the applicable legal standard, but there can be no assurance that such compliance will not be challenged.

In recent challenges, various states have sought to require companies to begin collection of use taxes and/or pay taxes from previous sales. The company has not received assessments from any state. The amount of potential assessments, if any, cannot be reasonably estimated.

The Supreme Court decision also established that Congress has the power to enact legislation that would permit states to require collection of use taxes by mail order companies. Congress has from time to time considered proposals for such legislation. The company anticipates that any legislative change, if adopted, would be applied only on a prospective basis.

In October 1998, The Internet Tax Freedom Act was signed into law. Among the provisions of this Act is a three-year moratorium on multiple and discriminatory taxes on electronic commerce. An Advisory Commission on Electronic Commerce has been appointed to study and report back to Congress on whether and, if so, how electronic commerce should be taxed.

We are monitoring the activities of the Commission, as well as any proposed changes in the sales and use tax laws and policies in general.

Note 12. Segment disclosure

The company organizes and manages its business segments (core, specialty and international) based on type of catalog, which focuses on specific customer needs and markets served. Certain catalogs are combined for purposes of assessing financial performance. Each business segment is separately evaluated by executive management with financial information reviewed to assess performance. The company evaluates the performance of its business segments based on net income before income taxes. The accounting policies of the company's segments are the same as those described in Note 1. The company is not dependent upon any single customer or group of customers, the loss of which would have a material effect on the company.

Core

The core segment is composed of adult apparel offered through our regular monthly catalogs, tailored catalogs and prospector catalogs. Sales for these catalogs that are received via the Internet, liquidation or export channels are included in this core segment. The regular monthly catalogs contain a full assortment of classically inspired, traditionally styled casual wear for adults. Some of these products include dress shirts, jeans, mesh knit shirts, women's knits, sweaters, outerwear and turtlenecks. The prospecting catalog is a condensed version of our monthly catalog featuring some of the company's best-selling products. The prospector catalogs are sent to active buyers, to those on the house file who have been inactive or have yet to make a purchase and to prospective customers. The tailored catalogs are Beyond Buttondowns, offering a broad assortment of fine tailored clothing for men, and First Person, featuring women's finely tailored clothing suitable for the workplace.

Specialty

The specialty segment is composed of Kids, Coming Home and Corporate Sales catalogs. Sales for these catalogs that are received via the Internet, liquidation or export channels are included in this specialty segment. The specialty catalogs have been developed over the years in response to customer requests for additional merchandise and are used to target specific needs that are important to Lands' End customers. The specialty businesses include the Kids catalog, which offers a collection of clothing for children of all ages. In addition, there is a uniform catalog that targets the growing uniform trend in many public and private schools. The Coming Home catalog offers home products, primarily bedding and bath items. The Corporate Sales catalog is a business-to-business catalog that utilizes the company's embroidery capabilities to design and apply unique emblems and logos on Lands' End product for corporations, clubs, teams and other groups.

International

The international segment consists of foreign-based operations located in Japan, the United Kingdom and Germany, which include catalogs, Internet and liquidation channels. Catalogs are denominated in local currencies and written in native languages. There are phone and distribution centers located in both Japan and the United Kingdom. Germany has its own phone and customer service center, but orders are packed and shipped from the distribution center in the United Kingdom.

Segment sales represent sales to external parties. Segment income before income taxes is revenue less direct and allocable operating expenses, which includes interest expense and interest income. Segment identifiable assets are those that are directly used in or identified with segment operations. "Other" includes corporate expenses, inter-company eliminations, and other income and deduction items that are not allocated to segments.

Notes to Consolidated Financial Statements

Pertinent financial data by operating segment for the three years ended January 28, 2000 are as follows:

	Fiscal year ended January 28, 2000				
(In thousands)	Core	Specialty	International	Other	Consolidated
Net sales	$780,298	$396,327	$143,198	$ –	$1,319,823
Income (loss) before income taxes[1]	$ 32,725	$ 43,144	$ 2,348	$(1,973)	$ 76,244
Identifiable assets	$262,397	$133,276	$ 60,523	$ –	$ 456,196
Depreciation and amortization	$ 12,165	$ 6,179	$ 2,371	$ –	$ 20,715
Capital expenditures	$ 17,573	$ 8,925	$ 1,515	$ –	$ 28,013
Interest expense	$ 848	$ 430	$ 612	$ –	$ 1,890
Interest income	$ 547	$ 278	$ 57	$ –	$ 882

	Fiscal year ended January 29, 1999				
(In thousands)	Core	Specialty	International	Other	Consolidated
Net sales	$860,891	$364,576	$145,908	$ –	$1,371,375
Income (loss) before income taxes[2]	$ 27,305	$ 23,016	$ 4,655	$(5,476)	$ 49,500
Identifiable assets	$273,929	$116,007	$ 65,983	$ –	$ 455,919
Depreciation and amortization	$ 11,310	$ 5,323	$ 2,098	$ –	$ 18,731
Capital expenditures	$ 24,828	$ 10,514	$ 11,408	$ –	$ 46,750
Interest expense	$ 3,910	$ 2,296	$ 1,528	$ –	$ 7,734
Interest income	$ 11	$ 5	$ –	$ –	$ 16

	Fiscal year ended January 30, 1998				
(In thousands)	Core	Specialty	International	Other	Consolidated
Net sales	$824,854	$306,986	$131,789	$ –	$1,263,629
Income before income taxes	$ 59,356	$ 30,225	$ 7,672	$ 4,572	$ 101,825
Identifiable assets	$275,764	$102,630	$ 55,078	$ –	$ 433,472
Depreciation and amortization	$ 9,805	$ 3,813	$ 1,509	$ –	$ 15,127
Capital expenditures	$ 27,585	$ 10,266	$ 9,808	$ –	$ 47,659
Interest expense	$ 714	$ 351	$ 930	$ –	$ 1,995
Interest income	$ 1,257	$ 468	$ –	$ –	$ 1,725

(1) Includes non-recurring credits of $0.5 million and $1.3 million allocated to the core and specialty segments, respectively.
(2) Includes non-recurring charges of $7.6 million and $5.0 million allocated to the core and specialty segments, respectively.
(3) Fiscal years 1999 and 1998 have been restated to conform to fiscal 2000 presentation.

Pertinent financial data by geographical location for the three years ended January 28, 2000 are as follows:

	Net Sales			Identifiable Assets		
(In thousands)	Jan. 28, 2000	Jan. 29, 1999	Jan. 30, 1998	Jan. 28, 2000	Jan. 29, 1999	Jan. 30, 1998
United States	$1,176,625	$1,225,467	$1,131,840	$395,673	$389,936	$378,394
Other countries	143,198	145,908	131,789	60,523	65,983	55,078
Total	$1,319,823	$1,371,375	$1,263,629	$456,196	$455,919	$433,472

Notes to Consolidated Financial Statements   Lands' End, Inc. & Subsidiaries

Note 13. Derivative instruments and hedging activities

The company's sales of merchandise to its subsidiaries in the United Kingdom, Japan and Germany are denominated in the subsidiary's local currency. To a lesser extent, the company has export sales to customers in Canada. The company incurs third-party expenses related to the Canadian export business, some of which are denominated in Canadian dollars. Accordingly, the future U.S. Dollar-equivalent cash flows may vary due to changes in related foreign currency exchange rates. To reduce that risk, the company enters into foreign currency forward contracts and purchases foreign currency put options. The company's sales to its foreign subsidiaries and its third-party purchases are on open account with settlement within approximately one month. Accordingly, the settlement dates of the forward contracts and put options fall approximately one month after the date of forecasted sales or purchases. The company has no other freestanding or embedded derivative instruments.

As of July 31, 1999, the company adopted the Financial Accounting Standards Board's (FASB's) Statement of Financial Accounting Standards No. 133, "Accounting for Derivative Instruments and Hedging Activities" (Statement 133). Statement 133 unifies accounting and financial reporting standards for forward contracts, put options, other derivative instruments and related hedging activities. Statement 133 requires, in part, that the company report all derivative instruments in the statement of financial position as assets or liabilities at their fair value. The treatment of subsequent changes in fair value depends on whether hedge accounting is available. Prior to the adoption of Statement 133 for fiscal 2000, a loss of $0.7 million was recognized in other expenses. For fiscal 2000, a loss of $0.8 million was recognized in other expenses, compared with a loss of $1.9 million in fiscal 1999. Before the effective date of Statement 133, hedge accounting was not available for the company's forward contracts. Those contracts were reported in the statement of financial position as assets or liabilities at their fair value and changes in fair value were reported currently in earnings. Hedge accounting for the company's put options involved reporting the put options initially at the amount of the premium paid, with amortization of the premium over the option period. Subsequent gains or losses on the put options through the date of the sale to the foreign subsidiary were deferred until the date the consolidated entity (through the foreign subsidiary) sold the merchandise to a third party. At the date merchandise is sold to a foreign subsidiary, the hedging relationship is terminated and subsequent gains and losses on the put option (including unamortized premium) were reported currently in earnings.

As part of its adoption of Statement 133 on July 31, 1999, the company designated all of its hedging relationships anew. Both forward contracts and put options can qualify for cash flow hedge accounting under Statement 133 if applicable hedging criteria are met. Under Statement 133's cash flow hedging model, gains and losses on the derivative instrument that occur through the date the company sells merchandise to a subsidiary or purchases from a foreign third party are deferred in a component of equity (accumulated other comprehensive income) to the extent the hedging relationship is effective. The maximum hedging period (the period between the company's designation and culmination of a hedging relationship) of the company's cash flow hedges is 24 months.

As required by Statement 133, the company assesses hedge effectiveness at least quarterly. The effectiveness of put options is assessed based on changes in intrinsic value of the options due to changes in spot foreign exchange rates. Because they are excluded from the company's assessment of hedge effectiveness, the company reports currently in earnings changes in the fair value of put options due to changes in time value of the options. For the year ended January 28, 2000, a net loss of $0.1 million was recognized in other expense due to hedge ineffectiveness and fair value changes excluded from the company's effectiveness assessments.

To the extent the company must discontinue cash flow hedge accounting because it is probable that original forecasted sales will not occur, Statement 133 requires that the company immediately reclassify the net gain or loss from accumulated other comprehensive income into earnings. During fiscal 2000, net losses of $0.2 million were so reclassified.

At the date merchandise is sold to a foreign subsidiary or purchased from a foreign third party, the hedging relationship is terminated and subsequent gains and losses on the hedging derivative instrument are reported currently in earnings. At the date of the ultimate sale of the merchandise by the foreign subsidiary to a third party or purchase from a foreign third party, the gain or loss previously deferred in equity is reclassified into earnings. The company estimates that net hedging gains of $0.1 million will be reclassified from accumulated other comprehensive income into earnings within the 12 months between January 29, 2000 and January 26, 2001.

Upon the company's adoption of Statement 133 on July 31, 1999, the company adjusted the carrying amount of the two put option contracts as assets at their fair value of $34 thousand. Because the put options had previously qualified in a cash-flow-type hedging relationship prior to adoption of Statement 133, an immaterial cumulative-effect-type transition adjustment and an immaterial transition adjustment related to the ineffective portion of the put options were reported in accumulated other comprehensive income and other expense, respectively. No transition adjustment was needed for the forward contracts, which were already being reported at their fair value with changes in fair value reported currently in earnings.

Notes to Consolidated Financial Statements

Note 14. Consolidated quarterly analysis (unaudited)

(In thousands, except per share data)	Fiscal 2000				Fiscal 1999			
	1st Qtr.	2nd Qtr.	3rd Qtr.	4th Qtr.	1st Qtr.	2nd Qtr.	3rd Qtr.	4th Qtr.
Net sales	$289,609	$254,616	$325,970	$449,628	$268,587	$239,194	$322,422	$541,172
Gross profit	125,434	118,216	140,813	208,069	124,740	115,478	145,262	231,234
Pretax income	10,332	7,068	13,890	44,954	8,266	(97)	551	40,780
Net income	$ 6,509	$ 4,453	$ 8,751	$ 28,321	$ 5,208	$ (61)	$ 347	$ 25,691
Basic earnings per share	$ 0.22	$ 0.15	$ 0.29	$ 0.94	$ 0.17	$ 0.00	$ 0.01	$ 0.85
Diluted earnings per share	$ 0.21	$ 0.14	$ 0.28	$ 0.92	$ 0.17	$ 0.00	$ 0.01	$ 0.84
Common shares outstanding	30,110	30,060	30,149	30,149	30,961	30,236	30,239	30,142

(In dollars)								
Market price of shares outstanding:								
Market high	39$^{15}/_{16}$	49½	78$^{7}/_{16}$	83½	44⅛	37⅞	30⅜	32$^{7}/_{16}$
Market low	28⅛	37$^{9}/_{16}$	39$^{9}/_{16}$	28	35	26⅛	15⅝	16¼

Quarterly earnings per share amounts are based on the weighted average common shares outstanding for each quarter and, therefore, might not equal the amount computed for the total year.

FIVE- OR TEN-YEAR SUMMARY

Usually presented in close proximity to the audited financial statements is a five- or ten-year summary of selected financial data. From such a summary, one can determine trends and growth patterns over a fairly long period of time. Lands' End presents eleven years of selected financial data that includes operating data, financial position data, and selected statistics and ratios.

Eleven-Year Consolidated Financial Summary (unaudited)

The following selected financial data have been derived from the company's consolidated financial statements, which have been audited by Arthur Andersen LLP, independent public accountants. The information set forth below should be read in conjunction with "Management's Discussion and Analysis" and the consolidated financial statements and notes thereto included elsewhere herein.

(In thousands, except per share data)	2000	1999	1998
Income statement data:			
Net sales	$1,319,823	$1,371,375	$1,263,629
Pretax income	76,244	49,500	101,825
Percent to net sales	5.8%	3.6%	8.1%
Net income before cumulative effect of change in accounting	48,034	31,185	64,150
Cumulative effect of accounting change	–	–	–
Net income	48,034	31,185	64,150
Per share of common stock: [1]			
Basic earnings per share before cumulative effect of change in accounting	$ 1.60	$ 1.02	$ 2.01
Cumulative effect of change in accounting	–	–	–
Basic earnings per share	$ 1.60	$ 1.02	$ 2.01
Diluted earnings per share	$ 1.56	$ 1.01	$ 2.00
Cash dividends per share	$ –	$ –	$ –
Common shares outstanding	30,149	30,142	30,979
Balance sheet data:			
Current assets	$ 289,408	$ 294,303	$ 299,146
Current liabilities	150,872	205,283	182,013
Property, plant, equipment and intangibles, net	166,788	161,616	134,326
Total assets	456,196	455,919	433,472
Noncurrent liabilities	9,117	8,133	8,747
Shareholders' investment	296,207	242,503	242,712
Other data:			
Net working capital	$ 138,536	$ 89,020	$ 117,133
Capital expenditures	28,013	46,750	48,228
Depreciation and amortization expense	20,715	18,731	15,127
Return on average shareholders' investment	18%	13%	28%
Return on average assets	11%	7%	16%

(1) Net income per share was computed after giving retroactive effect to the two-for-one stock split in May 1994.

(2) Effective January 30, 1993, the company adopted Statement of Financial Accounting Standards (SFAS) No. 109 "Accounting for Income Taxes," which was recorded as a change in accounting principle at the beginning of fiscal 1994 with an increase to net income of $1.3 million or $0.04 per share.

Lands' End, Inc. & Subsidiaries

	Fiscal year							
	1997	1996	1995	1994 [2]	1993	1992	1991	1990
	$1,118,743	$1,031,548	$992,106	$869,975	$733,623	$683,427	$601,991	$544,850
	84,919	50,925	59,663	69,870	54,033	47,492	29,943	47,270
	7.6%	4.9%	6.0%	8.0%	7.4%	7.0%	4.1%	8.7%
	50,952	30,555	36,096	42,429	33,500	28,732	14,743	29,071
	—	—	—	1,300	—	—	—	—
	50,952	30,555	36,096	43,729	33,500	28,732	14,743	29,071
	$ 1.54	$ 0.89	$ 1.03	$ 1.18	$ 0.92	$ 0.77	$ 0.38	$ 0.73
	—	—	—	0.04	—	—	—	—
	$ 1.54	$ 0.89	$ 1.03	$ 1.22	$ 0.92	$ 0.77	$ 0.38	$ 0.73
	$ 1.53	$ 0.89	$ 1.02	$ 1.21	$ 0.91	$ 0.76	$ 0.37	$ 0.73
	$ —	$ —	$ —	$ 0.10	$ 0.10	$ 0.10	$ 0.10	$ 0.10
	32,442	33,659	34,826	35,912	36,056	36,944	38,436	39,762
	$ 272,039	$ 222,089	$198,168	$192,276	$137,531	$131,273	$107,824	$ 99,714
	145,566	114,744	102,717	91,049	67,315	74,548	60,774	43,915
	106,006	101,408	99,444	81,554	74,272	74,527	77,576	67,218
	378,045	323,497	297,612	273,830	211,803	205,800	185,400	166,932
	9,474	7,561	5,767	5,496	5,100	4,620	7,800	8,413
	223,005	201,192	189,128	177,285	139,388	126,632	116,826	114,604
	$ 126,473	$ 107,345	$ 95,451	$101,227	$ 70,216	$ 56,725	$ 47,050	$ 55,799
	17,992	14,780	27,005	16,958	9,965	5,347	17,682	25,160
	13,558	12,456	10,311	8,286	7,900	7,428	7,041	5,251
	24%	16%	20%	28%	25%	23%	13%	28%
	15%	10%	13%	18%	16%	15%	8%	18%

SPECIMEN FINANCIAL STATEMENTS: Abercrombie & Fitch Co.

Abercrombie & Fitch Co.

FINANCIAL SUMMARY

(Thousands except per share and per square foot amounts, ratios and store and associate data)

Fiscal Year	1999	1998	1997	1996	1995*	1994	1993
Summary of Operations							
Net Sales	$1,042,056	$815,804	$521,617	$335,372	$235,659	$165,463	$110,952
Gross Income	$ 465,583	$343,951	$201,080	$123,766	$ 79,794	$ 56,820	$ 30,562
Operating Income (Loss)	$ 242,064	$166,958	$ 84,125	$ 45,993	$ 23,798	$ 13,751	$ (4,064)
Operating Income (Loss) as a Percentage of Sales	23.2%	20.5%	16.1%	13.7%	10.1%	8.3%	(3.7%)
Net Income (Loss)	$ 149,604	$102,062	$ 48,322	$ 24,674	$ 14,298	$ 8,251	$ (2,464)
Net Income (Loss) as a Percentage of Sales	14.4%	12.5%	9.3%	7.4%	6.1%	5.0%	(2.2%)
Per Share Results (1)							
Net Income (Loss) Per Basic Share	$ 1.45	$ .99	$ .47	$ .27	$ .17	$ .10	$ (.03)
Net Income (Loss) Per Diluted Share	$ 1.39	$ .96	$ .47	$ .27	$ .17	$ .10	$ (.03)
Weighted Average Diluted Shares Outstanding	107,641	106,202	102,956	91,520	86,000	86,000	86,000
Other Financial Information							
Total Assets	$ 458,166	$319,161	$183,238	$105,761	$ 87,693	$ 58,018	$ 48,882
Return on Average Assets	38%	41%	33%	26%	20%	15%	(4%)
Capital Expenditures	$ 83,824	$ 41,876	$ 29,486	$ 24,323	$ 24,526	$ 12,603	$ 4,694
Long-Term Debt	—	—	$ 50,000	$ 50,000	—	—	—
Shareholders' Equity (Deficit)	$ 311,094	$186,105	$ 58,775	$ 11,238	$(22,622)	$(37,070)	$(45,341)
Comparable Store Sales Increase	10%	35%	21%	13%	5%	15%	6%
Retail Sales Per Average Gross Square Foot	$ 512	$ 483	$ 376	$ 306	$ 290	$ 284	$ 243
Stores and Associates at End of Year							
Total Number of Stores Open	250	196	156	127	100	67	49
Gross Square Feet	2,174,000	1,791,000	1,522,000	1,229,000	962,000	665,000	499,000
Number of Associates	11,300	9,500	6,700	4,900	3,000	2,300	1,300

Fifty-three week fiscal year.

(1) Per share amounts reflect the two-for-one stock split on the Company's Class A Common Stock, paid on June 15, 1999.

Abercrombie & Fitch Co.

CONSOLIDATED STATEMENTS OF INCOME

(Thousands except per share amounts)	1999	1998	1997
Net Sales	$1,042,056	$815,804	$521,617
Cost of Goods Sold, Occupancy and Buying Costs	576,473	471,853	320,537
Gross Income	465,583	343,951	201,080
General, Administrative and Store Operating Expenses	223,519	176,993	116,955
Operating Income	242,064	166,958	84,125
Interest (Income)/ Expense, Net	(7,270)	(3,144)	3,583
Income Before Income Taxes	249,334	170,102	80,542
Provision for Income Taxes	99,730	68,040	32,220
Net Income	$ 149,604	$102,062	$ 48,322
Net Income Per Share:			
Basic	$ 1.45	$ .99	$ .47
Diluted	$ 1.39	$ .96	$ .47

The accompanying Notes are an integral part of these Consolidated Financial Statements.

Net Sales ($ in Millions)

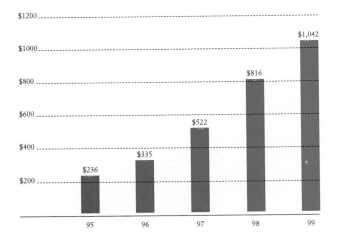

Sales per Gross Square Foot

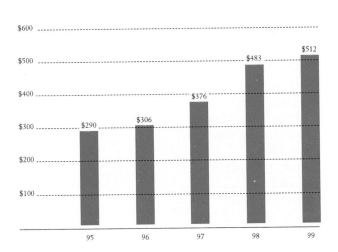

Abercrombie & Fitch Co.

CONSOLIDATED BALANCE SHEETS

(Thousands)	January 29, 2000	January 30, 1999
Assets		
Current Assets		
Cash and Equivalents	$147,908	$163,564
Marketable Securities	45,601	—
Accounts Receivable	11,447	4,101
Inventories	75,262	43,992
Other	19,999	6,578
Total Current Assets	300,217	218,235
Property and Equipment, Net	146,403	89,558
Deferred Income Taxes	11,060	10,854
Other Assets	486	631
Total Assets	$458,166	$319,278
Liabilities and Shareholders' Equity		
Current Liabilities		
Accounts Payable	$ 18,714	$ 24,759
Accrued Expenses	85,373	63,882
Income Taxes Payable	33,779	33,704
Total Current Liabilities	137,866	122,345
Other Long-Term Liabilities	9,206	10,828
Shareholders' Equity		
Common Stock	1,033	1,033
Paid-In Capital	147,305	143,626
Retained Earnings	192,735	43,131
	341,073	187,790
Less: Treasury Stock, at Average Cost	(29,979)	(1,685)
Total Shareholders' Equity	311,094	186,105
Total Liabilities and Shareholders' Equity	$458,166	$319,278

The accompanying Notes are an integral part of these Consolidated Financial Statements.

Abercrombie & Fitch Co.

CONSOLIDATED STATEMENTS OF SHAREHOLDERS' EQUITY

(Thousands)	Common Stock		Paid-In Capital	Retained Earnings (Deficit)	Treasury Stock, at Average Cost	Total Shareholders' Equity
	Shares Outstanding	Par Value				
Balance, February 1, 1997	102,100	$1,022	$117,469	$(107,253)	–	$ 11,238
Purchase of Treasury Stock	(100)	–	–	–	$ (929)	(929)
Net Income	–	–	–	48,322	–	48,322
Stock Options, Restricted Stock and Other	18	–	(8)	–	152	144
Balance, January 31, 1998	102,018	$1,022	$117,461	$ (58,931)	$ (777)	$ 58,775
Purchase of Treasury Stock	(490)	–	–	–	(11,240)	(11,240)
Net Income	–	–	–	102,062	–	102,062
Issuance of Common Stock	1,200	11	25,870	–	–	25,881
Stock Options, Restricted Stock and Other	86	–	295	–	10,332	10,627
Balance, January 30, 1999	102,814	$1,033	$143,626	$ 43,131	$ (1,685)	$ 186,105
Purchase of Treasury Stock	(1,510)	–	–	–	(50,856)	(50,856)
Net Income	–	–	–	149,604	–	149,604
Stock Options, Restricted Stock and Other	700	–	3,679	–	22,562	26,241
Balance, January 29, 2000	102,004	$1,033	$147,305	$ 192,735	$(29,979)	$ 311,094

The accompanying Notes are an integral part of these Consolidated Financial Statements.

Operating Income (%)

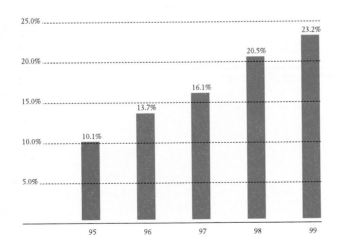

Earning Per Diluted Share

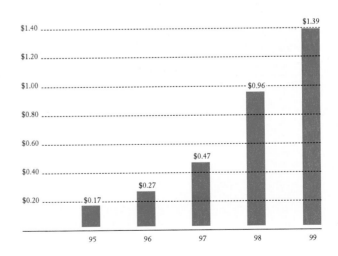

Abercrombie & Fitch Co.

CONSOLIDATED STATEMENTS OF CASH FLOWS

(Thousands)	1999	1998	1997
Cash Flows from Operating Activities			
Net Income	$149,604	$102,062	$ 48,322
Impact of Other Operating Activities on Cash Flows			
Depreciation and Amortization	27,721	20,946	16,342
Non Cash Charge for Deferred Compensation	5,212	11,497	6,219
Change in Assets and Liabilities			
Inventories	(31,270)	(10,065)	1,016
Accounts Payable and Accrued Expenses	15,446	37,530	22,309
Income Taxes	(131)	10,758	4,606
Other Assets and Liabilities	(12,773)	355	1,381
Net Cash Provided by Operating Activities	153,809	173,083	100,195
Investing Activities			
Capital Expenditures	(83,824)	(41,876)	(29,486
Proceeds from Maturities of Marketable Securities	11,332	–	–
Purchase of Marketable Securities	(56,933)	–	–
Note Receivable	(1,500)	–	–
Net Cash Used for Investing Activities	(130,925)	(41,876)	(29,486
Financing Activities			
Settlement of Balance with The Limited	–	23,785	–
Decrease in Receivable from The Limited	–	–	(29,202
Net Proceeds from Issuance of Common Stock	–	25,875	–
Repayment of Long-Term Debt	–	(50,000)	–
Purchase of Treasury Stock	(50,856)	(11,240)	(929
Other Changes in Shareholders' Equity	12,316	1,270	144
Net Cash Used for Financing Activities	(38,540)	(10,310)	(29,987
Net Increase/(Decrease) in Cash and Equivalents	(15,656)	120,897	40,722
Cash and Equivalents, Beginning of Year	163,564	42,667	1,945
Cash and Equivalents, End of Year	$147,908	$163,564	$ 42,667

The accompanying Notes are an integral part of these Consolidated Financial Statements.

PRESENT VALUE CONCEPTS

Business enterprises borrow and invest large sums of money. Both of these types of transactions involve the use of **present value computations**. A present value computation is based on the concept of the **time value of money**. For example, would you rather be given $1,000 today or be given $1,000 a year from today? If you get the $1,000 today and invest it to earn 10% per year, the $1,000 will accumulate to $1,100 ($1,000 plus the $100 interest) one year from today. The $1,000 received today is the present value amount that is equivalent to $1,100 one year from now. The present value, therefore, is based on three variables: (1) the dollar amount to be received (the future amount), (2) the length of time until the amount is received (the number of periods), and (3) the interest rate (the discount rate). The process of determining the present value is referred to as **discounting the future amount**. The relationship of these fundamental variables is depicted in the following time diagram.

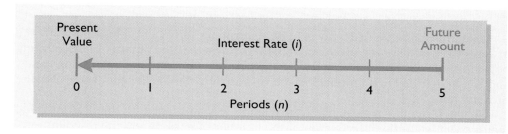

Illustration C-1

Time diagram

To better understand the variables involved in present value analysis, we encourage you to use time diagrams such as the one in Illustration C-1.

In this textbook, present value computations are used in measuring several items. For example, in Chapter 16, to determine the market price of a bond, the present value of the principal and interest payments is computed. In addition, finding the amount to be reported for notes payable and lease liability involves present value computations. And, in Chapter 27, the discounted cash flow technique and the net present value method for capital budget decisions use present value computations.

PRESENT VALUE OF A SINGLE FUTURE AMOUNT

To illustrate present value concepts, assume that you are willing to invest a sum of money that will yield $1,000 at the end of one year. In other words, what amount would you need to invest today to have $1,000 one year from now? If you want a 10% rate of return, the investment or present value is $909.09 ($1,000 ÷ 1.10). The computation of this amount is shown in Illustration C-2.

Present value × (1 + interest rate) = Future amount
Present value × (1 + 10%)   = $1,000
Present value   = $1,000 ÷ 1.10
Present value   = **$909.09**

Illustration C-2

Present value computation—$1,000 discounted at 10% for 1 year

The future amount ($1,000), the discount rate (10%), and the number of periods (1) are known. The variables in this situation can be depicted in the time diagram in Illustration C-3 on the next page.

Illustration C-3

Finding present value if discounted for one period

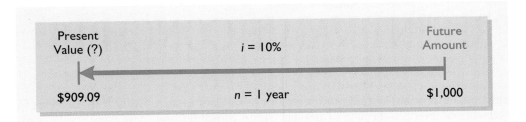

If the single future amount of $1,000 is to be received **in 2 years** and discounted at 10%, its present value is $826.45 [($1,000 ÷ 1.10) ÷ 1.10], depicted as follows.

Illustration C-4

Finding present value if discounted for two periods

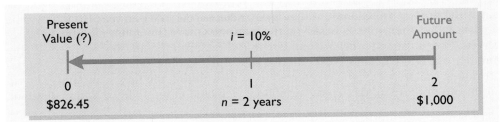

The present value of 1 may also be determined through tables that show the present value of 1 for *n* periods. In Table C-1 below, *n* is the number of discounting periods involved. The percentages are the periodic interest rates or discount rates, and the 5-digit decimal numbers in the respective columns are the factors for the present value of 1.

When Table C-1 is used, the future amount is multiplied by the present value factor specified at the intersection of the number of periods and the discount rate. For example, the present value factor for 1 period at a discount rate of 10% is .90909, which equals the $909.09 ($1,000 × .90909) computed in Illustration C-2.

TABLE C-1
Present Value of 1

(*n*) Periods	4%	5%	6%	8%	9%	10%	11%	12%	15%
1	.96154	.95238	.94340	.92593	.91743	.90909	.90090	.89286	.86957
2	.92456	.90703	.89000	.85734	.84168	.82645	.81162	.79719	.75614
3	.88900	.86384	.83962	.79383	.77218	.75132	.73119	.71178	.65752
4	.85480	.82270	.79209	.73503	.70843	.68301	.65873	.63552	.57175
5	.82193	.78353	.74726	.68058	.64993	.62092	.59345	.56743	.49718
6	.79031	.74622	.70496	.63017	.59627	.56447	.53464	.50663	.43233
7	.75992	.71068	.66506	.58349	.54703	.51316	.48166	.45235	.37594
8	.73069	.67684	.62741	.54027	.50187	.46651	.43393	.40388	.32690
9	.70259	.64461	.59190	.50025	.46043	.42410	.39092	.36061	.28426
10	.67556	.61391	.55839	.46319	.42241	.38554	.35218	.32197	.24719
11	.64958	.58468	.52679	.42888	.38753	.35049	.31728	.28748	.21494
12	.62460	.55684	.49697	.39711	.35554	.31863	.28584	.25668	.18691
13	.60057	.53032	.46884	.36770	.32618	.28966	.25751	.22917	.16253
14	.57748	.50507	.44230	.34046	.29925	.26333	.23199	.20462	.14133
15	.55526	.48102	.41727	.31524	.27454	.23939	.20900	.18270	.12289
16	.53391	.45811	.39365	.29189	.25187	.21763	.18829	.16312	.10687
17	.51337	.43630	.37136	.27027	.23107	.19785	.16963	.14564	.09293
18	.49363	.41552	.35034	.25025	.21199	.17986	.15282	.13004	.08081
19	.47464	.39573	.33051	.23171	.19449	.16351	.13768	.11611	.07027
20	.45639	.37689	.31180	.21455	.17843	.14864	.12403	.10367	.06110

For 2 periods at a discount rate of 10%, the present value factor is .82645, which equals the $826.45 ($1,000 × .82645) computed previously.

Note that **a higher discount rate produces a smaller present value.** For example, using a 15% discount rate, the present value of $1,000 due one year from now is $869.57. At 10%, it is $909.09. You also should recognize that **the further removed from the present the future amount is, the smaller the present value.** For example, using the same discount rate of 10%, the present value of $1,000 due **in 5 years** is $620.92. The present value of $1,000 due in **1** year is $909.09.

The following two demonstration problems (Illustrations C-5 and C-6) illustrate how to use Table C-1.

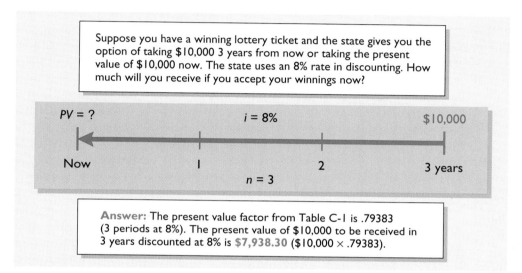

Illustration C-5

Demonstration Problem—
Using Table C-1 for PV of 1

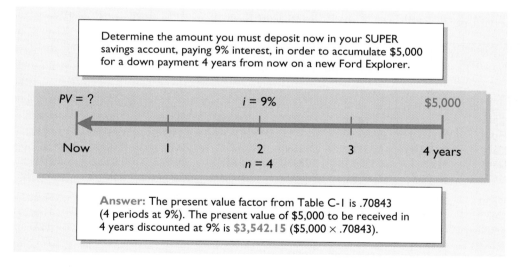

Illustration C-6

Demonstration Problem—
Using Table C-1 for PV of 1

PRESENT VALUE OF A SERIES OF FUTURE AMOUNTS (ANNUITIES)

The preceding discussion involved the discounting of only a single future amount. Businesses and individuals frequently engage in transactions in which a series of equal dollar amounts are to be received or paid periodically. Examples of a series of periodic receipts or payments are loan agreements, installment sales, mortgage notes, lease (rental) contracts, and pension obligations. These series of periodic receipts or payments are called **annuities.** In computing the present value of an annuity, it is necessary to know (1) the discount rate, (2) the number of discount periods, and (3) the amount of the periodic receipts or payments. To illustrate the computation of the present value of an annuity, assume that you will receive $1,000 cash annually for 3 years and the discount rate is 10%. This situation is depicted in the following time diagram.

Illustration C-7

Time diagram for a 3-year annuity

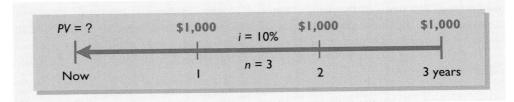

The present value in this situation may be computed as follows.

Illustration C-8

Present value of a series of future amounts computation

Future Amount	×	Present Value of 1 Factor at 10%	=	Present Value
$1,000 (1 year away)		.90909		$ 909.09
1,000 (2 years away)		.82645		826.45
1,000 (3 years away)		.75132		751.32
		2.48686		$2,486.86

This method of calculation is required when the periodic cash flows are not uniform in each period. When the future receipts are the same in each period, there are two other ways to compute present value. First, the annual cash flow can be multiplied by the sum of the three present value factors. In the example above, $1,000 × 2.48686 equals $2,486.86. Second, annuity tables may be used. As illustrated in Table C-2 below, these tables show the present value of 1 to be received periodically for a given number of periods.

TABLE C-2									
Present Value of an Annuity of 1									
(n) Periods	**4%**	**5%**	**6%**	**8%**	**9%**	**10%**	**11%**	**12%**	**15%**
1	.96154	.95238	.94340	.92593	.91743	.90909	.90090	.89286	.86957
2	1.88609	1.85941	1.83339	1.78326	1.75911	1.73554	1.71252	1.69005	1.62571
3	2.77509	2.72325	2.67301	2.57710	2.53130	2.48685	2.44371	2.40183	2.28323
4	3.62990	3.54595	3.46511	3.31213	3.23972	3.16986	3.10245	3.03735	2.85498
5	4.45182	4.32948	4.21236	3.99271	3.88965	3.79079	3.69590	3.60478	3.35216
6	5.24214	5.07569	4.91732	4.62288	4.48592	4.35526	4.23054	4.11141	3.78448
7	6.00205	5.78637	5.58238	5.20637	5.03295	4.86842	4.71220	4.56376	4.16042
8	6.73274	6.46321	6.20979	5.74664	5.53482	5.33493	5.14612	4.96764	4.48732
9	7.43533	7.10782	6.80169	6.24689	5.99525	5.75902	5.53705	5.32825	4.77158
10	8.11090	7.72173	7.36009	6.71008	6.41766	6.14457	5.88923	5.65022	5.01877
11	8.76048	8.30641	7.88687	7.13896	6.80519	6.49506	6.20652	5.93770	5.23371
12	9.38507	8.86325	8.38384	7.53608	7.16073	6.81369	6.49236	6.19437	5.42062
13	9.98565	9.39357	8.85268	7.90378	7.48690	7.10336	6.74987	6.42355	5.58315
14	10.56312	9.89864	9.29498	8.24424	7.78615	7.36669	6.98187	6.62817	5.72448
15	11.11839	10.37966	9.71225	8.55948	8.06069	7.60608	7.19087	6.81086	5.84737
16	11.65230	10.83777	10.10590	8.85137	8.31256	7.82371	7.37916	6.97399	5.95424
17	12.16567	11.27407	10.47726	9.12164	8.54363	8.02155	7.54879	7.11963	6.04716
18	12.65930	11.68959	10.82760	9.37189	8.75563	8.20141	7.70162	7.24967	6.12797
19	13.13394	12.08532	11.15812	9.60360	8.95012	8.36492	7.83929	7.36578	6.19823
20	13.59033	12.46221	11.46992	9.81815	9.12855	8.51356	7.96333	7.46944	6.25933

From Table C-2 you can see that the present value factor of an annuity of 1 for three periods at 10% is 2.48685.[1] This present value factor is the total of the three individual present value factors as shown in Illustration C-8. Applying this amount to the annual cash flow of $1,000 produces a present value of $2,486.85.

The following demonstration problem (Illustration C-9) illustrates how to use Table C-2.

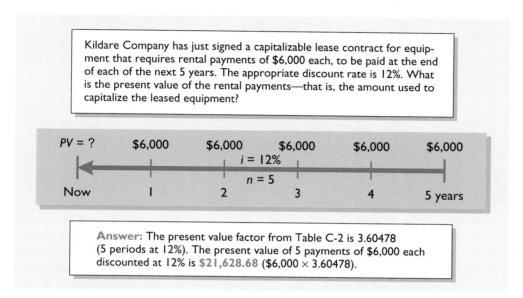

Kildare Company has just signed a capitalizable lease contract for equipment that requires rental payments of $6,000 each, to be paid at the end of each of the next 5 years. The appropriate discount rate is 12%. What is the present value of the rental payments—that is, the amount used to capitalize the leased equipment?

PV = ? $6,000 $6,000 $6,000 $6,000 $6,000
                              i = 12%
                              n = 5
Now   1   2   3   4   5 years

Answer: The present value factor from Table C-2 is 3.60478 (5 periods at 12%). The present value of 5 payments of $6,000 each discounted at 12% is **$21,628.68** ($6,000 × 3.60478).

TIME PERIODS AND DISCOUNTING

In the preceding calculations, the discounting has been done on an annual basis using an annual interest rate. Discounting may also be done over shorter periods of time, such as monthly, quarterly, or semiannually. When the time frame is less than one year, it is necessary to convert the annual interest rate to the shorter time frame. Assume, for example, that the investor in Illustration C-8 received $500 **semiannually** for 3 years instead of $1,000 annually. In this case, the number of periods becomes 6 (3 × 2), the discount rate is 5% (10% ÷ 2), the present value factor from Table C-2 is 5.07569, and the present value of the future cash flows is $2,537.85 (5.07569 × $500). This amount is slightly higher than the $2,486.86 computed in Illustration C-8 because interest is computed twice during the same year. That is, interest is earned on the first half year's interest.

COMPUTING THE PRESENT VALUE OF A BOND

The present value (or market price) of a bond is a function of three variables: (1) the payment amounts, (2) the length of time until the amounts are paid, and (3) the discount rate.

The first variable (dollars to be paid) is made up of two elements: (1) a series of interest payments (an annuity) and (2) the principal amount (a single sum). To

---

[1]The difference of .00001 between 2.48686 amd 2.48685 is due to rounding.

compute the present value of the bond, both the interest payments and the principal amount must be discounted. This is done in two different computations. The time diagrams for a bond due in 5 years are shown in Illustration C-10.

Illustration C-10

Time diagram for the present value of a bond

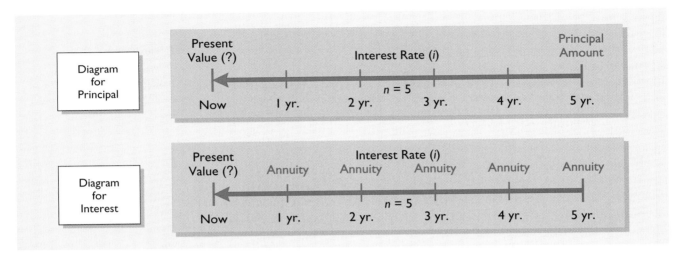

When the investor's discount rate is equal to the bond's contractual interest rate, the present value of the bonds will equal the face value of the bonds. To illustrate, assume a bond issue of 10%, 5-year bonds with a face value of $100,000 with interest payable **semiannually** on January 1 and July 1. If the discount rate is the same as the contractual rate, the bonds will sell **at face value**. In this case, the investor will receive (1) $100,000 at maturity and (2) a series of ten $5,000 interest payments [($100,000 × 10%) ÷ 2] over the term of the bonds. The length of time is expressed in terms of interest periods (in this case, 10) and the discount rate per interest period (5%). The following time diagram (Illustration C-11) depicts the variables involved in this discounting situation.

Illustration C-11

Time diagram for the present value of a 10%, 5-year bond paying interest semiannually

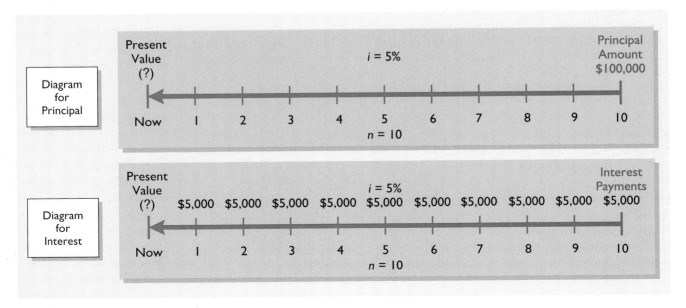

The computation of the present value of these bonds is shown below.

10% Contractual Rate—10% Discount Rate

Present value of principal to be received at maturity
$100,000 × PV of 1 due in 10 periods at 5%
$100,000 × .61391 (Table C-1) $ 61,391
Present value of interest to be received periodically
over the term of the bonds
$5,000 × PV of 1 due periodically for 10 periods at 5%
$5,000 × 7.72173 (Table C-2)   38,609*
Present value of bonds $100,000

*(Rounded).

Illustration C-12
Present value of principal and interest (face value)

Now assume that the investor's required rate of return is 12%, not 10%. The future amounts are again $100,000 and $5,000, respectively. But now a discount rate of 6% (12% ÷ 2) must be used. The present value of the bonds is $92,639, as computed below.

10% Contractual Rate—12% Discount Rate

Present value of principal to be received at maturity
$100,000 × .55839 (Table C-1) $55,839
Present value of interest to be received periodically
over the term of the bonds
$5,000 × 7.36009 (Table C-2)   36,800
Present value of bonds $92,639

Illustration C-13
Present value of principal and interest (discount)

If the discount rate is 8% and the contractual rate is 10%, the present value of the bonds is $108,111, computed as follows.

10% Contractual Rate—8% Discount Rate

Present value of principal to be received at maturity
$100,000 × .67556 (Table C-1) $ 67,556
Present value of interest to be received periodically
over the term of the bonds
$5,000 × 8.11090 (Table C-2)   40,555
Present value of bonds $108,111

Illustration C-14
Present value of principal and interest (premium)

TECHNOLOGY IN ACTION

As discussed in this appendix, the selling price of bonds can be determined by present value formulas. Many computer spreadsheets and computer programs can perform the discounting functions given the basic information of the situation.

USE OF CALCULATORS TO SOLVE PRESENT VALUE PROBLEMS

The above discussion relied on present value tables in solving present value problems. Electronic hand-held calculators may also be used to compute present values without the use of these tables. Some calculators, especially the "business" or "financial" type calculators, have present value (PV) functions that allow you to calculate present values by merely punching in the proper amount, discount rate, periods, and pressing the PV key. Whether you use a calculator or tables to solve present value problems, you should make sure that you fully understand the important concepts that underlie the calculations.

BRIEF EXERCISES (Use Tables to Solve Exercises)

Using present value tables.

BEC-1 For each of the following cases, indicate (a) to what interest rate columns and (b) to what number of periods you would refer in looking up the discount rate.

1. In Table C-1 (present value of 1):

	Annual Rate	Number of Years Involved	Discounts Per Year
(a)	12%	6	Annually
(b)	10%	15	Annually
(c)	8%	8	Semiannually

2. In Table C-2 (present value of an annuity of 1):

	Annual Rate	Number of Years Involved	Number of Payments Involved	Frequency of Payments
(a)	12%	20	20	Annually
(b)	10%	5	5	Annually
(c)	8%	4	8	Semiannually

Determining present values.

BEC-2 (a) What is the present value of $10,000 due 8 periods from now, discounted at 8%? (b) What is the present value of $10,000 to be received at the end of each of 6 periods, discounted at 9%?

Compute the present value of a single-sum investment.

BEC-3 Hernandez Company is considering an investment that will return a lump sum of $500,000 5 years from now. What amount should Hernandez Company pay for this investment in order to earn a 15% return?

Compute the present value of a single-sum investment.

BEC-4 Pizzeria Company earns 11% on an investment that will return $875,000 8 years from now. What is the amount Pizzeria should invest now in order to earn this rate of return?

Compute the present value of a single-sum noninterest-bearing note.

BEC-5 Slurpy Company sold a 5-year, noninterest-bearing $27,000 note receivable to Valley Inc. Valley wishes to earn 12% over the remaining 4 years of the note. How much cash will Slurpy receive upon sale of the note?

Compute the present value of a single-sum noninterest-bearing note.

BEC-6 Roberto Company issues a 3-year, zero-interest-bearing $66,000 note. The interest rate used to discount the zero-interest-bearing note is 8%. What are the cash proceeds that Roberto Company should receive?

Compute the present value of an annuity investment.

BEC-7 Bob Skabo Company is considering investing in an annuity contract that will return $20,000 annually at the end of each year for 15 years. What amount should Skabo Company pay for this investment if it earns a 6% return?

Compute the present value of an annuity investment.

BEC-8 Donald R. Hughes Enterprises earns 11% on an investment that pays back $110,000 at the end of each of the next 4 years. What is the amount Donald R. Hughes Enterprises invested to earn the 11% rate of return?

BEC-9   Dick Way Railroad Co. is about to issue $100,000 of 10-year bonds paying a 12% interest rate, with interest payable semiannually. The discount rate for such securities is 10%. How much can Dick Way expect to receive for the sale of these bonds?

Compute the present value of bonds.

BEC-10   Assume the same information as BEC-9 except that the discount rate is 12% instead of 10%. In this case, how much can Dick Way expect to receive from the sale of these bonds?

Compute the present value of bonds.

BEC-11   Cheryl Countryman Company receives a $50,000, 6-year note bearing interest of 11% (paid annually) from a customer at a time when the discount rate is 12%. What is the present value of the note received by Cheryl Countryman Company?

Compute the present value of a note.

BEC-12   Michael Mooney Enterprises issued 10%, 8-year, $2,000,000 par value bonds that pay interest semiannually on October 1 and April 1. The bonds are dated April 1, 2002, and are issued on that date. The discount rate of interest for such bonds on April 1, 2002, is 12%. What cash proceeds did Michael Mooney receive from issuance of the bonds?

Compute the present value of bonds.

BEC-13   Barney Googal owns a garage and is contemplating purchasing a tire retreading machine for $16,280. After estimating costs and revenues, Barney projects a net cash flow from the retreading machine of $2,790 annually for 8 years. Barney hopes to earn a return of 11% on such investments. What is the present value of the retreading operation? Should Barney Googal purchase the retreading machine?

Compute the value of a machine for purposes of making a purchase decision.

BEC-14   Hung-Chao Yu Company issues a 10%, 6-year mortgage note on January 1, 2002, to obtain financing for new equipment. Land is used as collateral for the note. The terms provide for semiannual installment payments of $112,825. What were the cash proceeds received from the issuance of the note?

Compute the present value of a note.

BEC-15   Denice Rode Company is considering purchasing equipment. The equipment will produce the following cash flows: Year 1, $30,000; Year 2, $40,000; Year 3, $50,000. Rode requires a minimum rate of return of 15%. What is the maximum price Rode should pay for this equipment?

Compute the maximum price to pay for a machine.

BEC-16   If Josey Rodriquez invests $1,827 now, she will receive $10,000 at the end of 15 years. What annual rate of interest will Josey earn on her investment? (*Hint*: Use Table C-1.)

Compute the interest rate on a single sum.

BEC-17   Jeri Delaney has been offered the opportunity of investing $24,719 now. The investment will earn 15% per year and at the end of that time will return Jeri $100,000. How many years must Jeri wait to receive $100,000? (*Hint*: Use Table C-1.)

Compute the number of periods of a single sum.

BEC-18   Janice Rahn purchased an investment for $11,469.92. From this investment, she will receive $1,000 annually for the next 20 years, starting one year from now. What rate of interest will Janice's investment be earning for her? (*Hint*: Use Table C-2.)

Compute the interest rate on an annuity.

BEC-19   Amy Sanchez invests $8,851.37 now for a series of $1,000 annual returns, beginning one year from now. Amy will earn a return of 8% on the initial investment. How many annual payments of $1,000 will Amy receive? (*Hint*: Use Table C-2.)

Compute the number of periods of an annuity.

STANDARDS OF ETHICAL CONDUCT FOR MANAGEMENT ACCOUNTANTS

Management accountants have an obligation to the organizations they serve, their profession, the public, and themselves to maintain the highest standards of ethical conduct. In recognition of this obligation, the **Institute of Management Accountants**, formerly the National Association of Accountants, has published and promoted the following standards of ethical conduct for management accountants. Adherence to these standards is integral to achieving the *Objectives of Management Accounting*.[1] Management accountants shall not commit acts contrary to these standards nor shall they condone the commission of such acts by others within their organizations.

COMPETENCE

Management accountants have a responsibility to:

- Maintain an appropriate level of professional competence by ongoing development of their knowledge and skills.

- Perform their professional duties in accordance with relevant laws, regulations, and technical standards.

- Prepare complete and clear reports and recommendations after appropriate analyses of relevant and reliable information.

CONFIDENTIALITY

Management accountants have a responsibility to:

- Refrain from disclosing confidential information acquired in the course of their work except when authorized, unless legally obligated to do so.

---

[1]Institute of Management Accountants, formerly National Association of Accountants, *Statements on Management Accounting: Objectives of Management Accounting,* Statement No. 1B, June 17, 1982.

- Inform subordinates as appropriate regarding the confidentiality of information acquired in the course of their work and monitor their activities to assure the maintenance of that confidentiality.
- Refrain from using or appearing to use confidential information acquired in the course of their work for unethical or illegal advantage either personally or through third parties.

INTEGRITY

Management accountants have a responsibility to:

- Avoid actual or apparent conflicts of interest and advise all appropriate parties of any potential conflict.
- Refrain from engaging in any activity that would prejudice their ability to carry out their duties ethically.
- Refuse any gift, favor, or hospitality that would influence or would appear to influence their actions.
- Refrain from either actively or passively subverting the attainment of the organization's legitimate and ethical objectives.
- Recognize and communicate professional limitations or other constraints that would preclude responsible judgment or successful performance of an activity.
- Communicate unfavorable as well as favorable information and professional judgments or opinions.
- Refrain from engaging in or supporting any activity that would discredit the profession.

OBJECTIVITY

Management accountants have a responsibility to:

- Communicate information fairly and objectively.
- Disclose fully all relevant information that could reasonably be expected to influence an intended user's understanding of the reports, comments, and recommendations presented.

Chapter 1
Opener: Warren Bolster/Stone. Page 5: Gary Hunter/Stone. Page 6: Jean Miele/The Stock Market. Page 8: Mike Cressy/Stock Illustration Source. Page 11: Roger Boehm/Stock Illustration Source. Page 24: Will Crocker/The Image Bank. Page 39: Courtesy of Nestle S.A.

Chapter 2
Opener: Rod Long/Stone. Page 50: Simon Battensby/Stone. Page 53: Mike Stewart/Corbis Sygma. Page 55: Joe Bator/The Stock Market. Page 62: Nora Hope/Stock Illustration Source. Page 66: Frank Wing/Stock, Boston/PNI.

Chapter 3
Opener: T. Kevin Smyth/The Stock Market. Page 90: ©AP/Wide World Photos. Page 94: Romily Lockyer/The Image Bank. Page 98: Dennis Galante/Stone. Page 103: Peter Poulides/Stone.

Chapter 4
Opener: Matthias/Kulka/The Stock Market. Page 137: William Whitehurst/The Stock Market. Page 142: Marc Francoeur/Liaison Agency, Inc. Page 144: M. Tcherevkoff/The Image Bank. Page 150: Miguel S. Salmeron/FPG International. Page 152: Leland Bobbe/Stone. Page 153 (top): John Fiordalisi/SUPERSTOCK. Page 153 (bottom): Zigy Kaluzny/Stone. Page 154 (top): Courtesy United Airlines. Page 154 (bottom): Courtesy Consolidated Freightways. Page 155: The Dell logo is a registered trademark of Dell Computer Corporation in the United States and other countries. Page 162: John Riley/Stone. Page 179: Courtesy Holmen.

Chapter 5
Opener: Rob Colvin/©2000 Artville, Inc. Page 186: Michael Simpson/FPG International. Page 190: Ed Honowitz/Stone. Page 191: Gregory Heislerban/The Image Bank. Page 193: Thierry Dosogne/The Image Bank. Page 201: Steve Taylor/Stone.

Chapter 6
Opener: Chris Noble/Stone. Page 226: John Turner/Stone. Page 227: Tom Tracey/FPG International. Page 241: Michael Rosenfeld/Stone. Page 242 (top): Courtesy The Quaker Oats Company. Page 242 (bottom): Bob Krist/Stone. Page 271 (top): Courtesy Fuji Photo Film U.S.A., Inc. Page 271 (bottom): Kodak corporate symbol is a trademark of Eastman Kodak Company. Used with permission.

Chapter 7
Opener: Elle Schuster/The Image Bank. Page 278: W. Cody/CORBIS. Page 281: Earl Glass/Stock, Boston/PNI.

Chapter 8
Opener: Robert Stanton/Stone. Page 319: Gary Buss/FPG International. Page 321: Ken Straiton/The Stock Market. Page 322: R. Michael Stuckey/Comstock, Inc. Page 324: Sean Kane/Stock Illustration Source. Page 330: Michael Murphy/The Image Bank. Page 334: Miachel A. Keller/The Stock Market. Page 336: J.W. Burkey/Stone. Page 341: Kodak corporate symbol is a trademark of Eastman Kodak Company. Used with permission.

Chapter 9
Opener: ©PhotoDisc. Page 364: David Gould/The Image Bank. Page 369: ©Zefa/Stock Imagery. Page 370: ©Yemi/Stock Illustration Source. Page 377: Brad Hamann/Stock Illustration Source. Page 379: ©Telegraph Colour Library/FPG International.

Chapter 10
Opener: Stewart Cohen/Stone. Page 405: Greg Probst/Stone. Page 411: Thierry Cariou/The Stock Market. Page 421: ©Schnepf/Liaison Agency, Inc. Page 422: Courtesy Grand Metropolitan. Page 441: Courtesy J Sainsbury.

Chapter 11
Opener: John Turner/Stone. Page 448: Ed Honowitz/Stone. Page 452: Peter Gridley/FPG International. Page 453: ©The Image Bank. Page 455: James Noble/The Stock Market. Page 463: ©1994 Turner & Devries/The Image Bank. Page 476: "Polaroid" is a registered trademark of the Polaroid Corporation.

Chapter 12
Opener: Andrew Olney/Stone. Page 489: Lonny Kalfus/Stone. Page 491: Comstock, Inc. Page 497: Henry Sims//The Image Bank. Page 498: Doug Armand/Stone. Page 499: Barbara Nessim/Stock Illustration Source. Page 503: Olney Vasan/Stone.

Chapter 13
Opener: ©2000 Razor & Tie Direct, LLC. Page 522: Jude Maceren/Stock Illustration Source. Page 524: Denis Scott/The Stock Market. Page 528: Robert Cattan/Index Stock.

Chapter 14
Opener: Rick Graves/Stone. Page 563: Stephen Johnson/Stone. Page 564: ©Josh Sohm; Chromosohm, Inc./CORBIS. Page 566: ©AP/Wide World Photos. Page 568 (top): Lands' End is a registered trademark of Lands' End, Inc. Used with permission. Page 568 (bottom): Seth Resnick/Stock, Boston/PNI. Page 575: Alex Fevzer/CORBIS. Page 579: Jaime Salles/The Stock

Chapter 15
Opener: Gregg Adams/Stone. Page 603: Sandra Baker/Stone. Page 609: John Labbe/The Image Bank. Page 611 (top): David Madison/Stone. Page 611 (bottom): Ken Whitmore/Stone. Page 617: Andy Sacks/Stone. Page 621: Charles Thomaidis/Stone.

Chapter 16
Opener: Leon Zeritsky/Stock Illustration Source. Page 642: ©AP/Wide World Photos. Page 656: Andy Levine/Stock Illustration Source. Page 667: Ken Whitmore/Stone. Page 678: Information suppplied courtesy of Apache Corporation.

Chapter 17
Opener: ©Photofest. Page 684: ©AP/Wide World Photos. Page 686: D. Boone/CORBIS.

Chapter 18
Opener: John Lund/Stone. Page 719: Jonathan Elderfield/Liaison Agency, Inc. Page 748: ©William Waldron. Page 775: Compliments of Saint-Gobaine.

Chapter 19
Opener: Jerry Driendl/FPG International. Page 782 & 783: Sears, Roebuck and Co. Page 788: Don Bishop/©2000 Artville, Inc. Page 790: Nora Good/ Masterfile. Page 792: Christopher Morris/Black Star. Page 793: Jay Ahrend/FoodPix. Page 799 (top): Michael Skott/The Image Bank. Page 799 (bottom): Eric Sander/Liaison Agency, Inc. Page 801: Laurie Rubin/The Image Bank. Page 802: Mark Wiens/Stone. Page 806: Jan Cobb/The Image Bank. Page 813: Courtesy Nordstrom.